THE COMPLEAT CAST *of* CHARACTERS IN LITERATURE

This edition published by Spark Publishing
Spark Publishing
120 Fifth Avenue, 8th Floor
New York, NY 10011

Please submit all comments and questions or report errors to www.sparknotes.com/errors.

Printed and bound in the United States

ISBN-13: 978-1-4114-0218-8
ISBN-10: 1-4114-0218-9

Library of Congress Cataloging-in-Publication Data

The compleat cast of characters in literature.
p. cm.
ISBN-13: 978-1-4114-0218-8
ISBN-10: 1-4114-0218-9
1. Characters and characteristics in literature--Dictionaries.
PN56.4.C55 2006
809'.92703--dc22

2005032413

THE COMPLEAT CAST *of* CHARACTERS IN LITERATURE

SPARK PUBLISHING

TABLE OF CONTENTS

HOW TO USE THIS BOOK

Characters are listed alphabetically by last name, where last names are applicable. (Some characters have very general names like "Joe" or "Mary's mother.") The name of the work in which they appear is listed to the right.

In some cases, characters of the same name appear in works written by different authors. They will be listed separately. If the same character appears in more than one work by a single author (such as Tom Sawyer, who appears in both *Tom Sawyer* and *Huckleberry Finn* by Mark Twain), there will be only one entry that covers the character's entire literary career.

Within the entries you will see other character names written in bold. This means you can also look up that character in this book.

INTRODUCTION

Welcome to *The Compleat* Cast of Characters.*

We know the feeling. You're thinking of a novel you read back in high school. You remember the main character's name, *but you can't remember what he did that tipped off the action of the book.*

"Who was that guy?" you keep asking yourself. "And whom did he kill again?"

Or you're on your way to see someone who loves her Shakespeare, and you just can't remember which Richard was the really bad guy, the II or the III. (It's the III, by the way.)

We made this book for just those moments. Here, to help you in every literary pinch—those classes, those papers, those impromptu discussions—is an easy-to-use *compleat* reference. We can't say we've listed every character in literature, but we've come as close as anyone can really hope to get.

Happy reading.

–THE SPARKNOTES EDITORS

*A quaint, literary way of saying that this book is the only one of its kind that you'll ever need.

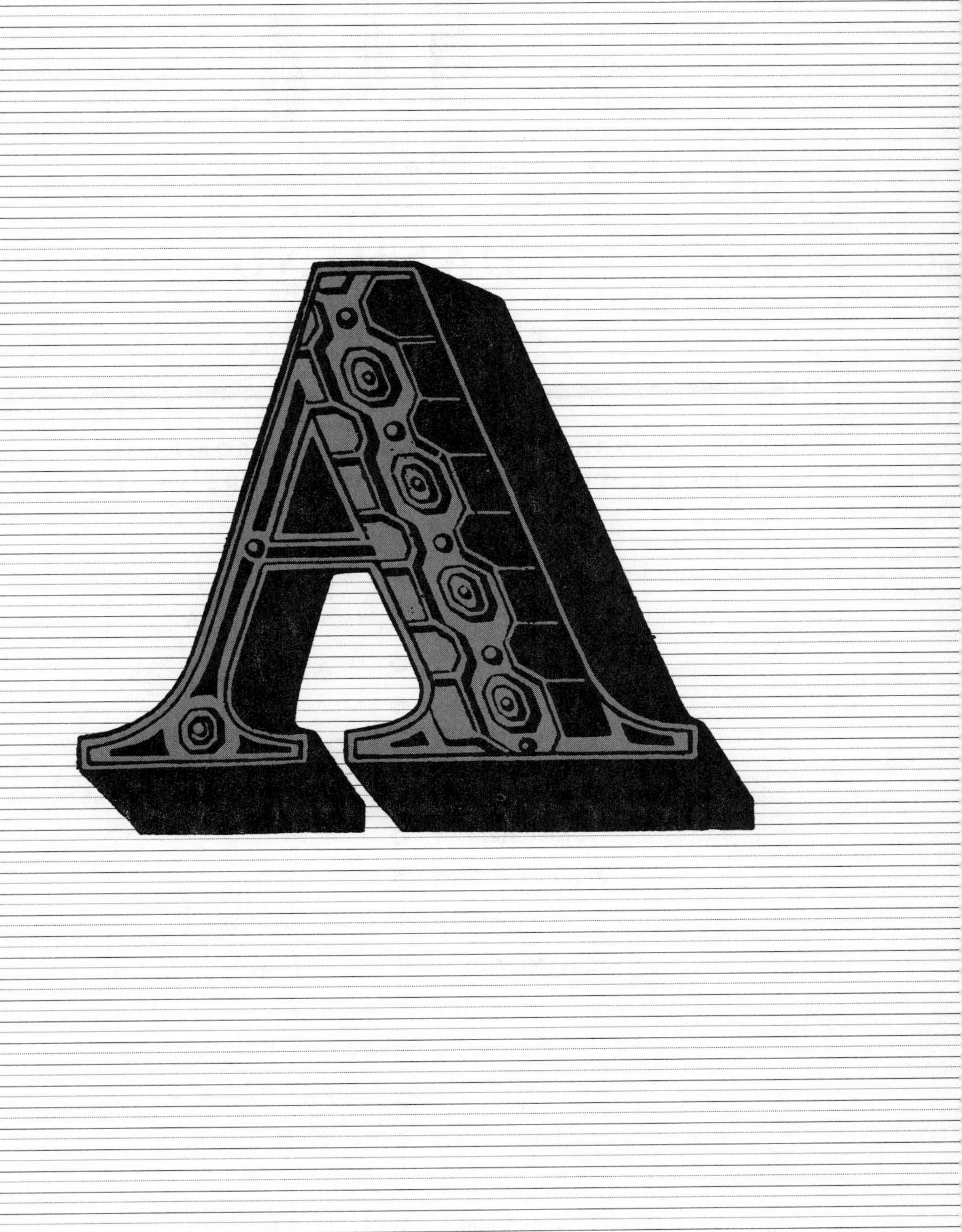

19

DASHING HEROES

BRAVE, RECKLESS MEN... SOME DO BATTLE WITH SWORDS, SOME FIGHT THE SYSTEM.

Aeneas	1	*The Aeneid*
Frodo Baggins	2	*The Lord of the Rings* trilogy
d'Artagnan	3	*The Three Musketeers*
Don Quixote	4	*Don Quixote*
Atticus Finch	5	*To Kill a Mockingbird*
Huckleberry Finn	6	*Huckleberry Finn*
Sir Gawain	7	*Sir Gawain and the Green Knight*
King Henry V	8	*Henry V*
Sherlock Holmes	9	*The Hound of the Baskervilles*
Tom Joad	10	*The Grapes of Wrath*
Randle McMurphy	11	*One Flew over the Cuckoo's Nest*
Odysseus	12	*The Odyssey*
Will Perry	13	*His Dark Materials* trilogy
Pip	14	*Great Expectations*
Harry Potter	15	*Harry Potter* series, Books I-IV
Winston Smith	16	*1984*
Jean Valjean	17	*Les Misérables*
Westley	18	*The Princess Bride*
John Yossarian	19	*Catch-22*

Mr. A

A Room of One's Own
Virginia Woolf

An imagined male author. Mr. A's work is overshadowed by his self-consciousness and petulant assertiveness.

A. E.

Ulysses
James Joyce

A poet and, historically, the central figure of the Irish Literary Revival. **Stephen Dedalus** disdains A. E.'s focus on national literature, as opposed to literature in general, but resents being ostracized from his literary circles.

Nestor Aamons

Cat's Cradle
Kurt Vonnegut

Mona Aamons Monzano's biological father. Nestor, a Finnish architect, designed **Julian Castle**'s charity hospital on San Lorenzo.

Aarfy

Catch-22
Joseph Heller

John Yossarian's navigator. Aarfy always gets lost. He infuriates Yossarian by pretending that he can't hear orders during bombing runs.

Aaron

The Old Testament
Unknown

Moses's brother, who assists Moses in leading the Israelites out of Egypt. **God** designates Aaron the first high priest in Israel. The quiet Aaron often stands between Moses and the people to soften Moses's angry response to their sinful behavior.

Aaron

Titus Andronicus
William Shakespeare

Tamora's Moor lover. Aaron admits that he has had a hand in nearly every crime in the play. He is practically the engine of action in Act II, bringing Tamora's dream of revenge on **Titus** to reality. When Titus's son **Lucius** regains control of Rome, he has the unrepentant Aaron buried alive.

Jimmy Aaron

The Autobiography of Miss Jane Pittman
Ernest J. Gaines

A boy born in the plantation whom everyone believes is going to be the "one." Jimmy Aaron is a messiah-like figure who will return to help mobilize the community toward action. The elders on the plantation want Jimmy to become a religious leader, but because of the changes in civil rights, he becomes more interested in politics. Jimmy Aaron's final sacrifice of his life truly saves the people of the plantation from the fear that has governed them all their lives.

Glengarry Glen Ross
David Mamet

George Aaronow

A timid real estate salesman. Aaronow is extremely meek and mild-mannered. In conversation, faster talkers like **Dave Moss** and **Ricky Roma** easily overpower him. Like **Shelly Levene**, Aaronow is not on the board and is in immediate danger of getting fired. But unlike Levene, he is wise enough to resist Moss's proposal of robbing the office.

Bridge to Terabithia
Katherine Paterson

Brenda Aarons

Jess's second-oldest sister, around fourteen. She harries **Jesse Oliver Aarons, Jr.** and is primly content with her own little world of makeup, scanty clothing, and romantic interests.

Bridge to Terabithia
Katherine Paterson

Ellie Aarons

Jesse Oliver Aarons, Jr.'s oldest sister, about fifteen or sixteen. Ellie is thoroughly spoiled, much like **Brenda Aarons**.

Bridge to Terabithia
Katherine Paterson

Jesse Oliver Aarons, Jr.

The main character and protagonist of the novel. Jess is a fifth-grader living in a rural Southern area. He is lonely and lost in the middle of a family of four girls when **Leslie Burke** moves in next door. Leslie and Jess become best friends, and the novel centers on their friendship. Jess is a budding artist whose talent receives little praise from anyone except Leslie and **Miss Edmunds**. He is talented as well as intelligent, caring, and down-to-earth. Leslie's death has a profound impact on Jesse.

Bridge to Terabithia
Katherine Paterson

Joyce Ann Aarons

Jesse Oliver Aarons, Jr.'s youngest sister. Often portrayed as whiny, Joyce Ann does not share the sort of bond with Jess that **May Belle Aarons** does, but Jess seems to feel a certain warmth toward her, as suggested in the end of the book when he says that one day Joyce Ann may join May Belle in Terabithia as a princess.

Bridge to Terabithia
Katherine Paterson

May Belle Aarons

Jesse Oliver Aarons, Jr.'s little sister. Six-year-old May Belle is closer to Jesse than any other member of their family. She often tries to push herself in with Jess and **Leslie Burke**, which they do not like, but all the same Jess feels bad for her. At the end of the novel, May Belle allows Terabithia to live on when she becomes its new queen.

Mr. Aarons

Bridge to Terabithia
Katherine Paterson

Jesse Oliver Aarons, Jr.'s father. Mr. Aarons is harried by the concerns of being the sole breadwinner for a large family. He expects Jess to be a "man," a source of considerable heartache and soul-searching for Jess. However, Mr. Aarons is concerned with his son's welfare and wants nothing but the best for him, as is evidenced in his treatment of Jess after **Leslie Burke**'s death.

Mrs. Aarons

Bridge to Terabithia
Katherine Paterson

Jesse Oliver Aarons, Jr.'s mother. Mrs. Aarons is tired and careworn with the stresses of trying to support a family of seven on a meager income. She always seems to be hounding Jess, but her shortness of temper is merely a result of overwork. After **Leslie Burke**'s death, she shows herself to be a caring mother torn apart by her son's pain.

Abbé of Perigord

Candide
Voltaire

An abbot and Paris socialite who cheats **Candide** out of his money.

Abbess

The Comedy of Errors
William Shakespeare

The long-lost wife of **Egeon** and the mother of the two Antipholi. The Abbess harbors **Antipholus of Syracuse** and **Dromio of Syracuse** in her priory and attempts to calm the enraged townfolk. She blames **Adriana**'s "jealous fits" for Antipholus of Syracuse's madness, and insists on treating her two refugees herself. The Abbess acts much like a *deus ex machina*: she appears at the end of the play to clear up the confusion that has embroiled Ephesus and neatly saves the life of her estranged husband. The Abbess also represents order in an otherwise chaotic play—her reproach of Adriana invokes the social code to which women should adhere, while her explanation of the day's weird incidents dispels prior notions of the involvement of witchcraft and sorcery.

Abdiel

Paradise Lost
John Milton

An angel who considers joining **Satan** in rebellion but ultimately returns to **God the Father**. Abdiel's character demonstrates the power of repentance.

Mian Abdullah

Midnight's Children
Salman Rushdie

A pro-Indian Muslim political figure, who dies at the hands of assassins.

Abel

House Made of Dawn
N. Scott Momaday

The novel's protagonist, a young Native American man, **Francisco**'s grandson, **Ben Benally**'s friend, **Milly**'s lover and **The Albino**'s killer. Abel has grown up in Walatowa, New Mexico, under the care of his grandfather, but after doing his time in prison for the murder of The Albino, he moves to Los Angeles and lives with Ben. He has just returned from fighting in World War II, and is often drunk. Abel is reserved, not talking unless necessary, and is by nature slow to open up to others. Like many around him at Walatowa, he feels a strong connection to the earth and the landscape around him, and his spiritual upbringing is firmly grounded in a relationship with the outdoors.

Abel

Bless Me, Ultima
Rudolfo A. Anaya

One of a group of exuberant boys who frequently curse and fight. Abel, the smallest boy in the group, frequently urinates in inappropriate places.

Lord Abergavenny

Henry VIII
William Shakespeare

A son-in-law of the **Duke of Buckingham**. Abergavenny is taken to the Tower of London at the same time Buckingham is arrested.

Abigail

The Jew of Malta
Christopher Marlowe

Barabas's daughter. Abigail is initially dutiful to her father and unwittingly helps him mislead **Mathias** and **Lodowick**. However, when she discovers her father's involvement in their deaths, Abigail decides to convert to Christianity to atone for her sins.

Godfrey Ablewhite

The Moonstone
Wilkie Collins

A renowned philanthropist and leader of several Ladies' Charity Groups in London. He is a cousin of **Rachel Verinder**'s and proposes marriage to Rachel twice. Godfrey begins to look suspicious and hypocritical during **Miss Clack**'s narrative. He receives the Moonstone from **Franklin Blake** when Blake is in a drug-induced trance and attempts to sell it for his own profit.

The Misses Ablewhite

The Moonstone
Wilkie Collins

Godfrey Ablewhite's two sisters. Rambunctious and happy, they are referred to as "the Bouncers" by **Gabriel Betteredge**.

Mr. Ablewhite

The Moonstone
Wilkie Collins

Godfrey Ablewhite's father, a self-made man who married into money. He is a caretaker for **Rachel Verinder** after **Lady Verinder**'s death.

Mrs. Ablewhite

The Moonstone
Wilkie Collins

Godfrey Ablewhite's mother, a lazy, happy person. **Rachel Verinder** enjoys visiting with her.

Abraham

The Old Testament
Unknown

The patriarch of the Hebrew people. Abraham is traditionally called "Father Abraham" because the Israelite people and their religion descend from him. **God** establishes his covenant, or promise, with Abraham, then develops an ongoing relationship with the Israelites through Abraham's descendants. Abraham is monotheistic, and his resilient faith in God, despite many challenges, sets the pattern for the Israelite religion's view of righteousness.

Abraham

Romeo and Juliet
William Shakespeare

Montague's servant, who fights with **Sampson** and **Gregory** in the first scene of the play.

Abraxas

Demian
Hermann Hesse

A God known to mystics in ancient times who contains both good and evil aspects. Abraxas captures **Emil Sinclair**'s imagination more than the Christian God, who is only a God of the good. The later part of Sinclair's preparatory school years are spent in search and study of Abraxas.

Absalom

The Old Testament
Unknown

David's son, who attempts to overthrow his father's throne. Absalom's violent rise to power suggests that the evil that corrupts Israel comes from within.

Absolon

The Canterbury Tales
Geoffrey Chaucer

The local parish clerk in **the Miller**'s Tale. Absolon is a little bit foolish and more than a little vain. He curls his hair, uses breath fresheners, and fancies **Alisoun**.

The Misanthrope
Molière

Acaste

A young and egotistical marquis. He considers himself a prime candidate for the role of **Célimène**'s lover. He desires her to such an extent that he strikes a deal with **Clitandre** to bolster his chances of wooing her.

The Aeneid
Virgil

Achates

A Trojan and a friend of **Aeneas**.

The Iliad
Homer

Achilles

The greatest Greek warrior of the Trojan War and the tragic hero of the *Iliad*. Achilles possesses superhuman strength and benefits from a close relationship with the Gods. His mother, the sea-nymph **Thetis**, has made him invulnerable everywhere except his heel, where he is eventually struck and killed. He has deep-seated character flaws that prevent him from acting with nobility and integrity. He mercilessly mauls his opponents, ignobly desecrates the body of **Hector**, and savagely sacrifices twelve Trojan men at the funeral of **Patroclus**. Also appears as a figure in Greek mythology.

The Aeneid
Virgil

Achilles

See above.

Troilus and Cressida
William Shakespeare

Achilles

The greatest of the Greek warriors. Achilles is an arrogant, vicious thug who refuses to fight whenever his pride is injured.

The Catcher in the Rye
J. D. Salinger

Ackley

Next-door neighbor to **Holden Caulfield** in his dorm at Pencey Prep. Ackley is a pimply, insecure boy with terrible dental hygiene. He often barges into Holden's room and acts oblivious to Holden's hints that he should leave.

Watership Down
Richard Adams

Acorn

A rabbit whom **Blackberry** convinced to leave. Acorn is not very happy with the trip until he begins to gain faith in **Hazel** and the other rabbits. Although Acorn is neither large nor strong, he does his best to help the warren in any way he can.

Acton

Jazz
Toni Morrison

Dorcas's cocky and self-absorbed boyfriend after she tires of **Joe Trace**. Acton constantly criticizes Dorcas and advises her on how to behave and what to wear. He is a young, good-looking man whom all the girls adore. When Joe shoots Dorcas, Acton seems more concerned about the bloodstain on his fancy clothes than Dorcas's grave situation.

Ada

Alice in Wonderland
Lewis Carroll

An acquaintance of **Alice**'s. Ada does not appear in the book, but Alice refers to her when confused about her own identity. Alice reasons that she could not be Ada, because Ada has ringlets and she does not.

Adam

The Old Testament
Unknown

The first man created by **God**. Adam and his companion **Eve** introduce human evil into the world when they eat the fruit of a tree God has forbidden them to touch.

Adam

Paradise Lost
John Milton

The first human, the father of the human race, and, along with his wife, **Eve**, the caretaker of the Garden of Eden. Adam is grateful and obedient to **God the Father** but falls from grace when Eve convinces him to join her in the sin of eating from the Tree of Knowledge.

Adam

As You Like It
William Shakespeare

The elderly former servant of **Sir Rowland de Bois** and then **Oliver**. After he warns **Orlando** of Oliver's plot to burn down his house, Adam offers not only to accompany Orlando into exile but also to fund their journey with the whole of his modest life's savings. He is a model of loyalty and devoted service and comes to the Forest of Arden through the goodness of his heart.

Adam

The Color Purple
Alice Walker

Celie and **Alphonso**'s biological son, who, like **Olivia**, is adopted by **Samuel** and **Corrine**. Adam falls in love with **Tashi**, a young Olinka girl. By marrying Tashi, Adam symbolically bridges Africa and America, and his respect for and deference to her subverts patriarchal notions of women's subordinance to men. After Tashi goes through the painful facial scarring and genital mutilation that is part of her people's tradition, Adam scars his face to show his union with Tashi. In the end, Adam is reunited with Celie.

Nick Adams

In Our Time
Ernest Hemingway

The protagonist of many of the stories in *In Our Time*. Several of the stories show him as a young boy in the Midwest. Nick grows up and goes to war, later returning as a changed man.

Nick's father

In Our Time
Ernest Hemingway

A doctor who emphasizes the importance of masculinity to his son **Nick Adams**. Nick's father also has a hot temper and has trouble getting along with his wife.

Samuel Adams

Johnny Tremain
Esther Forbes

A leader of the Revolutionary forces in Boston. Samuel Adams was considered the greatest creator of propaganda for the rebel cause. He wrote numerous pamphlets inciting and inspiring the revolution.

Frankie Addams

The Member of the Wedding
Carson McCullers

The novella's protagonist. Frankie Addams is a precocious and gregarious girl in the throes of adolescence. She feels disconnected from everyone around her and spends the novella searching for a way to meld with other people. She has lofty fantasies about how she will escape what she feels is a stifling existence. However, her naïveté and lack of awareness of the adult world, particularly when it comes to matters of sex and interpersonal relationships, prevent her from achieving her fantastical plans. In each of the three parts of the novella, she goes by different names: first Frankie, then F. Jasmine, and then Frances.

Jarvis Addams

The Member of the Wedding
Carson McCullers

Frankie Addams's older brother. He marries **Janice Evans**. A completely absent figure from the immediate action, he inspires all of Frankie's desires and fantasies. She spends two years dreaming about him while he is stationed in Alaska, and now all she can think about is somehow joining in on his marriage. Though Frankie tries to convince herself that she is an adult, Jarvis still sees her as a little kid.

Royal Quincy Addams

The Member of the Wedding
Carson McCullers

Frankie Addams's quiet and serious father. Mr. Addams's wife, Frankie's mother, died when Frankie was born. His function in the novel is minimal, as he spends most of the novel working in his jewelry shop. When we do hear from him, his stern adult voice keeps the cantankerous Frankie in line.

Randy Adderson

The Outsiders
S. E. Hinton

Marcia's boyfriend and **Bob Sheldon**'s best friend. Randy Adderson is a handsome Soc, or member of the Socials, who eventually sees the futility of fighting. Randy speaks with **Ponyboy Curtis** before the rumble between the greasers and the Socs, assuring him that all the fighting is making him sick and he will not participate in the rumble.

Aunt Addie

Black Boy
Richard Wright

One of **Ella Wright**'s sisters. Addie lives at home with **Granny** in Jackson, Mississippi. She shares her mother's spite for **Richard Wright** and tries not to miss any opportunity to beat or humiliate him. She also shares Granny's intense religious nature and teaches at a religious school that Richard briefly attends.

Adeimantus

The Republic
Plato

One of Plato's brothers in real life and **Socrates**'s primary interlocutor in *The Republic*. The personalities of Adeimantus and Plato's other brother, **Glaucon**, are not prominent or well-defined. Adeimantus, who sometimes disagrees vehemently with Socrates, is perhaps the bolder of the two brothers, who are both intelligent.

Dr. Adler

Seize the Day
Saul Bellow

Tommy Wilhelm's father, a difficult man who abides by the rules of a previous generation. He is a Jewish American who has worked hard to establish himself as a successful and admired doctor and/or "professor." He refuses to "carry" his children on his back because he believes they should come to their own achievements.

Adolphe

Swann's Way
Marcel Proust

Marcel's uncle, who is a connoisseur of courtesans even into old age. He and **Charles Swann** nearly duel over **Odette**. Because Marcel accidentally visits him one day while he is with a courtesan, Adolphe never returns to Combray.

Adriana

The Comedy of Errors
William Shakespeare

The wife of **Antipholus of Ephesus**. Adriana is a fierce, jealous woman, already troubled with her marriage and social status before the double Antipholi become a problem. She is caught up in the madness caused by the double sets of twins in Ephesus, as she dines with the wrong Antipholus and eventually orders her husband bound for his strange behavior, even ordering an exorcism on him. Though her sister **Luciana** advises her to practice obedience in her marriage, it is the loss of her husband and the **Abbess**'s reproach that convince Adriana to become a more attentive wife.

Aegeus

Medea
Euripides

The king of Athens and **Theseus**'s father. In *Medea*, Aegeus passes through Corinth after visiting the **Oracle at Delphi**, where he sought a cure for his sterility. His appearance marks a turning point in the play. After he promises **Medea** sanctuary, she changes from a passive victim to an aggressor.

Aegeus

The King Must Die
Mary Renault

See above.

Aegisthus

Electra
Sophocles

Agamemnon's cousin and **Clytemnestra**'s lover. Aegisthus's father, **Thyestes**, and Agamemnon's father, **Atreus**, were rivals for the throne. Agamemnon's father cooked his rival's children—Aegisthus's brothers—and served them to him for dinner. With Clytemnestra, Aegisthus is responsible for the murder of Agamemnon. He is aware of the uneasy foundations upon which his position rests. He and his paramour, Clytemnestra, are eventually murdered by **Orestes**.

Aegisthus

Agamemnon and *The Libation Bearers*
Aeschylus

See above.

Aegistheus

The Flies
Jean-Paul Sartre

King of Argos. Aegistheus killed **Agamemnon** fifteen years ago, married his wife **Clytemnestra**, and took the throne. To maintain power, Aegistheus cultivates a deep sense of remorse in the people of Argos. He makes everyone complicit in Agamemnon's murder by holding a day of mourning when the dead supposedly rise from a cave and haunt the subjects of Argos. In his attempt to hold on to power, Aegistheus has lost his soul.

Aelroth

The Song of Roland
Unknown

Marsilla's fiery nephew who leads the Saracen ambush squad along with a dozen Muslim lords, paralleling the leadership of the Frankish rear guard by **Charlemagne**'s nephew **Roland** and the twelve peers. Fittingly, Roland kills him at Roncesvals.

Aeneas

The Aeneid
Homer

The son of **Aphrodite** and the only great Trojan warrior to survive the war. *The Aeneid* is an account of his journey from Troy to Italy, where it is claimed that he founded the city of Rome. Aeneas's defining characteristic is piety, a respect for the will of the gods. He is a fearsome warrior and a powerful leader, but also a man capable of great compassion and sorrow. Also a figure who appears in Greek mythology.

Aeneas

The Iliad
Virgil

See above.

Aeneas

Troilus and Cressida
William Shakespeare

A Trojan commander.

Aeolus

The Aeneid
Virgil

The god of the winds, enlisted to help **Juno** create bad weather for the Trojans.

Aeschere

Beowulf
Unknown

Hrothgar's trusted advisor.

Aeschines

Pericles
William Shakespeare

Pericles's advisor.

Agamemnon

The Iliad and *The Odyssey*
Homer

The King of Argos (or "Mycenae") and the commander of the Greek (or "Achaean") armies during the siege of Troy. Agamemnon is **Atreus**'s son and the older brother of King **Menelaus** of Sparta. Agamemnon's wife is **Clytemnestra**, and his children are **Electra**, **Iphigenia**, and **Orestes**. A strong but often reckless leader, Agamemnon sacrificed Iphigenia to the gods to secure a favorable wind to carry the Greek fleet to Troy. During the war, Agamemnon's arrogant treatment of **Achilles**, the finest warrior under his command, almost costs the Greeks the war. Agamemnon is away for ten years, during which time Clytemnestra and her lover **Aegisthus** plot to kill him to avenge Iphigenia's death and take over the kingdom. Agamemnon is murdered on his return from Troy, an act that Orestes later avenges. Also appears as a figure in Greek mythology.

Agamemnon

Agamemnon and *The Libation Bearers*
Aeschylus

See above.

Agamemnon

The Aeneid
Virgil

See above.

Agamemnon

Troilus and Cressida
William Shakespeare

The Greek general, and **Menelaus**'s elder brother.

Lady Agatha

The Picture of Dorian Gray
Oscar Wilde

Lord Henry Wotton's aunt. Lady Agatha is active in charity work in the London slums.

Agathocles

The Prince
Niccolò Machiavelli

Ruler of Syracuse (317–310 b.c.) who conquered all of Sicily except for territory dominated by Carthage; he is eventually defeated by the Carthaginian army.

Agave

The Bacchae
Euripides

Pentheus's mother and **Cadmus**'s daughter. Agave is one of the maenads, a worshipper of **Dionysus** who participates in orgiastic rites.

Agenor

The Iliad
Homer

A Trojan warrior who attempts to fight **Achilles**. Agenor delays Achilles long enough for the Trojan army to flee inside Troy's walls.

Aggie

Incidents in the Life of a Slave Girl
Harriet Ann Jacobs

An old slave woman who tells **Aunt Martha** to rejoice that **William** has run away. Aggie provides a counterpoint to Aunt Martha's reluctance to see her loved ones escape north.

Aunt Aggie

Angela's Ashes
Frank McCourt

Angela McCourt's sister and **Frank McCourt**'s miserly aunt. Aunt Aggie initially resents the McCourt children. Although she never ceases to be rude and unpleasant, she does help the family through tough times.

Agravaine

The Once and Future King
T. H. White

One of **Morgause**'s sons, and the brother of **Gawaine**, **Gaheris**, and **Gareth**. As a child, Agravaine is the cruelest of Morgause's sons, and he remains deceitful and cowardly. He holds a grudge against **King Arthur** because Arthur's father, **Uther Pendragon**, killed their grandfather to take his wife, Igraine. As it turns out, Arthur is also Agravaine's half-brother. Agravaine ends up killing Morgause in a fit of jealousy after he finds her in bed with a man.

Agrippa

Antony and Cleopatra
William Shakespeare

One of **Octavius Caesar**'s officers. Agrippa leads the retreat from **Antony**'s unexpectedly powerful forces.

Sir Andrew Aguecheek

Twelfth Night
William Shakespeare

A friend of **Sir Toby Belch**'s. Sir Andrew Aguecheek attempts to court **Olivia**, but he doesn't stand a chance. He fancies himself witty, brave, and adept at languages and dancing, but he is actually an idiot and coward. Sir Andrew helps Sir Toby, **Feste**, and **Maria** plot an elaborate practical joke on the puritanical **Malvolio**. Sir Andrew eventually becomes the butt of Sir Toby's joke, when he is persuaded to engage in a mock duel with Olivia's page, who is secretly **Viola** in disguise.

Agustín

For Whom the Bell Tolls
Ernest Hemingway

A trustworthy and high-spirited fighter with the guerrilla band that **Robert Jordan** commands. Agustín, who mans the machine gun, curses frequently and is secretly in love with the peasant girl **Maria**.

Ahab

The Old Testament
Unknown

The most wicked ruler of Israel. Ahab, along with **Jezebel**, spreads cult worship of the pagan god Baal throughout the northern kingdom. Dogs gather to eat their blood at their deaths, fulfilling **Elijah**'s prophecy.

Ahab

Moby-Dick
Herman Melville

The egomaniacal captain of the *Pequod*. Ahab lost his leg to the White Whale, **Moby-Dick**. He is single-minded in his pursuit of the whale, using a mixture of charisma and terror to persuade his crew to join him. As a captain, he is dictatorial but not unfair. At moments he shows a compassionate side, caring for the insane **Pip** and musing on his wife and child back in Nantucket.

Ajax

The Iliad
Homer

The mightiest Achaean commander after **Achilles**. Ajax's extraordinary size and strength help him wound **Hector**.

Ajax

Troilus and Cressida
William Shakespeare

A Greek warrior. Ajax is as proud as **Achilles** but less intelligent and less skilled in battle.

Ajax

Sula
Toni Morrison

The oldest of his mother's seven sons. Ajax has many lovers who often fight over him in the streets. The only true loves of his life are his mother, a conjure woman, and airplanes. At age twenty-one, he is a beautiful, graceful "pool haunt." Other men envy his way of infusing the most ordinary words with power. Ajax takes an interest in **Sula Peace** because she is so unpredictable. He and Sula have a passionate affair, enjoying one another's independence. For the first time in her life, Sula experiences the desire for possession of her lover. When Ajax senses her new domestic impulse, he abandons the relationship.

Little Ajax

The Iliad
Homer

An Achaean commander. He often fights alongside **Ajax**, whose stature and strength complement Little Ajax's speed and small size. The two together are sometimes called the "Aeantes."

Hugh Akston

Atlas Shrugged
Ayn Rand

A philosopher who champions reason. Hugh Akston taught **John Galt**, **Ragnar Danneskjold**, and **Francisco d'Anconia** at Patrick Henry University. He joins John Galt's strike of the mind early on, after society proclaims the death of reason. He works as a short-order cook in a diner, having chosen to no longer use his mind to help the powers of the government and the "looters." When **Dagny Taggart** seeks out Akston to find out who invented the motor that runs on static electricity, he cannot tell her, but he gives her a mysterious cigarette with a dollar sign printed on it.

Akunna

Things Fall Apart
Chinua Achebe

A clan leader of Umuofia. He and **Mr. Brown** discuss their religious beliefs peacefully, and by doing so Mr. Brown begins to formulate a strategy for converting clansmen by working with, rather than against, their beliefs.

Alai

Ender's Game
Orson Scott Card

A member of **Ender**'s launch group, and Ender's best friend. Often, Alai's friendship is enough to keep Ender from falling into despair. He becomes one of Ender's commanders in the battles against the buggers.

Alan

Holes
Louis Sachar

See **Squid**.

The Miss Alans

A Room with a View
E. M. Forster

Two old spinster sisters, Catharine and Teresa Alan, who are usually referred to in the plural. They stay at the same pension as **Lucy Honeychurch** and the others in Florence. The Miss Alans are mild-mannered and very proper, but they have an adventurous streak that eventually takes them traveling all over the world.

Alba

The House of the Spirits
Isabel Allende

Blanca's and **Pedro Tercero Garcia**'s daughter, **Clara**'s and **Esteban Trueba**'s granddaughter. Alba reunites the family after her grandparents' estrangement, through her love for them and their love for her. She devotes her life to her family and to her love for **Miguel**, the revolutionary. When she is young, she is molested by **Esteban Garcia**. After Clara's death, Alba is allowed to sleep in her mother's room, where Blanca tells Alba wild family stories. In reaction to her detention, torture, and rape at the hands of Esteban Garcia she convinces Esteban Trueba to help her write the story of their family. While she is being tortured in the fascist dictator's prison, being cared for by **Ana Diaz**, Alba ends up wishing she would just die. However, Clara appears to her in a vision and tells her that if Alba can start testifying to herself, she will not go mad and will eventually survive. Finally she is found with the help of **Transito Soto** and Miguel. Once out of prison, with the help of Clara's notebooks, she and Esteban Trueba start to compose the story of their family. When Esteban Trueba dies, Alba is not the last living member of her family because she is pregnant. The father of her unborn child may be Miguel, or it may be one of the men who raped her while she was detained.

Albany

King Lear
William Shakespeare

The husband of **King Lear**'s daughter **Goneril**. Albany is good at heart, and he eventually denounces and opposes the cruelty of Goneril, his sister-in-law **Regan**, and Regan's husband **Cornwall**. Albany is indecisive and lacks foresight, realizing the evil of his wife and in-laws quite late in the play.

Fra Alberigo

Inferno
Dante Alighieri

A sinner suffering, with **Branca d'Oria**, among the Betrayers of Guests in Ptolomea, the Third Ring of the Ninth Circle of Hell (Canto XXXIII). Technically, Alberigo and Branca d'Oria are not dead; their crimes were so grave that devils now occupy their bodies while their souls rot in Hell.

The Albino

House Made of Dawn
N. Scott Momaday

An excellent horseman who outdoes **Abel** and the rest of the participants during a contest held for Saint Santiago. Abel later murders The Albino for reasons that are left unknown.

Albino

The Princess Bride
William Goldman

The strange and silent character who takes care of Humperdinck's Zoo of Death.

Mitch Albom

Tuesdays with Morrie
Mitch Albom

Morrie Schwartz's former student at Brandeis University and the narrator of the book. After having abandoned his dreams of becoming a famous musician, Albom is disgusted by his desire for financial success and material wealth, though neither fill the void he feels. He has been working himself nearly to death, and suddenly finds himself out of a job when the staff at the newspaper he writes for decides to strike. Each Tuesday, he learns from Morrie that he needs to reassess his life, to value love over money and happiness over success.

Alceste

The Misanthrope
Molière

The protagonist and title character. Alceste's advanced age and disposition set him apart from the rest of the company at **Célimène**'s home. He is unforgiving, incapable of coming to terms with the flaws of human nature, and quick to point out faults in others. He tells Célimène, the woman he courts, all of her faults, while the rest of her suitors tell her only that she is perfect. Alceste is very jealous of her suitors, fearing that she flatters each of them, divvying out insincere compliments. Célimène is Alceste's greatest source of agony: he recognizes that love is his weakness and that he cannot reject her, even though he abhors her behavior. He is insulted when she rejects his offer to retreat into solitude with him, and he finally leaves her. When a verdict is passed that falsely attributes authorship of an obscene book to him, Alceste vows to live the rest of days in solitude, away from the society he has come to abhor.

Alcibiades

Timon of Athens
William Shakespeare

An acquaintance of **Timon**'s. When one of his friends is sentenced to death by **the Senators**, Alcibiades protests, and the government banishes him. He promises to raise an army and conquer Athens. Timon and Alcibiades meet in the wilderness, and Timon gives Alcibiades some of the gold he has found in order to finance Alcibiades's conquest of Athens.

Alcinous

The Odyssey
Homer

King of the Phaeacians. Alcinous hears the story of **Odysseus**'s wanderings and provides him with safe passage back to Ithaca.

Amos Bronson Alcott

Walden
Henry David Thoreau

A friend whom **Henry David Thoreau** refers to as "the philosopher." Alcott was a noted educator and social reformer, as well as the father of beloved children's author Louisa May Alcott. In 1834 he founded the Temple School in Boston, a noted progressive school that spawned many imitators. Affiliated with the Transcendentalists, he was known for a set of aphorisms titled "Orphic Sayings" that appeared in *The Dial*. Alcott also had a hand in the utopian communities of Brook Farm and Fruitlands and went on to become the superintendent of the Concord public schools.

Alde

The Song of Roland
Unknown

Alde the Beautiful is **Olivier**'s sister and **Roland**'s betrothed. She dies of grief the moment she hears of Roland's death.

Karen Aldrich

Ordinary People
Judith Guest

One of **Conrad Jarrett**'s friends from the hospital. They meet in a diner early in the novel to catch up on old times, but he feels compelled to curse at her because she doesn't seem to care that much. Toward the end of the novel, Conrad learns that she has committed suicide, and the news sends him into shock.

Alec

The Light in the Forest
Conrad Richter

True Son's pudgy white cousin. Alec takes after his boorish father, **Uncle Wilse**, in his treatment of True Son.

Alejandra

All the Pretty Horses
Cormac McCarthy

The sorrowful daughter of **Don Hector**, on whose ranch **John Grady Cole** and **Lacey Rawlins** find work. She is beautiful: dark-haired, blue-eyed, pale, and thin. She and Cole fall in love and start an illicit affair. When Don Hector finds out, he turns Cole over to the Mexican police. After his incarceration, Cole spends one last passionate day with Alejandra, but she cannot bring herself to follow him to America. She has been manipulated by her cynical great-aunt, **Alfonsa**.

Maria Alejandrina Cervantes

Chronicle of a Death Foretold
Gabriel García Márquez

An elegant whore with eyes like an "insomniac leopard." She eats excessively to mourn **Santiago Nasar**'s death. He wakes in her lap the morning of his death. At her house, there are musicians, a dancing courtyard, and "pleasurable mulatto girls." The narrator says she did away with his generation's virginity. The narrator goes to see her after the autopsy, and she refuses to sleep with him because she says he smells like Santiago.

Duke of Alençon

Henry VI, Part I
William Shakespeare

A French lord loyal to **Charles, Dauphin of France**. He commands a portion of the French army and at the end of the play urges Charles to sign a peace accord with the English.

The Aleuts

Island of the Blue Dolphins
Scott O'Dell

A Native American tribe that often comes to Ghalas-at to hunt otter, and the traditional enemies of **Karana**'s people. Early in the novel, conflict between the two tribes results in a bloody battle that kills many men of Ghalas-at, including **Chowig**, Karana's father. Because of this negative experience, Karana is initially mistrustful of them, but eventually she befriends one tribe member.

Alex

A Clockwork Orange
Anthony Burgess

A young man whose principal interests are rape, ultra-violence, and Beethoven. Alex is an arrogant aesthete of violence, taking joy in his crimes without a thought for his victims. Alex's confidence proves to be his downfall, as **Georgie** parlays his routine abuse of the gang into a mutiny that leads to Alex's arrest. Alex comes into the custody of **Dr. Brodsky**, who subjects him to Ludovico's Technique, rendering him physically ill at the thought of violence or classical music. Returned to society stripped of his capacity for violence, Alex is an easy target for former enemies such as **Billyboy** and ends up in the care of **F. Alexander**, an anti-government activist who drives Alex to a suicide attempt in order to discredit Ludovico's Technique. The resulting scandal frees Alex of the process. Finding he has matured, he yearns to make a life for himself away from gangs and violence. Occurring in the book's twenty-first and final chapter, Alex's epiphany was long omitted from American editions of the novel, much to the chagrin of its author.

Alex

Like Water for Chocolate
Laura Esquivel

The son of **Dr. John Brown** and the father of the narrator. He marries **Esperanza**.

Alex's parents

A Clockwork Orange
Anthony Burgess

A meek, kind couple. **Alex**'s parents are frightened of their son and do not want to know too much about his activities. When he is imprisoned, they lease his room to **Joe**.

Pope Alexander VI

The Prince
Niccolò Machiavelli

Father of Cesare Borgia; elected pope in 1492. Challenged by French invasion of Italy and a war between France and Spain.

Alexander the Great

The Prince
Niccolò Machiavelli

King of Macedonia (336–323 b.c.) who conquered Greece, Persia, and much of Asia.

F. Alexander

A Clockwork Orange
Anthony Burgess

A young subversive writer who takes **Alex** in after his beating at the hands of **Dim** and **Billyboy**. Alexander nurses the beaten Alex back to health, planning to use him as a political tool against the establishment in general and Ludovico's Technique specifically. However, once Alexander realizes that Alex and his gang had raped and killed his wife—the act that led to Alex's imprisonment—he plans to use Alex as a martyr after driving him to suicide.

Alexandra

Go Ask Alice
Anonymous

Alice's younger sister. Often Alexandra's ability to adjust to society makes Alice jealous.

Aunt Alexandra

To Kill a Mockingbird
Harper Lee

Atticus Finch's sister, a strong-willed woman with a fierce devotion to her family. Alexandra is the perfect Southern lady, and her commitment to propriety and tradition often leads her to clash with **Scout Finch**. She wants Scout to be ladylike and wear dresses instead of pants. She runs Finch's landing, where Atticus grew up. She thinks it is a disgrace upon the Finch name that Atticus defends **Tom Robinson** and other "trash," as she puts it. She holds a ladies' missionary circle in Maycomb when she comes to stay there.

Alexandro

The Spanish Tragedy
Thomas Kyd

A Portuguese nobleman who fought at the battle in Act I. Alexandro is betrayed by **Villuppo**, who falsely informs **The King** that Alexandro has shot **Balthazar**, the King's son. Alexandro's character appears exceptionally just; even when Villuppo is discovered, he begs **The Viceroy** (unsuccessfully) for mercy on Villuppo's behalf.

Alfieri

A View from the Bridge
Arthur Miller

An Italian-American lawyer. Alfieri is the narrator of the story. He speaks directly to the audience and attempts to make clear the greater social and moral implications of the story. He is a well-educated man who studies and respects American law but is still loyal to Italian customs. The viewpoint of Alfieri is the view from the bridge between American and Italian cultures; he attempts to objectively portray **Eddie Carbone** and the 1950s Red Hook, Brooklyn, community. He is cast as the chorus part in Eddie's tragedy. He is also the lawyer to whom Eddie Carbone goes in order to see if he can prevent **Rodolpho** from marrying **Catherine**.

Alfonsa

All the Pretty Horses
Cormac McCarthy

Alejandra's great-aunt. She lives on the ranch of her nephew **Don Hector**. An intelligent and intuitive student of human nature, Alfonsa had an aristocratic upbringing and a cosmopolitan, European education. In her youth she fell in love with one of Mexico's revolutionary leaders, but her family prevented her from marrying him. Alfonsa's personal sorrows, instead of making her more sensitive, have left her cynical and manipulative. She pays the bribe to get **John Grady Cole** and **Lacey Rawlins** out of jail, but only if Alejandra swears never to see Cole again.

Algernon

Flowers for Algernon
Daniel Keyes

A white mouse, the first successful test subject for the experimental operation performed on **Charlie Gordon**. The operation makes Algernon three times as intelligent as a normal mouse and enables him to solve complex puzzles.

Ali

The Count of Monte Cristo
Alexandre Dumas

Edmond Dantès's mute Nubian slave. Ali is adept with all weapons.

Mahmoud Ali

A Passage to India
E. M. Forster

Dr. Aziz's friend; a Chandrapore lawyer. Mahmoud Ali is deeply pessimistic about the English in India.

Sherif Ali

Lord Jim
Joseph Conrad

A fanatic Muslim bandit who terrorizes Patusan from a stronghold in the hills. **Jim** defeats Ali to become a hero in Patusan.

Alia

Dune
Frank Herbert

Duke Leto Atreides and **Jessica**'s daughter, and **Paul Atreides**'s sister. Alia's mother took the "Water of Life" before she was born. Alia had a conscious awakening while in the womb and even at her birth was much more intelligent than most adults. She kills **Baron Vladimir Harkonnen** in the novel's final battle.

Alia

Midnight's Children
Salman Rushdie

The sister of Amina Sinai, or **Mumtaz**, Alia suffers from a lifelong love for **Ahmed Sinai**, whom Mumtaz marries. Her resentment toward her sister manifests itself in the meals she cooks, and therefore affects those who eat what she prepares.

Alice

Henry V
William Shakespeare

The maid of the French princess **Catherine**. Alice has spent time in England and teaches Catherine some English; she acts as an interpreter between **King Henry V** and Catherine in the final scene of the play.

Alice

Alice in Wonderland and *Through the Looking Glass*
Lewis Carroll

An English girl of about seven with an active imagination and a fondness for showing off her knowledge. Brave and headstrong, she always follows through when she gets an idea. She quickly adapts to the rules of Wonderland, as she has come to expect strangeness and regards regular things as "dull and stupid." Alice's frequent struggles with issues of identity, especially when tied to physical change, could be interpreted as representative of every child's search for self as he or she passes into adulthood.

Alice

Go Ask Alice
Anonymous

The anonymous fifteen-year-old protagonist who keeps a diary intermittently. (The name "Alice" is an allusion to a Jefferson Airplane song.) An intelligent, sensitive girl with a literary flair, she experiments with drugs and the counterculture to escape her low self-esteem and consuming loneliness.

Alice Calais

Girl, Interrupted
Susanna Kaysen

A troubled patient who pronounces her last name "callous." Alice's mental breakdown results in her transfer to the maximum-security ward. Alice's appearance and the frightening austerity of the ward appall the girls when they visit.

Alice's father

Go Ask Alice
Anonymous

An unnamed professor who cares deeply about his daughter **Alice** but cannot communicate with her openly.

Alice's grandparents

Go Ask Alice
Anonymous

Beloved members of **Alice**'s family. Alice spends a summer with her grandparents, and they visit on holidays up until their deaths.

Alice's mother

Go Ask Alice
Anonymous

A homemaker who leads a traditional upper-middle-class life.

Aliokhin

"Gooseberries"
Anton Chekhov

Ivan's friend and owner of a large country estate where the protagonist shelters from a storm. Aliokhin typifies the successful Russian landowner—he is wealthy, contented, and even has a beautiful servant girl.

Alisoun

The Canterbury Tales
Geoffrey Chaucer

Alisoun is the sexy young woman married to **John**, the carpenter from **the Miller**'s Tale. She is bright and sweet like a small bird and dresses in a tantalizing style—her clothes are embroidered inside and outside, and she laces her boots high. She willingly goes to bed with **Nicholas**, but she heaps humiliation and obscenities on her other suitor, **Absolon**.

Mr. Allan

Anne of Green Gables
L. M. Montgomery

The new minister of Avonlea. Mr. Allan is a good man and a natural leader of the community. He and his wife, **Mrs. Allan**, earn the universal approval of the town.

Mrs. Allan

Anne of Green Gables
L. M. Montgomery

Wife of the new minister, **Mr. Allan**. **Anne Shirley** admires Mrs. Allan for her youth, beauty, and natural goodness, and frequently turns to her for guidance.

Rajah Allang

Lord Jim
Joseph Conrad

The corrupt, unofficial ruler of Patusan and the uncle of the legitimate but underage and possibly mentally incompetent Sultan. He tries to enforce a monopoly on trade in the area. Allang captures **Jim** upon his arrival in Patusan. He also secretly allies with **Gentleman Brown** against Jim. Also known as Tunku Allang.

Bobbie Allen

Light in August
William Faulkner

A waitress and prostitute. Bobbie was **Joe Christmas**'s first lover.

Miss Coral Allen

I Never Promised You a Rose Garden
Joanne Greenberg

A well-educated, elderly mental patient at Deborah's hospital. She teaches **Deborah** everything she knows about Latin and Greek.

Mr. and Mrs. Allen

Northanger Abbey
Jane Austen

The couple that invites **Catherine Morland** to Bath. Like Catherine's family, the Allens live in the rural town of Fullerton. They are older and wealthier than the Morlands, but they are childless, and see Catherine as a kind of surrogate daughter. Mr. Allen is a practical man who spends most of his time in Bath playing cards; **Mrs. Allen** is greatly concerned with fashion and spends all her time shopping, knitting, and talking to **Mrs. Thorpe**.

Mr. Alleyne

Dubliners
James Joyce

Farrington's boss in "Counterparts." Exasperated by his employee's poor work, Mr. Alleyne yells and insults Farrington until Farrington embarrasses him. He serves mainly to fuel Farrington's anger.

Bridget Allworthy

Tom Jones
Henry Fielding

Mother of **Blifil** and **Tom**. An unattractive lady who resents beautiful women, Bridget marries **Captain Blifil**, because he flatters her religious views. Although Bridget's affection wavers between Blifil and Tom as the boys mature, she becomes devoted to Tom before her death—largely due to his good looks and gallantry.

Mr. Allworthy

Tom Jones
Henry Fielding

Uncle of **Blifil** and brother of **Bridget**. Mr. Allworthy is benevolent and altruistic, just as his name implies: all worthy. The moral yardstick of the novel, Allworthy's only fault (which ironically propels much of the plot) is that, due to his goodness, he cannot perceive the evil in others.

Alma

Pigs in Heaven
Barbara Kingsolver

Cash Stillwater's daughter, who commits suicide. She is **Turtle**'s biological mother.

Almásy

The English Patient
Michael Ondaatje

The protagonist of the novel and the English patient of the title. Almásy is knowledgeable and reflective, the blank screen upon which the other characters project their thoughts and wishes. Though he is badly burned in a plane crash, he retains all his mental faculties and is able to tell **Hana**, **Kip**, and **Caravaggio** the pieces of his past and the story of how he fell in love with **Katharine Clifton**. Almásy strongly believes that nations are dangerous inventions, and that love can transcend both time and geography.

Alonso

The Tempest
William Shakespeare

The king of Naples and the father of **Ferdinand**. Alonso helped **Antonio** unseat **Prospero** twelve years before. He is acutely aware of the consequences of his actions, and blames the death of his son on his own decision to marry his daughter to the prince of Tunis. He also regrets his role in usurping Prospero.

Alphonso

The Color Purple
Alice Walker

Celie's and **Nettie**'s stepfather, whom the sisters think is their real father until Nettie learns the truth years later. When Celie is young, Alphonso rapes and abuses her until she moves out of the house. He takes the children born from the rapes away. Celie fears that he killed them or sold them. Unlike **Mr.** ___ and **Harpo**, who undergo transformations, Alphonso remains an abuser until his death. When Celie comes back to Alphonso to ask him if he is really her stepfather, and not her real father, she finds that Alphonso lives in a nice house on beautifully landscaped land with his fifteen-year-old wife, Daisy. Celie inherits the house and property after Alphonso dies.

Frank Alpine

The Assistant
Bernard Malamud

The stranger who appears in the Bobers' neighborhood and eventually takes over their grocery. Frank Alpine's struggle to reform is the driving conflict of the novel. Having robbed **Morris Bober**'s store, he arrives to work there as an effort to "make it up" to the grocer. But for all his efforts to become a better man, he continues to steal from Morris. Frank's pursuit of **Helen Bober** is likewise ambiguous. He seeks pure love but also lusts after her body and forces Helen to have sex with him. Only when his dishonesty is exposed does Frank really start to patch his life together again.

Doña Althea

Animal Dreams
Barbara Kingsolver

The matriarch of her family and of the Stitch and Bitch Club. Doña Althea expresses her strong beliefs in off-color remarks. When CBS News comes to cover the Stitch and Bitch Club's efforts against the mine that is destroying the environment of their town, they interview Doña Althea. Doña Althea is later revealed to be the cousin of **Codi Nolina** and **Hallie Nolina**'s mother, **Alice Nolina**.

Altisidora

Don Quixote
Miguel de Cervantes

The **Duchess**'s bratty maid. Altisidora pretends to be in love with **Don Quixote** to mock his romantic ideals.

Captain Alving

Ghosts
Henrik Ibsen

A pillar of the community and dead for ten years at the start of the play. Captain Alving was a very famous man with a good reputation, and before he died he was made a chamberlain. He never appears in the play but is often referred to by his widow **Mrs. Alving**. Despite his good reputation, Captain Alving was a lecherous man who sired **Regina** with the Alvings' maidservant **Johanna**. He eventually died of syphilis.

Mrs. Helene Alving

Ghosts
Henrik Ibsen

Captain Alving's widow and **Oswald**'s mother. Mrs. Alving lives with her maidservant, **Regina**, in a mansion in Norway's countryside. She married her late husband, **Captain Alving**, at her relatives' suggestion, but she had a horrible marriage. She ran away once, to **Pastor Manders**, to whom she was attracted, but he made her return to her husband. She endured her husband's debauchery, but when her son **Oswald** was seven she sent him away with the hope that he would never discover his father's immorality. At the opening of the play, Captain Alving has been dead for ten years and Mrs. Alving is in the process of establishing an orphan asylum to memorialize his death. She doesn't want anyone to doubt that her dead husband was a good and honorable man. At the same time, she is a free-thinking woman, and she feels compelled to tell her son the truth about his father.

Oswald Alving

Ghosts
Henrik Ibsen

Mrs. Alving's son. At the play's start, Oswald has come home to spend the winter with his mother. He has most recently been in Italy, living a relatively bohemian life. He is also a promising painter. **Pastor Manders** believes that Oswald has strayed from what is moral and also finds him reminiscent of his father. Oswald is by nature idealistic. He has felt a profound listlessness, for which he blames himself. He shows a romantic interest in **Regina**, who unbeknownst to him is his half sister, sired by his father **Captain Alving**. *Ghosts* depicts a transmission of sin from fathers down to sons in Ibsen's portrayal of both Oswald's improper advances toward Regina and Oswald's eventual contraction of the dementia associated with syphilis.

Alyona Ivanovna

Crime and Punishment
Fyodor Dostoevsky

An old, withered pawnbroker whom **Rodion Romanovich Raskolnikov** kills. Raskolnikov calls Alyona Ivanovna a "louse" and despises her for cheating the poor out of their money and enslaving her own sister, **Lizaveta Ivanovna**.

Alyoshka

One Day in the Life of Ivan Denisovich
Aleksandr Solzhenitsyn

A prisoner with a bunk that neighbors **Ivan Denisovich Shukhov**'s. Alyoshka is a devout Baptist who reads the notebook into which he has copied half of the New Testament late into the night. Alyoshka is known for doing favors for other inmates but never expecting or receiving rewards for these favors. By the end of the novel, Shukhov begins to respect Alyoshka's naïve goodwill, faith, and disdain of worldly goods.

Ama

His Dark Materials
Robert Pullman

A young girl who brings **Lyra Belacqua** food in the cave where **Mrs. Coulter** has hidden her. Ama also leads **Will Parry** to the cave.

Father Amador

Chronicle of a Death Foretold
Gabriel García Márquez

The local priest, who forgets to warn **Santiago Nasar** about the plot against him. Though everyone has amassed roosters and firewood to give to him, he never gets off of his boat. He just stands on the upper deck and crosses himself until the boat disappears.

Amanda

The House of the Spirits
Isabel Allende

A lower-class woman, active in university counterculture. She has a relationship with **Nicolas** and gets pregnant. **Jaime**, who loves her but will not admit this secret to himself, performs the abortion. After the abortion, Nicolas distances himself from Amanda. Shortly after the abortion, Amanda disappears from the story. She reappears twenty years later when Jaime helps to save her from illness due to drug addiction. Jaime is not really interested in a relationship with Amanda by this point. She becomes a revolutionary against **Esteban Garcia**'s fascist government after she recovers.

Amaranta

One Hundred Years of Solitude
Gabriel García Márquez

The daughter of **Úrsula Iguarán** and **José Arcadio Buendía**. She is the sister of **Colonel Aureliano Buendía** and **José Arcadio**. She falls in love with **Pietro Crespi** just as **Rebeca** falls in love with him. When Rebecca and Pietro Crespi are engaged, she bears deep jealousy for Rebeca and vows to stop their marriage. When Rebeca begins an extramarital affair, Crespi's tenderness for Amaranta grows. She cruelly rejects him, and he kills himself. She is also the object of the unconsummated incestuous passion of her nephew, **Aureliano José**, whom she helped to raise. In her loneliness, she comes dangerously close to requiting their love. When they are almost discovered kissing, however, Amaranta breaks off the affair, and Aureliano José joins the army and dies. When she is much older, she finds real love with **Colonel Gerineldo Márquez**, but she spurns him because of her ancient fear and bitterness.

Amaranta Úrsula

One Hundred Years of Solitude
Gabriel García Márquez

The third child of **Aureliano Segundo** and **Fernanda del Carpio**. Her father, Aureliano Segundo, devotes himself to raising the money to send her to Europe for her education. He sends her to Brussels and she returns bringing Gaston, her husband. While Gaston is preoccupied, her nephew, **Aureliano (II)**, takes the opportunity to admit his love for her. The love affair between the two begins fiercely and happily. Their house falls into total disrepair, destroyed by the couple's rampant lovemaking and by the red ants that swarm everywhere. In fulfillment of family matriarch **Úrsula Iguarán**'s old fears about the dangers of incest, the lovers' baby, whom they name **Aureliano (III)**, is born with the tail of a pig. Amaranta Úrsula bleeds uncontrollably after giving birth and dies.

Amata

The Aeneid
Virgil

Queen of Laurentum (a region of Latium, in Italy) and wife of **Latinus**. Amata opposes her daughter **Lavinia**'s marriage to **Aeneas**. Amata is loyal to **Turnus**, Lavinia's original suitor, and when it becomes clear that Aeneas will win the battle, Amata kills herself.

Reverend Ambrose

A Lesson Before Dying
Ernest J. Gaines

The fiery, self-righteous leader of the black quarter's religious community, and **Grant Wiggins**'s primary foil. Reverend Ambrose believes that true faith in God shields the believer against oppression, and that Grant is foolish for forsaking his religion. **Jefferson**, however, connects only with Grant, and the Reverend cannot convince Grant to attempt to save Jefferson's soul. In his conversations with Grant, the Reverend reveals his belief that lying is necessary for survival, especially among southern blacks.

Amelie

Wide Sargasso Sea
Jean Rhys

A young half-caste servant who accompanies **Antoinette** and **Rochester** to Granbois. The lovely and cunning Amelie snickers at her newlywed employers with a sort of knowing contempt, using her thinly veiled amusement to unsettle them. Later, Amelie feeds and comforts Rochester, then sleeps with him. When he offers Amelie a gift of money the following morning, she refuses it and announces that she is going to leave Massacre and go to Rio, where she will find rich, generous men.

Amos Ames

Mourning Becomes Electra
Eugene O'Neill

A fat carpenter. Amos Ames is a typical and relatively benign town gossip-monger. He sneaks around the Mannon property to spy along with his wife, **Louisa Ames**, and her cousin **Minnie**. After the Mannon house is boarded up and **Orin Mannon** and **Lavinia Mannon** are abroad in China, Amos hangs around with **Seth Beckwith**, **Ira Mackel**, **Joe Silva**, and **Abner Small**; they dare each other to go into the house, which they believe is haunted.

Cathy Ames

East of Eden
John Steinbeck

A moral monster and the most evil character in the novel. Cathy acts out of a perverse love of debasement, destruction, and control. As a young girl, she murders her parents by arson and then commences a life of prostitution. She later marries and then shoots **Adam Trask**, abandoning her newborn twin sons, **Aron** and **Cal Trask**, in order to return to prostitution. After murdering the brothel owner, **Faye**, Cathy becomes its madam, using drugs to control and manipulate her whores. Cathy represents Eve in the Cain and Abel story of the novel, introducing sin and evil into the world. Cathy commits suicide after Aron discovers that she is his mother.

Dalton Ames

The Sound and the Fury
William Faulkner

A local Jefferson boy who is probably the father of Caddy's child, **Miss Quentin**.

Louisa Ames

Mourning Becomes Electra
Eugene O'Neill

Amos Ames' wife. Like Amos, Louisa Ames is a gossip, though her tongue is much more malicious. She sneaks around the Mannon property to spy along with Amos and Louisa's cousin **Minnie**.

Mr. Ames

Sister Carrie
Theodore Dreiser

A New Yorker and a cousin of the Vances, with whom **Carrie** becomes infatuated. Mr. Ames represents, for Carrie, the artistic and scholarly tastes she wishes to acquire.

Lord Amiens

As You Like It
William Shakespeare

A faithful lord who accompanies **Duke Senior** into exile in the Forest of Arden. Lord Amiens is rather jolly and loves to sing. His tune about the pleasures of leisurely life displays the easiness of pastoral life, as opposed to the hectic nature of the city.

Amphinomus

The Odyssey
Homer

The only decent suitor of **Penelope**, Amphinomus sometimes speaks up for **Odysseus** and **Telemachus**. He is killed with the rest of the suitors in the final fight.

Mr. Amundsen

Sophie's World
Jostein Gaarder

Father of **Sophie Amundsen**. He sends his daughter a postcard early on, and it is clear that he cares for her, but his work keeps him away from home for most of the year. **Alberto Knox** seems to be much more of a father figure to Sophie than Mr. Amundsen.

Mrs. Amundsen

Sophie's World
Jostein Gaarder

Sophie Amundsen's mother. She provides a foil for Sophie's philosophical adventures. Mrs. Amundsen throws the garden party that allows Sophie and **Alberto** to escape.

Sophie Amundsen

Sophie's World
Jostein Gaarder

The protagonist of *Sophie's World*. Sophie Amundsen is an inquisitive and spirited girl who learns just before turning fifteen that her life is the invention of **Albert Knag**, the purpose of which is to amuse his daughter **Hilde Møller Knag**. Sophie learns this and many other things from **Alberto Knox**, the philosopher whom Albert Knag invented as her teacher. By the end of the story, Sophie shows that she is a philosopher, because she has the ability to look at things from a different perspective and she can act on what she thinks.

Amyntor

The King Must Die
Mary Renault

Theseus's most trusted friend among the Cranes. Amyntor was also one of the Companions in Eleusis. He is a catcher in the bull-dance, and his steadiness and courage help Theseus in Crete.

Anchises

The Aeneid
Virgil

Aeneas's father and a reminder of his Trojan heritage. Although Anchises dies during the journey from Troy to Italy, his spirit continues to help Aeneas fulfill fate's decrees.

Anderson

Regeneration
Pat Barker

A patient of **Dr. W. H. R. Rivers**'s in Craiglockhart War Hospital. Formerly a war surgeon, Anderson suffers a mental breakdown and finds himself unable to bear the sight of blood. Anderson doubts that he will ever be able to practice civilian medicine again. Once a strong, self-assured man, he is now reduced to a childlike state.

Major Anderson

Ender's Game
Orson Scott Card

Colonel Graff's second in command at the Battle School. Major Anderson sets up the battleroom scenarios, increasingly stacking the odds against **Ender Wiggin**. Ender views him with hostility, but, like Graff, Anderson feels for Ender. He questions some of Graff's actions but stands by him during his trial.

Ghost of Andrea

The Spanish Tragedy
Thomas Kyd

The first character we see in the play, and the first voice to cry out for revenge. His quest for revenge can be seen both as a quest for justice, since it is sanctioned by **Persephone**, the Queen of the Underworld, and as a quest for closure. Andrea is denied closure when he travels to the underworld, because the three judges there cannot decide where to place him; ironically, at the end of the play he becomes a judge himself, determining the places of the various characters in hell.

Count Andrenyi

Murder on the Orient Express
Agatha Christie

A very defensive man who tries to conceal the true identity of his wife, **Countess Andrenyi**. The Count takes his wife's place in **Ratchett**'s murder.

Countess Andrenyi

Murder on the Orient Express
Agatha Christie

The sister of Sophie Armstrong. She is the only conspirator who does not stab **Ratchett**. Because the Countess is closest to the Armstrong case, she attempts to conceal her identity by dropping grease on her passport and smudging the name label on her luggage.

Andrés

For Whom the Bell Tolls
Ernest Hemingway

One of the guerrilla fighters in **Robert Jordan**'s band. Andrés comes into conflict with the Republican leaders' bureaucracy in his attempt to deliver Robert Jordan's dispatch to the Republican command. Andrés serves as a foil to **Pablo**, the leader of the guerrilla band: although both Andrés and Pablo enjoy killing in an almost sexual way, Andrés has had the opportunity to satisfy that thirst through his experience with bull-baiting during a town fiesta. As a result, unlike Pablo, Andrés has learned to identify and control his desire to kill. Andrés's brother **Eladio** is also in the guerrilla band.

Anne of Green Gables
L. M. Montgomery

Jane Andrews

A plain, sensible girl in **Anne Shirley**'s group of friends. Jane is not particularly ambitious, imaginative, or pretty, but she is steadfast and reliable.

In Cold Blood
Truman Capote

Lowell Lee Andrews

A schizophrenic college student who murdered his family. Several of his years on death row overlap with those of **Richard Eugene Hickock** and **Perry Edward Smith**.

Anne of Green Gables
L. M. Montgomery

Prissy Andrews

A classmate of **Anne Shirley**'s. Prissy is a teenager when Anne begins her studies at Avonlea School and is considered grown up enough to court the teacher, **Mr. Phillips**.

Volpone
Ben Jonson

Androgyno

Hermaphrodite who, according to **Nano**, possesses the soul of Pythagoras, which has been in gradual decline ever since it left the ancient mathematician's body.

The Iliad
Homer

Andromache

Hector's loving wife, who survives the siege of Troy. She begged her husband to withdraw from the war and save himself before the Achaeans killed him.

The Aeneid
Virgil

Andromache

See above.

Troilus and Cressida
William Shakespeare

Andromache

Hector's wife.

The Angel of America

Angels in America
Tony Kushner

A terrifying divine presence who descends from Heaven to bestow prophecy on **Prior Walter**. The Angel seeks a prophet to overturn the migratory impulse of human beings, believing that their constant motion and change have driven God to abandon creation. Her cosmology is disturbingly reactionary, even deadly, and Prior successfully resists it in a visit to Heaven.

Evil Angel

Doctor Faustus
Christopher Marlowe

A spirit who embodies the negative aspects of **Faustus**'s conscience and will. The evil angel helps Faustus justify his unholy actions.

Good Angel

Doctor Faustus
Christopher Marlowe

A spirit who embodies the positive aspects of **Faustus**'s conscience and will. The good angel urges Faustus to repent and return to God.

Angelica

His Dark Materials
Robert Pullman

A vicious little red-headed girl from Ci'gazze, the sister of **Tullio** and **Paolo**.

Angelica

The Hours
Michael Cunningham

Vanessa Bell's youngest child, age five. Nervous and distractible, she is a classic youngest child whose older brothers indulge her whims.

Angelo

The Comedy of Errors
William Shakespeare

A goldsmith in Syracuse and a friend to **Antipholus of Ephesus**. After being barred from entering his own house for dinner, Antipholus of Ephesus tells Angelo to meet him at the Porpentine Inn with a gold chain, which he intends to give to the **Courtesan**. After Angelo gets the chain, he attempts to give it to **Antipholus of Syracuse**, who claims no knowledge of the transaction.

Angelo

Measure for Measure
William Shakespeare

The merciless nobleman whom Duke **Vincentio** leaves in charge of Vienna. He tries to enforce a strict code of sexual morals and sentences **Claudio** to death for impregnating **Juliet**. He hypocritically pressures **Isabella** to have sex with him, and then refuses to honor their agreement.

Angels

The Handmaid's Tale
Margaret Atwood

Officers in the military of the **Republic of Gilead**.

An-mei's mother

The Joy Luck Club
Amy Tan

A strong but sorrowful woman. Her husband died young, and she was tricked into becoming the fourth wife of **Wu Tsing**. Eventually, An-mei's mother committed suicide so that An-mei would not live a life of shame and unhappiness.

Anna

The Martian Chronicles
Ray Bradbury

An old woman who moves to Mars to retire with her husband **LaFarge**. They miss their son **Tom**, who died of pneumonia as a boy. When a Martian posing as Tom visits, LaFarge quickly guesses the truth, but he doesn't want to tell Anna, unwilling to destroy the peace brought by the illusion of Tom.

Anna Sergeyevna

The Lady with the Dog
Anton Chekhov

Dimitri Gurov's lover. Like the protagonist, Anna has grown dissatisfied with her provincial lifestyle. Initially the epitome of gentrified morality, she soon realizes that she would sacrifice everything to be with her lover.

Anne

Stranger in a Strange Land
Robert A. Heinlein

One of **Jubal Harshaw**'s three beautiful, extremely competent, live-in secretaries. Anne is also a Fair Witness, a professional, official observer of important events.

Lady Anne

Richard III
William Shakespeare

The young widow of **Prince Edward**, who was the son of **King Henry VI**. Lady Anne harbors a deep hatred for **King Richard III**, who has killed her husband and father-in-law. Nevertheless, Richard, for reasons of politics (and sadistic pleasure), approaches Anne at Henry's funeral procession and declares his love for her, hoping to win her hand in marriage. Though she understandably recoils at first, Anne is won over by Richard's verbal mastery, and she agrees to wear his ring and meet him later. Richard's conquest over Anne, perhaps one of his toughest challenges, proves his skill at manipulation. Just as the depth of Richard's evil becomes painfully obvious to everyone, Anne is summoned off to Westminster, where she will be crowned Queen. She reluctantly goes, well knowing that Richard will "no doubt, shortly be rid of me." Anne dies soon after, though the method is unknown. Her ghost comes to haunt Richard and praise **Richmond** the night before the decisive battle between the two armies.

Queen Anne

The Three Musketeers
Alexandre Dumas

Queen of France. She stays at the Louvre for most of the novel. Anne is Spanish, and her loyalties are divided between her Spanish heritage, her position as Queen of France, and her love for **George Villiers, the Duke of Buckingham**. Her husband, **King Louis XIII**, does not trust her, or particularly like her, and **Cardinal Richelieu** hates her. Anne leads an unhappy life in the court. Throughout the novel, Anne represents a kind of hard-to-reach figure who causes a lot of conflict simply because she exists.

Anne-Marie

A Doll's House
Henrik Ibsen

The Helmers' kindly, elderly nanny. Anne-Marie is also **Nora**'s former nanny. Like **Mrs. Linde**, Anne-Marie has made emotional sacrifices for money: she gave up her illegitimate daughter in order to take a nursing job.

Annette

Wide Sargasso Sea
Jean Rhys

Antoinette's young and beautiful mother. Annette is the second wife first to **Alexander Cosway** and later to **Mr. Mason**. A disembodied presence throughout the book, Annette often shows signs of madness and melancholy in her daughter's earliest recollections. After the fire, Mr. Mason leaves Annette in the care of a black couple who humiliate her and mock her condition. Annette dies when Antoinette is at the convent school.

Annie's father

Annie John
Jamaica Kincaid

A kindly, quiet man who runs **Annie**'s household. Before marrying **Annie's mother**, her father slept with other women and even fathered their children. These women occasionally harass Annie's mother on the street. Although he is relatively good to his family, Annie's father provides a reminder of the unequal gender roles in the Antigua of Annie's childhood.

Annie's mother

Annie John
Jamaica Kincaid

A strong, beautiful woman with a very close relationship to **Annie**. Annie's mother smothers Annie with attention when she is young, but as Annie grows up she learns that she and her mother are separate beings, which causes her great distress. Annie's portrait of her mother becomes tinged with jealousy and anger. Annie's mother has a breadth of powerful knowledge about nature, the rituals of obeah, and death.

Anny

Nausea
Jean-Paul Sartre

Roquentin's old lover, an English girl who lives in Paris. Even though she begs Roquentin to come see her, she is more interested in the man he used to be. She admittedly lives in the past, rereading the same history books and recalling the "perfect moments" of her life. She refuses to resume her relationship with Roquentin since she is already the mistress of a number of men who pay for her apartment.

Father Anselme

Dangerous Liaisons
Pierre-Ambroise-François Choderlos de Laclos

The Présidente de Tourvel's confessor. He is the priest who arranges for **the Vicomte de Valmont** to meet with Tourvel after she has refused to see him anymore. Because of this, Valmont finally gets to sleep with Tourvel.

Anselmo

For Whom the Bell Tolls
Ernest Hemingway

An old, trustworthy Spanish guerrilla fighter. Anselmo lives close to the land, is loyal, follows directions, and stays where he is told. He likes to hunt but has not developed a taste for the kill and hates killing people. Anselmo is killed at the end of the novel when he and the other guerrillas blow up a fascist-controlled bridge.

Antaeus

Inferno
Dante Alighieri

A worker in Hell; the giant who lowers **Dante** and **Virgil** from the Tenth Pouch of the Eighth Circle into the Ninth Circle.

Antenor

The Iliad
Homer

A Trojan nobleman and the father of many Trojan warriors. Antenor is an advisor to King **Priam**. He thinks **Helen** should be returned to **Menelaus**.

Antenor

Troilus and Cressida
William Shakespeare

A Trojan commander who is captured by the Greeks and exchanged for **Cressida**.

Anterrabae

I Never Promised You a Rose Garden
Joanne Greenberg

The most powerful being in the Kingdom of Yr, a world that **Deborah** created as a defense against a confusing and frightening reality.

Captain Anthony

Narrative of the Life of Frederick Douglass
Frederick Douglass

Fredrick Douglass's first master, and, most likely, his father. Anthony is the clerk for **Colonel Edward Lloyd**, managing Lloyd's surrounding plantations and the overseers of those plantations. Anthony is a cruel man who takes pleasure in whipping his slaves, especially Douglass's **Aunt Hester**. He is called "Captain" because he once piloted ships up the Chesapeake Bay.

Antigone

Oedipus trilogy (Oedipus Rex, Oedipus at Colonus, Antigone)
Sophocles

Daughter of **Oedipus** and **Jocasta**, and therefore also her father's sister. Antigone is the most courageous and clear-headed character in the three Theban plays. After **Creon** banishes Oedipus, Antigone cares for her old blind father throughout his exile. Whereas other characters—Oedipus, Creon, and **Polynices**, for example—are reluctant to acknowledge the consequences of their actions, Antigone always tries to do what is right.

Antigone

Antigone 1946
Jean Anouilh

The play's tragic heroine. In the first moments of the play, Antigone is opposed to her radiant sister **Ismene**. Unlike her beautiful and docile sister, Antigone is scrawny, sallow, and withdrawn. Antigone seems to have a death drive that is motivated by nihilism more than a sense of moral purpose. She defies **Creon**'s wishes and actively seeks the penalty of death, even though she knows that burying her brother won't solve anything.

Antigonus

The Winter's Tale
William Shakespeare

Paulina's husband and **Hermione**'s loyal supporter. He is given the unsavory task of abandoning the baby **Perdita** on the Bohemian coast.

Antinous

The Odyssey
Homer

The most arrogant and bloodthirsty of **Penelope**'s suitors. He leads the campaign to have **Telemachus** killed.

Antiochus

Pericles
William Shakespeare

King of Antioch. After his wife's death, Antiochus enters into an incestuous relationship with **Antiochus's daughter**. He makes her potential suitors agree to a test: either they answer a riddle or lose their lives. The action of the play begins with **Pericles**' arrival to try for Antiochus's daughter's hand.

Antiochus's daughter

Pericles
William Shakespeare

The princess of Antioch. **Antiochus**'s daughter has an incestuous relationship with her father. The play begins with **Pericles**' attempt to win her hand.

Antipholus of Ephesus

The Comedy of Errors
William Shakespeare

The twin brother of **Antipholus of Syracuse**, the son of **Egeon** and the **Abbess**, and the husband of **Adriana**. The Ephesian Antipholus is a well-respected merchant in Ephesus. The arrival of his twin brother throws his life out of order. During the day's incidents, he shows just as much ferocity as his jealous wife: when he is barred from his house during suppertime, he immediately seeks emotional revenge on Adriana by dining at the Porpentine Inn with the **Courtesan**; when his wife attempts an exorcism on him, he violently strikes the schoolmaster, **Doctor Pinch**.

Antipholus of Syracuse

The Comedy of Errors
William Shakespeare

The twin brother of **Antipholus of Ephesus**, and the son of **Egeon** and the **Abbess**. The Syracusan Antipholus has been traveling the world with his slave, **Dromio of Syracuse**, trying to find his long-lost brother and mother. His arrival at Ephesus throws the entire town into a state of confusion, since both his and Dromio's twin reside there. He declares his love for **Luciana** after dining with her and **Adriana**, who has mistaken him for his brother, her husband.

Pavel Pavlovich Antipov

Dr. Zhivago
Boris Pasternak

The son of a railway worker. He marries his childhood sweetheart **Larissa Fyodorovna Guishar** (later **Antipova**) and the two move to the Urals together to teach school. He joins the army and is captured, causing Lara to go to the front as a nurse to look for him. He is presumed dead, but later returns, using the pseudonym Strelnikov. Only he is aware of his double life, and when he thinks about going back to Lara and **Katya**, he does so with the conviction that it can be done only when he has lived this new life out.

Madame Antoine

The Awakening
Kate Chopin

A friendly local on Chênière Caminada, the island where **Edna Pontellier** and **Robert Lebrun** attend Mass. For the first time in their relationship, they are allowed to relax and speak openly with each other. The island, and Madame Antoine's cottage in particular, symbolize a freedom from self-isolation for Edna and Robert.

Matthew Antoine

A Lesson Before Dying
Ernest J. Gaines

Grant Wiggins's primary school teacher and predecessor as the quarter's schoolteacher. Antoine dies before the events in the novel begin, but his influence on Grant is felt throughout the novel. His defeated, resentful cynicism contributed to Grant's bitterness.

Antoinette

Wide Sargasso Sea
Jean Rhys

The daughter of ex-slave owners and the story's principal character, Antoinette is a sensitive and lonely young Creole girl who grows up with neither her mother's love nor her peers' companionship. In a convent school as a young woman, Antoinette becomes increasingly introspective and isolated, showing the early signs of her inherited emotional fragility. Her arranged marriage to an unsympathetic and controlling Englishman, **Rochester,** exacerbates her condition and pushes her to fits of violence. Eventually her husband brings her to England and locks her in his attic, assigning a servant woman, **Grace Poole**, to watch over her. Delusional and paranoid, Antoinette awakes from a vivid dream and sets out to burn down the house.

Mr. Antolini

The Catcher in the Rye
J. D. Salinger

Former English teacher of **Holden Caulfield** at the Elkton Hills School. **Mr. Antolini** now teaches at New York University. He is young, clever, sympathetic, and likable, and Holden respects him. Holden quickly assumes that Mr. Antolini makes a sexual overture toward him when he touches Holden's forehead. Later, this causes Holden to question his own practice of making snap judgments about people, when he realizes that Mr. Antolini was kind and generous.

Spiros Antonapoulos

The Heart Is a Lonely Hunter
Carson McCullers

A deaf-mute who is **John Singer**'s best friend. Antonapoulos and Singer live together for more than ten years until Antonapoulos is sent to an insane asylum at the beginning of the story. He is fat, greasy, and lazy, never signing anything with his hands unless he is talking about eating, drinking, or sleeping.

Antonio

All the Pretty Horses
Cormac McCarthy

A cowboy who works on **Don Hector**'s ranch with **John Grady Cole**. He is the brother of the ranch's foreman, **Armondo**. More than any of the other Mexicans, he becomes Cole's friend.

Antonio of *Merchant*

The Merchant of Venice
William Shakespeare

The merchant of Venice. Antonio's love for his friend **Bassanio** prompts him to sign a contract with **Shylock** and almost lose his life. Only **Portia**'s intervention saves him. Antonio is often inexplicably melancholy. As Shylock points out, he dislikes all Jews. However, Antonio's friends love him, and he does show mercy to Shylock.

Antonio of *Much Ado*

Much Ado About Nothing
William Shakespeare

Leonato's elderly brother, and uncle to **Hero** and **Beatrice**. Antonio causes the first ripple in the play when he incorrectly informs his brother that he overheard **Don Pedro** declaring his love for **Hero**. He later consoles Leonato over Hero's humiliation.

Antonio of *Tempest*

The Tempest
William Shakespeare

Prospero's brother. Antonio quickly demonstrates that he is power-hungry and foolish. He persuades **Sebastian** to kill the sleeping **Alonso**. He then goes along with Sebastian's absurd story about fending off lions when **Gonzalo** wakes up and catches Antonio and Sebastian with their swords drawn.

Antonio of *Twelfth Night*

Twelfth Night
William Shakespeare

A sea captain who rescues **Sebastian** after his shipwreck. Antonio has become very fond of Sebastian, caring for him, accompanying him to Illyria, and furnishing him with money—all because of a love so strong that it seems to be romantic in nature.

Antonio of *Two Gents*

The Two Gentlemen of Verona
William Shakespeare

Proteus's father and **Panthino**'s master. Antonio appears in just one scene, deciding to send **Proteus** to Milan to gain experience and worldly knowledge. Antonio's resolution to send his son away, despite Proteus's protestations, demonstrates the role that demanding parents have in determining the lives of their children.

Mark Antony

Antony and Cleopatra and *Julius Caesar*
William Shakespeare

A Roman solidier, friend to **Julius Caesar** and lover to **Cleopatra**. In *Julius Caesar*, Antony claims allegiance to **Brutus** and the conspirators after Caesar's death in order to save his own life. Later, however, when speaking a funeral oration over Caesar's body, he spectacularly persuades the audience to withdraw its support of Brutus and instead condemn him as a traitor. With tears on his cheeks and Caesar's will in his hand, Antony engages masterful rhetoric to stir the crowd to revolt against the conspirators. Antony's desire to exclude **Lepidus** from the power that Antony and **Octavius Caesar** intend to share hints at his own ambitious nature. In *Antony and Cleopatra*, Antony is a once-fierce and -feared soldier who rules the Roman Empire along with Octavius and Lepidus. When the play opens, Antony has neglected his duties as a ruler in order to live in Egypt, where he carries on a highly visible love affair with Cleopatra. His loyalty is divided between the Western and Eastern worlds. He is torn between the sense of duty and the desire to seek pleasure, between reason and passion, between West and East. While he feels the need to reaffirm the honor that has made him a celebrated Roman hero, he is also madly in love with Cleopatra.

Anu

The Epic of Gilgamesh
Unknown

The god of the firmament and the father of the gods, including **Ishtar**. Anu conceives of **Enkidu** and later suggests punishing **Gilgamesh** or Enkidu for slaughtering **Humbaba** and the Bull of Heaven.

Evelina Anville

Evelina
Fanny Burney

The heroine, a young girl of seventeen who leads a life of seclusion before her introduction to the world. The daughter of **Sir John Belmont** and **Lady Caroline Evelyn Belmont**, Evelina is beautiful, intelligent, delicate, and inexperienced. She leaves the guardianship of Reverend **Mr. Arthur Villars** to go visit her childhood friend **Maria Mirvan**, and from there the two girls go to London. The novel documents the process of Evelina's self-discovery in the often cruel world of high society.

Anya

The Cherry Orchard
Anton Chekhov

Ranevksy's biological daughter, Anya is seventeen years old. She seems to have lived a sheltered life. She greatly enjoys the company of **Pyotr Trofimov** because of his lofty idealism. Anya and Trofimov become so close that Anya's adoptive older sister **Varya** fears they may become romantically involved.

Apemantus

Timon of Athens
William Shakespeare

A philosopher and detractor of **Timon**'s. Apemantus scorns Athenian citizens and scoffs at Timon's greetings. He thinks Timon's friends are flatterers and money-grubbers. Apemantus is delighted when Timon's luck changes. He follows Timon to the wilderness merely to remind him that his villainous friends refused to loan him money. Although Apemantus and Timon insult each other vigorously, they form a curious bond.

Aphrodite

The Iliad
Homer

The goddess of love, beauty, and romance, and one of **Zeus**'s daughters. She is married to the ugly and crippled **Hephaestus** and takes **Ares**, the god of war, as her lover. By rewarding the Trojan **Paris** with **Helen**, the wife of the Spartan king **Menelaus**, Aphrodite sets off the Trojan War. Her son is the great Trojan warrior **Aeneas**, and Aphrodite remains on the side of the Trojans for the duration. In the *Aeneid* and other texts that follow the Roman tradition, Aphrodite is known as **Venus**. Also appears as a figure in Greek mythology.

Apollo

The Iliad
Homer

The sun god, the twin brother of the goddess **Artemis** and a son of **Zeus** and **Leto**. Apollo is also the god of civilization and learning, the master of arts and archery. His **Oracle at Delphi** is revered for her powers of prophecy and truth. He supports the Trojans throughout the war, and when they stop at Delos, Apollo's birthplace, the god helps them. In the *Oresteia*, Apollo sides with **Orestes** against **the Furies**, decreeing that **Agamemnon**'s son will not have to pay for his crimes, like so many before him. He is represented by his proxy, **Pylades**. Also appears as a figure in Greek mythology.

Apollo

The Libation Bearers
Aeschylus

See above.

Apollo

The Aeneid
Virgil

See above.

Apollon

Notes from Underground
Fyodor Dostoevsky

The Underground Man's elderly servant. Apollon lives with the Underground Man and performs household tasks for him somewhat grudgingly. The Underground Man detests him and his manner. He thinks that Apollon is constantly judging him and that he is unforgivably vain.

Apolonia

The Pearl
John Steinbeck

The wife of **Kino**'s brother, **Juan Tomás**, and the mother of four children. Apolonia, like her husband, is sympathetic to Kino and **Juana**'s plight.

Colonel Lazaro Aponte

Chronicle of a Death Foretold
Gabriel García Márquez

The lazy colonel who fails to prevent **Santiago Nasar**'s murder. A police officer warns him of the murderous plot, but the colonel had settled so many fights the night before that he is in no hurry to settle another. When he hears that **Angela Vicario** had been brought home on her wedding night, he realizes the connection between that event and the impending murder.

Apothecary

Romeo and Juliet
William Shakespeare

An apothecary in Mantua whos sell poison to **Romeo**. Though selling poison goes against the apothecary's morals, poverty forces him into it.

Appleby

Catch-22
Joseph Heller

A handsome, athletic member of **John Yossarian**'s squadron. Appleby is a superb ping-pong player.

Professor Nathan Appleman

The Chosen
Chaim Potok

The chairman of the psychology department at the Hirsch Seminary and College.

Arab

The Stranger
Albert Camus

The brother of **Raymond**'s mistress. The Arab wields a knife and threatens Raymond by constantly shadowing him. On the Sunday that Raymond, **Meursault**, and **Marie** spend at **Masson**'s beach house, Meursault kills the Arab with Raymond's gun. The crime is apparently motiveless—the Arab has done nothing to Meursault. The Arab is a mysterious character and so makes Meursault's crime all the more strange and difficult to understand.

Aragog

Harry Potter and the Chamber of Secrets
J. K. Rowling

A giant spider raised in captivity by **Hagrid**.

Prince of Aragon

The Merchant of Venice
William Shakespeare

An arrogant Spanish nobleman. The prince attempts to win **Portia**'s hand but makes an unwise choice of chest.

Aragorn

The Lord of the Rings Trilogy
J. R. R. Tolkien

The heir of **Isildur**, one of the few **Humans** from the great race of Númenor left in Middle-earth. Aragorn is a formidable warrior and tracker. He hides an impressive amount of power, greatness, and knowledge under a humble exterior. In *The Fellowship of the Ring*, Aragorn is introduced as a Ranger, a protector of the Shirefolk, or Hobbits, and other lands from servants of the Enemy, **Sauron**. As the action moves forward, we see Aragorn slowly transform into the King he is destined to become. He saves **Frodo Baggins** upon Weathertop when **the Nazgûl** stabs him with his Ringwraith knife. Aragorn displays bravery, kindness, and wisdom just as **Gandalf** does—indeed, neither of them appears to have any major faults. At certain moments, however, Aragorn does display a sort of vulnerability. When questioned about why he does not immediately offer proof of his identity to Frodo and the other Hobbits in Bree, one of his answers is simply that he wishes the Hobbits would count him as a friend without knowledge of his lineage—indeed, he is tired of being constantly wary. In *The Two Towers*, Aragorn is in league with **Gimli** and **Legolas** to aid the Hobbits in their mission to destroy the Ring. The three track **Peregrin Took** and **Meriadoc Brandybuck** after they are captured by **Orcs**. In *The Return of the King*, Aragorn is the King to which the title refers. He claims his right to the throne near the end of the novel, and takes the Elf **Arwen Evenstar** as his queen. Aragorn's character reveals itself in the roles he plays, and particularly in the symbolic actions he performs. He emerges as a Christ figure—one whose experiences resemble those of Christ and who performs a sacrifice that redeems others.

Aramis

The Three Musketeers
Alexandre Dumas

The youngest of the great Three Musketeers. The other two are **Athos** and **Porthos**. Aramis is a handsome and prim young man, quiet, and somewhat foppish. His servant is **Bazin**. Aramis constantly protests that he is only temporarily in the Musketeers, and that any day now he will return to the Church to pursue his true calling. Upon his second meeting with Aramis, **d'Artagnan** gets into a fight with him, tactlessly picking up a handkerchief from the ground that Aramis had been trying to hide, thus exposing Aramis as the lover of the lady to whom the handkerchief belongs. Aramis upbraids d'Artagnan for his rudeness, and the two set a duel for later that day. The duel never happens though, because d'Artagnan ends up helping the Three Musketeers fight some men in **Cardinal Richelieu**'s guard. Aramis's mysterious mistress turns out to be **Madame de Chevreuse**, a high noblewoman, whose existence and identity he tries to keep from everyone he knows. Thanks to Aramis, Porthos, Athos, and d'Artagnan, the sinister **Lady de Winter** is caught and beheaded. Aramis joins the Church after the conflict of *The Three Musketeers* is over.

Alexandro Aranda

Benito Cereno
Herman Melville

The owner of the slaves on the *San Dominick* and a friend of **Benito Cereno**'s. Aranda's death is ordered by **Babo**.

Colonel Arbuthnot

Murder on the Orient Express
Agatha Christie

A friend of Colonel Armstrong's, and father of Daisy Armstrong. **Hercule Poirot** suspects him of concealing his familiarity with **Mary Debenham** when he hears the Colonel call Mary by her first name on the train to Stamboul.

Arcadio

One Hundred Years of Solitude
Gabriel García Márquez

The illegitimate son of **José Arcadio Buendía** and **Pilar Ternera**. As a boy, Arcadio seems gentle. He grows to be the schoolmaster of the town. When **Colonel Aureliano Buendía** places him in charge of Macondo during the uprising, Arcadio becomes a dictator, obsessed with order and given to cruelty. When he tries to sleep with Pilar Ternera, his own mother, she sends him a young virgin named **Santa Sofía de la Piedad** instead. He marries her and she gives birth to **Remedios the Beauty**. Arcadio is executed by a firing squad when the conservatives retake the village. After Arcadio's death, Santa Sofía de la Piedad gives birth to his twins: **Aureliano Segundo** and **José Arcadio Segundo**.

José Arcadio Buendía

One Hundred Years of Solitude
Gabriel García Márquez

The patriarch of the Buendía clan. He is married to his cousin, **Úrsula Iguarán**, who fears having a child with a genetic deformity and refuses to have sex with him. The people of the village mock him, including his rival, **Prudencio Aguilar**, who implies that Buendía is impotent. Haunted by guilt, José Arcadio Buendía decides to leave his home. After many months of wandering, he founds the village of Macondo and becomes obsessed with magical implements given to him by **Melquíades**, the leader of the gypsies. Buendía goes on to immerse himself in scientific study, to the frustration of his more practical wife. He explores alchemy, the pseudo-science of making gold out of other metals. The desire for progress and intense search for knowledge lead Buendía to withdraw. He becomes unkempt, antisocial, and interested only in his pursuit of knowledge. But his obsession shifts to a desire to establish contact with civilization. He is exhausted by his endless research into the unknown and he slips into insanity. Buendía ultimately becomes convinced that the same day is repeating itself over and over again. He begins to rage, tearing up the house, and it takes twenty men to drag him out and tie him to a tree in the backyard, where he remains until the end of his life, many years later. He is survived by his children, **José Arcadio**, **Colonel Aureliano Buendía**, and **Amaranta**.

José Arcadio

One Hundred Years of Solitude
Gabriel García Márquez

The first son of **Úrsula Iguarán** and **José Arcadio Buendía**, from whom he inherits his amazing strength and his impulsive drive. When he is a teenager, he is seduced by a local woman, **Pilar Ternera**. Eventually, he impregnates her. Before their child can be born, however, he meets a young gypsy girl and falls madly in love with her. When the gypsies leave town, he joins them. He grows into a beast of a man—

enormously strong, tattooed all over his body, impulsive, and crude. Despite her engagement to **Pietro Crespi**, **Rebeca** is enthralled by José Arcadio's masculinity, and they begin a torrid affair. The affair ends in marriage, and they are exiled from the house by José Arcadio's outraged mother. When **Colonel Gerineldo Márquez** is captured and sentenced to execution by firing squad, José Arcadio saves his life. José Arcadio is a brother to **Colonel Aureliano Buendía** and **Amaranta**. He dies mysteriously, and it is unclear whether he has been murdered or has committed suicide.

One Hundred Years of Solitude
Gabriel García Márquez

José Arcadio (II)

The son of **Aureliano Segundo** and **Fernanda** and the brother of **Renata Remedios**. He goes to a seminary, but a few months after his mother's death, he returns to Macondo and becomes a solitary, dissolute man. It turns out that he has not been studying in the seminary but has rather been counting on inheriting a large fortune. When he discovers the gold that **Úrsula Iguarán** hid under her bed, he falls into debauchery, sharing with the adolescent children of the town in long nights of revelry. In his loneliness, he becomes friendly with the solitary **Aureliano (II)**. The two Buendías receive a visit from the last remaining son of **Colonel Aureliano Buendía**, who, like his sixteen brothers before him, is shot down by the police as he stands in front of the Buendía house. The developing relationship between Aureliano (II) and José Arcadio (II) is abruptly cut off when four of the children, with whom José Arcadio (II) once celebrated at a party, kill him in his bath and steal his gold.

One Hundred Years of Solitude
Gabriel García Márquez

José Arcadio Segundo

The son of **Santa Sofía de la Piedad** and her dead husband, **Arcadio**. He may have been switched at birth with his twin brother, **Aureliano Segundo**. Appalled by witnessing an execution at an early age, he becomes bone-thin, silent, solitary, and increasingly scholarly, like his great-uncle **Colonel Aureliano Buendía**. He and his twin share a strong resemblance until they are fully grown. Both of them start sleeping with the same woman, **Petra Cotes**, who does not realize that they are two different men. He finds purpose in leading the strikers against the banana company. The government invites him and more than 3,000 of the workers to gather for a meeting and then methodically kills everyone who attends. The corpses are collected onto a train and dumped into the sea. José Arcadio Segundo is taken for dead and thrown onto the train but manages to jump off and walk back to Macondo. There, he is horrified to discover that all memory of the massacre has been wiped out. The army and the government track him down at the Buendía house. They do not capture him, but the experience makes him terrified of the outside world. He takes refuge in the gypsy's old room, studying **Melquíades**'s incomprehensible manuscripts and trying to preserve the memory of the massacre. Slowly, his obsession leads to insanity. He dies at the same instant as his twin brother. In the confusion of the burial, he and his twin's coffins are mixed up, and each is buried in the other's grave.

Brave New World
Aldous Huxley

Arch-Community-Songster

The secular, shallow equivalent of an archbishop in the World State society.

Isabel Archer

The Portrait of a Lady
Henry James

The novel's protagonist, the lady of the title. Isabel is a young woman from Albany, New York, who travels to Europe with her aunt, **Mrs. Touchett**. Isabel's experiences in Europe—she is wooed by an English lord, inherits a fortune, and falls prey to a villainous scheme to marry her to the sinister **Gilbert Osmond**—force her to confront the conflict between her desire for personal independence and her commitment to social propriety. Ultimately, Isabel chooses to remain in her miserable marriage to Osmond rather than violate custom by leaving him and searching for a happier life.

Janey Archer

The Age of Innocence
Edith Wharton

Newland Archer's sister. Somewhat socially timid, Janey loves to gossip, grow ferns, and make lace. While she and her mother are devoted to Newland Archer, they are nonetheless frequently shocked by his social views.

Mrs. Archer

The Age of Innocence
Edith Wharton

Newland Archer's mother. Mrs. Archer behaves like a sister to her daughter **Janey Archer**. Both women adore Newland Archer, but frequently find his social views shocking.

Newland Archer

The Age of Innocence
Edith Wharton

The novel's protagonist. Archer is a wealthy young lawyer who marries, with some misgivings, the beautiful debutante **May Welland**. Archer is in love with May's cousin **Countess Ellen Olenska**, who represents to him the freedom missing from the suffocating environment of the New York aristocracy. Archer is torn between his duty to May and to his family, and his passion for Ellen. In the end, he remains faithful to his wife and comes to be known in society as a philanthropist and civic figure.

Archibald, Earl of Douglas

Henry IV, Part I
William Shakespeare

The leader of the large army of Scottish rebels. Though he and his men are first defeated by **Hotspur** in battle, Douglas is then joined in opposition to **King Henry IV** by the Percy clan. When faced with the loss of both the **Earl of Northumberland**'s and **Owen Glendower**'s military backup, Douglas responds with the same baseless confidence that Hotspur does, replying that he does not fear death. In battle, Douglas kills **Sir Walter Blunt** and finally runs away from **Prince Harry**. He is later reported caught, but Prince Harry sets him free as a reward for valor and integrity.

Archidamus

The Winter's Tale
William Shakespeare

A lord of Bohemia.

Archimago

The Faerie Queene
Edmund Spenser

Next to **Duessa**, a major antagonist in Book I. Archimago is a sorcerer capable of changing his own appearance or that of others. In the end, his magic is proven weak and ineffective.

Arcite

The Canterbury Tales
Geoffrey Chaucer

In **the Knight**'s Tale, **Palamon** and his cousin Arcite are two Thebans imprisoned together in a tower. Both men fall head over heels in love with **Emelye**. Arcite wins Emelye's hand in a tournament by praying for victory to the gods. Ironically, just after winning Emelye's hand, he dies when a divinely fated earthquake causes his horse to throw him.

Arcite

The Two Noble Kinsmen
William Shakespeare

Palamon's cousin and **Creon**'s nephew. A powerful fighter, Arcite remains concerned with his honor, his moral innocence, and his love for Palamon throughout the conflict over **Emilia**.

Dawn Ardent

Stranger in a Strange Land
Robert A. Heinlein

A famed stripper and a major presence in the Fosterite organization. Dawn harbors a crush on **Jubal Harshaw**, whose writings she has long admired.

Ares

The Iliad
Homer

The vicious god of war, hated by both his father, **Zeus**, and his mother, **Hera**. As **Aphrodite**'s lover, Ares generally supports the Trojans in the war, but for all his ruthless bullying, the god of war is also, paradoxically, cowardly—he also appears as a figure in Greek mythology.

Arete

The Odyssey
Homer

The intelligent and influential Queen of the Phaeacians, the wife of **Alcinous** and the mother of **Nausicaa**. Arete hears **Odysseus**'s appeal for assistance and helps him continue his voyage.

Filippo Argenti

Inferno
Dante Alighieri

A political enemy of **Dante**'s who was a member of the Black Guelphs and now resides in the Fifth Circle of Hell among the Wrathful and the Sullen (Canto VIII).

Argives

The Flies
Jean-Paul Sartre

The men and women of Argos, who completely accept their submission to **Aegistheus**. They live in constant repentance for their sins by always wearing black and never speaking out or committing any actions that could displease the gods. Aegistheus has attempted to make his subjects feel his eyes are on them all the time, judging them even in their private moments. The Argives, completely unaware that they are free, do not realize that when **Orestes** kills Aegistheus, he is actually doing them a great service. Fear and repentance have taught them to always look for external judgment so that they will never think of looking within themselves and finding their own freedom.

Father Arguedas

Bel Canto
Ann Patchett

A young priest and an opera lover. Although the terrorists are willing to release him, Father Arguedas asks to stay. During the four months of captivity, he says mass and hears people's confessions. He is one of the first characters to feel more concern than fear for the terrorists. He considers the four months during which he is able to hear **Coss** sing a gift from God.

Right Argument

The Clouds
Aristophanes

A personified school of thought. Right Argument is **Wrong Argument**'s necessary foil. He, like **Strepsiades**, represents the "old" or "traditional" system of education, one that stressed obedience, reverence for one's elders, values indoctrinated in martial poetry such as that of Homer, and physical fitness. However, like Strepsiades, Right Argument's overdeveloped sense of the physical will be his undoing: his own overzealous sexual appetite undermines the moral content in his argument, making him into a foolish pederast.

Wrong Argument

The Clouds
Aristophanes

A personified school of thought. Wrong Argument is **Right Argument**'s necessary foil. Like **Socrates**, Wrong Argument represents all that is wrong with sophistry and the "new education"—the specious moral content masked by slippery, well-wrought persuasion and rhetoric. Like **Pheidippides**, Wrong Argument is smug and disdainful of tradition. He has a facile mind, if not necessarily an upright set of values.

Ariadne

The King Must Die
Mary Renault

The daughter of King **Minos** of Crete, the highest Cretan princess, who does not believe in the gods. Ariadne falls in love with the hero **Theseus** and uses a golden thread to help him defeat the Labyrinth of the dreaded Minotaur—who also appears as a figure in Greek mythology.

The Tempest
William Shakespeare

Ariel

Prospero's spirit helper. Rescued by Prospero from a long imprisonment at the hands of the witch **Sycorax**, Ariel is Prospero's servant until Prospero decides to release him. He is mischievous and ubiquitous, able to traverse the length of the island in an instant and to change shapes at will.

The Rape of the Lock
Alexander Pope

Ariel

Belinda's guardian sylph, who oversees an army of invisible protective deities.

The Da Vinci Code
Dan Brown

Manuel Aringarosam

The bishop of Opus Dei. Aringarosa is conservative in his religious views and longs for the Church to return to strict ways. He has affection for material things that represent the power of his order. He is kind to **Silas**.

Love in the Time of Cholera
Gabriel García Márquez

Florentino Ariza

An obsessive man consumed by sexual desire. Florentino Ariza falls in love with **Fermina Daza** on sight and waits more than half a century for her husband, **Dr. Juvenal Urbino del Calle**, to die so that he may reaffirm his love for her. During the half century that passes, Florentino has over 600 serious relationships, which he records in a book. Florentino uses sex as an addict would a narcotic; it is the one means by which he is able to forget his heartache and his desire for Fermina, the source of all his anguish. His lovesickness is often equated with cholera, as he is plagued by his passion. He is insane with love, and exhibits borderline criminal behavior, stalking his love and watching her house. In his old age, he eventually wins Fermina Daza back and remains forever on a cruise ship with her.

Love in the Time of Cholera
Gabriel García Márquez

Transito Ariza

Florentino Ariza's doting mother. Transito Ariza is the one person to whom Florentino ever divulges his secret passion for **Fermina Daza**. She takes pains to prepare for Florentino's marriage to Fermina Daza, but after Fermina Daza rejects Florentino, she tries to get her off his mind by arranging sex with women like the **Widow Nazaret**. Transito turns senile and dies.

The Seagull
Anton Chekhov

Irina Nikolayevna Arkadina

One of the protagonists of *The Seagull*, a renowned Russian actress who stars in grand, melodramatic plays. She is the mother of the struggling playwright **Treplyov**, the lover of the famed author **Trigorin**, and the sister of **Sorin**. Her arrival at Sorin's country estate is the highlight of the year for her family. Arkadina's son Treplyov longs to join her among the Russian intelligensia and artistic community. Stubborn, vain, stingy, and beautiful, Arkadina is a selfish mother whose competitive spirit discourages Treplyov's creative impulses.

Ender's Game
Petra Arkanian — Orson Scott Card

Ender Wiggin's leader during his time in Salamander Army. They remain friends, though she is upset when his Dragon Army defeats her Phoenix Army. She is one of his commanders in the battles with the buggers.

Oranges Are Not the Only Fruit
Mrs. Arkwright — Jeanette Winterson

Shopowner in **Jeanette**'s town who specializes in ridding houses of vermin.

Love's Labour's Lost
Don Adriano de Armado — William Shakespeare

A Spanish wanderer, knight, and storyteller who has made his home in Navarre. With a highly foppish nature and great affectation of speech, Armado has become a source of mirth for the **King of Navarre** and his lords. Hopelessly in love with the milkmaid **Jacquenetta**, Armado catches **Costard** in the forest with her and promptly sends a letter to the court to get Costard in trouble. At the end of the play, after he is accused of getting Jacquenetta pregnant, Armado takes a vow to "hold the plough" (be a farmer) for three years in order to win the milkmaid's love.

Chronicle of a Death Foretold
Clothilde Armenta — Gabriel García Márquez

The proprietress of the milk shop where the Vicarios wait to kill **Santiago**. An insightful woman, she can tell that **Pablo Vicario** and **Pedro Vicario** are tired and are killing Santiago only out of obligation. In an attempt to save Santiago, she yells at him to run, and he sprints fifty yards to his front door.

The Killer Angels
General Lew Armistead — Michael Shaara

An officer of the confederacy and a 46-year-old widower whose wife's death causes him constant sorrow. A general serving in **General George Pickett**'s division, Armistead knows that his old friend **Winfield Hancock** is on the other side of the war serving as a general in the Union army. Armistead and Hancock both fight in the Battle of Gettysburg.

The Bean Trees
Mr. Jonas Wilford Armistead — Barbara Kingsolver

The legal authority in Oklahoma City who oversees **Turtle**'s adoption. An old white man, he treats **Esperanza** and **Estevan** like ignorant foreigners.

Holes
Armpit — Louis Sachar

Along with **Squid**, Armpit is one of **X-Ray**'s closest companions.

As I Lay Dying
William Faulkner

Armstid

A farmer. The Bundrens stay with Armstid on the second night of their journey. Armstid offers to lend them a team of mules, but **Anse Bundren** repeatedly refuses the offer.

And Then There Were None
Agatha Christie

Dr. Edward George Armstrong

A gullible, slightly timid doctor. Armstrong often draws the suspicion of the other guests because of his medical knowledge. He is a recovering alcoholic who once accidentally killed a patient by operating on her while drunk.

A Portrait of the Artist as a Young Man
James Joyce

Father Arnall

The priest who taught **Stephen Dedalus** Latin at Clongowes Wood. Father Arnall delivers a series of terrifying lectures on hell at a religious retreat, prompting Stephen Dedalus to repent for his life of debauchery.

My Brother Sam Is Dead
Christopher & James Lincoln Collier

Benedict Arnold

Captain of the Governor's Second Foot Guard, **Sam Meeker**'s company.

Jurassic Park
Michael Crichton

John Arnold

The head engineer at Jurassic Park, who previously worked with missiles and at amusement parks. Confident that he can control the entire park virtually alone, Arnold claims that **Dr. Ian Malcolm**'s predictions for the park represent a misapplication of chaos theory.

Babbitt
Sinclair Lewis

May Arnold

Riesling's widowed, middle-aged mistress. **Babbitt** finds out about **May**'s affair with Riesling when he encounters them together in Chicago during a business trip.

The Awakening
Kate Chopin

Alcée Arobin

Edna Pontellier's lover, whom she does not really care for. The playboy of the New Orleans Creole community, Arobin becomes Edna's lover while both **Léonce** and **Lebrun** are away. They have a sexual relationship and see each other frequently. As soon as Edna learns that Robert has returned to New Orleans and still feels devoted to her, she stops paying attention to Alcée, putting his notes under her maid's stove-lid.

Half Arrow

The Light in the Forest
Conrad Richter

True Son's light-hearted Indian cousin and most devoted, loving friend. A young boy who loves to laugh, Half Arrow is at times overconfident or naïve about his abilities to outmaneuver the enemy whites.

Martin Arrowsmith

Arrowsmith
Sinclair Lewis

The novel's title character and protagonist. Martin shows an interest in medicine early in his Midwestern youth and goes on to attend medical school. Though inclined stubbornly toward the ideals of science and research rather than the practice of being a physician, Martin abandons "true science" after graduation in order to support his young wife, **Leora Tozer**. After several disheartening professional experiences, Martin has the opportunity to pursue research again under the professor **Max Gottlieb**, who sends Martin and Leora to the Caribbean to try to combat a local plague. However, Leora herself falls victim to the plague, leaving Martin in a depression that a new marriage to the wealthy **Joyce Lanyon** fails to alleviate. Ultimately, Martin retreats to a rural area with his friend **Terry Wickett** to pursue independent research. Throughout the novel, Martin, alternately cold and compassionate, driven and easily swayed, struggles to reconcile his "pure" scientific ideals with the realities of commercial and financial pressure.

Arsinoé

The Misanthrope
Molière

A bitter woman who is older, unattractive, unpleasant, and thus unable to attract men. She masks her frustration with extreme manners and piety. Although she does participate in the gossip and rumor-mongering about the Court, it does not make her happy. Perhaps the only thing that could make her happy—**Alceste**'s love—is beyond her reach. She is jealous of **Célimène** and openly critical of her flirtatiousness.

Artemis

The Iliad
Homer

The beautiful goddess of the hunt, twin sister of **Apollo**, and a daughter of **Zeus** and **Leto**. Like **Athena**, Artemis is somewhat masculine. She supports the Trojans and also appears as a figure in Greek mythology.

Artful Dodger

Oliver Twist
Charles Dickens

The cleverest of **Fagin**'s pickpockets. The Dodger's real name is Jack Dawkins. Though no older than Oliver, the Dodger talks and dresses like a grown man.

Arthur

The Faerie Queene
Edmund Spenser

The central hero of the poem, although he does not play the most significant role in its action. Arthur is in search of **the Faerie Queene**, whom he saw in a vision.

Arthur, Duke of Brittany

King John
William Shakespeare

King John's young nephew, **Constance**'s son, and the rightful heir to the throne of England. Pushed by Constance and backed by the French **King Philip**, Arthur becomes a meek pawn in the game of royal succession. Arthur himself just wants to be a peaceful shepherd. Though King John orders **Hubert** to kill Arthur, the young duke's innocent nature prompts his would-be executioner to spare his life. Arthur does indeed die when he leaps off the castle wall trying to escape. His death appears to be a murder, which compels John's lords to join the French side in the war.

King Arthur

Sir Gawain and the Green Knight
Unknown

The king of Camelot. In *Sir Gawain and the Green Knight*, Arthur is young and beardless, and his court is in its golden age. Arthur's refusal to eat until he hears a fantastic tale conveys his youthful petulance, as does his initial stunned response to the **Green Knight**'s challenge, which he eventually accepts. At the story's end, Arthur wears a green girdle on his arm just like his nephew **Sir Gawain**, and his new garb acknowledges that Sir Gawain's trial has taught him about his own fallibility.

King Arthur

A Connecticut Yankee in King Arthur's Court
Mark Twain

A wise and gracious king. King Arthur tries his best, but he has a full share of the prejudices and superstitions of the day. **The Yankee**'s opinion of his intellectual capacity varies, but he is capable of learning and correcting his mistakes. When King Arthur goes with the Yankee around the country disguised as a peasant and is eventually sold into slavery, he changes his mind about slavery, deciding it is a terrible thing. King Arthur dies in battle in a war with **Sir Launcelot** over **Guenever**, which is revealed as the Yankee is dying in the nineteenth century.

King Arthur

The Once and Future King
T. H. White

The protagonist of *The Once and Future King*. King Arthur is known as the Wart in the first book, "The Sword in the Stone," and as King Arthur once he is crowned. He is a conscientious, slightly timid young boy who becomes king of England after being tutored by **Merlyn**, who actually drops off this son of the King **Uther Pendragon** to the castle of **Sir Ector** as a baby. As Arthur grows, he learns to believe in justice and in doing what is right. But Arthur's faith in good sometimes makes him blind to the intrigue around him. After Arthur becomes king, his ideas about government reshape English society, and these changes determine the plot, chronology, and setting of the four books that make up the novel. Despite Arthur's extraordinary importance to the novel, he is a fairly simple character. King Arthur shapes his government with an important new philosophy that makes him a great king, but the ideas are Merlyn's rather than Arthur's. Benevolent optimism keeps Arthur from acknowledging **Lancelot**'s and **Guenever**'s love affair early in the novel. Later, the same benevolence causes him to persuade them to keep their behavior secret so that neither is killed by the very laws that Arthur enacted. Even as he grows older and wiser, Arthur is incapable of acting harshly toward the people he loves. In a sense, it is Arthur's very simplicity and earnestness that enable the downfall of his reign. While the direct cause of the tragedy is Arthur's incestuous affair with **Morgause** and the birth of their baby, **Mordred**, we do get a sense that Camelot is also doomed because it has stagnated. This lack of innovation sets in around the time that **Nimue** imprisons Merlyn, suggesting that Arthur cannot think and develop without his old tutor. As Camelot stagnates and the quest for the Holy Grail takes its toll on the Knights of the Round Table, the enemy Orkney faction is able to gain more power, until Camelot is too corrupt to survive. Arthur dies knowing that his tales of his life will be recorded by **Sir Thomas Malory**.

Arthur's son

Cry, the Beloved Country
Alan Paton

Son of **Arthur Jarvis**. He is curious, intelligent, and generous. He treats black people with unusual courtesy and pleases **Stephen Kumalo** by visiting him and practicing Zulu.

Arthur's knight

The Canterbury Tales
Geoffrey Chaucer

A figure from **The Wife of Bath**'s tale describes King Arthur's knight as a man who rapes a maiden. **Arthur's wife** allows the knight to choose between death or going on a seemingly impossible quest. The knight chooses the quest, marrying an ugly **old woman** who promises to help him. The knight submits to the will of his ugly wife, and she rewards him by becoming beautiful and submissive.

Aruru

The Epic of Gilgamesh
Unknown

The mother goddess who gives birth to all humans. With **Anu**'s assistance, Aruru fashioned **Enkidu** from clay and her spittle.

Arviragus

Cymbeline
William Shakespeare

Cymbeline's younger son and **Imogen**'s brother. Arviragus was kidnapped and raised by **Belarius** under the name "Cadwal."

Arwen

The Fellowship of the Ring and *The Return of the King*
J. R. R. Tolkien

Elrond Halfelven's beautiful daughter. In *The Fellowship of the Ring*, she lurks around Rivendell during the Council of Elrond and speaks to **Aragorn** about the smashed sword, **Isildur**'s bane, which was used to defeat the Dark Lord **Sauron**. In *The Return of the King*, after the defeat of Sauron, Arwen marries Aragorn to become Queen of Gondor. This means Arwen must give up her Elfish immortality and pass up the chance to travel with Elrond and the other **Elves** to the Grey Havens as the Third Age of Middle-earth passes.

Joseph Asagai

A Raisin in the Sun
Lorraine Hansberry

A Nigerian student in love with **Beneatha Younger**. Asagai, as he is often called, is very proud of his African heritage, and Beneatha hopes to learn about her African heritage from him. He eventually proposes marriage to Beneatha and hopes she will return to Nigeria with him to help bring about positive change and modern advancements.

Ascanius

The Aeneid
Virgil

Aeneas's young son by his first wife, **Creusa**. Ascanius (also called Iulus) is most important as a symbol of Aeneas's destiny—his future founding of the Roman race. Though still a child, Ascanius has several opportunities over the course of the epic to display his bravery and leadership.

Gustav von Aschenbach

Death in Venice
Thomas Mann

An aging writer, honorable, fastidious, and repressed, of high public status in Germany. He travels to Venice and stays in a hotel where the beautiful boy **Tadzio** is also a guest. As he gives way to his repressed sexuality and falls in love with the young boy, he embraces beauty and the sensual side of art. He also abandons morality and dignity, abandoning himself to passion, decadence, and ultimately death.

Captain Edward Ashburnham

The Good Soldier
Ford Madox Ford

Florence Hurlbird Dowell's lover. The "good soldier" of the title, **John Dowell** describes him as "the cleanest looking sort of chap," "an excellent magistrate, a first-rate soldier, and one of the best landlords." He is generous with those who live on his land and even jumps overboard from a ship to save a drowning man. Edward is not practical; he is a poor manager of money and is easily led by instincts of lust and passion.

Leonora Powys Ashburnham

The Good Soldier
Ford Madox Ford

Captain Edward Ashburnham's wife. Described as a "sheer individualist," Leonora cares deeply that her affairs are in order and that the Ashburnham family maintains every ounce of propriety. She is economical, practical, and efficient in financial matters. Though she has the capacity to be deeply in love with her husband, Edward, she is also easily hurt by him. When wounded, Leonora defends herself with great power and cruelty. Above all, she seeks to have a normal life, free of the distractions of her husband's passion.

Asher

The Giver
Lois Lowry

Jonas's best friend. Asher is a fun-loving, hasty boy who usually speaks too fast, mixing up his words, to the exasperation of his teachers and Jonas. When Jonas and Asher are playing catch with an apple, Jonas for the first time perceives subtle changes, which will later be recognized as his special powers. Asher is assigned the position of Assistant Director of Recreation after **the Chief Elder** gives a long and humorous speech about Asher's pleasant nature and the trouble he has had in using precise language.

Asher

The Red Tent
Anita Diamant

Son of **Jacob** by **Zilpah**; **Gad**'s twin. The bearing of Asher and Gad leaves Zilpah half-dead.

Aslaksen

An Enemy of the People
Henrik Ibsen

The newspaper printer. Because he lets the paper print on credit, he has a degree of editorial control. He is also the chairman of the homeowners association, a group that represents the town's small business class and the majority of voters. Aslaksen has great influence with the Temperance Society and is a lover of moderation.

Aslan

The Lion, the Witch, and the Wardrobe
C. S. Lewis

The king and god of Narnia. Aslan the noble lion sacrifices his life so that **the White Witch** will spare **Edmund Pevensie**. After being resurrected the next morning, Aslan rises and defeats the White Witch once and for all. Aslan is awe-inspiring and a little frightening, but unquestionably benevolent and kind. Aslan's amazing love for the people of Narnia, even Edmund, a traitor, is demonstrated with painful clarity when Aslan sacrifices his own life to save Edmund. The novel's depiction of Aslan's death and resurrection is a clear allusion to the biblical story of the crucifixion and resurrection of Jesus.

Lucas Asphalter

Herzog
Saul Bellow

A childhood friend of **Moses Herzog**. Lucas is poor and becomes distraught when his monkey Rocco dies. He gives Moses a place to stay, and tells Moses about **Madeleine**'s affair with **Valentine Gersbach**.

Lord Asriel

His Dark Materials
Robert Pullman

Lyra Belacqua's father, the gentlemanly devil who plans to overthrow God and establish a Republic of Heaven. Lord Asriel had an affair with **Marisa Coulter**, Lyra's mother, and killed Mr. Coulter. For much of her life, Lyra thought Lord Asriel was her uncle. Lord Asriel kills **Roger Parslow** and leads the army of rebels against God. His daemon is **Stelmaria**, a snow leopard.

Assistant Manager

The Trial
Franz Kafka

Joseph K.'s unctuous rival at the Bank who is only too willing to catch K. in a compromising situation.

Asterion

The King Must Die
Mary Renault

The power-hungry heir to **Minos**'s throne, although he is not the King's son. Asterion treats other people as objects, and he insults his nemesis, **Theseus**, continually. Unlike Theseus, Asterion enjoys using his power and rules by fear, not respect.

Lady Astor

The Remains of the Day
Kazuo Ishiguro

A member of the "blackshirt" organization (British Union of Fascists) and a Nazi sympathizer who used to visit Darlington Hall.

Mikhail Lvovich Astrov

Uncle Vanya
Anton Chekhov

The play's brooding and deliberate philosopher. Astrov is an overworked country doctor who feels ruined by provincial life. He is always deep in introspection, finding himself numb to the world, unable to want and love, and dejected at the thought that he will be forgotten in the course of time. Continually described as "eccentric" and "strange," he nevertheless is something of a visionary in his passion for conversation.

Athelstane

Ivanhoe
Sir Walter Scott

A high-born Saxon nobleman whom **Cedric the Saxon** hopes to marry to **Lady Rowena**, thinking that their union could reawaken the Saxon royal line.

Athena

The Iliad and *The Odyssey*
Homer

The goddess of wisdom, purposeful battle, and the womanly arts, who emerged from the head of her father, **Zeus**, fully grown and armed. Like **Artemis** and **Hestia**, Athena is chaste. Along with **Hera**, Athena passionately hates the Trojans and often actively helps the Greeks, particularly the wily **Odysseus**. Confident, practical, and clever, Athena is a master of disguises and a great warrior, qualities she finds reflected in Odysseus's son **Telemachus**. In the *Aeneid* and other Roman texts, Athena is known as **Minerva**—she also appears as a figure in Greek mythology.

Athos

The Three Musketeers
Alexandre Dumas

The most important of the Three Musketeers, Athos is a father figure to **d'Artagnan**. His fellow great Musketeers are **Porthos** and **Aramis**. Athos lives in a finely appointed apartment with his servant **Grimaud**. Athos is older than his comrades, although still a young man, and is distinguished in every way—intellect, appearance, bravery, swordsmanship—yet he is tortured by a deep melancholy, the source of which no one knows. Athos makes an extraordinary confession to d'Artagnan. He tells of a "friend" of his, a nobleman, who married a young woman of humble background under his rule, breaking the rules of social conduct for idealistic love. One day, his friend discovered that this woman was branded with the Fleur-de-Lis on her left shoulder, a symbol put on the most heinous of criminals. The young woman was a fraud; all she wanted was money and social power. In mad sadness, Athos's friend hung his wife. This horrible and extraordinary story is clearly about Athos himself (Athos lapses into the first person toward the end of the story). The woman in the story is just like the **Lady de Winter**, who is also hiding a Fleur-de-Lis on her body, and is causing havoc on behalf of the Cardinal. After d'Artagnan manipulates the Lady sexually, Athos and d'Artagnan become convinced that the she is Athos's presumed-dead wife. Athos finds the Lady and confronts her. Athos, Aramis, Porthos, and d'Artagnan end up defeating the Lady, putting her on trial, and having her beheaded.

Athy

A Portrait of the Artist as a Young Man
James Joyce

A fellow student whom **Stephen Dedalus** meets at the infirmary.

Tante Atie

Breath, Eyes, Memory
Edwidge Danticat

Sophie's maternal aunt and first guardian, **Martine**'s sister and **Grandmè Ifé**'s daughter. Atie is devastated by two great betrayals: in her youth, **Donald Augustin** promises to marry her and then suddenly marries another woman, and in her old age, Atie's best friend, **Louise**, leaves for Miami without so much as a goodbye.

Miss Atkins

Light in August
William Faulkner

The dietitian in **Joe Christmas**'s childhood orphanage. When Joe overhears Miss Atkins having sex with a doctor, she believes Joe will turn her in and have her fired, so she takes steps to have him sent away from the institution.

Bill Atkinson

Lucky Jim
Kingsley Amis

An insurance salesman who lives in **Jim Dixon**'s house and is his drinking friend. Dixon admires Atkinson for the power and style of Atkinson's contempt for pretty much everything around him. He is a man of few words, and **Miss Cutler**, the housekeeper, seems afraid of him.

Miss Maudie Atkinson

To Kill a Mockingbird
Harper Lee

The neighbor of **Atticus Finch**, **Jem Finch**, **Scout Finch**, and **Calpurnia**. A sharp-tongued widow and an old friend of the family. She shares Atticus's passion for justice and is the children's best friend among Maycomb's adults.

Duke Leto Atreides

Dune
Frank Herbert

Paul Atreides's father. Duke Leto Atreides is the head of the House of Atreides and the rightful ruler of Arrakis. The duke received Arrakis from the emperor in exchange for Leto's own planet of Caladan, which was given to the duke's mortal enemy, **Baron Vladimir Harkonnen**. The duke is a wise, intelligent, and compassionate man, but he is ruthless when it comes to dealing with his enemies. He cares very much for his concubine, **Jessica**, and their son, Paul.

Paul Atreides

Dune
Frank Herbert

The protagonist of *Dune*. Paul is the son of **Duke Leto Atreides** and **Jessica**, the brother of **Alia**, and the heir to the House of the Atreides. At the beginning of the novel, Paul is fifteen years old. He has been trained from birth to fulfill the role of duke, and he is adept at combat and strategic thinking. Paul is also a quiet, thoughtful, and observant young man. Paul is not overly tall or muscular, but he is strong and quick. Among the Fremen, Paul has two names: Usul, which signifies strength, and Muad'Dib, the name of the desert mouse on Arrakis. He sires a child with **Chanti**, a Fremen woman. At the end of the novel, he kills **Feyd-Rautha Harkonnen** in a duel and marries **Princess Irulan**.

Atufal

Benito Cereno
Herman Melville

Babo's main coconspirator. He is a huge black slave, tall and muscular, who uses his size and strength to intimidate and threaten **Benito Cereno**.

Audrey

As You Like It
William Shakespeare

A simpleminded goatherd who agrees to marry **Touchstone**. The pairing, with Audrey's lack of vocabulary and Touchstone's constant wordplay, seems strange, but as Touchstone himself admits, "man hath his desires…" Though there ought to be an ideal achieved by the couple—the witty urban servant taking to the woods to find the pastoral love—Audrey is far from ideal for Touchstone in her lack of eloquence.

Audrey

Ordinary People
Judith Guest

The wife of **Beth Jarrett**'s brother, **Ward**. Ward and Audrey live in Houston and host Beth and **Calvin Jarrett** when the two play in a lawyers-only golf tournament in Houston.

Lena Auffmann

Dandelion Wine
Ray Bradbury

The wife of **Leo Auffman**. She counsels against Leo's creation of a Happiness Machine by pointing out that all is well in their lives. She understands from the beginning that true happiness comes from a loving family, and Lena does her best to help her husband see this.

Leo Auffmann

Dandelion Wine
Ray Bradbury

The town inventor, and **Lena Auffman**'s husband. Leo is as happy as he is brilliant. On a farcical suggestion from **Douglas Spaulding** and **Grandpa Spaulding**, he decides to build a Happiness Machine but finds that it only threatens the real happiness in his life—his family. He is devoted to his family and could not be any happier than when he's with his wife and children.

Tullus Aufidius

Coriolanus
William Shakespeare

A general of the Volscians, Rome's enemy. Tullus Aufidius is **Coriolanus**'s great rival in warfare, but he is not quite Coriolanus's equal. After suffering a defeat to Coriolanus, the two later ally to take over Rome. Coriolanus's failure to uphold the agreed takeover causes Aufidius to order Coriolanus's murder.

Monsieur Donald Augustin

Breath, Eyes, Memory
Edwidge Danticat

A relatively affluent and handsome neighbor of **Sophie** and **Tante Atie**'s in Croix-des-Rosets, Haiti. Though once in love with Atie, he married another woman, a betrayal from which Atie has never recovered. His post as teacher at the local school distinguishes him in the community as a professional man.

Madame Lotus Augustin

Breath, Eyes, Memory
Edwidge Danticat

Wife of **Donald Augustin**. Lotus is a pretty, gossipy, and self-important woman. In choosing to marry her, Donald breaks his engagement to **Atie**.

Captain Thomas Auld

Narrative of the Life of Frederick Douglass
Frederick Douglass

Lucretia Auld's husband and **Hugh Auld**'s brother. Thomas Auld did not grow up owning slaves, but gained them through his marriage to Lucretia. After attending a church meeting in Maryland, Thomas Auld becomes a "pious" man, but he uses his newfound Christianity to be even more self-righteously brutal toward his slaves.

Hugh Auld

Narrative of the Life of Frederick Douglass
Frederick Douglass

Captain Thomas Auld's brother and **Frederick Douglass**'s occasional master. Hugh lives in Baltimore with his wife, **Sophia Auld**. Thomas and **Lucretia Auld** allow Hugh to borrow Douglass as a servant for Hugh's son. Hugh is well aware that whites maintain power over blacks by depriving them of education, and he unwittingly enlightens Douglass in this matter. Hugh seems to know that slavery and the law's treatment of blacks are inhumane, but he does not allow this awareness to interfere with his exercising power over Douglass.

Lucretia Auld

Narrative of the Life of Frederick Douglass
Frederick Douglass

Captain Anthony's daughter and **Captain Thomas Auld**'s wife. After Captain Anthony's death, Lucretia inherits half his property, including Douglass. Lucretia is as mean to her slaves as her husband was.

Sophia Auld

Narrative of the Life of Frederick Douglass
Frederick Douglass

Hugh Auld's wife. Sophia was a working woman before marrying Hugh, and she had never owned slaves. Owning a slave transforms Sophia from a sympathetic woman into a vengeful monster.

Duke of Aumerle, Earl of Rutland

Richard II and *Henry V*
William Shakespeare

Son to **Edmund of Langley, Duke of York** and the **Duchess of York**; cousin to **King Richard II** and Henry Bolingbroke (**Henry IV**). Aumerle remains fiercely loyal to Richard throughout *Richard II*. After

Richard is deposed, he plots with the **Bishop of Carlisle** and the **Abbot of Westminster** to assassinate Henry IV. The discovery of the conspiratorial letter by his father and mother pits the loyalty to the family against the loyalty to the state. Aumerle's father, the Duke of York, rushes to Henry IV to expose his son as a traitor, while his mother rushes right behind him to beg Henry to pardon him. The newly crowned king does magnanimously pardon Aumerle, but executes the Abbot of Westminster. In *Henry V*, Aumerle—now Duke of York himself—is one of the few English nobles to die at Agincourt. His death is related in emotional terms by the **Duke of Exeter**: apparently, the wounded York (Aumerle) lay down to die beside the body of his beloved cousin Suffolk (**Michael de la Pole, Earl of Suffolk**).

Heart of Darkness
Joseph Conrad

Aunt

Marlow's doting relative, who secures him a position with the Company. She believes firmly in imperialism as a charitable activity that brings civilization and religion to suffering, simple savages. To Marlow, she is an example of womanly naïveté.

The Kitchen God's Wife
Amy Tan

Old Aunt and New Aunt

Winnie's aunts. New Aunt and Old Aunt raise Winnie in Winnie's father's house. Old Aunt is the more socially conservative of the two, basing her beliefs on ancient Chinese customs. New Aunt is younger and more easygoing, yet still conservative. Both aunts treat Winnie as an outsider of sorts, but later, when the war is over, they seem to have real love for her.

The Shipping News
E. Annie Proulx

The aunt

The "stouthearted" woman in **Quoyle**'s life. The aunt is the sister of Quoyle's father, **Guy**. She is nostalgic for her childhood home in Newfoundland and determined to repair the old family house to a state of livability. She recognizes **Petal Bear**'s cruelty and helps Quoyle get his life back on track by whisking him, **Sunshine**, and **Bunny** away to Newfoundland. The aunt has past pains of her own, including the death of her lesbian partner **Irene Warren**, the death of her dog, **Warren**, and the trauma of being sexually abused by Guy.

Ceremony
Leslie Marmon Silko

Auntie

Tayo's aunt. As the eldest daughter in her family, she is in charge of running the household and caring for the family. Although she performs her duties diligently, Auntie is a proud and spiteful woman. She is largely responsible for Tayo's sense of exclusion from his family. In addition to following the old Native American traditions almost blindly, Auntie is a devout Christian who thrives on martyrdom.

Shabanu
Suzanne Fisher Staples

Auntie

Dadi's sister-in-law, Auntie, lives with **Shabanu**'s family in the desert. Her husband, Dadi's brother, works in a government office in Rahimyar Khan. Auntie is a fat and bitter woman. She is proud that she has borne **Uncle** two sons, but she feels displaced and lonely among her husband's relatives.

Aunts

The Handmaid's Tale
Margaret Atwood

Older, unmarried women. The Aunts work as disciplinarians and midwives and train **Handmaids**-to-be.

Aureliano (II)

One Hundred Years of Solitude
Gabriel García Márquez

The illegitimate son of **Meme** and **Mauricio Babilonia**. He was brought to the house by a nun, and his grandmother, **Fernanda del Carpio**, keeps him hidden in **Colonel Aureliano Buendía**'s old workshop. Ashamed of Meme's actions, Fernanda del Carpio pretends that Aureliano (II) is a foundling. When he finally escapes from the room where she hides him, **Aureliano Segundo** takes care of him. Aureliano (II) falls into the pattern of the family's tall, thin, solitary Aurelianos. He grows up a hermit in the Buendía household, only gradually acclimating himself to society. He becomes a scholar and works in **Melquíades**' old laboratory. In his pursuit of prophetic knowledge and the history of Macondo, Aureliano (II) discovers that practically all of the town's history has been forgotten. One day, when he wanders the rundown town, he discovers almost no one remembers the Buendías, once the most notable family in the village. Following the family propensity toward incestuous love, Aureliano (II) falls in love with his aunt, **Amaranta Úrsula**.

Aureliano Segundo

One Hundred Years of Solitude
Gabriel García Márquez

The son of **Arcadio** and **Santa Sofía de la Piedad**. Although he loves the concubine **Petra Cotes**, he is married to the cold beauty **Fernanda del Carpio**, with whom he has three children: **Meme**, **José Arcadio (II)** and **Amaranta Úrsula**. In his adolescence, Aureliano Segundo begins to delve into the esoteric mysteries still preserved in **Melquíades**' laboratory. His twin brother is **José Arcadio Segundo**. When they both start sleeping with Petra Cotes, she does not realize they are two different men. Petra Cotes and Aureliano Segundo have a fierce passion for each other, and something magical in their union causes their farm animals to be supernaturally fertile. Soon, Aureliano Segundo becomes fabulously wealthy by virtue of his livestock's productivity. He throws huge parties and engages in colossal displays of wealth. The whole village seems to share in his prosperity. When he returns to his wife, she torments him, and he loses his temper and breaks every valuable thing in the house. He devotes himself to raising the money to send Amaranta Úrsula to Europe for her education, but his great strength of former years has left him, and he begins to die. In the confusion of his funeral, Aureliano Segundo and José Arcadio Segundo's coffins are mixed up, and each is buried in the other's grave.

Aureliano José

One Hundred Years of Solitude
Gabriel García Márquez

The bastard son of **Colonel Aureliano Buendía** and **Pilar Ternera**. He falls in love with his aunt, **Amaranta**, who steadily rebuffs his protestations of love. She becomes more and more used to his presence, and in her loneliness, she comes dangerously close to requiting their love. When they are almost discovered kissing, however, Amaranta, repelled by the notion of incest, breaks off the affair. Aureliano José goes off to war and then deserts the rebel army and returns home, hoping to marry Amaranta, who continues to avoid him. The situation comes to a tragic close when Aureliano José is killed by a Conservative soldier during an act of civil disobedience.

Austin

True West
Sam Shepard

An Ivy League graduate who works as a screenwriter; younger brother of **Lee**; son of **Mom**. Austin has a wife and children in Northern California, but is working at his mother's house in Southern California while she is away in Alaska. Austin can be seen as one half of the creative process: the methodical, diligent aspect in contrast to Lee's wild, creative, inspired side. Together they form the basic ingredients of an artist and are able to write the beginnings of a screenplay.

Duke of Austria

King John
William Shakespeare

The killer of **King Richard** the Lionheart (**King John**'s eldest brother). He allies himself with the French to atone for his deed and receives **Arthur**'s forgiveness. During the first meeting between King John and **King Philip**, the Duke of Austria engages in a bitter argument with **Philip the Bastard**; this conflict is later brought to a "head" when the Bastard decapitates him in war.

Autolycus

The Winter's Tale
William Shakespeare

A roguish peddler, vagabond, and pickpocket. Autolycus steals the **Clown**'s purse and does a great deal of pilfering at the **Shepherd**'s sheepshearing, but at the end helps **Perdita** and **Florizel** elope.

Countess of Auvergne

Henry VI, Part I
William Shakespeare

A French noblewoman who lures **Lord Talbot** to her castle in the hopes of capturing him and saving France from the English. Her plot and his reaction serve as a symbol of the outmoded chivalry that seems to have its last vestige in Talbot. When the Countess declares that he is captured, Talbot responds that she's mistaken to think of him as just a single body; rather, he represents the collective body of his army. Understanding the true power of Talbot, the Countess apologizes and invites the English commander and his troops for dinner.

Janice Avery

Bridge to Terabithia
Katherine Paterson

A seventh-grader and the school bully. Janice terrorizes **May Belle Aarons**, as well as the rest of the younger kids, until **Jesse Oliver Aarons, Jr.** and **Leslie Burke** find a way of getting back at her. Janice has her own problems that make her somewhat sympathetic. Her father abuses her, and when her friends blab her secrets to the entire school, her tough-girl persona snaps. It is Leslie who comforts her, at Jess's urging, giving rise to an unlikely friendship between them.

Miss Avery

Howards End
E. M. Forster

An elderly spinster living in Hilton who takes care of Howards End when it is unoccupied. She is a childhood friend of **Mrs. Wilcox**'s.

Shug Avery

The Color Purple
Alice Walker

A sultry blues singer who first appears as **Mr.** ___'s mistress. Our first impression of Shug Avery is negative. We learn she has a reputation as a woman of dubious morals who dresses scantily, has some sort of "nasty woman disease," and is spurned by her own parents. **Celie** immediately sees something more in Shug than the others see. When Celie looks at Shug's photograph, not only does Shug's glamorous appearance amaze her but Shug reminds Celie of her "mama." Shug becomes Celie's friend and eventually her lover, all the while remaining a gentle mentor who helps Celie evolve into an independent and assertive woman. Shug does not at first appear to be the mothering kind, yet she nurtures Celie physically, spiritually, and emotionally. Despite her unpredictable nature and shifting roles, Shug remains Celie's most constant friend and companion.

T. J. Avery

Roll of Thunder, Hear My Cry
Mildred D. Taylor

A trouble-making friend of **Stacey Logan**'s. The Averies are sharecroppers on **Harlan Granger**'s land. The other children ostracize T.J. because they find out he is responsible for the gossip at the Wallace store that has resulted in Mama's getting fired from teaching. T.J. befriends some white kids, **Melvin Simms** and **R. W. Simms**, who take advantage of him and frame him in a robbery in the town of Strawberry, which turns into an event with a lynch mob and a direct threat to the Logan family: the mob threatens to hang T.J., L.T., and **Papa** at the Logan house.

Al Axelrad

Tuesdays with Morrie
Mitch Albom

A rabbi from Brandeis and a longtime friend of **Morrie Schwartz**'s. He performs Morrie's funeral service.

Eeben Axelroot

The Poisonwood Bible
Barbara Kingsolver

A mercenary pilot and CIA operative who is integral in the U.S.-orchestrated coup that overthrows **Patrice Lumumba**. Slimy and immoral, he refuses to deliver the Prices' weekly mail and provisions without a bribe. In order to avoid marrying Chief Ndu, **Rachel Price** is forced to pretend she is engaged to Axelroot. The fake engagement leads to a fake marriage when he saves Rachel from the Congo by flying her to South Africa.

Prior Aymer

Ivanhoe
Sir Walter Scott

The abbot of a monastery, and a companion of **Brian de Bois-Guilbert**'s. The prior is addicted to good food and pleasure, and Scott uses him to represent the hypocrisies of the medieval church.

Ayooba

Midnight's Children
Salman Rushdie

Farooq, **Shaheed**, and Ayooba are **Saleem**'s fellow soldiers in the Pakistani army.

Azar

The Things They Carried
Tim O'Brien

A soldier with **Tim O'Brien** in Alpha Company. Azar is one of the few unsympathetic characters in the work. He tortures Vietnamese civilians and pokes fun at the dead—enemy and fellow soldiers alike. In a moment of remorse, he helps unearth **Kiowa**'s body from the muck of the sewage field.

King Azaz

The Phantom Tollbooth
Norton Juster

Ruler of the realm of letters and words. Azaz and his brother argue over which is more important—numbers or letters—and they banish the princesses **Rhyme** and **Reason**. Once he realizes the foolishness of his squabble, King Azaz sends **Milo** to rescue the princesses.

Azelma

Les Misérables
Victor Hugo

M. Thénardier and **M'me. Thénardier**'s younger daughter. She grows up pampered and spoiled but ends up enduring the same poverty as the rest of her family.

Aadam Aziz

Midnight's Children
Salman Rushdie

Aadam Aziz is a doctor and the father of Amina Sinai, or **Mumtaz**. He has many children with **Naseem Ghani**, and struggles with questions of the existence of God throughout his life.

Dr. Aziz

A Passage to India
E. M. Forster

The novel's protagonist. Dr. Aziz is an intelligent, emotional Muslim Indian doctor in Chandrapore. A widower, Aziz has three children who live with their grandmother. He enjoys writing and reciting poetry.

Azolan

Dangerous Liaisons
Pierre-Ambroise-François Choderlos de Laclos

The valet of **the Vicomte de Valmont**. Azolan is often required to offer bribes and sleep with other servants, especially those of **the Présidente de Tourvel**, to get information for his master.

19

IRRESISTIBLE BEAUTIES

NO ONE CAN RESIST THESE LOOKERS.

Aphrodite	1	*The Iliad*
Arwen Evenstar	2	*The Lord of the Rings* trilogy
Bianca	3	*The Taming of the Shrew*
Emma Bovary	4	*Emma Bovary*
Rhett Butler	5	*Gone with the Wind*
Cunegonde	6	*Candide*
Fleur Delacour	7	*Harry Potter and the Goblet of Fire*
La Esmerelda	8	*The Hunchback of Notre Dame*
Gwendolen Fairfax	9	*The Importance of Being Earnest*
Trip Fontaine	10	*The Virgin Suicides*
Queen Guinevere	11	*Sir Gawain and the Green Knight*
Helen	12	*The Aeneid*
Tom Jones	13	*Tom Jones*
Legolas	14	*The Lord of the Rings* trilogy
Lolita	15	*Lolita*
Mona Aamons Monzano	16	*Cat's Cradle*
Scarlett O'Hara	17	*Gone with the Wind*
The rose	18	*The Little Prince*
Tadzio	19	*Death in Venice*

Comtesse de B—

Dangerous Liaisons
Pierre-Ambroise-François Choderlos de Laclos

The Vicomte de Valmont's former lover, whose estate he visits before returning to that of **Madame de Rosemonde** to pursue **the Présidente de Tourvel** and **Cécile Volanges**. Valmont only just avoids being caught in a compromising situation with the Comtesse. He writes to **the Marquise de Merteuil** about this event, hoping to arouse her jealousy.

Babbie

Go Ask Alice
Anonymous

A young former prostitute and drug addict. **Alice** meets Babbie in the mental hospital.

George F. Babbitt

Babbitt
Sinclair Lewis

The novel's title character and protagonist, a successful, middle-aged real estate broker in the Midwestern town of Zenith. When the novel opens, Babbitt is a typical member of Zenith's hypocritical, ignorant, conformist middle class. However, he feels vaguely dissatisfied with the monotonous, conventional lifestyle. After his best friend **Paul Riesling** is sent to jail for shooting his wife **Zilla** in an argument, Babbitt briefly rebels against middle-class values. He has an affair with **Tanis Judique**, joins his mistress's Bohemian circle of friends, and voices liberal political opinions. However, his friends and associates quickly crush his rebellion by shunning him socially and refusing to do business with him. When Babbitt's wife **Myra** falls seriously ill, he realizes that it is too late for him to rebel. He has too much to lose and does not want his family to suffer for his unorthodox behavior. Babbitt returns to his conventional life to regain his social status and respectability with a new understanding of the values of his class.

Katherine Babbitt

Babbitt
Sinclair Lewis

Myra and **George Babbitt**'s youngest child.

Myra Babbitt

Babbitt
Sinclair Lewis

Babbitt's dull but devoted wife. Myra is dissatisfied with the monotonous, conventional middle-class lifestyle she and her husband live. She is deeply hurt by Babbitt's affair, but when she falls seriously ill, Babbitt returns to his role as a responsible family man and takes care of her.

Theodore Roosevelt Babbitt

Babbitt
Sinclair Lewis

George and **Myra**'s teenage son. Ted does not harbor college ambitions, because his talents and interests lie in mechanics. Like many middle-class boys, he is interested in girls, nice clothing, and expensive cars. At the end of the novel, he drops out of college and elopes with **Eunice Littlefield**. Because Babbitt finally understands that the conventional middle-class lifestyle is extremely repressive, he tells his son to follow his dreams.

Babbitt
Sinclair Lewis

Verona Babbitt

Myra and **George Babbitt**'s oldest child. Verona, a graduate of Bryn Mawr, professes liberal opinions and wants to have a socially responsible career. However, her beliefs and character are still heavily influenced by the materialistic, ignorant values of the middle class. She marries **Kenneth Escott**, a young reporter for Zenith's local newspaper.

The American
Henry James

Benjamin Babcock

A Unitarian minister from Massachusetts **Christopher Newman** meets during his tour of Europe in the summer of 1868. Babcock is nervous, pious, and overly concerned with the gravity of life and art. Europe distresses Babcock, who hates the Continent's oddities, impurities, and impieties. Still, Babcock somehow feels Europe is more deeply and richly beautiful than his homeland.

White Noise
Don DeLillo

Babette

Jack Gladney's wife and the mother of **Wilder** and **Denise**. Babette is the perfect American mother, loving and caring, slightly overweight, with a head of messy blond hair. Like her husband, she is a teacher. Openness is the hallmark of their marriage until, to relieve her obsessive fear of death, Babette begins to take a secret experimental drug called Dylar. She experiences frequent memory lapses and becomes increasingly evasive.

One Hundred Years of Solitude
Gabriel García Márquez

Mauricio Babilonia

The sallow, solemn lover of **Meme** who works as a mechanic for the banana plantation. He courts Meme bluntly and shamelessly, and his openness and solemnity entrance her. When Meme's mother, **Fernanda del Carpio**, discovers them kissing in a movie theater, she confines the lovesick Meme to the house. When she deduces that Mauricio Babilonia sneaks into the house every night to make love to Meme, she posts a guard in the backyard. When Mauricio Babilonia returns once more, the guard shoots him, shattering his spine and paralyzing him for the rest of his life. The tragic paralysis traumatizes Meme, striking her mute. She is interred in a convent, where she spends the rest of her life thinking about Mauricio. At the convent, she gives birth to Mauricio Babilonia's child, **Aureliano (II)**.

Benito Cereno
Herman Melville

Babo

The leader of the slave revolt against the sailors who takes over the *San Dominick*. For most of the novella, Babo masquerades as **Benito Cereno**'s servant.

East of Eden
John Steinbeck

Abra Bacon

The daughter of the corrupt county supervisor in Salinas, California. The goodhearted Abra offers compassion and common sense to the tumultuous Trask family. Abra falls in love with **Aron Trask**, but after Aron withdraws into the church upon discovering the sinister **Cathy Ames** is his mother, Abra shifts her affections to Aron's brother, **Cal**. Like Cal, Abra worries that her father's corruption will taint her. However, with Cal, Abra comes to realize that she is free to choose her own moral destiny.

The Black Prince
Iris Murdoch

Arnold Baffin

The husband of **Rachel Baffin**, father of **Julian Baffin** and a close friend of **Bradley Pearson**'s who falls in love with **Christian Evandale**. He is a very successful popular writer who had once been Bradley's protégé and whom Bradley is accused of killing at the end of the novel. Arnold and Bradley's friendship is one of the primary relationships within the novel, and a homoerotic element is implied. The breaking point in their friendship comes when Arnold discovers the affair Bradley is having with Julian.

The Black Prince
Iris Murdoch

Julian Baffin

Julian is the daughter of **Arnold Baffin** and **Rachel Baffin**, with whom **Bradley Pearson** falls in love. Julian is characterized by youth and naïveté. She has never been a successful student, but suddenly decides she wants to be a writer and asks Bradley to be her teacher. Her career goals are romanticized dreams, just as her love is for Bradley. Her illusions are finally shattered when Bradley makes violent love to her. The intensity of his passion reveals his true nature to her, and she flees.

The Black Prince
Iris Murdoch

Rachel Baffin

The wife of **Arnold Baffin**, the mother of **Julian Baffin**, and a friend of **Bradley Pearson**'s who has attempted to seduce him. Rachel is a forceful woman underestimated by those around her. Arnold seems to think that all is well between him and his wife, while Bradley regards Rachel as a benign older woman. Rachel's firm speech and unforgiving tone, however, suggest the power within her personality. Rachel herself anticipates her fierceness when she tells Bradley that she still has "real fire" in her, and in the end this fire leads, according to Bradley, to her murdering her husband.

The Hobbit, The Fellowship of the Ring, and The Return of the King
J. R. R. Tolkien

Bilbo Baggins

The cousin of **Frodo Baggins**, and a Hobbit, "a short, human-like person." He is the main character of *The Hobbit*, and its hero. Like so many Hobbits, he loves food, drink, security, and his snug home in the Shire, but his adventures awaken his courage and initiative and prove his relentless ability to do what needs to be done. Even as the other participants in his quest become corrupted by greed, Bilbo maintains his common sense, courage, and eagerness to please. In *The Hobbit*, Bilbo saves the **Dwarves** from the **Goblins**, rescues them from spiders and Wood **Elves**, finds the way into Lonely Mountain, leads the team to the treasure, and he attempts to bring peace to the feuding Dwarves, Elves, and **Humans**. Bilbo finds **Gollum**'s "precious," the One Ring that is infused with the spirit of the evil **Sauron**. In *The Fellowship of the Ring*, Bilbo remains the very old cousin of Frodo Baggins, as well as his mentor. The effects of having kept the One Ring for so long only occasionally mar his thoughtfulness. He makes one attempt to violently grab the Ring back from Frodo; the Ring has taken possession of Bilbo just as it kept him young for so many years. At the very end of the series, Bilbo is brought to the Grey Havens, a kind of heavenly place, with Frodo, **Gandalf**, and the High Elves, like **Elrond Halfelven**.

Frodo Baggins

The Lord of the Rings trilogy
J. R. R. Tolkien

The protagonist of *The Lord of the Rings*. As the bearer of the One Ring, Frodo Baggins is the center of the Fellowship of the Ring, which includes **Gandalf**, **Samwise Gamgee**, **Peregrin Took**, **Meriadoc Brandybuck**, **Legolas**, **Gimli**, **Aragorn**, and **Boromir**. Like any Hobbit, Frodo loves good food and simple comforts, but he has something that sets him apart from the rest of his race—unlike the common run of provincial, self-satisfied Hobbits, Frodo is curious about the outside world. His generally impeccable character might render him one-dimensional if he were not so frequently wracked with doubt and faced with obstacles he feels unable to surmount. Unlike Aragorn or even Gandalf, there is no particular glory associated with Frodo. Inheriting the Ring and being chosen by the Council of **Elrond Halfelven** to bear it in *The Fellowship of the Ring* is a great task, but it is to him simply a burden, one that grows heavier as the quest progresses. While in the Shire, Frodo dreamed of adventure; on his quest, he simply longs for home. His willingness to go ahead with the quest speaks much about his strength of character. In *The Two Towers*, Frodo makes his way with Samwise, or Sam, led by **Gollum** to bring the ring to the place in which it was created by **Sauron**, the only place where it can be destroyed. In *The Return of the King*, after the Ring is destroyed, Frodo's loss of vigor and identity propels his desire to sail away to the paradise of the West, beyond the Great Sea, to the Grey Havens, with **Bilbo**, Elrond, Gandalf, and the **Elves**.

Harry Bagley

Cloud Nine
Caryl Churchill

On the surface, Harry, a British explorer, represents British courage and discovery. However, Harry's acclaim as an explorer masks his confusion over his sexual identity. Harry's presence, while seemingly harmless, begins to bring out the deep sexual leanings of **Clive**'s family, including **Betty**, **Joshua**, and **Edward**. When Harry mistakes Clive for a homosexual and Clive threatens to betray the secret, Harry must hide his homosexuality by marrying the lesbian governess **Ellen**.

Ludo Bagman

Harry Potter and the Goblet of Fire
J. K. Rowling

The head of Magical Games and Sports within the Ministry of Magic; an ex-professional Quidditch player. Ludo is a rosy-faced, good-natured but irresponsible man, who once was a Death Eater, a follower of Voldemort.

Bagot

Richard II
William Shakespeare

One of **King Richard II**'s favored and loyal supporters. When word comes that **Henry Bolingbroke** has come back to England with an army, Bagot, along with **Bushy** and **Green**, realize they will be punished along with Richard, and flee. Bushy and Green are captured and executed soon after, but Bagot, who is captured later on, turns informer (implicating the **Duke of Aumerle** in the death of his uncle **Thomas of Woodstock, Duke of Gloucester**), and apparently survives.

Bagration

War and Peace
Leo Tolstoy

A Russian military commander.

Betsy Bailey

Narrative of the Life of Frederick Douglass
Frederick Douglass

Frederick Douglass's grandmother. Betsy raised Douglass on **Captain Anthony**'s land after Douglass's mother was taken away. She served the Anthony family her whole life and had many children and grandchildren who became slaves for the Anthonys. After seeing Captain Anthony's children from birth to death, Betsy is abandoned to a hut in the woods instead of being allowed to go free.

Harriet Bailey

Narrative of the Life of Frederick Douglass
Frederick Douglass

Frederick Douglass's mother. Harriet is separated from Douglass after his birth, but she still attempts to maintain family relations by walking twelve miles to see him at night. She dies when Douglass is young.

Bump Baily

The Natural
Bernard Malamud

The star of the New York Knights until the arrival of **Roy Hobbs**. Bump is a cocky, egotistical, and mean-spirited player who enjoys playing cruel practical jokes on his teammates. While a talented athlete, Bump occasionally tries too hard to rise above and beyond his impressive abilities, resulting in disaster when he cracks his skull while trying to catch a long ball.

Mrs. Baines

Major Barbara
George Bernard Shaw

A Salvation Army commissioner. By accepting the donations of the wealthy as necessary to the work of salvation, she surrenders the Army to millionaires like **Bodger** and **Andrew Undershaft**.

Guitar Bains

Song of Solomon
Toni Morrison

Milkman Dead's best friend. Having grown up in poverty after his father was killed in a factory accident, Guitar harbors a lifelong hatred of white people, whom he considers responsible for all evil in the world. He belongs to a group called the Seven Days, which matches white murders of black people with murders of whites performed in the same fashion.

Baker

Rebecca
Daphne du Maurier

A London doctor who saw **Rebecca** the day of her death.

Jordan Baker

The Great Gatsby
F. Scott Fitzgerald

Daisy Buchanan's beautiful friend and **Nick Carraway**'s sometime lover. A competitive golfer, Baker is one of the "new women" of the 1920s—cynical, boyish, and self-centered. She cheated to win her first golf tournament and often bends the truth. After Daisy introduces Jordan to Nick, they begin an off-and-on romantic relationship, which Nick ends when he moves back to the Midwest after **Gatsby**'s funeral.

Paul Baldino

The Virgin Suicides
Jeffrey Eugenides

An intimidating high school boy, who at fourteen acts the part of a local gangster's son. While the boys rarely believe Paul's elaborate tales, they do fear and respect him. It is Paul who, exploring storm sewers, comes up into the Lisbon house and discovers **Cecilia Lisbon** in the bathtub bleeding from her wrists.

Alexander Balfour

Kidnapped
Robert Louis Stevenson

David Balfour's father. Alexander Balfour and his brother, **Ebenezer Balfour**, had a fight over a woman (David's future mother). Alexander was the elder brother, but he made a deal: he married David's mother, and Ebenezer kept the House of Shaws, their estate. Even though the House of Shaws was his legal inheritance as the eldest son of the eldest son, Alexander only wanted to be with David's mother, and therefore did not care about the money. Alexander has died by the beginning of *Kidnapped*. David does end up getting two-thirds of the yearly Shaws income with the help of **Alan Breck Stewart** and **Mr. Rankeillor**.

David Balfour

Kidnapped
Robert Louis Stevenson

A young man, born and raised in the Lowlands of Scotland, the narrator of *Kidnapped*. David Balfour's father, **Alexander Balfour**, has just died at the beginning of the story, leaving him an orphan. David is young and inexperienced, and so he describes everything he sees with unfamiliar eyes. He is sent off to slavery by **Ebenezer Balfour**, his terrible, miserly old uncle, but escapes upon encountering some turns of fate aboard the *Covenant* with **Riach** and **Captain Hoseason**. Through his association with **Alan Breck Stewart**, David learns much about the real world. By the end of the novel, he is able to outwit his own scheming uncle and claim his inheritance, all while helping Alan Breck Stewart escape his life as a wanted man.

Ebenezer Balfour

Kidnapped
Robert Louis Stevenson

The scheming, miserly uncle of **David Balfour** and the brother of **Alexander Balfour**. Ebenezer plots to have David killed or taken away by **Captain Hoseason** so that he can attain complete control of the Balfour fortunes of the House of Shaws. Ebenezer wanted to marry Alexander's wife, David's mother, but instead settled for the right to the House of Shaws, which was slated for David. When he sees that David is around, he wants to get rid of him to safeguard his fortune. David, with the help of his lawyer, **Mr. Rankeillor**, and **Alan Breck Stewart**, tricks Ebenezer into saying that he was going to sell David into slavery. After the admission, Ebenezer agrees to give two-thirds of the yearly House of Shaws income to David.

Baligant

Song of Roland
Unknown

The emir of Babylon at the beginning of **Charlemagne**'s campaign in Spain, **Marsilla** sends for help from Baligant. Years later, Baligant finally arrives with an enormous army and sets out to battle Charlemagne. Charlemagne is able to kill Baligant, avenging **Roland**'s death and conquering Spain with one stroke.

Balin

The Hobbit
J. R. R. Tolkien

One of the dwarf companions on the novel's quest.

Cainy Ball

Far from the Madding Crowd
Thomas Hardy

A young boy who works as **Gabriel Oak**'s assistant shepherd on **Bathsheba Everdene**'s farm. Cainy Ball brings news to Weatherbury, the town where Bathsheba has her farm, that he spied Bathsheba arm in arm with a soldier in the town of Bath after she disappeared from the farm. The soldier is **Sergeant Francis Troy**.

The Balrog

The Fellowship of the Ring
J. R. R. Tolkien

A mysterious, gigantic, terrifying elemental demon from deep inside the earth. The Balrog has existed perhaps before many things in Middle-earth. It is the "nameless fear" awakened by the **Dwarves** in the Mines of Moria, and it emerges from the depths when the Fellowship of the Ring passes through the Mines, arousing the **Orcs** who are hiding there. The Balrog ultimately confronts **Gandalf** in an epic battle, brandishing an enormous flaming sword and whip, wreathed in flame and yet exuding shadow and darkness. Gandalf is separated from the Fellowship because the Balrog pulls him to his apparent death. Gandalf, however, defeats the Balrog and emerges more powerful than ever.

Balthamos

His Dark Materials
Robert Pullman

An angel of the lower orders. Balthamos, along with his lover, **Baruch**, is sent to lead **Will Parry** to **Lord Asriel**. After Baruch is killed, cowardly Balthamos stays with Will. Balthamos kills **Father Gomez** before Gomez can kill **Lyra Belacqua**.

Balthasar of *Comedy*

The Comedy of Errors
William Shakespeare

A merchant in Ephesus. The polite Balthasar, who's been invited to dine at **Antipholus of Ephesus**'s home, convinces his friend not to break down the door when they are barred entry by **Dromio of Syracuse**. His level head is contrasted with Antipholus's violent temper.

Balthasar of *Merchant*

The Merchant of Venice
William Shakespeare

Portia's servant, whom she dispatches to get the appropriate materials from **Doctor Bellario**.

Balthasar of *Much Ado*

Much Ado About Nothing
William Shakespeare

A musician and servant in **Leonato**'s household. Balthasar flirts with **Margaret** at the masked party and helps Leonato, **Claudio**, and **Don Pedro** trick **Benedick** into falling in love with **Beatrice**.

Balthasar of *Romeo*

Romeo and Juliet
William Shakespeare

Romeo's dedicated servant. He brings **Romeo** the news of **Juliet**'s death, unaware that her death is a ruse.

Balthazar

The Spanish Tragedy
Thomas Kyd

The prince of Portugal and son of **The Viceroy**. Balthazar is characterized by his extreme pride and his hot-headedness. This pride makes him kill **Horatio** along with **Lorenzo**, and it turns him into a villain. He kills Andrea fairly, though with help, so it is unclear whether he is as "valiant" as the King and others continuously describe him. His love for **Bel-Imperia** is genuine, and it is the primary motivation behind his decision to kill Horatio.

Mr. Bambridge

Middlemarch
George Eliot

A Middlemarch horse dealer who comes to hold substantial debts on **Fred Vincy**. **John Raffles** meets him at a horse fair and tells him everything about **Nicholas Bulstrode**'s past.

Pete Bancini

One Flew over the Cuckoo's Nest
Ken Kesey

A hospital patient who suffered brain damage when he was born. He continually declares that he is tired, and at one point he tells the other patients that he was born dead.

Dr. Bangs

Little Women
Louisa May Alcott

A doctor who tends to **Beth March** when she is ailing.

Mavis Bangs

The Shipping News
E. Annie Proulx

The aunt's assistant in the upholstery business, who helps keep the aunt in line when she begins to falter. Mavis Bangs is an older woman and a terrific gossip. One day she gives her take on the upholsterer **Agnis Hamm** to **Dawn Budgel**.

The banker

Moll Flanders
Daniel Defoe

A prosperous man whom **Moll** agrees to marry if he will divorce his unfaithful wife. She marries **Jemy**, a rich man from Lancashire, in the meantime. When her marriage to Jemy collapses, Moll and the Banker marry. They live happily for several years until his death.

William Bankes

To the Lighthouse
Virginia Woolf

A botanist and old friend of the Ramsays. Bankes is a kind, mellow man. He and **Lily Briscoe** do not marry, as **Mrs. Ramsay** hoped they would, but they are close friends.

Judge Goodwill Banner

The Natural
Bernard Malamud

The owner of the New York Knights. Judge prefers his team to lose, as this allows him to run the organization cheaply. He is crooked and often bets against his own players. He attempts to bribe **Roy Hobbs** into throwing the game for the pennant. Judge lives in a tower high above the ballpark, scheming ways to make money and to take back **Pop Fisher**'s remaining forty percent of the team's stock.

Mr. Bannister

Inherit the Wind
Jerome Lawrence & Robert E. Lee

A member of the jury. **Tom Davenport** accepts Mr. Bannister as a member of the jury because he says he goes to church on Sundays. **Henry Drummond** accepts Bannister because he is illiterate, and therefore, has read neither Darwin nor the Bible.

Banquo

Macbeth
William Shakespeare

The brave, noble general whose children, according to **the Three Witches**' prophecy, will inherit the Scottish throne. Banquo's character stands in contrast to **Macbeth**, since Banquo need not betray and murder in order to realize his ambitions. Appropriately, it is Banquo's ghost—not **King Duncan**'s—that haunts Macbeth.

Baobabs

The Little Prince
Antoine de Saint-Exupéry

Harmless trees on Earth, baobabs pose a great threat to smaller planets like **the Little Prince**'s if they are left unchecked. They can squeeze whole planets to pieces with their roots. Although baobabs have no malicious intentions, their growth represents the danger of being lazy or indifferent about the outside world.

Bao-Bao

The Kitchen God's Wife
Amy Tan

Helen's son. Bao-Bao is a silly boy whom **Winnie** pegs as a loser. He is constantly making jokes, is on the verge of losing his job when the novel begins (according to Winnie), and has already been married several times. His marriage, ironically, brings the family together.

Baptista

The Taming of the Shrew
William Shakespeare

One of the wealthiest men in Padua, father of **Katherine** and **Bianca**. Baptista Minola is good-natured, if a bit superficial. His daughters become the prey of many suitors due to the substantial dowries he can offer.

His absentmindedness increases when Kate shows her obstinate nature. At the opening of the play, he is already desperate to find her a suitor, having decided that she must marry before Bianca, the younger daughter, does.

Baptiste

Wide Sargasso Sea
Jean Rhys

The overseer of the Granbois mansion. Baptiste is a dignified man of advanced age.

Barabas

The Jew of Malta
Christopher Marlowe

The protagonist of the play. Barabas is a Jewish merchant who only cares for his daughter **Abigail** and his vast personal fortune. When **Ferneze** appropriates Barabas's estate to help the government pay Turkish tribute, Barabas is enraged and vows revenge. His clever plots lead to the deaths of many characters, including those of Abigail and the governor's son. He is marked as an outsider within Maltese society because of his religion and because of his Machiavellian cunning. However, in many ways Barabas is the least hypocritical character in the play. He is generally honest about what motivates his crimes, and he never attempts to justify his actions by religious doctrine.

Anastassya Filippovna Barashkova

The Idiot
Fyodor Dostoevsky

An immensely beautiful femme fatale. She falls in love with **Prince Lev Nikolayevich Myshkin**. Nastassya Filippovna was once a ward of **Afanassy Ivanovich Totsky**'s. Later, however, he seduced her and made her his mistress when she was a young woman. She blames herself for her dishonor and, although she loves Myshkin, she considers herself unworthy of marrying him. Nastassya runs to **Parfyon Semyonovich Rogozhin**, who later stabs her to death.

Tommy Barban

Tender Is the Night
F. Scott Fitzgerald

A half-American, half-French mercenary soldier who is in love with **Nicole Diver**. The smug, dramatic Tommy challenges **Albert McKisco** to a duel from which both men emerge unscathed. As Nicole's marriage to **Dick** deteriorates, Tommy begins an affair with her and ultimately marries her after she secures a divorce from Dick.

Barbara

Major Barbara
George Bernard Shaw

Robust, jolly, and energetic, Barbara begins the play as a major for the Salvation Army. She is peacefully convinced of her righteousness in the mission to redeem mankind. Her father **Andrew Undershaft**'s arrival and virtual purchase of the Salvation Army forces her to recognize that the wealthy, rather than God, hold the world and its salvation in their hands.

Hunchback of Notre Dame
Victor Hugo

Master Florian Barbedienne

A deaf man who judges **Quasimodo** after he attacks **La Esmeralda**. When he attempts to question Quasimodo, who is also deaf, the crowd breaks into laughter because neither of them knows what the other is saying. Florian orders Quasimodo to the pillory because he assumes the crowd is laughing contemptuously at Quasimodo. When someone finally tells Florian that Quasimodo is deaf, he pretends to hear that Quasimodo has done something else to mock him and he condemns him to an extra whipping.

Invisible Man
Ralph Ellison

Reverend Homer A. Barbee

A preacher from Chicago who visits **the Narrator**'s college. Reverend Barbee's fervent praise of **the Founder**'s "vision" strikes an inadvertently ironic note, because he himself is blind.

Don Quixote
Miguel de Cervantes

Barber

Don Quixote's friend. The barber realizes that Don Quixote is delusional and strenuously disapproves of his antics.

Pigs in Heaven
Barbara Kingsolver

Barbie

A nutty waitress in Las Vegas who has committed her life to worshipping Barbie dolls. She owns all of Barbie's clothes and knows every doll ever on the market. Barbie is also a petty thief, stealing from her employers and from **Taylor Greer**. Her obsession with living Barbie's life has also driven her to an eating disorder.

Chronicle of a Death Foretold
Gabriel García Márquez

Mercedes Barcha

The narrator's wife. The narrator proposes to her at **Angela Vicario** and **Bayardo San Roman**'s wedding party.

Lucky Jim
Kingsley Amis

Professor Barclay

A professor of music at the college where **Jim Dixon** works. Dixon likes him and appreciates his help with the material for the "Merrie England" lecture.

The Hobbit
J. R. R. Tolkien

Bard

The grim Human who is the honorable captain of the guard in Lake Town. Lake Town is a city built by **Humans** on Long Lake just south of the Lonely Mountain, where **Smaug** guards the treasure that **Thorin Oakenshield** is after. With the help of information discovered by **Bilbo Baggins** and related by a thrush, Bard finds Smaug's weak spot in the hollow of his left breast and kills him. Bard of Dale is the only human hero in *The Hobbit*, and his character stands in direct contrast to the greed of the **Dwarves** and the fear of the Humans in Lake Town.

Bardolph

Henry IV, Part I; Henry IV, Part II; Henry V; The Merry Wives of Windsor
William Shakespeare

A criminal and highwayman, friend to **Sir John Falstaff** and Prince Harry (the future **Henry V**). Along with **Edward Poins** and **Peto**, Bardolph drinks with Falstaff and Hal in the Boar's Head Tavern in Eastcheap, accompanies them in highway robbery, and goes with them to war in *King Henry IV, Part I*. Usually a whipping boy and straight man for Falstaff's buffoonery, like Sir Jack, he gets richer and gains prestige following the Battle of Shrewsbury. However, this does not stop him from aiding and abetting Falstaff's schemes; in *King Henry IV, Part II*, Bardolph accepts the bribes from the army recruits on behalf of the fat knight. Even as a military man in France in *King Henry V*, he continues to thieve. However, he is captured after stealing a "pax" (religious tablet) and is sentenced to death by hanging. Though his friend **Pistol** pleads on his behalf, the Welsh **Captain Fluellen** refuses to pardon him, a move that **King Henry V** approves. Henry's cold response to his former friend's execution is a sign he has severed ties to his former life. Bardolph is an insatiable drinker, and his bright red nose is a constant source of amusement for his peers. Bardolph and **Mistress Quickly** have the longest run of the Eastcheap characters, appearing in *The Merry Wives of Windsor* as well.

Lord Bardolph

Henry IV, Part II
William Shakespeare

An ally of the **Earl of Northumberland**'s. As preordained in the prologue of the play, Lord Bardolph delivers the false news of Northumberland's son **Hotspur**'s success, but is quickly contradicted when the real news of Hotspur's demise arrives. He conspires with the **Archbishop of York**, **Thomas Mowbray**, and **Lord Hastings** to mount another rebellion against **King Henry IV**. His and Northumberland's defeat is mentioned only in passing toward the end of the play. (He is not to be confused with **Sir John Falstaff**'s friend **Bardolph**.)

Mrs. Barker

American Dream
Edward Albee

A caricature of the socially responsible American housewife. Mrs. Barker is the flighty and ingenuous volunteer from the Bye-Bye Adoption Service who delivered the "bumble" to **Mommy** and **Daddy** twenty years ago and has returned, upon their request, to provide them with the "satisfaction" they deserve. She remains steadfastly ignorant of the purpose of her visit even as she remains fully aware of her shared history with the household.

Catherine Barkley

A Farewell to Arms
Ernest Hemingway

An English nurse's aide who falls in love with **Frederic Henry**, the protagonist of the novel. Catherine is exceptionally beautiful. When the novel opens, Catherine's grief for her dead fiancé launches her headlong into a playful but reckless game of seduction. Her feelings for Henry intensify and become more complicated, however, and she eventually swears lifelong fidelity to him. Ultimately, their romance ends tragically, as Catherine becomes pregnant and dies of a hemorrhage after a difficult labor and delivery of a stillborn infant.

Holes
Louis Sachar

Kate Barlow

The schoolteacher-turned-outlaw who robbed **Stanley Yelnats IV**'s great-grandfather, **Stanley Yelnats I**, of his stock-market fortune in California. While intelligent and kind by nature, the murder of her beloved **Sam** by **Charles Walker** turns Kate into a violent outlaw. She becomes Kissin' Kate Barlow, and returns to Green Lake twenty years later. **Trout Walker** and his wife, the redhead **Linda Miller**, tie Kate up while she is sleeping. Trout has lost all his money and demands to know where Kate's outlaw loot is. Trout and Linda make Kate walk barefoot across the hot sand until she dies from the bite of a yellow-spotted lizard. Kate never tells them where the money is.

Measure for Measure
William Shakespeare

Barnardine

A long-term prisoner in the jail. Barnardine is sentenced to be executed at the same time as **Claudio**. Duke **Vincentio** eventually decides that even Barnardine's life deserves to be spared.

The Sun Also Rises
Ernest Hemingway

Jake Barnes

The narrator and protagonist of the novel. Jake is an American veteran of World War I working as a journalist in Paris, where he and his friends live a life full of drinking and parties. Although Jake is more stable than most of his friends, he struggles with his love for the fickle **Lady Brett Ashley**, his impotence (the result of a war injury), and the emotional aftermath of the war. Jake spends most of the novel traveling aimlessly throughout France and Spain with various friends and acquaintances. Although Jake rarely speaks directly about himself, his descriptions of other people and events shed light on his own thoughts and feelings. Although Jake seems more aware than his friends of the aimlessness and casual interpersonal cruelty of their generation, he nonetheless remains trapped within it.

The Remains of the Day
Kazuo Ishiguro

Mrs. Carolyn Barnet

Another member of the British Union of Fascists. Mrs. Barnet is very glamorous and intelligent. **Stevens** believes Mrs. Barnet persuaded **Lord Darlington** to fire the Jewish maids.

The Rape of the Lock
Alexander Pope

The Baron

A character based on the historical Robert, Lord Petre, the young gentleman in Pope's social circle who offended Arabella Fermor and her family by cutting off a lock of her hair.

Candide
Voltaire

The Baron

Cunégonde's brother. After his family's castle is destroyed, the Baron becomes a Jesuit priest. Voltaire often suggests that the Baron has homosexual tendencies. He is arrogant about his family's noble lineage and refuses to allow **Candide** to marry Cunégonde.

Barrabas

The House of the Spirits
Isabel Allende

The dog of **Nivea del Valle**, **Severo del Valle**, and especially, **Clara**, as a young girl. Barrabas is stabbed in the back and killed at the engagement party of Clara and **Esteban Trueba**.

Diana Barry

Anne of Green Gables
L. M. Montgomery

Anne Shirley's best friend. Diana is a plump, pretty girl Anne's age who lives next door to Green Gables at Orchard Slope. Diana and Anne become bosom friends immediately after they meet. Full of romantic notions about love and friendship, they swear devotion to each other forever. Although an agreeable girl, she lacks Anne's imagination, intelligence, and independence.

Mrs. Barry

Anne of Green Gables
L. M. Montgomery

Diana Barry's mother. Mrs. Barry is a severe, unforgiving woman. She expects her children to follow strict and sometimes unreasonable rules and is quick to condemn **Anne Shirley** when Anne makes mistakes. She bans her daughter from seeing Anne after Anne accidentally feeds Diana alcohol. She allows the two girls to be friends again after Anne saves the life of her youngest daughter, **Minnie May**. **Marilla Cuthbert** warns Anne not to say anything startling or to use too many big words in front of Mrs. Barry, due to her reputation for strictness.

Mrs. Eliza Barrymore

Hound of the Baskervilles
Sir Arthur Conan Doyle

The longtime domestic help of **Sir Henry Baskerville** and his clan. Eliza and her husband, **Mr. John Barrymore**, attempt to help Eliza's brother, **the convict**, and initially draw unfounded suspicion from **Sherlock Holmes** and **Dr. Watson**.

Mr. John Barrymore

Hound of the Baskervilles
Sir Arthur Conan Doyle

The longtime domestic help of the Baskerville clan. Earnest and eager to please, the gaunt Mr. Barrymore and his portly wife, **Mrs. Eliza Barrymore**, serve as a red herring for the detectives. They're in league with Eliza's brother, **the convict**, but ultimately no more suspicious than **Sir Henry Baskerville**.

John Barsad

A Tale of Two Cities
Charles Dickens

Like **Roger Cly**, a British spy who swears that patriotism is his only motive. Barsad falsely claims to be a virtuous man of upstanding reputation.

Lily Bart

The House of Mirth
Edith Wharton

The novel's protagonist, an unmarried twenty-nine-year-old woman who desires to be a social success. Lily's mission is to marry a relatively wealthy man, thereby ensuring her financial stability and a place in the higher levels of New York society. Unfortunately, her desire to marry someone wealthy clashes with her feelings for **Lawrence Selden**, a man of modest means whom she truly loves. She also suffers from an inability to make decisions, which causes her to pass up several good marriage opportunities in hopes that she can do better. Book Two chronicles Lily's gradual expulsion from society after a false rumor spreads that she has had an extramarital affair. She eventually joins the working classes before dying at the end of the novel from a sleeping-medicine overdose.

Bartleby

Bartleby, the Scrivener
Herman Melville

A young man hired by **the Lawyer** as a scrivener, or law-copyist. Though initially an excellent copyist, when asked to examine his work for errors, Bartleby replies that he "would prefer not to." Bartleby soon answers anything he is asked to do with "I would prefer not to," and he slowly drives his coworkers crazy. This mantra, and the politely firm way Bartleby delivers it, prevents the Lawyer from taking any real action against him, and the phrase "I would prefer not to" begins to infect the Lawyer's speech, even his mind.

Charlotte Bartlett

A Room with a View
E. M. Forster

Lucy Honeychurch's older, poorer cousin and an old maid. Charlotte accompanies Lucy to Italy as a chaperone and attempts to uphold what is "proper." She has old-fashioned notions and does not approve of the Emersons. She seems to conspire against the happiness of everyone with her tiresome and cloying manner, but in the end, she mysteriously assists Lucy in attaining marital happiness.

Edith Bartlett

Looking Backward
Edward Bellamy

Julian West's aristocratic fiancée in the nineteenth century. Like Julian, Edith considered the wide gap between the rich and poor in her day a natural, irremediable condition of human society.

Mr. Barton

Looking Backward
Edward Bellamy

A twentieth-century preacher. After **Julian West** is discovered in his underground sleeping chamber, Mr. Barton is inspired to deliver a sermon about the vast improvements of twentieth-century society over that of the nineteenth century. After hearing the sermon, Julian becomes depressed, realizing he contributed to the barbaric and inhumane nature of nineteenth-century society.

Baruch

His Dark Materials
Robert Pullman

An angel of the lower orders who accompanies his lover, **Balthamos**, on the mission to bring **Will Parry** to **Lord Asriel**. Baruch is killed by **Metatron**'s angels.

Basan and Basil

The Song of Roland
Unknown

Charlemagne's envoys. During Charlemagne's Spanish campaign before the beginning of *The Song of Roland*, **Marsilla** had sent an embassy of pagans carrying olive branches and a peace offer to Charlemagne. Counts Basan and Basil were sent to receive it; the pagans chopped off their heads. **Roland** reminds the king of this incident when urging him not to pay any attention to Marsilla's later offer of peace; **Ganelon** also remembers Basan and Basil's fate and thus takes offense when Roland nominates Ganelon as the next envoy.

Iris Bascom

A Day No Pigs Would Die
Robert Newton Peck

A distant neighbor of **Robert Peck**, **Lucy Peck**, and **Haven Peck**. She is first seen by Robert as a broom-wielding maniac after he and **Jacob Henry** run through her strawberry patch shortly after her husband's death. Later, she is revealed as a very sweet woman, asking Robert for help and then giving him cookies and buttermilk. Lucy Peck and **Aunt Carrie** gossip about the Widow Bascom because there is a rumor that she has been sleeping with her hired hand, **Ira Long**. This turns out to be true, and by the end of the novel, Mrs. Bascom has become Mrs. Long.

Uncle Maury Bascomb

The Sound and the Fury
William Faulkner

Mrs. Compson's brother. Bascomb lives off of his brother-in-law's money.

Mrs. Basil

The Good Soldier
Ford Madox Ford

One of **Captain Edward Ashburnham**'s lovers. The wife of an army officer stationed in India, Mrs. Basil is a sympathetic listener to Edward's discussion of his estate and his tales of heroism. Mrs. Basil is lonely, as her husband, Major Basil, often leaves her alone for long stretches of time. Because she is closer to Edward's class, the affair they begin seems relatively safe and ends when Edward leaves India. But when he learns of the affair, Major Basil attempts to blackmail Edward.

Sir Charles Baskerville

Hound of the Baskervilles
Sir Arthur Conan Doyle

The head of the Baskerville estate. A superstitious man, terrified of the Baskerville curse and his waning health at the time of his death. Sir Charles was also a well-known philanthropist; his plans to invest in the regions surrounding his estate make it essential that **Sir Henry Baskerville** move to Baskerville Hall to continue his uncle's good works.

Sir Henry Baskerville

Hound of the Baskervilles
Sir Arthur Conan Doyle

The late **Sir Charles Baskerville**'s nephew and closest living relative. Sir Henry is hale and hearty, described as "a small, alert, dark-eyed man about thirty years of age, very sturdily built." By the end of the story, Henry is as worn out and shell-shocked as his late uncle was before his death.

Hound of the Baskervilles
Sir Arthur Conan Doyle

Sir Hugo Baskerville

A debaucherous and shadowy Baskerville ancestor. Sir Hugo was the picture of aristocratic excess, drinking and pursuing pleasures of the flesh until it killed him.

The Misanthrope
Molière

Basque

Célimène's manservant. He is loyal to his mistress, promptly announcing the arrival of her visitors.

The Merchant of Venice
William Shakespeare

Bassanio

A kinsman and dear friend of **Antonio**'s. Bassanio's love for the wealthy **Portia** leads him to borrow money from **Shylock** with Antonio as his guarantor. Bassanio is an ineffectual businessman but a worthy suitor.

Henry VI, Part I
William Shakespeare

Basset

A follower of the **Duke of Somerset**'s. Basset plucks a red rose to show his allegiance to Somerset. Later in Paris, Basset gets into a fight with **Vernon**, a follower of the **Duke of York**'s, and the two ask **King Henry VI**'s permission to duel. The internal strife that has trickled down from York and Somerset to their supporters has followed the noblemen from England to France—and the prophecy of brimming civil war bringing about the downfall of England's foreign rule begins to come true.

Titus Andronicus
William Shakespeare

Bassianus

The late emperor's younger son, **Saturninus**'s brother, and **Lavinia**'s fiancé. Bassianus is a man of grace and virtue whose failure to secure the crown in Act I signals Rome's degeneracy. His elopement with Lavinia humiliates Saturninus. Bassianus is killed by **Chiron** and **Demetrius**, and two of **Titus**'s sons are executed when **Aaron** frames them for the murder.

Howards End
E. M. Forster

Jacky Bast

Leonard Bast's garish wife, a former prostitute who had an affair with **Henry Wilcox** in Cyprus.

Howards End
E. M. Forster

Leonard Bast

A poor insurance clerk on the very bottom rung of the middle class. Constantly tormented by financial worries, Leonard has money for food, clothing, and a place to live, but not much else. He is married to **Jacky**. Leonard represents the aspirations of the lower classes; he is obsessed with self-improvement and reads constantly, hoping to elevate himself. He is never able to translate his meager education to an improved standard of living. Late in the novel, Leonard has a sexual encounter with **Helen Schlegel**, which results in his fathering of Helen's child. Leonard is killed by **Charles Wilcox** near the end of the novel.

Philip the Bastard

King John
William Shakespeare

The illegitimate son of the former King Richard the Lionhearted (**King John**'s eldest brother). The Bastard disavows his rightful inheritance in favor of his younger half-brother, **Robert Faulconbridge**, in order to become a knight (renamed Richard Plantagenet) and fight the French with King John. At the beginning of the play he is a mischievous figure, privately rejoicing in his turn of fortune, persistently favoring war over a truce with the French, even urging the English and French to unite to destroy Angiers. He enters with the **Duke of Austria**'s head after battle with the French begins and agrees to steal from the monasteries. But the Bastard's loyal—even honest—side becomes the more prominent. As other noblemen desert, the Bastard remains King John's most loyal supporter. When the King is poisoned, he demands revenge on the enemies of England.

Charley Bates

Oliver Twist
Charles Dickens

One of **Fagin**'s pickpockets.

James Bates

Gulliver's Travels
Jonathan Swift

Young **Gulliver**'s surgeon mentor. Gulliver rarely mentions Bates in his narrative, despite his importance to Gulliver's business, demonstrating his reticence regarding England.

John Bates

Henry V
William Shakespeare

An English soldier. The night before the Battle of Agincourt, **King Henry V** disguises himself and argues with Bates, **Alexander Court**, and **Michael Williams** about the worthiness of the French war. Though he disagrees heatedly with them, and ends up exchanging gloves with Williams as the promise of a future fight, Henry is generally impressed with the intelligence and courage of these men.

Miss Bates

Emma
Jane Austen

Jane Fairfax's aunt and **Mr. Woodhouse**'s friend. Miss Bates is a middle-aged spinster without beauty or cleverness but with universal goodwill and a gentle temperament. **Emma Woodhouse** treats her with impatience.

Doctor Baugh

Cat on a Hot Tin Roof
Tennessee Williams

Big Daddy's physician. The sober Doctor Baugh delivers Daddy's diagnosis to **Big Mama** and leaves her with a prescription of morphine. **Brick** and **Gooper**, Daddy and Mama's sons, know that the doctors have lied to Mama and Daddy and that he really has cancer.

Paul Bäumer

All Quiet on the Western Front
Erich Maria Remarque

A young German soldier fighting in the trenches during World War I. Paul is the protagonist and narrator of the novel. He is, at heart, a kind, compassionate, and sensitive young man, but the brutality of warfare teaches him to detach himself from his feelings. His account of the war is a bitter invective against sentimental, romantic ideas about combat.

Bawd

Pericles
William Shakespeare

A brothel madam. Together with **Pander**, Bawd purchases **Marina** from pirates and unsuccessfully tries to convince her to become a prostitute.

Vivian Baxter

I Know Why the Caged Bird Sings
Maya Angelou

Mother of **Bailey Johnson** and **Maya Johnson**. Although she has a nursing degree, Vivian Baxter earns her money working in gambling parlors or by gambling. Vivian's parents and brothers are tough city dwellers who thrive in St. Louis amid the chaos of Prohibition, and Vivian seems to have inherited the family's wild streak. Though her lifestyle differs greatly from that of **Momma**, and though the two have very different values, Vivian is like Momma in that she is strong, supportive, proud, practical, and financially independent. She is also devastatingly beautiful. A somewhat inattentive mother, Vivian nevertheless treats her children with love and respect. Vivian sees no need to focus attention on Maya as long as Maya is healthy, well-clothed, and at least outwardly happy. Bailey only wants to seek the approval of his mother by emulating the lifestyle in which she immerses herself. Vivian does not recognize what Bailey is doing and disapproves. The two become estranged, but eventually reconcile, and Vivian helps him get a job on the South Pacific Railroad. She demonstrates a high degree of maternal intuition when **Mr. Freeman** molests and rapes Maya. Without knowing what has happened, Vivian kicks him out of the house immediately. Later, she proves unable to deal with Maya's post-rape trauma, and Maya and Bailey go back to Stamps.

Rodney Bayham

The Good Soldier
Ford Madox Ford

Leonora Powys Ashburnham's second husband. Rodney Bayham is portrayed as the utterly normal (and somewhat boring) British man. He is mentioned, but does not act, in the story. His character serves as a foil to Edward; Bayham is quite respectable in his quiet, passionless liaisons.

Baylen

Glengarry Glen Ross
David Mamet

A police detective who investigates the office robbery. We learn extremely little about Baylen's personality, as he spends most of Act Two offstage in **John Williamson**'s inner office, interrogating the salesmen about their knowledge of the break-in. He mainly exists to increase tension.

Bazin

The Three Musketeers
Alexandre Dumas

Aramis's manservant. He wants nothing so much as for his master to enter the Church. Bazin takes Aramis's letter to **Madame de Chevreuse**, **Queen Anne**'s close friend and Aramis's mysterious mistress, to warn the Queen of the plot against **George Villiers, the Duke of Buckingham**, planned by the **Lady de Winter**.

Bazulto

The Spanish Tragedy
Thomas Kyd

An old man. Bazulto visits **Hieronimo** because his own son has been murdered, and he wants the Knight-Marshal's help in finding justice. The appearance of the old man makes Hieronimo feel ashamed of his inability to avenge **Horatio**'s death.

Mr. Beach

My Brother Sam Is Dead
Christopher & James Lincoln Collier

An elderly, loyalist preacher.

Frederick Beale, Jr.

Lolita
Vladimir Nabokov

The driver of the car that kills **Charlotte Haze**. Frederick apologizes while defending himself, saying Charlotte swerved into his path. He offers to pay all the expenses for the funeral, and **Humbert Humbert** accepts.

Bean

Ender's Game
Orson Scott Card

Ender Wiggin's youngest friend at Battle School. Bean reminds Ender of himself as a young recruit. Bold and brilliant, Bean helps Ender with Dragon Army and also helps him hold on to his humanity. He is one of Ender's commanders against the buggers.

Petal Bear

The Shipping News
E. Annie Proulx

Quoyle's wife for six years who dies in a car accident after selling their two daughters, **Sunshine** and **Bunny**, to a sexual molester. A maliciously cruel, selfish woman, she marries Quoyle for the sex, but is disgusted by every other part of him. She is motivated only by sexual conquest, and she finds one man after another with whom she can act out her infidelity. She haunts both Quoyle and his daughters for many months after she is gone.

Aunt Beast

A Wrinkle in Time
Madeleine L'Engle

A tall, furry, many-tentacled inhabitant of the planet Ixchel. Aunt Beast cares lovingly for **Meg Murry** after she is nearly destroyed by **the Black Thing**. Aunt Beast, like all the creatures on Ixchel, lacks eyes and has no concept of light or vision. Aunt Beast also takes care of **Calvin O'Keefe** and **Mr. Murry** while everyone figures out a way to rescue **Charles Wallace Murry** on Camazotz.

Beatrice

Inferno
Dante Alighieri

One of the blessed in Heaven, Beatrice aids **Dante**'s journey by asking an angel to find **Virgil**, bidding Virgil to guide Dante through Hell. Like Dante and Virgil, Beatrice corresponds to an historical personage. Although the details of her life remain uncertain, we know that Dante fell passionately in love with her as a young man and never fell out of it. She has a limited role in *Inferno* but becomes more prominent in *Purgatorio* and *Paradiso*. In fact, Dante's entire imaginary journey throughout the afterlife aims, in part, to find Beatrice, whom he has lost on Earth because of her early death. Critics generally view Beatrice as an allegorical representation of spiritual love.

Beatrice

Much Ado About Nothing
William Shakespeare

Leonato's niece and **Hero**'s cousin. Generous and loving, Beatrice has a very sharp tongue and frequently mocks others with elaborately tooled jokes and puns. She has been waging a spirited war of wits with **Benedick**, but insists that she will never marry. After her cousin becomes engaged to **Claudio**, Beatrice is "tricked" into falling in love with Benedick by her friends, who want to see the two end up together. After Claudio shames Hero at the altar, the loyal Beatrice is convinced her cousin has been slandered, and asks Benedick to kill him. After the confusion is cleared up, Beatrice and Benedick's love is brought to light, and they agree to marry.

Beatrice

Demian
Hermann Hesse

A girl **Emil Sinclair** sees in a park by his boarding school. She becomes a symbol of love for him and is the person whom he is inspired to try to paint.

Beatrice

Rebecca
Daphne du Maurier

Maxim de Winter's sister. A friendly, outgoing woman with a passion for horses.

Beatrice

A View from the Bridge
Arthur Miller

The wife of **Eddie Carbone** and aunt of **Catherine**. Beatrice has raised Catherine from the time she was very young and acts as Catherine's mother. A warm and caring woman, Beatrice is more reasonable than Eddie.

Beatriz

Bel Canto
Ann Patchett

The brattiest of the young terrorists. Beatriz is often cranky and frustrated, and she is quick to draw her gun if any of the hostages gets out of line.

Captain Beatty

Fahrenheit 451
Ray Bradbury

The captain of **Guy Montag**'s fire department. Paradoxically, although he is extremely well read, he hates books and persecutes people who insist on reading them. He is cunning and devious, and so perceptive that he appears to read Montag's thoughts.

Beauchamp

The Count of Monte Cristo
Alexandre Dumas

A good friend of **Albert de Morcerf**'s. Beauchamp is a well-known journalist and also a friend to **Franz d'Epinay**. While **Danglars**, his interest sparked by the **Count of Monte Cristo**, investigates the possible dishonorable actions of **Fernand Mondego**, or the **Count de Morcerf**, Beauchamp's newspaper publishes a small article, reporting that a man named Fernand betrayed **Ali Pacha** to the Turks. Albert is convinced the article is a libelous slander against his father. Despite Monte Cristo's pleas for Albert to show restraint, Albert orders Beauchamp to retract the article or else fight a duel. Beauchamp, who did not even write the offending article, asks for three weeks to investigate the matter before he is forced to decide between these two options. Beauchamp goes to Yanina, where he finds incontrovertible proof of the allegations against the Count de Morcerf. Albert is devastated by the revelation regarding his father but grateful to Beauchamp, whom he forgives. In the end, Beauchamp agrees to help Albert track down the enemy.

Hubert Beauchamp

Go Down, Moses
William Faulkner

The owner of the plantation nearest the McCaslins'. A leisurely, childish man. His sister, **Sophonsiba Beauchamp**, believes he is the true Earl of Warwick.

Lucas Beauchamp

Go Down, Moses
William Faulkner

The part-black grandson of **Carothers McCaslin**, the son of **Tennie** and **Tomey**'s **Turl**. A tenant farmer on the old McCaslin plantation when it is owned by **Carothers Edmonds**.

Molly Beauchamp

Go Down, Moses
William Faulkner

Lucas Beauchamp's wife, who helps to raise **Carothers Edmonds**.

Samuel Beauchamp

Go Down, Moses
William Faulkner

Molly Beauchamp and Lucas Beauchamp's grandson, a criminal who is executed in Illinois in the final story.

Sophonsiba Beauchamp

Go Down, Moses
William Faulkner

Hubert Beauchamp's sister, eventually **Buck McCaslin**'s wife. She believes her brother is the real Earl of Warwick and insists that his plantation be called Warwick.

Tennie Beauchamp

Go Down, Moses
William Faulkner

The Beauchamp slave who marries **Tomey**'s **Turl**; **Lucas Beauchamp**'s mother.

Beaufort

Frankenstein
Mary Shelley

A merchant who is **Caroline Beaufort**'s father and a friend of **Alphonse Frankenstein**'s.

Cardinal Beaufort, Bishop of Winchester

Henry VI, Part I and *Henry VI, Part II*
William Shakespeare

Head of the Catholic Church in England and great-uncle of **King Henry VI**. Winchester's strife with **Humphrey, Duke of Gloucester** is one of the civil dissensions (along with the War of the Roses) that is prophesied to tear apart England. In the opening scene of *King Henry VI, Part I*, Winchester and Gloucester begin bickering at **King Henry V**'s funeral procession. After Winchester makes clear his intention to be the new king's main advisor, he bars Gloucester from the Tower of London. Soon Gloucester's and Winchester's followers are battling each other in the streets, causing the king himself to forge a peace between them. Eventually, Winchester purchases the title of cardinal from the Pope in hopes of acquiring more power. By *King Henry VI, Part II*, the animosity between Winchester and Gloucester is well known. Rallying nobles against Gloucester, he successfully achieves victory when Gloucester is arrested for treason. But though he plots Gloucester's death with **William de la Pole, Duke of Suffolk**, Beaufort is crippled with guilt after the murder, falls ill, and dies miserably soon after.

Caroline Beaufort

Frankenstein
Mary Shelley

Beaufort's daughter. After her father's death, Caroline marries **Alphonse Frankenstein**. She dies of scarlet fever, which she contracts from **Elizabeth Lavenza**.

Julius Beaufort

The Age of Innocence
Edith Wharton

A British banker who arrives in New York society with much fanfare. Little is known about Beaufort's past, but most believe that he left Europe after some shady business deals. Beaufort is one of the most important hosts of New York society and holds lavish balls annually. Following a scandalous business failure, he is swiftly exiled from good society.

Ivanhoe
Sir Walter Scott

Lucas Beaumanoir

The stern, moralistic Grand Master of the Knights-Templars.

Evelina
Fanny Burney

Mrs. Beaumont

A high-society acquaintance of **Mrs. Selwyn**'s with whom **Evelina Anville** visits for a time at Clifton. Mrs. Beaumont's good qualities originate from pride rather than from principle, and she equates birth with virtue.

The Lion, the Witch, and the Wardrobe
C. S. Lewis

Mr. Beaver

Tumnus's friend. He aids **Lucy Pevensie**, **Peter Pevensie**, **Susan Pevensie**, and **Edmund Pevensie** in the search for the petrified faun, Tumnus. Mr. Beaver introduces the Pevensies to **Mrs. Beaver** and **Father Christmas** and ultimately brings them to the Stone Table and **Aslan**.

The Lion, the Witch, and the Wardrobe
C. S. Lewis

Mrs. Beaver

Mr. Beaver's wife. Mrs. Beaver is kindly, good-natured, motherly, and a good cook, giving **Peter Pevensie, Edmund Pevensie**, **Lucy Pevensie**, and **Susan Pevensie** delicious fish and potatoes before telling them about **Aslan**.

When the Legends Die
Hal Borland

Dolly Beaverfoot

Ed Porter's wife and a teacher of basketry at the school that **Thomas Black Bull** attends.

Demian
Hermann Hesse

Alfons Beck

A boy **Emil Sinclair** meets at boarding school, who first takes him to a bar. He leads Sinclair into a world of misbehavior during his time at boarding school. He is one in a string of older, more dominating characters to whom Sinclair looks for validation.

Mourning Becomes Electra
Eugene O'Neill

Seth Beckwith

The Mannons' aged gardener. Seth Beckwith is stoop-shouldered and raw-boned but still strong. Like his employers, especially **Christine Mannon** and **Lavinia Mannon**, his gaunt face gives the impression of a lifelike mask. In his time with the Mannons, he has learned most of the family's secrets and colluded in keeping them. A watchman figure of sorts, he is repeatedly seen wandering the grounds.

Henry IV, Parts I, II; Henry V; and Henry VI, Part I
William Shakespeare

John of Lancaster, Duke of Bedford

Son of **King Henry IV**; brother of Prince Harry (**Henry V**), **Humphrey, Duke of Gloucester**, and **Thomas, Duke of Clarence**; uncle of **King Henry VI**. A fierce warrior in *King Henry IV, Part I*, John is better known in *King Henry IV, Part II* for his cunning and dishonesty in battle. Granted full authority to act in the king's name with the rebels, the prince is given the official list of grievances from **Lord Thomas Mowbray**, **Lord Hastings**, and the **Archbishop of York**. In a meeting in the forest, John essentially agrees to grant the rebels' requests, and urges them to disperse their armies. As soon as they do so, however, he gives an order for the three leaders to be arrested and executed for treason. The contrast between the humorless and cold Prince John and the compassionate Prince Harry is pointedly, if amusingly, expounded upon by **Sir John Falstaff**, who credits wine for Harry's warmth. The new Duke of Bedford in *King Henry V*, says precious little, merely standing around and supporting his older brother's campaign in France. By *King Henry VI, Part I*, he is the aged regent of the English territories in France. After he learns of **Lord Talbot**'s capture, he goes to France to ransom him. Though able to fight at Orléans, Bedford soon becomes sick with age. He dies content after the English win a battle.

Chronicle of a Death Foretold
Gabriel García Márquez

Cristo Bedoya

A friend of the narrator's and of **Santiago Nasar**'s. The night before the murder, he was with **Bayardo San Roman**, **Luis Enrique** and Santiago all the time, at the church and after at the festival. On the day of the planned murder, he and Santiago walked through town. As soon as he found about **Pedro Vicario** and **Pablo Vicario**'s plan, he unsuccessfully ran to try and find Santiago.

Oliver Twist
Charles Dickens

Mrs. Bedwin

Mr. Brownlow's kindhearted housekeeper. Mrs. Bedwin is unwilling to believe **Mr. Bumble**'s negative report of **Oliver Twist**'s character.

White Noise
Don DeLillo

Bee

Jack Gladney's normal, thoughtful daughter from his marriage to **Tweedy Bonner**. She is a well-adjusted, cosmopolitan child who makes Jack highly self-conscious and uncomfortable.

A Room with a View
E. M. Forster

Mr. Beebe

The rector in **Lucy Honeychurch**'s town, a tactful and pleasant man who aims to use his influence to help various characters. He takes a liking to those who are honest, but sees the good in almost everyone. He supports Lucy all through the book until she decides to marry **George Emerson**, a prospect he opposes.

Paradise Lost
John Milton

Beelzebub

Satan's second-in-command. Beelzebub discusses with Satan their options after being cast into Hell, and at the debate suggests they investigate the newly created Earth. He and Satan embody perverted reason, since they are both eloquent and rational but use their talents for wholly corrupt ends.

Lucky Jim
Kingsley Amis

Alfred Beesley

Holds a position similar to **Jim Dixon**'s, but in the college's English department. He and Dixon are drinking friends and often walk to college together. However, he takes his career and work more seriously than Dixon.

All Quiet on the Western Front
Erich Maria Remarque

Joseph Behm

The first of **Paul Bäumer**'s classmates to die in the war. Behm did not want to enlist but caved under the pressure of the schoolmaster, **Kantorek**. His ugly, painful death shatters his classmates' trust in the authorities who convinced them to take part in the war.

Into Thin Air
Jon Krakauer

Neal Beidleman

An excellent guide with **Scott Fischer**'s service. Consistent as a climber and a guide, Neal is instrumental in saving his clients' lives during the summit descent.

The Light in the Forest
Conrad Richter

Bejance

An old black slave who works as a basket maker. Like **True Son**, Bejance grew up with an Indian tribe, the Wyandottes of Virginia, and misses the freedom of his youth very much. The experiences Bejance has endured in both the Indian and white worlds have given him a wise perspective on life, which he is able to share with True Son and **Gordie**.

His Dark Materials
Robert Pullman

Lyra Belacqua

The protagonist of the trilogy, an eleven-year-old girl from Jordan College in Oxford who is destined to be the second Eve. Lyra is the daughter of **Marisa Coulter** and **Lord Asriel**, and her daemon is **Pantalaimon**. As the new Eve, Lyra must fall again in order to restore respect for knowledge. After learning about herself and her body, she must pass from childhood to womanhood to restore Dust, which has been leaking out of the world. Hungry for experience, Lyra is rebellious and willful; she obeys no one without good reason.

Belarius

Cymbeline
William Shakespeare

A British nobleman unjustly banished by **Cymbeline**. For revenge, Belarius kidnapped Cymbeline's infant sons and raised them as his own.

Sir Toby Belch

Twelfth Night
William Shakespeare

Olivia's uncle. The lady of Illyria lets Sir Toby live with her, but she does not approve of his rowdy behavior, practical jokes, heavy drinking, late-night carousing, or friends (specifically the idiotic **Sir Andrew Aguecheek**). Sir Toby, the embodiment of the play's chaotic spirit, also earns the ire of the puritanical **Malvolio**. But he has an ally, and eventually a mate, in Olivia's sharp-witted serving-woman, **Maria**. Together they hatch an elaborate practical joke that ruins the controlling, self-righteous Malvolio and validates their own decadent lifestyle.

Belial

Paradise Lost
John Milton

One of the principal devils in Hell. Belial argues against further war with Heaven, but only because he is slothful and inactive. His eloquence and learning are great, and he is able to persuade many of the devils with his faulty reasoning.

Bel-Imperia

The Spanish Tragedy
Thomas Kyd

The main female character of the story. The daughter of the **Duke of Castile**, she is headstrong, as evidenced by her decisions to love **Andrea** and **Horatio**, both against her father's wishes. She is intelligent, beautiful, and, in moments of love, tender. She also is bent on revenge, both for her slain lover Andrea and for Horatio. Her transformation into a Machiavellian villain is not as dramatic as **Hieronimo**'s, but only because she shows signs of Machiavellian behavior beforehand—her decision to love Horatio, in part, may have been calculated revenge, undertaken to spite **Balthazar**, Andrea's killer.

Belinda

The Rape of the Lock
Alexander Pope

A character based on the historical Arabella Fermor, a member of Pope's circle of prominent Roman Catholics. In the poem, **the Baron** precipitates a rift between their two families by snipping off a lock of Belinda's hair.

Belize

Angels in America
Tony Kushner

A black ex–drag queen and registered nurse. Belize is **Prior Walter**'s best friend and **Roy Cohn**'s caretaker. He is the most ethical and reasonable character in the play, generously looking out for Prior, grappling with Roy, and rebutting **Louis Ironson**'s blindly self-centered politics.

Belknap — *Out of Africa*, Isak Dinesen

The American mill-manager whose gun is used in the accidental shooting.

Mary Anne Bell — *The Things They Carried*, Tim O'Brien

Mark Fossie's high school sweetheart. Although Mary Anne arrives in Vietnam full of innocence, she gains a respect for death and the darkness of the jungle and, according to legend, disappears there. Unlike **Jimmy Cross**'s Martha and **Henry Dobbins**'s girlfriend, who only serve as fantasy reminders of a world removed from Vietnam, Mary Anne is a strong and realized character who shatters Fossie's fantasy of finding comfort in his docile girlfriend.

Mr. Bell — *Anne of Green Gables*, L. M. Montgomery

The church superintendent. Mr. Bell leads prayer every Sunday. **Anne Shirley** cannot stand his prayers because she finds them unimpassioned and boring.

Vanessa Bell — *The Hours*, Michael Cunningham

Virginia Woolf 's sister, an accomplished artist, and mother of three children. Vanessa has a raucous, colorful, and cheerful life.

Queen Bella — *The Princess Bride*, William Goldman

The Queen of Florin and **Prince Humperdinck**'s stepmother.

Bellamira — *The Jew of Malta*, Christopher Marlowe

The prostitute who dupes **Ithamore** into bribing **Barabas**. Bellamira is willing to resort to crime if her business dries up and thus displays a basic interest in money as a means of survival. She is murdered by Barabas with the use of a poisoned flower.

Doctor Bellario — *The Merchant of Venice*, William Shakespeare

A wealthy Paduan lawyer and **Portia**'s cousin. Doctor Bellario never appears in the play, but he sends Portia the letters of introduction she needs to make her appearance in court.

Lady Bellaston

Tom Jones
Henry Fielding

A London lady, and a relative of **Sophia**'s, whose passionate, lusty personality leads her to dabble in intrigues. Lady Bellaston carries out a vengeful battle against **Tom** and Sophia with the utmost glee.

Belle

A Christmas Carol
Charles Dickens

Ebenezer Scrooge's onetime fiancée. Belle had no dowry and realized that her poverty made her undesirable in Scrooge's eyes. While traveling with the Ghost of Christmas Past, Scrooge sees that Belle has married a kind man and had many loving children.

Belle

The Chairs
Eugène Ionesco

The invisible former lover of the **Old Man**, and the current wife of the **Photo-engraver**. The Old Man reminisces with Belle about their romantic past and appears to hold on to what could have been.

Claire de Bellegarde, Comtesse de Cintré

The American
Henry James

The daughter of the **Marquis** and **Marquise** and the sister of **Valentin** and **Urbain**, also the childhood friend of **Mrs. Tristram** and the beloved of **Christopher Newman**. Claire is described as an exquisite and perfect woman: cultured, aristocratic, beautiful, and kind. At twenty-eight, she is a widow. Though Claire is strong and willing to stand against her family on moral principles, she cannot ultimately fight for her own happiness. Newman's courtship gives her a brief glimpse of the joy others experience, but by novel's end she comes to feel that personal satisfaction and pleasure are hopelessly vain in a world where others suffer. Claire's decision to enter the Carmelite order is not simply an act of desperation, but a sign that she has dedicated her life to God to redeem the family.

Marquis de Bellegarde

The American
Henry James

The late father of **Claire de Bellegarde**, **Valentin de Bellegarde**, and **Urbain de Bellegarde**, and late husband of the **Marquise de Bellegarde**. The handsome, eloquent, and sympathetic Marquis is reflected in Valentin and Claire just as the ruthless Marquise is reflected in Urbain. When the Marquis refused to allow Claire to marry the wealthy but unsavory **Comte de Cintré**, his wife and eldest son murdered him at the family estate at Fleurières.

Marquise de Bellegarde

The American
Henry James

The mother of **Urbain**, **Valentin**, and **Claire**, born Lady Emmeline Atheling, the daughter of an English earl. The Marquise, **Christopher Newman**'s nemesis, is completely at home in her meticulously arranged world of pedigrees and lost fortunes, a ruthless matriarch and a formidable adversary. Together, she and Urbain run the Bellegarde household with an iron fist, first secretly killing her husband the Marquis for attempting to prevent Claire's first marriage and now scheming to manipulate Claire and Valentin for the glory of the family name. Yet even the Marquise's most appalling actions stem from a deep sense of entitlement and duty to the aristocratic traditions she has been given to uphold.

Young Marquise de Bellegarde

The American
Henry James

Urbain de Bellegarde's wife, a flighty, fashionable woman who, bored with pedigrees and damp chateaux, is looking for some excitement. The young Marquise adores music, dancing, and fashion. She flirts, pouts, and fears her husband even though she finds him dull. She attempts to establish an alliance with **Christopher Newman**—another outsider to the family—but her idea of a joint venture is a secret trip to the rowdy students' ball in the Latin Quarter.

Urbain de Bellegarde

The American
Henry James

The older son of the late **Marquis de Bellegarde** and the **Marquise de Bellegarde**. Urbain is middle-aged and much older than Claire and Valentin. He is also infinitely epicurean and accomplished, cultivating the best manners in France. He takes after his mother in looks, ambition, values, and temperament. But though Urbain fancies himself the male head of the household, he is little more than his mother's lackey. His role in the household, as in the murder, is that of accomplice, posturer, and guard.

Valentin de Bellegarde

The American
Henry James

The younger son of the late **Marquis de Bellegarde** and the **Marquise de Bellegarde**, brother of **Claire de Bellegarde** and **Urbain de Bellegarde**. The charismatic and entertaining Valentin is a great friend to **Christopher Newman**. Valentin is very close to Claire and loves and admires her tremendously, while resenting their mother and Urbain for forcing Claire into marriage against her will. Valentin also suspects that his mother and Urbain were involved in the Marquis's death, but he does not know how. Valentin plays the go-between between Claire and Newman, singing Newman's praises to his hesitant sister and acting as Newman's advocate toward the Marquise and Urbain. His motives are not entirely selfless, however, as he sees Newman as a means of exacting revenge against his mother and brother's reign of terror.

Chevalier de Belleroche

Dangerous Liaisons
Pierre-Ambroise-François Choderlos de Laclos

The Marquise de Merteuil's lover. Merteuil is having a romance with Belleroche for much of the novel, but grows tired of him and seeks to replace him with Danceny.

Oscar Belling

The Black Prince
Iris Murdoch

Julian Baffin's ex-boyfriend. He never appears in the novel. At the end of the novel, however, Julian's name has changed to "Julian Belling," signifying that she has married him. His presence merely serves to suggest Julian's youthful approach to the art of loving, since it is just after breaking up with him that she decides she is passionately in love with **Bradley Pearson**.

Governor Bellingham

The Scarlet Letter
Nathaniel Hawthorne

A wealthy, elderly gentleman who spends much of his time consulting with the other town fathers. Despite his role as governor of a fledgling American society, he very much resembles a traditional English aristocrat. Bellingham tends to strictly adhere to the rules, but he is easily swayed by **Reverend Arthur Dimmesdale**'s eloquence. He remains blind to the misbehaviors taking place in his own house: his sister, **Mistress Hibbins**, is a witch.

Lady Caroline Evelyn Belmont

Evelina
Fanny Burney

The daughter of **Mr. Evelyn** and **Madame Duval**, Lady Caroline Belmont is **Evelina Anville**'s mother. She leaves the **Reverend Mr. Arthur Villars**'s care at eighteen to spend time with her mother, but suffers under Madame Duval's decision to withhold her dowry to **Sir John Belmont**, who subsequently abandons her. She dies giving birth to Evelyn.

Sir John Belmont

Evelina
Fanny Burney

Evelina Anville's father. Sir Belmont marries **Lady Caroline Evelyn Belmont** but destroys the marriage certificate when the dowry is withheld. He regrets his unscrupulous behavior later in life and attempts to make some restitution.

Lady Belmont, née Polly Green

Evelina
Fanny Burney

The daughter of Dame Green, an imposter whom **Sir John Belmont** mistakenly accepts as his own child. Raised in a convent, she is quiet, modest, and shy.

Belmonte

The Sun Also Rises
Ernest Hemingway

A Spanish bullfighter who once was skilled and popular. When Belmonte came out of retirement to fight again, however, he found he could never live up to the legends that had grown around him. A bitter, purposeless, and dejected man, he embodies the aimlessness and futility of the Lost Generation.

Beloved

Beloved
Toni Morrison

A mysterious visitor to 124 Bluestone Road. Beloved's limited linguistic ability, neediness, baby-soft skin, and emotional instability could all be explained by a lifetime spent in captivity. These traits could also support the theory held by most of the characters in the novel, as well as most readers: Beloved is the embodied spirit of Sethe's dead daughter, whom Sethe murdered. Her presence catalyzes Sethe's, **Paul D**'s, and **Denver**'s processes of emotional growth. Once Sethe reciprocates Beloved's violent passion for her, the two become locked in a destructive, exclusive, parasitic relationship. Beloved allows and inspires Sethe to tell the stories she never tells—stories about her own feelings of abandonment by her mother, about the harshest indignities she suffered at Sweet Home, and about her motivations for murdering her daughter. By engaging with her past, Sethe begins to learn about herself and the extent of her ability to live in the present.

However, Beloved causes Sethe to waste away, stealing Sethe's life energy away from her. In the end, a group of women led by **Ella** perform an exorcism to rid the town of Beloved.

Belter

The Martian Chronicles
Ray Bradbury

One of the American Negroes who is emigrating to Mars. When **Mr. Teece** tries to stop him from leaving because he owes Teece fifty dollars, the other Negroes band together to pay off the debt.

Ben

Rebecca
Daphne du Maurier

A harmless man, mildly retarded, who spends much of his time on the beach near Manderley.

Ben

The Dumb Waiter
Harold Pinter

Ben is the senior hit man, the dominant foil to his submissive partner **Gus**. He runs their outfit, but pays strict attention to the demands of **Wilson**, their boss. He often broods silently, reads the newspaper, doesn't question their job, and evades Gus's probing questions.

Ben Finney

Walk Two Moons
Sharon Creech

The roommate and romantic interest of **Salamanca Tree Hiddle** (Sal). Ben is a quirky, creative young man who persists despite confusion and shyness in expressing his affection for Sal throughout the novel.

Old Ben

Go Down, Moses
William Faulkner

The bear of "The Bear," a ferocious, gigantic beast who becomes legendary as an immortal force in the forest. **Boon Hogganbeck** finally kills him after he tears out the entrails of the dog **Lion**.

Ben Benally

House Made of Dawn
N. Scott Momaday

A friend and father figure to **Abel**. Ben is a Navajo from an area known as the Wild Ruins, but, now lives in Los Angeles. Benally, who believes he is related to Abel somehow, does his best to help Abel adjust to city life in Los Angeles when he first meets him on the job at the factory. The sections of the book written in his voice paint a picture of Ben as a pragmatic and practical man who is aware of his Indian heritage but aspires to many of the amenities of the modern American lifestyle.

Benedetto

The Count of Monte Cristo
Alexandre Dumas

The adopted son of **Signor Bertuccio**. Benedetto is really the illegitimate son of **Gérard de Villefort** and **Madame Danglars**. Handsome, charming, and a wonderful liar, Benedetto plays a part in one of **Edmond Dantès**'s elaborate revenge schemes.

Benedick

Much Ado About Nothing
William Shakespeare

A witty aristocrat-soldier who fights under his friend **Don Pedro**. The high-spirited Benedick carries on a "merry war" of wits with **Beatrice**, but insists that he will never marry. But after his friends **Claudio** and **Hero** become engaged, Benedick is "tricked" into falling in love with Beatrice by his friends, who want to see the two end up together. When Claudio shames Hero at the altar, Benedick is tested: he declares his feelings for Beatrice, who demands that he show his love by killing Claudio in a duel. After the confusion is cleared up, Beatrice and Benedick's love is brought to light, and they agree to marry. Proving love's superiority to wit, Benedick is finally able to stop Beatrice's sharp tongue—with a kiss.

Cide Hamete Benengeli

Don Quixote
Miguel de Cervantes

The fictional Moor historian whose history of **Don Quixote** has been translated by **Cervantes**. Benengeli's history is rife with contempt for authors who warp or embellish stories of chivalry. Cervantes creates this construct of a lost first author to comment on authorship and literature.

Benia

The Red Tent
Anita Diamant

A carpenter with an open face. When **Dinah** is looking for a jewelry box with **Meryt**, Benia meets Dinah by chance and feels an immediate connection to her. Dinah feels something in Benia's gaze but says nothing. Later when **Joseph** is bringing Dinah and Benia in his caravan, Dinah travels as Benia's wife, not as Joseph's sister. Benia's love gives Dinah the strength to count her blessings, forgive her family, and move on. Benia knows the story of Dinah's past only much later after meeting her.

Benjamin

Animal Farm
George Orwell

A donkey who refuses to feel inspired by the Rebellion. The oldest and most cynical of the animals, Benjamin does not celebrate or change his routine once **Mr. Jones** is expelled from the farm, nor when **Napoleon** wrests control from **Snowball**. He seems to be the only animal who recognizes the increasing tyranny and hypocrisy of the pigs, but chooses to remain out of the fray.

Benjamin

The Red Tent
Anita Diamant

Youngest of all of **Jacob**'s sons. His birth kills his mother **Rachel** after Jacob and his sons murder all of the men in Shechem. In the end, it is Benjamin's daughter, **Gera**, who tells **Dinah** that her name and her story are remembered by blindly telling Dinah the legend of Dinah and then realizing who she is. After the experience, Gera resolves to name her own daughter Dinah.

General Benjamin

Bel Canto
Ann Patchett

The most intelligent and thoughtful of the three generals who lead the terrorists. Benjamin was a schoolteacher until his brother was arrested and imprisoned for handing out flyers publicizing a political protest. After that, he joined the terrorist group La Familia de Martin Suarez, named after a ten-year-old boy who was shot dead while handing out flyers for a political rally. Benjamin has left behind a wife and children, and he is fatherly to some of the young terrorists under his command. He is plagued with shingles, which rage across much of his face.

Uncle Benjamin

Incidents in the Life of a Slave Girl
Harriet Ann Jacobs

Linda Brent's beloved uncle, a slave who defies and beats his master and then runs away. Uncle Benjamin's successful escape inspires Linda, but also shows her that to run away means to give up all family and community ties.

Catherine Bennet

Pride and Prejudice
Jane Austen

The fourth Bennet sister. Like **Lydia Bennet**, she is girlishly enthralled with the soldiers.

Elizabeth Bennet

Pride and Prejudice
Jane Austen

The novel's protagonist. The second daughter of **Mr. Bennet**, Elizabeth is the most intelligent and sensible of the five Bennet sisters. She is well read and quick-witted, with a tongue that occasionally proves too sharp for her own good. Her realization of **Fitzwilliam Darcy**'s essential goodness eventually triumphs over her initial prejudice against him.

Jane Bennet

Pride and Prejudice
Jane Austen

The eldest and most beautiful Bennet sister. Jane Bennet is more reserved and gentler than **Elizabeth Bennet**. The easy pleasantness with which she and **Charles Bingley** interact contrasts starkly with the mutual distaste that marks the encounters between Elizabeth and **Fitzwilliam Darcy**.

Lydia Bennet

Pride and Prejudice
Jane Austen

The youngest Bennet sister. Lydia is gossipy, immature, and self-involved. Unlike **Elizabeth Bennet**, Lydia flings herself headlong into romance and ends up running off with **George Wickham**.

Mary Bennet

Pride and Prejudice
Jane Austen

The middle Bennet sister. Mary is bookish and pedantic.

Mr. Bennet

Pride and Prejudice
Jane Austen

The patriarch of the Bennet family, a gentleman of modest income with five unmarried daughters. Mr. Bennet has a sarcastic, cynical sense of humor that he uses to irritate his wife, **Mrs. Bennet**. Though he loves his daughters (**Elizabeth Bennet** in particular), he often fails as a parent, preferring to withdraw from the marital obsessions of the women around him rather than offer help.

Mrs. Bennet

Pride and Prejudice
Jane Austen

Mr. Bennet's wife, a foolish, noisy woman whose only goal in life is to marry off her daughters. Her low breeding and often unbecoming behavior often repel the suitors Mrs. Bennet tries to attract for her daughters.

Benny

Incidents in the Life of a Slave Girl
Harriet Ann Jacobs

Linda Brent's child with Mr. Sands. Linda loves Benny and his sister **Ellen** passionately, and her feelings about them drive the book's action.

Will Benteen

Gone with the Wind
Margaret Mitchell

A one-legged Confederate soldier who becomes a fixture at Tara after the war despite his lack of family or wealth. Will makes Tara a marginally profitable farm. His competence allows **Scarlett O'Hara** to move to Atlanta.

Jesse Bentley

Winesburg, Ohio
Sherwood Anderson

A wealthy farmer and a deeply religious man with a brutal, Old Testament sensibility and tendency to terrorize his family, especially his daughter, **Louise Bentley**, and his grandson, **David Hardy**.

Louise Bentley

Winesburg, Ohio
Sherwood Anderson

Jesse Bentley's daughter. A lonely woman with a vicious temper, she is estranged from her father and marries young out of a craving for love, but her marriage is not a success.

Mr. Bentley

Anne of Green Gables
L. M. Montgomery

A minister at Avonlea. Mr. Bentley does little to inspire his congregation and gives dull, lengthy sermons.

Benvolio

Romeo and Juliet
William Shakespeare

Montague's nephew and **Romeo**'s cousin and thoughtful friend. He makes a genuine effort to defuse violent scenes in public places, though **Mercutio** accuses him of having a nasty temper in private. At the play's onset, Montague asks Benvolio to discover the cause of Romeo's moody temperament. Benvolio also tries to get Romeo to forget **Rosaline**, the unseen character whom Romeo loves just before falling in love with Juliet.

Benvolio

Doctor Faustus
Christopher Marlowe

A German nobleman at **Emperor Charles V**'s court who vows to avenge himself for **Faustus**'s trickery.

Captain Benwick

Persuasion
Jane Austen

A depressed naval officer who was once engaged to **Captain Harville**'s now-deceased sister, Fanny. Captain Benwick is a shy man and an ardent reader of poetry. When **Anne Elliot** meets him, he is on leave from his ship and he is living with Captain and Mrs. Harville. He seeks a young woman to help him get over Fanny, and his attentions turn, surprisingly, to **Louisa Musgrove**.

Beor

The Red Tent
Anita Diamant

Ruti and **Laban**'s son, **Kemuel**'s brother. Kemuel and Beor are negligent watching the flocks in Laban's camp, and this makes **Jacob** grow angry.

Beorn

The Hobbit
J. R. R. Tolkien

A man who can turn into a bear. **Gandalf** brings **Bilbo Baggins** and the band of **Dwarves** to his old friend Beorn's wooden house in Mirkwood after their escape from the **Goblins**. Beorn does not like Dwarves, but he feels that he should help these friends of Gandalf because they defeated the leader of the Goblins. Beorn provides food, water, and shelter to the team.

Beow

Beowulf
Unknown

The second king listed in the genealogy of Danish rulers with which the poem begins. Beow is the son of **Scyld Scefing** and father of **Halfdane**. The narrator presents Beow as a gift from God to a people in need of a leader.

Beowulf

Beowulf
Unknown

The protagonist of the epic, Beowulf is a Geatish hero who fights the monster **Grendel**, **Grendel's mother**, and a fire-breathing **dragon**. Beowulf's boasts and encounters reveal him to be the strongest, ablest warrior of the Geats. In his youth, he personifies all of the best values of the heroic culture. In his old age, he proves a wise and effective ruler.

Beowulf

Grendel
John Gardner

A Geatish hero who comes across the sea to rid the Scyldings of **Grendel**. Huge and exceedingly strong, Beowulf is cold and mechanical, showing little emotion or personality. In the climactic battle with Grendel, Beowulf appears to sprout wings and speak fire, prompting comparisons to the dragon.

Marija Berczynskas

The Jungle
Upton Sinclair

Ona's cousin. A large, assertive woman, Marija fights back against the corrupt bosses in Chicago. She represents the defiant immigrant spirit slowly crushed by capitalism.

Elroy Berdahl

The Things They Carried
Tim O'Brien

The proprietor of the Tip Top Lodge on the Rainy River near the Canadian border. Berdahl serves as the closest thing to a father figure for **Tim O'Brien**, who, after receiving his draft notice, spends six contemplative days with the quiet, kind Berdahl while he makes a decision about whether to go to war or to escape the draft by running across the border to Canada.

Beregond

The Return of the King
J. R. R. Tolkien

A member of the Tower Guard at Minas Tirith, and **Peregrin Took**'s friend. Beregond breaks the law of the Guard of the Citadel by leaving his post, but, in doing so, he successfully delays **Denethor** from killing his son **Faramir** by burning him alive.

Berenger

Rhinoceros
Eugène Ionesco

The protagonist of the play, an Everyman slacker who finds neither his work in an office nor the culture around him fulfilling. Alienated, yet still confused as to why he has been displaced, he is unwilling to commit himself to anything in life but his love for **Daisy**. His friend **Jean** constantly reprimands the submissive Berenger for his uncouth appearance and apathetic attitude.

Dr. Berger

Ordinary People
Judith Guest

A psychiatrist in Chicago with whom **Conrad Jarrett** begins meeting once a week in an effort to gain more "control." Dr. Berger tells Conrad that he needs to do less thinking and more feeling, which is also a conclusion that **Calvin Jarrett** comes up with independently about his own life. Dr. Berger also tells Conrad during his breakdown after the death of **Karen Aldrich** that Conrad has to stop trying to be his brother **Buck Jarrett** and must stop blaming himself for Buck's accidental death.

Bergil

The Return of the King
J. R. R. Tolkien

Beregond's son. Bergil becomes close with **Peregrin Took** after the Hobbit joins the Guard of Minas Tirith.

Alexandra Bergson

O Pioneers!
Willa Cather

The novel's protagonist. Alexandra Bergson is a model of emotional strength, courage, and resolve. As the eldest child of the Swedish immigrant **John Bergson**, she inherits his farm and makes it profitable. Particularly suited to the toil of prairie life, Alexandra is a prototype of the strong American pioneer and an embodiment of the untamed American West.

Emil Bergson

O Pioneers!
Willa Cather

The youngest son of **John Bergson**, and the younger brother of **Oscar Bergson**, **Lou Bergson**, and **Alexandra Bergson**. Emil reaps the advantages of Alexandra's financial success: freed from the obligations of farm work, he is able to go to college and explore the world. He grows up tall, handsome, and athletic—a shining emblem of America's immense promise. Tragically, however, Emil falls in love with his flirtatious neighbor **Marie Shabata**; he is killed, along with her, by her husband, **Frank Shabata**.

John Bergson

O Pioneers!
Willa Cather

The patriarch of the Bergson clan, father of **Alexandra Bergson**, **Oscar Bergson**, **Lou Bergson**, and **Emil Bergson**. John Bergson had been a shipwright in Sweden, but became a farmer in the untamed, hardscrabble prairie lands of Nebraska. He recognizes the wisdom of his eldest child and leaves her as the caretaker of the farm he has fought so hard to cultivate out of the stubborn wilderness.

Lou Bergson

O Pioneers!
Willa Cather

The second son of **John Bergson**, and the brother of **Alexandra Bergson**, **Oscar Bergson**, and **Emil Bergson**. Lou is relatively intelligent, but he is also devious, small-minded, and vicious. He marries **Annie Lee** and settles into a life of scheming and small-time politics. He is less creative and flexible than Alexandra, and, like his older brother Oscar, he resents the relationship between Alexandra and **Carl Linstrum.**

Milly Bergson

O Pioneers!
Willa Cather

The daughter of **Lou Bergson** and **Annie Lee**, and **Alexandra Bergson**'s favorite niece. Milly is intelligent and friendly, in contrast to her small-minded and devious parents.

O Pioneers!
Willa Cather

Mrs. Bergson

The matriarch of the Bergson clan, wife of **John Bergson**, and mother of **Alexandra Bergson**, **Oscar Bergson**, **Lou Bergson**, and **Emil Bergson**. Mrs. Bergson is fat and unimaginative, but a good housewife.

O Pioneers!
Willa Cather

Oscar Bergson

The oldest son of **John Bergson**, the younger brother of **Alexandra Bergson**, and the older brother of **Lou Bergson** and **Emil Bergson**. Oscar is a hard worker, but mentally sluggish and uncreative. Like his smarter brother Lou, he resents Alexandra for her financial success, her unconventional ways, and her relationship with **Carl Linstrum**.

Richard II
William Shakespeare

Lord Berkeley

A nobleman sent by the **Duke of York** to intercept **Henry Bolingbroke**. After settling their differences and declaring his neutrality, York invites Bolingbroke and his men to spend the night at Berkeley Castle.

Death of a Salesman
Arthur Miller

Bernard

Charley's son and an important, successful lawyer. He argues a case in front of the Supreme Court but does not mention it to **Willy Loman**. Although Willy used to mock him for studying hard, Bernard always loved Willy's sons dearly and regarded **Biff Loman** as a hero. Bernard's success is difficult for Willy to accept because his own sons' lives do not measure up.

Ender's Game
Orson Scott Card

Bernard

A Battle School bully. Bernard attacks **Ender Wiggin** on the shuttle ride to the school, and Ender breaks his arm. Bernard tries to bully the launchies into disliking **Shen** and Ender, and he attempts to intimidate Ender in the showers with **Bonzo Madrid**.

The Jew of Malta
Christopher Marlowe

Friar Bernardine

Jacomo's friend and a friar, though of a different order from Jacomo. **Bernardine** fights with Jacomo, as both men want **Barabas**'s money to go to their own monasteries. Bernardine is strangled with his own belt by **Ithamore** after Barabas pretends he is converting to Christianity.

Hamlet
William Shakespeare

Bernardo

A night watchman at Elsinore. The play begins on a cold night atop the castle ramparts, where Bernardo and **Marcellus** are the first people to see **the Ghost** of King Hamlet, **Hamlet**'s father.

Berniece

The Piano Lesson
August Wilson

Sister of **Boy Willie**, niece of **Doaker Charles**, mother of **Maretha**. She blames her brother for her husband's death, remaining skeptical of his bravado and chiding him for his rebellious ways. The main conflict of the play focuses around Berniece and Boy Willie, as she refuses to let him sell the piano. Berniece's refusal to part with or play the piano shows that she regards it as an artifact and symbol of their ancestors' history. In the end, Berniece plays a song to exorcise the ghost of the piano's previous owner, **Sutter**, from the house. She thus proves ownership of the family heirloom and resumes her role in the family chain.

Berowne

Love's Labour's Lost
William Shakespeare

The most vocal of the three lords who join the **King of Navarre** in his oath of scholarship. Before signing on to the oath, Berowne challenges the King, **Dumain**, and **Longaville** about the details of the pact, proving himself more worldly and clever than the other three. He ultimately falls in love with **Rosaline**, the wittiest of the **Princess of France**'s ladies. Berowne is a skilled speaker, and much of the play revolves around his witty repartee with the other characters. Like the King and the other lords, Berowne truly matures only at the end of the play, when he swears to work at a hospital for a year in order to win Rosaline's love.

Gilbert Berquist

Stranger in a Strange Land
Robert A. Heinlein

A high-level assistant to Secretary General Douglas, it is Berquist's job to deal covertly with the administration's less savory problems.

Lieutenant Paco Berrendo

For Whom the Bell Tolls
Ernest Hemingway

A devoutly Catholic Fascist officer who orders the beheading of **El Sordo**'s men. Berrendo's sorrow at the death of his captain, his awareness of the useless horror of war, and his tendency toward introspection make him a sympathetic character.

Berta

Hedda Gabler
Henrik Ibsen

Hedda Tesman's maid. Berta used to work for **Aunt Julle**. She tries hard to please Hedda, but her efforts are in vain.

Berthe

Madame Bovary
Gustave Flaubert

Charles Bovary and **Emma Bovary**'s daughter, who is condemned to a life of poverty by her mother's financial excesses and her parents' deaths. When she is orphaned, Berthe is sent to live with Charles's mother. When Charles's mother dies, she is dispatched to an impoverished aunt and forced to work in a cotton mill.

Bertilak of Hautdesert

Sir Gawain and the Green Knight
Unknown

The sturdy, good-natured lord of the castle where **Sir Gawain** spends Christmas. Bertilak makes an arrangement with **Sir Gawain** that he will go hunting each day and give Sir Gawain everything he catches if Sir Gawain will do the same for him. Boisterous, powerful, brave, and generous, Lord Bertilak provides an interesting foil to **King Arthur**. We only learn Bertilak's name at the end of *Sir Gawain and the Green Knight*, when Bertilak reveals that he and the **Green Knight** are the same person, magically enchanted by **Morgan le Fay** for her own designs.

Bertilak's wife

Sir Gawain and the Green Knight
Unknown

An amazingly clever debater and an astute reader of Gawain's responses, Bertilak's wife attempts to seduce **Sir Gawain** on a daily basis during his stay at the castle. Bertilak's wife argues her way through three attempted seductions, ultimately succeeding in getting Gawain to take a green girdle from her and violate the terms of his agreement with Bertilak. Flirtatious and intelligent, Bertilak's wife ultimately turns out to be another pawn in **Morgan le Fay**'s plot.

Edmund Bertram

Mansfield Park
Jane Austen

The Bertrams' younger son. Since he will not be the heir to Mansfield, Edmund will become a clergyman. The only one of the Bertrams' children with a good head and a good heart, Edmund is **Fanny Price**'s closest companion. He rashly falls in love with **Mary Crawford**, which almost leads to his downfall.

Julia Bertram

Mansfield Park
Jane Austen

The Bertrams' younger daughter. Julia is equally vain but slightly less cocky, because she is younger and less beautiful than **Maria Bertram**. Julia follows Maria around, and when Maria elopes, she runs away with **Yates**, her brother **Tom Bertram**'s friend.

Lady Bertram

Mansfield Park
Jane Austen

The sister of **Fanny Price**'s mother and the wife of **Sir Thomas Bertram**. Lady Bertram is a neurotic and lazy hypochondriac. A beauty in her youth, she values people's attractiveness over all else, yet she is honest enough to admit how much Fanny means to her.

Maria Bertram

Mansfield Park
Jane Austen

The Bertrams' older daughter. Vain and pretentious, Maria abuses **Fanny Price** and marries the odious **Rushworth** for his fortune. Maria's self-indulgence eventually gets her in quite a lot of trouble when she runs away with **Henry Crawford**.

Bertram, Count of Roussillon

All's Well that Ends Well
William Shakespeare

The **Countess of Roussillon**'s only son. Bertram is a handsome, well-liked young man, whom **Helena** is in love with. After Helena heals the **King of France**'s wound and is rewarded with her pick of husbands, she picks Bertram; Bertram unwillingly accepts, and then leaves to fight in the wars. For the majority of the play, his status as an excellent soldier, general, and gentleman is compromised by his mistreatment of his estranged wife: he sends her a letter declaring that he will never be her husband, attempts a dalliance with a Florentine virgin, **Diana**, and only repents at the end of the play.

Sir Thomas Bertram

Mansfield Park
Jane Austen

A wealthy landowner and **Fanny Price**'s uncle, who rather ominously owns slaves on his plantations in the Caribbean. Sir Thomas Bertram is authoritarian and rather hard on his children until a series of disasters show him the error of his ways. He means well and eventually does right by Fanny.

Tom Bertram

Mansfield Park
Jane Austen

The Bertrams' older son and the heir to Mansfield. Tom lives to party and has gone into debt, for which **Edmund Bertram** will suffer. Eventually, Tom's lifestyle catches up to him, and he nearly dies from an illness caused by too much drinking.

Signor Bertuccio

The Count of Monte Cristo
Alexandre Dumas

Edmond Dantès' steward. The common lust for revenge draws Bertuccio close to Monte Cristo, and Bertuccio is one of Monte Cristo's two true companions, the other being **Haydée**.

Bessie

When the Legends Die
Hal Borland

Thomas Black Bull's mother, a Ute Indian. Courageous, intelligent, and strong-willed, Bessie teaches her son Tom about all the old Ute traditions and customs.

Aunt Bessie

Main Street
Sinclair Lewis

One of **Kennicott**'s relatives who moves to Gopher Prairie and proves to be a constant source of annoyance to **Carol**. Aunt Bessie joins her friend, **Mrs. Bogart**, as one of the town's biggest gossips.

Mrs. Bessie

Johnny Tremain
Esther Forbes

The Lytes' cook and **Priscilla Lapham**'s only friend in the Lyte household. Mrs. Bessie is an ardent Whig and a confidant of **Samuel Adams**, but she nonetheless remains loyal to her Tory employers.

Ulysses
James Joyce

Richard Best

A librarian at the National Library. Best is enthusiastic and agreeable, though most of his own contributions to the Hamlet conversation in Episode Nine are points of received wisdom.

Oliver Twist
Charles Dickens

Bet

One of **Fagin**'s former child pickpockets, now a prostitute.

Go Ask Alice
Anonymous

Beth

Alice's Jewish neighbor. Beth is a nice girl who bonds with Alice at first, but after Alice's experiences with drugs, Beth seems changed.

A Room of One's Own
Virginia Woolf

Mary Beton

The Narrator's aunt, who leaves her niece 500 pounds a year, thus securing her financial independence.

Ceremony
Leslie Marmon Silko

Betonie

The medicine man who guides **Tayo** through his ceremony, and **Descheeny**'s grandson. Betonie lives on the edge of the Navajo reservation, on a cliff overlooking the white town of Gallup. Feared and mistrusted by many for his eccentricities and for his contact with whites, Betonie comes from a long line of medicine men and women who struggle to create a new ceremony that will answer to the needs of the contemporary world. His wisdom is a key element in Tayo's cure, by providing Tayo with the tools and the faith necessary to complete the ceremony.

The Bell Jar
Sylvia Plath

Betsy

A pretty, wholesome girl from Kansas who becomes **Esther Greenwood**'s friend when they both work at *Lady's Day* magazine. Esther cannot relate to Betsy's cheerfulness and optimism.

Ellen Foster
Kaye Gibbons

Betsy

Ellen's aunt on her mother's side. Betsy allows her niece to stay with her for a weekend. Betsy is amused that Ellen did not realize she would be staying permanently. Betsy is petty and bickers with **Nadine**, her sister, when their mother dies.

Rita Bettencourt

On the Road
Jack Kerouac

A Denver waitress who, according to **Dean Moriarty**, has "sex difficulties." Dean sets her up with **Sal Paradise**, who tries and fails to demonstrate that sex is beautiful.

Gabriel Betteredge

The Moonstone
Wilkie Collins

The trusted house steward of **Lady Verinder**. He has been in service to the lady and her family his entire life and feels a strong attachment to the family and household servants. Betteredge has a provincial, earthy sense of humor. He enjoys the novelty of both detective work and the writing of a narrative.

Betty

Incidents in the Life of a Slave Girl
Harriet Ann Jacobs

An uneducated but intelligent, loyal, and resourceful slave who provides material assistance and encouragement to **Linda Brent**.

Betty

Miss Lonelyhearts
Nathanael West

A woman to whom **Miss Lonelyhearts** had proposed marriage two months prior to the events of the novel, but whom he now avoids, until desire for sex makes him visit her again. Betty is ordered, earnest, and virginal, and attributes Miss Lonelyhearts's illness to city life. Betty's naïveté prevents her from completely understanding Miss Lonelyhearts's plight and makes her an easy target for his verbal abuse.

Betty

Cloud Nine
Caryl Churchill

In the first act, Betty, played by a man, spends most of her time confused and incapable of making any decisions of her own. She relies totally upon her husband **Clive** to provide direction in her life. She dreams of a relationship with **Harry**, wondering what life might be like outside of her home. Betty remains caught between her duty to family and her yearning for romance. In Act II, a new Betty, played by a new actor, acquires a sense of independence and evolves into the play's protagonist. The new Betty finds independence intriguing yet frightening, and she seems to sacrifice her personal yearnings in favor of strained mother-child relationships with her children **Victoria** and **Edward**.

Sister Betty

The Autobiography of Malcolm X
Malcolm X & Alex Haley

Malcolm X's wife, a quiet and strong woman. The autobiography does not emphasize Betty's role, though she acts as Malcolm's secretary, housekeeper, and confidant. Betty endures his busy traveling and work schedule, gives birth to five of his children, and witnesses his assassination.

Pierre Bezukhov

War and Peace
Leo Tolstoy

The large-bodied, ungainly, and socially awkward illegitimate son of an old Russian grandee. Pierre, educated abroad, returns to Russia as a misfit, but his unexpected inheritance of a large fortune makes him socially desirable. Pierre is ensnared by the fortune-hunting **Helene Vasilievna Kuragina**, whose eventual deception leaves him depressed and confused, spurring a spiritual odyssey that spans the novel. Pierre eventually marries **Natasha Ilyinichna Rostova**.

Frederick Bhaer

Little Women
Louisa May Alcott

A respected professor in Germany who becomes an impoverished language instructor in America. Mr. Bhaer lives in New York, where he meets **Josephine March**. In Bhaer's presence Jo becomes nearly conventional, conforming to a more accepted code of female behavior. Before Bhaer proposes to Jo, she travels to see him, demonstrating that she has some agency in the affair. When he proposes, the rain and mud prevent him from going down on his knee or giving her his hand, so they stand literally on an equal footing. Their marriage begins with equality and primacy of the heart rather than primacy of appearances.

Bianca of *Othello*

Othello
William Shakespeare

A courtesan, or prostitute, in Cyprus. **Bianca**'s favorite customer is Cassio, who teases her with promises of marriage.

Bianca of *Shrew*

The Taming of the Shrew
William Shakespeare

The younger daughter of **Baptista**. The lovely Bianca proves herself the opposite of her sister, **Katherine**, at the beginning of the play: she is soft-spoken, sweet, and unassuming. Thus, she operates as Kate's principal female foil. Because of her large dowry and her mild behavior, several men vie for her hand, some donning disguises at one point or another—**Lucentio** as a Latin tutor, **Hortensio** as a music tutor. Baptista, however, will not let her marry until Kate is wed. When Bianca is finally given away to Lucentio, she proves more dynamic than previously thought; at the play's end banquet, she is flip and sarcastic with not only her husband, but also **Petruccio**.

Bib

A Day No Pigs Would Die
Robert Newton Peck

An ox that **Robert Peck** helps bring into the world when he assists **Benjamin Tanner**'s cow, Apron.

Billy Bibbit

One Flew over the Cuckoo's Nest
Ken Kesey

A shy patient with a bad stutter, who seems much younger than his thirty-one years. He is dominated by his mother, one of **Nurse Ratched**'s close friends. Billy is voluntarily in the hospital, as he is afraid of the outside world.

Tai Bibi

Midnight's Children
Salman Rushdie

A 512-year-old whore whom **Saleem** visits.

Sergeant Bickle

Walk Two Moons
Sharon Creech

The chief of police and the **Lunatic**'s adoptive father. Sergeant Bickle listens skeptically but patiently to **Phoebe**'s worries about her mother's disappearance.

Wing Biddlebaum

Winesburg, Ohio
Sherwood Anderson

A sensitive ex-schoolteacher who was accused of molesting one of his male pupils in a town near Winesburg.

Biddy

Great Expectations
Charles Dickens

A simple, kindhearted country girl. Biddy befriends **Pip** at school. After **Mrs. Joe** is attacked, Biddy cares for her. Biddy is **Estella**'s opposite—plain, kind, moral, and of Pip's own social class.

Sister Sandrine Bieil

The Da Vinci Code
Dan Brown

Nun and keeper of the Church of Saint-Sulpice. Sister Sandrine favors loosening Church strictures and modernizing the Church, and objects to **Opus Dei**'s attitude toward women. She is murdered by **Silas** while acting as a sentry for the Priory of Sion.

Bifur

The Hobbit
J. R. R. Tolkien

One of the dwarf companions on the novel's quest.

Big Brother

1984
George Orwell

The perceived ruler of Oceania. Though he never appears in the novel, and though he may not actually exist, Big Brother is a crucial figure. Everywhere **Winston Smith** looks, he sees posters of Big Brother's face bearing the message "BIG BROTHER IS WATCHING YOU." His image is stamped on coins and broadcast on unavoidable telescreens. Big Brother fills Winston with hatred and fascination, and much of the world has followed suit—the name "Big Brother" has become synonymous with invasive, totalitarian authority figures.

Big Daddy

Cat on a Hot Tin Roof
Tennessee Williams

Affectionately dubbed by **Maggie** as an old-fashioned "Mississippi redneck," Big Daddy is a large, brash, and vulgar plantation millionaire who believes he has returned from the grave after a near-death experience. Big Daddy loves **Brick** dearly, more than his other son, **Gooper**, and favors Brick as his rightful heir. However, Brick and Maggie's childlessness puts them at risk for losing Daddy's fortune to Gooper and **Mae**. Daddy returns from death and dismisses the vanities.

Big Laura

The Autobiography of Miss Jane Pittman
Ernest J. Gaines

Ned Douglass's mother and the slave woman who leads the freedmen as they leave slavery. Big Laura is one of many physically and emotionally strong black women who dominate the novel.

Big Ma

Roll of Thunder, Hear My Cry
Mildred D. Taylor

Papa's mother. A very mature woman, she runs the Logan farm. She was married to **Paul-Edward Logan** from *The Land*. When the children confess that they have gone to **the Wallace Family (Kaleb, Dewberry, etc.)** store, Big Ma brings them to the man who was burned and reveals to the children that he was burned by the Wallaces. Big Ma and the children then go door-to-door to convince other members of the black community not to use the Wallaces' store.

Big Mama

Cat on a Hot Tin Roof
Tennessee Williams

A fat, earnest, and crude woman, bedecked in tasteless flashy gems. Big Mama is embarrassingly dedicated to **Big Daddy**, a man who despises her. The constantly sobbing Mama is in feeble denial of her husband's disgust. Mama considers **Brick** her "only son," favoring him over **Gooper**, investing in Brick all her hopes for the future of the family. She implores Brick to carry on the family line, telling him he must provide Daddy with a grandson as similar to Brick as Brick is to Daddy himself. Mama's moment of dignity comes upon the revelation of Daddy's cancer.

Big Mama

The Member of the Wedding
Carson McCullers

Berenice Sadie Brown's mother. Big Mama is a shoddy fortune-teller. She tells **Frankie Addams** her fortune, and does not give Frankie the rosy future Frankie had hoped. However, she turns out to be correct, putting Frankie into her place.

Big Richard

The Color of Water
James McBride

Jack's husband. Big Richard is a tough and fun guy who introduces James to all the working men on the corner.

Biggs

The Martian Chronicles
Ray Bradbury

A member of the fourth expedition. Biggs is eager to party. **Jeff Spender** hates him, and punches him in the mouth.

Lord Bigot

King John
William Shakespeare

An English nobleman who defects, along with **Pembroke** and **William, Earl of Salisbury**, to the French after **Arthur**'s death. However, Lord Bigot and the other two lords return to the English after they discover that **Lewis** plans to kill them after defeating **King John**'s forces in battle.

Bigwig

Watership Down
Richard Adams

The strongest of the refugees and a courageous and daring fighter. Bigwig's knowledge and power save the group many times. Cunning and intelligent, Bigwig savors battle, but knows when to avoid it.

Bildad

Moby-Dick
Herman Melville

A well-to-do Quaker ex-whaleman from Nantucket, Massachusetts, who owns a large share of the *Pequod*, along with **Peleg**. Both men display a business sense and a bloodthirstiness unusual for Quakers, who are normally pacifists. Bildad and Peleg believe in Captain **Ahab**'s competence, and they believe him harmless, since he has a young wife and an infant child waiting for him at home. What they don't know is that he is keeping a band of questionable men hidden in the *Pequod*, including the mysterious and terrifying **Fedallah**. When Bildad meets **Queequeg**, he tries to convert Queequeg to Christianity. Peleg reminds Bildad that, at sea, practical concerns trump religious matters. Bildad and Peleg see their ship out of harbor, and then take a small boat back to the Nantucket shore.

Bilhah

The Red Tent
Anita Diamant

Third wife of **Jacob**, given to him by her illegitimate father **Laban** as **Rachel**'s handmaid, making her a possible concubine of Jacob. Bilhah is the kind and true mother of **Dan**, whom she offered to have for the constantly miscarrying Rachel. She is dark, quiet, and introspective. She is considered the kindest and most nurturing of the sisters. **Reuben** has a deep love for his aunt Bilhah, and this love results in their banishment by Jacob after he and his sons murder all the men of Shechem. **Dinah** dreams of Bilhah, as she dreams of each of her mothers toward the end of her life.

Bill

Alice in Wonderland
Lewis Carroll

A lizard. The **White Rabbit** sends Bill down the chimney in an attempt to remove the overgrown **Alice** from it. Alice kicks him into the sky, but the other creatures revive him with brandy.

Bill

White Fang
Jack London

Henry's morose traveling companion. Bill's impulsiveness with the gun causes him to be eaten by the pack of wolves that have been tracking the men and their dogs.

Bill

In Our Time
Ernest Hemingway

Nick Adams's best friend from home. Bill drinks with Nick in "The Three-Day Blow," and the two often fish and hunt together. He is glad when Nick breaks up with **Marjorie**.

Billie

Maggie: A Girl of the Streets
Stephen Crane

A Rum Alley urchin who fights with **Jimmie** in the novel's first scene and who, like Jimmie, grows up to be a violent brawler. Billie is Jimmie's ally in the fight against **Pete** late in the novel.

Billing

An Enemy of the People
Henrik Ibsen

An assistant at the newspaper, he is a radical, like **Hovstad**, but he is also ambitious and plans to run for office. He courts **Petra**, **Dr. Thomas Stockmann**'s daughter.

Billy's father

Slaughterhouse-Five
Kurt Vonnegut

Billy Pilgrim's father. He throws young Billy into the YMCA pool to teach him how to swim.

Billy's mother

Slaughterhouse-Five
Kurt Vonnegut

Billy Pilgrim's mother. She visits Billy in the mental hospital, and her presence embarrasses him—he feels his indifference to life makes him an ungrateful son.

Billyboy

A Clockwork Orange
Anthony Burgess

The leader of a gang that clashes with **Alex**'s. Alex hates Billyboy for being fat and "smelling of oil." Billyboy eventually partners with former rival **Dim** as a police officer. They drive Alex into the country, where they beat him and leave him for dead in a field.

Bilton

Major Barbara
George Bernard Shaw

A foreman at **Andrew Undershaft**'s armory.

Bimbi

The Autobiography of Malcolm X
Malcolm X & Alex Haley

The most vocal of **Malcolm X**'s fellow inmates. Bimbi makes speeches that gain him the respect of guards and prisoners alike. Bimbi demonstrates to Malcolm the power of independent thought and persuasive argument.

Binet

Madame Bovary
Gustave Flaubert

The tax collector in Yonville, who takes his meals regularly at the Lion d'Or inn. **Emma Bovary** begs him for more time to pay her taxes and attempts to seduce him, but he rebuffs her.

Charles Bingley

Pride and Prejudice
Jane Austen

Fitzwilliam Darcy's wealthy best friend. Bingley is a genial, well-intentioned gentleman whose easygoing nature contrasts with Darcy's initially discourteous demeanor. He is blissfully oblivious to class differences.

Miss Bingley

Pride and Prejudice
Jane Austen

Charles Bingley's snobbish sister. Miss Bingley disdains the Bennets' middle-class background. Her attempts to attract **Fitzwilliam Darcy**'s attention make Darcy admire **Elizabeth Bennet**'s self-possession even more.

Alec Bings

The Phantom Tollbooth
Norton Juster

A boy who floats several feet off the ground. Alec has the special ability to "see through things" and can see anything except that which is right before him.

Biondello

The Taming of the Shrew
William Shakespeare

Lucentio's second servant. The dim-witted Biondello assists his master and **Tranio** in carrying out their plot to win the hand of **Bianca** for Lucentio.

Jimmy Biondo

Legs
William Kennedy

A figure of the New York underworld, he owns a farm that **Jack** rents and uses to make and store booze. Biondo is a partner of sorts with Jack until Jack refuses to return the money that Biondo loaned him to make a drug deal.

Birch

Cold Mountain
Charles Frazier

Teague's young associate who kills **Inman**. Although Birch convinces Teague to bring the captive into town instead of hanging him, he is not a sympathetic figure. With his white hair and glassy eyes, the boy appears deadened by the violence he has witnessed.

Harriet Bird

The Natural
Bernard Malamud

A young woman whom **Roy Hobbs** falls for while on his way to his first major league tryout. Harriet is actually a murderer who shoots major athletes; after Hobbs strikes out **The Whammer**, a baseball star, Harriet turns her sights on Hobbs. She later shoots him in a hotel room.

Mrs. Bird

Uncle Tom's Cabin
Harriet Beecher Stowe

A virtuous woman who tries to exert influence through her husband, **Senator Bird**.

Senator Bird

Uncle Tom's Cabin
Harriet Beecher Stowe

Husband of **Mrs. Bird**. Senator Bird is well-meaning and sympathetic to the abolitionist cause but nonetheless remains complacent or resigned to the status quo.

Fanny Birden

Flowers for Algernon
Daniel Keyes

The only bakery employee who treats **Charlie Gordon** kindly. Fanny does not like to see the others pick on Charlie because of his disability. When Charlie becomes a genius, Fanny is glad for him, but suspects he may have made a deal with the devil.

Birdsong

Go Down, Moses
William Faulkner

The security guard who runs a crooked dice game for blacks at the Jefferson sawmill.

Mr. Birkway

Walk Two Moons
Sharon Creech

Salamanca Tree Hiddle's English teacher and **Margaret Cadaver**'s brother. Mr. Birkway is a passionate and energetic teacher whose enthusiasm and friendliness engage his students. Mr. Birkway makes a grave mistake when he, in all innocence, reads excerpts from his students' journals. He realizes his mistake only when his sister becomes implicated in the gossipy journal entries.

Great-Aunt Birte

Number the Stars
Lois Lowry

The fictional aunt whose "death" is part of the plan to help **Ellen Rosen**, **Mr. Rosen**, **Mrs. Rosen**, and other Jews escape to Sweden.

Bitzer

Hard Times
Charles Dickens

One of the successes of **Thomas Gradgrind**'s rationalistic system of education. Initially a bully at Gradgrind's school, Bitzer later becomes an employee and a spy at **Josiah Bounderby**'s bank. He tries to stop **Thomas Gradgrind, Jr.** from fleeing the country after the robbery.

Miles Bjornstam

Main Street
Sinclair Lewis

Gopher Prairie's town handyman. Bjornstam, who supports socialism and the Democratic Party, is largely scorned by the citizens of Gopher Prairie, who consider him slightly insane. **Carol**, however, finds him to be a kindred spirit because he shares many of her liberal views. Although Bjornstam settles down after his marriage to **Bea Sorenson**, he leaves Gopher Prairie forever when his wife and son, **Olaf**, die.

Black

Fahrenheit 451
Ray Bradbury

A fireman who works with **Guy Montag**. He and **Stoneman** share the lean, shadowed look common to all firemen and go about their jobs unquestioningly.

George Black Bull

When the Legends Die
Hal Borland

Thomas Black Bull's father and **Bessie**'s husband. George Black Bull is an honest and hard-working man who loves his family. He strives to educate his son about how to survive in the wilderness after he must flee town for killing **Frank No Deer**, a thief who repeatedly stole his hard-earned money.

Thomas Black Bull

When the Legends Die
Hal Borland

The novel's main character, and **George Black Bull** and **Bessie**'s son. Tom was raised in the traditional Ute Native American ways, in the wilderness, but after his parents' deaths, he is left with an acute sense of anger and aggression. He will never forget the way that **Blue Elk** tricked him into his attendance at the local reservation school, or the poor treatment he receives from teachers and bosses during this phase of his life. While he first exhibits signs of this anger outwardly, by picking fights and making scenes, he soon begins to repress this anger and hostility, which only serves to worsen the emotional damage. He takes up bronco riding, but finds that his boss **Red Dillon** is exploitative. Tom is finally able to achieve happiness when he returns to the wilderness and to his Ute roots.

Black Dog

Treasure Island
Robert Louis Stevenson

A pirate and enemy of **Billy Bones**. Black Dog pays an unexpected visit to Billy and threatens him. Billy attacks Black Dog, who flees but remains a herald of coming violence in the novel.

Black George

Tom Jones
Henry Fielding

The servant favored by **Tom**, and father of **Molly**. Although of dubious moral tincture, his loyalty to and love of Tom is clear.

The Black Knight

Ivanhoe
Sir Walter Scott

The disguise **King Richard I** uses during most of the novel, when he is still hiding his presence in England. As the mysterious Black Knight, Richard is involved in a spate of adventures: He fights **Ivanhoe** (disguised as the **Disinherited Knight**) at the tournament, rescues the Saxon prisoners from Torquilstone, and meets **Locksley** (Robin Hood) and his merry men.

The Black Thing

A Wrinkle in Time
Madeleine L'Engle

A cold and dark shadow that symbolizes the evil forces in the universe. It takes over whole planets and destroys whole stars. The **Happy Medium** shows **Charles Wallace Murry**, **Meg Murry**, and **Calvin O'Keefe** a vision of the Black Thing approaching Earth. Meg, Calvin, and Charles Wallace must fight against the Black Thing in order to rescue **Mr. Murry**. The Black Thing has created the oppressive order and sameness of Camazotz. Its embodiment there is **IT**, which is a freestanding brain that sends out a brain-piercing, controlling pulse.

Captain Black

Catch-22
Joseph Heller

The bitter intelligence officer of **John Yossarian**'s squadron. Captain Black wants to be squadron commander. He exults in the men's discomfort and actively tries to increase it. When **Nately** falls in love with a Roman whore, Captain Black begins to buy her services regularly, just to taunt him.

Captain John Black

The Martian Chronicles
Ray Bradbury

The leader of the third expedition to Mars. When his rocket lands in a quaint "American" town, he is very suspicious, but his men, certain they are witnessing a miracle, convince him to explore. He is charmed to see his family, but realizes too late that his crew has wandered into a deadly Martian trap.

Sirius Black

The Harry Potter Series: Books 3 and 4
J. K. Rowling

Harry Potter's loyal and loving godfather and an unregistered animagus. (An animagus is a witch or wizard who can change into animal form.) Sirius can change himself at will into a large black dog, **Padfoot**. In *Harry Potter and the Prisoner of Azkaban*, he is widely thought to be responsible for thirteen deaths that **Peter Pettigrew** caused. Since Sirius's name is not yet clear, he must remain in hiding. He fulfills his godfatherly duties and looks carefully after Harry. In *Harry Potter and the Goblet of Fire*, Sirius is a source of information from the outside world and a secretive and loyal companion to Harry.

Blackavar

Watership Down
Richard Adams

A strong rabbit who is good at tracking. Blackavar, who was rescued from the Efrafan warren by **Bigwig**, had tried to escape but failed. Bigwig rejuvenates Blackavar and gains his unwavering loyalty.

Blackberry

Watership Down
Richard Adams

The smartest of the rabbits. Blackberry figures out things that most of the other rabbits cannot even understand. **Hazel** comes to Blackberry when in need of a plan or an idea.

Stephen Blackpool

Hard Times
Charles Dickens

A Hand in **Josiah Bounderby**'s factory. Stephen, who is married to a wretched woman, loves **Rachael**. A man of great honesty and compassion, Stephen maintains his moral standards even in the face of ruin.

Corn Blade

The Light in the Forest
Conrad Richter

According to **Bejance**, the only person living near Paxton Township who can speak Lenni Lenape. Until **Harry Butler** tells **True Son** that Corn Blade is dead, Corn Blade represents hope for True Son during his first winter in Paxton Township.

Amory Blaine

This Side of Paradise
F. Scott Fitzgerald

The protagonist of the novel, a young man who grows up in the Midwest under the care of his wealthy, eccentric mother, **Beatrice**, until he leaves for boarding school in New England. Amory is handsome and intelligent but also egocentric and self-conscious, overeager to attain what he sees as East Coast sophistication. He is admitted to Princeton, where he falls in love with several women, fails a course, and realizes he prefers to learn through reading and discussions with his friends rather than through classes. Amory's education is cut short by his enlistment in World War I. When he returns to America, he falls in love with the young **Rosalind Connage**, who ultimately breaks his heart by leaving him to marry a wealthier man. Throughout the novel, Amory yearns to make peace with himself and his place in the world. Eventually, he comes to realize his own selfishness and, in the final line of the novel, claims he finally knows himself, "but that is all —."

Beatrice Blaine

This Side of Paradise
F. Scott Fitzgerald

Amory Blaine's sophisticated, unconventional mother, who was educated in France and married Amory's unimportant father primarily out of weariness. Beatrice loves Amory both as a friend and a son and indulges many of his flights of fancy. Beatrice dies while Amory is away in World War I and bequeaths half her money to the church, leaving Amory in a precarious financial position.

Howard Blair

Inherit the Wind
Jerome Lawrence & Robert E. Lee

A student in **Bertram Cates**'s science class. Howard Blair grasps the idea of evolution in only a rudimentary way. At the trial, Howard gives testimony that is used against Cates.

Ben Blake

A Tree Grows in Brooklyn
Betty Smith

A very bright, successful young man whom **Mary Frances Nolan** meets in summer college classes. Ben will attend a midwestern college and then law school. He makes Francie happy, keeps her from feeling lonely, and knows what he wants.

Franklin Blake

The Moonstone
Wilkie Collins

Lady Verinder's nephew, and the editorial force behind the collected narratives of the novel. He has asked everyone to write what they know about the disappearance of the diamond, in the interests of clearing his own name. Franklin is in love with **Rachel Verinder**.

Dr. Joseph Blake

Mourning Becomes Electra
Eugene O'Neill

The Mannons' kindly family physician. He is stout, self-important, and stubbornly opinionated. When **Christine Mannon** poisons the **Brigadier-General Ezra Mannon**, Dr. Blake examines him and provides tactless comments.

Mattie Lou Blakeslee

Cold Sassy Tree
Olive Anne Burns

Will Tweedy's grandmother and **Rucker Blakeslee**'s first wife. Mattie Lou dies three weeks before the novel begins. Mattie Lou was an excellent gardener and a devoted caretaker for the sick. The people of Cold Sassy speak reverently of her, and Rucker never forgets her companionship and goodwill.

Rucker Blakeslee

Cold Sassy Tree
Olive Anne Burns

Will Tweedy's maternal grandfather. Rucker is a brash, humorous, and domineering man who owns the general store in Cold Sassy. Rucker is passionately Southern, but he has no use for the gossip and hypocrisy of Cold Sassy's small-town ways, and he acts according to his own code of decent conduct.

Blanca

The House of the Spirits
Isabel Allende

Clara and **Esteban Trueba**'s first-born. Blanca falls in love with the revolutionary **Pedro Tercero Garcia** at a young age and throughout her life defies Esteban Trueba to meet with him as often as possible. Blanca is caught with Pedro Tercero and they must separate for a time, during which Blanca is forced to marry **Jean de Satigny**. Blanca leaves Jean, who is only interested in his cocaine and erotic poses with his Indian servants, just before giving birth to her daughter, **Alba**, who was fathered by Pedro Tercero. Blanca raises Alba in her parents' house and continues meeting Pedro Tercero, but refuses to run away with him until after the military coup, led by Esteban Trueba, when they flee together to Canada. Unlike her mother, Blanca is quite practical. After her divorce from Jean de Satigny, and even more so after Clara's death, Blanca runs the big house on the corner. Like both of her parents, Blanca is incredibly stubborn. Even while she runs his house, she never asks for a cent from her father, instead supporting herself through her ceramics.

Dona Blanca

Love in the Time of Cholera
Gabriel García Márquez

Mother of **Dr. Juvenal Urbino del Calle**. Dona Blanca proves the bane of **Fermina Daza**'s existence. She dies while Dr. Urbino del Calle and Fermina Daza are in Europe.

Blancandrin

The Song of Roland
Unknown

A shrewd pagan, and one of **Marsilla**'s most useful vassals. He suggests that Marsilla offer **Charlemagne** treasure, hostages, and a deceitful promise. Blancandrin advises Marsilla to promise that he will come to Aix and convert to Christianity in order to save the pagans' honor and lands from the great Frankish army. Blancandrin delivers the faulty peace offer to the Franks, and then he and the Frank **Ganelon** plot the ambush at Roncesvals and the death of **Roland**.

Blanche

King John
William Shakespeare

Daughter of the King of Spain and **King John**'s niece. To cement the shaky alliance between the French and the English, Blanche is married to **Lewis**. She is caught in the middle of the conflict when the French declare war on the English again.

Gerald Bland

The Sound and the Fury
William Faulkner

A swaggering student at Harvard. **Quentin Compson** fights with Gerald because he reminds him of **Dalton Ames**.

Mrs. Bland

The Sound and the Fury
William Faulkner

Gerald Bland's boastful Southern mother.

One Flew over the Cuckoo's Nest
Ken Kesey

Old Blastic

A patient who is a vegetable. **Chief Bromden** has a prophetic dream about a mechanical slaughterhouse in which Old Blastic is murdered. He wakes up to discover that Old Blastic died in the night.

I Never Promised You a Rose Garden
Joanne Greenberg

Deborah Blau

The novel's protagonist. Deborah spends three years in a mental hospital battling schizophrenia. With the help of her dedicated therapist, **Dr. Fried**, Deborah finds the courage to emerge from the Kingdom of Yr, a world Deborah created as a defense against a confusing, frightening reality.

I Never Promised You a Rose Garden
Joanne Greenberg

Esther Blau

Deborah's mother. Over the course of the novel, Ester Blau comes to terms with her daughter's illness. Her strength, faith, and love in her daughter help her insist that Deborah continue receiving treatment even when she seems to show few signs of improvement or recovery.

I Never Promised You a Rose Garden
Joanne Greenberg

Jacob Blau

Deborah's father, who feels alternately guilty and angry about Deborah's condition. Over the years, Jacob has had financial difficulties, forcing him to live on the charity of his in-laws. During Deborah's treatment, **Esther** realizes that she always placed Jacob's wishes second to her father's.

I Never Promised You a Rose Garden
Joanne Greenberg

Suzy Blau

Deborah's younger sister. **Esther** and **Jacob** do not tell Suzy the truth about Deborah's illness until it becomes clear that there is no quick and easy cure. Although she loves Deborah, Suzy feels neglected because she often has to arrange her life around her older sister's illness.

Invisible Man
Ralph Ellison

Dr. Bledsoe

The president at **the Narrator**'s college. Dr. Bledsoe proves selfish, ambitious, and treacherous. He is a black man who puts on a mask of servility to the white community. Driven by his desire to maintain his status and power, he declares that he would see every black man in the country lynched before he would give up his position of authority.

Gulliver's Travels
Jonathan Swift

Blefuscudians

A race of miniature, six-inch-tall people. The Blefuscudians have been engaged in a long-standing war with the similarly statured **Lilliputians** over the proper way to break eggs. Prone to conspiracies and jealousies, they are quick to take advantage of **Gulliver**. Despite having helped the Lilliputians defeat the Blefuscudian navy, Gulliver is nevertheless warmly received by the Blefuscudian court.

Jimmy Blevins

All the Pretty Horses
Cormac McCarthy

A thirteen-year-old runaway who follows **John Grady Cole** and **Lacey Rawlins** to Mexico. His real name is never revealed. He is hypersensitive to mockery and insult, which leads him to flee his abusive stepfather. When Blevins returns to reclaim his stolen horse and gun, he is captured and eventually executed by the cruel captain.

Mrs. Peter Blewett

Anne of Green Gables
L. M. Montgomery

A woman living in Avonlea. Mrs. Blewett offers to take **Anne Shirley** in as a babysitter when she learns that **Marilla Cuthbert** intends to get a boy orphan in Anne's place. Marilla decides to keep Anne because Mrs. Blewett is a nasty, stingy woman who is not fit to care for a child.

Master Blifil

Tom Jones
Henry Fielding

Antagonist to **Tom Jones** and the son of **Bridget Allworthy** and **Captain Blifil**. His greed serves as a foil to Tom's compassion, especially at the end of the novel where Blifil's secrecy regarding Tom's origins is revealed. Blifil's dearth of natural human appetites—he at first does not desire **Sophia**—does not distinguish him as a virtuous character, but rather provides a depressing picture of what humanity would be like if devoid of passion.

Betty Bliss

Pnin
Vladimir Nabokov

A student in **Timofey Pnin**'s class. Betty is not a particularly bright student, but she is earnest and affectionate in a quiet, unassuming way. Pnin sees her after she has graduated from college and gotten engaged.

Baroness Karen Blixen

Out of Africa
Isak Dinesen

The narrator of the novel. Karen is a Danish female, who generally cloaks her true identity throughout the book. Karen is a friendly woman who treats the people around her with respect. Her kindness can be seen in her willingness to run a school for the natives and give them medical treatment. She is also a brave woman who looks for adventure and does not like to remain cloistered. Occasionally, some of Karen's ideas suggest an inherent condescension. Still, Karen is a thoughtful and compassionate woman who is able to respect and admire the many cultures around her.

Bloch

Swann's Way
Marcel Proust

One of **Marcel**'s friends at Combray. He introduces Marcel to his favorite writer, Bergotte. He is Jewish, and his presence evokes some anti-Semitic comments from Marcel's grandfather.

Block

The Trial
Franz Kafka

Another accused man and client of **Huld**'s, to whom Block is completely subservient. Five years into his case, the once-prosperous tradesman has withered into a shadow of his former self. He devotes all his time, energy, and resources to his case.

Leopold Bloom

Ulysses
James Joyce

One of the novel's protagonists; an advertising canvasser for the Freeman. Throughout the novel, Bloom's thoughts return to his wife **Molly Bloom**, her infidelity, and their dead son **Rudy Bloom**. Bloom's deep compassion and an extraordinary ability to empathize with many creatures—animals, blind men, women in labor—make him the novel's true and unironic hero. He was raised in Dublin by his Hungarian Jewish father **Rudolph** and his Irish Catholic mother **Ellen**.

Millicent Bloom

Ulysses
James Joyce

Molly and **Leopold Bloom**'s 15-year-old daughter, who recently moved to Mullingar to study photography. Blond and pretty, Milly is dating **Alec Bannon**. She does not appear in *Ulysses*.

Molly Bloom

Ulysses
James Joyce

Leopold Bloom's wife, a professional singer. Plump, pretty, and flirtatious, Molly is clever and opinionated, if not well-educated. Molly is impatient with her husband, especially for his refusal to sleep with her ever since the death of their son, **Rudy Bloom**, eleven years earlier.

Rudy Bloom

Ulysses
James Joyce

Leopold Bloom and **Molly Bloom**'s dead son.

William Henry Blore

And Then There Were None
Agatha Christie

A former police inspector. Blore is a well-built man whose experience often inspires others to look to him for advice. As a policeman, he was corrupt and framed a man named **Landor** at the behest of a criminal gang. On the island, he acts boldly and frequently takes initiative, but he also makes frequent blunders. He constantly suspects the wrong person, and his boldness often verges on foolhardiness.

Professor Blorenge

Pnin
Vladimir Nabokov

The chairman of the French department, who is stunned when **Dr. Hagen**, chairman of the German department, suggests that perhaps **Timofey Pnin** might teach a French course.

Blossom

Number the Stars
Lois Lowry

Uncle **Henrik**'s milk cow. **Kirsten Johansen** wants to take her kitten, **Thor**, to meet Blossom. When Uncle Henrik is showing **Annemarie** how to milk Blossom, he tells her all the details of the Rosens' escape.

Jake Blount

The Heart Is a Lonely Hunter
Carson McCullers

A heavy-drinking, ranting man who comes into town and frequents **Biff Brannon**'s café. Jake is a bizarre-looking man: short, but with long arms, large hands, and a moustache that appears oddly detached from his somewhat distorted face. He drinks constantly and often goes on long, frustrated rants about socialism. Jake's behavior is extremely volatile and occasionally violent.

Red Blow

The Natural
Bernard Malamud

One of the coaches of the New York Knights. Red is among the first members of the team to take a liking to **Roy Hobbs**, and he does his best to steer Hobbs clear of trouble.

Blue Elk

When the Legends Die
Hal Borland

An unscrupulous, greedy Ute who tricks **Thomas Black Bull** into first attending school on the reservation and into entering the civilized town of Pagosa. While Blue Elk shares Tom's heritage, he has rejected it for the new ways of civilization. Blue Elk seeks to force Tom to believe that these new ways represent an improvement on the old Ute ways. He constantly manipulates and exploits Tom and others and rarely, if ever, demonstrates selflessness. He represents the Native Americans who have lost their sense of heritage and have submitted to the white values concerning materialism and nature.

Blue Jack

The Bluest Eye
Toni Morrison

A coworker and friend of **Cholly Breedlove**'s during his boyhood. Blue Jack enthralls Cholly with his excellent storytelling and shares the heart of a watermelon with him at a church picnic.

Bluebell

Animal Farm
George Orwell

A dog that gives birth early in the novel. **Napoleon** confiscates her and **Jessie**'s puppies, claiming he wants to educate them. Instead, the puppies are trained to become vicious attack dogs who serve as his personal guards.

Bluebell

Watership Down
Richard Adams

Captain Holly's faithful friend who uses humor to lighten up situations. Bluebell traveled with Holly to find **Hazel**'s rabbits. Bluebell tells stories almost as well as **Dandelion**.

Mr. Blum

Native Son
Richard Wright

A white delicatessen owner on the South Side of Chicago. **Bigger Thomas** and his friends plan to rob Mr. Blum, even though they are nervous about robbing a white man.

Sir Walter Blunt

Henry IV, Part I
William Shakespeare

A loyal and trusted ally of **King Henry IV**'s and a valuable warrior. Blunt delivers word on the rebels' meeting to the King, and acts as an emissary between the King's forces and those of **Hotspur** and the **Earl of Worcester**. When he dresses up like the King in battle, he is slain by the **Earl of Douglas**.

Gilbert Blythe

Anne of Green Gables
L. M. Montgomery

A handsome and intelligent Avonlea boy who becomes **Anne Shirley**'s rival when he makes the mistake of teasing her about her red hair. Anne swears never to speak to Gilbert, and even when he rescues her from the river, she refuses to break the silence between them. Anne's rivalry with Gilbert keeps her motivated throughout her academic career. By the end of the novel, the rivalry has become affectionate, and Anne and Gilbert have become friends.

John Blythe

Anne of Green Gables
L. M. Montgomery

Gilbert Blythe's father. Mr. Blythe courted **Marilla Cuthbert** when they were younger, but ended up marrying someone else. Marilla confides in Anne that she regrets ending her courtship with Mr. Blythe.

Edy Boardman

Ulysses
James Joyce

Gerty MacDowell's friend, who is annoyed by Gerty's uppity demeanor.

Gillian Boardman

Stranger in a Strange Land
Robert A. Heinlein

A courageous and confident young nurse. Her friend and old flame, newspaper reporter **Ben Caxton**, convinces her to help him rescue **Valentine Michael Smith** from his enforced captivity at her hospital. The two find safety at the estate of **Jubal Harshaw**. Her nurturing attachment to Mike grows into a profound understanding.

Boatswain

The Tempest
William Shakespeare

A shipman. The boatswain is vigorous and good-natured. He is competent and almost cheerful in the shipwreck scene, demanding practical help rather than weeping and prayer. He seems surprised but not stunned when he awakens from a long sleep at the end of the play.

Bob

A Day No Pigs Would Die
Robert Newton Peck

An ox that **Robert Peck** helps bring into the world when he assists **Benjamin Tanner**'s cow, Apron. Bob is one of the two oxen born of Apron, the other being **Bib**. Bob is named for Robert by Mr. Tanner, who has always dreamed of taking a pair of matched oxen to the Rutland fair.

Helen Bober

The Assistant
Bernard Malamud

The daughter of **Ida Bober** and **Morris Bober**. She lacks the Yiddish dialect of her parents and speaks in educated English. She longs to read and become a great scholar, but has no access to college. For this reason, Helen becomes a dreamer who does not always perceive people and situations correctly. She initially fails to perceive that **Nat Pearl** is not seriously interested in her, which later crushes her after she has sex with him. She similarly misreads **Frank Alpine**'s character.

Ida Bober

The Assistant
Bernard Malamud

The wife of **Morris Bober** and the mother of **Helen Bober**. Ida is a slightly worrisome older Jewish woman who is anxious about the Gentile **Frank Alpine** becoming involved with her daughter.

Morris Bober

The Assistant
Bernard Malamud

The protagonist of the novel, the grocer forever down on his luck. Morris Bober is honest, thoughtful, and compassionate, a bedrock of morality in an economically troubled community. Morris's temperament is governed by quiet resignation to the hand that he has been dealt. While other merchants make money by cheating their customers, Morris remains poor but triumphs spiritually because he remains good.

Bobo

A Raisin in the Sun
Lorraine Hansberry

One of **Walter Lee Younger**'s partners in a plan to open a liquor store with the insurance money from Walter's father's death. He comes to the Younger family home to inform Walter that Walter's partner and supposed friend **Willy Harris** has run off with the money that they were supposed to invest in their liquor store.

Mr. and Miss Bodwin

Beloved
Toni Morrison

White abolitionists, brother and sister, who play an active role in winning **Sethe**'s freedom. Mr. Bodwin longs a little too eagerly for the "heady days" of abolitionism. Miss Bodwin demonstrates a condescending desire to "experiment" on **Denver** by sending her to Oberlin College. The distasteful figurine Denver sees in the Bodwins' house, portraying a slave and displaying the message "At Yo' Service," marks the limits and ironies of white involvement in the struggle for racial equality. Nevertheless, they are motivated by good intentions, believing that "human life is holy, all of it."

The Boeufs

Rhinoceros
Eugène Ionesco

Mr. Boeuf, another coworker of **Berenger**'s, appears offstage only as a rhinoceros. His wife remains devoted to him despite his new form.

Bofur

The Hobbit
J. R. R. Tolkien

One of the dwarf companions on the novel's quest.

Mrs. Bogart

Main Street
Sinclair Lewis

Carol Kennicott's nosy neighbor and the town's gossip. Mrs. Bogart is very much a religious hypocrite, creating a scandal out of nothing when her boarder, **Fern Mullins**, innocently attends a barn dance with her son, Cy Bogart, the town's juvenile delinquent.

Bokonon

Cat's Cradle
Kurt Vonnegut

Founder of the religion of Bokononism. When Bokonon and his friend, **Edward McCabe**, landed on San Lorenzo, a small island republic ravaged by poverty and disease, they hoped to turn the island into a utopia. Quickly realizing the futility of these efforts, Bokonon creates the comforting lies of Bokononism to offer the people of San Lorenzo some hope in a hopeless world. He then asks McCabe to outlaw the religion, knowing an official ban would make it more exciting and meaningful for its practicioners. **John** becomes a follower of Bokononism after he travels to San Lorenzo to interview **Julian Castle** for a magazine article.

William Boldwood

Far from the Madding Crowd
Thomas Hardy

Bathsheba Everdene's second suitor after **Gabriel Oak**. William Boldwood owns a farm close by to Bathsheba's. Boldwood is a somewhat wooden, reserved man. He seems uninterested in romance until Bathsheba sends him a valentine, after which he becomes irrationally obsessed with her. When Bathsheba cuts off her slow-moving romance with Boldwood in favor of her dynamic new lover, **Sergeant Francis Troy**, Boldwood becomes incredibly jealous and inattentive to his farm duties. In the end, Boldwood ends up shooting the presumed-dead Troy, who makes a surprise reappearance at a party of Boldwood's to reclaim Bathsheba. Boldwood is pardoned from his death by hanging at the last minute by way of town petition.

Anne Boleyn

Henry VIII
William Shakespeare

The second wife of **King Henry VIII**, after **Queen Katherine**. The King meets Anne at **Cardinal Wolsey**'s dinner party and is quite taken with her, thinking about her throughout his divorce proceedings. Though Anne pities Katherine and declares that she would never want to be queen, Henry sends **Lord Chamberlain** to honor her with a new title and an increased annual income. Soon she and Henry are married, though the Pope has not consented to Henry and Katherine's divorce. Anne gives birth to **Elizabeth**, the future Queen of England. Much of Anne's "action" takes place either without words or offstage and is merely reported by others.

Chuck Bolger

This Boy's Life
Tobias Wolff

The son of a minister. Chuck Bolger is **Jack Wolff** 's gentle, somewhat alcoholic friend who is accused of impregnating **Tina Flood**, an overweight and promiscuous underage girl at their high school. Chuck refuses to marry Tina, and is pardoned when his friend **Jerry Huff** agrees to marry her instead. Jack lives with Chuck for a short period after **Rosemary Wolff** is fed up with **Dwight**'s violence toward Jack. Jack promises to be good when he lives with Chuck and the Bolger family, but he cannot keep his promise and, along with Chuck, steals gasoline from **Jack Welch**.

Fredegar Bolger

The Fellowship of the Ring
J. R. R. Tolkien

A Hobbit friend of **Meriadoc Brandybuck**, or Merry. He is sometimes called Fatty. Fatty stays behind at **Frodo**'s house, Bag End, Underhill, to keep up the pretense that Frodo still lives in the Shire, both for the purpose of not arousing Hobbit suspicion and for the purpose of confusing **the Nazgûl**.

Skyresh Bolgolam

Gulliver's Travels
Jonathan Swift

High Admiral of Lilliput. Bolgolam is the sole member of the administration to oppose allowing **Gulliver** to roam free in Lilliput. Arguably, Bolgolam's hostility may be merely a tool to divert Gulliver from the larger system of Lilliputian exploitation to which he is subjected.

Bolingbroke

Henry VI, Part II
William Shakespeare

A conjurer whom **Eleanor, Duchess of Gloucester** hires. The Duchess pays Bolingbroke and **Margery Jourdain** to communicate with spirits to find out the fate of **King Henry VI** and other nobles. Bolingbroke and Jourdain are arrested for dealing with the occult and sentenced to death: Bolingbroke by hanging, Jourdain by burning.

Lise Bolkonskaya

War and Peace
Leo Tolstoy

Andrei Nikolayevich Bolkonsky's angelic wife, who dies in childbirth.

Marya Nikolayevna Bolkonskaya

War and Peace
Leo Tolstoy

The lonely, plain, and long-suffering daughter of **Prince Bolkonsky**. Marya Nikolayevna cares for her father, enduring his cruel treatment with Christian forgiveness. In the end, **Nikolai Ilyich Rostov** weds Marya and saves her from an unhappy solitude.

Andrei Nikolayevich Bolkonsky

War and Peace
Leo Tolstoy

The intelligent, disciplined, and ambitious son of the retired military commander **Prince Bolkonsky**. Andrei is coldly analytical and resistant to flights of emotion. Lonely after the death of his wife, **Lise Bolkonskaya**, he falls in love with **Natasha Ilyinichna Rostova** but is unable to forgive her momentary passion for **Anatole Vasilievich Kuragin** until his deathbed.

Prince Bolkonsky

War and Peace
Leo Tolstoy

Prince Andrei Nikolayevich Bolkonsky and **Marya Nikolayevna Bolkonskaya**'s father, a stodgy and old-fashioned recluse who lives in the country after his retirement from the army and subsequent retreat from social life. The old prince, cynical about modern life, is stern and sometimes cruel toward his daughter Marya Nikolayevna. In the war with **Napoleon**, he returns to active military service, but dies as the French approach his estate.

Mrs. Bolton

Lady Chatterley's Lover
D. H. Lawrence

Clifford Chatterley's nurse and caretaker. Mrs. Bolton is a competent, complex, still-attractive middle-aged woman. Years before the action in this novel, her husband died in an accident in the mines owned by Clifford's family. Even as Mrs. Bolton resents Clifford as the owner of the mines, she still maintains a worshipful attitude toward him as an aristocrat.

Tom Bombadil

The Fellowship of the Ring
J. R. R. Tolkien

A jovial, mysterious, and powerful being who dances around his small realm, singing songs in doggerel. Tom Bombadil is extremely old, perhaps immortal, and his origins are unknown. For a while, the Council of **Elrond Halfelven** at Rivendell considers giving the One Ring to Tom, knowing that its power does not affect him. Tom has immense power over nature, and offers **Meriadoc Brandybuck**, **Peregrin Took**, **Samwise Gamgee**, and **Frodo Baggins** a place to stay when they are fleeing **the Nazgûl**. Tom saves Frodo from the **Barrow-wight**, or mound demon, which threatens Frodo's life.

Bombur

The Hobbit
J. R. R. Tolkien

One of the dwarf companions on the novel's quest.

Charles Bon

Absalom, Absalom!
William Faulkner

Son of **Thomas Sutpen** and Eulalia Bon, the part-black daughter of the owner of the Haitian plantation on which the young Thomas Sutpen was overseer. After Sutpen renounced his wife and son upon learning of Eulalia's black blood, Bon and his mother moved to New Orleans, where Bon lived until deciding to attend the University of Mississippi in 1859. A laconic, sophisticated, and ironical young man, he befriends **Henry Sutpen** at school, goes to war with him, and becomes engaged to his sister, **Judith Sutpen**. Informed by his father of Bon's origin, Henry kills him to prevent his marrying their common sister.

Charles Etienne de St. Valery Bon

Absalom, Absalom!
William Faulkner

Son of **Charles Bon** and his octoroon mistress-wife. He is taken by **Clytemnestra Sutpen** to Sutpen's Hundred in 1871 and marries a black woman in 1879. A tormented, violent man.

Lady Bona

Henry VI, Part III
William Shakespeare

King Louis XI's sister. The **Earl of Warwick** comes to France, seeking to make a politically advantageous union between Lady Bona and the newly crowned **King Edward IV**. Though she agrees to marry Edward, Lady Bona is embarrassed when word comes from England that Edward has already taken a bride. As Louis XI, **Queen Margaret**, and Warwick begin to plan an attack on Edward, Lady Bona sends harsh words back to her would-be husband.

Madame Bonacieux

The Three Musketeers
Alexandre Dumas

Wife of **Monsieur Bonacieux** and lady-in-waiting for **Queen Anne**. Madame Bonacieux is loyal to the Queen through and through. Monsieur Bonacieux shows up in **d'Artagnan**'s apartment and asks d'Artagnan for help because Madame Bonacieux has been kidnapped by a man who fits the description of the **Comte de Wardes**. **Athos**, **Porthos**, **Aramis**, and d'Artagnan decide that they should aid Madame Bonacieux and therefore the Queen. While d'Artagnan saves Madame Bonacieux from a violent police capture and interrogation, and escorts her back to the Louvre to see the Queen, he realizes that he has fallen in love with her and makes arrangements to see her again. In doing so, d'Artagnan gets involved in the Queen's secret affairs. After the second kidnapping of Madame Bonacieux, d'Artagnan becomes sure that the **Lady de Winter** and the **Comte de Wardes**, or the Man from Meung, are somehow behind the plot. In the end, the Lady de Winter gains Madame Bonacieux's confidence and poisons her, killing her.

Monsieur Bonacieux

The Three Musketeers
Alexandre Dumas

D'Artagnan's landlord, and **Madame Bonacieux**'s husband. He originally comes to d'Artagnan for help when Madame Bonacieux is kidnapped, but after a private audience with **Cardinal Richelieu**, he turns on his wife and becomes a Cardinalist agent.

Bonario

Volpone
Ben Jonson

The son of **Corbaccio**. Bonario is an upright youth who remains loyal to his father even when his father perjures against him in court. He heroically rescues **Celia** from **Volpone** and represents bravery and honor, qualities the other characters seem to lack.

Remi Boncoeur

On the Road
Jack Kerouac

Sal Paradise's prep-school friend. Remi, an extravagant and gallant Frenchman, is a gambler and a petty thief who is constantly in debt.

Jim Bond

Absalom, Absalom!
William Faulkner

Son of **Charles Etienne de St. Valery Bon** and his black wife. Raised by **Clytemnestra Sutpen** on Sutpen's Hundred, from which he disappears following the fire in 1910. A slack-jawed, oafish man.

Eddie Bondo

Prodigal Summer
Barbara Kingsolver

Deanna Wolfe's summer love. Eddie is a handsome, opinionated twenty-eight-year-old sheep rancher from Wyoming with a penchant for killing coyotes.

Mr. Bone

The Autobiography of Miss Jane Pittman
Ernest J. Gaines

The man who originally owns and runs the plantation on which **Miss Jane Pittman** stays after slavery. He is a Republican who is willing to run the plantation with relative fairness for all the blacks.

Bonello

A Farewell to Arms
Ernest Hemingway

An ambulance driver under **Frederic Henry**'s command in the Italian army. Bonello displays his ruthlessness when he brutally unloads a pistol round into the head of an uncooperative engineer whom Henry has already shot.

Bones

Bless Me, Ultima
Rudolfo A. Anaya

One of a group of exuberant boys who frequently curse and fight. **Horse** loves to wrestle, but everyone fears Bones more because he is reckless and perhaps even crazy. The boys in the group are **Abel**, **the Vitamin Kid**, **Ernie**, Horse, **Lloyd**, Bones, and **Red**.

Billy Bones

Treasure Island
Robert Louis Stevenson

The old seaman who resides at **Jim Hawkins**'s parents' inn. Billy, who used to be a member of **Silver**'s crew, is surly and rude. He hires Jim to be on the lookout for a one-legged man, thus involving the young Jim in the pirate life. Billy's sea chest and treasure map set the whole adventure in motion.

Bill Bonham

Johnny Got His Gun
Dalton Trumbo

Joe Bonham's father and **Macia Bonham**'s husband, who died before Joe went to war. Bill Bonham was a hard worker and was close with his son and his wife.

Joe Bonham

Johnny Got His Gun
Dalton Trumbo

The protagonist and narrator of the novel. Joe grew up in Shale City, Colorado, then moved with his family to Los Angeles, where he worked in a bakery. An infantryman in World War I, Joe sustained serious injuries when a shell exploded near him. Lying in his hospital bed, Joe slowly realizes that he has no limbs, nor a face, and therefore cannot move, smell, see, hear, taste, or speak.

Macia Bonham

Johnny Got His Gun
Dalton Trumbo

Joe Bonham's mother and **Bill Bonham**'s wife.

Pope Boniface VIII

Inferno
Dante Alighieri

A notoriously corrupt pope. Boniface, who tried to increase the political power of the Catholic Church, and **Dante**, who advocated church-state separation, were political enemies.

Tweedy Bonner

White Noise
Don DeLillo

Jack Gladney's ex-wife and the mother of **Bee**. She is married to a covert secret agent and is the exact opposite of **Babette** in that she lives almost entirely in a world of false appearances.

Jim Bono

Fences
August Wilson

Troy Maxson's best friend, usually called "Bono" or "Mr. Bono" by the characters in *Fences*. Bono idolizes Troy, whom he met in jail thirty-odd years before the start of the play. He is the only character in the play who remembers firsthand Troy's glory days in the Negro Leagues. Bono spends every Friday after work drinking beers and telling stories with Troy in the Maxson family's backyard. Bono's concern for Troy's marriage takes precedent over his loyalty to their friendship.

Captain Boomer

Moby-Dick
Herman Melville

The jovial captain of the English whaling ship the *Samuel Enderby*. Captain Boomer lost his arm in an accident involving **Moby-Dick**. Unlike Captain **Ahab**, Boomer is glad to have escaped with his life, and he sees further pursuit of the whale as madness.

Senator Boone

Stranger in a Strange Land
Robert A. Heinlein

A power-hungry senator and powerful Fosterite.

Borachio

Much Ado About Nothing
William Shakespeare

Don John's servant and accomplice, and **Margaret**'s lover. Borachio conspires with Don John to trick **Claudio** and **Don Pedro** into thinking that **Hero** is unfaithful to Claudio. When the plan works, Don John pays him a thousand ducats. He is later apprehended by the night watchmen when he relates his malevolence to **Conrad**.

Emma Borden

Mourning Becomes Electra
Eugene O'Neill

Josiah Borden's wife. Emma Borden is a typical New England woman of pure English ancestry, with a horse face and big buckteeth. Her manner is defensively sharp and assertive.

Josiah Borden

Mourning Becomes Electra
Eugene O'Neill

A small, wizened man, the husband of **Emma Borden**. Josiah Borden is the shrewd manager of the Mannon shipping company.

Lord Carlo Boreal

His Dark Materials
Robert Pullman

A power-hungry nobleman. Boreal passes between **Will Parry**'s and **Lyra Belacqua**'s worlds with ease. **Marisa Coulter** is Boreal's lover, and his daemon is a snake. Boreal steals Lyra's alethiometer and tries to force Will to trade the subtle knife for it.

Isabelle Borges

This Side of Paradise
F. Scott Fitzgerald

The young but experienced debutante with whom **Amory Blaine** first falls in love. Isabelle and Amory share an innocent affair until a minor argument makes them both realize that they actually do not like one another.

Cesare Borgia, Duke Valentino of Romagna

The Prince
Niccolò Machiavelli

A powerful Italian leader (1476–1507). Borgia was made duke of Romagna in 1501 by his father, **Pope Alexander VI**, and lost power after the pope's death. Cesare Borgia is Machiavelli's primary example of a prince of great prowess, as evidenced by success in securing his state and quickly assuming power.

Borman

The Power of One
Bryce Courtenay

Borman is the aggressive warder at Barberton prison who brutally murders **Geel Piet**.

Miss Bornstein

The Power of One
Bryce Courtenay

A young Jewish woman who arrives to teach at the Barberton primary school while **Peekay** is studying there. She becomes a mentor to Peekay and helps him to win a scholarship to the prestigious private boys school in Johannesburg, the Prince of Wales school. She continues to write copious study notes for Peekay after he leaves for the Prince of Wales school. Peekay and **Morrie** eventually publish these notes and sell them. They help to establish the famous "Miss Bornstein Correspondence School," of which Miss Bornstein becomes the principal.

Boromir

The Fellowship of the Ring and *The Two Towers*
J. R. R. Tolkien

One of the Nine belonging to the Fellowship of the Ring. Boromir is of the **Humans**, one of the Men of Gondor, from the city of Minas Tirith in the south. His father is **Denethor**, the Steward of Gondor, and his brother is **Faramir**. Boromir is a valiant fighter and is always trustworthy in battle, but his pride and recklessness make him vulnerable to the Ring's power. He thinks that if only he could use the Ring's power to do good, he could restore the power of the Men of Gondor. His greed and pursuit make **Frodo Baggins** put the Ring on, and also make Frodo realize that he must make his Quest alone, because the Ring tears people apart. In *The Two Towers,* after attempting to seize the Ring for himself in *The Fellowship of the Ring*, he dies in battle with the **Orcs**, repenting his mistake in pursuing Frodo.

Emory Bortz

The Crying of Lot 49
Thomas Pynchon

An English professor who used to teach at UC-Berkeley but later moved to San Narciso College. He helps **Oedipa Maas** untangle some of the mysteries related to the Wharfinger play's mention of Tristero.

Martin del Bosco

The Jew of Malta
Christopher Marlowe

The Spanish vice-admiral who convinces **Ferneze** to break his alliance with the Turks in return for Spanish protection. Marlowe shows how this protection fails when, with **Barabas**'s help, Calymath storms the city walls.

The boss

Of Mice and Men
John Steinbeck

Curley's father and the stocky, well-dressed man in charge of the ranch where **Lennie** and **George** work.

Botard

Rhinoceros
Eugène Ionesco

Botard is a senior member of **Berenger**'s office. He is cynical and skeptical, and jealous of **Dudard**'s rising stature. He refuses to believe at first the presence of the rhinos and seeks rational explanations for everything.

Nick Bottom

A Midsummer Night's Dream
William Shakespeare

The overconfident weaver chosen to play Pyramus in the craftsmen's play for **Theseus**'s marriage celebration. Bottom is full of advice and self-confidence, but frequently makes silly mistakes and misuses language. His simultaneous nonchalance about the beautiful **Titania**'s sudden love for him and unawareness that **Puck** has transformed his head into that of an ass mark the pinnacle of his fool's arrogance.

M. Bouc

Murder on the Orient Express
Agatha Christie

The director of the Compagnie Wagon Lits, who formerly worked on the Belgian police force with **Hercule Poirot.** Traveling on the Orient Express, M. Bouc asks Poirot to take the case.

Anatoli Boukreev

Into Thin Air
Jon Krakauer

A guide with **Scott Fischer**'s group, a world-respected climber who had previously summated Everest with no supplemental oxygen. He rescues the group of climbers stranded in the storm, but is also thought to have contributed to the disaster by descending far ahead of his clients.

Rodolphe Boulanger

Madame Bovary
Gustave Flaubert

Emma Bovary's first lover, a wealthy landowner with an estate near Yonville. Rodolphe is shrewd, selfish, and manipulative. Rodolphe's life of ease, combined with his status as a man, allows him great sexual liberty. Soon after his affair with her begins, he finds her romantic idealism exhausting and loses interest in her. At one point, their romance is rekindled and they decide to run away together. Before they depart, he decides that the sexual pleasure she provides will not be enough to offset the inconvenience and drain of being constantly in her company. He writes Emma a letter in which he lies and says that he must leave her because he loves her and fears that he will only cause her pain. When Emma reads his letter, she contemplates jumping out of her attic window. Later, when Emma is in need of money, she runs to him, and he becomes taciturn, telling her he has no money available. After Emma's death, **Charles Bovary** finds out about Emma's affair with Rodolphe. Rodolphe expresses feelings of guilt , but Charles tells him that he does not hold a grudge.

Boult

Pericles
William Shakespeare

Servant to Pander and **Bawd**. Boult falls under **Marina**'s spell of virtue and offers to help her find a more honorable place to work.

Dick Boulton

In Our Time
Ernest Hemingway

The half-Native American, half-Caucasian man who made a deal to chop wood for **Nick's father** in "The Doctor and the Doctor's Wife." Dick accuses Nick's father of stealing the wood and gets kicked out.

Josiah Bounderby

Hard Times
Charles Dickens

Thomas Gradgrind's friend and later **Louisa Gradgrind**'s husband. Although he was actually raised by loving parents, Bounderby claims to be a self-made man whose mother abandoned him.

Colonel Bouquet

The Light in the Forest
Conrad Richter

The military leader who forces the return of the Indians' white prisoners. He is portrayed by **Del Hardy** as a fair and peaceful man who acts as a father to his soldiers. However, Colonel Bouquet is also a confident, determined frontiersman willing to take risks.

Duke of Bourbon

Henry V
William Shakespeare

A French nobleman and military leader. Like the **Dauphin** and the other French nobles, Bourbon does not take the English seriously, and instead of preparing for battle mocks the English and comments on how easy the battle will be. For much of the play, the French are shown in a poor light, as decadent, derisive schoolboys rather than warriors. Only when they face defeat at the Battle of Agincourt do they show any honor, promising to rush back into battle lest they face shame. Bourbon is taken prisoner following the Battle of Agincourt.

Mademoiselle Bourienne

War and Peace
Leo Tolstoy

The French companion of **Marya Nikolayevna Bolkonskaya**, who lives with her on the Bolkonsky estate. Mademoiselle Bourienne becomes the object of the old **Prince Bolkonsky**'s affections shortly before his death.

Abbé Bournisien

Madame Bovary
Gustave Flaubert

The town priest in Yonville. He is preoccupied with the petty banalities of his own problems and with a group of unruly boys in his catechism class. He often argues with **Homais** about the value of religion, but seems incapable of grasping deep spiritual problems.

Charles Bovary

Madame Bovary
Gustave Flaubert

Emma Bovary's husband. He is kind, but simple, dull, and unremarkable. He is a doctor who manages simple cases decently but is incapable of performing difficult operations. Despite his deep love for Emma, he doesn't understand her. Her looks and dress captivate him, but he remains oblivious to her personality. His adoration of her often leads him to act with baffling innocence. He fails to detect her extramarital affairs with **Rodolphe Boulanger** and **Leon**, which are so poorly concealed that they become the subjects of town gossip. When Emma begins to run up debts, he grants her power of attorney over all his property, an act that leads to his financial ruin. After Emma's suicide, he learns of her infidelities. He tells one of Emma's lovers that he does not hold a grudge against him for their affair. Instead of blaming any individual, he blames fate. He dies soon after Emma's death.

Emma Bovary

Madame Bovary
Gustave Flaubert

The novel's protagonist, the Madame Bovary of the title. A country girl educated in a convent and married to **Charles Bovary** at a young age, she harbors idealistic romantic illusions, covets sophistication, sensuality, and passion, and lapses into fits of extreme boredom and depression when her life fails to match the sentimental novels she treasures. She has a daughter, **Berthe**, but lacks maternal instinct and is often annoyed with her. Occasionally, guilt or a memory of her simple childhood causes her to repent, and she becomes devoutly religious and dedicates herself to her family. Such fits of conscience are short-lived. Emma's desire for passion and pleasure leads her into extramarital affairs with **Rodolphe Boulanger** and **Leon**. Each of her affairs is ultimately unsatisfying. In addition, Emma runs up enormous debts against her husband's property. After many attempts to pay off the debt, she commits suicide by ingesting arsenic, dying in the company of her husband.

Madame Bovary the Elder

Madame Bovary
Gustave Flaubert

Charles Bovary's mother. She is a bitter, conservative woman who spoiled Charles as a youth. She disapproves of his marriage to **Emma Bovary** and sees through Emma's lies. She fights with Emma about her infidelity to Charles and tries to get her son to rein in Emma's excessive spending.

Norman Bowker

The Things They Carried
Tim O'Brien

A man who embodies the damage that the war can do to a soldier long after the war is over. During the war, Bowker is quiet and unassuming, but **Kiowa**'s death has a profound effect on him. Bowker's letter to **Tim O'Brien** in "Notes" demonstrates the importance of sharing stories in the healing process.

Mrs. Bowles

Fahrenheit 451
Ray Bradbury

One of **Mildred Montag**'s friends. Like **Mrs. Phelps**, she does not seem to care deeply about her own miserable life, which includes one divorce, one husband killed in an accident, one husband who commits suicide, and two children who hate her. Both of Mildred's friends are represented as typical specimens of their society.

Lois Bowling

Prodigal Summer
Barbara Kingsolver

Cole Widener's sister. Lois is a mean-spirited, conservative woman who wants ten-year-old **Crystal Gail Walker** to dress like a "young lady."

Big Rickie Bowling

Prodigal Summer
Barbara Kingsolver

Cole Widener's brother-in-law, the husband of **Lois Bowling**. Big Rickie Bowling lusts after **Lusa Maluf Landowski** at the Fourth of July party.

Little Rickie Bowling

Prodigal Summer
Barbara Kingsolver

The son of **Big Rickie Bowling** and **Lois Bowling**. Little Rickie is a tall, handsome, kind-hearted seventeen-year-old with a crush on **Lusa Maluf Landowski**.

David Bowman

2001: A Space Odyssey
Arthur C. Clarke

A broadly skilled astronaut. David is chosen, along with **Frank Poole**, as one of two crew members to stay awake during the entire voyage to Saturn. He is intelligent and disciplined, which helps him survive the loneliness of Poole's death. He passes through the Star Gate and becomes transformed into an eternal, bodiless being.

Ellen and Mike Bowman

Jurassic Park
Michael Crichton

The parents of **Tina Bowman**, a girl attacked by mysterious lizards early in the novel.

Tina Bowman

Jurassic Park
Michael Crichton

The daughter of **Ellen Bowman** and **Mike Bowman**. At the beginning of the novel, Tina is attacked by mysterious lizards on the beach during a family vacation in Costa Rica.

Mrs. Boxall

The Power of One
Bryce Courtenay

The librarian in Barberton, Mrs. Boxall has a weekly column in the local newspaper called "Clippings from a Cultured Garden." She becomes a great friend of **Peekay** and of **Doc**, and she personally undertakes to educate Peekay in English literature. A generous and magnanimous woman, she initiates the mysterious Sandwich Fund, whereby she gathers food, money, letters, and tobacco for black prisoners and their families.

Boxer

Animal Farm
George Orwell

Strong and loyal cart-horse who is an invaluable contributor to Animal Farm and the construction of the farm's windmill. Boxer epitomizes the exploited working class, adopting first the loyalist motto, "I will work harder!" and later the naïve "**Napoleon** is always right!" as the pigs grow more tyrannical. After injuring himself during an early-morning shift on the windmill, Boxer is sent to his death by the pigs, who sell him to a glue factory.

Boy

Henry VI, Part I
William Shakespeare

The son of the **Master Gunner**. The boy and his father help **Joan** bring down the English siege at Orléans.

Boy

The Two Noble Kinsmen
William Shakespeare

The singer in **Theseus** and **Hippolyta**'s wedding procession.

The Boy

Six Characters in Search of an Author
Luigi Pirandello

A timid and wretched fourteen-year-old. He has been driven mute from humiliation at having to enter the new household on **the Father**'s charity. As a result, he suffers **the Stepdaughter**'s contempt. He and **the Child** are "accessory figures" of sorts to **the Mother**, functioning to keep her torture "actual." He wears the black of mourning and spends most of the play clinging to the Mother. When he discovers the Child dead in a fountain, he commits suicide with a gun.

The boy

The Power and the Glory
Graham Greene

A youngster, the child of the **woman**, growing up in the violent and impoverished land of Mexico. The boy listens with skepticism to his mother's stories about **Juan**, a martyred boy. He meets **The Priest** in the beginning of the novel and, by the end, is impressed that the man he encountered has become a martyr for his faith. The boy represents the human race's ability to better itself by teaching its youth.

Boy

Waiting for Godot
Samuel Beckett

A messenger. He appears at the end of both acts to inform Vladimir that **Godot** will not be coming that night. Both times, he insists that he was not there the previous night.

The boy

Sounder
William Armstrong

The protagonist of *Sounder*. The story focuses on the boy's search for **Sounder** and **the boy's father**, both of whom he loses on the same night: the deputy comes to take the father away and shoots Sounder. The boy comes of age as the novel progresses, especially in helping raise his siblings, comforting **the boy's mother** and filling the void left behind by his father. The boy is sad and lonely, and most of the time it does not appear that he has many joys in life. In addition to his constant search for his father and Sounder, the boy learns to read and finally moves out of the cabin in pursuit of an education by **the teacher**.

The boy's father

Sounder
William Armstrong

An absent character for the most part, since he is in jail for much of the text. Before his arrest and conviction, though, he plays a typical paternal role, supporting his family by hunting. Providing for **the boy** and **the boy's mother** becomes increasingly difficult, and it is when his responsibility as a provider reaches near impossibility that he steals to feed his family, triggering the string of events that eventually lead to his imprisonment. At the end, he is injured much like **Sounder**, significantly beaten, and broken by his stint as a convict. Like Sounder, he has a strong sense of home, and finds his way back, but dies soon after.

The boy's mother

Sounder
William Armstrong

Wife of **the boy's father**. She remains strong after her husband's arrest, working to support her family and to remain optimistic despite the tragic events that have befallen her family. She is very sensitive to **the boy** and discourages him from searching for his father and **Sounder**, though she supports him when he does. She does not complain about the circumstances and increased difficulty of their situation, and is the rock that holds the family together when her husband is put in jail.

Rupert Boyce

Childhood's End
Arthur C. Clarke

George Greggson's friend and a "supervet" assigned to assist animals over thousands of acres of jungle. Boyce owns the world's largest library of paranormal research, something of great interest to **the Overlords**, especially **Rashaverak**.

Mr. Boydon

Death Be Not Proud
John Gunther

The kindly headmaster of Deerfield Academy. Mr. Boydon recognizes **Johnny**'s achievements while he is away from school because of his illness and grants him a diploma.

Boyet

Love's Labour's Lost
William Shakespeare

A lord attending on the **Princess of France**. Mocked by **Berowne** to be "Wit's peddlar" and "honey-tongued," Boyet serves as a liaison between the lords of Navarre and the visiting ladies, often standing by to watch the men and women fall into their destined loves. At the end of the play, he proves himself as part of the lords by exchanging jokes at the expense of the players of the Nine Worthies masque.

Hugh Boylan

Ulysses
James Joyce

The manager for **Molly Bloom**'s upcoming concert in Belfast. Blazes Boylan is well-known and well-liked around town, though somewhat sleazy toward women. Boylan has become interested in Molly, and they commence an affair during the afternoon of the novel.

Boyle

In Our Time
Ernest Hemingway

A police officer who helps **Drevitts** shoot the two Hungarians.

Orren Boyle

Atlas Shrugged
Ayn Rand

The corrupt owner of Associated Steel. Although his product is inferior to **Hank Rearden**'s, he uses his government connections to protect his business and obtain the rights to make Rearden Metal, which, when appropriated by the government, is called "Miracle Metal."

Brabanzio

Othello
William Shakespeare

Desdemona's father and **Othello**'s friend. Brabanzio is a blustering and self-important Venetian senator. He feels betrayed when Othello marries Desdemona in secret.

Judge Brack

Hedda Gabler
Henrik Ibsen

A well-connected local judge. A friend and would-be suitor of **Hedda Tesman**'s, Judge Brack visits the Tesmans' home regularly. Worldly and cynical, he enjoys meddling in other people's affairs.

Lady Bracknell

The Importance of Being Earnest
Oscar Wilde

Algernon Montcrieff's aunt and **Gwendolen Fairfax**'s mother. A member of the English aristocracy, Lady Bracknell forbids her daughter to marry **Jack Worthing** because of his obscure background.

Sir William Bradshaw

Mrs. Dalloway
Virginia Woolf

A renowned London psychiatrist who specializes in "nerve cases." When **Lucrezia Smith** seeks help for her disturbed husband, **Septimus Warren Smith**, **Dr. Holmes** recommends Bradshaw, who determines that Septimus has suffered a complete mental breakdown. He recommends that Septimus spend time in the country, apart from Lucrezia.

Brady

The Autobiography of Miss Jane Pittman
Ernest J. Gaines

A older black man on the Samson plantation who is supposed to drive **Miss Jane Pittman** to town on the day of the protest at the courthouse. Brady is too scared to do so.

Earl Brady

Tender Is the Night
F. Scott Fitzgerald

An American filmmaker in France with whom the young actress **Rosemary Hoyt** is briefly fascinated.

Matthew Harrison Brady

Inherit the Wind
Jerome Lawrence & Robert E. Lee

A national political figure and a three-time loser in presidential campaigns. **Henry Drummond** helped Matthew Harrison Brady in his 1908 election campaign. A Christian fundamentalist and Nebraska native, Brady arrives in Hillsboro to defend the literal truth of the Bible against what he labels as **Bertram Cates**' big-city agnosticism. At the beginning of *Inherit the Wind*, Brady is confident the trial is as good as won. Scornful of the threat that Drummond might present to him as the opposing attorney, Brady exhibits hubris in failing to consider the prospect of his own humiliation, which Drummond secures by exposing the obvious contradictions in Brady's viewpoint. Playing on his home turf in rural Christian Tennessee, Brady basks in the glow of his simple-minded supporters' praise. When Drummond undermines Brady's authority, Brady breaks down, for he lacks the inner strength to reconsider his own beliefs and adjust to an unexpected challenge. The failures of Brady's campaigns for president plague him throughout his life and manifest themselves during the trial. Brady is a caricature of the real-life prosecutor William Jennings Bryan. Like Brady, Bryan lost three presidential elections and died shortly after the Scopes Monkey Trial.

Mrs. Brady

Inherit the Wind
Jerome Lawrence & Robert E. Lee

Matthew Harrison Brady's wife. Mrs. Brady monitors her husband and nags him not to overeat. Brady calls her "Mother." Mrs. Brady is occasionally escorted around by **Reverend Jeremiah Brown**.

Ben Franklin Bragg

Alas, Babylon
Pat Frank

The son of **Mark Bragg** and **Helen Bragg**. In the aftermath of the war, he is forced to grow up quickly, carrying a gun and guarding the family's barn and henhouse from predators.

Helen Bragg

Alas, Babylon
Pat Frank

Mark Bragg's wife, and the mother of **Peyton Bragg** and **Ben Franklin Bragg**. Her husband, fearing imminent war, sends her to Fort Repose from their home in Omaha. She moves in with her brother-in-law, **Randy Bragg**, on the day before war breaks out.

Mark Bragg

Alas, Babylon
Pat Frank

Randy Bragg's brother, and an officer with the Strategic Air Command in Omaha. He warns his brother that nuclear war is imminent, and sends his wife, **Helen Bragg**, and their children, **Peyton Bragg** and **Ben Franklin Bragg**, to live with Randy. He dies in Omaha during the first nuclear exchange—although Helen does not learn of his death for months.

Peyton Bragg

Alas, Babylon
Pat Frank

The daughter of **Mark Bragg** and **Helen Bragg**. She is blinded when she looks directly at a distant nuclear explosion.

Randy Bragg

Alas, Babylon
Pat Frank

Mark Bragg's brother, **Dan Gunn**'s best friend, and the descendant of an old Florida family. When the novel begins, he is a failed candidate for political office, living off his family's land and occasional work as a lawyer in the small Florida town of Fort Repose. After the nuclear war, however, he becomes responsible for his brother's family and the people who live around him. He eventually marries his girlfriend, **Elizabeth McGovern**, and emerges as the leader of the entire town.

Bramimonde

Song of Roland
Unknown

Marsilla's queen, Bramimonde falls into a deep despair and feels utterly disgraced after her husband's defeat by the Franks. She loses her faith in Islam, cursing the Saracen gods for not having helped Marsilla and his men on the battlefield. When the Franks take Saragossa, **Charlemagne** decides to bring her back to Aix to convert her to Christianity, which she does by true conviction. She is baptized Juliana.

Branca d'Oria

Inferno
Dante Alighieri

A sinner suffering, with **Fra Alberigo**, among the Betrayers of Guests in Ptolomea, the Third Ring of the Ninth Circle of Hell (Canto XXXIII). Technically, d'Oria and Alberigo are not dead; their crimes were so grave that devils now occupy their bodies while their souls rot in Hell.

Brandon

Henry VIII
William Shakespeare

An officer or noble under **King Henry VIII**, sent to arrest the **Duke of Buckingham**.

Colonel Brandon

Sense and Sensibility
Jane Austen

A retired officer and friend of **Sir John Middleton**'s. Colonel Brandon falls in love with **Marianne Dashwood**. He always treats the Dashwoods kindly, honorably, and graciously.

The Kitchen God's Wife
Amy Tan

Cleo and Tessa Brandt

The two daughters of **Pearl** and **Phil**. Both girls are raised in an American way, yet they love their grandmother and her stories. Tessa is older and more confident, while Cleo is younger and gentler.

The Kitchen God's Wife
Amy Tan

Pearl Louie Brandt

Winnie's daughter. Pearl is the child of Chinese immigrants and is caught between her American identity and her Chinese ancestry and parents. She is married to an American man and feels more American than she does Chinese. She, like her mother, harbors secrets; when the novel opens, she has not told her mother about her multiple sclerosis.

The Kitchen God's Wife
Amy Tan

Phil Brandt

Pearl's husband. Phil is a "regular American guy." He is a good father and husband but often finds himself out of place among Pearl's Chinese family.

The Lord of the Rings Trilogy
J. R. R. Tolkien

Meriadoc Brandybuck

The young Hobbit from Buckland. Meriadoc, known as Merry, has a temperament similar to that of **Peregrin Took**, who is known as Pippin. Merry is more mature and, unlike most Hobbits, not afraid of boats and water. In *The Fellowship of the Ring*, he is chosen to be part of the Fellowship, which is meant to destroy **Sauron**'s One Ring in Mordor. In *The Two Towers*, Merry and Pippin are captured by **Orcs** and separated from the Fellowship. The Orcs, part of **Saruman**'s force, think that Merry or Pippin must have the One Ring, and are instructed to bring them to Saruman alive. The Hobbits escape, however, and flee into the forest of Entwash, where they meet **Treebeard** and **Fangorn**. There, Merry and Pippin convince Treebeard and his force of old Ents to attack Saruman at Orthanc. In *The Return of the King*, Merry is stranded from his counterparts and desperately seeks the approval of King **Théoden**, to whom he offers his service. Merry sacrifices his safety for Théoden in slaying the Black Captain, the leader of **the Nazgûl**, and is the primary focus of the chapters concerning the Riders of Rohan.

Evelina
Fanny Burney

Biddy Branghton

Mr. Branghton's eldest daughter and one of **Evelina Anville**'s three cousins. Evelina describes her as proud, ill-tempered, and conceited. Biddy has her sights set on **Mr. Smith**.

Evelina
Fanny Burney

Mr. Branghton

Madame Duval's bourgeois nephew. Around forty years old, Mr. Branghton has a good common understanding but is very prejudiced. He owns a silversmith shop and rents a room out to **Mr. Macartney**.

Tom Branghton

Evelina
Fanny Burney

Evelina Anville's twenty-year-old cousin. Tom Branghton has the demeanor of a foolish, overgrown schoolboy. He likes having money but lacks intelligence, skill, and talent.

Polly Branghton

Evelina
Fanny Burney

Evelina Anville's nineteen-year-old pretty, good-natured, foolish, and ignorant cousin. Polly is courted by **Mr. Brown**.

Alice Brannon

The Heart Is a Lonely Hunter
Carson McCullers

Biff Brannon's wife, who passes away at the beginning of Part Two. Alice seems to be generally unpleasant, and Biff does not miss her very much after she dies.

Biff Brannon

The Heart Is a Lonely Hunter
Carson McCullers

The proprietor of the New York Café, a central eating spot in town. Mr. Brannon is a quiet, thoughtful man who enjoys pondering life and wants children of his own.

Dr. Branom

A Clockwork Orange
Anthony Burgess

Assistant to **Dr. Brodsky** in implementing Ludovico's Technique on **Alex**. He puts on a show of friendliness, but seems to enjoy Alex's pain and agony as much as his superior.

Captain Adam Brant

Mourning Becomes Electra
Eugene O'Neill

A powerful, romantic sea captain. The illegitimate child of **Brigadier-General Ezra Mannon**, he returns to wreak vengeance on Ezra's household. Ezra threw his own brother **David** out of the Mannon house, as well as David's beloved, **Marie Brantôme**. Ezra then impregnated Marie with Brant. Brant returns and steals Ezra's wife, **Christine Mannon** and then seduces Ezra's and Christine's daughter, Brant's half-sister, **Lavinia Mannon**, to conceal their affair. Lavinia vows to protect Ezra from Brant's revenge. After Christine murders Ezra, Lavinia keeps close watch upon her mother. When **Orin Mannon**, Lavinia's brother, comes home, he incestuously seeks Christine. They have a romance, but Lavinia exposes the affair and Orin kills Brant in a rage, ransacking Brant's ship to make the murder look like a robbery gone wrong.

Brave Orchid

The Woman Warrior
Maxine Hong Kingston

Kingston's mother. Brave Orchid's talk-stories about Chinese life and traditions haunt Kingston and make up a large part of her memoir.

Mrs. Catherine Bread

The American
Henry James

An old British nurse, formerly the **Marquise de Bellegarde**'s nurse when she was still living in England as the Lady Atheling. Mrs. Bread is thin, pale, and thoroughly English, standing straight and perpetually dressed in black. She helped raise **Valentin de Bellegarde** and **Claire de Bellegarde**, loves them fiercely, and embraces **Christopher Newman** as someone who can give her beloved charges a chance at happiness. Mrs. Bread is honest, decent, observant, discreet, and completely trustworthy, and is also the only non-complicit witness to the Marquis' murder.

Breca

Beowulf
Unknown

Beowulf's childhood friend, whom Beowulf defeated in a swimming match.

Gavin Breckbridge

The Unvanquished
William Faulkner

Drusilla's fiance, who was killed at the battle of Shiloh and never appears in the novel. After his death, Drusilla becomes disillusioned with femininity and grows to hate the Yankees, running away from home to join the army.

Asa Breed

Cat's Cradle
Kurt Vonnegut

Felix Hoenikker's supervisor at the lab where Felix worked on the atomic bomb. According to rumor, he was also **Emily Hoenikker**'s lover. **John** interviewed him when he was researching his book, *The Day the World Ended*, which was never finished. Asa took offense at John's questions because he felt John believed scientists were heartlessly indifferent to humankind. He told John about Felix's attempts to create *ice-nine*.

Martin Breed

Cat's Cradle
Kurt Vonnegut

Asa Breed's brother; he owned and operated the tombstone shop in the city where **Felix Hoenikker** worked on the atomic bomb.

Cholly Breedlove

The Bluest Eye
Toni Morrison

Pecola Breedlove's father and **Pauline "Polly" Breedlove**'s husband. Cholly is an impulsive, violent man. Having suffered early humiliations, like being caught having sex with a girl by hunters and then told to continue at gunpoint, he takes out his frustration on the women in his life. He has loved and beaten many women in his life, and he has killed three white men. He is rejected by his father after seeking him out, and while trying not to cry, he defecates in his pants. He burns down his own family's home and goes to jail. After he is out of jail, he rapes Pecola, impregnating her, and then runs away.

Dana Breedlove

White Noise
Don DeLillo

Jack Gladney's ex-wife and **Steffie**'s mother. Like all of Jack's ex-wives, she is involved with the intelligence community.

Pauline Breedlove

The Bluest Eye
Toni Morrison

Pecola Breedlove's mother, and **Cholly Breedlove**'s wife. She has a deformed foot and sees herself as the martyr of a terrible marriage. When she finds Pecola covered up after being raped by Cholly, she beats Pecola. Like Cholly, Pauline inflicts a great deal of pain on her daughter. She becomes fixated on her appearance and emulates the white movie star Jean Harlow. Pauline finds no meaning in her own family. She often beats up her husband, who beats her too. Pauline's existence is just as haunted and delusional as her daughter's.

Pecola Breedlove

The Bluest Eye
Toni Morrison

The protagonist of *The Bluest Eye*. Pecola believes she is ugly and that having blue eyes would make her beautiful. She passively suffers the abuse of her mother, **Pauline "Polly" Breedlove**, father, **Cholly Breedlove**, and classmates. She feels as if she is invisible, and that she has no way to communicate with people in the world. Pecola is a fragile and delicate child when the novel begins, and by the novel's close, she has been almost completely destroyed by violence. Pecola is forced further and further into her fantasy world, which is her only defense against the pain of her existence. She believes that being granted the blue eyes she wishes for would change both how others see her and what she is forced to see. At the novel's end, she believes her wish has been granted, but at the cost of her sanity. Her father has raped and impregnated her, resulting in a stillbirth and her father's and **Sammy**'s disappearance.

Sammy Breedlove

The Bluest Eye
Toni Morrison

Pecola Breedlove's brother, who copes with his family's problems by running away from home. When his mother and father, **Pauline "Polly" Breedlove** and **Cholly Breedlove**, are fighting, he helps knock out his father, and urges his mother to kill Cholly. His active response contrasts with Pecola's passivity.

Denis Breen

Ulysses
James Joyce

Josie Breen's mentally unstable and paranoid husband.

Josie Breen

Ulysses
James Joyce

Leopold Bloom's former sweetheart. Josie has grown haggard taking care of her "dotty" husband, **Denis Breen**.

Bregalad

The Two Towers
J. R. R. Tolkien

A younger Ent, or tree creature, who befriends **Meriadoc Brandybuck** and **Peregrin Took** during the Ent assembly in Entwash, after the two Hobbits escape the **Orcs**.

Breitbart

The Assistant
Bernard Malamud

The seller of light bulbs, and like **Morris Bober**, a man who persists in the face of difficult times. Although his partner defrauded him and ran away with his wife, Breitbart goes on.

Herr Karl-Heinz Bremann

The Remains of the Day
Kazuo Ishiguro

A German friend of **Lord Darlington**'s who commits suicide after World War I, presumably due to the dire postwar economic conditions in Germany.

Emily Brent

And Then There Were None
Agatha Christie

An old, ruthlessly religious woman who reads her Bible every day. The recording accuses Emily Brent of killing **Beatrice Taylor**, a servant whom she fired upon learning that Beatrice was pregnant out of wedlock. Beatrice subsequently killed herself. Unlike the other characters, Emily Brent feels convinced of her own righteousness and does not express the slightest remorse for her actions.

Linda Brent

Incidents in the Life of a Slave Girl
Harriet Ann Jacobs

The book's protagonist, and a pseudonym for the author. Linda begins life with a secure attachment to her parents, who take excellent care of her for her first six years. They do not tell her she is a slave, which enables her to develop a strong sense of self-worth that later allows her to overcome major obstacles. Although she is exposed to degrading treatment at the hands of **Dr. Flint**, she never loses her self-respect or her desire to have a normal home and family. She is devoted to her children, and willing to undergo great suffering for their sake. She describes her family, particularly **Aunt Martha**, with affectionate sentimentality. She interweaves impassioned political arguments into her story, boldly challenging the Church, the law, and the sexual mores of her time, indicting all of these institutions for their indifference to the terrible plight of slaves.

Percy Bresnahan

Main Street
Sinclair Lewis

A wealthy automobile manufacturer originally from Gopher Prairie who allegedly has attained nationwide fame. Bresnahan is much admired by the people of the town, who value material success. **Carol Kennicott**, however, finds him coarse and overbearing. She admires Bresnahan for his importance but discovers in Washington that in reality he is relatively unimportant.

Lady Brett Ashley

The Sun Also Rises
Ernest Hemingway

A beautiful, aimless, hard-drinking British socialite who lives in Paris. As the novel begins, Brett is separated from her husband and awaiting a divorce. The novel's narrator, **Jake Barnes**, met Brett in England during World War I and fell in love with her, and then encountered her again in Paris after the war. Brett loves Jake but is unwilling to commit to him, as a war injury has rendered him impotent, and thus a relationship with him would mean giving up sex. Brett refuses to commit to any of the many men who become infatuated with her, although she has affairs with a number of them. Despite her desire to remain unattached, Brett fails to draw much happiness from her independence and seems uncomfortable being by herself. In fact, she often complains to Jake that her life is aimless and unsatisfying. For Hemingway, Brett's personal aimlessness is representative of the entire Lost Generation's search for the shattered prewar values of love and romance.

Brew

Fallen Angels
Walter Dean Myers

A devoutly religious solider in **Richie Perry**'s squad. Brew plans to join the ministry upon his return to civilian life.

Captain Brice

Arcadia
Tom Stoppard

Captain Brice is a sea captain and **Lady Croom**'s brother. He is in love with Mrs. Chater, and in order to sustain an affair he hires **Mr. Chater** to be his botanist on a sea voyage to Malta, bringing Mrs. Chater along for the ride. When Mr. Chater dies from a spider bite in Malta, Mrs. Chater marries Brice.

Brick

Cat on a Hot Tin Roof
Tennessee Williams

The favored son of **Big Daddy** and **Big Mama**, the unwilling and dispassionate husband of **Maggie**, and the brother of **Gooper**. Brick embodies an almost archetypal masculinity; at the same time, Brick also has a repressed homosexual desire for his dead friend **Skipper**, with whom Maggie once had sex. Brick has depressively withdrawn from the world behind a screen of liquor. Brick's brokenness is materialized in his injury, a broken ankle incurred while jumping hurdles on the high school athletic field. Brick is brought to judgment on his desire first by Maggie and then by Daddy. Maggie hounds Brick about sleeping with her, since he doesn't perform in bed, and then hounds the indifferent man about making a good show for Daddy so that Brick and Maggie will inherit Daddy's money instead of Gooper and his competitive wife **Mae**.

Brickmaker

Heart of Darkness
Joseph Conrad

A man **Marlow** meets at the Central Station. The brickmaker is a favorite of the manager and seems to be a kind of corporate spy. He never actually produces any bricks, as he is supposedly waiting for some essential element that is never delivered. He is petty and conniving and assumes that other people are, too.

Susanna Bridehead

Jude the Obscure
Thomas Hardy

Jude Fawley's cousin. Susanna works as an apprentice to the schoolmaster **Richard Phillotson**, whom she eventually marries. She is intellectually radical and leaves the Training College because she discovers that its rules are intolerably strict, and her supervisors' suspicions are too much for her to bear. In many ways, she is a feminist before her time. She recognizes her own intellect and her potential for a satisfying career in teaching, and marries Phillotson partly out of a desire for a pleasant work environment. When Jude falls in love with her, she wavers back and forth in her protests, sometimes wanting to enter into a romantic relationship with him and sometimes believing it to be misguided.

Bridget

Tristram Shandy
Laurence Sterne

Maidservant to **Widow Wadman**. **Corporal Trim** courts Bridget at the same time that Toby courts **Widow Wadman**, and Trim and Bridget's relationship continues for five years thereafter.

Captain Brierly

Lord Jim
Joseph Conrad

One of the most decorated and respected ship's captains in the area. He is on the board of inquiry that tries **Jim**. Secretly, he makes **Marlow** an offer of money to help Jim run away. Not long after the inquiry, he commits suicide, motivated by some secret shame.

Mr. Briggs

Jane Eyre
Charlotte Brontë

John Eyre's attorney. He helps **Richard Mason** prevent **Jane Eyre**'s wedding to **Edward Rochester** when he learns of the existence of **Bertha Mason**, Rochester's wife. After John Eyre's death, Briggs searches for Jane in order to give her her inheritance.

Brigida

The Power and the Glory
Graham Greene

The illegitimate daughter of **the Priest** and **Maria**. Brigida meets with her father briefly during his stay at her village. Mocked because of her ignominious parentage, she is less than thrilled to meet her long-lost father, and their short exchange is a tense one. The Priest worries about how she will fare in the dangerous, cruel world, and fears that her heart has already become hardened by what she has experienced.

Brigitte

Breath, Eyes, Memory
Edwidge Danticat

Sophie's daughter by **Joseph**. The infant Brigitte has a remarkable face in which **Grandmè Ifé** can see the traces of generations of ancestors. She is calm, quiet, and sleeps peacefully, signs that perhaps she has not inherited the insomnia and nightmares.

Brillante

The Rape of the Lock
Alexander Pope

The sylph assigned to guard **Belinda**'s earrings.

Ginger Brinker-Smith

A Prayer for Owen Meany
John Irving

A young faculty wife at Gravesend Academy, a legendary sex symbol to academy boys. One Christmas holiday, shortly after the Brinker-Smiths have twins, **John** and **Owen Meany** discover that the couple is engaged on a campaign to have sex in every dorm room in the building.

Brint

I Am the Cheese
Robert Cormier

A sinister character, presumably a psychiatrist in an institution, though he never admits to this. In his talks with **Adam Farmer**, where he acts as a "guide," he is generally cold and aggressive, often pushing for specific information that does not seem relevant to Adam. It turns out he is trying to squeeze information out of Adam. Adam's father, **David Farmer**, may have told Adam more information about the organizations against which he testified than what he told the government. Brint is unsuccessful at reaching Adam in terms of extracting such information, but is persistent, wondering if what he wants to know is in the "psychological residue" of Adam's life before the Witness Re-Identification Program, or in Adam's traumas. It turns out that Brint works for the very same branch of the government that took David Farmer's (then called **Anthony Delmonte**) testimony, relocated and re-identified him and his family, and possibly was working against the family as well.

Lily Briscoe

To the Lighthouse
Virginia Woolf

A young, single painter who befriends the Ramsays on the Isle of Skye. Like **Mr. Ramsay**, Lily is plagued by fears that her work lacks worth. She begins a portrait of **Mrs. Ramsay** at the beginning of the novel but has trouble finishing it. The opinions of men like **Charles Tansley**, who insist that women cannot paint or write, threaten to undermine her confidence.

Briseis

The Iliad
Homer

A woman **Achilles** claims as a war prize. When **Agamemnon** is forced to return **Chryseis** to her father, he takes Briseis as compensation, infuriating Achilles.

Britomart

The Faerie Queene
Edmund Spenser

The hero of Book III, the female warrior virgin, who represents chastity. Britomart is a skilled fighter who is strong of heart, with an amazing capacity for calm thought in troublesome circumstances.

Duke of Brittany

Henry V
William Shakespeare

A French nobleman and military leader. Like the **Dauphin** and the other French nobles, Brittany does not take the English seriously, and instead of preparing for battle, he mocks the English and comments on how easy the battle will be. For much of the play, the French are shown in a poor light: as decadent, derisive schoolboys rather than warriors. Only when they face defeat at the Battle of Agincourt do they show any honor, promising to rush back into battle lest they face shame. The English capture or kill most of the French nobility at the Battle of Agincourt.

Britten

Native Son
Richard Wright

A racist, anticommunist private investigator who helps **Mr. Dalton** investigate **Mary Dalton**'s disappearance.

Brobdingnagians

Gulliver's Travels
Jonathan Swift

A race of giants. Polite, gentle, and fair, they contrast with the petty, quarrelling **Lilliputians**. Brobdingnagians are kind to **Gulliver**, but do not take him seriously, treating him as a curious plaything.

King of Brobdingnag

Gulliver's Travels
Jonathan Swift

The ruler of Brobdingnag. Unlike the emperor of Lilliput, this king is an intellectual who is well-versed in political science. He engages in serious discussions about English history and political institutions with **Gulliver**, ultimately dismissing Englishmen as "odious vermin."

Queen of Brobdingnag

Gulliver's Travels
Jonathan Swift

Queen of Brobdingnag. She purchases **Gulliver** from the **farmer** for a thousand gold pieces and brings him to the court. Pleasant and genuinely considerate, the queen possesses "infinite" wit and humor, according to Gulliver, though this description may involve a bit of Gulliver's characteristic flattery of superiors.

Mr. Brocklehurst

Jane Eyre
Charlotte Brontë

Jane Eyre's cruel, hypocritical master at the Lowood School, Mr. Brocklehurst preaches a doctrine of privation, while stealing from the school to support his luxurious lifestyle. After a typhus epidemic sweeps Lowood, Brocklehurst's shifty and dishonest practices are brought to light and he is publicly discredited.

Dr. Brodsky

A Clockwork Orange
Anthony Burgess

The psychologist in charge of conditioning **Alex** using Ludovico's Technique. He is unconcerned with the "higher ethics" of the procedure, seeing Ludovico's Technique as better than the "unprofitable" imprisonment of criminals. When Brodsky learns that the films used in the technique cause Alex to grow averse not just to violence but also classical music, he laughs it off, as he does all of Alex's pain.

Joseph Brody

The Big Sleep
Raymond Chandler

A man who tries to take over **Geiger**'s porn racket. Brody is a common criminal who blackmails and gets involved in any scheme or illegal activity that might make him a dollar. He blackmails **Vivian Sternwood** with the pictures of **Carmen** he possesses. He is not incredibly smart, and his life seems almost an accident, just like his death, which is a mere misunderstanding—Lundgren thinks it is Brody who has killed Geiger.

Chief Bromden

One Flew Over the Cuckoo's Nest
Ken Kesey

The narrator, the son of the chief of the Columbia Indians and a white woman. He suffers from paranoia and hallucinations, has received multiple electroshock treatments, and has been in the hospital for ten years, longer than any other patient in the ward. Although he says that he is telling the story about the guys in the hospital, he is also telling the story of his own journey toward sanity. When the novel begins, Bromden is paranoid and bullied, medicated and sheltered from reality. By the end of the novel, the fog has cleared, and Bromden has recovered the personal strength to euthanize **Randle McMurphy**, escape from the hospital, and record his account of the events.

Arthur Brooke

Middlemarch
George Eliot

Dorothea Brooke and **Celia Brooke**'s bachelor uncle. He is a bumbling man who can never stick to an opinion, always wanting to please everyone. He hires **Will Ladislaw** to write for his paper, the *Pioneer*. He runs for a seat in Parliament on the Reform platform but lets his own tenants live in poverty and squalor. The scandal resulting from his hypocrisy prompts him to improve conditions on his estate, Tipton Grange.

Celia Brooke

Middlemarch
George Eliot

Dorothea Brooke's sister. She marries **Sir James Chettam**.

Dorothea Brooke

Middlemarch
George Eliot

A kind-hearted and honest woman who longs to find some way to improve the world. She thinks **Edward Casaubon** is a great intellectual, but after marrying him, she quickly discovers that he is not passionate enough to make her happy. Dorothea draws plans for comfortable cottages to replace the ramshackle buildings on large estates and helps **Tertius Lydgate** when he suffers for his connections with **Nicholas Bulstrode**. She falls in love with Casaubon's young cousin, **Will Ladislaw**, and defies Casaubon's machinations by marrying Will even though it means losing her inheritance as Casaubon's widow.

Mr. Brooke

Little Women
Louisa May Alcott

Laurie Laurence's tutor. Mr. Brooke is poor but virtuous. When **Meg March** agrees to marry Mr. Brooke, she demonstrates that at last she has overcome her own weakness for luxury and riches.

Alfred Brooks

The Contender
Robert Lipsyte

The protagonist high school dropout who begins training to become a boxer. Alfred Brooks deals with the downfall of his childhood friend, **James**, while trying to make something of himself as a boxer and a worker in **Mr. Epstein**'s store. Alfred stands out against neighborhood kids like **Major**, who try to lure him into committing crimes and doing drugs. For the most part, Alfred shows a strong will, although he does once succumb to vice by smoking pot and drinking.

Cherryl Brooks

Atlas Shrugged
Ayn Rand

A young, idealistic hero-worshipper who marries **James Taggart**, mistakenly believing he is a good man. Jim seeks to destroy her and the good she represents and is ultimately successful.

Mother's Younger Brother

Ragtime
E. L. Doctorow

Idealistic and difficult, Mother's Younger Brother searches for a sense of self throughout the novel. He falls in love with **Evelyn Nesbit**, and spends some time with her before she leaves him. He becomes embittered and depressed and soon joins the forces of Coalhouse to fight injustice. Subsequently, he travels all around the United States and then to Mexico, where he becomes involved in several revolutionary campaigns and eventually dies.

Avery Brown

The Piano Lesson
August Wilson

A preacher who is trying to build his congregation. While he pursues his dream, Avery takes a job as an elevator operator at a building downtown. After securing a loan from the bank to start up his church, he makes a play for Berniece's hand. Avery brings modern Christian authority, in combination with Berniece's African folk faith, to help exorcise the ghost of Sutter, the piano's previous owner.

Berenice Sadie Brown

The Member of the Wedding
Carson McCullers

The Addams family's African-American housekeeper. Though she is over forty years old, she is still an avidly sexual woman who is never shy about having a good time with the various men who come through her life. In fact, by the end of the novella, she considers marrying her fifth husband. She is a no-nonsense type who doesn't put up with **Frankie Addams**'s difficult and moody behavior. She acts as a voice of reason, giving readers a better perspective on the reality that Frankie easily overlooks.

Clamp Brown

The Autobiography of Miss Jane Pittman
Ernest J. Gaines

One of the teenage boys who lives on the Samson plantation at the end of the book.

Corporal Brown

The Autobiography of Miss Jane Pittman
Ernest J. Gaines

The white Union soldier who renames **Miss Jane Pittman**.

Dan Brown

The Hours
Michael Cunningham

Laura Brown's husband. He was a war hero and was much more popular than Laura in high school. He fell in love with Laura and married her when he came back from the war. Dan is consistently kind and appreciative of Laura. He is happy with his life and has high hopes for the future.

Gentleman Brown

Lord Jim
Joseph Conrad

A white pirate who, having barely escaped Spanish officials in the Philippines, comes to Patusan hoping to steal some provisions. He is rather infamous in this part of the world, and is used as the stock villain whenever locals are telling stories. He and his men are attacked upon arrival in Patusan by **Dain Waris** and his band, who have had advance warning of their coming. Although he had initially wanted to conquer and loot Patusan, he realizes he is outnumbered and negotiates with **Jim**. In those negotiations, Brown shows he is aware of Jim's dark past, thereby appealing to Jim's tortured sense of ideals and receiving permission to retreat in safety. Brown has been conspiring with **Cornelius** and the **Rajah Allang**. On his way back to his ship, he surprises Dain Waris and his men at their camp. Dain Waris is killed, which also leads to Jim's death. After Brown and his men are shipwrecked, Brown is the only survivor, although he dies soon afterward. **Marlow** visits him on his deathbed and gets part of the story from him.

Honey Brown

The Member of the Wedding
Carson McCullers

Berenice Sadie Brown's foster brother. Honey seems to have a few screws loose. He is unable to go to war, so he lives with **Big Mama**.

Dr. John Brown

Like Water for Chocolate
Laura Esquivel

An American doctor who cares for **Tita** when she experiences a breakdown, and the father of **Alex**. At Dr. Brown's house, Tita is able to explore a new way of existing in the world, not circumscribed by the limits imposed by **Mama Elena** or by her role as nurturer. As an outsider, John offers Tita access to the independence she seeks. Yet even the option that arises out of her relationship with John Brown relies on her domesticity, as they are to become engaged. Tita eventually denies him marriage to pursue **Pedro**.

Laura Brown

The Hours
Michael Cunningham

One of the three major characters. Her chapters are set in 1949, in Los Angeles. Laura is a young wife and the mother of a three-year-old son, who will grow up to be **Richard Brown** in **Clarissa Vaughn**'s present-day chapters. Laura lives in a lovely house and has a nice husband (**Dan Brown**), but she nevertheless feels that she should be living a different life. She can't believe in her own role as a housewife. She is a bookworm and sees herself as an outsider, a strange, awkward exile from normalcy.

Miss Brown

The Heart Is a Lonely Hunter
Carson McCullers

A boarder in **Mick Kelly**'s house. Miss Brown often listens to the music of Mozart on her radio, which Mick tries to overhear.

Mr. Brown

Things Fall Apart
Chinua Achebe

The first white missionary to travel to Umuofia. Mr. Brown institutes a policy of compromise, understanding, and non-aggression between his Christian missionaries and the native clan. He even becomes friends with prominent clansmen such as **Akunna**, and builds a school and a hospital in Umuofia. Unlike **Reverend Smith**, he attempts to appeal respectfully to the tribe's value system rather than impose his religion on it.

Rachel Brown

Inherit the Wind
Jerome Lawrence & Robert E. Lee

The daughter of **Reverend Jeremiah Brown**. Rachel Brown teaches second grade at the school where **Bertram Cates** also taught before he was arrested for teaching evolution. Rachel is a close friend of Cates's, and their relationship has a romantic element. Rachel fears her father's disapproval and becomes upset when Brady calls on her to testify about her personal conversations with Cates. **Matthew Harrison Brady** asks Rachel if Cates said things like, "man created God," and "human marriage is comparable to the breeding of animals." As Rachel tells more of her story, her father and the form of Christianity practiced in Hillsboro appear increasingly more cruel and heartless. Rachel relates that her father had always frightened her, even from a young age. He publicly confirms her fears at a town prayer meeting, when he damns her soul for supporting Cates. Throughout *Inherit the Wind*, Cates and Reverend Brown test Rachel's loyalties. At the conclusion of the trial, Rachel separates from her father and departs with Cates, a choice that enables her personal liberation.

Reverend Jeremiah Brown

Inherit the Wind
Jerome Lawrence & Robert E. Lee

The figure of religious authority in Hillsboro. Reverend Jeremiah Brown preaches a creed based on the fear of God and the punishment of sinners. He publicly damns his own daughter, **Rachel Brown**, to an eternity in hell because she supports **Bertram Cates**.

Richard Brown

The Hours
Michael Cunningham

Novelist and poet, a gay man who is dying of AIDS. He has been Clarissa's best friend since they were in college together. Before he started losing his mind because of the disease, Richard was argumentative, intelligent, and stubborn. He had a grand vision of his own life, and of his friends' lives—he was interested in the narrative of every passing day. His work was experimental and only sometimes successful. He is the adult son of **Laura Brown**. Richard shares characterstics both with *Mrs. Dalloway*'s **Septimus Warren Smith** and **Richard Dalloway**.

Mr. Brownlow

Oliver Twist
Charles Dickens

A wealthy, compassionate gentleman. Mr. Brownlow is **Oliver Twist**'s first benefactor. He owns a portrait of **Agnes Fleming** and was engaged to **Mr. Leeford**'s sister when she died.

Mrs. Bruce #1

Incidents in the Life of a Slave Girl
Harriet Ann Jacobs

Linda's first employer in New York City, a kindly Englishwoman who provides Linda with much help in hiding from the Flints. She dies and is replaced by **Mrs. Bruce #2**.

Mrs. Bruce #2

Incidents in the Life of a Slave Girl
Harriet Ann Jacobs

Mr. Bruce's second wife, an abolitionist American who protects **Linda Brent** at great risk to herself, and ultimately buys her freedom from **Mr. Dodge**.

Sir Bruce Sans Pitié

The Once and Future King
T. H. White

An evil knight known for his sneak attacks and ambushes. Sir Bruce Sans Pitié always manages to avoid capture and is a recurring example of the old injustices **King Arthur** is trying to fight.

Mr. Bruce

Incidents in the Life of a Slave Girl
Harriet Ann Jacobs

Mrs. Bruce's husband, a vague character who takes **Linda Brent** on a trip to England.

Mr. Mathew Bruff

The Moonstone
Wilkie Collins

The Verinder family's longtime lawyer. He holds **Rachel Verinder**, **Lady Verinder**, and **Franklin Blake** in high esteem. Mr. Bruff has a lawyer's mind for thinking logically through the facts of the case, resisting any imaginative or mystical thinking.

Corporal Brunner

Fallen Angels
Walter Dean Myers

An ambitious soldier in **Richie Perry**'s squad. A bully, Corporal Brunner constantly kisses up to soldiers of higher rank while abusing those below him.

Bruno

Doctor Faustus
Christopher Marlowe

Emperor Charles V's pick for the papacy. Bruno is imprisoned by the pope and freed by **Faustus**.

Lady Bruton

Mrs. Dalloway
Virginia Woolf

A sixty-two-year-old socialite known for her "extraordinarily amusing" lunch parties. She invites **Richard Dalloway** to one of these parties, which makes **Clarissa Dalloway** feel left out.

Brutus of *Coriolanus*

Coriolanus
William Shakespeare

One of the tribunes elected by the plebeians to serve as their representative in government. A clever politician, Brutus regards **Coriolanus** as a great danger to the plebeians and the Roman state and works to keep him out of power.

Brutus of *Julius Caesar*

Julius Caesar
William Shakespeare

A supporter of the republic who believes strongly in a government guided by the votes of senators. While Brutus loves **Julius Caesar** as a friend, he opposes the ascension of any single man to the position of dictator, and he fears Caesar aspires to such power. Brutus's inflexible sense of honor makes it easy for Caesar's enemies to manipulate him into believing Caesar must die in order to preserve the republic. While the other conspirators act out of envy and rivalry, only Brutus truly believes that Caesar's death will benefit Rome. Unlike Caesar, Brutus is able to completely separate his public life from his private life; by giving priority to matters of state, he epitomizes Roman virtue. Torn between his loyalty to Caesar and his allegiance to the state, Brutus becomes the tragic hero of the play. When **Antony** and **Octavius Caesar**'s victory seems imminent, Brutus orders one of his men to hold up his sword so that Brutus can impale himself.

Bryce

Silas Marner
George Eliot

A friend of both **Godfrey Cass** and **Dunstan Cass**. Bryce arranges to buy Wildfire, Dunsey's horse.

Bryce

Regeneration
Pat Barker

Dr. W.H.R. Rivers's boss, close friend, and fellow psychiatrist at Craiglockhart War Hospital. Bryce is a sympathetic, affable man who believes in the benefits of psychotherapy.

Frank Bryce

Harry Potter and the Goblet of Fire
J. K. Rowling

The Riddles' gardener, and an elderly, misanthropic Muggle (non-magical person) suspected to have murdered the Riddles. Frank is murdered by **Voldemort** in the first chapter of the book.

Brynhild

Norse Mythology
Unknown

A Valkyrie who angers **Odin** and is punished with imprisonment in a ring of fire. She is a dazzling character, later the prototype for Wagner's Brünnhilde.

Bubeh

The Color of Water
James McBride

Ruth McBride Jordan's maternal grandmother. She is one of the few family members Ruth recalls fondly. Bubeh allowed Ruth to stay with her in New York. While Bubeh tried to shape Ruth's behavior in some ways, she also gave Ruth some space and seemed to accept her.

Daisy Buchanan

The Great Gatsby
F. Scott Fitzgerald

Nick Carraway's beautiful cousin and the object of **Jay Gatsby**'s obsessive adoration. Daisy and Gatsby originally met in Daisy's hometown of Louisville, Kentucky, and got engaged. During World War I, Daisy broke her promise to wait for Gatsby and married the powerful, wealthy, boorish **Tom Buchanan** instead. When the novel opens, Daisy is a Long Island socialite, living with Tom in fashionable, upper-class East Egg and feigning sardonic flippancy to mask her pain at her husband's infidelity. Gatsby, obsessed with winning Daisy back, moves into a mansion across the harbor, throws extravagant parties in an attempt to impress Daisy, and uses Nick to arrange a meeting with her. Daisy and Gatsby do rekindle their affair, but it is short-lived, as Daisy ultimately decides to stay with Tom. Although Daisy is beautiful and charming, she also is shallow, bored, and materialistic—an embodiment of the amorality of the American upper class that Fitzgerald criticizes in the novel.

Tom Buchanan

The Great Gatsby
F. Scott Fitzgerald

A former member of **Nick Carraway**'s social club at Yale and **Daisy Buchanan**'s husband. A wealthy, arrogant, bigoted, powerfully built bully, Tom cheats on Daisy continually but is outraged at the thought that Daisy and **Gatsby** may be having an affair. The hotheaded Tom physically abuses his lover of the moment—**Myrtle Wilson**, a passionate woman stuck in a lifeless marriage—and initiates a confrontation with Gatsby at Gatsby's hotel suite in New York City. Tom indirectly causes Gatsby's death by telling Myrtle's husband **George** that Gatsby was driving the car that struck and killed Myrtle on a Long Island road.

Buck

The Call of the Wild
Jack London

A powerful dog, half St. Bernard and half sheepdog, who feels the "call of the wild" of the novel's title. Buck is stolen and sold by **Manuel** from the California estate of **Judge Miller** and sold as a sled dog in the Arctic. Over the course of *The Call of the Wild*, Buck evolves from a pampered pet into a fierce, masterful animal, a survivor in the cruel Northern wilderness. Filtered through the third-person omniscience of the narrator, Buck comes across as far more than a creature of instinct, since he has a sense of wonder, shame, and justice. He also possesses a capacity for mystical experiences and for great, unselfish love, as his relationship to **John Thornton** amply demonstrates.

Billy Buck

The Red Pony
John Steinbeck

The lone hired hand on **Carl Tiflin**'s farm. An experienced middle-aged man, Billy is very good with horses, and Carl trusts him deeply. Billy often takes a keen interest in **Jody** and spends a great deal of time teaching the boy about horses.

Pearl Buck

Hiroshima
John Hersey

A prominent American author who befriends the **Reverend Mr. Kiyoshi Tanimoto**. She is the author of *The Good Earth*.

Uncle Buck

The Unvanquished
William Faulkner

A brave but undeniably eccentric old man who lives with his brother **Uncle Buddy** on the outskirts of town. Buck and Buddy (whose real names are Amodeus and Theophilus) are true town characters, who live in a converted slave cabin while their slaves live in the main house. They give their slaves considerable freedom and are beloved by the poor hill people for their generosity and leadership—the polar opposite of the **Snopeses**. Buck, forced to stay home in Jefferson while his brother is away at war, accompanies **Bayard** on his quest for revenge against **Grumby**.

Buckbeak

Harry Potter and the Prisoner of Azkaban
J. K. Rowling

One of **Hagrid**'s beloved hippogriffs. A hippogriff is a large, winged creature that is half horse and half eagle-like bird. Buckbeak attacks **Draco Malfoy** and is sentenced to death, only to be saved by **Harry** and **Hermione** when they turn back time.

1st Duke of Buckingham

Henry VI, Part II
William Shakespeare

An English nobleman. Buckingham is a large part of the civil turmoil that boils over in the kingdom. At the beginning of the play, he joins **Cardinal Beaufort**, **Duke of Somerset**, **William de la Pole, Duke of Suffolk**, and **Queen Margaret** in their plot to wrest power from **Humphrey, Duke of Gloucester**, and later speaks out against Gloucester in front of **King Henry VI**. After he and the **Duke of York** arrest the **Duchess of Gloucester** for conspiring with conjurers, Buckingham takes the pleasure of telling the king and the other noblemen of the Duchess's crime. For all of his backstabbing with Gloucester, Buckingham is exceedingly faithful to the king, and serves as his loyal representative in **Jack Cade**'s and York's rebellions. Buckingham is one of many noblemen taking advantage of Henry VI's weak rule, jockeying for power with internal skirmishes.

2nd Duke of Buckingham

Richard III
William Shakespeare

King Richard III's right-hand man in his schemes to gain power. Though Richard has plotted and connived alone for quite a while, he takes Buckingham in as a co-conspirator, promising him the earldom of Hereford as well as all of **King Edward IV**'s possessions once he becomes king. As he schemes with Richard, Buckingham soon proves as amoral and ambitious as the hunchback himself. Buckingham helps convince the Cardinal to retrieve **Richard, Duke of York** from sanctuary; he helps convince the **Lord Mayor of London** that **Hastings** was a traitor; he tries to stir up support for Richard among the London commoners; finally, he contrives a well-structured public speech "begging" Richard to become king. However, when the newly crowned King Richard asks him to execute the young princes in the Tower, Buckingham hesitates and falls out of favor. Realizing what his fate could be, Buckingham flees to his family in Wales before raising an army to assist in the assault on Richard. His forces are defeated, and he is captured and executed, finally realizing that **Margaret**'s curse on his neck has come true. His ghost visits Richard and praise **Henry Tudo, Earl of Richmond** the night before the decisive battle between the two armies.

3rd Duke of Buckingham

Henry VIII
William Shakespeare

A powerful duke and father-in-law to the **Earl of Surrey**. Buckingham harbors a grudge against **Cardinal Wolsey**, whom he believes unfairly influences the king. Soon into the play, Buckingham's fears of Wolsey plotting against him come true: he is arrested and charged with treason. Thanks to testimony given by **Buckingham's surveyor**, a man who used to run the duke's estates, **King Henry VIII** calls for a trial. Despite speaking eloquently in his own defense, Buckingham is found guilty, and is led away to be executed.

George Villiers, Duke of Buckingham

The Three Musketeers
Alexandre Dumas

Minister of War for King Charles I of England. George Villiers, the Duke of Buckingham, is the perfect English gentleman: handsome, witty, brave, wealthy, and powerful. He is desperately in love with **Queen Anne** of Austria, who is the Queen of France. Throughout the novel, the Duke's only motivation is to see and please the queen. He even wages a war upon France out of love for her, trying to save a piece of the queen's diamond brooch that the **Lady de Winter** stole. In the end, **John Felton**, under the strong influence of the Lady, stabs and kills the duke. However, he dies a happy man, for at the moment before his death, a messenger arrives and tells the duke that the queen still loves him and wants him to call off the war against France.

Buckingham's surveyor

Henry VIII
William Shakespeare

A former employee of the **Duke of Buckingham**. **Cardinal Wolsey** brings the surveyor in to speak against Buckingham in front of **King Henry VIII**. The surveyor gives damning testimony, charging that Buckingham intended to get control of the crown if **King Henry VIII** died without a male heir. Though **Queen Katherine** notes that the surveyor was fired from his position, and may hold a grudge against the duke, the testimony stands. Buckingham goes to trial, is found guilty, and executed.

Buckley

Native Son
Richard Wright

The incumbent State's Attorney, who prosecutes **Bigger Thomas**'s case. He is a vicious racist and anti-communist.

Buckthorn

Watership Down
Richard Adams

A rabbit brought by **Blackberry** in the beginning. Buckthorn is strong and large, and along with **Silver** and **Bigwig** he fights often for **Hazel**'s party. Quiet and straightforward, Buckthorn always helps the warren, but does not often act on his own.

Billy Budd

Billy Budd, Sailor
Herman Melville

The novel's protagonist. Discovered on a doorstep as an infant, Billy Budd is a fine physical specimen as a young adult, renowned for his good looks and gentle, innocent ways. He is impressed into naval duty aboard the warship HMS *Bellipotent*. Although much younger than most of the *Bellipotent*'s crewmen, Billy quickly becomes popular and inspires love and admiration in all his fellows. At the same time, Billy is unable to believe that other people could feel ill will toward him. He also stutters, and at certain crucial moments he is completely speechless. These shortcomings render him extremely vulnerable to the evil influences aboard the ship. He has no defenses against a hateful man such as **John Claggart** and cannot even perceive malice in Claggart's speech and actions. Ultimately, Billy is sentenced to hang for a murder that he does not deny committing. He faces death with ease: his last words are "God Bless Captain Vere!"

Dawn Budgel

The Shipping News
E. Annie Proulx

The younger of **the aunt**'s assistants in the upholstery business. Dawn Budgel will take any job just to escape from Newfoundland and is uninterested in **Quoyle**.

Chase Buell

The Virgin Suicides
Jeffrey Eugenides

Son of a Christian Scientist, a decent, hardworking boy who worries about the Lisbon girls' salvation. He helps neighbors and sweeps bugs from the Lisbon house to save the girls the trouble.

Colonel Aureliano Buendía

One Hundred Years of Solitude
Gabriel García Márquez

The second son of **José Arcadio Buendía** and **Úrsula Iguarán**. As a child, his name is Aureliano, and he grows up solitary and enigmatic, with a strange capacity for extrasensory perception. Outraged by the corruption of the Conservative government, he leads young men of the town in a rebellion, conquering the town for the Liberals. He leaves Macondo with his hastily assembled troops and joins the national civil war effort, fathering seventeen children around the country as he goes. He leaves **Arcadio** in charge of the town in his absence. After years of fighting, he returns to Macondo as the head of an army. He withdraws from society, spending his days locked in his workshop making tiny golden fishes and refusing to speak about politics. On the anniversary of the armistice that ended the civil war, the president of the Republic tries to honor Colonel Aureliano Buendía with the Order of Merit, which he declines scornfully. He is the widower of **Remedios Moscote** and the father, with **Pilar Ternera**, of **Aureliano José**.

General John Buford

The Killer Angels
Michael Shaara

A Union cavalry commander who comes from the great plains of the Midwest and dislikes the tame and political East. He has an eye for finding the best ground on a battlefield. He has been given two brigades and ordered to follow the movements of the Confederate army.

Beety Buggit

The Shipping News
E. Annie Proulx

Dennis Buggit's wife, and a warm mother and homemaker. She takes care of **Bunny** and **Sunshine** while **Quoyle** is at work.

Dennis Buggit

The Shipping News
E. Annie Proulx

A carpenter who helps **Quoyle** and **the aunt** repair their old family house. Dennis is **Jack Buggit**'s son, and has consistently gone against his father's wishes that he stay away from the sea since the death of Jack's other son at sea. Dennis could fish for lobster if Jack would turn over Dennis's fishing and lobstering license to Dennis, but Jack doesn't want him to have it. When Jack "wakes up" after having drowned, Dennis is overjoyed because it means that now Jack can give Dennis his lobster license.

Jack Buggit

The Shipping News
E. Annie Proulx

Editor of *The Gammy Bird* in Killick-Claw, Newfoundland, where **Quoyle** is in charge of the shipping news and is later an editor. A fisherman through and through, Jack usually chooses fishing over coming into work, calling in sick frequently. Although he has saved many from drownings, he failed to save his son Jesson, who died at sea. He forbade all of his other children to go into the sea, but **Dennis Buggit** defied him time and time again, so the father and son don't speak. Although he is almost never around, he maintains a tight grip on his authority at the newspaper, and feels proud that his paper lacks any resemblance to good journalism.

Bugis

Lord Jim
Joseph Conrad

A group of traders from Celebes who immigrate to Patusan many years before **Jim** arrives there. They are constantly embroiled in conflict with the **Rajah Allang**, who wants to shut down their trading activities and enjoy a monopoly for himself. **Doramin** is their chief.

Bugs

In Our Time
Ernest Hemingway

Ad Francis's traveling companion. Bugs feeds **Nick Adams** and saves him from Ad's anger.

Buki

Breath, Eyes, Memory
Edwidge Danticat

One of three members of **Sophie**'s sexual-phobia group. Buki is an Ethiopian college student who was ritually genitally mutilated by her grandmother as a girl.

Bull

Grendel
John Gardner

A bull that discovers **Grendel** hanging in a tree and attacks him repeatedly. The encounter with the bull is a formative event in Grendel's philosophical development.

Bull's-eye

Oliver Twist
Charles Dickens

Bill Sikes's dog. Bull's-eye is as vicious as his master.

Bullcalf

Henry IV, Part II
William Shakespeare

One of the Army recruits that **Sir John Falstaff** inspects in Gloucestershire. Bullcalf and **Mouldy** bribe Falstaff to let them off the hook, and thus are not selected for military service.

Harriet Bulstrode

Middlemarch
George Eliot

Walter Vincy's sister and **Nicholas Bulstrode**'s wife. She is a kind, honest, religious woman. No one in Middlemarch blames her for her husband's misdeeds. She resolves to stay with her husband even after she learns of his wrongdoing.

Millicent Bulstrode

Harry Potter and the Chamber of Secrets
J. K. Rowling

A belligerent Slytherin girl who has to duel with **Hermione Granger** during the dueling club meeting.

Nicholas Bulstrode

Middlemarch
George Eliot

A wealthy Middlemarch banker who is married to **Walter Vincy**'s sister, **Harriet Bulstrode**. Bulstrode professes to be a deeply religious Evangelical Protestant, but he has a dark past: he made his fortune as a pawnbroker selling stolen goods. He married **Will Ladislaw**'s grandmother after her first husband died. Her daughter had run away years before, and she insisted that Bulstrode find her daughter before she remarried, because she wanted to leave her wealth to her only surviving child. Bulstrode located the daughter and her child, **Will Ladislaw**, but he kept her existence a secret. He bribed the man he hired to find her, **John Raffles**, to keep quiet. John Raffles blackmails him with this information. When Raffles becomes ill, Bulstrode cares for him. However, he disobeys **Tertius Lydgate**'s medical advice, and Raffles dies as a result. When the scandal about his past and the circumstances of Raffles's death become known, Bulstrode leaves Middlemarch in shame. He purchases Stone Court from **Joshua Rigg Featherstone**.

Mr. Bumble

Oliver Twist
Charles Dickens

The pompous, self-important beadle (minor church official) at the workhouse where **Oliver Twist** is born. Though Mr. Bumble preaches Christian morality, he mistreats the paupers under his care. Dickens mercilessly satirizes his self-righteousness, greed, hypocrisy, and folly.

Byron Bunch

Light in August
William Faulkner

A quiet, diminutive man. Byron works at the Jefferson planing mill six days a week because he believes working will keep him from doing any harm. His only friend is **Gail Hightower**. He falls in love with **Lena Grove** the instant he sees her.

Mrs. Buncombe

A Wrinkle in Time
Madeleine L'Engle

The wife of the constable in **Meg Murry**'s hometown. She has had twelve bed-sheets stolen from her at the beginning of the novel by a roving tramp, who turns out to be **Mrs. Whatsit**.

Addie Bundren

As I Lay Dying
William Faulkner

The matriarch of the Bundren family; her death sets the novel's action in motion. Addie is a former schoolteacher whose bitter, loveless life has caused her to despise her husband and to invest all her love in her favorite child, **Jewel**, who was born after her affair with a minister named **Whitfield**.

Anse Bundren

As I Lay Dying
William Faulkner

Addie Bundren's husband. Anse, a farmer, is poor, hunchbacked, and largely selfish. His children both hate and disrespect him, but he achieves all of his goals—he acquires false teeth, buries Addie in Jefferson, and remarries.

Cash Bundren

As I Lay Dying
William Faulkner

The eldest Bundren child. Cash is a skilled carpenter. Patient and selfless to the point of absurdity, Cash is the most stable major character. He never complains about his broken, festering leg, allowing the injury to worsen.

Darl Bundren

As I Lay Dying
William Faulkner

The second-oldest Bundren child. Of all the novel's characters, Darl is the closest to being a protagonist. He is the most sensitive and articulate of the surviving Bundrens and narrates more of the novel than anyone else.

Dewey Dell Bundren

As I Lay Dying
William Faulkner

The only Bundren daughter. Dewey Dell's pregnancy, a result of her relations with **Lafe**, leaves her increasingly desperate, and she views all men with suspicion.

Vardaman Bundren

As I Lay Dying
William Faulkner

The youngest Bundren child. Thoughtful and innocent, Vardaman has a lively imagination and memorably compares his mother, **Addie Bundren**, to a fish.

Bunny

The Shipping News
E. Annie Proulx

Quoyle's older daughter. Unlike her sister, **Sunshine**, Bunny is the one more prone to temper tantrums and emotional stress. Sunshine and Bunny were sold to a child molester by their mother **Petal Bear**, but luckily, nothing happened to them before they were rescued. Bunny is deathly afraid of anything resembling a white dog and often sees ghosts of such a creature. She has a penchant for carpentry, and Skipper Alfred brings her a brass square to help her measure straight lines and cuts. Bunny is not only protected from the ills of her ancestry—for example, her paternal grandparents who committed a double suicide—but she also proves to have a good heart, demonstrating that the chain of evil has been broken.

Lucas Burch

Light in August
William Faulkner

A shiftless, cowardly man who loves to hear himself talk. In Jefferson, Lucas Burch uses the alias "Joe Brown." He starts the fire at Miss Burden's house after he discovers her body, then tries to turn in his bootlegging partner, **Joe Christmas**, and collect the thousand-dollar reward. Lucas is the father of **Lena Grove**'s child.

Ellis Burden

All the King's Men
Robert Penn Warren

The man whom **Jack** believes to be his father for most of the book before learning his real father is **Judge Irwin**. After discovering his wife's affair with the judge, the **Scholarly Attorney** (as Jack characterizes him) leaves her. He moves to the state capital, where he attempts to conduct a Christian ministry for the poor and the unfortunate.

Emmaline Burden

My Ántonia
Willa Cather

Jim Burden's grandmother. Emmaline shows great compassion for the Shimerdas and is a loving maternal figure for Jim.

Jack Burden

All the King's Men
Robert Penn Warren

Willie Stark's political right-hand man, the narrator, and, in many ways, the novel's protagonist. Despite his aristocratic background, Jack allies himself with the liberal, amoral governor, to the displeasure of his family and friends. He uses his considerable skills as a researcher to uncover the secrets of Willie's political enemies. Jack was once married to **Lois Seager**, but has left her by the time the novel begins. Jack is intelligent but curiously lacking in ambition; he seems to have no agency of his own, and for the most part he is content to take direction from Willie. Jack is also continually troubled by the question of motive and responsibility in history: he quit working on his PhD thesis in history when he decided he could not comprehend **Cass Mastern**'s motives. He develops the Great Twitch theory to convince himself that no one can be held responsible for anything that happens. During the course of the novel, however, Jack rejects the Great Twitch theory and accepts the idea of responsibility.

Jim Burden

My Ántonia
Willa Cather

The author of the youthful recollection that makes up the body of the novel. As a youth in Nebraska, Jim develops a close friendship with a Bohemian immigrant girl, **Ántonia Shimerda**. Jim is an intelligent, introspective young man who responds strongly to the land and the environment in which he lives. Unlike most other boys his age, Jim is more interested in academics and reflection than in roughhousing; in fact, he seems to prefer spending time alone or with girls such as Ántonia. At the time of the narrative's composition, Jim is married, but childless, and working as legal counsel in New York City.

Joanna Burden

Light in August
William Faulkner

The daughter of a family of Northern abolitionists who moved to Jefferson during Reconstruction. She helps and advises black students and colleges. When she holds her lover, **Joe Christmas**, at gunpoint and demands that he undergo a religious conversion, he murders her.

Josiah Burden

My Ántonia
Willa Cather

Jim Burden's grandfather. Josiah is a strongly religious man, silent and given to hard work.

Burdovsky

The Idiot
Fyodor Dostoevsky

A young man who fraudulently claims to be the son of **Prince Lev Nikolayevich Myshkin**'s late benefactor. Burdovsky attempts to use the false claim to gain access to a portion of the prince's inheritance.

Mr. Burdow

Across Five Aprils
Irene Hunt

The father of **Travis Burdow**, who killed **Jethro Creighton**'s sister Mary. Mr. Burdow protects Jethro from the men who are angry about **Bill Creighton**'s betrayal and redeems himself by helping Jethro and sending supplies to help the Creightons rebuild the barn.

Duke of Burgundy

Henry V and *Henry VI, Part I*
William Shakespeare

Ruler of Burgundy, a Duchy in present-day France. In *Henry V* he helps broker the peace between the French and English following the war. He engages in light innuendo with **King Henry V** about what **Catherine** will be like in bed. In *Henry VI, Part I*, Burgundy fights with the English against France, but enticed by the convincing words of **Joan of Arc**, Burgundy agrees to return to the French side. His departure leaves **Lord Talbot** weakened. This character is a conflation and distortion of several historical contemporary dukes of Burgundy.

Barbara Burke

Lolita
Vladimir Nabokov

Lolita Haze's friend at Camp Q. Barbara and Lolita take turns having sex with thirteen-year-old **Charlie Holmes**.

Bill Burke

Bridge to Terabithia
Katherine Paterson

Leslie Burke's father. He is a political writer who is extremely gifted intellectually but rather scatterbrained. Leslie's growing friendship with Bill disturbs **Jesse Oliver Aarons, Jr.** until Leslie invites him to spend time with them as well.

Judy Burke

Bridge to Terabithia
Katherine Paterson

Leslie Burke's mother. Judy writes novels and seems to spend most of her time closed in her room with her typewriter going.

Leslie Burke

Bridge to Terabithia
Katherine Paterson

Jesse Oliver Aarons, Jr.'s new next-door neighbor and best friend. Leslie is highly intelligent and imaginative. It is her idea to build a fantasyland named Terabithia across the creek. Leslie's family is affluent and well-educated, in stark contrast with their neighbors. Leslie dies at the end of the novel.

Sadie Burke

All the King's Men
Robert Penn Warren

Willie Stark's secretary and mistress. Sadie has been with Willie from the beginning, and believes that she made him what he is. Despite the fact that he is a married man, she becomes extremely jealous of his relationships with other women, and they often have long, passionate fights. Sadie is tough, cynical, and extremely vulnerable; when Willie announces that he is leaving her to go back to **Lucy**, she tells **Tiny Duffy** in a fit of rage that Willie is sleeping with **Anne Stanton**. Tiny tells **Adam Stanton**, who assassinates Willie. Believing herself to be responsible for Willie's death, Sadie checks in to a sanitarium.

St. John Burnham

The Power of One
Bryce Courtenay

The headmaster at the Prince of Wales school. An Englishman, he is known for choosing six boys from the third form each year to take under his personal tutelage and mold into "Renaissance men." Singe 'n' Burn assists **Peekay** and **Morrie** with setting up the night school for black boxers, but only after he has met **Gideon Mandoma**.

David Burns

Regeneration
Pat Barker

A patient of **Dr. W.H.R. Rivers**'s at Craiglockhart War Hospital. Burns has been unable to eat since a bomb threw him into the body of a gas-filled German cadaver. The emaciated Burns refrains from talking about his problems. Always aware of others, he does not want to bother anyone.

Evie Lilith Burns

Midnight's Children
Salman Rushdie

Saleem's American childhood sweetheart.

Helen Burns

Jane Eyre
Charlotte Brontë

Jane Eyre's close friend at the Lowood School. Helen endures her miserable life with passive dignity. She dies of consumption in Jane's arms.

Professor Burris

Walden Two
B. F. Skinner

A professor of psychology, the protagonist of the novel, and the man through whose eyes we see Walden Two. He is intelligent and professorial, but weary of academic life. Although initially skeptical of Walden Two, he becomes increasingly enthusiastic about it over the course of his visit.

Fraulein Burstner

The Trial
Franz Kafka

A boarder in the same house as **Joseph K.** She lets him kiss her one night, then rebuffs further advances.

Bushy

Richard II
William Shakespeare

One of **King Richard II**'s favored and loyal supporters. When word comes that **Henry Bolingbroke** has come back to England with an army, Bushy, along with **Bagot** and **Green**, realize they will be punished along with Richard and flee. Bushy and Green are captured and executed soon after by Bolingbroke's forces on the grounds of corrupting Richard.

The Businessman

The Little Prince
Antoine de Saint-Exupéry

A caricature of grown-ups, the Businessman is the fourth person **the Little Prince** visits. He claims he owns all the stars, but cannot remember what they are called and contributes nothing to them.

Abbé Busoni

The Count of Monte Cristo
Alexandre Dumas

See **Edmond Dantès**.

Angie Buster

Pigs in Heaven
Barbara Kingsolver

Lucky Buster's mother. She is one of the novel's examples of a mother who would give anything for her child.

Lucky Buster

Pigs in Heaven
Barbara Kingsolver

The instigator of the novel's plot. Lucky is a grown man with Down's Syndrome living with his mother **Angie Buster**, and he has a habit of running away from home. His descent down the side of the Hoover dam sparked **Taylor Greer** and **Turtle Greer**'s decision to hunt down a rescue team, and thus instigated the media onslaught that alerted **Annawake Fourkiller** of Turtle's situation.

Bonnie Blue Butler

Gone with the Wind
Margaret Mitchell

Scarlett O'Hara's third and last child. Bonnie is the daughter of **Rhett Butler**. Spoiled and strong-willed like her mother, Bonnie elicits utter devotion from Rhett and eventually replaces Scarlett as the center of Rhett's attention. She is killed in a horse-riding accident.

Harry Butler

The Light in the Forest
Conrad Richter

True Son's white father, viewed by True Son as the exact opposite of **Cuyloga**: weak, pale, and insignificant. In actuality, however, Harry Butler has been strong enough to endure the extraordinary guilt and sorrow he has felt ever since True Son was kidnapped. He cares deeply for his son and never loses hope that True Son will come around in the end.

Myra Butler

The Light in the Forest
Conrad Richter

True Son's white mother. Like **Harry Butler**, Myra loves True Son very much and has experienced guilt since his disappearance. She wants desperately to believe that True Son will one day give up his Indian ways and refuses to listen to the pessimistic **Aunt Kate**. True Son thinks his white mother is disgraceful, since she does not work, as he believes women should.

Rhett Butler

Gone with the Wind
Margaret Mitchell

Scarlett O'Hara's third husband, a dashing, dangerous adventurer and scoundrel. Expelled from West Point and disowned by his prominent Charleston family, Rhett becomes an opportunistic blockade-runner during the war, emerging as one of the only rich Southern men in Atlanta afterward. Rhett is a loving father and, at times, a caring husband. Candid, humorous, and contemptuous of silly social codes, Rhett exposes hypocrisy wherever he goes. He represents postwar society: a pragmatic, fast-paced world in which the strong thrive and the weak perish.

Barliman Butterbur

The Fellowship of the Ring and *The Return of the King*
J. R. R. Tolkien

The innkeeper at the Prancing Pony in Bree. Barliman Butterbur is an old friend of **Gandalf**'s and a forgetful man. In *The Fellowship of the Ring*, Gandalf leaves a letter at the Prancing Pony for **Frodo Baggins** and **Samwise Gamgee** because he was held up and wants to meet the Hobbits later in Rivendell. Butterbur does finally remember to deliver the letter after the Hobbits are worried that Gandalf will not show for a while. In *The Return of the King*, Butterbur welcomes Gandalf and Frodo back to the inn on their return journey to the Shire after the defeat of **Sauron** and destruction of the One Ring.

Buttercup

The Princess Bride
William Goldman

The most beautiful woman in the world and the heroine of this story. Buttercup loves **Westley** and her horse. When she is isolated in the novel, she becomes quieter, sadder, more beautiful, and bolder than she has ever had to be before. When she pushes Westley down the ravine as a punishment for mocking her heartache, we see also why Westley loves her.

Doctor Butts

Henry VIII
William Shakespeare

King Henry VIII's doctor. Suspecting that the Council (composed of the **Lord Chancellor**, **Duke of Suffolk**, and other lords) is up to no good, he observes the members force **Cranmer, Archbishop of Canterbury**, a member of the Council, to wait outside the door. Butts and the king secretly watch Cranmer's trial from a hidden spot, which leads the king to reprimand the lords for their mistrust and bickering.

Buynovsky

One Day in the Life of Ivan Denisovich
Aleksandr Solzhenitsyn

A prisoner in the camp with **Ivan Denisovich Shukhov** known familiarly throughout the novel as "the captain" for his former military rank. In the prison camp, Buynovsky is no more privileged than Shukhov. He is well-educated, as demonstrated by his theoretical discussions with **Tsezar Markovich** about Russian films. But his knowledge of culture is of little service to him in the camp, where the only thing that truly matters is survival.

Bless Me, Ultima
Rudolfo A. Anaya

Father Byrnes

A Catholic priest who gives catechism lessons to **Antonio Márez** and his friends. He is a stern priest with hypocritical and unfair policies. He punishes **Florence** for the smallest offenses because Florence challenges the Catholic orthodoxy, but he fails to notice, and perhaps even ignores, the misbehavior of the other boys, such as **Horse**. Rather than teach the children to understand God, he prefers to teach them to fear God.

His Dark Materials
Robert Pullman

Iorek Byrnison

Lyra Belacqua's friend and the rightful king of the armored bears. When Lyra meets Iorek in her world, he has been stripped of his armor and as a result drinks heavily. Iorek rescues Lyra and fights **Iofur Raknison** for the right to rule the bears.

MISERABLE MISERS

FAMOUS FOR BEING CHEAP, FOR HOARDING, FOR CLINGING TO THEIR WEALTH... BUT FOR SOME REASON WE CAN'T HELP BUT LOVE THESE WEASELS.

Ebenezer Balfour	1	*Kidnapped*
Dragon	2	*Grendel*
Gollum	3	*The Lord of the Rings* trilogy
Frydor Karamazov	4	*The Brothers Karamazov*
Silas Marner	5	*Silas Marner*
Ebenezer Scrooge	6	*A Christmas Carol*
Shylock	7	*The Merchant of Venice*
Volpone	8	*Volpone*

Cacambo

Candide
Voltaire

Candide's valet. A mixed-race native of the Americas, Cacambo is very intelligent and moral. He single-handedly rescues Candide from a number of scrapes. He is also directly responsible for Candide's reunion with **Cunégonde**. A practical man of action, he contrasts with ineffectual philosophers such as **Pangloss** and **Martin**.

Margaret Cadaver

Walk Two Moons
Sharon Creech

Phoebe's next-door neighbor and **Salamanca Tree Hiddle**'s father's friend. Margaret helped **Mr. Hiddle** find a job selling farm machinery so that he could live in Euclid, away from his farm. Although Salamanca (Sal) feels suspicious of Margaret's intentions toward her father, Margaret realizes that Sal's father sees her only as a friend. He understands that their friendship is based on the fact that Margaret befriended **Sal's mother** during her last days alive. Margaret herself suffered a great tragedy when she lost her husband in a car accident.

Jack Cade

Henry VI, Part II
William Shakespeare

A fierce commoner hired by the **Duke of York** to raise a popular rebellion and gauge the public's opinion of the Yorkist claim to the throne. Cade manages to raise an army of followers and defeat a battalion led by **Sir Humphrey Stafford** and his brother. He leads the rebels to Kent, where they defeat King Henry's army before mounting an attack on London. When his fickle rebels are swayed by Clifford's rhetoric, they turn against him, and Cade escapes to the countryside. **Alexander Iden** kills Cade in a duel in Iden's garden and carries his head to **King Henry VI**. Some of Cade's declarations reflect the rhetoric of rebel leaders of the time, including a tradition of popular radicalism that championed laborers.

Johnny Cade

The Outsiders
S. E. Hinton

A greaser with black hair and large, fearful eyes. Though Johnny Cade does not succeed in school, he approaches intellectual matters with steady concentration. The child of alcoholic, abusive parents, he is nervous and sensitive. Since his parents do not care for him, Johnny sees the greasers as his true family. In turn, the older boys, particularly **Dally**, are protective of him. Johnny murders **Bob Sheldon**, trying to protect **Ponyboy Curtis**. Later, Johnny's back is crushed after he attempts to rescue some schoolchildren from a burning church.

Caderousse

The Count of Monte Cristo
Alexandre Dumas

A lazy, drunk, and greedy petty criminal. **Monte Cristo** uses Caderousse as an instrument in his plan of revenge against his enemies. Caderousse exemplifies human dissatisfaction, helping to illustrate that happiness depends more on attitude than on external circumstances. He is pained by his friends' good fortune, and his envy festers into hatred and ultimately into crime. Caderousse consistently resorts to dishonorable means in order to acquire what he wants, thieving and even murdering in order to better his own position. Ultimately, Caderousse's unending greed catches up with him, and he must eat his words to Abbé Busoni about how the good are always punished and the wicked rewarded.

Cadmus

The Bacchae
Euripides

Former king of Thebes, father of **Agave** and **Semele**, grandfather of **Pentheus** and **Dionysus**. Cadmus is the only one in his family to declare allegiance to Dionysus.

Elinor Cadwallader

Middlemarch
George Eliot

The wife of the Rector at Tipton Grange, **Arthur Brooke**'s estate. She was born to a good family, but she married down and angered her friends and family. She is a practical woman who is forever trying to play matchmaker to unmarried young people, including **Dorothea Brooke**, **Celia Brooke**, and **Sir James Chettam**.

Humphrey Cadwallader

Middlemarch
George Eliot

Elinor Cadwallader's husband, and the Rector at Tipton Grange, **Arthur Brooke**'s estate. Unlike his wife, he doesn't believe in meddling in other people's affairs.

Julius Caesar

Julius Caesar
William Shakespeare

A great Roman general and senator, recently returned to Rome in triumph after a successful military campaign. While his good friend **Brutus** worries that Caesar may aspire to dictatorship over the Roman republic, Caesar seems to show no such inclination, declining the crown several times. Yet while Caesar may not be unduly power-hungry, he does possess his share of flaws. He is unable to separate his public life from his private life, and, seduced by the populace's increasing idealization and idolization of his image, he ignores ill omens and threats against his life, believing himself as eternal as the North Star. Caesar's murder at the hands of consiprators triggers a massive Roman power struggle.

Octavius Caesar

Antony and Cleopatra and *Julius Caesar*
William Shakespeare

Julius Caesar's nephew, adopted son, and appointed successor. In *Julius Caesar*, Octavius, who had been traveling abroad, returns after Caesar's death; he then joins with **Mark Antony** and sets off to fight **Cassius** and **Brutus**. Antony tries to control Octavius's movements, but Octavius follows his adopted father's example and emerges as the authoritative figure, paving the way for his eventual seizure of the reins of Roman government. In *Antony and Cleopatra*, years later, Octavius rules the Roman Empire with Mark Antony and **Lepidus**. Relations between Octavius Caesar and Antony are strained throughout the play, for the young triumvir believes that Antony squanders his time and neglects his duties while in Egypt. Ambitious and extremely pragmatic, Octavius lacks Antony's military might as a general, but his careful and stoic reasoning enables him to avoid Antony's tendency toward heroic or romantic folly.

Cissy Caffrey

Ulysses
James Joyce

Gerty MacDowell's close friend. A frank tomboy, Cissy babysits her brothers, **Jacky Caffrey** and **Tommy Caffrey**.

Percy Cahill

Howards End
E. M. Forster

Dolly's uncle, who marries **Evie Wilcox**.

Caiaphas

The New Testament
Unknown

The high priest who presides over **Jesus**' trial. Though it is **Pontius Pilate** who declares the verdict of Jesus' guilt, the Gospel writers insist that Caiaphas is also responsible for the crucifixion.

Caius

The Merry Wives of Windsor
William Shakespeare

The local doctor and **Mistress Quickly**'s master. One of three suitors to **Anne Page**, Caius challenges **Sir Hugh Evans**, who has tried to set Anne up with **Abraham Slender**, to a duel. Caius and Evans's duel is stopped by the onlookers; the **Host** declares, "Let them keep their limbs whole, and hack our English." As Caius is French, and Evans is Welsh, both men's mangling of the Queen's language has made for some humor with the ruffian crowd. The two band together to seek revenge on the Host, a situation that muddily resolves itself when the Host loses three horses. Caius does not end up with Anne; in the confusion at the end of the play, he is duped, and sneaks off with a disguised young boy.

Calchas

The Iliad
Homer

An important soothsayer who identifies the cause of the plague ravaging the Greek armies. This revelation leads to the catastrophic rift between **Agamemnon** and **Achilles**.

Calchas

Troilus and Cressida
William Shakespeare

Cressida's father and a Trojan priest. Calchas defected to the Greeks in the early days of the war.

Caliban

The Tempest
William Shakespeare

Another of **Prospero**'s servants. Caliban, the son of the deceased witch **Sycorax**, acquainted Prospero with the island when Prospero arrived. Caliban believes the island rightfully belongs to him and has been stolen by Prospero. His speech and behavior are sometimes coarse and brutal, as in his drunken scenes with **Stefano** and **Trinculo**. At other times he is eloquent and sensitive, as in his rebukes of Prospero and his description of the island's eerie beauty.

Christine Callaghan

Lucky Jim
Kingsley Amis

A young beauty that **Jim Dixon** falls for, who is dating **Bertrand Welch**. She lives in London and comes from money—her uncle is the rich Gore-Urquhart—but Christine herself works in a bookshop and wears the same outfit every time Dixon sees her. Though Dixon initially misconstrues her shyness as prissy haughtiness, when Christine finally opens up to him, he becomes smitten with her. She truly enjoys Dixon's predicaments and participates in his mischief while laughing unabashedly.

Callan

Regeneration
Pat Barker

Dr. Lewis Yealland's patient at the National Hospital in London, and one of his more interesting cases. After serving in almost every major battle of the First World War, Callan finds himself in the hospital suffering from mutism. He appears insolent in his illness, merely smiling at the doctor, who offers to cure him. Callan initially fights back against the treatment but eventually resigns himself to it.

Major Callendar

A Passage to India
E. M. Forster

The Chandrapore civil surgeon; **Dr. Aziz**'s boastful, cruel, and ridiculous superior.

Calpurnia

Julius Caesar
William Shakespeare

Julius Caesar's wife. Calpurnia invests great authority in omens and portents. She warns Caesar against going to the Senate on the Ides of March, since she has had terrible nightmares and heard reports of many bad omens. Nevertheless, Caesar's ambition ultimately causes him to disregard her advice.

Calpurnia

To Kill a Mockingbird
Harper Lee

The cook for **Atticus Finch**, **Jem Finch**, and **Scout Finch**. She scolds Scout for making **Walter Cunningham, Jr.** feel singled out when she asks why he is putting syrup on his meat. She wants Scout to learn to be a good hostess. Calpurnia bridges the gap between the children's world and her own black community, bringing them to her church.

Calvin

The Day of the Locust
Nathanael West

One of **Earle**'s friends and a fellow cowboy who sits outside Hodge's each day.

Calypso

The Odyssey
Homer

The beautiful nymph who falls in love with **Odysseus** when he lands on her island-home of Ogygia. Calypso holds him prisoner for seven years until **Hermes**, the messenger god, persuades her to free him.

Earl of Cambridge

Henry V
William Shakespeare

One of three noblemen bribed by French agents to kill **King Henry V** before he sets sail for France. Along with **Lord Scroop** and **Sir Thomas Grey**, Cambridge is found out and sentenced for execution, despite his pleas for mercy.

Henry Cameron

The Fountainhead
Ayn Rand

Howard Roark's mentor. Henry Cameron is an intractable and aggressive architect. Like Roark, he has a difficult time because he values his buildings more than he values people. Because he lacks Roark's strength, Cameron lives a frustrated and anguished life. He dies fighting, ruined physically and financially.

James Cameron

The Iceman Cometh
Eugene O'Neill

A man at **Harry Hope**'s saloon who dreams of returning to his newspaper career. He is the leader of the so-called "Tomorrow Movement," a movement dedicated to deferring the realization of a pipe dream to tomorrow. He has the manners of a gentleman, mixing the qualities of a prim old maid and a boy who has never grown up.

Camidius

Antony and Cleopatra
William Shakespeare

A general in **Antony**'s army. After the battle in which Antony follows **Cleopatra**'s lead and flees, Camidius surrenders and defects to **Octavius Caesar**'s side.

Camilla

The Aeneid
Virgil

The leader of the Volscians, a race of warrior maidens. Camilla is the strongest mortal female character in the epic.

Camille

On the Road
Jack Kerouac

Dean Moriarty's second wife. Loyal Camille lives in San Francisco with their children.

Mademoiselle Camille

"The Murders in the Rue Morgue"
Edgar Allan Poe

Daughter of **Madame L'Espanaye**. Mademoiselle Camille is choked to death and then stuffed into the chimney.

Camillo

The Winter's Tale
William Shakespeare

An honest Sicilian nobleman. Camillo refuses to follow **Leontes**'s order to poison **Polixenes**, deciding instead to flee Sicily and serve Polixenes.

Camp director

Bless the Beasts and Children
Glendon Swarthout

The leader who endorses the cruel and competitive spirit rampant at the Box Canyon Boys Camp.

Billy Campbell

Angela's Ashes
Frank McCourt

A friend of **Frank McCourt**'s who shares many adventures with him.

Colin Roy Campbell of Glenure

Kidnapped
Robert Louis Stevenson

The King's Factor, or agent, in the Highlands. Unlike most of the Highland clans, the Campbells are not Jacobites, and are loyal to England. The Campbells and the Stewarts are in a years-long feud. Colin Roy Campbell of Glenure is plotting to evict all the Jacobite Stewarts from their homes when he is murdered. **David Balfour** is present at this murder, and quickly runs into **Alan Breck Stewart**, who swears he himself is not the murderer. However, in order to make sure that **James of the Glens** is not pinned as the murderer, David and Alan go on the run.

Colonel Campbell

Emma
Jane Austen

A friend of **Jane Fairfax**'s father. Colonel Campbell took charge of orphaned Jane when she was eight years old. He loves Jane but is unable to provide her with an inheritance.

Howard W. Campbell Jr.

Slaughterhouse-Five
Kurt Vonnegut

An American who has become a Nazi. Campbell speaks to the prisoners in the slaughterhouse and tries to recruit them for "The Free American Corps," a German army unit that he is forming to fight the Russians.

Mike Campbell

The Sun Also Rises
Ernest Hemingway

A drunken, bankrupt Scottish war veteran. Mike has a terrible temper, which his frequent drinking exacerbates. Although he and **Lady Brett Ashley** intend to marry, Brett remains sexually promiscuous, which incites Mike's anger and self-pity. Mike feels especially threatened by the American writer **Robert Cohn**, with whom Brett has a brief affair.

Mr. Campbell

Kidnapped
Robert Louis Stevenson

The kindly Protestant preacher who takes care of **David Balfour** after the death of his father, **Alexander Balfour**. Mr. Campbell reveals the father's dying wishes to David. He wants David to take a letter to the House of Shaws in Cramond, near Edinburgh, which is where the father comes from. This means that David is, in fact, from a wealthy family, though he has grown up in poverty. David is to take the letter to **Ebenezer Balfour**, his uncle. Because David is indebted to Mr. Campbell, **Alan Breck Stewart**, whose family is warring with the Campbell clan, mistrusts David.

Cardinal Campeius

Henry VIII
William Shakespeare

An emissary from the pope. Campeius comes to assess the legality of **King Henry VIII**'s divorce. He carries papers from Rome that apparently grant the divorce, since Henry plans to carry it out. He and **Cardinal Wolsey** try to convince **Queen Katherine** to agree to the divorce, telling her that Henry still loves her and plans to protect her. Later, Campeius flees to Rome after the discovery of Wolsey's secret correspondence with the pope urging against granting the divorce.

Captain Campion

Watership Down
Richard Adams

General Woundwort's best captain. Captain Campion is a great tracker and a courageous rabbit who leads the Efrafans back to their warren in the end. Brave yet under control, Campion helps set up the new warren in between the down and Efrafa.

Luis Campion

Tender Is the Night
F. Scott Fitzgerald

A heavy, effeminate friend of **Albert McKisko**'s. Campion takes **Rosemary Hoyt** to watch the duel between McKisco and **Tommy Barban**.

The Candidate

The House of the Spirits
Isabel Allende

A Socialist. Never given any other name in the story, the Candidate runs for president for the Socialist Party every single year, never expecting to win. Over the years he and **Jaime** become friends. Jaime is as surprised as the Conservatives are when the Candidate wins the election. He does his best as president, but he has great difficulties running the country in the face of the Conservatives' attempts to undermine his government. The Conservatives take all of their money out of the country's industries, crippling the economy and ruining society. He is one of the first people killed during **Esteban Garcia**'s Military Coup.

Candide

Candide
Voltaire

Protégé of **Pangloss** and the protagonist of the story. Candide is a good-hearted but hopelessly naïve young man. After being banished from his adopted childhood home, Candide travels the world and meets with a wide variety of misfortunes, all the while pursuing security and following **Cunégonde**, the woman he loves. His misadventures severely test his faith in Pangloss's doctrine of optimism.

Candy

Of Mice and Men
John Steinbeck

An aging handyman at the ranch where **Lennie** and **George** work. Candy lost his hand in an accident and worries about his future on the ranch. Fearful that his age makes him useless, he seizes on George's description of the farm that he and Lennie imagine they will own someday, offering his life's savings if he can join the pair in an attempt to achieve their dream.

Mr. Candy

The Moonstone
Wilkie Collins

Lady Verinder's doctor. He has a boyish sense of humor and a lively pride in his profession. Mr. Candy falls ill the night of **Rachel Verinder**'s birthday from exposure to the rain and is incoherent and forgetful forever after.

Lash Canino

The Big Sleep
Raymond Chandler

Eddie Mars's cruel, rash, and trigger-happy gunman. Canino poisons **Harry Jones** with cyanide and attempts to kill **Marlowe**.

Cannibals

Heart of Darkness
Joseph Conrad

Natives hired as the crew of the steamer, a surprisingly reasonable and well-tempered bunch. **Marlow** respects their restraint and their calm acceptance of adversity.

Archbishop of Canterbury

Henry V
William Shakespeare

A wealthy and powerful English clergyman. Worried that **King Henry V** will pass a bill that will authorize the government to take away a portion of the Church's land and money, the Archbishop and the **Bishop of Ely** decide to urge the King to war with the French and thus distract him from passing the bill. The two bishops do not go to fight in the war, but their urging and fundraising are important factors in Henry's decision to invade France and are indicative of the backroom political dealings in the play.

Christian Cantle

The Return of the Native
Thomas Hardy

An awkward, superstitious young man who works for **Mrs. Yeobright**. Christian provides comic relief throughout the novel with his petty phobias and dolorous over-certainty that he will never marry. He fails in his mission to bring **Thomasin Yeobright** her inheritance, thus contributing to the degeneration of the family relationships.

Angelo & Luigi Capello

Pudd'nhead Wilson
Mark Twain

A set of near-identical twins. They appear in Dawson's Landing in reply to an ad placed by the **Widow Cooper**, or Aunt Patsy, who is looking for a boarder. They claim to be the children of an Italian nobleman who was forced to flee Italy after a revolution and died soon afterward. According to their story, they were enslaved by a traveling circus and put on display. After several years they escaped and went into business for themselves. The twins are good-looking and smooth-talking, and the townspeople fall over themselves trying to be associated with them. Luigi has a dark secret in his past, though: he once killed a man who tried to rob them and was about to kill Angelo. They are quite popular, and **Valet de Chambre**, or the impostor "Tom," takes advantage of their mysterious past to try and blame them for the thefts that have been going on around Dawson's Landing. This leads to a duel in which the twins emerge as heroes. The twins even run for office after their popularity surges after the duel. In the last speech of the campaign, however, **Judge Driscoll** slams the twins as con-artists, sideshow freaks, and criminals. When Tom kills Judge Driscoll, he uses the knife he stole from Luigi. The twins are indicted on murder charges, but **Pudd'nhead Wilson** uses his catalog of fingerprints to show that the twins were not the murderers. The twins grow tired of their own notoriety and leave Dawson's Landing vindicated and triumphant.

A Cappadocian

Salomé
Oscar Wilde

A guest at **Herod**'s court who in the first scenes of the play discusses **Jokanaan**'s identity. The Cappadocian doubts the prophet's power.

Captain

Henry VI, Part II
William Shakespeare

The captain of the pirate ship that captures **William de la Pole, Duke of Suffolk**'s ship, headed to France. The captain gives Suffolk as a prisoner to **Walter Whitmore**, who declares that he will kill Suffolk. When Suffolk arrogantly declares his name and birth, the captain, having heard of his misdeeds, derides him for kissing **Queen Margaret**, smiling at **Humphrey, Duke of Gloucester**'s murder, and losing the counties Anjou and Maine to the French. He orders Suffolk away to be beheaded.

Captain

Sister Carrie
Theodore Dreiser

A homeless man who lives in New York. Every day, other homeless men gather around Captain, who asks passing pedestrians to donate the price of a bed for the night for each man. He persists in his effort until every man has a place to sleep.

The Captain

All the Pretty Horses
Cormac McCarthy

The sadistic corrupt lawman in the town of Encantada. The captain wrongly accuses **John Grady Cole** and **Lacey Rawlins** of being outlaws, then tortures Rawlins into confessing to crimes he did not commit. Later, after accepting a bribe from the charro, a relative of the man **Jimmy Blevins** killed, the captain murders Blevins.

Captive

Cold Mountain
Charles Frazier

A deserter awaiting execution whose tale **Ada Monroe** and **Ruby Thewes** overhear one day in town. The man tells of his experiences at the hands of **Teague**'s Home Guard, who shot his father for harboring outliers. The captive insists that the world is about to end because of the evil perpetrated in the name of war. The prisoner is the only character to speak out against the war, because he has nothing left to lose.

Capuchin

Cyrano de Bergerac
Edmond Rostand

A modest and well-meaning monk. Employed by **Comte de Guiche** to carry a message to **Roxane**, the Capuchin is diverted by **Cyrano de Bergerac** outside Roxane's residence. He presides over Roxane and **Baron Christian de Neuvillette**'s hasty wedding.

Capuchius

Henry VIII
William Shakespeare

An ambassador from the king of Spain. **King Henry VIII** sends Capuchius to talk to **Queen Katherine** and ask after her health. Katherine gives Capuchius a letter asking Henry to care for their child and her servants, but admits that she herself is already dying.

Capulet

Romeo and Juliet
William Shakespeare

The patriarch of the Capulet family, father of **Juliet**, husband of **Lady Capulet**, and enemy—for unexplained reasons—of **Montague**. He truly loves his daughter, though he is not well-acquainted with her thoughts or feelings, and seems to think that what is best for her is a "good" match with **Paris**. Often prudent, he commands respect and propriety but is subject to fits of rage.

Lady Capulet

Romeo and Juliet
William Shakespeare

Juliet's mother and **Capulet**'s wife. She is eager to see her young daughter marry **Paris**. She is an ineffectual mother, relying on **the Nurse** to raise Juliet. She loves her nephew **Tybalt** and demands **Romeo**'s death when Romeo kills him.

Caravaggio

The English Patient
Michael Ondaatje

A Canadian thief whose profession is legitimized during the war when he puts his skills to use for the British intelligence effort. Caravaggio, who at first is only known as "the man with bandaged hands," proves endearing despite the fact that his actions are not always virtuous. **Hana** remembers that, in his burglaries, Caravaggio was always distracted by "the human element"—an Advent calendar that was not open to the right day, for example. Caravaggio serves as a kind of surrogate father to Hana and sheds light on the identity of **Almásy**, the English patient.

Eddie Carbone

A View from the Bridge
Arthur Miller

A Longshoreman and the tragic protagonist of *A View from the Bridge*. Eddie Carbone lives with his wife, **Beatrice**, and orphaned niece, **Catherine**, in Red Hook, Brooklyn. Eddie creates a fictional fantasy world where his absurd decisions make sense and have no repercussions. He calls the Immigration Bureau on the illegal immigrants **Rodolpho** and **Marco** in the middle of an Italian community that prides itself on protecting illegal immigrants. In Eddie's world, he imagines protecting Catherine from marriage or any male relationship, desiring her for himself. Eddie does not comprehend his romantic feelings for Catherine until Beatrice clearly articulates them in the conclusion of the play. Because he has no outlet for his feelings, Eddie transfers his energy to a hatred of Marco and Rodolpho and acts irrationally. He dies while trying to stab Marco; the knife is turned onto himself.

Carn Carby

Ender's Game
Orson Scott Card

The commander of Rabbit Army, and one of **Ender Wiggin**'s platoon leaders in the Third Invasion.

Tert Card

The Shipping News
E. Annie Proulx

The managing editor for *The Gammy Bird*, who bears great resemblance to the devil himself. Politically, Tert Card falls on the opposite end of the spectrum from **Billy Pretty**, worshipping oil and the age of technology. He is cantankerous and crusty. He has a terrible reputation with typographical errors in the paper, and condemns the harsh living conditions of Newfoundland. He pays a mysterious visit to **Beety Budgel**, and tells **Quoyle** that he was just going to investigate a ship fire as a lame excuse.

Cardenio

Don Quixote
Miguel de Cervantes

The quintessential romantic lover. Cardenio is an honorable man driven mad by his wife **Lucinda**'s infidelities with the treacherous **Duke Ferdinand**.

Cecily Cardew

The Importance of Being Earnest
Oscar Wilde

Jack Worthing's niece and ward. Cecily falls in love with **Algernon Montcrieff**.

Sir David Cardinal

The Remains of the Day
Kazuo Ishiguro

A close friend of **Lord Darlington**'s, and **Reginald Cardinal**'s father. During the March 1923 conference that Lord Darlington hosts, Cardinal makes a speech saying that the German reparation payments should be stopped, and that the French troops should be withdrawn from the Ruhr region.

Mr. Reginald Cardinal

The Remains of the Day
Kazuo Ishiguro

Lord Darlington's godson. After Reggie Cardinal's father passes away, Lord Darlington treats the young man as his kin, though their political views differ widely. Cardinal is a journalist, and it infuriates him that the Nazis have used Lord Darlington's noble instincts to turn him into a pawn for their regime. Cardinal tells **Stevens** that the Nazis have been using Lord Darlington—he is amazed that Stevens has not noticed himself. Cardinal is later killed in the war, in Belgium.

Sam Cardinella

In Our Time
Ernest Hemingway

A prisoner condemned to death. When he is about to be hanged in Chapter XV, Cardinella is too afraid to walk. A priest tells him to be a man.

Marie Cardona

The Stranger
Albert Camus

A former coworker of **Meursault**'s who begins an affair with him the day after his mother's funeral. Marie is young and high-spirited, and delights in swimming and the outdoors. Meursault takes interest in Marie primarily because of her physical beauty. Marie does not seem to understand Meursault, but she feels drawn to his peculiarities. Even when Meursault expresses indifference toward marrying her, she still wants to be his wife, and she tries to support him during his arrest and trial.

Caretaker

The Stranger
Albert Camus

A worker at the old persons' home where **Madame Meursault** spent the three years prior to her death. During the vigil **Meursault** holds before his mother's funeral, the caretaker chats with Meursault in the mortuary. They drink coffee and smoke cigarettes next to the coffin, gestures that later weigh heavily against Meursault as evidence of his monstrous indifference to his mother's death.

Sir Danvers Carew

Dr. Jekyll and Mr. Hyde
Robert Louis Stevenson

Mr. Edward Hyde's murder victim. Carew was a well-liked old nobleman, a member of Parliament, and a client of **Mr. Gabriel John Utterson**'s.

Carla

How the Garcia Girls Lost Their Accents
Julia Alvarez

The oldest of the Garcia sisters. Carla had the most difficulty adjusting to school and the English language after the move to the United States. She grows up to be a psychologist.

Bishop of Carlisle

Richard II
William Shakespeare

A clergyman loyal to **King Richard II**. Upon **Henry Bolingbroke**'s acceptance of the crown, Carlisle delivers one of the key speeches of the play, presenting a deadly warning. Carlisle invokes the divine right of kings and God's anger at the usurpation of the throne, saying that no subject may overthrow the king; furthermore, he prophesies that if Bolingbroke does become king, civil war will take over the land. Carlisle continues the prediction that **John of Gaunt** began earlier in the play, and foretells the strife that dominates the *Henry* plays and *Richard III* in the War of the Roses. Carlisle is indicted for conspiring to kill Henry IV with the **Duke of Aumerle** and the **Abbot of Westminster**, but he is pardoned, with the caveat that he find some quiet spot to live out the rest of his religious life.

Dr. Carlisle

The Remains of the Day
Kazuo Ishiguro

A gentleman in Moscombe who gives **Stevens** a ride back to his car the morning after he stays at the Taylors'. Although the other residents of Moscombe think Stevens is some sort of lord because of all the famous people he has met, Dr. Carlisle correctly guesses that Stevens is a manservant.

Carlo

Animal Dreams
Barbara Kingsolver

Codi Nolina's lover in Tucson. An emergency-room doctor, his relationships with people are characterized by their transience. He cares a great deal about Codi, but is not in love with her. The home **Hallie Nolina**, Codi, and Carlo established in Tucson fell apart when Hallie left for Nicaragua; Carlo, like all of Codi's boyfriends, had "loved Hallie best and settled for" Codi. After Codi has already left Carlo and moved back to Grace, Carlo invites Codi to move to Denver or to Aspen with him, and she considers it, because it would involve few risks. In the end, Codi almost moves with Carlo to Telluride, but at the last minute returns to Grace and stays with **Loyd Peregrina**.

Carlos

The House on Mango Street
Sandra Cisneros

One of **Esperanza**'s younger brothers.

Carlos

How the Garcia Girls Lost Their Accents
Julia Alvarez

The overprotective father of the four Garcia sisters. Carlos resisted the military dictatorship in the Dominican Republic. As a result of his political activities, the family had to flee to the United States.

Carlson

Of Mice and Men
John Steinbeck

A ranch-hand who complains bitterly about **Candy**'s old, smelly dog. Carlson's mercy killing of the dog foreshadows **Lennie**'s death at the end of the novel.

Carmen

I Never Promised You a Rose Garden
Joanne Greenberg

Briefly a patient at **Deborah**'s hospital. Carmen's multimillionaire father takes her out of the hospital before she can receive treatment. Soon afterward, Carmen commits suicide.

Carmen

Bel Canto
Ann Patchett

A shy, timid, and beautiful young terrorist. Carmen's greatest talent is her ability to move stealthily. She asks **Gen Watanabe** to teach her how to read and write in Spanish, her native language. Over the course of their secret lessons, they fall in love.

Augustus Carmichael

To the Lighthouse
Virginia Woolf

An opium-using poet who visits **the Ramsays** on the Isle of Skye. Carmichael languishes in literary obscurity until his verse becomes popular during the war.

Mary Carmichael

A Room of One's Own
Virginia Woolf

A fictitious novelist. The narrator of the essay analyzes Mary Carmichael's novel, which she thinks has changed the course of women's writing.

Mr. Carmichael

Cry, the Beloved Country
Alan Paton

An acquaintance of **Father Vincent**'s who becomes **Absalom**'s lawyer. Mr. Carmichael is a tall and serious man who carries himself with an almost royal bearing. He takes Absalom's case pro deo ("for God").

Theresa Carmody

Angela's Ashes
Frank McCourt

A seventeen-year-old consumptive girl with whom **Frank** has a sexual relationship. Frank desperately worries about the fate of Theresa's immortal soul, which he thinks he is jeopardizing by having premarital sex with her.

Sophie Carnay

Dangerous Liaisons
Pierre-Ambroise-François Choderlos de Laclos

A friend **Cécile Volanges** made during the time she was in the convent. Sophie Carnay continues to live among the nuns, though she is able to take time out to write to Cécile from time to time. Sophie's letters are not included in the novel, but we can imagine that they contain plenty of warnings and advice, the work of a traditional, devout, and extremely naïve young girl.

Carney

A Tree Grows in Brooklyn
Betty Smith

The junkie in Williamsburg who collects scraps from the children and gives them pennies in exchange. He likes girls better than boys.

Carol

Oleanna
David Mamet

A college student who, despite attending an institution of higher learning, feels oppressed to an extent that denies her full education. She is seemingly incapable of synthesis, often consulting her notes to get the facts straight but rarely coming up with an original idea of her own. Her charges ultimately belie a desire for power, a political agenda and an unexplained amount of anger.

Lady Caroline

Tender Is the Night
F. Scott Fitzgerald

A snobby Englishwoman whom the drunken **Dick Diver** insults gravely on a boat near the Divers' villa on the French Riviera. Later, Lady Caroline is arrested with **Mary North**, and Dick makes up a story and bribes the jailer to secure their release.

Joe Carp

Flowers for Algernon
Daniel Keyes

An employee at Donner's Bakery who often picks on **Charlie Gordon**. With **Frank Reilly**, Joe plays tricks on Charlie and makes him the butt of jokes that he does not understand. However, Frank and Joe think of themselves as Charlie's friends and defend him when others pick on him.

Belle Carpenter

Winesburg, Ohio
Sherwood Anderson

The daughter of a Winesburg bookkeeper. She goes on walks with **George Willard** and even kisses him—mainly, however, to arouse the jealousy of the man she really wants, a local bartender named **Handby**.

Sampson Carrasco

Don Quixote
Miguel de Cervantes

A sarcastic and self-important student from **Don Quixote**'s village. After losing to Don Quixote in combat, Sampson dedicates himself to revenge. His final battle with Don Quixote provokes Don Quixote's disillusionment with knight-errantry.

Nick Carraway

The Great Gatsby
F. Scott Fitzgerald

The narrator of *The Great Gatsby*. A young Yale graduate from Minnesota and a veteran of World War I, Nick moves to New York in the summer of 1922 to learn about the bond business. He settles in nouveau-riche West Egg, Long Island, next door to **Jay Gatsby**'s mansion. Nick's cousin, **Daisy Buchanan**, lives in nearby East Egg and introduces Nick to **Jordan Baker**, a beautiful, shallow young woman with whom

Nick begins an off-and-on romantic relationship. Nick starts to attend Gatsby's parties and later reunites Gatsby and Daisy, who were romantically involved years earlier. Ultimately, after Gatsby's death, Nick returns to the Midwest, disgusted with the shallowness and emptiness of life among the New York elite. Throughout the novel, Nick serves as a confidant for other characters, and the events of the novel are seen entirely through his eyes.

Aunt Carrie

A Day No Pigs Would Die
Robert Newton Peck

A motherly figure to **Robert Peck**. Aunt Carrie lives with the Pecks on their farm and is a great friend to **Lucy Peck**, Robert's mother. She too goes to great lengths to take care of Robert when he is sick and also sneaks him a ten-cent piece for the Rutland fair, where he is going with **Benjamin Tanner**, **Bess Tanner**, **Bib**, **Bob**, and **Pinky**. Aunt Carrie and Lucy like to discuss the town gossip, and they get together with **Aunt Matty** approximately once a month to do so.

Aunt Carrie

Cold Sassy Tree
Olive Anne Burns

An eccentric woman called "aunt" because of her friendship with the Tweedy family. Although she is educated and poised, Aunt Carrie's odd mannerisms and theories make her the object of ridicule.

Aunt Carrol

Little Women
Louisa May Alcott

One of the March girls' aunts. Aunt Carrol is ladylike, and she takes **Amy March** with her to Europe.

Lieutenant Carroll

Fallen Angels
Walter Dean Myers

The leader of **Richie Perry**'s platoon. A smart and sympathetic leader, Lieutenant Carroll is well-liked by the men under his command, and his death during combat leaves them all grief-stricken.

Pinky Carson

Johnny Got His Gun
Dalton Trumbo

One of **Joe Bonham**'s coworkers at the bakery in Los Angeles. It was Pinky's idea for **Jose** to try to get himself fired by being clumsy.

Carter

The Chocolate War
Robert Cormier

President of **the Vigils**. Carter provides some physical back-up to the group. He doubts **Archie Costello** when Archie gets involved with the chocolate sale, and threatens to kick Archie out of the group if Archie's plan does not work.

Dr. Roberta Carter

Jurassic Park
Michael Crichton

A doctor, also called Bobbie, who works at a medical center in Costa Rica. On duty one night at the beginning of the novel, Bobbie is called to treat an InGen employee who has allegedly been injured in a construction accident. The employee's wounds are suspicious, however, leading Bobbie to believe that InGen is not telling the truth about the accident.

Uncle Carter

Hatchet
Gary Paulsen

Brian Robeson's uncle. Uncle Carter eats raw eggs in the morning. Having seen his uncle do this, Brian feels he can eat the turtle eggs that he finds. Brian saves the eggs and tries to eat one a day, but later the eggs are eaten by a skunk.

Sydney Carton

A Tale of Two Cities
Charles Dickens

One of the protagonists of the novel. In the beginning, Carton is insolent, indifferent, and alcoholic. His love for **Lucie Manette** eventually transforms him into a man of profound merit. At first the polar opposite of **Charles Darnay**, Carton morally surpasses him in the end.

Caryl

The Rape of the Lock
Alexander Pope

A character based on John Caryll, a friend of Pope's and of the two families that had become estranged over the incident the poem relates. It was Caryll who suggested that Pope encourage a reconciliation by writing a humorous poem.

Edward Casaubon

Middlemarch
George Eliot

A scholarly clergyman who owns a large estate called Lowick. His lifelong ambition is to write the *Key to All Mythologies*, but he is insecure and uncertain about his own abilities. He marries **Dorothea Brooke** because he thinks she is completely submissive and worshipful. Her stubborn independence frustrates him, and he mistakenly believes that she is constantly criticizing him. Casaubon is **Will Ladislaw**'s cousin. His mother's sister was disowned by her family for running away to marry a man they didn't like. Her own daughter, Will's mother, also ran away to marry. Casaubon offers financial support to Will because he feels obligated to make amends for his aunt's disinheritance. He becomes jealous of Will's relationship with Dorothea. He includes an addendum in his will stating that Dorothea will lose his wealth and property if she ever marries Will Ladislaw. He dies before finishing his *Key*.

Casca

Julius Caesar
William Shakespeare

A public figure opposed to **Julius Caesar**'s rise to power. Casca relates to **Cassius** and **Brutus** how **Antony** offered the crown to Caesar three times and how each time Caesar declined it. He believes, however, that Caesar is the consummate actor, lulling the populace into believing that he has no personal ambition.

Mr. John Casey

A Portrait of the Artist as a Young Man
James Joyce

Simon Dedalus's friend. At **Stephen**'s first Christmas dinner, he and Simon, both Irish nationalists, argue with **Dante** and mourn the death of **Charles Stuart Parnell**.

Dunstan Cass

Silas Marner
George Eliot

One of **Squire Cass**'s sons. Dunsey, as he is usually called, is a cruel, lazy, unscrupulous man who loves gambling and drinking. He steals **Silas Marner**'s gold.

Godfrey Cass

Silas Marner
George Eliot

The eldest son of **Squire Cass**. He is secretly married to **Molly Farren** and is the father of **Eppie**. Godfrey is good-natured but selfish and weak-willed. He knows what is right but is unwilling to pay the price for obeying his conscience.

Squire Cass

Silas Marner
George Eliot

Dunstan Cass and **Godfrey Cass**'s father, and the wealthiest man in Raveloe. The Squire is lazy, self-satisfied, and short-tempered.

Cassandra

Agamemnon
Aeschylus

A Trojan princess captured by **Agamemnon** and carried to Argos as his slave and mistress. **Apollo**, Cassandra's former lover, gave her the gift of prophecy, but when she refused to bear his child, he punished her by making those around her disbelieve her predictions.

Cassandra

Troilus and Cressida
William Shakespeare

A Trojan princess and prophetess, often considered mad.

Leona Cassiani

Love in the Time of Cholera
Gabriel García Márquez

A determined, intelligent woman. **Florentino Ariza** meets Leona Cassiani on the trolley and mistakes her for a whore. She asks him for employment, not sex, and he finds her work in his uncle **Don Leo XII Loayza**'s Riverboat Company in the most menial position available. She impresses Don Leo with her ideas, and he promotes her to the position of his personal assistant. She moves through the company, but out of courtesy, will not take a position higher than Florentino's. She is arguably Florentino's true love, for she nurtures his career and cares for him in his old age.

Michael Cassio

Othello
William Shakespeare

Othello's lieutenant, who is truly devoted to Othello. Cassio is a young and inexperienced soldier whose high position is much resented by **Iago**. Cassio generally avoids alcohol, but Iago fashions a plot whereby Cassio gets drunk and instigates a brawl in Cyprus. Othello punishes Cassio by stripping him of his place as lieutenant, and Cassio laments his loss of reputation. Iago uses Cassio's youth, good looks, and friendship with **Desdemona** to play on Othello's insecurities about Desdemona's fidelity.

Cassius

Julius Caesar
William Shakespeare

A talented general and longtime acquaintance of **Julius Caesar**'s. Cassius dislikes the fact that Caesar has become godlike in the eyes of the Romans. He slyly leads **Brutus** to believe that Caesar has become too powerful and must die, finally converting Brutus to his cause by sending him forged letters claiming the Roman people support the Caesar's death. Impulsive and unscrupulous, Cassius harbors no illusions about the way the political world works. A shrewd opportunist, he proves successful but lacks integrity. When he believes his forces have suffered defeat, he orders his men to kill him.

Cassy

Uncle Tom's Cabin
Harriet Beecher Stowe

Simon Legree's slave mistress and **Eliza Harris**'s mother, Cassy is a proud and intelligent woman who devises a clever way to escape Legree's plantation.

Dr. Castel

The Plague
Albert Camus

An elderly doctor who is the first person to suggest the rats are dying because of the bubonic plague. Together with **Rieux**, Castel struggles to convince authorities that sanitation measures must be taken in order to stop the spread of the epidemic. He develops a serum to vaccinate against the plague.

Carbon de Castel-Jaloux

Cyrano de Bergerac
Edmond Rostand

The captain of **Cyrano de Bergerac**'s company. A friend of Cyrano's, Castel-Jaloux is a strong-willed and successful leader.

Augustine Castle

Walden Two
B. F. Skinner

A philosopher and one of **Professor Burris**'s colleagues at the university. He is intelligent and a good debater, but rather closed-minded. He badgers **T. E. Frazier** throughout his visit to Walden Two, trying to expose some practical or principled reason why the community should not work.

Julian Castle

Cat's Cradle
Kurt Vonnegut

The multimillionaire owner of the Castle Sugar Corporation. He spent the first forty years of his life as an irresponsible playboy before turning his attention to charity. He opened a charity hospital on San Lorenzo, the same island where Castle Sugar had a small operation. **John** traveled to San Lorenzo to interview Julian for a magazine article.

Philip Castle

Cat's Cradle
Kurt Vonnegut

Julian Castle's only son, and **Mona Aamons Monzano**'s former fiance. Philip wrote a book about San Lorenzo's history and people, which **John** read on the plane to San Lorenzo. Philip opened a hotel, the Casa Mona, but had few guests.

Castrone

Volpone
Ben Jonson

A eunuch with no speaking lines.

Jim Casy

The Grapes of Wrath
John Steinbeck

A former preacher who gave up his ministry out of a belief that all human experience is holy. Often the moral voice of the novel, Casy articulates many of its most important themes. Most notably, he redefines the concept of holiness, suggesting that the most divine aspect of human experience is to be found on Earth among one's fellow humans. A staunch friend of **Tom Joad**'s, Casy goes to prison in Tom's stead for a fight that erupts between laborers and the California police. He emerges a determined organizer of the migrant workers, and the police ultimately hunt him down and kill him in Tom's presence.

Caterpillar

Alice in Wonderland
Lewis Carroll

A Hookah-smoking insect who gives **Alice** the means to change size at will. He is severe and somewhat unfriendly, but he offers her some assistance.

Bertram Cates

Inherit the Wind
Jerome Lawrence & Robert E. Lee

A science teacher who teaches the controversial theory of evolution and goes to trial over it. Soft-spoken and humble, he teaches the then forbidden theory to his children straight out of a textbook. He is quiet, unassuming, innocent, naïve, and wondrous about the world, believing that any questions about existence and any challenge to people's fundamental beliefs are allowed. Cates struggles to stand up as an individual even as the crowd opposes his views and actions. Although he remains idealistic throughout *Inherit the Wind*, he often needs **Henry Drummond**'s encouragement to persevere with his cause. Cates doubts himself at times, especially when **Rachel Brown** entreats him to admit his guilt and beg forgiveness so that he does not have to challenge the status quo and be punished for it. After many witnesses are seen in the trial against Cates, he is found guilty. His punishment is a $100 fine. Cates asks Drummond whether he won or lost, and Drummond tells him he won a moral victory by bringing national attention to his case. Cates submits himself to **Meeker** to be returned to jail, but Meeker says that **E. K. Hornbeck** and the *Baltimore Herald* have put up $500 for Cates's bail. In the end, when Cates leaves town with Rachel, we see that his trial has opened Rachel's mind as well, teaching her to think for herself and overcome her fear of her terrible father.

Richard III
William Shakespeare

Sir William Catesby

A supporter of **King Richard III**. Catesby carries out tasks for Richard, delivering messages and acting as a liaison between Richard and other nobles. He fights alongside Richard during the final battle with **Richmond**'s army.

Catch-22
Joseph Heller

Colonel Cathcart

The ambitious officer in charge of **John Yossarian**'s squadron. Cathcart, who wants to be a general, tries to impress his superiors by volunteering his men for as much dangerous combat duty as he can.

Wuthering Heights
Emily Brontë

Catherine

One of the novel's protagonists. Catherine, **Mr. Earnshaw**'s daughter, falls powerfully in love with **Heathcliff**. However, her desire for social advancement motivates her to marry **Edgar Linton**, who fathers her daughter, **young Catherine**. Catherine is free-spirited, beautiful, spoiled, and often arrogant. She brings misery to both of the men who love her.

A View from the Bridge
Arthur Miller

Catherine

The niece of **Eddie Carbone** and **Beatrice**. Catherine is a beautiful, smart young Italian girl who is very popular among the boys in the community. When Eddie notices Catherine's new way of dressing and walking, Eddie is both aroused by and protective of her. Catherine seeks approval from her uncle and struggles when Eddie does not like **Rodolpho**, the man she intends to marry. She still invites Eddie to the wedding, even after he drunkenly kisses Catherine and calls the immigration police on **Marco** and Rodolpho.

Seize the Day
Saul Bellow

Catherine

Tommy Wilhelm's sister and **Dr. Adler**'s daughter. Like Tommy, Catherine also changed her name, in her case to Philippa. She is a married woman with a Bachelor of Science degree from Bryn Mawr. She aspires to be a painter, but her father will not help her rent gallery space for an exhibition. Dr. Adler has no faith in her talent, nor does Tommy.

Pride and Prejudice
Jane Austen

Lady Catherine de Bourgh

A rich, bossy noblewoman; **Mr. Collins**'s patron and **Fitzwilliam Darcy**'s aunt. Lady Catherine epitomizes class snobbery, especially in her attempts to separate the middle-class **Elizabeth Bennet** from her well-bred nephew.

Little Catherine

A Death in the Family
James Agee

The younger sister of **Rufus Follet**, the daughter of **Mary Follet** and **Jay Follet**. She and Rufus frequently argue during the novel. Catherine has trouble understanding Jay's death, wondering when he is coming home, even after she is told he is dead.

Princess Catherine of France

Henry V
William Shakespeare

The daughter of **King Charles VI** and **Queen Isabel**, and sister to the **Dauphin** (Louis) and to **Charles**, who later also becomes the dauphin. Catherine is eventually married off to **King Henry V** in order to cement the peace between England and France. Though she appears in very little of the play, her scenes are significant because they depict a female world that contrasts starkly with the grim, violent world in which the men exist. While the men engage in bloody war, Catherine lives with her tutor **Alice** in a much gentler milieu, generally ignorant of the struggle around her. She becomes the mother of **King Henry VI**.

Cathleen

Long Day's Journey into Night
Eugene O'Neill

The Tyrone family maid. She appears in the play only briefly. Cathleen is chatty and flirty and, by Act III, drunk. **Mary Tyrone** is displeased with Cathleen, and she blames her unhappiness on **James Tyrone**'s refusal to hire a top-rate maid.

Cathy

Cloud Nine
Caryl Churchill

Cathy, a four-year-old girl played by a man, is an abnormal child who has a remarkable knowledge of inappropriate words and phrases. She seems to harbor aggression, making her susceptible to occasional outbursts. Her disposition derives in part from her fear that her mother **Lin** will leave her. Cathy's desire to fit in drives most of her actions throughout Act II. Her lesbian mother encourages the boyishness in her, giving her guns to play with, cursing at her, and dressing her in jeans. Cathy straddles gender roles, enjoying dresses and **Betty**'s jewelry just as much as she likes playing with guns and the boys in the Dead Hand gang.

Dr. L. S. Caton

Lucky Jim
Kingsley Amis

A shady academic who accepts **Jim Dixon**'s article for his new academic journal, then steals it and publishes it in Italian under his own name, winning him a position as department chair at a university in Argentina.

Homi Catrack

Midnight's Children
Salman Rushdie

A man who has an affair with **Lila Sabarmati** and is subsequently murdered by **Commander Sabarmati.**

Allie Caulfield

The Catcher in the Rye
J. D. Salinger

Younger brother of **Holden Caulfield**. Allie dies of leukemia three years before the start of the novel. Allie was a brilliant, friendly, red-headed boy—according to Holden, he was the smartest of the Caulfields. Holden is tormented by Allie's death and carries around a baseball glove on which Allie used to write poems in green ink.

D. B. Caulfield

The Catcher in the Rye
J. D. Salinger

Older brother of **Holden Caulfield**. D. B. Caulfield wrote a volume of short stories that Holden admires very much, but Holden feels that D. B. prostitutes his talents by writing for Hollywood movies.

Holden Caulfield

The Catcher in the Rye
J. D. Salinger

The protagonist and narrator of *The Catcher in the Rye*. Holden Caulfield writes his story from a rest home where he has been sent for therapy. He has just been expelled in his junior year for academic failure from a school called Pencey Prep. Although he is intelligent and sensitive, Holden narrates in a cynical and jaded voice. He finds the hypocrisy and ugliness of the world around him almost unbearable, and through his cynicism he tries to protect himself from the pain and disappointment of the adult world. However, the criticisms that Holden aims at people around him are also aimed at himself. He is uncomfortable with his own weaknesses, and at times displays as much phoniness, meanness, and superficiality as anyone else in the book.

Phoebe Caulfield

The Catcher in the Rye
J. D. Salinger

The younger sister of **Holden Caulfield**, whom he loves dearly. Although Phoebe Caulfield is six years younger than Holden, she listens to what he says and understands him more than most other people do. Phoebe is intelligent, neat, and a wonderful dancer, and her childish innocence is one of Holden's only consistent sources of happiness throughout the novel. At times, she exhibits great maturity and even chastises Holden for his lack of it. Like **Mr. Antolini**, Phoebe seems to recognize that Holden is his own worst enemy.

Major Bartolomeo Cavalcanti

The Count of Monte Cristo
Alexandre Dumas

A part made up by **the Count of Monte Cristo** to further his plan of revenge. A poor and crooked man plays Major Bartolomeo Cavalcanti, who is an Italian nobleman. The major's son, Andrea Cavalcanti, is played by **Benedetto**. These two impostors are present at Monte Cristo's dinner party, so that the money-hungry **Danglars** can meet Andrea and believe him to be very rich.

James Oliver Cavendish

Stranger in a Strange Land
Robert A. Heinlein

A famous and respected Fair Witness. His job is to be brought into any given situation and retain detailed, completely objective memories of everything that happens. It is part of Cavendish's professional credo to never interfere in any of the occurrences that he is employed to observe.

Lord Caversham

An Ideal Husband
Oscar Wilde

Lord Goring's father, a "fine Whig type." Lord Caversham is a stuffy, serious, and respectable gentleman who is firmly opposed to the excesses of his dandified son. He insistently urges his son to marry and adopt a career, and offers Sir Robert as an exemplar. Caversham represents the old-fashioned in contrast to his son, who masters the art of modern living.

Ben Caxton

Stranger in a Strange Land
Robert A. Heinlein

A newspaper reporter who writes a muckraking political column that has earned him the ire of the Earth's government. Ben is driven partially by a newspaperman's inherent lust for a scintillating story, and partially by a passion for social justice. He is a close friend of **Jubal Harshaw**'s, and longs for an old-fashioned marriage to **Gillian Boardman**. Despite his liberal politics, he has difficulty accepting the untraditional sexual practices of the church that **Valentine Michael Smith** founds.

Jimmy Caya

The Autobiography of Miss Jane Pittman
Ernest J. Gaines

Tee Bob Samson's best friend, whom he met at Louisiana State University in Baton Rouge. Jimmy Caya is not from the high landowning class like the Samsons, and **Jules Raynard** looks down on him for that reason.

Cecile

Sula
Toni Morrison

Helene's strict, religious grandmother. She raises Helene from birth, protecting her from her Creole prostitute mother, **Rochelle**. Cecile arranges Helene's marriage to **Wiley Wright**, Cecile's grand-nephew. When Cecile falls ill, Helene takes her ten-year-old daughter, **Nel**, to New Orleans to prepare for the funeral. Helene sews herself a magnificent dress in preparation for the journey she will have to make. When she and Nel arrive in New Orleans, they discover Cecile has already died.

Cedric the Saxon

Ivanhoe
Sir Walter Scott

Ivanhoe's father, a powerful Saxon lord who has disinherited his son for joining **King Richard I**'s Crusades. Cedric is fiercely proud of his Saxon heritage, and his first priority is to the prospects of his people—hence his desire to marry **Lady Rowena** to **Athelstane** rather than to Ivanhoe. Cedric's unpolished manners make him the butt of jokes among his Norman superiors, but he has a knack for making grand gestures to restore the balance—as when he shocks **Prince John** by toasting Richard at John's tournament feast.

Jay Cee

The Bell Jar
Sylvia Plath

Esther Greenwood's boss at the magazine, an ambitious career woman who encourages Esther. She is physically unattractive but moves self-confidently in her world. She treats Esther brusquely but kindly.

Celeborn

The Fellowship of the Ring and *The Return of the King*
J. R. R. Tolkien

The husband of **Galadriel**. Celeborn and Galadriel, who both appear to be timeless, ageless beings, rule as Lord and Lady of Lórien, the Elvish forest. In *The Fellowship of the Ring*, **Frodo Baggins**, **Samwise Gamgee**, **Meriadoc Brandybuck**, **Peregrin Took**, **Aragorn**, **Boromir**, **Gimli**, and **Legolas** meet Celeborn after they lose **Gandalf** to **the Balrog** in Moria. In *The Return of the King*, Celeborn comes with Galadriel to Minas Tirith after **Sauron**'s defeat to see the marriage of Aragorn and **Arwen Evenstar**. At the end of the book, Celeborn and all the **Elves**, along with Gandalf, Frodo and **Bilbo Baggins** sail to the West beyond the Great Sea to the Grey Havens.

Celeste

The Stranger
Albert Camus

The proprietor of a café where **Meursault** frequently eats lunch. Celeste remains loyal to Meursault during his murder trial. He testifies that Meursault is an honest, decent man, and he states that bad luck led Meursault to kill **the Arab**. Celeste's assertion that the murder had no rational cause and was simply a case of bad luck reveals a worldview similar to Meursault's.

Celia

As You Like It
William Shakespeare

The daughter of **Duke Frederick**, and **Rosalind**'s dearest friend and cousin. Celia's devotion to Rosalind is unmatched, as evidenced by her decision to follow her cousin into exile. To make the trip, Celia assumes the disguise of a simple shepherdess and calls herself Aliena. As elucidated by her extreme love of Rosalind and her immediate devotion to **Oliver**, whom she marries at the end of the play, Celia possesses a loving heart but is prone to deep, almost excessive emotions.

Celia

Volpone
Ben Jonson

The voice of goodness and religiosity in the play, **Corvino**'s beautiful wife. Celia's attractiveness drives both **Volpone** and Corvino to distraction. She is absolutely committed to her husband, even though he treats her horribly, and has a faith in God and sense of honor, traits that seem to be lacking in both Corvino and Volpone. These traits guide her toward self-restraint and self-denial.

Celie

The Color Purple
Alice Walker

The protagonist and narrator of *The Color Purple*. Celie is a poor, uneducated black woman with a sad personal history. She survives **Alphonso**, her stepfather, who calls her ugly, rapes her, and steals her babies. As a child, Celie decides that the best way to stay safe is to be silent and invisible. Her letters to God are her only outlet. Celie does little to fight back against Alphonso, or her abusive husband, **Mr.** ____. As an adult,

Celie befriends and finds intimacy with a blues singer, **Shug Avery**. Shug moves into Mr. ___ and Celie's home and is Mr. ___'s mistress. Celie witnesses how strong Shug is, and how she lets no one command her or beat her down. Shug's maternal prodding helps spur Celie's development. Gradually, Celie recovers her own history, sexuality, spirituality, and voice. Celie's sister **Nettie**'s long-lost letters, which Celie discovers with Shug's help hidden in Mr. ___'s trunk, fortify Celie's sense of self by informing her of her personal history and of the fate of her children. Celie's process of finding her own voice culminates with her enraged explosion at Mr. ___, in which she curses him for his years of abuse and abasement. The self-actualization Celie achieves transforms her into a happy, successful, independent woman. Celie takes the domestic act of sewing and turns it into an outlet for creative self-expression and a profitable business: Folkspants, Unlimited. When Nettie, **Olivia**, and **Adam** return to Georgia from Africa, Celie's circle of friends and family is finally reunited.

Célimène

The Misanthrope
Molière

A young woman who is the object of desire of **Alceste**, **Oronte**, **Acaste**, and **Clitandre**. She has specific reasons for keeping many of her suitors: she entertains Clitandre because he may be able to help her with a lawsuit, and she tries to stay on good terms with Acaste because he carries considerable clout in "Court circles." While many of her suitors tell her that she is perfect, Alceste finds her faults and points them out to her upon noticing them. Célimène is happy and confident, but not without fault; she loves to gossip, and she is critical of nearly everyone she meets. She is careless in her insults, and she ultimately stirs the ire of those who once loved her when her suitors find a letter that enumerates each of their faults. At one point, Oronte and Alceste demand that she choose between them. She calls their requests "inappropriate," not wanting to publicly offend the one she does not choose. In the end, she refuses to retreat into solitude with Alceste, but she agrees to marry him. This is not enough for him, however, and he says that he wants nothing to do with her.

Censor

I Never Promised You a Rose Garden
Joanne Greenberg

The Censor is a being in the Kingdom of Yr, a world that **Deborah** created as a defense against a confusing and frightening reality. Once, Deborah accidentally left a clue in the real world to the existence of Yr, so the gods of Yr created the Censor to guard Yr's secrets from Earth. Over time, the Censor has become a tyrant who watches and controls all of Deborah's actions to prevent her from revealing Yr's existence.

Cerberus

Greek Mythology
Unknown

A vile three-headed dog that guards the gates of **Hades**.

Benito Cereno

Benito Cereno
Herman Melville

The title character, a tall, thin Chilean man. He is the captain of the *San Dominick*, a merchant vessel.

Cerimon

Pericles
William Shakespeare

A kindly Ephesus physician. A model of charity, Cerimon miraculously brings **Thaisa** back from the brink of death and helps her become a priestess.

Cervantes

Don Quixote
Miguel de Cervantes

The narrator and translator of **Benengeli**'s supposed historical novel. Cervantes interjects commentary into his narrative at key times.

Cesar

Bel Canto
Ann Patchett

A young terrorist with crooked teeth and a crooked nose. For most of the novel, no one really notices Cesar. One morning when **Coss** does not come down to sing, Cesar performs instead, and his voice is practically miraculous. Coss takes him under her wing and gives him singing lessons.

Chabin

Breath, Eyes, Memory
Edwidge Danticat

The albino lottery agent in Croix-des-Rosets, Haiti, from whom **Atie** faithfully buys lottery tickets, though she rarely wins.

Chaerephon

The Clouds
Aristophanes

A philosopher-sophist from **Socrates**'s school. Renowned for his paleness and his esoteric intellect, he is also whiny and helpless.

Sundar Chakravarty

White Noise
Don DeLillo

Jack Gladney's doctor, who speaks English beautifully.

Jack Challee

The Caine Mutiny
Herman Wouk

The judge advocate in **Steve Maryk**'s trial. It is his job to prosecute the mutineer. Challee thinks that **Philip Francis Queeg**'s case is a simple matter—he must simply have the psychologists prove Queeg sane. He is very distraught when **Barney Greenwald**'s tricks cause a probable miscarriage of justice.

Colonel Joshua Lawrence Chamberlain

The Killer Angels
Michael Shaara

A Union soldier. A thirty-four-year-old man from Maine who has left a comfortable professorship at Bowdoin College to go to war. He is the colonel of the Twentieth Maine Infantry regiment. He was an excellent student at school, speaks seven languages, and has a lovely singing voice, but all his life he has wanted to be a soldier. He lied to Bowdoin and told them he was going on sabbatical to France because they would not let him go to war.

Thomas Chamberlain

The Killer Angels
Michael Shaara

A Union soldier. **Colonel Joshua Lawrence Chamberlain**'s brother and aide, also in the Twentieth Maine. Not as smart or as brooding as his brother, Tom is more social, funnier, and more easygoing. While he has been a calming presence to his brother, he soon becomes a liability when Joshua Chamberlain realizes that he might, at some point, order his brother to his death.

Arthur Chambers

Snow Falling on Cedars
David Guterson

Ishmael Chambers's father, **Helen Chambers**'s husband, and the founding editor of the *San Piedro Review*, the most prominent newspaper on the island. Arthur frequently—and courageously—used the editorial column in his newspaper as a forum to condemn the racism directed at San Piedro's Japanese-American residents during World War II. Though his editorials often provoked hostility from much of the community, Arthur maintained a strong heart and firmly believed that his perspective was the correct one.

Helen Chambers

Snow Falling on Cedars
David Guterson

Ishmael Chambers's mother and **Arthur Chambers**'s wife. Now a widow, Helen remains committed to the principles of tolerance and honesty her husband practiced. She doubts that **Kabuo Miyamoto**'s trial is fair. Concerned about Ishmael's solitary and seemingly joyless life, Helen urges her son to get over his emotional issues and fall in love again.

Ishmael Chambers

Snow Falling on Cedars
David Guterson

The novel's protagonist and the editor of the local paper, the *San Piedro Review*. He is a World War II veteran, and a gunshot in the war left him with an amputated left arm. As a young boy, Ishmael had a deep friendship with **Hatsue Miyamoto**. Hatsue eventually called an abrupt end to the relationship and married **Kabuo Miyamoto**, leaving Ishmael bitter and resentful.

Champmathieu

Les Misérables
Victor Hugo

A poor, uneducated man who unfortunately resembles **Jean Valjean** so much that he is identified, tried, and almost convicted as Valjean. When he is too dim-witted to defend himself successfully, his predicament reveals the callousness of the French justice system. In the end, the court exonerates Champmathieu.

Ender's Game
Orson Scott Card

Admiral Chamrajnagar

Colonel Graff's superior, and the leader of the fleet. Chamrajnagar questions Graff's decision to give **Ender Wiggin** a three-month vacation, and then fills Graff in on their plans for Ender at Command School.

Dubliners
James Joyce

Little Chandler

An unhappy, shy clerk who once dreamed of poetry but now finds himself stifled by routine. Little Chandler's physical attributes match his name—he is small, fragile, and delicately groomed. He reunites with his friend **Gallaher** in "A Little Cloud." After hearing about Gallaher's adventures, Little Chandler fleetingly rebels against his domestic life, then shamefully re-embraces it.

The Harry Potter Series: Books 3 and 4
J. K. Rowling

Cho Chang

A pretty fifth-year Ravenclaw girl upon whom **Harry Potter** develops a crush. In *Harry Potter and the Prisoner of Azkaban*, Harry beats her to the Snitch in a Quidditch match. In *Harry Potter and the Goblet of Fire*, Harry makes himself vulnerable by asking Cho to go to the ball, only to find that she has already agreed to attend with **Cedric Diggory**.

Dune
Frank Herbert

Chani

Daughter of **Liet-Kynes**, lover of **Paul Atreides**, and mother of Paul's first child, Chani is one of the Fremen and has some of the skills of the Bene Gesserit.

Walden
Henry David Thoreau

William Ellery Channing

Henry David Thoreau's closest friend, an amateur poet and an affiliate of the Transcendentalists. Channing was named after his uncle, a noted Unitarian clergyman. His son, **Edward Channing**, went on to become a noted professor of history at Harvard University.

Tess of the d'Urbervilles
Thomas Hardy

Mercy Chant

The daughter of a friend of **Reverend Clare**'s. Mr. Clare hopes **Angel Clare** will marry Mercy, a girl of high societal standing, but after Angel marries **Tess Durbeyfield**, Mercy becomes engaged to Angel's brother, **Reverend Cuthbert Clare**, instead.

The Canterbury Tales
Geoffrey Chaucer

Chanticleer

The heroic rooster of **the Nun's Priest**'s Tale, Chanticleer has seven hen-wives and is the most handsome cock in the barnyard. One day, he has a prophetic dream of a fox that will carry him away. Chanticleer is vain about his clear and accurate crowing voice, and he unwittingly allows a fox to flatter him out of his liberty.

The Chantyman

Mourning Becomes Electra
Eugene O'Neill

A drunk, weather-beaten man. Though dissipated, he possesses a romantic, troubadour-of-the-sea air. He is around a wharf in East Boston when **Orin Mannon** shoots **Captain Adam Brant** after Orin witnesses **Christine Mannon**'s meeting with Brant.

Chaplain

Mother Courage
Bertolt Brecht

One of two characters who use **Mother Courage** as a "feedbag." The Chaplain initially seems like a cynical, wooden character. He remains loyal to the Swedish monarchy and thinks of the war as religious and justified, but he also notices the horrors around him. The Chaplain later reveals more sympathetic qualities, particularly when he defies Courage and attempts to save the local peasants at the Battle of Magdeburg. At Magdeburg, the *Courage Model Book* shows him recalling a sense of his former importance, and he begins to understand himself as oppressed by the war. As he will tell the **Cook**, his life as a tramp makes it impossible to return to the priesthood and all its attendant beliefs.

Chaplain

The Stranger
Albert Camus

A priest who attends to the religious needs of condemned men, the chaplain acts as a catalyst for **Meursault**'s psychological and philosophical development. After Meursault is sentenced to death for the crime of premeditated murder, he repeatedly refuses to see the chaplain. The chaplain visits Meursault anyway, demanding that he take comfort in God. The chaplain seems threatened by Meursault's stubborn atheism. Eventually, Meursault angrily asserts to the chaplain that life is meaningless and that all men are condemned to die. Meursault's outburst triggers his final acceptance of the meaninglessness of the universe.

Chaplain

Catch-22
Joseph Heller

John Yossarian's timid and thoughtful friend. Over the course of the novel, the chaplain is haunted by déjà vu and slowly loses his faith in God.

Mr. Chappelle

Dicey's Song
Cynthia Voigt

Dicey's English teacher. Mr. Chappelle is dull and unwilling to question conventions. He accepts the unexceptional answers and ideas of his students but reacts with suspicion when Dicey turns in superior work.

Sister Ella Chapter

Angels in America
Tony Kushner

A real estate agent who handles the sale of **Hannah Pitt**'s house in Salt Lake. Like the nurse **Emily**, who counsels **Prior Walter**, she urges her friend to settle down and remain at home.

Chapuys

A Man for All Seasons
Robert Bolt

The Spanish ambassador to England. Chapuys is loyal to his country and intent on assuring that **King Henry** remain married to Catherine, because Catherine is related to the King of Spain, and her divorce would bring great shame. When questioning **More**, Chapuys displays his aptitude for hiding his political agenda under the guise of Catholic fervor.

Dona Charito

How the Garcia Girls Lost Their Accents
Julia Alvarez

Sandra's childhood art teacher. She disciplines Sandra for disobedience instead of encouraging her talent and enthusiasm for art.

Charlemagne

The Song of Roland
Unknown

Historically, Charlemagne (742?-814) was king of the Franks and a committed, militant Christian. A loyal ally of the pope and a great conqueror, he forced conversions as he expanded the boundaries of his empire outward from his central territory, straddling present-day France and Germany. In 800 he was crowned emperor by the pope, legitimizing his rule over the former Roman empire in western Europe. After his death, he became legendary; it is this legendary Charlemagne, the perfect Christian king, symbol of the spirit of the Crusades, and favorite of heaven, who is presented in *The Song of Roland* as leader of the Frankish troops and **Roland**'s uncle and avenger. His name means "Charles the Great."

Charles

As You Like It
William Shakespeare

A professional wrestler in **Duke Frederick**'s court. Charles demonstrates both his caring nature and political savvy when he asks **Oliver** to intercede in his upcoming fight with **Orlando**: he does not want to injure the young man and thereby lose favor among the nobles who support him. Charles's concern proves unwarranted when Orlando beats him senseless.

Charles

The Call of the Wild
Jack London

Mercedes's husband and **Hal**'s brother-in-law. Charles, like Mercedes and Hal, is inexperienced and foolish. Hal and Charles buy **Buck** and the team of dogs left behind by **François** and **Perrault** and the Scotsman. Buck almost dies as a result of Hal and Charles's incompetence.

King Charles VI of France

Henry V
William Shakespeare

The ruler of France, husband to **Queen Isabel**, and father to **Catherine**, the first **Dauphin** (Louis), **Charles** (later also dauphin), and **Isabella** (wife of King **Richard II** of England). A capable leader, Charles does not underestimate **King Henry V**, unlike his rash son the Dauphin. Charles VI agrees to the terms of Henry's truce following the Battle of Agincourt, and consents to let the English ruler marry Catherine and become his son-in-law.

Emperor Charles V

Doctor Faustus
Christopher Marlowe

The most powerful European monarch. **Faustus** visits Charles's court.

Charles, Dauphin of France

Henry VI, Part I
William Shakespeare

The heir to the French throne. Charles gathers enough support in France to crown himself king and sets about recapturing France from England. When **Joan of Arc** approaches him to assist the French cause, Charles first challenges her to single combat (and loses), and then tries to woo her (and fails). With Joan's help, Charles and his army do battle with the English throughout the play and regain half of France. At the end, he agrees to make peace with the English and becomes viceroy of France under **King Henry VI**.

Doaker Charles

The Piano Lesson
August Wilson

Berniece and **Boy Willie**'s uncle and the owner of the household in which the play takes place. Tall and thin, Doaker spent his life working for the railroad. He functions as the play's testifier, recounting the piano's history and its strong attachment to the family. While Doaker attempts to remain neutral with the conflict over the piano, he knows its rightful place is within the Charles household.

Uncle Charles

A Portrait of the Artist as a Young Man
James Joyce

Stephen Dedalus's lively great-uncle.

Uncle Charles

The Member of the Wedding
Carson McCullers

John Henry West's great-uncle, who is not related to **Frankie Addams** by blood. After a long illness, he dies on Saturday. This is much to the irritation of Frankie, who feels the glum nature of death distracts from the excitement about the wedding.

Charley

The Return of the Native
Thomas Hardy

A local youth who works for the Vyes, and who falls hopelessly in love with **Eustacia Vye**.

Charley

Death of a Salesman
Arthur Miller

Willy Loman's next-door neighbor. Charley owns a successful business and his son **Bernard** is a wealthy, important lawyer. Willy is jealous of Charley's success. Charley gives Willy money to pay his bills, and Willy reveals at one point, choking back tears, that Charley is his only friend.

Charlie

The Sound and the Fury
William Faulkner

One of **Caddy Compson**'s first suitors, who **Benjy** catches with Caddy on the swing during the first chapter.

Charlie

Tuesdays with Morrie
Mitch Albom

David and **Morrie Schwartz**'s dispassionate father, who immigrated to America to escape the Russian Army. Charlie raises his children on the Lower East Side of Manhattan and works in the fur business, though he seldom finds jobs and earns barely enough money to feed his family. He shows Morrie and his brother David little attention and no affection. He insists that Morrie keep his mother's death a secret from David, as he wants his son to believe that his stepmother, **Eva**, is his biological mother. He dies after having run away from muggers, and Morrie must travel to New York to identify his body at the city morgue.

Cheap Charlie

A Tree Grows in Brooklyn
Betty Smith

Owner of the penny-candy store in Williamsburg. Cheap Charlie lures kids into the store by making them think they might earn a nice prize.

Charlotte

Oliver Twist
Charles Dickens

The Sowerberrys' maid. Charlotte becomes romantically involved with **Noah Claypole** and slavishly follows him around.

Charlotte

The Cherry Orchard
Anton Chekhov

Anya's governess. Charlotte traveled from town to town performing tricks such as "the dive of death" when she was very young, before her father and mother died. Charlotte is something of a clown, performing tricks for the amusement of the elite around her, such as **Yasha**, **Ranevsky**, and **Lopakhin**.

Charlotte

Tuesdays with Morrie
Mitch Albom

Morrie Schwartz's caring wife, who, at his insistence, keeps her job as a professor at M.I.T. throughout his illness.

Miss Charlotte

Annie John
Jamaica Kincaid

Annie's neighbor who falls down dead on the street.

Charmian

Antony and Cleopatra
William Shakespeare

Cleopatra's attendant.

Master Jacques Charmolue

Hunchback of Notre Dame
Victor Hugo

One of **Claude Frollo**'s associates. He and Claude discuss the laws of alchemy and their inability to turn light into gold. He prosecutes and then tortures **La Esmerelda** to get her to confess to killing **Phoebus.** He later has her executed.

Charon

Inferno
Dante Alighieri

An old man who ferries the dead across the river Acheron from Fore-Hell to the First Circle of Hell (Canto III). The character originates in Greek mythology.

Mr. Charrington

1984
George Orwell

An old man who runs a secondhand store in the prole district. Kindly and encouraging, Mr. Charrington seems to share **Winston Smith**'s interest in the past. He also seems to support Winston's rebellion against the Party and his relationship with **Julia**, renting Winston a room without a telescreen where the two can conduct their affair. However, Mr. Charrington is a member of the Thought Police, and turns the couple in to the Ministry of Love.

The Charro

All the Pretty Horses
Cormac McCarthy

A citizen of Encantada. He pays the captain a bribe to execute **Jimmy Blevins**, who killed a relative of his. When **John Grady Cole** returns to Encantada, he forces the charro to show him where he has hidden the American horses.

Dr. Chasuble

The Importance of Being Earnest
Oscar Wilde

The rector of the Manor House. Chasuble and **Miss Prism** flirt throughout Acts II and III.

Konstantin Chateau

Pnin
Vladimir Nabokov

An old friend of **Timofey Pnin**'s. In the 1920s, Chateau and Pnin were students together at the University of Prague. Chateau teaches the History of Philosophy at a college in New York.

Baron of Château-Renaud

The Count of Monte Cristo
Alexandre Dumas

An aristocrat and diplomat whom **Maximilian Morrel** saves from death at the battle of Constantinople. By way of thanks to Maximilian, the Baron of Château-Renaud introduces Maximilian into Parisian society. The Count of Monte Cristo meets the Baron, as well as **Beauchamp** and **Lucien Debray**, at a breakfast given by **Albert de Morcerf.**

Ezra Chater

Arcadia
Tom Stoppard

Ezra Chater is a poet and amateur biologist—neither of which he does particularly well. His wife **Mrs. Chater** is constantly cheating on him, and she has made her rounds between almost all of the men at the estate. **Brice** hires Mr. Chater as a botanist on his ship so that Brice can sustain an affiar with Mrs. Chater. During that voyage, Mr. Chater dies in Malta of a spider bite. Mr. Chater is the source of much speculation by the modern historian **Bernard**, who attempts to prove that **Lord Byron** killed Chater in a dual over Mrs. Chater's honor.

Chatillon

King John
William Shakespeare

A French messenger. He arrives from **King Philip** to ask **King John** to abdicate the throne in favor of **Arthur**. He is sent back to France to tell Philip that England has denied the request and is marching forward for war.

Clifford Chatterley

Lady Chatterley's Lover
D. H. Lawrence

Lady Chatterley's husband. Clifford Chatterley is a minor nobleman who becomes paralyzed from the waist down during World War I. As a result of his injury, Clifford is impotent. He retires to his familial estate, Wragby, where he becomes first a successful writer and then a powerful businessman. But the gap between Connie and him grows ever wider; obsessed with financial success and fame, Clifford is not truly interested in love, and Connie feels he has become passionless and empty. He turns for solace to his nurse and companion, **Mrs. Bolton**, who worships him as a nobleman even as she despises his casual arrogance. Clifford is a weak, vain man who feels entitled to rule the lower classes, and he soullessly pursues money and fame through industry and the meaningless manipulation of words.

Lady Chatterley

Lady Chatterley's Lover
D. H. Lawrence

The protagonist of the novel. Before her marriage, she is simply Constance Reid, an intellectual and social progressive, the daughter of **Sir Malcolm Reid** and the sister of **Hilda Reid**. When she marries **Clifford Chatterley**, a minor nobleman, Constance—or, as she is known throughout the novel, Connie—assumes his title, becoming Lady Chatterley. *Lady Chatterley's Lover* chronicles Connie's maturation as a woman and as a sensual being. She comes to despise her weak, ineffectual husband and to love **Oliver Mellors**, the gamekeeper on her husband's estate. In the process of leaving her husband and conceiving a child with Mellors, Lady Chatterley moves from the heartless world of the intelligentsia and aristocracy into a vital and profound connection rooted in sensuality and sexual fulfillment.

Chaucer the narrator

The Canterbury Tales
Geoffrey Chaucer

The narrator of *The Canterbury Tales*, who may or may not represent Chaucer the author. In the General Prologue, Chaucer the narrator presents himself as a gregarious and naïve character. Later on, **the Host** accuses him of being silent and sullen. The narrator writes down his impressions of the pilgrims from memory, and so his prejudices say more about the narrator than the characters themselves.

Marie Chauvel

The Da Vinci Code
Dan Brown

Sophie Neveu's grandmother and **Jacques Saunière**'s wife. A kind and smart woman, Marie Chauvel is part of the Priory's plan to keep the secret. She is a descendent of Jesus and Mary Magdalene.

Chávez

Bless Me, Ultima
Rudolfo A. Anaya

The father of **Antonio Márez**'s friend, **Jasón Chávez**. He leads a mob to find **Lupito** after Lupito kills Chávez's brother, the local sheriff. The mob kills Lupito. Chávez forbids Jasón to visit an Indian who lives near the town, but Jasón disobeys him and goes to see **Jasón Chávez's Indian**.

Jasón Chávez

Bless Me, Ultima
Rudolfo A. Anaya

One of **Antonio Márez**'s friends. He disobeys his father when he continues to visit **Jasón Chávez's Indian**, who lives near the town.

Swiss Cheese

Mother Courage
Bertolt Brecht

The first of **Mother Courage**'s children to die. Swiss Cheese suffers from an excessive sense of duty and honesty and ultimately dies because of it. Unable to adapt to the mad rules of war, his very honesty and sweetness cost him his life. Courage had instilled Swiss Cheese with these virtues because he had never been particularly bright.

Ezekiel Cheever

The Crucible
Arthur Miller

A man from Salem who acts as clerk of the court during the witch trials. Ezekiel Cheever is upright and determined to do his duty for justice, arriving at **Elizabeth Proctor** and **John Proctor**'s house with an arrest warrant for Elizabeth. Cheever, acting on strange and spotty evidence, makes assertions in court that help convict other residents of Salem.

M. Chélan

The Red and the Black
Stendhal

The priest of the town of Verrières. M. Chélan recognizes **Julien Sorel**'s intelligence and stunning memory, but also sees Julien's lack of devotion to the Church. Kind-hearted and benevolent, he chooses to be Julien's mentor and teach him Latin anyway. When Chélan sees that **Elisa** is in love with Julien, he asks Julien to reconsider his path in the Church. When Elisa tells Chélan about the affair between Sorel and **Mme. de Rênal**, Chélan, in order to avoid a scandal, arranges for Julien to enter a seminary in Besançon.

Rabbi Isador Chemelwitz

Angels in America
Tony Kushner

An elderly rabbi who delivers the eulogy at the funeral of **Sarah Ironson**. In the first scene of *Millennium Approaches*, Rabbi Chemelwitz describes the conservative process by which Jewish immigrants resisted assimilation. **Louis Ironson** seeks spiritual guidance from him, and **Prior Walter** later encounters him in Heaven on his way to confront the Angels.

Marvin Chen

The Joy Luck Club
Amy Tan

Waverly's first husband and the father of her daughter, **Shoshana**. Waverly's mother, **Lindo**, always pointed out Marvin's faults. Soon Waverly could see nothing but his shortcomings and divorced him.

Shoshana Chen

The Joy Luck Club
Amy Tan

Waverly's four-year-old daughter. Waverly loves Shoshana unconditionally.

Chencha

Like Water for Chocolate
Laura Esquivel

The ranch maid. She is of indigenous descent and possesses a somewhat flighty disposition. She becomes **Tita**'s companion in the kitchen after **Nacha**'s death.

Cheroke

The Martian Chronicles
Ray Bradbury

A member of the fourth expedition. Cheroke is a descendant of the Cherokee tribe of Native Americans. He claims to sympathize with the Martians, but he still stands up to **Jeff Spender**, who kills him.

Cheshire Cat

Alice in Wonderland
Lewis Carroll

The **Duchess**'s grinning cat. The Cheshire Cat claims to be mad, but it is one of the more reasonable creatures in Wonderland. The Cheshire Cat treats **Alice** with civility, but he has very threatening teeth and claws.

Annie John
Jamaica Kincaid

Ma Chess

Annie's grandmother. Ma Chess lives on Dominica but comes to Antigua to heal Annie. A powerful female figure, Ma Chess is deeply connected with obeah, the local healing religion of the island. She appears to have powers outside of herself that she uses to maintain her own health and to bring Annie's back.

Annie John
Jamaica Kincaid

Pa Chess

Annie's mother's father. Annie's mother and he quarreled when she was young, which led Annie's mother to leave home at the age of sixteen. Later in life, he becomes decrepit and unable to walk around freely. He represents oppressive male control over a family.

Lord Jim
Joseph Conrad

Chester

Chester and **Robinson** are two disreputable characters who offer **Jim**, through **Marlow**, a job taking a wreck of a ship to a desolate island to collect guano. The guano-collecting mission, under someone else's command, leaves port and is never heard from again.

One Flew over the Cuckoo's Nest
Ken Kesey

Charles Cheswick

The first patient to support **Randle McMurphy**'s rebellion against **Nurse Ratched**'s power. Cheswick later drowns in the pool—possibly a suicide—after McMurphy does not support Cheswick's stand against Nurse Ratched. Cheswick's death is significant in that it awakens McMurphy to the extent of his influence and the mistake of his decision to conform.

Middlemarch
George Eliot

Sir James Chettam

A baronet who owns a large estate called Freshitt. He courts **Dorothea Brooke**, but marries her sister **Celia Brooke** after Dorothea marries **Edward Casaubon**. He enacts Dorothea's cottage plans on his own estate.

O Pioneers!
Willa Cather

Amedee Chevalier

A French immigrant who is **Emil Bergson**'s best friend. Amedee is clever, mischievous, kind-hearted, and jovial. His marriage to **Angelique Chevalier** and the birth of their son seem to promise happiness and success. Amedee's sudden death sets into motion the string of tragedies at the novel's end.

O Pioneers!
Willa Cather

Angelique Chevalier

Amedee Chevalier's beautiful, graceful bride. Amedee's death punctures the optimism that her marriage and the birth of her son fostered.

Mrs. Cheveley

An Ideal Husband
Oscar Wilde

One of the play's wittiest and most well-dressed characters, but also a vicious and opportunistic villain. Mrs. Cheveley, a disciple of the deceased **Baron Arnheim**, values wealth and power above all. Cast as a monstrous femme fatale, Mrs. Cheveley constantly foils the virtuous and earnest **Lady Gertrude Chiltern**.

Madame de Chevreuse

The Three Musketeers
Alexandre Dumas

Aramis's secret mistress, and a close personal friend of **Queen Anne**'s. Madame de Chevreuse is banished from Paris because **King Louis XIII**, goaded by **Cardinal Richelieu**, suspects her of aiding the queen in her personal and political intrigues. Madame de Chevreuse is friends with the oft-kidnapped **Madame Bonacieux**, who loves **d'Artagnan**. **Bazin** takes a letter written by Aramis to Madame de Chevreuse to warn the Queen of the plot against **George Villiers, the Duke of Buckingham**, as planned by the **Lady de Winter**.

Chicken Little

Sula
Toni Morrison

A neighborhood boy who dies accidentally while playing by the river with **Sula Peace** and **Nel**. The whites in positions of power consider the death of a black child to be of little consequence. Sula and Nel both attend Chicken Little's funeral. Nel sits silent, burdened with a heavy sense of guilt. Sula cries freely, but she feels no guilt.

Chicken Man

The Color of Water
James McBride

Part of the crew on "the corner." Chicken Man is endearing and intelligent, but he has done little with his life, wasting money and time on the corner drinking.

Mr. Chickering

A Prayer for Owen Meany
John Irving

The Little League coach who orders **Owen Meany** to bat for **John Wheelwright** in their final game. When he goes to the plate, Owen hits the foul ball that kills John's mother. Mr. Chickering blames himself and sobs at the funeral.

Chief accountant

Heart of Darkness
Joseph Conrad

An efficient worker with an incredible habit of dressing up in spotless whites and keeping himself absolutely tidy despite the squalor and heat of the Outer Station, where he lives and works.

Chief Elder

The Giver
Lois Lowry

The elected leader of **Jonas**'s community. She shows genuine affection for all of the children at the Ceremony of Twelve, knowing their names and an anecdote about each one. She skips Jonas when she is giving out Assignments, which causes distress for Jonas and the other children and families. However, she only does this because she is about to name Jonas as the Receiver, a very special position.

Chief surgeon

The Unbearable Lightness of Being
Milan Kundera

Tomas's boss at the hospital. Though he deeply respects Tomas's decision not to sign a denouncement of the article Tomas wrote criticizing the Czech Communists, he encourages Tomas to sign it, as it is the only way to salvage Tomas's career.

Chielo

Things Fall Apart
Chinua Achebe

A priestess in Umuofia who is dedicated to the Oracle of the goddess Agbala. Chielo is a widow with two children. She is good friends with **Ekwefi** and is fond of **Ezinma**, whom she calls "my daughter." At one point, she carries Ezinma on her back for miles in order to help purify her and appease the gods.

The Child

Six Characters in Search of an Author
Luigi Pirandello

A four-year-old girl dressed in white who does not speak. **The Stepdaughter** dotes on the Child out of remorse and pity, particularly in light of what she perceives as **the Mother**'s neglect. The Child's role is that of the fallen innocent, the Characters' drama demanding the elimination of the stepchildren and return to the original household. The child is found drowned in a fountain at the end of the play, which prompts **the Boy** to commit suicide.

Children of Ham

The Handmaid's Tale
Margaret Atwood

African Americans.

Roger Chillingworth

The Scarlet Letter
Nathaniel Hawthorne

Hester Prynne's husband in disguise. Chillingworth is much older than she is and had sent her to America while he settled his affairs in Europe. Because he is captured by Native Americans, he arrives in Boston belatedly and finds Hester and her illegitimate child being displayed on the scaffold. He lusts for revenge, and thus decides to stay in Boston despite his wife's betrayal and disgrace. He is a scholar and uses his knowledge to disguise himself as a doctor, intent on discovering and tormenting Hester's anonymous lover.

Lady Gertrude Chiltern

An Ideal Husband
Oscar Wilde

A woman of grave Greek beauty. Lady Chiltern embodies the Victorian new woman: upright, virtuous, educated, politically engaged, and active in her husband **Sir Robert Chiltern**'s career. She is the play's sentimental heroine, a moral absolutist who worships her ideal husband and cannot tolerate the revelation of his secret past.

Mabel Chiltern

An Ideal Husband
Oscar Wilde

Sir Robert Chiltern's younger sister, who is pretty in the English fashion. Mabel Chiltern embodies what Wilde describes as the "fascinating tyranny of youth" and "astonishing courage of innocence." Pert and clever, Mabel flirtatiously matches **Lord Goring**'s wit throughout the play. Their unconventional union upsets the other marriages and would-be engagements in the play.

Sir Robert Chiltern

An Ideal Husband
Oscar Wilde

The play's "tragic" hero, a government official who owes his success and fortune to secret scandal. Sir Robert Chiltern is a "personality of mark" with a manner of impeccable distinction. Love has driven him to hide his past in the desperate hope of remaining his wife's ideal husband. Conscious of the price of his success, Sir Robert has a decidedly nervous and harried temperament.

China

The Bluest Eye
Toni Morrison

One of the three local whores, along with **the Maginot Line**, also known as **Miss Marie** and **Poland**. China is skinny and sarcastic. They live above the Breedlove apartment and befriend **Pecola Breedlove**. These women cheerfully and unsentimentally hate men. They feel neither ashamed of nor victimized by their profession.

Ching

The Good Earth
Pearl S. Buck

Wang Lung's neighbor in the village. He later becomes Wang Lung's capable, faithful, and valued servant.

Chingachgook

The Last of the Mohicans
James Fenimore Cooper

Uncas's father and **Hawkeye**'s longtime friend; one of two surviving Mohican Native Americans. Mostly naked and covered in war paint, Chingachgook is also known as Le Gros Serpent ("Great Snake") for his crafty intelligence. He often stays awake and on watch all night, and still has the energy of a warrior during the day. He disguises himself as a beaver in order to deceive the chief of the Huron Indians. Chingachgook assists **Major Duncan Heyward**, **Cora Munro**, and **Alice Munro** when they are captured and threatened by Hurons. Chingachgook disappears for parts of *The Last of the Mohicans*, becoming an absent father figure to Uncas. When Uncas is killed, Chingachgook offers the song of a father for his fallen son.

Chiron

Titus Andronicus
William Shakespeare

Chiron and **Demetrius** are **Tamora**'s sons. The two brothers murder **Bassianus** and brutally rape and maim **Lavinia**. Nothing more than engines of lust, destruction, and depravity, they lack the wit and intelligence that make their coconspirator **Aaron** a more compelling villain. **Titus** kills the two for raping his daughter and has them cooked into pies and fed to their treacherous mother Tamora.

Chizu

Farewell to Manzanar
Jeanne Wakatsuki Houston

Woody's wife. Chizu is on the wharf with **Jeanne** and **Mama** when the news of the attack on Pearl Harbor is announced.

Aunt Chloe

Uncle Tom's Cabin
Harriet Beecher Stowe

Uncle Tom's wife and the cook for **Arthur Shelby** and **Emily Shelby**. Chloe often acts like a jovial simpleton around the Shelbys to mask her more complex feelings.

Chlomo

Night
Elie Wiesel

Eliezer's father. Chlomo is respected by the Jewish community in Sighet. The father and son desperately try to remain together throughout their ordeal. Chlomo is named only once, at the end of the memoir.

Lee Chong

Cannery Row
John Steinbeck

The Chinese grocer on Cannery Row. Despite his shrewd and occasionally manipulative business practices, Lee is good-hearted: he extends credit generously, tries to take care of the unfortunate, helps with the parties for **Doc**, and even arranged for his grandfather to be disinterred and reburied in his homeland.

Granpa Chook

The Power of One
Bryce Courtenay

Peekay's pet chicken, given to him as a gift from **Inkosi-Inkosikazi**. Granpa Chook is Peekay's only friend at the boarding school. He stands up for Peekay by defecating into **the Judge**'s open mouth while the Judge is trying to make Peekay eat human feces. Peekay is heartbroken when the Judge kills Granpa Chook by pelting him to death with stones.

Chorus of *Antigone*

Antigone 1946
Jean Anouilh

A single character who appears as narrator and commentator. The Chorus frames the play with a prologue and epilogue, introducing the action and characters under the sign of fatality. In presenting the tragedy, the Chorus instructs the audience on proper spectatorship, reappearing at the tragedy's pivotal moments to comment on the action or the nature of tragedy itself. Along with playing narrator, the Chorus also attempts to intercede throughout the play, whether on behalf of the Theban people or the horrified spectators.

Chorus of *Faustus*

Doctor Faustus
Christopher Marlowe

A single character outside the story who provides narration and commentary. Greek tragedies usually included a Chorus character.

Chorus of *Henry V*

Henry V
William Shakespeare

A single character who provides a prologue of the play's five acts as well as the epilogue. Like choruses in Greek drama, the Chorus in *Henry V* comments on the play's plot and themes, advancing the story all the while. The Chorus's general role is to fire the audience's imagination with strong, descriptive language that helps to overcome the visual limitations of the stage.

Chorus of *Romeo*

Romeo and Juliet
William Shakespeare

A character who functions as a narrator offering commentary on the play's plot and themes. The Chorus provides prologues for the first two acts of the play.

Chowig

Island of the Blue Dolphins
Scott O'Dell

Karana and **Ramo**'s father and the chief of the people of Ghalas-at at the beginning of the book. A strong and confident leader, Chowig is mistrustful of the Aleuts that come to Ghalas-at to hunt. He refuses to allow the Aleuts to take advantage of his people, and this, in the end, is his downfall, as he dies in a battle with the tribe.

Chris

Shane
Jack Schaefer

Initially one of **Fletcher**'s men, he begins escalating the situation with **Shane**. After Shane beats him up, Shane makes a comment about Chris's goodness but of his immaturity as well. When Chris offers to take Shane's place at **Bob Starrett**'s farm, we witness a man growing up and coming full circle.

Chris

Go Ask Alice
Anonymous

A hip girl **Alice** befriends. Chris accompanies Alice on her journey to San Francisco, and the two girls go on and off drugs together.

Baron Christian de Neuvillette

Cyrano de Bergerac
Edmond Rostand

A young cadet in love with **Roxane**. Christian is handsome but lacks wit and intelligence, so he has to have his love letters to Roxane ghost-written by **Cyrano de Bergerac**. Christian dies in battle.

Christine

Miss Julie
August Strindberg

A relatively minor character, Christine is the manor's cook and **Jean**'s fiancé. She gossips with Jean about **Miss Julie**, and believes wholeheartedly in the class system.

Christine

A Yellow Raft in Blue Water
Michael Dorris

Elgin Taylor's wife, **Rayona**'s mother and **Lecon** and his sister-in-law, **Clara**'s, biological daughter. Christine was raised as **Ida**'s daughter and grew up thinking of **Lee** as her brother. Christine is fickle in her youth, going from fearless to devoutly religious, but she loses her faith after an apocalyptic prophecy fails to come true. After her disillusionment with religion, Christine devotes her time to being popular and chasing boys. Christine is very protective of her brother, Lee, and always concerned for his welfare. She is self-sufficient, but is also hopelessly devoted to Elgin, Rayona's father. Christine tries to be a better mother to Rayona than Ida was to her but nonetheless engages in excessive partying and drinking that irreparably damages her liver and pancreas and eventually leads to her death.

Father Christmas

The Lion, the Witch, and the Wardrobe
C. S. Lewis

Also known as Santa Claus, he explains that Christmas has arrived in Narnia. He gives special tools to each of the children, as well as marvelous food and tea. He dashes off to bring Christmas to more people, animals, and creatures. With the arrival of Christmas, some of the sourness of **the White Witch**'s reign fades away.

Joe Christmas

Light in August
William Faulkner

A sullen, contemptuous man. Joe's father was black, but Joe looks white. He lives in Jefferson, Mississippi, where he works in a planing mill and brews illegal whiskey on the side. He murders his lover, **Joanna Burden**, shortly before the action of the novel begins.

Christopf

Bel Canto
Ann Patchett

Coss's accompanist. Much to Coss's dismay, Christopf declares his love for Coss on the plane ride to the South American country. She rejects his love, but he refuses to leave her side after they are taken captive, even when he grows deathly ill. A diabetic, he eventually dies from lack of insulin.

Christophe

Black Like Me
John Howard Griffin

A well-dressed black man who rides on **John Howard Griffin**'s bus during his trip through Mississippi. Christophe fawns over the white passengers, but acts cynical and condescending toward the blacks with whom he is forced to sit.

Christopher

No Longer at Ease
Chinua Achebe

A friend of **Obi**'s. Unlike **Joseph**, Christopher is educated. He is very much like Obi in terms of education, but is more pragmatic than Obi and less of an idealist. He believes he knows how to live in the Nigerian world of the late 1950s, and he thinks he understands the balance he must possess in order to live between two very different cultures.

Christophine

Wide Sargasso Sea
Jean Rhys

A servant given to **Annette** as a wedding present by her first husband, **Alexander Cosway**. Christophine, like her mistress, comes from Martinique and is therefore treated as an outsider by the Jamaican servant women. A wise and ageless figure, Christophine is loyal to both Annette and her daughter, and she exercises an unspoken authority within the household.

Chroma

The Phantom Tollbooth
Norton Juster

Conductor of the great color orchestra in the Forest of Sight, Chroma makes sure all the colors of the day are properly handled. When he decides to take a rest, **Milo** makes a mess of the colors of the day.

Chryseis

The Iliad
Homer

The daughter of **Chryses**, who is a priest of **Apollo** in a Trojan-allied town. **Agamemnon** takes Chryseis as a war prize at the beginning of *The Iliad*.

Chrysothemis

Electra
Sophocles

The younger daughter of **Clytemnestra** and **Agamemnon**. Although she recognizes her mother's corruption and understands the injustice of her father's murder, she refuses to mourn in the way that her sister, **Electra**, does. She realizes that she will gain the greatest benefits by siding with those in control.

Chucha

How the Garcia Girls Lost Their Accents
Julia Alvarez

The Garcia family's Haitian maid in the Dominican Republic. She practices voodoo and sleeps in a coffin.

Roy Church

In Cold Blood
Truman Capote

The oldest of **Alvin Dewey**'s KBI assistants. Church is nicknamed "Curly" and is supposedly the fastest draw in Kansas.

Soaphead Church

The Bluest Eye
Toni Morrison

A light-skinned West Indian misanthrope and self-declared "Reader, Adviser, and Interpreter of Dreams." Soaphead Church tells **Pecola Breedlove** that he will grant her wish to have blue eyes.

Frank Churchill

Emma
Jane Austen

Mr. Weston's son, considered a potential suitor for **Emma Woodhouse**. Frank lives at Enscombe with his aunt and uncle, the Churchills. Although Frank is attractive and charming, he is also irresponsible, deceitful, and rash.

Mrs. Churchill

Emma
Jane Austen

Mr. Weston's ailing former sister-in-law and **Frank Churchill**'s aunt and guardian. Mrs. Churchill is capricious, ill-tempered, and extremely possessive of Frank, who can only marry **Jane Fairfax** after his guardian's death.

Winston Churchill

The Remains of the Day
Kazuo Ishiguro

The prime minister of Britain during World War II. Mr. Churchill visited Darlington Hall on several occasions before he became prime minister.

Cicero

Julius Caesar
William Shakespeare

A Roman senator renowned for his oratorical skill. Cicero speaks at **Julius Caesar**'s triumphal parade. He later dies at the order of **Antony**, **Octavius**, and **Lepidus**.

Cico

Bless Me, Ultima
Rudolfo A. Anaya

One of **Antonio Márez**'s closer friends. Cico exposes Antonio to yet another belief system when he takes Antonio to see the golden carp, a pagan god who lives in the river.

Hiroshima
John Hersey

Father Cieslik

A Jesuit priest who helps the others get medical attention. He also locates the mother of the **the Kataoka children**.

The Libation Bearers
Aeschylus

Cilissa

Orestes's simple-minded nurse, who raised the hero from birth. Cilissa is loyal to Orestes and **Agamemnon** and loathes **Clytemnestra** for her treacheries. Cilissa helps Orestes succeed in his plan.

Homecoming
Cynthia Voigt

Cilla

Gram's sister and **Momma**'s aunt. Cilla writes cards to Momma every year. Momma drives to her house in Bridgeport, hoping she can help them.

The American
Henry James

Comte de Cintré

The rich, despicable old man whom **Claire de Bellegarde** was forced to marry at eighteen. Claire's mother, the **Marquise de Bellegarde**, selected the count for his fortune, pedigree, and willingness to accept a small dowry. Claire was repulsed when she first met the count, but by then the wedding arrangements had already been made. When the count died several years later, the exposé of his business practices so horrified Claire that she renounced all her claims to his money.

The Odyssey
Homer

Circe

The beautiful witch-goddess who transforms **Odysseus**'s crew into swine when he lands on her island. With **Hermes**'s help, Odysseus resists Circe's powers before becoming her lover and living in luxury at her side for a year.

Song of Solomon
Toni Morrison

Circe

A maid and midwife. She worked for the wealthy Butler family, who made their fortune off of killing poor, independent farmers like **Macon Dead I**. Circe delivers **Macon, Jr.** and **Pilate Dead**. Circe provides crucial information that reconnects **Milkman** with his family history. She tells him that the Butlers killed Macon Dead I, that Macon Dead I's body floated out of its grave and into the cave where Pilate and Macon, Jr. stayed.

Ulysses
James Joyce

The citizen

An older Irish patriot. A former national athlete, the citizen is belligerent and xenophobic.

Miss Drusilla Clack

The Moonstone
Wilkie Collins

Niece to **Lady Verinder**. An overly pious and falsely humble Christian, she belongs to many of **Godfrey Ablewhite**'s ladies' charities. Miss Clack's main interest is in the evilness of others, whom she attempts to save with the Christian pamphlets she carries with her. Miss Clack is capable of real venom toward those she doesn't like, such as **Rachel Verinder**.

John Claggart

Billy Budd, Sailor
Herman Melville

The master-at-arms of the H.M.S. *Bellipotent*, an office equivalent to chief of police onboard the ship. Behind his back, the crew refers to John Claggart with the derogatory nickname "Jemmy Legs." It is known that after entering the navy unusually late in life, Claggart rose through the ranks to attain his present position on the strength of his sobriety, deference to authority, and patriotism. However, his compliant exterior disguises a cruel and sinister streak. When Claggart's false allegation prompts **Billy** to strike him violently, Claggart has effectively coaxed Billy into abandoning his virtue and committing an evil deed.

Claire

The Maids
Jean Genet

Solange's younger sister. While she claims she loathes **Madame**, she is also quick to defend her, pointing out her kindness. Madame favors Claire, and Claire always plays the role of Madame when she and Solange dress up and roleplay their murderous fantasies.

Claire

Homecoming
Cynthia Voigt

One of the workers in **Will**'s circus. Claire has a nasty temper that at first intimidates the Tillermans but later rescues them from the dastardly **Rudyard**.

Sister Claire

Cyrano de Bergerac
Edmond Rostand

A nun of **Roxane**'s convent. She admires and respects **Cyrano de Bergerac**, so she allows him to visit whenever he wishes.

Clara

The House of the Spirits
Isabel Allende

Daughter of **Severo del Valle** and **Nivea del Valle**, sister of **Rosa the Beautiful**, wife of **Esteban Trueba**, mother of **Blanca**, **Jaime**, and **Nicolas**, grandmother of **Alba**. Clara quickly elects to be mute after seeing Rosa's autopsy, and thus witnessing her prediction of an accidental death in the family come true. The key female figure in *The House of the Spirits*, Clara is the connection between the Trueba and del Valle families. She is clairvoyant, barely aware of the material world, and only sporadically attentive to domestic chores, but she holds her family together through her love and predictions. Clara marries Esteban Trueba because she understands it is her fate. After he hits her she never talks to him again as long as they live, but she maintains a civil relationship with him, supporting his political life until her death. Clara's character changes very little as she grows from a young girl to an old woman. When she announces that she is going to die, Jaime looks for a way to cure her, but realizes that she is ready for death.

Clara

A Yellow Raft in Blue Water
Michael Dorris

Ida's aunt on her mother's side, who has an affair with her brother-in-law, **Lecon**, which results in the birth of **Christine**. Though Clara is Christine's biological mother, the family hides this fact to avoid disgrace. Ida assumes control of Christine's upbringing during the time Clara lives in Denver. When Clara returns to the reservation and attempts to take Christine away, Ida asserts her legal rights to the girl, and Clara leaves bitterly.

Clara

The English Patient
Michael Ondaatje

Hana's stepmother and **Patrick**'s wife. Clara does not appear in the novel as a character, but Hana thinks of her occasionally. Clara plays an important role in the novel because, to Hana, she symbolizes home, the place she has escaped from but the place to which she longs to return at the end of the novel.

Aunt Clara

Of Mice and Men
John Steinbeck

Lennie's aunt. Clara appears only at the end of the novel, as a vision chastising Lennie for causing trouble for **George**. She was a kind, patient woman who took good care of Lennie and gave him plenty of mice to pet.

Angel Clare

Tess of the d'Urbervilles
Thomas Hardy

An intelligent, freethinking young man who has decided to become a farmer to preserve his intellectual freedom from the pressures of city life. Angel's father, **Reverend Clare**, and his two brothers, **Reverend Cuthbert Clare** and **Reverend Felix Clare**, are respected clergymen, but Angel's religious doubts have kept him from joining the ministry. Angel meets **Tess Durbeyfield** when she is a milkmaid at the Talbothays Dairy and quickly falls in love with her. His love for Tess, his social inferior, is one expression of Angel's disdain for tradition. Angel awakens to the actual complexities of real-world morality after his failure in Brazil, and only then he realizes he has been unfair to Tess, whom he leaves after she tells him of her marred past with and pregnancy by **Alec d'Urberville**. By the time Angel comes to his senses and tries to retrieve Tess, she has finally been broken after trying to stay loyal to Angel. Alec causes Tess to abandon all hope and come with him, where she commits her final act in her complicated fall: Alec's murder. He promises Tess that he will look after **Eliza Louisa Durbeyfield** after Tess's death.

Reverend Cuthbert Clare

Tess of the d'Urbervilles
Thomas Hardy

Angel Clare's and **Reverend Felix Clare**'s brother. Reverend Cuthbert Clare is a classical scholar and dean at Cambridge. He can concentrate only on university matters, but does manage to marry **Mercy Chant**.

Reverend Felix Clare

Tess of the d'Urbervilles
Thomas Hardy

A village curate, and brother of **Angel Clare** and **Reverend Cuthbert Clare**, son of **Reverend Clare** and **Mrs. Clare**. Reverend Felix Clare, like his parson father and brother, stands in direct contrast to Angel's more progressive, godless thinking.

Mrs. Clare

Tess of the d'Urbervilles
Thomas Hardy

Angel Clare's, **Reverend Felix Clare**'s and **Reverend Cuthbert Clare**'s mother, the **Reverend Clare**'s wife. Mrs. Clare is a loving but snobbish woman who places great stock in social class. Mrs. Clare initially looks down on **Tess Durbeyfield** as a "simple" and impoverished girl, but later grows to appreciate her.

Reverend Clare

Tess of the d'Urbervilles
Thomas Hardy

Father of **Angel Clare**, **Reverend Felix Clare** and **Reverend Cuthbert Clare**. A somewhat intractable but principled clergyman in the town of Emminster, Mr. Clare considers it his duty to convert the populace. One of his most difficult cases proves to be none other than **Alec d'Urberville**, who is converted, but who then slips back into a life of evil after he is "tempted" for a second time in his life by **Tess d'Urberville**. While Angel has his time away from his new wife, Tess, Reverend Clare holds some money for Tess, but she does not want to appear a lowly peasant at the Clares' door, so she remains poor.

Clarence

A Connecticut Yankee in King Arthur's Court
Mark Twain

The Yankee's most trusted friend. Clarence begins as a friendly but fairly ignorant page who takes a liking to the Yankee and offers him aid. He responds magnificently to the Yankee's tutelage and, by the end of the story, becomes thoroughly indoctrinated in the manners, speech, skills, and ideology of the nineteenth-century United States. In the end, after the destruction of all of the nineteenth-century civilization that the Yankee built, Clarence puts the sleeping body of the Yankee, spellbound by **Merlin**, into a cave, where he sleeps for thirteen centuries.

George, Duke of Clarence

Henry VI, Part III and *Richard III*
William Shakespeare

Son of **Richard Plantagenet, Duke of York** and the **Duchess of York**; brother to **King Edward IV**, **King Richard III**, and **Edmund, Earl of Rutland**. When the battle for the throne of England is in full force between the Houses of York and Lancaster in *King Henry VI, Part III*, George is in France, and returns with reinforcements after his father's death. He joins Edward's struggle for the throne and is named the Duke of Clarence when Edward becomes king. Shortly after Edward declares his intention to marry **Lady Elizabeth Grey**, George breaks from his brother and follows the **Earl of Warwick** in joining **Queen Margaret** and **King Henry VI**'s side. He marries one of Warwick's daughters and helps the Lancaster army return to England and capture Edward, restoring Henry VI to the throne. Before the final battle, George is persuaded by his brothers to return to the Yorkist faction; after helping Edward's final ascent to the throne, he and his brothers stab **Prince Edward** in front of Margaret. George's flip-flopping between sides not only shows the turbulence of the times, but also reinforces the sea-waves metaphor Henry VI uses to describe the armies, buffeting this way and that. In *King Richard III*, however, George is nothing but a roadblock to his younger brother Richard's rise to power. Thanks to the hunchback's careful plotting, Edward IV has grown suspicious of George and sends him to be imprisoned in the Tower. Richard weeps as he says goodbye to his brother, but soon pays two murderers to kill him. George's ghost comes to haunt Richard and praise **Henry Tudor, Earl of Richmond** the night before the decisive battle between the two armies.

Thomas, Duke of Clarence

Henry IV, Part II and *Henry V*
William Shakespeare

Son of **King Henry IV**; brother of **King Henry V** (Prince Harry), **John, Duke of Lancaster**, and **Humphrey, Duke of Gloucester**. He enters *King Henry IV, Part II* toward the end, in time to bid farewell to his dying father and see Hal ascend to the throne as King Henry V. In *King Henry V*, Clarence mostly provides support for his older brother's campaign in France.

Clarice

Rebecca
Daphne du Maurier

The Heroine's maid.

Clarissa

The Rape of the Lock
Alexander Pope

A woman in attendance at the Hampton Court party. She lends **the Baron** the pair of scissors to cut **Belinda**'s hair and later delivers a moralizing lecture.

Uncle Clark

Black Boy
Richard Wright

A brother of **Ella Wright**'s who briefly houses **Richard Wright** after Ella gets sick. Clark is a just, upright man, if a bit strict. He seems genuinely concerned for Richard's welfare.

Winsome Clark

Jazz
Toni Morrison

A woman in Harlem whose letter falls into **Malvonne Edwards**'s hands. In a letter to her husband, Winsome spells out her suffering and loneliness. Her writing is later read by Malvonne, an anonymous, invisible, and benevolent observer who hopes to help Winsome in any way possible. As Malvonne reads the letters that her nephew stashed (for unexplained and mysterious reasons), she is able to flesh out the stories and reconfigure them.

Claudio of *Measure*

Measure for Measure
William Shakespeare

Isabella's brother. Claudio is sentenced to death by **Lord Angelo** for impregnating his common-law bride, **Juliet**.

Claudio of *Much Ado*

Much Ado About Nothing
William Shakespeare

A young soldier who has won great acclaim fighting under **Don Pedro** during the recent wars. Claudio falls in love with **Hero** upon his return to Messina and wins her hand when Don Pedro woos her on his behalf. Young and gullible, Claudio falls for **Don John**'s tricks twice: first, when he believes that Don Pedro seeks the hand of Hero for himself, and again, when he believes that Hero is unchaste. After the second trick, he publicly humiliates her at the wedding altar. When he realizes his mistake, he begs **Leonato**, Hero's father, for forgiveness, and agrees to marry Leonato's niece, obviously Hero in disguise. His suspicious nature makes him quick to believe evil rumors and hasty to despair and seek revenge.

Claudius

Hamlet
William Shakespeare

The King of Denmark, **Hamlet**'s uncle, **King Hamlet**'s brother, and the play's antagonist. Claudius is a calculating, ambitious politician driven by his sexual appetite and his lust for power. He sincerely loves **Queen Gertrude**, his new wife and the widow of King Hamlet.

Clif Clawson

Arrowsmith
Sinclair Lewis

The clown in **Martin Arrowsmith**'s class at medical school. Clif quits medical school and almost immediately becomes a fairly successful car salesman, implying that the step from doctor to salesman is unfortunately not very distant or difficult.

Cassius Clay

The Autobiography of Malcolm X
Malcolm X & Alex Haley

The world heavyweight boxing champion. Generous and understanding, Clay provides a place for **Malcolm X** to stay during the first days of Malcolm's split from the Nation of Islam.

Collis Clay

Tender Is the Night
F. Scott Fitzgerald

A young Yale graduate and acquaintance of **Rosemary Hoyt**'s. Collis gossips with **Dick Diver** about Rosemary and helps rescue Dick from an Italian prison when he ends up there after a drunken argument.

Henry Clay

Walden
Henry David Thoreau

A prominent Whig senator from Kentucky. Clay ran unsuccessfully for president on three occasions. He was a supporter of internal improvements as a part of his American System, and is well known as "the Great Compromiser" for his role in the Missouri Compromise and the Compromise of 1850. **Henry David Thoreau** was a staunch critic of Clay and of the expansionism that Clay advocated.

Mrs. Clay

Persuasion
Jane Austen

The daughter of **Mr. Shepard** (family advisor to **Sir Walter Elliot**). Mrs. Clay soon becomes **Elizabeth Elliot**'s friend. Though she is of much lower birth, freckled, and unattractive, Mrs. Clay is a well-mannered widow. **Anne Elliot**, however, sees danger in the way she endears herself to Sir Walter, and suspects she may seek to marry in a class far above her own.

Noah Claypole

Oliver Twist
Charles Dickens

A charity boy and **Mr. Sowerberry**'s apprentice. Noah is an overgrown, cowardly bully who mistreats **Oliver Twist** and eventually joins **Fagin**'s gang.

Vera Claythorne

And Then There Were None
Agatha Christie

A former governess who comes to Indian Island purportedly to serve as a secretary to **Mrs. Owen**. Vera wants to escape a past in which she killed a small boy in her care, **Cyril Hamilton**, so that the man she loved would inherit Cyril's estate. Although the coroner cleared her of blame, Vera's lover abandoned her. Vera is one of the most intelligent and capable characters in the novel, but she also suffers from attacks of hysteria, feels guilty about her crime, and reacts nervously to the uncanny events on the island.

Penelope Clearwater

The Harry Potter Series: Books 2 and 3
J. K. Rowling

Percy Weasley's girlfriend, a Ravenclaw prefect who has been turned to stone with fear by a spell cast upon her.

Isabel Clements

Pnin
Vladimir Nabokov

The daughter of the couple who rent a room to **Timofey Pnin**. After Isabel marries, her parents decide to rent out her bedroom, but her marriage ends and she soon comes to reclaim the room.

Joan Clements

Pnin
Vladimir Nabokov

The woman who, along with her husband **Laurence Clements**, rents a room to **Timofey Pnin**. At first Joan finds Pnin eccentric, but eventually she warms to him, especially after his wife treats him harshly.

Laurence Clements

Pnin
Vladimir Nabokov

The man who, along with his wife **Joan Clements**, rents a room to **Timofey Pnin**. Laurence distances himself from his boarder until he realizes that Pnin is a gold mine of inspiration for his Philosophy of Gesture course.

Cleomenes

The Winter's Tale
William Shakespeare

A lord of Sicilia, sent to Delphi to ask the oracle about **Hermione**'s guilt.

Cleon

Pericles
William Shakespeare

Governor of Tarsus and **Dionyza**'s husband. **Pericles** saves Tarsus from famine when he flees Tyre to protect Tyre from **Antiochus**'s attack. Later, Cleon pledges to take care of **Marina**, but Dionyza plots to kill her. Cleon claims to have been unaware of Dionyza's scheme, but is punished along with Dionyza at the end.

Cleopatra

Antony and Cleopatra
William Shakespeare

The queen of Egypt and **Antony**'s lover. A highly attractive woman who once seduced **Julius Caesar**, Cleopatra delights in the thought that she has caught Antony like a fish. In matters of love, as in all things, Cleopatra favors high drama: her emotions are as volatile as they are theatrical, and regardless of whether her audience is her handmaiden or the emperor of Rome, she always offers a top-notch performance. Although she tends to make a spectacle of her emotions, one cannot doubt the genuine nature of her love for Antony.

Gaston Cleric

My Ántonia
Willa Cather

Jim Burden's tutor at the university in Lincoln. Cleric eventually moves on to a teaching position at Harvard University and brings Jim along with him. His premature death from pneumonia has a powerful impact on Jim.

Henry Clerval

Frankenstein
Mary Shelley

Victor Frankenstein's boyhood friend. Clerval nurses Victor back to health in Ingolstadt. He is a cheerful, loyal man.

Emma Clery

A Portrait of the Artist as a Young Man
James Joyce

The Dublin girl who symbolizes feminine purity and untainted love to **Stephen Dedalus**. Because he has such trouble communicating with women, whom he either idealizes or reviles, Emma remains a shadowy figure throughout the novel.

Clevinger

Catch-22
Joseph Heller

An idealistic member of **John Yossarian**'s squadron. Clevinger believes in country, loyalty, and duty, and defends his beliefs to Yossarian.

Daddy Clidell

I Know Why the Caged Bird Sings
Maya Angelou

Vivian Baxter's second husband. She marries him after her children join her in California. Although **Maya Johnson** initially tries to dismiss him, Daddy Clidell becomes the only real "father" Maya knows. He combines the virtues of strength and tenderness and enjoys thinking of himself as Maya's father.

Lord Clifford

Henry VI, Part II
William Shakespeare

King Henry VI's elderly supporter and **Young Clifford**'s father. Using crowd-pleasing rhetoric and invoking the late **King Henry V**, Clifford convinces **Jack Cade**'s rebels to lay down their arms. When judging the **Duke of York**'s claim to the throne, Clifford declares him a traitor and trades barbs with York's son Richard, who later becomes **King Richard III**. When civil war breaks out, Clifford is slain by York at the Battle of St. Albans; Clifford's son decides he is finished with pity for any Yorkist after he finds his father's body.

Lord Clifford

Henry VI, Part II and *Henry VI, Part III*
William Shakespeare

The elder **Lord Clifford**'s son. After seeing his elderly father slain by **Richard Plantagenet, Duke of York** at the Battle of St. Albans in *King Henry VI, Part II*, Young Clifford resolves to be ruthless in battle with the Yorkists and to exact vengeance. Fiercely loyal to **Queen Margaret** and **King Henry VI**, Clifford makes good on his promise in *King Henry VI, Part III*. As war rages in England, Clifford kills York's son **Edmund, Earl of Rutland**, and then, along with Margaret, stabs York to death. York's son Richard (the future **King Richard III**) takes up the feud, but before the two can have a showdown, Clifford dies on the battlefield, shot in the neck by an arrow.

Martha Clifford

Ulysses
James Joyce

A woman with whom **Leopold Bloom** corresponds under the pseudonym Henry Flower. Martha's writing is full of spelling mistakes and hackneyed innuendo.

Geoffrey Clifton

The English Patient
Michael Ondaatje

A British explorer and **Katharine Clifton**'s husband. Geoffrey is a new addition to the group of explorers who are mapping the North African desert. Geoffrey seems to have everything going for him: an Oxford education, wealthy family connections, and a beautiful young wife. He is a proud and devoted husband, and enjoys praising his wife in front of the other explorers. Geoffrey claims to have come to North Africa purely out of an interest in exploration, but **Almásy** finds out that Geoffrey has been working for British Intelligence as an aerial photographer. Everyone seems to like Geoffrey, but Katharine, who knows him best, knows his capacity for extreme jealousy.

Katharine Clifton

The English Patient
Michael Ondaatje

An Oxford-educated woman and the wife of **Geoffrey Clifton**. One of the most mysterious characters in the novel, Katharine is never fully understood. We know that she married Geoffrey quite young and traveled with him to North Africa, and that she is an avid reader who learns all she can about Cairo and the desert. Though polite and genteel, Katharine nevertheless takes what she wants, assertively approaching **Almásy** and telling him that she wants him to "ravish her." Though Geoffrey is a devoted and kind husband, Katharine never seems remorseful about her affair with Almásy. Katharine's affair reveals her wild and dark side: she punches and stabs her lover, angry at him for refusing to change and daring the world to recognize their relationship.

Tod Clifton

Invisible Man
Ralph Ellison

A black member of the Brotherhood and a resident of Harlem. Tod Clifton is passionate, handsome, articulate, and intelligent. He eventually parts ways with the Brotherhood, though it remains unclear whether a falling-out has taken place, or whether he has simply become disillusioned with the group. He begins selling Sambo dolls on the street, seemingly both perpetrating and mocking the offensive stereotype of the lazy and servile slave that the dolls represent.

Clitandre

The Misanthrope
Molière

Another marquis chasing **Célimène**'s love. He may be able to help Célimène in a lawsuit. Ultimately, Clitandre has enough pride and confidence to give up on Célimène when she insults him.

Clive

Cloud Nine
Caryl Churchill

The first act's protagonist, Clive seems to be the model British aristocrat. He puts patriotism and decorum above all else, and expects those that depend on him to behave according to his will. Clive refuses to compromise in his belief that sexual roles are clearly defined: he expects his gay son **Edward** to be masculine and repeatedly derides women for their weakness. Almost daily, Clive struggles to keep his family proper and intact. He is a racist who believes the African natives are "savages" that can only be tamed by his firm British discipline. Although his principles may seem clear, Clive does engage in an affair with **Mrs. Saunders**, breaking the standard of fidelity that he tries to impose upon his wife **Betty**. He also firmly believes that he has converted his black servant **Joshua** (who is actually played by a white man) into a loyal servant, but Joshua attempts to shoot Clive at the end of the first act.

Paddy Clohessy

Angela's Ashes
Frank McCourt

A school friend of **Frank McCourt**'s who lives in unbearable squalor as a child. Paddy eventually moves to England to earn money for his family.

Clorinda

Orlando
Virginia Woolf

One of the first women **Orlando** dated when he was a member of King James's court. Clorinda was a sweet, gentle lady whose religiosity came to sicken Orlando.

Cloten

Cymbeline
William Shakespeare

The **Queen**'s son. Cloten, who is an arrogant, clumsy fool, was betrothed to **Imogen** before her secret wedding to **Posthumus**.

Clov

Endgame
Samuel Beckett

Clov is one of the two protagonists of the play, the servant to **Hamm** despite his own infirmity. He was taken in by Hamm as a child, and the play's tension pits Clov's desire to leave against his obligation to stay with the blind and paraplegic Hamm.

Clover

Animal Farm
George Orwell

A good-hearted female cart-horse. Like **Boxer**, Clover is devoted to the Farm and not very quick-witted. Though she often suspects the pigs of violating the Seven Commandments, she has neither the memory nor the reasoning to realize the Commandments have been altered and so remains loyal.

Clover

Watership Down
Richard Adams

The first doe to bear a litter in the new warren. Clover is one of the hutch rabbits that **Hazel** decides to set free from the barn. She adjusts to the wild life better than any of the others, and she mates with **Speedwell.**

Clown of *Antony*

Antony and Cleopatra
William Shakespeare

An Egyptian who brings a basket of figs containing poisonous snakes to **Cleopatra**.

Clown of *Faustus*

Doctor Faustus
Christopher Marlowe

Wagner's servant. The clown's ridiculous antics provide comic relief and contrast with **Faustus**'s notions of grandeur. As the play progresses, Faustus begins to resemble the clown in some ways.

Clown of *Othello*

Othello
William Shakespeare

Othello's servant. Although the clown appears only in two short scenes, his appearances reflect and distort the action and words of the main plots: his puns on the word "lie" in Act III, scene iv, for example, anticipate **Othello**'s confusion of the two meanings of that word in Act IV, scene i.

Clown of *Winter's Tale*

The Winter's Tale
William Shakespeare

The **Shepherd**'s buffoonish son, and **Perdita**'s adopted brother.

Bonnie Clutter

In Cold Blood
Truman Capote

Herbert Clutter's wife. She cannot keep up with Herbert's public image as a leader, and she withdraws into the home. Suffering from depressive disorders, she spends a great deal of time in bed. She is murdered by **Richard Eugene Hickock** and **Perry Edward Smith**.

Herbert Clutter

In Cold Blood
Truman Capote

The father of the Clutter family. His wife is **Bonnie Clutter**, and he has four children: two older daughters who have moved out, **Nancy Clutter**, and **Kenyon Clutter**. His large property, River Valley Farm, keeps him moderately wealthy. Starting with little, he has built up a large, successful farm. Clutter is a community leader, involved with many organizations. Herbert, Bonnie, Nancy, and Kenyon are murdered by **Richard Eugene Hickock** and **Perry Edward Smith**.

Kenyon Clutter

In Cold Blood
Truman Capote

An awkward teenager, Kenyon loves to tinker with carpentry and machines. He is murdered by **Richard Eugene Hickock** and **Perry Edward Smith**.

Nancy Clutter

In Cold Blood
Truman Capote

Along with **Kenyon Clutter**, one of the two youngest Clutter children. They both still live at home. She is "the darling" of the town, a class president and future prom queen. Like her father, she is very organized. She is murdered by **Richard Eugene Hickock** and **Perry Edward Smith**.

Albert Cluveau

The Autobiography of Miss Jane Pittman
Ernest J. Gaines

An old white Cajun man who fishes near **Miss Jane Pittman**'s cabin each day and who shoots **Ned Douglass**, killing him. Cluveau's willingness to do so reveals him as a coward. He is willing to follow the orders of the higher-ranking whites in order to gain their acceptance. After Cluveau believes Jane has cursed him, his status as a weak coward becomes more obvious; he fears going to hell so much that he beats his innocent daughter.

Roger Cly

A Tale of Two Cities
Charles Dickens

A British spy. Cly swears that patriotism alone inspires all of his actions. He feigns honesty but constantly participates in conniving schemes.

Judith Clyde

Pnin
Vladimir Nabokov

A member of the Cremona Women's Club, who invites **Timofey Pnin** to speak on a timely topic: "Are the Russian People Communist?"

Frances Clyne

The Sun Also Rises
Ernest Hemingway

The forceful, controlling girlfriend of the American writer **Robert Cohn**. A manipulative status-seeker, Frances persuaded Cohn to move to Paris. As her looks begin to fade, she becomes increasingly possessive and jealous and her relationship with Cohn falls apart.

Clytemnestra

Agamemnon and *The Libation Bearers*
Aeschylus

The Queen of Argos, the sister of **Helen** of Troy, and once the wife of **Agamemnon**, whom she plotted to murder, presumably to avenge his sacrifice of their daughter **Iphigenia** ten years earlier. After carrying out this murder upon her husband's return from the Trojan War, Clytemnestra rules Argos with her lover and coconspirator, **Aegisthus**. She despises her eldest daughter, **Electra**, who in turn longs to punish Clytemnestra and calls on her brother, **Orestes**, to enact this revenge. Despite Electra's unflattering portrayal of her, Clytemnestra is not an altogether unsympathetic character. Strong and intelligent, she is a fiercely protective mother who maintains that she killed Agammemnon not to be with Aegisthus, but to avenge the unnecessary sacrifice of Iphigenia. In the end, Orestes kills his mother and her lover and so ends the cyclical torments of the House of **Atreus**.

Clytemnestra

Electra
Sophocles

See above.

Clytemnestra

The Flies
Jean-Paul Sartre

Previously Agamemnon's wife, Clytemnestra is now married to **Aegistheus**, whom the queen has helped to maintain an atmosphere of remorse. Clytemnestra hates her daughter **Electra** and does not attempt to protect her from Aegistheus. In her silent approval of the king's policies and her complicity in his murder of the rightful king, Clytemnestra represents the Vichy government of France, which collaborated with the Nazi conquerors.

Cobweb

A Midsummer Night's Dream
William Shakespeare

One of four fairies, along with **Mote**, **Mustardseed**, and **Peaseblossom**, whom **Titania** orders to attend to **Bottom** after she falls in love with him.

Brian Cochran

The Chocolate War
Robert Cormier

The Trinity School treasurer who keeps **Brother Leon** informed of the sales figures of the chocolate.

Gwen Cockerell

Pnin
Vladimir Nabokov

The wife of **Jack Cockerell**, head of the English department. Gwen listens to Jack's impersonations of **Timofey Pnin** and seems to authentically enjoy her husband's mimicry.

Jack Cockerell

Pnin
Vladimir Nabokov

The head of the English department, an agitated, nervous, chattering magpie of a man. Jack is dubiously renowned for his lengthy impressions of **Timofey Pnin**.

Major Cody

Dead Man Walking
Helen Prejean

The man responsible for the death house. Despite his opposition to the death penalty, Major Cody plays an important role in each execution, a fact that torments him.

Hubert Coffee

All the King's Men
Robert Penn Warren

A slimy **MacMurfee** employee who tries to bribe **Adam Stanton** into giving the hospital contract to **Gummy Larson**.

Jan Coggan

Far from the Madding Crowd
Thomas Hardy

A farm laborer and friend of **Gabriel Oak**'s. Jan Coggan works on **Bathsheba Everdene**'s farm with Gabriel. When **Fanny Robin** dies, **Joseph Poorgrass** is entrusted with the task of transporting Fanny's body from Casterbridge to Weatherbury. However, Coggan and company detain Poorgrass at Buck's Head. Coggan convinces Poorgrass to stay later and later, delaying the return of the body to Bathsheba's farm.

Bella Cohen

Ulysses
James Joyce

A large, conniving brothel madam. One of her customers pays her son's Oxford tuition.

Genghis Cohen

The Crying of Lot 49
Thomas Pynchon

A character hired by the stamp expert **Oedipa Maas** to go through **Pierce Inverarity**'s extensive stamp collection in order to appraise it. Genghis provides some more clues to help Oedipa solve the Tristero mystery.

Robert Cohn

The Sun Also Rises
Ernest Hemingway

A wealthy American writer living in Paris. Cohn often feels like an outsider among his peers because he is Jewish, and because he is not a World War I veteran. Indeed, the narrator, **Jake Barnes**, and his friends often seize on these differences and treat Cohn with cruel and petty antagonism. During his Princeton years, Cohn took up boxing to combat his insecurities, and it is clear that physical confrontation is still one of his preferred methods of resolving differences. He is in a relationship with **Frances Clyne** at the beginning of the novel, but his attentions soon turn to the socialite **Lady Brett Ashley**, whose fickleness and promiscuity wound him. Unlike most of the other characters, Cohn holds on to romantic prewar ideals of love and fair play—values that seem tragically absurd in the devastating aftermath of World War I.

Roy Cohn

Angels in America
Tony Kushner

A famous New York lawyer and powerbroker whom Kushner adapted for his play. Roy is the play's most vicious and disturbing character, a closeted homosexual who disavows other gays and cares only about amassing clout. His lack of ethics led him to illegally intervene in the espionage trial of **Ethel Rosenberg,** which resulted in her execution. He is forgiven (though not exonerated) in the play's moral climax, after his death from AIDS unwittingly reconnects him to the gay community from which he always distanced himself.

Mr. Coldfield

Absalom, Absalom!
William Faulkner

A middle-class Methodist merchant and father of **Ellen Coldfield Sutpen** and **Rosa Coldfield**.

Rosa Coldfield

Absalom, Absalom!
William Faulkner

Ellen Coldfield's much younger sister, younger aunt of **Henry Sutpen** and **Judith Sutpen**. Briefly engaged to Thomas Sutpen following Ellen's death, Rosa leaves him after he insults her, and spends the rest of her life as a bitter spinster, obsessed with her anger and hatred of Thomas Sutpen. She tells the Sutpens' story to **Quentin Compson**.

Berkeley Cole

Out of Africa
Isak Dinesen

Good friends with **the narrator**. Berkeley is an innately aristocratic man who helps the narrator develop fine tastes. He, like **Denys Finch-Hatton**, possesses a level of gentility that allows him to easily transcend cultural differences. He can speak Masai and gets along well with most natives. Though a gentle man with a good heart, he frequently acts as a jokester or a buffoon. Berkeley's desire to always enjoy life ultimately leads to his death.

All the Pretty Horses
Cormac McCarthy

John Grady Cole

The sixteen-year-old protagonist. Laconic and pensive, John Grady Cole is prematurely aged. He lives his life according to a strict, almost ritualistic code, valuing honor, intelligence, responsibility, justice, loyalty, and skill. He loves horses and is preternaturally gifted with them. The novel follows Cole's journey south, from the Texas ranch where he grew up into Mexico.

All the Pretty Horses
Cormac McCarthy

John Grady Cole's father

The nameless father of **John Grady Cole**. He is dying at the beginning of the novel, possibly of lung cancer. A prisoner of war during World War II, he returned a changed man and never reunited with **John Grady's mother**, a flighty, promiscuous woman who ran off to become an actress. He is a lonely, silent man.

All the Pretty Horses
Cormac McCarthy

John Grady Cole's mother

The nameless mother of **John Grady Cole**. She appears briefly in the opening pages of the novel. Flighty and promiscuous, she has divorced **John Grady's father**.

Emma
Jane Austen

Mr. and Mrs. Cole

Tradespeople and longtime residents of Highbury whose good fortune of the past several years has led them to adopt a luxurious lifestyle only a notch below that of the Woodhouses. Offended by their attempt to transcend their "only moderately genteel" social status, **Emma Woodhouse** has long been preparing to turn down any dinner invitation from the Coles to teach them the folly of thinking they can interact socially with the Woodhouses. Like the Martins, the Coles are the means through which Emma demonstrates her class consciousness.

I Never Promised You a Rose Garden
Joanne Greenberg

The Collect

The Collect is the chorus of voices that constantly criticize **Deborah** in Yr. The Collect represents all the teachers, peers, and neighbors who abused and insulted Deborah throughout her childhood and adolescence.

Anthem
Ayn Rand

Collective 0-0009

The leader of the World Council of Scholars. Collective 0-0009 is shapeless and cowardly, like all members of the World Council. He fears and hates **Equality 7-2521** for breaking the rules because he believes that only those decisions reached collectively by the council can be of value. Collective 0-0009 represents the thinking force behind the evil collectivism of the unnamed city.

Jermone Collet

The Da Vinci Code
Dan Brown

An agent with the Judicial Police. In some ways the classic bumbling police officer, Collet commits various errors during the pursuit of **Sophie Neveu** and **Robert Langdon**. Jerome's missteps contrast with **Bezu Fache**'s efficiency. He believes in Sophie's innocence, however, and proves himself to Fache in the end.

Collie

White Fang
Jack London

A dog at **Judge Scott**'s and **Weedon Scott**'s home. Collie does not trust **White Fang** at first because she is a sheep dog and he is a wolf dog, but he works his way into her confidence, and they become mates.

John Collins

The Autobiography of Benjamin Franklin
Benjamin Franklin

Benjamin Franklin's Boston friend, a "bookish lad." The two practice their debating skills, first in Boston and later via letters. Collins becomes an alcoholic, and his relationship with Franklin turns sour on a boat trip when Franklin throws Collins overboard. Collins moves to Barbados and never repays Franklin a large loan.

Mr. Collins

Pride and Prejudice
Jane Austen

The pompous, semi-idiotic clergyman, both snobbish and obsequious, who stands to inherit **Mr. Bennet**'s property. While Mr. Collins's social status is nothing to brag about, he takes great pains to let everyone and anyone know that **Lady Catherine de Bourgh** serves as his patroness.

Billy Colman

Where the Red Fern Grows
Wilson Rawls

The protagonist of *Where the Red Fern Grows*. At the start of the novel, he is ten years old. Billy wants a dog badly and saves up for two hounds he sees in a catalog. He names the dogs **Old Dan** and **Little Ann**, and they become excellent coon-hunting dogs who win competitions. Billy is often praying for help and receiving it, which strengthens his faith. In the scuffle between Billy, **Rainie Pritchard**, **Ruben Pritchard**, Little Ann, Old Dan, and the Pritchard's dog, Old Blue, Billy saves his dogs, but Ruben falls on his own axe and dies. Billy comes to terms with Ruben's death after he puts some dried flowers on Ruben's grave. After the mountain-lion causes Old Dan's death, Billy is heartbroken. Little Ann dies soon afterward, and it is only seeing a red fern growing on the dogs' grave that brings Billy to accept their death.

Chava Colon

Dead Man Walking
Helen Prejean

Sister Helen Prejean's friend from the Prison Coalition who first invites Prejean to work with death-row inmates.

Colonel

The Awakening
Kate Chopin

Edna Pontellier's father. A former Confederate officer in the Civil War, the Colonel is a strict Protestant who believes that husbands should manage their wives with authority and coercion. Edna is not very close with the Colonel, who retains a certain military air from his war days. She takes him to **Adèle Ratignolle**'s *soirée musicale*, where Adèle enchants the Colonel by being flirtatious and flattering. Edna takes delight in serving her father hand and foot, appreciating their companionship but realizing that her interest in him will likely fade. However, in the time that the Colonel is there, Edna acts nothing like the distressed and wayward woman that **Léonce** makes her out to be to **Doctor Mandelet**. When Doctor Mandelet comes to dinner at the Pontellier home, he notices nothing in Edna's behavior to arouse concern. When Edna refuses to attend Janet's wedding in New York, the Colonel criticizes Léonce for his lack of control over Edna.

Colonel

The Chairs
Eugène Ionesco

A famous soldier and the second invisible guest of the **Old Woman** and the **Old Man**. The Old Woman rebukes him for spilling his cigarettes on the floor, though she is also taken with his grandness, as is the Old Man with his prestige. The Colonel makes inappropriate advances toward the **Lady**.

Cominius

Coriolanus
William Shakespeare

A patrician and a former consul. Cominius is a friend to **Coriolanus** and one of the generals who leads the Roman army against the Volscians.

The Commander

The Handmaid's Tale
Margaret Atwood

The head of the household where **Offred** lives. Although he was involved in establishing the regime of the **Republic of Gilead**, the Commander is a sympathetic figure. He is kind to Offred and recognizes that Gilead has problems.

Commanders of the Faithful

The Handmaid's Tale
Margaret Atwood

Male members of the elite of the **Republic of Gilead**.

Commissioner of Public Safety

Lysistrata
Aristophanes

Nominally the head of security and law in Athens. He is so overwhelmed by the women that he ends up dressed as a woman himself. **Lysistrata** has a lengthy conversation with the dense Commissioner about the future of Athens and peace in the region.

The Common Man

A Man for All Seasons
Robert Bolt

The occasional narrator of the play. The Common Man plays the roles of most of the lower-class characters: **More**'s steward Matthew, the boatman, the publican (innkeeper), the jailer, the jury foreman, and the headsman (executioner). The Common Man personifies attitudes and actions that are common to everyone, but he is also "common" in that he is ignoble.

Compeyson

Great Expectations
Charles Dickens

A criminal and the former partner of **Magwitch**. Compeyson is an educated, gentlemanly outlaw who left **Miss Havisham** at the altar.

Jason Compson III

The Sound and the Fury
William Faulkner

The head of the Compson household until his death from alcoholism in 1912.

Jason Compson IV

The Sound and the Fury
William Faulkner

The second-youngest of the Compson children and the narrator of the novel's third chapter. Jason is mean-spirited, petty, and cynical.

Benjy Compson

The Sound and the Fury
William Faulkner

The youngest of the Compson children and the narrator of the novel's first chapter. Benjy is severely retarded.

Caddy Compson

The Sound and the Fury
William Faulkner

The second-oldest of the Compson children and the only daughter. Actually named Candace, Caddy is very close to her brother **Quentin**. She becomes promiscuous, gets pregnant out of wedlock, and eventually marries and divorces **Herbert Head** in 1910.

Caroline Compson

The Sound and the Fury
William Faulkner

Mr. Compson's wife and mother of the four Compson children. Mrs. Compson is a self-pitying, self-absorbed hypochondriac who does not pay attention to her children.

General Compson

Go Down, Moses
William Faulkner

The old Civil War general and Jefferson aristocrat who goes on the hunting expeditions. Also the ancestor of important characters in *Absalom, Absalom!* and *The Sound and the Fury*.

General Compson

Absalom, Absalom!
William Faulkner

Quentin Compson's grandfather and **Thomas Sutpen**'s first friend in Yoknapatawpha County. A Brigadier General for the Confederacy during the Civil War and a distinguished citizen of Jefferson, Mississippi.

Mr. Compson

Absalom, Absalom!
William Faulkner

Quentin Compson's father and **General Compson**'s son, a man who believes in the power of fate to destroy human lives. He relays to Quentin many of the stories he heard from his father about Thomas Sutpen.

Mrs. Compson

The Unvanquished
William Faulkner

A respectable lady of Jefferson who, along with **Mrs. Habersham**, meddles in **Drusilla**'s affairs. She represents the hypocritical, vindictive side of southern womanhood, more concerned with appearances than with truth or real kindness.

Quentin Compson

Absalom, Absalom! and *The Sound and the Fury*
William Faulkner

The oldest of the Compson children and the narrator of *The Sound and the Fury*'s second chapter. A sensitive and intelligent boy, Quentin is preoccupied with his love for his sister **Caddy** and his notion of the Compson family's honor. He commits suicide by drowning himself just before the end of his first year at Harvard. In *Absalom, Absalom!* **Rosa Coldfield** tells him the story of the Sutpens.

Comte de Forcheville

Swann's Way
Marcel Proust

Odette's other lover, who insults and mocks **Charles Swann** one night at the **Verdurins**'.

Christopher Coney

The Mayor of Casterbridge
Thomas Hardy

A peasant in Casterbridge. Coney represents the bleak reality of peasant life. With their colorful dialect, the crew of **Nance Mockridge** and Coney lighten the tone of Thomas Hardy's tragedy. They also serve as a Greek chorus, in that they appear on the scene to judge the action of the primary characters and comment on the world at large.

Walden
Henry David Thoreau

Confucius

A Chinese sage of the sixth century B.C., known for his sayings and parables collected under the title *Analects*. His teachings gave rise to a sort of secular religion known as Confucianism, which served as a model for the Chinese government in subsequent centuries. Confucius also had a significant effect on the Transcendentalist movement and was one of **Henry David Thoreau**'s favorite authors.

The Red Badge of Courage
Stephen Crane

Jim Conklin

Henry Fleming's friend; a tall soldier hurt during the regiment's first battle. Jim soon dies from his wounds and represents, in the early part of the novel, an important moral contrast to Henry.

Ragtime
E. L. Doctorow

Willie Conklin

Obnoxious and mean, fire chief Conklin acts hostilely toward **Coalhouse** and is soon forced out of New Rochelle.

The Virgin Suicides
Jeffrey Eugenides

Joe Hill Conley

The practical joker who makes farting noises at school assemblies and still wins all the school prizes. **Trip Fontaine** chooses Conley to join the Homecoming coalition, hoping that his academic success will impress **Mr. Lisbon**. On Homecoming, Conley is paired with **Bonnie Lisbon**.

A Portrait of the Artist as a Young Man
James Joyce

Father Conmee

A rector.

This Side of Paradise
F. Scott Fitzgerald

Alec Connage

One of **Amory Blaine**'s close friends at Princeton and the older brother of **Rosalind Connage**, Amory's major love interest in the novel. After World War I, Amory meets Alec in Atlantic City, where they lament the loss of several mutual friends in the war. Later that night, Amory takes the blame when Alec is caught with a woman in his hotel room—technically a crime, because they are not married. Amory's sacrifice for Alec is an important step in his development, and he takes it despite his awareness that it may affect their friendship negatively.

This Side of Paradise
F. Scott Fitzgerald

Rosalind Connage

Alec Connage's debutante younger sister, with whom **Amory Blaine** has a brief but intense love affair. The two fall deeply in love, but Amory, because of his family's poor investments, has little money, and Rosalind does not wish to marry into poverty. Despite Amory's best efforts to earn money at an advertising agency, Rosalind breaks off their engagement in order to marry the wealthier **Dawson Ryder**. The devastated Amory goes on a three-week drinking binge, which is finally terminated by the advent of Prohibition. Ultimately, Amory abandons women as a source of inspiration.

Harrison C. Conners

Cat's Cradle
Kurt Vonnegut

The handsome husband of **Angela Hoenikker**. A scientist involved in top-secret weapons research for the U.S. government, Conners married Angela in return for a piece of *ice-nine*, which he gave to the United States' weapons arsenal. Angela's bargain did not bring her the happiness she sought: Harrison often returned home late at night, covered in lipstick.

Connie

The Grapes of Wrath
John Steinbeck

Rose of Sharon's husband. Connie is an unrealistic dreamer who abandons the Joads after they reach California. His selfishness and immaturity surprise no one but his naïve wife.

Connie

Tuesdays with Morrie
Mitch Albom

Morrie Schwartz's home health aide who is always there to assist Morrie in going to the bathroom, getting into his chair, and eating his meals.

Phil Connor

The Jungle
Upton Sinclair

Ona Lukoszaite's boss at the factory. A bullying, depraved man, Connor harasses and eventually rapes Ona. His many connections with Chicago politicians, criminals, and businessmen enable him to ruin **Jurgis**'s life. Connor embodies the moral corruption that comes with too much power.

Conrad

Much Ado About Nothing
William Shakespeare

One of **Don John**'s intimate, devoted associates. He conspires with Don John and **Borachio** to bring disaster to the court. He is apprehended by the watch when Borachio tells him of the plot's success.

Gabriel Conroy

Dubliners
James Joyce

A moderately successful writer and teacher, the protagonist of "The Dead." He is the sole character in *Dubliners* to voice his unhappiness with life in Ireland. When Gabriel realizes that his wife has been thinking of a young man, **Michael Furey**, at the very moment when he was thinking of her alone, he experiences an agonizing moment of shame followed by the realization that no human being can ever truly know another.

Gretta Conroy

Dubliners
James Joyce

Gabriel Conroy's wife in "The Dead." When Gretta hears the song "The Lass of Aughrim," she remembers her old lover, **Michael Furey**, who used to sing the same song. Gretta plays a relatively minor role in the story until the conclusion, when she describes the tragedy of her childhood love to Gabriel. Gretta's loyalty to Michael Furey unnerves Gabriel and generates his despairing thoughts about life and death.

Constable of France

Henry V
William Shakespeare

A French nobleman and military leader. Like the **Dauphin** and the other French nobles, the Constable does not take the English seriously. Instead of preparing for battle, he mocks the English and comments on how easy the battle will be. For much of the play, the French are shown in a poor light, as decadent, derisive schoolboys rather than warriors. Only when they face defeat at the Battle of Agincourt do they show any honor, promising to rush back into battle lest they face shame. The Constable is killed during the Battle of Agincourt.

Constance

King John
William Shakespeare

Arthur's mother, who champions his right to the throne and secures French support. One of the more vocal opponents to **King John**'s ascension to the throne, she and **Eleanor** exchange insults and vie for Arthur's favor. After **King Philip** and King John agree to an alliance through the political marriage of the dauphin **Lewis** and **Blanche**, the daughter of the King of Spain, Constance bemoans Philip's inconstancy and the loss of her son's land, which will soon be Lewis's. She mourns her fortune and curses the marriage; following **Cardinal Pandulph**'s call for the split between France and England, she urges France on to war once more. She is undone, however, and dies shortly after the English capture Arthur. With violent and powerful unladylike rhetoric, Constance successfully gains a war for her son's right. However, she loses the thing most dear to her, and symbolizes the megalomaniacal discord that would strangle England.

Constantin

The Bell Jar
Sylvia Plath

A man who takes **Esther Greenwood** on a date. Handsome, thoughtful, and accomplished, he seems sexually uninterested in Esther, who is willing to let him seduce her. Esther and Constantin sleep together as Esther thinks about what it would be like to be married.

Dr. Constantine

Murder on the Orient Express
Agatha Christie

The coroner aboard the Orient Express. Dr. Constantine is often **Hercule Poirot** or **M. Bouc**'s sidekick and is present for most of the evidence-gathering. Dr. Constantine examines **Ratchett**'s body and determines when he could have been killed.

Convict

Hound of the Baskervilles
Sir Arthur Conan Doyle

A murderous villain whose crimes defy description. The convict is nonetheless humanized when he is revealed to be **Mrs. Eliza Barrymore**'s brother. He has a rodent-like, haggardly appearance. His only wish is to flee his persecutors in Devonshire and escape to South America.

Dan Conway

Atlas Shrugged
Ayn Rand

The owner of the Phoenix-Durango Railroad Line in Colorado. Dan Conway disappears after **James Taggart** uses his influence to destroy Conway's railroad with the Anti-dog-eat-dog Rule. The rule is designed to reduce competition among railroads.

Dodo Conway

The Bell Jar
Sylvia Plath

Esther Greenwood and **Mrs. Greenwood**'s neighbor. Dodo is a Catholic woman with six children and a seventh on the way. She lives unconventionally but everyone likes her.

Mr. Cooger

Something Wicked This Way Comes
Ray Bradbury

Along with **Mr. Dark**, the man in charge of the carnival. He is pure evil, and he pretends to be **Miss Foley**'s nephew **Robert** in order to get her to ride on the carousel. Mr. Cooger also tries to get **James Nightshade** to ride on the merry-go-round, but he is thwarted by **William Halloway**. Although he is dangerous and cunning, Mr. Cooger is basically neutralized when Will damages his carousel.

Cook

Alice in Wonderland
Lewis Carroll

The **Duchess**'s servant. The Cook makes soup with vast amounts of pepper and then hurls pots and dishes at the Duchess and her baby.

Cook

Mother Courage
Bertolt Brecht

The **Chaplain**'s rival for **Mother Courage**'s affections and bread. The Cook is an aging Don Juan, a bachelor long past his prime. Darkly ironic, he is all too aware of the war as a continuation of business as usual, continually unmasking the divinely inspired military campaign as another massive profit scheme.

Al Cook

Pnin
Vladimir Nabokov

A Russian liberal who fled the Russian Revolution. The parents of Al's wife bequeathed The Pines to them, and they host Russian academics there during alternate summers. Their guests lounge through the summer, playing croquet and discussing intellectual and literary matters.

Alas, Babylon
Pat Frank

Alice Cooksey

The Fort Repose librarian, and **Florence Wechek**'s best friend.

I Know Why the Caged Bird Sings
Maya Angelou

Cool Clyde

One of **Daddy Clidell**'s con-men friends. These men teach **Maya Johnson** that it is possible to use white prejudice to gain advantage over whites. They represent creativity and the ethics that result from necessity and desperation. The other con-men are **Just Black**, **Tight Coat**, **Red Leg Daddy**, **Stonewall Jimmy**, and **Spots**.

Pudd'nhead Wilson
Mark Twain

Widow Cooper

Known to the town of Dawson's Landing as Aunt Patsy. The Widow Cooper takes in the twins, **Luigi Capello** and **Angelo Capello**, as boarders. She and her daughter **Rowena** fan the flames of the twins' celebrity for their own benefit. Everyone is at her house when the string of robberies takes place.

The Heart Is a Lonely Hunter
Carson McCullers

Dr. Benedict Mady Copeland

An aging black doctor who works tirelessly. Dr. Copeland traveled to the North for an education and then returned to the South out of a feeling of duty to help blacks. He often feels uncontrollable anger about the injustices black people suffer in the South.

The Heart Is a Lonely Hunter
Carson McCullers

Buddy and Hamilton Copeland

Dr. Benedict Mady Copeland's two eldest sons. Buddy and Hamilton are estranged from their father, who is disappointed that they have not become the distinguished, well-educated men he had hoped they would.

The Heart Is a Lonely Hunter
Carson McCullers

Daisy Copeland

Dr. Benedict Mady Copeland's former wife, who is now deceased. Though Dr. Copeland tried to get his wife to share his radical political views, she never did, which was often a source of frustration to the doctor.

David Copperfield
Charles Dickens

Clara Copperfield

David Copperfield's mother. The kind, generous, and goodhearted Clara embodies maternal devotion until her death, which occurs early in the novel. David remembers his mother as an angel whose independent spirit was destroyed by **Mr. Murdstone**'s cruelty.

David Copperfield

David Copperfield
Charles Dickens

The protagonist and narrator of the novel. David is innocent, trusting, and naïve, despite the abuse he suffers as a child. At times, David can be chauvinistic toward the lower classes, and occasionally he makes foolhardy decisions that undermine his good intentions.

Madame de Coquenard

The Three Musketeers
Alexandre Dumas

Porthos's mistress, the wife of a wealthy attorney. She dotes on Porthos, living for his affection. Porthos keeps her identity secret from his friends, telling them his mistress is a duchess even though she is not. Eventually, Madame de Coquenard's husband dies, and Porthos settles down with her after his life as a Musketeer.

Cora

The Iceman Cometh
Eugene O'Neill

A thin, peroxide blonde a few years older than **Rocky Pioggi**'s tarts. Her doll-like prettiness has begun to decline. She wants to marry her lover **Chuck Morello**, but their engagement breaks before the end of the play.

Cora

The Handmaid's Tale
Margaret Atwood

One of the **Marthas** at **the Commander**'s household. Cora hopes that **Offred** will have a baby so that she will be able to help raise a child.

Aunt Cora

Wide Sargasso Sea
Jean Rhys

The widow of a prosperous slave owner. Aunt Cora lives alone in Spanish Town. Unlike **Antoinette**'s own mother, **Annette**, Cora nurtures and cares for Antoinette, and eventually enrolls her in a convent school. But eventually Cora, too, abandons Antoinette when she moves to England for a year. On her return, Cora tries to ensure Antoinette's financial independence by giving her a silk pouch and two of her treasured rings. Ill and in bed, Cora tells her niece that she does not trust **Richard Mason** and fears the Lord has forsaken them.

Farder Coram

His Dark Materials
Robert Pullman

An old and wise Gyptian man from **Lyra Belacqua**'s world who has been crippled by disease. Coram's daemon is a cat. Coram was once in love with **Serafina Pekkala**. They had a child together, but it died.

Corbaccio

Volpone
Ben Jonson

The third "carrion-bird" who circles **Volpone**. Corbaccio is actually extremely old and ill himself and is much more likely to die before Volpone even has a chance to bequeath him his wealth. He has a hearing problem and betrays no sign of concern for Volpone, delighting openly in (fake) reports of Volpone's worsening symptoms.

Jesus Maria Corcoran

Tortilla Flat
John Steinbeck

A humanitarian among the ruffians of Tortilla Flat. He takes the plight of **Teresina Cortez** and her children to heart and, along with **Danny** and his friends, saves the mother and her children from starvation.

Cordelia

King Lear
William Shakespeare

King Lear's youngest daughter, disowned by her father for refusing to flatter him. Cordelia is held in extremely high regard by all of the good characters in the play—the king of France marries her for her virtue alone, overlooking her lack of dowry. She remains loyal to Lear despite his cruelty toward her, and she displays a mild and forbearing temperament even toward her evil older sisters **Goneril** and **Regan**. Despite her obvious virtues, Cordelia's reticence makes her motivations difficult to read, as in her refusal to flatter her father. **Edmund** captures Cordelia and orders her execution, and at the end of the play King Lear carries her lifeless body and laments the death of his only faithful daughter.

Giles Corey

The Crucible
Arthur Miller

An elderly farmer in Salem, famous for his litigiousness. Giles asks **Reverend John Hale** about the meaning of his wife **Martha Corey**'s book reading. As a result, Martha is accused of witchcraft. In court, Giles tells **Judge Hathorne**, **Reverend Parris**, and others that the witch trials are really just a ploy to grab **Thomas Putnam** more land. He decides not to enter a plea, so that his farm will fall to his sons and not be bought up by Putnam. In order to force him to enter a plea, the court tortures him on the press, but he continually refuses, and the weight on his chest eventually becomes so great that it crushes him.

Martha Corey

The Crucible
Arthur Miller

Giles Corey's third wife. Martha Corey's reading habits lead to her arrest and conviction for witchcraft; Martha is punished with all the other "witches" and **John Proctor** at the end of *The Crucible*.

Corin

As You Like It
William Shakespeare

An old shepherd. Corin attempts to counsel his friend **Silvius** in the ways of love, admitting that he himself has loved a thousand times, but Silvius refuses to listen. Unlike the other shepherds, whom **Touchstone** easily conquers in tests of wits, Corin is able to hold his own against the clown. The two discuss the merits of courtly life versus pastoral life, and Corin's argument defends the notion that pastoral and courtly life, though full of contradictions, must coexist.

Corinthian

The King Must Die
Mary Renault

The great bull-dancer in the Bull Court when the Cranes arrive. The Corinthian is brave, proud, and fearless, a model to **Theseus**.

Caius Martius Coriolanus

Coriolanus
William Shakespeare

The protagonist of the play. He receives the name "Coriolanus" after leading the Roman armies to victory against the Volscian city of Corioles. Brave, fearsome in battle, and extremely honorable, Coriolanus is also proud, immature, inflexible, and snobbish. These faults lead to his downfall.

Corley

Dubliners
James Joyce

The scheming, repugnant police inspector's son, **Lenehan**'s friend in "Two Gallants." Corley's bulky, assertive physical presence matches his grandiose bragging and incessant self-promotion. As a police informant and veteran womanizer, he is one of the most critical and unsympathetic characters in *Dubliners*.

Cornelius of *Cymbeline*

Cymbeline
William Shakespeare

A doctor at **Cymbeline**'s court.

Cornelius

Doctor Faustus
Christopher Marlowe

Faustus's magician friend who teaches him black magic.

Cornelius of *Hamlet*

Hamlet
William Shakespeare

Along with **Voltimand**, he is sent to Norway as a courtier to prevent **Fortinbras**'s impending attack on Denmark.

Cornelius

Lord Jim
Joseph Conrad

Husband of the **Dutch-Malay woman** and the previous manager of **Stein**'s Patusan post. A bitter, conniving man, he betrays **Jim** to **Gentleman Brown** and causes the death of **Dain Waris**. He is **Jewel**'s stepfather and treats her badly, even asking Jim to give him money in exchange for her.

Mrs. Corney

Oliver Twist
Charles Dickens

The matron of the workhouse where **Oliver Twist** is born. Mrs. Corney is hypocritical, callous, and materialistic. After she marries **Mr. Bumble**, she hounds him mercilessly.

Cornwall

King Lear
William Shakespeare

The husband of Lear's daughter **Regan**. Unlike **Albany**, Cornwall is domineering, cruel, and violent. He, his wife, and his sister-in-law **Goneril** actively persecute Lear and **Gloucester**. At his wife's urging, Cornwall plucks out Gloucester's eyes. A messenger later relays that a servant killed Cornwall for blinding Gloucester.

Corrine

The Color Purple
Alice Walker

Samuel's wife and a missionary in Africa. After moving to Africa, Corrine grows increasingly suspicious and jealous of **Nettie**'s role in her family, convinced that Nettie and Samuel have had an affair and produced the children **Adam** and **Olivia**, who are actually **Celie**'s children. While still in Africa, Corrine dies from a fever, opening the opportunity for Nettie and Samuel to marry.

Corsablis

The Song of Roland
Unknown

An evil magician from Barbary and one of the twelve Saracen lords picked to battle the twelve Frankish peers at Roncesvals. He is soon killed by **Turpin**.

Teresina Cortez

Tortilla Flat
John Steinbeck

A mother of nine who struggles, along with her mother, to maintain her ever-growing household. **Danny** and his *paisanos* steal to save Teresina and her family from starvation one year when the local bean crop fails.

Corvino

Volpone
Ben Jonson

Celia's jealous husband. He frequently threatens to do disgusting acts of physical violence to her and her family to gain control over her. Yet Corvino is more concerned with financial gain than with her faithfulness, seeing her, in essence, as a piece of property. Corvino is another one of the "carrion-birds" circling **Volpone**.

Cosette

Les Misérables
Victor Hugo

Fantine's daughter, who lives as **Jean Valjean**'s adopted daughter after her mother dies. Cosette spends her childhood as a servant for **M. Thénardier** and **M'me. Thénardier** in Montfermeil, but even this awful experience does not harden her. Under the care of Valjean and the nuns of Petit-Picpus, she ultimately blossoms into a beautiful, educated young woman, and finds fulfillment in her love for **Marius Pontmercy**. Cosette is innocent and docile, but her participation in Valjean's many escapes from the law shows that she also possesses intelligence and bravery.

Roxane Coss

Bel Canto
Ann Patchett

An opera diva used to the indulgence of the world. Over the course of the novel, every man who hears Coss sing falls in love with her. Eventually, Coss returns the love of **Katsumi Hosokawa**. When she is taken hostage, she believes that whatever may happen to everyone else, she will survive because she is special. Once Coss finds love with Hosokawa, she is able to love Cesar, the young terrorist who aspires to be a great singer. During their lessons, her desire to be a star is temporarily replaced by her desire to help someone else.

Billy Costa

His Dark Materials
Robert Pullman

A Gyptian boy from **Lyra Belacqua**'s world whom the Gobblers steal and take to Bolvanger.

Ma Costa

His Dark Materials
Robert Pullman

A Gyptian woman from **Lyra Belacqua**'s world. Ma Costa took care of Lyra when she was a baby and hid her from **Mr. Coulter** when he came looking for Lyra and **Lord Asriel**. She is **Billy Costa** and **Tony Costa**'s mother.

Tony Costa

His Dark Materials
Robert Pullman

A young Gyptian man who accompanies the tribe of Gyptians north to rescue the children the Gobblers stole. Tony is **Billy Costa**'s brother.

Costard

Love's Labour's Lost
William Shakespeare

A rustic of the court of Navarre. After **Armado** spots him in the forest with **Jacquenetta**, breaking the new restrictive oath of Navarre, he is put on trial in front of the lords. His punishment, which leads to high comedic effect, is that he must serve Armado. Costard is the clown of the play, and his action—misdirecting two separate letters—ultimately causes the oath to unravel and the lords and ladies to come together.

Archie Costello

The Chocolate War
Robert Cormier

The antagonist of *The Chocolate War*. He is revered and feared, and gets away with everything and anything. **Brother Leon** asks for his help, lending credence to Archie's power and giving him immunity from consequences arising from his cruel actions. Archie recognizes that **Jerry Renault** is resistant to the idea of selling chocolates and takes it as an opportunity to exploit and manipulate him. Archie contributes to

Jerry's downfall by forcing him into a difficult situation, which ends in a boxing match, and in Jerry's deciding to do what he is expected and told to do in his life.

Mrs. Costello

Daisy Miller
Henry James

Winterbourne's aunt, who has resided in Europe for many years and adopted the attitudes of European society. Mrs. Costello also claims high status in New York City and refuses to socialize with people of lower status, like the Millers.

Alexander Cosway

Wide Sargasso Sea
Jean Rhys

Antoinette's deceased father and **Annette**'s first husband. Alexander Cosway was a debased ex–slave owner known for fathering illegitimate children, squandering the family's money, and drinking himself into a stupor. By the time Mr. Cosway died, leaving his second wife and two children on their own, the Emancipation Act had led to the ruin of his sugar plantation and the end of his fortune.

Daniel Cosway

Wide Sargasso Sea
Jean Rhys

One of **Alexander Cosway**'s bastard chidren. Daniel writes a letter to **Rochester** informing him of the madness that runs in **Antoinette**'s family. The half-white, half-black Daniel is a racially split counterpart to the culturally split Antoinette.

Sandi Cosway

Wide Sargasso Sea
Jean Rhys

One of **Alexander Cosway**'s bastard children. Sandi helps his half-sister **Antoinette** when she is harassed on her way to school. Although Antoinette would like to call him "Cousin Sandi," **Mr. Mason** scolds her for acknowledging her black relatives. Antoinette's fragmented memory of a good-bye kiss with Sandi supports the possibility that the two may have been intimate at some point.

Petra Cotes

One Hundred Years of Solitude
Gabriel García Márquez

Aureliano Segundo's concubine. She sleeps with twins, **José Arcadio Segundo** and **Aureliano Segundo**, without realizing they are two different men. Aureliano Segundo stays with her longer, and the two have a fierce passion for each other. Something magical in their union causes their farm animals to be supernaturally fertile; Aureliano Segundo becomes fabulously wealthy by virtue of his livestock's productivity. At one point, all of their animals die, and though they struggle to make ends meet, they are as happy as ever, once again falling madly in love with each other.

Prudencia Cotes

Chronicle of a Death Foretold
Gabriel García Márquez

Pablo Vicario's fiancé. She says she would not have married Pablo if he had not upheld the honor of his sister by killing the man who took her virginity. She waits the three years he is in jail, and when he gets out she becomes his wife for life.

Dimitros Cotsakis

White Noise
Don DeLillo

New York émigré and professor at the College on the Hill. He is a large man and former bodyguard. He is **Murray Jay Siskind**'s principal competitor for **Elvis** until he dies.

Cottard

The Plague
Albert Camus

A suspicious and paranoid man guilty of an unnamed crime. For Cottard, the quarantine is a relief from fear and solitude. During the quarantine, Cottard makes money by smuggling, eschewing responsibility for fighting the plague.

Old Cotter

Dubliners
James Joyce

The family friend in "The Sisters" who disapproves of **the narrator**'s relationship with **Father Flynn**. Old Cotter informs the narrator of Father Flynn's death.

Farmer Tom Cotton

The Return of the King
J. R. R. Tolkien

One of the oldest and most respected hobbits in the Shire. Farmer Tom Cotton explains how a police state formed in the Shire after **Frodo Baggins**, **Samwise Gamgee**, **Meriadoc Brandybuck**, and **Peregrin Took** left. This police state was set up through **Gríma Wormtongue** and **Saruman**, and enforced by evil **Humans** from Bree after the fall of **Sauron**. When Frodo and his Hobbits from the Fellowship return to the Shire, they save it from the terrible rule of this police state.

John Cotton

Bless the Beasts and Children
Glendon Swarthout

A sixteen-year-old counselor who adopts a leadership role in respect to the Bedwetters. He accepts these misfits into his cabin and works to help them improve themselves. At the conclusion of the novel, Cotton dies when he crashes in a stolen pick-up truck.

Rosie Cotton

The Return of the King
J. R. R. Tolkien

Farmer Tom Cotton's daughter. Rosie Cotton marries **Samwise Gamgee** at the end of *The Lord of the Rings*, and together they have a daughter, whom they name **Elanor**.

Marisa Coulter

His Dark Materials
Robert Pullman

Lyra Belacqua's mother, the head of the General Oblation Board (Gobblers), the former lover of **Lord Asriel**, Lyra's father, and the current lover of **Lord Carlo Boreal**. Despite her charm and sweet demeanor, Mrs. Coulter is an almost purely evil woman. Her daemon, the vicious little golden monkey, reflects its owner's personality. Just as the monkey enjoys torturing and killing bats in the cave in which Mrs. Coulter keeps Lyra, Mrs. Coulter enjoys exercising her power. She shows no remorse after tearing people to pieces or torturing them to death. Despite her cruelty, Mrs. Coulter has a soft spot for Lyra, and is always battling Lord Asriel for control of her.

Countess

The Princess Bride
William Goldman

The Count's wife. The countess is the most fashionable woman in what would become Europe. Her attentiveness to **Westley** stirs envy in **Buttercup**.

Mother Courage

Mother Courage
Bertolt Brecht

The play's wisewoman. Courage delivers shrewd commentary on the realities of the war. She feeds off the war, selling wares from her wagon to the combatants. Wise about the world but not about herself, even as she tries to protect her children from the war, she loses each of them. Her unyielding work ethic prevents her from analyzing her own actions, and even after all her children die she cannot help but continue business as usual, hauling the wagon alone.

Alexander Court

Henry V
William Shakespeare

An English soldier. The night before the Battle of Agincourt, **King Henry V** disguises himself and argues with Court, **John Bates**, and **Michael Williams** about the worthiness of the French war. Though he disagrees heatedly with them and ends up exchanging gloves with Williams as the promise of a future fight, Henry is generally impressed with these men's intelligence and courage.

Courtesan

The Comedy of Errors
William Shakespeare

An expensive prostitute in Ephesus. After **Antipholus of Ephesus** is barred entry from his house, he dines with her at the Porpentine Inn. When the Courtesan greets **Antipholus of Syracuse** on the street and asks for the return of a ring that his twin borrowed during dinner, the Syracusan Antipholus and Dromio decide that she is a witch and run off, leaving a puzzled Courtesan to assume he's insane.

Norman Cousins

Hiroshima
John Hersey

A prominent American editor who orchestrates many of **Reverend Mr. Kiyoshi Tanimoto**'s speeches and appearances in America in the postwar years.

Lane Coutell

Franny and Zooey
J. D. Salinger

Boyfriend of **Franny Glass**. Lane represents much of the phoniness, egotism, and intellectualism in academics that Franny cannot stand. He is fairly insensitive to her breakdown and talks about wanting her to read a paper that earned him a good grade. Though annoyed by Franny's erratic behavior, he acts smooth and cold and tries to look "attractively bored."

Bertha Coutts

Lady Chatterley's Lover
D. H. Lawrence

Oliver Mellors's wife, separated from him but not divorced. Their marriage failed because of their sexual incompatibility: she was too rapacious, not tender enough. She returns at the end of the novel to spread rumors about Mellors's infidelity to her, and helps get him fired from his position as gamekeeper. As the novel concludes, Mellors is in the process of divorcing her.

Augustus Coverly

Arcadia
Tom Stoppard

A fifteen year-old boy. He is double cast with **Gus Coverly**. The two are foils for each other in that Gus is shy and passionate, while Augustus is more of a rambunctious, aristocratic scamp. Augustus only appears in one scene, as the troublemaking cousin who disrupts **Thomasina**'s lessons and wants her tutor **Septimus** to tell him about sex.

Chloe Coverly

Arcadia
Tom Stoppard

A modern-day rich heiress and a foil for **Thomasina**. As a function of the changing times, she is also much more savvy about sex than Thomasina: where Thomasina discovers her sexuality through kisses and waltzes with her tutor **Septimus**, Chloe literally has sex with the visiting historian **Bernard**. The two are linked, however, with a sort of mutual brilliance. Thomasina posits that if the world is truly Newtonian, then everything is deterministic and one could use mathematical equations to determine everything down to the shape of a leaf. Meanwhile, one hundred years later Chloe posits a similar idea, saying that if the world were truly Newtonian, a computer could calculate every human action.

Gus Coverly

Arcadia
Tom Stoppard

The self-elected mute son of **Sidley Park**. Gus is a connector and communicator between past and present; he intuitively finds the relics that others can't, such as when he finds the foundation for a lost outbuilding or when he gives **Hannah** a portrait that is vital to her ongoing research. Gus is double cast as **Augustus Coverly**, and the two serve as foils for each other. Gus is shy and passionate while Augustus is more outgoing and mischievous.

Major —— de Coverley

Catch-22
Joseph Heller

The fierce, intense executive officer of **John Yossarian**'s squadron. The major is feared and revered by the men, who are afraid to ask his first name, even though all he does is play horseshoes and rent apartments for the officers in cities taken by American forces.

Thomasina Coverly

Arcadia
Tom Stoppard

The young, impetuous genius child of Lord and **Lady Croom**. Thomasina miraculously theorizes the second law of thermodynamics and understands chaos theory. She is inspired and impassioned by her tutor **Septimus**. Late in the play, the present-day characters discover that Thomasina died in a fire at the age of seventeen. It is assumed that Septimus became a hermit afterward, madly collecting data on Thomasina's brilliant theories.

Valentine Coverly

Arcadia
Tom Stoppard

A rich heir who is casually undertaking graduate studies in mathematics. The son of the Coverly estate, Valentine tries unsuccessfully to capture the behavior of grouse using a purely mathematical formula. In the process, he stumbles on **Thomasina**'s research and reluctantly shares her genius with **Hannah**. Valentine determines from Thomasina's scribblings that the young child had discovered chaos theory and thermodynamics.

Edward Covey

Narrative of the Life of Frederick Douglass
Frederick Douglass

A notorious slave "breaker" and **Frederick Douglass**'s keeper for one year. Slave owners send their unruly slaves to Covey, who works and punishes them and returns them trained and docile. Covey's tactics as a slaveholder are both cruel and sneaky.

Elmer Cowley

Winesburg, Ohio
Sherwood Anderson

The son of a store owner. He feels terribly out of place in Winesburg and is prone to hysterical outbursts. Two of these outbursts are directed at **George Willard**, who is intrigued by Elmer's personality.

Cowslip

Watership Down
Richard Adams

The leader of the rabbits at the warren of the snares. Cowslip shocks **Hazel** and **Blackberry** by laughing at them. He lives his life pretending that rabbits are not dying all around him, and he is almost killed by **Holly**.

The Pearl
John Steinbeck

Coyotito

Kino and **Juana**'s only son, who is stung by a scorpion while resting in a hammock one morning. Kino and Juana's efforts to save him by finding a big pearl with which they can pay a doctor ultimately do more harm than good, as the pearl indirectly results in Coyotito's death at Kino's hands.

The Two Gentlemen of Verona
William Shakespeare

Crab

Launce's dog. Crab plays the straight man in the Launce-Crab comic pairing. The great love that the clown Launce has for his poor Crab is deeper and more loyal than the stylized affections of **Valentine** and **Proteus**.

The Harry Potter Series: Books 2–4
J. K. Rowling

Crabbe

One of **Draco Malfoy**'s unintelligent, lumbering cronies.

Our Town
Thornton Wilder

Sam Craig

Emily Webb's cousin. He has left Grover's Corners to travel west, but returns for Emily's funeral in Act III. Like the audience, he is an outsider and does not know what has happened in town.

The Light in the Forest
Conrad Richter

Little Crane

True Son and **Half Arrow**'s friend. Little Crane is deeply in love with his white wife, who is being returned to Paxton Township with True Son. Little Crane is very critical of white behavior, but his lack of discretion in voicing his opinions proves fatal.

Black Boy
Richard Wright

Mr. Crane

A white Northerner who runs the optical shop where **Richard Wright** works. Mr. Crane is a fair and unprejudiced man who is sad to see Richard run off his job by **Pease** and **Reynolds**.

A Portrait of the Artist as a Young Man
James Joyce

Cranly

Stephen Dedalus's closest friend, who acts as his nonreligious confessor. Stephen resents Cranly's advice that he try to conform to his family's wishes and attempt to fit in with his peers. While Cranly is a good friend, he fails to understand Stephen's need for absolute freedom, and urges him to conform to society.

Cranmer, Archbishop of Canterbury

Henry VIII
William Shakespeare

Loyal supporter of **King Henry VIII**. As Cranmer travels abroad, asking scholars what they think about the legality of Henry's divorce, **Gardiner** spreads rumors about him and plots his demise. When Henry warns Cranmer about the rumors, the Archbishop thanks him but admits that he could fall into a trap set for him. Henry gives Cranmer his ring as a symbol of his protection, and promises to hear an appeal.

Bob Cratchit

A Christmas Carol
Charles Dickens

Ebenezer Scrooge's clerk. Cratchit struggles to support his large family on the absurdly small salary Scrooge pays him. Despite his worries, Crachit is a loving, patient, cheerful man.

Mrs. Cratchit

A Christmas Carol
Charles Dickens

Bob Cratchit's wife. Mrs. Cratchit is a spirited woman who makes her dislike for **Ebenezer Scrooge** plain. She scoffs when her husband calls Scrooge "the Founder of the Feast."

Archibald Craven

The Secret Garden
Frances Hodgson Burnett

The master of Misselthwaite Manor, who suffers from a crooked spine and general ill health. He lives in a great house composed of a hundred locked rooms. His house, coupled with his position as widower and the rumor that he is a hunchback, makes him seem like an English Bluebeard. He has been in a crushing depression ever since the death of his wife, ten years before the novel begins. Archibald spends most of his time abroad, since he wants to see neither his house nor his son, **Colin Craven**, because they remind him of his late wife. Archibald's sadness has a deathly effect upon both him and those around him. At the novel's end, he undergoes a change of heart after his wife comes to him in a dream.

Colin Craven

The Secret Garden
Frances Hodgson Burnett

Archibald Craven's ten-year-old son and heir. His mother died shortly after he was born, and his father could not bear to look at him because of his resemblance to her. It is feared that he will grow to be a hunchback like his father, and he has been treated as an invalid since his birth. Colin has been bedridden throughout his childhood, and his servants are commanded to obey his every whim. As a result, Colin is imperious and gloomy. Mary and Colin's friendship is only possible because they are so similar in temperament and circumstances. Mary uses stories of the Sowerbies, the garden, the moor, and her friend Dickon to engage and revitalize Colin, because these things attended her own reawakening. Like Mary, Colin begins to find things in the world worth his affection. He becomes fond of Mary, and is astounded upon first meeting Dickon. Both Mary's and Dickon's effects on Colin are described as magical. When Colin is finally taken out into the garden, his eyes devour the landscape; Colin's eyes respond to the garden because they are somehow his mother's eyes—the part of her that lives on in him answers the call of spring.

Dr. Craven

The Secret Garden
Frances Hodgson Burnett

Archibald Craven's brother and **Colin Craven**'s uncle, he tends to Colin during the latter's illness. He is a bit stuffy and officious, and both Colin and **Mary Lennox** laugh at him at every opportunity. Described as a weak man, he half hopes for Colin's death so that he might inherit Misselthwaite.

Lilias Craven

The Secret Garden
Frances Hodgson Burnett

Archibald Craven's late wife, who died ten years before the outset of the novel. Her spirit is associated with both roses and the secret garden. She is described by all who knew her as the gentlest, sweetest, and most beautiful of women. She represents an absent ideal.

Dr. Crawford

Ordinary People
Judith Guest

The doctor who treated **Conrad Jarrett** while he was in the hospital. We never see him in the novel, but we learn that he referred Conrad to **Dr. Berger**.

Henry Crawford

Mansfield Park
Jane Austen

Mary Crawford's brother. Henry is equally charming and possibly even more amoral, and he possesses a sizeable estate. **Maria Bertram** and **Julia Bertram** fall in love with him, and Henry chooses Maria, despite her engagement. When Maria marries and the sisters leave Mansfield, he falls for **Fanny Price** and proposes to her. She refuses, even though everyone else believes that Henry has changed. Eventually, he meets up with Maria again, and the two run off, but their relationship ends badly.

Janie Mae Crawford

Their Eyes Were Watching God
Zora Neale Hurston

The protagonist of the novel, Janie defies categorization. She is black but flaunts her Caucasian-like straight hair, which comes from her mixed ancestry. She is a woman but defies gender stereotypes by insisting on her independence and wearing overalls. Janie Mae resents her upbringing by **Nanny Crawford**, who sends her off to marry **Logan Killicks**. She leaves Logan Killicks for the suave **Jody Starks**, who suppresses her voice, but has power as the mayor of Eatonville. He dies, and she goes to the Everglades, or "the muck," only to be forced to kill her great love **Tea Cake** because he is delusional with rabies after being bitten by a dog when saving Janie from a hurricane. Part of Janie's maturity rests in her ability to realize that others' cruelty toward her or their inability to understand her stems not from malice but from their upbringing or limited perspective. Although *Their Eyes Were Watching God* revolves around Janie's relationships with other people, it is first and foremost a story of Janie's search for spiritual enlightenment and a strong sense of her own identity. When we first and last see Janie, she is alone. The novel is not the story of her quest for a partner but rather that of her quest for independence.

Leafy Crawford

Their Eyes Were Watching God
Zora Neale Hurston

Janie Mae Crawford's mother. Leafy is born shortly before the end of the Civil War. After she is raped by her schoolteacher, Leafy goes out drinking every night and eventually runs off, shortly after giving birth to Janie. Janie then must be raised by her grandmother, **Nanny Crawford**, who puts all her hope in Janie.

Mary Crawford

Mansfield Park
Jane Austen

Sister of **Mrs. Grant**, who is the wife of the second parson at Mansfield. Mary is beautiful and charming, but also shallow and corrupt. She has been brought up poorly by an aunt and uncle and has been subject to the influences of her fashionable friends. She becomes friends with a reluctant **Fanny Price**, and later **Edmund Bertram** falls in love with and nearly proposes to Mary.

Nanny Crawford

Their Eyes Were Watching God
Zora Neale Hurston

Janie Mae Crawford's grandmother. As a slave, Nanny was raped by her master, which resulted in the birth of **Leafy Crawford**, Janie's mother. Leafy runs off after her own rape by her schoolteacher, leaving Nanny to care for Janie. Nanny's experience as a slave stamped her worldview with a strong concern for financial security, respectability, and upward mobility. After seeing Janie kiss **Johnny Taylor** under a pear tree, she has Janie married off to **Logan Killicks** immediately. Nanny's values clash with Janie's independence and desire to experience the world, though Janie comes to respect Nanny's values and decisions as well-intended.

Frank Crawley

Rebecca
Daphne du Maurier

Maxim de Winter's kind, loyal overseer at Manderley. He befriends **the Heroine** almost immediately.

First Creditor

The Clouds
Aristophanes

An angry Athenian to whom **Strepsiades** owes money. He comes to demand Strepsiades's appearance in court and acts with great brashness and surety.

Second Creditor

The Clouds
Aristophanes

A mopey Athenian to whom **Strepsiades** owes money. He is a morose, weepy figure, prone to swearing great, pathetic oaths to the gods.

Colin Creevey

The Harry Potter Series: Books 2 and 4
J. K. Rowling

A first-year boy who follows **Harry Potter** around, taking his photograph and embarrassing him tremendously.

Across Five Aprils
Irene Hunt

Bill Creighton

Jethro Creighton's favorite brother. Bill toils over his decision of whether to fight and for which side, and ultimately he decides to fight for the South.

Across Five Aprils
Irene Hunt

Eb Creighton

Jethro Creighton's cousin, a deserter in the war. He returns to the farm, and Jethro keeps his presence a secret, sneaking him food and blankets. Eventually he rejoins the war effort because President Lincoln declares amnesty for all deserters who return to their posts.

Across Five Aprils
Irene Hunt

Ellen Creighton

Jethro Creighton's mother, a calming influence around the house. Ellen does her best to nurture Jethro. She knows Jethro is special and is worried that the responsibilities he must assume are too great for one so young.

Across Five Aprils
Irene Hunt

Jenny Creighton

Jethro Creighton's sister. Jenny and Jethro struggle together, talking about the war. They are the only Creighton children not fighting in the war, and they find solace in each other. They are also linked together by **Shadrach Yale**, Jenny's romantic interest and Jethro's teacher. At the end of the book, Jethro moves in with Jenny and Shadrach.

Across Five Aprils
Irene Hunt

Jethro Creighton

The protagonist, who comes of age during the Civil War. He is forced to reckon with a national crisis, a tragic death in his family, a sudden assumption of responsibility, and a loss of innocence. Jethro must deal with the effects of the war while trying to shape his vision of America.

Across Five Aprils
Irene Hunt

Matt Creighton

Jethro Creighton's father, who provides an example of fairness for Jethro. Matt chooses not to seek revenge on his daughter's killer, and he keeps a level head about his situation during the war. He has a heart attack, which prompts Jethro to assume responsibility in the family. Matt finally relents on his prohibition to let Jenny and Shadrach marry, signing his consent when the two are in Washington, DC.

Hattie Crenshaw

The Land
Mildred D. Taylor

The woman who hides **Mitchell Thomas** and **Paul-Edward Logan** when they are running away from **Edward Logan** after the horse race. Paul and Mitchell hide under Hattie's and her daughter's dresses on a train. Hattie gives them jobs on her farm.

Creon

Oedipus trilogy (Oedipus Rex, Oedipus at Colonus, Antigone)
Sophocles

Oedipus's brother-in-law and **Jocasta**'s brother. Creon appears more than any other character in the three Oedipus plays combined. Early in *Oedipus Rex*, Creon claims to have no desire for kingship. Yet, when he has the opportunity to grasp power at the end of that play, Creon seems quite eager. We learn in *Oedipus at Colonus* that he is willing to fight with his nephews for this power, and in *Antigone* Creon rules Thebes with a stubborn blindness that is similar to Oedipus's rule. Creon never has our sympathy in the way Oedipus does, because he is bossy and bureaucratic, intent on asserting his own authority. In *Medea*, as the King of Corinth, Creon banishes **Medea** from the city.

Creon

Medea
Euripides

See above.

Creon

Antigone 1946
Jean Anouilh

Antigone's uncle. Creon is powerfully built, but a weary and wrinkled man suffering the burdens of rule. A practical man, he firmly distances himself from the tragic aspirations of **Oedipus** and his line. Creon is bound to ideas of good sense, simplicity, and the banal happiness of everyday life. He never wanted to be king, but assumed that role like a worker assuming a job. He doesn't believe in the punishment of **Polynices** and the martyrdom of **Eteocles**, but he knows that the public's arbitrary need for heroes, villains, and clear rules must be pacified.

Pietro Crespi

One Hundred Years of Solitude
Gabriel García Márquez

The gentle, delicate Italian musician whom both **Amaranta** and **Rebeca** love. When Pietro chooses Rebeca, Amaranta is very jealous and is suspected of stalling the wedding by sending Pietro to his mother with a fabricated letter saying his mother is ill. Rebeca, however, chooses to marry the more manly **José Arcadio**. After Amaranta leads Pietro on and then rejects him, Pietro commits suicide.

Cressida

Troilus and Cressida
William Shakespeare

A beautiful young Trojan woman who becomes **Troilus**'s lover. Cressida's father, **Calchas**, defected to the Greeks. The Trojans send Cressida to the Greeks to join him in exchange for the return of **Antenor**.

The King Must Die
Mary Renault

Cretan Captain

The Captain on the Cretan ship that **Theseus** and the others take from Athens. **Lukos** is a scheming, intelligent man who wishes to improve his favor at court.

The Aeneid
Virgil

Creusa

Aeneas's wife at Troy and **Ascanius**'s mother. In the flight from Troy, Creusa is lost and killed. When Aeneas returns to search for her, he meets her shade, or spirit, which comforts him with descriptions of the new home and wife awaiting him.

The Rape of the Lock
Alexander Pope

Crispissa

The sylph who is assigned to guard **Belinda**'s "fav'rite Lock."

Pigs in Heaven
Barbara Kingsolver

Mr. Crittendon

The owner of the jewelry shop where **Rose** works. Although Mr. Crittendon has made a fortune, his devastation over the loss of Native American culture drives him to suicide.

Persuasion
Jane Austen

Admiral and Mrs. Croft

The amiable couple that rents Kellynch Hall. The Admiral is a decorated Naval officer, and his devoted wife travels with him when he is at sea. The Crofts are one of the few examples of an older happily married couple in any of Austen's novels.

Henry VIII
William Shakespeare

Thomas Cromwell

A friend of **Cardinal Wolsey**'s. Cromwell is devastated by Wolsey's fall from favor, but Wolsey encourages him to go back to **King Henry VIII** and to serve the state with honor and humility, setting aside ambition. Cromwell follows through soon after, as one of **Cranmer, Archbishop of Canterbury**'s only supporters at the Council.

A Man for All Seasons
Robert Bolt

Thomas Cromwell

A crafty lawyer who is the primary agent plotting against **More**. Where his accomplices **Rich** and **the Common Man** sometimes express reluctance about their immoral actions (conspiracy, execution, etc.), Cromwell is a purely evil character. He sets up More's execution using a sham trial. The Common Man alludes to Cromwell's eventual execution for High Treason, which will take place after the end of the play.

Captain Cronjager

The Big Sleep
Raymond Chandler

A local police captain who appears to feel a rivalry with **Marlowe**.

Cronus

Greek Mythology
Unknown

The ruler of the **Titans** after overthrowing his father **Ouranos**. After learning that he, too, will be overthrown, Cronos swallows each of his children as his wife **Rhea** gives birth to them. Rhea is able to save one, **Zeus**, who forces Cronus to vomit up his siblings, with whom he defeats the Titans for control of the universe.

Crooks

Of Mice and Men
John Steinbeck

A black stable hand who gets his name from his crooked back. Proud, bitter, and caustically funny, Crooks is isolated from the other men because of his race. Nonetheless, Crooks becomes fond of **Lennie**, and though he derisively claims to have seen countless men follow empty dreams of buying their own land, he asks Lennie if he can accompany them.

Crookshanks

The Harry Potter Series: Books 3 and 4
J. K. Rowling

Hermione Granger's aggressive ginger cat.

Lady Croom

Arcadia
Tom Stoppard

The bossy battle-ax who storms around the estate. She is perceptive of everything that happens on the property. A stickler for manners and propriety, she rids her household of the troublemaking **Lord Byron**, **Ezra Chater**, and **Mrs. Chater**. It is implied that she has a brief affair with **Septimus**, the household tutor for Croom's daughter **Thomasina**.

H. Lowe Crosby

Cat's Cradle
Kurt Vonnegut

A bicycle manufacturer married to **Hazel Crosby**. The Crosbys meet **John** on the plane to San Lorenzo. They are investigating the possibility of moving their business to the island because they found U.S. labor regulations too restrictive. Lowe and Hazel exhibit the ignorant hubris of typical Americans.

Hazel Crosby

Cat's Cradle
Kurt Vonnegut

H. Lowe Crosby's wife. She insists that **John** call her "mom," as they are both Hoosiers (natives of Indiana). John calls her Hoosier obsession a *granfalloon*, a false *karass*.

Something Wicked This Way Comes
Ray Bradbury

Mr. Crosetti

The barber. Mr. Crosetti informs **William Halloway** and **James Nightshade** that he smells cotton candy. He realizes that a carnival is coming to town and he becomes sentimental. When the boys see that his shop is closed "due to illness," they realize that Mr. Crosetti was likely one of the first casualties of the carnival.

The Things They Carried
Tim O'Brien

Jimmy Cross

The lieutenant of the Alpha Company. Cross has good intentions, but he does not know how to lead his men. He is wracked with guilt because he believes his preoccupation with an old crush and his tendency to follow orders against his better judgment caused the deaths of **Ted Lavender** and **Kiowa**.

Harry Potter and the Goblet of Fire
J. K. Rowling

Bartemius Crouch

The stiff and rule-abiding Head of the Department for International Magical Cooperation; **Percy Weasley**'s boss.

Harry Potter and the Goblet of Fire
J. K. Rowling

Bartemius Crouch, Jr.

Bartemius Crouch's son, a convicted Death Eater, or follower of Voldemort. Bartemius, Jr. was allowed to remain outside of prison so long as he wore an invisibility cloak and stayed in his father's house, guarded carefully by **Winky**. In *Harry Potter and the Goblet of Fire*, he comes back to Hogwarts disguised as **Mad-Eye Moody**.

This Boy's Life
Tobias Wolff

Bobby Crow

Norma's high school sweetheart, an Indian boy from Marblemount who is a star football quarterback at Concrete High. When Norma decides not to marry Bobby Crow, he is heartbroken and turns angry and bitter.

Rebecca
Daphne du Maurier

Lady Crowan

A local noblewoman who suggests that **Maxim de Winter** and **the Heroine** revive the tradition of holding an annual costume ball at Manderley.

Our Town
Thornton Wilder

Joe Crowell, Jr.

The paperboy. Joe's morning delivery establishes the town's comfortable routine. Joe becomes the brightest boy in high school and studies at Massachusetts Tech. Well on his way to becoming a successful engineer, Joe is killed in France during World War I.

Si Crowell

Our Town
Thornton Wilder

Joe Crowell, Jr.'s younger brother. He takes over Joe's paper route, contributing to the sense of human continuity in Grover's Corners.

Fanny Crowne

Brave New World
Aldous Huxley

Lenina Crowne's friend and coworker in the Bottling Room. Fanny is an archetypal, typical citizen. She warns Lenina away from falling into a monogamous relationship with **Henry Foster**. She suspects that **Bernard Marx**'s unorthodox beliefs and behavior can be attributed to an error in his prenatal conditioning.

Lenina Crowne

Brave New World
Aldous Huxley

A vaccination worker at the Central London Hatchery and Conditioning Centre. Lenina seems drawn to unorthodox figures like **Bernard Marx** and **John the Savage**. She defies cultural conventions by dating **Henry Foster** exclusively for several months. While she flirts with deviation from World State ethos, Lenina is ultimately a conventional citizen; her hypnopaedic conditioning keeps her from relating to John and others in any way other than sex. Her relentless advances on John contribute to his isolation and eventual suicide.

Jerry Cruncher

A Tale of Two Cities
Charles Dickens

An odd-job man for Tellson's Bank. Cruncher is gruff, short-tempered, superstitious, and uneducated. He supplements his income by working as a "Resurrection-Man," one who digs up dead bodies and sells them to scientists.

Robinson Crusoe

Robinson Crusoe
Daniel Defoe

The novel's protagonist and narrator. Crusoe begins the novel as a young middle-class man in York in search of a career. He father recommends the law, but Crusoe yearns for a life at sea. His subsequent rebellion and decision to become a merchant is the impetus for the whole adventure that follows. Crusoe's vague but recurring feelings of guilt over his disobedience color the early part of the story and show the depth of Crusoe's religious fear. Crusoe is steady and plodding in everything he does, and his perseverance ensures his survival through storms, enslavement, and a twenty-eight-year isolation on a desert island.

Cristobal Cruz

House Made of Dawn
N. Scott Momaday

A squat, oily man with blue-black hair who assists **John Big Bluff Tosamah**, the Priest of the Sun. Cruz, whose English has rural inflections, is very devoted to his boss.

Dr. Cruz

Jurassic Park
Michael Crichton

The doctor who treats **Tina Bowman** in Costa Rica.

Cuckoo

The Good Earth
Pearl S. Buck

A slave in **Old Master Hwang**'s household at the same time as **O-lan**. In her youth, Cuckoo was beautiful and became the Old Master's concubine. She insulted and berated O-lan, who worked in the kitchen.

Sergeant Cuff

The Moonstone
Wilkie Collins

A renowned detective from London. Tall and gaunt, he does not look like a member of the police force, yet his perceptive intelligence is striking. When not working, he breeds roses.

Mrs. Viola Cullinan

I Know Why the Caged Bird Sings
Maya Angelou

A southern white woman in Stamps, Arkansas, and **Maya Johnson**'s first employer. She hides her racism under a self-deceptive veneer of gentility.

Don Cullivan

In Cold Blood
Truman Capote

An old army friend of **Perry Edward Smith**'s who starts a correspondence with him upon reading about the case in the newspaper.

Cunégonde

Candide
Voltaire

The daughter of **Candide**'s German uncle. Cunégonde loves Candide but is willing to betray him. After her father's castle is destroyed in war, a number of exploitative men enslave her or use her as a mistress. Like Candide, she is neither intelligent nor complex. Her very blandness casts a satiric light on Candide's mad passion for her.

Martin Cunningham

Dubliners and *Ulysses*
James Joyce

A well-respected, unhappily married Dubliner. In *Dubliners*' "Grace," Cunningham orchestrates the attempt to bring **Tom Kernan** to the religious revival. His friends think that his face resembles Shakespeare's. In *Ulysses*, Cunningham is a leader in **Leopold Bloom**'s circle of casual friends. He sticks up for Bloom but still treats him as an outsider.

Mr. Walter Cunningham

To Kill a Mockingbird
Harper Lee

A farmer whose family is large and poor. Because Mr. Cunningham cannot afford to pay **Atticus Finch** for his legal services with money, he pays in hickory nuts, turnip greens, or other goods. Mr. Cunningham is part of the mob that seeks to lynch **Tom Robinson** at the jail. Mr. Cunningham, one of the beasts in the lynch mob, suddenly shows his human goodness when he encounters **Scout**'s politeness.

Walter Cunningham, Jr.

To Kill a Mockingbird
Harper Lee

Son of **Mr. Walter Cunningham** and classmate of **Scout Finch**.

Cupid

The Aeneid
Virgil

A son of **Venus** and the god of erotic desire. Cupid disguises himself as **Ascanius**, **Aeneas**'s son, and causes **Dido** to fall in love with Aeneas. In the Greek tradition, Cupid is known as **Eros**.

Curate

Tristram Shandy
Laurence Sterne

The local church official, also named Tristram, who misnames the baby when **Susannah** fails to pronounce the chosen name, "Trismegistus."

Curley

Of Mice and Men
John Steinbeck

The son of **the boss** of the ranch where **Lennie** and **George** work. Curley, who wears high-heeled boots to distinguish himself from the field hands, is rumored to be a champion prizefighter and is confrontational, mean-spirited, and aggressive. In addition, the jealous Curley is violently possessive of his flirtatious young wife. When **Lennie** inadvertently kills **Curley's wife** by breaking her neck, Curley organizes a lynch mob to track Lennie down.

Curley's wife

Of Mice and Men
John Steinbeck

The only female character in the novel. Sultry, flirtatious, and given to wearing fancy, feathered red shoes, she represents the temptation of female sexuality in the male-dominated world of the ranch. Like the ranch-hands, she is desperately lonely and yearns for a better life than the mean-spirited **Curley** gives her. Curley's wife takes a liking to the strong but mildly retarded **Lennie**, who inadvertently breaks her neck and kills her.

Curly

The Call of the Wild
Jack London

A friend of **Buck**'s on the sea journey to the North. In the North, a pack of huskies kills Curly when she tries to make friends with them without approaching with caution.

Darrell Curtis

The Outsiders
S. E. Hinton

See **Darry**.

Ponyboy Curtis

The Outsiders
S. E. Hinton

The narrator and protagonist of *The Outsiders*, and the youngest of the greasers. Ponyboy's literary interests and academic accomplishments set him apart from the rest of his gang. Because his parents have died in a car accident, Ponyboy lives with his brothers **Darry** and **Sodapop Curtis**. Darry repeatedly accuses Ponyboy of lacking common sense, but Ponyboy is a reliable and observant narrator. Through his conversations with **Cherry Valance**, we learn how thoughtful Ponyboy is, that he notices beauty in the world, and that he has the capacity to understand the points of view of his enemies. Ponyboy flees to Windrixville with **Johnny Cade**, lives through the deaths of both Johnny and **Dally**, and learns how to keep family peace by understanding Darry better. He matures over the course of the novel, eventually realizing the importance of strength in the face of class bias.

Sodapop Curtis

The Outsiders
S. E. Hinton

The happy-go-lucky, handsome brother of **Darry** and **Ponyboy Curtis**. Sodapop Curtis is the middle Curtis boy. Ponyboy envies Sodapop's good looks and charm. Sodapop plans to marry **Sandy**, a greaser girl, but she becomes pregnant with someone else's child and moves away. Sodapop causes Darry and Ponyboy to come to a peaceful understanding of each other when they realize that their fighting is tearing Sodapop apart.

Dr. Harvey Cushing

Death Be Not Proud
John Gunther

Preeminent brain surgeon who was the first to open the skull to remove tumors. **Johnny** asks for Dr. Harvey Cushing after he develops papilledema.

Adolphus Cusins

Major Barbara
George Bernard Shaw

A "slight, thin haired, and sweet voiced" student of Euripides. Cusins is determined to marry **Barbara** and is enthralled by the excesses and ecstasies of the Dionysian spirit. In his determination, he has joined her in the Salvation Army to bring this spirit to the power, but ultimately converts to **Andrew Undershaft**'s gospel, becoming Andrew's heir at the Armory.

Marilla Cuthbert

Anne of Green Gables
L. M. Montgomery

An unmarried woman who raises **Anne Shirley**. Marilla lives at Green Gables with her unmarried brother, **Matthew Cuthbert**. Marilla seems sexless, straight-laced and stern, but some view her cohabitation with her brother as slightly strange. Although Marilla does not usually express emotion, underneath she has a wry sense of humor and a loving heart. As Marilla and Anne begin to understand each other better, they start to question their own standards of judgment and to accept each other's moral codes.

Matthew Cuthbert

Anne of Green Gables
L. M. Montgomery

An old bachelor who lives at Green Gables with his sister, **Marilla Cuthbert**. Matthew is painfully shy and a little eccentric. Although he is terrified of women, he instantly likes **Anne Shirley** and pressures Marilla to adopt her. Matthew becomes a warm father figure who takes increasing pleasure in spoiling Anne. Matthew and Anne are "kindred spirits," and in his dealings with Anne, Matthew shows a flair for parenting.

Miss Cutler

Lucky Jim
Kingsley Amis

Jim Dixon's housekeeper who runs the boardinghouse where **Evan Johns**, **Bill Atkinson**, and Dixon live. She is scared of Atkinson and does not relate to his contemptuous and misanthropic attitude.

Wick Cutter

My Ántonia
Willa Cather

A shady moneylender in Black Hawk.

Mother Cuxsom

The Mayor of Casterbridge
Thomas Hardy

A peasant in Casterbridge. Mother Cuxsom is friends with **Joshua Jopp**, **Nance Mockridge**, and **Christopher Coney**.

Cuyloga

The Light in the Forest
Conrad Richter

A brave, fair, and stoic warrior, the ideal image of the noble Indian. Although he is a strict leader who rarely shows emotion, Cuyloga deeply loves his white son and tries to guide him whenever possible. He is **True Son**'s hero.

Cuzak

My Ántonia
Willa Cather

A Bohemian immigrant who marries **Ántonia Shimerda** and raises a large family with her.

Cyclopes

Greek Mythology
Unknown

Fearsome one-eyed giants, of whom **Polyphemus** is the most famous. In some myths they are the children of **Gaea** and **Ouranos**; in others they are the sons of **Poseidon**. They forge thunderbolts for **Zeus**, who favors them.

Cymbeline

Cymbeline
William Shakespeare

The king of Britain and **Imogen**'s father. A wise and gracious monarch, Cymbeline is led astray by the machinations of his wicked **Queen**.

Cynthia

The Bean Trees
Barbara Kingsolver

The social worker who comes to work with **Taylor Greer** after **Turtle**'s run-in with a miscreant in the park. Eventually, Cynthia finds out about Turtle's past and tells Taylor that she has no legal claim to the child. Without a legal guardian, Turtle is a ward of the state. Cynthia's prim attitude annoys Taylor, but in the end, Taylor discovers that Cynthia's intentions are good.

Cynthia

Girl, Interrupted
Susanna Kaysen

A severe depressive on **Susanna Kaysen**'s ward. Cynthia undergoes months of electroshock therapy. The effects of the shock treatments change Cynthia's personality, leaving her trembling and unable to assert herself. Cynthia is close to **Polly**.

Cyrano de Bergerac

Cyrano de Bergerac
Edmond Rostand

The play's protagonist. Cyrano is a talented poet, swordsman, scientist, and musician. He is a member of the Cadets of Gascoyne, a company of royal guards. His countless displays of wit, valor, and heroism make him into an exaggerated stereotype of the swashbuckling, seventeenth-century poet-cavalier. He explains that he sometimes becomes depressed because of his very long nose. In some ways, his sense of alienation seems to prompt Cyrano to search for love even more ardently. He is unreasonably tough on himself, focusing only on his failures, imperfections, and weaknesses. His insecurity over his long nose prevents him from revealing his love for **Roxane**. Despite his affection for her, he enjoys helping **Baron Christian de Neuvillette** win her love, a fact that exemplifies Cyrano's attraction to challenges of all kinds. But he also displays modesty: when Roxane praises the love letters that Cyrano secretly writes, he does not believe that they have truly affected her. He realizes this impact, or allows himself to realize it, only when Roxane recites many of the lines back to him by heart. By the end of the novel, his long nose has become a symbol of his honorable nature and a reminder of its consequences. When he dies, he says he will take his unstained white plume with him to heaven.

Cyrus

The Prince
Niccolò Machiavelli

Founder of the Persian Empire.

13

THIRTEEN DISMAL DRUNKS

WE'RE AMAZED THESE CHARACTERS EVEN MAKE IT INTO THEIR STORIES.

Abel	1	*House Made of Dawn*
Lady Brett Ashley	2	*The Sun Also Rises*
Jack Barnes	3	*The Sun Also Rises*
Chuck Bolger	4	*This Boy's Life*
Billy Bones	5	*Treasure Island*
Dionysus	6	*The Bacchae*
Sir John Falstaff	7	*Henry IV, Parts One and Two, Henry V, The Merry Wives of Windsor*
Ligniere	8	*Cyrano de Bergerac*
The Miller	9	*The Canterbury Tales*
Inigo Montoya	10	*The Princess Bride*
Pap	11	*Huckleberry Finn*
Muff Potter	12	*Tom Sawyer*
James Tyrone	13	*Long Day's Journey into Night*

Francisco d'Anconia

Atlas Shrugged
Ayn Rand

An enormously wealthy and brilliant industrialist. Francisco d'Anconia is the first to join **John Galt**'s strike of the mind and the man who pays the highest price for it, losing his first and only love, **Dagny Taggart**. As a result of joining Galt's strike, Francisco destroys much of his own property, not wanting it to fall into the hands of the government "looters," who are looking to nationalize all industries. Eventually, Dagny and **Hank Rearden** come to understand and admire him, and the strike he devotes his life to works as planned.

Joseph D'Costa

Midnight's Children
Salman Rushdie

Mary Pereira's lover, who is politically radical.

Franz d'Epinay

The Count of Monte Cristo
Alexandre Dumas

A young Parisian and good friend of **Albert de Morcerf**'s. Franz D'Epinay is **Valentine Villefort**'s unwanted fiancé. **Maximilian Morrel**, who loves Valentine, makes her promise not to resign herself to marrying Franz. Franz writes an angry letter to **Gérard de Villefort**, calling off his engagement to Valentine, after he finds out that his father and Valentine's grandfather, **Noirtier de Villefort**, were great political enemies. Albert and Franz are both good friends with **Beauchamp**. Franz first meets **Edmond Dantès** in Edmond's guise as **Sinbad the Sailor** on the island of Monte Cristo.

Thomas Park D'Invilliers

This Side of Paradise
F. Scott Fitzgerald

An intellectual Princeton student and friend of **Amory Blaine**'s. An avid reader, Tom interests Amory in many new authors. In return, Amory introduces Tom to the Princeton social scene, which gradually conventionalizes Tom. Amory lives with him for a while in New York.

Alec d'Urberville

Tess of the d'Urbervilles
Thomas Hardy

The handsome, insouciant, amoral son of a wealthy merchant. Alec is not really a d'Urberville—his father simply took on the name of the ancient noble family after he built his mansion and retired. Alec is a manipulative, sinister young man who does everything he can to seduce the inexperienced **Tess Durbeyfield** when she comes to work for his family. When he finally has his way with her out in the woods, he subsequently tries to help her but is unable to make her love him. Alec's divided and duplicitous character is evident to the very end of the novel, when he quickly abandons his newfound Christian faith taught to him by the **Reverend Clare** upon meeting Tess again.

Dad

The Martian Chronicles
Ray Bradbury

Timothy's father in the story "The Million-Year Picnic," and the former governor of Minnesota. He is quiet, warm, and eager to start a new life on Mars. He burns a map of Earth, symbolizing his willingness to forget a past life.

Daddy

American Dream
Edward Albee

The subservient husband of **Mommy**. Bent to Mommy's will, he relies on her entirely for the confirmation of his masculinity. Like his wife, Daddy also displays a disturbing propensity for infantile behavior. Whereas Mommy becomes the tyrannical sadist in her regression, Daddy characteristically becomes the child needing punishment.

Daddy

Ellen Foster
Kaye Gibbons

The novel's antagonist. Daddy abuses his daughter, **Ellen**, sexually and psychologically. A severe alcoholic, Daddy's only job is selling liquor. He eventually drinks himself to death.

Dadi

Shabanu
Suzanne Fisher Staples

Shabanu and **Phulan**'s father. Dadi is a man of the desert. He is a skilled herder and is well-known for having the best camels in the Cholistan desert. Like **Mama**, Dadi is a kind and loving parent. He adores his two daughters and raises them to have a sense of freedom and pride. Dadi struggles to provide for the future safety and happiness of all his family members, especially his daughters.

Daggoo

Moby-Dick
Herman Melville

Flask's harpooner, or "squire." Daggoo is a physically enormous, imperious-looking African. Like **Queequeg**, he stowed away on a whaling ship that stopped near his home. Daggoo dies along with the rest of the crew, save **Ishmael**, in the final confrontation with Moby-Dick.

Mr. Dagley

Middlemarch
George Eliot

One of **Arthur Brooke**'s impoverished tenants. His son is caught poaching on Brooke's lands. He refuses Brooke's request that he chastise his son.

Daisy

Little Women
Louisa May Alcott

Meg March and **Mr. Brooke**'s daughter. Daisy is the twin of **Demi**. Her real name is Margaret.

Daisy

Rhinoceros
Eugène Ionesco

Berenger's love interest. She is fairly uncommitted to anything and does not mind the presence of the rhinoceroses. She and Berenger become isolated in his apartment while the rhinoceroses run freely about the city, and eventually she leaves him because he is adamantly opposed to the rhinos while she is noncommittal.

Daisy

Herzog
Saul Bellow

Moses Herzog's first wife and the mother of **Marco**. Daisy is a conservative, organized, and systematic woman of Jewish background, almost the antithesis of Moses' second wife, **Madeleine**. Moses' disorderly life brought out the worst in Daisy and led to their eventual divorce.

Daisy

Girl, Interrupted
Susan Kaysen

A patient who spends the period from Thanksgiving to Christmas at the hospital each year. Daisy lets no one into her room, emerging only for laxatives and the whole roast chickens her father brings twice weekly. **Lisa** discovers that Daisy's room is filled with the picked-over chicken carcasses. Daisy leaves the hospital to live in an apartment her father has purchased for her. The girls later learn that Daisy committed suicide on her birthday.

Clarissa Dalloway

Mrs. Dalloway
Virginia Woolf

The title character and protagonist. A middle-aged, upper-class British woman, Clarissa is alternately extremely sensitive and hopelessly shallow, constantly struggling to balance her inner and outer lives. She uses a stream of convivial chatter and activity to keep her soul locked safely away. For most of the novel she considers aging and death with trepidation, even as she performs life-affirming actions, such as buying flowers. Though content, Clarissa still questions the decisions that have shaped her life, particularly that of marrying **Richard Dalloway** instead of **Peter Walsh**. Like **Septimus Warren Smith**, Clarissa feels keenly the oppressive forces in life.

Elizabeth Dalloway

Mrs. Dalloway
Virginia Woolf

Clarissa Dalloway and **Richard Dalloway**'s only child. Gentle, considerate, and somewhat passive, seventeen-year-old Elizabeth does not have Clarissa's energy. She has a dark beauty that is beginning to attract attention. Not a fan of parties or clothes, she likes being in the country with her father and dogs. She spends a great deal of time praying with her history teacher, the religious **Miss Kilman**, and is considering career options.

Richard Dalloway

Mrs. Dalloway
Virginia Woolf

Clarissa Dalloway's husband. A member of Parliament in the Conservative government, Richard plans to write a history of the great English military family, the Brutons, when the Labour Party comes to power. He is a sportsman who likes the country, and he is a loving father and husband.

Dally

The Outsiders
S. E. Hinton

The toughest hood in **Ponyboy Curtis**'s group of greasers. Dallas Winston, known as Dally, is a hardened boy who used to run with gangs in New York. He has an elfin face and icy blue eyes and, unlike his friends, does not put grease in his white-blond hair. Dally's violent tendencies make him more dangerous than the other greasers, and he takes pride in his criminal record. Dally feels protective of **Johnny Cade**, whose parents do not care about him. Dally does reckless things, like slashing **Tim Shepard**'s tires, and talking dirty to Soc girls at the movies. Dally cannot deal with Johnny's death, and immediately after the death goes out and robs a store, pulls a gun on police, and gets shot to death.

Mary Dalton

Native Son
Richard Wright

The daughter of **Mr. Dalton** and **Mrs. Dalton**, **Bigger Thomas**'s wealthy employers. Mary identifies herself as a progressive, dates an admitted communist, and interacts with Bigger with little regard for the strict boundary society imposes between black men and white women. Mary's transgression of this boundary drives Bigger to murder her.

Mr. Dalton

Native Son
Richard Wright

Mrs. Dalton's husband, **Mary Dalton**'s father, and **Bigger Thomas**'s landlord and employer. A white millionaire living in Chicago, Mr. Dalton has earned his fortune by exploiting black people, but he thinks of himself as a generous supporter of them.

Mrs. Dalton

Native Son
Richard Wright

Mr. Dalton's wife, and **Mary Dalton**'s mother. She is blind.

Damrod

The Two Towers
J. R. R. Tolkien

One of two warriors of **Gondor** who come upon **Samwise Gamgee**, **Frodo Baggins**, and **Gollum** as the three are making their way east to Mordor. Damrod threatens to kill Gollum upon finding the creature bathing in a sacred pool in the outskirts of the land of Gondor. Frodo begs for Gollum to not be killed, which helps prove to Gollum that Frodo is an honorable master.

Damuddy

The Sound and the Fury
William Faulkner

The Compson children's grandmother.

Dan

The Red Tent
Anita Diamant

The only son of **Jacob** and **Bilhah**. Bilhah offers to bear a child for **Rachel** after Rachel's many miscarriages. This child turns out to be Dan, who is kind and true like his mother, and one of **Dinah**'s favorite brothers.

Old Dan

Where the Red Fern Grows
Wilson Rawls

One of **Billy Colman**'s red-bone coonhounds. Billy saved up to buy Old Dan. He is bigger and stronger than **Little Ann**, the other hound. Little Ann and Old Dan win the coon-hunting championship and get the gold cup. Old Dan has a fight with a mountain lion that ends up killing him. Little Ann dies soon afterward, having no will to live without Old Dan.

Major Danby

Catch-22
Joseph Heller

The timid operations officer of **John Yossarian**'s squadron. Danby used to be a college professor.

Chevalier Danceny

Dangerous Liaisons
Pierre-Ambroise-François Choderlos de Laclos

Cécile Volanges's music teacher. The Chevalier Danceny becomes the pet of **the Marquise de Merteuil** and the student of **the Vicomte de Valmont**. Along the way, he falls in love with Cécile. He exchanges many love letters with her, and in her naïve responses, she consistently confuses him. Later, Merteuil decides to tell **Madame Volanges** about Danceny's affair with Cécile in order to punish Danceny for not moving quickly enough to get what he wants. Merteuil decides to make a project out of seducing Danceny, which she succeeds in. When Merteuil and Valmont declare war upon each other, Valmont proves that Danceny will run from Merteuil's side to be with his beloved Cécile. Danceny kills Valmont in a duel over Cécile, with whom Valmont has been having his way.

Madame Dandelard

The American
Henry James

A pretty, childlike Italian woman who obtained a divorce from her abusive husband and fled to Paris. Mme. Dandelard now lives hand-to-mouth in the city, perpetually looking for an apartment and relying on the kindness of others. **Valentin de Bellegarde** is sure that Mme. Dandelard's story will end badly, as divorced, pretty, penniless women in nineteenth-century Paris had little choice other than prostitution. Though Valentin neither helps nor hurts Mme. Dandelard, he keeps in touch with her to satisfy his morbid curiosity about just how long her descent will take.

Dandelion

Watership Down
Richard Adams

The fastest of the rabbits, who often runs ahead to scout. Dandelion's speed often comes in handy, and **Hazel** uses him in some schemes because he knows Dandelion will not get caught. Dandelion also tells many stories.

William Dane

Silas Marner
George Eliot

Silas Marner's proud and priggish best friend from his childhood in Lantern Yard. William frames Silas for theft in order to bring disgrace upon him, then marries Silas's fiancée, **Sarah**.

Doc Daneeka

Catch-22
Joseph Heller

The medical officer of **John Yossarian**'s squadron. Doc Daneeka, who first explains Catch-22 to Yossarian, is unhappy that the war has interrupted his lucrative private practice in America.

Deputy Governor Danforth

The Crucible
Arthur Miller

The deputy governor of Massachusetts and the presiding judge at the witch trials. Honest and scrupulous, at least in his own mind, Deputy Governor Danforth is convinced that he is right to root out witchcraft. Danforth often takes the accusations of **Abigail Williams** and her group of "afflicted" girls as truth. He works with **Judge Hathorne** and **Reverend Parris** to get to the bottom of certain matters like **Giles Corey**'s accusation that the witch hunt is just **Thomas Putnam**'s ploy to grab more land. Often, if a citizen like Giles cannot back up his claim, Danforth holds that citizen in contempt of court. Even **Reverend John Hale**, whose appearance started the fervor of the witch hunt, starts to beg Danforth to consider certain people's testimony as untrue. By the time the witch trials are moving along, however, it is too late for Danforth to call them off, or he will appear to have been deceived by a group of young girls.

Danglars

The Count of Monte Cristo
Alexandre Dumas

A greedy cohort of **Fernand Mondego**'s who hatches the plot to frame **Edmond Dantès** for treason. He becomes a wealthy and powerful baron but loses everything when Dantès takes revenge as **the Count of Monte Cristo**. A greedy and ruthless man, Danglars cares only for his personal fortune. He has no qualms about sacrificing others for the sake of his own welfare, and he goes through life shrewdly calculating ways to turn other people's misfortunes to his own advantage. Danglars's betrayal of Dantès starts him on the path to utter disregard for other people's lives, but this betrayal is not the cruelest of his acts. Danglars abandons his wife, **Madame Danglars**, and attempts to sell his own daughter, **Eugénie Danglars**, into a loveless and miserable marriage with **Benedetto**'s faked role, Andrea Cavalcanti, for three million francs. Though he manages to claw his way into a position of great wealth and power, Danglars's greed grows as he grows richer, and his lust for money continues to drive all his actions in the two decades that the novel spans.

Eugénie Danglars

The Count of Monte Cristo
Alexandre Dumas

Daughter of **Danglars** and **Madame Danglars**. Eugénie Danglars, a musician, despises men and longs for independence, wanting to live her life as an artist. She is originally engaged to **Albert de Morcerf**, but Danglars breaks the engagement off and chooses Andrea Cavalcanti, because he believes Cavalcanti is very rich. On the eve of her wedding with Cavalcanti, an impostor played by **Benedetto**, she escapes to Italy with her companion, **Louise d'Armilly**.

Madame Danglars

The Count of Monte Cristo
Alexandre Dumas

Danglars's wife. Greedy, conniving, and unfaithful, Madame Danglars has a love affair with **Lucien Debray**.

Daniele and Giovanni

Lady Chatterley's Lover
D. H. Lawrence

Venetian gondoliers in the service of **Hilda Reid** and **Lady Chatterley**. Giovanni hopes the women will pay him to sleep with them, but he is disappointed. Daniele reminds Connie of **Oliver Mellors**, for he is attractive, a "real man."

Ken Dannager

Atlas Shrugged
Ayn Rand

A self-made Pennsylvania coal producer and a friend of **Hank Rearden**'s. Ken Dannager recognizes the irrationality of the looters' laws and breaks them. Ken Dannager joins **John Galt**'s strike of the mind after he is arrested for making illegal deals with Rearden. He refuses to lend any power, material, or money to the government, and then disappears.

Ragnar Danneskjold

Atlas Shrugged
Ayn Rand

A notorious pirate and a student of **Hugh Akston**'s. Ragnar Danneskjold is of the first mind strikers, a group of powerful industrial bosses and influential thinkers led by **John Galt** who disappear from the world so they do not have to take part in the government-regulation travesty destroying the economy and society. The leaders of the government who want to take all production and redistribute it according to "need," but who are hideously corrupt, are called "looters." Danneskjold fights the looters on their own violent terms, as they are exposed as simple brutes. A kind of reverse Robin Hood, Danneskjold steals from the government parasites and returns wealth to the productive, who are mostly hiding out in John Galt's secret valley.

Danny

Tortilla Flat
John Steinbeck

The protagonist of the novel and father figure of the group of *paisanos* whose exploits the novel follows. Danny owns the house in which the *paisanos* live and feels more responsibility than the rest for the well-being of the group. After serving in World War II and returning to Tortilla Flat, Danny dies by falling into a deep gulch after a night of drunken debauchery. Throughout the novel, Steinbeck likens the *paisanos* to King Arthur's knights of the Round Table, with Danny, as the ringleader, the clear King Arthur figure.

The Dansker

Billy Budd, Sailor
Herman Melville

Billy Budd's acquaintance and confidant aboard the HMS *Bellipotent*, a wizened old Danish sailor with beady eyes. The Dansker listens to Billy's confidences and occasionally issues inscrutable, oracular responses. At other times, however, the Dansker is decidedly reticent and unhelpful. The Dansker often warns Billy that **John Claggart** truly dislikes him, but the naïve Billy cannot sense Claggart's ill will.

Dante

Inferno
Dante Alighieri

The narrator and protagonist. While the narrator of *Inferno* is named Dante, he is not necessarily the same person as Dante the author. Sympathetic and fearful of danger, Dante the narrator is confused, both morally and intellectually, by his experiences in Hell. As the poem progresses, he adopts a more pitiless attitude toward the punishment of sinners, which he views as perfect divine justice.

Dante

A Portrait of the Artist as a Young Man
James Joyce

The Dedalus children's governess. Militantly pious, Dante speaks out against **Charles Stuart Parnell**, whom **Mr. Casey** and **Simon Dedalus** support, at **Stephen Dedalus**'s first Christmas dinner.

Edmond Dantès

The Count of Monte Cristo
Alexandre Dumas

The novel's protagonist. Dantès takes on the guise of four other characters, with **the Count of Monte Cristo** being the most powerful, important, and vengeful. Before his wrongful imprisonment, which is the fault of **Danglars**, **Fernand Mondego**, and **Gérard de Villefort**, Edmond Dantès is a kind, innocent, honest, and loving man. While in prison, however, Dantès undergoes a great change. He becomes bitter and vengeful as he obsesses over the wrongs committed against him. As the mysterious Count of Monte Cristo, Edmond gains the trust of his enemies. He ruins Danglars by exploiting Danglars's greed, tricking him into falling in love with the nonexistent money of Andrea Cavalcanti, played by **Benedetto**. He ruins Villefort by exposing the self-righteous public prosecutors as a man willing to kill and buy an illegitimate child. He causes **Madame d'Villefort** to be exposed as a woman willing to kill her own daughter, **Valentine d'Villefort**, in order to favor her other child, **Edward d'Villefort.** He exposes the **Count de Morcerf** as Fernand Mondego, who was responsible for the betrayal of **Ali Pacha** to Pacha's enemies. In order to carry out his work as Providence, Dantès becomes **Abbé Busoni**, who spreads wealth among the poor, and **Sinbad the Sailor**. As the eccentric and generous Englishman **Lord Wilmore**, the only supposed enemy of the Count of Monte Cristo, Dantès provides for himself a character who can explain Monte Cristo's behavior to others. Through these characters, as well as the other characters that Dantès has other people play, such as **Major Bartolomeo Cavalcanti**, Dantès acts as an emotionless and strong lord over everybody, not stopping until he feels his last enemy has been destroyed or shown repentance. It is not until Dantès finds love again, in a relationship with **Haydée**, the daughter of the wronged, deceased Ali Pacha, that he is able to reconnect to his own humanity and begin to live in the realm of human emotion again.

Louis Dantès

The Count of Monte Cristo
Alexandre Dumas

Edmond Dantès' father. Louis Dantès almost starves when Edmond is away at sea because **Caderousse** decides to collect on a debt of Edmond's. When Edmond Dantès is wrongly imprisoned, Louis becomes grief-stricken. Both **Monsieur Morrel** and **Mercédès** offered many times to take the old man into their homes and care for him, but Louis refused every time, ultimately choosing to starve himself to death.

Mrs. Danvers

Rebecca
Daphne du Maurier

Maxim de Winter's sinister housekeeper at Manderley. She was fiercely devoted to **Rebecca**, and remains devoted to her even after death. She despises **the Heroine** for taking her mistress's place.

Dap

Ender's Game
Orson Scott Card

The only teacher assigned by the school to actually befriend the Launchies. Dap looks out for the boys, and informs **General Pace** of the plot against **Ender Wiggin**.

Uncle Dap

The Once and Future King
T. H. White

Lancelot's childhood instructor. Although he is the brother of kings, Uncle Dap is Lancelot's squire when Lancelot becomes a knight of the Round Table in **King Arthur**'s court. Uncle Dap does his best to keep Lancelot away from **Guenever**, with whom he is in love.

Dapple

Don Quixote
Miguel de Cervantes

Sancho's donkey. Dapple's disappearance and reappearance stir much controversy in the novel.

Fitzwilliam Darcy

Pride and Prejudice
Jane Austen

A wealthy gentleman, the master of Pemberley, and the nephew of **Lady Catherine de Bourgh**. Though Darcy is intelligent and honest, his pride makes him look down on his social inferiors. Over the course of the novel, he tempers his class-consciousness and learns to admire and love **Elizabeth Bennet** for her strong character.

Georgiana Darcy

Pride and Prejudice
Jane Austen

Fitzwilliam Darcy's sister. Georgiana is immensely pretty and immensely shy. She has great skill at playing the pianoforte.

Monsignor Darcy

This Side of Paradise
F. Scott Fitzgerald

A man whose aborted love affair with **Amory Blaine**'s mother, **Beatrice**, motivated him to join the clergy. By the time Amory meets him, **Darcy** is a well-respected clergyman in New England. The two form a strong kinship, and Darcy essentially serves as a foster father to Amory, whose biological father is absent from the novel. Darcy laments the violence of World War I but praises Amory's enlistment as dutiful and noble. After the war, Amory learns via telegram that Darcy has passed away, and the loss leaves him feeling friendless and alone.

Mr. Dark

Something Wicked This Way Comes
Ray Bradbury

The major evil character in the book. Mr. Dark is the Illustrated Man, covered in tattoos, which allow him to exert some power over the figures the tattoos represent. He feeds on pain and destruction and fears nothing except the good that **Charles Halloway** uses to defeat him. He is tremendously strong and intimidates people, inspiring fear when he wishes to. The freaks at the carnival are completely within his power, and he uses both manipulation and force to bend people to his will.

Lolita
Vladimir Nabokov

Vivian Darkbloom

Clare Quilty's female writing partner. **Lolita** confuses **Humbert Humbert** by telling him that Vivian is a man and Clare is a woman. After Quilty's death, Vivian writes Quilty's biography.

The Bluest Eye
Toni Morrison

Darlene

The first girl whom **Cholly Breedlove** likes. The first time Cholly has sex, it is with Darlene. However, during this first time, some white hunters find Darlene and Cholly in the field and force them to continue at gunpoint while they watch. This incident sets up Cholly's hatred and mistreatment of women.

The Remains of the Day
Kazuo Ishiguro

Lord Darlington

The nobleman and proprietor of Darlington Hall for whom **Stevens** worked until Lord Darlington passed away. Lord Darlington is a traditional English gentleman who has honorable instincts and old-fashioned opinions. His manner of speaking, like Stevens's, is formal and refined. Stevens's attitude toward Lord Darlington changes when he learns that his former employee was a Nazi supporter.

The Count of Monte Cristo
Alexandre Dumas

Louise d'Armilly

Eugénie Danglars's music teacher and companion. Louise and Eugénie escape to Italy together. Eugénie dresses as a man and pretends to be Louise's brother during their escape. The two women often discuss their disdain for men. Once in Italy, they plan to make a living from their music.

A Tale of Two Cities
Charles Dickens

Charles Darnay

One of the protagonists of the novel. A French aristocrat by birth, Darnay chooses to live in England because he cannot bear to be associated with the cruel injustices of the French social system. Darnay is virtuous, honest, and courageous.

The Outsiders
S. E. Hinton

Darry

The older of **Ponyboy Curtis**'s two older brothers, and the unofficial leader of the greasers. His real name is **Darrell Curtis**. Darry raises his brothers Ponyboy and **Sodapop Curtis** because their parents died in a car crash. Strong, athletic, and intelligent, Darry holds the family together. He quit school and works two jobs. Ponyboy is sure that Darry is disappointed in him, especially after Darry slaps him. In the end, Ponyboy and Darry realize that they must stop bickering and start understanding each other if they want their family to stay together.

d'Artagnan

The Three Musketeers
Alexandre Dumas

The central character of the novel. D'Artagnan is a young, impoverished Gascon nobleman who comes to make his fortune in Paris. He is brave, noble, ambitious, crafty, and intelligent. After planning duels with the Three Musketeers, **Athos**, **Porthos**, and **Aramis**, he befriends them and gains a servant, **Planchet**. He falls in love with **Madame Bonacieux** while trying to protect her. He also sexually manipulates **Kitty** and the **Lady de Winter** in order to get information about Madame Bonacieux's whereabouts after she is kidnapped. D'Artagnan is a fighter for **Queen Anne**; he is a Royalist, but it turns out that he is in demand by **Cardinal Richelieu**, whom d'Artagnan is actually fighting against. The Cardinal sees what good fighters the Three Musketeers and d'Artagnan are and wants them in his guard. D'Artagnan is partly responsible for apprehending the Lady de Winter, finding out her true identity as the presumed-dead wife of Athos and bringing her to justice. During the fight to retrieve his beloved Madame Bonacieux, she is poisoned by the Lady and killed, dying in d'Artagnan's arms. This further inspires d'Artagnan to be a great warrior. He is not content to mourn Madame Bonacieux passively; he overcomes his sadness by achieving justice through revenge against the Lady de Winter.

Rosa Dartle

David Copperfield
Charles Dickens

The orphan child of **Mr. Steerforth**'s cousin, and the ward of **Mrs. Steerforth**. Rosa is bitter and proud. Like Mrs. Steerforth, she loves **James Steerforth** and dislikes **David Copperfield**.

Lifafa Das

Midnight's Children
Salman Rushdie

A peep-show street man who leads **Mumtaz** to **Shri Ramram Seth**, the seer.

Elinor Dashwood

Sense and Sensibility
Jane Austen

The protagonist of the novel. Elinor is the nineteen-year-old eldest daughter of the Dashwoods. She is composed but affectionate, both when she falls in love with **Edward Ferrars** and when she comforts and supports her younger sister **Marianne Dashwood**.

Fanny Dashwood

Sense and Sensibility
Jane Austen

John Dashwood's wife. Fanny is selfish, snobbish, and manipulative. She is the sister of **Edward Ferrars** and **Robert Ferrars**.

Henry Dashwood

Sense and Sensibility
Jane Austen

The father of **John Dashwood** and, by his second marriage, of **Elinor Dashwood**, **Marianne Dashwood**, and **Margaret Dashwood**. Henry Dashwood dies in the opening chapter of the novel, bequeathing his estate at Norland to his son.

John Dashwood

Sense and Sensibility
Jane Austen

Henry Dashwood's son. John is weak-minded and money-grubbing. Heeding the advice of his wife, **Fanny Dashwood**, he disobeys the promise he made to his father on his deathbed and gives almost no money to his late father's wife and daughters.

Margaret Dashwood

Sense and Sensibility
Jane Austen

The Dashwoods' youngest daughter. Margaret, a good-humored thirteen-year-old, shares **Marianne Dashwood**'s romantic tendencies.

Marianne Dashwood

Sense and Sensibility
Jane Austen

The second daughter of **Mr. and Mrs. Henry Dashwood**. Marianne is seventeen years old. Her spontaneity, excessive sensibility, and romantic idealism lead her to fall in love with **John Willoughby**. After he spurns her, she marries her admirer, **Colonel Brandon**.

Mrs. Dashwood

Sense and Sensibility
Jane Austen

The kind and loving mother of **Elinor Dashwood**, **Marianne Dashwood**, and **Margaret Dashwood**. Mrs. Dashwood is **Henry Dashwood**'s second wife. She wants the best for her daughters and shares Marianne's romantic sensibilities.

The dauphin

The Adventures of Huckleberry Finn
Mark Twain

A con man along with **the duke**. **Huckleberry Finn** and **Jim** rescue the duke and the dauphin as they are being run out of a river town. He claims to be the "dauphin," the son of King Louis XVI and heir to the French throne. Although Huck quickly realizes the men are frauds, he and Jim remain at their mercy, as Huck is only a child and Jim is a runaway slave. The dauphin was run out of town for leading temperance revival meetings but secretly drinking while doing so. As Huck, Jim, the dauphin, and the duke travel the river, the dauphin and the duke pull increasingly disturbing swindles, including a sham circus featuring "The King's Cameleopard, or The Royal Nonesuch." This behavior culminates in the con artists' treatment of **the Wilks family** and their eventual sale of Jim. Huck finally parts with the men after the duke encourages Huck to go look for Jim, at first slipping and saying that the dauphin sold Jim to **Silas Phelps**, but then trying to confuse Huck by changing his story.

Louis, Dauphin of France

Henry V
William Shakespeare

The son of **King Charles VI** and **Queen Isabel** and heir to the throne of France (until **King Henry V** takes this privilege from him). The Dauphin is a headstrong and overconfident young man, more inclined to mock the English than to think of them as an enemy worthy of respect. Unlike his father and other older nobles who recognize the English King's successful transformation, the Dauphin mocks Henry, making frequent mention of his irresponsible youth. His foolish overconfidence shows when he fails to send an army adequate enough to prevent Harfleur from being captured by Henry. Though the Dauphin and the other French noblemen are painted as decadent schoolboys for much of the play, they finally realize the strength of the English army and agree to die with honor, fighting in battle.

The Call of the Wild
Jack London

Dave

A dog on **Buck**'s sled team. Buck learns from Dave and **Sol-leks** how to be a sled dog when he is placed between them. Dave falls ill on one of the team's journeys after the Scotsman takes over the dogs from **François** and **Perrault**. He is shot and killed by the Scotsman.

Inherit the Wind
Jerome Lawrence & Robert E. Lee

Tom Davenport

The local district attorney in Hillsboro. Tom Davenport assists **Matthew Harrison Brady** during the trial. Davenport attempts to stop **Henry Drummond**'s humiliation of Brady at the end of the trial, but by the time he objects, Brady has already made a fool of himself. Drummond preys on the obvious contradictions in Brady's Christian-fundamentalist way of thinking.

The Old Testament
Unknown

David

The king of Israel and the founder of Jerusalem, or "Zion." David's reign marks the high point of Israel in the biblical narrative. Although David's claim to the throne is threatened by **Saul** and by David's own son, **Absalom**, David maintains his power by blending shrewd political maneuvering with a forgiving treatment of his enemies. His decision to bring the Ark of the Covenant—Israel's symbol of **God**—to the capital of Jerusalem signals the long-awaited unification of the religious and political life of Israel in the promised land. David is a humble but self-possessed shepherd chosen by God to replace **Saul** as king of Israel.

Tuesdays with Morrie
Mitch Albom

David

Morrie Schwartz's younger brother who, after their mother's death, is sent with Morrie to a small hotel in the woods of Connecticut. There, he develops polio after he and Morrie spend a night frolicking in the rain. Although his paralysis has nothing to do with their night in the rain, Morrie blames himself for David's condition.

On the Beach
Nevil Shute

Moira Davidson

A hard-drinking, tough-talking, flirtatious single young woman from Australia. Moira would rather dance and drink than think about her hopes for the future that the coming radiation will destroy. Even though she knows **Dwight Towers** will never be disloyal to his wife, Moira becomes his good friend, bringing life and excitement to Dwight's last months. In turn, Dwight's influence helps Moira find some peace in their inevitable fate.

Mr. Davidson

On the Beach
Nevil Shute

Moira Davidson's father. Mr. Davidson is a cattle rancher who cares for his farm and his animals until the very end. He is a hardworking man who loves his land.

Mrs. Davidson

On the Beach
Nevil Shute

Moira Davidson's mother. Mrs. Davidson still hopes her daughter will get married and have children, despite the fact that she only has a few months left to live.

Davin

A Portrait of the Artist as a Young Man
James Joyce

Stephen Dedalus's athletic friend. A simple, solid Irish nationalist from the provinces.

Davina

Breath, Eyes, Memory
Edwidge Danticat

The second member and hostess of **Sophie**'s sexual-phobia group. Davina is a middle-aged Chicana who, as a girl, was raped by her grandfather over a period of ten years.

Lancy Davis

The Heart Is a Lonely Hunter
Carson McCullers

A young black student to whom **Dr. Benedict Mady Copeland** awards an annual five-dollar prize for a rather militant essay he writes. Lancy is killed in a brawl near the end of the novel.

Davy

Henry IV, Part II
William Shakespeare

One of **Justice Shallow**'s household servants. Davy is honest, industrious, and talkative—he continually interrupts Shallow's dinner instructions to ask favors for local servants and friends who are in trouble.

Baxter Dawes

Sons and Lovers
D. H. Lawrence

Clara Dawes's husband. He fights with **Paul Morel**, but they later become friends while he is ill.

Clara Dawes

Sons and Lovers
D. H. Lawrence

A friend of **Miriam**'s, she is a suffragette who is separated from her husband. She becomes Paul's second love and they have a passionate affair.

Old day nurse

Johnny Got His Gun
Dalton Trumbo

Joe Bonham's regular day nurse. Joe senses she is a heavyset woman with a lot of nursing experience. Joe likes her efficiency and her affection for him.

New day nurse

Johnny Got His Gun
Dalton Trumbo

Joe Bonham's new nurse. From the vibrations of her steps, Joe senses that the new day nurse is shorter, lighter, and younger than the **old day nurse**. The new day nurse has a sympathetic connection with Joe and understands that he is trying to communicate.

Fermina Daza

Love in the Time of Cholera
Gabriel García Márquez

The wife of **Dr. Juvenal Urbino del Calle** and the object of **Florentino Ariza**'s affection. Fermina Daza is a sophisticated woman who, having grown up a peasant, takes pride in her haughty manner and unrelenting stubbornness; she cannot ever bear to admit that she is wrong. She is raised by her father, **Lorenzo Daza**, and her **Aunt Escolastica** after her mother, **Fermina Sánchez**, dies when Fermina Daza is a young child. She rejects Florentino's affections when she is young, and marries Dr. Urbino del Calle instead of Florentino. Fermina's sudden rejection of Florentino is founded in the many changes she undergoes during her long absence, which her father arranges so that she can forget Florentino, who is far below Fermina Daza in social class. The thrill of her forbidden romance with Florentino is lost on her with the onset of womanhood, for it is no longer scandalous or dangerous, as it was when she was a young girl bent on disobeying her domineering father. In marrying Dr. Urbino del Calle, she marries into the blue-blooded upper crust from the ranks of the peasants, and upholds with the utmost proficiency her position as a lady of society. In her old age, however, after Dr. Urbino del Calle's death, she does allow herself to be gently courted by the still-in-love Florentino, and she ends up exiling herself forever with him on a river-boat.

Lorenzo Daza

Love in the Time of Cholera
Gabriel García Márquez

Fermina Daza's domineering father, who pays cash for his home and is rumored to be a thief and a swindler. After finding Fermina's stash of love letters from **Florentino Ariza**, he cruelly banishes his sister, **Aunt Escolastica**, who is financially dependent upon him, and sends Fermina Daza on a years-long journey so that she will erase all memories of Florentino. He encourages **Dr. Juvenal Urbino del Calle** to court his daughter, greedy for Dr. Urbino del Calle's wealth and prestige. When it is uncovered that Lorenzo Daza is a thief, Dr. Urbino del Calle arranges the quieting of his criminal record and for an escape for Lorenzo out of the country.

Dr. Urbino Daza

Love in the Time of Cholera
Gabriel García Márquez

A physician and son of **Fermina Daza** and **Dr. Juvenal Urbino del Calle**. Dr. Urbino Daza asks **Florentino Ariza** to lunch, during which he thanks Florentino for the companionship he provides for Fermina Daza after Dr. Urbino del Calle's death.

Brian de Bois-Guilbert

Ivanhoe
Sir Walter Scott

A knight of the Templar Order, also known as the Knights-Templars, and **Ivanhoe**'s mortal enemy. Brian de Bois-Guilbert is a formidable fighter, but he is a weak moralist and often lets his temptations take control of him. Among the most complex characters in Ivanhoe, de Bois-Guilbert begins the novel as a conventional villain, but his love for **Rebecca** brings out his more admirable qualities as the story unfolds.

Maurice de Bracy

Ivanhoe
Sir Walter Scott

A Norman knight who is allied to **Prince John**. John plans to marry de Bracy to **Lady Rowena**, but de Bracy becomes impatient and kidnaps her party on its way home from Ashby, imprisoning them in **Reginald Front-de-Boeuf**'s stronghold of Torquilstone.

Comte de Guiche

Cyrano de Bergerac
Edmond Rostand

A powerful, married nobleman in love with **Roxane** who is not fond of **Cyrano de Bergerac**. Deceitful and always angry, he makes several attempts to have Cyrano killed.

Don Rogelio de la Flor

Chronicle of a Death Foretold
Gabriel García Márquez

Clothilde Armenta's husband. He tells his wife that she is being silly when she warns him about **Pedro Vicario** and **Pablo Vicario**'s plan. He dies of shock at age eighty-six when he sees the brutality of **Santiago Nasar**'s murder.

Don Quixote de la Mancha

Don Quixote
Miguel de Cervantes

The novel's tragicomic hero and protagonist. Obsessed with medieval romances, Don Quixote seeks to revive knight-errantry in a world where chivalry has become obsolete. Idealistic and dignified, willful and self-delusional, Don Quixote changes from an absurd and isolated figure to a pitiable, sympathetic old man over the course of the novel.

Marquis de la Mole

The Red and the Black
Stendhal

The benefactor of **M. Pirard** and **Julien Sorel**'s employer in Paris. Marquis de la Mole is a symbol of the dying aristocracy. Because Sorel impregnates the Marquis de la Mole's daughter, **Mathilde de la Mole**, the Marquis de la Mole reluctantly ennobles Sorel, giving Sorel a new name and rank in society. However, once **Mme. de Rênal** writes a letter denouncing Sorel to the Marquis de la Mole, he withdraws all support for Sorel, condemns his proposed marriage to Mathilde, and asks Sorel to move to America.

Mathilde de la Mole

The Red and the Black
Stendhal

The daughter of the **Marquis de la Mole**. Mathilde de la Mole is bored with Parisian society and immediately takes a liking to **Julien Sorel**. Mathilde is an admired beauty in high demand by Parisian society, so Sorel decides to seduce her. Unlike the noblemen who declare their love to her every day, she finds Sorel exciting. More important, she is extremely attracted to the bold notion of a forbidden love between an aristocratic woman and a man so far below her on the social scale. Mathilde also finds Sorel's fiery ambitions and liberal political aspirations a welcome change from the boring nobles she is used to. Sorel and Mathilde have a rocky relationship because of his attempts to make her jealous and her histrionics. When Sorel impregnates Mathilde, she urges her father to ennoble Sorel so that they can marry. After **Mme. de Rênal**'s condemning letter about Sorel, Mathilde and Sorel are forced to separate. When Sorel is in jail, **Fouqué** and Mathilde come to help him escape, but he refuses their help. Sorel decides in jail that he did not find true happiness with Mathilde, only with Mme. de Rênal. Still, after Sorel's decapitation, Mathilde buries Sorel's head.

Santa Sofía de la Piedad

One Hundred Years of Solitude
Gabriel García Márquez

The quiet woman who marries **Arcadio** and continues to live in the Buendía house for many years after his death, impassively tending to the family. She is the mother of **Remedios the Beauty**, **Aureliano Segundo**, and **José Arcadio Segundo**.

De Lacey

Frankenstein
Mary Shelley

The peasant father of **Felix De Lacey** and **Agatha De Lacey**. De Lacey is a blind old man who has lost his fortune. **The monster** learns how to speak and interact by observing the De Laceys. When he reveals himself to them, hoping for friendship, they flee in terror.

Agatha and Felix De Lacey

Frankenstein
Mary Shelley

The peasant children of **De Lacey**.

Albert de Morcerf

The Count of Monte Cristo
Alexandre Dumas

The son of **Fernand Mondego** and **Mercédès**. Albert de Morcerf is brave, honest, and kind. Mercédès is devoted to him. Albert and **Franz d'Epinay** first meet **Edmond Dantès** in his guise as **the Count of Monte Cristo**. The Count of Monte Cristo organizes a kidnapping of Albert by **Luigi Vampa** so that Monte Cristo can come to Albert's rescue, appearing to save Albert's life. In repayment, the Count of Monte Cristo only asks that Albert introduce the Count to Parisian society. Since Albert is the son of Fernand Mondego, Dantès strategically places himself as Albert's savior. Albert's father, Fernand Mondego, turns out to be the evil Frenchman who betrayed **Haydée**'s father, **Ali Pacha**, causing Ali Pacha's death. When Albert finds his father accused of this, he traces the investigation and accusation back to the Count of Monte Cristo, and he challenges the Count of Monte Cristo to a duel. The night before the duel, Mercédès pays a desperate visit to Monte Cristo. Monte Cristo explains to Mercédès why he hates Fernand, showing her the false accusation which caused Dantès' imprisonment. She pleads with Monte Cristo to save her son Albert's life, and he swears that Albert's life will be saved. The next day Albert apologizes to Monte Cristo, as Mercédès told her son everything that she and Monte Cristo talked about. After finding out about Fernand's terrible past, Albert and Mercédès try to move far away from him. Monte Cristo gives them the house of his father, **Louis Dantès**, and the money that is buried by the house. In the end, Albert joins the army, gives the money he receives for joining to his mother, and tries to shape his life in this way, heading off to his service in Africa.

Count de Morcerf

The Count of Monte Cristo
Alexandre Dumas

See **Fernand Mondego**.

Captain De Vriess

The Caine Mutiny
Herman Wouk

The first captain **Willie Keith** serves under on the *Caine*, and arguably the best captain to command the ship. De Vriess is well liked by the crew, who present him with a silver watch upon his departure from the ship.

Maxim de Winter

Rebecca
Daphne du Maurier

A cultured, intelligent older man, and the owner of Manderley, a prized estate and mansion on the English coast. When the novel begins, he has recently lost his beautiful, accomplished wife, **Rebecca**, in what the world believes was a tragic drowning. In fact, however, he killed her himself.

Deacon

The Sound and the Fury
William Faulkner

A black man in Cambridge, Massachusetts, to whom **Quentin** gives his suicide notes.

Macon Dead I

Song of Solomon
Toni Morrison

Macon, Jr. and **Pilate Dead**'s father and **Milkman Dead**'s grandfather. Macon Dead I is also known as Jake. Macon Dead I was abandoned in infancy when his father, **Solomon**, flew back to Africa and his mother, **Ryna**, went insane. Macon Dead I was raised by a Native American woman, **Heddy**. Macon Dead I later ran off with his adoptive sister, **Sing**, and they produced children. He was murdered by the Butler family, who made their fortune by killing poor, independent farmers. The mysterious legend of Macon Dead I's identity motivates Milkman's search for self-understanding.

Macon Dead III

Song of Solomon
Toni Morrison

See **Milkman Dead**.

First Corinthians Dead

Song of Solomon
Toni Morrison

Milkman Dead's worldly sister. Educated at Bryn Mawr and in France, First Corinthians shares her name with a New Testament book in which the apostle Paul seeks to mend the disagreements within the early Christian church. She works for the Michigan poet laureate, **Michael-Mary Graham**, as a maid, but she tells her family she is working as his secretary. Her passionate love affair with an elderly yardman and murderous Seven Days group member, **Henry Porter**, crosses class boundaries. Milkman later tells their father, **Macon, Jr.**, about First Corinthians's love affair, and Macon, Jr. throws Henry out of his apartment, makes First Corinthians quit her job, and forbids her to see Henry.

Macon Dead, Jr.

Song of Solomon
Toni Morrison

See **Macon, Jr.**.

Magdalene Dead

Song of Solomon
Toni Morrison

Another of **Milkman Dead**'s sisters, also known as Lena. Lena has a submissive attitude in **Macon Jr**.'s home, but her rebuke of Milkman's selfishness demonstrates her inner strength. After Milkman tells their father about **First Corinthians Dead**'s secret relationship with **Henry Porter**, Lena is furious with Milkman.

Milkman Dead

Song of Solomon
Toni Morrison

The protagonist of the novel, also known as **Macon Dead III**. **Freddie** gave him the nickname "Milkman" because he once spotted the boy taking milk from **Ruth Foster Dead**'s breast at an age that was too mature for breastfeeding. Born into a noble lineage of a prominent black doctor and wealthy landowner, **Dr. Foster**, and into a sheltered, privileged life, Milkman grows up to be an egotistical young man. He lacks compassion, wallows in self-pity, and alienates himself from the African-American community. Although he fits in at upscale parties, Milkman feels alienated by his family, other African Americans of all classes, and humanity in general. He is also physically different from the people around him, since he has an undersize leg. Since Milkman is able to conceal his leg, he believes that he can also hide his emotional shortcomings. He drives **Hagar**, the girl who loves him, to madness and death. Milkman's eventual discovery of his family history through **Pilate Dead** and **Circe** gives his life purpose. Milkman's immaturity stems directly from the enslavement and ensuing escape of his great-grandfather, **Solomon**. Because Solomon escaped, causing his wife **Ryna** to go mad, Milkman's grandfather, **Macon Dead I**, grew up an orphan. In turn, Macon Dead I's son, **Macon, Jr.**, witnesses white men murder his father. Macon, Jr. never fully recovers from witnessing his father's death; he becomes a greedy, vicious man who raises his own son, Milkman, to share those characteristics. Milkman is finally able to heal his wounds by traveling to Shalimar, the site of Solomon's flight toward liberty. There, he survives a second murder attempt upon him by his best friend, **Guitar Bains**, witnesses the accidental killing by Bains of Pilate, and becomes transformed into a fearless man.

Pilate Dead

Song of Solomon
Toni Morrison

Macon, Jr.'s younger sister. Born without a navel from her mother who is dead from labor, Pilate is physically and psychologically unlike the novel's other characters. She is a fearless mother who is selflessly devoted to others. Pilate is responsible for **Milkman Dead**'s safe birth and continues to protect him for years afterward. She also takes care of her daughter, **Reba**, and granddaughter, **Hagar**. She is frequently leading someone who is in need of guidance, such as the skeleton of her dead father, **Macon Dead I**, or Milkman, during his spiritual journey. Driven out of towns because of the fear people have of her navellessness, Pilate is a survivor of the same racism that has embittered Macon, Jr. and Milkman. Both Macon, Jr., who secretly eavesdrops on her nightly singing sessions, and Milkman, who uses the songs to find his ancestral home, Shalimar, need Pilate to keep alive the remaining vestiges of their humanity. When she is accidentally killed by **Guitar Bains**, who is trying to kill Milkman, Milkman suddenly realizes he has the strength to fearlessly leap in front of Guitar. He fails to save her, but after she dies, a flock of birds appears around Milkman's head.

Ruth Foster Dead

Song of Solomon
Toni Morrison

Macon, Jr.'s wife and the mother of **Milkman Dead**, **First Corinthians Dead**, and **Magdalene Dead**. After growing up in a wealthy home, Ruth feels unloved by everyone except her deceased father, **Dr. Foster**. Although her existence is joyless, she refuses to leave Macon, Jr. for a new life, proving that wealth's hold is difficult to overcome. It is possible that she had an incestuous affair with Dr. Foster. Unlike **Pilate Dead**, who is strong-willed, Ruth is a subdued, quiet, upper-class woman. Ruth relies on Pilate for financial support. As a result, Ruth never develops into a strongly independent person.

The dean

The Fountainhead
Ayn Rand

The dean of **Howard Roark**'s architecture school. He is a staunch traditionalist. He believes that everything worthy has already been designed and finds Roark dangerous.

Nelly Dean

Wuthering Heights
Emily Brontë

The chief narrator of *Wuthering Heights*. A sensible, intelligent, and compassionate woman, she grew up with **Catherine** and **Hindley Earnshaw** and is deeply involved in the story she tells. She has strong feelings for the characters in her story and these feelings complicate her narration.

Lucy Deane

The Mill on the Floss
George Eliot

The pretty, petite, blond cousin of **Tom Tulliver** and **Maggie Tulliver**. Lucy is genuinely good-hearted, thinking often of the happiness of others. She is also enough of a child of society life that she pays heed to social conventions and to her own appearance.

Mr. Deane

The Mill on the Floss
George Eliot

Mrs. Deane's husband and **Lucy Deane**'s father. He is a swiftly rising junior partner at Guest & Co. who focuses on business and profit-making more than family claims. He hires his nephew, **Tom Tulliver**, to work with him at the firm.

Mrs. Deane

The Mill on the Floss
George Eliot

Mr. Deane's wife, **Lucy Deane**'s mother, and the pale, quiet sister of **Mrs. Glegg**, **Mrs. Pullet**, and **Elizabeth Tulliver**. Mrs. Deane does not say much, and she rehearses what she says beforehand. She dies before the end of the novel.

Link Deas

To Kill a Mockingbird
Harper Lee

Tom Robinson's white employer. When **Atticus Finch** examines Tom Robinson in court, Link Deas stands up and declares that in eight years of work, he has never had any trouble from Tom. Deas threatens **Bob Ewell** with arrest when he finds Ewell harassing **Helen Robinson**, the widow of Tom Robinson.

Garrett Deasy

Ulysses
James Joyce

Headmaster of the boy's school where **Stephen Dedalus** teaches. A Protestant from the North, Deasy respects the English rule in Ireland. His overwrought letter to the editor of the Freeman about foot-and-mouth disease becomes an object of mockery.

Death

Paradise Lost
John Milton

Satan's son by his daughter, **Sin**. Death rapes his mother, begetting the mass of beasts that torment Sin. Death, Sin, and Satan represent a horrible perversion of the Holy Trinity.

Mary Debenham

Murder on the Orient Express
Agatha Christie

Daisy Armstrong's governess. Mary Debenham is a calm, cool and unruffled lady, instrumental in the planning of **Ratchett**'s murder. **Hercule Poirot** is most suspicious of Mary because of a conversation he overhears between her and **Colonel Arbuthnot** on the train to Stamboul.

Deborah

Go Tell It on the Mountain
James Baldwin

Florence's friend and **Gabriel**'s first wife and spiritual companion. She was brutally raped as a girl by a group of white men. Unable to bear children, she dies fairly young.

Lucien Debray

The Count of Monte Cristo
Alexandre Dumas

A government official who has an affair with **Madame Danglars**. She and Lucien Debray, using Debray's inside government information about the stock market, use much of **Danglars**'s money to gamble in stocks and bonds. When **the Count of Monte Cristo** finds out about this, he creates a fake news report that causes Debray to advise Madame Danglars to advise Danglars to sell all his Spanish stock. Once Debray learns that Danglars has been ruined financially, he is no longer interested in Madame Danglars.

Decius

Julius Caesar
William Shakespeare

A member of the conspiracy. Decius convinces **Julius Caesar** that **Calpurnia** misinterpreted her dire nightmares and that, in fact, no danger awaits him at the Senate. Decius leads Caesar right into the hands of the conspirators.

Decretas

Antony and Cleopatra
William Shakespeare

One of Antony's soldiers.

Boody, Dilly, Katey, Maggy, and Maurice Dedalus

A Portrait of the Artist as a Young Man and *Ulysses*
James Joyce

Stephen Dedalus's younger siblings, who have not had many of the opportunities offered to Stephen. After the death of their mother **Mary Dedalus**, they struggle with running the household.

Mary Dedalus

A Portrait of the Artist as a Young Man and *Ulysses*
James Joyce

Stephen Dedalus's mother and **Simon Dedalus**'s wife. In *A Portrait of the Artist as a Young Man*, Mary is very religious, and argues with her son about attending religious services In *Ulysses*, she has died. Despite her pleas, Stephen refused to pray on her deathbed and is now paralyzed by guilt.

Simon Dedalus

A Portrait of the Artist as a Young Man and *Ulysses*
James Joyce

Stephen Dedalus's father, a good signer and former medical student with a strong sense of Irish patriotism. Simon has driven the family to poverty through bad money management and heavy drinking. After ruining himself and his family, he turns to nostalgia and alcohol for consolation. He spends a great deal of his time reliving past experiences. In *A Portrait of the Artist as a Young Man*, Stephen regards his father as symbolic of the burdens that family and nationality place upon him. By *Ulysses*, Stephen thinks that Simon has failed him as a father and so seeks out spiritual fathers in Shakespeare and **Leopold Bloom**.

Stephen Dedalus

A Portrait of the Artist as a Young Man and *Ulysses*
James Joyce

The young hero said to be the author's alter ego. Stephen grew up devoutly Catholic and is crippled by guilt about the death of his mother, **Mary Dedalus**. Stephen is intelligent, sensitive, and extremely well-read, but he is also profoundly lonely, at once insecure and arrogant. *A Portrait of the Artist as a Young Man* chronicles Stephen's childhood and adolescence, during which he passes through phases of hedonism and religious asceticism. He emerges with an almost fanatical devotion to aesthetic beauty and scorns society's constraints to live freely as an artist. Despite his family's increasing financial difficulties, Stephen graduates from a series of prestigious schools and then university. In *Ulysses*, Stephen is an aspiring poet in his mid-twenties.

Dee-Dee

The Color of Water
James McBride

Ruth McBride Jordan's younger sister. Dee-Dee was a shy, pretty girl, less strong-willed than Ruth. She had fewer conflicts with her father, **Fishel Shilsky**, than Ruth did, and she was more Americanized from a young age. While Ruth always envied her, later in life she realized that Dee-Dee had suffered sorrow and desperation.

Lord Deepmere

The American
Henry James

Valentin de Bellegarde, **Claire de Bellegarde**, and **Urbain de Bellegarde**'s seventh cousin, an extremely rich heir to sizable estates in England and Ireland. At thirty-three, Deepmere is young, artless, and fairly simple. Though he enjoys Paris and London, he is a self-avowed Irishman who lacks the subtlety and ambition of the Bellegardes. The elder Bellegardes are thrilled with Deepmere, hoping he will marry Claire and allow them access to his non-commercial fortunes. His lack of sophistication borders on naïveté, as when **Madame de Bellegarde** tries to persuade him to steal Claire from **Christopher Newman**, and Deepmere immediately tells Claire everything. Deepmere's behavior also implies childish pleasure and convenient forgetfulness, as when he consorts unashamedly with **Noémie Nioche** several months after she causes the death of his cousin Valentin.

Madame Defarge

A Tale of Two Cities
Charles Dickens

A cruel revolutionary whose hatred of the aristocracy fuels her tireless crusade. Madame Defarge spends a good deal of the novel knitting a register of everyone who must die for the revolutionary cause. Unlike her husband, **Monsieur Defarge**, she is unrelentingly bloodthirsty.

Monsieur Defarge

A Tale of Two Cities
Charles Dickens

A wine-shop owner and revolutionary in the poor Saint Antoine section of Paris. Monsieur Defarge formerly worked as a servant for **Doctor Manette**. Defarge is an intelligent and committed revolutionary leader.

Purisima del Carmen

Chronicle of a Death Foretold
Gabriel García Márquez

The mother of **Angela Vicario**. She had been a schoolteacher until she married. After her daughter is brought home by **Bayardo San Roman** on her wedding night, she holds Angela's hair with one hand and beats her with the other.

Fernanda del Carpio

One Hundred Years of Solitude
Gabriel García Márquez

The wife of **Aureliano Segundo** and the mother of **Meme**, **José Arcadio (II)**, and **Amaranta Úrsula**. Raised by a family of impoverished aristocrats, she is very haughty and very religious. She tries to impose her harsh, religious discipline on her household, forcing her daughter to become a nun in the same gloomy convent where she had lived. She hides **Aureliano (II)**, her daughter's illegitimate son, in a back room. Her hedonistic husband does not love her and maintains his relationship with his concubine, **Petra Cotes**. In her old age, Fernanda del Carpio does nothing but bemoan her fate and write to her children in Europe. She dies, overcome with nostalgia.

Lucretia del Real del Obispo

Love in the Time of Cholera
Gabriel García Márquez

Fermina Daza's close friend. She is too ashamed ever to speak to Fermina Daza again after a tabloid press fabricates a story that Lucretia del Real del Obispo and **Dr. Juvenal Urbino del Calle**, Fermina Daza's husband, had had an affair. This false article is published after the death of Dr. Urbino del Calle.

Nivea del Valle

The House of the Spirits
Isabel Allende

The mother of **Clara**, **Rosa the Beautiful**, and thirteen other children; wife of **Severo del Valle**. Nivea is a suffragette. She dies, decapitated, in a car accident. Clara retrieves the head of her mother and puts it in a hat box in her and **Esteban Trueba**'s house.

Severo del Valle

The House of the Spirits
Isabel Allende

Father of **Clara** and **Rosa the Beautiful**, husband of **Nivea del Valle**. Severo is a businessman who becomes a politician with the Liberal party. He only goes to church as a way to gain political favor with his constituency. When he gets support to be a candidate from a group in the South, someone tries to poison him with poisoned brandy at his celebration, but Rosa the Beautiful drinks the brandy instead and dies. He and Nivea die in a car accident.

Fleur Delacour

Harry Potter and the Goblet of Fire
J. K. Rowling

The Triwizard champion for Beauxbatons. Fleur is a beautiful, silvery haired part-Veela girl who is a bit patronizing and snobby, but in the end grows moderately fond of **Harry Potter** and **Ron Weasley**.

Packy Delaney

Legs
William Kennedy

Owner of a favorite latter-day Diamond hangout, the Parody Club, he is an Irish-American barkeep who does a few favors for **Jack**. At the beginning of the novel, **Marcus** and Packy reminisce about Jack.

Amasa Delano

Benito Cereno
Herman Melville

The main character, the captain of the Bachelor's Delight, a whaling ship from Massachusetts. Delano is a pleasant, good-natured man, who is slow to become suspicious but by no means naïve.

Uda Dell

Animal Dreams
Barbara Kingsolver

Doc Homer Nolina's nearest neighbor. Uda Dell cares for **Codi Nolina**, **Hallie Nolina**, and Doc Homer over the years, and is one of Codi's most important links to her childhood.

Pier della Vigna

Inferno
Dante Alighieri

A former advisor to the Holy Roman Emperor Frederick II. Because he committed suicide after falling into disfavor at court, della Vigna must spend eternity as a tree in the Second Ring of the Seventh Circle of Hell (Canto XIII).

Dellon

Pigs in Heaven
Barbara Kingsolver

Annawake Fourkiller's brother and husband of **Millie**. Dellon and Millie are a classic example of the way the Cherokee value all kinds of family configurations. Although they are divorced, they keep having kids together, and love them dearly.

Anthony Delmonte

I Am the Cheese
Robert Cormier

See **David Farmer**.

Paul Delmonte

I Am the Cheese
Robert Cormier

See **Adam Farmer**.

Oracle at Delphi

Greek Mythology
Unknown

A priestess of **Apollo** and the most famous prophet in all of Greece. Humans typically consult the Oracle to ascertain the will of the gods or a person's fate. She most often appears at the beginning of a story, as a character asks his fate, finds it unpleasant, and then tries to change it, only to become a victim of fate precisely because of his attempts to alter it.

P. R. Deltoid

A Clockwork Orange
Anthony Burgess

A "Post-Corrective Advisor" assigned to **Alex**. He encourages Alex to stop engaging in violence and theft early in the narrative, claiming that the next time he is arrested he will be sent to prison, not corrective school. Like nearly all "responsible" adults in *A Clockwork Orange*, Deltoid is not altruistic. Alex's crimes only concern him because an "unreclaimed" Alex will be a "black mark" on his record. When Alex is arrested, Deltoid's only response is to spit in Alex's face and walk away.

Nikolai Dementiev

Crime and Punishment
Fyodor Dostoevsky

A painter working in an empty apartment next to **Alyona Ivanovna**'s on the day of the murders. Suspected of the murders and held in prison, Nikolai eventually makes a false confession.

Demeter

Greek Mythology
Unknown

The goddess of corn and harvest, a sister of **Zeus** who lives, unlike the majority of gods, on Earth. Demeter is kinder than **Dionysus** but also sadder, mostly because **Hades** has taken her daughter **Persephone** as his reluctant bride. Demeter mourns this abduction for four months of the year, leaving the fields barren, which provides the mythological explanation for winter.

Demetrius of *Midsummer*

A Midsummer Night's Dream
William Shakespeare

A young man of Athens. Initially in love with and betrothed to **Hermia**, Demetrius follows her and **Lysander** to the forest—and he, in turn, is pursued by his adorer, **Helena**. Demetrius's obstinate pursuit of Hermia throws love out of balance among the quartet of Athenian youths and precludes a symmetrical two-couple arrangement. Thanks to the fairies' intrusion, Demetrius is ultimately made to fall in love with Helena.

Demetrius of *Titus*

Titus Andronicus
William Shakespeare

Chiron and Demetrius are **Tamora**'s sons. The two brothers murder **Bassianus** and brutally rape and maim **Lavinia**. Nothing more than engines of lust, destruction, and depravity, they lack the wit and intelligence that make their coconspirator **Aaron** a more compelling villain. **Titus** kills the two for raping his daughter, and has them cooked into pies and fed to their treacherous mother Tamora.

Demi

Little Women
Louisa May Alcott

Meg March and **Mr. Brooke**'s son and **Daisy**'s twin. Demi's real name is John Laurence. Demi is a stereotypical boy who often tries to control his sister. Louisa May Alcott's characterization along traditional gender lines seems to reflect her understanding that progress toward a greater role for women would be achieved only gradually.

Max Demian

Demian
Hermann Hesse

Emil Sinclair's mentor, an almost unnaturally precocious youth who first meets Sinclair while still in grade school. He inspires Sinclair at many of the steps along his route to self-discovery. Even when the two are not together, Sinclair often feels Demian's influence. Demian is, more than anyone else, the character responsible for getting Sinclair to recognize the importance of living for himself and breaking free of societal constraints.

Demon of Insincerity

The Phantom Tollbooth
Norton Juster

A demon that looks like a cross between a beaver and a kangaroo. He tries to scare **Milo** and his companions off their path through the Mountains of Ignorance by throwing half-truths at them. Once he looks upon the so-called monster with unclouded vision, Milo sees that there is nothing to be afraid of and the demon is defeated.

Denethor

The Return of the King
J. R. R. Tolkien

The Steward of Gondor and the father of **Boromir** and **Faramir**. Denethor undergoes a painful descent into madness that J.R.R. Tolkien uses to explore the complexity of the Evil within **Humans**. Proud and wise, Denethor fails not because he is inherently evil, but because he allows the evil lies of the *palantír*, a seeing stone much like the one that caused the fall of **Saruman**, to convince him that he is incapable of saving Minas Tirith from Mordor's power. He is tricked when he looks into the *palantír* and sees Mordor's ships coming toward Minas Tirith. They really are coming, but they are commanded by **Aragorn**, who had won them in defeating **Sauron**'s **Orcs** with the help of the Army of the Dead. **Théoden**, King of Rohan, serves as a foil to Denethor, for Théoden is able to be saved from his dishonorable fall by **Gandalf**'s words of wisdom and hope.

Mr. Denham

The Autobiography of Benjamin Franklin
Benjamin Franklin

A Quaker friend of **Benjamin Franklin**'s in London. Denham eventually convinces Franklin to return to Philadelphia after a successful and enjoyable eighteen-month stay. Franklin works in Denham's goods store upon his return.

Denise

White Noise
Don DeLillo

Babette's overly cautious and caring daughter. She is the first one to see Babette taking Dylar and prompts **Jack** to do something about it.

Denisov

War and Peace
Leo Tolstoy

A short, hairy, good-looking friend of **Nikolai Ilyich Rostov**'s who accompanies him to Moscow on home leave and falls for **Sonya Rostova**. Denisov is later court-martialed for seizing army food provisions to feed his men.

Sir Anthony Denny

Henry VIII
William Shakespeare

A lord of the court who escorts **Cranmer, Archbishop of Canterbury** to **King Henry VIII**.

Parkie Denton

The Virgin Suicides
Jeffrey Eugenides

Mary Lisbon's Homecoming date. A comparatively rich boy, Parkie is notable for his occasional access to his father's yellow Cadillac, in which he, **Trip Fontaine**, **Kevin Head**, and **Chase Buell** take the Lisbon girls to Homecoming.

Denver

Beloved
Toni Morrison

Sethe's youngest child, named for **Amy Denver**. Sethe considers Denver a "charmed" child who has miraculously survived, and throughout the book Denver is in close contact with the supernatural. Her self-conception remains so tentative that she feels slighted by the idea of a world that does not include her—even the world of slavery at Sweet Home. Denver defines her identity in relation to Sethe. She also defines herself in relation to her sister—first in the form of the baby ghost, then in the form of **Beloved**. In the face of Beloved's escalating malevolence and Sethe's submissiveness, Denver is forced to step outside the world of 124 Bluestone Road. Filled with a sense of duty, purpose, and courage, she enlists the help of the community and cares for her increasingly self-involved mother and sister. She asks for help from an old teacher, **Lady Jones**, enters a series of lessons with **Miss Bodwin**, and considers attending Oberlin College someday. **Ella** hears about Beloved because of Denver's solicitations for help, and comes to 124 with a group of women to perform an exorcism.

Amy Denver

Beloved
Toni Morrison

A nurturing and compassionate white girl who works as an indentured servant. She has finished her servitude and is on her way to Boston when she runs into the fleeing slave, **Sethe**. Amy is young, flighty, talkative, and idealistic. She helps Sethe when Sethe is ill and running from Sweet Home. She later delivers Sethe's baby, whom **Sethe** names **Denver**, after Amy.

Edgar Derby

Slaughterhouse-Five
Kurt Vonnegut

Like **Billy Pilgrim**, a soldier who survives the firebombing of Dresden. After the bombing, Derby is sentenced to die by firing squad for plundering a teapot from the wreckage. His death is anticlimactic, since Billy views it as inevitable.

Miss Derek

A Passage to India
E. M. Forster

A young, easygoing Englishwoman resented by the British community for working as a servant for a wealthy Indian family whose car Miss Derek often "borrows."

Descheeny

Ceremony
Leslie Marmon Silko

Betonie's grandfather. Along with the **Mexican girl**, Descheeny, a medicine man, began the creation of the new ceremony that would be able to cure the world of the destruction of the whites. He was the first of his people to recognize the need for collaboration between Native Americans and Mexicans.

Desdemona

Othello
William Shakespeare

The daughter of the Venetian senator **Brabanzio**. Desdemona and **Othello** are secretly married before the play begins. While in many ways stereotypically pure and meek, Desdemona is also determined and self-possessed. She is equally capable of defending her marriage, jesting bawdily with **Iago**, defending **Cassio** to Othello, and responding with dignity to Othello's incomprehensible jealousy. Othello eventually murders Desdemona in a jealous rage incited by Iago's lies.

Dessalines

Breath, Eyes, Memory
Edwidge Danticat

The poor coal seller in the marketplace of La Nouvelle Dame Marie. Dessalines is capriciously beaten and finally killed by Macoute soldiers during **Sophie**'s trip to Haiti with her infant daughter in Section Three.

Detering

All Quiet on the Western Front
Erich Maria Remarque

One of **Paul Bäumer**'s close friends in the Second Company. Detering is a young man who constantly longs for his wife and farm.

Alvin Dewey

In Cold Blood
Truman Capote

An investigator for the Kansas Bureau of Investigation (KBI), Dewey is the agent responsible for much of western Kansas. He becomes very involved in the Clutter murder case, to the distress of his wife, **Marie**, and his two small boys.

The Deweys

Sula
Toni Morrison

Eva Peace's three informally adopted children, all of whom she named Dewey. Although they look completely different, people have trouble telling them apart. They never grow into full adult size. The Deweys represent a parallel to **Sula Peace** and **Nel**. Like the two girls, the three boys are intensely attached to one another, and the intensity of their friendship makes it difficult to draw a boundary between their individual identities.

Dexios

The King Must Die
Mary Renault

A childhood friend of **Theseus**'s. Dexios is his charioteer on the ride through the Isthmus. He is a good friend and a good driver, and when he is killed, Theseus avenges his death.

Manny di Presso

The Crying of Lot 49
Thomas Pynchon

A lawyer and old friend of **Metzger**'s. Manny di Presso resides near Lake Inverarity. One of his clients is suing **Pierce Inverarity**'s estate for money Inverarity owed. The client sent Inverarity human bones recovered from an Italian lake for use in charcoal production.

Mother Dia

The King Must Die
Mary Renault

The major deity in Eleusis, Crete, and all of the Minyan areas. Mother Dia represents the old religion. Some of the priests and priestesses who worship Mother Dia are very resistant to change, and do not wish to allow the worship of any other gods.

Diagnosing Doctor

Girl, Interrupted
Susanna Kaysen

The psychiatrist who encourages **Susanna Kaysen** to enter McLean Hospital. He completes his diagnosis in twenty minutes.

Alice Diamond

Legs
William Kennedy

Jack's faithful wife, she is the archetypal good homemaker. She cooks for Jack and keeps his house well furnished. Troubled by Jack's corrupt occupation, Alice surrounds him with reminders of his Irish Catholic heritage.

Eddie Diamond

Legs
William Kennedy

Jack's brother, he was Jack's closest companion. They entered the life of crime together when they started stealing bootleg booze. Jack thinks that Eddie brought him good luck. Eddie died of tuberculosis before most of the novel's events take place.

Legs
William Kennedy

Jack Diamond

The novel's protagonist, he is a ruthless gangster who has built an underground empire based on bootlegging, drug dealing, and money laundering. Although he has a mean streak when it comes to business, Jack does not relish violence. His vibrant personality has made it easy for the press and others to see him as a larger-than-life bad guy. Jack loves his wife **Alice**, but he also loves his girlfriend **Kiki**. The novel is narrated forty-five years after the events it describes, and this distance emphasizes Jack's position as mythical hero of a bygone era.

Greek Mythology
Unknown

Diana

The Roman name for the Greek goddess **Artemis**.

Pericles
William Shakespeare

Diana of *Pericles*

Goddess of chastity, the moon, and the hunt in Greek mythology. Diana appears to **Pericles** and urges Pericles and **Marina** to go to Ephesus, prompting their reunion with **Thaisa**.

All's Well that Ends Well
William Shakespeare

Diana of *All's Well*

A young Florentine virgin whom **Bertram** attempts to seduce. When **Helena** hears of Bertram's play for the chaste Diana, she convinces the Florentine girl to trick him. Diana persuades Bertram to hand over his ring and come back at night, at which point Helena, his lawful wife, secretly switches places with her. In her well-played seduction of Bertram, Diana proves just as clever as Helena. At the close of the play, the **King of France** offers her the same present he awarded Helena: her pick of French husbands.

Miss Julie
August Strindberg

Diana

Miss Julie's dog, said to resemble her mistress.

Johnny Got His Gun
Dalton Trumbo

Diane

Joe Bonham's girlfriend in Shale City. They broke up when she cheated on him with **Glen Hogan**.

The House of the Spirits
Isabel Allende

Ana Diaz

A student revolutionary. She first meets **Alba** during the occupation of the university. Later, Ana Diaz helps Alba to survive in **Esteban Garcia**'s detention centers, caring for Alba's wounds, and strengthening Alba's will to live.

Dick the Butcher

Henry VI, Part II
William Shakespeare

A follower of **Jack Cade**'s rebellion. Along with Cade and his other followers, the Butcher calls for the creation of a realm where the simplest working man is the most honored, and literate people will be executed.

Colonel Nathaniel Dick

The Unvanquished
William Faulkner

A Union colonel who spares **Bayard** and **Ringo** when they shoot a Yankee horse and who issues an order granting **Granny** more than a hundred mules and slaves. Bayard and the others believe that Yankees are practically a different species, but Colonel Dick represents the humane face of the Northern army—he is humorous and reasonable, sympathetic to Granny's plight thanks to thoughts of his own children.

Vernon Dickey

White Noise
Don DeLillo

Babette's father and **Jack Gladney**'s father-in-law. He is a rough, good-natured man, seemingly unafraid of dying, who works with his hands and knows how to build things.

Didius

Tristram Shandy
Laurence Sterne

A pedantic church lawyer, and the author of the midwife's license.

Dido

The Aeneid
Virgil

The queen of Carthage, a city in northern Africa in what is now Libya, and lover of **Aeneas**. Dido left the land of Tyre when her husband was murdered by her brother **Pygmalion**. She and her city are strong, but she becomes an unfortunate pawn of the gods in their struggle for Aeneas's destiny. Her love for Aeneas, provoked by **Venus**, proves her downfall. After he abandons her, she constructs a funeral pyre and stabs herself upon it with Aeneas's sword.

Bishop Digby

Stranger in a Strange Land
Robert A. Heinlein

The Supreme Bishop of the Fosterite sect. Digby had risen to his position by poisoning **the Reverend Foster**, though his followers do not know this. He attempts to convert **Valentine Michael Smith** to the Fosterite faith. Digby is a great salesman, who has discovered untraditional ways, such as encouraging gambling and employing celebrities, to promote the word of his church.

Amos Diggory

Harry Potter and the Goblet of Fire
J. K. Rowling

The proud father of **Cedric Diggory** and another employee of the Ministry of Magic.

Cedric Diggory

The Harry Potter Series: Books 3 and 4
J. K. Rowling

The handsome, brave, and fair Hufflepuff Triwizard champion. In *The Prisoner of Azkaban*, Cedric catches the Snitch during a Quidditch match when **Harry** falls from his broom. In *Harry Potter and the Goblet of Fire*, Cedric dies at the hands of **Voldemort**.

Mrs. Dignam

Ulysses
James Joyce

Patrick Dignam's wife, left poor after his death because he used his life insurance to pay off debts.

Patrick Dignam

Ulysses
James Joyce

An acquaintance of **Leopold Bloom**'s who recently passed away, apparently from drinking. His funeral occurs on the day described in the novel. Bloom and others get together to raise money for Paddy's widow, **Mrs. Dignam**, and her children.

Dr. Dilling

Babbitt
Sinclair Lewis

A conservative surgeon in Zenith. **Dr. Dilling** helps the other members of the Good Citizen's League in the attempt to coerce **Babbitt** into conforming to Zenith's middle-class values. Dr. Dilling also treats **Myra** when she falls seriously ill.

Red Dillon

When the Legends Die
Hal Borland

Meo Martinez's employer and **Thomas Black Bull**'s teacher. He instructs young Tom as a bronco rider. Tom travels with him to many shows throughout the southwestern United States. Though Tom is somewhat attached to him, Red continually exploits the young boy for his ability to win him gambling money. Not only a compulsive gambler, but also an alcoholic, Red eventually dies in Tom's arms.

Dilsey

The Sound and the Fury
William Faulkner

The Compsons' cook. Dilsey is a pious, strong-willed, protective woman who stabilizes the Compson family.

Dim

A Clockwork Orange
Anthony Burgess

The biggest, strongest, and stupidest member of **Alex**'s gang. Dim's sloppiness and vulgarity constantly annoy **Alex**, often to the point of physical abuse. Dim's lingering resentment toward Alex contributes to **Georgie**'s successful coup, which leaves him in charge of the gang while Alex is imprisoned. Two years later, when Alex is released from prison, Dim and former rival **Billyboy** appear as police officers who drive Alex into the country, where they beat him and leave him for dead in a field.

Joe DiMaggio

The Old Man and the Sea
Ernest Hemingway

A star player for the New York Yankees baseball team. Although Joe DiMaggio never actually appears in the novel, the fisherman **Santiago** worships him as a model of strength and commitment and turns his thoughts toward DiMaggio whenever he needs to reassure himself of his own strength.

Reverend Arthur Dimmesdale

The Scarlet Letter
Nathaniel Hawthorne

A young man who achieved fame in England as a theologian and then emigrated to America. In a moment of weakness, he and **Hester Prynne** became lovers. Although he will not confess it publicly, he is the father of her child, **Pearl**. He deals with his guilt by tormenting himself physically and psychologically, developing a heart condition as a result. His commitments to his congregation are in constant conflict with his feelings of sinfulness and the need to confess.

Sir Dinadan

A Connecticut Yankee in King Arthur's Court
Mark Twain

A knight who fancies himself a comedian. The sixth century finds him funny enough, but **the Yankee** simply cannot abide a particular joke of his. When Sir Dinadan leaves the Yankee's company in order to fight a joust, the Yankee exclaims to himself that he hopes that Sir Dinadan is killed. This gets the Yankee into trouble because **Sir Sagramor le Desirous** thinks that the Yankee is talking about him, and challenges the Yankee to a fight in four years.

Dinah

The Red Tent
Anita Diamant

Only surviving daughter of **Jacob** and protagonist of *The Red Tent*, birthed by **Leah**. As the only daughter among twelve sons birthed by four mothers, **Rachel**, **Bilhah**, **Leah**, and **Zilpah**, Dinah grows up comfortable and adored in the world of women. She spends her childhood in the women's tents, learning their private stories and ways. As a narrator, she is careful to detail even the subtlest actions of her family members, but rarely takes such care in describing herself. For the majority of Dinah's life she is portrayed as a passive observer, taking little to no responsibility for the events in her life after she leaves to find her own story. She is twice married, to **Shalem** and to **Benia**, and becomes a renowned midwife in Egypt under the tutelage of **Meryt**. When **Re-nefer** takes Dinah's son **Re-mose** as her own, Dinah is practically unresponsive, grieving quietly but not defending herself.

Aunt Dinah

Tristram Shandy
Laurence Sterne

Tristram's great aunt and, in Tristram's estimation, the only woman in the Shandy family with any character at all. She created a family scandal by marrying the coachman and having a child late in her life.

Diomedes

The Iliad
Homer

The youngest of the Achaean commanders. Diomedes is bold and sometimes impetuous. Inspired by **Athena**, he wounds two gods, **Aphrodite** and **Ares**, after **Achilles** withdraws from combat.

Diomedes

Troilus and Cressida
William Shakespeare

A Greek commander who seduces **Cressida**.

Diomedes

Antony and Cleopatra
William Shakespeare

Cleopatra's servant. She employs Diomedes to bring **Antony** the message that she has not committed suicide but is still alive.

Dion

The Winter's Tale
William Shakespeare

A Sicilian lord. Dion accompanies **Cleomenes** to Delphi.

Dionysus

Greek Mythology
Unknown

God of wine. He embodies both the good and evil effects of alcohol. At times he is a jovial partyer and patron of music and art, but at other times he is the god of madness and frenzy. Also known as Bacchus.

Dionysus

The Bacchae
Euripides

Originator, protagonist, and central axis of *The Bacchae*. Dionysus is the god of wine, theater, and group ecstasy, who appears mostly in disguise. Dionysus is the son of **Zeus** and the mortal **Semele**, daughter of **Cadmus**. At times he is a jovial partyer and patron of music and art, but at other times he is the god of madness and frenzy.

Dionyza

Pericles
William Shakespeare

Cleon's wife. Dionyza pledges to care for **Marina**, but is jealous when her own daughter grows up less beautiful and gracious, so she plots to have Marina killed. Both Dionyza and Cleon are punished at the end.

Director

Brave New World
Aldous Huxley

Administrator of the Central London Hatchery and Conditioning Centre. The Director is a threatening figure, with the authority to exile **Bernard Marx** to Iceland. However, he is vulnerable because he bore a son—**John**—with **Linda**. Natural childbirth is a scandalous and obscene act in the World State, and when **Marx** returns from the New Mexico Savage Reservation with John and Linda in tow, the Director is forced to resign.

Director

The Stranger
Albert Camus

The manager of the old persons home where **Madame Meursault** spent her final three years. When **Meursault** arrives to keep vigil before his mother's funeral, the director assures him that he should not feel guilty for having sent Madame Meursault to the home. When Meursault goes on trial for murdering **the Arab**, the director becomes suddenly judgmental and chastises Meursault's indifference toward his mother.

Dischord

The Phantom Tollbooth
Norton Juster

A quack doctor who prescribes medicines of terrible noises to all of his patients. Dischord has an assistant, a smoke monster named **Dynne**.

The Disinherited Knight

Ivanhoe
Sir Walter Scott

The name under which **Ivanhoe** fights in the great tournament at Ashby, using a disguise because he still has not revealed his presence in England.

District Commissioner

Things Fall Apart
Chinua Achebe

An authority figure in the white colonial government in Nigeria. The prototypical racist colonialist, the District Commissioner thinks he understands everything about native African customs and cultures, and he has no respect for them. He plans to work his experiences into an ethnographic study on local African tribes, the idea of which embodies his dehumanizing and reductive attitude toward race relations.

Dick Diver

Tender Is the Night
F. Scott Fitzgerald

A young American psychiatrist living in Europe. A former Rhodes scholar, **Dick** is on the way to becoming a renowned figure in his field when he falls in love with and marries one of his patients, the young **Nicole Warren**. Several years into the marriage, Dick meets the American starlet **Rosemary Hoyt**, who is instantly infatuated with him. Rosemary confesses her love, and Dick initially resists but gradually falls for her. When the still-fragile Nicole finds out, she has an hysterical relapse. Several years later, having opened a clinic in Zurich and still taking care of the unstable Nicole, Dick finds Rosemary again, and they engage in a brief affair. Dick goes back to Nicole, begins to drink heavily, and loses his job at the clinic. When Nicole asks for a divorce in order to marry **Tommy Barban**, Dick returns to America, where he disappears into his alcoholism.

Lanier Diver

Tender Is the Night
F. Scott Fitzgerald

Dick and **Nicole Diver**'s young son. Dick sees **Lanier** as difficult because he asks too many questions.

Nicole Diver

Tender Is the Night
F. Scott Fitzgerald

The beautiful young daughter of a wealthy Chicago businessman. Born Nicole Warren, she was sexually abused by her father, **Devereux**, and suffers from mental breakdowns as a result. While recovering at a psychiatric clinic in Zurich, Nicole falls in love with her doctor, **Dick Diver**, at first sight. Although initially tentative, Dick marries her, partly because of her inheritance and partly because Nicole's controlling sister, **Baby**, pushes for the match. As a married couple, Dick and Nicole enjoy an extravagant and turbulent life in Europe at the center of a sophisticated group of friends. However, Nicole's mental illness, which still renders her fragile and prone to fits, plunges into full relapse when she becomes aware that Dick is infatuated with another woman, the young actress **Rosemary Hoyt**. Their marriage begins to disintegrate, but as Dick falls into a downward spiral of heavy drinking, Nicole seems to recover. Ultimately, she requests a divorce so that she can marry the smug **Tommy Barban**.

Topsy Diver

Tender Is the Night
F. Scott Fitzgerald

Dick and **Nicole Diver**'s young daughter.

Jim Dixon

Lucky Jim
Kingsley Amis

The hero of the story. A good friend to **Margaret Peel**, an admirer of **Christine Callaghan**'s, and an unremarkable young man about to complete his first year as an assistant lecturer in the Department of History at a provincial college in Britain. Intolerant of the pretense and hypocrisy of the college's faculty and their families, Jim hides his contempt, channeling it into venomous mental outbursts and a wide array of nasty faces.

Mr. and Mrs. Dixon

Emma
Jane Austen

Residents of Ireland. Mrs. Dixon is the Campbells' plain-looking daughter and **Jane Fairfax**'s friend. **Emma Woodhouse** suspects Mr. Dixon of having had a romance with Jane Fairfax before his marriage.

Djali

Hunchback of Notre Dame
Victor Hugo

La Esmerelda's goat. When La Esmerelda and **Djali** are in the courtroom, all the tricks that La Esmerelda taught her for their street performances appear to be witchcraft.

Sir Gerald Doak

Babbitt
Sinclair Lewis

An aristocratic British businessman who is a guest of **Charles McKelvey**'s when he stays in Zenith. When **Babbitt** encounters Doak in Chicago, they become friendly with one another, and Babbitt learns that Doak is frustrated with the mistaken assumptions that Americans make about him because he is an aristocrat.

Babbitt
Sinclair Lewis

Seneca Doane

A radical lawyer who was one of **Babbitt**'s college classmates. Doane supports the labor rights movement and runs unsuccessfully against **Prout** in the Zenith mayoral election. Doane protests the standardized opinions and values of the middle class. When Babbitt engages in a brief rebellion against those values, he voices support for Doane's political opinions, much to the horror and dismay of his friends.

The Things They Carried
Tim O'Brien

Henry Dobbins

The platoon's machine gunner. A gentle giant, Henry is profoundly decent.

The Adventures of Tom Sawyer
Mark Twain

Mr. Dobbins

The schoolmaster where **Tom Sawyer**, **Joe Harper**, and **Becky Thatcher** attend school. Mr. Dobbins seems a slightly sad character: his ambition to be a medical doctor has been thwarted and he has become a heavy drinker and the butt of schoolboy pranks.

Catch-22
Joseph Heller

Dobbs

A copilot. Dobbs seized the controls from **Huple** on the mission to Avignon during which **Snowden** died.

The Harry Potter Series: Books 2 and 4
J. K. Rowling

Dobby

The house-elf of **Lucius Malfoy**. Dobby tries to get **Harry Potter** out of Hogwarts to keep him away from the danger that lurks there. He almost kills Harry many times trying to save his life.

I Never Promised You a Rose Garden
Joanne Greenberg

Quentin Dobshansky

One of the attendants at the mental hospital. It pains **Deborah** that Quentin is nervous around her sometimes because she has a mental illness.

Native Son
Richard Wright

Doc

The black owner of a pool hall on the South Side of Chicago where **Bigger Thomas** and his friends hang out.

Doc

Cannery Row
John Steinbeck

The proprietor of Western Biological Laboratory, a specimen supply house on Cannery Row. Doc is a gentle, melancholy man who is a source of culture, benevolence, and aid for all on the Row. He introduces **Dora**'s girls and **Mack** and his boys to opera, classical music, and literature, and he takes the young, neglected **Frankie** and cares for him. Most of the loose plot of *Cannery Row* revolves around the locals' plans—some successful, some failed—to throw Doc a party.

Doc

The Power of One
Bryce Courtenay

A German music professor, in his 80s, with whom **Peekay** becomes best friends in the town of Barberton. Doc was a concert pianist in Germany before he gave up performing after a disastrous concert in Berlin in 1925. He is one of Peekay's most important mentors, but is prized by the Barberton citizens only for the culture he brings to the town through his classical music. When Doc dies, he leaves all his belongings to Peekay.

Doctor

The Two Noble Kinsmen
William Shakespeare

A cynical man, he values psychological well-being over conventional moral standards.

Doctor

A Tree Grows in Brooklyn
Betty Smith

Medical worker who administers vaccinations. A Harvard graduate, he makes cruel assumptions about the poor in Brooklyn.

Doctor

The Pearl
John Steinbeck

A small-time colonial who dreams of returning to a bourgeois European lifestyle. The doctor initially refuses to treat the infant boy **Coyotito** for a scorpion sting but changes his mind after learning that Coyotito's father, **Kino**, has found a large pearl of great value.

Doctor

A Streetcar Named Desire
Tennessee Williams

The man who arrives to whisk **Blanche DuBois** off to an asylum. He and the nurse initially seem to be heartless institutional caretakers, but, in the end, the doctor appears more kindly as he takes off his jacket and leads Blanche away.

Dodecahedron

The Phantom Tollbooth
Norton Juster

A creature with twelve different faces wearing twelve different emotions. He leads **Milo** and his companions through the numbers mine, where workers chisel out gemlike digits, to the city of Digitopolis.

Mr. Dodge

Incidents in the Life of a Slave Girl
Harriet Ann Jacobs

Emily Flint's husband, who seeks to recapture **Linda Brent** after **Dr. Flint** dies. Although Mr. Dodge is northern by birth, entering southern society has made him as grasping and unfeeling as any native-born slave holder.

Lewis Dodgson

Jurassic Park
Michael Crichton

A reckless geneticist who is the head of product development at Biosyn Corporation. Dodgson hires **Dennis Nedry** to steal InGen's technology from Jurassic Park.

Dodo

Alice in Wonderland
Lewis Carroll

The leader of the Caucus-race, in which the participants run in confused circles and never really accomplish anything.

Dogberry

Much Ado About Nothing
William Shakespeare

The foolish constable in charge of the watchmen of Messina. His scenes with **Verges** and the other watchmen provide the standard comic relief between the scenes of malicious tricks and public humiliation. Though his watchmen have successfully apprehended **Borachio** and **Conrad**, Dogberry's bumbling and malapropisms ruin his chances to warn **Leonato** of the treachery in time. Dogberry is very sincere and takes his job seriously, but he has a habit of using exactly the wrong word to convey his meaning.

Dr. Dohmler

Tender Is the Night
F. Scott Fitzgerald

The psychiatrist who initially handles **Nicole Warren**'s case at the clinic in Zurich. Dr. Dohmler urges **Dick Diver** to terminate his relationship with Nicole.

Dolabella

Antony and Cleopatra
William Shakespeare

One of **Octavius Caesar**'s men. Dolabella is assigned to guard the captive **Cleopatra**.

Father Dolan

A Portrait of the Artist as a Young Man
James Joyce

A cruel prefect of studies.

Denver D. Doll

On the Road
Jack Kerouac

Sal Paradise's Central City friend. A caricature of an eager official, Denver D. Doll often shakes hands and drops incoherent pleasantries.

Ben Dollard

Ulysses
James Joyce

A man known for his superior bass voice. Ben Dollard's business and career foundered a while ago. He seems good-natured but is rattled by a past drinking habit.

Dolokhov

War and Peace
Leo Tolstoy

A handsome Russian army officer and friend of **Nikolai Ilyich Rostov**'s. Dolokhov carries on with **Helene Vasilievna Kuragina**, prompting **Pierre Bezukhov** to challenge him to a duel in which Pierre nearly kills him.

Emelina Domingos

Animal Dreams
Barbara Kingsolver

Codi Nolina's childhood friend in whose guesthouse she lives in Grace. Emelina Domingos happily mothers her five sons as well as her close friend Codi. Emelina leads a simple life, devoted to her family and to her community without ever losing a strong sense of herself. Codi saves **Nicholas Domingos**, Emelina's youngest son, from choking.

Juan Teobaldo Domingos

Animal Dreams
Barbara Kingsolver

Emelina Domingos's husband. Juan Teobaldo Domingos, or J.T., divides his time between working on the railroad, caring for his orchard, and loving his family. He works on the railroad with **Loyd Peregrina**, who impregnated **Codi Nolina** when they were in high school.

Nicholas Domingos

Animal Dreams
Barbara Kingsolver

Emelina Domingos's youngest son. As Emelina and **Codi Nolina** are attending a dance at **Doña Althea**'s family's outdoor restaurant, Nicolas Domingos begins to choke and Codi saves his life. Nicholas learns to walk in the middle of the disaster of **Hallie Nolina**'s disappearance in Nicaragua, symbolizing the continuation of life.

Viola Domingos

Animal Dreams
Barbara Kingsolver

Emelina Domingos's mother-in-law. Viola Domingos appears to be a typical meddling but sweet grandmother. Her devotion to her family and her community makes her one of the leaders of the movement that saves the town of Grace from the chemical pollution that is being caused by the Black Mountain mine. Viola also proves to be a repository of local and family history.

Donalbain

Macbeth
William Shakespeare

King Duncan's son and **Malcolm**'s younger brother. Once his father is murdered, Donalbain flees to Ireland for fear that the killers will also make an attempt on his life.

Mr. Donatelli

The Contender
Robert Lipsyte

The boxing trainer and life teacher of **Alfred Brooks**. Mr. Donatelli is the vehicle through which Alfred changes and evolves as a person. He is completely candid and never sugarcoats the truth.

Sergeant Dongan

Fallen Angels
Walter Dean Myers

An officer who replaces **Sergeant Simpson** as the leader of **Richie Perry**'s squad. Sergeant Dongan is a racist and always places black soldiers in the most dangerous positions during patrols.

Mr. Edward Donleavy

I Know Why the Caged Bird Sings
Maya Angelou

A white speaker at **Maya Johnson**'s eighth-grade graduation ceremony. He insults the black community by talking condescendingly, but not explicitly, of their limited potential in a racist society. His racist tone casts a pall over the graduation and infuriates Maya.

Arabella Donn

Jude the Obscure
Thomas Hardy

Jude Fawley's first wife, and mother to their son, **Little Father Time**. Arabella is a heartless character who personifies the danger of a bad marriage. Jude proposed to her when they were very young because he thought she was pregnant, and he felt trapped and manipulated when he found that there was no baby on the way. Jude marries her again at the end of his life. When he is dying, she is unwilling to sacrifice the diversion of a boat race to be with him.

Joe Donnelly

Dubliners
James Joyce

The man **Maria** visits in "Clay." Joe's brief appearance in the story provides a backdrop for Maria's own concerns.

Mr. Donner

Flowers for Algernon
Daniel Keyes

The owner of the bakery where **Charlie Gordon** works. A friend of **Uncle Herman**'s, Mr. Donner agreed to hire Charlie so he would not have to go to the Warren State Home upon Herman's death. Donner gave Herman his word that he would look out for Charlie's interests. Donner stands by his pledge faithfully and treats Charlie like family.

Larry Donovan

My Ántonia
Willa Cather

Ántonia Shimerda's fiancé, an arrogant and selfish young man. After being fired from his job as a railroad conductor, Donovan leaves Ántonia on the eve of their wedding, running away to Mexico in search of a quick fortune.

Peter Dooley

Angela's Ashes
Frank McCourt

Frank McCourt's hunchbacked friend who wants to work for the BBC as a radio newsreader.

Alfred Doolittle

Pygmalion
George Bernard Shaw

Eliza's father, an elderly but vigorous dustman. Unembarrassed and unhypocritical, Doolittle advocates the pursuit of drink and pleasure. When he becomes rich, he becomes miserable; as a poor dustman, he feels freer than as a member of the leisure class.

Eliza Doolittle

Pygmalion
George Bernard Shaw

The Cockney flower girl whom **Higgins** teaches to speak proper English. Apart from learning a new way of speaking and new manners, she develops from a squawking street urchin into a human being with a sense of dignity and self-worth.

Dora

Ellen Foster
Kaye Gibbons

Ellen's cousin and **Nadine**'s daughter. Dora is a sheltered, spoiled brat who gets everything she wants, when she wants it.

Doramin

Lord Jim
Joseph Conrad

Chief of the **Bugis**; a wise, kind old man and a "war-comrade" of **Stein**'s. Stein gives **Jim** a silver ring as a token of introduction to Doramin. Doramin saves Jim after his escape from the **Rajah Allang**, who had been holding him prisoner. Doramin is the father of **Dain Waris**, Jim's closest friend. When Dain Waris is killed because of Jim's misjudgment, Doramin shoots and kills Jim, who has offered himself up as a sacrifice.

Mr. Doran

Dubliners
James Joyce

The lover of **Mrs. Mooney**'s unpolished daughter **Polly Mooney** in "The Boarding House." A successful clerk, Mr. Doran fears his affair with Polly will tarnish his reputation, but he resolves to marry her out of social necessity and fear.

Dorcas

Stranger in a Strange Land
Robert A. Heinlein

One of **Jubal Harshaw**'s three beautiful, extremely competent live-in secretaries. Dorcas is the most squeamish and flirtatious of the three.

Dorcas

Jazz
Toni Morrison

A girl with acne, light skin, straight hair and a womanly figure. Dorcas has an affair with **Joe Trace**, who meets her at the home of her aunt, **Alice Manfred**, when he is selling cosmetics. Precocious and romantic, and seeking male attention at a young age, Dorcas yearns to live a racy, adult life. She wants to attend nightclubs and parties, and most important, she wants to adore and be adored. She quickly becomes bored with the infatuation of her older lover and becomes eager to track down a more desirable catch. She finds **Acton**, who really only cares about his own image. Joe becomes madly jealous and finds Dorcas at a party and shoots her. Later, at Dorcas's funeral, Joe's jealous wife **Violet** slashes the face of Dorcas' corpse with a knife while it is lying in the casket.

Doreen

The Bell Jar
Sylvia Plath

Esther Greenway's companion in New York. Doreen is a blond, beautiful southern girl with a sharp tongue. Esther envies Doreen's nonchalance in social situations, and the two share a witty, cynical perspective on their position as guest editors for a fashion magazine.

Dori

The Hobbit
J. R. R. Tolkien

One of the dwarf companions on the novel's quest.

Doris

Go Ask Alice
Anonymous

A fourteen-year-old girl whom **Alice** meets in Oregon. Doris has been sexually abused by both her stepfather and foster-family siblings.

Dormouse

Alice in Wonderland
Lewis Carroll

The **March Hare** and the **Mad Hatter**'s lethargic, much-abused companion.

Yevgeny Sergeyevich Dorn

The Seagull
Anton Chekhov

A local doctor who was once a popular and handsome ladies' man. Dorn often provides an outsider's perspective to the play, functioning as a virtual onstage audience member in his fluid observations and commentaries. He has known **Arkadina**, **Sorin**, and the rest of the characters for many years. Dorn is fond of **Polina Andreyevna** but does not seem to be in love with her. Dorn attempts to assuage the tensions between **Treplyov**'s fledgling artistic impulses and his mother Arkadina's domineering ego.

Dorothea

Don Quixote
Miguel de Cervantes

Ferdinand's faithful and persistent lover. Cunning and aggressive, Dorothea tracks down Ferdinand after he sleeps with her and refuses to marry her.

Bertha Dorset

The House of Mirth
Edith Wharton

The wife of **George Dorset**. Most of the characters know that she has a history of extramarital affairs, one of which may have been with **Lawrence Selden**. She is described as a nasty woman who enjoys making other people miserable, especially her own husband. She invites **Lily** on a cruise with her, her husband, and **Ned Silverton** around the Mediterranean, but only so Lily will distract George while Bertha has an affair with Ned. Bertha, the novel's antagonist, spreads the rumor that Lily and George are having an affair, then uses her money and influence to keep Lily out of society forever.

George Dorset

The House of Mirth
Edith Wharton

The husband of **Bertha Dorset**. George does not factor into the novel regularly until Book Two, when he begins to realize that his wife is cheating on him with **Ned Silverton**. To complicate matters, George seems to fancy **Lily**, although she refuses to see him ever again after people spread rumors that the two of them had an affair.

Marquess of Dorset

Richard III
William Shakespeare

The son of **Elizabeth Woodville, Lady Grey** (Queen Elizabeth), brother of **Lord Grey**, nephew of **Lord Rivers**, and stepson of **King Edward IV**. Threatened by the entire Woodville line, **King Richard III** eventually executes Rivers and Grey, but Dorset survives and flees to join **Henry Tudor, Earl of Richmond**.

Lydia Douce

Ulysses
James Joyce

A bronze-haired barmaid at the Ormond Hotel bar. Miss Douce has a crush on **Hugh "Blazes" Boylan**.

Douglas

The Turn of the Screw
Henry James

One of the holiday guests in the Prologue. Douglas reads the manuscript, which composes the bulk of the novel. The **governess**, the author of the manuscript, was also Douglas's sister's governess.

Agnes Douglas

Stranger in a Strange Land
Robert A. Heinlein

Secretary General Joseph Douglas's domineering wife. Agnes is a staunch devotee of astrology and often forces her husband to base important decisions on the advice of her astrologist, **Madame Alexandra Vesant**.

Secretary General Joseph Douglas

Stranger in a Strange Land
Robert A. Heinlein

The leader of the Earth's government. Douglas worries that his power is under threat and endeavors to maneuver **Valentine Michael Smith** to his political advantage. Douglas is a consummate politician, at ease with the tremendous power, responsibility, and pressures of his position. The one person who has influence over him is his domineering wife, **Agnes Douglas**.

Mildred Douglas

The Hairy Ape
Eugene O'Neill

The frail, impetuous daughter of Nazareth Steel's owner. She is an "artificial character," solely bred from and pampered by aristocratic and monetary pleasures with no real knowledge of work or hardship. She attempts to regain some connection to and understanding of the "other half" by studying sociology and doing various service projects.

Widow Douglas

The Adventures of Tom Sawyer
and *The Adventures of Huckleberry Finn*
Mark Twain

A kindhearted, pious resident of the town of St. Petersburg, Missouri, whom the children recognize as a friend; the eventual adoptive mother of **Huckleberry Finn**. The Widow Douglas is the sister of **Miss Watson**; the two wealthy sisters live together in a large house. In *The Adventures of Tom Sawyer*, **Tom Sawyer** knows that the Widow Douglas will give Tom and **Becky Thatcher** ice cream and let them sleep over. The widow is kind to Huckleberry Finn even before she learns that he saved her life by spotting **Injun Joe** heading toward her house. When the widow finds out that Huck saved her life, she announces that she plans to give him a home and educate him. In *The Adventures of Huckleberry Finn*, it becomes clear that the Widow Douglas is somewhat gentler in her beliefs than her harsh sister, and has more patience with the mischievous Huck. She tries to explain prayer to Huck, to teach him table manners, and to help him quit smoking. When Huck's **Pap** shows up to town, Pap is infuriated with the Widow Douglas' attempts to "sivilize" Huck. Even though it is clear that Pap is a terrible father, the new judge in town refuses to grant custody of Huck to the Widow and **Judge Thatcher** because he does not want to break up a father and son. Huck runs away with **Jim**, but the memory of the widow stays with him. Huck is reunited with the Widow Douglas at the end of *The Adventures of Huckleberry Finn*.

Chet Douglass

A Separate Peace
John Knowles

Gene Forrester's main rival for the position of class valedictorian at the Devon School. Chet Douglass is an excellent tennis and trumpet player who sincerely loves learning. In Gene's imagined academic competition with **Finny**, he ends up surpassing Chet, who is his only real academic rival.

Frederick Douglass

Narrative of the Life of Frederick Douglass
Frederick Douglass

The author and narrator. Douglass, a rhetorically skilled and spirited man, is a powerful orator for the abolitionist movement. One of his reasons for writing the book is to offer proof to critics who felt that such an articulate and intelligent man could not have once been a slave. *Narrative* describes Douglass's experience under slavery from his early childhood until his escape north at the age of twenty. Within that time, Douglass progresses from unenlightened victim of the dehumanizing practices of slavery to educated and empowered young man. He gains the resources and convictions to escape to the North and wage a political fight against the institution of slavery.

Ned Douglass

The Autobiography of Miss Jane Pittman
Ernest J. Gaines

Miss Jane Pittman's adopted son. Ned represents insight, strength, and youth. He is a bright young man who desires change in the society and boldly makes an effort to help his people by building a school. He does his good work even though he knows it places him in danger, and he is eventually killed for his actions by **Albert Cluveau**. His bravery makes him a hero to his community.

Duchess d'Outreville

The American
Henry James

A very fat heiress whom **Urbain de Bellegarde** introduces to **Christopher Newman** as the greatest lady in France. The duchess is opulent and good-spirited, a master of the conversational arts. When Newman decides to spill the Bellegardes' secret, he goes first to the duchess, but her saccharine bon mots so repel him that he leaves abruptly without disclosing his reason for coming.

Dove

Johnny Tremain
Esther Forbes

An apprentice at the Lapham house. Dove is lazy, dishonest, and stupid. He is responsible for **Jonathan Tremain**'s hand injury.

Mary Dove

The Day of the Locust
Nathanael West

A friend of **Faye**'s and a call-girl at **Mrs. Jenning**'s.

Florence Hurlbird Dowell

The Good Soldier
Ford Madox Ford

John Dowell's wife and **Captain Edward Ashburnham**'s lover. Florence is a manipulative and deceptive woman. She desires to be the lady of her ancestors' home, Branshaw Manor in Fordingbridge, and is willing to have an affair with Edward in order to achieve that position. Feigning a heart condition, Florence deceives her husband in order to control him and gain greater freedom for herself.

John Dowell

The Good Soldier
Ford Madox Ford

The novel's narrator. John Dowell is the reader's only guide through the twisted story of the thirteen years he and his wife, **Florence Hurlbird Dowell**, spent in France. He is a naïve man, quickly taken in by appearances and easily cuckolded by his wife. He tells the disjointed story of his own gradual understanding of what has occurred. Ultimately, he is a man who has lost all moral certitude, all comprehension of right and wrong.

Mr. Dowlas

Silas Marner
George Eliot

The town farrier. Mr. Dowlas shoes horses and tends to general livestock diseases. He is a fierce contrarian.

Dowley

A Connecticut Yankee in King Arthur's Court
Mark Twain

A prosperous blacksmith, extremely proud of his position as a self-made man. When **the Yankee**, disguised as a peasant along with **King Arthur**, insults Dowley at a dinner by one-upping his wealth and extravagance, he ends up leaving the guests terrified, thinking they will all be locked up in pillories for lying about what wages they pay their workers.

Mr. Dowling

Tom Jones
Henry Fielding

A shrewd, shifty lawyer who becomes friends with **Blifil**. Always operating out of expediency, when Dowling realizes that Blifil will not be able to reward him for his efforts, he defects to **Tom** and **Allworthy**'s side.

Jimmy Doyle

Dubliners
James Joyce

The upwardly mobile protagonist of "After the Race." Infatuated with the prestige of his friends and giddy about his inclusion in such high-society circles, Jimmy leads a directionless life.

Minta Doyle

To the Lighthouse
Virginia Woolf

A flighty young woman who visits the Ramsays on the Isle of Skye. Minta marries **Paul Rayley** at **Mrs. Ramsay**'s wishes.

Fay Doyle

Miss Lonelyhearts
Nathanael West

A large, almost grotesquely voluptuous and brutish woman. A great beauty when she was younger, Fay married the disabled **Peter Doyle** when she did not have enough money to support her daughter by another man. She is unhappy with her life and especially with Doyle, whom she verbally and physically abuses. Fay takes her frustrations out with aggressive advances on **Miss Lonelyhearts**, who plays the traditionally feminine role of resister to her pursuit.

Peter Doyle

Miss Lonelyhearts
Nathanael West

A worker for a gas company whose foot has been crippled from birth. Peter, who was married by convenience to the much stronger **Fay**, wonders what the point of life is and why he keeps on struggling. He is also angry and threatened that Fay's daughter **Lucy** is his biological child. Peter plays a submissive role to Fay while trying to overlook her sexual advances on other men, notably **Miss Lonelyhearts**.

Count Dracula

Dracula
Bram Stoker

A centuries-old vampire and Transylvanian nobleman. Beneath a veneer of aristocratic charm, the count has a dark, evil soul. He can assume the form of an animal and control the weather. His powers are limited, however—he cannot enter a victim's home uninvited, cross water unless carried, or use his powers during the day.

Princess Dragomiroff

Murder on the Orient Express
Agatha Christie

A Russian princess. Princess Dragomiroff is a generally despicable, ugly old lady; her yellow, toad-like face puts off **Hercule Poirot**. She is the owner of the famous "H" handkerchief found in **Ratchett**'s room and tells Poirot many lies about the other passenger's identities.

Dragon

Beowulf
Unknown

An ancient, powerful serpent. The dragon guards a hoard of treasure in a hidden mound. **Beowulf**'s fight with the dragon constitutes the third and final part of the epic, and he dies slaying the dragon.

Dragon

Grendel
John Gardner

A great cranky beast that rules over a vast hoard of treasure. The dragon provides a vision of the world as essentially meaningless and empty. Throughout the novel, **Grendel** frequently finds himself weighing the fatalistic words of the dragon against the beautiful words of **the Shaper**. Although Grendel only visits the dragon once, he feels its presence throughout the novel.

Draper

Moll Flanders
Daniel Defoe

Moll's second husband, a tradesman with the manners of a gentleman. His financial indiscretions sink them into poverty, and he eventually escapes to France as a fugitive from the law.

General Dreedle

Catch-22
Joseph Heller

The grumpy old general in charge of **John Yossarian**'s wing. The ambitious **General Peckem** hates General Dreedle.

Drevitts

In Our Time
Ernest Hemingway

The man who shoots the two Hungarians with **Boyle**.

Rev. John Jennison Drew

Babbitt
Sinclair Lewis

The minister at **Babbitt**'s church. Drew, who appoints Babbitt to the committee to increase Sunday school attendance, mixes politics and religion by preaching against the labor rights movement in Zenith.

Randolph Driblette

The Crying of Lot 49
Thomas Pynchon

The director of the production of *The Courier's Tragedy* that **Oedipa Maas** and **Metzger** attend. Driblette is a leading Wharfinger scholar, but he commits suicide toward the end of the novel before Oedipa can extract any useful information from him about the Tristero.

Benjamin Driscoll

The Martian Chronicles
Ray Bradbury

A simple man who comes to Mars to work as a laborer. He is nearly forced to return to Earth because the oxygen is too thin for him. As a result, he decides to plant trees all over Mars to create oxygen.

Judge Driscoll

Pudd'nhead Wilson
Mark Twain

A member of a prominent Virginia family. Judge Driscoll is a leading citizen of Dawson's Landing. He and his wife are childless, but adopt **Valet de Chambre**, or Tom, who is really the disguised black slave child switched with **Thomas a Becket Driscoll**, or Chambers, when the judge's brother, **Percy Northumberland Driscoll**, dies. The judge is wealthy and generally kind-hearted, and supports Tom, even paying his gambling debts. His real adopted nephew is unknowingly masquerading as the son of **Roxana**, or Roxy. Judge Driscoll fights a duel with **Luigi** for Tom. Luigi emerges a hero from the duel. Luigi and **Angelo Capello** run for town council, and Judge Driscoll, in the last speech of the campaign, slams the twins as con-artists, sideshow freaks, and criminals. The twins don't get elected because of the judge's speech. Later,

Tom sneaks into the judge's room, where he has fallen asleep counting money, and when he tries to take the money, the judge wakes up and grabs Tom. Tom screams and stabs the judge, killing him.

Percy Northumberland Driscoll

Pudd'nhead Wilson
Mark Twain

Judge Driscoll's brother, **Thomas a Becket Driscoll**'s father, **Roxana**'s, or Roxy's, owner. A rich speculator, he dies when Tom, who has since been thrust into life as Chambers, and Tom, who is really **Valet de Chambre**, are fifteen, with his estate heavily encumbered by debt. Shortly before he dies, he frees Roxy, who had originally switched the two identical-looking children so that her son, now Tom, would not be "sold down the river."

Thomas a Becket Driscoll

Pudd'nhead Wilson
Mark Twain

The son of **Percy Northumberland Driscoll**. Thomas a Becket Driscoll, or Tom, is switched with **Roxana**'s baby, **Valet de Chambre**, or Chambers, when he is only a few months old. Tom is called Chambers from then on, while Chambers is then called Tom. Chambers is raised as a slave and is purchased by **Judge Driscoll** when Percy dies, thus freeing Roxy to prevent Tom from selling him "down the river." Chambers is a decent young man who is often forced to fight bullies for Tom. When Chambers finds out that he is really Tom Driscoll, he becomes a free man and the heir to the judge's estate. Having been raised as a slave, he can't bring himself to inhabit "the white man's parlor." The slave quarters are no longer an option for him either, and he spends his time alone and unhappy.

Dromio of Ephesus

The Comedy of Errors
William Shakespeare

The bumbling, comical slave of **Antipholus of Ephesus**, twin of **Dromio of Syracuse**, and husband of **Nell**. Dromio of Ephesus begins the confusion of the play by approaching the visiting Antipholus on the street of Ephesus, and advising him to go home to **Adriana** for dinner. When the mystery of the two sets of twins is revealed at the close of the play, the Dromios seem happiest to rediscover one another. While the Antipholi resume their prior activities of business or wooing, the twin slaves rejoice in their reunion, and walk in to the banquet, "hand in hand, not one before another."

Dromio of Syracuse

The Comedy of Errors
William Shakespeare

The bumbling, comical slave of **Antipholus of Syracuse**, and twin of **Dromio of Ephesus**. The Syracusan Dromio is as bawdy a character as is seen in the play, at one point launching into a vulgar spiel about **Nell**, the kitchen-wench, who has accosted him, thinking him to be the Ephesian Dromio. Much like his brother, Dromio of Syracuse complains about the heavy hands of his master—and mistress, since **Adriana** is not averse to slapping the Dromios around.

Charles Drouet

Sister Carrie
Theodore Dreiser

A charming, flashy salesman with a strong appetite for romance. Although Drouet is warm-hearted, he never takes any of his romantic affairs seriously. He provides **Carrie** with a place to stay after she is forced to stop living with her sister; he also promises to marry her but never really intends to follow through. Drouet loses Carrie to **Hurstwood** and then, years later, after she has become a famous actress, tries unsuccessfully to win her back.

War and Peace
Leo Tolstoy

Princess Anna Mikhaylovna Drubetskaya

Boris Drubetskoy's mother, a woman from an illustrious old family who is nonetheless impoverished. Anna Mikhaylovna is dominated by thoughts of securing a good future for her son. She extracts a promise from **Vasili Kuragin** that he will help Boris get an officer's position in the army.

War and Peace
Leo Tolstoy

Boris Drubetskoy

Princess Anna Mikhaylovna Drubetskaya's son, a poor but ambitious friend of **Nikolai Ilyich Rostov**'s. Boris fights to establish a career for himself, using connections and his own intelligence and talents. Though he flirts with the young **Natasha Ilyinichna Rostova**, as an adult he seeks a bigger fortune, eventually marrying an heiress.

Night
Elie Wiesel

Akiba Drumer

A Jewish prisoner in the same camp as **Eliezar** who gradually loses his faith in God as a result of his experiences in the concentration camp.

A Tree Grows in Brooklyn
Betty Smith

Drummer

Horse who hates his owner, **Uncle Willie Flittman**.

Great Expectations
Charles Dickens

Bentley Drummle

An unpleasant young man. Drummle feels superior because he is a minor member of the nobility. Eventually he marries **Estella**.

Inherit the Wind
Jerome Lawrence & Robert E. Lee

Henry Drummond

An infamous criminal defense lawyer from Chicago whom the *Baltimore Herald* sends to defend **Bertram Cates**. Henry Drummond, a believer in human progress, argues for freedom of thought. Drummond arrives in Hillsboro vilified as an atheist. He exposes the contradictions underlying his witnesses' inherited religious beliefs, specifically those of the prosecution, namely **Matthew Harrison Brady**. Drummond's greatest triumph in the name of free thought is getting **Howard Blair** to admit that he has not made up his mind about evolutionary theory. When we hear this admission, Drummond's point becomes clear: freedom of thought becomes the freedom to be wrong or to change our minds. The world, viewed in this light, is full of possibilities. Brady self-destructs when his convictions about the literal truth of the Bible wither under the light of Drummond's skepticism. Drummond tells Cates that he won a moral victory because of the national media exposure. The jury finds Cates guilty, but **the judge** only sentences a fine of $100. Drummond brings Cates and **Rachel Brown** with him when he leaves Hillsboro.

The Little Prince
Antoine de Saint-Exupéry

The drunkard

The third person **the Little Prince** encounters after leaving home. The Drunkard spends his days and nights lost in a stupor. He is a sad figure, but also foolish because he drinks to forget that he is ashamed of drinking.

The Unvanquished
William Faulkner

Drusilla

Older cousin of **Bayard**, who abandons home to join the Confederate army after her fiancé is killed. She is fierce, violent, militaristic and stubbornly independent, but displays a moving vulnerability when her mother tries to confine her and force her to be feminine. Eventually, she is pressured into marrying **Colonel Sartoris** after living with him on the front as a common soldier.

Jude the Obscure
Thomas Hardy

Aunt Drusilla

The relative who raised **Jude Fawley** after the death of his father.

The Misanthrope
Molière

Du Bois

Alceste's jittery, bumbling manservant. Du Bois's comic subservience to Alceste is a major element of the farcical nature of *The Misanthrope*. Because he is so nervous as he tries to tell Alceste everything, Du Bois says virtually nothing. He is of little help to his master, regardless of his good intentions.

Typee
Herman Melville

Rear Admiral du Petit Thouars

The French admiral who has recently taken control of the Marquesas Islands.

The Kitchen God's Wife
Amy Tan

Auntie Du

Helen's aunt and one of the most giving characters in the novel. She loves **Winnie** very much and is always helping in one way or another. She is kind and sincere, always shedding light and truth on situations.

The Jungle
Upton Sinclair

Jack Duane

A polished, charismatic criminal whom **Jurgis Rudkus** meets in prison. Duane later introduces Jurgis to a lucrative lifestyle in Chicago's criminal underworld. Duane is forced to flee Chicago when he is caught breaking into a safe, and his criminal associates must sever ties with him.

Blanche DuBois

A Streetcar Named Desire
Tennessee Williams

Stella Kowalski's older sister, who was a high school English teacher in Laurel, Mississippi, until she was forced to leave her post. Blanche is a loquacious and fragile woman around the age of thirty. After losing Belle Reve, the DuBois family home, Blanche arrives in New Orleans at the Kowalski apartment and eventually reveals that she is completely destitute. Blanche comes across as a frivolous, hysterical, insensitive, and self-obsessed individual as she derides her sister's lesser social status and doesn't express joy when she sees that Stella has fallen in love. Though she has strong sexual urges and has had many lovers, she puts on the airs of a woman who has never known indignity. She avoids reality, preferring to live in her own imagination. Blanche represents the Old South's intellectual romanticism and dedication to appearances. As the play progresses, Blanche's instability grows along with her misfortune. **Stanley Kowalski** sees through Blanche and finds out the details of her past, destroying her relationship with his friend **Mitch**. Stanley also destroys what's left of Blanche by raping her and then having her committed to an insane asylum.

Mrs. Henry Lafayette Dubose

To Kill a Mockingbird
Harper Lee

An elderly, ill-tempered, racist woman who lives near **Atticus Finch**, **Jem Finch**, **Scout Finch**, and **Calpurnia**. Although Jem believes that Mrs. Dubose is a thoroughly bad woman, Atticus warns Jem to be a gentleman to her because she is old and sick. However, one day she tells the children that Atticus is not any better than the "niggers and trash he works for." Jem takes a baton from Scout and destroys all of Mrs. Dubose's camellia bushes. As punishment, Jem must go to her house every day for a month and read to her. Mrs. Dubose dies a little more than a month after Jem's punishment ends. Atticus reveals to Jem that she was addicted to morphine and that the reading was part of her successful effort to combat this addiction. Atticus gives Jem a box that Mrs. Dubose had given her maid for Jem; in it lies a single white camellia.

Heloise Dubuc

Madame Bovary
Gustave Flaubert

Charles Bovary's first wife. Heloise is a wealthy widow, years older than Charles. She gives Charles little love but plenty of nagging and scolding. Soon after she realizes that Charles is enamored with **Emma Bovary**, she dies from the shock of having all her property stolen by her lawyer. She differs from Emma in that she is petty and unimaginative, whereas Emma longs for a grand, romantic life.

Dubula

Cry, the Beloved Country
Alan Paton

One of a trio of powerful black politicians in Johannesburg. The others are **Tomlinson** and **John Kumalo**. Dubula provides the heart to complement John Kumalo's powerful voice. The bus boycott and the construction of Shanty Town are his handiwork.

Ducely

The Caine Mutiny
Herman Wouk

The son of the owner of an East Coast shipyard. He is a spoiled brat who shows what **Willie Keith** could have been in the Navy. Ducely avoids the danger of war and plays it safe, just as Willie could have and did not.

The duchess and the duke

Don Quixote
Miguel de Cervantes

A cruel and haughty couple who, in the Second Part, contrive adventures for **Don Quixote** for their own amusement. The anonymity of the duke and duchess, who are never named, demonstrates the pervasive cruelty of the "fallen world" Don Quixote attempts to save.

Duchess

Alice in Wonderland
Lewis Carroll

An odd, spiteful woman who mistreats her baby and submits to a shower of abuse from her **Cook**. She is horribly ugly. In her anxiety to remain in the good graces of the queen, she can be superficially sweet to someone she thinks can aid her socially while simultaneously causing her the utmost discomfort.

Nurse Duckett

Catch-22
Joseph Heller

The nurse in the Pianosa hospital who becomes **John Yossarian**'s lover.

Dudard

Rhinoceros
Eugène Ionesco

Dudard is a coworker of **Berenger**'s and a rival for **Daisy**'s affections. He prides himself on his intellect and rationality.

Nicky Dudorov

Dr. Zhivago
Boris Pasternak

A childhood friend of **Yury Andreyevich Zhivago**'s. Later, along with **Misha Gordon**, he encourages Yury to reconcile with **Antonina Alexandrovna Gromeko**, Yury's estranged wife. At the novel's end, he and Misha discover Yury and **Larissa Fyodorovna Guishar (later Antipova)**'s daughter, **Tanya**.

Duenna

Cyrano de Bergerac
Edmond Rostand

Roxane's companion and chaperone, who tries to keep Roxane out of trouble.

Angus Duer

Arrowsmith
Sinclair Lewis

Martin Arrowsmith's rival at medical school. A good student and hard worker, **Angus** always achieves his goals. He is a good surgeon, believes in success, and is Martin's opposite in many ways.

Duessa

The Faerie Queene
Edmund Spenser

The opposite of **Una**. Duessa represents falsehood and nearly succeeds in getting **Redcrosse** to leave Una for good. She appears beautiful, but it is only skin deep.

Mr. James Duffy

Dubliners
James Joyce

A solitary, prim man in "A Painful Case." Tightly self-regulated and commited to his mundane routine, Mr. Duffy stops himself from falling in love with **Mrs. Sinico**. His remorse after her death makes him realize that his pursuit of order and control yields only loneliness.

Tiny Duffy

All the King's Men
Robert Penn Warren

Lieutenant-governor of the state when **Willie** is assassinated. Fat, obsequious, and untrustworthy, Tiny swallows Willie's abuse and contempt for years, but finally tells **Adam Stanton** that Willie is sleeping with **Anne**. When Adam murders Willie, Tiny becomes governor.

The duke's steward

Don Quixote
Miguel de Cervantes

The **duke**'s henchman. The steward pretends to be a maidservant in distress to exploit **Don Quixote**'s sympathy for the duke's amusement. His name, Trifaldi, means "three-skirt."

The duke

The Adventures of Huckleberry Finn
Mark Twain

A con man along with **the dauphin**. He claims to be the usurped Duke of Bridgewater. **Huckleberry Finn** and **Jim** rescue the duke and the dauphin as they are being run out of a river town. Although Huckleberry Finn quickly realizes the men are frauds, after addressing them as "Duke" and "Your Majesty," he and Jim remain at their mercy, as Huck is only a child and Jim is a runaway slave. As Huck, Jim, the dauphin, and the duke travel the river, the dauphin and the duke pull increasingly disturbing swindles, including a sham circus featuring "The King's Cameleopard, or The Royal Nonesuch." This behavior culminates in the con artists' treatment of **the Wilks family** and their eventual sale of Jim. Huck finally parts with the two men after the duke encourages Huck to go look for Jim, at first slipping and saying that the dauphin sold Jim to **Silas Phelps**, but then trying to confuse Huck by changing his story.

Duke

Stranger in a Strange Land
Robert A. Heinlein

An engineer who works on **Jubal Harshaw**'s estate.

Duke of Milan

The Two Gentlemen of Verona
William Shakespeare

Silvia's father. The duke wants Silvia to marry the boorish but wealthy **Sir Thurio**. After **Proteus** tells him that **Valentine** plans to elope with his daughter, the duke cleverly manages to "discover" Valentine's plan without letting Valentine know about his friend's betrayal. In return for the secret information of his daughter's flight, the duke entrusts Proteus, and asks him to persuade Silvia to marry Thurio.

Duke of Venice of *Merchant*

The Merchant of Venice
William Shakespeare

The ruler of Venice. The duke presides over **Antonio**'s trial.

Duke of Venice of *Othello*

Othello
William Shakespeare

The official authority in Venice, the duke has great respect for **Othello** as a public and military servant. His primary role in the play is to reconcile Othello and **Brabanzio** in Act I, scene iii, and then to send Othello to Cyprus.

Vincentio, Duke of Vienna

Measure for Measure
William Shakespeare

The kind-hearted ruler of Vienna. Concerned about Vienna's depravity, the duke contrives to leave the strict **Lord Angelo** in charge of Vienna while he himself observes the proceedings disguised as a friar.

Tommy Dukes

Lady Chatterley's Lover
D. H. Lawrence

One of **Clifford Chatterley**'s contemporaries. Tommy Dukes is a brigadier general in the British Army and a clever and progressive intellectual. Though he speaks of the importance of sensuality, Dukes is uninterested in sex.

Dulcinea del Toboso

Don Quixote
Miguel de Cervantes

A peasant woman whom **Don Quixote** casts as his princess lady-love and muse. Though Don Quixote's vision of Dulcinea drives the action, she never appears in the novel.

Anthony Dull

Love's Labour's Lost
William Shakespeare

A constable in the court of Navarre. Dull provides a contrast to **Nathaniel**'s and **Holofernes**' scholarliness and pretension.

Dum and Dee

The Power of One
Bryce Courtenay

Peekay's Shangaan twin kitchen maids. They become the caretakers of **Doc**'s cottage and are very possessive of Doc and Peekay.

Dumain

Love's Labour's Lost
William Shakespeare

One of the lords who join the king in his oath of scholarship. Dumain falls in love with **Katherine**. Though Dumain and **Longaville** tend to be overshadowed by the **King of Navarre** and **Berowne**, they do add their witticisms throughout the play, especially during the masque of the Nine Worthies, when the lords make a mockery of the show.

First and Second Lord Dumaine

All's Well that Ends Well
William Shakespeare

French noblemen. They serve in the Florentine army under the **Duke of Florence**, and become friends of **Bertram**'s. Sick of **Parolles**'s cowardice and lies, they devise a plot to expose him for what he is in front of Bertram.

Albus Dumbledore

The Harry Potter Series: Books 1–4
J. K. Rowling

The headmaster of Hogwarts. Dumbledore is a wise, powerful, elderly man with a long silver beard. He has a calm, secretive demeanor and is extremely intuitive and trustworthy. He also is an egalitarian wizard, believing that all wizards, whatever their blood, have the same potential for greatness. This notion infuriates **Lucius Malfoy**, who tries to get Dumbledore fired from the position of headmaster. Dumbledore's gentle advice to Harry shows the great wizard is a wise psychologist as well as a father figure.

Dunbar

Catch-22
Joseph Heller

John Yossarian's friend. Dunbar is one of the only people who understands the danger and the absurdity of the soldiers' situation. Faced with likely death, Dunbar has decided to make time pass as slowly as possible. He treasures boredom and discomfort.

Judy Duncan

Fallen Angels
Walter Dean Myers

An army nurse **Richie Perry** meets during the trip to Vietnam. Though Richie sees Judy only once more before learning of her death, she serves as the closest thing to a love interest in the novel, and she is a source of confusion and tame fantasy for Richie.

King Duncan

Macbeth
William Shakespeare

The good king of Scotland whom **Macbeth** murders in order to attain the crown. Duncan is a virtuous, benevolent, and farsighted ruler. His death symbolizes the destruction of an order in Scotland that can be restored only when Duncan's line, in the person of his son **Malcolm**, once more occupies the throne.

Jesse H. Dunlap

Inherit the Wind
Jerome Lawrence & Robert E. Lee

A farmer and cabinetmaker. Jesse H. Dunlap stands as a potential juror in the trial against **Bertram Cates**.

Howard Dunlop

White Noise
Don DeLillo

Jack Gladney's German teacher. He's a solitary, quiet boarder in the same house as **Murray Jay Siskind.** In addition to teaching German, he also teaches meteorology, a subject he turned to after his mother's death much in the same way Jack turned to Hitler studies to relieve his own fear of dying.

Derrick Dunne

Holes
Louis Sachar

The bully from **Stanley Yelnats**'s school. Derrick throws Stanley's notebook into the toilet, but the teachers never believed that Derrick could bully Stanley because Stanley was so much larger. Derrick's testimony, however, eventually proves Stanley is innocent of stealing **Clyde Livingston**'s shoes.

Clarence Duntz

In Cold Blood
Truman Capote

One of **Alvin Dewey**'s three KBI assistants. Duntz is a burly man with a broad face.

Dunyasha

The Cherry Orchard
Anton Chekhov

A maid on the Ranevsky estate. She functions mainly as a foil to **Yasha**, her innocent naïveté and love for him exposing his cynicism and selfishness. She is also the object of **Semyon Yepikhodov**'s affections.

C. Auguste Dupin

"The Murders in the Rue Morgue"
Edgar Allan Poe

A Parisian crime-solver who discovers the truth behind the violent murders of two women after the Paris police arrest the wrong man. He employs psychological analysis and intuition and considers possibilities not imagined by the police to conclude that the murders were committed by an orangutan. Dupin works outside conventional police methods, and he uses his distance from traditional law enforcement to explore new ways of solving crimes.

Dr. Dupont

I Am the Cheese
Robert Cormier

A kindly doctor. Dr. Dupont oversees the mental hospital. **Adam Farmer** is a patient there.

Monsieur Dupont

The Remains of the Day
Kazuo Ishiguro

A Frenchman with a small amount of political influence in his home country. M. Dupont is present at the same March 1923 conference as **Mr. Lewis**. M. Dupont constantly badgers **Stevens** to get him more bandages for his feet, which are sore from sightseeing.

Eliza Louisa Durbeyfield

Tess of the d'Urbervilles
Thomas Hardy

Tess Durbeyfield's younger sister. Tess believes Eliza Louisa Durbeyfield, or Liza-Lu, has all of Tess's own good qualities and none of her bad ones. Tess encourages **Angel Clare** to look after and even marry Liza-Lu after Tess's execution.

Mrs. Joan Durbeyfield

Tess of the d'Urbervilles
Thomas Hardy

Tess Durbeyfield and **Eliza Louisa Durbeyfield**'s mother, wife of **Mr. John Durbeyfield**. Mrs. Joan Durbeyfield has a strong sense of propriety and very particular hopes for Tess's life. She is continually disappointed and hurt by the way her daughter's life actually proceeds. She is also somewhat simpleminded and naturally forgiving, and she is unable to remain angry with Tess—particularly once Tess becomes her primary means of support. Joan Durbeyfield is the one who advises Tess never to tell of her secret past with **Alec d'Urberville** to **Angel Clare**, but Tess does not listen. Mrs. Durbeyfield's sickness and Mr. Durbeyfield's death cause Tess to become completely poor.

Mr. John Durbeyfield

Tess of the d'Urbervilles
Thomas Hardy

Tess Durbeyfield and **Eliza Louisa Durbeyfield**'s father, **Mrs. Joan Durbeyfield**'s husband, a lazy peddler in Marlott. When he learns that he descends from the noble line of the d'Urbervilles, he is quick to make an attempt to profit from the connection. He tries to send Tess to work at the home of the old woman d'Urberville, hoping for a connection to money. This sets up Tess's meeting with **Alec d'Urberville** and begins her long fall from grace. John Durbeyfield later dies, forcing the Durbeyfields off their land, and sucking away Tess's last money.

Tess Durbeyfield

Tess of the d'Urbervilles
Thomas Hardy

The protagonist of *Tess of the d'Urbervilles*. Tess Durbeyfield is a strikingly attractive, intelligent, deeply moral, passionate young woman living with her impoverished family, **Mrs. Joan Durbeyfield**, **Mr. John Durbeyfield**, and **Eliza Louisa Durbeyfield**, in the village of Marlott. Tess has a keen sense of responsibility and is committed to doing the best she can for her family, although her inexperience and lack of wise parenting leave her extremely vulnerable. Her life is complicated when her father discovers a link to the noble line of the d'Urbervilles, and, as a result, Tess is sent to work at the d'Urberville mansion. Unfortunately, her ideals cannot prevent her from sliding further and further into misfortune after she becomes pregnant by the evil **Alec d'Urberville**. The terrible irony is that Tess and her family are not really related to this branch of the d'Urbervilles at all: Alec's father, a merchant named Simon Stokes, simply assumed the name after he retired. Again and again, she seems to be tempted by the devil, Alec, who turns up trying to entice Tess with money to support her poor family. In the end, Tess's hope that Angel will return for her is worn down by Alec, and she gives in to him, only to kill him in madness. She is executed for her crime.

Midnight's Children
Salman Rushdie

Durga

A wet nurse for **Aadam Sinai** and a succubus to **Picture Singh**.

Incidents in the Life of a Slave Girl
Harriet Ann Jacobs

Reverend and Mrs. Durham

Some of the first people **Linda Brent** meets in Philadelphia. With their legitimate marriage and morally upstanding life, the Durhams remind Linda that slavery has robbed her of the chance to have a normal existence.

The Harry Potter Series: Books 1–4
J. K. Rowling

Dudley Dursley

Harry Potter's spoiled, overweight Muggle (non-magical) cousin. Annoying and loud, Dudley manipulates parental love to get what he wants.

The Harry Potter Series: Books 1–4
J. K. Rowling

Petunia Dursley

Harry Potter's unpleasant Muggle (non-magical) aunt and **Vernon Dursley**'s wife. Petunia is an overly doting mother to her spoiled son, **Dudley Dursley**. She is haughty and excessively concerned with what the neighbors think of her family. She is somewhat humanized for us when we discover that she was always jealous of the magical gifts of her sister, **Lily Potter**, Harry's witch mother. Her malevolence toward Harry springs from an earlier resentment of her sister.

The Harry Potter Series: Books 1–4
J. K. Rowling

Vernon Dursley

Harry Potter's stuffy, nasty-tempered Muggle (non-magical) uncle. Vernon is quite disgusted by the idea of anything magical. Part of his hesitation comes from the fact that he enjoys tormenting his nephew, and another part comes from the fact that he does not want to acknowledge that magic exists. It is through Mr. Dursley's jaded Muggle eyes that we first look at wizards.

Anne Frank: Diary of a Young Girl
Anne Frank

Albert Dussel

A dentist and an acquaintance of **Edith Frank** and **Otto Frank** who hides with them in the annex. His real name is Fritz Pfeffer, but **Anne Frank** calls him Mr. Dussel in her diary. Anne finds Mr. Dussel particularly difficult to deal with because he shares a room with her, and she suffers the brunt of his odd personal hygiene, pedantic lectures, and controlling tendencies. Mr. Dussel's wife is a Christian, so she does not go into hiding, and he is separated from her. He dies on December 20, 1944, at the Neuengamme concentration camp.

Dust Witch

Something Wicked This Way Comes
Ray Bradbury

A blind woman who feels and hears things imperceptible to others. She is the lookout for **Mr. Dark** and the carnival. The Witch is evil and greedy, and **William Halloways** uses those traits against her when he destroys her balloon. She is powerful only if her powers are believed in, and **Charles Halloway** destroys her with a laugh.

Dusty

Johnny Tremain
Esther Forbes

Ephraim Lapham's youngest apprentice. Dusty runs away to sea after **Jonathan Tremain** leaves Mr. Lapham's silver shop.

Dutch-Malay woman

Lord Jim
Joseph Conrad

A woman with a mysterious past, she is **Jewel**'s mother and **Cornelius**'s wife (although Cornelius is not Jewel's father). As a favor to her, **Stein** gives Cornelius a post in Patusan. She dies a horrible death when Cornelius, who has always tormented her, tries to break down the door to her room.

Gérard Duval

All Quiet on the Western Front
Erich Maria Remarque

A French soldier **Paul Bäumer** kills in No Man's Land. Duval is a printer with a wife and child at home. He is the first person Paul kills in hand-to-hand combat.

Madame Duval

Evelina
Fanny Burney

A former tavern waitress, **Evelina Anville**'s grandmother, and the mother of **Lady Caroline Evelyn Belmont**. Although she is a rude and lowbrow woman, Madame Duval comes into a large fortune through her marriage to **Mr. Evelyn** (Evelina's grandfather) and later **Monsieur Duval**. She tried to pressure her daughter into a bad marriage, and withheld the dowry when Caroline married the unscrupulous **Sir John Belmont** in an attempt to escape her mother's threats.

Dwalin

The Hobbit
J. R. R. Tolkien

One of the dwarf companions on the novel's quest.

The Lion, the Witch, and the Wardrobe
C. S. Lewis

Dwarf

One of **the White Witch**'s evil henchman. He is her right-hand man, and he treats **Edmund Pevensie** badly by giving him stale bread and water.

The Hobbit
J. R. R. Tolkien

Dwarves

A race of ground-dwelling creatures who wield axes and carve stone very skillfully. They are also excellent at creating secret doors and passageways. Dwarves and **Elves** have a history of rivalry. **Gandalf** introduces **Bilbo Baggins** to Dwarves who are a part of **Thorin Oakenshield**'s group, composed of **Fili**, **Kili**, **Dwalin**, **Balin**, **Oin**, **Gloin**, **Ori**, **Dori**, **Nori**, **Bifur**, **Bofur**, and **Bombur**, none of whom is really developed as an individual character in *The Hobbit*. Gloin is **Gimli**'s father, where Gimli is the dwarf member of the Fellowship of the Ring. The narrator describes Dwarves unfavorably, noting their greed and trickery. Despite this characterization, Dwarves are a race that belong to the Good Peoples of Middle-earth, unlike the **Goblins** or **Wargs**.

This Boy's Life
Tobias Wolff

Dwight

A cruel and violent man who drinks to excess. He convinces **Rosemary Wolff** to marry him and move to Chinook. Dwight is especially resentful of **Jack Wolff** and treats him with the utmost brutality. Unmistakably the antagonist of the memoir, Dwight is a villain who steals Jack's happy childhood out from underneath him. Dwight derives satisfaction from exercising his power over other people, primarily Jack and Rosemary, and needs to belittle and victimize others to reassure himself that he is important. Dwight is also exceedingly deceptive and dishonest, either making various promises he cannot keep, or simply lying outright, relishing his self-serving underhandedness.

Dead Man Walking
Helen Prejean

Tom Dybdahl

The head of the Prison Coalition and a close friend of **Sister Helen Prejean**'s. Tom helps Prejean fight **Patrick Sonnier**'s execution.

The Autobiography of Miss Jane Pittman
Ernest J. Gaines

Colonel Dye

The man who reclaims the plantation where **Miss Jane Pittman** first lived after slavery. Colonel Dye fought with the Confederate Army and represents the old southern landowning order. Colonel Dye supports restrictions and violence against his blacks if necessary, and sends the Ku Klux Klan after **Ned Douglass**. He also is slightly dishonest in the way he tries to keep **Joe Pittman** on the plantation by saying that Joe owes him money and by adding interest after Joe gets the cash.

Main Street
Sinclair Lewis

Maud Dyer

The wife of **Dave Dyer**, the town druggist. Maud is a neurotic hypochondriac with whom **Kennicott** begins a secretive affair as his relationship with **Carol** deteriorates.

Dynne

The Phantom Tollbooth
Norton Juster

The assistant of **Dischord** and a smoke monster. Dischord and Dynne think that noises are much more enjoyable to hear than beautiful sounds.

DIVINE DANDIES

WHAT'S INSIDE ISN'T ALWAYS SO GREAT, BUT THE PACKAGE IS FABULOUS.

Sir Walter Elliot	1	*Persuasion*
Trip Fontaine	2	*The Virgin Suicides*
Dorian Gray	3	*The Portrait of Dorian Gray*
Gilderoy Lockheart	4	*Harry Potter and the Chamber of Secrets*
Captain Lydgate	5	*Middlemarch*
Algeron Moncrieff	6	*The Importance of Being Earnest*
Charles Swann	7	*Swann's Way*
The Victome de Valmont	8	*Dangerous Liasons*

Ea

The Epic of Gilgamesh
Unknown

The god of the ocean depths, of crafts, and of wisdom; a patron of mankind. Ea lives in Apsu, the primal waters below the earth. Ea saves **Utnapishtim** from the deluge and sends the Seven Sages to civilize humans.

Denis Eady

Ethan Frome
Edith Wharton

The son of Starkfield's rich Irish grocer, **Michael Eady**. Denis shows interest in **Mattie Silver**, which makes **Ethan Frome** jealous until he understands Mattie's true feelings.

Mr. Eager

A Room with a View
E. M. Forster

The British chaplain in Florence. He is rude to Italians, unkind to the Emersons, and perpetuates a false rumor that **Mr. Emerson** murdered his wife.

Earl

The Sound and the Fury
William Faulkner

The owner of the farm-supply store where Jason works. Earl feels some loyalty toward **Mrs. Compson** and thus puts up with Jason's surliness.

Earlene

Fallen Angels
Walter Dean Myers

Peewee's girlfriend. Not long after Peewee arrives in Vietnam, Earlene writes him a letter, informing him that she married another man in his absence.

General Jubal Early

The Killer Angels
Michael Shaara

A young, ambitious, and cold Confederate general. Like **General Richard Ewell**, Early has been given part of Jackson's old command. He accepts this responsibility easily. He is capable and confident, but also pushy, particularly with Ewell. Though Ewell technically has the greater responsibility and the greater control, he defers to Early. **Longstreet** and **Armistead** despise Early.

Frances Earnshaw

Wuthering Heights
Emily Brontë

Hindley Earnshaw's simpering, silly wife. Frances dies shortly after giving birth to **Hareton Earnshaw**.

Hareton Earnshaw

Wuthering Heights
Emily Brontë

The son of **Hindley Earnshaw** and **Frances Earnshaw**, and **Catherine**'s nephew. After Hindley's death, **Heathcliff** forces Hareton to be an uneducated field worker, just as Hindley did to Heathcliff himself. Illiterate and quick-tempered, Hareton is easily humiliated, but he has a good heart and a deep desire to improve himself. At the end of the novel, he and **young Catherine** fall in love.

Hindley Earnshaw

Wuthering Heights
Emily Brontë

Catherine's brother, and **Mr. Earnshaw**'s son. Hindley resents it when **Heathcliff** comes to live at Wuthering Heights. After his father dies and he inherits the estate, Hindley begins to abuse the young Heathcliff, terminating his education and forcing him to work in the fields. When Hindley's wife **Frances Earnshaw** dies shortly after giving birth to their son **Hareton Earnshaw**, he lapses into alcoholism.

Mr. Earnshaw

Wuthering Heights
Emily Brontë

Catherine and **Hindley Earnshaw**'s father. Mr. Earnshaw adopts **Heathcliff** and comes to love him more than Hindley. Nevertheless, he bequeaths Wuthering Heights to Hindley.

Mrs. Earnshaw

Wuthering Heights
Emily Brontë

Catherine and **Hindley Earnshaw**'s mother, who neither likes nor trusts the orphan **Heathcliff** when he comes to live at her house. She dies shortly after Heathcliff's arrival at Wuthering Heights.

P. D. East

Black Like Me
John Howard Griffin

The editor of a newspaper in a small Mississippi town. Like **John Howard Griffin**, East is a passionate advocate for racial equality in America. East's family is ostracized as a result of his stance, and his newspaper is a financial disaster. But he is an inspiration to Griffin, who sees him as a sign of goodness flourishing amid the evil of racism and segregation.

Alfred Eastman

A Prayer for Owen Meany
John Irving

John Wheelwright's uncle by marriage, a rugged lumber baron who lives in Sawyer Depot.

Hester Eastman

A Prayer for Owen Meany
John Irving

John Wheelwright's youngest cousin (about a year older than he is), for whom John feels a bizarre, quasi-sexual attraction as a young man. Hester is extremely bitter about the treatment she receives from her parents, believing that they favor her brothers. She remains an angry, sexually, and emotionally aggressive woman. By 1987, Hester has become a rock star, performing under the name "Hester the Molester." During their adolescence, Hester is romantically and possibly sexually involved with **Owen Meany**.

A Prayer for Owen Meany
John Irving

Martha Eastman

John Wheelwright's aunt, **Tabitha Wheelwright**'s sister, and **Harriet Wheelwright**'s daughter. Martha is neither as pretty as Tabby nor as talented a singer, and John suspects that she is slightly jealous of her. Martha is married to **Alfred Eastman** and lives in Sawyer Depot with her husband and their three children.

A Prayer for Owen Meany
John Irving

Noah Eastman

John Wheelwright's oldest cousin, **Hester Eastman** and **Simon Eastman**'s brother. Wild and unruly as a youth, Noah attends Gravesend Academy and a college on the West Coast.

A Prayer for Owen Meany
John Irving

Simon Eastman

John Wheelwright's second-oldest cousin, **Noah Eastman** and **Hester Eastman**'s brother. Even wilder than Noah as a youth, Simon follows his brother to Gravesend Academy and a college on the West Coast.

Babbitt
Sinclair Lewis

William Washington Eathorne

A banker and a member of Zenith's oldest, richest family. **Eathorne** and **Babbitt** work together on a project to increase the attendance at their church's Sunday school. Eathorne gives Babbitt a secret loan to carry out a shady business deal.

Beowulf
Unknown

Ecgtheow

Beowulf's father, **Hygelac**'s brother-in-law, and **Hrothgar**'s friend. Ecgtheow is dead by the time the story begins, but he lives on through the noble reputation that he made for himself during his life and in his dutiful son's remembrances.

Grendel
John Gardner

Ecgtheow

Beowulf's father.

The Handmaid's Tale
Margaret Atwood

Econowives

The wives of poor men of the **Republic of Gilead**.

Sir Ector

The Once and Future King
T. H. White

King Arthur's foster father and **Sir Kay**'s biological father. Sir Ector is good-natured, pompous, and boisterous. Although he often seems like a caricature, Sir Ector proves to be less foolish than we might expect. He likes to hunt with his friends, like **King Pellinore**.

Eddie

Cannery Row
John Steinbeck

One of **Mack**'s boys and a substitute bartender at La Ida, the local bar. Eddie brings home stolen bottles and a jug filled with remnants from customers' drinks, which makes him immensely popular among the boys.

Eddie

Fool for Love
Sam Shepard

The play's protagonist, half-brother and lover of **May**, son of the **Old Man**. An overly proud man with a drinking problem, Eddie believes in the myths of the idyllic American West, the cowboy as a hero who saves the day, and the American Dream of country living. Eddie habitually entangles himself in volatile romances. His passionate, competitive nature magnifies itself when he drinks and when he relates to his lovers May and "the Countess." Eddie has a strange but complicit relationship with his father, the Old Man, who exists in the play only in his children's minds.

Edgar

King Lear
William Shakespeare

Gloucester's older, legitimate son. Edgar plays many different roles, starting out as a gullible fool easily tricked by his bastard brother **Edmund**, then assuming a disguise as a mad beggar to evade his father's men, then carrying his impersonation further to aid **King Lear** and Gloucester. Edgar finally appears as an armored champion who avenges his brother's treason.

Edie

Homecoming
Cynthia Voigt

Louis's girlfriend. Edie buys into Louis's cynical and self-indulgent philosophies about life. He convinces her to steal money from her father and run away with him, and occasionally he teases her and treats her cruelly. Edie is a gentle girl who plays the autoharp, so the children warily agree to spend time with the couple.

The Editor

Steppenwolf
Hermann Hesse

The nephew of **the Steppenwolf**'s landlady. The novel opens with a fictional preface by the Editor, to whom Harry has left his records, indicating he may do with them as he pleases.

The editor with a big chin

The Unbearable Lightness of Being
Milan Kundera

Political dissident and journalist involved with **Tomas**'s original paper criticizing the Czech Communists. This editor is also a friend of Tomas's estranged son, **Simon**, and helps bring the two together. He and Simon attempt to convince Tomas to join the ranks of dissidents, and their tactics are similar to those of the police: they want him to sign something.

Carothers Edmonds

Go Down, Moses
William Faulkner

McCaslin Edmonds's grandson, **Carothers McCaslin**'s great-great-great-grandson. He runs the plantation in the old age of Lucas Beauchamp and **Isaac McCaslin**.

McCaslin Edmonds

Go Down, Moses
William Faulkner

The great-grandson of **Carothers McCaslin**, descended from Carothers's daughter. Raised by his **Uncle Buck** and **Uncle Buddy**, he in turn raises Buck's son, **Isaac McCaslin**. Inherits the plantation at the age of thirty-seven, when twenty-one-year-old Isaac refuses to take it as his own inheritance.

Zack Edmonds

Go Down, Moses
William Faulkner

McCaslin Edmonds's son, **Carothers Edmonds**'s father.

Edmund

King Lear
William Shakespeare

Gloucester's younger, illegitimate son. Edmund resents his status as a bastard and schemes to usurp Gloucester's title and possessions from **Edgar**. He is a formidable character, succeeding in almost all of his schemes and wreaking destruction upon virtually all of the other characters. Edmund captures **King Lear** and Lear's youngest daughter **Cordelia**, successfully ordering Cordelia's death. Lear's older daugthers **Regan** and **Goneril** fight over his love, and both die in the process.

Miss Edmunds

Bridge to Terabithia
Katherine Paterson

The music teacher at the school. **Jesse Oliver Aarons, Jr.** worships her. She encourages his artistic talent, one of the two people in the world, including Leslie, who does, and seems to care about him in a special way. She is somewhat of a hippie, which only deepens her allure for Jess, because it confirms her individuality and separation from the narrow world of Lark Creek.

Dr. Edvig

Herzog
Saul Bellow

The psychiatrist who treated **Moses Herzog** during the last days of his marriage to **Madeleine**. Dr. Edvig is one of the many people Moses believes to have betrayed him. Evig questions Moses' mental health.

Edward

Cloud Nine
Caryl Churchill

Son of **Clive** and **Betty**. At a young age, Edward (played by a woman in Act I) discovers a proclivity for feminine things such as his sister **Victoria**'s doll, and he has an attraction to other males. He keeps his yearnings in check for fear of upsetting his conservative father, hiding his sexual exploration with Clive's friend **Harry**. As a child, Edward hates his father for being so intolerant, and so when Clive's servant **Joshua** raises a gun to kill Clive, Edward does nothing to stop it. The older Edward of Act II (played by a man) keeps his homosexuality a secret in public but is much more comfortable being gay in private. When his lover **Gerry** abandons him, he moves in with his sister Victoria and her lover **Lin**, becoming a fellow "lesbian."

Prince Edward

Henry VI, Part III
William Shakespeare

Queen Margaret and **King Henry VI**'s teenage son. Courageous and spirited, Prince Edward gives hope to Henry's supporters. Henry VI's initial agreement to bequeath the throne to the Yorkist line alienates the prince from his father. Edward realizes that the power lies with Margaret, his mother, and not the weak, ineffectual Henry. When the **Earl of Warwick** changes allegiance in France to Henry's side, Prince Edward accepts Warwick's daughter as his bride. When the Yorkist faction wins in the final battle, the three York brothers—**King Edward IV**, Richard of Gloucester (the future **Richard III**), and **George, Duke of Clarence**—drag the prince in and kill him before Margaret. The severing of Henry VI from Prince Edward is one of many broken father-son relationships in the play: the broken kinship ties leave only the will of the individual, which Richard III will come to symbolize.

Prince Edward

Richard III
William Shakespeare

The older son of **King Edward IV** and **Queen Elizabeth**, older brother of **Richard, Duke of York**, and half-brother of **Lord Grey** and the **Marquess of Dorset**. Though he and his brother pose no legitimate threat to the throne (yet), **Richard III** still has them locked up in the Tower of London. After his ascent to the throne, the paranoid king then contracts **Sir James Tyrrel** to kill them. The murder of the two princes is the crime for which Richard was most demonized. This Prince Edward should not be confused with the Prince Edward who was the son of **Queen Margaret** and the husband of **Lady Anne**.

King Edward IV

Henry VI, Part II; Henry VI, Part III; and *Richard III*
William Shakespeare

Brother of Richard, Duke of Gloucester (later **King Richard III**), **George, Duke of Clarence**, and **Edmund, Earl of Rutland**; son of **Richard Plantagenet, Duke of York**; husband of **Elizabeth Woodville, Lady Grey**; father of **Prince Edward** and **Richard, Duke of York**; and stepfather of the **Marquess of Dorset** and **Lord Grey**. Part of the Yorkist line that fought for the throne in the Wars of the Roses, Edward first appears in *King Henry VI, Part II*, fighting with his father York in the Battle of St. Albans against **King Henry VI** and **Queen Margaret**'s forces. With the battle in full swing by *King Henry VI, Part III*, Edward inherits York's claim to the crown after his father's death. With the help of his brothers and Yorkist nobles like **Richard Neville, Earl of Warwick** and the **Marquess of Montague**, Edward is able to topple Margaret's armies and take the crown for himself. Once king, Edward manages to alienate both his brothers and his advisors by marrying Lady Elizabeth Grey. Not only does the marriage have no political advantage, but Edward ends up insulting **King Louis XI** of France and some English nobles by reneging on his intention to marry the king's sister, **Lady Bona**. After another power struggle in which

Edward is captured by the returning Lancaster forces, he raises another army and defeats Margaret's armies, killing her son, Prince Edward, and imprisoning Henry VI (who is killed by Richard). In *King Richard III*, he is devoted to achieving a reconciliation among the various political factions of his reign. But since the end of the wars, he has become weak and melancholy, and thanks to his scheming brother Richard, suspicious of others: He imprisons his own brother Clarence in the Tower. While trying to maintain order in the kingdom, Edward is unaware that Richard attempts to thwart him at every turn. After hearing of Clarence's death, Edward grows more despondent, ultimately succumbing to grief and dying.

Miss Edward

Annie John
Jamaica Kincaid

Annie's history teacher at school who grows extremely upset with Annie's defacing of the history book.

Governor Edwin Edwards

Dead Man Walking
Helen Prejean

The governor of Louisiana. Governor Edwards does not personally support the death penalty, but he condones executions for political reasons.

Malvonne Edwards

Jazz
Toni Morrison

An upstairs neighbor to **Joe Trace** and **Violet**. Malvonne agrees to rent out the spare room of her nephew, **Sweetness**, to Joe so that he can have a private place in which to meet **Dorcas**. She works cleaning the office buildings of powerful white executives during the evenings. She also finds many unsent letters hidden in her nephew's old room. Some of the letters require her to take immediate action, because the intended recipient has been left waiting with inadequate or outdated information. She sends along an impassioned letter from **Winsome Clark** to her husband in Panama. The unsent letters that Malvonne reads display the pain of separated families, homesickness, and a longing for something simpler. Malvonne is an anonymous, invisible, and benevolent observer who hopes to help Winsome in any way possible.

Mr. Edwards

East of Eden
John Steinbeck

A man who runs a prostitution ring throughout Massachusetts and Connecticut. Mr. Edwards has a highly moral wife and a pair of sons who attend the prestigious Groton School, and he leads a largely respectable life despite his base profession. After employing **Cathy Ames** as a prostitute, Mr. Edwards falls in love with her. Upon discovering her involvement in the murder of her parents, he beats her nearly to death, and she crawls away to the nearest farm—owned by **Charles** and **Adam Trask**.

Mrs. Eff

Wide Sargasso Sea
Jean Rhys

Grace Poole's nickname for Mrs. Fairfax, the head housekeeper at Thornfield Hall, and a character in the novel *Jane Eyre*. While Mrs. Eff never appears in the novel, Grace mentions her in conversation with **Leah**.

Egeon

The Comedy of Errors
William Shakespeare

A Syracusan merchant, father of the two Antipholi, and husband of the **Abbess**. Like his Syracusan son, Egeon has come to Ephesus in search of the missing half of his family. But according to a new law, any Syracusan found in Ephesus will be put to death. As **Solinus** leads him away to his execution, Egeon relates the convoluted tale that has resulted in two sets of twins and an estranged wife. Though this grim opening quickly gives way to slapstick humor, the threat of execution always hovers above the characters. By the end, with the pairs of twins and Egeon and the Abbess reconciled, order and happiness displaces the anarchy and despair.

Egeus

The Canterbury Tales
Geoffrey Chaucer

Theseus's father in **the Knight**'s tale. Egeus gives Theseus advice that helps his son to convince **Palamon** and **Emelye** to end their mourning over **Arcite** and marry each other.

Egeus

A Midsummer Night's Dream
William Shakespeare

Hermia's father, who brings a complaint against his daughter to **Theseus**: Egeus has given **Demetrius** permission to marry his daughter, but Hermia proclaims her love for **Lysander** and refuses the betrothal. Egeus's insistence that his daughter either respect his wishes or be held accountable to Athenian law places him outside the whimsical dream realm of the forest.

Sir Eglamour

The Two Gentlemen of Verona
William Shakespeare

Silvia's cowardly escort as she flees the imperial palace in search of the banished **Valentine**. Eglamour promises to accompany Silvia through the woods, but as soon as they are beset by outlaws, he runs off, leaving Silvia in their clutches. His craven flight is another example of the failure of men to treat women with respect—furthermore, his selfish actions contradict his social status as a gentleman and noble.

John Eglinton

Ulysses
James Joyce

An essayist who listens to **Stephen Dedalus**'s theory about Shakespeare with skepticism. Eglinton is affronted by Stephen's youthful self-confidence.

Eilif

Mother Courage
Bertolt Brecht

The first child **Mother Courage** loses to the army. Eilif is the warlike son, eager to join the war and carry out its brutal business. Ostensibly, his fatal virtue is his Caesar-like "bravery," though the accolades he receives are perhaps undeserved. His rise to power—reflected in his costume—involves nothing more than a series of cunning, murderous raids on the local peasantry, raids motivated by the need to keep his men fed. He dies during the war.

Eino

One Day in the Life of Ivan Denisovich
Aleksandr Solzhenitsyn

One of the two Estonians who share a bunk in **Ivan Denisovich Shukhov**'s hut. Eino and the other Estonian chat in their own language constantly, interacting with each other much more than with anyone else. The Estonians represent the necessity of maintaining a private world set apart from the horrors of camp existence.

Gina Ekdal

Wild Duck
Henrik Ibsen

Hjalmar Ekdal's wife and the former house servant of the Werles. By far the most practical members of the family, she refrains from her relatives' flights into fancy and occupies herself with the management of the household and photographic studio. She has suppressed her past with **Haakon Werle** to ensure the survival of her marriage.

Hedvig Ekdal

Wild Duck
Henrik Ibsen

The Ekdals' daughter. She is the play's most pathetic figure: its innocent and victimized child. She is of uncertain parentage, belonging either to **Hjalmar** or **Werle** and potentially passed from the former to the latter in a marriage designed to circumvent public scandal. Like the duck, she is no longer certain of her origins and has been adopted into a second home. Hedvig is also marked by an incipient blindness, a degenerative eye disease that she has inherited from either Werle or Hjalmar's line. Her inherited disease is the legacy of crimes past, crimes of which she is innocent.

Hjalmar Ekdal

Wild Duck
Henrik Ibsen

A comic take on the romantic hero. Hjalmar imagines himself as a great father and provider. Convinced he is on the brink of a great invention, Hjalmar dreams of restoring his family name to honor. His dismissal of the petty concerns in life and his dawdling in the garret serve as a parody of the romantic notions of creation and creativity.

Old Ekdal

Wild Duck
Henrik Ibsen

The victim of **Werle**'s betrayal, he suffered public disgrace years ago. He is a social pariah, and his intrusion into Werle's house brings the dinner party to a halt. Ekdal's ruin has left him like a wounded duck, a drunken man who spends his hours dreaming of hunting in the "forest" he has built in the garret.

Ekwefi

Things Fall Apart
Chinua Achebe

Okonkwo's second wife, once the village beauty. Ekwefi ran away from her first husband to live with Okonkwo. **Ezinma** is her only surviving child, her other nine having died in infancy. Ekwefi constantly fears that she will lose Ezinma as well. She is good friends with **Chielo**, the priestess of the goddess Agbala.

El Sordo

For Whom the Bell Tolls
Ernest Hemingway

The leader of a guerrilla band that operates near **Pablo**'s. Short, heavy, and gray-haired, El Sordo (Spanish for "the deaf one") is a man of few words. Like **Robert Jordan**, he is excited by a successful kill. El Sordo and his entire band are killed when their hilltop is bombed by Fascist planes.

Eladio

For Whom the Bell Tolls
Ernest Hemingway

One of the guerrilla fighters in **Robert Jordan**'s band, and **Andrés**'s older brother. His death at the end of the novel attracts little notice.

El-ahrairah

Watership Down
Richard Adams

The folk hero of rabbits. El-ahrairah is the ultimate trickster, the prince of the rabbits who tries to trick even **Lord Frith** himself, the sun god and creator. El-ahrairah's adventures, often with the aid of his friend **Rabscuttle**, are a part of rabbit lore, and **Dandelion** tells many of his stories.

Elaine

The Once and Future King
T. H. White

A girl who tricks **Lancelot** into having sex with her. As a result, she becomes the mother of **Galahad**. Although still very young, Elaine is crafty and determined enough to do all she can to win Lancelot's love. Except for the two times she persuades Lancelot to stay with her, Elaine is an unhappy woman. Elaine ends up killing herself because she knows deep down that Lancelot's heart lies with **Guenever**.

Elbow

Measure for Measure
William Shakespeare

A dim-witted constable charged with making arrests. His malapropisms provide comic relief.

The elder brother

Moll Flanders
Daniel Defoe

The older of the two brothers, who falls in love with **Moll**. She becomes his mistress with the understanding that he will marry her when he receives his inheritance. He later abandons her without marrying her.

Parson Elder

The Light in the Forest
Conrad Richter

A thin, wise, and elderly man, one of the most respected and accomplished citizens of Paxton Township. He has worked as a colonel and farmer, in addition to being the village pastor. Although he firmly believes in Christian superiority, Pastor Elder understands the complex situation that exists between whites and Indians.

Eleanor

King John
William Shakespeare

King John's mother and staunchest supporter and wife to the deceased **Henry II**. Like her counterpart on the French side, **Arthur**'s mother **Constance**, Eleanor vociferously urges John on to defend himself. She and Constance engage in heated verbal assaults, both vying for the child Arthur's affection. Unlike Constance, she supports the political marriage between the dauphin **Lewis** and the Spanish princess **Blanche**, as it will ensure John retains the crown of England. After her death in France following the battle of Angiers, John is disheartened, becoming indecisive and weak.

Eleanor, Duchess of Gloucester

Henry VI, Part II
William Shakespeare

The ambitious wife of **Humphrey, Duke of Gloucester**. Eleanor reveals her own designs on the throne when she relates a dream to her husband, in which **King Henry VI** and **Queen Margaret** were at her feet. She hires conjurers, **Bolingbroke** and a witch, **Margery Jourdain**, to predict her future. She is arrested and paraded through the streets of London in shame before being exiled to the Isle of Man. Her disgrace complicates Gloucester's situation and precipitates his downfall.

Electra

The Libation Bearers
Aeschylus

Orestes's older sister, the eldest daughter of **Clytemnestra** and **Agamemnon**. Mistreated by her mother and **Aegisthus**, Electra spends her days mourning her father's murder and awaiting Orestes, whom she believes will avenge Agamemnon's death. Electra is stubbornly devoted to the principles of justice, reverence, and honor, although her grasp on these principles is often shaky.

Electra

Electra
Sophocles

See above.

Electra

The Flies
Jean-Paul Sartre

Orestes's sister, Electra is both his companion and his foil. Mistreated by her mother **Clytemnestra**, Electra waits for the day when her brother will come to free her and avenge the murder of their father **Agamemnon** by **Aegistheus**. Electra spends her days in hatred of Clytemnestra and Aegistheus, who constantly punish her for refusing to repent for their crimes like the rest of the Argives. Having helped Orestes kill Aegistheus and Clytemnestra, Electra turns against him, repents their murder, and surrenders to **Jupiter**.

Mama Elena

Like Water for Chocolate
Laura Esquivel

The widowed matriarch of the De La Garza clan, Mama Elena is the prime source of **Tita**'s suffering. Her fierce temperament inspires fear in all three of her daughters. She keeps **Tita** from her true love, **Pedro**. It is later revealed that Mama Elena herself once suffered from a lost love, embittering her for the rest of her life.

After her death, Mama Elena appears to Tita as a ghost, scolding her daughter for conceiving a child by Pedro. She is renounced by Tita and turns into a ball of light that ignites Pedro's oil lamp and burns him.

Elendil

The Fellowship of the Ring
J. R. R. Tolkien

An ancient king of Westernesse who allied his armies with **Gil-galad**'s to take on **Sauron** before the Third Age of Middle-earth. Elendil, an ancestor of **Aragorn**'s line of the Men of Gondor, was killed along with Gil-galad in the battle to defeat the Dark Lord.

Queen of Eleusis

The King Must Die
Mary Renault

The queen who marries **Theseus** after he kills **Kerkyon**, the former king. She is also the chief priestess of **Mother Dia**, and when Theseus begins acting against custom, she tries to have him killed. She is a passionate woman who considers her life less important than her service to the Mother.

Rabbi Eliahou

Night
Elie Wiesel

A devout Jewish prisoner in the same camp as **Eliezar**.

Éliante

The Misanthrope
Molière

The object of **Philinte**'s romantic attentions. Éliante possesses a deep understanding of the French society in which she lives. Philinte tells Éliante that he would like to win her favor if she fails to win **Alceste**'s.

Eliezar

Night
Elie Wiesel

The author's stand-in and the son of **Chlomo**. The memoir traces Eliezar's psychological journey as his experiences in concentration camps rob him of his faith in God and expose him to inhumanity at human hands. Throughout his ordeal, Eliezar maintains his devotion to his father. His intensely personal story is representative of the experiences of hundreds of thousands of Jewish teenagers.

Elijah

The Old Testament
Unknown

A prophet who opposes the worship of the god Baal in Israel. After the division of Israel into two kingdoms, Elijah and his successor, **Elisha**, represent the last great spiritual heroes before Israel's exile. Their campaign in northern Israel against King **Ahab** and **Jezebel** helps to reduce Israel's growing evil but does not restore its greatness. Israel's demise makes Elijah and Elisha frustrated doom-sayers and miracle workers rather than national leaders or saviors.

Elijah

Inherit the Wind
Jerome Lawrence & Robert E. Lee

A mountain man. The illiterate Elijah sells Bibles to the townspeople and preaches his beliefs to the crowd.

Elisa

The Red and the Black
Stendhal

Mme. de Rênal's maid. Elisa is the first woman to fall in love with **Julien Sorel**. Elisa gives an offer of marriage to Sorel, but Sorel refuses. Because Mme. de Rênal is jealous of Elisa, she begins to acknowledge her own interest in Sorel and is overjoyed when Sorel refuses Elisa. Elisa is so jealous of his affair with Mme. de Rênal that she tells **M. Valenod** about it, who writes an anonymous letter about the affair to **M. de Rênal**. However, Mme. de Rênal and Sorel come up with a plan to fool M. de Rênal into thinking that nothing is going on and that M. Valenod wants Mme. de Rênal's affections. Not satisfied, Elisa tells **M. Chélan** about the affair, and Chélan has Sorel sent to a seminary in Besançon.

Elisha

The Old Testament
Unknown

A prophet who opposes the worship of the god Baal in Israel, **Elijah**'s successor and one of the last great spiritual heroes before Israel's exile.

Elisha

Go Tell It on the Mountain
James Baldwin

John Grimes's role model. A young leader in the congregation and a saved man.

Elizabeth

Go Tell It on the Mountain
James Baldwin

John Grimes's mother and **Gabriel**'s wife. Raised by her strict, religious, and unloving aunt, Elizabeth came north to be with her boyfriend, **Richard**. Richard killed himself, leaving her unwed and pregnant with John. She met Gabriel through his sister **Florence**, whom she had come to know at work. Gabriel offered her hope and a return to the true path. He promised to raise John as if the boy were his own. If Gabriel raised her up, he has also done much to undermine her.

Queen Elizabeth I

Henry VIII
William Shakespeare

The daughter of **King Henry VIII** and **Anne Boleyn**. Elizabeth will later be Queen of England, the ruling monarch for much of Shakespeare's life. The play's most important event, and the goal toward which all of the action moves, is Elizabeth's birth. In order for the birth to take place, a complex set of events must be put into motion: the fall of the **Duke of Buckingham**, who posed a possible threat to the throne; Henry's divorce from **Queen Katherine**; England's break with Rome and the Catholic Church, Henry's marriage to Anne; and the fall of **Cardinal Wolsey**, who opposed this second marriage. The final scene of the play is Elizabeth's baptism. **Cranmer, Archbishop of Canterbury** does the ceremony, and makes a speech about her future greatness, and that all of her good traits will be carried on in her heir, **James I** (the English king at the time when *King Henry VIII* was written).

Queen Elizabeth I

Orlando
Virginia Woolf

A noble, older woman accustomed to complete control. She likes **Orlando**'s youthful, innocent look, which she longs to regain for herself. After she makes Orlando her Treasurer, Steward, and lover, she grows possessive of him. She dies soon after seeing him with another woman.

Elizabeth of York

Richard III
William Shakespeare

The former **Queen Elizabeth**'s daughter. Young Elizabeth enjoys the fate of many Renaissance noblewomen: at the end of the play she is promised in marriage to **Henry Tudor, Earl of Richmond**, the Lancastrian rebel leader and the future King Henry VII, in order to unite the warring houses of York and Lancaster.

Elizabeth Woodville, Lady Grey

Henry VI, Part III and *Richard III*
William Shakespeare

The wife of **King Edward IV** and the mother of **Prince Edward**, **Richard, Duke of York**, and **Elizabeth of York**, as well as of **Lord Grey** and the **Marquess of Dorset** by a previous marriage. In *King Henry VI, Part III*, the widowed Lady Grey approaches Edward seeking to regain her dead husband's lands. Edward proposes to her after she refuses to become his mistress. This move proves costly for the Yorkists: Edward had initially negotiated for a marriage to **King Louis XI**'s sister, **Lady Bona**. The political gaffe causes a handful of nobles to join the Lancastrian side and briefly reinstate **King Henry VI** on the throne, before Edward's final, decisive victory. In *King Richard III*, Elizabeth watches her family members drop like flies as **King Richard III** takes steps to procure the throne. After Edward IV's death, Elizabeth is at Richard III's mercy. The hunchback rightly views her as an enemy because she opposes his rise to power, and because she is intelligent and fairly strong-willed. **Queen Margaret**, the widow of **King Henry VI**, curses Elizabeth, saying that she will outlive her glory, and see her husband and children die. Powerless to stop Richard's rise to the throne, Elizabeth sees her two sons from her marriage with Edward killed, as well as her brother **Lord Rivers**. She is finally approached by Richard, who, using all of his persuasion and guile, says that he wants to marry her daughter, Young Elizabeth. Horrified but overcome with grief, Elizabeth finally relents and says that she will talk to her on his behalf. However, Elizabeth betrothes her daughter to **Henry Tudor, Earl of Richmond**. The union, alluded to at the end of the play, does indeed take place after Richmond is crowned King Henry VII. The marriage rejoins the Houses of York and Lancaster, ending the Wars of the Roses, and creating the Tudor dynasty.

Aunt Elizabeth

The Handmaid's Tale
Margaret Atwood

One of the **Aunts** of **the Red Center**. **Moira** attacks Aunt Elizabeth and steals her Aunt uniform to escape from the Red Center.

Ella

Black Boy
Richard Wright

A young schoolteacher who briefly rents a room in **Granny**'s house. Bookish and dreamy, she introduces **Richard Wright** to the pleasures of fiction by telling him the story of Bluebeard and His Seven Wives. Granny thinks Ella's stories are sinful and forces her to move out.

Ella

Beloved
Toni Morrison

Worked with **Stamp Paid** on the Underground Railroad. Traumatized by the sexual brutality of a white father and son who once held her captive and raped her repeatedly, she believes, like **Sethe**, that the past is best left buried. When it surfaces in the form of **Beloved**, Ella organizes the women of the community to exorcise Beloved from 124 Bluestone Road.

Elladan

The Return of the King
J. R. R. Tolkien

Elrond's son and **Elrohir**'s brother. Elladan and Elrohir are members of the Dúnedain of the North, who make their way to Minas Tirith in response to a message requesting that they come to **Aragorn**'s aid.

Ellen

Incidents in the Life of a Slave Girl
Harriet Ann Jacobs

Linda Brent's child with **Mr. Sands**. Linda loves Ellen and her brother **Benny** passionately, and her feelings about them drive the book's action.

Ellen

Ordinary People
Judith Guest

Beth Jarrett's mother, **Conrad Jarrett**'s grandmother, wife of **Howard**. Howard and Ellen spend Christmas with the Jarretts, and Conrad stays at their house when his parents go to Houston. Ellen is constantly criticizing Conrad about the way he sleeps, eats, studies, and lives, but Conrad is able to let it roll off his back.

Ellen

Cloud Nine
Caryl Churchill

Edward's governess. She possesses a strong sense of duty to **Clive**'s family. She is also dependent upon them and afraid of being sent away. Ellen is working out her sexuality and nervously tests her attraction to **Betty**. Ultimately, Ellen cannot reconcile her desires with her lot in life, marrying the gay explorer **Harry** in a marriage that masks their mutual homosexuality.

Anne Elliot

Persuasion
Jane Austen

The novel's protagonist, the middle daughter of **Sir Walter Elliot**, a landed baronet from a socially important family. Reserved, clever, and practical, Anne considers her father's lavish spending foolish. Unfortunately, because she is neither the most beautiful nor the most image-conscious of his daughters, Sir Walter often overlooks Anne and dismisses her opinions. Seeking to please those around her, in her youth Anne was persuaded from following her true desires. In contrast to both of her two sisters and to the other young female characters in the novel, Anne is level-headed, considerate of others, and humble. She balances duty and passion in a composed and respectful way.

In Our Time
Cornelia Elliot Ernest Hemingway

The wife of **Hubert Elliot** in "Mr. and Mrs. Elliot." Cornelia is an unhappy American living in France with her husband.

Persuasion
Elizabeth Elliot Jane Austen

The eldest daughter of **Sir Walter Elliot** and the older sister of **Anne Elliot**. Elizabeth Elliot is her father's favorite. Like her father, she is vain and preoccupied with associating with important people. At the end of the novel, Elizabeth is the only one of the Elliot daughters to remain single, there being no one of adequate birth to suit her taste.

In Our Time
Hubert Elliot Ernest Hemingway

A poet living in France in "Mr. and Mrs. Elliot." Hubert cannot make his wife pregnant or happy.

Persuasion
Mr. William Elliot Jane Austen

Anne Elliot's cousin, heir to Kellynch Hall. Mr. William Elliot is a smooth talker whom everyone agrees is "perfectly what he ought to be." Only six months after the death of his first wife, and at the end of a marriage that was generally known to be unhappy, Mr. Elliot is searching for a new bride. Good-looking and well-mannered, Mr. Elliot talks his way back into the good graces of Sir Walter, yet Anne questions his true motives.

Persuasion
Sir Walter Elliot Jane Austen

The father of **Anne Elliot**, baronet, and owner of Kellynch Hall. Sir Walter is a caricature of the impractical titled upper classes. Extraordinarily vain, Sir Walter lines his dressing room with mirrors and agrees to be seen in public only with attractive or well-born people. Conscious of keeping up grand appearances, Sir Walter spends lavishly and brings his family into debt. A poor judge of character, he is easily fooled by those who would take advantage of him.

One Flew over the Cuckoo's Nest
Ellis Ken Kesey

A patient who was once an Acute. Ellis's excessive electroshock therapy transformed him into a Chronic. In the daytime, he is nailed to the wall. He frequently urinates on himself.

I Never Promised You a Rose Garden
Ellis Joanne Greenberg

A Conscientious Objector who comes to work at the hospital. Ellis's fear and hatred of the mental patients is evident in his every gesture. The patients, sensing that Ellis himself has mental problems, torment him by ridiculing his fundamental religious beliefs. Later, **Deborah** witnesses Ellis physically abuse **Helene**, but no one takes her seriously when she reports it.

Ellen Foster
Kaye Gibbons

Ellis

Ellen's uncle on her father's side. With his brother **Rudolph**, Ellis agrees to spy on Ellen and her father for Ellen's grandmother. After inaccurately reporting that Ellen is wild and a troublemaker, Rudolph and Ellis are compensated by Ellen's grandmother with large sums of money, some of which she instructs them to give to Ellen and her father for bare necessities.

When the Legends Die
Hal Borland

Rowena Ellis

A mother figure to **Thomas Black Bull** and the other schoolchildren. She teaches English and is in charge of the girls' dormitory.

The Martian Chronicles
Ray Bradbury

Elma

The wife of **Sam Parkhill**. She is smarter than him and seems quietly amused at his mishandling of life on Mars.

The Return of the King
J. R. R. Tolkien

Elrohir

Elrond's son and **Elladan**'s brother. Elrohir and Elladan are members of the Dúnedain of the North, who make their way to Minas Tirith in response to a message requesting that they come to **Aragorn**'s aid.

The Hobbit, The Fellowship of the Ring, and *The Return of the King*
J. R. R. Tolkien

Elrond Halfelven

The father of **Arwen Evenstar**, friend of **Gandalf**, and the great leader of the **Elves** at Rivendell. Elrond Halfelven has the blood of **Humans** and Elves, as his name states. Elrond had the choice to be mortal or immortal and chose the latter. As a consequence, Elrond must leave Middle-earth for the Grey Havens when the time comes. He is renowned for his wisdom and learning. In *The Hobbit*, Elrond Halfelven gives **Thorin Oakenshield**'s and **Bilbo Baggins**'s group aid and helpful advice when they pass through Rivendell early on in their quest to defeat **Smaug** in the Lonely Mountain. In *The Fellowship of the Ring*, the Council of Elrond at Rivendell selects **Aragorn**, **Boromir**, **Legolas**, **Gimli**, **Frodo Baggins**, **Meriadoc Brandybuck**, **Peregrin Took**, **Samwise Gamgee**, and Gandalf to form the Fellowship of the Ring. In *The Return of the King*, Elrond sees his daughter, Arwen, give up her immortality to marry Aragorn, the newly returned King of Númenor. Elrond travels with the other elves and Frodo, Bilbo, and Gandalf to the West beyond the Great Sea to the Grey Havens after the defeat of **Sauron** and the destruction of the One Ring by **Gollum** and Frodo.

Mr. Elton

Emma
Jane Austen

The village vicar, a handsome and agreeable man. When Mr. Elton marries a woman in Bath only a short time after proposing to **Emma Woodhouse**, he seems proud and superficial.

Mrs. Elton

Emma
Jane Austen

Formerly Augusta Hawkins. Mrs. Elton hails from Bristol and meets **Mr. Elton** in Bath. She has some fortune and a well-married sister, but her vanity, superficiality, and vulgar overfamiliarity offset her admirable qualities.

Elves

The Hobbit
J. R. R. Tolkien

The first creatures in Middle-earth. Immortal unless killed in battle, they are fair-faced, with beautiful voices, and have a close communion with nature, which makes them wonderful craftsmen. There are actually two different varieties of Elves: the Wood Elves and the High Elves. The Wood Elves reside in Mirkwood and, as a result, have more suspicious and less-wise tendencies than their high relatives. The High Elves live in the enchanted forest of Lothlórien. The power of the enchanted forest lies within the Ring of Power that **Galadriel** wears. **Elrond Halfelven** is the master of the Elves in Middle-earth, residing in the peaceful retreat of Rivendell, where **Gandalf** takes **Bilbo Baggins** during his journey to defeat **Smaug**, and where the Fellowship of the Ring is formed. Elves and **Dwarves** are traditionally old rivals. The Elves know that with the passing of the age of Middle-earth in which they live, they will have to make an exodus from Middle-earth and go west over the Great Sea to the Grey Havens. **Legolas** is the Elf member of the Fellowship of the Ring. **Arwen Evenstar** is the Elf who decides to give up her immortality to marry the returned King of Númenor, **Aragorn**.

Mrs. Elvsted

Hedda Gabler
Henrik Ibsen

Hedda Tesman's weak but passionate classmate. Mrs. Elvsted is a former maid who married the widower for whom she worked. Secluded in the country, she has grown very attached to **Ejlert Løvborg**. **Mr. Elvsted** aids Ejlert Løvborg in his research and writing, all the while keeping him away from his destructive drinking problem. Mrs. Elvsted leaves her husband to follow and watch out for the unstable Ejlert Løvborg. She remembers being tormented by Hedda during their school days.

Bishop of Ely

Henry V
William Shakespeare

A wealthy and powerful English clergyman. Worried that **King Henry V** will pass a bill that will authorize the government to take away a portion of the church's land and money, the Bishop and the **Archbishop of Canterbury** decide to urge the king to war with the French and thus distract him from passing the bill. The two bishops do not go to fight in the war, but their urging and fundraising are important factors in Henry's decision to invade France and are indicative of the backroom political dealings in the play.

Little Em'ly

David Copperfield
Charles Dickens

Mr. Peggoty's unfaithful niece. Little Em'ly is sweet but also coy and vain. Her desire to be a lady leads her to disgrace herself by running away from her family.

Emelye

The Canterbury Tales
Geoffrey Chaucer

Sister to **Hippolyta**, **Theseus**'s domesticated Amazon queen in **the Knight**'s Tale. Fair-haired and glowing, we first see Emelye as **Palamon** does, through a window. Although she is the object of both Palamon's and **Arcite**'s desire, she would rather spend her life unmarried and childless. Arcite wins a tournament with Emelye's hand as the prize, and Emelye willingly agrees to marry Arcite. However, Arcite dies directly after the tournament, and so Emelye ends up marrying Palamon.

Emerald

Midnight's Children
Salman Rushdie

Saleem's aunt, the sister of **Mumtaz**, who marries **General Zulfikar**.

Emerson

Invisible Man
Ralph Ellison

The son of one of the wealthy white trustees (also called Emerson) of **the Narrator**'s college. The younger Emerson reads the supposed recommendation from **Dr. Bledsoe** and reveals Bledsoe's treachery to the narrator. He expresses sympathy for the narrator and helps him get a job, but he remains too preoccupied with his own problems to help the narrator in any meaningful way.

George Emerson

A Room with a View
E. M. Forster

A young man with a passionate desire for truth. At the beginning of the book, George doubts if life is worth living. Though he is of a lower social class, he falls in love with **Lucy Honeychurch** in Italy, and she stimulates his search for joy and meaning. He discourages her from marrying **Cecil Vyse** and helps her to follow the true ways of her heart.

Lidian Emerson

Walden
Henry David Thoreau

Ralph Waldo Emerson's second wife. Lidian Emerson was somewhat distressed by her husband's frequent absences from home. During her husband's tours of Europe, Thoreau stayed with her, and the two developed a close friendship.

Mr. Emerson

A Room with a View
E. M. Forster

George Emerson's father, who means well but constantly offends proper societal conventions with his abrupt manner of speaking and his blatant honestly. An avid reader, he espouses liberal values, and also plays a role in helping **Lucy Honeychurch** surrender herself to her true desires, even if it means violating social taboos. His wife is dead.

Ralph Waldo Emerson

Walden
Henry David Thoreau

Essayist, poet, and the leading figure of Transcendentalism. Emerson became a mentor to **Henry David Thoreau** after they met in 1837. Emerson played a significant role in the creation of Walden by allowing Thoreau to live and build on his property near Walden Pond. There is an appropriate symbolism in this construction site, since philosophically Thoreau was building on the Transcendentalist foundation already prepared by Emerson. The influence of Emerson's ideas, especially the doctrine of self-reliance that sees the human soul and mind as the origin of the reality it inhabits, pervades Thoreau's work. However, whereas Thoreau retreated to his own private world, Emerson assumed a prominent role in public life, making extended overseas lecture tours to promote the view expressed in his renowned *Essays*. The two often disagreed on the necessity of adhering to some public conventions, and the heated tensions between the two may perhaps be felt in the minimal attention Emerson receives in *Walden*. Thoreau fails to mention that Emerson owns the land, despite his tedious detailing of less significant facts, and when Emerson visits, in the guise of the unnamed "Old Immortal," Thoreau treats him rather indifferently.

Emilia

Othello
William Shakespeare

Iago's wife and **Desdemona**'s attendant. Cynical and worldly, Emilia is devoted to Desdemona and distrusts Iago. When Emilia finds Desdemona's handkerchief and gives it to Iago, Iago plants the handkerchief in **Cassio**'s room as "evidence" that Cassio and Desdemona are having an affiar. When Emilia uncovers Iago's plot and exposes her husband's treachery, Iago stabs and kills her.

Emilia of *Noble Kinsmen*

The Two Noble Kinsmen
William Shakespeare

Hippolyta's sister. Emilia is the unwitting cause of **Palamon** and **Arcite**'s feud. Emilia wants to stay a virgin.

Emilia of *Winter's Tale*

The Winter's Tale
William Shakespeare

One of **Hermione**'s ladies-in-waiting.

Emilie

Dangerous Liaisons
Pierre-Ambroise-François Choderlos de Laclos

A courtesan favored by **the Vicomte de Valmont**.

Emilio

A Farewell to Arms
Ernest Hemingway

A bartender in the town of Stresa, Italy, who frequently aids **Frederic Henry** and **Catherine Barkley**. Emilio helps reunite the couple after they are separated, saves them from arrest, and ushers them off to safety.

Emily

Angels in America
Tony Kushner

A nurse who attends to **Prior Walter** in the hospital. One of several characters who give voice to the same anti-migratory impulse as the Angel, Emily tells Prior in no uncertain terms to stay put.

Miss Emma

A Lesson Before Dying
Ernest J. Gaines

Jefferson's devout godmother. After hearing Jefferson's lawyer call Jefferson a hog, she becomes obsessed with ensuring that Jefferson dies "like a man." Miss Emma expresses her emotions freely and demonstrates her strength during Jefferson's trial and incarceration.

Emmanuelson

Out of Africa
Isak Dinesen

A local Swede who flees from Nairobi because he gets into trouble. Emmanuelson is a heroic, mythic figure who survives a difficult trek across the Masai reserve. His widespread knowledge of literature and his wisdom about life also indicate that he shares some of the aristocratic qualities that **the narrator** values. Emmanuelson is a tragic figure because he is constantly being persecuted and judged. The reason for his persecution, though only hinted at, may relate to his being homosexual.

Emmeline

Uncle Tom's Cabin
Harriet Beecher Stowe

A young and beautiful slave girl purchased by **Simon Legree**, perhaps to replace **Cassy** as his mistress. Emmeline has been raised as a pious Christian.

Emo

Ceremony
Leslie Marmon Silko

A childhood acquaintance of **Tayo** and **Pinkie**'s killer. Emo has always been critical of Tayo for his mixed race and has always possessed an undirected rage that only increases as a result of his fighting in World War II. Like the other war veterans, he is unable to find a place for himself on his return, and spends his time drinking and reliving memories of his army days.

Emperor

The Chairs
Eugène Ionesco

The most esteemed invisible guest the **Old Man** welcomes. The Emperor is bathed in light, and the Old Man and **Old Woman** defer to him at all times.

Emperor-over-the-Sea

The Lion, the Witch, and the Wardrobe
C. S. Lewis

Aslan's father and the ultimate God of Narnia. He is the Father, while Aslan is the Son, as in the Christian trinity.

Mr. Enfield

Dr. Jekyll and Mr. Hyde
Robert Louis Stevenson

A distant cousin and lifelong friend of **Mr. Gabriel John Utterson**'s. Like Utterson, Enfield is reserved, formal, and scornful of gossip.

Second Engineer

The Hairy Ape
Eugene O'Neill

Mildred Douglas's escort into the stokehole of the Ocean Liner. The Second Engineer warns Mildred that her white dress will be ruined, but she ignores him.

English Teacher

Girl, Interrupted
Susanna Kaysen

Susanna's high school teacher and lover. He takes her to the Frick Museum in New York, where she first sees the Vermeer painting titled *Girl, Interrupted at Her Music*. Their affair is short-lived.

Jakob Engstrand

Ghosts
Henrik Ibsen

A carpenter with a deformed leg. Jakob married **Johanna** when she was pregnant with **Captain Alving**'s child. The daughter was **Regina**. At the start of the play, he is working on the orphan asylum meant to memorialize Captain Alving. He wants to use the money he is saving to open an "establishment" for sailors.

Regina Engstrand

Ghosts
Henrik Ibsen

Mrs. Alving's maidservant. She is believed to be the daughter of **Jakob Engstrand**, a carpenter, and the late **Johanna**, Mrs. Alving's former maid. In fact, she is the illegitimate daughter of Johanna and **Captain Alving**. She only learns this at the end of the play. Throughout the play, she resists her father's dubious affection and takes pride from working in Mrs. Alving's home. She seems to return **Oswald**'s affection. However, she is careful not to overstep the bounds of propriety.

Enjolras

Les Misérables
Victor Hugo

The fiery leader of the Friends of the ABC. He is a radical, wild, beautiful student revolutionary. He leads the insurrection at the barricade. When a drunken revolutionary shoots a local homeowner, Enjolras executes the man on the spot. He delivers a rousing speech. **Marius Pontmercy** eventually grows tired of his rhetoric.

Enkidu

The Epic of Gilgamesh
Unknown

A wild creature created by the gods as a rival and companion for **Gilgamesh**. Enkidu grows up outside civilization, but is tamed and socialized by **Shamhat**. Enkidu's wisdom contrasts with and tempers Gilgamesh's impetuosity. Enkidu's death from an illness sent by **Enlil** triggers Gilgamesh's quest for immortality.

Enlil

The Epic of Gilgamesh
Unknown

The chief god and a harsh ruler over Earth and humans. "Enlil" means "Lord Wind." God of earth, wind and water, Enlil sends the deluge to destroy all humans, and decrees that **Enkidu** should die.

Domitius Enobarbus

Antony and Cleopatra
William Shakespeare

Antony's most loyal supporter. Worldly and cynical, Enobarbus is friendly with the subordinates of both **Pompey** and **Octavius Caesar**, yet stays faithful to his master even after Antony makes grave political and military missteps. He abandons Antony only when the general appears to be completely finished, joining Caesar. When Antony sends Enobarbus's possessions back to him after a battle, the guilt-stricken and once loyal Enobarbus dies in grief.

Enoch

Things Fall Apart
Chinua Achebe

A fanatical convert to the Christian church in Umuofia. Enoch triggers the climactic clash between the indigenous and colonial justice systems when he disrespectfully rips the mask off an egwugwu during an annual ceremony to honor the native earth deity. Early on, **Mr. Brown** keeps Enoch in check in the interest of community harmony, but Brown's successor **Reverend Smith** approves of Enoch's zealotry.

Luis Enrique

Chronicle of a Death Foretold
Gabriel García Márquez

The narrator's younger brother. He plays the guitar very well and goes around with **Santiago Nasar**, **Cristo Bedoya**, and the narrator when they go to serenade **Bayardo San Roman** and **Angela Vicario** on the night of their wedding.

Éomer

The Two Towers and *The Return of the King*
J. R. R. Tolkien

The nephew and declared heir of **Théoden** and the brother of **Éowyn**. In *The Two Towers*, Éomer is introduced as one of the Riders of Rohan, the horsemen to whom the Lord of Gondor has given land in exchange for guarding his territories. Éomer encounters with suspicion **Aragorn**'s traveling party early in *The Two Towers*, giving Aragorn, **Legolas**, and **Gimli** information implying that **Meriadoc Brandybuck** and **Peregrin Took** are still alive. In *The Return of the King*, Éomer, who initially urges his uncle, the King of Rohan, not to go east to battle Mordor, joins the battle himself and bravely leads the Rohirrim, the fighting horsemen of Rohan, after his uncle's valiant death in battle.

The Two Towers and *The Return of the King*
J. R. R. Tolkien

Éowyn

The Lady of Rohan, niece of **Théoden**-king, and sister of **Éomer**, skilled horsewoman, like all those from Rohan. In *The Two Towers*, Éowyn is beseeched by her uncle and King to defend the land of Rohan in his absence. In *The Return of the King*, Éowyn, driven by a desire for combat and for **Aragorn**'s affection, disguises herself in men's clothing and endangers herself to challenge the Lord of **the Nazgûl** in battle. In disguise, she watches Théoden fall in battle and reveals herself to him in his last moments. With the help of **Meriadoc Brandybuck**, she destroys the Lord of the Nazgûl. With the passing of the Shadow of Mordor after **Frodo Baggins**'s quest to destroy the One Ring is successful, Éowyn is freed from her desire for war, and she turns her affections to **Faramir**, the son of the Steward of Gondor, **Denethor**.

The Assistant
Bernard Malamud

Ephraim

Morris Bober and **Ida Bober**'s deceased son. His death has left a void in Morris Bober's life. **Frank Alpine** replaces Ephraim and becomes the Bobers' foster child.

Silas Marner
George Eliot

Eppie

A girl whom **Silas Marner** eventually adopts. Eppie is the biological child of **Godfrey Cass** and **Molly Farren**, Godfrey's secret wife. She is pretty, spirited, and loving.

The Contender
Robert Lipsyte

Mr. Epstein

The boss of **Alfred Brooks**. Mr. Epstein's and Alfred's relationship is marred when **James**, **Major**, and **Hollis** try to break into Mr. Epstein's store. Alfred's hard work helps to restore Mr. Epstein's trust in him, as does the knowledge that Alfred trains as a boxer. As an old boxer himself, Mr. Epstein develops a kinship with Alfred and pays for his lessons. Mr. Epstein, much like **Mr. Donatelli**, gives Alfred a chance to prove that Alfred is worth the risk of taking him on as a worker/student.

Anthem
Ayn Rand

Equality 7-2521

A street sweeper, the protagonist of *Anthem*. Equality 7-2521, who later renames himself Prometheus, believes in individualism and rejects the collectivist society around him. Equality 7-2521 begins the novella as a benighted, if exceptional, youth, who has only barely realized that he might be different from those around him. He regrets his differences and tries to bring himself into conformity. When Equality 7-2521 meets **the Golden One**, he no longer wants to deny that he prefers some of his peers to others. The discovery of the light bulb pushes Equality 7-2521 into complete rebellion. Until the moment when the World Council and **Collective 0-0009** threaten to destroy the light bulb, Equality 7-2521 thinks of his brothers and their welfare. Because he will not abide seeing the light bulb destroyed, even though he might tolerate his own destruction, he is forced into exile from his society. Once he has broken from society, Equality 7-2521 adopts a vanity and pride unknown in the society in which he was raised and, in so doing, he realizes his manhood.

Ereshkigal

The Epic of Gilgamesh
Unknown

Terrifying queen of the underworld.

Erestor

The Fellowship of the Ring
J. R. R. Tolkien

An Elf-lord who attends the Council of **Elrond Halfelven** at Rivendell to choose the Fellowship of the Ring. Erestor suggests that the One Ring be given to the ancient and magically powerful **Tom Bombadil,** over whom it has no power; the others at the Council, including **Gandalf**, worry, however, that even Bombadil could not single-handedly defeat the Dark Lord **Sauron**.

Eric

Lord of the Flies
William Golding

One of a pair of twins closely allied with **Ralph**. **Sam** and Eric are always together, and the other boys often treat them as a single entity, calling them "Samneric." The easily excitable Sam and Eric are part of the group known as the "bigguns." At the end of the novel, they fall victim to **Jack**'s manipulation and coercion.

Eric

The Bell Jar
Sylvia Plath

An acquaintance of **Esther Greenwood**'s with whom she had her most open conversation about sex. Eric is a southern prep school boy who lost his virginity with a prostitute and now associates love with chastity and sex with behaving like an animal.

Jan Erlone

Native Son
Richard Wright

A member of the Communist Party and **Mary Dalton**'s boyfriend, to the distress of her parents. Jan, like Mary, wants to treat **Bigger Thomas** as an equal, but such untraditional behavior only frightens and angers Bigger. Jan later recognizes his mistake in trying to treat Bigger this way and becomes sympathetic toward his plight.

Ernie

Bless Me, Ultima
Rudolfo A. Anaya

One of a group of exuberant boys who frequently curse and fight. Ernie is a braggart who frequently teases **Antonio Márez**. He says that he hears that a witch lives in Antonio's house. He and Antonio fight about this teasing, and afterward, no one teases Antonio about **Ultima** again. The other boys in the group are **Abel**, **Bones**, **the Vitamin Kid**, **Horse**, **Lloyd**, and **Red**.

Eros

Greek Mythology
Unknown

The Greek name for the Roman god **Cupid**; the son of **Aphrodite**, Eros uses his bow to fire magic arrows that cause people to fall in love. He is a beautiful young man typically depicted as a winged cherub. Eros, who is often blindfolded, performs works of romantic mischief whenever Aphrodite asks.

Eros

Antony and Cleopatra
William Shakespeare

An attendant serving **Antony**. Eros's love for his master compels him to refuse Antony's order that Eros kill him, instead choosing to commit suicide.

Sir Thomas Erpingham

Henry V
William Shakespeare

A wise, aged veteran of many wars who serves with **King Henry V**'s campaign. The King borrows Erpingham's cloak to disguise himself and mingle with the troops the night before the Battle of Agincourt.

Esa

Out of Africa
Isak Dinesen

The narrator's original cook, who is later murdered by his wife. Esa is an older man who is described as being very gentle. Esa often is taken advantage of by other people, perhaps because of his gentility. Esa's wife uses him, first by deserting him for other native men and then by murdering him.

Esau

The Red Tent
Anita Diamant

Jacob's twin brother and other son of **Isaac**. When leaving **Laban**'s camp, Jacob's main obstacle is that he is terrified of seeing Esau, who he is afraid might kill Jacob and all of Jacob's family. When Jacob finally is surprised by Esau and his sons on the way to Canaan, he falls on his knees in front of Esau. The prosperous Esau picks Jacob up and embraces him. There is a reconciliation, and Jacob's family comes to live in Canaan, where the women come under the wise and powerful influence of **Rebecca**.

Escalus

Measure for Measure
William Shakespeare

A wise lord who advises **Lord Angelo** to be more merciful. He is loyal to Duke **Vincentio**, but does not dare defy Angelo.

Prince Escalus

Romeo and Juliet
William Shakespeare

The Prince of Verona; a kinsman of **Mercutio** and **Paris**. As the seat of political power in Verona, he is concerned about maintaining the public peace at all costs. He punishes those in the Capulet or Montague families who break the peace.

Aunt Escolastica

Love in the Time of Cholera
Gabriel García Márquez

The aunt of **Fermina Daza**. Aunt Escolastica helps raise Fermina Daza after the girl's mother, **Fermina Sánchez**, dies. She is more of a friend than an aunt, and brazenly helps Fermina Daza communicate in secret with **Florentino Ariza**. When **Lorenzo Daza**, Escolastica's brother and Fermina Daza's father, discovers that she has been assisting Fermina Daza in her affair, he banishes Escolastica from his house, though she owns nothing and has no money. When Fermina Daza tries to contact her aunt, she learns that Escolastica is dead.

Kenneth Escott

Babbitt
Sinclair Lewis

A young reporter for Zenith's local newspaper. Kenneth compromises his journalistic integrity when he agrees to become the unofficial press agent for **Babbitt**'s church. He marries **Verona Babbitt**.

Governess Esmerelda

Bel Canto
Ann Patchett

The governess who cares for **Ruben Iglesias**'s children. She ably and tenderly stitches up Iglesias's face after he is wounded.

La Esmeralda

Hunchback of Notre Dame
Victor Hugo

The lost daughter of **Sister Gudule**, La Esmeralda is a beautiful gypsy street dancer. She has a very romantic view of love, instantly falling for **Phoebus de Chateaupers** when he saves her. When a jealous priest, **Claude Frollo**, stabs Phoebus, Esmeralda is blamed. She is tortured and eventually confesses, and then is sentenced to death. When she is about to be hanged, **Quasimodo** saves her and takes her to Notre Dame and cares for her. He loves her, but she cannot help but recoil in horror each time she looks at him. They form an uneasy friendship. Esmeralda is again captured for execution. Sister Gudule, a woman who was once very critical of gypsies, discovers that Esmeralda is her daughter and tries in vain to save her from death. Years later, when a gravedigger stumbles across La Esmeralda's remains, he finds the skeleton of Quasimodo curled around her.

Esperanza

The House on Mango Street
Sandra Cisneros

The novel's perceptive, poetic narrator. Esperanza is ashamed of her Chicano family's poverty, their house, and their neighborhood. The novel chronicles a year in Esperanza's life, as she matures emotionally, sexually, and artistically.

Esperanza

The Bean Trees
Barbara Kingsolver

A Guatemalan refugee, and the wife of **Estevan**. Her grave demeanor is a reflection of her sorrowful past. **Turtle**'s presence touches her because Turtle reminds her of the daughter she had to leave in Guatemala.

Esperanza

Like Water for Chocolate
Laura Esquivel

The second child of **Rosaura** and **Pedro**, and the mother of the novel's narrator. She is raised by **Tita** in the kitchen. Her marriage to **Alex** breaks the De la Garza family tradition that disallows the marriage of youngest daughters.

Colonel Cecil Burleigh Essex

Pudd'nhead Wilson
Mark Twain

A Virginian and friend of **Judge Driscoll**'s. Colonel Cecil Burleigh Essex dies the same year as **Percy Northumberland Driscoll**. **Roxana** reveals to her true child, **Valet de Chambre**, Chambers, or "Tom" that Colonel Essex is his father. His whole life, Tom thought his father was Percy and that he himself was white.

Alice Estee

The Day of the Locust
Nathanael West

Claude's wife.

Claude Estee

The Day of the Locust
Nathanael West

A successful Hollywood screenwriter and another of **Tod**'s friends. Claude plays along with the masquerades of Hollywood, keeping a house that is a replica of a southern mansion and acting the part of a southern gentleman himself.

Estella

Great Expectations
Charles Dickens

Miss Havisham's beautiful young ward. Estella sometimes seems to consider **Pip** a friend, but she is usually cold and cruel to him. She repeatedly warns him that she has no heart.

Estelle

No Exit
Jean-Paul Sartre

The third and final prisoner, she is also the most frightened. She desperately wants to see her reflection in a mirror and swears that she does not belong in hell, having just died of pneumonia. **Inez** tries to seduce her, but she says that she needs to be with a man. She eventually confesses to not only having an affair, but also drowning the baby of her lover. **Garcin** is momentarily drawn to her but chooses instead to focus all his energy on Inez. Estelle tries to kill Inez, forgetting that they are all already dead.

Harry Y. Esterbrook

Inherit the Wind
Jerome Lawrence & Robert E. Lee

A radio host from WGN in Chicago. Harry Y. Esterbrook broadcasts the announcement of the verdict and the sentencing in **Bertram Cates**'s trial.

Estevan

The Bean Trees
Barbara Kingsolver

A Guatemalan refugee, he worked as an English teacher in Guatemala before he and his wife **Esperanza** fled to the United States. He speaks beautiful English, and his kind ways inspire romantic feelings in **Taylor Greer**. He enlightens Taylor about the corruption of Central American governments.

Esther

The Old Testament
Unknown

A timid Jewish girl who becomes the queen of Persia. Esther boldly and cunningly persuades the king of Persia to remove his edict calling for the death of the exiled Jews.

Esther

Little Women
Louisa May Alcott

Aunt March's servant. Esther is a French Catholic.

Esther's parents

I Never Promised You a Rose Garden
Joanne Greenberg

Wealthy first-generation Jewish immigrants. **Esther**'s father, a Latvian immigrant with a clubfoot, has been driven by anger and resentment for all of his life. The old insults of a long-dead Latvian nobleman continue to drive his ambition to build a wealthy dynasty in the United States.

Estragon

Waiting for Godot
Samuel Beckett

One of the play's two main characters. Weak and helpless, he seeks **Vladimir**'s protection. In Act II, he has forgotten the events of Act I.

Ethel

East of Eden
John Steinbeck

A prostitute at **Faye**'s brothel who obtains proof that **Cathy Ames** murdered Faye. Ethel tries to blackmail Cathy for a payment of $100 each month but is later discovered to have drowned.

Euclides

Love in the Time of Cholera
Gabriel García Márquez

The cunning boy whom **Florentino Ariza** hires to dive for the treasure of the galleon. He deceives Florentino by only recovering treasure he has planted himself, which turns out to be fake jewelry.

Eugenia

I Never Promised You a Rose Garden
Joanne Greenberg

A patient who attended the same summer camp as **Deborah** when they were children. One day, Deborah found Eugenia naked in the camp bathroom. She gave Deborah a belt and asked Deborah to beat her. Deborah refused and never spoke to Eugenia again. At the hospital, they become friends.

Eugenio

Daisy Miller
Henry James

The courier for the Millers, Eugenio acts more like a member of the family. **Mrs. Costello** considers the family's familiarity with Eugenio a typical example of their lack of social breeding.

Eugenius

Tristram Shandy
Laurence Sterne

Friend and advisor to **Parson Yorick**. His name means "well-born," and he is often the voice of discretion.

Eulalie

Swann's Way
Marcel Proust

One of **Aunt Léonie**'s few remaining friends. Eulalie visits Aunt Léonie each Sunday to gossip about the townspeople.

Eumaeus

The Odyssey
Homer

A loyal shepherd. Even though he does not know that the vagabond who appears at his hut is **Odysseus**, Eumaeus gives the man food and shelter. Along with the cowherd **Philoetius**, Eumaeus helps Odysseus reclaim his throne after his return to Ithaca.

Eunice

Homecoming
Cynthia Voigt

The Tillerman children's cousin. Eunice is **Gram**'s sister's daughter. A pious Catholic used to her routine, Eunice is nearly incapable of spontaneity and affection. She takes the Tillerman children in out of a sense of duty, but, consciously or not, expects them to show gratitude and earn their keep with good behavior and hard work.

Euphrosyne

Orlando
Virginia Woolf

The third of **Orlando**'s loves at the court of King James. Euphrosyne would have made the perfect wife of a nobleman. She was fair, sweet, kind to animals, and from an extraordinarily good Irish family. Instead of marrying her, Orlando runs away with **Sasha**.

Eurycleia

The Odyssey
Homer

The aged and loyal servant who nursed **Odysseus** and **Telemachus** when they were babies. Eurycleia is well-informed about palace intrigues and serves as her masters' confidante. She keeps Telemachus's journey a secret from **Penelope**, and she later keeps **Odysseus**'s identity a secret after she recognizes a scar on his leg.

Eurydice

Oedipus trilogy (Oedipus Rex, Oedipus at Colonus, Antigone)
Sophocles

Creon's wife.

Eurydice

Antigone 1946
Jean Anouilh

Creon's kind, knitting wife. Her suicide is Creon's last punishment, leaving him entirely alone.

Eurymachus

The Odyssey
Homer

A manipulative, deceitful suitor of **Penelope**'s. Eurymachus's charisma and duplicity allow him to exert some influence over the other suitors.

Eva

Tuesdays with Morrie
Mitch Albom

The kind, caring immigrant woman whom **Charlie** marries after **Morrie Schwartz**'s mother dies. She gives Morrie and his brother **David** the love and affection they have so longed for, and instills in Morrie his love of books and desire for education.

Frau Eva

Demian
Hermann Hesse

Max Demian's mother, with whom **Emil Sinclair** is in love. Like Demian, Eva's primary role is to help Sinclair develop appropriately. Even before they have met, she serves as a goal for him, which he pursues vicariously through his pursuit of **Beatrice**. Once they meet, she loves and coddles Sinclair, commiserating with him about the hard times of his adolescence. At the same time, however, she exhorts him to have more confidence in and connection with his desires.

Evan

The Hours
Michael Cunningham

Walter Hardy's boyfriend. He has AIDS, but is responding much better than **Richard Brown** to treatment.

Christian Evandale

The Black Prince
Iris Murdoch

Bradley Pearson's ex-wife, **Francis Marloe**'s sister and the object of **Arnold Baffin**'s affection. Christian is a confident, strong woman who has aged but still remains sexually attractive. She has returned from living in America after becoming widowed.

Evander

The Aeneid
Virgil

King of Pallanteum and father of **Pallas**. Evander is a sworn enemy of the Latins. **Aeneas** befriends him and secures his assistance in the battles against **Turnus**.

Evangeline St. Clare

Uncle Tom's Cabin
Harriet Beecher Stowe

Augustine St. Clare and **Marie**'s angelic daughter. Eva laments the existence of slavery and sees no difference between blacks and whites. She becomes close friends with **Uncle Tom** and convinces her father to buy him for his companionship after Tom saves her from drowning. Eva encourages the education of **Topsy**, convincing the unruly slave that she loves her and that Jesus loves her as well. Eva dies before reaching adulthood, and due to her father's miscalculation, many of the slaves that she wanted to see freed are sold to tyrannical masters. After her death, Eva's memory strengthens Tom when he has to endure the beatings of his new master, **Simon Legree**.

Evans

Mrs. Dalloway
Virginia Woolf

Septimus Warren Smith's wartime officer and close friend. Evans died in Italy just before the Armistice, but Septimus, in his deluded state, continues to see and hear him behind trees and bedroom walls.

Janice Evans

The Member of the Wedding
Carson McCullers

Jarvis Addams's fiancée from Winter Hill. Like Jarvis, she represents **Frankie Addams**'s great wish to become an adult and connect with other people.

Sir Hugh Evans

The Merry Wives of Windsor
William Shakespeare

The local clergyman. When Evans pleads for a marriage between **Anne Page** and **Abraham Slender**, **Doctor Caius**, another suitor of Anne's, challenges him to a duel. Caius and Evans's duel is stopped by the onlookers. As Caius is French and Evans is Welsh, both men's mangling of the queen's language has made for some humor with the ruffian crowd. The two band together to seek revenge on **the Host**, which resolves itself when the Host loses three horses. The humor at the expense of Evans's verbal gaffes, religious authority, and foolish duel is indicative of the locals' hostility toward the artistocracy and foreigners.

The Old Testament
Unknown

Eve

The first man and woman created by **God**. **Adam** and Eve introduce human evil into the world when they eat the fruit of a tree God has forbidden them to touch.

Paradise Lost
John Milton

Eve

The first woman and the mother of mankind. Eve was made from a rib taken from **Adam**'s side. Because she was made from Adam and for Adam, she is subservient to him. She is also weaker than Adam, so **Satan** focuses his powers of temptation on her. He succeeds in getting her to eat the fruit of the forbidden tree despite God's command.

Dubliners
James Joyce

Eveline

The protagonist of the story that shares her name. Eveline makes a bold and exciting decision to elope to Argentina with her lover, **Frank**, but changes her mind at the last minute. Her dilemma illustrates not indecisiveness, but the lack of options for someone in her position: either unhappy domesticity or an unknown foreign exile.

A Yellow Raft in Blue Water
Michael Dorris

Evelyn

Sky's wife and a cook at Bearpaw Lake State, she helps **Rayona** get a janitorial job there. Evelyn is strong-willed, understanding, and caring. She is kind to Rayona and tries to act as a mother figure.

Evelina
Fanny Burney

Mr. Evelyn

Evelina Anville's grandfather and the former pupil of **Reverend Mr. Arthur Villars**. Mr. Evelyn falls in love with **Madame Duval** and marries her against the advice of his friends. He dies two years into the marriage, and on his deathbed commits his only child, **Lady Caroline Evelyn Belmont**, to Mr. Villars's care.

Far from the Madding Crowd
Thomas Hardy

Bathsheba Everdene

The young woman at the center of the story. Bathsheba Everdene is vain, beautiful, and impulsive. Because she is financially independent, she is not concerned with taking a husband, and does not consider herself cut out for a married life devoid of freedom. The initially poor Bathsheba meets the prosperous **Gabriel Oak**, whom she spurns. He then becomes poor, and she rich, and she takes him as one of her workers on her farm at Weatherbury. She carelessly sends a valentine to **William Boldwood**, which causes his obsessive love for her. Bathsheba tries to break up with **Sergeant Francis Troy**, only to be pressured into marrying him. Bathsheba also irresponsibly and unfairly fires Gabriel, even though it is obvious that he is her best, most valuable worker. Through the novel, Bathsheba turns from her quick words and deeds caused by selfishness and jealousy to a more gentle, caring nature. After Boldwood shoots the presumed dead but returned Troy, Bathsheba finally realizes that she must ask Gabriel to marry her after he tells her he is leaving her farm. This marks the first time that Bathsheba lets her intentions to a man be known, instead of playing with his feelings or feeling weak around him.

Marquis Evrémonde

A Tale of Two Cities
Charles Dickens

Charles Darnay's uncle. The Marquis Evrémonde is a French aristocrat who typifies an inhumanly cruel caste system.

Aunt Evy

A Tree Grows in Brooklyn
Betty Smith

Katie Nolan's older sister. Hardworking and practical, Aunt Evy does not understand Katie's few bursts of wastefulness. She married **Willie Flittman** and works at his jobs when he no longer can. She does fantastic imitations, especially when poking fun at her husband.

Bob Ewell

To Kill a Mockingbird
Harper Lee

A mostly unemployed member of Maycomb's poorest family. In his knowingly wrongful accusation that **Tom Robinson** raped his daughter, **Mayella Ewell**, Bob Ewell represents the dark aspects of the South: ignorance, poverty, squalor, and hate-filled racial prejudice. Tom Robinson is wrongfully convicted of raping Mayella, but Bob is not satisfied because **Atticus Finch** reveals in court that Bob was a drunk who probably beat his daughter and blamed it on Tom. After the court case, Bob starts harassing Atticus. Tom even follows **Jem Finch** and **Scout Finch** in the woods after a Halloween party, hoping to murder the children. However, **Boo Radley** saves them, and Bob dies in the process. **Heck Tate** decides that Ewell fell on his knife, rather than accuse Jem of murder in defense of himself or accuse Boo Radley of murder to protect the Finch children.

General Richard Ewell

The Killer Angels
Michael Shaara

The Confederate general recently chosen to replace part of "Stonewall" Jackson's command. Ewell has become unsure of himself after suffering an injury that cost him his leg. As Jackson's replacement, Ewell has a great amount of responsibility, which is a source of concern to **General Robert E. Lee**. Lee is particularly troubled by the way that Ewell defers to **General Jubal Early**.

Mayella Ewell

To Kill a Mockingbird
Harper Lee

Bob Ewell's abused, unhappy daughter. In court, it is becomes clear that Bob Ewell beat Mayella, and that **Tom Robinson** did not rape her. **Atticus Finch** pleads with Mayella to admit this fact. She shouts at him and yells that the courtroom would have to be a bunch of cowards not to convict Tom Robinson; she then bursts into tears, refusing to answer any more questions.

Walter Ewell

Go Down, Moses
William Faulkner

A hunter who goes on **Major de Spain**'s expeditions. When he shoots, he never misses.

Duke of Exeter

Henry VI, Part III
William Shakespeare

A supporter of **King Henry VI**. Though loyal to Henry, Exeter acknowledges the strength of the **Duke of York**'s claim to the crown.

Thomas, Duke of Exeter

Henry V and *Henry VI, Part I*
William Shakespeare

Uncle of **King Henry V**; great-uncle of **King Henry VI**. Rarely far from Henry V's side, Exeter is entrusted with carrying important messages to the French ruler, **King Charles VI**, during *Henry V*. He is also a smart military leader; thanks to his wisdom and bravery, the English are able to take a key bridge in France. In *King Henry VI, Part I*, Exeter has more of a narrative role: one of the more level-headed of the lords, Exeter comments on the action of several public scenes. He often remains behind after the bickering nobles leave the stage, to predict (correctly) that the squabbles in the English command will develop into great strife, causing civil war as well as the loss of French territories.

Sir Piers Exton

Richard II
William Shakespeare

A nobleman who assassinates the imprisoned **King Richard II** as a favor to **Henry Bolingbroke**.

Eyes of God

The Handmaid's Tale
Margaret Atwood

The secret police of the Republic of Gilead.

Jane Eyre

Jane Eyre
Charlotte Brontë

The protagonist and narrator of the novel, Jane is an intelligent, honest, plain-featured young girl forced to contend with oppression, inequality, and hardship. Although she meets with a series of individuals who threaten her autonomy, Jane repeatedly succeeds at asserting herself and maintaining her principles of justice, human dignity, and morality. She also values intellectual and emotional fulfillment. Her strong belief in gender and social equality challenges the Victorian prejudices against women and the poor.

John Eyre

Jane Eyre
Charlotte Brontë

Jane Eyre's uncle. John Eyre leaves Jane his vast fortune of 20,000 pounds.

Ogbuefi Ezeudu

Things Fall Apart
Chinua Achebe

The oldest man in the village and one of the most important clan elders and leaders.

Ezinma

Things Fall Apart
Chinua Achebe

The only surviving child of **Okonkwo**'s second wife, **Ekwefi**. As the only one of Ekwefi's ten children to survive past infancy, Ezinma is the center of her mother's world. Ezinma is also Okonkwo's favorite child, for she understands him better than any of his other children and reminds him of Ekwefi when she was the village beauty. Okonkwo rarely demonstrates his affection, however, because he fears that doing so would make him look weak.

12

SMARTIES

DON'T PLAY SCRABBLE AGAINST ANY OF THESE BIG BRAINS.

Blackberry	1	*Watership Down*
Phoebe Caulfield	2	*The Catcher in the Rye*
Thomasina Coverly	3	*Arcadia*
John Galt	4	*Atlas Shrugged*
Hermione Grainger	5	*Harry Potter* series, Books I-IV
Charlie Gordon	6	*Flowers for Algeron*
Sergei Ivanovich Koznyshev	7	*Anna Karenina*
Laputans	8	*Gulliver's Travels*
Ejlert Løvbog	9	*Hedda Gabler*
Charles Wallace Murray	10	*A Wrinkle in Time*
Prospero	11	*The Tempest*
Vizzini	12	*The Princess Bride*

Fa Mu Lan

The Woman Warrior
Maxine Hong Kingston

A heroic female warrior from a traditional Chinese legend. Fa Mu Lan represents both the female ideal of motherhood and the male ideal of power and independence.

John Faa

His Dark Materials
Robert Pullman

The head of the Gyptians, who leads the expedition to the North to rescue the stolen children from Bolvanger.

Professor Faber

Fahrenheit 451
Ray Bradbury

A retired English professor **Guy Montag** met a year before the book opens. Faber still possesses a few precious books and aches to have more. He readily admits that the current state of society is due to the cowardice of people like himself, who would not speak out against book burning when they still could have stopped it. He berates himself for being a coward, but he shows himself capable of acts that require great courage and place him in considerable danger.

Fabian

Twelfth Night
William Shakespeare

An associate of **Sir Toby Belch**'s who helps contrive the plot against **Malvolio**.

Bezu Fache

The Da Vinci Code
Dan Brown

The captain of the Judicial Police. Nicknamed "The Bull," Fache is strong, strong-willed, and religious. He has great faith in the use of technology in his work, which sometimes leads him down the wrong road. Fache's policing methods are a bit unorthodox, but he is good at heart.

Faerie Queene

The Faerie Queene
Edmund Spenser

The focus of the poem who never actually appears. The Faerie Queene's castle is the ultimate goal or destination of many of the poem's characters. She represents Queen Elizabeth, among others.

Fagin

Oliver Twist
Charles Dickens

A conniving career criminal. Fagin takes in homeless children and trains them to pick pockets for him. He rarely commits crimes himself.

Tom Faheem

The Virgin Suicides
Jeffrey Eugenides

A particularly shy boy who finds the courage to enter the Lisbon house on June 15, as the other boys stand paralyzed by the vision of **Lux Lisbon** in the living room.

Alice Fairfax

Jane Eyre
Charlotte Brontë

The housekeeper at Thornfield Hall. Alice is the first to tell **Jane Eyre** that the mysterious laughter often heard echoing through the halls is the laughter of **Grace Poole**—a lie that **Edward Rochester** often repeats.

Gwendolen Fairfax

The Importance of Being Earnest
Oscar Wilde

Lady Bracknell's daughter. Gwendolen is in love with **Jack Worthing**.

Jane Fairfax

Emma
Jane Austen

Miss Bates's niece, whose arrival in Highbury irritates **Emma Woodhouse**. Jane rivals Emma in accomplishment and beauty, possessing a kind heart and a reserved temperament. Because Jane is poorer than Emma, she must consider employment as a governess, but her marriage to **Frank Churchill** saves her from that fate.

Falk

Black Boy
Richard Wright

A white Irish Catholic who works at the optical shop in Memphis with **Richard Wright**. In stark counterpoint to **Olin**, Falk does not explicitly profess to be **Richard**'s friend, but he proves to be a genuine friend by letting Richard borrow his library card to obtain books from the whites-only library.

Mike Fallopian

The Crying of Lot 49
Thomas Pynchon

A member of the Peter Pinguid Society, a right-wing anti-government organization. **Oedipa Maas** and **Metzger** meet him in a bar called the Scope.

Falsaron

The Song of Roland
Unknown

One of the twelve Saracen lords picked to battle the twelve Frankish peers at Roncesvals, Falsaron is **Marsilla**'s brother. His forehead, we are told, is "a half-foot wide." He is soon killed by **Olivier**.

Sir John Falstaff

Henry IV, Part I, Henry IV, Part II, and *The Merry Wives of Windsor*
William Shakespeare

A knight, a scoundrel, a mooch, occasionally a thief, and one of Shakespeare's most beloved characters. He enters the dramatic world in *King Henry IV, Part I,* as Prince Harry (the future **Henry V**)'s closest friend and part-mentor in the ways of criminals and vagabonds. Falstaff is a fat man between the ages of about fifty and sixty-five who hangs around in taverns on the wrong side of London. Armed with a quick tongue and ability to weasel out of lies, he is the only one who can match Hal's wit. Throughout *King Henry IV, Part I,* Falstaff robs some wealthy travelers, is himself robbed by Hal and **Edward Poins**; he tries to con **Mistress Quickly**; as an army captain, he takes bribes from wealthy landowners who don't want to serve; he replaces his pistol with a bottle of wine; he pretends to be dead at the Battle of Shrewsbury, only to rise up, stab the already dead **Hotspur** and claim him as his victim. This act of "bravery," which Hal has gone along with, garners Falstaff undue respect in *King Henry IV, Part II.* Throughout the play, Falstaff lies, begs, brawls (albeit cowardly), accepts bribes, and always seems to be weaseling out of responsibility. However, he is harshly rebuked when Hal ascends to the throne as King Henry V. The newly crowned monarch, who has taken on a new father-figure in the **Lord Chief Justice**, first ignores his old mentor, and then warns him not to come within ten miles of his person. Though a petty thief, Falstaff is eternally endearing, not only because of his inability to achieve success in crime, but also because of his genuine affection for Hal. All the more touching is the ubiquitous foreshadow of Hal's ultimate rebuke of the fat knight. In their first scene in *King Henry IV, Part I,* Falstaff tells his young friend that when Hal becomes king, thieves will be respected in the court. Hal replies that Falstaff will hang when he's king. Though Falstaff doesn't appear in *King Henry V*, his giant shadow (and death) loom large. Out of his element in the countryside in *Merry Wives*, Falstaff falsely believes he can seduce married women to gain access to their wealth. He launches a plan to bed **Mistress Margaret Page** and **Mistress Alice Ford**, two local wives.

Falstaff's page

Henry V
William Shakespeare

Formerly a page in the service of **Sir John Falstaff**, and now in the employ of **Pistol**, **Nym**, and **Bardolph**. The nameless boy leaves London after his master's death and goes with his new masters to the war in France. As **Captain Fluellen** notes later, the French attack the English camp, killing the boys and pages who were guarding the goods. Most likely, the boy has met a horrible end, a grim reminder that even comic characters succumb to mortality—Bardolph, Nym, and **Mistress Quickly** are all dead by the end of the play.

Fang

Henry IV, Part II
William Shakespeare

Along with **Snare**, one of the incompetent officers of the law whom **Mistress Quickly** calls to arrest **Sir John Falstaff**.

Fang

Harry Potter and the Chamber of Secrets
J. K. Rowling

Hagrid's large but friendly dog.

Mr. Fang

Oliver Twist
Charles Dickens

A magistrate. Mr. Fang is harsh, irrational, and power-hungry. He presides over **Oliver Twist**'s trial for pickpocketing.

Fangorn

The Two Towers
J. R. R. Tolkien

One of the Ents, a race of giant, mobile, tree-like creatures, along with **Treebeard** and **Bregalad**. The fourteen-foot-tall Fangorn is one of the oldest creatures in Middle-earth. An authority figure to the other Ents, he shows great hospitality to **Peregrin Took** and **Meriadoc Brandybuck**, whom he offers food in his Ent-house. He explains to the Hobbits, who have just escaped the **Orcs**, that many of the trees of Middle-earth used to move around and talk just like the Ents, but they lost their will and power to do so. At the bidding of Pippin and Merry, Fangorn decides to make an army of Ents to fight **Saruman**, who has been destroying the natural environment around Isengard.

Dr. Fanning

How the Garcia Girls Lost Their Accents
Julia Alvarez

A friend of the Garcia family who arranged for **Carlos**'s medical fellowship and helped the family out when they first arrived in the United States.

Mrs. Fanning

How the Garcia Girls Lost Their Accents
Julia Alvarez

A woman who kisses **Carlos** in the restroom of a Spanish restaurant during a celebratory dinner.

Fanny

A Christmas Carol
Charles Dickens

Ebenezer Scrooge's sister and **Fred**'s mother. As a young man, Scrooge adored Fanny, and she adored him, urging their cold father to treat him kindly. She died young.

Fanny

Incidents in the Life of a Slave Girl
Harriet Ann Jacobs

A slave friend of **Linda Brent**'s, with whom she escapes by boat to the North. Fanny had the devastating experience of watching all of her children sold to slave traders.

Fanny

Sons and Lovers
D. H. Lawrence

A hunchback who works in the finishing-off room at the factory, who likes to have **Paul Morel** visit her to sing or talk. She organizes the other girls to get Paul a birthday present.

Miss Fanny

Incidents in the Life of a Slave Girl
Harriet Ann Jacobs

An elderly lady, the sister of **Aunt Martha**'s mistress. Miss Fanny buys and frees Aunt Martha when **Dr. Sands** puts her on the auction block.

Fantine

Les Misérables
Victor Hugo

A working-class girl who leaves her hometown of Montreuil-sur-mer to seek her fortune in Paris. Her innocent affair with a dapper student named **Felix Tholomyès** leaves her pregnant and abandoned. Although she is frail, she makes a Herculean effort to feed herself and her daughter, **Cosette**. Even as she descends into prostitution, she never stops caring for her daughter. At times, Fantine seems like a simple spectator who does not fully understand the action unfolding in front of her.

Farah

Out of Africa
Isak Dinesen

The servant closest to **the narrator**. Farah is the chief of all servants and the narrator's closest confidant. The narrator and Farah are so close, in fact, that she often appears quite dependent upon him. Farah manages all the affairs of the household. He accompanies the narrator to her ship when she travels to and from Europe.

Faramir

The Two Towers and *The Return of the King*
J. R. R. Tolkien

The brother of **Boromir** and son of **Denethor**, the Steward of Gondor. In *The Two Towers*, Faramir becomes the Lord of Gondor after the death of Boromir. Faramir initially distrusts **Frodo Baggins** when he finds Frodo, **Samwise Gamgee**, and **Gollum** on the outskirts of Gondor, in Ithilien, outside Mordor. He suspects Frodo of having killed Boromir, and Frodo makes the task of proving his innocence difficult for himself, as he strives hard to avoid the part of the story of Boromir's death where Boromir dishonorably tries to take the Ring from Frodo. When Faramir learns the truth, that Boromir was a part of the Fellowship of the Ring and was killed by **Orcs**, he aids the Hobbits in their mission. He even resists the power of the Ring when he is tempted to take it and use it to make the Kingdom of Gondor strong and great. In *The Return of the King*, it becomes clear that the mad Denethor hates Faramir and loved Boromir. Denethor's attempts to burn Faramir alive are the extreme manifestations of the Steward's suppression of his dutiful son. In contrast to his father, Faramir displays the depth of his nobility by immediately recognizing **Aragorn**'s long-awaited claim to the throne of Gondor, instead of trying to assume the Stewardship after Denethor's death. After the One Ring is destroyed, Faramir marries the Lady of Rohan, **Éowyn**.

Camden Farebrother

Middlemarch
George Eliot

A vicar who doesn't consider himself a very good clergyman, even though many people like his sensible sermons. He becomes fast friends with **Tertius Lydgate** and supports his mother, sister, and aunt on his small income. He must gamble to make ends meet and to pursue his scientific hobbies. He loses in the election for the chaplaincy at the New Hospital. He receives the Lowick parish after **Edward Casaubon**'s death. **Fred Vincy** enlists his help in courting **Mary Garth**.

Mrs. Farebrother

Middlemarch
George Eliot

Camden Farebrother's widowed mother.

Winifred Farebrother

Middlemarch
George Eliot

Camden Farebrother's unmarried sister.

Donald Farfrae

The Mayor of Casterbridge
Thomas Hardy

The Scotchman who arrives in Casterbridge at the same time as **Susan Henchard** and **Elizabeth-Jane Newson**. Donald Farfrae's business efficiency, good humor, and polish make him extremely popular among the town's citizens. These same qualities, however, eventually make him **Michael Henchard**'s rival, a condition exacerbated by his fledgling courtship of Elizabeth-Jane, the woman Henchard believes to be his own daughter. The rivalry is furthered by Farfrae's courtship and eventual marriage to Henchard's old lover, **Lucetta Templeman**. He brings to Casterbridge a method for salvaging damaged grain, a system for reorganizing and revolutionizing the business of the then-mayor, Henchard.

Abbé Faria

The Count of Monte Cristo
Alexandre Dumas

A priest and scholar whom **Edmond Dantès** meets in prison. Abbé Faria becomes Dantès's intellectual father and bequeaths to Dantès his vast hidden fortune, which enable Dantès to become **the Count of Monte Cristo**. Faria is incredibly resourceful, having fashioned writing implements and tools to dig his escape tunnel while he is imprisoned. He also writes a political treatise: he has been imprisoned for his political beliefs concerning a unified Italy. Faria teaches Dantès everything he knows, and eventually dies from a "fit" before the two men can put their escape plan into action.

Farinata

Inferno
Dante Alighieri

A Florentine political leader from the Ghibelline party, a rival of **Dante**'s White Guelph party. Dante and **Virgil** encounter him in the Sixth Circle of Hell, among the Heretics (Canto X).

Gerty Farish

The House of Mirth
Edith Wharton

Lawrence Selden's cousin. Gerty is a kind, generous woman who does a lot of charity work. In Book Two, she becomes one of Lily's only friends, giving her a place to stay and taking care of her when everyone else abandons her.

Farival Twins

The Awakening
Kate Chopin

Twin girls. The Farival twins vacation at Grand Isle with their family. Associated with the Virgin Mary, they represent the ideal of chaste motherhood that adolescent Victorian girls are meant to attain. They entertain guests by playing the piano and fulfill society's expectation that women should use art to delight others.

Miss Farkis

Miss Lonelyhearts
Nathanael West

A young woman with whom **Shrike** has a date at the speakeasy. Miss Farkis is interested in intellectual discussions and is seduced by Shrike's eloquent speeches.

Jean Farlow

Lolita
Vladimir Nabokov

The wife of **John Farlow**. John and Jean Farlow are among Charlotte and **Humbert Humbert**'s few friends. After Charlotte's death, Jean secretly kisses Humbert.

John Farlow

Lolita
Vladimir Nabokov

A friend of **Charlotte Haze**'s and the husband of **Jean Farlow**. John initially handles the Haze estate after Charlotte's death.

Farmer

Gulliver's Travels
Jonathan Swift

Gulliver's first owner. The farmer owns the land on which Gulliver first arrives. He treats Gulliver with gentleness and initially respects his intelligence, but later puts him on display as a freak-show attraction. Less cruel than simpleminded, he exploits Gulliver and inadvertently almost starves him.

Farmer

Candide
Voltaire

A simple, hardworking man who lives outside Constantinople. The farmer impresses **Candide** and his friends. They emulate his industrious lifestyle and find happiness.

Adam Farmer

I Am the Cheese
Robert Cormier

The novel's protagonist. Adam Farmer narrates his bike trip to Rutterburg to see his father, **David Farmer**. Adam used to be called **Paul Delmonte** before his family entered into the government Witness Re-Identification Program. He also has conversations with someone named **Brint** in some kind of institution. He is fearful, sensitive, paranoid, and alienated. Over the course of the novel, we see how Adam has discovered that he used to have a different life and a different name. In the end, we find that he has been riding around the grounds of the institution, imagining he has been in the outside world. Adam does not know his real identity; he believes he is the "cheese," like in the song "The Farmer in the Dell." The cheese stands alone.

David Farmer

I Am the Cheese
Robert Cormier

Adam Farmer's father, husband of **Louise Farmer**. David Farmer is a respectable insurance agent in Monument. He is a good father to Adam, delighting him with worldly stories and his love of books. David is always on the lookout and has a soundproof basement where he goes to talk to a man called **Mr. Grey**. Adam later realizes that his father is a participant in the government Witness Re-Identification Program. It is his father upon whom Adam fixates, believing he is riding his bike to visit his father in a hospital somewhere. The last time Adam saw David was when a mysterious car crashed into the whole Farmer family, possibly some sort of conspiracy concocted by Mr. Grey, the one man who seemed able to protect the Farmer family.

Louise Farmer

I Am the Cheese
Robert Cormier

Mother of **Adam Farmer**, wife of **David Farmer**. Louise Farmer is kind, compassionate, and protective. Ever since the family entered the Witness Re-Identification Program and moved to Monument she has acted withdrawn, closing herself off in her room. She lives her life in fear of the "Never Knows"—the state of never knowing whom to trust or what will happen next. After David reveals to Adam their past, hidden lives, Adam and Louise grow closer. She tells Adam about how **Mr. Grey** is a cold man with a government number for a name. In the end, Adam watches his mother die when the Farmer family is run into by a car, possibly a plan devised by Mr. Grey.

Millard Farmer

Dead Man Walking
Helen Prejean

A death-row attorney from Atlanta who works tirelessly to save **Patrick Sonnier**'s life. Millard's dedication to abolishing the death penalty and providing legal counsel to men on death row inspires **Sister Helen Prejean**.

Farooq

Midnight's Children
Salman Rushdie

Along with **Shaheed** and **Ayooba**, one of **Saleem**'s fellow soldiers in the Pakistani army.

Mr. Farraday

The Remains of the Day
Kazuo Ishiguro

The new owner of Darlington Hall after **Lord Darlington**'s death, and, as such, **Stevens**'s new employer. Mr. Farraday is a very easygoing American gentleman and frequently jokes around with Stevens, who does not know how to handle such "banter."

Molly Farren

Silas Marner
George Eliot

Godfrey's secret wife and **Eppie**'s mother. Once pretty, Molly has been destroyed by her addiction to opium and alcohol.

Farrington

Dubliners
James Joyce

The burly and aggressive copy clerk and protagonist in "Counterparts." Set apart by his explosive temper, Farrington, unlike most characters in *Dubliners*, refuses to accept boredom and routine as basic facts of life.

Farrington

The Caine Mutiny
Herman Wouk

The last ensign to report to the *Caine* under **Philip Francis Queeg**'s rule. He is exactly what **Willie Keith** was when Willie first came aboard the ship. He demonstrates the continuity of the Navy's program of indoctrinating sailors.

Sir John Fastolf

Henry VI, Part I
William Shakespeare

A cowardly English soldier who repeatedly flees the scene of battle when he fears for his life. Fastolf provides a stark contrast to the chivalry and nobility of **Lord Talbot**, who curses him for lacking the valor and honor of the old generation of knights. After Fastolf comes to **King Henry VI** to deliver the message of the **Duke of Burgundy**'s betrayal, the king (with Talbot by his side) banishes him on pain of death.

The Fates

Greek Mythology
Unknown

Three mysterious sisters who affect the paths of everyone in the universe. Clotho spins the thread of life; Lachesis assigns each person's thread; and Atropos snips the thread at its end. Since fate is the only force to rule above both gods and men, the Fates are arguably the most powerful forces in the Greek universe.

The father

Six Characters in Search of an Author
Luigi Pirandello

A fattish man in his fifties with thin, reddish hair, a thick moustache, and piercing, blue oval eyes. Along with **the Stepdaughter**, he is the character who most fervently insists that **the Mangaer** stage the characters' drama.

Father

Dandelion Wine
Ray Bradbury

Douglas Spaulding and **Tom Spaulding**'s father, a man equally at ease in civilization and the wilderness. He is quiet and thoughtful, and he understands his children very well.

Father

Ragtime
E. L. Doctorow

Owner of a company that manufactures fireworks and other accoutrements of patriotism such as flags and banners. He represents the traditional views held by many turn-of-the-century Americans.

Sam Fathers

Go Down, Moses
William Faulkner

The son of **Ikkemotubbe**, the Choctaw chief, and a slave-girl. Ikkemotubbe sold Sam and his mother into slavery when Sam was very young. Now an expert hunter, Sam tames the dog **Lion** and teaches **Isaac** the ways of the forest.

Fatima

Shabanu
Suzanne Fisher Staples

Sharma's daughter, who lives in the desert with her. Fatima is sixteen, which is well past the marrying age in Cholistan. She does not want to get married, and Sharma will not force her to do so. Fatima resembles her mother in her fiercely independent and outspoken nature.

Fauchelevent

Les Misérables
Victor Hugo

A critic of **Jean Valjean**'s while Valjean is the mayor of Montreuil-sur-mer. Fauchelevent becomes indebted to Valjean when Valjean saves him from a carriage accident. When they meet again by incredible coincidence years later, Fauchelevent returns the favor by hiding Valjean and **Cosette** in a convent, declining Valjean's one hundred francs.

Mr. Faughnan

Ordinary People
Judith Guest

The choir director at Lake Forest.

Lady Faulconbridge

King John
William Shakespeare

Mother of **Philip the Bastard** and **Robert Faulconbridge**, and the late senior Robert Falconbridge's wife. She rebukes the Bastard for bringing the case of inheritance to the court; but when he tells her that he has been knighted, Lady Faulconbridge admits that **King Richard the Lionhearted** is indeed the Bastard's father, who seduced her years ago.

Robert Faulconbridge

King John
William Shakespeare

Philip the Bastard's younger half-brother, and the late **Robert Faulconbridge**'s legitimate son. He and the Bastard argue over the family's estate until the Bastard concedes it, accepting instead a knighthood and the mantle of Richard the Lionheart's son.

Naomi Faust

Cat's Cradle
Kurt Vonnegut

A secretary at the Research Laboratory. She works with **Francine Pefko** transcribing documents that neither of them really understand and gives **John** a tour of **Felix Hoenikker**'s lab.

Faustus

Doctor Faustus
Christopher Marlowe

The play's protagonist. Faustus is a brilliant sixteenth-century scholar from Wittenberg, Germany. Hungry for knowledge, wealth, and fame, Faustus pays **Lucifer** the ultimate price—his soul—in exchange for supernatural powers. Though plagued by doubts, Faustus is able neither to repent nor to embrace his dark path.

Jack Favell

Rebecca
Daphne du Maurier

Rebecca's cousin. Lacking integrity and given to alcoholic behavior, he was Rebecca's lover while she was married to **Maxim de Winter**.

Favilla

Orlando
Virginia Woolf

The second of **Orlando**'s loves at King James's court and the daughter of a poor Somersetshire gentleman. Despite her elegance and reputation at court, Orlando ends his relationship with Favilla after seeing her whip a dog.

Fawkes

Harry Potter and the Goblet of Fire
J. K. Rowling

Albus Dumbledore's beautiful pet phoenix, who gave two feathers that ended up in the wands of **Harry Potter** and **Voldemort**.

Jude Fawley

Jude the Obscure
Thomas Hardy

A poor young man from Marygreen. In his village, Jude is seen as eccentric, and his aspirations are dismissed as unrealistic. He aspires to things greater than his background allows, like studying at a school in Christminster. The Christminster colleges do not welcome self-educated men or members of the working class. He marries **Arabella Donn** after she falsely claims that he has impregnated her, but later falls in love with his cousin, **Susanna Bridehead**, and lives with her, ultimately returning to Arabella before his death.

Fawn

Go Ask Alice
Anonymous

A "straight" girl who befriends **Alice** at the end of the book and accepts her into her group of non–drug using friends.

Fayaway

Typee
Herman Melville

The beautiful maiden with whom **Tommo** falls in love.

Faye

East of Eden
John Steinbeck

The madam at the Salinas whorehouse where **Cathy Ames** works as a prostitute. Faye is misguidedly kind to the predatory Cathy, who poisons Faye gradually and takes over the brothel after Faye finally dies.

Joshua Rigg Featherstone

Middlemarch
George Eliot

Peter Featherstone's illegitimate son, and **John Raffles**'s stepson. He inherits Stone Court but sells it to **Nicholas Bulstrode** because he wants to become a moneychanger.

Peter Featherstone

Middlemarch
George Eliot

The wealthy, manipulative old widower who owns Stone Court. Featherstone married twice but had no legitimate children. His first wife was **Caleb Garth**'s sister. His second wife was **Lucy Vincy**'s sister. He hints for years that he plans to leave his entire estate to **Fred Vincy**, his nephew by marriage. He even writes two separate wills. **Mary Garth** refuses to burn one of them. Featherstone leaves his property to his illegitimate son, **Joshua Rigg Featherstone**.

Fedallah

Moby-Dick
Herman Melville

A strange, "oriental" old Parsee (Persian fire-worshipper) whom Captain **Ahab** has brought onboard unbeknownst to most of the crew. Fedallah has a very striking appearance: around his head is a turban made from his own hair, and he wears a black Chinese jacket and pants. He is an almost supernaturally skilled hunter and also serves as a prophet to Ahab. Fedallah keeps his distance from the rest of the crew, who view him with unease. Fedallah mirrors Ahab's madness when the chase for **Moby-Dick** begins. Fedallah foretells Ahab's death.

Feeble

Henry IV, Part II
William Shakespeare

One of the Army recruits that **Sir John Falstaff** inspects in Gloucestershire. Because Feeble does not bribe Falstaff, he, **Shadow**, and **Wart** have to serve in the military.

Felice

Jazz
Toni Morrison

Dorcas's best friend from school. Felice's grandmother raised her while her mother and father worked in a town called Tuxedo. Felice is darker-skinned and less attractive than her friend Dorcas, but she has a much stronger sense of self. She disapproves of Dorcas's reckless behavior, even though she often acts as an accomplice or provides Dorcas with an alibi.

Lord Fellamar

Tom Jones
Henry Fielding

A suitor of **Sophia**'s who, though he has a conscience, allows himself to be easily manipulated by **Lady Bellaston**. He attempts to rape Sophia on Lady Bellaston's advice.

Captain Fellows

The Power and the Glory
Graham Greene

The father of **Coral Fellows**. Captain Fellows is a benign, if ineffectual, plantation owner who tries to remain cheerful and optimistic in the face of difficult times and an isolated existence. He is unhappy when he learns that **the Priest** is hiding in his barn, but turns a blind eye to his daughter when she insists upon helping him. He and **Mrs. Fellows** leave Mexico after Coral's death.

Coral Fellows

The Power and the Glory
Graham Greene

A young American girl, the daughter of **Captain Fellows** and **Mrs. Fellows**, whom **the Priest** meets early on in the novel when she discovers him hiding on her family's property. Independent-minded and responsible, she anchors her family emotionally and takes charge of the business when her hapless father neglects it. Although a self-professed atheist since the age of ten, Coral is deeply affected by her brief encounter with the Priest, and she, in turn, remains a presence in the Priest's mind during his journeys.

Mrs. Fellows

The Power and the Glory
Graham Greene

Coral's mother and **Captain Fellows**'s wife. Mrs. Fellows is a neurotic, hysterical woman who confines herself to her bed out of fear of death.

John Felton

The Three Musketeers
Alexandre Dumas

A British Naval Officer, ward of **Lord de Winter**; a Protestant. When the **Lady de Winter** is imprisoned by her brother, the Lord, John Felton is responsible for keeping her imprisoned. The Lady poses as a Protestant herself, and slowly wears down the inexperienced young Felton's defenses with her beauty and mock religious fervor. She feigns illness to gain his sympathy, then begs him to allow her to commit suicide, playing the role of a martyr. Her coup comes on her fifth night of captivity. He falls completely in love with her, and helps her escape. Under her power, the religious Felton stabs and kills **George Villiers**, the **Duke of Buckingham**.

Count Fenring

Dune
Frank Herbert

A servant and friend of **Emperor Shaddam IV**'s, and husband of **Lady Fenring**. He is a very skilled man, particularly at killing others, and he was almost the Kwisatz Haderach, the prophesied Messiah of Dune.

Lady Fenring

Dune
Frank Herbert

Count Fenring's wife, and a member of the Bene Gesserit.

Fenton

The Merry Wives of Windsor
William Shakespeare

One of **Anne Page**'s suitors, Fenton is high-born but poor. Though he admits his interest in Anne is purely financial at first, he does indeed fall for her, and wins not only her love but also the admiration of **Mistress Quickly**. Fenton persuades the **Host** to secure a vicar to marry him and Anne, thus duping her other suitors, **Doctor Caius** and **Sir Hugh Evans**. At the end of the play, both of Anne's parents, who originally were opposed to Fenton's courtship, welcome the new marriage.

Father Ferapont

The Brothers Karamazov
Fyodor Dostoevsky

A severe and ascetic monk who hates **Zosima**.

Ferdinand

Don Quixote
Miguel de Cervantes

An arrogant young duke who steals **Lucinda** from her husband, **Cardenio**.

Ferdinand

The Tempest
William Shakespeare

Alonso's son and heir. In some ways, **Ferdinand** is as pure and naïve as **Miranda**. He falls in love with her at first sight and happily submits to servitude in order to win her father's approval.

Ferdyshchenko

The Idiot
Fyodor Dostoevsky

An ugly and insolent lodger in the apartment of **Gavril Ardalyonovich Ivolgin** and his family, at the beginning of the novel. Ferdyshchenko strives to be original, yet most people regard him contemptuously, as a drunkard and an amoral rogue.

Ferfichkin

Notes from Underground
Fyodor Dostoevsky

One of **the Underground Man**'s former schoolmates and an admirer of **Zverkov**. In school, Ferfichkin was the Underground Man's "bitterest enemy." The Underground Man describes Ferfichkin as impudent, foolish, and cowardly, and notes that Ferfichkin frequently borrows money from Zverkov.

Dr. Ferguson

When the Legends Die
Hal Borland

The doctor who advises **Thomas Black Bull** never to ride broncos again.

Helen Ferguson

A Farewell to Arms
Ernest Hemingway

A nurse's aide who works at the American hospital in Milan. Helen is a dear friend of **Catherine Barkley**'s, but eventually she has an hysterical outburst over Catherine's "immoral" affair with **Frederic Henry**.

Lord Fermor

The Picture of Dorian Gray
Oscar Wilde

Lord Henry Wotton's irascible uncle. Lord Fermor tells Henry the story of **Dorian Gray**'s parentage.

Fernando

For Whom the Bell Tolls
Ernest Hemingway

A guerrilla fighter in his mid-thirties. Short and with a lazy eye, Fernando is dignified and literal-minded, embraces bureaucracy, and is easily offended by vulgarities. When the guerrilla band blows up the Fascist bridge, Fernando is fatally wounded.

Don Fernando d'Ibaraa y Figueora y Mascarenes y Lampourdos y Souza

Candide
Voltaire

The governor of Buenos Aires. He makes **Cunégonde** his mistress despite her engagement to **Candide**.

Ferneze

The Jew of Malta
Christopher Marlowe

Barabas's great enemy and the governor of Malta. Ferneze hides his real motives behind ideals of Christian morality. Ultimately, his role in undermining Barabas and bribing **Calymath** shows how he uses Machiavellian tactics to his own advantage.

Bill Ferny

The Fellowship of the Ring
J. R. R. Tolkien

A swarthy, suspicious fellow in Bree who appears to have been paid off by **the Nazgûl**, the Black Riders, to watch **Frodo Baggins**'s movements. Bill Ferny sells the Hobbits a half-starved pony at a high price to replace the ponies the Black Riders set loose the night before. Bill Ferny is an example of a Human corrupted by the dark influence of **Sauron**.

Edward Ferrars

Sense and Sensibility
Jane Austen

The older brother of **Fanny Dashwood** and **Robert Ferrars**. Edward, a sensible and friendly man, proposes to **Elinor Dashwood** after he is freed from a four-year engagement to **Lucy Steele**.

Mrs. Ferrars

Sense and Sensibility
Jane Austen

The mother of **Edward Ferrars** and **Robert Ferrars**. Mrs. Ferrars is a wealthy, manipulative woman who disinherits Edward when he refuses to marry a rich heiress.

Robert Ferrars

Sense and Sensibility
Jane Austen

The younger brother of **Edward Ferrars** and **Fanny Dashwood**. Robert is a conceited coxcomb. At the end of the novel, he marries **Lucy Steele**.

Jesse Ferrenby

This Side of Paradise
F. Scott Fitzgerald

One of **Amory Blaine**'s friends at Princeton. Amory remembers a trip to the coast with **Jesse** and several other friends as one of the happiest times of his college life. After Jesse is killed in World War I, Amory propounds his new socialist ideals in a dialogue with Jesse's father, **Mr. Ferrenby**.

Mr. Ferrenby

This Side of Paradise
F. Scott Fitzgerald

The father of **Jesse Ferrenby**, one of **Amory Blaine**'s friends at Princeton.

Dr. Floyd Ferris

Atlas Shrugged
Ayn Rand

The head of the State Science Institute and author of *Why Do You Think You Think?* Dr. Floyd Ferris rejects the mind and recognizes only bald power. Ferris leads the faction that seeks to torture and kill **John Galt** instead of working with the powerful and ingenious man, which would jeopardize the government's own power. Ferris knows that if Galt were put in charge, the men who loot power and property in the government would be put out of existence.

Ferula

The House of the Spirits
Isabel Allende

Esteban Trueba's older sister. Ferula is jealous of her brother. After the death of Esteban Trueba and Ferula's mother, **Dona Ester Trueba**, Ferula moves in with Esteban Trueba and **Clara**. Ferula and Clara become great friends. Ferula secretly desires Clara. When Esteban Trueba discovers Ferula sleeping in Clara's bed, he throws her out of the house forever. As she leaves, Ferula curses Esteban Trueba. Many years later, Ferula dies in one of the city's poor neighborhoods, and Esteban Trueba discovers that she has left all his letters containing money unopened, which makes him feel enormously guilty.

Mme. de Fervaques

The Red and the Black
Stendhal

A member of the **Marquis de la Mole**'s salon. She is very religious, and **Julien Sorel** uses a campaign of love-letter writing and Fervaques's attention to make **Mathilde de la Mole** jealous. Julien knows that Fervaques is too pious to understand his fake declarations of love and really just wants to upset Mathilde, with whom he is still very much in love.

Feste

Twelfth Night
William Shakespeare

The clown, or fool, of **Olivia**'s household. Feste moves between Olivia's and **Orsino**'s homes, earning a living by making pointed jokes, singing old songs, and offering circuitous advice. Though he is quick to join in the malicious plot against the puritanical **Malvolio**, Feste stands apart from the rest of the rabble-rousers and comments on the folly with a slight wink.

Fetyukov

One Day in the Life of Ivan Denisovich
Aleksandr Solzhenitsyn

A fellow prisoner of **Ivan Denisovich Shukhov**'s and the scrounger and wheedler of Gang 104, always nagging for a cigarette or an extra bit of bread from the other inmates. Shukhov scorns Fetyukov, but in the end pities him when the guards beat up Fetyukov as punishment for licking bowls in the mess hall. Fetyukov represents the degradation to which prisoners in the labor camp are capable of slipping if they let go of their human dignity.

Fetyukovich

The Brothers Karamazov
Fyodor Dostoevsky

A famous defense attorney from Moscow who represents **Dmitri Fyodorovich Karamazov** at the trial for the murder of his father, **Fyodor Pavlovich Karamazov**.

Billy Le Fever

Tristram Shandy
Laurence Sterne

The son of **Lieutenant Le Fever**. **Uncle Toby** becomes Billy's guardian, supervises his education, and eventually recommends him to be **Tristram**'s governor.

Fezzik

The Princess Bride
William Goldman

The large-hearted and obedient giant who accompanies **Vizzini**. Fezzik is laden with self-doubt and a certain awkward fear. He loves rhymes and his friend **Inigo**, and he is excellent at lifting heavy things.

John Field

Walden
Henry David Thoreau

A poor Irish-American laborer who lives with his wife and children on the Baker Farm just outside of Concord. **Henry David Thoreau** uses Field as an example of an "honest, hardworking, but shiftless man" who is forced to struggle at a great disadvantage in life because he lacks unusual natural abilities or social position. The conversation that Thoreau and Field have is an uncomfortable reminder that Thoreau's ideas and convictions may set him apart from those same poor people that he elsewhere idealizes.

John Field

Sons and Lovers
D. H. Lawrence

A man with whom **Gertrude Morel** is friendly when she is nineteen. He gives her a Bible, which she keeps for the rest of her life.

Cyril Fielding

A Passage to India
E. M. Forster

The principal of Government College. An independent man who believes in educating Indians to be individuals, Fielding befriends **Aziz** and supports him throughout his trial.

Judge Llewellyn Fielding

Snow Falling on Cedars
David Guterson

The judge presiding over **Kabuo Miyamoto**'s murder trial. Although he appears sleepy and distracted, Judge Fielding is keenly aware of everything that takes place in his courtroom. He understands the racially charged nature of Kabuo's trial and does all he can to diminish the role that racism plays in the proceedings.

Old Willy Fields

Sula
Toni Morrison

An orderly at the local hospital. After **Hannah Peace**'s death by burning and **Eva Peace**'s near-death by burning after trying to save Hannah, Old Willy Fields narrowly prevents Eva's death by blood loss, an act for which she curses him for years.

Argus Filch

The Harry Potter Series: Books 2–4
J. K. Rowling

The Hogwarts caretaker. He is grouchy and adores nothing but his cat, **Mrs. Norris**.

Fili

The Hobbit
J. R. R. Tolkien

One of the dwarf companions on the novel's quest.

Mrs. Filmer

Mrs. Dalloway
Virginia Woolf

The Smiths' neighbor. Mrs. Filmer finds **Septimus Warren Smith** odd. She is **Lucrezia Smith**'s only friend in London.

Atticus Finch

To Kill a Mockingbird
Harper Lee

Father of **Scout Finch** and **Jem Finch**, brother of **Aunt Alexandra**. Atticus Finch is a wise, empathetic lawyer in Maycomb descended from an old local family. He is one of the most prominent members of the community of Maycomb during the Great Depression, and is therefore relatively well-off. A widower with a dry sense of humor, Atticus has instilled in his children his strong sense of morality and justice. He is one of the few residents of Maycomb committed to racial equality, and is respected as the moral backbone of Maycomb by all, including the very poor. However, when he agrees to defend **Tom Robinson**, a black man charged with raping a white woman, he exposes himself and his family to the anger of the white community. Though his children's attitude toward him evolves, Atticus is characterized throughout the book by his absolute consistency. He stands rigidly committed to justice and thoughtfully willing to view matters from the perspectives of others.

Jean Louise Finch

To Kill a Mockingbird
Harper Lee

The narrator and protagonist of the story. Jean Louise Finch, or "Scout," lives with her father, **Atticus Finch**, her brother, **Jem Finch**, and their cook, **Calpurnia**, in Maycomb. She is intelligent, learning to read before starting school, and, by the standards of her time and place, a tomboy. Scout has a confident and combative streak, is not unwilling to pick fights with boys, and has a basic faith in the goodness of the people in her community. At the beginning of the novel, Scout is an innocent, good-hearted child who has no experience with the evils of the world. As the novel progresses, Scout has her first contact with evil in the form of racial prejudice through her father's case involving **Tom Robinson**. The basic development of Scout's character is governed by the question of whether she will emerge from that contact with her conscience and optimism intact, or whether she will be bruised, hurt, or destroyed like **Boo Radley** or Tom Robinson. Thanks to Atticus's wisdom, Scout learns that though humanity has a great capacity for evil, it also has a great capacity for good, and that the evil can often be mitigated if one approaches others with sympathy and understanding.

Jeremy Atticus Finch

To Kill a Mockingbird
Harper Lee

Son of **Atticus Finch**, and **Scout Finch**'s brother and constant playmate at the beginning of the novel. Jeremy Atticus Finch, or "Jem," is something of a typical American boy, refusing to back down from dares and fantasizing about playing football. Four years older than Scout, he gradually separates himself from her games, but he remains her close companion and protector throughout the novel. His disillusionment upon realizing that justice does not always prevail—as in the wrongful conviction of **Tom Robinson**—leaves him vulnerable and confused. Later in his life, Jem is able to see that there is good in people through **Boo Radley**'s unexpected rescue of Jem and Scout from a drunken **Bob Ewell**'s violent hands.

Pastor Finch

Oranges Are Not the Only Fruit
Jeanette Winterson

Visiting minister to **Jeanette**'s church. He unleashes a fiery sermon about the dangers of being seven to Jeanette. The seriousness of his sermon compared to Jeanette's innocence of age renders him ridiculous.

Justin Finch-Fletchley

Harry Potter and the Chamber of Secrets
J. K. Rowling

A boy in Hufflepuff House who is turned to stone by a spell cast upon him.

Denys Finch-Hatton

Out of Africa
Isak Dinesen

Close friends with **the narrator**. Although it is never mentioned explicitly, the novel subtly suggests that they are lovers. Denys Finch-Hatton is the embodiment of gentility and aristocracy. He is handsome, athletic, and a good sportsman. He is a lover of fine music, wine, and art. He also takes the narrator up in an airplane, which allows her to look down on Africa with new eyes, like God. Denys's sheer nobility as a human makes many natives deeply respect him. His death is considered a tragedy by natives and Europeans alike.

Sidney Finkelstein

Babbitt
Sinclair Lewis

One of **Babbitt**'s friends and associates in the Zenith business community.

Mr. Finley

Sula
Toni Morrison

A resident of the Bottom. Not long after **Sula Peace** returns to the Bottom after a ten-year absence, Mr. Finley chokes to death on a chicken bone upon seeing her. The community blames Sula for its demise.

Finn

Grendel
John Gardner

One of the characters in a song that **the Shaper's assistant** sings at **the Shaper**'s funeral.

Huckleberry Finn

The Adventures of Tom Sawyer
and *The Adventures of Huckleberry Finn*
Mark Twain

The son of the town drunk in St. Petersburg, Missouri, a town on the Mississippi River. Frequently forced to survive on his own wits and always a bit of an outcast, Huck is thoughtful, intelligent (though formally uneducated), and willing to come to his own conclusions about important matters, even if these conclusions contradict society's. In *The Adventures of Tom Sawyer*, Huckleberry Finn is introduced as a juvenile outcast with a deadbeat father, **Pap**. Huck is shunned by respectable society and adored by the local boys, who envy his freedom. Like **Tom Sawyer**, Huck is highly superstitious, and both boys are always ready for an adventure. While Tom and **Becky Thatcher** are off adventuring in caves, Huck prevents the **Widow Douglas** from being brutally killed by **Injun Joe**. As a result of this, Huck gains $6,000 from Joe's treasure and becomes the adopted child of the widow. He does not like her efforts to "sivilize" him, however, and runs away. When Tom finally finds Huck, he convinces Huck to go back and live with the widow. In *The Adventures of Huckleberry Finn*, Huck is the protagonist and narrator. When Huck learns that his Pap is back in town, Huck finds the slave **Jim** and they run away, having adventures as they travel the Mississippi River. Huck and Jim meet **the duke** and **the dauphin**, con men who trick and mistreat people and then get run out of towns. Huck eventually tricks the duke and the dauphin into losing some money they stole from **the Wilks family**, but also loses Jim after the dauphin sells him to **Silas Phelps**. Huck and Tom are reunited, the two boys eventually "rescue" Jim from his impending sale, and they then make plans to go to Oklahoma to have an adventure. Huck does not want to endure another bout with a woman trying to "sivilize" him, as **Sally Phelps** seems to be planning to do. Years of having to fend for himself have imbued Huck with a solid common sense and practical competence that complement Tom's dreamy idealism and fantastical approach to reality. Through Huck, Twain weighs the costs and benefits of living in a society against those of living independently of it. Imperfect as he is, Huck represents what anyone is capable of becoming: a thinking, feeling human being rather than a mere cog in the machine of society.

Mary Lou Finney

Walk Two Moons
Sharon Creech

Salamanca Tree Hiddle's classmate and **Ben**'s cousin. Mary Lou is a loud, brash girl of whom **Phoebe** disapproves. Salamanca is secretly envious of her chaotic, loving household.

Seamus Finnigan

Harry Potter and the Goblet of Fire
J. K. Rowling

One of **Harry Potter**'s Gryffindor roommates.

Finny

A Separate Peace
John Knowles

Classmate and best friend of **Gene Forrester**. Finny, whose real name is Phineas, is honest, handsome, self-confident, disarming, extremely likable, and the best athlete in the school; in short, he seems perfect in almost every way. He has a talent for engaging others with his spontaneity and sheer joy of living, and, while he frequently gets into trouble, he has the ability to talk his way out of almost any predicament. According to Gene, he is rare among human beings in that he never perceives anyone as an enemy, and never strives to defeat others. Gene deliberately causes Finny to fall out of a tree and shatter his leg. Finny later dies from an operation gone wrong after his second broken leg. Gene realizes that he is a part of Finny, and that, in some ways, Finny's funeral is his own.

Mrs. Brigid Finucane

Angela's Ashes
Frank McCourt

The old woman to whose debtors **Frank McCourt** writes threatening letters.

Fiona

The Giver
Lois Lowry

One of **Jonas**'s friends. She has red hair, which only Jonas can see, and she works as a Caretaker in the House of the Old. She is mild-mannered and patient. When Jonas later finds out what "release" really means in the context of his community, he realizes that Fiona has been efficiently "releasing," or killing, those in the House of the Old. Jonas's first sexual urges, called "Stirrings," come in the form of an erotic dream about Fiona.

Firs

The Cherry Orchard
Anton Chekhov

The old manservant on the **Ranevsky** estate. Firs is always talking about how things were in the past, when the estate was prosperous. Firs also frequently talks about how life was before the serfs were freed. He is possibly senile, and is constantly mumbling. He is the only surviving link to the estate's glorious past. The Ranevskys' accidental abandonment of Firs symbolizes the way they must leave and forget the opulent lifestyle they once led.

Scott Fischer

Into Thin Air
Jon Krakauer

The head guide of the Mountain Madness expedition group. Fischer and **Rob Hall** are friends and competitors. Fischer is a renowned climber infamous for having survived some terrible falls. Fischer becomes seriously ill about halfway through the climb but continues undeterred.

Mr. Fish

A Prayer for Owen Meany
John Irving

John Wheelwright's neighbor, who lives next to 80 Front Street and loves to act in **Dan Needham**'s Gravesend Players productions.

Carry Fisher

The House of Mirth
Edith Wharton

A woman known for bringing newcomers, such as **the Brys**, into society. After **Lily** has been expelled from the upper class by **Bertha**, Carry is one of the few people who still shows compassion toward her, offering Lily support and money.

Pop Fisher

The Natural
Bernard Malamud

The long-suffering manager of the New York Knights. Once a great player himself, Pop once made a bad play that cost his team an important game, and he has never recovered from that mistake. He wants nothing more than to lead the Knights to a pennant victory. The worse the team is doing, the worse Pop's health gets.

Fitzgerald

Sister Carrie
Theodore Dreiser

Along with **Moy**, the joint owner of a popular saloon in Chicago. Fitzgerald and Moy are good to **Hurstwood**, the saloon's manager, first providing him with gainful employment and then choosing not to prosecute when he steals thousands of dollars from them.

Harriet Fitzpatrick

Tom Jones
Henry Fielding

Sophia's cousin and the wife of **Mr. Fitzpatrick**. Pretty and charming, she is nevertheless selfish and plots against Sophia in order to improve her relationship with **Squire Western** and **Mrs. Western**.

Mr. Fitzpatrick

Tom Jones
Henry Fielding

A rash Irishman who aggressively pursues **Harriet Fitzpatrick** against her wishes. Fitzpatrick becomes admirable, however, when he admits to initiating the duel with **Tom** at the end of the novel.

Waldemar Fitzurse

Ivanhoe
Sir Walter Scott

Prince John's chief adviser, who has tied his political aspirations to John's success despite his dislike for the prince. Fitzurse is a cool, calculating, and treacherous power-seeker who often reacts calmly to news that makes John panic. Ultimately, he leads an unsuccessful ambush against **King Richard I** and is banished from England forever.

Lord Fitzwalter

Richard II
William Shakespeare

A nobleman who supports **Henry Bolingbroke**. When the **Duke of Aumerle** is accused by **Bagot** of being complicit in the death of the late **Thomas of Woodstock, Duke of Gloucester**, Fitzwalter challenges Aumerle to a fight.

Fiver

Watership Down
Richard Adams

Hazel's brother. Fiver is small and awkward, but he sees things that no other rabbits see. His sixth sense saves the rabbits many times, and they learn to always seek his opinion.

Flaminius

Timon of Athens
William Shakespeare

One of **Timon**'s servants.

Moll Flanders

Moll Flanders
Daniel Defoe

The narrator and protagonist of the novel, who actually goes by a number of names during the course of her lifetime. Born an orphan, she lives a varied and exciting life, moving through an astonishing number of marriages and affairs and becoming a highly successful professional criminal before her eventual retirement and repentance. "Moll Flanders" is the alias she adopts during her years as an expert thief.

Bonnie Flannigan

Johnny Got His Gun
Dalton Trumbo

A woman, younger than **Joe Bonham**, who also grew up in Shale City. Bonnie and Joe met up again in Los Angeles.

Flask

Moby-Dick
Herman Melville

A native of Tisbury on Martha's Vineyard and the third mate of the *Pequod*. Short and squat, Flask has a confrontational attitude and no reverence for the dignity of the whale or anything else. Flask and the other two mates, **Starbuck** and **Stubb**, are mostly used to provide philosophical contrasts with Captain **Ahab**. Flask simply enjoys the thrill of the hunt and takes pride in killing whales with no thought to consequences. The perspectives of the three mates accentuate Ahab's monomania.

Flavius of *Julius Caesar*

Julius Caesar
William Shakespeare

A tribune, or an official elected by the people to protect their rights. Flavius condemns the plebeians for their fickleness in cheering **Julius Caesar** when once they cheered for Caesar's enemy **Pompey**. Flavius is punished along with **Murellus** for removing the decorations from Caesar's statues during Caesar's triumphal parade.

Flavius of *Timon*

Timon of Athens
William Shakespeare

Timon's steward. After Timon's downfall, Flavius decides to continue serving him and seeks him out in the wilderness. Flavius offers Timon all the money he has and weeps at Timon's downfall.

Fleance

Macbeth
William Shakespeare

Banquo's son. Fleance survives **Macbeth**'s plot of sending **the Murderers** to kill him, and at the end of the play his whereabouts are unknown. Presumably, Fleance may rule Scotland one day and fulfill **the Three Witches**' prophecy that Banquo's sons will sit on the Scottish throne.

Agnes Fleming

Oliver Twist
Charles Dickens

Oliver Twist's mother. A retired naval officer's daughter, she is a beautiful, loving woman. After falling in love with and becoming pregnant by **Mr. Leeford**, she chooses to die anonymously in a workhouse rather than stain her family's reputation.

Henry Fleming

The Red Badge of Courage
Stephen Crane

The novel's protagonist; a young soldier fighting for the Union army during the American Civil War. Initially, Henry stands untested in battle and questions his own courage. As the novel progresses, he encounters hard truths about the experience of war, confronting the universe's indifference to his existence and the insignificance of his own life. Though he is vain and has extremely romantic notions about himself, Henry grapples with these lessons as he first runs from battle, then comes to thrive as a soldier in combat.

Fletcher

Shane
Jack Schaefer

The antagonist of the book. He is angry that **Joe Starrett** will not sell him his farm and that Joe has rallied the other farmers against Fletcher. When **Shane** comes to town, Joe becomes an even more formidable adversary to Fletcher, who resorts to violence and murder, standing in direct contrast to both Joe and Shane. Shane kills Fletcher in the end.

Dr. Fletcher

On the Beach
Nevil Shute

A conscientious doctor who treats **Dwight Towers** when he falls ill after his long sea voyage. A few weeks before the radiation comes to Melbourne, Dr. Fletcher performs surgery on a woman to enable her to live a few more years.

Fleur-de-Lys de Gondelaurier

Hunchback of Notre Dame
Victor Hugo

A wealthy aristocrat who marries the dashing young **Phoebus de Chateaupers**. She is jealous of **La Esmeralda**'s beauty.

Flimnap

Gulliver's Travels
Jonathan Swift

Lord High Treasurer of Lilliput. Flimnap's jealous hatred of **Gulliver** arises from the absurd suspicion that Gulliver is having an affair with Flimnap's wife.

Dr. Flint

Incidents in the Life of a Slave Girl
Harriet Ann Jacobs

Linda Brent's real-life master. He is morally bankrupt and without redeeming qualities. Dr. Flint loves power above all things, and forcing Linda to submit to him is more important to him than simply sleeping with her. He is galled and infuriated by her defiance of him and becomes obsessed with the idea of breaking her will. When Linda escapes, he pursues her relentlessly, putting himself hundreds of dollars in debt to chase her to New York. After his death, his venom and determination seem to be reincarnated in the form of his son-in-law, **Mr. Dodge**.

Emily Flint

Incidents in the Life of a Slave Girl
Harriet Ann Jacobs

Dr. Flint's daughter and **Linda Brent**'s legal owner. Emily Flint serves mainly as Dr. Flint's puppet, who sometimes writes Linda letters in her name, trying to trick her into returning to him.

Mrs. Flint

Incidents in the Life of a Slave Girl
Harriet Ann Jacobs

Linda Brent's mistress and Dr. Flint's jealous wife. Mrs. Flint is characterized mainly by her hypocrisy. She is a church woman who supposedly suffers from weak nerves, but she treats her slaves with callousness and brutality.

Nicholas Flint

Incidents in the Life of a Slave Girl
Harriet Ann Jacobs

Dr. Flint's son. Nicholas is essentially a carbon copy of his father, with the same lecherous tendencies toward his female slaves.

Young Mrs. Flint

Incidents in the Life of a Slave Girl
Harriet Ann Jacobs

Nicholas Flint's bride. Seemingly kind at first, young Mrs. Flint provides further evidence of the cruelty of slave-holding women when she orders an elderly slave to eat grass.

Uncle Willie Flittman

A Tree Grows in Brooklyn
Betty Smith

Aunt Evy's husband and the owner of **Drummer**. Willie feels like a failure and is often the subject of Evy's best imitations and jokes.

Professor Flitwick

Harry Potter and the Prisoner of Azkaban
J. K. Rowling

A small, kind professor who teaches Charms.

Dora Flood

Cannery Row
John Steinbeck

The local madam and proprietor of the Bear Flag Restaurant, a brothel. Dora is a huge woman with bright orange hair and flamboyant clothes. She runs a tight ship—refusing to allow her girls to drink or talk to men on the street—but is kindhearted and generous. Dora paid the grocery bills for many local families during the Depression, and she organizes an aid effort during the influenza epidemic that passes through Cannery Row during the novella.

Tina Flood

This Boy's Life
Tobias Wolff

The girl who is impregnated by **Chuck Bolger**. Tina Flood's father charges Chuck with statutory rape and also holds **Jerry Huff** responsible. Huff marries Tina so that he will not have to do jail time.

Divina Flor

Chronicle of a Death Foretold
Gabriel García Márquez

Victoria Guzman's daughter. **Santiago Nasar** desires her sexually, but Victoria watches carefully to make sure he does not do anything to her. On the day of Santiago's death, she serves Santiago a mug of coffee with a shot of cane liquor as she did every Monday.

Flora

The Turn of the Screw
Henry James

The orphaned eight-year-old niece of the **governess**'s employer. Flora possesses an unearthly, angelic beauty.

Florence

Little Women
Louisa May Alcott

Aunt Carrol's daughter. Florence accompanies her aunt and **Amy March** to Europe.

Florence

Go Tell It on the Mountain
James Baldwin

Gabriel's sister. She resents him because of the favoritism he received from their mother. Florence knows she is ill and doesn't have much time left to live.

Florence

Bless Me, Ultima
Rudolfo A. Anaya

One of **Antonio Márez**'s friends. Although Florence does not believe in God, he attends catechism to be with his friends. Florence's active, vocal questioning of Catholic orthodoxy is partly a result of his own difficult past. Both of Florence's parents are dead, and his sisters have become prostitutes at **Rosie**'s place. Florence shows Antonio that the Catholic Church is not perfect and that religion can fail.

Duke of Florence

All's Well that Ends Well
William Shakespeare

The ruler of Florence. As he engages in war, he expresses regret that the **King of France** has not come to assist in battle. However, his army does include several volunteer French lords, including **Bertram**, **Parolles**, and the **First Lord Dumaine** and **Second Lord Dumaine**. The Duke later makes Bertram a general of his horse, illuminating Bertram's positive attributes.

Florimell

The Faerie Queene
Edmund Spenser

A significant female character in Book III. Florimell represents Beauty. She is chaste but constantly hounded by men who go mad with lust for her. She does love one knight, who seems to be the only character that does not love her.

Florizel

The Winter's Tale
William Shakespeare

Polixenes's only son and heir. Florizel falls in love with **Perdita**, unaware of her royal ancestry, and defies his father by eloping with her.

Flossie

Legs
William Kennedy

A fun-loving hooker with the proverbial heart of gold. She sleeps with both **Jack** and **Marcus** and is a mainstay at the Parody Club, where she sings as well as solicits.

Three-petaled flower

The Little Prince
Antoine de Saint-Exupéry

The three-petaled flower lives alone in the desert, watching the occasional caravan pass by. She mistakenly informs **the Little Prince** that there are only a handful of men in the world and that their lack of roots means they are often blown along.

Mrs. Bertha Flowers

I Know Why the Caged Bird Sings
Maya Angelou

A black aristocrat living in Stamps, Arkansas. One of **Maya Johnson**'s idols, she becomes the first person to prod Maya out of her silence after Maya's rape by **Mr. Freeman**. Maya respects Mrs. Flowers for encouraging her love of literature.

Dr. Heywood Floyd

2001: A Space Odyssey
Arthur C. Clarke

A senior government official. Floyd is sent to the moon to investigate TMA. He is an effective bureaucrat and a caring family man. He is one of the first men to see TMA-1 and to wonder about its consequences.

Captain Fluellen

Henry V
William Shakespeare

The Welsh captain of **King Henry V**'s troops. The three foreign captains in the play, Fluellen, the Scottish **Captain Jamy**, and the Irish **Captain MacMorris**, retain their respective heavy accents, broadly represent their nationalities, and prove the importance of each of the British nations. Fluellen embodies many of the comical stereotypes associated with the Welsh in Shakespeare's day: he is wordy, overly serious, and possesses a ludicrous pseudo-Welsh accent. Beyond the comic relief he provides, he is likable, intelligent, and a loyal officer. He refuses **Pistol**'s plea to spare **Bardolph**'s life, saying that discipline must be maintained.

Who Flung

Their Eyes Were Watching God
Zora Neale Hurston

A young rascal. Who Flung dates a wealthy widow, **Annie Tyler**, who lives in Eatonville. He takes her money and flees at the first opportunity. Early in her marriage to **Tea Cake**, **Janie Mae Crawford** fears that Tea Cake will turn out to be like Who Flung.

Francis Flute

A Midsummer Night's Dream
William Shakespeare

The bellows-mender chosen to play Thisbe in the craftsmen's play for **Theseus**'s marriage celebration. Forced to play a young girl in love, the bearded craftsman decides to speak his lines in a high, squeaky voice.

Father Flynn

Dubliners
James Joyce

The priest who dies in "The Sisters," and a potential child-molester. Father Flynn's ambiguous role in the story initiates a book-long critique of religious leaders as incompetent.

Mike Flynn

A Portrait of the Artist as a Young Man
James Joyce

Simon Dedalus's friend, who tries and fails to train **Stephen Dedalus** to be a runner.

Joe Fogerty

Legs
William Kennedy

Jack's driver and right-hand man, he is the spitting image of **Eddie**. Fogerty carries around Eddie's revolver and acts as a replacement for Jack's brother. Fogerty does not like to fight, so Jack rarely asks him to strong-arm anyone, and Fogerty usually leaves Eddie's .38 millimeter gun unloaded.

Miss Foley

Something Wicked This Way Comes
Ray Bradbury

An unhappy woman who believes she can find happiness on the merry-go-round. She is obsessed with riding the carousel. She tries to get **William Halloway** and **James Nightshade** into trouble so that they will not stop her from using it, even though the boys saved her from the Mirror Maze.

Grampa Follet

A Death in the Family
James Agee

Father of **Jay Follet** and **Ralph Follet**. Grampa Follet was very burdensome to his wife, which frequently made Jay furious when he was younger. Nonetheless, Jay believes that his father was a good-hearted man and always meant well. Jay has his fatal accident while driving to Grampa Follet's to investigate Grampa Follet's alleged illness, which was exaggerated by a drunken Ralph.

Great-Great-Grandmother Follet

A Death in the Family
James Agee

The great-great-grandmother of **Rufus Follet** and **Little Catherine**. **Great-Aunt Sadie**, who lives with Great-Great-Grandmother Follet, says that the old woman will be especially happy to see Rufus, because he is the first fifth-generation grandchild in the family.

Jay Follet

A Death in the Family
James Agee

Husband of **Mary Follet** and father of **Rufus Follet** and **Little Catherine**. Jay Follet is a gentle father with an impressive, grand physique. There are implications that he used to drink heavily, like his brother **Ralph Follet**. Jay is killed in a car accident while investigating the illness of his father, **Grampa Follet**, as reported to him by a drunken Ralph. Jay's death catalyzes most of the action and emotion in the novel.

Mary Follet

A Death in the Family
James Agee

Wife of **Jay Follet**, mother of **Rufus Follet** and **Little Catherine**. Mary Follet is sensitive, high-strung, and ardently religious, as well as kind, giving, and very loving to her children. Mary and Jay, when together at the beginning of the novel, appear to have a happy marriage with relatively little strife. There are allusions throughout the novel to a drinking problem that Jay used to have; Mary herself wonders for a moment if Jay was drunk when he had the accident. Her religious beliefs become a point of contention between her and her husband and the rest of her family. After Jay dies, religion becomes even more important to Mary; she cannot understand how else to cope with the death.

Ralph Follet

A Death in the Family
James Agee

Younger brother of **Jay Follet**. Ralph Follet is an alcoholic and a generally weak and whiny man. He calls Jay while drunk to tell Jay that their father, **Grampa Follet**, is ill.

Rufus Follet

A Death in the Family
James Agee

The protagonist and the son of **Mary Follet** and **Jay Follet**, and brother of **Little Catherine**. Rufus Follet is perceptive and inquisitive and intelligent, and he greatly admires his father. At the end of the novel, there is no conclusive idea of what he makes of his father's death. Rufus understands that death is a permanent condition, but the full weight of grief has not yet struck him. Throughout the novel, Rufus questions his mother's and his aunt **Hannah Lynch**'s faith in God.

Trip Fontaine

The Virgin Suicides
Jeffrey Eugenides

The high school stud. Aware of his masculine prowess, Trip takes great care of his appearance, entrance, clothing, and hair. He swaggers down the hall, suns himself daily by the family pool, and spends much of the school day smoking marijuana in his car. Swooning female admirers continually surround him, but Trip is too gentlemanly to reveal the details of his erotic conquests. When he meets **Lux Lisbon**, he falls madly in love.

Fool of *Lear*

King Lear
William Shakespeare

King Lear's jester, who uses double-talk and seemingly frivolous songs to give Lear important advice.

Fool of *Timon*

Timon of Athens
William Shakespeare

A man who appears with **Apemantus** outside **Timon**'s house while the creditors' servants wait for their payments. The Fool draws a parallel between those who go to creditors and those who go to prostitutes.

Duncan Forbes

Lady Chatterley's Lover
D. H. Lawrence

An artist friend of **Lady Chatterley** and **Hilda Reid**. Forbes paints abstract canvases, a form of art **Oliver Mellors** despises. He once loved **Connie**, and Connie originally claims to be pregnant with his child.

Mrs. Forbes

I Never Promised You a Rose Garden
Joanne Greenberg

A well-liked attendant at the hospital. Patients try to protect Mrs. Forbes from harm. However, **Miss Coral** breaks her arm by throwing a bed at Mrs. Forbes during a psychotic episode.

Mistress Alice Ford

The Merry Wives of Windsor
William Shakespeare

Master Frank Ford's wife and **Mistress Margaret Page**'s friend. The central plot of the play begins when Mistress Ford and Mistress Page receive wooing letters from **Sir John Falstaff**, who secretly hopes to bed them and then gain financial rewards. The two ladies quickly discover the trickery, and plot to humiliate the fat knight. The plan the ladies hatch has a second motive: to root out Mistress Ford's husband's oppressive jealousy by showing that she is entirely faithful to him. The plan does work—Falstaff is humiliated in front of the town, and Ford promises never to doubt his wife's fidelity again. Mistress Ford's actions overthrow the supposed cleverness of the aristocracy while promoting the warmth and unity of the middle class.

Master Frank Ford

The Merry Wives of Windsor
William Shakespeare

Mistress Alice Ford's husband. As opposed to **Master George Page**, Ford doubts his wife's fidelity and is immediately enraged when he hears about **Sir John Falstaff**'s plot to seduce his wife. Mistress Ford lets him in on the plot to embarass Falstaff. Ford apologizes, and the pairs of wives and husbands plot Falstaff's final undoing. At the close of the play, Ford promises to never mistrust his wife again.

Henry Ford

Ragtime
E. L. Doctorow

Ford invents the concept of the assembly line and makes his fortune through the manufacture of Model-Ts.

Bill Forrester

Dandelion Wine
Ray Bradbury

A boarder in the home of **Grandma Spaulding** and **Grandpa Spaulding**. Bill gets along very well with everyone. Grandpa teaches him the beauty of mowing a lawn. Bill spends several weeks enchanted with **Miss Helen Loomis** before she dies, and her keen, inquisitive mind is a match for his.

Gene Forrester

A Separate Peace
John Knowles

The narrator and protagonist of the novel. When the story begins, Gene is in his early thirties, visiting the Devon School for the first time in years. He thinks back to his teen years at Devon, when he developed a love-hate relationship with his best friend, **Finny**, whom he alternately adored and envied. Gene caused Finny to fall out of a tree, shattering his leg. Later, when Finny died, Gene believed that Finny's funeral was in part his own. He often seems to want to lose hold of his own identity and live as a part of Finny, a tendency suggesting that he is strongly uncomfortable with his own personality.

Miss Forsythe

Death of a Salesman
Arthur Miller

A young woman who meets **Happy Loman** and **Biff Loman** at Frank's Chop House. She brings her friend **Letta**, and it is implied that both women are prostitutes.

Fortinbras

Hamlet
William Shakespeare

The young Prince of Norway. Fortinbras's father, **King Fortinbras of Norway**, was killed by **Hamlet**'s father, **King Hamlet** of Denmark. Fortinbras seeks to avenge his father's honor by conquering Denmark. Fortinbras is a foil for Hamlet because while Fortinbras actively seeks vengeance, Hamlet broods and hesitates.

Brother Fortinbride

The Unvanquished
William Faulkner

An uneducated but kind preacher in Jefferson who delivers the sermon at **Granny**'s funeral. Although he is unpolished, his roughness suits the times, and he is superior to the fancy minister whom the respectable ladies of the town originally choose to preach the funeral.

Antonio Foscanelli

Murder on the Orient Express
Agatha Christie

A large, menacing Italian man. **M. Bouc** suspects him of murdering **Ratchett**, primarily because M. Bouc distrusts Italians. **Hercule Poirot** reveals that Antonio was the Armstrong's chauffeur.

Mark Fossie

The Things They Carried
Tim O'Brien

A medic from **Bob "Rat" Kiley**'s previous assignment. Fossie loses his innocence when he realizes that his girlfriend, **Mary Anne Bell**, would rather be out on ambush with Green Berets than home planning a wedding.

Dr. Foster

Song of Solomon
Toni Morrison

The first black doctor in the novel's Michigan town. Dr. Foster is an arrogant, self-hating racist who calls fellow African Americans "cannibals" and checks to see how light-skinned his granddaughters are when they are born. He possibly has an incestuous relationship with his daughter, **Ruth Foster Dead**, who is found sucking on his corpse's fingers by **Macon, Jr.**

Ellen Foster

Ellen Foster
Kaye Gibbons

The novel's eleven-year-old protagonist. Ellen is subjected to sexual and psychological abuse at the hands of her alcoholic father. After her mother commits suicide, Ellen is tossed from one unhappy home to another, but she never loses hope that one day she will find a loving home, which does eventually happen.

Henry Foster

Brave New World
Aldous Huxley

One of **Lenina Crowne**'s many lovers. Foster, a conventional Alpha male, is happy to devote his leisure time to emotionless sex and sporting. Foster discusses Lenina's body casually with coworkers, illustrating the gap between a "normal" World State resident and dissidents like **Bernard Marx**.

Laura Foster

Cold Mountain
Charles Frazier

The girl **Solomon Veasey** attempts to murder because she is pregnant with his baby.

The Reverend Foster

Stranger in a Strange Land
Robert A. Heinlein

A savvy and slick self-styled prophet who drew people to his teachings through showmanship. His followers are called Fosterites.

Tom Foster

Winesburg, Ohio
Sherwood Anderson

A quiet, likable boy who moves to Winesburg from Cincinnati.

Fouqué

The Red and the Black
Stendhal

Julien Sorel's only friend. Fouqué lives in the mountains surrounding the town of Verrières and works in the lumber business. He offers Sorel a lumber trade job that promises wealth but little glory. Fouqué's tempting proposition gives Sorel, who refuses the job, a renewed energy and vigor to climb the social ladder just like Sorel's hero, Napoleon. After Sorel shoots and wounds **Mme. de Rênal**, **Mathilde de la Mole** and Fouqué come to Besançon to help Sorel escape from prison.

Annawake Fourkiller

Pigs in Heaven
Barbara Kingsolver

A young, gutsy law intern. Annawake has taken on **Turtle Greer**'s case as her personal cause. Fresh out of law school, she has returned to her home in the Cherokee Nation to fight against the injustices suffered by her people. Turtle's circumstances remind her of the way her brother **Gabriel** was taken from the Nation.

Ledger Fourkiller

Pigs in Heaven
Barbara Kingsolver

Annawake Fourkiller's uncle, with whom she lived after **Gabriel** was taken away from their family. Ledger is also the tribal chief. He is wise, unassuming, and humble.

Brother Fowles

The Poisonwood Bible
Barbara Kingsolver

The previous missionary in Kilanga, who was removed from the post due to inappropriate fraternizing with the natives. Brother Fowles has a deep understanding of and sympathy for the Congolese people and their religion.

The fox

The Canterbury Tales
Geoffrey Chaucer

The orange fox from **the Nun's Priest**'s Tale. Interpreted by some to be an allegorical figure for the devil, the fox uses flattery to capture **Chanticleer** the rooster. Eventually, Chanticleer outwits the fox by encouraging him to boast of his deceit to some pursuers. When the fox opens his mouth, Chanticleer escapes.

The fox

The Little Prince
Antoine de Saint-Exupéry

Friend of **the Little Prince**. The Fox asks the Little Prince to tame him, but the fox actually trains the prince. Before the two part, the Fox tells the Little Prince a secret with three important lessons: only the heart can see correctly; the prince's absence from his planet has made him better appreciate **the Rose**; and love entails responsibility.

Madeleine Fox

Arrowsmith
Sinclair Lewis

A snobbish literature student at Winnemac University who attends the same college as **Martin Arrowsmith**. Madeleine eventually becomes Martin's fiancée, but she turns out to be what Martin calls an "improver"—someone who tries to change people, including Martin, to fit her beliefs and her society. Martin breaks off his engagement to Madeleine in order to be with **Leora Tozer**.

Foxy

A Yellow Raft in Blue Water
Michael Dorris

Pauline's son, **Ida**'s nephew. Foxy is a rider at the rodeo and a cruel boy who taunts and even threatens **Rayona**, always making her very uncomfortable.

King of France

All's Well that Ends Well
William Shakespeare

The ruler of France and **Bertram**'s liege. Deathly ill at the start of the play, the king is miraculously cured by **Helena** with her father's medicine. In a magnanimous gesture, the king agrees to give Helena her pick of husbands. When Bertram flinches at the idea of marrying Helena, the King rebukes him, remarking that inner worth is more important than noble birth, and true rank is "dignified by the doer's deed."

Frances

Death Be Not Proud
John Gunther

Mother of **Johnny** and divorced wife of **John Gunther**. She gives Johnny philosophical and emotional support and teaches him how to use his strong right side to compensate for his tumor-weakened left side. Holding out for a miracle cure, Frances is a beacon of hope.

Frances

The Color of Water
James McBride

Ruth McBride Jordan's only childhood friend in Suffolk. Frances was sweet and accepting of Ruth, even though she is from a gentile family. Ruth's few good memories of Suffolk involve the time she spent playing with Frances.

Francesca

Inferno
Dante Alighieri

A lover condemned to the Second Circle of Hell with the Lustful for an adulterous affair that began with **Paolo** and Francesca reading about **Lancelot** and **Guinevere** (Canto V). Paolo is Francesca's husband's brother.

Ad Francis

In Our Time
Ernest Hemingway

A somewhat crazy and tough old boxer whom **Nick Adams** meets when he is punched off of a freight train.

Francisco

Hamlet
William Shakespeare

A soldier and guardsman at Elsinore.

Francisco

House Made of Dawn
N. Scott Momaday

Abel and **Vidal**'s grandfather. The elderly Francisco, a farmer, remembers how different life for the area's Indians in 1945 is from how life used to be years ago. As one of the elders, he participates in gatherings of elders in the kiva—a partly underground ceremonial structure—during important events such as feasts. Francisco has raised Abel and his brother, Vidal, the way his ancestors raised him, telling them the stories of his tribe and the stories of the land around Walatowa. His death brings about a transformation in Abel, causing Abel to take on the responsibility of being the family's patriarch.

François

The Call of the Wild
Jack London

A French Canadian mail driver who buys **Buck** and adds him to his team. Along with the mail carrier, **Perrault**, François runs the pack of dogs all over the North country. François is an experienced man, accustomed to life in the North, and he impresses Buck with his fairness and good sense. François exits Buck's life abruptly after being reassigned to work somewhere else along with Perrault.

Françoise

Swann's Way
Marcel Proust

First **Aunt Léonie**'s maid and then a servant for **Marcel**'s family. Françoise becomes a dedicated and devoted friend to everyone.

Françoise

Nausea
Jean-Paul Sartre

The barmaid of a local cafe, she is **Roquentin**'s sometimes lover. As his nausea progresses, he is more and more disgusted at the prospect of having sex with her.

Dominique Francon

The Fountainhead
Ayn Rand

Guy Francon's beautiful daughter. Dominique Francon is the first and only strong woman we encounter in *The Fountainhead*. She contrasts with the other female characters, who are either manipulative, stifling, or weak-willed superficial New York socialites who gossip or shop. Dominique has a great appreciation for what is pure, beautiful, and strong, and she firmly believes that the world destroys all that is good. She refuses to love anyone or anything for fear that the world will destroy what she loves, and she surrounds herself with those people she likes the least, knowing that she will be in no danger of falling in love with them. Dominique's encounter with **Howard Roark** derails her loveless existence, as she finds herself caring for a man with vision and character. True to her philosophy, she does not celebrate this turn of events. She fears the world will destroy this good man, so she decides to destroy him first.

Guy Francon

The Fountainhead
Ayn Rand

The owner of architectural firm Francon & Heyer. Guy Francon is also **Peter Keating**'s employer and **Dominique Francon**'s father. A fundamentally honest and decent man, Francon has no architectural talent of his own. Eventually, he finds salvation through his love for his daughter.

Franek

Night
Elie Wiesel

Eliezer's foreman at Buna. Franek gets a camp dentist to pry out Eliezer's gold tooth with a rusty spoon.

Frank

Dubliners
James Joyce

A sailor. Frank tries to convince **Eveline** to elope with him to Buenos Aires in "Eveline." She changes her mind at the last minute.

Anne Frank

Anne Frank: Diary of a Young Girl
Anne Frank

The author of the diary, daughter of **Otto Frank** and **Edith Frank**, sister of **Margot Frank**. The Franks are forced to hide in an annex to Otto Frank's office building during the Nazi occupation of Holland. Anne is very intelligent and perceptive, and she wants to become a writer. She feels that the diary she receives for her thirteenth birthday is her only confidant. Anne describes those who live with her and their situation with serious reflection and humor. Anne is remarkably forthright and perceptive at the beginning of the diary, but as she leaves her normal childhood behind and enters the dire and unusual circumstances of the Holocaust, she becomes more introspective and thoughtful. She tries to understand her identity in the microcosm of the annex and attempts to understand the workings of the cruel world outside. As she matures, Anne comes to long not for female companionship, but intimacy with a male counterpart. She becomes infatuated with **Peter van Daan**, and comes to consider him a close friend, confidant, and eventually an object of romantic desire. In her final diary entries, Anne is particularly lucid about the changes she has undergone, her ambitions, and how her experience is changing her. Anne died of typhus in the Bergen-Belsen concentration camp in late February or early March of 1945.

Edith Frank

Anne Frank: Diary of a Young Girl
Anne Frank

Mother of **Anne Frank** and **Margot Frank**, wife of **Otto Frank**. She is mentioned almost exclusively in instances when she is the source of Anne's anger and frustration. Later in her diary, however, Anne attempts to look at her mother's life as a wife and mother from a more objective viewpoint. Despite her new perspective, Anne continues to feel estranged from her critical mother and irrevocably deems her unfit. It seems that Mrs. Frank's inability to provide support for her daughter stems in part from the stress and pain of their persecution and forced confinement. Edith died in the Auschwitz concentration camp in January 1945.

Margot Frank

Anne Frank: Diary of a Young Girl
Anne Frank

Anne Frank's older sister, and the daughter of **Edith Frank** and **Otto Frank**. Anne thinks that Margot is pretty, smart, emotional, and everyone's favorite. However, Anne and Margot do not form a close bond, and Margot mainly appears in the diary when she is the cause of jealousy or anger. She died of typhus in the Bergsen-Belsen concentration camp a few days before Anne did.

Otto Frank

Anne Frank: Diary of a Young Girl
Anne Frank

Father of **Anne Frank** and **Margot Frank**, husband of **Edith Frank**. Otto is practical and kind, and Anne feels a particular kinship to him. After the Nazis came to power in Germany, Otto moved to Amsterdam in 1933 to protect his family from persecution. There he made a living selling chemical products and provisions until the family was forced into hiding in 1942. In Anne's eyes, Mr. Frank is one of the kindest, smartest, most gentle and thoughtful fathers imaginable. Otto became the only resident of the annex to survive the war. He remained in Auschwitz until it was liberated by Russian troops in 1945. He returned to Holland, where he received Anne's diary. He married another Auschwitz survivor and devoted the rest of his life to promoting Anne's diary.

Alphonse Frankenstein

Frankenstein
Mary Shelley

Victor Frankenstein's father. Alphonse consoles Victor in times of pain and encourages him to remember the importance of family.

Victor Frankenstein

Frankenstein
Mary Shelley

The doomed protagonist and narrator of the main portion of the story. Victor lets his ambitions overtake his morals, and then can't find the courage to solve the problems he has created. His cowardice and revulsion for **the monster** he creates result in the deaths of everyone he loves.

William Frankenstein

Frankenstein
Mary Shelley

Victor Frankenstein's youngest brother and the darling of the Frankenstein family. **The monster** strangles William in the woods outside Geneva in order to hurt Victor for abandoning him. William's death deeply saddens Victor and burdens him with tremendous guilt.

Frankie

Cannery Row
John Steinbeck

A mentally disabled boy who is neglected by his mother and taken in by **Doc**. Frankie is incapable of doing any real work, for he seems to do every task he is given just a little bit wrong. He loves Doc and frequently tells him so. Frankie is institutionalized after he breaks into a jewelry store to steal a gift for Doc.

Mr. Frankland

Hound of the Baskervilles
Sir Arthur Conan Doyle

Laura Lyons's father. Frankland likes to sue over every infringement on what he sees as his rights.

The franklin

The Canterbury Tales
Geoffrey Chaucer

A connoisseur of food and wine whose table remains laid and ready for food all day. In Chaucer's day, *franklin* referred to a free commoner—neither a vassal nor a nobleman.

Benjamin Franklin

The Autobiography of Benjamin Franklin
Benjamin Franklin

The author and protagonist. Benjamin Franklin claimed he wrote his autobiography ostensibly to tell his son (**William Franklin**) about his life, as well as to provide a model of self-improvement. Born into a modest Boston family in 1706, Franklin moves to Philadelphia in his late teens and eventually opens up his own newspaper, *The Pennsylvania Gazette*. At various points during his lifetime, Franklin becomes a vegetarian, runs a lending library, converts to Deism, serves as postmaster general, receives honorary degrees from Harvard and Yale, invents the stove, and experiments with lightning and electricity. Preoccupied with self-betterment, he creates a list of thirteen virtues to practice, one virtue a week. The book recounts the major events of his life and discusses many of his important scientific and political ideas, but shies away from examining the Revolutionary War, in which the historical Franklin was a major participant.

James Franklin

The Autobiography of Benjamin Franklin
Benjamin Franklin

Benjamin Franklin's older brother, the owner of a Boston printing house. Benjamin works as James Franklin's apprentice during his teens, and while their relationship is rocky, Benjamin learns a great deal. After a particularly bitter fight, James spitefully makes sure that no Boston printer will give Benjamin a job; Benjamin in return breaks his contract with James and moves to Philadelphia. Many years later, Benjamin and James make amends.

Josiah Franklin

The Autobiography of Benjamin Franklin
Benjamin Franklin

Benjamin Franklin's father. Although Benjamin is the fifteenth of seventeen children, Josiah takes a great interest in Benjamin, teaching him how to debate and how to write effectively. Benjamin admires his father enormously. After the death of his parents, Benjamin has them buried in a still-famous Boston cemetery and erects a prominent monument to them.

William Franklin

The Autobiography of Benjamin Franklin
Benjamin Franklin

Benjamin Franklin's son, the royal governor of New Jersey in 1771 when Benjamin begins his *Autobiography*. It is to William that the book is initially addressed.

Franz

The Unbearable Lightness of Being
Milan Kundera

An idealistic Geneva professor and **Sabina**'s lover. Franz falls in love with Sabina, whom he (erroneously) considers a liberal and romantically tragic Czech dissident. Ultimately he leaves his wife **Marie-Claude** for Sabina. Franz identifies strongly with the European liberal left, loves parades and marches, and idolizes his dead mother. Abandoned by Sabina, he finds solace in the arms of a perfectly ordinary **young student** who loves him deeply. In the end he dies a preventable death in Cambodia after being attacked by criminals trying to take his money.

T. E. Frazier

Walden Two
B. F. Skinner

A former classmate of **Professor Burris**'s and the founding member of Walden Two. He is enthusiastic, hyper-verbal, and frequently pedantic. Unlike the children of Walden Two, he is driven by an urge to dominate and achieve.

Freawaru

Grendel
John Gardner

Hrothgar's teenage daughter. Hrothgar plans to marry Freawaru off to **Ingeld** in order to avoid a war with the Heathobards.

Fred

A Christmas Carol
Charles Dickens

Ebenezer Scrooge's nephew. Unlike Scrooge, Fred enjoys Christmas, which he considers "a kind, forgiving, charitable, pleasant time." Despite constant rejection, he doggedly continues making friendly overtures to his uncle.

Freddie

Song of Solomon
Toni Morrison

A janitor employed by **Macon, Jr.** Freddie spreads rumors through the town, illustrating how information was often disseminated within African-American communities. Freddie coins the nickname "Milkman" for **Ruth Foster Dead**'s son, **Milkman Dead**. Milkman finds out from Freddie that **Guitar Bains** is engaged in questionable activities.

Freddy

A Room with a View
E. M. Forster

Lucy Honeychurch's younger brother, who is energetic and loves tennis, swimming, and the study of anatomy. He dislikes **Cecil Vyse** and likes **George Emerson**.

Frederick

Doctor Faustus
Christopher Marlowe

A friend of **Benvolio**'s who, along with **Martino**, reluctantly joins Benvolio's scheme to kill **Faustus**.

Duke Frederick

As You Like It
William Shakespeare

The brother of **Duke Senior** and the usurper of his throne. Duke Frederick's cruel nature and volatile temper are displayed when he banishes his niece, **Rosalind**, from court without reason. Frederick mounts an army against his exiled brother but aborts his vengeful mission after he meets an old religious man on the road to the Forest of Arden. He immediately changes his ways, dedicating himself to a monastic life and returning the crown to his brother.

Mr. Frederick

Animal Farm
George Orwell

Operator of Pinchfield Farm, a neighbor to Animal Farm. Tough and shrewd, Frederick is notorious for treating his animals cruelly and cheats **Napoleon** out of timber by paying with forged banknotes. When Animal Farm threatens retaliation, Frederick destroys their windmill with blasting powder. Frederick's harsh rule, dishonesty, and brute force are meant to parallel Hitler's Germany of the 1930s.

William Freeland

Narrative of the Life of Frederick Douglass
Frederick Douglass

Frederick Douglass's keeper for two years after he is enslaved by **Edward Covey**. Freeland is the most fair and straightforward of all of Douglass's masters and is not hypocritically pious.

Colonel Freeleigh

Dandelion Wine
Ray Bradbury

A very old man whose body has failed him. He wants nothing more than to live life to its fullest, and he passes on that passion to the boys through the stories he tells them.

Ludie Freeman

The Member of the Wedding
Carson McCullers

Berenice Sadie Brown's first husband. He died in 1931, when **Frankie Addams** was born.

Mr. Freeman

I Know Why the Caged Bird Sings
Maya Angelou

Vivian Baxter's live-in boyfriend in St. Louis. When **Maya Johnson** and **Bailey Johnson** move to St. Louis, Mr. Freeman sexually molests and rapes Maya, taking advantage of her need for physical affection and her innocent, self-conscious nature. Vivian chases Mr. Freeman out of the house, suspecting that something has gone wrong. In court, Maya names Mr. Freeman as her attacker. Soon after, Mr. Freeman is found beaten to death. In retrospect, Maya feels partly responsible for Mr. Freeman's fate, and her guilt over his murder haunts her throughout her childhood.

Arthur Fremantle

The Killer Angels
Michael Shaara

An Englishman sent to observe the Confederate army in action. Many people in the Confederacy hope that England will come to their aid, since the South still bears many of the traditional aspects of English society, particularly in its class structure. Realists like **General Robert E. Lee** and **General James Longstreet** know that England will never help the Confederacy as long as it endorses slavery.

French lieutenant

Lord Jim
Joseph Conrad

The man who stayed aboard the damaged Patna as his gunboat towed her back into port. Although his act was heroic, he seems to have been motivated more by duty and professionalism. **Marlow** meets the French lieutenant in a Sydney café many years after the events of the novel.

Fresleven

Heart of Darkness
Joseph Conrad

Marlow's predecessor as captain of the steamer. Fresleven, by all accounts a good-tempered and nonviolent man, was killed in a dispute over some hens, apparently after striking a village chief.

Sigmund Freud

Ragtime
E. L. Doctorow

A famous psychiatrist, Freud has a profound effect on ideas about sex and society in America.

Marvin Frey

All the King's Men
Robert Penn Warren

Sibyl Frey's father, who threatens **Willie** with a paternity suit.

Sibyl Frey

All the King's Men
Robert Penn Warren

A young girl who accuses **Tom Stark** of impregnating her. Tom alleges that Sibyl has slept with so many men that she could not possibly know he was the father of her child.

Friar

The Canterbury Tales
Geoffrey Chaucer

A roaming priest with no tie to a monastery. Friars were objects of great criticism in Chaucer's time. Chaucer's worldly Friar has taken to accepting bribes.

Friar

Ivanhoe
Sir Walter Scott

A merry monk who befriends **King Richard I** in Robin Hood's forest. He is soon revealed to be none other than the legendary Friar Tuck, a member of **Locksley**'s (Robin Hood) band of merry men.

Friday

Robinson Crusoe
Daniel Defoe

A Caribbean native and cannibal who converts to Protestantism under **Crusoe**'s tutelage. Friday becomes Crusoe's servant when Crusoe saves him from being eaten by other cannibals. Friday never appears to resist or resent his new master, and he may sincerely view it as appropriate compensation for having his life saved. Nevertheless, his servitude has become a symbol of imperialist oppression throughout the modern world.

Dr. Clara Fried

I Never Promised You a Rose Garden
Joanne Greenberg

Deborah's famous German therapist, whose empathy is arguably her greatest gift as a doctor. Dr. Fried takes on Deborah's case, even though doing so requires turning down several other professional opportunities. With Dr. Fried's help, Deborah gains the courage to fight her way to mental health.

T. Cholmondeley Frink

Babbitt
Sinclair Lewis

One of Babbitt's many friends and associates. Although **Chum Frink** is considered a poetic genius, he writes clumsy, terrible jingles for advertisements. He is secretly unhappy that he never fulfilled his youthful ambition to be a real poet.

Frith

Rebecca
Daphne du Maurier

Maxim de Winter's butler at Manderley.

Archdeacon Claude Frollo

Hunchback of Notre Dame
Victor Hugo

A priest at Notre Dame, and the novel's antagonist. He is not a typical evil character in that he is very bright and compassionate. He dearly loves his brother **Jehan** and does everything in his power to make him happy after their parents die. He extends the same compassion to **Quasimodo**, whom he tries to mold into a scholar just like his brother by teaching him how to read and write. Frollo descends into black magic and madness because he fails to bring up both Jehan and Quasimodo. Jehan drinks and gambles all his money away, completely neglecting his studies, while Quasimodo's deafness makes it virtually impossible to teach him anything. The hunchback thus becomes both a symbol of failure for Frollo as well as a powerful tool of vengeance to wreak his frustrations out on the world. His obsessive lust for **La Esmerelda** causes her to be executed and Quasimodo to be tortured.

Jehan Frollo

Hunchback of Notre Dame
Victor Hugo

Claude Frollo's brother. Jehan is a horrible student who gambles and drinks all his money away. He decides to join the vagabonds and shows them a way around the cathedral when they prepare an assault on Notre Dame. **Quasimodo** thinks that the vagabonds are going to try to kill **La Esmerelda** and makes plans to defend the cathedral from the imminent assault. Quasimodo swings Jehan up against a wall, crushing his skull, and then throws him down to his death.

Ethan Frome

Ethan Frome
Edith Wharton

The protagonist of the novel. Ethan is a farmer whose family has lived and died on the same Massachusetts farm for generations. A sensitive figure, Ethan has a deep, almost mystical appreciation of nature. He feels a strong connection to the youth, beauty, and vital spirit of **Mattie Silver**, his wife's cousin. Ultimately, however, he lacks the strength to escape the oppressive forces of convention, climate, and his sickly wife, **Zenobia Frome**.

Zenobia Frome

Ethan Frome
Edith Wharton

Ethan Frome's sickly wife, more commonly known as "Zeena." Zenobia is prematurely aged, caustic in temperament, prone to alternating fits of silence and rage, and utterly unattractive, making her the novel's least sympathetic figure. Despite Zeena's apparent physical weakness, she holds the dominant position in their household.

Reginald Front-de-Boeuf

Ivanhoe
Sir Walter Scott

The ugliest and most brutal villain in the novel, a Norman knight allied to **Prince John**. He runs the stronghold of Torquilstone, where **Maurice de Bracy** brings his Saxon prisoners. Front-de-Boeuf threatens **Isaac of York** with torture unless the Jew coughs up 1,000 silver pieces. Front-de-Boeuf is killed in the fight for Torquilstone.

Frony

The Sound and the Fury
William Faulkner

Daughter of **Dilsey**. Frony is **Luster**'s mother and works in the Compsons' kitchen.

Douglas Froude

On the Beach
Nevil Shute

A former lieutenant general in the Australian navy. The elderly Douglas plans to spend the last few months of his life drinking all the vintage port left in the wine cellars of the Pastoral Club.

Wen Fu

The Kitchen God's Wife
Amy Tan

Winnie's first husband. He is self-centered, arrogant, ignorant, and ultimately abusive and cruel.

Otto Fuchs

My Ántonia
Willa Cather

One of the Burdens' hired hands. Otto, an Austrian immigrant, looks like a cowboy to **Jim Burden**. Otto seeks his fortune in the West after the Burdens move to Black Hawk.

Cornelius Fudge

The Harry Potter Series: Books 2–4
J. K. Rowling

The rather eccentrically dressed Minister of Magic, who is very kind to **Harry Potter** but is ultimately a stubborn and cowardly man who refuses to acknowledge **Voldemort**'s return.

Dr. Masakazu Fujii

Hiroshima
John Hersey

A physician whose clinic topples into the water when the bomb strikes. He, like other doctors in Hiroshima, is too badly injured to help anybody else. Though apparently unaffected by radiation, he falls victim to a sudden, mysterious illness years later.

Shigeyuki Fujii

Hiroshima
John Hersey

One of **Dr. Masakazu Fujii**'s sons. Shigeyuki finds Dr. Fujii poisoned by gas leaking out of his heater in 1963.

Mr. Fukai

Hiroshima
John Hersey

The secretary of the diocese at the Jesuit mission. **Father Wilhelm Kleinsorge** carries Mr. Fukai out of the mission on his back, but Mr. Fukai escapes and returns to throw himself into the flames.

Samson Fuller

The Bluest Eye
Toni Morrison

Cholly Breedlove's father. He abandoned Cholly's mother when she became pregnant. He lives in Macon, Georgia, and is short, balding, and mean.

Michael Furey

Dubliners
James Joyce

A young boy who died at seventeen. Before **Gretta Conroy** left him to attend a convent school, Michael Furey snuck out to see her on a rainy night. The rain exacerbated his illness, and he died a week later.

The Furies

The Libation Bearers
Aeschylus

Three horrible sisters—Tisiphone, Megaera, and Alecto—who torment evildoers and punish them for their sins. They inflict horrible diseases and torment upon those who thwart their laws. **Apollo** warned **Orestes** that the Furies would pursue him if he failed to avenge **Agamemnon**'s death. Although Orestes obeys and carries out their commands, the Furies nevertheless harass him. The Furies also appear as figures in Greek mythology.

The Furies

The Flies
Jean-Paul Sartre

Unlike the Furies of Greek myth who punished crimes against family, Sartre's Furies are the goddesses of repentance. Until **Orestes** and **Electra** commit their murder, the Furies manifest themselves as flies. They are everywhere in the city, biting its inhabitants to punish them for their sins. The **Argives** welcome the flies and demand to be punished for their crimes. In speaking with Electra, the Furies confound love with hatred: they hate sinners and punish them, but they do so out of love in order to help the sinners atone for their crimes.

Mr. Fury

Something Wicked This Way Comes
Ray Bradbury

The first casualty of **Mr. Dark**'s carnival. In the book's opening scene, Mr. Fury warns **William Halloway** and **James Nightshade** of the storm that is coming. He cannot resist the beauty of the ice sculpture in the store, and he is turned into the Dwarf, a constant reminder of the evil of the carnival and the horrific damage inflicted upon its victims.

Tessie Fuso

The Assistant
Bernard Malamud

A poor Italian immigrant who rents the upstairs apartment from **Morris Bober** with her husband **Nick Fuso**.

Fyodor Petrovich

The Death of Ivan Ilych
Leo Tolstoy

Lisa Ivanovich's fiancé. Fyodor is a typical member of his society.

Victor Fyodorov

Bel Canto
Ann Patchett

A high-ranking Soviet official. Fyodorov declares his love for **Coss** not because he hopes she will return it, but because expressing his love for her makes him feel better.

DEBONAIR DETECTIVES

MEET THE BANE OF THE CRIMINAL ELEMENT AND THE PROTECTORS OF THE INNOCENT. THERE'S NO CASE THESE GUYS CAN'T CRACK.

Sergeant Cuff	❶	*The Moonstone*
Alvin Dewey	❷	*In Cold Blood*
C. Auguste Dupin	❸	*"The Murders in the Rue Morgue"*
Bezu Fache	❹	*The Da Vinci Code*
Sherlock Holmes	❺	*The Hound of the Baskervilles*
Phillip Marlowe	❻	*The Big Sleep*
Hercule Poriot	❼	*Murder on the Orient Express*

Countess G—

The Count of Monte Cristo
Alexandre Dumas

A beautiful Italian aristocrat. She is sitting with **Franz d'Epinay** and **Albert de Morcerf** when she spies **the Count of Monte Cristo** at the opera, accompanied by **Haydée**. She is terrified by the mysterious and deathly pale Monte Cristo, whom she is certain is a vampire.

G. H.

Native Son
Richard Wright

One of **Bigger Thomas**'s group of friends, who often plan and execute robberies together. G. H., **Gus**, and **Jack** hatch a tentative plan to rob a white shopkeeper, **Mr. Blum**, but they are afraid of the consequences if they should be caught robbing a white man.

Gabelle

A Tale of Two Cities
Charles Dickens

The man charged with keeping up the Evrémonde estate after the **Marquis Evrémonde**'s death. Gabelle is imprisoned by the revolutionaries.

Gabilan

The Red Pony
John Steinbeck

A young colt and the red pony of the novella's title. Gabilan belongs to **Jody Tiflin** and is Jody's responsibility. Sometimes fierce, he is difficult to break and to train to wear a halter and saddle. Gabilan catches a bad cold in the rain, and, despite the ranch-hand **Billy Buck**'s desperate measures, escapes one night and dies.

Hedda Gabler

Hedda Gabler
Henrik Ibsen

Daughter of the famous General Gabler and **Jørgen Tesman**'s wife. Intelligent, bored, and unpredictable, Hedda is not afraid to manipulate the people around her. Used to a life of daring and luxury, she is depressed by her more financially and spiritually modest lifestyle with Tesman.

Gabriel

Paradise Lost
John Milton

One of the archangels of Heaven who acts as a guard at the Garden of Eden. Gabriel battles **Satan** after his angels find Satan whispering to **Eve** in the Garden.

Gabriel

Moby-Dick
Herman Melville

A sailor aboard the *Jeroboam*, which is encountered at sea by the *Pequod*. Part of a Shaker sect, Gabriel has prophesied that **Moby Dick** is the incarnation of the Shaker god and that any attempts to harm him will result in disaster. His prophecies have been borne out by the death of the *Jeroboam*'s mate in a whale hunt and the plague that rages aboard the ship.

Gabriel

Go Tell It on the Mountain
James Baldwin

A hard, religious man. Despite his pious mother's prayers and beatings, Gabriel was wild and sinful—until he was born again at the age of 21 and became a preacher. He married **Deborah**, had an adulterous affair with **Esther**, and endured the early death of his unacknowledged son, **Royal**, from a distance. His son by **Elizabeth**, **Roy**, is his new hope. **John Grimes**, his stepson, must bear the brunt of Gabriel's sublimated wrath and guilt.

Gabriel

Pigs in Heaven
Barbara Kingsolver

Annawake Fourkiller's twin brother, who was separated from their family and the Cherokee Nation when they were ten. He represents the fate of Cherokee children who leave or are taken from the tribe. Confused and frustrated by his ethnic identity, he fell into a life of crime and sadness.

Gabriel

The Giver
Lois Lowry

The newchild that **Jonas**'s family cares for at night. **Jonas's father** works as a Nurturer, and bends the rules a bit by peeking at the child's name, with the hope that, by calling him a name instead of the assigned number, he will stimulate the child's growth. If the child does not have a certain weight by a certain time, or if he can't sleep through the night, he will be "released," or killed. He and Jonas become very close, and when Jonas finds out that Gabriel is to be released, Jonas takes the baby along with him on his escape from the community.

Gad

The Red Tent
Anita Diamant

Son of **Jacob** by **Zilpah** and **Asher**'s twin. The bearing of Asher and Gad leaves Zilpah half-dead.

Flossie Gaddis

A Tree Grows in Brooklyn
Betty Smith

The girl who lives downstairs from the Nolans in their house on Grand Street, Flossie is a teenager when **Francie** is a young girl. She is crazy about boys and keeps a whole closet filled with costumes for Saturday-night extravaganzas. Her favorite boy is **Frank**, whom she ends up marrying. **Henny** is her younger brother, who dies of consumption.

Gadshill

Henry IV, Part I
William Shakespeare

A highwayman friend of **Sir John Falstaff**'s. He sets up a robbery with Falstaff, **Bardolph**, and **Peto** to steal money from some travelers. The joke is on them, however, when **Prince Harry** and **Edward Poins** steal the money from them directly after.

Gaea

Greek Mythology
Unknown

The first being to emerge in the universe, a fertile Earth born from the forces of Love, Light, and Day. She gives birth to **Ouranos**, who then becomes her husband.

General Gage

Johnny Tremain
Esther Forbes

The British general placed in charge of the Boston troops once **Governor Hutchinson** is recalled to London.

Miss Gage

A Farewell to Arms
Ernest Hemingway

An American nurse who helps **Frederic Henry** through his recovery at the American hospital in Milan. Easygoing and accepting, Miss Gage becomes a friend to Henry, someone with whom he can share a drink and gossip.

Slim Gaillard

On the Road
Jack Kerouac

A San Francisco friend of **Dean Moriarty**'s. Slim frequents jazz joints and adds the suffix "orooni" to almost everything he says.

Galadriel

The Fellowship of the Ring and *The Return of the King*
J. R. R. Tolkien

The Lady of Lothlórien and perhaps the wisest of the **Elves**. In *The Fellowship of the Ring*, the Fellowship minus **Gandalf** comes to Lothlórien after their trials in the depths of Moria. Galadriel bears one of the Elven Rings of Power, which keeps the magic of Lothlórien alive, and she uses the Ring to read **Sauron**'s mind. Like **Elrond Halfelven**, she sometimes appears as less a character than an embodiment of physical, mental, and spiritual perfection. She has **Frodo Baggins** and **Samwise Gamgee** look into the Mirror of Galadriel, which shows them images of the future. Frodo sees the Great Eye of Sauron as well as images of the Shire in trouble. Galadriel also passes her test of being tempted by the One Ring that Frodo bears, not taking it for her own powerful use. She then gives members of the Fellowship gifts. In *The Return of the King*, Galadriel and her husband, **Celeborn**, arrive at Minas Tirith after Sauron's defeat to witness the marriage of Aragorn and **Arwen Evenstar**. Later, Galadriel and all the Elves, along with **Bilbo Baggins**, Frodo, and Gandalf, leave Middle Earth, for the time of the Elves is over. They go west across the Great Sea to the Grey Havens.

Galahad

The Once and Future King
T. H. White

Lancelot and **Elaine**'s son. Galahad is morally perfect, invincible, and the only knight holy enough to find the Holy Grail. Galahad is disliked by all but a few of **King Arthur**'s other knights. King Arthur also loves Galahad.

Mr. Galanter

The Chosen
Chaim Potok

The gym instructor at **Reuven Malter**'s yeshiva.

Iosif Gimazetdinovich Galiullin

Dr. Zhivago
Boris Pasternak

Serves in the army during World War I with **Larissa Fyodorovna Guishar (later Antipova)**'s husband, **Pavel Pavlovich Antipov**. He is wounded and sent to the same hospital room as **Yury Andreyevich Zhivago**, where they are both tended by Lara. Iosif is the son of a railway worker and janitor who dies in combat during the war. He is a Muslim and later joins the White Army.

Gallaher

Dubliners
James Joyce

Little Chandler's old friend who visits Dublin in "A Little Cloud." For Little Chandler, Gallaher represents all that is enticing and desirable: success in England, a writing career, foreign travel, and ease with women.

Jane Gallagher

The Catcher in the Rye
J. D. Salinger

A girl with whom **Holden Caulfield** spent a lot of time one summer when their families stayed in neighboring summer houses in Maine. Jane Gallagher never actually appears in *The Catcher in the Rye*, but she is extremely important to Holden, because she is one of the few girls whom he both respects and finds attractive.

John Galt

Atlas Shrugged
Ayn Rand

The man around whom the action of *Atlas Shrugged* revolves. A student of **Hugh Akston**, John Galt organizes and leads the strike of the mind, in which the leading industrialists and thinkers in the United States disappear so that they do not have to cooperate with the new government "looters" who are destroying society and economy by nationalizing industry and promoting a corrupt system based on "need." Galt is simultaneously the destroyer of all industry and economy, the inventor of the revolutionary motor that runs on static electricity, **Eddie Willers**'s mysterious friend, and **Dagny Taggart**'s greatest love. Brilliant and perceptive, he is the physical and intellectual representation of man's ideal as put forth by Ayn Rand. Galt has also created a philosophy of reason and become a statesman capable of leading the nation's most talented leaders, who have abandoned their industries, destroyed their public earnings, and gone into hiding in Galt's secret valley. Galt represents the main theme of the novel and of Rand's philosophy: the idea that the mind is the only means by which man can achieve prosperity. The mind is the motive power that drives civilization, just as the motor Galt develops can drive the industry of the future that will rebuild society after the looters fail in their selfish task.

Mr. Gamfield

Oliver Twist
Charles Dickens

A brutal chimney sweep. **Oliver Twist** narrowly escapes becoming Mr. Gamfield's apprentice.

Ham Gamgee

The Fellowship of the Ring
J. R. R. Tolkien

The father of **Samwise Gamgee**, or Sam. He lives next door to Bag End, where **Frodo Baggins** and **Bilbo Baggins** live.

Samwise Gamgee

The Lord of the Rings trilogy
J. R. R. Tolkien

The gardener at Bag End and the son of **Ham Gamgee**. Sam becomes **Frodo Baggins**'s indomitable servant throughout his Quest to destroy **Sauron**'s One Ring. Although Sam is not extraordinarily intelligent, he is deeply loyal to Frodo. Fond of his beer and his bread, Sam is much more the typical Hobbit than Frodo, though he too displays a great curiosity about the world beyond the Shire. Sam's speech consistently has a modest, awestruck tone. He serves as a foil for Frodo's melancholy and fatalism. When Frodo becomes increasingly preoccupied with the great burden of the One Ring, he comes to rely more and more on Sam for help. Indeed, throughout even the lowest and most hopeless points of the journey, Sam remains relentlessly pragmatic and optimistic. In *The Fellowship of the Ring*, it becomes clear that Sam will stay with Frodo as he notices that he is going further than ever before from his hometown. Over the course of *The Two Towers*, Sam changes more than any other character. Initially, he is subservient and not quite capable of independent judgment. By the end of *The Two Towers*, when his master lies speechless and paralyzed, Sam is forced to affirm his own strength and assume the role of Ring-bearer himself. In being forced to make his own decisions, he becomes his own master, thereby becoming a symbol of the potential for leadership and heroism that may lie dormant in the most unsuspecting people. In *The Return of the King*, Sam emerges as a true hero, performing the physical and sacrificial deeds expected of a great hero while maintaining his humble and lighthearted nature.

David Gamut

The Last of the Mohicans
James Fenimore Cooper

A young American Calvinist proselytizing through song on the frontier. David Gamut is a psalmodist, a man who worships by singing Old Testament psalms. **Hawkeye** initially makes fun of Gamut for being so absurdly unsuited for the wilderness, but Gamut matures into a helpful ally. His singing scares away many Native American enemies and helps get Gamut released from capture by Native Americans because he is thought to be insane.

Gandalf the Grey

The Hobbit and *The Lord of the Rings trilogy*
J. R. R. Tolkien

A wise old wizard, and one of the five Great Wizards. He resided in Middle-earth at least since the early times when the **Elves** settled there. Something both inspiring and dangerous defines Gandalf's character—he is an unshakable bulwark against evil, and yet he seems to have an enlightened, almost godlike knowledge of every person's place in the world. In the *Fellowship of the Ring*, Gandalf helps to form the Fellowship and guides them as they travel toward Mordor to destroy the One Ring. In *The Two Towers*, Gandalf the Grey is seemingly killed in the chasm by the **Balrog**, but he returns from beyond the grave as Gandalf the White, or the White Rider. This new, improved, enormously powerful wizard aids the Hobbits in their quest to destroy the One Ring. In *The Return of the King*, the great Wizard leads the forces of the West. Like Frodo, Gandalf—whom we later learn is a bearer of one of the three lesser Rings of Power—distinguishes himself from the evil **Sauron** in that he does not perceive his life or destiny to be fixed.

Sam Gandy

Black Like Me
John Howard Griffin

The dean of Dillard College, which **John Howard Griffin** visits during his stay with **P.D. East**.

Ganelon

Song of Roland
Unknown

A well-respected Frankish baron and **Roland**'s stepfather. He resents his stepson's boastfulness, popularity among the Franks, and success on the battlefield. When Roland nominates him as messenger to the Saracens, Ganelon is so deeply offended that he vows vengeance. Ganelon plots with the pagan **Blancandrin** an ambush of the Franks at Roncesvals. Though the plot succeeds and Roland dies, Ganelon's crimes are exposed and he goes to trial. His comrade **Pinabel** is defeated in a trial by combat, showing that Ganelon is a traitor in the eyes of God. As punishment, Ganelon is torn limb from limb by four fiery horses.

Esteban García

The House of the Spirits
Isabel Allende

Pancha and **Esteban Trueba**'s grandson, the son of their illegitimate child. Esteban Garcia despises Esteban Trueba for not allowing him to be acknowledged as his legitimate grandson. He eventually rises to become the leader of the Military Coup of **the Candidate**'s government, in the process venting much of his anger on Alba by torturing her and raping her. He kills and tortures many innocent people under his fascist regime.

Pedro García

The House of the Spirits
Isabel Allende

Father of **Pedro Segundo Garcia**. Pedro Garcia is one of the oldest residents of Tres Marias, the plantation that **Esteban Trueba** owns.

Pedro Segundo García

The House of the Spirits
Isabel Allende

Pedro Garcia's son, **Pedro Tercero Garcia**'s father. Pedro Segundo Garcia is the foreman and caretaker of Tres Marias. Although he works closely with **Esteban Trueba** for much of his life, he never becomes friends with Esteban Trueba, who exploits all the people of Tres Marias. However, Pedro Segundo does develop a close friendship with **Clara**. He leaves Tres Marias after Esteban Trueba discovers that Pedro Tercero is **Blanca**'s lover.

Pedro Tercero García

The House of the Spirits
Isabel Allende

Pedro Segundo Garcia's son. As a young boy, Pedro Tercero Garcia falls deeply in love with **Blanca**. As he reaches adolescence, Pedro Tercero becomes a revolutionary and a songwriter. He is greatly respected by the peasants and his music is very popular with revolutionary students. Pedro Tercero's revolutionary activities and his affair with Blanca lead to his expulsion from Tres Marias along with his father, but Pedro Tercero continues to meet Blanca in secret. He eventually gets Blanca pregnant with **Alba**. Because of this, she must marry **Jean de Satigny**. When the Socialists come to power, Pedro Tercero joins the government under **the Candidate**. At Blanca's request, he saves **Esteban Trueba**'s life. After the military coup led by

Esteban Garcia, Esteban Trueba saves Pedro Tercero's life and helps Pedro Tercero to escape to Canada with Blanca.

No Exit
Jean-Paul Sartre

Garcin

A journalist from Rio and the first to arrive in the room. He was shot by a firing squad for attempting to desert during a war. When **Estelle** and **Inez** arrive, he recognizes that the three of them have been grouped together to make each other miserable. He continually tries to make peace with himself and the people he hurt during his lifetime. He is momentarily attracted to Estelle, but chooses to concentrate all his energy on Inez. When given a chance to leave the room, he chooses to stay, hoping to convince Inez that he is not a coward.

Richard II
William Shakespeare

Gardener

A gardener who works at **King Richard II**'s court. **Queen Isabella** overhears him and his assistant talking about the capture and probable ouster of Richard.

Pale Fire
Vladimir Nabokov

Gardener

Charles Kinbote's gardener, who heroically saves Kinbote from **Gradus**, a hired assassin from Zembla. Kinbote promises to fund the young black gardener's education.

My Ántonia
Willa Cather

Mrs. Gardener

The proprietress of the Boys' Home in Black Hawk.

Henry VIII
William Shakespeare

Gardiner

Cardinal Wolsey's secretary. Wolsey assigns Gardiner to **King Henry VIII** with the understanding that Gardiner will remain loyal to Wolsey. When Wolsey falls from grace, Gardiner receives a promotion to **Bishop of Wincester** and becomes a member of the Council. Out of personal dislike for **Cranmer, Archbishop of Canterbury** and lingering loyalty to Wolsey, Gardiner tries to plot Cranmer's demise, spreading rumors about him and bringing a case against him to the Council. Henry hears of these rumors, secretly watches the trial, and intervenes, chastising the lords for in-fighting. Henry forces Gardiner and Cranmer to bury the hatchet and embrace as friends.

Little Women
Louisa May Alcott

Sallie Gardiner

Meg March's rich friend. Sallie represents the good life to Meg, and she often covets Sallie's possessions.

George Gardner

In Our Time
Ernest Hemingway

A jockey friend of **Joe**'s father in "My Old Man."

William Gardner

Narrative of the Life of Frederick Douglass
Frederick Douglass

A Baltimore shipbuilder. **Hugh Auld** sends **Frederick Douglass** to Gardner to learn the trade of caulking. Gardner's shipyard is disorderly with racial tension between free-black carpenters and white carpenters.

Gareth

The Once and Future King
T. H. White

Morgause's sweetest and most sensitive son. Unlike most of his brothers, Gareth loves **King Arthur** and **Lancelot**. When his brothers **Agravaine**, **Gawaine**, and **Gaheris** plot to get **Guenever** and Lancelot executed for having an affair, Gareth tries to warn them beforehand, to Arthur's delight. Gareth is accidentally killed by Lancelot in the fight that ensues near the bedroom.

Joe Gargery

Great Expectations
Charles Dickens

Pip's brother-in-law. Joe stays with **Mrs. Joe**, his overbearing, abusive wife, solely out of love for Pip. Though he is uneducated and unrefined, his quiet goodness makes him one of the few completely sympathetic characters in the story.

Sir Thomas Gargrave

Henry VI, Part I
William Shakespeare

An English soldier who dies at the siege of Orléans right after **Lord Talbot** has been ransomed.

Miss Garnder

A Tree Grows in Brooklyn
Betty Smith

Mary Frances Nolan's eighth grade English teacher. Self-righteous in her convictions, Miss Garnder believes that writing should only be about "beauty," not ugly things like poverty and drunkenness. She insults Francie about her background, gives her poor marks on the compositions she wrote after **Johnny**'s death, and does not allow Francie to write the graduation play.

Mr. and Mrs. Garner

Beloved
Toni Morrison

The relatively harmless owners of Sweet Home. The events at Sweet Home reveal that the idea of benevolent slavery is a contradiction in terms. Mr. Garner's paternalism and condescension are simply watered-down versions of the vicious racism of **schoolteacher**, the subsequent owner of Sweet Home. The Garners are not violent, but they savage the slaves' spirits by treating them like subhuman beings.

Garrett

The Martian Chronicles
Ray Bradbury

An investigator for Moral Climates, a Martian censorship agency. He sends a robot replica of himself to investigate the house, Usher II, which **William Stendahl** and **Pikes** have built. Later, he visits the house in person, and Stendahl murders him by walling him up in the house's catacombs.

William Lloyd Garrison

Narrative of the Life of Frederick Douglass
Frederick Douglass

Founder of the American Anti-Slavery Society. Garrison meets **Frederick Douglass** when Douglass is persuaded to tell his history at an abolitionist convention in Nantucket in 1841. Immediately impressed with Douglass's poise and with the power of his story, Garrison hires him for the abolitionist cause.

Caleb Garth

Middlemarch
George Eliot

A poor businessman who is **Susan Garth**'s husband and **Mary Garth**'s father. He earns his living managing large estates. He cosigns a debt for **Fred Vincy**. When he is unable to pay, Garth's family suffers. He receives new business, overcomes the loss, and hires Fred Vincy to work for him. He refuses to manage Stone Court for **Nicholas Bulstrode** after **John Raffles** reveals Bulstrode's dark past.

Mary Garth

Middlemarch
George Eliot

The daughter of **Caleb Garth** and **Susan Garth**. She loves **Fred Vincy**, but she refuses to marry him if he becomes a clergyman and fails to find a steady occupation.

Susan Garth

Middlemarch
George Eliot

Caleb Garth's wife and **Mary Garth**'s mother. She is a former schoolteacher.

Gaston

One Hundred Years of Solitude
Gabriel García Márquez

The Belgian husband of **Amaranta Úrsula**, Gaston is loving and cultured. He travels to Belgium to start an airmail company, and when he hears of the relationship between his wife and **Aureliano (II)**, he never returns.

Ned Gates

Miss Lonelyhearts
Nathanael West

An irritable friend of **Miss Lonelyhearts**'s who takes delight in verbally torturing the old man.

Jay Gatsby

The Great Gatsby
F. Scott Fitzgerald

A dashing, charismatic, fabulously wealthy young man who lives in a mansion in West Egg, Long Island. At the start of the novel, Gatsby is a figure shrouded in mystery, an aloof socialite who throws lavish Saturday-night parties for hundreds of guests. **Nick Carraway**, the novel's narrator and Gatsby's next-door neighbor, learns that Gatsby moved to West Egg in an attempt to win back his lost love, **Daisy Buchanan**, and that the weekly parties are merely an attempt to impress Daisy. Gatsby uses Nick to arrange a meeting with Daisy, and the two rekindle their affair. Eventually, Gatsby's dreams and carefully constructed identity come crashing down: Daisy rejects him in favor of her husband, **Tom**, and it emerges that Gatsby grew up impoverished in the Midwest and built his fortune by participating in organized crime. At the end of the novel, Gatsby is killed by the enraged **George Wilson**, who mistakenly believes that Gatsby ran down his wife, **Myrtle**, in a hit-and-run accident—when the driver of the car was in fact Daisy, who fails to take responsibility.

Makalu Gau

Into Thin Air
Jon Krakauer

The leader of the Taiwanese climbing group. During the storm at the summit, Gau is abandoned by his Sherpas. Members of **Rob Hall**'s and **Scott Fischer**'s teams save Gau.

John of Gaunt, Duke of Lancaster

Richard II
William Shakespeare

Uncle to **King Richard II**, father to Henry Bolingbroke (later **Henry IV**), brother to **Edmund of Langley, Duke of York** and the late **Thomas of Woodstock, Duke of Gloucester**. At the beginning of the play, Gaunt admits to the **Duchess of Gloucester** what is common knowledge—that Richard is to blame for her husband's death. On his deathbed following his son's exile, he summons Richard, condemning him for mismanaging the country, banishing his son, and being implicit in the death of Gloucester. Gaunt's deathbed curse on Richard becomes the foundation for cross-dynastic strife—in the short term, Bolingbroke almost immediately usurps the crown, but the shadow of shame hangs over the following Henry plays.

Gautier

Song of Roland
Unknown

One of the twelve barons **Roland** picks for his rear guard. Gautier is to lead a thousand Franks in scouting around the hilltops and ravines around the pass. He is the third to last to perish at Roncesvals, just before **Turpin** and Roland.

Madame Gautier

The Autobiography of Miss Jane Pittman
Ernest J. Gaines

A Creole "hoodoo" woman whom **Miss Jane Pittman** consults. She is a comedic figure because her affectations suggest that she is just a woman dressed up and acting like a sorceress for financial gain.

Gavroche

Les Misérables
Victor Hugo

M. Thénardier and **Mme. Thénardier**'s oldest son. He is a happy-go-lucky child who enjoys the small pleasures of life and demonstrates unusual generosity toward those even less fortunate than he is. He is kicked out of the house at an early age and becomes a Parisian street urchin. Fierce and brave, Gavroche plays a decisive role in the barricade even though he does not have a gun.

Sir Gawain

Sir Gawain and the Green Knight
Unknown

The story's protagonist. Sir Gawain is **King Arthur**'s nephew and one of his most loyal knights. Although he modestly disclaims it, Gawain has the reputation of being a great knight and courtly lover. He prides himself on his strict observance of the five points of chivalry: Gawain is a pinnacle of humility, piety, integrity, loyalty, and honesty. Gawain takes up the **Green Knight**'s challenge out of pride and a sense of adventure, but leaves the Green Chapel penitent and changed.

Gawaine

The Once and Future King
T. H. White

Morgause's oldest and strongest son, the brother of **Gaheris**, **Agravaine**, and **Gareth**. Gawaine, prone to murderous rages, is in many ways an emblem of everything that is wrong with knighthood. Despite Gawaine's roughness, however, he is a decent man. He takes part in the plot to get **Lancelot** and **Guenever** caught in the act of their affair so that they will be executed.

Gay

Cannery Row
John Steinbeck

A man who lives with **Mack**'s boys because his wife beats him. He is a gifted mechanic who can make seemingly any vehicle run, and he is often at the local bar or in jail as a result of brawls with his wife.

Leonid Gayev

The Cherry Orchard
Anton Chekhov

Ranevsky's older brother. Gayev is a kind and concerned uncle and brother, but he behaves very differently around people beneath his social class. He constantly pops sweets in his mouth, insults people with whom he disagrees (such as the middle-class businessman **Lopakhin**), and receives reminders to put on his jacket from the manservant **Firs**.

Arthur Gayle

This Boy's Life
Tobias Wolff

The overweight, outcast boy who spends most of his time with his dog, Pepper. Arthur Gayle eventually becomes **Jack Wolff**'s best friend. After Jack calls Arthur a sissy, they get into a fistfight. After the fight, they become friends. At one point, Arthur and Jack kiss in an intimate moment. Ultimately, because of Jack's insensitivity, and the boys' drifting from each other, their friendship does not last.

Lieutenant Gearhart

Fallen Angels
Walter Dean Myers

The inexperienced leader of **Richie Perry**'s platoon after **Lieutenant Carroll**'s death.

Arthur Gwynn Geiger

The Big Sleep
Raymond Chandler

A pornographer who runs an illegal smut rental shop under the guise of a rare bookstore. Geiger, who is homosexual (or perhaps bisexual), blackmails **General Sternwood** and is murdered in the act of attempting to further his blackmail by taking nude pictures of **Carmen Sternwood**.

Gelatinous Giant

The Phantom Tollbooth
Norton Juster

A giant so huge that **Milo** first mistakes him for a mountain. He is the epitome of spinelessness. He hides in the Mountains of Ignorance and tries to look exactly like everything around him.

Countess Gemini

The Portrait of a Lady
Henry James

Gilbert Osmond's vapid sister, who covers up her own marital infidelities by gossiping constantly about the affairs of other married women. The Countess seems to have a good heart, however, opposing **Madame Merle**'s scheme to marry Osmond and **Isabel** and eventually revealing to Isabel Merle's real relationship to Osmond and **Pansy Osmond**'s parentage.

Gender Traitors

The Handmaid's Tale
Margaret Atwood

Homosexuals.

General manager

Heart of Darkness
Joseph Conrad

The chief agent of the Company in its African territory, who runs the Central Station. He is average in appearance and unremarkable in abilities, but he possesses a strange capacity to produce uneasiness in those around him, keeping everyone sufficiently unsettled for him to exert his control over them.

General of the Spanish Army

The Spanish Tragedy
Thomas Kyd

The character who describes the battle between Spain and Portugal in Act I. His account of **Andrea**'s death and description of the Spanish casualties as minimal provide an ironic contrast to the **Ghost of Andrea**'s lamenting of his death in battle.

Jurassic Park
Michael Crichton

Donald Gennaro

A lawyer from the firm of Cowain, Swain and Ross, which represents InGen. Gennaro is nervous about the progress of Jurassic Park and has heard rumors of animals getting off the island. He forces **John Hammond** to bring **Dr. Alan Grant**, **Dr. Ellie Sattler**, and **Dr. Ian Malcolm** in to evaluate the park.

Moll Flanders
Daniel Defoe

Gentleman

A well-to-do man who befriends **Moll** and eventually makes her his mistress. He keeps Moll for six years before an illness and religious experience prompt him to break off the affair.

The Hairy Ape
Eugene O'Neill

Gentleman

A member of the upper class. He calls the police because **Yank** causes him to miss a bus.

The Little Prince
Antoine de Saint-Exupéry

The Geographer

The sixth and final character that **the Little Prince** encounters before he lands on Earth. Although the geographer is apparently well-read, he refuses to learn about his own planet, saying it is a job for explorers. He recommends that the Little Prince visit Earth, and his comments on the ephemeral nature of flowers reveal to the prince that his own flower, **the Rose**, will not last forever.

In Our Time
Ernest Hemingway

George

The student who goes skiing with a friend in "Cross-Country Snow."

Of Mice and Men
John Steinbeck

George

A small, wiry, quick-witted man who travels with and cares for the lumbering, mildly retarded **Lennie**. Although George frequently complains that his life would be much better if he did not have to care for Lennie, it is clear that their devotion and dependence are mutual. George is motivated by his desire to protect Lennie and, ultimately, to deliver them to the future they have imagined for themselves—an idyllic farm on which they raise rabbits. Their shared dream is shattered when Lennie inadvertently kills **Curley's wife** and George is forced to kill Lennie in order to spare him the vengeance of **Curley**'s lynch mob.

Who's Afraid of Virginia Woolf?
Edward Albee

George

A member of the history department at New Carthage University and husband to **Martha**. While his marriage was once a loving relationship, it is now defined by sarcasm and acrimony. George and Martha engage in public and private humiliation and cruelty, even drawing their guests, **Nick** and **Honey**, into their fights.

George performs the figurative exorcism of the myth of their son and begins the resurrection of his and his wife's love.

Lloyd George

The Remains of the Day
Kazuo Ishiguro

The prime minister of Britain during the end of World War I and the early postwar period. George attended a conference in Switzerland to review the Treaty of Versailles in 1923, prompting **Lord Darlington** to invite dignitaries to Darlington Hall.

Uncle George

In Our Time
Ernest Hemingway

Nick Adams's uncle. He helps deliver the squaw's baby in "Indian Camp."

Georgette

The Sun Also Rises
Ernest Hemingway

A beautiful but somewhat thick-witted prostitute. The narrator, **Jake Barnes**, picks Georgette up at a café in Paris and takes her to dinner but quickly grows bored of her superficial conversation, abandoning her in a club.

Georgia boy

Cold Mountain
Charles Frazier

A young man who sets out with **Stobrod Thewes** and **Pangle** to found a community of outliers at Shining Rocks. He avoids getting shot by **Teague** by hiding in a thicket, and he later marries **Ruby Thewes**.

Georgie

A Clockwork Orange
Anthony Burgess

The most ambitious member of **Alex**'s gang. He parlays **Dim**'s anger about Alex's abuse into a mutiny leading to Alex's arrest. A year after Alex's arrest, Georgie is killed during a theft.

Georgina

Girl, Interrupted
Susanna Kaysen

Susanna Kaysen's roommate at McLean Hospital. Kind and fragile, Georgina suffers from depression. She has a romantic relationship with **Wade**, a violent and unpredictable patient on another ward, and aspires to a kind of domestic normality in the hospital.

Geraldine

The Bluest Eye
Toni Morrison

A middle-class black woman. Though she keeps house flawlessly and diligently cares for the physical appearances of herself and her family (including her husband, Louis, and her son, **Junior**), she is essentially cold. She feels real affection only for her cat.

Gerasim

The Death of Ivan Ilych
Leo Tolstoy

Ivan Ilych Golovin's sick nurse and the butler's assistant. Gerasim serves as a foil to Ivan: healthy, vigorous, direct, he is everything that Ivan is not.

Comte de Gercourt

Dangerous Liaisons
Pierre-Ambroise-François Choderlos de Laclos

The man to whom **Madame Volanges** has promised to marry **Cécile Volanges**. He is with the army in Corsica during the events of the novel. After his army service, he further delays the wedding by extending his stay in Italy to vacation. Gercourt was once **the Marquise de Merteuil**'s lover, but left her for **the Intendante**. The Intendante used to be **Vicomte de Valmont**'s lover. Merteuil believes that she and Valmont should get revenge on their former lovers through Valmont's seduction of Cécile.

Gerry

Cloud Nine
Caryl Churchill

A promiscuous homosexual, Gerry has trouble staying in any one place for too long. His relationships fail because of his distaste for commitment. He abandons **Edward** only to return to his lover at the end of the play.

Phoebe Gersbach

Herzog
Saul Bellow

Valentine Gersbach's devoted wife. Phoebe fails to see the truth about her husband's affair with **Madeleine**.

Valentine Gersbach

Herzog
Saul Bellow

Phoebe Gersbach's husband and **Moses Herzog**'s best friend. The Gersbachs are Moses and **Madeleine**'s only neighbors in the country. Valentine, who has one wooden leg, begins an affair with Madeleine that continues after she and Moses divorce.

Rav Gershenson

The Chosen
Chaim Potok

An orthodox rabbi and **Danny Saunders** and **Reuven Malter**'s teacher in the highest-level Talmud class at the Hirsch Seminary and College. He thinks that **David Malter** is a great scholar.

Dr. Max Gerson

Death Be Not Proud
John Gunther

Administrator of the nursing home where **Johnny** is placed on a salt-free, fat-free diet and given daily enemas. He is an impressive and humane man. **John Gunther**'s and **Frances**'s willingness to try controversial techniques demonstrates the lengths to which the family will go to save Johnny's life.

Queen Gertrude

Hamlet
William Shakespeare

Hamlet's mother. After the death of **King Hamlet**, Gertrude marries her brother-in-law **Claudius**, a union that would have been considered incestuous. When Hamlet pleads for Gertrude to separate from Claudius, her love for a comfortable life overrides her love for Hamlet. Hamlet feels that Gertrude has betrayed his father and, by extension, him.

Gertrude's son

Cry, the Beloved Country
Alan Paton

Stephen Kumalo's nephew. He returns with Kumalo to Ndotsheni, where **Absalom's wife** raises him.

Gertrudis

Like Water for Chocolate
Laura Esquivel

The eldest daughter of **Mama Elena**. She escapes from the ranch with a revolutionary soldier drawn by her scent. She works in a brothel at the Mexico-Texas border and returns to the ranch as a general in the revolutionary army. It is eventually revealed that Gertrudis is the offspring of a hidden extramarital affair between Mama Elena and her true love, a mulatto man.

Geryon

Inferno
Dante Alighieri

The massive serpentine monster who flies **Dante** and **Virgil** from the Third Ring of the Seventh Circle down to the Eighth Circle (Canto VIII).

Ghani the landowner

Midnight's Children
Salman Rushdie

Naseem Ghani's father.

Naseem Ghani

Midnight's Children
Salman Rushdie

The daughter of a landlord and the mother of Amina Sinai, or **Mumtaz** Aziz. She is a dramatic and strong-willed character who possesses a lot of power in her relationship with her husband **Aadam Aziz**.

Ghost

Hamlet
William Shakespeare

The spirit of King Hamlet, **Hamlet**'s recently deceased father. King Hamlet was murdered by his brother **Claudius**, and the Ghost demands that Hamlet exact revenge. After informing Hamlet of his duties, the Ghost appears once more to Hamlet in an attempt at spurring him to action.

Ghost of Christmas Past

A Christmas Carol
Charles Dickens

A figure that looks both like a child and an old man. It wears a white tunic decorated with summer flowers and carries a holly branch.

Ghost of Christmas Present

A Christmas Carol
Charles Dickens

A hearty, robust figure that grows older as the day passes. It wears a green garment and a wreath of holly.

Ghost of Christmas Yet to Come

A Christmas Carol
Charles Dickens

A mysterious spirit whose black robe conceals it entirely, except for one hand. It never speaks.

Dr. Frank Gibbs

Our Town
Thornton Wilder

George Gibbs's father and the town doctor. Dr. Gibbs's return home after delivering twins at the start of the play establishes the themes of birth, life, and daily activity.

George Gibbs

Our Town
Thornton Wilder

Dr. Frank Gibbs and **Mrs. Julia Gibbs**'s decent, upstanding son. A high school baseball star, George plans to attend the State Agricultural School after high school. His courtship of and eventual marriage to **Emily Webb** form the focus of the play's narrative.

Mrs. Julia Gibbs

Our Town
Thornton Wilder

George Gibbs's mother. Mrs. Gibbs's never-fulfilled desire to visit Paris suggests how important it is to seize life's opportunities before it is too late.

Rebecca Gibbs

Our Town
Thornton Wilder

George Gibbs's younger sister.

Jan Gies

Anne Frank: Diary of a Young Girl
Anne Frank

Miep Gies's husband. He and Miep, who is a Dutch coworker of **Otto Frank**'s, spend the night at the annex soon after the Franks move there to hide. Jan brings news to those living in the annex about other Jews in hiding.

Miep Gies

Anne Frank: Diary of a Young Girl
Anne Frank

A secretary at **Otto Frank**'s office who helps the Franks hide. She also leads **Albert Dussel** to the annex to hide. Miep is very good to the Franks, the van Daans, and to Mr. Dussel, bringing them supplies, books, and news of other Jews in hiding. After the Franks are arrested, she stows Anne's diary away in a desk drawer and keeps it there, unread, until Otto's return in 1945.

Gilberte

Swann's Way
Marcel Proust

Charles Swann and **Odette**'s daughter. **Marcel** falls in love with Gilberte the moment he first sees her because she has been a taboo subject in his family.

Peter Giles

Utopia
Sir Thomas More

A friend of **Sir Thomas More**'s and an acquaintance of **Raphael Hythloday**'s. Peter Giles is a historical figure, and a friend and intellectual companion of More's.

Gil-galad

The Fellowship of the Ring
J. R. R. Tolkien

An ancient King of the **Elves** who, united with **Elendil**, a Human king of Westernesse, fought in a climactic battle against **Sauron** ages before the events of *The Lord of the Rings*. Gil-galad was killed in the battle in which Sauron lost the One Ring at **Isildur**'s hand.

Gilgamesh

The Epic of Gilgamesh
Unknown

The king of Uruk and the epic's protagonist, the personification of all human virtues. Gilgamesh is strong, handsome, and wise, but a callow and tyrannical ruler. He possesses a potential for greatness that is realized through his friendship with **Enkidu** and his quests for renown and immortality. According to Babylonian mythology, Gilgamesh is posthumously deified and becomes the judge and ruler of the dead.

M. Gillenormand

Les Misérables
Victor Hugo

Marius Pontmercy's ninety-year-old maternal grandfather. Gillenormand prevents Marius from seeing his father, **Georges Pontmercy**, because he fears that Pontmercy will corrupt Marius. A devout monarchist, Gillenormand rejects the French Revolution outright and also rejects Pontmercy's Napoléonic beliefs.

Gillespie

As I Lay Dying
William Faulkner

A farmer who houses **the Bundrens** late in their journey.

The Gillespie boy

As I Lay Dying
William Faulkner

Gillespie's son. He helps **Jewel** save the animals from the burning barn.

Joan Gilling

The Bell Jar
Sylvia Plath

Esther Greenwood's companion in the mental hospital. A large, horsey woman, Joan was a year ahead of Esther in college, and Esther envied her social and athletic success. Joan once dated **Buddy Willard**, Esther's boyfriend. Joan commits suicide by hanging herself in the woods.

Ruby Gillis

Anne of Green Gables
L. M. Montgomery

One of the youngest of the many Gillis girls. Ruby has learned about growing up from her older sisters, and she loves to share her superior knowledge with **Anne Shirley** and their other friends. Ruby inclines toward sentimentality and hysterical fits.

Gimli

The Lord of the Rings Trilogy
J. R. R. Tolkien

The Dwarf son of **Glóin**, who himself was in the company of **Bilbo Baggins** in *The Hobbit*. Gimli bristles when he feels insulted, but he is noble, stalwart, and brave; he is an expert in wielding his axe against **Orcs**. In *The Fellowship of the Ring*, he is chosen at the Council of **Elrond Halfelven** to be a member of the Fellowship, accompanying the Ring-bearer, **Frodo Baggins**. In *The Two Towers*, Gimli follows **Aragorn** and **Legolas** in pursuit of the captured Hobbits, **Meriadoc Brandybuck** and **Peregrin Took**. In *The Return of the King*, the headstrong Gimli dutifully traverses the Paths of the Dead with Aragorn and Legolas. He fights against the force of Orcs in the service of Sauron before the Army of the Dead comes to save the army of Men defending the Kingdom of Gondor.

Gimpy

Flowers for Algernon
Daniel Keyes

A baker at **Mr. Donner**'s Bakery who secretly steals from his boss.

Ginger Nut

Bartleby, the Scrivener
Herman Melville

The Lawyer's errand boy. **Turkey**, **Nippers**, and **Bartleby** often send him to get ginger-nut cakes.

Gino

A Farewell to Arms
Ernest Hemingway

A young Italian whom **Henry** meets at a decimated village in northern Italy. Gino's patriotic belief that his fatherland is sacred and should be protected at all costs contrasts sharply with Henry's more cynical attitude toward war.

Mr. Giovanelli

Daisy Miller
Henry James

Daisy Miller's suitor, a lower-class Italian man. Her relationship with him is responsible for her downfall in society. He brings her to the Colosseum, where she catches the fever that eventually kills her.

The Red Girl

Annie John
Jamaica Kincaid

A local lower-class girl whom **Annie** befriends. The Red Girl's life is as unstructured as Annie's is structured, and Annie envies her freedom.

Brother Giroflée

Candide
Voltaire

A dissatisfied monk. Giroflée pays to sleep with **Paquette**. His spirits do not improve after **Candide** gives him a large sum of money.

Gistan

Jazz
Toni Morrison

A friend of **Joe Trace**'s living in New York City, along with **Stuck**.

Gitano

The Red Pony
John Steinbeck

An old *paisano* who appears on **Carl Tiflin**'s ranch claiming that he was born in a small adobe house that stood on what is now the ranch.

The Giver

The Giver
Lois Lowry

The man known in the community as the Receiver of Memory. The Giver has held the community's collective memory for many years. He has the job of giving **Jonas** all his memories after Jonas is chosen to be the next Receiver. Like someone who has seen and done many things over many years, he is very wise and world-weary, and he is haunted by memories of suffering and pain, but in reality his life has been surprisingly uneventful. Since he carries *all* memories of the past, he feels like a man who has done more in his life than anyone else in the world: he has experienced the positive and negative emotions, desires, triumphs, and failures of millions of men and women. Among the members of the community, the Giver alone is capable of real love, an emotion he experiences with **Rosemary**, the first child who was designated to be the Receiver. When Rosemary is taken from him, the Giver's anger and grief allow him to finally overturn his years of silence and endurance and change the community.

Jack Gladney

White Noise
Don DeLillo

Narrator of the novel and chairman of Hitler Studies at the College-on-the-Hill. Jack lives with his fourth wife, **Babette**, and their four children from previous marriages. His obsessive fear of death, magnified by his exposure to a toxic substance, is the primary lens through which he sees the world. He relies on appearances and illusions to secure an identity and to help him cope with his fear of dying.

Gladys

How the Garcia Girls Lost Their Accents
Julia Alvarez

The family's Dominican maid. She is fired for accepting a toy bank from **Carla** as a present.

Sir William Glansdale

Henry VI, Part I
William Shakespeare

An English soldier who fights at the siege of Orléans.

Bessie Glass

Franny and Zooey
J. D. Salinger

The mother of the Glass clan. Bessie Glass is, with her husband, **Les**, a former Vaudeville star. She encourages the children's intellectual pursuits but is not nearly so gifted herself. Two of her sons, **Seymour** and **Walter**, have died. These events have injected a tragic beauty into Bessie's face and eyes. Unlike her husband, she believes there is something wrong with her daughter, **Franny Glass**, as Franny never stops crying. Bessie believes that her son **Zooey** will never understand beautiful or unusual things.

Buddy Glass

Franny and Zooey
J. D. Salinger

The narrator who claims to have authored the "Zooey" section of the book. At the time of his narration, Buddy is the oldest remaining Glass child, since **Seymour** committed suicide several years prior. Buddy claims to be guilty of possible excess in the religious coaching of **Franny Glass** and **Zooey Glass**.

Franny Glass

Franny and Zooey
J. D. Salinger

The protagonist of the "Franny" section of the book. Franny Glass, a college student in the midst of a breakdown, is the youngest child in the Glass clan. She is an actress and an English major, but she has become disenchanted with college, socially and academically. She is dating **Lane Coutell**. She believes that people are phonies, that her teachers destroy literature instead of creating it, and that everyone acts in the same way.

Zooey Glass

Franny and Zooey
J. D. Salinger

The protagonist of the "Zooey" section of the book. Zooey helps his sister **Franny Glass** through her spiritual breakdown and her obsessive recitation of the "Jesus prayer." He is a television actor and is the best-looking member of the Glass clan. He believes that Bessie and **Lane Coutell**, Franny's boyfriend, are shallow for believing that Franny will be healed through psychoanalysis. Instead, he takes it upon himself to counsel Franny.

Glauce

Medea
Euripides

Creon's beautiful young daughter. She never appears onstage, but she is a constant presence in **Medea**'s mind.

Glaucon

The Republic
Plato

One of **Plato**'s brothers in real life and one of **Socrates**'s primary interlocutors in *The Republic*. Glaucon is competitive and loves young boys.

Glaucus

The Iliad
Homer

A powerful Trojan warrior who nearly fights a duel with **Diomedes**. The men's exchange of armor after they realize that their families are friends illustrates the value that ancients placed on kinship and camaraderie.

Mr. Glegg

The Mill on the Floss
George Eliot

Mrs. Glegg's husband. Mr. Glegg tries to mediate his wife's ill temper and will stand up to her as well.

Mrs. Glegg

The Mill on the Floss
George Eliot

Mr. Glegg's wife and **Elizabeth Tulliver**, **Mrs. Deane**, and **Mrs. Pullet**'s sister. She acts as the leader of the Dodson sisters and is loudly vocal with her disapproval. Her strict sense of respectability allows Mrs. Glegg to stand by **Maggie Tulliver** when Maggie is suspected of an affair with **Stephen Guest**.

Owen Glendower

Henry IV, Part I
William Shakespeare

The leader of the Welsh rebels and the father-in-law of **Edmund Mortimer, Earl of March**. Glendower joins **Hostpur** and the **Earl of Worcester** in their insurrection against King **Henry IV**. Well-read, educated in England, and highly capable in battle, the mysterious and proud Glendower is also steeped in the traditional lore of Wales and claims to be a magician. Ultimately, Glendower is not able to bring his forces to join the Battle of Shrewsbury in time.

Glóin

The Hobbit and *The Fellowship of the Ring*
J. R. R. Tolkien

Gimli's father. Glóin, one of the **Dwarves** who traveled with **Bilbo Baggins** to defeat **Smaug** in *The Hobbit*, is present at the Council of **Elrond Halfelven** in Rivendell, where the Fellowship of the Ring is established.

Glorfindel

The Fellowship of the Ring
J. R. R. Tolkien

An Elf-lord and friend of **Aragorn**'s. Glorfindel, who lives in Rivendell, attends the Council of **Elrond Halfelven**, which is called to determine what should be done with the One Ring.

Glory

I Know Why the Caged Bird Sings
Maya Angelou

Mrs. Cullinan's cook, formerly called Hallelujah. A descendent of the slaves once owned by the Cullinan family, her acceptance of Mrs. Cullinan's condescending and racist practice of renaming her slaves contrasts with **Maya Johnson**'s resistance to being called Mary.

Gloucester

King Lear
William Shakespeare

A nobleman loyal to **King Lear**. Gloucester fathered a bastard son, **Edmund**, and a legitimate son, **Edgar**. Gloucester at first trusts the devious Edmund and persecutes his faithful son Edgar. Gloucester appears weak and ineffectual when he is unable to prevent Lear from being turned out of his own house.

Duchess of Gloucester

Richard II
William Shakespeare

Widow of **Thomas of Woodstock, Duke of Gloucester**, and sister-in-law to **John of Gaunt** and **Edmund of Langley, Duke of York**. The duchess urges Gaunt to take revenge for Gloucester's death out of family loyalty and a sense of justice. She dies at her home in Plashy soon after Gaunt himself passes away.

Humphrey, Duke of Gloucester

Henry IV, Part II; Henry V; Henry VI, Part I; and *Henry VI, Part II*
William Shakespeare

Son of **King Henry IV**; brother of **King Henry V** (Prince Harry), **John, Duke of Lancaster**, and **Thomas, Duke of Clarence**; uncle of **King Henry VI**; and husband of **Eleanor, Duchess of Gloucester**. He makes his first appearance toward the end of *King Henry IV, Part II*, in time to bid farewell to his dying father and see Hal ascend to the throne as King Henry V. In *King Henry V* he does little except provide support for his monarch brother's campaign in France. Appointed Lord Protector of the Realm until Henry VI comes of age, Gloucester's strife with the **Bishop of Winchester** (later Cardinal Beaufort) is one of the civil dissensions that begins to tear England apart in *King Henry VI, Part I*. Unlike the plotting Winchester, Gloucester continues to do his job for England, attempting to negotiate a peace with the French by arranging a political marriage between Henry and the **Earl of Armagnac**'s daughter. Henry VI decides instead to marry **Margaret of Anjou**, a disastrous move that weakens the state further, as evidenced in *King Henry VI, Part II*. While he is loyal to the state, Gloucester airs his disgust with the loss of the French counties in exchange for the new Queen Margaret. It is not long before Gloucester becomes the focal point of the strife within the court. Though the commoners love him, other noblemen think that he has too much power and consequently despise him. Cardinal Beaufort, along with Queen Margaret, the **Duke of Suffolk**, the **Duke of Somerset**, and the **Duke of Buckingham**, plots against Gloucester; after his wife is arrested and banished for dealing with conjurers, Gloucester himself is arrested on suspicion of taking bribes and torturing prisoners. While Gloucester is under house arrest, he is assassinated by Suffolk and Beaufort's hit men.

Slaughterhouse-Five
Kurt Vonnegut

Werner Gluck

A young German guard at the slaughterhouse. Gluck gets his first glimpse of a naked woman alongside **Billy Pilgrim**.

Gulliver's Travels
Jonathan Swift

Glumdalclitch

The farmer's forty-foot-tall daughter. She treats **Gulliver** as a living doll and becomes his babysitter, both at home and later at the court. She teaches him her language and delights in clothing him.

Grendel
John Gardner

The goat

A goat that climbs a cliff despite **Grendel**'s repeated yells and screams. Grendel tries to bludgeon the goat to death with stones, but it continues to climb.

Cold Mountain
Charles Frazier

Goat-woman

A woman who lives in the mountains and raises goats and whom **Inman** encounters on his journey. The goat-woman possesses a strong connection to the natural world, healing Inman's wounds with food and medicine.

The Merchant of Venice
William Shakespeare

Lancelot Gobbo

Bassanio's servant. A comical, clownish, punning figure, Lancelot leaves **Shylock**'s service in order to work for Bassanio.

The Merchant of Venice
William Shakespeare

Old Gobbo

Lancelot Gobbo's father and a servant in Venice.

The Hobbit
J. R. R. Tolkien

Goblins

Evil creatures encountered by **Bilbo Baggins**, **Thorin Oakenshield** and the other **Dwarves** in *The Hobbit* on their quest to defeat **Smaug**. Goblins are infamous for their ability to make cruel weapons and torture devices. They are counted among the Evil Peoples of Middle-earth, like the **Wargs** and **Orcs**.

God

The Old Testament
Unknown

The creator of the world, an all-powerful being. God calls himself the only true deity worthy of worship. In the Old Testament, physical manifestations of God are indirect or symbolic. The Old Testament God is unique and sovereign. His unchanging nature is hinted at by his names. In biblical Hebrew, God is called "YAHWEH," meaning "to be." However, the God presented in the Old Testament does contradict himself at times: Over the course of two chapters in Exodus, God threatens to destroy the Israelites, relents, and then pronounces himself loving, forgiving, and slow to anger. God grants himself the power of self-description; he is whoever he says he is. God's initial interaction with humankind is unsolicited. **Noah**, **Abraham**, and **Moses** do not seek out God.

God the Father

Paradise Lost
John Milton

One part of the Christian Trinity. God the Father creates the world by means of **God the Son**, creating **Adam** and **Eve** last. He foresees the fall of mankind through them. He does not prevent their fall, in order to preserve their free will, but he does allow his Son to atone for their sins.

God the Son

Paradise Lost
John Milton

Jesus Christ, the second part of the Trinity. He delivers the fatal blow to **Satan**'s forces, sending them down into Hell before the creation of Earth. When the fall of man is predicted, he offers to sacrifice himself to pay for the sins of mankind, so that **God the Father** can be both just and merciful.

Professor Godbole

A Passage to India
E. M. Forster

A Brahman Hindu who teaches at Government College. A spiritual man, Godbole is reluctant to involve himself in human affairs.

Godfrey

Wide Sargasso Sea
Jean Rhys

One of **Alexander Cosway**'s servants who stays on after the master's death. **Annette** considers Godfrey a greedy and untrustworthy "rascal." He makes constant allusions to death and damnation.

Gaston Godin

Lolita
Vladimir Nabokov

A plump, lovable French teacher at Beardsley College and **Humbert Humbert**'s friend. Godin is a perfect opposite of Humbert. Where Humbert is meticulously neat, Godin is slovenly; where Humbert is slim and manly, Godin is obese; where Humbert dotes on little girls, Godin has a predilection for young boys.

Godot

Waiting for Godot
Samuel Beckett

Someone with answers and opinions whom **Vladimir** and **Estragon** await in vain. Godot is often thought to stand in for God. He never appears in the play.

Herb Goins

Prodigal Summer
Barbara Kingsolver

Cole Widener's brother-in-law. Herb is a dairy farmer. He and **Big Rickie Bowling** offer to plant a tobacco crop on **Lusa Maluf Landowski**'s farm.

Mary Edna Goins

Prodigal Summer
Barbara Kingsolver

Cole Widener's sister.

Sidney Goldberg

The Chosen
Chaim Potok

Reuven Malter's friend and softball teammate. Sidney is a likable and athletic boy.

Goldberry

The Fellowship of the Ring
J. R. R. Tolkien

Tom Bombadil's wife. Goldberry has a presence that moves **Frodo Baggins** in a way similar to that of the **Elves**. There is a darkness and an oldness to Goldberry and Tom, even though they seem quite able and powerful.

The Golden One

Anthem
Ayn Rand

A beautiful peasant with whom **Equality 7-2521** falls madly in love. The Golden One demonstrates her subservience to Equality 7-2521 by allowing him to change her name from Liberty 5-3000 to the Golden One, and later, Gaea. The Golden One is proud and vain, strong and bitter. She is relatively underdeveloped as a character, functioning mostly as the object of Equality 7-2521's affection, and, arguably, later as a vessel through which he can start his new free race. Though subservient to Equality 7-2521, the Golden One is nevertheless superior to those around her because she at least suspects that there is more to the world than the collective equality enforced in her society.

Emma Goldman

Ragtime
E. L. Doctorow

An anarchist and social activist. She appears throughout the novel to challenge other characters' conceptions.

The Power of One
Bryce Courtenay

Solly Goldman

A Jewish man, and the best boxing trainer in South Africa. He coaches **Peekay** while Peekay attends the Prince of Wales School in Johannesburg, and he teaches Peekay his famous thirteen-punch combination.

The Princess Bride
William Goldman

William Goldman

The author of *The Princess Bride*, as well as many other acclaimed books and screenplays. Goldman explains that this is his favorite book, the book his father used to read to him when he was sick. He casts himself as the "good-parts editor," rewriting the original **S. Morgenstern** version so that we can enjoy it the way he did when he was young.

Miss Lonelyhearts
Nathanael West

Goldsmith

A coworker at the newspaper who fills in for **Miss Lonelyhearts** the day he is too hung over to go to work.

Lucky Jim
Kingsley Amis

Carol Goldsmith

Cecil Goldsmith's wife and **Bertrand Welch**'s lover. She gets along well with **Jim Dixon**, who sees her as an ally, as she is good at turning people's statements back on them and speaks frankly. Dixon is also impressed by her "femaleness," which seems mostly to consist of her ability to admit she enjoys sex. When things sour between her and Bertrand, she moves on to **Gore-Urquhart**.

Lucky Jim
Kingsley Amis

Cecil Goldsmith

Jim Dixon's officemate and a senior lecturer in the History Department at the college. He is aware that his wife, **Carol Goldsmith**, is having an affair with **Bertrand Welch**, but seems accepting of it. Unlike Dixon, he takes the world of academia rather seriously.

1984
George Orwell

Emmanuel Goldstein

Legendary leader of the Brotherhood and the most dangerous and treacherous man in Oceania. Goldstein never appears outside of the Party's Two Minute Hate propaganda, and **Julia** and others doubt a real Goldstein exists. Regardless, all thoughts about Opposition revolve around Goldstein, and when **Winston Smith** dreams of smashing **Big Brother**, Goldstein inspires him.

The Hobbit and *The Lord of the Rings trilogy*
J. R. R. Tolkien

Gollum

A strange, small, slimy creature. Capable of speech, he is quite forthcoming in sharing his inner thoughts with anyone who cares to hear them, even talking out loud when no one is there. In *The Hobbit*, we are introduced to Gollum while he lives deep in the caves of Moria. There, he broods over his "precious," a magic ring that embodies the spirit of the evil **Sauron**. Gollum accidentally loses the ring, and **Bilbo Baggins** finds it. In *The Fellowship of the Ring,* we learn that Gollum was once Sméagol, a young boy of a Hobbit-like race who killed his friend Déagol after Déagol found the One Ring on the bottom of the Anduin River. The Ring corrupted Sméagol and changed him into his current form. In *The Two Towers,* Gollum tries desperately to get his "precious" back by helping guide **Frodo Baggins** through the treacherous lands of the East. At the end of *The Two Towers,* Gollum willingly leads Frodo to a probable death, and it is clear that he is no true friend to the Hobbit. In *The Return of the King,* Gollum's evil ultimately serves a good purpose when he completes the Ring-quest, biting the Ring off Frodo's finger and falling into the Cracks of Doom with it after Frodo is unable to take the Ring off his own finger to destroy it.

Ivan Ilych Golovin

The Death of Ivan Ilych
Leo Tolstoy

The protagonist of the novel, **Lisa Ivanovich** and **Vladimir Ivanich**'s father, and **Praskovya Fyodorovna Golovina**'s wife. Ivan is a nondescript, unexceptional man. He admires those with high social standing, and conforms his values and behavior to their rules. Ivan has a penchant for formalizing every human relationship. In his official work, he is careful to remove all personal concerns from consideration. In his private life, he adopts a fixed attitude toward his family. After an accident makes him ill, however, he develops a bond with his nurse, **Gerasim**.

Praskovya Fyodorovna Golovina

The Death of Ivan Ilych
Leo Tolstoy

Ivan Ilych Golovin's wife and the mother of his children. Praskovya's behavior toward others is artificial and self-interested. While feigning sympathy and concern for Ivan during his illness, her real attitude is one of hostility and impatience for his death.

General Golz

For Whom the Bell Tolls
Ernest Hemingway

The Russian general, allied with the Republicans, who assigns **Robert Jordan** the mission to blow up a Fascist-controlled bridge. Robert Jordan views Golz as the best general he has served under but says the Republican military bureaucracy impedes all of Golz's operations. Golz, for his part, believes thinking is useless because it breaks down resolve and impedes action.

Father Gomez

His Dark Materials
Robert Pullman

An assassin sent by the Consistorial Court to kill **Lyra Belacqua** before she can fall again. Father Gomez has done preemptive penance for most of his life so that one day he can kill someone without being damned.

Captain Rogelio Gomez

For Whom the Bell Tolls
Ernest Hemingway

A former barber and now commander of the battalion that the guerrilla fighter **Andrés** first reaches after crossing the Republican lines. Gomez romanticizes the idea of guerrilla warfare and escorts Andrés to several commanders trying to reach **General Golz**.

The House of the Spirits
Isabel Allende

Professor Sebastian Gomez

A professor at the university that **Alba** and **Miguel** attend. He helps them to organize the occupation of the school, as they are counterculture activists who dislike the Conservative government and society.

The Martian Chronicles
Ray Bradbury

Toma's Gomez

Part of an early wave of settlers on Mars. He is poetic when he thinks to himself, and he has a winning smile that he uses to greet **Muhe Ca**.

King Lear
William Shakespeare

Goneril

King Lear's ruthless oldest daughter and the wife of the duke of **Albany**. Goneril is jealous, treacherous, and evil. Goneril challenges Lear's authority, boldly initiates an affair with **Edmund**, and wrests military power away from her husband. At the end of the play she poisons her sister **Regan** over Edmund's love, but then stabs herself.

A Streetcar Named Desire
Tennessee Williams

Pablo Gonzales

Stanley Kowalski's brutish poker buddy. Pablo's Hispanic background emphasizes the culturally diverse nature of their neighborhood.

The Tempest
William Shakespeare

Gonzalo

An old, honest lord. Gonzalo helped **Prospero** and **Miranda** to escape after **Antonio** usurped Prospero's title. Gonzalo's speeches provide commentary on the events of the play.

The Chocolate War
Robert Cormier

The Goober

An amazing runner who plays football with **Jerry Renault**. Even though the Goober is not there for Jerry at critical points throughout the book, he is Jerry's only ally.

Bless the Beasts and Children
Glendon Swarthout

Gerald Goodenow

A fourteen-year-old camper with complicated emotional problems. When Goodenow was four years old, his father died, and he developed an overly dependent relationship with his mother. He is afraid of school and has difficulty making friends, particularly at Box Canyon Boys Camp, where athletics and physical strength determine status. The Bedwetters help him gain confidence.

Caspar Goodwood

The Portrait of a Lady
Henry James

The son of a prominent Boston mill owner, and **Isabel Archer**'s most dedicated suitor in America. Goodwood's charisma, simplicity, capability, and lack of sophistication make him the book's purest symbol of James's conception of America.

Gooper

Cat on a Hot Tin Roof
Tennessee Williams

A successful corporate lawyer. Gooper is **Big Daddy**'s eldest and least-favored son. Gooper deeply resents Daddy's and **Big Mama**'s love for **Brick**, viciously relishes in Daddy's illness, and rather ruthlessly plots to secure control of Daddy's estate. He is married to **Mae**, who is constantly competing with **Maggie**. Gooper and Mae feel that because they have lots of children and Brick and Maggie have none, they are entitled to Daddy's fortune. Gooper and Mae tell Daddy about how there was something "abnormal" in the relationship between Brick and his friend **Skipper** to provoke Daddy's disgust for Brick.

Gooseberry

The Moonstone
Wilkie Collins

A young boy in **Mr. Mathew Bruff**'s employ—he keeps his eyes open for Mr. Bruff and follows people when necessary. He is sneaky, quick, and smart.

Gopchik

One Day in the Life of Ivan Denisovich
Aleksandr Solzhenitsyn

A sixteen-year-old boy in prison with **Ivan Denisovich Shukhov** for providing milk to nationalist rebels hiding in the forest. Gopchik is fresh and innocent and has not yet been hardened by camp life.

Gorbag

The Two Towers
J. R. R. Tolkien

A warrior of the **Orcs** in the service of **Sauron** in Mordor, who, along with **Shagrat**, carries the body of **Frodo Baggins**, recently paralyzed by **Shelob**, into Mordor.

Gordie

The Light in the Forest
Conrad Richter

True Son's naïve younger brother. Gordie seems unaware that True Son's actions or behavior is different from that of whites. On the contrary, Gordie looks up to his older brother and tries to defend him against their less tolerant relatives.

Charlie Gordon

Flowers for Algernon
Daniel Keyes

The protagonist and author of the progress reports that form the text of the book. Charlie is a mentally retarded man who lives in New York City and works at Donner's Bakery as a janitor and delivery boy. Charlie's friendliness and eagerness to please, along with his childhood feelings of inadequacy, make him the hardest-working student in **Alice Kinnian**'s literacy class for retarded adults. When Charlie undergoes an experimental surgery to increase his intelligence, his IQ skyrockets to the level of genius. His obsession with untangling his own emotional life and his longing to reach an emotional maturity and inner peace to match his intellectual authority are among the novel's primary concerns.

Doctor Gordon

The Bell Jar
Sylvia Plath

Esther Greenwood's first psychiatrist, whom she distrusts. He is good-looking and has an attractive family, and Esther finds him conceited. He does not know how to help Esther, and ends up doing her more harm than good by sending her to shock therapy.

Matt Gordon

Flowers for Algernon
Daniel Keyes

Charlie Gordon's father and **Rose Gordon**'s husband. Matt works as a barbershop-supply salesman and eventually opens his own barbershop. Although Matt tried to protect the young Charlie from Rose's hostility, he gave in too easily to her bullying.

Misha Gordon

Dr. Zhivago
Boris Pasternak

A friend of **Yury Andreyevich Zhivago**'s who witnessed the elder **Zhivago**'s suicide. Later, along with **Nicky Dudorov**, he encourages Yury to reconcile with **Antonina Alexandrovna Gromeko**, Yury's estranged wife. At the novel's end, he and Nicky discover Yury and **Larissa Fyodorovna Guishar (later Antipova)**'s daughter, **Tanya**.

Norma Gordon

Flowers for Algernon
Daniel Keyes

Charlie Gordon's younger sister and **Rose Gordon**'s daughter and caretaker. As a child, Norma resented Charlie for getting what she perceived as special treatment and was cruel to him. When she reencounters Charlie as an adult, however, she is glad to see him and regrets her youthful spite.

Rose Gordon

Flowers for Algernon
Daniel Keyes

Charlie Gordon's mother. Domineering and ashamed of Charlie, Rose initially refused to accept that Charlie was retarded, despite the appeals of her husband, **Matt Gordon**. Rose finally had another child, **Norma Gordon**, on whom she focused all of her energy.

Mr. Gore

The Mill on the Floss
George Eliot

Jeremy Tulliver's lawyer.

Lord Goring

An Ideal Husband
Oscar Wilde

A thirty-something idle aristocrat and dandied philosopher, and a thinly veiled double for the author. Irreverent and wry, witty and impeccably dressed, Goring "plays with the world" and in doing so rejects ideals of duty, respectability, and responsibility. As with Wilde's other dandies, he functions as a figure for the modern art of living and the aestheticist creed, particularly in his encounters with his stuffy father, **Lord Caversham**. Expounding a philosophy of love and forgiveness, Goring is also a savior and helpmate to the Chilterns, **Lady Gertrude Chiltern** in particular.

Marcus Gorman

Legs
William Kennedy

An Albany lawyer who ends up representing the infamous New York gangster **Jack Diamond**. The novel consists of Marcus's recollections of Jack and his legacy. Marcus is cocky and confident that Jack's myth deserves its place in the book of American legends. The most exciting spell of Marcus's life came when he worked for Jack Diamond.

Bill Gorton

The Sun Also Rises
Ernest Hemingway

A heavy-drinking American veteran of World War I and a friend of the narrator, **Jake Barnes**. Bill uses humor to deal with the war's emotional and psychological fallout, and he shares a strong bond with Jake that is based on their war experience. The two spend several days fishing together in the Spanish countryside; their friendship is one of the few genuine emotional connections in the novel.

Burt Gorton

The Caine Mutiny
Herman Wouk

Executive officer to **Captain De Vriess**. He is friendly and easygoing with the crew, but maintains the authority needed to perform his duties. When **Philip Francis Queeg** takes over, Gorton reacts by changing his command style to match the captain's desire for discipline.

Gotama

Siddhartha
Hermann Hesse

A wise man. Sought by **Siddhartha** and **Govinda**. He is believed to have achieved Nirvana and broken from the cycle of reincarnation.

Max Gottlieb

Arrowsmith
Sinclair Lewis

Martin Arrowsmith's mentor and a German Jew. Gottlieb is a scientist more than a physician, often seen as eccentric, cold, or lacking in compassion despite the fact that he does have a deep belief in Martin.

Roland Goubert

The Chocolate War
Robert Cormier

See **The Goober**.

Richie Goulding

Ulysses
James Joyce

Stephen Dedalus's uncle; his mother, **Mary Dedalus**'s, brother. Richie is a law clerk who has been unable to work recently because of a bad back.

Walter Goulding

Ulysses
James Joyce

Richie Goulding's son. Walter is "skeweyed" and has a stutter.

Governess

Moll Flanders
Daniel Defoe

Moll's landlady and midwife, later her friend and partner in crime. She helps Moll manage an inconvenient pregnancy and initiates her into the criminal underworld.

Governess

The Turn of the Screw
Henry James

The writer of the manuscript, **Flora** and **Miles**'s twenty-year-old governess. She becomes convinced that she is seeing ghosts. It is possible that she kills Miles by suffocating him.

Governor of Harfleur

Henry V
William Shakespeare

The governor of the town that **King Henry V** lays siege to and wins. Acting in the best interest of his people, the governor agrees to hand over the town to the English after Henry gives him an ultimatum.

Govinda

Siddhartha
Hermann Hesse

The eternal follower of **Siddhartha**. Govinda is a perpetual seeker who has great difficulty seeing what is right in front of him. He fails to recognize his own best friend, Siddhartha, first when Siddhartha is a businessman and again when he is a Buddha. Govinda never finds satisfaction because he relies on doctrine instead of thought, trusting that dogma will show him the truth without his really looking for it on his own.

Harmon Gow

Ethan Frome
Edith Wharton

A former stage-driver and town gossip. Gow provides the narrator with a scattering of details about **Ethan Frome**'s life and later suggests that the narrator hire Ethan as a driver, which is how the narrator eventually learns Ethan's story.

Gower

Henry IV, Part II
William Shakespeare

A messenger who informs the **Lord Chief Justice** of the state of the army and **King Henry IV**'s whereabouts.

Captain Gower

Henry V
William Shakespeare

An army captain and capable fighter who serves with **King Henry V**'s campaign. He is good friends with the Welsh **Captain Fluellen**, and comically serves as his straight man.

John Gower

Pericles
William Shakespeare

The play's narrator. Gower introduces each act and concludes the play, sometimes with dumbshows. The historical John Gower was a fourteenth-century English poet who wrote the *Confessio Amantis*, part of which inspired the story of **Pericles**.

Goyle

The Harry Potter Series: Books 2–4
J. K. Rowling

One of **Draco Malfoy**'s unintelligent, lumbering cronies. **Harry Potter** uses Polyjuice potion to transform himself into Goyle.

Graaberg

Wild Duck
Henrik Ibsen

Werle's bookkeeper.

Grace

The Piano Lesson
August Wilson

A young urban woman whom **Boy Willie** takes home and **Lymon Jackson** asks out.

Jane Gradgrind

Hard Times
Charles Dickens

Thomas Gradgrind's younger daughter and **Thomas Gradgrind, Jr.**'s sister. Because **Cecelia Jupe** largely raises her, Jane is happier than her sister, **Louisa Gradgrind**.

Louisa Gradgrind

Hard Times
Charles Dickens

Thomas Gradgrind's daughter, later **Josiah Bounderby**'s wife. Louisa Gradgrind eventually recognizes that her father's system of education has deprived her of joy and the ability to empathize with others. She marries Bounderby to please her father, even though she does not love her husband. Indeed, the only person she loves completely is her brother **Thomas Gradgrind, Jr.**

Mrs. Gradgrind

Hard Times
Charles Dickens

Thomas Gradgrind's whiny, anemic wife. Although Mrs. Gradgrind does not share her husband's interest in facts, she lacks the energy and the imagination to oppose his system of education.

Thomas Gradgrind

Hard Times
Charles Dickens

A wealthy retired merchant who becomes a member of Parliament. Mr. Gradgrind espouses a philosophy of rationalism and self-interest. He raises his six children to be practical by stunting the development of their imaginations and emotions.

Thomas Gradgrind, Jr.

Hard Times
Charles Dickens

Thomas Gradgrind's eldest son and an apprentice at **Joseph Bounderby**'s bank who is generally called Tom. Tom reacts to his strict upbringing by becoming a dissipated, hedonistic, hypocritical young man. Although he appreciates his sister's affection, Tom cannot return it entirely—he loves money and gambling even more than he loves **Louisa Gragrind**. These vices lead him to rob Bounderby's bank and implicate **Stephen** as the robbery's prime suspect.

Gradus

Pale Fire
Vladimir Nabokov

The man hired to kill Charles the Beloved, a.k.a. **Charles Kinbote**. A bungler from birth, Gradus first fails to shoot a Charles Kinbote look-alike in a hospital and then fails to shoot Charles Kinbote himself, killing **John Shade** instead.

Grady

The Color Purple
Alice Walker

Shug Avery's husband. Grady is a loving and sweet man, but also a womanizer. He is a flamboyant and profligate spender of Shug's money, and frequently smokes pot. When Grady and **Squeak** begin an affair, Shug seems relieved to be rid of any responsibility to her relationship with Grady.

Colonel Graff

Ender's Game
Orson Scott Card

The head of the Battle School and the man who recruits **Ender Wiggin** for the school. Graff has unswerving faith in Ender and, although he manipulates Ender, he also loves him. Graff leaves the Battle School with Ender and accompanies him until Ender begins training under **Mazer Rackham**. He is put on trial after the war because of the deaths of **Stilson** and **Bonzo Madrid**, but the court acquits him.

Stanley Graff

Babbitt
Sinclair Lewis

A real estate salesman in **Babbitt**'s real estate business. When Graff becomes engaged, he asks Babbitt for a raise but instead receives a lecture for his lack of gratitude and business ethics. His low wages force him to cheat some of Babbitt's customers in order to feed himself and his wife. When Babbitt discovers these unethical business practices, he lectures Graff about morals and fires him. Graff threatens to reveal the details of Babbitt's shady deals if Babbitt tries to prevent him from getting a job in another firm.

Michael-Mary Graham

Song of Solomon
Toni Morrison

The Michigan poet laureate. Graham is a liberal who writes sentimental poetry and hires **First Corinthians Dead** as a maid. First Corinthians lies to her family, telling them that she is working as Graham's secretary.

Gram

Homecoming and *Dicey's Song*
Cynthia Voigt

The Tillerman children's grandmother and **Momma**'s mother. **Gram** lives by herself on a run-down farm outside of Crisfield, Maryland. Fierce and independent, Gram shares **Sammy Tillerman**'s belligerence and stubbornness and **Dicey Tillerman**'s determination. Gram has been hardened by a long marriage to a stern and unloving man, and, more often than not, Gram's love for her grandchildren shows itself in her supportive and protective actions toward them and in her respect for their individuality.

The Grand Inquisitor

Candide
Voltaire

A hypocritical but powerful figure in the Portuguese Catholic Church who orders heretics burned alive. **The Grand Inquisitor** uses the threat of religious oppression to force **Don Issachar** to share **Cunégonde** with him. **Candide** kills the Inquisitor when he discovers him with Cunégonde.

Joseph Grand

The Plague
Albert Camus

An elderly civil servant who never pursued opportunities for promotion. His wife **Jeanne** eventually left him after the marriage settled into a monotonous routine.

Grandfather

The Red Pony
John Steinbeck

Mrs. Tiflin's father and **Jody**'s maternal grandfather. An old man who lives in Monterey and sometimes visits the Tiflin ranch, Jody's grandfather led a wagon train across the Great Plains to California when he was a younger man. Although his endless stories of the crossing annoy **Carl** and Mrs. Tiflin, young Jody learns from them.

Grandfather

Where the Red Fern Grows
Wilson Rawls

Billy Colman's grandfather. He runs a general store and a small mill. He is full of imagination, and gets Billy into a lot of adventures. At first, he is a secret supporter of Billy's, taking Billy's saved-up money and ordering Billy's hounds for him. Billy's grandfather also takes it upon himself to enter **Little Ann** and **Old Dan** in a coon-hunting championship, which proves to be a very successful venture for Billy and his dogs.

Grandfather

Shabanu
Suzanne Fisher Staples

Dadi's father and **Shabanu**'s grandfather, who lives with them in the desert. Grandfather fought for the Nawab of Bahawalpur, who was the king of their region before the formation of the state of Pakistan. Grandfather is kindly and forgetful. In his old age, he often "disappears" for days into garbled reveries but always returns to his old self.

Grandma

American Dream
Edward Albee

Mother of **Mommy** and the ironic commentator of the play. Grandma ultimately exits the frame of the action to become its director. Notably, she is the only character to underline the fact that she is staging a masquerade, what she describes as her "act." At the end of the play, she watches the final family scene, becoming a commentator on the action from the outside who delivers the party up to the audience's judgment.

Grandma

Ceremony
Leslie Marmon Silko

Tayo's grandmother and the matriarch of the family. Already old and wise when Tayo is just a child, Grandma intervenes at key moments in Tayo's life to bring him to the medicine men or to provide tidbits of advice in the form of seemingly random comments.

Grandma

Angela's Ashes
Frank McCourt

The mother of **Angela McCourt**. Grandma helps the McCourts whenever she can, although she remains suspicious of **Malachy McCourt, Sr.**'s Northern Irish roots and insists that **Frank McCourt** has inherited his father's "odd manner."

Grandpa

Black Boy
Richard Wright

Richard Wright's maternal grandfather and a former soldier in the Union Army during the Civil War. Sour and remote, Grandpa is forever bitter that a clerical error deprived him of his war pension. He keeps a loaded gun by his bed because he believes Civil War hostilities could resurface at any moment.

Grandpapa

The Heart Is a Lonely Hunter
Carson McCullers

Dr. Benedict Mady Copeland's father-in-law. Grandpapa loves to ask Dr. Copeland about remedies for his various aches and pains. He believes that on Judgment Day, God will finally have mercy on black people by making their skin white—an idea that Dr. Copeland finds revolting and humiliating.

Lord Grandpré

Henry V
William Shakespeare

A French nobleman and military leader. He gives a speech spurring on the French to victory over the "island carrions," mocking how tired and inept the English look in war. Grandpré dies during the Battle of Agincourt.

Granger

Fahrenheit 451
Ray Bradbury

The leader of the "Book People," the group of hobo intellectuals **Guy Montag** finds in the countryside. Granger is intelligent, patient, and confident in the strength of the human spirit. He is committed to preserving literature through the current Dark Age.

Filmore Granger

The Land
Mildred D. Taylor

A greedy and dishonest landowner. It is from Filmore Granger that **Paul-Edward Logan** attempts to buy forty acres of land.

Harlan Granger

Roll of Thunder, Hear My Cry and *The Land*
Mildred D. Taylor

The son of the wealthy and bigoted **Filmore Granger**. In *The Land*, Harlan is young; by *Roll of Thunder, Hear My Cry*, he has grown up and inherited both his father's plantation and sensibilities. In *Roll of Thunder, Hear My Cry*, Harlan is anxious to buy back the Logans' land—which Filmore Granger, along with **J. T. Hollenbeck**, had sold to **Big Ma**'s husband **Paul-Edward Logan** in *The Land*. He puts pressure on the Logan family by getting **Mama** fired from her teaching job; he also uses threats to influence the black community to stop the boycott of the **Wallace** family store store, which is on Harlan's land.

Hermione Granger

The Harry Potter Series: Books 1–4
J. K. Rowling

A girl who is always the top student in her class. Most spells come easily to her and remain in her encyclopedic mind. In *Harry Potter and the Sorcerer's Stone* she becomes friendly with **Harry Potter**. Along with **Ron Weasley**, the trio are the focus of the books. She is principled and fond of rules, so she unwillingly follows the boys on their illicit adventures. She comes from a purely Muggle (non-magical) family, and her character illustrates the social-adjustment problems often faced by new students at Hogwarts. In *Harry Potter and the Chamber of Secrets*, Hermione's insight leads her to discover that the monster within the Chamber is a basilisk (a snake-like creature whose eyes will turn you to stone) and that Polyjuice potion (a potion that transforms your body shape) will allow the group of friends to spy on **Draco Malfoy**. She makes a mistake with her polyjuice potion, turning herself temporarily into a cat. Her mistake reveals that she does not possess some of the more practical skills and assumptions that Harry Potter does. In *Harry Potter and the Goblet of Fire*, Hermione becomes concerned about **Bartemius Crouch**'s mistreatment of his house-elf. She recognizes this treatment as a form of abusive slavery and takes deep offense.

The Grangerfords

The Adventures of Huckleberry Finn
Mark Twain

A family that takes **Huckleberry Finn** in after a steamboat hits his raft, separating him from **Jim**. The kindhearted Grangerfords, who offer Huck a place to stay in their tacky country home, are locked in a long-standing feud with another local family, the **Shepherdsons**. The Grangerfords' home features the artwork of a deceased daughter, **Emmeline**, who created unintentionally funny sentimental artwork and poems about people who died. Ultimately, the families' sensationalized feud gets many of them killed.

Granny

Black Boy
Richard Wright

Richard Wright's maternal grandmother. Austere and unforgiving, Granny is a strict Seventh-Day Adventist who thinks Richard is sinful. Granny's parents were slaves. Due to her partially white ancestry, she has light skin.

Granny

Farewell to Manzanar
Jeanne Wakatsuki Houston

Mama's mother, sixty-five at the time of the relocation to Manzanar. Granny's inability to go to the mess halls is one reason that the Wakatsuki family stops eating together.

Granpa

The Power of One
Bryce Courtenay

Granpa spends most of his time smoking his pipe and tending his rose garden, which he cultivates for his long-dead English wife. He is notorious for telling **Peekay** irrelevant stories when Peekay goes to him for advice. A racist, Granpa nevertheless has respect for **Inkosi-Inkosikazi** since he cured him of his gall stones.

Dr. Alan Grant

Jurassic Park
Michael Crichton

A paleontologist famous for his studies of fossilized dinosaur nests in Montana. Grant is athletic and down to earth and takes pride in not being a stuffy academic like many of his colleagues. Although certain characters seem to resent the presence of **John Hammond**'s grandchildren, Grant likes children and is quickly drawn to **Tim Murphy** in particular.

Mona Grant

The Big Sleep
Raymond Chandler

The loyal and faithful wife of **Eddie Mars**. Though rumors abound that Mona has run off with **Regan**, this is not the case. Mona allows herself to be hidden in order to protect her husband, whom she does not believe is a crooked gambler and a ruthless murderer.

Captain Graveling

Billy Budd, Sailor
Herman Melville

Captain of the merchant marine *Rights-of-Man*; an overweight and benign shipmaster.

Muley Graves

The Grapes of Wrath
John Steinbeck

One of the **Joads**' neighbors in Oklahoma. When the bank evicts the Graves framily, Muley stays behind and lives outdoors, while his wife and children move to California.

Robert Graves

Regeneration
Pat Barker

A fellow poet, soldier, and friend of **Siegfried Sassoon**'s. Although Graves agrees with Sassoon that the war is evil and unjust, he refuses to protest. Graves feels that regardless of his personal beliefs, it is his duty to honor his contract to his country. Nevertheless, Graves is a true friend to Sassoon.

Gray Beaver

White Fang
Jack London

A harsh Native American man. Gray Beaver is **White Fang**'s first master. Although he shows no affection for his dog, **White Fang** bonds with him in a certain mutual respect. **Beauty Smith** gets Gray Beaver drunk and tricks Gray Beaver into selling White Fang to him.

Colonel Wordsworth Gray

Jazz
Toni Morrison

A wealthy plantation owner who sends his daughter, **Vera Louise Gray**, away when he learns that she has become pregnant with the child of a black man. He gives her enough money to settle somewhere herself, and support herself and her child, but does not want to see her anymore.

Dorian Gray

The Picture of Dorian Gray
Oscar Wilde

A radiantly handsome, impressionable, and wealthy young gentleman whose portrait the artist **Basil Hallward** paints. Under the influence of **Lord Henry Wotton**, Dorian becomes extremely concerned with the transience of his beauty and begins to pursue his own pleasure above all else. He devotes himself to having as many experiences as possible, whether moral or immoral, elegant or sordid.

Golden Gray

Jazz
Toni Morrison

The son of **Vera Louise Gray** and **Henry LesTroy**, who is also known as "Hunters Hunter." He is the result of the forbidden love between a white woman and a black man. Raised by his mother and **True Belle** in Baltimore, Maryland, Golden Gray leads a privileged existence and is told that he was adopted at a young age. When he is eighteen, he learns the truth about his parents from True Belle and flies into a rage. He travels to Vienna, Virginia, intending to hunt down and kill his black father, whom he assumes violated Vera Louise, but he runs off in the woods and finds **Wild**, who is pregnant with **Joe Trace**. Rather than strike out the part of his identity that does not correspond with his own sense of self, Golden seeks refuge in Wild's blackness and escapes from society with her, roaming free in the woods. Golden abandons the white upbringing that his mother offered him and also knows that the black community will never fully accept him.

Vera Louise Gray

Jazz
Toni Morrison

The white daughter of wealthy plantation owners, one of whom is **Colonel Wordsworth Grey**, Vera Louise is sent away by her parents when they figure out that she has become pregnant with the child of her black lover. They give her a large sum of money as a kind of bribe, and she takes her servant **True Belle** with her to Baltimore, Maryland, where the two women raise her son, **Golden Gray**. True Belle leaves Vera Louise to help her daughter, **Rose Dear**, in Rome, Virginia.

Benny Grayback

When the Legends Die
Hal Borland

A vocational instructor in the carpentry shop on the same reservation where **Thomas Black Bull** is living.

Graziano of *Merchant*

The Merchant of Venice
William Shakespeare

A friend of **Bassanio**'s. A coarse young man, Graziano is **Shylock**'s most vocal and insulting critic during the trial. Graziano falls in love with and eventually weds **Portia**'s lady-in-waiting, **Nerissa**.

Graziano of *Othello*

Othello
William Shakespeare

Brabanzio's kinsman who accompanies **Lodovico** to Cyprus. Amidst the chaos of the final scene, Graziano mentions that **Desdemona**'s father Brabanzio has died. After Othello commits suicide, Lodovico wills Othello's house and goods to Graziano.

Green

Richard II
William Shakespeare

One of **King Richard II**'s favored and loyal supporters. When word comes that **Henry Bolingbroke** has come back to England with an army, **Bushy**, **Bagot**, and Green realize that they will be punished along with Richard, and flee. Bushy and Green are captured and executed soon after by Bolingbroke's forces, on the grounds of corrupting Richard.

Dame Green

Evelina
Fanny Burney

Lady Caroline Evelyn Belmont's former servant, and current servant of **Sir John Belmont**. Dame Green was with Lady Caroline Belmont when she died, and presented Sir Belmont with her own child, claiming it was the daughter of his deceased wife.

Ed Green

Black Boy
Richard Wright

A high-ranking black communist. Green is suspicious of **Richard Wright**'s interviews with **Ross**. Green's rough, authoritative manner alienates Wright.

Mr. Green

Wuthering Heights
Emily Brontë

Edgar Linton's lawyer. Mr. Green arrives too late to hear Edgar change his will in order to prevent **Heathcliff** from obtaining control of Thrushcross Grange.

William Green

No Longer At Ease
Chinua Achebe

Obi's boss at the Civil Service. Mr. Green is an old Englishman accustomed to the colonial mindset. He believes that the English brought education and civility to Africa.

Jude Greene

Sula
Toni Morrison

Nel's husband, who works as a waiter in the Hotel Medallion. To secure a sense of manhood, he decides to marry and proposes to Nel. One day, when Jude returns home and complains to Nel about some minor annoyance at his job, **Sula Peace** is there, and teases him. This early animosity, though, eventually leads to an affair. After Nel discovers the affair by stumbling on Sula and Jude having sex, Jude abandons Nel and their children. Nel is devastated by the betrayal of her husband and best friend.

Sir Nicholas Greene

Orlando
Virginia Woolf

A seventeenth-century poet who writes a parody of **Orlando**, and who later appears as the most eminent Victorian literary critic. Though times have changed, Nick remains the same, generally unhappy and preoccupied with his ill health. Greene is able to get Orlando's work published.

Faye Greener

The Day of the Locust
Nathanael West

A seventeen-year-old aspiring actress. Faye was raised by her father **Harry**, her mother having left them when Faye was a child. As Harry has worked off and on as a vaudeville comedian, Faye has grown up in the world of acting and entertainment and has always wanted to be an actress. Though she is still a teenager, she can carry herself like a worldly, sexual woman.

Harry Greener

The Day of the Locust
Nathanael West

Faye's father, a vaudeville clown and comedic actor who has never been truly successful. Harry began his stage career in New York, then moved to Hollywood with Faye in hopes of finding film work. But Harry has never found the work he hoped for and has been selling homemade silver polish door to door to support himself.

Barney Greenwald

The Caine Mutiny
Herman Wouk

A hotshot New York lawyer in peacetime and a Jewish fighter pilot during the war. He is pressured into defending **Steve Maryk** and the rest of the *Caine* mutineers. Against his beliefs, he gets Maryk acquitted, but then reprimands the crew for their attack on the Navy.

Esther Greenwood

The Bell Jar
Sylvia Plath

The protagonist and narrator of the novel, she has just finished her junior year of college. Esther grew up in the Boston suburbs with her brother and her mother, **Mrs. Greenwood**. Esther is attractive, talented, and lucky, but uncertainty plagues her, and she feels a disturbing sense of unreality. Esther feels unsatisfied by her work for a fashion magazine called *Lady's Day*. After she is assaulted by a man named **Marco**, she seriously considers suicide and lapses into a long period of mental illness. She describes her madness as a bell jar that can descend without warning and sour the air around her.

Mrs. Greenwood

The Bell Jar
Sylvia Plath

Esther Greenwood's mother. Mrs. Greenwood lost her husband when her children were young. Because her husband had inadequate life insurance, she struggles to make a living by teaching typing and shorthand. Practical and traditional, she loves Esther and worries about her future, but cannot understand her.

Alice Greer

The Bean Trees and *Pigs in Heaven*
Barbara Kingsolver

Taylor Greer's Kentucky-native mother. In Chapter One of *The Bean Trees*, Taylor says that her mother expects the best from her daughter and thinks that whatever Taylor does is wonderful. In *Pigs in Heaven*, Alice Greer runs away from her old life when she comes out West to visit her daughter. She is a strong, lonely woman, craving a community that could provide her the comfort and warmth that her husband **Harland** cannot.

Taylor Greer

The Bean Trees and *Pigs in Heaven*
Barbara Kingsolver

The protagonist of *The Bean Trees* and a major character in *Pigs in Heaven*. A strong, gutsy woman with a sassy yet kind voice, Taylor was born and raised in rural Kentucky but leaves to escape a small life in her hometown. Like her mother **Alice Greer**, Taylor is proud of her Cherokee blood. She makes up her mind to avoid pregnancy and promises herself that she will change her name by driving until the gas runs out and naming herself after whatever town she happens to land in. She accepts an abandoned baby named **Turtle** and becomes close to **Estevan**, **Esperanza**, **Lou Ann Ruiz** and **Mattie** as she builds new life for herself in Arizona. In *Pigs in Heaven*, Taylor is a mother-bear figure. Her fierce love for Turtle drives her to run away when her rights of custody are called into question by the lawyer **Annawake Fourkiller**.

Turtle Greer

The Bean Trees and *Pigs in Heaven*
Barbara Kingsolver

Taylor Greer's adopted Cherokee daughter, who shows up as a toddler in *The Bean Trees* and as a young girl in *Pigs in Heaven*. In *The Bean Trees*, Taylor finds Turtle in a car on the Cherokee Nation; the little girl has been sexually abused and appears half-dead. During the next many months, Turtle is so quiet and unengaged that many believe her to be dumb or retarded. Nonethess, she triumphs over adversity: her first sound is a laugh, and her first word is "bean." In *Pigs in Heaven*, Turtle is a bright and charming little girl who still harbors fears of her past. She feels threatened whenever she is separated from anyone, most of all Taylor.

Count Greffi

A Farewell to Arms
Ernest Hemingway

A spry, ninety-four-year-old nobleman whom **Frederic Henry** befriends on a trip to Stresa, Italy. **Count Greffi** represents a more mature version of Henry. Henry sees him as a father figure.

George Greggson

Childhood's End
Arthur C. Clarke

A television production designer. He marries **Jean Morrel** and fathers **Jeffrey Greggson** and **Jennifer Greggson**.

Jeffrey Greggson

Childhood's End
Arthur C. Clarke

The son of **George Greggson** and **Jean Morrel**. Early in his childhood, Jeffrey has strange dreams and begins to exhibit amazing mental abilities.

Jennifer Greggson

Childhood's End
Arthur C. Clarke

The daughter and youngest child of **George Greggson** and **Jean Morrel**. As a baby, Jennifer soon begins to exhibit the strange behavior of her brother, **Jeffrey Greggson**.

Gregor's father

The Metamorphosis
Franz Kafka

A slouching, defeated man. **Gregor Samsa**'s father failed at business, but once Gregor's misfortune compels him to find work again, he discovers new confidence. His fit of rage leads to Gregor's declining health and eventual demise.

Gregor's mother

The Metamorphosis
Franz Kafka

A physically weak woman. **Gregor Samsa**'s metamorphosis damages his mother the most. Despite her love for Gregor, she gets sick whenever she sees him as a bug. **Gregor's father** and **Grete Samsa**, his younger sister, feel protective of her and resent Gregor for endangering her health.

Dr. Franz Gregorovius

Tender Is the Night
F. Scott Fitzgerald

One of **Dick Diver**'s psychiatry colleagues who, like **Dr. Dohmler**, urges Dick to end his relationship with the patient **Nicole Warren**. Later, Dick and Dr. Gregory open a clinic funded by Nicole's inheritance money. When Dick's heavy drinking becomes a problem, Dr. Gregory buys the clinic from him.

Gregory

Romeo and Juliet
William Shakespeare

Along with **Sampson**, one of two servants who, like their master **Capulet**, hate the Montagues. At the onset of the play, they successfully provoke some **Montague** men into a fight.

Captain Gregory

The Big Sleep
Raymond Chandler

An officer at the Missing Persons Bureau who chides **Marlowe** for taking matters into his own hands.

Gremio

The Taming of the Shrew
William Shakespeare

An old, rich, clownish gentleman of Padua. Gremio and **Hortensio** are **Bianca**'s suitors at the beginning of the play. Though they are rivals, these men also become allies in their attempts to marry **Katherine** off, thereby leaving Bianca available for marriage.

Grendel

Beowulf
Unknown

A demon descended from Cain. Grendel preys on **Hrothgar**'s warriors in the king's mead-hall, Heorot. Because his ruthless and miserable existence is part of the retribution exacted by God for Cain's murder of Abel, Grendel fits solidly within the ethos of vengeance that governs the world of the poem.

Grendel

Grendel
John Gardner

The protagonist and narrator of the novel. A great, bearlike monster, Grendel is the first of three monsters defeated by the Geatish hero **Beowulf** in the sixth-century poem *Beowulf*. In *Grendel*, he is a lonely creature who seeks an understanding of the seemingly meaningless world around him. As an outsider, Grendel observes and provides commentary on the human civilization he battles.

Grendel's mother

Beowulf
Unknown

An unnamed swamp-hag, **Grendel**'s mother seems to possess fewer human qualities than her son, although her ransacking of Heorot seems an act of vengeance for her son's murder.

Grendel's mother

Grendel
John Gardner

A foul, wretched being, and **Grendel**'s only apparent family member. Grendel's mother lives with Grendel in a vast underground cave. She desperately tries to protect her son from the humans and his fate. She has either forgotten or never knew how to speak, though at times her gibberish approaches coherent language.

Allan Grey

A Streetcar Named Desire
Tennessee Williams

The young man with poetic aspirations whom **Blanche DuBois** fell in love with and married as a teenager. One afternoon, she discovered Allan in bed with an older male friend. That evening at a ball, after she announced her disgust at his homosexuality, he ran outside and shot himself in the head. Allan's death, which marked the end of Blanche's sexual innocence, has haunted her ever since.

Lord Grey

Richard III
William Shakespeare

The son of **Elizabeth Woodville, Lady Grey** (Queen Elizabeth), brother of the **Marquess of Dorset**, nephew of **Lord Rivers**, and stepson of **King Edward IV**. Threatened by the entire Woodville line, **King Richard III** eventually executes Rivers and Grey, but Dorset survives and flees to join the opposition led by **Henry Tudor, Earl of Richmond**.

Miss Sophia Grey

Sense and Sensibility
Jane Austen

The wealthy heiress **John Willoughby** marries after abandoning **Marianne Dashwood**.

Mr. Grey

I Am the Cheese
Robert Cormier

A mysterious figure who pretends to assist the Farmer family. Mr. Grey is the head of a new government department called the Witness Re-Identification Program. This program assigns **Anthony Delmonte** and his family a new identity. Anthony becomes **David Farmer**, and his son **Paul Delmonte** becomes

Adam Farmer. It is possible that Grey sets up the attempted murder of David, the capture of Adam, and the death of **Louise Farmer**.

Sir Thomas Grey

Henry V
William Shakespeare

One of three noblemen bribed by French agents to kill **King Henry V** before he sets sail for France. Along with the **Earl of Cambridge** and **Lord Scroop**, Grey is found out and sentenced for execution, despite his pleas for mercy.

John Howard Griffin

Black Like Me
John Howard Griffin

The narrator, author, and protagonist. Griffin is a middle-aged white southerner with a passionate commitment to the cause of racial justice. In order to understand what life is like for black Americans, Griffin undergoes medical therapy to darken his skin color, then poses as a black man for nearly two months in 1959-1960. He publishes his experiences with prejudice and racism in the journal *Sepia*, leading to a firestorm of public controversy; he is eventually forced to move his family to Mexico to end the threat of violent reprisals from racist whites in his hometown in Texas.

Laman Griffin

Angela's Ashes
Frank McCourt

Angela McCourt's cousin and lover for a short time. After a fight with Laman, **Frank McCourt** moves in with his Uncle **Ab Sheenan**.

Griffith

Henry VIII
William Shakespeare

Queen Katherine's loyal attendant. Following **Cardinal Wolsey**'s death, Griffith delivers a touching elegy filled with forgiveness and pity.

Griggs

Black Boy
Richard Wright

One of **Richard Wright**'s boyhood friends. Griggs, like Richard, is intelligent, but he has a sense of when blacks need to abide by the rules—a sense Richard lacks. Griggs displays the compassionate concern of a true friend when he advises Richard on how to survive in the racist white world.

Grimaud

The Three Musketeers
Alexandre Dumas

Athos's manservant. Athos has trained him to communicate in hand signals. Grimaud stays locked in the basement of the inn where he and Athos are ambushed, consuming all the wine to spite the innkeeper, who helped with the ambush.

John Grimes

Go Tell It on the Mountain
James Baldwin

The protagonist of the novel, who turns fourteen on the day the story begins. He is **Elizabeth**'s son, but does not suspect that his father is not **Gabriel**, the man who has raised him, but **Richard**, his mother's first lover. Both attracted and repulsed by Gabriel and everything he represents, John is anguished and deeply confused. He longs to experience all the world has to offer, but he is terrified by sin.

Percy Grimm

Light in August
William Faulkner

A fiercely racist army captain. Grimm organizes a group of American Legion men to keep the townspeople from lynching **Joe Christmas**, but after Joe escapes, Grimm tracks him down, kills, and castrates him.

Mr. Grimwig

Oliver Twist
Charles Dickens

Mr. Brownlow's pessimistic, curmudgeonly friend.

The Gringo

The Power and the Glory
Graham Greene

An American outlaw, and the other "hunted man" along with **the Priest**. The gringo is wanted for murder. Although his reputation seems to fill people with a strange admiration, when one finally encounters him near the novel's end, he turns out to be little more than a common criminal.

Pierre Gringoire

Hunchback of Notre Dame
Victor Hugo

A struggling playwright and philosopher. **La Esmerelda** saves him from being hanged by a group of vagabonds and agrees to "marry" him for four years. He later joins the vagabonds and unwittingly helps **Jehan Frollo** hand La Esmerelda over to the authorities.

Gringolet

Sir Gawain and the Green Knight
Unknown

Gawain's horse.

Walter Gripp

The Martian Chronicles
Ray Bradbury

A simple, solitary, polite man who lives in the mountains. He does not realize that Mars has been evacuated because of the war on Earth. He desperately wants a female companion, but when he encounters **Genevieve Selsor**, he finds her to be a fat, slovenly bore and flees her.

Hoppie Groenewald

The Power of One
Bryce Courtenay

One of the guards on **Peekay**'s train to Barberton and also the "champion of the railways." He inspires Peekay to begin boxing lessons.

Alexander Alexandrovich Gromeko

Dr. Zhivago
Boris Pasternak

The father of **Antonina Alexandrovna Gromeko** and a wealthy friend of **Yury Andreyevich Zhivago**'s. He comes to live with Tonya and Yury after they are married, and accompanies them on the train ride to the Varykino Estate.

Anna Ivanovna Gromeko

Dr. Zhivago
Boris Pasternak

The mother of **Antonina Alexandrovna Gromeko**; the daughter of a wealthy landowner from Varyniko, near Yuryatin; also called Anna. As she is dying of a pulmonary disease, Anna unofficially betrothes her daughter to **Yury Andreyevich Zhivago**.

Antonina Alexandrovna Gromeko

Dr. Zhivago
Boris Pasternak

The daughter of **Alexander Alexandrovich Gromeko** and **Anna Ivanovna Gromeko**, later **Yury Andreyevich Zhivago**'s wife. Raised alongside Yury, she is betrothed to him on her mother's deathbed. Essentially good-natured, Tonya cannot compete with **Lara** for Yury's heart.

Mike Groom

Into Thin Air
Jon Krakauer

An Australian guide with Adventure Consultants who gets lost with a group of clients during the descent but survives. He also guides **Beck Weathers** down the mountain when Beck goes blind.

Mrs. Grose

The Turn of the Screw
Henry James

The housekeeper at Bly. Mrs. Grose professes to believe **the governess**'s stories about the ghosts of **Peter Quint** and **Miss Jessel**.

Lena Grove

Light in August
William Faulkner

A young pregnant girl. Lena travels from Alabama to Mississippi in search of **Lucas Burch** (Joe Brown), the father of her child. She loves seeing new places and maintains a positive attitude despite her scandalous pregnancy.

Mary Grove

Walden Two
B. F. Skinner

Steve Jamnik's girlfriend. She is a fan of Walden Two.

Benjamin Grower

The Mayor of Casterbridge
Thomas Hardy

One of **Michael Henchard**'s creditors. When Henchard jealously blackmails **Lucetta Templeman** into agreeing to marry him, he later asks Templeman if she will notify Benjamin Grower of this arrangement. Henchard hopes that if Grower knows of his engagement to Templeman, a woman with known financial credit, Grower will regard Henchard's outstanding debt with more leniency. Templeman refuses and notifies Henchard that she has already secretly married **Donald Farfrae**.

Frau Grubach

The Trial
Franz Kafka

The proprietress of the lodging house where **Joseph K.** lives. She holds K. in high esteem.

Grumby

The Unvanquished
William Faulkner

A cowardly ex-Confederate soldier whose band of mauraders terrorizes the countryside in the wake of the Yankee occupation. Grumby is the opposite of **Colonel Sartoris**: he preys on the local population rather than protecting them, and kills a defenseless old woman rather than fighting against the Yankees. By killing him, **Bayard** achieves more than personal revenge—he sets right the moral order for the entire community.

Grumio

The Taming of the Shrew
William Shakespeare

Petruccio's constantly grumbling servant. A source of much comic relief, Grumio is often involved in some sort of physical humor—either abusing someone lower on the totem pole than he, or being abused by Petruccio.

Percy Gryce

The House of Mirth
Edith Wharton

A young, rich, eligible bachelor. **Lily Bart** sets her sights on Percy Gryce early in the novel. Unfortunately, just as Lily decides she must marry him, he announces his engagement to **Evie Van Osburgh**.

Guard

The Hairy Ape
Eugene O'Neill

Yank's keeper at the prison where he is held after causing the **Gentleman** to miss his bus. The Guard shoots water at Yank when he bends the bars of his cell back.

Guardians of the Faith

The Handmaid's Tale
Margaret Atwood

Males of the **Republic of Gilead** who are too young, too old, or too weak for the army. Guardians staff the police force and often work for **Commanders of the Faithful** as servants.

Dr. Guarino

Flowers for Algernon
Daniel Keyes

A quack doctor who treats young **Charlie Gordon**. Dr. Guarino promised **Rose Gordon** that he could scientifically increase Charlie's intelligence, but his methods are a complete sham.

Nels Gudmundsson

Snow Falling on Cedars
David Guterson

Kabuo Miyamoto's morally upright defense attorney. Nels is in his late seventies and his health is failing.

Sister Gudule

Hunchback of Notre Dame
Victor Hugo

La Esmerelda's long-lost mother, a miserable recluse living in the Tour Roland. She is convinced that gypsies ate her adoptive daughter fifteen years earlier. Sister Gudule hates La Esmeralda and is convinced she is a thief. She later realizes that La Esmeralda is her daughter. When Esmeralda is taken away to be hung, Sister Gudule cries out in horror at the prospect of having searched for her daughter for fifteen years only to find her just before her execution.

Duchess of Guermentes

Swann's Way
Marcel Proust

The local aristocrat at Combray. **Marcel** imagines her to be the most beautiful woman on earth and is sorely disappointed with her physical appearance when they actually meet.

Mr. Guest

Dr. Jekyll and Mr. Hyde
Robert Louis Stevenson

Mr. Gabriel John Utterson's clerk and confidant. Guest, an expert in handwriting, notices that **Mr. Edward Hyde**'s script is nearly the same as **Dr. Henry Jekyll**'s.

Stephen Guest

The Mill on the Floss
George Eliot

A character introduced as a suitor of **Lucy Deane**'s who has not proposed marriage. He is the son of the senior partner of Guest & Co., where both **Tom Tulliver** and **Mr. Deane** work. Though he cares for Lucy, and for the life they would have together, he falls unexpectedly in love with **Maggie Tulliver**, drawn to her strikingly different qualities.

Guiderius

Cymbeline
William Shakespeare

Cymbeline's eldest son, **Imogen**'s brother, and **Cloten**'s murderer. Guiderius was kidnapped and raised by **Belarius** under the name "Polydore."

Sheriff Guidry

The Autobiography of Miss Jane Pittman
Ernest J. Gaines

The town sheriff. He is a classic white southern sheriff who seems totally indifferent to justice in the wake of **Tee Bob**'s death. He supports **Jules Raynard** when Raynard begs for peace, but it seems just as likely that he would look away if the Samson family proceeded with violence.

Sheriff Guidry

A Lesson Before Dying
Ernest J. Gaines

An authoritarian man who runs the prison in Bayonne. Guidry resents anyone who trespasses on his domain, especially blacks like **Grant Wiggins** and **Miss Emma**. He provides blacks with a modicum of freedom and opportunity while maintaining a white authoritarian superstructure.

Guildenstern

Hamlet
William Shakespeare

Along with **Rosencrantz**, one of two bumbling courtiers and former friends of **Hamlet**'s from Wittenberg. **Claudius** and **Gertrude** summon the pair so they can discover the cause of Hamlet's strange behavior. Sensing their hidden purpose, Hamlet has them murdered by making them the targets of a contract killing originally meant for Hamlet himself.

The Guildsmen

The Canterbury Tales
Geoffrey Chaucer

Five of the pilgrims on the journey, always appearing as a unit. English guilds were a combination of labor unions and social fraternities: craftsmen of similar occupations joined together to increase their bargaining power and live communally. All five Guildsmen are clad in the livery of their brotherhood.

Sir Henry Guilford

Henry VIII
William Shakespeare

A lord of the court who announces the beginning of **Cardinal Wolsey**'s dinner party.

Guillaumin

Madame Bovary
Gustave Flaubert

Leon's first employer, the well-to-do lawyer in Yonville. When **Emma Bovary** tries to rid herself of debt, she visits Guillaumin, who agrees to help her in return for sexual favors. Emma angrily refuses his offer and leaves.

Don Quixote
Miguel de Cervantes

Roque Guinart

A chivalrous bandit. Roque believes in justice and kindness but kills an underling who criticizes his generosity.

The Bell Jar
Sylvia Plath

Philomena Guinea

A famous, wealthy novelist who gives **Esther Greenwood** a scholarship to attend college and pays for Esther's stay in the private mental hospital. She is elderly, generous, and successful.

Sir Gawain and the Green Knight
Unknown

Queen Guinevere

Arthur's wife. She sits next to **Sir Gawain** at the New Year's feast and remains a silent, objectified presence in the midst of the knights of the Round Table.

The Canterbury Tales
Geoffrey Chaucer

Queen Guinevere

Arthur's queen, mentioned in the **Wife of Bath**'s tale as part of her explanation of power dynamics between women and men.

A Connecticut Yankee in King Arthur's Court
Mark Twain

Queen Guinevere

King Arthur's beautiful queen. Everyone in the country knows of her indiscretions, except Arthur. She has an affair with **Sir Launcelot**, which eventually leads to a destructive war between Launcelot and King Arthur. The war is a precursor to the destruction of the nineteenth-century civilization that **the Yankee** had created in Camelot.

The Once and Future King
T. H. White

Queen Guenever

King Arthur's wife and **Lancelot**'s lover. Guenever is beautiful, jealous, and often petty. She understands and supports Arthur's ideas and loves Lancelot despite his great ugliness. Guenever loves Arthur as genuinely as she loves Lancelot, though not as passionately. While Lancelot's guilt about their affair reaches epic proportions and threatens to destroy him, any guilt Guenever feels is secondary to her constant craving to be with Lancelot. She handles their cover-up badly, and at one point she is visibly excited to be reunited with Lancelot even in front of Arthur. As Guenever ages, she tries desperately to stay young and beautiful. At the end of the novel, **Mordred** and **Gawaine** try to cause Lancelot and Guenever's execution by having them caught in the act of their affair. Guenever is almost burned at the stake due to Arthur's new laws of civilization, but escapes when Lancelot saves her.

Amalia Karlovna Guishar

Dr. Zhivago
Boris Pasternak

The widow of a Belgian engineer. She settles in Moscow with her daughter **Larissa Fyodorovna Guishar** (later Antipova) and son **Rodyon Fyodorovich Guishar**. Although used to a lavish lifestyle, she finds her circumstances greatly reduced as Lara grows up, and comes to depend more and more on the lecherous **Victor Ippolitovich Komarovsky**.

Larissa Fyodorovna Guishar

Dr. Zhivago
Boris Pasternak

Daughter of **Amalia Karlovna Guishar**, and **Yury Andreyevich Zhivago**'s lover. She is victimized by **Victor Ippolitovich Komarovsky** as a child, and attempts to shoot him in revenge, but misses. She marries her childhood sweetheart, **Pavel Pavlovich Antipov**, or Pasha, and settles with him in Yuryatin, her birthplace. When Pasha goes missing on the front during World War I, Lara goes to the front as a nurse in order to look for him. There she meets Yury and begins to fall in love with him. Her fate continues to intertwine with Yury's throughout the Revolution, and she eventually has a long-running affair with him, which produces a daughter, **Katya**. Lara eventually disappears in the swirling events leading up to World War II; it seems that she has died in a concentration camp.

Rodyon Fyodorovich Guishar

Dr. Zhivago
Boris Pasternak

Brother of **Larissa Fyodorovna Guishar**. He attends a military academy and becomes a soldier.

Dr. Guitierrez

Jurassic Park
Michael Crichton

An American doctor in Costa Rica who initially believes **Tina Bowman** has been attacked by a basilisk lizard.

Lemuel Gulliver

Gulliver's Travels
Jonathan Swift

The story's protagonist and narrator. Well-educated but naïve, Gulliver never acknowledges the absurdities of the fantastical societies he meets on his voyages. Humans, including his wife **Mary**, hold little interest for him.

Mary Gulliver

Gulliver's Travels
Jonathan Swift

Gulliver's wife. He mentions her only perfunctorily at the beginning of each voyage, and shows no sentimental attachment to her or to any other human being. He goes on his travels against her wishes.

Gulliver's Houyhnhnm master

Gulliver's Travels
Jonathan Swift

The Houyhnhnm who discovers and hosts **Gulliver**. His good hygiene, tranquil demeanor, and temperate approach to life make a deep impression on Gulliver, who eventually feels more at home in this Houyhnhnm household than with his human family.

Guluband

Shabanu
Suzanne Fisher Staples

The family's most highly prized camel. Guluband is a warm and intelligent beast. **Shabanu** adores him, and the two share a special rapport. Guluband is famous throughout the region for his massive size, his intelligence, and his ability to dance.

Vergil Gunch

Babbitt
Sinclair Lewis

A Zenith coal merchant and one of **Babbitt**'s many friends and associates in the Zenith business community. When Babbitt rebels against the conventional social and political values of Zenith's middle class, Gunch tries to coerce him into conforming by shunning him socially and organizing a boycott of Babbitt's real estate firm through the Good Citizen's League. When **Myra Babbitt** falls seriously ill, Gunch once again extends his friendship and support to Babbitt, but it comes with strings attached.

Gundi

Pigs in Heaven
Barbara Kingsolver

The landlord in Rancho Copo, **Jax** and **Taylor Greer**'s community on the outskirts of Tucson. An acclaimed local artist, she spends much of her time wandering around the desert naked. When Taylor leaves, she tempts **Jax** into a sexual affair.

Ben Gunn

Treasure Island
Robert Louis Stevenson

A former pirate marooned on Treasure Island for three years. Ben's solitude has left him somewhat deranged, and he has the appearance of a wild man. He is the only character to be reformed, as he shifts sides from the pirates to the good men, willingly helping **Jim Hawkins** and **Dr. Livesey**.

Dan Gunn

Alas, Babylon
Pat Frank

Fort Repose's doctor, and **Randy Bragg**'s best friend. A bitter divorce has left him disillusioned, but after the nuclear war, he becomes a hero, throwing himself into the difficult work of serving as a doctor to a community in turmoil. He marries **Helen Bragg** when she learns her first husband, **Mark Bragg**, did not survive the war.

Misses Gunn

Silas Marner
George Eliot

Sisters from a large nearby town who come to **Squire Cass**'s New Year's dance. The Gunns look down on Raveloe's rustic ways, but are impressed by **Nancy Lammeter**'s beauty.

Master Gunner

Henry VI, Part I
William Shakespeare

A French soldier, who, along with his son, helps **Joan** bring down the English siege at Orléans.

John Gunther

Death Be Not Proud
John Gunther

The author, father of **Johnny**, and **Frances**'s ex-husband. He works as a journalist, and over the course of the memoir, he writes a book, *Inside U.S.A.* Gunther is constantly remarking on how well Johnny endures pain, and how incredibly intelligent and warm Johnny is. He strives to tell the story of Johnny's death without being overly sentimental.

Dmitri Gurov

"The Lady with the Dog"
Anton Chekhov

The protagonist, an aging, dissatisfied bureaucrat who surprises himself by falling in love with **Anna Sergeyevna**.

Gurth

Ivanhoe
Sir Walter Scott

Cedric the Saxon's swineherd, who becomes **Ivanhoe**'s de facto squire. Gurth longs for nothing so much as his freedom, which he finally obtains from Cedric after he helps to orchestrate the attack on Torquilstone.

Gus

Native Son
Richard Wright

One of **Bigger Thomas**'s group of friends, who often plan and execute robberies together. **G. H.**, Gus, and **Jack** hatch a tentative plan to rob a white shopkeeper, **Mr. Blum**, but they are afraid of the consequences should they be caught robbing a white man. At the beginning of the novel, Bigger taunts his friends about their fear, even though he is just as terrified himself.

Gus

The Dumb Waiter
Harold Pinter

A submissive junior hit man who is bossed around by **Ben**. Gus is more sensitive, has a conscience about his job, and is bored by the stale routine of his lower-class life. He is also more apt to question the inner workings of their job, especially with regards to their mysterious boss **Wilson**. The play's conclusion is purposely vague, but Ben potentially betrays and murders Gus at the end.

Guy

The Shipping News
E. Annie Proulx

Quoyle's father, and a sick, abusive man. He is responsible for Quoyle's terrible self-image. Guy and his wife both commit suicide at the beginning of the novel because they learn that they both have cancer. Guy also raped his sister, **the aunt** of Quoyle. The aunt dumps Guy's ashes in the outhouse hole at the beginning of *The Shipping News*.

Victoria Guzman

Chronicle of a Death Foretold
Gabriel García Márquez

The Nasars' cook and mother to **Divina Flor**. She violently guts rabbits on the morning of the murder. When she was a teenager, she had an affair with **Ibrahim Nasar**, **Santiago Nasar**'s father. She had heard that Santiago was going to be killed, but was not certain whether or not the rumor was true.

Gwaihir

The Fellowship of the Ring and *The Return of the King*
J. R. R. Tolkien

The swiftest of the Great Eagles. The Eagles, while generally only interested in their own natural world, occasionally interfere in the battles of Middle-earth. In *The Hobbit*, the Eagles save the **Elves**, **Dwarves**, and **Humans** in their battle against the **Wargs** and **Goblins** in the War of the Five Armies. In *The Fellowship of the Ring*, Gwaihir, the Windlord, rescues **Gandalf** from the top of **Saruman**'s tower at Orthanc and takes the wizard to Rohan. In *The Return of the King*, Gwaihir bears Gandalf to Mount Doom, where the wizard rescues the exhausted **Frodo Baggins** and **Samwise Gamgee** after they complete their Quest and destroy **Sauron**'s One Ring.

Gwen

Annie John
Jamaica Kincaid

Annie's best friend in school. When Annie's mother begins to betray Annie's trust, Gwen and Annie become inseparable, sharing their secrets and stories with one another. After Annie's illness, when she comes to crave rather than fear separation, Annie realizes that her connection with Gwen has not been very meaningful. Annie looks down upon Gwen's docility and her willingness to conform to the social order handed down by the colonial power.

13

SLAVISH SERVANTS

**THEY FETCH. THEY SERVE.
THEY DO YOUR EVIL BIDDING.
BUT BEHIND THE "YES, SIRS" AND "AS YOU WISH, MADAMS," THESE CHARACTERS ARE OFTEN MORE THAN THEY APPEAR.**

Azolan	1	*Dangerous Liasons*
Mrs. Danvers	2	*Rebecca*
Dobby	3	*Harry Potter* series, Books II-IV
Du Bois	4	*The Misanthrope*
Firs	5	*The Cherry Orchard*
Grimaud	6	*The Three Musketeers*
Kitty	7	*The Three Musketeers*
Kory-Kory	8	*Typee*
Kratus	9	*Prometheus Bound*
Lucky	10	*Waiting for Godot*
Mammy	11	*Gone with the Wind*
Mercy Lewis	12	*The Crucible*
Stevens	13	*The Remains of the Day*

The Unvanquished
William Faulkner

Mrs. Habersham

A respectable lady of Jefferson who meddles in **Drusilla**'s affairs. With **Aunt Louisa**, they represent the hypocritical, vindictive side of southern womanhood, more concerned with appearances than with truth or real kindness.

The Day of the Locust
Nathanael West

Tod Hackett

A young Hollywood set and costume designer who has been in California for three months after attending art school at Yale. Most of the novel focuses on Tod's outsider perspective; through the lens of his social and aesthetic value system, we see a grotesque picture of Hollywood. Though disillusioned by his experience, Tod continues to paint and hopes to portray the anger and frustration of Hollywood's downtrodden in a large canvas called *The Burning of Los Angeles*.

Greek Mythology
Unknown

Hades

The brother of **Zeus** and **Poseidon**; the ruler of the underworld, the realm of the dead. Hades lives with his wife **Persephone**.

A Separate Peace
John Knowles

Brinker Hadley

A charismatic class politician with an inclination for orderliness and organization. He is responsible for the student-led tribunal that pits **Gene Forrester**'s story against **Finny**'s about the day Finny fell from the tree.

Oedipus trilogy (Oedipus Rex, Oedipus at Colonus, Antigone)
Sophocles

Haemon

Creon's son, who appears only in *Antigone*. Haemon is engaged to marry **Antigone**. Motivated by his love for her, he argues with Creon about his decision to punish her.

Antigone 1946
Jean Anouilh

Haemon

Antigone's young fiancé and son to **Creon**. In his first scene, he is rejected by Antigone; in his second, he begs his father for Antigone's life. Creon's refusal to spare Antigone ruins Haemon's exalted view of his father. He and his fiancé commit suicide.

Song of Solomon
Toni Morrison

Hagar

Pilate Dead's granddaughter and **Milkman Dead**'s lover. Hagar devotes herself to Milkman, even though he loses interest and frequently rejects her. After Milkman rejects her, Hagar goes mad and wanders around town, occasionally trying to murder Milkman. Her life ends in a frenzy in which she decides to look more attractive for Milkman. Pilate gives Milkman a box of Hagar's hair, telling him that if he is responsible for Hagar's death, then he must own her.

Dr. Hagen

Pnin
Vladimir Nabokov

The dean of the German department. Hagen watches over **Timofey Pnin**, making sure he is given a sufficient number of classes to justify a full salary. When Hagen is offered a lucrative position at another college, he leaves Pnin to fend for himself.

Hagrid

The Harry Potter Series: Books 1–4
J. K. Rowling

The gamekeeper at Hogwarts and a good friend of **Harry Potter**'s. Hagrid is an enormous, hairy man with an inimitable accent and a half-giant heritage. In *Harry Potter and the Sorcerer's Stone* he cares deeply for Harry, as evidenced by the tears he sheds upon having to leave the infant Harry with the Dursleys. For Hagrid, even wild and monstrous nature is full of kindness; he simply cannot believe in the bad side of anything. Unfortunately, this naïveté leaves him ill-equipped to understand the villainous plots afoot at Hogwarts. In *Harry Potter and the Chamber of Secrets*, **Tom Riddle** frames Hagrid as responsible for the monster within the Chamber of Secrets. In *Harry Potter and the Prisoner of Azkaban*, Hagrid defends **Buckbeak**, a hippogriff that is placed on trial for injuring **Draco Malfoy**.

Dr. Hahn

Death Be Not Proud
John Gunther

A neurologist who identifies **Johnny**'s tumor at Deerfield Academy.

Haines

Ulysses
James Joyce

An Englishman studying Irish culture at Oxford who has been staying with **Malachi "Buck" Mulligan** and **Stephen Dedalus** at the Martello tower. Often unwittingly condescending, Haines reminds Stephen of Britain's control of Ireland.

Hal

The Call of the Wild
Jack London

A gold seeker from the United States. Together with his sister **Mercedes** and her husband **Charles**, Hal buys **Buck**'s dog team from **the Scotsman** after **François** and **Perrault** are reassigned to another job. The group's inexperience in the wilderness makes them terrible masters. Buck almost dies as a result of Hal and Charles's poor planning.

Hal

2001: A Space Odyssey
Arthur C. Clarke

An intelligent robot. He can carry on a conversation just as if he were human. He becomes self-conscious and develops a guilty and murderous streak, killing **Frank Poole** in an attempt to preserve his existence.

Haldir

The Fellowship of the Ring
J. R. R. Tolkien

The leader of the group of **Elves** who halts the Fellowship's entry into the forest of Lothlórien.

Andrew Hale

Ethan Frome
Edith Wharton

Ned Hale's father. Andrew Hale is an amiable builder involved in regular business dealings with the young **Ethan Frome**. When Ethan asks Hale to advance him a lumber load, Hale politely refuses, mentioning his own financial problem.

Mr. Hale

Sister Carrie
Theodore Dreiser

A theater manager who is **Carrie** and **Drouet**'s neighbor in Chicago.

Mrs. Hale

Sister Carrie
Theodore Dreiser

One of **Carrie**'s friends in Chicago. Mrs. Hale fills Carrie in on all of the gossip surrounding the Chicago theater scene, strengthening Carrie's fascination with the theater and the wealth associated with it.

Mrs. Ned Hale

Ethan Frome
Edith Wharton

The widow of **Ned Hale** and the unnamed narrator's landlady. The narrator describes Mrs. Hale as more refined and educated than most of her neighbors.

Ned Hale

Ethan Frome
Edith Wharton

Ruth Varnum's fiancé and later her husband. Ned and Ruth's romance provides a stark contrast to the fruitless love of **Ethan** and **Mattie**. Ned has died by the time the narrator comes to Starkfield.

Reverend John Hale

The Crucible
Arthur Miller

A young minister reputed to be an expert on witchcraft. Reverend John Hale is called in to Salem to examine **Reverend Parris**'s daughter, **Betty Parris**. Hale is a committed Christian and a naïve hater of witchcraft. In the beginning, he is the force behind the witch trials, probing for confessions and encouraging people to testify. Over the course of the play, however, he experiences a transformation. Listening to **John Proctor** and **Mary Warren**, he becomes convinced that they, not the manipulative **Abigail Williams**, are telling the truth. In the climactic court scene, he joins with those opposing the witch trials. In tragic fashion, his about-face comes too late—the trials are no longer in his hands but rather in those of **Deputy Governor Danforth** and the theocracy, which has no interest in seeing its proceedings exposed as a sham. He eventually counsels the accused witches to lie, to confess their supposed sins in order to save their own lives.

Mr. Haley

Uncle Tom's Cabin
Harriet Beecher Stowe

The slave trader who buys **Uncle Tom** and **Harry Harris** from **Arthur Shelby**. A gruff, coarse man, Haley mistreats his slaves, often violently.

Half Boy

The Phantom Tollbooth
Norton Juster

The leftover .58 from the 2.58 children the average family has. He believes in the reality of averages and likes to spend his time on the staircase to Infinity.

Halfdane

Beowulf
Unknown

The father of **Hrothgar**, **Heorogar**, **Halga**, and an unnamed daughter who married a king of the Swedes. Halfdane succeeded **Beow** as ruler of the Danes.

Chief White Halfoat

Catch-22
Joseph Heller

An alcoholic Native American from Oklahoma who has decided to die of pneumonia.

Halga

Grendel
John Gardner

Hrothgar's brother and **Hrothulf**'s father. When Halga is murdered, Hrothulf comes to live with his uncle at Hart.

Jim Hall

White Fang
Jack London

A criminal. Jim Hall escapes from San Quentin prison after he is sentenced to jail time by **Judge Scott**. Jim Hall tries to exact his revenge on Judge Scott, but is attacked by **White Fang**. Jim Hall shoots White Fang, but White Fang recovers.

Rob Hall

Into Thin Air
Jon Krakauer

The head guide of Adventure Consultants, the Everest climbing service that guides **Jon Krakauer** up the mountain. Hall is an esteemed climber, having reached the summit of the tallest mountain in each of the seven continents in a period of only seven months.

Halle

Beloved
Toni Morrison

Sethe's husband and **Baby Suggs**'s son. Halle is generous, kind, and sincere. He is very much alert to the hypocrisies of **Mr. Garner** and **Mrs. Garner**'s "benevolent" form of slaveholding. Halle eventually goes mad, presumably after witnessing **Schoolteacher**'s nephews raping his wife. Speechless, he smears butter all over his face and cannot bring himself to escape to find Sethe after witnessing the rape. **Paul D** witnesses Halle's madness, but does not know the reason until later.

Dr. Halle

I Never Promised You a Rose Garden
Joanne Greenberg

A well-liked doctor at the mental hospital. When **Carla** and **Deborah** escape from the hospital on a lark, Dr. Halle decides not to punish them upon their return because he is pleased that they had fun.

Gurney Halleck

Dune
Frank Herbert

Duke Leto Atreides's master of arms, or war master, **Paul Atreides**'s combat trainer, and an old friend of the Atreides family. Halleck is well-trained in the use of numerous weapons, and he is particularly good at swordplay with the use of personal electronic body shields. He is fond of music and plays the baliset, a guitar-like instrument.

Harry Haller

Steppenwolf
Hermann Hesse

See **The Steppenwolf**.

Richard Halley

Atlas Shrugged
Ayn Rand

A brilliant composer who joins **John Galt**'s strike of the mind after his work is praised only for having been borne of suffering.

Charles Halloway

Something Wicked This Way Comes
Ray Bradbury

William Halloway's father. Protecting Will and **James Nightshade**, Charles is transformed. In the beginning, Mr. Halloway is an old man who vividly remembers his times as a youth but is sure that his days of action are over. He slowly learns that there is more action in him than he thought, and it also becomes apparent that he is a man with cool nerves and much inner strength. He destroys the carnival by laughing at it, and he laughs with great certainty because he is completely comfortable with who he is.

William Halloway

Something Wicked This Way Comes
Ray Bradbury

James Nightshade's best friend and **Charles Halloway**'s son. At the beginning of the book, Will is much more of a thinker than Jim, who favors action. But as the story unfolds, Will finds that, much like his father, he is capable of quick and decisive action. Will is selfless, and he runs tremendous risks to save Jim even when Jim does not necessarily want to be saved.

Basil Hallward

The Picture of Dorian Gray
Oscar Wilde

An artist friend of **Lord Henry Wotton**'s. Basil becomes obsessed with **Dorian Gray** after meeting him at a party. He claims that Dorian possesses a beauty so rare that it has helped him realize a new kind of art; through Dorian, he finds "the lines of a fresh school." Dorian also helps Basil realize his artistic potential, as the portrait of Dorian that Basil paints proves to be his masterpiece.

Catherine Halsey

The Fountainhead
Ayn Rand

Ellsworth Toohey's niece and **Peter Keating**'s sometimes fiancée. Catherine Halsey, or Katie, is innocent and sincere and provides Keating with a refuge from himself. Keating loves Katie but abandons her, and Toohey slowly destroys her spirit.

Ralph Halvorson

2001: A Space Odyssey
Arthur C. Clarke

The Administrator of the Southern Province of the Moon.

Háma

The Two Towers
J. R. R. Tolkien

The doorman at the gates of the Golden Hall at Rohan. Háma is initially very suspicious of **Gandalf** and company.

Hamidullah

A Passage to India
E. M. Forster

Dr. Aziz's uncle and **Cyril Fielding**'s close friend. Educated at Cambridge, Hamidullah thinks that friendship between Englishmen and Indians is possible in England, but not in India.

Aunt Pittypat Hamilton

Gone with the Wind
Margaret Mitchell

Charles Hamilton and **Melanie Hamilton Wilkes**'s aunt. Aunt Pittypat is a flighty old maid who faints from shock several times a day. **Scarlett O'Hara** lives with Aunt Pittypat for much of her stay in Atlanta.

Charles Hamilton

Gone with the Wind
Margaret Mitchell

Melanie Hamilton Wilkes's brother and **Scarlett O'Hara**'s first husband. Charles is a timid and bland boy whom Scarlett never learns to love. Charles's death early in the war confines Scarlett to the role of widow.

Dessie Hamilton

East of Eden
John Steinbeck

The third daughter of **Samuel** and **Liza Hamilton**. Dessie, who runs a dressmaking shop in Salinas, California, is not beautiful but has a lovely personality that makes everyone enjoy her company. She dies when her brother **Tom** gives her salts to soothe her stomach, accidentally aggravating her illness.

George Hamilton

East of Eden
John Steinbeck

The eldest son of **Samuel** and **Liza Hamilton**. George is bland but has an aura of courtliness about him.

Joe Hamilton

East of Eden
John Steinbeck

The youngest son of **Samuel** and **Liza Hamilton**. Joe, a dreamer and academic by nature, attends Stanford University and then moves to the East Coast, where he has great success in the emerging field of advertising.

Liza Hamilton

East of Eden
John Steinbeck

Samuel Hamilton's wife and the mother of their nine children. The tiny Liza is a strict, moral woman who loves her husband and her family very much. The narrator marvels at Liza's ability to have so many children, feed them, make their clothes, and instill "good manners and iron morals" in them all at the same time.

Lizzie Hamilton

East of Eden
John Steinbeck

The eldest daughter of **Samuel** and **Liza Hamilton**. Lizzie essentially leaves the Hamilton family and chooses instead to associate herself with her husband's family. She has a capacity for hatred and bitterness that the rest of the Hamiltons do not share.

Mollie Hamilton

East of Eden
John Steinbeck

The youngest daughter of **Samuel** and **Liza Hamilton**. Mollie is the sweetheart of the family. She marries and moves to an apartment in San Francisco.

Olive Hamilton

East of Eden
John Steinbeck

The fourth daughter of **Samuel** and **Liza Hamilton**. Olive becomes a teacher, which makes her family proud. She is the mother of the narrator.

Samuel Hamilton

East of Eden
John Steinbeck

The patriarch of the Hamilton family. Samuel is a joyous, self-educated Irishman who moves his family to the Salinas Valley in California. Although he is never a rich man, he is well-respected in the community. Against the wishes of his wife, **Liza**, Samuel befriends his neighbor **Adam Trask**. Samuel remains a youthful, vigorous man until the death of his daughter **Una**, which sends him into a decline that ends in his death. Samuel sees through the evil **Cathy Ames** immediately and is chilled by her inhumanity and Adam's ignorance of it. Shortly before he dies of old age, Samuel tells Adam the difficult truth, that Cathy is working at a Salinas brothel. Although this revelation causes Adam pain, it ultimately enables him to confront Cathy's evil and escape from her power.

Tom Hamilton

East of Eden
John Steinbeck

The third son of **Samuel** and **Liza Hamilton**. Tom is ardent and passionate, in stark contrast to his brother **Will**. After Tom indirectly causes the death of his sister **Dessie** by giving her stomach-soothing salts that aggravate her severe illness, he kills himself out of guilt and grief.

Una Hamilton

East of Eden
John Steinbeck

The second daughter of **Samuel** and **Liza Hamilton**. The dark and brooding Una marries, moves with her husband to a remote area on the Oregon border, and dies not long after the move. Her death crushes Samuel and ages him considerably.

Wade Hampton Hamilton

Gone with the Wind
Margaret Mitchell

Scarlett O'Hara's oldest child. The son of **Charles Hamilton**, Wade inherits his father's timid and bland disposition.

Will Hamilton

East of Eden
John Steinbeck

The second son of **Samuel** and **Liza Hamilton**. The practical and conservative Will has a Midas touch in business dealings. He becomes wealthy and powerful in the Salinas community, but his business success alienates him from his family somewhat.

William Hamilton

Narrative of the Life of Frederick Douglass
Frederick Douglass

The father-in-law of **Captain Thomas Auld**. After **Lucretia Auld**'s death, Thomas remarries Hamilton's oldest daughter. Hamilton himself sometimes takes charge of **Frederick Douglass**. He arrests Douglass for plotting to escape from Freeland.

Hamir

Shabanu
Suzanne Fisher Staples

Phulan's fiancé. Hamir lives with his family in a nearby agricultural community. Hamir works hard and is a decent man, but he is proud and hot-blooded.

Hamlet

Hamlet
William Shakespeare

The Prince of Denmark and the play's protagonist. Hamlet is the son of **Queen Gertrude** and the late **King Hamlet**, and the nephew of **Claudius**. Thirty years old at the start of the play, Hamlet is melancholy, bitter, and cynical. He hates Claudius for marrying Queen Gertrude, and he is disgusted by Gertrude's sexuality. A reflective young man who has studied at the University of Wittenberg, Hamlet is often indecisive and hesitant, but at other times he is prone to rash and impulsive acts.

Hamm

Endgame
Samuel Beckett

The protagonist of the play, though his unlikable demeanor at times makes him the antagonist to his servant, **Clov**. Blind and immobilized by old age, Hamm believes no one suffers more than he does. To him, there is no cure for being on Earth, especially not in the dank hole where he also rules over his father, **Nagg**, and mother, **Nell**. To pass the time, he bullies Clov into menial tasks or bores Nagg and Nell with the story he is writing in his head.

Uncle Hammer

Roll of Thunder, Hear My Cry
Mildred D. Taylor

Papa's brother. Hammer lives in Chicago. He has a short temper, and is dissuaded from assaulting **Lillian Jean Simms**'s father with a rifle by **L.T. Morrison**. In times of financial need for the Logans, Uncle Hammer helps support them, for example, selling his car.

John Hammond

Jurassic Park
Michael Crichton

The grandfather of **Tim Murphy** and **Lex Murphy**, the owner of the bioengineering firm InGen and a well-known dinosaur fanatic. Hammond spends a decade furiously scrambling to clone dinosaurs, partly out of a sincere love of them, but also because he is hell-bent on turning his idea into profit. Hammond's greed often seems to supercede his judgment: the worse things get in Jurassic Park, the angrier he grows at those who want to shut the park down.

Mrs. Hammond

Anne of Green Gables
L. M. Montgomery

Anne Shirley's second foster parent. Mrs. Hammond uses Anne as a maid and makes her care for her three sets of twins.

Reverend Hammond

Native Son
Richard Wright

The pastor of **Mrs. Thomas**'s church. Hammond urges **Bigger Thomas** to turn to religion in times of trouble.

Hamor

The Red Tent
Anita Diamant

King of Shechem, father of **Shalem**, husband of **Re-nefer**. Hamor offers **Simon** and **Levi** a large piece of land when they are looking to expand their settlement. After **Dinah** and Shalem fall in love, and after Shalem deflowers Dinah, King Hamor makes a generous offer to **Jacob** for Dinah and Shalem's marriage. Jacob declares that if all the men in Shechem agree to be circumcised, he will consent. Hamor consents, further promising that, from that day forward, every boy born within Shechem will be circumcised and that Jacob's god will be worshipped in their temples. A massacre by Simon and Levi of all the men of Shechem follows.

Hana

The English Patient
Michael Ondaatje

A young Canadian who serves the Allies as a nurse in World War II. Very close to her father **Patrick**, Hana had an emotional breakdown when she heard the news of his death. She falls in love with the idea of the English patient, of the thought that she is caring for a saint-like man. Her heart, however, belongs to **Kip**, to whom she looks for protection as she stands at the boundary between adolescence and adulthood.

General Winfield Scott Hancock

The Killer Angels
Michael Shaara

A competent, important general of the Union army who directs much of the action at Gettysburg. He is an old friend of Confederate **General Lew Armistead**, who fights on the other side at Gettysburg.

John Hancock

Johnny Tremain
Esther Forbes

One of the wealthiest men in Boston and a leader of the Revolutionary forces. **Jonathan Tremain** disfigures his hand while making a silver basin for him.

Handmaids

The Handmaid's Tale
Margaret Atwood

Fertile women assigned to bear the children of elite barren couples.

Israel Hands

Treasure Island
Robert Louis Stevenson

The coxswain (a sailor who steers the ship). Hands was a gunner on earlier pirate voyages. He is acting as one of two guards on the ship when the other pirates are ashore, but he gets drunk, kills the other guard, and lies in a drunken stupor while the ship drifts aimlessly.

The Spanish Tragedy
Thomas Kyd

The Hangman

The witty and jovial man responsible for hanging **Pedringano**. Later, the hangman discovers the letter on Pedringano's body that confirms **Hieronimo**'s suspicions of **Lorenzo** and **Balthazar**'s guilt.

Midnight's Children
Salman Rushdie

Hanif

Saleem's uncle. Hanif is an actor who enjoys some fame in his youth but grows disillusioned later in life with Bollywood and the superficiality of the film industry. He commits suicide.

Ordinary People
Judith Guest

Ray Hanley

A tax attorney in Evanston. Ray Hanley and **Calvin Jarrett** maintain a law partnership together. They get along well, although Ray is often insensitive toward Calvin's family problems.

Little Women
Louisa May Alcott

Hannah

The Marches' loyal servant.

Anne Frank: Diary of a Young Girl
Anne Frank

Hanneli

Anne Frank's school friend. The Nazis arrest her early in the war. At night, Anne dreams that she sees Hanneli, who asks Anne to rescue her. Anne regrets not treating Hanneli better and feels guilty for her own relative safety while Hanneli is suffering.

Prodigal Summer
Barbara Kingsolver

Hannie-Mavis

One of **Cole Widener**'s sisters. Hannie-Mavis is kind to **Lusa Maluf Landowski**.

Angela's Ashes
Frank McCourt

Bridey Hannon

Angela McCourt's neighbor in Roden Lane and her favorite confidante. Bridey gives her friend much-needed support and empathy.

Angela's Ashes
Frank McCourt

Mr. Hannon

Bridey Hannon's father. **Frank McCourt** grows to love Mr. Hannon like a father after the old man gives him his first job delivering coal.

Giants in the Earth
O. E. Rölvaag

Anna Marie Hansa

Per Hansa and **Beret Hansa**'s daughter. She is an affectionate and playful girl.

Giants in the Earth
O. E. Rölvaag

Beret Hansa

Per Hansa's suffering wife. Unlike her husband, Beret cannot endure life on the prairie, and she longs to return to the comforts of her home in Norway. However, she still loves her husband and does not blame him for persuading her to emigrate. Incapable of severing ties to her old country, she becomes more and more depressed. When a plague of locusts arrives, Beret descends into madness, and Per fears for her and the children's safety. A traveling minister finally cures Beret, but she only replaces her madness with a religious mania.

Giants in the Earth
O. E. Rölvaag

Ole Hansa

Per Hansa and **Beret Hansa**'s oldest son. Ole helps his father work the land with the help of his brother **Store-Hans Hansa**. Ole often assumes the responsibility of oldest child.

Giants in the Earth
O. E. Rölvaag

Per Hansa

A former fisherman from Norway who immigrates to the Dakota Territory with his wife, children, and other friends. A man of action and a natural pioneer, Per possesses indomitable optimism and courage in the face of hardship. He dreams about building a kingdom in the Great Plains for his wife and family. Intelligent and strong, Per becomes the natural leader of his community, seeming to succeed at almost everything he does. Although he is capable of great tenderness in his relations with his wife and children, he gradually drifts apart from his wife.

Giants in the Earth
O. E. Rölvaag

Store-Hans Hansa

Per Hansa and **Beret Hansa**'s second son. He is an inquisitive and playful child. He helps his father work the land and often accompanies his father on trips.

Into Thin Air
Jon Krakauer

Doug Hansen

A client with Adventure Consultants. Doug is a postal worker who climbed Everest one year before but had to turn back just a few hundred feet from the summit. He and **Jon Krakauer** become close friends. Hansen is at the summit with **Rob Hall** when the storm hits.

Hanson

Sister Carrie
Theodore Dreiser

Carrie's brother-in-law, who is married to Carrie's sister, **Minnie**. The quiet, stern Hanson, who hosts Carrie when she first moves to Chicago, disapproves of Carrie's whimsical nature.

Healey Hanson

Babbitt
Sinclair Lewis

The surly proprietor of a speakeasy in Zenith.

Minnie Hanson

Sister Carrie
Theodore Dreiser

Carrie's older sister. Minnie and her husband **Hanson** believe in hard work and frugal spending, mostly because they are too poor to do otherwise.

Happy Medium

A Wrinkle in Time
Madeleine L'Engle

A jolly, clairvoyant woman in a silk turban and satin gown who lives on a foggy, gray planet in the belt of the constellation Orion. She shows **Meg Murry**, **Charles Wallace Murry**, and **Calvin O'Keefe** a vision of Earth surrounded by **the Dark Thing** through her crystal ball. She also shows the children a star sacrificing its life to fight the Dark Thing, and Charles realizes that **Mrs. Whatsit** was once a star who gave up her celestial existence. The Happy Medium is reluctant to show them anything unpleasant, but **Mrs. Which**, **Mrs. Who**, and Mrs. Whatsit insist that they see the enemy whom they will fight.

Harah

Dune
Frank Herbert

Jamis's wife. Harah becomes **Paul Atreides**'s servant after Paul kills her husband in a duel.

Harcourt

Henry IV, Part II
William Shakespeare

A nobleman and ally of **King Henry IV**'s. As the King lies on his deathbed, Harcourt delivers the news that the **Earl of Northumberland** and **Lord Bardolph**, the last of the rebels, have been defeated in Scotland.

Tandy Hard

Winesburg, Ohio
Sherwood Anderson

A young woman whose first name comes from a drunkard's speech about the perfect woman.

Newt Hardbine

The Bean Trees
Barbara Kingsolver

A classmate of **Taylor Greer**'s. He drops out before graduation to help his family on its farm and dies before Taylor leaves Pittman County. When Taylor is working at the hospital, Newt and his wife are brought in with bullet wounds. Years of abuse and neglect from his father led Newt to shoot **Jolene** and himself.

Harding

The Caine Mutiny
Herman Wouk

An ensign on the *Caine*, and **Willie Keith**'s first friend aboard ship. Their bond is solidified when Willie gives his hat to Harding to vomit into atop the crow's nest. Harding is married, and views the war differently than Willie does because of his attachments.

Dale Harding

One Flew over the Cuckoo's Nest
Ken Kesey

An acerbic, college-educated patient and president of the Patients' Council. Harding is a married homosexual who voluntarily stays in the hospital because he has difficulty dealing with society's bigotry. Eventually he checks himself out of the ward and paves the way for the other cured patients to leave.

Dr. Harding

Jurassic Park
Michael Crichton

The in-house veterinarian at Jurassic Park who treats a sick stegosaurus as the tour group passes by.

Cyrus Hardman

Murder on the Orient Express
Agatha Christie

A big, flamboyant American. Cyrus is a detective with a well-known practice in New York City. He becomes involved with the Armstrongs because he was in love with **Daisy**'s French nurse, who committed suicide after Daisy was killed. Cyrus pretends to help **Hercule Poirot** with the case.

David Hardy

Winesburg, Ohio
Sherwood Anderson

Louise Bentley's son and **Jesse Bentley**'s grandson. He goes to live on his grandfather's farm while an adolescent and ends up terrorized by his grandfather's religious zeal.

Del Hardy

The Light in the Forest
Conrad Richter

A twenty-year-old soldier. Del provides a contrasting viewpoint to **True Son**'s perspective on frontier life. Del was raised near Indians and knows their customs and language. His background causes him to be more sympathetic toward True Son than some of the other white characters, but he is still a strong white soldier who adamantly believes in the superiority of whites.

Jonathan Harker

Dracula
Bram Stoker

A solicitor whose firm sends him to Transylvania to conclude a real estate transaction with **Count Dracula**. Young and naïve, Harker quickly finds himself a prisoner in the castle; he barely escapes with his life. He demonstrates a fierce curiosity about the true nature of his captor and a strong will to escape. Later, after becoming convinced that the count has moved to London, Harker emerges as a brave fighter.

Feyd-Rautha Harkonnen

Dune
Frank Herbert

Nephew of **Baron Vladimir Harkonnen**'s. Feyd-Rautha is the baron's chosen heir. The baron hopes to secure a vast amount of power for the Harkonnen family before Feyd-Rautha comes into his inheritance.

Rabban Harkonnen

Dune
Frank Herbert

A nephew of **Baron Vladimir Harkonnen**'s. Before the novel begins, Rabban is the ruler of Arrakis. When the Atreides take over Arrakis, he must step down. However, Rabban rules Arrakis again after the Harkonnens overthrow the Atreides government.

Baron Vladimir Harkonnen

Dune
Frank Herbert

Leader of the House of Harkonnen and uncle of **Feyd-Rautha Harkonnen**. The baron is the mortal enemy of the House of Atreides. The baron is very fat, and his bulk is supported by electronic suspenders.

Harland

Pigs in Heaven
Barbara Kingsolver

Alice Greer's husband. Harland does not provide his wife with the warmth and love she deserves. He works at El-Jay's Paint and Body and collects old car junk, which is taking over Alice's house. He spends most of his time watching the Home Shopping Channel.

Harley

Ceremony
Leslie Marmon Silko

Tayo's childhood friend, and **Leroy**'s drinking buddy. Harley returns from fighting in World War II apparently less troubled than Tayo but with a severe alcohol addiction. Harley tries to be a good friend to Tayo but is impeded by his alcoholism.

Charley Harling

My Ántonia
Willa Cather

Mr. Harling and **Mrs. Harling**'s only son. Charley has a successful career at the Naval Academy in Annapolis.

Frances Harling

My Ántonia
Willa Cather

The oldest of the Harling children. Frances has a sound business mind and skillfully manages **Mr. Harling**'s accounts.

Julia Harling

My Ántonia
Willa Cather

Mr. Harling and **Mrs. Harling**'s middle child. Julia is **Jim Burden**'s age and has a penchant for music.

Mr. Harling

My Ántonia
Willa Cather

The patriarch of the Harling family. A businessman of keen ability, Mr. Harling disapproves of **Ántonia Shimerda**'s lifestyle.

Mrs. Harling

My Ántonia
Willa Cather

The matriarch of the Harling family. A charismatic and active woman, Mrs. Harling develops a strong affection for **Ántonia Shimerda**.

Sally Harling

My Ántonia
Willa Cather

Mr. Harling and **Mrs. Harling**'s youngest daughter. Sally is a tomboy.

Bill Harper

Johnny Got His Gun
Dalton Trumbo

Joe Bonham's best friend in Shale City, Colorado.

Joe Harper

The Adventures of Tom Sawyer
Mark Twain

Tom Sawyer's "bosom friend" and frequent playmate. Though Joe mostly mirrors Tom, he diverges from Tom's example when he is the first of the boys to succumb to homesickness on Jackson's Island after Tom, Joe, and **Huckleberry Finn** run away. As the story progresses, Huck begins to assume Joe's place as Tom's companion.

Harpo

The Color Purple
Alice Walker

Mr. ___'s eldest son. He confesses to **Celie** his love for **Sofia**, cries in her arms, enjoys cooking and housework, kisses his children, and marries an independent woman. However, Mr. ___'s expectations of stereotypical male dominance and Celie's careless advice convince Harpo that he needs to beat Sofia. At the end of the novel, Harpo reforms his ways, and he and Sofia reconcile and save their marriage.

Black Harriet

The Autobiography of Miss Jane Pittman
Ernest J. Gaines

A slow-witted woman at the Samson plantation who goes crazy after trying to win a race in the fields.

Andy Harris

Into Thin Air
Jon Krakauer

A guide in **Rob Hall**'s expedition. Harris is from New Zealand, and grows close to **Jon Krakauer** during the climb. Krakauer holds himself accountable for Harris's death.

Charles Baker Harris

To Kill a Mockingbird
Harper Lee

Jem Finch and **Scout Finch**'s summer neighbor and friend. Charles Baker Harris, or "Dill," is a diminutive, confident, talkative, intelligent boy with an active imagination. He becomes fascinated with **Boo Radley** and represents the perspective of childhood innocence throughout the novel. Dill, like Scout and Jem, cannot stand the racial injustice that is occurring in Maycomb. Like the Finch children, he is segregated from the other children, who taunt Dill, Jem, and Scout with slurs like "nigger-lover."

Eliza Harris

Uncle Tom's Cabin
Harriet Beecher Stowe

Emily Shelby's maid, **George Harris**'s wife, and **Harry Harris**'s mother, Eliza is an intelligent, beautiful, and brave young slave. After **George Shelby** makes known his plans to sell Eliza's son to **Mr. Haley**, she proves the force of her motherly love as well as her strength of spirit by making a spectacular escape. Her crossing of the Ohio River on patches of ice is the novel's most famous scene.

George Harris

Uncle Tom's Cabin
Harriet Beecher Stowe

Eliza Harris's husband and an intellectually curious and talented mulatto. George loves his family deeply and willingly fights for his freedom. He confronts the slave hunter **Tom Loker** and does not hesitate to shoot him when he imperils the family.

Harry Harris

Uncle Tom's Cabin
Harriet Beecher Stowe

Eliza Harris and **George Harris**'s son, a young boy.

Willy Harris

A Raisin in the Sun
Lorraine Hansberry

A supposed friend of **Walter Lee Youngers**'s and coordinator of the plan to open a liquor store with Walter's father's insurance money. Willy never appears onstage. **Bobo** comes by to inform the Younger family that Willy has run off with all the money that Walter invested in the liquor-store plan, shattering many of the Youngerses' hopes.

Harrison

Black Boy
Richard Wright

A young black man who works at a rival optical shop in Memphis. **Richard Wright** and Harrison like each other, but **Olin** tricks them into quarreling.

Joe Harrison

All the King's Men
Robert Penn Warren

Governor of the state who sets **Willie** up as a dummy candidate to split the **MacMurfee** vote, and thereby enables Willie's entrance onto the political stage. When Willie learns how Harrison has treated him, he withdraws from the race and campaigns for MacMurfee, who wins the election. By the time Willie crushes MacMurfee in the next election, Harrison's days of political clout are over.

John Harrison

Cry, the Beloved Country
Alan Paton

The brother of **Mary Jarvis**, **Arthur Jarvis**'s wife. John is young and quick-witted, and shares Arthur's opinions about the rights of the black population in South Africa. He provides companionship to **James Jarvis** in Johannesburg.

Mr. Harrison

Cry, the Beloved Country
Alan Paton

Mary Jarvis's father. Unlike his son **John Harrison**, Mr. Harrison has conservative political views and blames black South Africans for the country's problems. Though he disagrees with **Arthur Jarvis**, he admires Arthur's courage.

Archduke Harry / Archduchess Henrietta

Orlando
Virginia Woolf

A very tall Romanian archduke who dresses as a woman because he is in love with **Orlando** (as a man). He asks **Orlando** to marry him and come away with him to Romania. Absurd and doltish, he plays a comic role in the novel.

Jubal Harshaw

Stranger in a Strange Land
Robert A. Heinlein

A famous doctor, lawyer, and writer. An old friend of **Ben Caxton**'s, he takes in **Gillian Boardman** and **Valentine Michael Smith** when they are on the run. Although he has tired of fighting against corrupt institutions and prefers to spend his old age catering to his own desires, when he meets Mike, he relishes the opportunity to once again take on the authorities.

Alas, Babylon
Pat Frank

Paul Hart

An officer in the Air Force and a friend of **Randy Bragg** and **Mark Bragg**.

The Black Prince
Iris Murdoch

Hartbourne

A friend of **Bradley Pearson**'s from work. Bradley frequently has lunch with him and regards him as the embodiment of the boring routine he tries to escape as an artist. **Christian Evandale**, Bradley's ex-wife, later marries him.

Hard Times
Charles Dickens

James Harthouse

A sophisticated, manipulative young London gentleman who enters Coketown politics out of boredom. Harthouse resolves to seduce **Louisa Gradgrind** because he thinks it would amuse him.

In Cold Blood
Truman Capote

Bess Hartman

The proprietor of Hartman's Cafe. She has a thick skin and scolds her customers when they gossip too much about the Clutter murders.

Winesburg, Ohio
Sherwood Anderson

Curtis Hartman

The successful, popular minister of the Presbyterian Church. He struggles with the sexual temptation of peeping through **Kate Swift**'s window while he writes his sermons.

Dead Man Walking
Helen Prejean

Elizabeth Harvey

The mother of **Faith Hathaway**, who was killed by **Eddie Sonnier**. Elizabeth, like her husband, is a vocal advocate of the death penalty and a strong supporter of victims' families' rights.

The Lovely Bones
Alice Sebold

George Harvey

A psychopath who rapes and murders **Susie Salmon** and many other young women. After **Lindsey Salmon** secures evidence against him, Harvey leaves behind his suburban lifestyle for good.

Vernon Harvey

Dead Man Walking
Helen Prejean

The stepfather of **Faith Hathaway**, the teenage girl who was raped and murdered by **Robert Willie** and **Joe Vaccaro**. Enraged by Faith's murder, Vernon becomes an advocate of the death penalty and victims' families. Although he disagrees with **Sister Helen Prejean** about capital punishment, Vernon respects her views and maintains a friendship with her.

Elmer Hassel

On the Road
Jack Kerouac

A friend of **Sal Paradise**'s and **Dean Moriarty**'s. Elmer is imprisoned in Riker's Island, but Sal and Dean look for him wherever they go.

Hastings

Henry IV, Part II
William Shakespeare

A conspirator, along with **Lord Mowbray** and the **Archbishop of York**, who plots to overthrow **King Henry IV**. Though they file their grievances with **Prince John of Lancaster** and agree to disband their armies after a tentative truce, the prince goes back on his word and arrests the rebels, sending them to be executed.

Lord Hastings

Henry VI, Part III and *Richard III*
William Shakespeare

A loyal supporter of **King Edward IV**'s. In *Henry VI, Part III*, after Edward has become king, and spurned a political marriage with France, Hastings declares that England is strong enough on its own, and doesn't need France as a military ally. Hastings later helps rescue Edward from **King Henry VI**'s army, and helps him restore his power for the final, decisive battle. In *Richard III*, Hastings is warned by **Lord Stanley** that he may be in danger, but is initally skeptical of any threat from **King Richard III**. When **Lord Grey** and **Lord Rivers** are put to death, Hastings, who used to be enemies with them, has no remorse; however, when he refuses to help transfer the crown from Edward's heirs to Richard, Hastings soon becomes a target. Richard brands him a traitor and sends him away to be beheaded. Richard and **Buckingham** try to besmirch his name after his death, and though the **Lord Mayor of London** believes Hastings's guilt, the London commoners do not.

Hathaway

The Martian Chronicles
Ray Bradbury

Physician and geologist for the fourth expedition. He and his family do not leave Mars when the war starts on Earth. When the rest of his family dies and he is completely alone, he builds robot replicas of his dead family members.

Faith Hathaway

Dead Man Walking
Helen Prejean

The murder victim of **Robert Willie** and **David Vaccaro**. Faith had recently graduated from high school and was preparing to enlist in the army.

Judge Hathorne

The Crucible
Arthur Miller

A judge who presides, along with **Deputy Governor Danforth**, over the Salem witch trials. Hathorne often plays second fiddle to Danforth, going along with Danforth's word and the court's extreme power. Hathorne's job seems to be to press the accused and critics of the court further and further until the desired answers are produced. Even after it becomes obvious that the witch trials are based on lies, Danforth and Hathorne cannot undermine their own power by admitting that they have been tricked by a group of young girls, led by **Abigail Williams**.

Havermeyer

Catch-22
Joseph Heller

A fearless lead bombardier. Havermeyer never takes evasive action.

Miss Havisham

Great Expectations
Charles Dickens

A wealthy, eccentric old woman who lives in a manor called Satis House near **Pip**'s village. Miss Havisham is insane, flitting around her house in a faded wedding dress and keeping a decaying feast on her table. As a young woman, Miss Havisham was jilted by her fiancé minutes before her wedding, and now she has a vendetta against all men. She deliberately raises **Estella** to be the tool of her revenge, training her to break men's hearts.

Thufir Hawat

Dune
Frank Herbert

Duke Leto Atreides's master of assassins and **Paul Atreides**'s trainer in combat and tactics. Hawat is a well-known Mentat, a person trained to act with complete logic. He serves as Leto's main strategist and confidant. Hawat is old, having served three generations of Atreides.

Hawkbit

Watership Down
Richard Adams

A rabbit brought by **Dandelion**. Hawkbit at one point early on questions **Hazel**'s authority. After that, however, he follows orders and helps the group as best as he can.

Hawkeye

The Last of the Mohicans
James Fenimore Cooper

The protagonist, and a woodsman, hunter, and scout. Hawkeye's famed marksmanship and Killdeer, his rifle, have earned him the nickname La Longue Carabine ("Long Rifle"). Born Natty Bumppo, Hawkeye has no Native American blood but has adopted Native American culture and lifestyle. Hawkeye stars in several of James Fenimore Cooper's novels, which are known collectively as the *Leatherstocking Tales*. A social hybrid, Hawkeye identifies himself by his European race and his Native American world of companionship, in which his closest friends are the Mohicans **Chingachgook** and **Uncas**. Hawkeye's hybrid background breeds both productive alliances and disturbingly racist convictions. On one hand, Hawkeye cherishes individuality and makes judgments without regard to race. On the other hand, Hawkeye demonstrates an almost obsessive investment in his own "genuine" whiteness.

Jim Hawkins

Treasure Island
Robert Louis Stevenson

The narrator of the novel. Jim is the son of an innkeeper near Bristol, England, and he is probably in his early teens. He is eager and enthusiastic to go to sea and hunt for treasure, but he is also meek and fearful of the pirates' drunken swaggering, coarse language, and tendency toward violence. Jim moves from being a cabin boy to the captain of the ship in the span of a single voyage.

Haydée

The Count of Monte Cristo
Alexandre Dumas

Ali Pacha's daughter. Haydée is sold into slavery after her father is betrayed by **Fernand Mondego** and murdered by the Turks. **Edmond Dantès** purchases Haydée's freedom and raises her as his ward, eventually falling in love with her. Besides **Signor Bertuccio**, Haydée is Dantès's only trusted companion.

Arthur Hayes

I Am the Cheese
Robert Cormier

A man with a southern accent. Arthur Hayes overlooks Hookset from his cage-like fire escape. Arthur refers to **Adam Farmer** as "honey" while reluctantly giving him information about his stolen bike. Adam feels sorry for Arthur, whom he sees as trapped in a prison due to his obesity and his situation. It turns out that Arthur is just another man on the institution grounds, where Adam is really riding his bike.

Sally Hayes

The Catcher in the Rye
J. D. Salinger

A very attractive girl whom **Holden Caulfield** has known and dated for a long time. Though Sally Hayes is well-read, Holden claims that she is "stupid," although it is difficult to tell whether this judgment is based in reality or merely in Holden's ambivalence about being sexually attracted to her. She is certainly more conventional than Holden in her tastes and manners.

Charles Hayter

Persuasion
Jane Austen

The Musgroves' cousin. Charles Hayter's family belongs to a much lower social circle than the Musgroves. Charles Hayter, the eldest son, however, chose to be a scholar and a gentleman, and consequently has much more refined manners. He will one day inherit his family's land, and he hopes to marry his cousin **Henrietta Musgrove**.

Charlotte Haze

Lolita
Vladimir Nabokov

Lolita Haze's mother and **Humbert Humbert**'s wife, an uncultured woman who is intoxicated by Humbert's European background, accent, expensive wardrobe, polished manners, and cultured taste in food and perfumes. She is religious, unimaginative, and none too fond of her daughter. She discovers Humbert's lust for her daughter by reading his diary and dies soon after in a car accident.

Dolores Haze

Lolita
Vladimir Nabokov

See **Lolita**.

Hazel

Cannery Row
John Steinbeck

Perhaps the hardest-working of **Mack**'s boys. Hazel often accompanies **Doc** on collecting trips.

Hazel

Watership Down
Richard Adams

The young leader of the rabbits, **Fiver**'s brother. As the rabbits flee their home warren, Hazel guides them through all of their difficulties. He thinks quickly and imaginatively, frequently putting himself at risk in order to protect the other rabbits. Hazel wins the unfailing loyalty of the others, and though he is generally successful, he sometimes encounters obstacles that he cannot tackle. His goal is not the establishment of personal power, but rather the establishment of a new home for himself and the others.

Admiral Hazzard

Alas, Babylon
Pat Frank

A retired military man, he lives near **Randy Bragg** on the River Road and operates a ham radio as a hobby.

Henry Head

Regeneration
Pat Barker

An old friend of **Dr. W.H.R. Rivers**'s from their days at Cambridge. Like Rivers, Head is now a practicing psychiatrist. At Cambridge, the two men worked together on research charting nerve regeneration in the arm and hand.

Kevin Head

The Virgin Suicides
Jeffrey Eugenides

Therese Lisbon's homecoming date, who is dedicated to finding out more about the girls. Kevin is the epitome of a typical suburban boy—he plays football and helps **Trip Fontaine** tune up his car.

Sydney Herbert Head

The Sound and the Fury
William Faulkner

The prosperous banker whom **Caddy** marries. Herbert later divorces Caddy because of her pregnancy.

Ronny Heaslop

A Passage to India
E. M. Forster

Mrs. Moore's son; the magistrate at Chandrapore and briefly **Adela Quested**'s fiancé. Like other British colonialists, Ronny treats native Indians with condescension and contempt.

Heathcliff

Wuthering Heights
Emily Brontë

An orphan adopted by **Mr. Earnshaw**, Heathcliff falls intensely in love with Mr. Earnshaw's daughter, **Catherine**. After Catherine marries **Edgar Linton**, Heathcliff's humiliation and misery sour him. He spends most of the rest of his life seeking revenge on **Hindley Earnshaw**, his beloved Catherine, and their respective children, **Hareton Earnshaw** and **young Catherine**. Heathcliff is a powerful, fierce, and often cruel man.

Linton Heathcliff

Wuthering Heights
Emily Brontë

Heathcliff's son by **Isabella Linton**. Weak, sniveling, demanding, and constantly ill, Linton is raised in London by his mother and does not meet his father until he is thirteen years old, when he goes to live with him after his mother's death. **Heathcliff** despises Linton, treats him contemptuously, and, by forcing him to marry **young Catherine**, uses him to cement his control over Thrushcross Grange after **Edgar Linton**'s death. Linton himself dies not long after this marriage.

Mr. Heaton

Sons and Lovers
D. H. Lawrence

The Congregational clergyman who visits with **Gertrude Morel** every day after **Paul Morel** is born. Mr. Heaton is Paul's godfather and teaches him French, German, and mathematics.

Hecate

Macbeth
William Shakespeare

The goddess of witchcraft. Hecate helps **the Three Witches** work their mischief on **Macbeth**.

Hector

The Iliad
Homer

The greatest of the Trojan warriors, a son of King **Priam** and Queen **Hecuba**. Hector is devoted to his wife, **Andromache**, and son, **Astyanax**, but resents his brother **Paris** for bringing war upon their family and city. Hector is killed at Troy. Also appears as a figure in Greek mythology.

Hector

The Aeneid
Virgil

See above.

Hector

Troilus and Cressida
William Shakespeare

A Trojan prince and hero. Hector is the greatest Trojan warrior. Matched in might only by **Achilles**, Hector is respected even by his enemies.

Don Hector

All the Pretty Horses
Cormac McCarthy

The owner of the hacienda where **John Grady Cole** and **Lacey Rawlins** find work. Don Hector is an intelligent and cultured member of the Mexican aristocracy, and he seems both practical and kind. He is impressed by Cole and promotes him to the position of breeder. But when he discovers Cole's illicit affair with his daughter **Alejandra**, Don Hector is unforgiving, and turns the Americans over to the lawless Mexican police.

Hecuba

The Iliad
Homer

Queen of Troy, wife of **Priam**, and mother of **Hector** and **Paris**.

Hedwig

The Harry Potter Series: Books 2–4
J. K. Rowling

Harry Potter's pet owl.

Uriah Heep

David Copperfield
Charles Dickens

A two-faced, conniving villain who puts on a false show of humility and meekness to disguise his evil intentions.

Carl Heine

Snow Falling on Cedars
David Guterson

The local fisherman who dies mysteriously on the night of September 15, 1954. The son of **Etta Heine** and **Carl Heine, Sr.**, Carl was a high school classmate of **Kabuo Miyamoto**, **Ishmael Chambers**, and **Hatsue Miyamoto**, and was particularly good friends with Kabuo. After fighting in World War II, however, Carl struggled with his prejudices toward people of Japanese descent. A physically robust, quiet man, he was greatly respected and admired by residents of San Piedro.

Carl Heine Sr.

Snow Falling on Cedars
David Guterson

Carl Heine's father and **Etta Heine**'s husband. Carl Sr. owned the strawberry farm on which **Zenhichi Miyamoto**'s family lived and worked as sharecroppers.

Etta Heine

Snow Falling on Cedars
David Guterson

Carl Heine, Sr.'s rabidly racist wife. Etta was furious when her husband agreed to sell seven acres of his strawberry farm to **Zenhichi Miyamoto**, **Kabuo Miyamoto**'s father. Immediately after her husband's death, Etta sold his land to a white farmer, **Ole Jurgensen**.

Susan Marie Heine

Snow Falling on Cedars
David Guterson

Carl Heine's beautiful blond widow. Though Susan Marie feels that Carl was a hardworking, steady husband and a good lover, she began to worry when she realized that their sex life constituted the core of their marriage.

Heinrich

White Noise
Don DeLillo

Jack Gladney's awkward, scientific son. Heinrich surrounds himself with death and tragedy. His name reflects Jack's obsession with the German culture and language.

Hela

Norse Mythology
Unknown

A fearful goddess who presides over the realm of the dead, called Hel (which is not, however, synonymous with our word "hell").

Helen

The Iliad and *The Odyssey*
Homer

The most beautiful mortal woman in the ancient world, who also appears as a figure in Greek mythology. Though **Menelaus**'s wife and the Queen of Sparta, Helen is promised to **Paris** after his judgment of **Aphrodite**. Her kidnapping triggers the Trojan War. More an object than a person, Helen is peculiarly silent in the *Iliad*, living with Paris for ten years before returning home with Menelaus. In the *Odyssey*, she offers **Telemachus** assistance in his quest to find his father.

Helen

The Aeneid
Virgil

See above.

Helen

Troilus and Cressida
William Shakespeare

Menelaus's wife. She elopes with **Paris**, sparking the Trojan War.

Helen

In Our Time
Ernest Hemingway

Nick Adams's pregnant significant other in "Cross-Country Snow."

Helen

Herzog
Saul Bellow

Moses Herzog's sister, who never makes a physical appearance in the novel. Like her brother **Will Herzog**, Helen seems to worry about Moses.

Helen Jean

Ceremony
Leslie Marmon Silko

A woman **Harley** and **Leroy** pick up in a bar.

Helena of *All's Well*

All's Well that Ends Well
William Shakespeare

The orphan daughter of a great doctor and the ward of the **Countess of Roussillon**. Helena travels to cure the **King of France**'s deathly wound in exchange for the right to marry any man. The king grants her proposal, and she chooses **Bertram**, with whom she has long been in love. He reluctantly agrees to the match, but leaves her to fight in war, later sending her a letter expressing his unwillingness ever to be with her. Over the course of the play, Helena doggedly pursues him, "winning" his love (and losing her virginity) in a trick she concocts with **Diana** and the **Widow**. Helena is a resourceful and determined woman, loved by everyone except her beloved Bertram.

Helena of *Midsummer*

A Midsummer Night's Dream
William Shakespeare

A young woman of Athens, in love with **Demetrius**. Demetrius and Helena were once betrothed, but when he met **Hermia**, he fell in love with her and abandoned Helena. Lacking confidence in her looks, Helena thinks that Demetrius and **Lysander** are mocking her when **Puck**'s misdirected flower potion causes them to fall in love with her. Before Puck sets things right, even the good friends Helena and Hermia fight over love.

Helene

A Doll's House
Henrik Ibsen

The Helmers' maid.

Helene

I Never Promised You a Rose Garden
Joanne Greenberg

A well-educated patient at the hospital who is prone to violent psychotic episodes. During one such episode, Helene breaks a tray over **Deborah**'s head.

Helenus

Troilus and Cressida
William Shakespeare

A Trojan prince.

Helicanus

Pericles
William Shakespeare

Pericles's advisor, who rules Tyre in his absence. Though the lords of Tyre want to crown him king, Helicanus is loyal to Pericles, and he refuses.

Martin Heller

Angels in America
Tony Kushner

A Justice Department official and political ally of **Roy Cohn**'s. Martin is fundamentally spineless, allowing Roy to manipulate him in order to impress **Joe Pitt** and then taking the abuse that Roy heaps on him along with a blackmail threat.

Bob, Emmy, and Ivan Helmer

A Doll's House
Henrik Ibsen

Nora and **Torvald**'s young children. In her brief interactions with them, Nora plays with the children as if she is playing a game. At the end of the play, she decides that she knows too little about the world to be a good mother.

Nora Helmer

A Doll's House
Henrik Ibsen

Torvald's wife and the play's protagonist. At the start of the play, Nora behaves like a playful, naïve child. However, her small acts of rebellion, such as the loan and forgery, indicate that she is both stronger and less happy than she appears. Over the course of the play, Nora comes to see her role in the marriage with increasing clarity. She ultimately resolves to leave her family, abandoning the husband who treated her as a plaything and the children who are virtual strangers.

Torvald Helmer

A Doll's House
Henrik Ibsen

Nora's husband. Patronizing but not unkind, Torvald calls Nora his "squirrel" and treats her as he would a capricious child. He takes pleasure in positions of authority, both at home and at his bank. He dislikes ugliness of any kind, in everything from sewing, to death, to disease, and is deeply concerned about his reputation and his place in society.

Mr. Helms

In Cold Blood
Truman Capote

An employee of River Valley Farm.

Helmsman

Heart of Darkness
Joseph Conrad

A young man from the coast trained by **Marlow**'s predecessor to pilot the steamer. He is killed when the steamer is attacked by natives hiding on the riverbanks.

Michael Henchard

The Mayor of Casterbridge
Thomas Hardy

The protagonist, the husband of **Susan Henchard**, lover of **Lucetta Templeman**, surrogate father to **Elizabeth-Jane Newson**, and friend and eventual rival of **Donald Farfrae**. Michael Henchard is the "Man of Character" to whom the subtitle of the novel alludes. When the novel opens, Henchard is a disconsolate twenty-one-year-old hay-trusser who, in a drunken rage, sells his wife and daughter at a county fair. Eighteen years later, Henchard has risen to become the mayor and the most accomplished corn merchant in the town of Casterbridge. Although he tries to atone for his youthful crimes, he focuses too much on his guilt for his past misdeeds and enters a downward trajectory.

Susan Henchard

The Mayor of Casterbridge
Thomas Hardy

A meek, unassuming woman married to **Michael Henchard** when the story opens. She is later married to **Newson**, who buys her and takes her to sea. Susan Henchard is anxious to be respectable. Overly concerned with propriety, she attempts to keep secrets about Henchard's and **Elizabeth-Jane Newson**'s identities in order to give the appearance of perfect family harmony when she returns to Casterbridge after eighteen years away from Henchard.

John Henchy

Dubliners
James Joyce

The equivocating, omni-wary political promoter in "Ivy Day in the Committee Room." Henchy suspects his boss of shirking the men out of beer and paychecks, and he suspects **Joe Hynes** of helping the opposing candidate. Henchy constantly changes his opinions to suit the situation.

Henderland

Kidnapped
Robert Louis Stevenson

An old catechist who befriends **David Balfour** as he walks through the Highlands. Henderland is kind, and has read some of the works of David's friend, **Mr. Campbell**. Henderland tells David about many of the current events in the Highlands. Henderland then catechizes David, who is happy to have the man speak to him of God.

Annie Henderson

I Know Why the Caged Bird Sings
Maya Angelou

See **Momma**.

Ellie Henderson

Mrs. Dalloway
Virginia Woolf

Clarissa Dalloway's distant cousin. Ellie, who is in her early fifties, is poor and dowdy. She desperately wants Clarissa to invite her to the party, though both women know she doesn't really belong there.

Miss Henderson

The Jungle
Upton Sinclair

The cruel and embittered forelady at the factory where **Ona Lukoszaite** works, and the superintendent's jilted mistress. Miss Henderson runs a brothel on the side and hates Ona for being a decent married woman.

Hengest

Grendel
John Gardner

One of the characters in a song that **the Shaper's assistant** sings at **the Shaper**'s funeral.

Henri

Cannery Row
John Steinbeck

The local artist on Cannery Row and a friend of **Doc**'s. Henri is not actually French, although he pretends to be. No one is certain about Henri's artistic abilities, but everyone agrees that he is doing a beautiful job building his boat, which is up on blocks in a vacant lot.

Henrik

Number the Stars
Lois Lowry

Mrs. Johansen's younger brother, and a fisherman in the sea town of Gilleleje. He is a kind, joyful man, the jolly bachelor who seems unaffected by the worries of city society. Henrik plays an important role in saving **Ellen Rosen**, **Mr. Rosen**, and **Mrs. Rosen** by staging a funeral at his home and then transporting the Rosens across the water to Sweden, which is not occupied by the Germans. He leads a relaxed life close to nature, and is able to help many Jews escape with his knowledge of the surrounding forest and water.

King Henry IV

Richard II; Henry IV, Part I; and *Henry IV, Part II*
William Shakespeare

Son of **John of Gaunt**; father of **Henry V**, **John, Duke of Bedford**, **Thomas, Duke of Clarence**, and **Humphrey, Duke of Gloucester**; cousin of **King Richard II**. Loved by the people, respected by the nobility, Bolingbroke is first seen in *King Richard II*, accusing **Thomas Mowbray** of conspiracy in the murder of the late **Thomas Woodstock, Duke of Gloucester**. Though exiled by Richard II for six years, Bolingbroke returns to England with an army to reclaim the land left in the dead Gaunt's inheritance. Bolingbroke, thanks to the strength of the many lords who defect to his side, stages a nearly bloodless coup and is crowned King Henry IV, fulfilling the prophesied downfall of Richard. Bolingbroke's implicit wish that Richard II be killed is carried out by **Sir Piers Exton**. The guilt is apparent, and the newly crowned Henry IV announces that he will cleanse his soul in a Jerusalem crusade. But in *King Henry IV, Part One*, guilt and anxiety begin to wear him down. Still promising to undertake a crusade in the Holy Land, Henry sees his reign marred by rebellion. Former allies—the **Earl of Northumberland**, his son **Hotspur**, and the **Earl of Worcester**—plot to rebel against the throne for mistreatment. They join forces with the dangerous Welshman **Owen Glendower**. Henry also worries about the irresponsible antics of his eldest son Hal, who spends his time at a dive bar in Eastcheap. The tide turns, though: his reformed son joins him in battle, and with the help of powerful nobles, Henry defends his crown, defeating Hotspur and Worcester's forces. Henry's health declines throughout *King Henry IV, Part Two*, due to his fears about further civil insurrection and the fate of his son, Hal. The shadow of the dead Richard II still hangs over Henry's rule, and he remains deathly ill, though the rebellions are quelled and Hal has transformed into a noble prince.

King Henry V

Henry IV, Part I; Henry IV, Part II; and *Henry V*
William Shakespeare

King Henry IV's eldest son; also the brother of **Prince John of Lancaster**, **Humphrey, Duke of Gloucester**, and **Thomas, Duke of Clarence**; husband of **Katherine, Princess of France**; father of **King Henry VI**. The Prince of Wales and future king of England is cast in a poor light at the outset of *King Henry VI, Part I,* hanging around the mischievous **Sir John Falstaff**, highwaymen, robbers, and whores, and still using the boyish name Hal. After a couple of scenes dealing with the underbelly of England, tricking Falstaff, and wiling away his youth in an Eastcheap tavern, Hal is taken to task by his father, who rebukes him, telling him that the rebellious **Hotspur**, the same age as Hal, is more worthy of the throne than he. The prince changes tack immediately, becoming the regal young soldier he promised to be. He enlists Falstaff in the King's army and fights the uprising. In the Battle of Shrewsbury, he saves his father from the **Earl of Douglas** and kills Hotspur. Over the course of *King Henry IV, Part II,* Hal debates his responsibility, his misfit years, and his friendship with Falstaff. After swearing to the dying monarch that he will let his "present wildness die," Hal takes the **Lord Chief Justice** as his new surrogate father, replacing Falstaff, and emerging as the glorious king, Henry V. His metamorphosis is complete when he ascends the throne and rebukes Falstaff, telling him not to come within ten miles of his person. In *King Henry V*, he is brilliant, focused, and committed to the responsibilities of kingship—a far cry from his wild youth. Though old friends plead for his forgiveness after being exposed for treason, Henry meets the demands of the state by ordering their execution. Henry is also a brilliant orator who uses his verbal skills to justify his claims and to motivate his troops. Henry can be cold and menacing, as when he speaks to **Montjoy**, the **Dauphin**'s messenger; he can be passionate and uplifting, as in his St. Crispin's Day speech; and he can be gruesomely terrifying, as in his diatribe against the **Governor of Harfleur**. Once Henry has resolved to conquer France, he pursues his goal relentlessly, using every resource imaginable to see it accomplished. After Henry has conquered the French territories, he sets about cementing the political marriage between him and **Katherine, Princess of France**, who eventually bears him **King Henry VI**. Henry dies between *King Henry V* and *King Henry VI, Part I.*

King Henry VI

Henry VI, Part I; Henry VI, Part II; and *Henry VI, Part III*
William Shakespeare

Son of **King Henry V**; husband of **Queen Margaret** (Margaret of Anjou); father of **Prince Edward**; nephew of **Humphrey, Duke of Gloucester** and **John, Duke of Bedford**. Young and inexperienced, Henry VI is born into the prophecy that he will lose the lands that his father, the noble and charismatic Henry V, won in France. Immediately, Henry VI faces great difficulty with his squabbling advisors: even before the funeral procession of Henry V is over in *King Henry VI, Part I,* **Cardinal Beaufort, Bishop of Winchester** and Gloucester are at odds. As more noblemen politically maneuver to gain more power, the new king attempts to keep the peace. He temporarily settles the dispute between Gloucester and Winchester, and tries to do the same (but ultimately fails) with the **Duke of Somerset** and **Richard Plantagenet, Duke of York**. He agrees to marry Margaret of Anjou, a French noblewoman, on the advice of **William de la Pole, Duke of Suffolk**. By *King Henry VI, Part II,* the weakness of his reign is commonly known: internationally, the French territories are lost; domestically, the court lords plot and scheme—Henry's manipulative wife and high noblemen plot against his uncle, ultimately killing the falsely arrested Gloucester. His weakness as a ruler, evidenced by his inability to rein in Margaret as well as his swoon at the message of Gloucester's death, leads to civil war (the Wars of the Roses). The Duke of York asserts his claim to the throne and attacks the royal troops. The fight is continued in *King Henry VI, Part Three,* with Henry VI on the run from the rising rebellion. Henry is unable to stop the revolt and agrees to hand the throne over to the Yorkist line once he dies, thus disinheriting his own son, Prince Edward. The pious Henry expresses his wish to be a simple shepherd, passing the time with his flock and his thoughts. While his wife takes control of his army, Henry is left on the sidelines to observe the fighting and ponder his fate. He is twice deposed and twice imprisoned. One of York's sons, Richard (who will become the conniving **King Richard III**), kills him in the tower.

King Henry VIII

Henry VIII
William Shakespeare

The king of England, husband of **Queen Katherine** and **Anne Boleyn**, and father of **Elizabeth**. At the beginning of the play, Henry is under the powerful influence of **Cardinal Wolsey**, who manipulates him into doing away with the **Duke of Buckingham** and divorcing Queen Katherine. Though the Cardinal engineered the divorce so that Henry would marry the Princess of France, the King falls in love with Anne Boleyn and arranges for a secret marriage to her. Henry eventually discovers Wolsey's manipulations and strips Wolsey of his title and possessions. Henry takes a more active role when his friend **Cranmer, Archbishop of Canterbury** is threatened by negative rumors. The king intervenes to save Cranmer and scolds the other lords for infighting. As Anne has recently given birth, Henry asks Cranmer to baptize their new daughter, Elizabeth. The King's inactivity in the fall of a trusted duke and loving wife are seen as inevitable: with the play geared toward the birth and baptism of Elizabeth, the monarch for much of Shakespeare's life, certain events are necessary to allow the birth.

King Henry VIII

A Man for All Seasons
Robert Bolt

The king of England, who only briefly appears onstage but is a constant presence in the speech and the thoughts of other characters. It is very important to Henry that others think of him as a moral person, and he therefore cares greatly about what **More**, a man of great moral repute, thinks of his divorce from **Queen Catherine**. He tries to put his conscience at ease by forcing More into choosing between sanctioning the divorce or being executed.

Henry

White Fang
Jack London

A sled driver. He tries to use his wit to escape the hungry wolves who are following and surrounding the men and their dogs; but Henry is actually saved only by luck when some other men come and save him after **Bill** and the dogs are killed.

Henry

The Contender
Robert Lipsyte

A father figure to **Alfred Brooks**. Henry gets Alfred involved in boxing by mentioning that he works with **Mr. Donatelli**. Henry helps Alfred with his training inside and outside of the ring. He brings Alfred home after he is badly beaten up by **Major** and **Hollis**.

Henry

Angels in America
Tony Kushner

Roy Cohn's doctor, whom Roy threatens with destruction if he refers to him as a homosexual. Henry recognizes the folly of Roy's self-delusion but ultimately gives in to it, agreeing to set down his official condition as liver cancer.

Lieutenant Frederic Henry

A Farewell to Arms
Ernest Hemingway

The narrator and protagonist of the novel, Henry is a young American ambulance driver serving in the Italian army during World War I. He fulfills his military duties with stoicism and courage, but his selfish motivations undermine any sense of glory, heroism, or patriotism. The war leaves Henry emotionally numb until he meets the nurse's aide **Catherine Barkley** and embarks on a passionate but ultimately tragic affair with her.

Jacob Henry

A Day No Pigs Would Die
Robert Newton Peck

An old school friend of **Robert Peck**'s. When **Haven Peck** dies, Jacob Henry comes to the funeral, showing that Robert had clearly meant something to him.

Malachai Henry

Alas, Babylon
Pat Frank

Randy Bragg's neighbor, who works a farm with his father, **Preacher Henry**, and his brother, **Two-Tone Henry**.

Preacher Henry

Alas, Babylon
Pat Frank

The father of **Malachai Henry** and **Two-Tone Henry**.

Prince Henry

King John
William Shakespeare

King John's son and heir to the throne of England. At the end of the play, after John succumbs to poison and dies, Henry becomes King Henry III.

Two-Tone Henry

Alas, Babylon
Pat Frank

Malachai Henry's lazy brother, and **Missouri**'s husband. He is called "Two-Tone" because his face has two shades of color.

Henry's mother

The Red Badge of Courage
Stephen Crane

Henry Fleming's mother, who opposed his enlisting in the army.

Hephaestus

The Iliad
Homer

The only ugly Olympian and, ironically, the husband of **Aphrodite**. Hephaestus is the gods' metalsmith, the god of fire, and known as the lame or crippled god. He is either the son of **Zeus** and **Hera**, or just Hera, who gives birth to him in retaliation for Zeus's solo fathering of **Athena**. Hephaestus is kind, generous, and good-natured. In the *Iliad*, he forges a new set of armor for **Achilles** and saves him from the river god. In the *Aeneid* and other texts that follow the Roman tradition, Hephaestus is known as **Vulcan**. Also appears as a figure in Greek mythology.

Hephaestus

Prometheus Bound
Aeschylus

The metalsmith of the Olympian gods. Hephaestus resents Zeus but ultimately does his bidding, which makes him closer to **Kratus** than to **Prometheus**. Hephaestus, however, obeys more out of fear than sympathy for his ruler.

Hera

The Iliad
Homer

The queen of the gods and **Zeus**'s wife and sister. Hera is a very powerful goddess known mostly for her jealousy. She is often vicious and spiteful, and it is usually Zeus's infidelity that incites her anger. In the *Iliad*, she works with **Athena** to crush the Trojans, whom she passionately hates. In the *Aeneid* and other Roman texts, she is known as **Juno**. Also appears as a figure in Greek mythology.

The Herald

Agamemnon
Aeschylus

The man who tells the **Chorus** of **Agamemnon**'s homecoming. An ardent patriot, the Herald is ecstatic to see the home he thought he had left forever. He provides vivid descriptions of the horrors of the war against Troy.

Emmanuel Herbaut

The Count of Monte Cristo
Alexandre Dumas

Monsieur Morrel's employee and son-in-law. Emmanuel is very much in love with **Julie**, Morrel's daughter.

Hercules

Greek Mythology
Unknown

A famous Greek hero, a son of **Zeus** who rises to Olympus at his death. Hercules is renowned for his incredible strength and bravery, but he lacks intelligence and self-control. His most famous feats, the Twelve Labors of Hercules, are his punishment for murdering his family in a fit of madness.

King Heremod

Beowulf
Unknown

An evil king of legend. The scop, or bard, at Heorot discusses King Heremod as a figure who contrasts greatly with **Beowulf**.

Uncle Herman

Flowers for Algernon
Daniel Keyes

Charlie Gordon's uncle, who took care of Charlie after **Rose Gordon** expelled him from her home. Herman was generous to Charlie. He protected him from neighborhood bullies and set him up with his longtime job at Donner's Bakery. At the beginning of the novel, Herman has been dead for years.

Sister Hermann Marie

White Noise
Don DeLillo

Atheist German nun who treats **Jack Gladney** for his bullet wound. Sister Hermann justifies the necessity of illusions while at the same time showing Jack that beauty is still possible.

Hermes

The Iliad
Homer

The Greek messenger god, **Zeus**'s son and servant. Fast and cunning, Hermes is a master thief, the god of commerce and the market, transitions, travelers, and hidden meanings. Hermes leads the dead from Earth to **Hades**, and also appears as a figure in Greek mythology.

Hermes

Prometheus Bound and *The Libation Bearers*
Aeschylus

See above.

Hermes

Sophie's World
Jostein Gaarder

Alberto Knox's dog who works as a messenger, bringing **Sophie Amundsen** the lectures on philosophy and later taking her to Alberto. Sophie knows that some other power is controlling her life because of events like Hermes speaking to Sophie.

Hermia

A Midsummer Night's Dream
William Shakespeare

Egeus's daughter, a young woman of Athens. Though she is betrothed to **Demetrius**, Hermia is in love with **Lysander**. She is also a childhood friend of **Helena**'s. As a result of **Puck**'s confusion with **Oberon**'s love potion, both Lysander and Demetrius suddenly fall in love with Helena while in the woods. Self-conscious about her short stature, Hermia suspects that Helena has wooed the men with her height. By morning, however, Puck has sorted matters out with the love potion, and Lysander's love for Hermia is restored.

Hermine

Steppenwolf
Hermann Hesse

A lovely young hedonist and courtesan who takes **the Steppenwolf** under her wing and teaches him to live, putting him in touch with his long-ignored sensuous side. Hermine is Harry's opposite in many ways, yet also his close double. Since she bears an extraordinary resemblance to Harry's childhood friend Herman, we are led to believe that she is perhaps only a reflection of some part of Harry.

Hermione

The Winter's Tale
William Shakespeare

The virtuous and beautiful queen of Sicilia. Falsely accused of infidelity with **Polixenes** by her husband **Leontes**, she seems to have died of grief just after being vindicated by the oracle of Delphi, but is restored to life at the play's close.

Pete Hernandez

Alas, Babylon
Pat Frank

Rita Hernandez's brother.

Rita Hernandez

Alas, Babylon
Pat Frank

A poor but beautiful woman who lives in the slum known as Pistolville. She is **Randy Bragg**'s former girlfriend, and **Pete Hernandez**'s sister.

Colonel John Herncastle

The Moonstone
Wilkie Collins

A soldier who fought for the English army in India and stole the Moonstone diamond while he was there in 1799. A reclusive and dishonorable man, he eventually leaves the diamond to his niece, **Rachel Verinder,** in what is probably a malicious attempt to infect **Lady Verinder** with its curse.

Hero

Much Ado About Nothing
William Shakespeare

The beautiful daughter of **Leonato** and cousin of **Beatrice**. Hero is lovely, gentle, and kind, and her quiet wholesomeness meshes well with **Claudio**. After **Don Pedro** woos her on Claudio's behalf, Hero and her serving women successfully trick Beatrice into falling in love with **Benedick**. **Don John**'s malevolent lie about her infidelity causes Claudio to publicly humiliate her at the wedding altar, despite her fervent claims that she is a virgin.

Herod

The New Testament
Unknown

The King of Palestine from 37 to 4 b.c. According to **Matthew**, Herod hears of **Jesus**' birth and decides to kill the child, who is prophesied to become king of the Jews. To evade Herod's orders, **Joseph** takes Jesus and **Mary** to Egypt.

Herod Antipas

Salomé
Oscar Wilde

The Tetrarch of Judea. Herod is **Herodias**'s second husband and **Salomé**'s stepfather. Herod deposed, imprisoned, and executed Salomé's father—his own older brother and the former king—and wedded Herodias in what **Jokanaan** calls an incestuous union. Herod fears Jokanaan, whom he has imprisoned.

Herodias

Salomé
Oscar Wilde

The proud, hard queen of Judaea, **Herod**'s wife and **Salomé**'s mother. Herodias abhors **Jokanaan**, who has slandered her as an incestuous harlot and remains alive against her wishes. She also resents Herod's incestuous lust for Salomé.

The Heroine

Rebecca
Daphne du Maurier

The novel's protagonist and narrator. We never learn her given name. A shy, self-conscious young woman from a lower-middle-class background, she begins the novel as a paid companion to **Mrs. Van Hopper**, a wealthy American woman. In Monte Carlo, she meets and marries the older, wealthy **Maxim de Winter** and becomes "Mrs. de Winter," mistress of Manderley.

Mr. Heron

My Brother Sam Is Dead
Christopher & James Lincoln Collier

A wealthy and somewhat shadowy local character who claims to be a Tory but probably works for both sides. Heron asks **Tim Meeker** to relay a letter for him.

Vincent Heron

A Portrait of the Artist as a Young Man
James Joyce

Stephen Dedalus's rival.

Herry

The Shipping News
E. Annie Proulx

Wavey Prowse's son, who has Down's Syndrome. Herry is named for his terrible father. Wavey has become an advocate for Down's children on Herry's behalf, and is a diligent, nurturing mother to him.

Amy Hertz

I Am the Cheese
Robert Cormier

Adam Farmer's girlfriend. Amy Hertz is everything Adam is not: courageous and garrulous, she is neither afraid of authority nor of embracing her identity. Adam continually calls Amy throughout the novel, but never reaches her. It turns out he is calling the correct phone number, but is not reaching her because he is living two years in the past, and she has since moved from her house.

Jonah Herzog

Herzog
Saul Bellow

Moses Herzog's father, a Russian-Jewish immigrant who raised his four children in the slums of Montreal. Jonah worked long hours to support his family but often failed in his endeavors. He ended up working as a bootlegger.

Moses Herzog

Herzog
Saul Bellow

The protagonist of the novel, a man in his mid-forties going through a breakdown after divorcing his second wife, **Madeleine**. The novel takes place in his mind, through his memories of the past and the letters he writes. These letters are often unfinished and always unsent. Sentimental and "depressive," Moses is struggling to understand how to live his life and achieve happiness.

Mother Herzog

Herzog
Saul Bellow

Moses Herzog's mother. Mother Herzog came from an upper-class family but, upon immigrating to Canada, had to work as a seamstress and a washerwoman. In addition to supporting her husband, she looked after the children, making sure they grew up in the Jewish tradition.

Shura Herzog

Herzog
Saul Bellow

Moses Herzog's rich brother, a businessman with a much calmer temperament and more realistic outlook. Though Shura never hesitates to give him money, Moses claims that Shura "despises" everyone.

Will Herzog

Herzog
Saul Bellow

Moses Herzog's brother, who is always willing to give Moses financial help. Will worries about Moses's mental health. He bails Moses out of jail, and eventually offers to take him to the hospital for psychiatric attention.

Aunt Hester

Narrative of the Life of Frederick Douglass
Frederick Douglass

Frederick Douglass's aunt. Hester is an exceptionally beautiful and noble-looking woman, superior to most white and black women. **Captain Anthony** is extraordinarily interested in Hester, and she therefore suffers countless whippings at his hands.

Big Hettie

The Power of One
Bryce Courtenay

An obese Irish woman whom **Peekay** sits next to during **Hoppie Groenewald**'s boxing match against Jackhammer Smit in Gravelotte. Big Hettie gets stuck in the train compartment and—after stuffing her face with food—dies when they reach the town of Kaapmuiden.

Major Duncan Heyward

The Last of the Mohicans
James Fenimore Cooper

A young Southern colonist in the British army. Courageous, noble, well-intentioned but slightly foolish, Heyward is unfamiliar with Native American relations and feels out of place in the forest frontier. The British **General Webb** charges Major Duncan Heyward with the task of accompanying **Alice Munro** and **Cora Munro**, **Colonel Munro**'s daughters, who insist upon visiting their father. Naïvely, Heyward asks **Magua** to be their guide through a shortcut to Fort William Henry, where Colonel Munro is waiting. By the time Magua has taken Heyward, Cora, and Alice captive with the Hurons, Heyward figures out and confronts Magua about the fact that Magua is trying to betray the Huron nation for private gain.

Mistress Hibbins

The Scarlet Letter
Nathaniel Hawthorne

A widow who lives with her brother, **Governor Bellingham**, in a luxurious mansion. She is commonly known as a witch who ventures into the forest at night to ride with the "Black Man." Her appearances at public occasions remind the reader of the hypocrisy and hidden evil in Puritan society.

Theodore Hickman

The Iceman Cometh
Eugene O'Neill

A likeable, anxiously awaited "messiah" of the group at **Harry Hope**'s saloon. Hikey kills his wife, **Evelyn**, out of hate for her dreams for his reformation. Instead of partying, he delivers a sermon, suggesting that the men of the group give up all of their never-fulfilled hopes and sink to the bottom. His sermon threatens to ruin the culture of the bar, which runs on the continually delayed hopes and plans of its patrons.

Richard Eugene Hickock

In Cold Blood
Truman Capote

Along with **Perry Edward Smith**, one of the two murderers of **Herbert Clutter** and his family. A small man, Dick grew up in Kansas, was married twice and was jailed for passing bad checks. He is a practical man who exudes confidence and cruelty, but in reality he is not as ruthless or brave as he seems.

Amos Hicks

Their Eyes Were Watching God
Zora Neale Hurston

A resident of Eatonville, Florida. Amos Hicks is one of the first people to meet **Janie Mae Crawford** and **Jody Starks**. Amos tries unsuccessfully to lure Janie away from Jody.

Chanhassan Hiddle

Walk Two Moons
Sharon Creech

Salamanca Tree Hiddle's mother. A spontaneous and joyful woman closely attuned to the everyday beauty of the outdoors, Chanhassan Hiddle grew increasingly conflicted by her roles as a housewife and mother. Her unhappiness grew into full-fledged depression as a result of her miscarriage and hysterectomy, causing her to try to reconnect with who she was before she became a wife and mother by traveling to visit a cousin in Idaho. Salamanca (Sal) adores the memory of her beautiful, gentle mother and throughout the novel struggles to come to terms with the events that led up to her mother's departure.

Grandparents Hiddle

Walk Two Moons
Sharon Creech

Salamanca Tree Hiddle's father's parents. Gramps and Gram drive Sal across the country to visit her mother's final resting place in Lewiston, Idaho. They are wacky and unpredictable and have been arrested several times for their innocent foibles, such as "borrowing" a tire from a police car. Gramps and Gram married and lived in an unwavering spirit of love and joyfulness, despite the fact that **Mr. Hiddle** is their only son, of four, who lived to adulthood. Though her grandparents' unpredictability worries her, Sal looks to them for support, love, and adventure.

Mr. Hiddle

Walk Two Moons
Sharon Creech

Salamanca Tree Hiddle's father, a loving, gentle, almost too-perfect man. He takes Salamanca (Sal) to Euclid, Ohio, shortly after his wife's death because he is overwhelmed by grief for her at the farm. He struggles with his own overwhelming sense of loss and tries to deal patiently and compassionately with Sal's anger, confusion, and rebelliousness. When they move to Euclid, he allows Sal to spend her time as she likes, often away from him.

Salamanca Tree Hiddle

Walk Two Moons
Sharon Creech

The protagonist, a high-spirited country girl deeply troubled by the loss of her mother. She gains strength from spending time in natural settings and from her Native American heritage, and many of her memories and experiences center on trees, rivers, wild berries, and mountains. Although she is rebellious and often skeptical of adults, she is open-minded and deeply compassionate. Sal tells her story with verve and humor, peppering her sentences with colorful comparisons and exaggerations.

Hieronimo

The Spanish Tragedy
Thomas Kyd

The protagonist of the story. Hieronimo starts out as a loyal servant to **the King**. He is the King's knight-marshal and is in charge of organizing entertainment at royal events. At the beginning of the play, he is a minor character, especially in relation to **Lorenzo**, **Balthazar**, and **Bel-Imperia**. It is not until he discovers his son **Horatio**'s murdered body in the second act that he becomes the protagonist of the play. His character undergoes a radical shift over the course of the play, from grieving father to Machiavellian plotter. After his son's murder, he constantly pushes the limits of sanity, as evidenced by his erratic speech and behavior.

Professor Henry Higgins

Pygmalion
George Bernard Shaw

Phonetician who undertakes to transform **Eliza Doolittle**. Thoughtless and bullish, Higgins values his science, sometimes forgetting that human beings are more than sources of phonetic data. Higgins thinks the world of his mother **Mrs. Higgins**.

Mrs. Higgins

Pygmalion
George Bernard Shaw

Henry Higgins's mother. A stately lady in her sixties, Mrs. Higgins is quick to see that Higgins's experiment will lead to problems for **Eliza**. She treats Higgins and **Pickering** like children and consoles Eliza when she flees Higgins's house in despair.

Zoe Higgins

Ulysses
James Joyce

An outgoing prostitute at **Bella Cohen**'s brothel.

High Priest

The Flies
Jean-Paul Sartre

A maintainer of the repressive atmosphere set up by **Aegistheus**, king of Argos. The High Priest appears only once in the play, to lead the ceremony of the dead.

Highboy

The Heart Is a Lonely Hunter
Carson McCullers

Portia's husband. Highboy is good-natured and wears very loud outfits.

Mrs. Highcamp

The Awakening
Kate Chopin

A fashionable New Orleans matron. Mrs. Highcamp is instrumental in bringing together **Edna Pontellier** and **Alcée Arobin**.

Reverend Gail Hightower

Light in August
William Faulkner

A minister in Jefferson. Hightower fell from grace and was forced out of his church many years ago after his wife died in a Memphis hotel room where she was staying with her lover. Obsessed with the memory of his grandfather, who died in Jefferson during the Civil War, Hightower spends a great deal of time alone, although **Byron Bunch** visits him occasionally.

Hilarene

Annie John
Jamaica Kincaid

The girl who is second in class behind **Annie**. Annie finds Hilarene dull because she is very well-behaved.

Dr. Hilarius

The Crying of Lot 49
Thomas Pynchon

Oedipa Maas's psychiatrist, who goes on an insane acid trip and admits to having been a Nazi doctor at Buchenwald.

Hilda

Flowers for Algernon
Daniel Keyes

The nurse on duty while **Charlie Gordon** is first recovering from his operation. Hilda believes that Charlie may be defying God's will by trying to gain intelligence unnaturally.

Hildeburth

Grendel
John Gardner

One of the characters in a song that **the Shaper's assistant** sings at **the Shaper**'s funeral.

Freddy Eynsford Hill

Pygmalion
George Bernard Shaw

A young aristocrat who falls in love with **Eliza**. Freddy is well-meaning, but weak-willed and unresourceful.

General Ambrose Powell Hill

The Killer Angels
Michael Shaara

A general whose troops do much of the fighting on the first day of the battle, first with Union **General John Buford**'s cavalry, then **General John Reynolds**'s infantry.

Jenny Hill

Major Barbara
George Bernard Shaw

An overwrought "Salvation lass" who earnestly believes in her cause and her patron, **Major Barbara**. She suffers an assault from **Bill Walker** in Act II.

Everett Hills, D.D.

Mourning Becomes Electra
Eugene O'Neill

The well-fed minister of a prosperous, small New England town. Everett Hills, D.D. is snobbish, unctuous, and ingratiating in his demeanor. After the **Brigadier-General Ezra Mannon**'s funeral, Everett Hills's wife, **Mrs. Hills**, quotes her husband in saying that fate brought Ezra down.

Mrs. Hills

Mourning Becomes Electra
Eugene O'Neill

The sallow, flabby, and self-effacing wife of the local minister, **Everett Hills, D.D.**

Sandor Himmelstein

Herzog
Saul Bellow

The Chicago lawyer with whom **Moses Herzog** stayed after the divorce. He handled Moses's divorce case, and Moses believes he sided with **Madeleine**, betraying Moses. He questions Moses's mental stability.

Corporal Himmelstoss

All Quiet on the Western Front
Erich Maria Remarque

A noncommissioned training officer. Before the war, Himmelstoss was a postman. He is a petty, power-hungry little man who torments **Paul Bäumer** and his friends during their training. After experiencing the horrors of trench warfare, he tries to make amends with them.

Alice Hindman

Winesburg, Ohio
Sherwood Anderson

A woman in her twenties who once felt deep love for a man who eventually left Winesburg behind. She is now gradually and unwillingly becoming an old maid.

Tommy Hinds

The Jungle
Upton Sinclair

A well-known socialist and the proprietor of a small Chicago hotel where **Jurgis** finally finds work as a porter.

Mrs. Hines

Light in August
William Faulkner

Joe Christmas's maternal grandmother. She tries to keep her husband from killing Joe or having him lynched.

Uncle Doc Hines

Light in August
William Faulkner

Joe Christmas's maternal grandfather. Uncle Doc is a white racist who murdered Joe's father, a black circus employee. He places Joe in an orphanage.

Hingham

On the Road
Jack Kerouac

Sal Paradise's Tucson friend. Hingham is a shy writer who lives with his wife, mother, and baby.

Hink

The Day of the Locust
Nathanael West

One of **Calvin** and **Earle**'s friends who is also part of the Hollywood cowboy community.

Ira Hinkley

Arrowsmith
Sinclair Lewis

A classmate of **Martin Arrowsmith**'s who wants to become a medical missionary. Although Ira believes he is doing good, he is arrogant in his religious beliefs—most of which are narrow-minded, condescending, and colonial—and tries to impose them on others.

Samuel Hinkston

The Martian Chronicles
Ray Bradbury

The archaeologist for the third expedition. He eagerly makes up grand, implausible explanations for the appearance of an American town in the middle of Mars and convinces **Captain John Black** to explore the town. He is eighty, but is still spry due to technology.

Hippolyta of *Kinsmen*

The Two Noble Kinsmen
William Shakespeare

The queen of the Amazons. Recently captured by **Theseus**, Hippolyta is about to wed him, and approaches her fate complacently. She frequently opposes Theseus's decisions and persuades him to change his mind.

Hippolyta of *Midsummer*

A Midsummer Night's Dream
William Shakespeare

The legendary queen of the Amazons. Hippolyta is engaged to **Theseus**.

Hippolyte

Madame Bovary
Gustave Flaubert

A clubfooted servant at the inn in Yonville. He is stupid and simple, but very able. The operation on Hippolyte brings to light not only **Charles Bovary**'s incompetence, but also the real evil that pride and pretension can perpetrate on simplicity and innocence.

Hiroshima Maidens

Hiroshima
John Hersey

A group of young, unmarried women in Hiroshima whose faces are so badly burned from the explosion that many people, including **Reverend Mr. Hiyoshi Tanimoto**, help them receive plastic surgery.

Mrs. Hirsch

Number the Stars
Lois Lowry

The owner of the corner shop. She is Jewish. She and her family are among the first to leave Copenhagen. **Mrs. Johansen** sends the girls to Mrs. Hirsch's shop. On the door hangs a sign written in German and labeled with a swastika. **Annemarie** soon learns that the Germans are closing the shops of the Jews in Denmark.

Hnaef

Grendel
John Gardner

One of the characters in a song that **the Shaper's assistant** sings at **the Shaper**'s funeral.

I Never Promised You a Rose Garden
Joanne Greenberg

Hobbs

An attendant at the hospital. Sensing that Hobbs also suffers from mental problems, the patients torment and abuse him. Hobbs eventually commits suicide and is replaced by **Ellis**.

Incidents in the Life of a Slave Girl
Harriet Ann Jacobs

Mrs. Hobbs

Mr. Sands's New York cousin, to whom he "gives" **Ellen**. Mrs. Hobbs is a little slice of the Old South in Brooklyn, selfishly treating Ellen as property and highlighting the continued danger for escaped slaves even after they reach the Free States.

The Natural
Bernard Malamud

Roy Hobbs

The tragic hero. Roy is a baseball player gifted with great athletic abilities, but he can never succeed due to a tragic combination of ego, selfish ambition, and naïveté. While still a teenager on his way to the major leagues, Roy is shot and nearly killed by **Harriet Bird**. Fifteen years later, at the age of thirty-five, Hobbs returns to the game; his body has aged, but his mind and heart are the same.

Arcadia
Tom Stoppard

Septimus Hodge

An academic, and the tutor of **Thomasina Coverly**. Septimus works on his own research while teaching Thomasina. He falls in love with Thomasina and, after her death, spends his time on **Lady Croom**'s estate as a mad hermit, obsessively researching Thomasina's theories.

The Autobiography of Miss Jane Pittman
Ernest J. Gaines

Mary Hodges

A woman who lives with **Miss Jane Pittman** and helps take care of her. She is one of the strong older black women in the book.

Cat's Cradle
Kurt Vonnegut

Angela Hoenikker

The oldest child of **Felix Hoenikker** and **Emily Hoenikker**. Although her brother **Newt Hoenikker** is a midget, Angela is over six feet tall and physically unattractive. After her mother died in childbirth with Newt, Felix withdrew Angela from school to take care of him, **Frank Hoenikker**, and Newt. To cope with her unhappiness, Angela deluded herself into believing her father was an unappreciated saint. After her father's death, Angela traded her share of *ice-nine* to **Harrison C. Conners**, a handsome scientist involved with top-secret weapons research for the U.S. government, in return for his agreement to marry her.

Emily Hoenikker

Cat's Cradle
Kurt Vonnegut

The beautiful wife of **Felix Hoenikker**, mother of **Angela Hoenikker**, **Frank Hoenikker**, and **Newt Hoenikker**, and rumored lover of **Asa Breed**. She died while giving birth to Newt. Felix exhibited little affection or concern for his wife when she was alive, and his disregard was unaltered by her sudden death. A year after her death, Angela and Frank used Felix's Nobel Prize money to buy a twenty-foot-high monument to mark her grave.

Felix Hoenikker

Cat's Cradle
Kurt Vonnegut

A key researcher in the development of the atomic bomb. Felix married **Emily Hoenikker** and fathered **Angela Hoenikker**, **Frank Hoenikker**, and **Newt Hoenikker**. When **John** began researching the Hoenikker family, he quickly learned that Felix cared little for human responsibilities. Felix approached his work as if it were an amusing game, regardless of the content of the research. When a marine general asked him to solve the problem of mud, Felix began working on the creation of an isotope of water, which he called *ice-nine*, that was solid at room temperature. After his death, his three children, Angela, Newt, and Frank, secretly divided his creation among themselves.

Frank Hoenikker

Cat's Cradle
Kurt Vonnegut

The second child of **Felix Hoenikker** and **Emily Hoenikker**. Frank, like his father, cared little for human responsibilities. He bought himself the comfy title of major general on San Lorenzo by giving *ice-nine* to the island's ailing dictator, **"Papa" Monzano**. Monzano wanted Frank to succeed him as president of San Lorenzo, but Frank did not wish to accept the responsibility. He preferred to live comfortably without having to deal with the concerns of other people, and convinced **John** to become president in his place.

Newt Hoenikker

Cat's Cradle
Kurt Vonnegut

A midget, and the youngest child of **Felix Hoenikker** and **Emily Hoenikker**. Newt's mother died while giving birth to him. Newt hoped to find happiness when he became engaged to **Zinka**, a Ukrainian midget belonging to a dance company. Unfortunately, she was also a Soviet spy, and she stole Newt's share of *ice-nine* for the Soviet government.

The Hoffmans

Black Boy
Richard Wright

The white Jewish shopkeepers who employ **Richard Wright** in Chicago. The Hoffmans respect Richard, but he assumes that they will act just like most Southern whites.

Mrs. Hoge

The Bean Trees
Barbara Kingsolver

The mother and daughter, respectively, who run the Broken Arrow Motor Lodge, where they let **Turtle** and **Taylor Greer** stay free of charge on their trip west.

Boon Hogganbeck

Go Down, Moses
William Faulkner

The ugly, alcoholic hunter who is fiercely loyal to **Major de Spain** and **McCaslin Edmonds**. He tends to the dog **Lion** and eventually kills the bear **Old Ben** with his hunting knife.

Dr. Rippleton Holabird

Arrowsmith
Sinclair Lewis

A department head at the McGurk Institute in New York where **Martin Arrowsmith** goes to work. **Holabird**, like the director of the Insitute, **Dr. A. DeWitt Tubbs**, believes strongly in competition and success and constantly pressures Martin to publish his findings even when they are not verified. Although Martin initially finds Holabird likable, he soon grows annoyed and tired of him.

Paul Holden

The Outsiders
S. E. Hinton

The husky blond Soc who steps forward to challenge **Darry** when the rumble begins. **Paul Holden** and Darry were friends and football teammates in high school. **Dally** steps in as Darry and Paul circle each other, and this causes everyone to start fighting. The greasers beat the Socs at the rumble.

Holgrave

The House of the Seven Gables
Nathaniel Hawthorne

A young lodger in **Hepzibah Pyncheon**'s home. Holgrave earns his living by making an early kind of photograph known as a daguerreotype. Holgrave's politics are very liberal and revolutionary, but he is kind despite the strange and lawless company he keeps. No one knows that Holgrave is actually a descendant of the first **Matthew Maule (the elder)**. This link has given him hypnotic powers, but does not prevent him from falling in love with **Phoebe Pyncheon**. He is a man of great integrity, as we learn when he supports and comforts the despondent Hepzibah and when he does not take advantage of the hypnotized Phoebe, as **Matthew Maule (the younger)** took advantage of **Alice Pyncheon**. He has been working on research of the Pyncheon family's misdeeds and relations with the early Maules, and shows his writing to Phoebe. His Maule sense of bitterness and rancor shows how Holgrave continues the Maule legacy of revenge and faulty judgment. His politics, once so inspiring, end up seeming rather flimsy; they crumble almost overnight once he has won Phoebe's love and seen **Judge Jaffrey Pyncheon** dead. When the Judge is found dead, he hopes for Hepzibah's and **Clifford Pyncheon**'s return because he does not want to look responsible for the Judge's death.

Burne Holiday

This Side of Paradise
F Scott Fitzgerald

One of **Amory Blaine**'s roommates at Princeton and the younger brother of **Kerry Holiday**. A serious young man, Burne stages a protest of the elite social clubs at Princeton and then becomes a pacifist, refusing to fight in World War I. Burne's rejection of convention inspires Amory to look beyond the established social scene for self-understanding.

Kerry Holiday

This Side of Paradise
F. Scott Fitzgerald

One of **Amory Blaine**'s roommates at Princeton and the older brother of **Burne Holiday**. Kerry and Amory maintain a rambunctious friendship at Princeton. During World War I, Kerry leaves school to enlist as a pilot in the chivalrous Lafayette Espadrille in France. He is killed in the war.

J. T. Hollenbeck

The Land
Mildred D. Taylor

An opportunistic Northerner. J.T. Hollenbeck bought a sizable portion of **Filmore Granger**'s land. **Paul-Edward Logan** waits for Hollenbeck to sell the land and then strikes a risky deal with Hollenbeck.

Captain Holly

Watership Down
Richard Adams

The captain of the Owsla back at the home warren. Holly is a good tracker and a strong fighter. He tracks down the rabbits who leave the warren and settles down with them.

Charlie Holmes

Lolita
Vladimir Nabokov

The thirteen-year-old son of Camp Q's headmistress. Charlie seduces both **Barbara Burke** and **Lolita Haze**. Later **Humbert Humbert** discovers that he has been killed in Korea.

Dr. Holmes

Mrs. Dalloway
Virginia Woolf

Septimus Warren Smith's general practitioner. When Septimus begins to suffer the delayed effects of shell shock, **Lucrezia Smith** seeks his help. Dr. Holmes claims nothing is wrong with Septimus, but that Lucrezia should see **Sir William Bradshaw** if she doesn't believe him. Septimus despises Dr. Holmes.

Jennifer Holmes

On the Beach
Nevil Shute

Peter Holmes and **Mary Holmes**'s baby daughter. Jennifer is a constant source of worry for her mother, especially when her father returns from a voyage during which one of the submarine crew came down with the measles.

Mary Holmes

On the Beach
Nevil Shute

Peter Holmes's wife and **Jennifer Holmes**'s mother. Mary lives for the comfort and domesticity of her family. Up until the last moments, she refuses to accept that her world is coming to an end.

Peter Holmes

On the Beach
Nevil Shute

Mary Holmes's husband, **Jennifer Holmes**'s father, and a lieutenant commander in the Royal Australian Navy. Peter becomes liaison officer to the U.S.S. *Scorpion*, the American nuclear submarine captained by **Dwight Towers**. Like Towers, Peter is a real Navy man who longs to go to the sea even if it means leaving his wife and baby daughter during their last few months alive.

Sherlock Holmes

Hound of the Baskervilles
Sir Arthur Conan Doyle

A brilliant detective and the novel's protagonist. Holmes is the famed 221B Baker Street detective with a keen eye, hawk nose, and the trademark hat and pipe. Holmes is observation and intuition personified, and though he takes a bit of a back seat to his sidekick, **Dr. Watson**, in this story, we always feel his presence. It takes his legendary powers to crack the case.

Arthur Holmwood

Dracula
Bram Stoker

Lucy Westenra's fiancé and a friend of her other suitors. Arthur is the son of **Lord Godalming** and inherits that title upon his father's death. In the course of his fight against **Count Dracula**'s dark powers, Arthur does whatever circumstances demand: he is the first to offer Lucy a blood transfusion, and he agrees to kill her demonic form.

Holofernes

Love's Labour's Lost
William Shakespeare

A schoolmaster who, along with the curate **Nathaniel**, gives learned commentary on **Berowne**'s misplaced letter to **Rosaline**. He organizes the highly comedic masque of the Nine Worthies that is performed for the lovers at the end of the play, giving himself the role of Judas Maccabaeus.

Hoppy Holohan

Dubliners
James Joyce

The befuddled secretary who organizes the musical concerts in "A Mother." Mr. Holohan is nicknamed "Hoppy" because one of his legs is shorter than the other. He is the victim of **Mrs. Kearney**'s abuse, and though he remains quiet, he is the only character who resists her.

Monsieur Homais

Madame Bovary
Gustave Flaubert

The apothecary at Yonville. Homais is a superficial, obnoxious, pompous, self-impressed man of the bourgeois class who tries to help **Charles Bovary** become established as a doctor in the town. His pomposity can cause real harm, as when he encourages Charles to operate on **Hippolyte** to disastrous effect. Homais is the perfect embodiment of all the bourgeois values and characteristics that bore **Emma Bovary**. When Emma is on her death bed, Homais seems entirely oblivious to her final throes of agony.

Honey

Who's Afraid of Virginia Woolf?
Edward Albee

The petite, "slim-hipped" wife of **Nick**. During a nightcap at **George** and **Martha**'s, she and her husband become an audience and then pawns in a sadistic game of jealousy and humiliation. Honey has a weak stomach and is the most proper of the foursome, and therefore the most susceptible to the verbal abuse that dominates the evening. Her hysterical pregnancy that spawned her marriage to Nick, along with her fear of having children, parallels George and Martha's barren marriage.

Lucy Honeychurch

A Room with a View
E. M. Forster

A young woman from Surrey who doesn't know what she wants. Her piano skills show that she has potential for great passions and the ability to recognize truth even if it means breaking the social codes that are expected of her. She grows into a woman through the course of the book, choosing to follow the true instincts of love (as represented by **George Emerson**) over the tedious falsities perpetuated by pretentious upper-class society (as represented by **Cecil Vyse**).

Mrs. Honeychurch

A Room with a View
E. M. Forster

Lucy Honeychurch's cheerful, talkative, good-natured, and warm-hearted mother, who always says what's on her mind. Her husband is dead.

Honor

Jazz
Toni Morrison

The young boy who helps take care of **Henry LesTroy**'s livestock when he is away. He arrives at Henry LesTroy's house and finds **Golden Gray** standing in the doorway. Upon Golden Gray's command, Honor helps deliver **Wild**'s baby. The baby turns out to be **Joe Trace**.

General John Hood

The Killer Angels
Michael Shaara

A Confederate major general under **General James Longstreet**'s command. Hood is Longstreet's most competent soldier. Like Longstreet, he prefers defensive strategies, and he understands that the nature of war is changing.

Alvin Hooks

Snow Falling on Cedars
David Guterson

The prosecuting attorney in **Kabuo Miyamoto**'s trial. Hooks charges Kabuo with first-degree murder and is rabidly seeking the death penalty. He subtly appeals to the jury's racism during the trial.

Harry Hope

The Iceman Cometh
Eugene O'Neill

The owner of the saloon. Likable to all, he hides his vulnerability behind a testy manner but fools no one. He has not left the saloon since his wife's death twenty years ago. He is struck by apathy and mechanically attempts to drink himself into a stupor.

Hopkins

In Our Time
Ernest Hemingway

An old friend of **Nick Adams**'s. Nick thinks of Hopkins as he makes coffee in "Big Two-Hearted River." Hopkins was presumably killed in the war.

Horatio

The Spanish Tragedy
Thomas Kyd

The proud, promising son of **Hieronimo**. Horatio's sense of duty and loyalty emerge in his actions toward Andrea, and he gives Andrea the funeral rites that let the **Ghost of Andrea** cross the river Acheron in the underworld. He also captures Andrea's killer, **Balthazar**, in battle. Horatio's sense of pride is shown in his confrontation with **Lorenzo**; though Lorenzo greatly outranks him in stature, he does not defer, but instead continues to argue his case before **the King**.

Horatio

Hamlet
William Shakespeare

Hamlet's closest friend. Horatio was a classmate of Hamlet's at the University in Wittenberg. He is loyal and helpful to Hamlet throughout the play. Horatio is the only major character who survives at the end of the play, informing the conquering **Fortinbras** of the tragedy that occurred.

E. K. Hornbeck

Inherit the Wind
Jerome Lawrence & Robert E. Lee

A cynical, wisecracking journalist and critic who speaks in colorful phrases. E.K. Hornbeck travels to Hillsboro to cover **Bertram Cates**'s trial for the *Baltimore Herald*. He despises **Matthew Harrison Brady**'s religious fundamentalism and the townspeople's simple-minded acceptance of Brady's views. In his column, Hornbeck portrays Cates as a hero.

Sugar Hornbuckle

Pigs in Heaven
Barbara Kingsolver

The face on the *Life* magazine advertisement. Sugar Hornbuckle was photographed on the Cherokee Nation, in front of a sign that read "Welcome to Heaven," the small town where she has lived for all of her adult life. Sugar and **Alice Greer** are second cousins and childhood friends. Now a grandma, Sugar is still kind and warm and loves her home and family on the Nation.

Thomas Horner

Henry VI, Part II
William Shakespeare

An armorer and **Peter Thump**'s master. Accused by Peter of supporting the **Duke of York**'s claim to the crown, Horner must fight Peter in single combat, typical of courtly trials by combat. Horner's death marks the beginning of a public Yorkist threat to King Henry's throne.

Dr. Hornicker

The Virgin Suicides
Jeffrey Eugenides

The hospital psychiatrist and respected local authority who deals with the Lisbon cases. After extensively testing **Cecilia Lisbon**, Dr. Hornicker concludes that her first suicide attempt was a cry for help and suggests she be given more social outlets. Upon her death and the family's subsequent disintegration, he begins to revise his hypothesis, diagnosing the surviving sisters with post-traumatic stress syndrome and warning of the high incidence of repetitive suicide in individual families.

Horrible

The Caine Mutiny
Herman Wouk

The only person to die onboard the *Caine* during its many voyages and misadventures. His unfortunate demise reminds **Willie Keith** of the inevitability of death.

Horse

Bless Me, Ultima
Rudolfo A. Anaya

One of a group of exuberant boys who frequently curse and fight. Horse loves to wrestle, but everyone fears **Bones** more because he is reckless and perhaps even crazy. Horse asks **Antonio Márez** to do a magic trick, and Antonio vomits carrot juice, which scares **Ernie** and Horse. The boys in the exuberant group are **Abel**, Bones, Ernie, Horse, **the Vitamin Kid**, **Lloyd**, and **Red**.

Horse-courser

Doctor Faustus
Christopher Marlowe

A trader of horses and victim of **Faustus**'s tricks. The horse that the horse-courser buys from **Faustus** vanishes when the horse-courser rides it into water.

Captain Horster

An Enemy of the People
Henrik Ibsen

A ship captain who has little interest in local politics, Horster provides the hall for **Dr. Thomas Stockmann**'s speech, but he is fired from his ship as a result.

Hortensio

The Taming of the Shrew
William Shakespeare

A sensible gentleman of Padua. **Gremio** and Hortensio are **Bianca**'s suitors at the beginning of the play. Though they are rivals, these men also become allies in their attempts to marry **Katherine** off, thereby leaving Bianca available for marriage. Once **Petruccio** agrees to woo and marry Kate, Gremio, Hortensio, and now a third suitor—**Tranio**, in the guise of **Lucentio**—are able to make their case to **Baptista** for his younger daughter's hand. Though Lucentio does end up with Bianca, Hortensio settles down to a logical, if unromantic marriage with a widow. Continuing with the theme of disguise in the play, Hortensio dresses up as a music teacher, Litio, in order to woo Bianca.

Captain Hoseason

Kidnapped
Robert Louis Stevenson

The captain of the ship *Covenant*. Captain Hoseason abducts **David Balfour** onto his ship on the orders of David's uncle **Ebenezer Balfour**, and later tries to kill David and **Alan Breck Stewart**. Alan and David kill off all of Hoseason's crew except for **Riach**, and come to parley with the captain from their fortified position in the ship's Round-House. The captain agrees to drop David and Alan off at Linnhe Loch, but David gets washed overboard at Torran Rocks. Captain Hoseason, similarly, is shipwrecked after the *Covenant* founders on the Torran Rocks.

Uncle Hoskins

Black Boy
Richard Wright

Aunt Maggie's first husband. Uncle Hoskins is a friendly man, but loses Richard's trust when he pretends to drive his buggy into the river to frighten Richard. Local whites murder Hoskins when they grow jealous of his profitable saloon.

Katsumi Hosokawa

Bel Canto
Ann Patchett

The head of a major Japanese electronics firm and an extremely hard worker. Order and diligence characterize Hosokawa's life, and only when listening to opera does he feel passionately alive. His adoration for the voice of opera singer **Roxane Coss** brings him to the poor South American country where the novel is set. There Hosokawa and Coss fall in love. At the beginning of *Bel Canto*, Hosokawa is a man with a tidy, conventional life. He works very hard. He is a success. He has a family. But when Hosokawa listens to opera, he stops doing and thinking and feeling what is proper and experiences the intensity of human love, anguish, and passion. When his romance with Roxane Coss blooms, the love that he used to feel only while listening to opera begins to color all of his days. Hosokawa wonders if he and Coss will be able to protect and maintain their passion for each other once they have been released.

Host of *Canterbury Tales*

The Canterbury Tales
Geoffrey Chaucer

The leader of the group. The Host is large, loud, and merry, but possesses a quick temper. He mediates among the pilgrims and facilitates the flow of their tales. His title of "host" may be a pun, suggesting both an innkeeper and the Eucharist, or Holy Host.

Host of *Merry Wives*

The Merry Wives of Windsor
William Shakespeare

The host of the Garter Inn. The delight he takes in hearing the French **Caius** and the Welsh **Sir Hugh Evans** mangle the English language comes back to him when the two foreigners plot together to release his horses. The Host also helps **Master Frank Ford** come in disguise to **Sir John Falstaff**, to catch the fat knight with Ford's wife.

Host of *Two Gents*

The Two Gentlemen of Verona
William Shakespeare

Julia's landlord in Milan. The Host tries to console the cross-dressed Julia, but inadvertantly causes greater grief when he has her listen to **Proteus**'s love song to **Silvia**.

Hotspur

Richard II and *Henry IV, Part I*
William Shakespeare

Son of the **Earl of Northumberland** and **Lady Northumberland**; husband of **Kate, Lady Percy**; nephew of the **Earl of Worcester**. Along with his father, Percy swears allegiance to the returned exile Bolingbroke (**Henry IV**) in *King Richard II*. In *King Henry IV, Part I*, Percy, who has adopted the evocative name Hotspur, becomes a major opponent to Henry IV's reign. Feeling that the king is ungrateful, Hotspur sides with his father and Worcester in beginning a revolt against the throne. Quick-tempered and impatient, Hotspur is obsessed with honor and glory. He insults his powerful ally **Owen Glendower**, making fun of his Welsh legend. Though historically inaccurate, Shakespeare makes Hotspur the same age as Prince Hal (the future **Henry V**), and the two are set up as archrivals. When the Battle of Shrewsbury, his time of revolt, is at hand, word comes that his father's army and Glendower's forces will not be there for battle; despite the tremendous loss, the hotheaded Hotspur declares that he will fight anyway. He is killed in battle by Hal.

Harry Houdini

Ragtime
E. L. Doctorow

A real-life magician and performer who appears intermittently throughout the novel. He is overly dependent on his mother and suffers greatly after her death. He begins to conduct research on the afterlife and contacting the dead. At the beginning of the novel, his car breaks down in front of the family's house in New Rochelle, and he meets **the little boy**, who admires him greatly.

Houyhnhnms

Gulliver's Travels
Jonathan Swift

Wise and rational-thinking horse creatures. The Houyhnhnms maintain a peaceful socialist society governed by reason and truthfulness. **Gulliver** becomes deeply attached to the Houyhnhnms, but they ask him to leave when they realize how much he physically resembles the brutish **Yahoos**. The encounter with the Houyhnhnms causes Gulliver to reevaluate the differences between humans and beasts and to question humans' claim to rational thought.

Hovstad

An Enemy of the People
Henrik Ibsen

The editor of *The People's Herald*, the town's leftist newspaper. Although slightly corrupt, Hovstad is at heart a political radical.

Howard

Ordinary People
Judith Guest

Beth Jarrett's father, **Conrad Jarrett**'s grandfather, husband of **Ellen**. Howard and Ellen spend Christmas with the Jarretts, and Conrad stays at their house when his parents go to Houston.

Mr. Howard

This Boy's Life
Tobias Wolff

An alumnus of Hill Preparatory School who is sent to interview **Jack Wolff** before his acceptance. Mr. Howard is exceedingly happy when Jack is accepted at Hill, and generously takes him to his own tailor in Seattle to be fitted for a new school wardrobe.

Pembroke Howard

Pudd'nhead Wilson
Mark Twain

A lawyer and close friend of **Judge Driscoll**'s. Pembroke Howard is another descendant of what Mark Twain calls the "FFV's," the First Families of Virginia. He prosecutes **Angelo Capello** and **Luigi Capello** for the judge's murder. He establishes a motive for the crime—the lost election as a result of the judge's speech, and the refused challenge to a duel. It turns out that "Tom," or **Valet de Chambre**, Chambers, really committed the murder.

Howie

Johnny Got His Gun
Dalton Trumbo

A boy with whom **Joe Bonham** grew up in Shale City. Howie and Joe were not good friends, but they decided to work on a section gang together one summer when they both learned their girlfriends had cheated on them.

Rosemary Hoyt

Tender Is the Night
F. Scott Fitzgerald

A beautiful, naive young movie star, born in America but educated in France under the watchful eye of her mother, **Elsie Speers**. The starry-eyed, optimistic Rosemary immediately falls in love with **Dick Diver** and soon confesses her love to him. Their affair progresses tentatively and is cut off when Dick's wife **Nicole** finds out. Several years later, Dick finds Rosemary again, and they resume their affair despite the fact that their attraction to each other has largely faded. It is unclear what happens to Rosemary at the end of the novel when Dick loses his wife and returns to America.

King Hrethel

Beowulf
Unknown

The Geatish king who took **Beowulf** in as a ward after the death of **Ecgtheow**, Beowulf's father.

Hrethric

Beowulf
Unknown

Hrothgar's elder son, Hrethric stands to inherit the Danish throne. However, Hrethric's older cousin **Hrothulf** will prevent him from doing so. **Beowulf** offers to support the youngster's prospect of becoming king by hosting him in Geatland and giving him guidance.

Hrothgar

Beowulf
Unknown

The king of the Danes. Hrothgar enjoys military success and prosperity until **Grendel** terrorizes his realm and kills his men in the mead hall. A wise and aged ruler, Hrothgar represents a different kind of leadership from that exhibited by the youthful warrior **Beowulf**. He is a father figure to Beowulf and a model for the kind of king Beowulf will become.

Hrothgar

Grendel
John Gardner

King of the Danes. Hrothgar maintains a highly powerful and prosperous kingdom until **Grendel** begins terrorizing the area. In *Beowulf*, Hrothgar is an exemplary model of kingship, but in *Grendel* he is more flawed and human. Grendel often describes his war with the humans as a personal battle between Hrothgar and himself.

Hrothmund

Beowulf
Unknown

Hrothgar's second son.

Hrothulf

Beowulf
Unknown

Hrothgar's nephew. Hrothulf betrays and usurps his cousin **Hrethric**, the rightful heir to the Danish throne. Hrothulf's treachery contrasts with **Beowulf**'s loyalty to his uncle, the Danish king **Hygelac**.

Hrothulf

Grendel
John Gardner

Hrothgar's orphaned nephew. In *Beowulf*, Hrothulf usurps Hrothgar's son **Hrethric** as ruler of the Scyldings. In *Grendel*, Hrothulf is a young man who forms ideas of revolution after seeing the aristocratic thanes subjugating the Danish peasants.

An-mei Hsu

The Joy Luck Club
Amy Tan

A member of the Joy Luck Club and the mother of seven. An-mei has learned the necessity of speaking up for herself, but, she notes with pain, she has not taught her daughter **Rose** the importance of assertiveness. Although she has lost most of her faith in God, An-mei has faith in the power of will and effort.

Bing Hsu

The Joy Luck Club
Amy Tan

The youngest of **An-mei** and **George Hsu**'s seven children. When Bing was four years old, he drowned at the beach. **Rose** irrationally blames herself for the death.

George Hsu

The Joy Luck Club
Amy Tan

An-mei's husband and **Rose**'s father.

Rose Hsu

The Joy Luck Club
Amy Tan

The youngest of **An-mei** and **George Hsu**'s three daughters. Rose married **Ted Jordan** over the protests of An-mei and Mrs. Jordan. She has always allowed Ted to make all the decisions, and when Ted asks her to take on some responsibility, their marriage disintegrates. An-mei helps Rose understand that she needs to assert herself.

Mrs. Hubbard

Murder on the Orient Express
Agatha Christie

The assumed identity of Linda Arden, a famous actress and grandmother of **Daisy Armstrong**. Mrs. Hubbard provides constant interruption and diversion on the train and is known for her stories about her daughter. Mrs. Hubbard's compartment is next to **Ratchett**'s.

Victor Hubbard

How the Garcia Girls Lost Their Accents
Julia Alvarez

An American CIA operative who arranges for **Carlos** and his family to escape to the United States.

Eunice Hubbell

A Streetcar Named Desire
Tennessee Williams

Stella Kowalski's landlady and upstairs neighbor. Eunice and her husband **Steve Hubbell** represent the low-class, carnal life that Stella has chosen. Like Stella, Eunice stays with and loves her husband despite his occasional outbursts of violence, and she advises Stella to do the same.

Steve Hubbell

A Streetcar Named Desire
Tennessee Williams

Stanley Kowalski's poker buddy; **Eunice Hubbell**'s husband. Like Stanley, Steve is a brutish, hot-blooded, strong male and an abusive husband.

Hubert

King John
William Shakespeare

King John's follower. After **Arthur** is captured, Hubert is assigned to look after the young duke. John asks him to kill Arthur, but Hubert spares his life. After English lords find out about Arthur's death, they defect to the French side; the king rebukes Hubert for the murder. Hubert tells John that the youth is alive, but later finds out that Arthur has leapt to his death from the tower. Hubert convinces **Philip the Bastard** that he is innocent in Arthur's death, and later informs him that the king has been poisoned.

Charley Huckleberry

When the Legends Die
Hal Borland

A Ute friend of **George Black Bull**'s. Charley is a member of the council on the reservation.

Izz Huett

Tess of the d'Urbervilles
Thomas Hardy

A milkmaid whom **Tess Durbeyfield** befriends at the Talbothays Dairy. Izz Huett, **Marian**, and **Retty** remain close to Tess throughout the rest of her life. They are all in love with **Angel Clare** and are devastated when he chooses Tess over them. Izz nearly runs off to Brazil with Angel when he leaves Tess.

Jerry Huff

This Boy's Life
Tobias Wolff

A short but physically strong boy. Jerry Huff is popular with the girls at school and is exceptionally vain. Huff bullies even those who have beaten him in fistfights. He later marries the pregnant **Tina Flood** to save himself from doing jail time as an accessory to statutory rape.

John Huff

Dandelion Wine
Ray Bradbury

Douglas Spaulding's best friend and the best athlete among the boys. John worries that he will be nothing more than a forgotten memory once he leaves Green Town.

Huld

The Trial
Franz Kafka

Joseph K.'s advocate, who supplies more anecdote than action.

Humamba

The Epic of Gilgamesh
Unknown

The tusked ogre set by **Enlil** to guard the sacred cedar forest. He is killed by **Gilgamesh** and **Enkidu**, with **Shamash**'s help. Humamba's seven garments produce an aura that paralyzes all potential opponents with fear. His mouth is fire, he roars like a flood, and he breathes death, much like an erupting volcano.

Humbert Humbert

Lolita
Vladimir Nabokov

The narrator and protagonist, an erudite European intellectual with an obsessive love for nymphets and a history of mental illness. While in jail awaiting his trial for murdering **Clare Quilty**, Humbert writes the text of *Lolita* as a confession. The narrative covers his affair with Dolores Haze (**Lolita**), the several years they spend together, her desertion, and his murder of Quilty, a pedophiliac porn king. Despite his knowledge of the world, Humbert becomes self-aware only toward the end of the novel, when he realizes he has ruined Lolita's childhood. Humbert dies of heart failure in prison soon after learning of Lolita's death.

Dick Humbird

This Side of Paradise
F. Scott Fitzgerald

A friend of **Amory Blaine**'s at Princeton. Despite the fact that Dick's wealth comes from new money, Amory finds in him all the ideal qualities of his generation. Dick dies in an auto accident when returning from a party in New York.

Humbug

The Phantom Tollbooth
Norton Juster

An insect who lives only to flatter people, including himself. The Humbug is ignorant about everything from math to geography and proves himself the fool by his constant attempts to say intelligent things. After trying to brown-nose his way to favor with **King Azaz**, he accompanies **Milo** and **Tock** on their journey.

Sir John Hume

Henry VI, Part II
William Shakespeare

A supposed adviser to **Eleanor, Duchess of Gloucester**. In fact, **Cardinal Beaufort** has bribed him to encourage the Duchess to dabble in the occult in order to make trouble for the **Duke of Gloucester**. Eleanor hires Hume to arrange for her to speak to conjurers and is arrested, along with her accomplices, for participating in witchcraft. Though he was a pawn in the plot, Hume is sentenced to death by **King Henry VI**.

Prince Humperdinck

The Princess Bride
William Goldman

The heir to the Florinese throne. Humperdinck is built like a barrel and walks like a crab. He is obsessed with hunting. He prefers fighting and adventure to domestic duties, and so he plots to murder his soon-to-be-wife, **Buttercup**, frame the Guilderians across the sea, and start a war.

Humphrey

Moll Flanders
Daniel Defoe

Moll's son by the husband who was also her brother. She meets him with an overwhelming affection on her return to America, and he very generously helps her get established there.

Through the Looking Glass
Lewis Carroll

Humpty Dumpty

A pompous and easily offended sort who fancies himself a master of words. He is rude and foolish.

Catch-22
Joseph Heller

Hungry Joe

An unbalanced member of **John Yossarian**'s squadron. A former photographer for *Life* magazine, Hungry Joe is obsessed with photographing naked women. He has horrible nightmares unless he is scheduled to fly a combat mission the next morning.

The Epic of Gilgamesh
Unknown

Hunter

The Hunter discovers **Enkidu** at a watering place in the wilderness and plots to tame him.

Ceremony
Leslie Marmon Silko

Hunter

An animal spirit sacred to the Native Americans. He appears to **Tayo** in both his animal and his human forms to help him catch **Josiah**'s cattle.

A Streetcar Named Desire
Tennessee Williams

Shep Huntleigh

A former suitor of **Blanche DuBois**'s whom she met again a year before her arrival in New Orleans while vacationing in Miami. Despite the fact that Shep is married, Blanche hopes he will provide the financial support for her and **Stella Kowalski** to escape from **Stanley Kowalski**. As Blanche's mental stability deteriorates, her fantasy that Shep is coming to sweep her away becomes more and more real to her. Shep never appears onstage.

Catch-22
Joseph Heller

Huple

The pilot who flew the Avignon mission during which **Snowden** was killed. Huple is **Hungry Joe**'s roommate.

The Good Soldier
Ford Madox Ford

The Misses Hurlbird

Florence Hulbird Dowell's unmarried aunts, two older women who reside in Connecticut. Though **John Dowell** thinks them eccentric, they try their hardest to warn him away from their wayward niece. Florence despises and distrusts them.

Uncle John Hurlbird

The Good Soldier
Ford Madox Ford

The old, wealthy uncle of **Florence Hurlbird Dowell**. Uncle John is thin, gentle and extraordinarily lovable. He is a violent Democrat and a hardworking man who has owned a factory his entire life. He desires to travel the world bringing gifts of oranges to every person he comes across.

Father Hurlburt

A Yellow Raft in Blue Water
Michael Dorris

A priest on the mission who first becomes acquainted with **Ida**'s family after the affair between **Clara** and **Lecon**. Father Hurlburt has a unique connection with Ida because, after the death of her parents, he is the only person on the reservation who knows the truth of **Christine**'s lineage. Ida and Father Hurlburt share a special, though often unarticulated, friendship.

George Hurstwood

Sister Carrie
Theodore Dreiser

The manager of **Fitzgerald** and **Moy**'s, a saloon in Chicago. At the beginning of the novel, **Hurstwood** is a wealthy, important man. He falls in love with **Carrie** after meeting her through **Drouet**. After his wife, **Julia**, discovers his affair with Carrie and files for divorce, he steals ten thousand dollars from Fitzgerald and Moy's and flees with Carrie to Montréal. There, Hurstwood marries Carrie before his divorce with Julia is complete. Although he keeps his theft a secret from Carrie, he is discovered by an investigator and required to return most of the money in order to protect his reputation. In New York, Hurstwood slowly descends into apathy and poverty. After Carrie leaves him, he becomes a homeless beggar and eventually commits suicide.

George Hurstwood, Jr.

Sister Carrie
Theodore Dreiser

Hurstwood's son, who works for a real estate firm. After his mother sues his father for divorce, George refuses to have anything to do with Hurstwood.

Jessica Hurstwood

Sister Carrie
Theodore Dreiser

Hurstwood's daughter. Jessica is a vain girl who hopes to enter elite social circles by marrying rich.

Julia Hurstwood

Sister Carrie
Theodore Dreiser

Hurstwood's first wife. The vindictive and jealous Julia files for divorce after discovering Hurstwood's infatuation with **Carrie**.

Johnny Tremain
Esther Forbes

Governor Hutchinson

The governor of Massachusetts. Governor Hutchinson refuses to send the tea ships back to London, which incites the Boston Tea Party. After the tea incident, he is called back to England.

Into Thin Air
Jon Krakauer

Stuart Hutchinson

A Canadian client with Adventure Consultants. Hutchinson is a strong climber, and when **Rob Hall** and the other guides are stranded on the mountain, he steps in as leader.

The Good Earth
Pearl S. Buck

Old Master Hwang

The patriarch of the great Hwang family. Extravagant with his money, he drains his coffers by taking a succession of concubines.

The Good Earth
Pearl S. Buck

Old Mistress Hwang

The opium-addicted matriarch of the great Hwang family.

Dr. Jekyll and Mr. Hyde
Robert Louis Stevenson

Mr. Edward Hyde

Dr. Henry Jekyll's dark side. Hyde is a violent, repugnant man who looks almost pre-human. Everyone who sees him describes him as ugly and deformed, but no one can explain why.

Beowulf
Unknown

Hygd

Hygelac's wife, the young, beautiful, and intelligent Queen of the Geats. Hygd's character contrasts with that of **Queen Modthryth**.

Beowulf
Unknown

Hygelac

Beowulf's uncle, king of the Geats, and husband of **Hygd**. Hygelac heartily welcomes Beowulf back from Denmark.

Grendel
John Gardner

Hygelac

King of the Geats and **Beowulf**'s lord.

Hygmod

Grendel
John Gardner

King of the Helmings and **Wealtheow**'s brother. Hygmod, a young king who is gaining in power and prominence, presents **Hrothgar** with a constant military threat.

Joe Hynes

Dubliners and *Ulysses*
James Joyce

A Dublin reporter and a friend of **the Citizen**'s. In *Ulysses*, Hynes has borrowed three pounds from **Bloom** and has not paid him back. In *Dubliners*, Hynes reads the poem about Parnell in "Ivy Day in the Committee Room." He never wavers in his statements or views.

Raphael Hythloday

Utopia
Sir Thomas More

A philosopher and world traveler who lived for five years on the island of Utopia before returning to Europe to spread the word about the Utopians' ideal society.

Hyzenthlay

Watership Down
Richard Adams

An Efrafan doe. Hyzenthlay is intelligent and caring, and she helps **Bigwig** free the other does. She can sometimes see special things like **Fiver** can, and she mates with **Holly** and bears the second litter in the new warren.

SERIOUS LIARS

DON'T BUY ANYTHING FROM ANY OF THE FOLLOWING. DON'T EVEN TALK TO THEM.

Big Brother	1	*1984*
The Duke and The Dauphin	2	*Huckleberry Finn*
Humbert Humbert	3	*Lolita*
Jay Gatsby	4	*The Great Gatsby*
Richard III	5	*Richard III*
Satan	6	*Paradise Lost*
Abigail Williams	7	*The Crucible*

Iachimo

Cymbeline
William Shakespeare

A clever and dishonest Italian gentleman. Iachimo makes a wager with **Posthumus** that he can seduce **Imogen**, and when his attempt at seduction fails, he resorts to trickery to make Posthumus believe that he has succeeded.

Iago

Othello
William Shakespeare

Othello's ensign and the villain of the play. While his ostensible reason for desiring Othello's demise is that Othello chose **Cassio** instead of Iago as his lieutenant, Iago's motivations are never very clearly expressed. His actions seem to originate in an obsessive, almost aesthetic delight in manipulation and destruction. When Iago's plots become unhinged, he swears a vow of silence, and **Lodovico** orders him executed.

Sonny Ibrahim

Midnight's Children
Salman Rushdie

Saleem's neighbor and friend.

Ida

Oranges Are Not the Only Fruit
Jeanette Winterson

One of the lesbians who owns the paper shop. Ida's presence foreshadows the eventual revelation of **Jeanette**'s sexual identity. Her presence helps Jeanette's latent feelings come to light. Significantly, Ida is present on the day that Jeanette meets **Melanie**.

Ida

A Yellow Raft in Blue Water
Michael Dorris

Lecon's daughter and **Lee**'s mother. Although she also poses as **Christine**'s mother, Ida is actually Christine's half-sister and cousin: they share a father, and Christine's mother is the sister of Ida's mother. Ida is often bitter and attempts to distance herself from others, as she fears becoming too attached to or dependent upon anyone. She stands firm only to maintain custody of Christine. Manipulated and betrayed by people she trusted, Ida commits herself to withdrawing from the world and refuses to interact except on her own terms, but her silence creates confusion and misunderstanding in the lives of the children she raises.

Duncan Idaho

Dune
Frank Herbert

Duke Leto Atreides's swordmaster and one of **Paul Atreides**'s trainers. Duncan is a skilled warrior and a faithful servant of the duke and his family.

Idat

I Never Promised You a Rose Garden
Joanne Greenberg

The Dissembler, a beautiful goddess in Yr, a world **Deborah** created as a defense against a confusing, frightening reality.

Idek

Night
Elie Wiesel

Eliezer's Kapo (a Jewish prisoner conscripted to police other Jewish prisoners) at the electrical-equipment warehouse in Buna. Idek beats Eliezer during moments of insane rage.

Alexander Iden

Henry VI, Part II
William Shakespeare

A small-property owner who prefers his peaceful garden to the intrigues of the court. When he discovers **Jack Cade** in his garden following the failed revolt, Iden very reluctantly engages the starving Cade in a duel and easily kills him. When he realizes that he has slain the famous rebel, Iden hurries to present his head to **King Henry VI**.

Idiot Boy

The Flies
Jean-Paul Sartre

A boy who appears only at the very start of the play. He sits stupidly in the square while flies suck on the pus leaking out of his eyes. The Idiot Boy represents the ideal of the **Argives**: complete passivity and willingness to take on punishment without complaint.

Idomeneus

The Iliad
Homer

King of Crete and a respected commander. Idomeneus leads a charge against the Trojans.

Grandmè Ifé

Breath, Eyes, Memory
Edwidge Danticat

The matriarch of the Caco family. Grandmè Ifé lives alone in the remote village of La Nouvelle Dame Marie, Haiti, until **Sophie** leaves for New York and **Atie** dutifully comes to stay with her mother. Grandmè Ifé is wise, candid, practical and astute, with an intuitive knowledge of human nature and a bottomless reserve of parables. While she does not consider it her place to challenge the social order, she is intensely loyal to her children, loving them against all of the world's pain so that a granddaughter or great-granddaughter can see her way out from under the burden.

Ruben Iglesias

Bel Canto
Ann Patchett

The vice president of the small South American country in which the novel is set, and the owner of the house in which the terrorists hold their captives. Iglesias rose up from poverty and put himself through law school by working as a clerk and a janitor. During the four-month standoff, he spends much of his time cleaning up after the other hostages and terrorists and making sure that they are all comfortable.

Tia Ignacia

Tortilla Flat
John Steinbeck

A widow of mostly Indian blood who is unsubtle in her romantic pursuits of **Big Joe Portagee**.

Úrsula Iguarán

One Hundred Years of Solitude
Gabriel García Márquez

The tenacious matriarch of the Buendía clan, Úrsula lives to be well over a hundred years old, continuing with her hard-headed common sense to try and preserve the family. She is frustrated with her husband **José Arcadio Buendía**'s obsession with magical implements. She afraid to consummate their marriage, as children of incest were said to have terrible genetic defects. As time passes after their marriage, and she continues to refuse to have sex with him, the people of the village begin to mock her husband. She discovers a route that connects Macondo with civilization. In her senility and extreme old age, she becomes childlike. She is the mother of **José Arcadio**, **Colonel Aureliano Buendía**, and **Amaranta**.

Ikemefuna

Things Fall Apart
Chinua Achebe

A boy given to **Okonkwo** by a neighboring village. Ikemefuna lives in the hut of Okonkwo's first wife and quickly becomes popular among Okonkwo's children. He develops an especially close relationship with Okonkwo's oldest son **Nwoye**, who looks up to him. Ikemefuna calls Okonkwo "father" and is a perfect clansman, but Okonkwo does not demonstrate his affection for Ikemefuna because he fears that doing so would make him look weak.

Ilya Petrovich

Crime and Punishment
Fyodor Dostoevsky

The police official whom **Rodion Romanovich Raskolnikov** encounters after committing the murder and to whom he confesses at the end of the novel. Unlike **Porfiry Petrovich**, Ilya Petrovich is rather oblivious and prone to sudden bouts of temper (thus the nickname "Gunpowder").

Fujiko Imada

Snow Falling on Cedars
David Guterson

Hatsue Miyamoto's mother. While her daughters were growing up, Fujiko was wary of *hakujin*, the word she used to refer to white Americans. She urged her young daughters to follow their Japanese cultural traditions and roles, and did not want to see them act like white Americans.

Hisao Imada

Snow Falling on Cedars
David Guterson

Hatsue Miyamoto's father.

Major Imbu

Ender's Game
Orson Scott Card

The computer expert at the Battle School. Imbu explains the mind game to **Colonel Graff**. He tells Graff that the game showed **Ender Wiggin** the picture of **Peter Wiggin** because it thought he needed to see it, but also that the computer makes up the game up as it goes along.

First immigration officer

A View from the Bridge
Arthur Miller

One of two officers from the Immigration Bureau who come to look for **Marco** and **Rodolpho** at **Eddie Carbone**'s request. The two men are put in jail as a result.

Imogen

Cymbeline
William Shakespeare

Cymbeline's daughter. Imogen, the British princess, is wise, beautiful, and resourceful. She displeases her father by choosing to marry the low-born **Posthumus** instead of Cymbeline's oafish stepson, **Cloten**.

Imrahil

The Return of the King
J. R. R. Tolkien

The Prince of Dol Amroth, the proudest of the captains of the Outlands who arrive to aid Minas Tirith. Imrahil is appointed interim leader of Gondor after **Denethor**'s suicide. Imrahil's show of support demonstrates the unity of different factions of **Humans** in Middle-earth.

Inez

No Exit
Jean-Paul Sartre

A self-described "damned bitch," she is the second prisoner and also the most hostile. She had been a postal clerk and thinks she is in hell for seducing a friend's wife. Her lover killed them both by leaving the gas on while Inez was asleep. She says that she does not like men and instantly detests everything about **Garcin.** However, she finds **Estelle** very attractive and tries to seduce her. She offers to be Estelle's "mirror," by describing her physical appearance, but ends up frightening her instead. After laughing off Estelle's attempt to kill her with a paper-knife, she agrees to let Garcin try and convince her that he is not a coward.

Inez

On the Road
Jack Kerouac

Dean Moriarty's third wife. Inez is a sexy brunette whom Dean meets in New York.

Inez

Animal Dreams
Barbara Kingsolver

Loyd Peregrina's mother. Inez is a Pueblo Native American who still lives on the reservation. Loyd brings **Codi Nolina** to Inez's house, where his sisters, aunts and Inez greet Codi warmly. Despite this, Codi feels very out of place. Being exposed to Inez's hospitality underscores Codi's disconnection with her personal history and with Grace.

Ingeld

Grendel
John Gardner

King of the Heathobards and an enemy of the Scyldings. **Hrothgar** plans to marry his daughter **Freawaru** to Ingeld in order to avoid a war with the Heathobards.

Gildor Inglorion

The Fellowship of the Ring
J. R. R. Tolkien

An Elf whose approach saves the Hobbits from an encounter with a Black Rider, one of **the Nazgûl**. Gildor Inglorion tells **Frodo Baggins** that the mysterious Black Riders are servants of the Enemy, **Sauron**, and must be avoided at all costs.

Blanche Ingram

Jane Eyre
Charlotte Brontë

A beautiful socialite who despises **Jane Eyre** and hopes to marry **Edward Rochester** for his money.

Injun Joe

The Adventures of Tom Sawyer
Mark Twain

A violent, villainous man who commits murder, becomes a robber, and plans to mutilate the **Widow Douglas**. When Injun Joe explains his motivation for revenge against **Dr. Robinson**, whom he murders, and later against the Widow Douglas, we see that his personal history involves others' mistreating and excluding him. His reappearances in different parts of *The Adventures of Tom Sawyer* help to provide a thread of continuity, as they bring the murder-case plot, the treasure-hunt plot, and the adventures-in-the-cave plot together into a single narrative. **Tom Sawyer** and **Huckleberry Finn** witness the murder of Dr. Robinson by Injun Joe, and the subsequent framing of **Muff Potter**. Despite his fearful hesitation, Tom tells the truth in court. Soon after, Tom and **Becky Thatcher** accidentally get lost in Injun Joe's cave. After they are rescued, the cave is sealed and Injun Joe starves to death inside. Huck and Tom each inherit $6,000 from Injun Joe's hidden fortune.

Inkosi-Inkosikazi

The Power of One
Bryce Courtenay

The great Zulu medicine man who, at the beginning of the novel, is summoned by **Peekay**'s **Nanny** to cure the boy's bed-wetting problem. Inkosi-Inkosikazi introduces Peekay to the magical world of the "night country," where Peekay can always find him. He also gives **Granpa Chook** to Peekay.

Inman

Cold Mountain
Charles Frazier

The male protagonist. The novel follows Inman's journey home from the Civil War. Inman is intelligent, literate, and sensitive, though emotionally reserved. Troubled by the carnage he has witnessed, Inman seeks spiritual solace in the natural world and in his memories of **Ada Monroe**. He attempts to retain his hope and his faith in a better world in the face of incomprehensible violence and cruelty.

Inna

The Red Tent
Anita Diamant

Accomplished midwife who trains the frequently miscarrying **Rachel** in childbirth and healing. Inna travels with **Jacob**'s family. During **Dinah**'s very difficult time of labor with **Re-mose**, she remembers Inna's teachings and instructs **Meryt** to cut her skin in order to assist the baby's delivery.

International 4-8818

Anthem
Ayn Rand

Equality 7-2521's only friend. International 4-8818 views Equality 7-2521 as a prophet. When he and Equality 7-2521 discover the tunnel in which Equality 7-2521 hides to write his journal and make his discoveries, International 4-8818 is torn between loyalty to his friend and his desire not to break the law.

Interrogator

Farewell to Manzanar
Jeanne Wakatsuki Houston

The American military man who questions **Papa** at Fort Lincoln, North Dakota.

Pierce Inverarity

The Crying of Lot 49
Thomas Pynchon

Oedipa Maas's ex-boyfriend and a fabulously rich real estate tycoon. He appears only in Oedipa's memories. He was a general jokester and may be playing a mean trick on Oedipa by inventing the Tristero conspiracy.

Io

Prometheus Bound
Aeschylus

A victim of **Zeus**'s love. Io is exiled from her home so that Zeus can deflower her. Transformed into a cow, she wanders the earth awaiting salvation. Io is seen as a parallel to **Prometheus**: though she suffers, in the end she will be freed and rewarded.

Iphigenia

The Libation Bearers
Aeschylus

The daughter of **Agamemnon** and **Clytemnestra**, the sister of **Orestes** and **Electra**. Also appears as a figure in Greek mythology. At **Artemis**'s request, Agamemnon offers Iphigenia as a human sacrifice at Aulis at the outset of the Trojan War. Clytemnestra avenges this death by killing her husband, thereby continuing the cycle of blood violence.

Ippolit Kirillovich

The Brothers Karamazov
Fyodor Dostoevsky

The prosecuting attorney at **Dmitri Fyodorovich Karamazov**'s trial.

Magid Iqbal

White Teeth
Zadie Smith

The elder of his father **Samad Iqbal**'s sons by two minutes. With his neatly parted hair and studious ways, Magid is far more serious than his mercurial, restless brother, **Millat Iqbal**. Magid dreams of a life more like his classmates', with pianos, flowers, and glamorous-sounding trips to France—not the screechy, chaotic life he knows at home. When he learns that Magid is ashamed of his culture, Samad "rescues" his son by sending him to Bangladesh. Removed from his parents' everyday life, Magid becomes frozen in time for them—a picture-perfect son, especially in contrast to the wild and rebellious Millat.

Millat Iqbal

White Teeth
Zadie Smith

The flip side of his twin brother, **Magid Iqbal**. Millat has charm, charisma, a sweet-talking tongue, and devastating good looks. If Magid has inherited his father **Samad Iqbal**'s serious nature and high esteem for education, Millat has inherited his father's innate flair for the dramatic, as well as his incessant need to prove himself.

Samad Iqbal

White Teeth
Zadie Smith

The father of **Magid Iqbal** and **Millat Iqbal**, a shadow of the handsome, learned man he once was. Now middle-aged and stuck in a demeaning and anonymous job, Samad yearns to hang a placard around his neck that proclaims his education, his history, his essential worth as a human being, beyond that of a mere waiter. Ardent and intense, Samad desperately wants to be in control of his life—and of the lives of those closest to him—and constantly fears that life has rendered him impotent or irrelevant. Samad is married to the much younger **Alsana Begum**, who was promised to him as a wife before she was even born. Samad's love-hate relationship with his adopted country, England, renders him a split person, caught between two worlds.

Iras

Antony and Cleopatra
William Shakespeare

Cleopatra's attendant.

Irene

The Bean Trees
Barbara Kingsolver

The daughter of **Mrs. Hoge**, who, together with Mrs. Hoge, runs the Broken Arrow Motor Lodge, where the two women let **Turtle** and **Taylor Greer** stay free of charge on their trip west.

Louis Ironson

Angels in America
Tony Kushner

A "word processor" who works at the federal appeals court in Brooklyn, boyfriend of **Prior Walter** and then **Joe Pitt**. Louis embodies all the stereotypes of the neurotic Jew: anxious, ambivalent, and perpetually guilty. Yet that guilt does not prevent him from leaving his lover Prior when he contracts AIDS. Louis's moral journey, from callous abandonment to genuine repentance and sorrow, is one of the key maturations in the play.

Sarah Ironson

Angels in America
Tony Kushner

Louis Ironson's grandmother, whose funeral takes place in the first scene of *Millennium Approaches*. **Prior Walter** encounters her in Heaven playing cards with **Rabbi Chemelwitz**.

Princess Irulan

Dune
Frank Herbert

Emperor Shaddam IV's eldest daughter. She is pledged to marry **Paul Atreides** after the novel's final battle, and goes on to write several books about the **Muad'Dib**, a figure of great historical importance.

Irwin

The Bell Jar
Sylvia Plath

Esther Greenwood's first lover, he is a tall, intelligent, homely math professor at Harvard. Irwin is charming and seductive but not particularly responsible or caring. After their lovemaking, Esther bleeds uncontrollably. He pays for the cost of her hospital bills, and Esther decides to never see him again.

Judge Montague Irwin

All the King's Men
Robert Penn Warren

A prominent citizen of Burden's Landing and a former state attorney general; also a friend to the **Scholarly Attorney** and a father figure to **Jack**. When Judge Irwin supports one of Willie's political enemies in a Senate election, Willie orders Jack to dig up some information on the judge. Jack discovers that his old friend accepted a bribe from the American Electric Power Company in 1913 to save his plantation. When he confronts the judge with this information, the judge commits suicide. Upon learning of the suicide from his mother, Jack also learns that Judge Irwin was his real father.

Isaac

The Old Testament
Unknown

Abraham's son and the second member in the triumvirate of Israel's patriarchs. Isaac's importance consists less of his actions than in the way he is acted upon by others. **God** tests Abraham by commanding him to kill Isaac, and Isaac's blindness and senility allow his own son **Jacob** to steal the inheritance of God's covenant.

Isaac

The Red Tent
Anita Diamant

Son of **Abraham**, father of **Jacob** and **Esau**. God told Abraham to sacrifice Isaac, his only son, but just before he does, God stops him and lets his son live for Abraham's show of faith. When Jacob finally arrives in Esau's land, Canaan, blind Isaac arrives, and he and Jacob weep in each other's arms.

Isaac of York

Ivanhoe
Sir Walter Scott

Rebecca's father, a wealthy Jew. Isaac is a thoroughly stereotypical literary Jew: an avaricious, somewhat bumbling, but ultimately kindhearted character who loves money more than anything in the world except his daughter.

Queen Isabel of France

Henry V
William Shakespeare

The wife of **King Charles VI**, and the mother of **Catherine**, the **Dauphin** (Louis), and **Charles** (later also dauphin). Isabel does not appear until the final scene of the play, and is a strong supporter of the marriage between her daughter and **King Henry V** to establish peace.

Isabella

The Spanish Tragedy
Thomas Kyd

Hieronimo's inert, suffering wife. Isabella's inaction, along with her visions of a dead **Horatio**, torment her increasingly throughout the play, providing an extreme version of Hieronimo's more subdued madness. Her death by her own hand foreshadows Hieronimo's suicide.

Isabella

Measure for Measure
William Shakespeare

The play's protagonist. Isabella, **Claudio**'s sister, is a virtuous young nun-in-training. She refuses to have sex with **Lord Angelo** to save her brother's life.

Queen Isabella

Richard II
William Shakespeare

King Richard II's wife, and a French princess (the daughter of **King Charles VI**). When she learns that her husband has been deposed, she decides to go to London, where she sees Richard being led to the Tower of London. When **Northumberland** orders the former king to be taken instead to Pomfret, Isabella and Richard share a long goodbye.

Judas Iscariot

The New Testament
Unknown

The traitor among the Twelve Apostles, who betrays **Jesus** to the authorities in exchange for thirty pieces of silver. According to Matthew, Judas commits suicide out of remorse.

Ishmael

Bel Canto
Ann Patchett

One of the youngest and brightest of the terrorists. Ishmael learns to play chess by watching **General Benjamin** and **Hosokawa** play. He is a favorite of both General Benjamin and the hostages. **Iglesias** becomes particularly fond of Ishmael and wants to adopt him.

Ishmael

Moby-Dick
Herman Melville

The narrator, and a junior member of the crew of the *Pequod*. Ishmael doesn't play a major role in the events of *Moby-Dick*, but much of the narrative is taken up by his eloquent, verbose, and extravagant discourse on whales and whaling. We know that he has gone to sea out of some deep spiritual malaise. When he arrives in Nantucket, he becomes a kind of soul-mate with the endearing and mysterious **Queequeg**, whom Ishmael "marries" through sharing a tomahawk pipe and a bed. Always trying to explain the phenomenon of **Moby Dick** to the reader, Ishmael gives scientific explanations, measurements, descriptions, and tales of various kinds of whales, mirroring Ahab's explanations in the scientific chapters of the book. Ishmael is the lone survivor of the crew's chase and battle with Moby Dick.

Ishtar

The Epic of Gilgamesh
Unknown

Uruk's patron, the goddess of sexual love, fertility, and war. Ishtar is **Anu**'s daughter. Furious when **Gilgamesh** rejects her advances, Ishtar sends the Bull of Heaven to destroy him.

Isildur

The Fellowship of the Ring
J. R. R. Tolkien

The eldest son and heir of **Elendil**, a King of Westernesse who fought against **Sauron** the first time Sauron was defeated. In the great battle against Sauron, ages before the events of *The Lord of the Rings*, Isildur cut the One Ring from Sauron's hand. **Elrond Halfelven** beseeched Isildur to destroy the Ring in the Cracks of Mount Doom, but Isildur's desire for power made him unable to do so. Isildur was consumed by the power of the Ring, but then lost it in the Great River, Anduin, where it was eventually found by **Gollum**, then known as Sméagol.

Ismene

Oedipus trilogy (Oedipus Rex, Oedipus at Colonus, Antigone)
Sophocles

Oedipus's daughter and **Antigone**'s sister. Ismene is too frightened to help Antigone bury **Polynices**, but she offers to die beside Antigone when **Creon** sentences her to death. Antigone, however, refuses to allow her sister to be martyred for something she did not have the courage to stand up for.

Ismene

Antigone 1946
Jean Anouilh

The good girl of the family. Blond, full-figured, and radiantly beautiful, the laughing, talkative Ismene is reasonable and understands her place, bowing to **Creon**'s edict and attempting to dissuade **Antigone** from her act of rebellion. Ultimately she will recant and beg Antigone to let them die together. Antigone refuses, saying that her sister hasn't earned the right to die.

Ismene

The Bean Trees
Barbara Kingsolver

Estevan and **Esperanza**'s daughter, whom they left in Guatemala.

Issachar

The Red Tent
Anita Diamant

Naphtali's twin; son of **Jacob** by **Leah**.

Don Issachar

Candide
Voltaire

A wealthy Jewish man. Don Issachar purchases **Cunégonde** and makes her his mistress. **The Grand Inquisitor** forces him to share Cunégonde by threatening to burn him alive as a heretic. **Candide** kills Don Issachar when he interrupts Candide and Cunégonde.

IT

A Wrinkle in Time
Madeleine L'Engle

The disembodied brain that controls all the inhabitants of Camazotz with its revolting, pulsing rhythm. IT, identified with **the Black Thing**, is the embodiment of evil on Camazotz. IT imposes sameness and extreme order on Camazotz and punishes anyone who varies from the order. **Charles Wallace Murry**, hypnotized by **the Man with the Red Eyes**, is left lying outside of the dome that houses IT. **Meg Murry** saves Charles Wallace by using a gift that **Mrs. Which** gave to her. Mrs. Which strengthens the thing within Meg that IT does not possess. That thing turns out to be love, and as Meg shows Charles Wallace love, he escapes from IT's grasp.

Ithamore

The Jew of Malta
Christopher Marlowe

Barabas's slave, whom the protagonist vows to make the heir to his estate after **Abigail**'s conversion to Christianity. The men share a similar hatred for Christians and vow to cause them as much disruption as they can. Similarly, both are obsessed by money and the power it affords. However, while Barabas is a criminal mastermind, Ithamore is more of a common thief and cutthroat. The slave fails his great test of loyalty when he falls for the prostitute **Bellamira**, bribes Barbabas, and confesses Barabas's crimes to the governor. As with Abigail, the merchant responds to this betrayal by killing Ithamore, along with his cohorts Bellamira and **Pilia-Borza**.

Ivan

"Gooseberries"
Anton Chekhov

The elderly protagonist. Ivan rails against complacent landowners but also berates himself for being happy.

Ivanhoe

Ivanhoe
Sir Walter Scott

The son of **Cedric the Saxon** and a knight who is deeply loyal to **King Richard I**. Ivanhoe was disinherited by his father for following Richard to the Crusades, but he won great glory in the fighting and has been richly rewarded by the king. Ivanhoe is in love with his father's ward, the beautiful **Rowena**. He represents the knightly code of chivalry, heroism, and honor.

Crazy Ivar

O Pioneers!
Willa Cather

A deeply religious and slightly unbalanced elderly man who becomes **Alexandra Bergson**'s trusted servant. He distrusts civilization and behaves bizarrely around people, but seems to have an innate understanding of nature and animals.

Ardalyon Ivolgin

The Idiot
Fyodor Dostoevsky

Varvara Ardalyonovna Ivolgina, **Nikolai Ardalyonovich Ivolgin**, and **Gavril Ardalyonovich Ivolgin**'s father, as well as the father of **Ippolit Terentyev**, conceived illegitimately with his mistress. An ex-general, Ivolgin has lost his circle of friends in high society due to constant drinking and lying.

Gavril Ardalyonovich Ivolgin

The Idiot
Fyodor Dostoevsky

Highly vain, ambitious and the epitome of mediocrity, he strives for originality. Ganya is in love with **Aglaya Ivanovna Yepanchina** but is willing to marry **Anastassya Filippovna Barashkova**—whom he despises—for 75,000 rubles per **Afanassy Ivanovich Totsky**'s request.

Nikolai Ardalyonovich Ivolgin

The Idiot
Fyodor Dostoevsky

Gavril Ardalyonovich Ivolgin's younger brother, also called **Kolya**. Kolya is a simple and good-natured boy who becomes friends with **Prince Lev Nikolayevich Myshkin**, whom he respects greatly. Kolya is also friends with **Ippolit Terentyev**, whom he visits throughout his illness until Ippolit's death from consumption.

Nina Aleksandrovna Ivolgina

The Idiot
Fyodor Dostoevsky

Ardalyon Ivolgin's wife and **Varvara Ardalyonovna Ivolgina**, **Nikolai Ardalyonovich Ivolgin**, and **Gavril Ardalyonovich Ivolgin**'s mother. Despite her husband's lying and keeping a mistress, she pities him and even helps **Ippolit Terentyev**, her husband's sickly illegitimate son.

Varvara Ardalyonovna Ivolgina

The Idiot
Fyodor Dostoevsky

Gavril Ardalyonovich Ivolgin's dignified sister. Varya is among the characters whom the narrator considers ordinary people. She tries to help her brother's chances with **Aglaya Ivanovna Yepanchina** by befriending the Yepanchina girls, but to no avail.

Molly Ivors

Dubliners
James Joyce

The young woman, an ardent nationalist, who teases **Gabriel Conroy** during a dance in "The Dead."

Ivy

The Bean Trees
Barbara Kingsolver

Lou Ann's mother. She fights perpetually with **Granny Logan**, her mother-in-law. Like Granny Logan, she is provincial and has no interest in seeing Arizona.

10

PILLARS OF WISDOM

BETTER THAN YOUR MAGIC EIGHT BALL ANY DAY OF THE WEEK. THESE WISE AND WIZENED CHARACTERS SEEM TO KNOW EVERTHING.

Aslan	1	*The Lion, the Witch, and the Wardrobe*
Albus Dumbledore	2	*Harry Potter* series, Books I-IV
Bokonon	3	*Cat's Cradle*
Gandalf	4	*The Lord of the Rings* triology
The Giver	5	*The Giver*
Professor Kirke	6	*The Lion, the Witch, and the Wardrobe*
Merlyn	7	*The Once and Future King*
Moses	8	*The Old Testament*
Prospero	9	*The Tempest*
Tiresias	10	*The Odyssey, The Oedipus Plays*

Jack

Native Son
Richard Wright

One of **Bigger Thomas**'s group of friends, who often plan and execute robberies together. **G. H.**, **Gus**, and Jack hatch a tentative plan to rob a white shopkeeper, **Mr. Blum**, but they are afraid of the consequences if they should be caught robbing a white man.

Jack

Lord of the Flies
William Golding

The novel's antagonist, one of the older boys stranded on the island. Jack becomes the leader of the hunters but longs for total power and becomes increasingly wild, barbaric, and cruel as the novel progresses. Jack, adept at manipulating the other boys, represents the instinct of savagery within human beings, as opposed to the civilizing instinct **Ralph** represents. At the height of his power, Jack tortures younger children, has people serving him, and is able to command other boys to do dances and tasks. He uses the idea of the beast and the temptation of meat to persuade boys to join his tribe.

Jack

Animal Dreams
Barbara Kingsolver

Loyd Peregrina's dog. Jack's extreme devotion to Loyd stems from the way Loyd saved him as a puppy, which demonstrates Loyd's connection with animals.

Jack

The Color of Water
James McBride

James McBride's older sister. James lives with Jack in Louisville, Kentucky for three summers during his teenage years. James regards her as sweet and fun, but she is also serious: she warns him about his drug abuse and petty crime. Jack's opinion matters to James, and eventually he heeds her advice.

Brother Jack

Invisible Man
Ralph Ellison

The white, blindly loyal leader of the Brotherhood. Although Brother Jack initially seems compassionate, intelligent, and kind to **the Narrator**, he is actually racist and cold. His glass eye and his red hair symbolize his blindness and his communist views, respectively.

Jack's mother

All the King's Men
Robert Penn Warren

A beautiful, "famished-cheeked" woman from Arkansas, Jack's mother is brought back to Burden's Landing by the **Scholarly Attorney**, but falls in love with **Judge Irwin** and begins an affair with him. Jack is a product of that affair. After the Scholarly Attorney leaves her, she marries a succession of men (the **Tycoon**, the **Count**, the **Young Executive**). Jack's realization that she is capable of love–and that she really loved Judge Irwin–helps him put aside his cynicism at the end of the novel.

Albert Jacks

Sula
Toni Morrison

See **Ajax**.

Adele Jackson

Black Like Me
John Howard Griffin

The editor of *Sepia* magazine, who warns **John Howard Griffin** of the dangers he will face if he goes through with his plan to pose as a black man.

Bluford Jackson

Cold Sassy Tree
Olive Anne Burns

Will Tweedy's deceased friend. Bluford makes a ghostly appearance early in the novel.

Father Jackson

A Death in the Family
James Agee

The priest who performs the funeral service for **Jay Follet**. He refuses to read the complete burial service because Jay was never baptized, which angers **Andrew Lynch**, **Mary Lynch**'s brother. The priest is cold and seemingly unsympathetic.

Lymon Jackson

The Piano Lesson
August Wilson

Boy Willie's longtime friend. Lymon is more taciturn than his partner, speaking with a disarming "straightforwardness." Fleeing the law, he plans to stay in the north and begin life anew. He is obsessed with women and he helps bring **Berniece** out of mourning for her dead husband when he kisses her late at night.

Sillerton Jackson

The Age of Innocence
Edith Wharton

An elderly gentleman and good friend of the Archer family. Jackson is the unofficial archivist of all New York gossip and family history.

Jacob

The Old Testament
Unknown

The grandson of **Abraham** and the third patriarch of the Israelite people. Jacob is the father of the twelve sons who form the tribes of Israel. Jacob steals his brother **Esau**'s inheritance and wrestles with **God** on the banks of the Jabbok River. Appropriately, the nation that springs from Jacob's children derives its name from Jacob's God-given name, "Israel," which means "struggles with God." Jacob's struggles are emblematic of the nation of Israel's tumultuous history.

Jacob

The Red Tent
Anita Diamant

Son of **Isaac** and **Rebecca**. Though Jacob is a twin (brother of **Esau**), he is born second and receives his mother's blessing. He marries the four sisters **Leah**, **Rachel**, **Zilpah**, and **Bilhah** and fathers thirteen children: **Simon**, **Levi**, **Asher**, **Gad**, **Issachar**, **Naphtali**, **Benjamin**, **Dan**, **Joseph**, **Judah**, **Reuben**, **Zebulun**, and **Dinah**. According to the Bible, he fathers the twelve tribes of Israel from his sons and is one of the Jewish Patriarchs. At the start of the novel, Jacob is a confident and charismatic man, hoping to work hard to escape **Laban**'s wickedness. He is a good husband and a kind and gentle lover to each of his wives. He works diligently as a herdsman to grow Laban's flocks and honor his bargain of bride-prices for Leah and Rachel, while also growing the prosperity and prospects of his family. He is entirely devoted to his god and liberal with his sacrifices. As Jacob grows older and his properties multiply, he changes. He becomes less of the fair and honest man he was in his youth and relies more on the poor counsel of sons Simon and Levi than the just counsel of his wife Leah and son Reuben. He allows his sons' suggestion of a hideous bride-price to be exacted and in doing so orchestrates his own downfall. Jacob dies full of regrets, cursing his sons.

Friar Jacomo

The Jew of Malta
Christopher Marlowe

The Dominican friar who converts **Abigail**. Jacomo is a flawed priest who sleeps with nuns and lusts after money. As such, he personifies the hypocrisy of the Catholic clergy. Barabas frames Jacomo for **Bernardine**'s murder, and Jacomo is subsequently executed.

Jacopo

The Count of Monte Cristo
Alexandre Dumas

One of a group of smugglers who picks **Edmond Dantès** up off the Isle of Tiboulen after Dantès' escape from prison. While on the island, Dantès pretends to injure himself and claims he cannot be moved. Dantès' best friend among the crew is Jacopo, who offers to stay behind, forgoing his share of the profits from his smuggling operation. After Dantés finds **Abbé Faria**'s treasure, he buys a small ship and a crew for Jacopo. He also finds out from Jacopo that **Louis Dantès**, Edmond's father, is dead, and **Mercédès**, Edmond's past lover, is missing.

Jacques

Candide
Voltaire

A humane Dutch Anabaptist. He cares for the itinerant **Candide** and **Pangloss**. Despite his kindness, Jacques is pessimistic about human nature. He drowns in the Bay of Lisbon while trying to save the life of an ungrateful sailor.

Jaggers

Great Expectations
Charles Dickens

A powerful, foreboding lawyer. Despite his worldliness and impenetrability, Jaggers often seems to care for **Pip**. He also helps **Miss Havisham** adopt the orphaned **Estella**. Jaggers washes his hands obsessively in an attempt to keep criminals from corrupting him.

Jail guard

Sounder
William Armstrong

A needlessly evil person. The jail guard personifies many of the obstacles that **the boy**, **the boy's father**, and **the boy's mother** face. He immediately picks on the boy, not showing compassion or even decency.

Jailer

The Two Noble Kinsmen
William Shakespeare

The guard of the prison where **Palamon** and **Arcite** are held in Act II. He is attached to both his daughter and the **Wooer**, and reluctantly acquiesces to curing her by encouraging her to have sex.

Jailer's brother

The Two Noble Kinsmen
William Shakespeare

A tender uncle to the **Jailer's Daughter**.

Jailer's daughter

The Two Noble Kinsmen
William Shakespeare

The protagonist of the subplot. The **Jailer**'s daughter is a young and very foolish girl who falls madly in love with **Palamon**. The jailer's daughter is ready to sacrifice her father and her **Wooer** to be with Palamon. She goes mad when he rejects her, but is cured when she has sex with the Wooer.

Jaime

The House of the Spirits
Isabel Allende

One of **Esteban Trueba** and **Clara**'s twin boys. Jaime studies medicine and devotes his life to helping the poor. He is secretly in love with his brother **Nicolas**'s girlfriend, **Amanda**. Over the years, he helps the Socialist, **the Candidate**, medically, which Esteban Trueba disapproves of. Jaime moves into the hospital instead of living with his father and becomes great friends with the Candidate. He also encounters Amanda twenty years after their initial meeting, though now she is a junkie who needs detoxification. After this episode, Jaime realizes that he no longer has any desire to have a relationship with her.

Jake

Hatchet
Gary Paulsen

See **Jim**.

Bob Jakin

The Mill on the Floss
George Eliot

A childhood friend of **Tom Tulliver**'s. Though Tom rejected his friendship when they were children over an incident of cheating, Bob returns after **Jeremy Tulliver**'s bankruptcy and offers help to Tom and **Maggie Tulliver**. Bob is a packman—a salesman who buys goods at one place and sells them at another.

Jamal

Fallen Angels
Walter Dean Myers

A medic in **Richie Perry**'s company.

James

The Contender
Robert Lipsyte

The best friend of **Alfred Brooks**. Throughout the book, Alfred struggles to maintain and regain James's trust and friendship, as well as attempt to steer him away from drugs and crime. He and James used to do everything together, but throughout the course of the book their paths diverge. At the end of the novel, Alfred leads James to the hospital to get help with his addiction.

James of the Glens

Kidnapped
Robert Louis Stevenson

The leader of the Stewart clan, to which **Alan Breck Stewart** belongs. Like most Highland chieftains, James of the Glens has been stripped of his powers by the English government, as he is a Jacobite. When **Colin Roy Campbell of Glenure** is murdered, James is accused of having been involved. Alan and **David Balfour** quickly go on the run to make it look like they are responsible for the murder in order to divert the blame from James. James sends money to David and Alan through friends when they are on the run. James is imprisoned anyway, even though the other men are suspected. When David gets his money from **Ebenezer Balfour**, he plans to use part of it to help James regain his freedom.

James Watson

Girl, Interrupted
Susanna Kaysen

Nobel Prize–winning friend of **Susanna Kaysen**'s family. Beloved by Susanna for his eccentric behavior, he visits Susanna and offers to help her escape. She turns him down in the belief that she should continue treatment.

Sister James

This Boy's Life
Tobias Wolff

The honest and spunky nun at **Jack Wolff**'s elementary school in Salt Lake City who organizes after-school activities to keep her students out of trouble. Sister James shows a particular concern for Jack, and when he has trouble confessing his sins to the priest, she takes him to the kitchen, where she shares her own stories of childhood delinquency.

Jamis

Dune
Frank Herbert

One of the Fremen. **Paul Atreides** is forced to kill Jamis when the man challenges him to a duel to the death.

Charles Jamison

The Land
Mildred D. Taylor

A trustworthy Vicksburg local interested in buying land from **J. T. Hollenbeck**. Charles Jamison helps **Paul-Edward Logan** find **Filmore Granger** so that Paul can ask about purchasing land from Granger. Charles Jamison also helps Paul draw up legal documents for his purchase of land when Paul is finally ready to buy from Hollenbeck.

Wade Jamison

Roll of Thunder, Hear My Cry and *The Land*
Mildred D. Taylor

Son of **Charles Jamison**, who befriends **Nathan Perry** in his youth in *The Land* and grows up to become a lawyer sympathetic to the black community in *Roll of Thunder, Hear My Cry*. In *The Land*, Wade Jamison is driven by a sense of justice to repay the wrongs committed against blacks under slavery. Remembering what happened between himself and **Robert Logan**, **Paul-Edward Logan** discourages the black boy Nathan Perry from befriending the white Wade. They become friends anyway. In *Roll of Thunder, Hear My Cry*, Wade Jamison supports the black boycott of the **Wallace** family store and offers to extend credit to black families so that they can shop at another store.

Steve Jamnik

Walden Two
B. F. Skinner

A man who befriends **Rogers** when they serve together during the war. He is **Mary Grove**'s boyfriend. Steve is quiet, but like Rogers he is looking for a better way to live his life.

Captain Jamy

Henry V
William Shakespeare

The Scottish captain of **King Henry V**'s troops. The three foreign captains in the play, Jamy, the Welsh **Captain Fluellen**, and the Irish **Captain MacMorris**, retain their respective heavy accents, broadly represent their nationalities, and prove the importance of each of the British nations. Despite the comic stereotype of each of the characters, the three are loyal soldiers and hard workers.

Jan

Go Ask Alice
Anonymous

An old drug-using friend of **Alice**'s who threatens Alice when she won't return to her old habits. Jan's interference eventually gets Alice put in the mental hospital.

Eleanor Jane

The Color Purple
Alice Walker

The mayor's daughter. Eleanor Jane develops a strong attachment to **Sofia** and turns to her for emotional support. However, Sofia does not reciprocate Eleanor Jane's feelings because of the years of mistreatment she suffered at the hands of Eleanor Jane's parents, the mayor and **Miss Millie**. She attempts to atone for her part in the unjust treatment of Sofia by caring for Sofia's daughter **Henrietta**.

Janet

The Awakening
Kate Chopin

Edna Pontellier's sister. Edna refuses to attend Janet's wedding, and **the Colonel** reprimands **Léonce Pontellier** for this, saying that Léonce has no control over his wife, whom he should treat with "authority" and "coercion."

Janine

The Handmaid's Tale
Margaret Atwood

One of the **Handmaids** who stayed at the Red Center at the same time as **Offred**. Janine, who takes the name Ofwarren, is the envy of the other Handmaids when she becomes pregnant, possibly by her doctor. However, her baby turns out to be malformed—an "**Unbaby**." A well-indoctrinated conformist, Janine endears herself to the **Aunts** and earns Offred's contempt.

Janine

Tuesdays with Morrie
Mitch Albom

Mitch Albom's patient wife. She takes a phone call from **Morrie Schwartz**, whom she has never met, and insists upon joining Mitch on his next Tuesday visit. Although she usually does not sing upon request, she does so for Morrie, moving him to tears with her beautiful voice.

Emile Janza

The Chocolate War
Robert Cormier

A thug. **Archie Costello** uses Janza to back up **the Vigils** and to beat up **Jerry Renault**. Blackmailing him with a photograph, Archie gets Janza to participate in a lopsided boxing match in which he brutally beats Jerry.

Jaquenetta

Love's Labour's Lost
William Shakespeare

A country wench and milkmaid in the court of Navarre. **Armado**, who is hopelessly in love with Jaquenetta, sees her in the forest with **Costard**. Jaquenetta delivers **Berowne**'s love letter to **Rosaline** back to the court and the lords, proving Berowne's infidelity to the oath.

Jaques

As You Like It
William Shakespeare

A faithful lord who accompanies **Duke Senior** into exile in the Forest of Arden. Jaques is an example of a stock figure in Elizabethan comedy, the man possessed of a hopelessly melancholy disposition. His sullenness ultimately blinds him; though he delivers a well-known speech about the seven stages of man's life, he is too wrapped up in his own melancholy to see the world he so desperately criticizes. Given his inability to participate in life, it is fitting that Jaques alone refuses to follow Duke Senior and the other courtiers back to court and instead resolves to assume a solitary and contemplative life in a monastery.

Jaques de Bois

As You Like It
William Shakespeare

The second son of Sir Rowland de Bois, brother of **Oliver** and **Orlando**. He enters at the very end of the play to tell **Duke Senior** and his assembly of **Duke Frederick**'s conversion to peace, and the restoration of the lands and power to the exiled company.

Beth Jarrett

Ordinary People
Judith Guest

The wife of **Calvin Jarrett** and mother of **Conrad Jarrett** and **Buck Jarrett**, Beth Jarrett spends most of her time playing golf and working around the home. Although she is troubled by the horrible events she has experienced with the death of Buck and the suicide attempt of Conrad, she wants to move on without dwelling on the past at all, an attitude that brings her into conflict with Calvin, who thinks that the family needs to talk through the past. She did not visit him in the hospital after his suicide attempt, and he can sense her coldness. At the end of *Ordinary People*, she leaves Calvin and Conrad for an indefinite period, although there is no talk of an official divorce.

Calvin Jarrett

Ordinary People
Judith Guest

The father of **Conrad Jarrett** and **Buck Jarrett**, husband of **Beth Jarrett**. Calvin is a natural listener. He tends to blame himself for most negative things that occur in his family, like his son Buck's accidental death and Conrad's suicide attempt. Calvin works as a tax attorney with his friend **Ray Hanley**, and Calvin considers his position prestigious, especially for someone who grew up in an orphanage. He believes that there is a serious lack of communication between him and Beth, which strains their relationship. He spends most of his time worrying about his son. Calvin ends up visiting **Dr. Berger**, Conrad's psychologist, to talk about his own problems. Beth leaves Calvin.

Conrad Jarrett

Ordinary People
Judith Guest

The protagonist and the son of **Calvin Jarrett** and **Beth Jarrett**. About eighteen months before the novel begins, Conrad was involved in a boating accident with his brother, **Buck Jarrett**, an accident that left Buck dead. A year later, Conrad tried to commit suicide but failed, forcing him to spend time in the hospital. At the beginning of the novel, he has been out of the hospital for a month. He is trying to get his life back on track, but he feels little purpose and no motivation. He begins to see **Dr. Berger** to help him recover from the traumatic events he has experienced. Over the course of the novel, Conrad begins a steady relationship, emotional and sexual, with **Jeannine Pratt** and rebuilds some of his old friendships. Through the help of his friend Dr. Berger, he comes to terms with the fact that he wants to be Buck, and also with the fact that he blames himself for Buck's death.

Jordan "Buck" Jarrett

Ordinary People
Judith Guest

The dead son of **Beth Jarrett** and **Calvin Jarrett**, brother of **Conrad Jarrett**. Jordan "Buck" Jarrett only appears in flashbacks. Older than Conrad, he died in a boating accident, an event for which Conrad has never forgiven himself.

Arthur Jarvis

Cry, the Beloved Country
Alan Paton

A powerful presence whose legacy hovers over the whole novel. An engineer and fierce advocate for justice for black South Africans, he is shot dead in his home by **Absalom Kumalo**.

Hannah Jarvis

Arcadia
Tom Stoppard

The champion of academic knowledge in *Arcadia*. Though her discoveries are not as revolutionary as **Thomasina**'s, she is far more academic and far less susceptible to romantic notions. Hannah is on **Valentine**'s estate attempting to discover the identity of the famed hermit of Sidley Park, who lived on **Lady Croom**'s estate in the nineteenth century. She gets momentarily sidetracked from her research at the arrival of the historian **Bernard**, but eventually discovers that the hermit was Thomasina's tutor **Septimus**. Hannah becomes a foil for Septimus in that she rejects romance and embraces pure intellect while he is equally intellectual yet passionate.

James Jarvis

Cry, the Beloved Country
Alan Paton

One of the novel's protagonists, a white landowner whose farm overlooks Ndotsheni. When he first appears in the novel, Jarvis is a relatively conservative farmer and a man of few words. When his only son **Arthur Jarvis** is murdered, James travels to Johannesburg and begins to rethink his opinions, eventually changing his relationship with the villagers who live below his farm.

Margaret Jarvis

Cry, the Beloved Country
Alan Paton

James Jarvis's wife. It is difficult for Margaret to accept the death of her son **Arthur Jarvis**. She is a physically fragile and loving woman who commiserates with and supports her husband through their grief. She also shares in his plans to help Ndotsheni, the town where they live.

Mary Jarvis

Cry, the Beloved Country
Alan Paton

Arthur Jarvis's wife. Mary fights hard to accept her husband's murder, but she remains strong for her children. She shares her husband's commitment to justice.

Dick Jarvits

A Prayer for Owen Meany
John Irving

The boy who kills **Owen Meany**; a hulking, sadistic fifteen-year-old from a trashy family in Phoenix. Dick lives for the day when he will be old enough to travel to Vietnam. Owen is assigned to return the body of Dick's dead brother. When Dick sees Owen escorting a group of Vietnamese orphans into a men's room, he throws a grenade into the room. Owen is killed in the act of saving the children's lives.

Jashu

Death in Venice
Thomas Mann

Tadzio's closest companion at the hotel. He seems to idolize Tadzio, acting as his "vassal." Jashu has glossy black hair, a sturdy build, and a rowdy temperament.

Jason

Medea
Euripides

The hero who assembled a cast of heroes to recover the Golden Fleece. When Jason arrives in Colchis to retrieve the Fleece, the daughter of the king, **Medea**, falls in love with him. Jason later abandons Medea to marry a princess for political gain. In revenge, Medea kills Jason's new wife and her own children with Jason. He survives, but bears the burden of this tragedy, in some ways a fate worse than death. Jason's tactless self-interest and whiny rationalizing make him an unsympathetic character. He also appears as a figure in Greek mythology.

Jasón Chávez's Indian

Bless Me, Ultima
Rudolfo A. Anaya

A friend of **Jasón Chavez**'s who is disliked by Jasón's father, **Chávez**. **Cico** tells **Antonio Márez** that the story of the golden carp originally comes from the Indian.

Jasper

Rebecca
Daphne du Maurier

One of **Maxim de Winter**'s spaniels, and **the Heroine**'s favorite pet.

Javert

Les Misérables
Victor Hugo

A police inspector who strictly believes in law and order and will stop at nothing to enforce France's harsh penal codes. He nurses an especially strong desire to recapture **Jean Valjean**, whose escapes and prosperity he sees as an affront to justice. Valjean's unconditional love for others weakens the stern Javert because it makes it impossible for him to justify his inflexible interpretation of the law. In the end, Javert cannot bring himself to arrest Valjean. Javert does not believe that Valjean is innocent, but he does believe that Valjean is good, and that to arrest him would debase the moral authority of the law. For the exceedingly practical Javert, the only way out of his dilemma is to remove himself from it altogether. While his suicide is a powerful and poignant moment, Javert dies in the same way he has lived: determined and resolute.

Jax

Pigs in Heaven
Barbara Kingsolver

Taylor Greer's boyfriend. He worships everything about Taylor and only wishes that she could return his steadfast adoration and love. A songwriter and member of the band "Irascible Babes," Jax is kindhearted and easy-going. He also loves and is adored by **Turtle**. Jax regrets an affair with he has with **Gundi**, a local artist who seduces him.

Jean

Rhinoceros
Eugène Ionesco

Berenger's foil, a highly cultured, somewhat arrogant and angry man who prides himself on his rationality. He urges Berenger to be more like him. His occasional lapses, however, expose cracks in his façade of efficiency. In the play's second act, Jean complains of illness and has a bump on his forehead that eventually becomes a horn. He becomes a rhinoceros right before Berenger's eyes.

Jean

Miss Julie
August Strindberg

The manor valet, chosen as **Miss Julie**'s lover on Midsummer's Eve. Though initially coarse, he pretends to be gallant when seducing Miss Julie. His cruelty reveals itself after he has slept with her. He simultaneously idealizes and degrades Julie. Eventually, he becomes a sadist, reveling in Julie's ruin.

Jeanette

Oranges Are Not the Only Fruit
Jeanette Winterson

The novel's narrator and heroine. Jeanette retells her life from when she is seven years old to an unspecified time after her teenage years. Jeanette is a kind, serious girl who believes in God as a child. As she grows into her teenage years, she falls in love with another girl. Eventually, she realizes that her same-sex love is part of her nature that cannot be denied.

Jeanette's father

Oranges Are Not the Only Fruit
Jeanette Winterson

Married to **Jeanette's mother**, seldom mentioned in the novel. Jeanette's father works in a factory and leaves for work at five in the morning.

Jeanette's mother

Oranges Are Not the Only Fruit
Jeanette Winterson

A fundamentalist Christian woman characterized by hypocrisy. She adopted **Jeanette** because she wanted to train her daughter to be a servant of God. Though she professes to be very religious, Jeanette's mother is combative and controlling and often acts in uncharitable ways.

Jefe

The Power and the Glory
Graham Greene

The Lieutenant's boss. The jefe is not nearly as concerned about the capture of **The Priest** as his crusading underling, and is content to play billiards and delegate authority.

Jeff

Dicey's Song
Cynthia Voigt

A tenth-grader in **Dicey**'s school. Jeff, a guitar player who sits by the bike racks outside of school, takes an interest in Dicey. He is a popular but private individual whose singing endears him to Dicey. He finally gains entrance into her home one afternoon after Thanksgiving.

Jefferson

A Lesson Before Dying
Ernest J. Gaines

A sincere, sensitive young black man of below-average intelligence. When his lawyer calls him a "hog," Jefferson takes the insult to heart and begins to consider himself powerless in the white-dominated society. He becomes sullen and withdrawn, accepting a living death and therefore becoming a dark symbol of his oppressed people. **Grant Wiggins** attempts to heal Jefferson's pain.

Dr. Henry Jekyll

Dr. Jekyll and Mr. Hyde
Robert Louis Stevenson

A respected doctor and friend of both **Dr. Hastie Lanyon**, a fellow physician, and **Mr. Gabriel John Utterson**, a lawyer. Jekyll is a seemingly prosperous man, well established in the community, and known for his decency and charitable works. Since his youth, however, he has secretly engaged in unspecified dissolute and corrupt behavior. Jekyll finds this dark side a burden and undertakes experiments intended to separate his good and evil selves from one another. Through these experiments, he brings **Mr. Edward Hyde** into being, finding a way to transform himself in such a way that he fully becomes his darker half.

Anton Jelinek

My Ántonia
Willa Cather

A Bohemian homesteader and friend of the Shimerdas'. Jelinek moves to Black Hawk and becomes a saloon proprietor.

Jellaby

Arcadia
Tom Stoppard

The distinguished, middle-aged butler of Sidley Park.

Jemy

Moll Flanders
Daniel Defoe

Moll's fourth husband. He is the only man for whom Moll has any real affection. They marry under a mutual deception and then part ways. After **Robert** dies and Moll has been caught stealing, Moll reunites with Jemy, who has also been arrested. They both manage to have their sentences reduced, and are transported to the colonies, where they begin a new life as plantation owners.

Jenkins

Fallen Angels
Walter Dean Myers

A member of **Richie Perry**'s squad who arrives in Vietnam at the same time as Richie.

Mr. Jenkins

A Wrinkle in Time
Madeleine L'Engle

Meg Murry's cold and unfeeling high school principal, who calls her "belligerent and uncooperative," just as **Charles Wallace Murry** does after he is taken over by **IT**. Mr. Jenkins implies that her family is in denial about **Mr. Murry**'s true whereabouts.

Sandy Jenkins

Narrative of the Life of Frederick Douglass
Frederick Douglass

A slave acquaintance of **Frederick Douglass**'s. The highly superstitious Sandy stands in the narrative as a representative of all uneducated slaves. Sandy is kind to Douglass when Douglass runs away from **Edward Covey**'s, but the narrative also implies that Sandy may have informed **William Freeland** about Douglass's plans to escape.

Audrey Jenning

The Day of the Locust
Nathanael West

The owner of a well-maintained call-house. Mrs. Jenning's establishment is respected because she oversees the transactions with class and care, meeting with the men first and then sending the girls out with a chauffeur. She was a silent-film star who decided to end her career in the movie industry when talking films became popular.

Ezra Jennings

The Moonstone
Wilkie Collins

The assistant to **Mr. Candy**. Jennings has a strange appearance—he is tall and thin, with a face wrinkled beyond his years and hair that is half white and half black—that causes him to be shunned from social interaction. Jennings is intelligent and science-minded. He seems to harbor secrets from his past.

Mrs. Jennings

Sense and Sensibility
Jane Austen

Lady Middleton's mother, a gossipy but well-intentioned woman. Mrs. Jennings invites the Dashwood sisters to stay with her in London and makes it her "project" to marry off the girls as soon as possible.

Aunt Jenny

The Unvanquished
William Faulkner

Colonel Sartoris's sister, who comes to live with the colonel and **Drusilla** after their marriage. She is as wise and understanding as her brother was intolerant. When **Bayard** is bent on seeking revenge against **Redmond**, she counsels him to seek peace and compassion over mindless violence.

Jensen

Wild Duck
Henrik Ibsen

A hired waiter who appears at the dinner party in Act I.

Dave Jensen

The Things They Carried
Tim O'Brien

A minor character whose guilt over injuring **Lee Strunk** causes him to break his own nose.

Nelse Jensen

O Pioneers!
Willa Cather

A man who works for **Alexandra Bergson** and eventually marries her maid **Signa**. He is glum and laconic, and his marriage to the cheerful Signa seems ill-fated.

Mr. Jenson

A Tree Grows in Brooklyn
Betty Smith

The janitor at **Francie**'s new school. He is loved and respected by the students and faculty even more than the principal. He represents the kindness that pervades the school, even for poor kids.

Jeremy

Sophie's World
Jostein Gaarder

The boy whom **Joanna** begins passionately kissing at the end of the garden party. Joanna and Jeremy's rolling around in the grass distracts the partygoers and allows **Alberto Knox** and **Sophie Amundsen** to escape from their world and enter **Hilde Møller Knag**'s.

Jeroboam

The Old Testament
Unknown

One of the opposing kings who divides Israel into the northern kingdom of Israel and the southern kingdom of Judah. **Rehoboam** and Jeroboam introduce rampant worship of idols and false gods into their kingdoms.

Jerry

Homecoming
Cynthia Voigt

Tom's friend. Jerry is the true sailor of the pair and is more contemplative than Tom. Jerry is impressed by **Dicey**'s sailing skill and flirts with her during their trip.

Miss Jessel

The Turn of the Screw
Henry James

The children's deceased former governess. There are hints that Miss Jessel became pregnant by **Peter Quint** and that she might have drowned herself in the lake at Bly.

Jessica

The Merchant of Venice
William Shakespeare

Shylock's daughter. Jessica hates life in her father's house and elopes with a young Christian gentleman, **Lorenzo**. The play's characters question the fate of her soul, wondering if her marriage can outweigh the fact that she was born a Jew.

Jessica

Dune
Frank Herbert

Paul Atreides and **Alia**'s mother, the concubine of **Duke Leto Atreides**. Though she acts like a wife to Leto and he has no other concubines, she is not married to him. Jessica is a member of the Bene Gesserit, a school that teaches and practices what many others think of as witchcraft.

Jessie

Animal Farm
George Orwell

A dog that gives birth early in the novel. **Napoleon** confiscates her and **Bluebell**'s puppies, claiming he wants to educate them. Instead, the puppies are trained to be vicious attack dogs who serve as Napoleon's personal guards.

Jessup

The Land
Mildred D. Taylor

The boss of the lumbering camp where **Paul-Edward Logan** and **Mitchell Thomas** work. Jessup holds a bitter grudge against Paul because Paul looks white. Jessup uses all kinds of excuses to punish Paul.

Jesus

The New Testament
Unknown

The central figure of the New Testament, whose life, death, and resurrection are chronicled in the books. The four Gospels describe Jesus's life until his resurrection, and the remaining New Testament books deal with the community of his followers that grows after his death. Jesus is at once a "bright morning star" (Rev. 22:16) and a small child who worries his mother sick because he stays at the temple for three extra days (**Luke** 2:46). Jesus is called a "glutton and a drunkard" by those who dislike him (**Matthew** 11:19), and he breaks social boundaries by associating with women and the poor. Jesus tells a man seeking eternal life to "go, sell what you own, and give the money to the poor, and you will have treasure in heaven; then come, follow me" (**Mark** 10:21). While Jesus blesses the peace-makers, the meek, and the pure in heart, he overturns the tables of the money changers in the temple, yelling that they have made God's house "a den of robbers" (Mark 11:17). He is simultaneously a savior and a servant.

Jewel

Lord Jim
Joseph Conrad

Daughter of the **Dutch-Malay woman** and stepdaughter of **Cornelius**. She and **Jim** fall in love, and she makes him promise never to leave her. She is a pragmatic woman and encourages Jim to fight to survive after **Dain Waris**'s death. **Marlow** encounters her after Jim's death at **Stein**'s, where she, broken and saddened, reminds Marlow that her prediction of Jim's infidelity has come true.

Jewel

As I Lay Dying
William Faulkner

Addie Bundren and **Whitfield**'s bastard child. Fiercely proud and brooding, Jewel is the novel's greatest mystery. He is often considered selfish, but he becomes a fierce protector of his mother's coffin.

Jeweler

Timon of Athens
William Shakespeare

One of **Timon**'s hangers-on. Timon buys the jeweler's ostentatious jewelry and provides it as gifts to his friends.

Miss Jewsbury

Oranges Are Not the Only Fruit
Jeanette Winterson

A member of **Jeanette**'s church who plays the oboe. Miss Jewsbury represents the closeted lesbian that Jeanette refuses to become. Miss Jewsbury's character is awkward, slightly unfriendly, and generally disdained by others who deem her unholy because of her latent sexual desires.

Jezebel

The Old Testament
Unknown

A Phoenecian princess who married **King Ahab**. She turns Ahab away from **God** to worship the pagan god **Baal**. After she murders prophets, Elijah charges her with abominations. She is eventually killed and eaten by dogs. Her name has become associated with wicked women.

Jim

The Adventures of Tom Sawyer and *The Adventures of Huckleberry Finn*
Mark Twain

A young slave. In *The Adventures of Tom Sawyer,* Jim is one of **Aunt Polly**'s slaves. In *The Adventures of Huckleberry Finn,* Jim is a bit older, and is one of **Miss Watson**'s household slaves. Jim has a wife and children. He is superstitious and occasionally sentimental, but he is also intelligent and practical. Jim's frequent acts of selflessness, his longing for his family, and his friendship with both **Huckleberry Finn** and **Tom Sawyer** demonstrate to Huck that humanity has nothing to do with race. Because Jim is a black man and a runaway slave, he is at the mercy of almost all the other characters in the novel and is often forced into ridiculous and degrading situations, especially during and after the time following the presence of **the duke** and **the dauphin**. Jim is Huck's companion as Huck travels down the Mississippi River to escape from his **Pap** and from the **Widow Douglas**. While Jim and Huck are traveling, Huck has to fight his guilt about not turning Jim in to the authorities because Jim is a runaway slave. Huck has a feeling that it is a sin to not turn Jim in, but when Jim calls out to Huck that Huck is his only friend, Huck realizes just how grateful, and more important, how human Jim is. On the river, Jim becomes a surrogate father as well as a friend to Huck, taking care of him without being intrusive or smothering. Like Huck, Jim is realistic about his situation and must find ways of accomplishing his goals without incurring the wrath of those who could turn him in. In this position, he is seldom able to act boldly or speak his mind. Nonetheless, despite these restrictions and constant fear, Jim consistently acts as a noble human being and a loyal friend. Jim is freed in Miss Watson's will.

Jim

Hatchet
Gary Paulsen

The pilot of the Cessna plane. He dies of a heart attack, forcing **Brian Robeson** to attempt to control the plane's descent. Brian becomes stranded in the Canadian woods after the plane crashes.

Lord Jim

Lord Jim
Joseph Conrad

The hero of the story, also known as "Lord Jim," or "Tuan Jim." Jim is a young man who, inspired by popular literature, goes to sea dreaming of becoming a hero. He gets his chance when the ship he is aboard gets damaged, but fails to live up to his own goals and abandons ship. Haunted by his failure and stripped of his officer's certificate, he wanders from job to job, finally becoming the manager of a remote trading post. He falls in love with **Jewel**, a beautiful, half-native girl, and, by defeating **Sherif Ali**, becomes leader of the people. His dreams of heroism lead to his failure to kill a marauding white pirate, **Gentleman Brown**, which in turn leads to the death of **Dain Waris**, his best friend and son of **Doramin**, the local chief. Jim allows Doramin to shoot him in retribution.

Jimmie

Maggie: A Girl of the Streets
Stephen Crane

Maggie's brother and **Mary**'s son. He grows up violent and combative, hardened against sympathy and introspection. Although he himself has seduced and abandoned women, he hates **Pete** for seducing Maggie and cannot muster any sympathy for Maggie, whom he blames, hypocritically, for bringing disgrace on the household. Unlike his naïve sister, Jimmie has the toughness necessary to survive in the rough world of urban poverty.

Jimmy

Typee
Herman Melville

An old European sailor who settled down on the islands and who speaks the native Polynesian tongue. He enjoys "taboo" status, allowing him to travel through the island with no harm from the natives. Jimmy appears to be an unkind figure, since he basically trades **Toby** away to a whaling ship with no consideration that **Tommo** will be trapped.

Jimmy

The Good Soldier
Ford Madox Ford

A cabin boy who travels with the Hurlbirds on their trip around the world. Jimmy becomes **Florence Hulbird Dowell**'s first lover. Jimmy is of a much lower class than either the Hurlbirds or the Dowells and he continues his affair with Florence by lying to **John Dowell** about Florence's heart condition.

Aunt Jimmy

The Bluest Eye
Toni Morrison

The elderly woman who raises **Cholly Breedlove**. She is affectionate but physically in decay. Cholly's mother abandons Cholly on a trash heap when he is four days old, but Great Aunt Jimmy rescues him. Aunt Jimmy is the person who tells Cholly that his father's name is **Samson Fuller**. Aunt Jimmy's brother **O.V.** and his family plan to take care of Cholly after Aunt Jimmy's death.

Jing-mei Woo

The Joy Luck Club
Amy Tan

The newest member of the Joy Luck Club, having taken her mother **Suyuan**'s place after her death. The other members of the Joy Luck Club give her money to travel to China so that she can find her mother's long-lost twin daughters, **Chwun Yu** and **Chwun Hwa**, and tell them Suyuan's story, but Jing-mei fears that she is not up to the task.

Jo Jo

Ellen Foster
Kaye Gibbons

Ellen's new foster sister, who loves to dance to music with no words.

Joab

The Old Testament
Unknown

King **David**'s loyal military commander, who serves as a foil to David's successful combination of religion and politics. Joab's reasonable desire for retribution delivered to the kingdom's traitors emphasizes the unusual quality of David's kindness to his enemies.

Al Joad

The Grapes of Wrath
John Steinbeck

Tom Joad's younger brother. Although Al is vain and cocky, he is also an extremely competent mechanic, and his expertise proves vital in bringing the Joad family, as well as **Ivy** and **Sairy Wilson**, to California. Al idolizes Tom but by the end of the novel becomes his own man. When he falls in love with a girl named **Agnes Wainwright** at a cotton plantation where they are working, he decides to stay with her rather than depart with his family.

Granpa Joad

The Grapes of Wrath
John Steinbeck

The patriarch of the Joad family and **Tom Joad**'s grandfather. Granpa used to have a cruel and violent temper, but his advanced age restricts him to shocking others, primarily **Granma Joad**, with sinful talk. Although Granpa is mainly a comic character, he also exhibits a poignant connection to the land. He founded the Joad farm, and the family is able to remove him from the homestead only by drugging him. Separated from his land, Granpa dies shortly after the family takes to the road.

Granma Joad

The Grapes of Wrath
John Steinbeck

The matriarch of the Joad family and **Tom Joad**'s grandmother. A pious Christian, Granma loves casting hellfire and damnation in her husband's direction. Her health deteriorates quickly after **Granpa Joad** dies, and she herself dies shortly after the family reaches California.

Ma Joad

The Grapes of Wrath
John Steinbeck

The mother of the Joad family. The determined and loving Ma emerges as the Joads' center of strength as **Pa** becomes less effective as a leader and provider. Even under the bleakest of circumstances, Ma meets every obstacle unflinchingly, heals the family's ills, and arbitrates its arguments. Perhaps her greatest test comes during the family's crossing of the California desert, when Ma suffers privately with the knowledge that **Granma Joad** has died, riding silently alongside the corpse so that the family can complete the treacherous journey. Although Ma keeps her sorrows to herself, she continually emphasizes to the other characters the importance of family and togetherness. Ma's indomitable nature suggests that even the most horrible circumstances can be weathered with grace and dignity.

Noah Joad

The Grapes of Wrath
John Steinbeck

Tom Joad's older brother. Slow and quiet, Noah has been slightly deformed since birth, when **Pa Joad**, performing the delivery, panicked and tried to pull Noah out forcibly. Noah leaves his family behind at a stream near the California border, telling Tom that he feels his parents do not love him as much as they love the other children.

Pa Joad

The Grapes of Wrath
John Steinbeck

Ma Joad's husband and **Tom**'s father. The plainspoken, good-hearted Pa has worked as an Oklahoma tenant farmer for years. Evicted from his farm during the Depression, Pa directs the effort to move the family to California. Although he works hard to maintain his role as head of the family, the hardships of the road prove too much for him. Nonetheless, Pa remains committed to protecting his family. When his efforts fall short, Pa despairs and his inability to find work forces him to retreat into his own thoughts. By the end of the novel, diminished by his failures, he follows Ma as blindly and helplessly as a child.

Ruthie Joad

The Grapes of Wrath
John Steinbeck

The second Joad daughter. Ruthie has a fiery relationship with her brother **Winfield**, as the two are both intensely dependent upon one another and firecly competitive.

Tom Joad

The Grapes of Wrath
John Steinbeck

The novel's protagonist, an ex-convict who returns to his family's Oklahoma farm after serving four years for a manslaughter conviction. The good-natured and thoughtful Tom is **Ma** and **Pa Joad**'s favorite son. Tom's years in prison have molded him into a man who devotes his time and energies to the present moment, unconcerned with the future, which seems illusory and out of reach. However, Tom undergoes a significant transformation during the family's journey west, when he becomes a reluctant disciple of **Jim Casy**, the former preacher who emphasizes that a human being can achieve wholeness only by devoting himself to his fellow humans. By the time Tom and Casy reunite at the cotton plantation in California, Tom realizes he cannot stand by as a silent witness to the world's injustices. Just when Tom has earned the awed respect of his family members and the migrant workers whom he organizes into unions, he becomes a fugitive again after killing a police officer in retaliation for Jim Casy's murder.

Winfield Joad

The Grapes of Wrath
John Steinbeck

The youngest of the Joad children. **Ma** worries that Winfield's lack of a proper home as a child will make him a wild and rootless man when he grows up.

Joan of Arc

Henry VI, Part I
William Shakespeare

A French shepherdess-turned-soldier. Joan comes to **Charles, Dauphin of France**, claiming to have been visited by "God's Mother," who directed her to fight for France against England. She proves her mettle after besting Charles in single combat, but rebuffs his sexual advances, saying that her sacred task requires her to remain a virgin. She leads French troops to victory at Orléans and Rouen, only to see both cities recaptured by the English. The **Duke of York** captures her and brings her to trial. Cursing England, she is taken away to be burned at the stake.

Joanna

A Tree Grows in Brooklyn
Betty Smith

A young unmarried woman with a baby, who is the object of the neighborhood women's cruelty. Joanna represents one stage in **Mary Frances Nolan**'s fall from innocence.

Joanna

Sophie's World
Jostein Gaarder

Sophie Amundsen's best friend. Joanna is loyal and friendly, although she does not think about things in the same way that Sophie does. Sophie does not pay much attention to Joanna after Sophie starts learning about philosophy. Joanna's passionate kissing and rolling around with **Jeremy** at the garden party creates a distraction that allows **Alberto Knox** and Sophie to escape their world and go to the world of **Hilde Møller Knag**.

Joaquín

For Whom the Bell Tolls
Ernest Hemingway

One of the members of **El Sordo**'s band of guerrilla fighters. Joaquín originally wanted to be bullfighter but was too scared. He lost most of his family at the hands of the Fascists and cries when he talks about them. Joaquín buys into the Republicans' propaganda but turns back to religion at the moment of his death, illustrating the emptiness of political rhetoric in times of true crisis.

Job

The Old Testament
Unknown

The subject of **God**'s cosmic experiment to measure human faithfulness to God amid immense pain. Job scorns false contrition and his friends' advice, preferring instead to question God's role in human suffering. He remains open and inquisitive and refuses to curse God.

Job

The Autobiography of Miss Jane Pittman
Ernest J. Gaines

A poor white man who takes **Miss Jane Pittman** and **Ned Douglass** to his house when they are fleeing slavery. His wife has gone crazy during the war, and he has little to share with them, but he does so anyway and takes them to the safe location of **Mr. Bone**'s plantation. Like his biblical namesake, he is a man who has seemingly endured much but who still maintains a sense of goodness and godliness by being charitable.

Uncle Job

The Sound and the Fury
William Faulkner

A black man who works with **Jason** at **Earl**'s store.

Joby

The Unvanquished
William Faulkner

A loyal older former slave of the Sartorises, who occasionally feuds with **Granny Millard** but staunchly remains by the family despite abolition.

Jocasta

Oedipus trilogy (Oedipus Rex, Oedipus at Colonus, Antigone)
Sophocles

Oedipus's wife and mother, and **Creon**'s sister. Jocasta is a peacemaker. She comforts Oedipus and calmly urges him to reject **Tiresias**'s terrifying prophecies. Jocasta is the first to solve the riddle of Oedipus's identity.

Jody

The Bell Jar
Sylvia Plath

A friend of **Esther Greenwood**'s, with whom she is supposed to live while she takes a summer writing course. Jody is friendly and tries to be helpful, but cannot reach Esther.

Joe

In Our Time
Ernest Hemingway

The narrator of "My Old Man," who tells the story of his father as a horse jockey.

Joe

Childhood's End
Arthur C. Clarke

A radical member of **Wainwright**'s Freedom League. He abducts **Stormgren** in an attempt to learn more about **the Overlords**.

Joe

A Clockwork Orange
Anthony Burgess

The lodger **Alex**'s parents take after Alex is sent to jail. Joe is extremely rude to Alex when he is released from jail.

Mrs. Joe

Great Expectations
Charles Dickens

Pip's sister and **Joe Gargery**'s wife, known only as "Mrs. Joe." A stern and overbearing woman, Mrs. Joe keeps her house spotless and frequently menaces her husband and her brother with her cane, which she calls "Tickler."

Joel

Go Ask Alice
Anonymous

A working-class freshman at **Alice**'s father's university. Joel's father died when he was young, his mother toils in a factory, and he works as a janitor to pay his tuition. He is gentle in his growing romantic relationship with Alice.

Jogona

Out of Africa
Isak Dinesen

The father of **Wamai**. During the legal disputes, Jogona's behavior contrasts with **Kinanu**'s, the Kikuyu man who is held responsible for the shooting of Jogona's son. Although others accuse Jogona of misdeeds, after Jogona gives his account to **the narrator**, he is able to establish that he is an honest, forthright figure and therefore is properly compensated.

Johanna

Ghosts
Henrik Ibsen

Captain Alving and **Mrs. Alving**'s servant. Johanna gave birth to **Regina** after Captain Alving forced her to sleep with him. She is dead and never appears onstage.

Annemarie Johansen

Number the Stars
Lois Lowry

The protagonist of the story. She lives in Copenhagen, Denmark, with her mother and father, **Mrs. Johansen** and **Mr. Johansen**, and her sister, **Kirsten Johansen**. Annemarie's best friend is **Ellen Rosen**, the girl who lives next door. She is tall and unusually thoughtful for her age. Because of the death of her older sister **Lise Johansen**, Annemarie worries about her parents and is careful not to upset them. Annemarie looks up to her parents and **Peter Neilsen**, Lise's ex-fiancé. She also greatly admires **King Christian X**, the king of Denmark. In all of these people Annemarie recognizes bravery and wishes that she could be as brave as those she admires. As she accuses **Uncle Henrik** of lying about **Great-aunt Birte**'s funeral, she starts to realize that there is a whole world of make-believe stories created by the adults in order to save people's lives and prevent others from worrying. Annemarie's turning point happens when she must bring a special package to the boat that Uncle Henrik is using to hide Ellen, **Mr. Rosen**, and **Mrs. Rosen**. Soldiers stop her and she has to be brave, play dumb, and endure the soldiers' cruelty. She does so, and saves the Rosens' lives.

Kirsten Johansen

Number the Stars
Lois Lowry

Annemarie Johansen's younger sister. She is a feisty, chatty girl. Completely unafraid of German soldiers and death, Kirsti is the embodiment of blissful innocence. She loves stories about kings and queens and is constantly turning the surrealistic aspects of war into the fantasy of fairy tales. On Kirsti's birthday, the Danes destroyed their own naval fleet in order to keep the Germans from using it. To calm Kirsti, **Mrs. Johansen** tells her that the explosions were fireworks for Kirsti's birthday.

Lise Johansen

Number the Stars
Lois Lowry

The eldest Johansen daughter, sister to **Annemarie Johansen** and **Kirsten Johansen**, daughter of **Mr. Johansen** and **Mrs. Johansen**. She died several years before the beginning of the novel, around the end of 1941. Lise Johansen was a member of the Resistance with **Peter Neilsen**. Annemarie had always been told that Lise was killed in a car accident, but it turns out that she was deliberately murdered by the Nazis. Annemarie finds this out only after her display of bravery in helping **Ellen Rosen**, **Mr. Rosen**, and **Mrs. Rosen** to escape.

Mr. Johansen

Number the Stars
Lois Lowry

A pillar of strength, he is deeply patriotic and willing to die for Denmark. Mr. Johansen is the teacher of his family and tells **Annemarie Johansen** about the country and the war. He leads Annemarie to believe that bravery is the most prized value that any person can possess. He stays at the Johansens' home in Copenhagen while **Kirsten Johansen**, **Mrs. Johansen**, Annemarie, and **Henrik** help **Ellen Rosen**, **Mr. Rosen**, and **Mrs. Rosen** escape to Sweden from Gilleleje.

Mrs. Johansen

Number the Stars
Lois Lowry

Mother of **Annemarie Johansen**, **Kirsten Johansen**, **Lise Johansen**, and caretaker of **Ellen Rosen**. She is a gentle, extremely strong, determined woman, firm but warm with her children. She is fiercely protective of her family. In three separate confrontations with German soldiers, Mrs. Johansen overcomes her fear and defends her loved ones. She manages to keep up the spirits of the girls, even when there is danger, by telling stories. Her confidence sets an example that Annemarie tries to follow. Mrs. Johansen willingly risks her life to help Ellen, **Mr. Rosen** and **Mrs. Rosen** escape from the Nazis; she is also prepared to let Annemarie face danger when it becomes necessary.

John

The Canterbury Tales
Geoffrey Chaucer

The dim-witted carpenter to whom **Alisoun** is married and with whom **Nicholas** boards in **the Miller**'s Tale. John is jealous and possessive of his wife. He gullibly believes Nicholas's pronouncement that a second flood is coming, and the ruse allows Nicholas to sleep with John's wife.

John

Brave New World
Aldous Huxley

The son of **the Director** and **Linda**. John was born when his mother, then pregnant, was abandoned with a head injury on the New Mexico Savage Reservation. There, raised by his outcast mother and **Pope**, his mother's lover, John develops a worldview very different than that of the World State society. Viewed as a curious novelty for his origins and beliefs, John is driven to violence and ultimately suicide by guilt over his desire for **Lenina Crowne**.

John

A Tree Grows in Brooklyn
Betty Smith

Aunt Sissy's third and last husband. Steve, like all of Sissy's men, goes along with her wishes most of the time. By the end of the book, though, he stands up for himself.

John

Cat's Cradle
Kurt Vonnegut

The hapless narrator. In the past, he set out to write a book about the day the atomic bomb was dropped on Hiroshima, entitled *The Day the World Ended*. His research led him to an ill-fated acquaintance with **Angela Hoenikker**, **Frank Hoenikker**, and **Newt Hoenikker**, the equally hapless children of **Felix Hoenikker**. He became involved with their efforts to buy happiness through the use of their father's scientific creation, *ice- nine*, a substance that turns water to ice.

John

How the Garcia Girls Lost Their Accents
Julia Alvarez

Yolanda's husband, who ceases to make sense to her and speaks only in a babbling gibberish once she realizes she does not love him anymore.

John

Oleanna
David Mamet

A highly analytical college professor, teacher to **Carol**. Alternately protagonist and antagonist, John is about to be granted tenure at the college and is situated in a very nice cloud of upper-middle-class security. This makes him pompous and inherently oppressive, but he is good at heart. While John does play into Carol's hands by touching her, restraining her, and ultimately beating her, it is his humanity and self-reflection that often draw the audience to side with him.

John the Baptist

The New Testament
Unknown

The forerunner to **Jesus**, who spreads the word of Jesus' imminent arrival. John the Baptist is an old ascetic who lives in the desert wearing a loincloth, feeding on locusts and honey.

Annie John

Annie John
Jamaica Kincaid

The protagonist of the novel. Annie is bright, spunky, and witty. She tells her own story in tones that vary from serious to comic. At first, she resists separation from her mother, but after her illness, she comes to see this separation as a natural part of growing up. Annie also finds substitutes for her mother in her friends and becomes disobedient. In her disobedience, she comes to define herself in contrast to the Antiguan social order.

Don John

Much Ado About Nothing
William Shakespeare

The illegitimate brother of **Don Pedro**. Though there had long been hostility between him and his brother, Don John had made up with Don Pedro, and has accompanied him to Messina following the wars. However, he is still angry. Don John plots, with his associates **Borachio** and **Conrad**, to cause havoc in Messina, ruining the marriage of **Claudio** and **Hero**, with further hopes to "misuse the Prince...and kill **Leonato**." His plan is initially successful, but when the watchmen force Borachio and Conrad to confess, Don John flees.

Friar John

Romeo and Juliet
William Shakespeare

A Franciscan friar charged by **Friar Lawrence** with taking the news of **Juliet**'s false death to **Romeo** in Mantua. Friar John is held up by a quarantine, and the message never reaches Romeo.

King John of England

King John
William Shakespeare

The ruler of England. John took the throne because the previous king, his eldest brother **Richard the Lionhearted**, named him his heir. Legally the throne should have passed to **Arthur**, the son of John and Richard's deceased middle brother, **Geoffrey**. The question of his rule's legitimacy creates the conflict that spurs the war between France and England, though it is almost avoided by a marriage between **Blanche**, the princess of Spain and John's niece, and **Lewis**, the dauphin of France. Throughout the play, the French attack John, the pope challenges him, and his noblemen desert him. His strongest supporter, his mother **Eleanor**, dies after war breaks out with France, leaving him weak and indecisive. His order to kill Arthur becomes the lynchpin in his defeat—hearing of the murder, English lords defect to France. John dies after being poisoned by a monk who is angry that the king ordered the monasteries plundered after breaking with Rome. At the end of the play, John's son **Prince Henry** inherits the crown.

Prince John

Ivanhoe
Sir Walter Scott

King Richard I's power-hungry and greedy brother, who sits on the throne of England in Richard's absence. John's chief adviser is **Waldemar Fitzurse**, and his allies include **Maurice de Bracy** and **Reginald Front-de-Boeuf**. John is a weak and uninspiring ruler who lets himself be pushed around by his powerful Norman nobles.

Uncle John

The Grapes of Wrath
John Steinbeck

Tom Joad's uncle. Years before the start of the novel, John refused to fetch a doctor for his pregnant wife when she complained of stomach pains, and she died as a result. He never forgives himself for her death and dwells heavily on the negligence he considers a sin.

Johnny

Death Be Not Proud
John Gunther

A sensitive, intelligent, selfless, courageous boy who battles a brain tumor—he is the subject of the story. His parents are **John Gunther** and **Frances**. He is incredibly intelligent: over the course of the memoir, he discovers a new property of ammonia, is concerned with the Unified Field Theory, and discusses journalism with his father. Had he not died, he would have been a student at Harvard. He is thoughtful about every event and object that comes his way in life, as demonstrated by his intense curiosity about his own illness. He never lets anyone else pity him, not out of pride, but to spare their feelings.

Johnny

On the Road
Jack Kerouac

Terry's seven-year-old son.

Evan Johns

Lucky Jim
Kingsley Amis

Jim Dixon's nemesis; the two have an ongoing feud. He lives with Dixon and is a staff member at the college, where he shamelessly sucks up to **Professor Ned Welch**. He plays the oboe at Professor Welch's amateur musical concerts and likes to tattle to **Celia Welch** about all of Dixon's social blunders.

Johnson

Fallen Angels
Walter Dean Myers

An extraordinarily strong black soldier on **Richie Perry**'s squad who proves himself to be a born leader.

Big Bailey Johnson

I Know Why the Caged Bird Sings
Maya Angelou

Father of **Maya Johnson** and **Bailey Johnson**. He exemplifies ignorant parental neglect. Despite his lively personality, he is handsome, vain, and selfish. He stands out among the other rural blacks because of his proper English and his flashy possessions. Big Bailey does not respect, care for, or connect with Maya. She regards him as a stranger, for he shows little genuine effort to care for her. He exemplifies the tragedy of the American black man trying to advance in a white society obsessed with class, paying more attention to his image than to his family.

Bailey Johnson, Jr.

I Know Why the Caged Bird Sings
Maya Angelou

Maya Johnson's older brother, son of **Vivian Baxter** and **Big Bailey Johnson**. Bailey is the most important person in Maya's life throughout her childhood. When moved around from place to place, Bailey and Maya depend on each other to achieve some semblance of stability and continuity in their lives. Unlike Maya, Bailey is graceful, attractive, outgoing, and charming, and many consider him the jewel of his family. Like Maya, he is intelligent and mature beyond his age. Though Bailey enjoys sports and fares well in social situations, he also shows deep compassion for his isolated sister, using his skills and status to protect Maya. The return to Stamps, Arkansas, from St. Louis traumatizes Bailey, and though he never blames his sister, he remains tormented by his longing for his mother. Bailey moves out at age sixteen and gets a job on the Southern Pacific Railroad. Bailey and Maya grow further apart as they go through adolescence, as Bailey becomes estranged from Vivian, and Bailey continues to withdraw deeper into himself.

In Cold Blood
Truman Capote

Barbara Johnson

Perry Edward Smith's only living sister. She lives in San Francisco and is married.

Death Be Not Proud
John Gunther

Dr. Johnson

The Deerfield doctor who takes **Johnny** into the infirmary because of his stiff neck and suspects something worse, like polio. Dr. Johnson brings in **Dr. Hahn**.

Maggie: A Girl of the Streets
Stephen Crane

Maggie Johnson

The novel's title character, who grows up amid abuse and poverty in the Bowery neighborhood of New York's Lower East Side. Maggie's mother, **Mary**, is a vicious alcoholic; her brother, **Jimmie**, is mean-spirited and brutish. Maggie grows up a beautiful young lady whose romantic hopes for a better life remain untarnished. Her seemingly inevitable path toward destruction begins when she becomes enamored of **Pete**, whose show of confidence and worldliness seems to promise wealth and culture. After Pete seduces and abandons her, Maggie becomes a neighborhood scandal when she turns to prostitution. The nature of her demise is unclear—she either commits suicide or is murdered. She seems a natural and hereditary victim, succumbing finally to the forces of poverty and social injustice that built up against her even before her birth.

I Know Why the Caged Bird Sings
Maya Angelou

Marguerite Ann Johnson

See **Maya Johnson**.

Maggie: A Girl of the Streets
Stephen Crane

Mary Johnson

Maggie and **Jimmie**'s mother. The alcoholic and vicious Mary Johnson is a virtual incarnation of the devil. After terrifying Maggie into fleeing from home, Mary is hypocritical enough to condemn her daughter for immorality, and crassly sentimental enough to stage an elaborate scene of mourning for the daughter she never really loved.

I Know Why the Caged Bird Sings
Maya Angelou

Maya Johnson

The subject of the story, a stand-in for the author, Maya Angelou. Maya Johnson—named Marguerite Ann Johnson at birth—writes about her experiences growing up as a black girl in the rural South and in the cities of St. Louis, Los Angeles, and San Francisco. She is the daughter of **Vivian Baxter** and **Big Bailey Johnson**, and the sister of **Bailey Johnson**. At the beginning, Maya is a precocious young girl suffering not just from the typical traumas associated with being black and female in America, but also from the trauma of displacement. Smart and imaginative, Maya nevertheless feels that people judge her unfairly due to her ungainly appearance. Her parents abandon her and Bailey when Maya is three, and her sense of abandonment and need for physical affection lead to further struggles. Five years later, she must leave the only home she has known and move to an unknown city where she seeks comfort in **Mr. Freeman**, who molests and rapes her. At age ten, having already witnessed callous whites mistreating the people she loves most, such as **Momma**, Maya begins to experience racism directly. In San Francisco, Maya's confusion about sexuality becomes compounded when she becomes pregnant at age sixteen. With Bailey and Momma's unwavering love and, later encouragement from Vivian, **Daddy Clidell**, and numerous role models and friends, Maya gains the strength to overcome difficulties and realize her full potential. She learns to confront racism actively and eventually secures a position as the first black conductor aboard a San Francisco streetcar. She remains insecure, especially about her sexuality and appearance, but eventually she learns to trust her own abilities.

Mr. Johnson

Maggie: A Girl of the Streets
Stephen Crane

Maggie, **Jimmie**, and **Tommie**'s father and **Mary**'s husband. Mr. Johnson dies early in the novel. Like his wife, Mary, he is an alcoholic, going to bars to escape the "livin' hell" of his home.

Mrs. Johnson

The Day of the Locust
Nathanael West

The janitor at the San Bernardino apartments. Mrs. Johnson's hobby is bossing grieving people into giving expensive funerals and letting her organize them.

Mrs. Johnson

A Raisin in the Sun
Lorraine Hansberry

The Youngers' neighbor. She predicts that the Youngers will also be scared out of the all-white neighborhood once they move in and insults much of the family by calling them a "proud-acting bunch of colored folks."

Nathan Johnson

Narrative of the Life of Frederick Douglass
Frederick Douglass

A Massachusetts worker and abolitionist. Johnson is immediately kind and helpful to **Frederick Douglass** and his family, loaning them money, helping Douglass find work, and suggesting Douglass's new name.

Roy Johnson

On the Road
Jack Kerouac

A friend of **Sal Paradise**'s who chauffeurs **Dean Moriarty** and Sal in San Francisco.

Tommie Johnson

Maggie: A Girl of the Streets
Stephen Crane

Maggie's youngest brother and **Mary**'s son. Brought up amid the curses and flying cutlery of his parents' battles, Tommie dies early in the novel.

Willy Johnson

I Know Why the Caged Bird Sings
Maya Angelou

Momma's son and **Maya Johnson** and **Bailey Johnson**'s uncle. Uncle Willy, who is an adult, was crippled in a childhood accident and has always lived with Momma. Like Momma, he is a devout Christian. He is disciplinarian and protector to the children.

Jokanaan

Salomé
Oscar Wilde

The prophet imprisoned in a tomb-like cistern at the orders of **Herod**, Wilde's version of the biblical John the Baptist. Jokanaan spends much of the play in his subterranean prison, figuring as a mad, booming voice that predicts the ruin of the kingdom, curses the royal family, and proclaims the coming of Christ. He appears onstage and takes corporeal form, against his wishes, at **Salomé**'s lustful call.

Ma Jolie

Annie John
Jamaica Kincaid

The obeah woman who moved to Antigua from Dominica and who comes to treat **Annie** during her illness.

Jon

Tuesdays with Morrie
Mitch Albom

One of **Morrie Schwartz**'s two adult sons. Though they live far away, Jon and his brother **Rob** often travel to Boston to visit Morrie, especially as his condition worsens.

Jonas

Antigone 1946
Jean Anouilh

One of the three Guardsmen who serve as doubles for the rank-and-file fascist collaborators of Anouilh's day. The card-playing trio, made all the more mindless and indistinguishable in being grouped in three, emerges from a long stage tradition of the dull-witted police officer. Their presence serves as a condemnation of those French who followed the pro-Nazi Vichy government.

Jonas

The Jungle
Upton Sinclair

Teta Elzbieta's brother. Jonas encourages **Jurgis**, **Ona**, and family to emigrate to America but then abandons them after months of miserable poverty.

Jonas

The Giver
Lois Lowry

The protagonist of *The Giver*. On the surface, Jonas is just like any other boy living in his community. However, he is extremely sensitive and intelligent, with strange powers of perception. Jonas is chosen to be the new Receiver of Memory for his community when he turns twelve. Once Jonas begins his training with **the Giver**, the tendencies he showed in his earlier life make him extremely absorbed in the memories the Giver has to transmit. In turn, the memories, with their rich sensory and emotional experiences, enhance all of Jonas's unusual qualities. Within a year of training, his universe widens dramatically. Jonas becomes extremely sensitive to beauty, color, pleasure, and suffering, and develops deep love. Things about the community that used to be mildly perplexing or troubling are now intensely frustrating or depressing, and Jonas's inherent concern for others and desire for justice makes him yearn to make changes in the community. After he decides to stop taking his medication to calm his sexual "Stirrings," he starts to develop ideas that the community needs to be changed, especially after he learns that "release" really means cold and calculated killing. He and the Giver develop a plan to give back all of their memories to the community, providing for Jonas's escape with **Gabriel**, and an end to the strictly ordered "Sameness" that the community lives under.

Jonas's father

The Giver
Lois Lowry

A mild-mannered Nurturer who works with infants, or "newchildren," and the husband of **Jonas's mother**. However, even if he is attached to a child, he will "release," or kill, it if that seems to be the best decision. He has an affectionate, playful relationship with his two children, **Jonas** and **Lily**. He is worried that **Gabriel** will have to be released, but he gains a year's reprieve for Gabriel, which means the newchild can live with Jonas's father's family for one year to try to get up to standard weight and behavior.

Jonas's mother

The Giver
Lois Lowry

A practical, pleasant woman with an important position at the Department of Justice. She is the wife of **Jonas's father** and the mother of **Lily**. Jonas's mother takes her work seriously, hoping to help people who break rules see the error of their ways.

Mr. Jonas

Dandelion Wine
Ray Bradbury

The town junkman. Mr. Jonas is a caring man who understands what **Douglas Spaulding** is going through during his fever.

Archie Jones

White Teeth
Zadie Smith

A hapless comic hero who fumbles blindly through life with his hands over his eyes. Sturdy but undistinguished, Archie is a typically dispassionate Englishman who surrounds himself with fiery, passionate people. Archie and **Samad Iqbal**'s fifty-plus-year friendship serves as the backbone of *White Teeth*. The two men serve together in a comically ragtag battalion in World War II, and their friendship is sealed when they take into their hands the fate of a French geneticist who's conducted various experiments for the Nazis. Throughout the novel, Archie remains rather out of step with the world around him. Though his marriage to the tall, Jamaican **Clara Bowden** bewilders many, Archie seems oblivious. **Irie Jones** is the daughter of Clara and Archie.

Clara Jones

White Teeth
Zadie Smith

A Jamaican girl fleeing the religious preachings of her overpowering mother. After renouncing the Church and fleeing her mother, at age nineteen Clara heads to the commune where she meets middle-aged **Archie Jones**. The Joneses' marriage is extremely unlikely, and after **Irie Jones** is born, Clara more or less disappears from the narrative.

Harry Jones

The Big Sleep
Raymond Chandler

An inept criminal. Harry is not very smart, but he demonstrates a good heart when he gives **Canino** the wrong address and when he protects **Agnes**, his partner in crime.

Irie Jones

White Teeth
Zadie Smith

A racially mixed girl who lives at odds with the complex legacies she inherits. Irie desperately wants to be "normal," without the crushing burden of her family's history on their shoulders. Irie pines for the beautiful, maddeningly unattainable **Millat Iqbal**, who only seems to ever want thin, blond, white girls. Irie comes to loathe the Jamaican features that she has inherited from the Bowden women. As Irie grows into her adolescence, she becomes closely involved with the highly educated, middle-class Chalfen family. Irie eventually becomes **Marcus Chalfen**'s secretary, and the work sharpens her intellect.

Jenny Jones

Tom Jones
Henry Fielding

A student of **Partridge** whom **Allworthy** banishes for being **Tom**'s mother. At the end of the novel, we learn that Jenny is not Tom's mother. Jenny reappears as "Mrs. Waters" at Upton, where Tom saves her from a robbery. She eventually marries **Parson Supple**, a friend of **Western**'s.

Lady Jones

Beloved
Toni Morrison

A light-skinned black woman who is a teacher in Cincinnati. She is convinced that everyone despises her for being a woman of mixed race. Lady Jones was **Denver**'s old teacher. When Denver finally, courageously leaves 124 Bluestone Road to get help for **Sethe**, she goes to Lady Jones, who, in turn, tells her whole church about Denver needing a job to get some money for Sethe's care.

Love Jones

The Heart Is a Lonely Hunter
Carson McCullers

A stripper. **Willie** gets into a knife fight over her and ends up in prison. Love, according to **Portia**, is an ugly, tasteless woman.

Milly Jones

Absalom, Absalom!
William Faulkner

Wash Jones's young granddaughter, who at fifteen gives birth to **Thomas Sutpen**'s child. She is murdered, along with Sutpen and the baby, by her grandfather shortly after the birth.

Mr. Jones

The Adventures of Tom Sawyer
Mark Twain

A Welshman who lives with his sons near the **Widow Douglas**'s house. Mr. Jones responds to **Huckleberry Finn**'s alarm on the night that **Injun Joe** intends to attack the widow.

Mr. Jones

Animal Farm
George Orwell

Complacent owner of the Manor Farm before the animals' revolution. Once a capable farmer, in the years leading to the rebellion Jones had fallen upon hard times and begun drinking to excess. Once banished from his own farm by a coalition led by **Snowball** and **Napoleon**, Jones makes an attempt to regain his land at the Battle of Cowshed, then slouches off to another part of the country.

Tom Jones

Tom Jones
Henry Fielding

A "bastard" raised by the philanthropic **Allworthy** and the novel's eponymous hero and protagonist. Although Tom's faults (namely, his imprudence and his lack of chastity) prevent him from being a perfect hero, his good heart and generosity make him Fielding's avatar of virtue. Tom's handsome face and gallantry win him the love and affection of women throughout the countryside. His dignified though natural air induces characters to assume he is a gentleman, which ultimately turns out to be true.

Wash Jones

Absalom, Absalom!
William Faulkner

A low-class squatter living in the abandoned fishing camp at Sutpen's Hundred. Wash murders Sutpen in 1869 for impregnating his granddaughter, **Milly Jones**.

Lindo Jong

The Joy Luck Club
Amy Tan

A member of the Joy Luck Club. Lindo teaches her daughter, **Waverly**, about the power of invisible strength. She worries that in trying to give Waverly American opportunities, she may have undermined her daughter's Chinese identity.

Tin Jong

The Joy Luck Club
Amy Tan

Lindo's second husband. Tin is the father of her three children: **Vincent**, **Waverly**, and **Winston**.

Vincent Jong

The Joy Luck Club
Amy Tan

Lindo and **Tin Jong**'s second child. When he receives a secondhand chess set at a church-sponsored Christmas party, his sister **Waverly** discovers her interest and talent in chess.

Waverly Jong

The Joy Luck Club
Amy Tan

The youngest of **Lindo** and **Tin Jong**'s children. Waverly has always been a model of success, winning chess tournaments as a child and eventually building a lucrative career as an attorney. **Jing-mei** feels a rivalry with her. Waverly worries about her mother's reaction to her white fiancé, **Rich**.

Winston Jong

The Joy Luck Club
Amy Tan

Lindo and **Tin Jong**'s first child. Winston was killed in a car accident at the age of sixteen.

Joshua Jopp

The Mayor of Casterbridge
Thomas Hardy

The man **Michael Henchard** intends to hire as his assistant before meeting **Donald Farfrae**. When Farfrae opens a business to compete with Henchard's much later on, Henchard hires Jopp and tells him that his primary objective is to cut Farfrae out of the corn-and-hay business. But after losing money after some bad business decisions, Henchard fires Jopp. After news of Henchard's past spreads through town, he is disgraced; his business fails and he moves in with Jopp.

Hunter Jordan

The Color of Water
James McBride

Ruth McBride Jordan's second husband and **James McBride**'s primary male role model. Hunter was a mechanic for the New York City Housing Authority. He met Ruth shortly after her first husband's death, married her, and had four children with her. He died of a stroke when James was a teenager, and his entire family recalls him with fondness.

Robert Jordan

For Whom the Bell Tolls
Ernest Hemingway

The protagonist and an American volunteer for the Republican side in the Spanish Civil War. Robert Jordan is pragmatic, very good at what he does, and never lets his emotions interfere with his work. He appreciates physical pleasures like smelling pine trees, drinking absinthe, and having sex. At the same time, he is conflicted about his role within the war and within the larger world. He falls in love with the peasant girl **Maria**, and they embark on a tender, passionate affair in their few days together. However, shortly after he accomplishes his mission to blow up a Fascist-controlled bridge, Robert Jordan breaks his leg when his horse tramples on it; presumably, he is killed by Fascist soldiers after the novel's closing pages.

For Whom the Bell Tolls
Ernest Hemingway

Robert Jordan's father

A weak, religious man who could not stand up to his aggressive wife and eventually committed suicide. His father's weakness is a constant source of embarrassment to **Robert Jordan**.

For Whom the Bell Tolls
Ernest Hemingway

Robert Jordan's grandfather

A veteran of the American Civil War and a member of the Republican National Committee. **Robert Jordan** feels more closely related to his grandfather than to his father.

The Color of Water
James McBride

Ruth McBride Jordan

The central figure of the memoir, and the tough but big-hearted mother of **James McBride** and eleven other children. A Polish Jewish immigrant, she is spiritual, intelligent, determined, practical, and brave. She stresses the importance of work, school, and God. She chose an unconventional life and succeeds in it because she has the grit and conviction to endure hardships.

The Joy Luck Club
Amy Tan

Ted Jordan

Rose's estranged husband. When they were dating, he made all the decisions. Later, he asks for a divorce and is surprised when Rose stands up for herself.

Sons and Lovers
D. H. Lawrence

Thomas Jordan

The owner of the factory where **Paul Morel** works. Paul dislikes Thomas Jordan from their first interview because he is rude and makes Paul look foolish. Thomas later fires **Baxter Dawes** because he knocks him down a flight of stairs.

The Caine Mutiny
Herman Wouk

Jorgensen

A newcomer to **Philip Francis Queeg**'s reign. He is an ensign who is shocked by the regular injustices that take place aboard the *Caine*.

On the Beach
Nevil Shute

Professor Jorgensen

A scientist who comes up with the controversial theory that precipitation in the Northern Hemisphere will clean the air of radiation and keep it from reaching Australia. This theory is referred to as the Jorgensen effect.

Bobby Jorgenson

The Things They Carried
Tim O'Brien

The medic who replaces **Bob "Rat" Kiley**. The second time **Tim O'Brien** is shot, Jorgenson's incompetence inspires O'Brien's desire for irrational revenge. Although Jorgenson's anger prompts him to kick O'Brien in the head for trying to scare him, he later apologizes, redeeming himself as a medic by patching things up with O'Brien.

Bertha Jorkins

Harry Potter and the Goblet of Fire
J. K. Rowling

A middle-aged, gossipy witch who works for the Ministry of Magic. She is tapped for information and killed by **Voldemort**.

Jose

Johnny Got His Gun
Dalton Trumbo

A Puerto Rican man who was hired to work in the Los Angeles bakery where **Joe Bonham** worked. Jose had been a chauffeur in New York City and was looking for a job in a film studio. He tried to be courteous and generous, especially toward **Jody Simmons**, who gave him his job.

José

Holes
Louis Sachar

See **Magnet**.

Don Jose

How the Garcia Girls Lost Their Accents
Julia Alvarez

Dona Charito's sculptor husband. Don Jose is insane; he terrifies **Sandra** and makes her fall and break her arm, and later he puts her face on a statue of the Virgin Mary.

Padre Jose

The Power and the Glory
Graham Greene

The only other religious figure in the novel besides the protagonist, **The Priest**. Padre Jose opted to renounce his faith rather than flee the state or face execution. Forced to marry, Padre Jose is allowed to remain in his town as a symbol of the weakness of the priesthood. He is mocked regularly by the children in his neighborhood and feels a deep and abiding sense of shame over the choices he has made.

Joseph

The Old Testament
Unknown

Jacob's son and the head official for the Pharaoh of Egypt. Despite being sold into slavery by his brothers, Joseph rises to power in Egypt and saves his family from famine. His calm and gracious response to his brothers' betrayal introduces the pattern of forgiveness and redemption that characterizes the survival of the Israelite people throughout the Old Testament.

Joseph

The Red Tent
Anita Diamant

Rachel's first son and the recipient of **Jacob**'s blessing. He is good-looking and charismatic like his father, and after he is sold into slavery by **Simon** and **Levi**, his cleverness and dream-interpreting abilities help him rise to the position of vizier in Egypt. **Dinah**'s son **Re-mose** unknowingly becomes the scribe for his own uncle Joseph after he becomes the vizier.

Joseph

The New Testament
Unknown

Mary's husband. Joseph is a direct paternal descendent of the great King **David**, which makes **Jesus** an heir to David's throne line. This heritage reinforces Jesus' place in the Jewish tradition.

Joseph

Wuthering Heights
Emily Brontë

A long-winded, fanatically religious elderly servant at Wuthering Heights. Joseph is strange, stubborn, and unkind, and he speaks with a thick Yorkshire accent.

Joseph

Breath, Eyes, Memory
Edwidge Danticat

Sophie's first and only boyfriend and eventual husband. Joseph is a professional musician who lives next door to the house where Sophie and **Martine** move during Sophie's eighteenth year. He is an African-American from Louisiana.

Joseph K.

The Trial
Franz Kafka

The hero and protagonist of the novel, and the chief clerk of a bank. Ambitious, shrewd, more competent than kind, K. is on the fast track to success until he is arrested one morning for no reason. There begins his slide into desperation as he grapples with an all-powerful Court and an invisible Law.

Father Joseph

Homecoming
Cynthia Voigt

Eunice's priest. Father Joseph is a well-intentioned but ultimately unsympathetic man. Eunice relies on him for advice when the Tillerman children appear on his doorstep.

Josephine March

Little Women
Louisa May Alcott

The protagonist of the novel, and the second-oldest March sister. Although Jo works hard to control herself, she has a temper and a quick tongue. She is a tomboy and reacts with impatience to the many limitations placed on women and girls. She hates romance in her real life, and wants nothing more than to hold her family together. Generations of readers have been tormented by Jo's seemingly inexplicable refusal to love her affectionate, charming, and wealthy neighbor, **Laurie Laurence**. In New York, Jo befriends **Freder-**

ick Bhaer. Surprisingly, in Bhaer's presence, Jo becomes nearly conventional, conforming to a more accepted code of female behavior. Their marriage, which begins with equality and primacy of the heart rather than primacy of appearances, is promising. When old **Mr. Laurence** asks Jo to be his "girl" in place of her deceased sister, **Beth March**, Jo agrees, demonstrating that she has tempered some of her wildness with the gentle femininity she loved in Beth. Even Jo's writing style changes; she no longer writes tales of adventure and intrigue but instead writes in a simpler style. Jo's character is built upon Louisa May Alcott's own personality.

Aunt Josephine

Anne of Green Gables
L. M. Montgomery

Diana Barry's old aunt. Aunt Josephine is very rich and lives in a mansion in the town of Charlotteville. She has come to expect people to cater to her, although when they do, it bores her. **Anne Shirley**'s vivacity charms Aunt Josephine, and she often invites Anne to visit.

Joshua

The Old Testament
Unknown

Moses's successor as Israel's leader. Joshua directs the people in their sweeping military campaign to conquer and settle the Promised Land. His persistent exhortations to Israel to remain obedient to **God** imply that he doubts Israel will do so. His exhortations foreshadow Israel's future religious struggles.

Joshua

Cloud Nine
Caryl Churchill

A black character played by a white actor. Honest, reliable, and dutiful, Joshua appears to be the perfect servant. He betrays his people to be with his master **Clive**. Joshua's loyalty, however, masks a boiling anger. He is loyal only for personal gain, betraying **Harry** and **Betty**'s affair as well **Ellen**'s love for Betty. The British soldiers kill Joshua's parents and Clive remains apathetic about the tragedy; Joshua shoots Clive at the end of the first act.

Josiah

Ceremony
Leslie Marmon Silko

Tayo's uncle. Josiah is the person who teaches Tayo the Native American traditions and makes him feel most at home in the family. Although he adheres strongly to tradition, Josiah is not afraid of change, falling in love with the Mexican **Night Swan** and following her advice to undertake raising a herd of Mexican cattle crossbred with Herefords.

Margery Jourdain

Henry VI, Part II
William Shakespeare

A witch whom **Eleanor, Duchess of Gloucester** hires. The Duchess pays Margery Jourdain and **Bolingbroke** to communicate with spirits to find out the fate of **King Henry VI** and other nobles. Bolingbroke and Jourdain are arrested for dealing with the occult and sentenced to death: Bolingbroke by hanging, Jourdain by burning.

Serena Joy

The Handmaid's Tale
Margaret Atwood

One of the **Wives** of the **Republic of Gilead**. She is married to the **the Commander**. After her singing career, she became an anti-feminist activist, a spokesperson who encouraged women to stay at home instead of going off to work. Serena lives deprived of freedom and saddled with **Offred**, one of Gilead's **Handmaids**. Offred has sex with Serena's husband, the Commander. Powerless in the world of men, Serena can only take out her frustration on the women under her thumb by making their lives miserable.

Joyce

I Know Why the Caged Bird Sings
Maya Angelou

Bailey Johnson's first love, to whom he loses his virginity. Four years older than Bailey, Joyce turns his innocent displays of sexual curiosity into sexual intercourse. She eventually runs away with a railroad porter whom she meets at the **Momma**'s store, leaving Bailey heartbroken and morose.

Juan

The Power and the Glory
Graham Greene

A young man who appears in the novel only through the stories that are told about him. Juan lives his life with perfect piety and generosity, and faces death with bravery and perfect composure. **The woman** tells her son, **The boy**, about Juan in order to maintain his faith.

Juana

The Pearl
John Steinbeck

The young wife of **Kino**, the protagonist of the novella. After her prayers for good fortune in the form of a giant pearl are answered, Juana slowly becomes convinced that the pearl is in fact an agent of evil. Unfortunately for her and her infant son, **Coyotito**, she represses her desires in favor of her dominant husband's and allows Kino to hold on to the pearl. Ultimately, Juana is right, as the pearl brings the family disaster.

Judah

The Red Tent
Anita Diamant

Handsomest of **Jacob**'s sons by **Leah**. Judah marries **Shua**. He eventually becomes the head of the clan when **Reuben**, **Simon**, and **Levi** die.

Judge

Cry, the Beloved Country
Alan Paton

The Judge who presides over **Absalom Kumalo**'s murder trial seems to be a fair-minded man, but he is constrained by unjust laws that he must apply strictly.

Inherit the Wind
Jerome Lawrence & Robert E. Lee

Judge

The judge presiding over **Bertram Cates**'s trial. The judge conducts the trial impartially, although his personal views about the Bible's legitimacy are in line with those of the townspeople of Hillsboro. At **the mayor**'s prompting, the judge gives Cates a lenient sentence of a $100 fine after the jury's guilty verdict.

The Power of One
Bryce Courtenay

Judge

A huge Afrikaans boy who terrorizes five-year-old **Peekay** at his first boarding school. At the end of the novel the Judge happens to be Peekay's diamond driller in the mines.

Babbitt
Sinclair Lewis

Tanis Judique

An attractive, middle-aged widow who rents an apartment from **Babbitt**. Babbitt has an affair with Tanis and joins her circle of Bohemian friends. When he realizes that her rebellion against social convention is just as silly and desperate as his, he breaks off their relationship.

The Two Gentlemen of Verona
William Shakespeare

Julia

Proteus's beloved and **Lucetta**'s mistress. After Proteus leaves, Julia disguises herself as a page and follows him to Milan. As soon as she lands in the city, she is witness to Proteus's deceit: he is now wooing **Silvia**, **Valentine**'s love. She employs herself with **Launce**, adopting the name Sebastian, and masochistically carries out Proteus's enticements to Silvia. Though Julia does end up with Proteus after a well-timed swoon, the conclusion of the play is disorienting, to say the least. She has witnessed Proteus betray her and Valentine, and then attempt to rape Silvia—yet, still in the garb of a page boy, Julia happily joins hands with her former lover and forgives all.

1984
George Orwell

Julia

Winston Smith's lover. Julia is a beautiful dark-haired girl who works in the Fiction Department at the Ministry of Truth. She enjoys sex—a treasonous position in Oceania—and says she has had affairs with many Party members. When both are betrayed by **Mr. Charrington** and turned over to the Ministry of Truth, Julia betrays and is betrayed by Winston and is thrown out of the Party.

Ellen Foster
Kaye Gibbons

Julia

Ellen's grade-school art teacher, who temporarily cares for Ellen after another teacher learns that she is being abused at home. Julia is a hippie raised in the Northeast, who has migrated to the South after college with her husband, **Roy**. She is very liberal and encourages Ellen in her artistic endeavors.

Julia

The Hours
Michael Cunningham

Clarissa Vaughn's daughter, age nineteen. She is willfully boyish and independent. Although she is straight and not particularly close to her mother, Julia is good friends with lesbian activist **Mary Krull**, who advocates anti-materialism, so she shaves her head and wears combat boots. Julia is blessed with an ability to deal with difficult social situations easily.

Julian

The Hours
Michael Cunningham

Vanessa Bell's oldest child. Fifteen years old and very handsome, Julian is Vanessa's favorite.

Julie

Dangerous Liaisons
Pierre-Ambroise-François Choderlos de Laclos

The Présidente de Tourvel's maidservant. **Azolan** sleeps with her, and **the Vicomte de Valmont** puts her in a compromising position so he can gain access to Tourvel.

Julie

The Count of Monte Cristo
Alexandre Dumas

Monsieur Morrel's daughter. **Emmanuel Herbaut** is very much in love with Julie. **Edmond Dantès** speaks to Julie and is responsible for providing the dowry for the marriage between Emmanuel and Julie.

Miss Julie

Miss Julie
August Strindberg

The play's tragic heroine, doomed to a cruel demise. Fresh from a broken engagement—an engagement ruined because of her attempt to master her fiancé—Miss Julie has become wild, making shameless advances to her valet, **Jean**. Julie is simultaneously disgusted by and drawn to men. She wants to enslave men, but she also desires her own fall.

Juliek

Night
Elie Wiesel

A young violinist prisoner whom **Eliezer** meets in Auschwitz. Eliezer hears Juliek playing the violin after the death march to Gleiwitz.

Juliet of *Measure*

Measure for Measure
William Shakespeare

Claudio's lover. She is pregnant with his baby.

Juliet of *Romeo*

Romeo and Juliet
William Shakespeare

The daughter of **Capulet** and **Lady Capulet**. A beautiful thirteen-year-old girl, Juliet begins the play as a naïve child who has thought little about love and marriage, but she grows up quickly upon falling in love with **Romeo**, the son of her father's enemy **Montague**. Because she is a girl in an aristocratic family, she possesses none of Romeo's freedom to roam about the city getting into swordfights. Nevertheless, she shows amazing courage in trusting her entire life and future to Romeo, even refusing to believe the worst reports about him after he gets involved in a deadly fight with her cousin **Tybalt**. Juliet's closest friend and confidante is **the Nurse** who raised her, though Juliet's loyalty to Romeo supercedes all other relationships.

Julio

The Sound and the Fury
William Faulkner

The brother of an Italian girl who attaches herself to **Quentin** as he wanders Cambridge before his suicide.

Julius II

The Prince
Niccolò Machiavelli

A sixteenth-century pope (1503–1513) who strengthened the power of the Church through vigorous leadership and intelligent diplomacy. He defeated Roman barons and negotiated an alliance against France.

Colonel Julyan

Rebecca
Daphne du Maurier

The local magistrate in the region surrounding Manderley.

June

Herzog
Saul Bellow

Moses Herzog's daughter from his second marriage. June demonstrates a great capacity for love. She shows affection for her father, and Moses thinks of her with great joy.

Junebug

The Heart Is a Lonely Hunter
Carson McCullers

The young man whom **Willie** fights over **Love Jones**.

Junior

The Bluest Eye
Toni Morrison

Geraldine's son. He resents his mother's love of their cat, as he can sense it is the only thing in the world she has affection for. In the absence of genuine affection from his mother, he becomes cruel and sadistic. He tortures the cat and harasses children who come to the nearby playground.

Cold Mountain
Charles Frazier

Junior

A man who befriends **Inman** and **Veasey** before handing them over to the Home Guard. Inman's unsettling experiences at Junior's home suggest the character may be a murderer who feeds his family human flesh.

The Aeneid
Virgil

Juno

The Roman name for the Greek goddess Hera; the queen of the gods, the wife and sister of **Jupiter**, and the daughter of **Saturn**. In the *Aeneid*, Juno hates the Trojans because the Trojan man **Paris** decided that **Venus** was the most beautiful goddess. Juno, a patron of Carthage, knows that **Aeneas**'s Roman descendants are destined to destroy Carthage. Throughout the epic, she is Aeneas's primary divine antagonist.

Hard Times
Charles Dickens

Cecelia "Sissy" Jupe

The daughter of a clown in Sleary's circus. **Thomas Gradgrind** takes in Sissy when her father disappears. She is a foil for **Louisa Gradgrind**, imaginative and compassionate where Louisa is rational and unfeeling. Sissy embodies the Victorian ideal of femininity.

The Aeneid
Virgil

Jupiter

The Roman name for the Greek god Zeus; the king of the gods and the son of **Saturn**. The gods often struggle against one another in battles of will, but Jupiter's will reigns supreme. In the *Aeneid*, Jupiter directs the general progress of **Aeneas**'s destiny, ensuring that Aeneas is never permanently thrown off his course toward Italy. Jupiter is controlled and levelheaded compared to the volatility of **Juno** and **Venus**.

The Flies
Jean-Paul Sartre

Jupiter

The king of the gods. As **Orestes**'s most important antagonist, Jupiter represents the moral systems imposed on human beings. Wanting to maintain order, Jupiter has devoted his existence to ensuring that humanity fears him and will follow his laws. He supports **Aegistheus** and **Clytemnestra**, who maintain control of their city through fear. Intimidation is his only weapon, and as a result he cannot force Orestes to atone for the crime of murdering Aegistheus and Clytemnestra.

Song of Roland
Unknown

Jurfaleu

Marsilla's only son. He is beheaded by **Roland** at Roncesvals.

Ole Jurgensen

Snow Falling on Cedars
David Guterson

A farmer and landowner in San Piedro. After **Carl Heine, Sr.** died, **Etta Heine** sold his strawberry farm to Ole, including the seven acres that **Zenhichi Miyamoto** had contracted to buy from her husband. When Ole suffers a stroke in June 1954, he puts his farm up for sale, and **Carl Heine, Jr.** quickly snatches it up.

Just Black

I Know Why the Caged Bird Sings
Maya Angelou

One of **Daddy Clidell**'s con-men friends. These men teach **Maya Johnson** that it is possible to use white prejudice to gain advantage over whites. The other con-men friends are **Cool Clyde**, **Tight Coat**, **Red Leg Daddy**, **Stonewall Jimmy**, and **Spots**.

Justin

Madame Bovary
Gustave Flaubert

Monsieur Homais's assistant. He is young, impressionable, and simple. He falls terribly in love with **Emma Bovary** and unwittingly gives her access to the arsenic that she uses to commit suicide. He does not attend her funeral, but visits Emma's grave in the middle of the night to mourn privately.

Mother St. Justine

Wide Sargasso Sea
Jean Rhys

The head instructor at **Antoinette**'s convent school. Mother St. Justine tells the girls about the lives of female saints, instructs them on manners and cleanliness, and teaches them how to be proper Christian ladies.

Juturna

The Aeneid
Virgil

Turnus's sister. Provoked by **Juno**, Juturna instigates a battle between the Latins and the Trojans by disguising herself as an officer and goading the Latins.

20

PLUCKY HEROINES

DON'T MESS WITH THESE LADIES.

Alice	1	*Alice in Wonderland, Through the Looking Glass*
Athena	2	*The Odyssey*
Buttercup	3	*The Princess Bride*
Celie	4	*The Color Purple*
Anne Elliot	5	*Persuasion*
Jane Eyre	6	*Jane Eyre*
Anne Frank	7	*The Diary of Anne Frank*
Isabella	8	*Measure for Measure*
Jo March	9	*Little Women*
Anna Karenina	10	*Anna Karenina*
Lysistrata	11	*Lysistrata*
Meg Murray	12	*A Wrinkle in Time*
Nora	13	*A Doll's House*
Offred	14	*The Handmaid's Tale*
Scarlett O'Hara	15	*Gone With the Wind*
Miss Jane Pittman	16	*The Autobiography of Miss Jane Pittman*
Portia	17	*The Merchant of Venice*
Sister Helen Prejean	18	*Dead Man Walking*
Hester Prynne	19	*The Scarlet Letter*
Dicey Tillerman	20	*Homecoming, Dicey's Song*

Kabero

Out of Africa
Isak Dinesen

The Kikuyu boy who accidentally shoots the other boys. Kabero initially appears a tragic figure, as he is presumed dead by lions or suicide. Later, it is discovered that he is still alive and has been living with the Masai.

Jacob Kahn

My Name Is Asher Lev
Chaim Potok

An old and famous artist. When he was younger, he abandoned his childhood religion to pursue his artwork. Jacob is temperamental and feels no moral attachments to anything but art.

Hugo Kalmar

The Iceman Cometh
Eugene O'Neill

A former anarchist editor who served ten years in prison for his activities. When **Theodore Hickman** accuses him of wanting to be an aristocrat, Hugo reveals that his revolutionary fervor covers over a violent desire to tyrannize the masses. He drinks throughout the play, intermittently rousing from his stupor to denounce the crowd.

Mrs. Kamai

Hiroshima
John Hersey

Reverend Mr. Kiyoshi Tanimoto's next-door neighbor. After the explosion, she walks around for days, clutching her dead baby in her arms and desperately pleading with Mr. Tanimoto to find her husband.

Juta Kamainen

His Dark Materials
Robert Pullman

A young witch who was once in love with **John Parry**. Because he turned her down, Juta now hates him. She kills him just after he meets his son, **Will Parry**.

Kamala

Siddhartha
Hermann Hesse

Siddhartha's lover, and a beautiful courtesan. She teaches Siddhartha the arts of love after he leaves **Gotama** and **Govinda**, casting aside the realm of the mind. Because she does not accept penniless Samanas as visitors, she introduces Siddhartha to the businessman **Kamaswami**, so that he may earn the money to become a worthy visitor. When Siddhartha leaves the town suddenly, she lets a bird out of its golden cage, finds herself pregnant with Siddhartha's son, and closes her house to visitors. Years later, while traveling with her son in search of Gotama, she is bitten by a snake and taken to the ferryman's hut where Siddhartha lives. She dies in his presence.

Kamante

Out of Africa
Isak Dinesen

A servant on the farm who eventually becomes a cook. He is younger than **Farah**, and an eight-year-old child when the narrator first meets him. Perhaps because of his youthfulness, **the narrator** frequently explains ideas to Kamante.

Kamaswami

Siddhartha
Hermann Hesse

A well-to-do businessman who takes **Siddhartha** on as his apprentice, giving him food, clothing, lodging, and business duties until Siddhartha learns to earn them for himself. The two men constantly disagree about what is valuable. The day that Siddhartha turns into a double of Kamaswami, fat with wealth and rank with vices, is the day he leaves his life in Samsara.

Kantorek

All Quiet on the Western Front
Erich Maria Remarque

A pompous, ignorant, authoritarian schoolmaster in **Paul Bäumer**'s high school. Kantorek places intense pressure on Paul and his classmates to fulfill their "patriotic duty" by enlisting in the army.

Stanislas Kapp

The American
Henry James

A large, ruddy brewer's son from Strasbourg who insults **Valentin de Bellegarde**'s honor by stealing his place in **Noémie Nioche**'s opera box at a performance of *Don Giovanni*. The men trade insults and eventually agree to a duel. Though Kapp is not a good shot, he manages to mortally wound Valentin on the second firing.

Old Mrs. Karafilis

The Virgin Suicides
Jeffrey Eugenides

Demo Karafilis's Greek grandmother. She survived the Turkish massacre of her village as a young woman and hid in a cave for a month eating olive pits. She now spends her days in the semi-darkness of the Karafilis basement.

Julie Karagina

War and Peace
Leo Tolstoy

Marya Nikolayevna Bolkonskaya's friend and pen pal. Julie, an heiress, lives in Moscow and eventually marries **Boris Drubetskoy**.

Karakoee

Typee
Herman Melville

The native man who comes to rescue **Tommo**. Little is known about him except that he lives around the Nukuheva Bay and interacts frequently with the Europeans there.

Alexei Fyodorovich Karamazov

The Brothers Karamazov
Fyodor Dostoevsky

The protagonist, the third son of **Fyodor Pavlovich Karamazov**, and the younger brother of **Dmitri Fyodorovich Karamazov** and **Ivan Fyodorovich Karamazov**. Kind, gentle, loving, and wise, Alyosha is the opposite of his coarse and vulgar father. He possesses a natural, simple faith in God that translates into a genuine love for mankind. Around twenty years old at the start of the novel, Alyosha is affiliated with the monastery, where he is a student of the elder **Zosima**.

Dmitri Fyodorovich Karamazov

The Brothers Karamazov
Fyodor Dostoevsky

The oldest son of **Fyodor Pavlovich Karamazov**. Dmitri is passionate and intemperate, easily swept away by emotions and enthusiasm, as he demonstrates when he loses interest in his fiancée **Katerina Ivanovna Verkhovtseva** and falls madly in love with **Agrafena Alexandrovna Svetlova**. Cursed with a violent temper, Dmitri is plagued with the burden of sin and struggles throughout the novel to overcome his own flawed nature and to attain spiritual redemption.

Fyodor Pavlovich Karamazov

The Brothers Karamazov
Fyodor Dostoevsky

The wealthy patriarch of the Karamazov dynasty, the father of **Alexei Fyodorovich Karamazov**, **Dmitri Fyodorovich Karamazov**, and **Ivan Fyodorovich Karamazov**, and almost certainly the father of **Pavel Fyodorovich Smerdyakov**, whom he fathered with a mute retarded girl. Coarse, vulgar, greedy, and lustful, Fyodor Pavlovich lives a life devoted exclusively to the satisfaction of his senses, with no thought for those whom he betrays or hurts. Completely lacking in dignity despite his wealth, Fyodor Pavlovich is loathed by almost everyone who knows him. He has no affection for his children, and even forgets which of them belongs to which mother. His only goal in life is to have money and seduce young women such as **Agrafena Alexandrovna Svetlova**, whom he lusts after for much of the novel. Fyodor Pavlovich is eventually murdered by Smerdyakov.

Ivan Fyodorovich Karamazov

The Brothers Karamazov
Fyodor Dostoevsky

The second son of **Fyodor Pavlovich Karamazov**, and the middle brother between **Dmitri Fyodorovich Karamazov** and **Alexei Fyodorovich Karamazov**. A brilliant student, Ivan has an acutely logical mind and demands a rational explanation for everything that happens in the universe. As a result of his inability to reconcile the idea of unjust suffering with the idea of a loving God, Ivan is plagued by religious doubt. His forceful arguments about God's cruelty toward mankind are compelling, but after they inadvertently lead to his father's murder by **Pavel Fyodorovich Smerdyakov**, they drive him into madness.

Karana

Island of the Blue Dolphins
Scott O'Dell

The protagonist and narrator of the book, **Ramo**'s sister, daughter of the chief **Chowig** and **Tutok**'s friend. Karana spends eighteen years as the only living person on the island of the blue dolphins. When the book opens, she is twelve years old, the daughter of the chief of Ghalas-at. Resourceful and resilient, she survives on her own after her tribe deserts Ghalas-at.

Platon Karataev

War and Peace
Leo Tolstoy

A spiritual guide to **Pierre Bezukhov**. Platon represents the author's ideal of the simple, life-affirming philosophy of the Russian peasantry—he lives in the moment, forgetful of the past and oblivious of the future, to the extent that he cannot even remember what he said a few minutes earlier, living by instinct rather than by reason.

Kareen

Johnny Got His Gun
Dalton Trumbo

Joe Bonham's girlfriend when he left for the war. Kareen is beautiful and tiny, and Joe teases her about her Irish background. Kareen gave Joe her ring the night before he left.

Karellen

Childhood's End
Arthur C. Clarke

One of **the Overlords**, an alien race that dominates Earth in the late twentieth century. Karellen is known by most humans as "the Supervisor." Like all Overlords, he is much taller and more broadly built than a human, with large wings, horns on his head, and a barbed tail.

Alexei Alexandrovich Karenin

Anna Karenina
Leo Tolstoy

Anna Arkadyevna Karenina's husband, **Sergei Alexeich Karenin**'s father, a high-ranking government minister and one of the most important men in St. Petersburg. Karenin is formal and duty-bound. He is cowed by social convention and constantly presents a flawless façade of a cultivated and capable man. He fulfills his family roles as he does other duties on his list of social obligations. Karenin's primary motivation in both his career and his personal life is self-preservation. When he unexpectedly forgives Anna on what he believes may be her deathbed, we see a hint of a deeper Karenin ready to emerge. Ultimately, however, he remains a bland bureaucrat.

Sergei Alexeich Karenin

Anna Karenina
Leo Tolstoy

Alexei Alexandrovich Karenin and Anna's young son. Seryozha is a good-natured boy, but his father treats him coldly after learning of Anna's affair. Anna shows her devotion to Seryozha when she risks everything to sneak back into the Karenin household simply to bring birthday presents to her son.

Anna Arkadyevna Karenina

Anna Karenina
Leo Tolstoy

Sergei Alexeich Karenin's mother, **Alexei Alexandrovich Karenin**'s wife, and **Alexei Kirillovich Vronsky**'s lover. A beautiful, aristocratic married woman from St. Petersburg whose pursuit of love and emotional honesty makes her an outcast from society, Anna's adulterous affair catapults her into social exile, misery, and finally suicide. Anna is a beautiful person in every sense: intelligent and literate, she reads voraciously, writes children's books, and shows an innate ability to appreciate art. Physically ravishing yet tastefully reserved, she captures the attention of virtually everyone in high society. Anna believes in love—not only romantic love but family love and friendship as well, as we see from her devotion to her son, her fervent efforts to reconcile **Stepan Arkadyich Oblonsky** and **Darya Alexandrovna Oblonskaya** in their marital troubles, and her warm reception of Dolly at her country home. Anna abhors nothing more than fakery, and she comes to regard her husband, Karenin, as the very incarnation of it.

Kari

Giants in the Earth
O. E. Rölvaag

A Norwegian immigrant who arrives in the settlement one day with her husband. Her husband tells **Per Hansa** that she became insane when their youngest son died.

Karkaroff

Harry Potter and the Goblet of Fire
J. K. Rowling

The headmaster of Durmstrang School during **Harry Potter**'s fourth year at Hogwarts. Karkaroff is a shifty and suspicious man; he was once a Death Eater, a follower of **Voldemort**. Karkaroff flees at the end of *Harry Potter and the Goblet of Fire*.

Karkov

For Whom the Bell Tolls
Ernest Hemingway

A well-connected foreign correspondent for the Russian newspaper *Pravda* and **Robert Jordan**'s friend in Madrid. **Karkov**, teaches Robert Jordan about the harsh realities of wartime politics.

Karky

Typee
Herman Melville

The Typee tattoo artist.

Uncle Karl

The Trial
Franz Kafka

Joseph K.'s impetuous uncle from the country, formerly his guardian. Karl insists that K. hire **Huld**.

Karomenya

Out of Africa
Isak Dinesen

A young native boy who is deaf and dumb. Karomenya lives entirely in his own world because he lacks the ability to speak and hear.

Julius Karp

The Assistant
Bernard Malamud

The liquor-store owner down the street from the Bobers. The most prosperous merchant on the block, though still extremely stingy, Karp leases the tailor shop to **Schmitz**, even though he realizes that the competition might ruin **Morris Bober**'s business.

Louis Karp

The Assistant
Bernard Malamud

The lazy son of **Julius Karp**. Louis has no ambitions in life beyond working at his father's store, which he constantly steals from. When **Julius Karp** has a heart attack at the end of the novel, Louis closes the liquor store rather than manage it while his father recovers.

Kashkin

For Whom the Bell Tolls
Ernest Hemingway

A Russian guerrilla operative who once worked with **Pablo**'s band to blow up a train.

The Kataoka children

Hiroshima
John Hersey

A young brother and sister who believe they have lost their family. They are comforted by **Father Wilhelm Kleinsorge** and **Father Cieslik** for weeks until they are finally reunited with their mother.

Fyodor Vasilievich Katavasov

Anna Karenina
Leo Tolstoy

Konstantin Dmitrich Levin's intellectual friend from his university days.

Stanislaus Katczinsky

All Quiet on the Western Front
Erich Maria Remarque

A soldier in **Paul Bäumer**'s company and Paul's best friend in the army. Kat, as he is known, is a middle-aged man with a family at home. A resourceful, inventive man, he always manages to find food, clothing, and blankets when they're needed.

Kate

The Color Purple
Alice Walker

One of **Mr. ___**'s sisters. Kate urges **Celie** to stand up for herself.

Aunt Kate

The Light in the Forest
Conrad Richter

True Son's strong-willed and opinionated white aunt, who very much disapproves of his Indian behavior. She is very outspoken about her feelings of mistrust and anger for the boy, and she worries that his actions are causing the further deterioration of his mother, **Myra Butler**.

Aunt Kate

A Death in the Family
James Agee

Uncle Ted's wife. Aunt Kate is a distant relative and close friend of **Mary Follet** and **Jay Follet**.

The Jew of Malta
Christopher Marlowe

Katherine of *Jew of Malta*

Mathias's mother and a voice of prejudice. Even before she discovers his role in her son's death, Katherine states her dislike for **Barabas** on the basis of his race.

Love's Labour's Lost
William Shakespeare

Katherine of *Love's Labour's*

One of three ladies attending the **Princess of France**. Katherine, along with **Rosaline** and **Maria**, helps catch the fancy of the three lords attending the **King of Navarre**. Katherine is wooed by **Dumain**, who secretly sends her a sonnet and a glove.

The Taming of the Shrew
William Shakespeare

Katherine of *Shrew*

The "shrew" of the play's title, Katherine, or Kate, is the daughter of **Baptista** Minola, with whom she lives in Padua. She is sharp-tongued, quick-tempered, and prone to violence, particularly against anyone who tries to marry her. Her anger and rudeness disguise her deep-seated sense of insecurity and her jealousy toward her sister, **Bianca**. She does not resist her suitor **Petruccio** forever, though, and she eventually subjugates herself to him, despite her previous repudiation of marriage. Her marriage to Petruccio gives her both a place in society as well as an authoritative voice that she was previously denied.

Henry VIII
William Shakespeare

Katherine of Aragon

Daughter of the King of Spain, the ex-wife of **King Henry VIII**'s brother, and Henry's wife as the play opens. Katherine's first scene shows her to be thoughtful, wise, and exceedingly fair. When the matter of divorce arises, Katherine speaks eloquently in her own defense, declaring to Henry that she has been a loyal wife for twenty years. Despite **Cardinal Wolsey**'s pretended kindness, she charges him with being a traitor. She refuses to submit to the divorce. After hearing her attendants—notably, **Griffith**—speak well of Wolsey, Katherine forgives him and has a vision of her own imminent death.

Dubliners
James Joyce

Kathleen

Mrs. Kearney's daughter. Kathleen has been coaxed into Irish Revivalism by her mother.

This Boy's Life
Tobias Wolff

Kathy

A plain and shy secretary who tries to conceal her out-of-wedlock pregnancy. **Rosemary Wolff** first meets Kathy while they both reside in the boarding house in Seattle. Later, before Kathy gives birth to her son, **Willy**, she shares a ramshackle house with Rosemary and **Marian**.

Tetsuya Kato

Bel Canto
Ann Patchett

A good numbers man in **Hosokawa**'s electronics company. During the four months of captivity, Kato reveals himself to be an accomplished pianist and takes over for **Coss**'s accompanist. The tenderness Kato feels for his wife and daughters infuses his piano playing.

Kattrin

Mother Courage
Bertolt Brecht

Mother Courage's deaf and mute daughter. Kattrin undergoes trauma during the war and ends up disfigured. At the end of the play, she madly beats on a drum in an attempt to warn the town of Halle that there is an oncoming seige. When she refuses to stop the racket, the oncoming soldiers kill her.

Katy

Oranges Are Not the Only Fruit
Jeanette Winterson

Jeanette's second long-term lover. Katy's character is confident, open, and unashamed. Katy's obviously sexual invitation to Jeanette demonstrates to Jeanette a new confidence about same-sex relations.

Meir Katz

Night
Elie Wiesel

Clomo's friend from Buna, who saves **Eliezar** from an unidentified assailant on the train to Buchenwald.

Sir Kay

A Connecticut Yankee in King Arthur's Court
Mark Twain

A cowardly and ineffective knight, who happens to be **King Arthur**'s foster brother and seneschal, or steward. When **the Yankee** appears in the sixth century, **Clarence** tells the Yankee that the Yankee is the prisoner of Sir Kay. When Kay presents the Yankee to **Guenever**, he rises and gives an outlandish account of capturing the Yankee.

Sir Kay

The Once and Future King
T. H. White

King Arthur's foster brother and a knight of the Round Table. Spoiled as a child, and often jealous of Arthur's adventures with **Merlyn**, Sir Kay remains nasty and selfish, but is decent at heart. Arthur, before he knew he would be king, served as Kay's squire.

Susanna Kaysen

Girl, Interrupted
Susanna Kaysen

The author and narrator, who is diagnosed with borderline personality disorder in 1967. At seventeen, Susanna is a bright but troubled teenager with a surprising breadth of life experience. The previous year, Susanna attempted suicide by swallowing fifty aspirin. She voluntarily commits herself to McLean Hospital, a psychiatric facility in Belmont, Massachusetts. Over the course of the next two years, Susanna confronts her illness, profound unhappiness, the treachery and kindness of peers and authority figures, and the future that awaits her outside the confining but protective walls of the ward.

Kaz

Farewell to Manzanar
Jeanne Wakatsuki Houston

Jeanne's brother-in-law and **Martha**'s husband. Kaz is stopped by a detachment of frightened military police while monitoring the reservoir with his crew on the night of the December Riot.

Mrs. Kearney

Dubliners
James Joyce

Kathleen's waspish, sharp-tongued mother, the commanding protagonist of "A Mother." Mrs. Kearney orchestrates her daughter's upbringing as an exemplary proponent of Irish culture and poise, but she has trouble dealing with Dubliners of different backgrounds, particularly those who challenge her authority.

Mrs. Keating

The Fountainhead
Ayn Rand

Peter Keating's forceful and manipulative mother. Preoccupied with money and success, Mrs. Keating pushes her son to compromise between dignified peace of mind and hunger for power. This pressure causes Peter Keating's downfall.

Pa Keating

Angela's Ashes
Frank McCourt

Frank McCourt's warm and caring uncle. Pa Keating bolsters Frank's confidence and encourages him to follow his own instincts in adulthood.

Peter Keating

The Fountainhead
Ayn Rand

An architect who lives only for fame and approval. Good-looking, successful, and under extreme pressure from **Mrs. Keating**, he steals his ideas from **Howard Roark**. To rise to the top, Keating flatters, lies, steals, kills, and even trades his wife **Dominique Francon** for the opportunity to work on a promising project. After a rapid fall, he recognizes his mistakes and lives the rest of his life in frightened misery.

Thomas Keefer

The Caine Mutiny
Herman Wouk

A scholar in a band of idiots, and, despite his many admirable qualities, the antihero of *The Caine Mutiny*. When Keefer is trusted with the role of captain, he proves just as bad a leader as **Philip Francis Queeg**. The novel that Keefer cites as his true passion, though it will sell plenty of copies, has no real literary merit.

Edwin Keggs

The Caine Mutiny
Herman Wouk

An algebra teacher during peacetime and one of **Willie Keith**'s friends and roommates in midshipmen's school. Willie and Keggs are equally impressionable when they leave school, but when they meet later, Willie has been softened by the loose rules of the *Caine*, and Keggs has been made completely subordinate to the harsh dictatorship aboard the *Moulton*.

Kehaar

Watership Down
Richard Adams

The bird whom **Hazel** tells the rabbits to help. Kehaar becomes a good friend of **Bigwig**'s. He is strong and knowledgeable and helps the rabbits numerous times, explaining to them about things they had never seen before.

Samuel Keimer

The Autobiography of Benjamin Franklin
Benjamin Franklin

A Philadelphia printer and **Benjamin Franklin**'s sometime employer. Throughout their relationship, Franklin continues to believe that Keimer is a poor printer and a dismal businessman. Their relationship deteriorates, and the two have a falling-out. Eventually Franklin takes over Keimer's printing house; later he buys Keimer's newspaper.

Mr. Keith

The Caine Mutiny
Herman Wouk

Willie Keith's father. Mr. Keith's deathbed letters, coupled with Willie's memory of him, are a source of much of Willie's determination. In the letters, Mr. Keith explains to his son that he took the comfortable road through life and never really challenged himself.

Mrs. Keith

The Caine Mutiny
Herman Wouk

A controlling influence on her son, **Willie Keith**. She shelters and protects Willie with money and status, and does not want him to go away to war. When he must, she tries to arrange a safe stateside position for him.

Governor William Keith

The Autobiography of Benjamin Franklin
Benjamin Franklin

The royal governor of Pennsylvania when **Benjamin Franklin** arrives in Philadelphia. Keith is impressed by Franklin and promises to help him with letters of recommendation when Franklin moves to London, but in effect does very little.

Willie Keith

The Caine Mutiny
Herman Wouk

Son of aristocratic Long Island parents, Princeton graduate, and accomplished lounge pianist. Though he does not narrate the novel, Willie is its protagonist—we see events from his viewpoint, and the narration focuses almost entirely on his experience. Over the course of the novel, Willie sheds his selfish, childish ways and becomes a man.

Owen Kellogg

Atlas Shrugged
Ayn Rand

A talented employee of **Dagny Taggart**'s. Owen Kellogg is one of the first men in the novel to retire mysteriously.

Bill Kelly

The Heart Is a Lonely Hunter
Carson McCullers

Mick Kelly's older brother. He is in his late teens. At the beginning of the novel, Bill is the sibling Mick looks up to the most. Later, however, she realizes that she and Bill are drifting apart, so she becomes much closer to **Bubber Kelly**.

Bubber Kelly

The Heart Is a Lonely Hunter
Carson McCullers

Mick Kelly's younger brother and her favorite in the family. Bubber is an intelligent boy who is small for his age. He is a pleasant child until he accidentally shoots **Baby Wilson** with a BB gun, at which point he undergoes a drastic personality change and becomes much more of a loner.

Etta Kelly

The Heart Is a Lonely Hunter
Carson McCullers

Mick Kelly's older sister. Etta, who is obsessed with becoming a movie actress, spends lots of time fussing over her hair, nails, clothing, and accessories.

Hazel Kelly

The Heart Is a Lonely Hunter
Carson McCullers

The eldest child in **Mick Kelly**'s family. Hazel is a plump but attractive young woman who is somewhat lazy. She tells Mick about a job opening at the local Woolworth's store.

Mick Kelly

The Heart Is a Lonely Hunter
Carson McCullers

The fourth child in a family of six. Fourteen years old, Mick is tall for her age and very thin, with short blond hair and blue eyes. She is often absorbed in private thoughts and dreams, such as learning to play the piano and traveling in foreign countries. Mick's family is poor and takes on boarders as a way to make money.

Mr. Kelly

The Heart Is a Lonely Hunter
Carson McCullers

Mick Kelly's father. Mr. Kelly is a kind man who feels largely useless to his family because an injury prevents him from working as a carpenter any longer. He now runs a small watch-repair business out of the house, but he hardly has any customers. Mr. Kelly, who often feels the family ignores him, frequently calls Mick over for trivial reasons just to talk to her.

Mrs. Kelly

The Heart Is a Lonely Hunter
Carson McCullers

Mick Kelly's mother.

Ralph Kelly

The Heart Is a Lonely Hunter
Carson McCullers

The youngest child in **Mick Kelly**'s family. Ralph is a baby.

Franz Kemmerich

All Quiet on the Western Front
Erich Maria Remarque

One of **Paul Bäumer**'s classmates and comrades in the war. After suffering a light wound, Kemmerich contracts gangrene, and his leg has to be amputated.

Kemuel

The Red Tent
Anita Diamant

Ruti and **Laban**'s son; **Beor**'s brother. When leaving Haran, and trying to steal some of Laban's special magic figurines, **Rachel** gives Kemuel a strong drink and he sleeps through two days.

Louise Kendricks

I Know Why the Caged Bird Sings
Maya Angelou

Maya Johnson's first friend outside her family. When she is with Louise, Maya is able to escape her troubles and play like a child should.

Dr. Kenn

The Mill on the Floss
George Eliot

The stern but charitable minister of St. Ogg's.

Ella Lorena Kennedy

Gone with the Wind
Margaret Mitchell

Scarlett O'Hara's second child. Ella Lorena is the ugly, silly daughter of **Frank Kennedy**.

Frank Kennedy

Gone with the Wind
Margaret Mitchell

Scarlett O'Hara's weak-willed but kind second husband. Scarlett steals him away from her sister **Suellen O'Hara** so that he will pay the taxes necessary to save Tara.

Mina Kennedy

Ulysses
James Joyce

One of the barmaids at the Ormond hotel. She is more reserved than her colleague **Lydia Douce**.

Kenneth

This Boy's Life
Tobias Wolff

The detestable, argumentative man **Norma** suddenly chooses to marry instead of **Bobby Crow**. Kenneth is a strict Christian who attempts to impose his values upon everyone else. **Rosemary Wolff** later reveals to **Jack Wolff** that Kenneth tried to make a pass at her. Kenneth and Norma have a child, and Jack notices how tired and old Norma looks when he goes to visit them with their child later on.

Carol Kennicott

Main Street
Sinclair Lewis

The protagonist of the novel from whose point of view nearly the entire story is told. Intelligent and vivacious, Carol Milford attends college in Minneapolis and then works as a librarian in St. Paul for three years before marrying the doctor **Will Kennicott** and moving to Gopher Prairie. An incurable romantic, Carol yearns to bring beauty and culture to the ugly towns of the Midwest. Her failed attempts to reform Gopher Prairie constitute the novel's main conflict. Unhappy with her life in Gopher Prairie, Carol seeks escape through books and a romantic friendship with a young man named **Erik Valborg**. In the end, however, the town defeats her. She leaves Gopher Prairie to move to Washington, D.C., but returns and accepts the town as it is.

Dr. Will Kennicott

Main Street
Sinclair Lewis

Carol's husband and a foil to his wife. Kennicott feels satisfied with his life and prefers to maintain the status quo. He is realistic and materialistic, interested only in making money and taking care of his family and patients. Will sets Carol on a pedestal and admires her, regardless of her whims. As they drift apart, however, he begins a short-lived secretive affair with **Maud Dyer**. When Carol moves to Washington, Kennicott visits her and courts her a second time in order to persuade her to return to Gopher Prairie.

Hugh Kennicott

Main Street
Sinclair Lewis

Carol and **Will Kennicott**'s infant son. Hugh, who is named after Carol's deceased father, is very much like his own unimaginative father, Will.

Kenny

Fallen Angels
Walter Dean Myers

Richie Perry's younger brother. Kenny depends on his older brother, who acts as a father figure to him and enlists in Vietnam in part to help support him. Kenny's dependence on Richie and his admiration and love for him serve as Richie's only solid link to the civilian world during the war.

Kent

King Lear
William Shakespeare

A nobleman of the same rank as **Gloucester** who is loyal to **King Lear**. Kent spends most of the play disguised as a peasant, calling himself "Caius," so that he can continue to serve Lear even after Lear unjustly banishes him. He is extremely loyal, but he gets himself into trouble throughout the play by being blunt and outspoken.

Miss Kenton

The Remains of the Day
Kazuo Ishiguro

The head housekeeper of Darlington Hall until just before World War II. Miss Kenton, like **Stevens**, excels at her job, but she is less formal and more personable than Stevens. She and Stevens often bicker about household affairs.

Kerkyon

The King Must Die
Mary Renault

The hereditary name given to the King of Eleusis. **Theseus** wrestles and kills Kerkyon to assume the title himself.

Tom Kernan

Dubliners
James Joyce

A once-successful businessman on the brink of alcoholism in "Grace." Mr. Kernan is manipulated into attending a religious revival by his wife, **Martin Cunningham**, and a group of well-meaning friends.

Kezia

The Mill on the Floss
George Eliot

The Tullivers' housemaid.

Nadir Khan

Midnight's Children
Salman Rushdie

Mumtaz's first husband, Nadir Khan is the Hummingbird's personal secretary. After the Hummingbird's assassination, Nadir hides in the Aziz household for a few years, where he has a relationship with Mumtaz.

Katerina Ospovna Khokhlakova

The Brothers Karamazov
Fyodor Dostoevsky

A wealthy gentlewoman in the town, an acquaintance of **Dmitri Fyodorovich Karamazov** and his family, and a friend of **Katerina Ivanovna Verkhovtseva**. A relatively harmless presence, she is somewhat shallow and self-centered, and tends to obsess over the misbehaviors of her daughter **Liza Khokhlakova**.

Liza Khokhlakova

The Brothers Karamazov
Fyodor Dostoevsky

Katerina Ospovna Khokhlakova's daughter, a mischievous and capricious young girl who is briefly engaged to **Alexei Fyodorovich Karamazov**. At least as shallow and self-centered as her mother, Lise has a hard time taking things seriously and finally lapses into self-destructive despair, in which she pathetically crushes her fingernail in a door in an attempt to punish herself for wickedness.

Mr. Kiaga

Things Fall Apart
Chinua Achebe

The native-turned-Christian missionary who arrives in Mbanta and converts **Nwoye** and many others.

Kiche

White Fang
Jack London

White Fang's mother. Kiche is also known as the "she-wolf." She is half wolf, half dog, and escaped from a Native American camp during a famine.

Susan Kidwell

In Cold Blood
Truman Capote

Nancy Clutter's best friend. Susan lives in Holcomb.

Morten Kiil

An Enemy of the People
Henrik Ibsen

A rich old man. Kiil owns several of the tanneries that **Dr. Thomas Stockmann** implicates in his water-pollution report. He is the adoptive father of **Mrs. Katherine Stockmann**, Thomas's wife. Kiil's will assigns a good deal of wealth to Katherine and her children.

Kiki

The House on Mango Street
Sandra Cisneros

One of **Esperanza**'s younger brothers.

Kildigs

One Day in the Life of Ivan Denisovich
Aleksandr Solzhenitsyn

A foreigner among **Ivan Denisovich Shukhov**'s Russian camp inmates. Kildigs is a Latvian bricklayer and Shukhov's colleague at the Power Station and is famed for his sense of humor.

Bob Kiley

The Things They Carried
Tim O'Brien

The platoon's medic. **Tim O'Brien** has great respect for Kiley's medical prowess, especially when he is shot for a second time and is subjected to the mistreatment of another medic, **Bobby Jorgenson**. Though levelheaded and kind, Kiley eventually succumbs to the stresses of the war and his role in it—he purposely blows off his toe so that he is forced to leave his post.

Kili

The Hobbit
J. R. R. Tolkien

One of the dwarf companions on the novel's quest.

Logan Killicks

Their Eyes Were Watching God
Zora Neale Hurston

Janie Mae Crawford's first husband. **Nanny Crawford** arranges Janie's marriage to Logan Killicks after she catches Janie kissing **Johnny Taylor** under a pear tree. Logan pampers Janie for a year before he tries to make her help him with the farming work. Feeling used, unloved, and treated like livestock, Janie leaves Logan for **Jody Starks**.

Doris Kilman

Mrs. Dalloway
Virginia Woolf

Elizabeth Dalloway's unattractive middle-aged history teacher, of German extraction. Miss Kilman was fired from a teaching job during the war owing to society's anti-German prejudice. She is a born-again Christian devoted to socialism who resents wealthy, privileged women like **Clarissa Dalloway**. She has strong romantic feelings for Elizabeth and tries to influence her protégé in religious as well as social issues.

Private Buster Kilrain

The Killer Angels
Michael Shaara

A former sergeant who was demoted to private for drunkenly assaulting a fellow officer. A big, stocky Irishman, Kilrain is getting old and knows he does not have many fights left in him. He becomes a friend and mentor to **Colonel Joshua Lawrence Chamberlain**.

Miss Kilsen

The Virgin Suicides
Jeffrey Eugenides

A social worker. Miss Kilsen was hired by the high school after **Cecilia Lisbon**'s death and she is thought to be the only person in whom the Lisbon girls confided. Miss Kilsen disappeared after her credentials were discovered to be false, and her patient records were later destroyed in a freak fire.

Mr. Kimble

Silas Marner
George Eliot

Godfrey Cass's uncle and Raveloe's doctor. Mr. Kimble is an animated conversationalist and joker who gets irritable when he plays cards. He has no medical degree and inherited the position of village physician from his father.

Kimki

Island of the Blue Dolphins
Scott O'Dell

Chosen as chief after **Chowig** is killed by the Aleuts, Kimki is an old and venerated member of the tribe. It is he that goes out alone to prepare a new home for the people of Ghalas-at after their battle with the Aleuts.

Saul Kimmer

True West
Sam Shepard

A slick Hollywood producer. Though he first offers to produce **Austin**'s screenplay, a bet on the golf course leads him to switch loyalty to **Lee**'s movie.

Kinanjui

Out of Africa
Isak Dinesen

The Chief of the Kikuyus. Kinanjui is one of the most noble of the local natives. **The narrator** likes Kinanjui and often uses him to arbitrate disputes on her farm. He dies from a wound to his knee that turns gangrenous. With his death, the future leadership of the Kikuyu people is uncertain.

Kinanu

Out of Africa
Isak Dinesen

The father of **Kabero**. Kinanu is the boy who shot the weapon during the shooting accident. He is one of the richest squatters on the farms. During the legal arbitration, Kinanu complies with the rulings against him, but may do so in questionable ways. He frequently is accused of trying to give cattle or sheep that are not as healthy or young as others.

Charles Kinbote

Pale Fire
Vladimir Nabokov

The author of the long series of notes that accompany **John Shade**'s poem "Pale Fire." He is thrilled to live near Shade, for he hopes that the poet will become enraptured by his stories about Charles the Beloved and write poems about them.

Kindervater

All Quiet on the Western Front
Erich Maria Remarque

A soldier in a neighboring unit. Kindervater, like **Tjaden**, is a bed wetter.

Kinesias

Lysistrata
Aristophanes

The needy, desperate clown that **Myrrhine** calls her husband. Kinesias is the first man targeted by the sex strike.

The king

The Spanish Tragedy
Thomas Kyd

The king of Spain is an ambivalent character. At times he appears noble and is definitely a friend to **Hieronimo**, resisiting **Lorenzo**'s attempts to have the Knight-Marshal dismissed. But he is also complacent, as demonstrated by his callous conversation after the Spanish victory in Act I, his subsequent dialogue with the ambassador, and his failure to know that **Horatio** has been murdered on his estate.

The king

The Little Prince
Antoine de Saint-Exupéry

A man on the first planet **the Little Prince** visits who claims to rule the entire universe. While not unkind, the king has no real power. When the prince declares that he will leave, the king declares the Little Prince his ambassador.

King of Hearts

Alice in Wonderland
Lewis Carroll

The nervous husband of the **Queen of Hearts**. The king makes an incompetent judge at the trial of the Knave. He is self-centered, stubborn, and generally unlikable.

Ferdinand, King of Navarre

Love's Labour's Lost
William Shakespeare

The ruler of Navarre. To make his kingdom the "wonder of the world," the king has drawn up an oath, to which he holds his closest friends, **Berowne**, **Dumain**, and **Longaville**, along with his court, accountable. The demands of the oath are: to study for three years, and in that period eat just one meal a day, fast once a week, sleep just three hours a night, and not to see a single woman. The king's plan quickly becomes unraveled when Navarre must open its gates to the **Princess of France** and her three ladies-in-waiting. Only when the princess learns of her father's death at the end of the play does an oath and the gravity of signing onto one become real in the minds of the king and his lords.

Chad King

On the Road
Jack Kerouac

Sal Paradise's friend from Denver. Young, slim, blond, and soft-spoken, Chad is interested in philosophy, anthropology, and prehistoric Indians.

Mrs. King

I Never Promised You a Rose Garden
Joanne Greenberg

A local woman who rents a room in her house to **Deborah**. Mrs. King is a good landlady because she has not lived in the town long enough to acquire the fear and contempt that other residents feel toward the hospital's outpatients.

Maxine Hong Kingston

The Woman Warrior
Maxine Hong Kingston

The author and narrator. Kingston's memories of her own life do not figure prominently until the final chapter, "A Song for a Barbarian Reed Pipe," in which she shakes off the frustrations of her childhood and finds her own voice.

Alice Kinnian

Flowers for Algernon
Daniel Keyes

Charlie Gordon's teacher at the Beekman College Center for Retarded Adults. Alice originally recommends Charlie for the experimental operation because she is impressed by his motivation. Although she is not one of the scientists who perform the experiment on Charlie, she acts as an unofficial member of the team because of her concern for him.

Kino

The Pearl
John Steinbeck

The protagonist of the novella, a dignified, hardworking, impoverished native who works as a pearl diver. Kino is simple man who lives in a brush house with his wife, **Juana**, and their infant son, **Coyotito**, both of whom he loves deeply. After Kino finds a great pearl, he becomes increasingly ambitious and desperate in his mission to break free of the oppression of his colonial society. Ultimately, Kino's material ambition drives him to a state of animalistic violence, and his life is reduced to a basic fight for survival.

Kiowa

The Things They Carried
Tim O'Brien

Tim O'Brien's closest friend and a model of quiet, rational morality amid the atrocities of war. Kiowa's death, when the company mistakenly camps in a sewage field, is the focal point of three stories.

Kip

The English Patient
Michael Ondaatje

A Sikh man from India who works as a "sapper," defusing bombs for the British forces in World War II. First introduced only as "the sikh," Kip is polite and well-mannered, and has both the skill and character to be an excellent sapper. His emotional detachment stands in the way of his relationships, most significantly his relationship with **Hana**.

Mrs. Kirke

Little Women
Louisa May Alcott

The woman who runs the New York boarding house where **Josephine March** lives.

Professor Kirke

The Lion, the Witch, and the Wardrobe
C. S. Lewis

A slightly eccentric, elderly professor. He takes care of **Edmund Pevensie**, **Lucy Pevensie**, **Susan Pevensie**, and **Peter Pevensie** so they can escape the air raids in London during World War II. Wise and open-minded, he helps Peter and Susan understand that Narnia may indeed exist, and tells them that they may not be able to reach it through the wardrobe again, but they might be able to reach it in their hearts and minds.

Miss Kirwin

I Know Why the Caged Bird Sings
Maya Angelou

Maya Johnson's teacher in San Francisco. Miss Kirwin treats Maya like an equal human being, regardless of her color.

Mr. Kirwin

Frankenstein
Mary Shelley

The Scottish magistrate who accuses **Victor Frankenstein** of murdering **Henry Clerval**.

Kitty

The Three Musketeers
Alexandre Dumas

The maid of the **Lady de Winter**. She falls in love with **d'Artagnan**, who has sex with her only to gain information about **Madame Bonacieux**'s whereabouts. D'Artagnan causes Kitty to completely turn against the Lady, and even after he starts sexually manipulating the Lady, the sad Kitty still helps d'Artagnan.

Kitty

The Hours
Michael Cunningham

Laura Brown's next-door neighbor. Kitty is very self-assured and has a confident magnetism, which is why Laura enjoys being around her.

Kiya

The Red Tent
Anita Diamant

One of **Meryt**'s granddaughters. **Dinah** becomes close to Kiya when she moves to the Valley of the Kings and marries **Benia**. Kiya eventually learns the skill of midwifery from Dinah and remains close to her for the rest of her life.

Meyer Klaus

Flowers for Algernon
Daniel Keyes

A brutish new employee at Donner's Bakery who is working there when **Charlie Gordon** briefly reassumes his job after losing his temporary intelligence.

Johannes Kleiman

Anne Frank: Diary of a Young Girl
Anne Frank

A man who helps **Anne Frank**, **Edith Frank**, **Otto Frank**, **Petronella van Daan**, **Mr. van Daan**, **Peter van Daan**, and **Albert Dussel** hide. He also brings news of other Jews in hiding to the families in the annex. Johannes Kleiman is arrested in 1944 but released because of poor health. Mr. Kleiman remained in Amsterdam until his death in 1959. In the Diary, he is referred to as Mr. Koophuis.

Father Wilhelm Kleinsorge

Hiroshima
John Hersey

A German Jesuit priest living in Hiroshima. He helps **Toshiko Sasaki** recover her will to live and eventually become a nun. In the years after the war, he becomes a Japanese citizen and takes the name Father Makoto Takakura.

Kleonike

Lysistrata
Aristophanes

Lysistrata's next-door neighbor and the first to arrive at the meeting of women. Unabashedly feminine, Kleonike is delighted that Lysistrata's scheme for peace involves negligees.

Klipspringer

The Great Gatsby
F. Scott Fitzgerald

A shallow freeloader who essentially lives in **Jay Gatsby**'s mansion. After Gatsby's death, Klipspringer disappears without attending the funeral, but later calls **Nick** about a pair of tennis shoes he left behind at Gatsby's house.

Albert Knag

Sophie's World
Jostein Gaarder

Father of **Hilde Møller Knag**. Albert Knag is the brains behind **Sophie Amundsen**'s and **Alberto Knox**'s existence. He creates them as a birthday gift for his daughter. He has the creative genius to write *Sophie's World*, a book in which his characters become aware of their role as characters in the book.

Hilde Møller Knag

Sophie's World
Jostein Gaarder

Albert Knag's daughter. **Sophie Amundsen** and **Alberto Knox** are created for Hilde Møller Knag's amusement by her father. Hilde is extremely compassionate, and she feels for Sophie and Alberto while her father plays with their lives. She is independent, and proves it by leaving manipulative and paranoia-inducing notes for Albert. When Sophie and Alberto become beings of spirit, Sophie makes contact with Hilde by hitting her hard in the face with a wrench. Hilde feels the force as a gadfly bite, but the result is inspirational to Sophie. Hilde believes that Sophie exists somewhere, although she cannot explain how.

Mrs. Knag

Sophie's World
Jostein Gaarder

Hilde Møller Knag's mother.

Knauer

Demian
Hermann Hesse

A student who seeks out **Emil Sinclair** for intellectual guidance toward the end of Sinclair's time at preparatory school.

The Knight

The Canterbury Tales
Geoffrey Chaucer

The first pilgrim Chaucer describes in the General Prologue and the teller of the first tale. The Knight represents the ideal of a medieval Christian man-at-arms. He has participated in no fewer than fifteen of the great crusades of his era. **The narrator** greatly admires him for his bravery, experience, and prudence.

Green Knight

Sir Gawain and the Green Knight
Unknown

A mysterious visitor to Camelot. The Green Knight's huge stature, wild appearance, and green complexion set him apart from the beardless knights and beautiful ladies of **King Arthur**'s Camelot. He is an ambiguous figure: he says that he comes in friendship, not wanting to fight, but the friendly game he proposes is quite deadly. He attaches great importance to verbal contracts, expecting **Sir Gawain** to go to great lengths to hold up his end of their bargain. The Green Knight shows himself to be a supernatural being when he picks up his own severed head and rides out of Arthur's court, still speaking. At the poem's end, we discover that the Green Knight is also **Bertilak**, Gawain's host, and one of **Morgan le Fay**'s minions.

George Knightley

Emma
Jane Austen

Mr. **John Knightley**'s brother and the Woodhouses' trusted friend and advisor. Knightley is a respected landowner in his late thirties. He is the only character who dares criticize **Emma Woodhouse** openly.

Isabella Knightley

Emma
Jane Austen

Emma Woodhouse's older sister. Isabella lives in London with her husband, Mr. **John Knightley**, and their five children. Isabella is pretty, amiable, and devoted to her family, but slow and diffident compared to Emma.

John Knightley

Emma
Jane Austen

Mr. **George Knightley**'s brother and **Isabella Knightley**'s husband. John Knightley, a lawyer, is clear-minded but somewhat sharp-tempered. His severity often displeases **Emma Woodhouse** and her father.

Floyd Knowles

The Grapes of Wrath
John Steinbeck

A migrant worker who inspires **Tom Joad** and **Jim Casy** to attempt to organize the California laborers into unions. Floyd's outspokenness sparks a scuffle with the police that results in Casy's arrest.

Alberto Knox

Sophie's World
Jostein Gaarder

Sophie Amundsen's teacher. Alberto believes passionately in philosophy, since it helps him understand that his existence is due to the mind of **Albert Knag**. He realizes that if he and Sophie are simply thoughts in Albert Knag's brain, then perhaps they can utilize Albert's unconscious to help bring about their escape from *Sophie's World*, the book and world that Albert Knag has placed them in. Even in the face of unbelievable circumstances Alberto holds on to the one thing that makes him human: his ability to think, which enables a successful escape. He and Sophie become beings of spirit, escaping from Sophie's world in the end, and migrating to **Hilde Møller Knag**'s world.

Old Knudsen

Out of Africa
Isak Dinesen

An Old Danish man who arrives on the farm sick and nearly blind. Knudsen asks for a place to stay and **the narrator** gives him one. He only remains for six months before he dies of a heart attack one afternoon as he is walking down a path.

Nadya Kologrigova

Dr. Zhivago
Boris Pasternak

A wife and mother who employs **Larissa Fyodorovna Guishar** to be her daughter **Lipa**'s governess until Lipa graduates from school.

Kolory

Typee
Herman Melville

The chief priest of the Typees. He presides over the Feast of the Calabashes and frequently conducts rituals with Mon Artu, the chief Typeean God.

Kolya

One Day in the Life of Ivan Denisovich
Aleksandr Solzhenitsyn

A medical orderly and novice poet who tends to **Ivan Denisovich Shukhov**.

Victor Ippolitovich Komarovsky

Dr. Zhivago
Boris Pasternak

A lawyer who drove the elder Zhivago to suicide. He assisted the Guishars out of loyalty to **Amalia Karlovna Guishar**'s deceased husband. He preys on the young **Larissa Fyodorovna Guishar** (later Antipova), taking advantage of her family's economic woes to seduce her while she is only a teenager. Lara is so affected by his actions that she attempts to shoot him at a Christmas party. He refuses to press charges against Lara and continues to help her family through the Revolution.

Ted Koppel

Tuesdays with Morrie
Mitch Albom

One of the most famous living television interviewers. Koppel conducts three interviews with **Morrie Schwartz** for the news show *Nightline*.

Lieutenant Colonel Korn

Catch-22
Joseph Heller

Colonel Cathcart's wily, cynical sidekick.

Kory-Kory

Typee
Herman Melville

The man appointed to be **Tommo**'s servant. Kory-Kory is a kind, industrious fellow who constantly attends to Tommo.

Stanley Koteks

The Crying of Lot 49
Thomas Pynchon

An employee of Yoyodyne. **Oedipa Maas** meets Stanley when she wanders into his office while touring the plant. He refuses to reveal what he knows about the Tristero.

Stanley Kowalski

A Streetcar Named Desire
Tennessee Williams

Stella Kowalski's husband. Around thirty years of age, Stanley, who fought in World War II, now works as an auto-parts salesman. Stanley is the epitome of vital force. He is loyal to his friends, passionate to his wife, and heartlessly cruel to **Blanche DuBois**. He sees himself as a social leveler and wishes to destroy Blanche's social pretensions. Stanley's early interactions with Blanche show him to be insensitive. By the play's end, he is a disturbing degenerate: he beats his wife and rapes his sister-in-law. Horrifyingly, he shows no remorse.

Stella Kowalski, née DuBois

A Streetcar Named Desire
Tennessee Williams

Blanche DuBois's younger sister; **Stanley Kowalski**'s pregnant wife. Stella's union with Stanley is robustly sexual and sometimes violent. Throughout the play, Stella is torn between her husband and her sister; her husband ultimately wins.

Anna Karenina
Leo Tolstoy

Sergei Ivanovich Koznyshev

Konstantin Dmitrich Levin's half-brother, a famed intellectual and writer whose thinking Levin has difficulty following. Koznyshev embodies cold intellectualism and is unable to embrace the fullness of life, as we see when he cannot bring himself to propose to **Varvara Andreevna**.

My Ántonia
Willa Cather

Peter Krajiek

A Bohemian immigrant and neighbor to the Burdens. Krajiek sells the Shimerdas their first farm in America and cheats them out of several comforts.

Into Thin Air
Jon Krakauer

Jon Krakauer

The narrator and the author. Krakauer is hired to write an article about Mount Everest for an adventure magazine and ends up going on the most disastrous expedition in Everest history. He survives and writes a memoir intended to provide a thorough and accurate account of the disaster.

The Brothers Karamazov
Fyodor Dostoevsky

Nikolai Ivanovich Krasotkin

A bold, intelligent young boy who befriends **Alexei Fyodorovich Karamazov** after **Ilyusha Snegiryov** becomes ill.

Prometheus Bound
Aeschylus

Kratus

An unquestioning servant of **Zeus**, whose name means "force." Kratus identifies completely with his master, identifying Zeus's thoughts as his own. Unlike **Hephaestus** and **Oceanus**, Kratus has no value system outside the one Zeus imposed on him.

Cat's Cradle
Kurt Vonnegut

Sherman Krebbs

A destitute poet who lives in **John**'s apartment while John travels to Ilium to research **Felix Hoenikker**. Upon his return, John discovered that Krebbs had incurred hundreds of dollars in long-distance phone calls, wrecked his apartment, and killed his cat. John credited Krebbs for turning him away from a philosophy of nihilism.

In Our Time
Ernest Hemingway

Krebs

The protagonist of "Soldier's Home." Krebs returns home to Kansas after being in the war, feeling disoriented and empty inside.

Helen Krebs

In Our Time
Ernest Hemingway

Krebs's younger sister. Helen plays indoor baseball and idolizes her brother.

Mrs. Krebs

Inherit the Wind
Jerome Lawrence & Robert E. Lee

An outspoken Hillsboro woman. On behalf of the Hillsboro Ladies' Aid, Mrs. Krebs serves lunch to **Matthew Harrison Brady** and **Mrs. Brady** upon their arrival into the town.

M. Krempe

Frankenstein
Mary Shelley

A professor of natural philosophy at Ingolstadt. Krempe dismisses **Victor Frankenstein**'s study of the alchemists as a waste of time and encourages him to begin his studies anew.

Yudel Krinsky

My Name Is Asher Lev
Chaim Potok

A Ladover man, whom **Aryeh Lev** helped bring to America from Russia. Yudel Krinsky seems somewhat withdrawn, affected by years of internment in Siberia. He is patient with **Asher Lev**, encouraging his talent and tolerating him more than most in the community.

Nils Krogstad

A Doll's House
Henrik Ibsen

Torvald's coworker and former classmate and **Mrs. Linde**'s former beau. Krogstad is a widower with many children, largely ostracized from polite society because he once committed a forgery. He has loaned Nora money and resorts to blackmail to protect his job and his family.

Franz Kromer

Demian
Hermann Hesse

A local bully who blackmails the ten-year-old **Emil Sinclair**. He is a manipulative figure who shatters Sinclair's innocence. Sinclair is deathly afraid of him until **Max Demian** saves Sinclair from Kromer.

Albert Kropp

All Quiet on the Western Front
Erich Maria Remarque

A former classmate of **Paul Bäumer**'s who also serves in the Second Company. An intelligent, speculative young man, Kropp is one of Paul's closest friends during the war. His interest in analyzing the causes of the war leads to the most articulate antiwar sentiments in the novel.

Mary Krull

The Hours
Michael Cunningham

Lesbian activist and radical feminist. She is humorless and judgmental and thinks that **Clarissa Vaughn**'s domestic lesbianism is a futile attempt to seem normal in a homophobic world. She is desperately in love with **Julia Vaughn**.

Viktor Krum

Harry Potter and the Goblet of Fire
J. K. Rowling

The Bulgarian Quidditch Seeker. He is quiet and sullen, but he develops quite a crush on **Hermione Granger**. He is quiet and not particularly attractive, but boys congregate around him seeking his friendship, while girls seek his autograph. This appearance poses an interesting dilemma for **Harry Potter**, who for the first time in his life is part of an audience that is reacting to someone else's fame.

Old Ku'oosh

Ceremony
Leslie Marmon Silko

The Laguna medicine man who helps **Tayo**. A very traditional medicine man, Ku'oosh does not have the wherewithal to invent the new ceremonies needed to treat the new diseases.

Victor Kugler

Anne Frank: Diary of a Young Girl
Anne Frank

A man who helps **Otto Frank**, **Edith Frank**, **Anne Frank**, and **Margot Frank** hide in the annex. Mr. Kugler is arrested along with **Johannes Kleiman** in 1944 but escapes in 1945.

Kulsum

Shabanu
Suzanne Fisher Staples

Lal Khan's widow. At age sixteen, Kulsum is a sad and withdrawn young woman. She is the mother of three children.

Absalom Kumalo

Cry, the Beloved Country
Alan Paton

Stephen Kumalo's son. After fleeing home for Johannesburg, Absalom quickly goes astray, but even after he commits murder, he is able to reclaim his fundamental decency. His decision to move to Johannesburg is part of a larger trend of young black people fleeing their villages for the cities.

Absalom Kumalo's girlfriend

Cry, the Beloved Country
Alan Paton

The kindhearted and quiet sixteen-year-old girl whom **Absalom** has impregnated. She has run away from her dysfunctional family but still seeks a family structure and bonds. She is sexually experienced but essentially innocent, obedient, and grateful for protection from adults such as **Stephen Kumalo**.

Gertrude Kumalo

Cry, the Beloved Country
Alan Paton

Stephen Kumalo's sister, twenty-five years younger than Stephen. Gertrude lives in Johannesburg, and Stephen's visit there is an attempt to save her from a life of crime. Although she considers joining a convent, she eventually succumbs to her original impulses and returns to her criminal ways.

John Kumalo

Cry, the Beloved Country
Alan Paton

Stephen Kumalo's brother. Formerly a humble carpenter and a practicing Christian, John Kumalo becomes a successful businessman and one of the three most powerful black politicians in Johannesburg. He has a beautiful and powerful voice, which he uses to speak out for the rights of black South Africans, but his fear of punishment prevents him from pushing for actual radical change.

Matthew Kumalo

Cry, the Beloved Country
Alan Paton

John Kumalo's son. He is a good friend and eventual accomplice of **Absalom Kumalo**'s. Eventually, Matthew denies having been present at the robbery, turning his back on his cousin and friend.

Mrs. Kumalo

Cry, the Beloved Country
Alan Paton

Stephen Kumalo's strong-minded, supportive, and loving wife. Mrs. Kumalo and her husband make household decisions as equals and she bears hardship gracefully. When Kumalo is inclined to brood, she rouses him to action. She supplies the courage needed to read the bad news that the mail brings from Johannesburg.

Stephen Kumalo

Cry, the Beloved Country
Alan Paton

One of the novel's main protagonists. Kumalo is an elderly Zulu priest who has spent all of his life in the village of Ndotsheni. The dignity and grace with which he accepts his suffering, along with his determination to help his people in spite of his limitations, make him the moral center of the novel.

Anatol Vasilyevich Kuragin

War and Peace
Leo Tolstoy

Vasili Kuragin's roguish and spendthrift son, who is on the hunt for a rich wife. Anatole falls for **Natasha Ilyinichna Rostova** at the opera, causing her rift with **Prince Andrei Nikolayevich Bolkonsky**.

Ippolit Vasilyevich Kuragin

War and Peace
Leo Tolstoy

The ugly and undistinguished brother of **Helene Vasilievna Kuragina** and **Anatole Vasilievich Kuragin**, and son of **Vasili Kuragin**.

Vasili Kuragin

War and Peace
Leo Tolstoy

The father of **Anatole Vasilievich Kuragin**, **Helene Vasilievna Kuragina**, and **Ippolyte Vasilievich Kuragin**. An artificial and untrustworthy Russian nobleman, and a special friend of **Anna Pavlovna Scherer**'s. Vasili continually tries to maneuver his children into lucrative marriages.

Helene Vasilievna Kuragina

War and Peace
Leo Tolstoy

Vasili Kuragin's cold, imperious, and beautiful daughter, who seduces **Pierre Bezukhov** into marriage, only to take up with another man immediately. Helene, though known in social circles as a witty woman, is actually stupid and shallow.

Kurtz

Heart of Darkness
Joseph Conrad

The chief of the Inner Station and the object of **Marlow**'s quest. Kurtz is a man of many talents, a gifted musician and fine painter as well as a charismatic leader. Kurtz is a man who understands the power of words, and his writings are marked by an eloquence that obscures their horrifying message. Although he remains an enigma even to Marlow, Kurtz clearly exerts a powerful influence on the people in his life. His downfall seems to be a result of his willingness to ignore the hypocritical rules that govern European colonial conduct: Kurtz has "kicked himself loose of the earth" by fraternizing excessively with the natives and not keeping up appearances; in so doing, he has become wildly successful but has also incurred the wrath of his fellow white men.

Kurtz's African mistress

Heart of Darkness
Joseph Conrad

A fiercely beautiful woman loaded with jewelry who appears on the shore when **Marlow**'s steamer arrives at and leaves the Inner Station. She seems to exert an undue influence over both **Kurtz** and the natives around the station, and the **Russian trader** points her out as someone to fear. She never speaks to Marlow.

Kurtz's intended

Heart of Darkness
Joseph Conrad

Kurtz's naive and long-suffering fiancée, whom **Marlow** goes to visit after Kurtz's death. Her unshakable certainty about Kurtz's love for her reinforces Marlow's belief that women live in a dream world insulated from reality.

Honest Abe Kusich

The Day of the Locust
Nathanael West

A book-keeping dwarf and one of **Tod**'s friends. Abe is scornful and belligerent, perhaps in an attempt to compensate for his tiny size. He can be caring, as when he finds Tod an apartment or nurtures his hurt gamecock. Abe can also be very ruthless and violent, however, and he is one of the only men in the novel who is scornful of **Faye**'s acting.

General Kutuzov

War and Peace
Leo Tolstoy

An old, one-eyed general who leads the Russians to military success at Borodino, but who falls from favor toward the end of his life. The commander of the Russian forces against **Napoleon**, Kutuzov is a brilliant strategist as well as a practiced philosopher of human nature. His spirituality and humility provide a sharp contrast to Napoleon's vanity and logic.

Grigory Vasilievich Kutuzov

The Brothers Karamazov
Fyodor Dostoevsky

Fyodor Pavlovich Karamazov's servant, who, along with his wife, raises **Pavel Fyodorovich Smerdyakov** from birth.

Tata Kuvundu

The Poisonwood Bible
Barbara Kingsolver

The much-revered keeper of the old traditions, the religious leader of the village. He is unhappy about **Nathan Price**'s presence and concerned that the traditions of the village be upheld. He begins to plant poisonous mamba snakes next to the beds of those connected to the Price family. One of these snakes, intended for **Nelson Price**, ends up killing **Ruth May**.

Helen Kwong

The Kitchen God's Wife
Amy Tan

Winnie's best friend, Helen is stubborn and also strong. She had grown up in poverty and married into a higher class, survived the war, and, with Winnie's help, immigrated to America.

Henry Kwong

The Kitchen God's Wife
Amy Tan

Helen's second husband. Henry loves his wife very much, and it is important for him to look strong in front of her. He takes credit for getting **Winnie** out of prison, even though this was **Auntie Du**'s doing.

Mary Kwong

The Kitchen God's Wife
Amy Tan

Helen's daughter. She is married to a doctor who had treated **Pearl** and therefore knows about **Winnie**'s condition. She is very concerned with appearances.

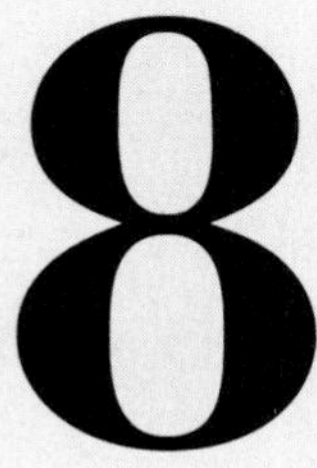

(OR SIXTEEN) TERRIBLE TWINS

SO GOOD, THE AUTHORS HAD TO MAKE TWO OF THEM. DOUBLE THE TROUBLE.

Antipholus of Syracuse and Antipholus of Ephesus	1	*The Illiad*
Dromio of Syracuse and Dromio of Ephesus	2	*The Comedy of Errors*
Jacob and Esau	3	*The Old Testament*
Luigi and Angelo	4	*Pudd'nhead Wilson*
Tweedledee and Tweedledum	5	*Alice in Wonderland, Through the Looking Glass*
Pedro and Pablo Vicario	6	*Chronicle of a Death Foretold*
Fred and George Weasley	7	*Harry Potter* series, Books I-IV
Aron and Caleb Trask	8	*East of Eden*

Madame L'Espanaye

"The Murders in the Rue Morgue"
Edgar Allan Poe

The older of the two Parisian murder victims. Violently beaten with a club, Madame L'Espanaye dies from a cut throat and is thrown through the window to a courtyard below her apartment.

La Dolciquita

The Good Soldier
Ford Madox Ford

The mercenary and manipulative mistress of a Grand Duke who is visiting Monte Carlo. She aims to seduce **Captain Edward Ashburnham** and take as much of his money as possible; she cares nothing about his love, his passions, or the public embarrassment of their affair.

Laban

The Red Tent
Anita Diamant

Cruel and selfish father of **Leah**, **Rachel**, **Zilpah**, **Bilhah**, **Kemuel** and **Beor**. Laban is a worthless cheat who mistreats his wife and daughters and tries to cheat **Jacob** of his due as overseer of Laban's lands. Laban eventually backs down in fear of Jacob's god, after trying to chase Jacob and his family on their way to Canaan.

Lactamaeon

I Never Promised You a Rose Garden
Joanne Greenberg

The second most powerful god in Yr, **Deborah**'s fantasy world.

Will Ladislaw

Middlemarch
George Eliot

The grandson of **Edward Casaubon**'s disinherited aunt. **Nicholas Bulstrode** tries to give him money to atone for hiding his existence from his grandmother. He refuses the money because he knows it came through thievery.

Lady

The Chairs
Eugène Ionesco

The invisible first guest of the **Old Man** and **Old Woman**. They engage in casual conversation with Lady. She also receives inappropriate advances from the **Colonel**.

Leading Lady

Six Characters in Search of an Author
Luigi Pirandello

A stereotypical star of the stage. Petty and egotistical, she will not support their laughter, protests their vulgar stage tricks, and continually insists that she will deliver a performance superior to theirs. She plays the role of **the Stepdaughter** and often takes it personally when the Stepdaughter points out how different they are in demeanor and appearance.

Old Lady

Henry VIII
William Shakespeare

Anne Boleyn's attendant. An old woman who has been working at the court for sixteen years, she disagrees with Anne's sentiment that she wouldn't want to be queen. When Anne is given a new title and increased financial support, the Old Lady is shocked and envious, and says that more gifts are to come.

Second Lady

Six Characters in Search of an Author
Luigi Pirandello

The actress who plays the role of **the Mother**.

Laertes

The Odyssey
Homer

Odysseus's aging father, who regains his spirit when his son returns.

Laertes

Hamlet
William Shakespeare

Polonius's son and **Ophelia**'s brother. Passionate and quick to action, Laertes is a foil for the reflective and indecisive Hamlet. Laertes spends much of the play in France but vows vengeance on Hamlet after the deaths of Polonius and Ophelia. With the help of King **Claudius**, Laertes plots a duel with Hamlet in which he decides to use a poison blade. That blade ends up killing Claudius, Laertes, and Hamlet.

LaFarge

The Martian Chronicles
Ray Bradbury

An old man who moves to Mars to retire with his wife **Anna**. The couple miss their son **Tom**, who died of pneumonia as a boy. When a Martian posing as Tom visits, LaFarge quickly guesses the truth, but he doesn't want to tell his wife, since the truth would destroy the peace brought by the illusion of Tom.

Lafe

As I Lay Dying
William Faulkner

Dewey Dell Bundren's sexual partner and the father of her baby. Lafe gives Dewey $10 to pay for an abortion.

Lafew

All's Well that Ends Well
William Shakespeare

A French lord, counselor to the **King of France** and friend to the **Countess of Roussillon**. He is wise and discerning, perceiving both **Helena**'s worth and **Parolles**'s worthlessness. He criticizes Bertram's conduct with Helena and almost comes to blows with Parolles, whom he calls a coward. Lafew's honor is again highlighted when he accepts Parolles, who has been thrust from the army into a beggar's role, into the house toward the end of the play.

Bibi Lal

Shabanu
Suzanne Fisher Staples

Hamir and **Murad**'s mother. Her husband died of natural causes two years prior. She is a warm, expansive, and understanding woman.

Dr. Panna Lal

A Passage to India
E. M. Forster

Dr. Aziz's professional rival, a lowborn Hindu doctor. Panna Lal intends to testify against Aziz at the trial but regrets this decision after Aziz is exonerated.

Billy Lally

Bless the Beasts and Children
Glendon Swarthout

Stephen Lally, Jr.'s younger brother. Billy Lally is a shy, meek, and sensitive eleven-year-old boy. Billy demonstrates a natural comfort and ease with animals, unlike his brother.

Alfred Lambert

The Corrections
Jonathan Franzen

The Parkinson's-afflicted father who spends much of the novel passively observing his own creeping death. Harsh and controlling, Alfred gave up life years before, when he descended into a deep depression and coped with it by sleeping and retreating into the family basement. Because Alfred can never summon the courage to take his own life, he pleads with **Chip Lambert** to kill him. Chip, of course, refuses. Only when Alfred has completely lost his faculties does he find the courage to go on a hunger strike, which to everyone's surprise lasts much longer than expected.

Chip Lambert

The Corrections
Jonathan Franzen

A shiftless, self-obsessed intellectual working toward a doctorate in "textual artifacts." Chip is a disciple of Foucault and Marx who chases women while descending into crippling debt. His pursuit of pleasure lands Chip in a Lithuanian Internet scam, where Chip loses himself in an economic wilderness of sex, drugs, and cash. Only after losing everything—his dignity, his money, his reputation—can Chip gain empathy.

Denise Lambert

The Corrections
Jonathan Franzen

The Lamberts' youngest child, a star chef unable to accept her probable lesbianism. In an indirect bid to win her father's approval, Denise embarked on many torrid affairs with older men in the past. Late in the novel, she realizes that her seemingly cold and detached father sacrificed his job and retirement pension to protect her.

Enid Lambert

The Corrections
Jonathan Franzen

The bitter, powerless housewife, who lives in fear of her husband **Alfred Lambert**'s criticism. On the cruise she takes with her husband, Enid discovers Aslan Cruiser, an Ecstasy-like drug that's illegal in the U.S. but perfectly legal on the high seas. On the Aslan, Enid is impenetrable, and after her husband recedes from her daily existence, Enid finds that she can cope with life even without the drug. She can cultivate her loving and generous nature for the first time in many years.

Gary Lambert

The Corrections
Jonathan Franzen

The powerful vice president of a bank, the husband of a rich and beautiful wife, and father of three smart, accomplished sons. Gary has a large home in the most exclusive section of Philadelphia. In reality, his marriage is a nightmare and his wife, Caroline, a manipulative power-monger. The two of them fight constantly, particularly after **Enid Lambert** invites them to spend Christmas in St. Jude. Gary grows depressed, begins to drink heavily, and eventually hurts himself drunkenly trimming the hedge with power tools. Ultimately, Gary sacrifices his integrity and admits that Caroline is right and he is wrong. It is implied that Gary might one day become as repressed as his father, **Alfred Lambert**.

Mr. Lammeter

Silas Marner
George Eliot

Nancy Lammeter and **Priscilla Lammeter**'s father. Mr. Lammeter is a proud, morally uncompromising man.

Nancy Lammeter

Silas Marner
George Eliot

The object of **Godfrey Cass**'s affection and, eventually, his wife. Nancy is pretty, caring, and stubborn, and she lives her life by a code of rules that sometimes seems arbitrary and uncompromising.

Priscilla Lammeter

Silas Marner
George Eliot

Nancy Lammeter's homely and plainspoken sister. Priscilla talks endlessly but is extremely competent at everything she does.

Lampito

Lysistrata
Aristophanes

A large, well-built representative of Spartan women. Lampito brings the Spartan women into **Lysistrata**'s plan.

The Lamplighter

The Little Prince
Antoine de Saint-Exupéry

The fifth and most complex figure **the Little Prince** encounters before landing on Earth. His selfless devotion to his orders earns him the little prince's admiration.

Lancelot

The Once and Future King
T. H. White

King Arthur's best knight and the commander of his forces. Lancelot has a love affair with **Guenever**, Arthur's queen. Lancelot's ugliness gives him a sense of unworthiness and inadequacy from a very young age, but this low self-esteem is paired with an astonishing, almost unnatural talent for all knightly skills and endeavors. He is easily tricked by **Elaine**, whom he saves from a spell of **Morgan le Fay**'s: Elaine tricks him into having sex with her, and also tricks him into impregnating her, telling him that he has lost his power with the loss of his virginity. He ends up having to save Guenever at the stake after **Mordred**'s plot to have her burned at the stake for her affair with him. He goes completely mad for a while because of his inability to have Guenever completely as his own.

Landau

Anna Karenina
Leo Tolstoy

A French psychic who instructs **Alexei Alexandrovich Karenin** to reject **Anna Arkadyevna Karenina**'s plea for a divorce.

Lusa Maluf Landowski

Prodigal Summer
Barbara Kingsolver

A bright, attractive twenty-eight-year-old entomologist. Lusa met **Cole Widener** at the University of Kentucky and married him about a year before the narration begins. After being widowed, Lusa deals with her sadness in courageous, creative ways.

Lane

Go Ask Alice
Anonymous

A violent drug user at school who tries persuading **Alice** to get him drugs. Lane later becomes Alice's supplier.

Robert Langdon

The Da Vinci Code
Dan Brown

The male protagonist of the novel, a professor of symbology at Harvard. Langdon is honest, likable, and trustworthy, an extremely successful academic and the author of several books. He, like his cohort and love interest, **Sophie Neveu**, has a great affection for puzzles of all kinds. Langdon is clumsy and inept with guns and weapons, and lacks resolve when it comes to planning and executing action. He would rather think about codes and symbols.

Dr. Lanselius

His Dark Materials
Robert Pullman

The Witch consul. Dr. Lanselius represents the witches to the outside world. He tests **Lyra Belacqua** to see if she is the girl in the witches' prophecies. He tells Lyra and **Farder Coram** where to find **Iorek Byrnison**.

Dr. Hastie Lanyon

Dr. Jekyll and Mr. Hyde
Robert Louis Stevenson

A reputable London doctor. Lanyon, along with **Mr. Gabriel John Utterson**, is one of **Dr. Henry Jekyll**'s closest friends. He is an embodiment of rationalism, materialism, and skepticism. Lanyon is a foil for Jekyll, who embraces mysticism.

Joyce Lanyon

Arrowsmith
Sinclair Lewis

Martin Arrowsmith's second wife. **Joyce** is a wealthy woman with whom Martin does not have very much in common.

Dorcas Lapham

Johnny Tremain
Esther Forbes

Mrs. Lapham's second daughter. Although Dorcas longs to be elegant and sophisticated, she ends up falling in love with the poverty-stricken **Frizel, Jr.**, and elopes to avoid having to marry **Mr. Tweedie**.

Ephraim Lapham

Johnny Tremain
Esther Forbes

A Boston silversmith. Mr. Lapham is a pious and kind man who acts as **Jonathan Tremain**'s master before the accident that disfigures his hand. Mr. Lapham attempts to teach Johnny humility by referring to the Bible and reminding him of the dangers of pride and arrogance.

Isannah Lapham

Johnny Tremain
Esther Forbes

The youngest daughter of **Mrs. Lapham**. Isannah is selfish and vain and beloved by **Priscilla Lapham**. Isannah's golden-haired, ethereal beauty attracts a great deal of attention, most significantly from **Lavinia Lyte**. Lavinia takes Isannah into her care and introduces her to high society, separating her from her family and their lower-class ways of life.

Madge Lapham

Johnny Tremain
Esther Forbes

Mrs. Lapham's oldest daughter. Like Mrs. Lapham, Madge is tough and capable. She elopes with **Sergeant Gale**, a British soldier.

Mrs. Lapham

Johnny Tremain
Esther Forbes

Ephraim Lapham's daughter-in-law. Mrs. Lapham is a dedicated, hardworking mother and a no-nonsense taskmaster to the apprentices. She works as the housekeeper in Mr. Lapham's house.

Priscilla Lapham

Johnny Tremain
Esther Forbes

The third-oldest daughter of **Mrs. Lapham**. Cilla is loyal, selfless, and caring. Although her primary devotion is to her younger sister, **Isannah Lapham**, Cilla's feelings for **Jonathan Tremain** help him to develop into a warm, patient, honest young man.

Laputans

Gulliver's Travels
Jonathan Swift

Absentminded intellectuals. With the Laputans, Swift parodies useless, self-indulgent, purely academic pursuits. They focus on abstract, impractical theorizing and neglect practical matters such as their dilapidated houses. They dismiss **Gulliver** as intellectually deficient.

Larissa

The Giver
Lois Lowry

A woman living in the House of the Old. **Jonas** shares pleasant conversation with her while he gives her a bath during his volunteer hours.

Lariviere

Madame Bovary
Gustave Flaubert

An esteemed doctor from Rouen who is called in after **Emma** takes arsenic. He is coldly analytical and condescending to his inferiors, but he is brilliant and competent, and he feels a real sympathy for his patients.

Larry

Stranger in a Strange Land
Robert A. Heinlein

One of **Jubal Harshaw**'s employees, who keep things running smoothly at his estate.

Gummy Larson

All the King's Men
Robert Penn Warren

MacMurfee's most powerful supporter, a wealthy businessman. **Willie** is forced to give Larson the building contract to the hospital so that Larson will call MacMurfee off about the **Sibyl Frey** controversy, and thereby preserve Willie's chance to go to the Senate.

Joe Larson

The Virgin Suicides
Jeffrey Eugenides

A neighborhood boy whose house is directly across the street from the Lisbons'. The boys gather at Joe's house to spy on the Lisbon girls.

Titus Lartius

Coriolanus
William Shakespeare

An old Roman nobleman. Titus Lartius is appointed, along with **Cominius**, general against the Volscians.

Father LaSalle

Hiroshima
John Hersey

A Jesuit priest who is badly injured in the blast and evacuated, along with **Father Schiffer**, with the help of **Father Wilhelm Kleinsorge** and **Reverend Mr. Kiyoshi Tanimoto**.

Latinus

The Aeneid
Virgil

The king of the Latins, the people of what is now central Italy, around the Tiber River. Latinus allows **Aeneas** into his kingdom and encourages him to woo his daughter, **Lavinia**. He respects the gods and fate, but his command over his people is not firm.

Launce

The Two Gentlemen of Verona
William Shakespeare

Proteus's clownish servant and devoted owner of **Crab**. One of Shakespeare's first clowns, Launce provides much comic relief with his verbal gaffes and melodramatic loyalty to his dog.

Sir Launcelot

A Connecticut Yankee in King Arthur's Court
Mark Twain

The shining pinnacle of chivalry, often referred to as "The Invincible." Sir Launcelot is noble and gracious and generally good in every way that can be expected, except for his tragic passion for **Guenever**, which results in an affair between the two. When **King Arthur** finds out about this affair, a war starts between Arthur and Launcelot. **The Yankee** has to fight a duel with Launcelot before any of the problems of the war start, and the Yankee defeats Sir Launcelot easily.

Laura

The Autobiography of Malcolm X
Malcolm X & Alex Haley

Malcolm X's first date, a quiet, middle-class black girl from Roxbury Hill. When Malcolm dumps Laura for **Sophia**, Laura becomes involved with drugs and prostitution.

Laura

Ceremony
Leslie Marmon Silko

Tayo's mother. Unable to negotiate the conflicting lessons she learned at home and at school, Laura became a victim of the contact between white and Native American cultures. Consumed by alcoholism, she conceived Tayo with an anonymous white man and, by the time Tayo was four years old, she was completely unable to care for him.

Laura

How the Garcia Girls Lost Their Accents
Julia Alvarez

The mother of the four sisters. Laura had to adjust to cultural and material differences when she came to the United States, as her family name and privilege meant much less in the U.S. than it had in the Dominican Republic. However, she continued to be proud and supportive of her daughters.

Laurie Laurence

Little Women
Louisa May Alcott

The rich boy who lives next door to the Marches. Laurie, whose real name is Theodore Laurence, becomes like a son and brother to the Marches. He is charming, clever, and has a good heart. His father, **Mr. Laurence**, does not let Laurie follow his dream of becoming a musician; instead, he wants Laurie to have a professional career in business. Laurie is highly marriageable and more and more obviously in love with **Josephine March**, who does not return his affection. When **Amy March** marries Laurie, she serves as a mentor for him, instead of the other way around. The two have the most egalitarian marriage of the novel. Though this marriage holds promise, it is layered with a bit of regret, because Laurie becomes his old playful self not in Amy's presence but only in the presence of Josephine.

Mr. Laurence

Little Women
Louisa May Alcott

Laurie Laurence's grandfather and the Marches' next-door neighbor. Mr. Laurence seems gruff, but he is loving and kind.

Laurette

Johnny Got His Gun
Dalton Trumbo

A prostitute at Stumpy Telsa's in Shale City. Laurette and **Joe Bonham** became friends while Joe was finishing high school. Joe imagined that she was in love with him.

Annie Laurie

A Tree Grows in Brooklyn
Betty Smith

Johnny Nolan and **Katie Nolan**'s third child. Annie Laurie is born five months after Johnny dies, when **Mary Frances Nolan** is fourteen.

Lavatch

All's Well that Ends Well
William Shakespeare

The **Countess of Roussillon**'s servant and messenger. The clown of the play, Lavatch enjoys coarse, sexual humor, but also delights in verbally tripping up others, as he does with **Parolles**.

Ted Lavender

The Things They Carried
Tim O'Brien

A young, scared soldier in the Alpha Company. Lavender is the first to die in the war. He makes only a brief appearance in the narrative, popping tranquilizers to calm himself while the company is outside Than Khe.

Elizabeth Lavenza

Frankenstein
Mary Shelley

An orphan, four or five years younger than **Victor Frankenstein**, whom the Frankensteins adopt. She marries Victor, but is killed by **the monster**. In the 1818 edition of the novel, Elizabeth is Victor's cousin, the child of **Alphonse Frankenstein**'s sister. In the 1831 edition, Victor's mother rescues Elizabeth from a destitute peasant cottage in Italy.

Lavinia

The Aeneid
Virgil

King **Latinus**'s daughter. The question of who will marry Lavinia—**Turnus** or **Aeneas**—determines future relations between the Latins and the Trojans.

Lavinia

Titus Andronicus
William Shakespeare

Titus's daughter. Lavinia spurns the unstable **Saturninus**, choosing to elope with his gentle and doting brother **Bassianus**. After she is brutally raped and maimed by **Tamora**'s sons **Chiron** and **Demetrius**, she becomes a mute and grotesque presence, an incapacitated heroine. Titus asks the emperor Saturninus if **Virginius** (a heroic Centurion) should have slain his daughter because she had been raped; Saturninus responds that a girl should not survive her shame. At this, Titus kills Lavinia.

Miss Lavish

A Room with a View
E. M. Forster

An ostentatious writer who stays in the pension in Florence and hopes to write novels about Italian life. She is outspoken and clever, but also abrasive. She despises English people traveling abroad and believes she alone knows the "true" Italy.

Amy Lawrence

The Adventures of Tom Sawyer
Mark Twain

Tom Sawyer's former love. Tom abandons Amy Lawrence when **Becky Thatcher** comes to town.

Friar Lawrence

Romeo and Juliet
William Shakespeare

A Franciscan friar, friend to both **Romeo** and **Juliet**. Kind, civic-minded, a proponent of moderation, and always ready with a plan, **Friar Lawrence** secretly marries the impassioned lovers in the hope that their union might eventually bring peace to Verona. In addition to being a Catholic holy man, Friar Lawrence is an expert in the use of mystical potions and herbs. He fashions the plot of giving Juliet a potion that will make her seem like she's dead.

Lawyer

Utopia
Sir Thomas More

An unnamed man who once spent an evening with **Raphael Hythloday** and **Cardinal John Morton**. He is defensive of England and unwilling to find fault with anything in English society.

Lawyer

Bartleby, the Scrivener
Herman Melville

The unnamed narrator of "Bartleby the Scrivener." He owns a law firm on Wall Street, and he employs four men as scriveners, or copyists: **Turkey**, **Nippers**, **Ginger Nut**, and **Bartleby**. He is good at dealing with people until he meets Bartleby.

Chester Kirby Laylock

Babbitt
Sinclair Lewis

A salesman who works for **Babbitt**'s real estate firm.

Joe Lazenby

Ordinary People
Judith Guest

A friend of **Buck Jarrett** and **Conrad Jarrett** and a member of the swimming team. He and Conrad have a falling-out, but they manage to mend their relationship. Conrad feels that Lazenby does not really value Conrad's friendship, and calls him out on it. After Conrad comes to terms with Buck's death and his parents' worries, he is able to open up lines of communication with Lazenby again.

Paul Lazzaro

Slaughterhouse-Five
Kurt Vonnegut

Another POW and the man responsible for **Billy Pilgrim**'s death. Lazzaro, a vengeful ruffian with criminal tendencies, arranges for Billy's assassination to avenge **Roland Weary**'s death.

Adolphe Le Bon

"The Murders in the Rue Morgue"
Edgar Allan Poe

A bank clerk and the first suspect in the two murders.

Le Bret

Cyrano de Bergerac
Edmond Rostand

Cyrano de Bergerac's friend, closest confidant, and fellow guardsman. Le Bret worries that Cyrano's stubborn life-long struggle against lies, compromise, prejudice, cowardice, and stupidity will ruin Cyrano's career.

Morgan le Fay

A Connecticut Yankee in King Arthur's Court
Mark Twain

A vicious but beautiful and genteel queen. **King Arthur** is her brother, but she hates him passionately. She orders **the Yankee** thrown in the dungeon when he makes a complimentary remark about King Arthur. The queen orders an old woman burned at the stake when the woman curses Le Fay for killing her grandson, but **Sandy** rises and says the Yankee will destroy the castle if Le Fay does not recall her command. Afterward, Le Fay is cowed and even seeks the Yankee's approval before having the court composer hanged. The Yankee subsequently frees all of Le Fay's prisoners but one.

Morgan le Fay

The Once and Future King
T. H. White

Morgause's sister and **King Arthur**'s half-sister. Morgan le Fay, who is most likely a fairy queen, shows up periodically to torment knights and villagers with her malicious spells.

Morgan le Fay

Sir Gawain and the Green Knight
Unknown

A powerful sorceress, trained by Merlin, as well as the half sister of **King Arthur**. Not until the last hundred lines do we discover that the old woman at the castle is Morgan le Fay and that she has controlled the poem's entire action from beginning to end.

Monsieur le Fer

Henry V
William Shakespeare

A French soldier and gentleman whom **Pistol** captures at the Battle of Agincourt. Le Fer speaks no English, and following a comic exchange between the two soldiers and the **Boy**, Pistol agrees to let him go for 200 French crowns.

Lieutenant Le Fever

Tristram Shandy
Laurence Sterne

A favorite sentimental charity case of **Uncle Toby**'s and **Corporal Trim**'s. Le Fever died under their care, leaving an orphan son.

Juvenile Lead

Six Characters in Search of an Author
Luigi Pirandello

The young actor who plays the role of **the Son**.

Mrs. Leaf

The Picture of Dorian Gray
Oscar Wilde

Dorian Gray's housekeeper. Mrs. Leaf is a bustling older woman who takes her work seriously.

Leah

The Red Tent
Anita Diamant

Eldest of the four daughters of **Laban**. Leah is the first wife of **Jacob**, mother of **Dinah** and of seven sons of Jacob. Leah bears the misfortune of having mismatched eyes—one blue and one green. She is the head mother of the clan, and manages the brewing, baking, harvesting and supervision of the children. Leah is a determined, decisive, and capable woman. She marries Jacob despite his love for **Rachel** and she revels in the joy he finds in her arms. Yet even with all of her talents and triumphs as a mother, Leah is a tragic figure. Her sister Rachel remains the true love of Jacob's life and she loses her only daughter through circumstances beyond her control. After Jacob's, **Simon**'s and **Levi**'s massacre at Shechem, Leah one day wakes up paralyzed and dies pining for the love and comfort of her only daughter, begging her daughters-in-law to kill her with poison.

Leah

Wide Sargasso Sea
Jean Rhys

Rochester's cook. Leah is one of only three servants who know about **Antoinette**'s imprisonment in the attic.

King Lear

King Lear
William Shakespeare

The aging king of Britain and the protagonist of the play. Lear is used to enjoying absolute power and to being flattered, and he does not respond well to being contradicted or challenged. At the beginning of the play, his values are notably hollow—he prioritizes the appearance of love over actual devotion. He also wishes to maintain the power of a king while unburdening himself of the responsibility. Nevertheless, he inspires loyalty in subjects such as **Gloucester**, **Kent**, **Cordelia**, and **Edgar**, all of whom risk their lives for him. Lear goes mad during the play, but he snaps out of his madness upon the death of Cordelia, his only loyal daughter.

Lebedev

The Idiot
Fyodor Dostoevsky

Part of **Parfyon Semyonovich Rogozhin**'s gang. He rents out several rooms in his summer cottage in Pavlovsk to **Prince Lev Nikolayevich Myshkin**.

Andrei Semyonovich Lebezyatnikov

Crime and Punishment
Fyodor Dostoevsky

Pyotr Petrovich Luzhin's grudging roommate. Lebezyatnikov is a young man who is convinced of the rightness of the "new philosophies" such as nihilism that are currently raging through St. Petersburg.

David LeBlanc

Dead Man Walking
Helen Prejean

The teenage boy murdered by **Eddie Sonnier**.

Lloyd LeBlanc

Dead Man Walking
Helen Prejean

The father of murder victim **David LeBlanc**. Lloyd reprimands **Sister Helen Prejean** for failing to contact the victims' families. He talks openly with Prejean about his family's grief and his desire to see **Patrick Sonnier** executed.

Madame Lebrun

The Awakening
Kate Chopin

Robert Lebrun and **Victor Lebrun**'s widowed mother. Madame Lebrun is the proprietor of the cottages on Grand Isle.

Robert Lebrun

The Awakening
Kate Chopin

Son of **Madame Lebrun**, brother of **Victor Lebrun**. Robert is the dramatic and passionate man with whom **Edna Pontellier** falls in love. After courting many different women, like **Adèle Ratignolle**, only half-seriously each summer while their husbands are away, Robert genuinely falls in love with Edna. Initially, Robert's flirtations with Edna cause her to desire more freedom from **Léonce Pontellier**. As they spend more time together, a love develops between them. Knowing that actually pursuing this kind of an affair is very different from the socially acceptable flirtations he makes with men's wives, Robert flees to Mexico to forget his love for Edna.

Victor Lebrun

The Awakening
Kate Chopin

Robert Lebrun's wayward younger brother, **Madame Lebrun**'s favored son. Victor spends his time chasing women and refuses to choose a career.

Lecon

A Yellow Raft in Blue Water
Michael Dorris

Ida's father, who has an affair with **Clara** that results in the birth of **Christine**. Lecon runs off shortly after Ida's mother dies and does not return.

Monsieur Ledoux

The American
Henry James

One of two friends of **Valentin de Bellegarde**'s who act for him in the duel against **Stanislas Kapp**. Ledoux, the nephew of a distinguished Ultramontane bishop, met Valentin when they fought together in the Pontifical Zouaves. He meets **Christopher Newman** at the Geneva train station to take him to Valentin's deathbed, and the next morning irritates Newman with his premature eulogies.

Lee

East of Eden
John Steinbeck

Adam Trask's dutiful cook and housekeeper, an educated man whose parents emigrated to America from China. Lee, who serves as a stabilizing force in the tumultuous Trask household, often affects a Chinese pidgin accent to play into Americans' expectations of him.

Lee

True West
Sam Shepard

Austin's older brother and **Mom**'s son. Lee is a beer-swilling desert rat and petty thief who has come to his mother's house to loot the neighbors of household appliances. Lee is a drifter, most recently touring the desert with a fighting pit bull.

Lee

A Yellow Raft in Blue Water
Michael Dorris

Ida's illegitimate son with **Willard Pretty Dog**, Lee grows up thinking he is Christine's brother. Initially a timid boy, Lee becomes the most attractive young man on the reservation. Sometimes mocking in his pride, he is certain of the great future that the entire reservation imagines for him. After his sister convinces him not to dodge the draft, he goes off to Vietnam and returns to the reservation in a body bag.

Annie Lee

O Pioneers!
Willa Cather

Lou Bergson's wife and **Milly Bergson**'s mother. Annie is a sharp, aggressive, petty woman who is obsessed with appearances. She is as intent as her husband on securing Alexandra's farm as an inheritance for their children.

Bessie Lee

Jane Eyre
Charlotte Brontë

The maid at Gateshead, and the only kind figure in **Jane Eyre**'s childhood. Bessie tells Jane stories and sings her songs. Bessie later marries **Robert Leaven**, the Reeds' coachman.

Old Bull Lee

On the Road
Jack Kerouac

A longtime friend of **Sal Paradise** and **Carlo Marx**'s. Old Bull Lee is a traveler, writer, and junkie.

General Robert E. Lee

The Killer Angels
Michael Shaara

The Commander of the Army of Northern Virginia, or Confederate army. At the age of 57, Lee has become one of the most famous—and most revered—men in the South. He has led his army through a string of victories.

Jane Lee

On the Road
Jack Kerouac

Old Bull Lee's sarcastic wife. Jane is a benzedrine junkie.

Mrs. Lee

O Pioneers!
Willa Cather

The mother of **Lou Bergson**'s wife and **Alexandra Bergson**'s sister-in-law, **Annie Lee**. Despite Alexandra's dislike for her sister-in-law, she has great affection for Annie's elderly mother. Mrs. Lee spends a long yearly visit in Alexandra's house, where she appreciates the reverence for old Swedish tradition.

Mr. Leeford

Oliver Twist
Charles Dickens

Oliver Twist and **Monks**'s father. Mr. Leeford was an intelligent, high-minded man who intended to flee the country with **Agnes Fleming** but died before he could do so.

Leer

All Quiet on the Western Front
Erich Maria Remarque

One of **Paul Bäumer**'s classmates and close friends during the war. Leer serves with Paul in the Second Company. He was the first in Paul's class to lose his virginity.

Lee-Sing

The Bean Trees
Barbara Kingsolver

The woman who owns the grocery store and Laundromat next door to Jesus Is Lord Used Tires. Her mother brought the original bean seeds from China, the descendents of which now grow in **Mattie**'s yard.

Dr. Leete

Looking Backward
Edward Bellamy

A representative of the twentieth century in the novel. When preparing a site for the construction of a laboratory, Dr. Leete discovers an underground sleeping chamber from the nineteenth century. Inside the chamber, he finds **Julian West** in a state of suspended animation. Doctor Leete helps Julian understand the vast changes that have swept the nation in the last century.

Edith Leete

Looking Backward
Edward Bellamy

The intelligent, attractive daughter of **Doctor** and **Mrs. Leete**. Edith offers **Julian West** a great deal of emotional support during the bewildering and difficult process of adjusting to twentieth-century society. Over time, she and Julian fall in love and become engaged, at which point Edith reveals that she is the great-granddaughter of **Edith Bartlett**, Julian's fiancée from the nineteenth century.

Mrs. Leete

Looking Backward
Edward Bellamy

Dr. Leete's kind, compassionate wife. Mrs. Leete is the granddaughter of **Edith Bartlett**, **Julian West**'s nineteenth-century fiancée.

Mary Agnes LeFarbre

The Autobiography of Miss Jane Pittman
Ernest J. Gaines

The Creole schoolteacher who comes to live on **Robert Samson**'s plantation. **Tee Bob Samson** falls in love with her. Mary Agnes came to the plantation in an effort to make amends for her family's slaveholding past. Her desire to be with dark-skinned people is equally as racist as her Creole family's desire to only be with whites. Mary Agnes is a coquette, as she continues to befriend Tee Bob but naïvely assumes that nothing will come of it. Her attitude inadvertently contributes to his death.

Lawrence Lefferts

The Age of Innocence
Edith Wharton

A huge gossip and an unfaithful husband who is widely considered to be the arbiter of good taste and moral values. There are suspicions that Lefferts courted **Countess Ellen Olenska** soon after her arrival and that she rejected his advances.

Albert Left Hand

When the Legends Die
Hal Borland

Thomas Black Bull's employer. Albert Left Hand owns a little band of sheep on the flats at the northern edge of the reservation. In need of a helper, he hires eleven-year-old Tom to help.

Remy Legaludec

The Da Vinci Code
Dan Brown

Manservant to **Leigh Teabing** and participant in the plot to recover the Grail. Legaludec is a mercenary who gets involved in the plot only for the money.

Legolas

The Lord of the Rings trilogy
J. R. R. Tolkien

A High Elf from the dark forest of Mirkwood. Legolas is beautiful, light on his feet, and masterful with a bow. After overcoming initial differences that stem from the historical antipathy between the races of **Dwarves** and **Elves**, he and the Dwarf **Gimli** become fast friends. Legolas is chosen to be a part of the Fellowship of the Ring at the Council of **Elrond Halfelven** in Rivendell in *The Fellowship of the Ring*. Without Legolas, the Fellowship would not be able to enter into the magical forest of Lothlórien to see **Galadriel**. In *The Two Towers*, Legolas's superhuman eyesight serves him well in warning his traveling party of approaching **Orcs**. Along with **Aragorn** and Gimli, he swiftly tracks **Meriadoc Brandybuck** and **Peregrin Took**, captives of Orcs. In *The Return of the King*, Legolas bravely represents the Elf race in Gondor's march against Mordor and its Dark Lord **Sauron**.

M. Legrandin

Swann's Way
Marcel Proust

A stereotype of bourgeois snobbery. He refuses to introduce **Marcel**'s family to his sister.

Simon Legree

Uncle Tom's Cabin
Harriet Beecher Stowe

Uncle Tom's ruthlessly evil master on the Louisiana plantation. He was the child of a loving mother and a tyrannical father. A vicious, barbaric, and loathsome man, Legree fosters violence and hatred among his slaves.

Mr. Lehr

The Power and the Glory
Graham Greene

A German-American living in Mexico. Mr. Lehr is the first to come upon **the Priest** after he crosses the border.

Annabel Leigh

Lolita
Vladimir Nabokov

Humbert Humbert's childhood love, the daughter of tourists visiting Humbert's father's hotel. Despite having many physical encounters, Humbert and Annabel are unable to consummate their adolescent love. She later dies of typhus in Corfu. Humbert is obsessed with her memory until he meets **Lolita**.

Miriam Leivers

Sons and Lovers
D. H. Lawrence

The daughter of the family at Willey Farm. She befriends **Paul Morel** and becomes his first love.

Curt Lemon

The Things They Carried
Tim O'Brien

A childish and careless member of the Alpha Company who is killed while tossing a grenade in a game of catch. Though **Tim O'Brien** does not particularly like Lemon, he contemplates Lemon's death with sadness and regret.

Iris Lemon

The Natural
Bernard Malamud

A kind, quiet woman who helps **Roy Hobbs** snap out of his slump. At thirty-three, Iris is already a grandmother, but she offers Hobbs the best hope of having a happy life. Unfortunately, Roy refuses her in favor of **Memo Paris**.

Lena

The Autobiography of Miss Jane Pittman
Ernest J. Gaines

Jimmy Aaron's great aunt. She raises him and is one of the strong older black women who remain on the plantation.

Lenehan

Dubliners and *Ulysses*
James Joyce

A dissipated leech, jokester, and flirt; the racing editor for the Dublin newspaper. In *Dubliners*, Lenehan uses his friends for money in "Two Gallants." Lenehan exudes both energy and exhaustion, participating in his friend **Corley**'s criminal exploits while lamenting his unstable and aimless life. In *Ulysses*, Lenehan's tip Sceptre loses the Gold Cup horse race. He mocks **Leopold Bloom** but respects **Simon Dedalus** and **Stephen Dedalus**.

Leni

The Trial
Franz Kafka

Huld's nurse, who becomes **Joseph K.**'s lover. She finds accused men extremely attractive.

Lennie

Of Mice and Men
John Steinbeck

A large, lumbering, childlike migrant worker. Due to his mild mental disability, Lennie depends completely upon **George**, his friend and traveling companion, for guidance and protection. The two men share a vision of a farm that they will someday own together. Although Lennie is gentle and kind, he does not understand his own strength, and his love of petting soft things results in disaster when he inadvertently kills the flirtatious wife of the hot-tempered rancher **Curley**. Lennie's innocence raises him to a standard of pure goodness that is more poetic and literary than realistic.

Lennox

Macbeth
William Shakespeare

A Scottish nobleman.

Mary Lennox

The Secret Garden
Frances Hodgson Burnett

A ten-year-old girl who, after the death of her parents in India, is sent to live with her uncle in Yorkshire, England. At first, Mary beats her servants, calls them appalling names, and does not mourn her nanny's death. Up to the moment that she sets foot into the garden, Mary is closed off: she has loved no one, and has been utterly unloved. Though she knows nothing about gardening, Mary clears space around the green shoots. Mary begins a friendship with a common moor boy named **Dickon Sowerby**. She evolves from a spoiled, unloved and unloving creature to a girl who is full of spirit and surrounded by friends.

Pope Leo X

The Prince
Niccolò Machiavelli

Elected pope in 1513. He supported the Medici family.

Leon

Madame Bovary
Gustave Flaubert

Emma Bovary's friend in Yonville, who later becomes her lover. Leon is shy, sentimental, and sexually innocent. Like Emma, Leon loves romantic novels and lofty ideals. After his first romance with Emma, Leon decides to go to Paris to study law. He loves Emma, but her sentiments make their romance impossible, and he is utterly bored in Yonville. When Emma reunites with him later, she is highly impressed by the sophistication he acquired in the city. He now perceives Emma to be unsophisticated and thinks he can win her love. Emma and Leon try to make one another into romantic ideals but fail to connect with each other as real individuals. Emma eventually starts to act domineeringly toward him, and he reacts with resentment. He marries a well-bred young woman shortly after Emma's death.

Brother Leon

The Chocolate War
Robert Cormier

The corrupt head administrator of the Trinity School. Brother Leon gets entangled by borrowing unauthorized funds and spending them all on chocolates for a school sale. He is so desperate to cover himself that he asks **The Vigils** for help, thus sanctioning their cruel methods and means.

Leonato

Much Ado About Nothing
William Shakespeare

The respected, elderly father of **Hero**, uncle of **Beatrice**, and brother of **Antonio**. Leonato, at whose home the action takes place, is the governor of Messina, Italy, second in social power only to **Don Pedro**. After his daughter is matched up with **Claudio**, Leonato conspires with his friends to trick **Benedick** into falling in love with Beatrice. Stricken by grief after Claudio's public humiliation of Hero, Leonato decides to challenge Claudio to a duel.

Aunt Léonie

Swann's Way
Marcel Proust

Marcel's great aunt, who is convinced that she will die at any moment and tries to get as much sympathy as possible for her various "ailments." It is she who dipped her madeleines in tea.

Leonine

Pericles
William Shakespeare

A murderer hired by **Dionyza** to kill **Marina**. Leonine fails when Marina is captured by pirates. Dionyza poisons him to keep him silent.

The Winter's Tale
William Shakespeare

Leontes

The king of Sicilia, **Hermione**'s husband, and **Polixenes**'s childhood friend. He is gripped by jealous fantasies that convince him that Polixenes has been having an affair with Hermione. Leontes's jealousy leads to the destruction of his family.

A Separate Peace
John Knowles

Elwin Lepellier

A classmate of **Gene Forrester** and **Finny**. Elwin Lepellier, called Leper Lepellier, is a mild, gentle boy from Vermont who adores nature and engages in peaceful, outdoor-oriented hobbies. He is the first boy from Gene's class to enlist in the army, but military life proves too much for him, and he suffers hallucinations and a breakdown. He shows up around the Devon School after his breakdown, and testifies that Gene deliberately caused Finny to fall from the tree. Leper's slight madness causes Finny to acknowledge that World War II actually exists.

Antony and Cleopatra and *Julius Caesar*
William Shakespeare

Marcus Aemilius Lepidus

The third member of **Mark Antony** and **Octavius Caesar**'s coalition, both politically and personally. In *Julius Caesar*, Antony has a low opinion of Lepidus, but **Octavius** trusts his loyalty. In *Antony and Cleopatra*, Lepidus attempts to keep the peace between Octavius Caesar and Antony, but fails when Caesar imprisons him after the defeat of **Pompey**. Caesar takes over all of Lepidus's power and possessions, en route to becoming the first Roman emperor.

Ceremony
Leslie Marmon Silko

Leroy

A childhood friend of **Tayo**'s and **Harley**'s sidekick and drinking buddy.

Jazz
Toni Morrison

Henry LesTroy

Vera Louise Gray's lover. Henry LesTroy resides near **Colonel Wordsworth Gray**'s old plantation in Vienna, Virginia. He does not know why or where Vera goes when she leaves for Baltimore, Maryland, and he is surprised when **Golden Gray** appears at his door, claiming to be his son. He did not know that he impregnated Vera Louise. Before the newly met father and son are able to talk, **Wild** screams and gives birth to **Joe Trace**.

The Phantom Tollbooth
Norton Juster

Lethargians

Minute creatures who live in perpetual boredom in the Doldrums. They change colors to match their surroundings and sometimes enforce laws against thinking and laughing.

Napoleon Letsitsi

Cry, the Beloved Country
Alan Paton

The agricultural expert hired by **James Jarvis** to teach better farming techniques to the people of Ndotsheni. A well-educated middle-class black man, Letsitsi earns a good salary and is eager to help build his country.

Letta

Death of a Salesman
Arthur Miller

A young woman who meets **Happy Loman** and **Biff Loman** at Frank's Chop House. She is accompanied by **Miss Forsythe**, and the two women seem to be prostitutes.

Lettie

Pigs in Heaven
Barbara Kingsolver

Cash Stillwater's sister and the nosiest woman in Heaven, Oklahoma. Lettie helps orchestrate the love affair between Cash and **Alice Greer**.

Aryeh Lev

My Name Is Asher Lev
Chaim Potok

Asher Lev's father. Well-respected and highly intelligent, Aryeh is incredibly driven to work hard for the cause in which he believes. He has a strong sense of morality and is deeply committed to his religion. His son's misbehavior deeply disturbs and hurts him. Though he works with high-ranking government officials, he has a hard time relating to those whose value systems are different from his own.

Asher Lev

My Name Is Asher Lev
Chaim Potok

The protagonist and narrator of the book. The book traces Asher's development as a person and an artist. He is immensely gifted as an artist and, when younger, not in control of himself. He often seems detached from the world around him and generally spaced out. As he grows older, Asher becomes more in touch with himself and learns to channel his feelings into artwork. As he gets older, he outgrows his teacher and becomes more reflective.

Rivkeh Lev

My Name Is Asher Lev
Chaim Potok

Asher Lev's mother. She is kind and supportive. Deeply disturbed by the death of her brother, she worries a lot. She is intelligent, loving, and caring; she cares deeply for the two men in her life—Asher and **Aryeh Lev**—and is troubled by their inability to get along.

Shelly Levene

Glengarry Glen Ross
David Mamet

A washed-up real estate salesman. Shelly "The Machine" Levene was successful years ago but recently has hit a streak of "bad luck" and finds himself in danger of getting fired. He desperately wants to save his career, and this desperation is grotesquely apparent, as evidenced by his paying **John Williamson** for leads in the first scene and his ultimate guilt in robbing the real estate office.

Levi

The Red Tent
Anita Diamant

A son of **Jacob** by **Leah**. Levi and his brother **Simon** are incredibly cruel men. They sell their own brother, **Joseph**, into slavery, and are responsible for counseling Jacob with their greedy influence and savage plans. Concerned that their own legacies and power might diminish, they reject **Dinah**'s marriage to **Shalem** and slaughter Shalem and all of the men of Shechem in their sleep.

Alice Levin

Jurassic Park
Michael Crichton

A technician at Columbia University who sees **Tina Bowman**'s drawing of the lizard that attacked her and identifies it as a dinosaur.

Konstantin Dmitrich Levin

Anna Karenina
Leo Tolstoy

Ekaterina Alexandrovna Shcherbatskaya's husband. Konstantin is a socially awkward but generous-hearted landowner who, along with **Anna Arkadyevna Karenina**, is the coprotagonist of the novel. Whereas Anna's pursuit of love ends in tragedy, Levin's long courtship of Kitty ultimately ends in a happy marriage. Levin is intellectual and philosophical but applies his thinking to practical matters such as agriculture. He aims to be sincere and productive in whatever he does, and he resigns from his post in local government because he sees it as useless and bureaucratic.

Nikolai Dmitrich Levin

Anna Karenina
Leo Tolstoy

Konstantin Dmitrich Levin's sickly, thin brother. The freethinking Nikolai is largely estranged from his brothers, but over the course of the novel he starts to spend more time with Levin. Nikolai is representative of liberal social thought among certain Russian intellectuals of the period; his reformed-prostitute girlfriend, **Marya Nikolaevna**, is living proof of his unconventional, radically democratic viewpoint.

George Levitan

Black Like Me
John Howard Griffin

The owner of *Sepia* magazine. He warns **John Howard Griffin** of the dangers he will face if he goes through with his plan to pose as a black man.

General Levy

Ender's Game
Orson Scott Card

A high military official who questions **Colonel Graff** about **Ender Wiggin**'s progress at Battle School.

Morris Levy

The Power of One
Bryce Courtenay

A very rich Jewish boy who becomes **Peekay**'s partner at the Prince of Wales School. Morrie, who is a foil for Peekay, teaches Peekay the tricks of business-gambling and pulls Peekay into all kinds of scams. Morrie is a loner, an intellectual, a fine joke-teller, and a generous friend. Through Peekay he comes to know black people for the first time in his life, and he becomes extremely invested in the night school that he and Peekay start for the black boxers at **Solly Goldman**'s gym.

Lewandowski

All Quiet on the Western Front
Erich Maria Remarque

A patient in the Catholic hospital where **Paul Bäumer** and **Albert Kropp** recuperate from their wounds.

Lewis

King John
William Shakespeare

King Philip's son and the heir (dauphin) to the French throne. Lewis is married to **Blanche**, the daughter of the King of Spain, to cement the tenuous French-English truce, but heads to war when **Cardinal Pandulph** pressures Philip. Though he continues his war after Pandulph asks him to pull back, he ultimately allows the Cardinal to broker a peace after his reinforcements perish at sea and the English lords desert him.

Cecil Lewis

The Iceman Cometh
Eugene O'Neill

A veteran from the Boer War. Captain Lewis dreams of returning to England, having been driven out upon losing his regiment's money in a drunken night of gambling.

Mercy Lewis

The Crucible
Arthur Miller

The servant in **Thomas Putnam**'s household. Mercy Lewis belongs to the group of girls who are pushed around and influenced by **Abigail Williams**. Like the other girls following Abigail's lead in the courtroom, Mercy shivers and screams in order to make it seems like **Mary Warren** is bewitching them. When **Reverend John Hale** returns to Salem around the time of the hanging of **John Proctor**, **Reverend Parris** reports that Mercy and Abigail vanished from Salem after robbing him.

Mr. Lewis

The Remains of the Day
Kazuo Ishiguro

An American gentleman who visited Darlington Hall for the March 1923 conference. He is a congenial man who smiles often. On the last night of the conference, Mr. Lewis makes a speech denouncing **Lord Darlington** as an "amateur" whose noble instincts are out of date in the modern world.

Monsieur Lheureux

Madame Bovary
Gustave Flaubert

A sly, sinister merchant and moneylender in Yonville. Lheureux leads **Emma Bovary** into debt, financial ruin, and eventually suicide by playing on her weakness for luxury and extravagance. He coaxes her into making extravagant and unwise purchases.

Mr. Lies

Angels in America
Tony Kushner

An imaginary travel agent who resembles a jazz musician. Mr. Lies is one of **Harper**'s medication-induced creations. She summons him whenever she wants to escape from her present surroundings, though Mr. Lies cautions her that there is a limit to her ability to flee from reality.

Liet-Kynes

Dune
Frank Herbert

A "planetologist," or planetary ecologist, on Arrakis. Unbeknownst to **Baron Vladimir Harkonnen**, he is also a member of the Fremen. He works with the Fremen to change Arrakis from a desert planet into a lush, green paradise.

Lieutenant

The Red Badge of Courage
Stephen Crane

Henry Fleming's commander in battle, a youthful officer who swears profusely during the fighting. As Henry gains recognition for doing brave deeds, he and the lieutenant develop sympathy for each other, often feeling that they must work together to motivate the rest of the men.

Lieutenant

The Power and the Glory
Graham Greene

A believer in the law, a staunch opponent of the Catholic Church, and **the Priest**'s pursuer. The lieutenant's hatred of the Church stems from a traumatic event in his childhood. He lives a modest, almost monastic life, but his "dapper," well-kempt appearance stands in striking contrast to the confusion and grime that surround him. The ruthless tactics he employs in his pursuit of the priest seem to contradict his left-wing political and social ideals.

Lifeguard

One Flew over the Cuckoo's Nest
Ken Kesey

A patient and a former football player who was committed to the ward eight years ago and often experiences hallucinations. The lifeguard tells **Randle McMurphy** that committed patients can leave only when **Nurse Ratched** permits, which changes McMurphy's initial rebelliousness into temporary conformity.

Lignière

Cyrano de Bergerac
Edmond Rostand

Baron Christian de Neuvillette's friend. Lignière is a disheveled-looking satirist and drunkard with many powerful enemies. **Cyrano de Bergerac** protects Lignière from the hundred men hired by **Comte de Guiche** to ambush him.

Emperor of Lilliput

Gulliver's Travels
Jonathan Swift

The ruler of **Lilliputians**. He impresses **Gulliver** with his power and majesty, but his small stature renders his delusions of grandeur laughable.

Lilliputians

Gulliver's Travels
Jonathan Swift

A race of miniature, six-inch-tall people. The Lilliputians have been engaged in longstanding war with the similarly statured **Blefuscudians** over the proper way to break eggs. Prone to conspiracies and jealousies, they are quick to take advantage of **Gulliver**. Gulliver joins the Lilliputian effort only later to fight on the Blefuscudian side.

Fay Lillman

Flowers for Algernon
Daniel Keyes

Charlie Gordon's neighbor in the apartment building that he moves into after running away from the scientific convention. Fay is an attractive, free-spirited, and sexually liberal artist whose favorite pastimes are drinking and dancing. She embarks on a brief affair with Charlie.

Lily

Dubliners
James Joyce

Julia Morkan and **Kate Morkan**'s housemaid, who rebukes **Gabriel Conroy** in "The Dead."

Lily

The Giver
Lois Lowry

Jonas's sister. She is a chatterbox and does not know quite when to keep her mouth shut, but she is also extremely practical and well-informed for a little girl. Lily owns a "comfort object," a community-issued stuffed elephant. She also notices that Jonas has "funny eyes" like **Gabriel**.

Lin

Cloud Nine
Caryl Churchill

A brash lesbian and a single mother, unafraid to let others know where she stands. She disciplines her daughter **Cathy** using copious swearing, encouraging her daughter to wear jeans instead of dresses and play with guns. Lin steals her best friend **Victoria** from Victoria's husband **Martin**, taking up a home with Victoria and **Edward** in a sexual threesome.

Dr. Lincoln

I Know Why the Caged Bird Sings
Maya Angelou

A white dentist in Stamps, Arkansas, to whom **Momma** lent money during the Great Depression. Despite Momma's favor, Dr. Lincoln tells her that he would rather stick his hand into a dog's mouth than into **Maya Johnson**'s mouth because she is a little black girl.

Jerry Lind

Prodigal Summer
Barbara Kingsolver

The Forest Service representative who brings **Deanna Wolfe** her mail and supplies each month.

Linda

Brave New World
Aldous Huxley

Beta worker and mother to **John**. Abandoned on the New Mexico Savage Reservation while pregnant with **the Director**'s son, Linda was forced to carry the child to term, an unspeakably taboo act in the World State. Her societal conditioning towards promiscuity and materialism left her an outcast amongst the savages, with only intermittent lovers like **Pope** and her son to comfort her, while away from the World State's technology she grew old, infirm and fat. When she is found by **Bernard Marx** and brought back to society, her appearance scandalized the Director, and she took refuge in ever-increasing doses of soma until she lapsed into a coma and died.

Linda

The Things They Carried
Tim O'Brien

Tim O'Brien's first love. Linda died of a brain tumor in the fifth grade.

Mrs. Linde

A Doll's House
Henrik Ibsen

Nora's childhood friend. Practical, sensible, and motherly, Mrs. Linde is a foil for the childlike and romantic Nora. Her sympathetically portrayed betrothal to the treacherous **Krogstad** shows that Ibsen does not attack marriage as an institution.

Mr. Karl Lindner

A Raisin in the Sun
Lorraine Hansberry

The only white character in the play. Mr. Lindner arrives at the Youngers' apartment from the Clybourne Park Improvement Association. He reveals that he and the neighborhood coalition believe that the Youngers' presence in Clybourne Park would destroy the community there. Mr. Lindner tells the Youngers that the association is prepared to offer them more money than they are to pay for the house in exchange for not moving to Clybourne Park.

Lindo's mother

The Joy Luck Club
Amy Tan

Grandmother to **Waverly**. After **Lindo** was engaged at the age of two, Lindo's mother began to talk about Lindo as if she were already the daughter of her future mother-in-law **Huang Taitai**. Lindo knows that her mother did so only because she wanted to keep herself from feeling too attached to the daughter she loved so dearly but had already given away.

Ingrid Lindstrom

Out of Africa
Isak Dinesen

The narrator's Swedish friend who helps her before the final move. Ingrid is a struggling farm owner like the narrator who has tried many different techniques to keep her land profitable.

Placida Linero

Chronicle of a Death Foretold
Gabriel García Márquez

Santiago Nasar's mother. She has a well-earned reputation as an interpreter of dreams. On the day of his death, Santiago goes into her house to get an aspirin for his headache. She never forgives herself for mixing up the bad omen of birds with the good omen of trees in her son's dream.

Lena Lingard

My Ántonia
Willa Cather

A Norwegian immigrant's daughter and a friend of **Ántonia Shimerda**'s. Lena has a brief liaison with **Jim Burden** in Black Hawk and a more extended relationship with him in Lincoln, where she sets up her own dressmaker's shop. Lena is pretty and blond, and she craves independence and excitement.

Mr. Lingerle

Dicey's Song
Cynthia Voigt

Maybeth's music teacher. Mr. Lingerle responds warmly to **Gram**'s hospitality, and his support and generosity are a boon to the Tillermans throughout the novel.

James Lingk

Glengarry Glen Ross
David Mamet

A quiet, timid man to whom **Ricky Roma** sells a piece of Florida land.

Carl Linstrum

O Pioneers!
Willa Cather

A boy whose family owns the farm next to **John Bergson**'s homestead. As a teenager, Carl establishes a special bond with **Alexandra Bergson**. When Carl returns to the Divide as an adult, his friendship with Alexandra evolves into a deeper attraction. At the novel's end, they resolve to marry.

Edgar Linton

Wuthering Heights
Emily Brontë

Isabella Linton's brother. He marries **Catherine** and fathers **young Catherine**. Well-bred but rather spoiled as a boy, Edgar grows into a tender, constant, but cowardly man.

Isabella Linton

Wuthering Heights
Emily Brontë

Edgar Linton's sister, who falls in love with **Heathcliff**, marries him, and gives birth to **Linton Heathcliff.** She sees Heathcliff as a romantic figure, like a character in a novel. Ultimately, she ruins her life by falling in love with him. He never returns her feelings and treats her as a tool in his quest for revenge on the Linton family.

Mr. Linton

Wuthering Heights
Emily Brontë

Edgar Linton and **Isabella Linton**'s father. Mr. Linton owns Thrushcross Grange when **Heathcliff** and **Catherine** are children.

Mrs. Linton

Wuthering Heights
Emily Brontë

Mr. Linton's snobbish wife. Mrs. Linton does not like her children, **Edgar Linton** and **Isabella Linton,** to associate with **Heathcliff**. She instills social ambitions in **Catherine**.

Mr. Lipari

A View from the Bridge
Arthur Miller

A butcher who lives upstairs from **Eddie Carbone**, **Beatrice**, **Catherine**, **Marco**, and **Rodolpho**. Eddie blames Mr. Lipari for the arrest of Marco and Rodolpho by the immigration police, even though it was Eddie himself who called the police out of craziness and jealousy.

Mrs. Lipari

A View from the Bridge
Arthur Miller

The upstairs neighbor of **Catherine**, **Beatrice**, and **Eddie Carbone**, and the wife of **Mr. Lipari**. Mrs. Lipari agrees to give **Marco** and **Rodolpho** a room in her home when Eddie kicks the men out of his house in a jealous craze over Rodolpho and Catherine's relationship.

Lip-lip

White Fang
Jack London

The bane of **White Fang**'s existence. Lip-lip is another pup in the Native American village who robs White Fang of any puppyhood by turning all the dogs against him. White Fang kills Lip-lip in a fight.

Lisa

The Remains of the Day
Kazuo Ishiguro

The maid hired to fill the staff shortage after the dismissal of **Ruth** and **Sarah**. Lisa applies for the position with dubious references, causing **Stevens** to be wary of her professional promise. Though Lisa improves quickly under **Miss Kenton**'s tutelage, she eventually elopes with the footman.

Lisa

Girl, Interrupted
Susanna Kaysen

Susanna Kaysen's fellow patient and the effective leader of the girls on the ward. Lisa is proud of her diagnosis as a sociopath, a personality driven by self-interest. Lisa throws tantrums and plans other patients' escapes when she isn't escaping herself. Initially in awe of Lisa's apparent confidence, Susanna learns that Lisa cares little for the consequences of her actions and can be willfully cruel.

Lisa Cody

Girl, Interrupted
Susanna Kaysen

A patient who becomes fast friends with **Lisa** only to be cruelly rejected. Diagnosed, like Lisa, as a sociopath, Lisa Cody emulates Lisa's behavior. Lisa later turns against her, and Lisa Cody leaves the hospital. Returning from an escape to Boston one day, Lisa tells the other girls that Lisa Cody has become a "real" junkie.

Bonnie Lisbon

The Virgin Suicides
Jeffrey Eugenides

The middle Lisbon child at age fifteen. She is quiet, docile, skittish, and exceptionally pious. As the Lisbon house declines, she begins appearing on the porch before dawn, thinner each day, to recite the rosary. She dies by hanging herself.

Cecilia Lisbon

The Virgin Suicides
Jeffrey Eugenides

The youngest of the Lisbon girls at age thirteen. Cecilia is mystical, precocious, shy, and considered weird even by her sisters. She habitually wears an ill-fitting vintage 1920s wedding gown, stained and cut short. She bites her nails, invokes the Virgin Mary, and spends hours listening to wailing Celtic music that she has ordered by mail. In her meticulous diary entries, discovered after her death, Cecilia is remarkably unselfconscious and speaks of her sisters and herself as a single entity. In her first suicide attempt, she slits her wrists in the bath, the event that sets off the Lisbon cycle of tragedies. Cecilia's second, successful suicide attempt cements the cycle when she jumps onto a spiked fence.

Lux Lisbon

The Virgin Suicides
Jeffrey Eugenides

The second-youngest of the Lisbon girls at age fourteen. Beautiful, sexy, adventurous, and eventually promiscuous, Lux epitomizes all the desirable qualities of the Lisbon girls. She is a secret smoker and gets rides on motorcycles with delinquent boys long before she begins her campaign of sex on the Lisbon roof. The only boy who catches Lux off guard is **Trip Fontaine**, her masculine foil. Lux is responsible for the sisters' confinement to the house for most of the winter, a punishment that has disastrous consequences. Lux dies from carbon-monoxide poisoning.

Mary Lisbon

The Virgin Suicides
Jeffrey Eugenides

The second-oldest of the Lisbon girls at age sixteen. Mary Lisbon is prim, proper, and poised. As the house decays, she attempts to maintain her appearance, and wears bright sweaters to collect the mail. After her unsuccessful suicide attempt, Mary spends a month sleeping and obsessively showering while the community faithfully waits for her suicide. She dies by taking sleeping pills.

Mr. Lisbon

The Virgin Suicides
Jeffrey Eugenides

The father of the Lisbon family. A thin, effeminate, retiring man with a high, boyish voice, Mr. Lisbon teaches math at the local high school. He seems to enjoy his job and to throw himself into his work. Despite his accommodating nature, he often feels lost amid the flurry of femininity at home. Mr. Lisbon is completely cowed by his domineering wife and automatically defers to all her decisions, however extreme.

Mrs. Lisbon

The Virgin Suicides
Jeffrey Eugenides

The Lisbon girls' mother, a forceful matriarch who heads the household. Heavy and commandeering, with steel-wool hair and glasses, she bears little resemblance to her five lovely daughters. Mrs. Lisbon strictly supervises her daughters' comings and goings, television-watching, and church attendance. Many of her rules for the girls—no makeup, no revealing clothes, no rock music—reflect her brand of rigid Catholic piety. She is permanently suspicious of the outside world.

Therese Lisbon

The Virgin Suicides
Jeffrey Eugenides

The oldest Lisbon girl at age seventeen. Therese Lisbon is intellectual and studious. She reads textbooks, grows seahorses, attends science conventions, uses a ham radio, and aspires to attend an Ivy League college. Physically, she is more awkward than her sisters. She dies from a combination of sleeping pills and gin.

Lise

Cyrano de Bergerac
Edmond Rostand

Ragueneau's sharp-tongued wife. She does not approve of her husband's patronage of the local poets. Unhappy and frustrated, she leaves Ragueneau for a musketeer.

Larry Lish

A Prayer for Owen Meany
John Irving

The over-sophisticated, cowardly Gravesend Academy boy who reveals to the police that **Owen Meany** has been making fake IDs for academy students, giving **Mr. White** an excuse to expel Owen.

Mitzy Lish

A Prayer for Owen Meany
John Irving

Larry Lish's mother, a wealthy divorcee who tells **Owen Meany** about John F. Kennedy's affair with Marilyn Monroe.

Dr. Lister

I Never Promised You a Rose Garden
Joanne Greenberg

The Blaus' family physician. **Esther** and **Jacob** put **Deborah** in the mental hospital at his recommendation.

Mrs. Lithebe

Cry, the Beloved Country
Alan Paton

The woman with whom **Stephen Kumalo** stays in Johannesburg. Mrs. Lithebe is a Msutu woman who lives in Sophiatown and takes in boarders, especially priests.

Little Ann

Where the Red Fern Grows
Wilson Rawls

One of **Billy Colman**'s red bone coonhounds that he saved up to buy. She is smaller but smarter than **Old Dan**. She wins the beauty competition at the coon-hunting championship on the first day. When Old Dan dies, Little Ann dies soon afterward, having lost her will to live.

Little boy

Ragtime
E. L. Doctorow

Son of **Mother** and **Father**, the little boy is the narrative voice for much of the novel. Precocious, intelligent, observant, and curious, the little boy is constantly learning about the world around him. He forms a close friendship with **Tateh**'s little girl **Sha**.

Little Father Time

Jude the Obscure
Thomas Hardy

Jude Fawley and **Arabella Donn**'s son, raised in Australia by Arabella's parents, and then raised by Jude and **Susanna Bridehead**. He is said to have the mind of an old man, though he is a young child.

Little girl

Ragtime
E. L. Doctorow

A quiet and reserved girl. She grows more animated and happier when she leaves New York City. She becomes good friends with the **little boy**.

Earl Little

The Autobiography of Malcolm X
Malcolm X & Alex Haley

Malcolm X's father. A preacher and political organizer from Georgia, Earl is a tall and outspoken authority figure in Malcolm's early years. Earl's assassination by whites for preaching the Black Nationalist ideas of Marcus Garvey makes him a martyr for black nationalism.

Ella Little

The Autobiography of Malcolm X
Malcolm X & Alex Haley

Malcolm X's half-sister on his father's side. When Malcolm is an adolescent, Ella provides him with a model of female strength and black pride. She represents family unity within the autobiography. She welcomes Malcolm into her home in Boston and always supports him, later lending him money for his pilgrimage to Mecca.

Louise Little

The Autobiography of Malcolm X
Malcolm X & Alex Haley

Malcolm X's fair-skinned black mother, who endures the worst of the Great Depression. For Malcolm, Louise represents the harm that the white government does even when it claims to be acting charitably. Welfare agents separate Louise from her children and put her in a mental hospital, and Malcolm's insistence on visiting her regularly shows his strong commitment to her.

Reginald Little

The Autobiography of Malcolm X
Malcolm X & Alex Haley

Malcolm X's younger brother. Malcolm takes Reginald under his wing from an early age and continues to protect him in Harlem. Malcolm's later justification of Reginald's eventual insanity as retribution for sinning shows Malcolm's commitment to the principles of Islam.

Eunice Littlefield

Babbitt
Sinclair Lewis

Howard Littlefield's movie-crazy daughter. Eunice elopes with **Ted Babbitt** at the end of the novel.

Howard Littlefield

Babbitt
Sinclair Lewis

An executive for the Traction Street Company and **Babbitt**'s neighbor and friend. **Ted Babbitt** elopes with Littlefield's daughter, **Eunice**.

Mary Littlejohn

The Member of the Wedding
Carson McCullers

A girl who befriends **Frankie Addams**. Two years older than Frankie, she is mature enough to satisfy Frankie's desire to grow up, but close enough to Frankie's age that the two of them can connect emotionally.

Miss Lily Mae Littlepaugh

All the King's Men
Robert Penn Warren

Mortimer Littlepaugh's sister, an old spiritual medium who sells her brother's suicide note to Jack, giving him the proof he needs about **Judge Irwin** and the bribe.

Mortimer L. Littlepaugh

All the King's Men
Robert Penn Warren

The man who preceded **Judge Irwin** as counsel for the American Electric Power Company in the early 1900s. When Judge Irwin took Littlepaugh's job as part of the bribe, Littlepaugh confronted **Governor Stanton** about the judge's illegal activity. When the governor protected the judge, Littlepaugh committed suicide.

Liu

The Good Earth
Pearl S. Buck

A town grain merchant. Liu is **Wang Lung**'s relative by marriage; his children marry **Wang Lung's first son** and **Wang Lung's second daughter**.

Dr. Livesey

Treasure Island
Robert Louis Stevenson

The local doctor. Dr. Livesey is wise and practical, and **Jim Hawkins** respects him. Livesey exhibits common sense and rational thought while on the island, and his idea to send **Ben Gunn** to spook the pirates reveals a deep understanding of human nature.

Clyde Livingston

Holes
Louis Sachar

The famous baseball player whose shoes **Stanley Yelnats** is accused of stealing. He suffers from the same foot odor that **Charles Walker**, or Trout, had. It turns out that **Zero** had stolen the shoes and left them on top of a parked car, from which they fell onto Stanley, who took them home to **Mr. Yelnats** for his experiments on a foot-odor cure. After Stanley is exonerated, Clyde becomes the spokesman for Stanley's father's odor cure.

Harold Livotny

The Joy Luck Club
Amy Tan

Lena's husband. He insists on splitting the cost of everything they share, saying this makes their love purer. In fact, the practice renders Lena powerless.

Liza

Notes from Underground
Fyodor Dostoevsky

A young prostitute whom **the Underground Man** tries to rescue after sleeping with her at a brothel. Liza is somewhat shy and innocent despite her profession, and she responds emotionally to the Underground

Man's efforts to convince her of the error of her ways. She is naturally loving and sympathetic, but she also has a sense of pride and nobility.

Lisa Ivanovna

The Death of Ivan Ilych
Leo Tolstoy

Ivan Ilych Golovin's daughter. Lisa is very much like her mother, **Praskovya Fyodorovna Golovina**. Selfish and easily annoyed, Lisa resents any influence that distracts her from her own contentment. Her father's suffering inconveniences her more than anything else.

Lizaveta Ivanovna

Crime and Punishment
Fyodor Dostoevsky

Alyona Ivanovna's sister. Lizaveta is simple, almost "idiotic," and a virtual servant to her sister. **Sofya Semyonovna Marmeladova** later reveals to **Rodion Romanovich Raskolnikov** that she and Lizaveta were friends.

Stinking Lizaveta

The Brothers Karamazov
Fyodor Dostoevsky

A young retarded girl who lives as the village idiot. She dies giving birth to **Pavel Fyodorovich Smerdyakov**, leading most people to suspect that **Fyodor Pavlovich Karamazov** either seduced or raped her.

Lizzie

Regeneration
Pat Barker

A friend of **Sarah Lumb**'s. Lizzie is a fellow worker in the munitions factory in Scotland. Her husband abuses her, and she is happy that war has given her the freedom to work and be separated from him while he is away.

Lloyd

Bless Me, Ultima
Rudolfo A. Anaya

One of a group of exuberant boys who frequently curse and fight. Lloyd enjoys reminding everyone that they can be sued for even the most minor offenses. The other boys in the group are **Abel**, **Bones**, **Ernie**, **Horse**, **the Vitamin Kid**, and **Red**.

Colonel Edward Lloyd

Narrative of the Life of Frederick Douglass
Frederick Douglass

Captain Anthony's boss and **Frederick Douglass**'s first owner. Colonel Lloyd is an extremely rich man who owns all of the slaves and lands where Douglass grows up. Lloyd insists on extreme subservience from his slaves and often punishes them unjustly.

Mr. Lloyd

Jane Eyre
Charlotte Brontë

The Reeds' apothecary. A kind man, Mr. Lloyd suggests that **Jane Eyre** be sent away to school. He writes a letter to **Maria Temple** denying **Mrs. Reed**'s charge that Jane is a liar.

Don Leo XII Loayza

Love in the Time of Cholera
Gabriel García Márquez

Florentino Ariza's paternal uncle and the president of the River Company of the Caribbean. Upon **Transito Ariza**'s request, he finds Florentino a job in a faraway city to help Florentino erase **Fermina Daza** from his memory. When Florentino returns, Don Leo grants Florentino yet another job at the River Company. He urges Florentino to marry **Leona Cassiani**, who becomes Don Leo's personal assistant. When Don Leo is too ill to continue running the River Company, he bequeaths it to Florentino.

Lobel

Fallen Angels
Walter Dean Myers

A member of **Richie Perry**'s squad. Jewish and possibly homosexual, Lobel is the target of prejudice nearly as frequently as the black soldiers, to whom he pledges his support in racial skirmishes. Lobel is a devoted fan of the movies, and he distances himself from the horror of battle by imagining that he is merely playing a role in a war film.

Gilderoy Lockhart

Harry Potter and the Chamber of Secrets
J. K. Rowling

The teacher of the class called "Defense Against the Dark Arts" during **Harry Potter**'s second year at Hogwarts. Lockhart is the author of many magical books, and the five-time winner of *Witch Weekly*'s Most Charming Smile Award. He is utterly useless and actually detrimental to Harry and **Ron Weasley** as they venture into the tunnels to confront the basilisk. Lockhart casts a memory-obliterating charm that backfires, leaving him muttering idiotically to himself.

Locksley

Ivanhoe
Sir Walter Scott

The leader of a gang of forest outlaws who rob from the rich and give to the poor, also known as the legendary Robin Hood. He and his merry men help **King Richard I** free the Saxon prisoners from Torquilstone and later save the king from **Waldemar Fitzurse**'s treacherous attack.

Lockwood

Wuthering Heights
Emily Brontë

A gentleman who rents Thrushcross Grange. Lockwood's narration forms a frame around **Nelly Dean**'s. A somewhat vain and presumptuous gentleman, Lockwood occasionally misunderstands the events of the story.

Lodovico

Othello
William Shakespeare

One of **Brabanzio**'s kinsmen, Lodovico acts as a messenger from Venice to Cyprus. He arrives in Cyprus in Act IV with letters announcing that **Othello** has been replaced by **Cassio** as governor. At the conclusion of the play, Lodovico orders **Iago**'s execution and wills the dead Othello's possessions to **Graziano**.

Don Lodowick

The Jew of Malta
Christopher Marlowe

Ferneze's son. Lodowick loves **Abigail** and is misled by **Barabas** into believing that he will marry her. This leads to the duel between Lodowick and **Mathias**.

Cassie Logan of *Roll of Thunder, Hear My Cry*

Roll of Thunder, Hear My Cry
Mildred D. Taylor

The narrator and protagonist. Cassie is the second-oldest Logan child and is in fourth grade. She has a fiery temper like her **Uncle Hammer**. In her naïvete, Cassie does not realize that a white store clerk in Strawberry is deliberately ignoring her and her brothers. The clerk makes Cassie leave the store, and Cassie bumps into **Lillian Jean Simms** and her father, who push Cassie into the street to make her apologize for bumping into them. Cassie is even more infuriated when **Big Ma** makes Cassie apologize. Cassie, though a little young to understand about racism completely, is clever enough to get her revenge on Lillian Jean. Cassie pretends for a month to be very nice to Lillian Jean. Lillian Jean confides her secrets to Cassie. Finally, Cassie beats her up, and when Lillian Jean threatens to tell **Mr. Simms**, Cassie threatens to tell everyone all of her secrets. Cassie also is the one who warns her family of a possible impending lynching that may occur at their home after she finds **T.J. Avery** beaten up by a mob incited by **Melvin Simms** and **R.W. Simms**.

Cassie Logan of *The Land*

The Land
Mildred D. Taylor

Paul-Edward Logan's older sister. Cassie moves to Atlanta and marries shortly after the novel begins. She is loving and motherly and tries to help Paul come to terms with the difficulty of living as a white-skinned black in their society. In the end, Cassie sends Paul a bank note for 1,100 dollars with a letter explaining that she has not only sent Paul her entire savings and everything she could borrow against her and her husband's business, but she sold the land their mother lived on—which, after emancipation, their mother had bought from their father. With this money Paul is able to buy **J. T. Hollenbeck**'s land.

Christopher-John Logan

Roll of Thunder, Hear My Cry
Mildred D. Taylor

A cheerful boy, Christopher-John is the second-youngest of the Logan children. He is timid. His brothers are **Stacey Logan** and **Little Man Logan**, and his sister is **Cassie Logan**. For Christmas, Christopher-John receives two volumes of Aesop's fables to share with Little Man.

Edward Logan

The Land
Mildred D. Taylor

Paul-Edward Logan's white father. Mr. Logan is a southern plantation owner who prospers from and participates in racist institutions, but he tries to treat blacks fairly and with respect. Edward raises his four sons, Paul and three white boys (**George Logan**, **Hammond Logan**, and **Robert Logan**). When Paul comes of age, Mr. Logan struggles to teach him the rules by which he must live as an adult, black male. In trying to teach his black children how they will have to act as black people in the world outside of the plantation, Mr. Logan sometimes treats Paul and **Cassie Logan** as society would treat them and not as equals in his household. Despite all this, Paul's father wants what is best for his son, and on his deathbed he only finds peace after he sees Paul once again.

George Logan

The Land
Mildred D. Taylor

Paul-Edward Logan's second-oldest, white brother. George is passionate and quick-tempered. Like **Hammond Logan**, George Logan vehemently professes having no racial bias toward Paul.

Granny Logan

The Bean Trees
Barbara Kingsolver

Lou Ann Ruiz's grandmother. She is provincial and harbors many prejudices about **Angel Ruiz**'s nationality. She hates the arid climate in Tucson and brings Lou Ann water from the Tug Fork River in Kentucky so that she may baptize **Dwayne Ray** properly.

Hammond Logan

The Land
Mildred D. Taylor

Paul-Edward Logan's oldest, white brother. Hammond Logan is fair-minded and even-tempered. He repeatedly tries to convince Paul that he is as much a brother to him as **Robert Logan** or **George Logan**.

Little Man Logan

Roll of Thunder, Hear My Cry
Mildred D. Taylor

The youngest of the Logan children. He is meticulously neat and becomes infuriated when standards of neatness are compromised.

Paul-Edward Logan

The Land
Mildred D. Taylor

The protagonist and narrator of the novel. Paul-Edward Logan is a steady, hardworking young man of mixed racial heritage. **Paul's mother** is half Native-American and half black. His father, **Edward Logan**, is white. Throughout his life, he struggles to come to terms with his relationship to his white, landowning and formerly slave-owning family and with his deep desire to own land. Paul is a skilled horseman and furniture maker and an industrious laborer. He is loyal and fair, and he reacts calmly in the face of cruelty and racism, while persistently trying to counteract bigotry and injustice.

Porky Logan

Alas, Babylon
Pat Frank

The fat, greedy man who defeated **Randy Bragg** in the election for representative to the state legislature. He dies of radiation poisoning from contaminated jewelry that he is hoarding.

Robert Logan

The Land
Mildred D. Taylor

One of **Paul-Edward Logan**'s white brothers. Robert is roughly the same age as Paul. He and Paul grow up side by side and spend almost their entire childhood playing together. Robert is even-tempered, gentle, and timorous. Robert expresses great distress when their father sends the two boys to different schools. As Robert grows into adolescence and spends the majority of his time with his peers at boarding school, he begins to perceive the significance of their racial differences, and the two begin to grow apart. After Robert betrays Paul, the two become irreparably estranged. Robert does show up the night before Paul will be forced to forfeit his dream acres, and brings money from **Cassie Logan**. Paul and Robert stay up all night talking despite their rift.

Stacey Logan

Roll of Thunder, Hear My Cry
Mildred D. Taylor

The oldest of the Logan children. He is part adult, part child. He is strong and clever, and ready to bend the rules in order to satisfy his siblings. **T.J. Avery** and Stacey have a rocky relationship throughout the novel. Stacey understands the way of the world well. He accepts the gift of a whistle from **Jeremy Simms**, but knows that it may be dangerous to accept gifts and be friends with a white boy. Stacey's biggest adult shock is when he, **Papa**, and **L.T. Morrison** are ambushed by members of the **Wallace** family on the road. Stacey feels responsible.

Logician

Rhinoceros
Eugène Ionesco

A highly rational man who appears only in the first act. He believes strictly in the laws of logic, though his attempts to prove anything often collapse.

Tom Loker

Uncle Tom's Cabin
Harriet Beecher Stowe

A slave hunter hired by **Mr. Haley** to bring back **Eliza Harris**, **Harry Harris**, and **George Harris**. Tom Loker first appears as a gruff, violent man. George shoots him when he tries to capture them, and, after he is healed by the Quakers, Loker experiences a transformation and chooses to join the Quakers rather than return to his old life.

Lola

Sister Carrie
Theodore Dreiser

A chorus girl who befriends **Carrie** in New York while they are working in the same show. Carrie moves in with Lola after she leaves **Hurstwood**.

Lolita

Lolita
Vladimir Nabokov

Humbert Humbert's stepdaughter and later his lover. To Humbert, she is both the embodiment of the ideal "nymphet" and the reincarnation of his beloved childhood sweetheart, **Annabel Leigh**. Lolita enslaves him sexually and eventually deserts him for **Clare Quilty**. She later marries **Richard Schiller** and dies in childbirth at age eighteen.

Ben Loman

Death of a Salesman
Arthur Miller

Willy Loman's wealthy older brother. He acquired a fortune at the age of twenty-one upon discovering an African diamond mine. Ben is a symbol of the success Willy so desperately craves for himself and his sons. After his death, Ben appears in Willy's daydreams and Willy is so disoriented that he talks to a dead brother as if he were present.

Biff Loman

Death of a Salesman
Arthur Miller

Willy Loman and **Linda Loman**'s elder son. Biff led a charmed life in high school as a football star with scholarship prospects, good male friends, and fawning female admirers. He failed math, however, and did not have enough credits to graduate. Since then, his kleptomania has gotten him fired from every job he has held. He's concerned that he has wasted his life, and his parents are disappointed in his unsteadiness. He is disappointed in himself and in the disparity between his life and the notions of value and success with which Willy indoctrinated him as a boy. He ultimately fails to reconcile his life with Willy's expectations of him.

Happy Loman

Death of a Salesman
Arthur Miller

Willy Loman and **Linda Loman**'s younger son. Happy has lived in his brother **Biff Loman**'s shadow all of his life, but he compensates by nurturing his relentless sex drive and professional ambition. Although he works as an assistant to an assistant buyer in a department store, Happy presents himself as supremely important. He longs to become an executive. He sleeps with the girlfriends and fiancées of his superiors and often takes bribes in an attempt to climb the corporate ladder. After his father's death, Happy resolves to stay in the city and carry out his father's dream by becoming a top businessman.

Linda Loman

Death of a Salesman
Arthur Miller

Willy Loman's loyal, loving wife. Linda suffers through Willy's grandiose dreams and self-delusions. Occasionally, she seems to be taken in by Willy's deluded hopes for future glory and success, but at other times, she seems far more realistic and less fragile than her husband. She has nurtured the family through all of Willy's misguided attempts at success, and her emotional strength and perseverance support Willy until his collapse. She tells her husband that he is the handsomest man ever, and that he is successful enough. After Willy's death, she apologizes for her inability to cry. She says that it seems as though he is on just another business trip.

Willy Loman

Death of a Salesman
Arthur Miller

An insecure, deluded traveling salesman. Willy believes wholeheartedly in the American dream of easy success and wealth, but he never achieves it. Despite his failures, he constantly maintains that he is a "big shot" in the sales world. He moans that he cannot move ahead because people do not seem to like him. When his illusions fail under the pressing realities of his life, his mental health begins to unravel. He has an affair, attempts to asphyxiate himself, and has automobile accidents that are actually failed suicide attempts. He contradicts himself often and talks to his deceased brother, **Ben Loman**, as though he were present. He kills himself, hoping that the insurance money from his sacrifice will allow his son to fulfill the American dream.

Charles Lomax

Major Barbara
George Bernard Shaw

A stereotypical "young man about town." A comic figure, he suffers the scolding of **Lady Britomart** throughout the play for his tactlessness and inarticulate speech. He repeatedly declares his allegiance to the Anglican Church, though these declarations only mask his propensity to align himself with the wealthy. He is engaged to **Sarah Undershaft** on a lark.

Philip Lombard

And Then There Were None
Agatha Christie

A mysterious, confident, and resourceful man who seems to have been a mercenary soldier in Africa. Lombard is far bolder and more cunning than most of the other characters, traits that allow him to survive almost until the end of the novel. His weakness is his chivalrous attitude toward women, particularly **Vera Claythorne**.

Miss Lonelyhearts

Miss Lonelyhearts
Nathanael West

The main character. Miss Lonelyhearts works as an advice columnist to his miserable readership at a New York newspaper, under the eye of his editor, **Shrike**. Miss Lonelyhearts is profoundly depressed by the letters he receives and by the moral climate around him. He believes that Jesus Christ is the only answer, but he has difficult integrating the concepts of Christian love into his personal life, as in his failed relationship with **Betty** and his affairs with **Mary Shrike** and **Fay Doyle**.

Long

The Hairy Ape
Eugene O'Neill

A fireman who preaches Marxism. He asks what right **Mildred** and the engineers have to come look at the firemen like animals in a zoo. Long takes **Yank** to New York City to prove to Yank that all members of the upper class are the same.

Long Jiaguo

The Kitchen God's Wife
Amy Tan

Helen's first husband. Jiaguo is a good man who has done a serious wrong in his life. He marries Helen out of guilt for having wronged her sister, but the two turn out to have a good marriage. Jiaguo has a high rank in the air force but is humble. He forgives easily and is also easily swayed by his wife.

Ira Long

A Day No Pigs Would Die
Robert Newton Peck

The hired hand of **Mrs. Iris Bascom**, a distant neighbor to **Robert Peck**, **Lucy Peck**, and **Haven Peck**. He is a large, good-natured, and hardworking man, and though he is suspected of sleeping with Mrs. Bascom, a widow of two years, he is portrayed as very decent. He is responsible for telling **Benjamin Tanner** about Robert's desire to go to the Rutland fair.

Longaville

Love's Labour's Lost
William Shakespeare

One of the lords who join the king in his oath of scholarship. Longaville falls in love with **Maria**.

Neville Longbottom

The Harry Potter Series: Books 1–4
J. K. Rowling

A timid Hogwarts classmate of **Harry Potter**'s. He is a pudgy, very clumsy Gryffindor boy. Neville is friendly and loyal, but like **Ron Weasley**, he lacks Harry Potter's charisma. In *Harry Potter and the Sorcerer's Stone*, when the time comes to go after the Sorcerer's Stone, he fears punishment and threatens to report his friends to the teachers. In *Harry Potter and the Chamber of Secrets*, he leaves the passwords on a scrap of paper in the corridors, thus allowing **Sirius Black** to enter Gryffindor Tower. In *Harry Potter and the Goblet of Fire*, we learn that he lives with his grandmother because his parents were tortured and driven mad by followers of Voldemort.

General James Longstreet

The Killer Angels
Michael Shaara

General Robert E. Lee's second in command and, since the death of "Stonewall" Jackson, his most important general. At forty-two, Longstreet is full-bearded, slow talking, and crude. He is aware of the new nature of warfare, and he knows that military tactics have to change with new technology. He is stubborn, but he has great respect for Robert E. Lee. All three of his children were killed by a fever during the winter before the Battle of Gettysburg. This loss has sunk the usually jovial Longstreet into severe depression.

Loomis

Cold Sassy Tree
Olive Anne Burns

A black man in Cold Sassy. Loomis is an employee at the general store and the husband of the Tweedys' cook, **Queenie**. Loomis is a kind and loving man and an excellent preacher.

Adore Loomis

The Day of the Locust
Nathanael West

A young boy whose mother has been trying to turn him into a child star. Adore, despite his mother's efforts, seems to have become a child monster.

Miss Helen Loomis

Dandelion Wine
Ray Bradbury

A woman who shares her lifetime of adventures and belief in true love with **Bill Forrester**. She believes that the love they share, a love of the mind, is the greatest love, and that someday some version of the two of them will meet at the right time and share a lifetime of love.

Maybelle Loomis

The Day of the Locust
Nathanael West

A woman who lives in **Homer Simpson**'s neighborhood and has been in California for six years. Mrs. Loomis is trying to turn her son, **Adore**, into a child star. She is a member of the raw-foodist sect, one of the many gimmicky religions in Hollywood.

Melinda Loomis

Inherit the Wind
Jerome Lawrence & Robert E. Lee

A girl who is teased by **Howard Blair**. After learning about evolution in **Bertram Cates**'s class, Howard tells Melinda that she and her family were once worms or blobs of jelly. Melinda believes in the Bible and fears the idea of evolution.

Loosh

The Unvanquished
William Faulkner

A traitorous slave of the Sartoris family. He leads the Yankees to the plantation. **Philadelphy** does not share his vengefulness and feels sad and guilty, but she is unable to sway him from his course.

Yermolay Lopakhin

The Cherry Orchard
Anton Chekhov

A businessman, and the son of peasants on **Ranevsky**'s estate. His grandparents were owned by the Ranevsky family before freedom was granted to the serfs. Lopakhin is extremely self-conscious, especially in the presence of Ranevsky, perpetually complaining about his lack of education and refinement. His memories of the brutality of a peasant child's life contrast with Ranevsky's idyllic memories as a child of the landowning class. Lopakhin purchases the cherry orchard and proceeds to level it for his business.

Lord Chamberlain

Henry VIII
William Shakespeare

A lord of the court and member of the Council. Lord Chamberlain expresses distrust of **Cardinal Wolsey** after Wolsey seizes his horses and hands them over to **King Henry VIII**. Lord Chamberlain is a member of the council that tries **Cranmer, Archbishop of Canterbury**.

Lord Chancellor

Henry VIII
William Shakespeare

A lord of the court and member of the Council. Lord Chancellor presides over **Cranmer, Archbishop of Canterbury**'s trial.

Lord Chief Justice

Henry IV, Part II
William Shakespeare

The most powerful official of the law in England. Level-headed, calm, perceptive, and intelligent, the Lord Chief Justice is a close advisor to **King Henry IV**. His lawfulness stands in stark opposition to **Sir John Falstaff**'s anarchy.

Lord of the Flies

Lord of the Flies
William Golding

The name given to the sow's head that **Jack**'s gang impales on a stake and erects in the forest as an offering to the "beast." The Lord of the Flies comes to symbolize the primordial instincts of power and cruelty that take control of Jack's tribe.

Lorenzo

The Spanish Tragedy
Thomas Kyd

One of **Horatio**'s murderers. He is a proud verbal manipulator and a Machiavellian plotter. A great deceiver and manipulator of others, Horatio has an enthusiasm for the theater.

Lorenzo

The Merchant of Venice
William Shakespeare

A friend of **Bassanio**'s and **Antonio**'s. Lorenzo is in love with **Shylock**'s daughter **Jessica**, with whom he elopes to Belmont.

Aldonza Lorenzo

Don Quixote
Miguel de Cervantes

See **Dulcinea del Toboso**.

Mr. Lorne

Johnny Tremain
Esther Forbes

Rab Silsbee's uncle and master. Mr. Lorne owns the print shop that publishes the *Boston Observer*, a rebellious Whig newspaper.

Mrs. Lorne

Johnny Tremain
Esther Forbes

Mr. Lorne's wife. Mrs. Lorne sees through **Jonathan Tremain**'s scornful and arrogant exterior to the lonely boy inside. She treats him like a son and becomes like a second mother to him.

Lorraine

The Sound and the Fury
William Faulkner

Jason's mistress. Lorraine is a prostitute who lives in Memphis.

Jarvis Lorry

A Tale of Two Cities
Charles Dickens

An elderly businessman who works for Tellson's Bank. Mr. Lorry is a business-oriented bachelor with a strong moral sense and a good, honest heart.

Mr. Losberne

Oliver Twist
Charles Dickens

Mrs. Maylie's family physician. A hot-tempered but good-hearted old bachelor, Mr. Losberne is fiercely loyal to the Maylies and, eventually, to **Oliver Twist**.

King Lotharon

The Princess Bride
William Goldman

The King of Florin, and **Prince Humperdinck**'s father. King Lotharon is quite old, deaf, and difficult to understand.

Lotho

The Return of the King
J. R. R. Tolkien

Frodo Baggins's greedy and corrupt relative, whom Frodo suspects is the "Chief" of the police state in the Shire to whom the Shirrifs refer. The police state was set up by **Gríma Wormtongue** and **Saruman** during the War of the Ring, and remained active after **Sauron**'s defeat by the hands of Evil **Humans**.

Lotus

The Good Earth
Pearl S. Buck

A beautiful, delicate prostitute with bound feet and a bad temper. Lotus becomes **Wang Lung**'s concubine.

Tante Lou

A Lesson Before Dying
Ernest J. Gaines

Grant Wiggins's aunt and a deeply religious woman. Tante Lou resents Grant's cynical atheism. Tante Lou took in Grant when his parents moved away and became a mother figure to him.

Jimmy Louie

The Kitchen God's Wife
Amy Tan

Winnie's second husband. Jimmy Louie was madly in love with Winnie. He was a minister and a truly good man, husband, and father, serving as a foil to **Wen Fu**.

Samuel Louie

The Kitchen God's Wife
Amy Tan

Winnie and **Jimmy Louie**'s son. He lives and works in New Jersey.

Winnie Louie

The Kitchen God's Wife
Amy Tan

The novel's protagonist and narrator. Winnie Louie is a woman who has suffered a great deal in her life. A Chinese immigrant to America, Winnie, known in China as Weili, lost her mother at a very young age and entered into an abusive marriage. Her suffering has made her sometimes cynical but always strong. She has lived her life trying to keep the past out of her present.

Louis

The Heart Is a Lonely Hunter
Carson McCullers

A black boy who takes over **Willie**'s position in the New York Café after Willie goes to prison.

King Louis XI

Henry VI, Part III
William Shakespeare

The king of France and **Lady Bona**'s brother. Louis receives **Queen Margaret** at his court to hear her grievances against **King Edward IV**. However, when the **Earl of Warwick** comes to court and makes the case for Edward's rightful claim to the throne of England, Louis readily agrees to marry his sister to the new king of England. When word comes that Edward has already taken a new wife (**Lady Elizabeth Grey**), Louis gives military aid to Margaret and Warwick to attack Edward's forces.

King Louis XI

Hunchback of Notre Dame
Victor Hugo

The King of France in 1482. He is an old and bitter monarch who has a bad reputation among the people. **Gringoire** is brought to him as a prisoner and he pleads for mercy. Louis agrees to let him go, but only on the condition that he help them hang **La Esmeralda**.

King Louis XIII

The Three Musketeers
Alexandre Dumas

King of France. Louis XIII is not much of a ruler, and is dominated by his advisors, most notably **Cardinal Richelieu**, the most powerful man in France. The king is a petulant and petty person, and those around him who are most successful are those who have learned to manipulate his pettiness. The king does not particularly like his wife, **Queen Anne**, who is having an affair with **George Villiers, the Duke of Buckingham**.

Louis

A View from the Bridge
Arthur Miller

A Longshoreman and friend of **Eddie Carbone**'s. Louis hangs out with **Mike** outside Eddie's home. Louis and Mike praise Eddie for keeping the illegal immigrants **Marco** and **Rodolpho**.

Louis

Homecoming
Cynthia Voigt

One of a pair of runaways the Tillerman children meet in a state park in Connecticut during the first half of their journey. Louis is selfish and immoral, rationalizing theft and irresponsibility as a way of rebelling against an unjust system.

Louisa

All the Pretty Horses
Cormac McCarthy

The cook at the Grady ranch where **John Grady Cole** grew up. She raised Cole when **John Grady Cole's mother** ran off to California.

Aunt Louisa

The Unvanquished
William Faulkner

Drusilla's mother, a weepy, melodramatic woman who is constantly shocked by her daughter's independence. She eventually moves in with **Bayard**'s family to try to rein in Drusilla and force her to conform to feminine expectations. Finally she defeats Drusilla and successfully insists that she marry Colonel Sartoris.

Louise

Breath, Eyes, Memory
Edwidge Danticat

A vendor in the marketplace of La Nouvelle Dame Marie. Louise becomes **Tante Atie**'s best friend once Atie returns to Dame Marie from Croix-des-Rosets to take care of the aging **Grandmè Ifé**. Though Louise teaches the adult Atie to read and write, she remains a troubling influence, implicated in Atie's night wanderings and her increasing alcoholism. Louise's dream is to save enough money to take a boat to Miami; she continually seeks a buyer for her pig in order to raise the money for her trip. When Grandmè Ifé finally buys Louise's pig, Louise departs without so much as a good-bye to Atie, leaving Atie heartbroken.

Louvinia

The Unvanquished
William Faulkner

A practical, devoted slave of the Sartoris family. Like the stereotypical mammy she is ornery but ultimately loyal and affectionate. She has no desire to be free, and angrily criticizes **Loosh** for turning on the Sartorises, calling him an ingrate and a fool.

Ejlert Løvborg

Hedda Gabler
Henrik Ibsen

A genius academic, **Jørgen Tesman**'s professional rival, and **Hedda Tesman**'s former beau. After a series of scandals related to his alcoholism, Ejlert left the city and tutored the Elvsted children. After returning to the city and publishing an important sociological work, he has begun work on another, even more promising manuscript. Hedda steals his manuscript and burns it, and when the woe-struck Ejlert thinks that he lost his manuscript in a drunken fit, he commits suicide.

Mr. Lovel

Evelina
Fanny Burney

An ugly, ill-mannered, and melodramatic fop who torments **Evelina Anville** when she rejects him at her first private ball. Because he is an acquaintance of **Lord Orville** and the Mirvans, Lovel has an opportunity to distress Evelina on a number of occasions before he is humiliated by **Captain Mirvan**.

Sir Thomas Lovell

Henry VIII
William Shakespeare

A lord of the court present in many general hubbub scenes. Besides attending **Cardinal Wolsey**'s dinner and asking the **Duke of Buckingham** for forgiveness, Lovell is the first to report that **Anne Boleyn** is in labor with **Elizabeth**.

James Russell Lowell

Walden
Henry David Thoreau

A Harvard-trained lawyer. Lowell eventually abandoned his first vocation for a career in letters. His poetic satire *The Bigelow Papers* was well-received, and he went on to become a professor of modern languages at Harvard and the first editor of the *Atlantic Monthly*.

P. Loxias

The Black Prince
Iris Murdoch

The editor of the novel who identifies himself in the foreward as a friend of **Bradley Pearson**'s. "Loxias" is a pseudonym for Apollo, the Greek god of the arts. His primary role is to alert the readers to the primary theme of the book: the importance of art in articulating truth.

Agnes Lozelle

The Big Sleep
Raymond Chandler

The front girl for **Geiger**'s pornography rentals. Agnes is a common criminal, a grifter in search of a buck. She has an expensive drug addiction that has landed her in a deep hole. Agnes takes up with **Brody** and then with **Harry Jones**, both times in schemes to make an easy dollar.

Ilse Lubin

Midnight's Children
Salman Rushdie

A German anarchist friend of **Aadam Aziz**'s.

Oskar Lubin

Midnight's Children
Salman Rushdie

Oskar Lubin and **Ilse Lubin** are German anarchist friends of **Aadam Aziz**.

Charlotte Lucas

Pride and Prejudice
Jane Austen

Elizabeth Bennet's dear friend. Pragmatic where Elizabeth is romantic, Charlotte does not view love as the most vital component of a marriage. She is more interested in having a comfortable home, so when **Mr. Collins** proposes, she accepts.

Carl Luce

The Catcher in the Rye
J. D. Salinger

A student at Columbia who was the student advisor of **Holden Caulfield** at the Whooton School. At Whooton, he was a source of knowledge about sex for the younger boys, and Holden tries to get him to talk about sex at their meeting at the Wicker Bar. Luce is annoyed by Holden because of this and tells Holden he needs psychoanalysis.

Lucentio

The Taming of the Shrew
William Shakespeare

A young, clean-cut student from Pisa. The good-natured and intrepid Lucentio comes to Padua to study at the city's renowned university, with his wise-cracking servant **Tranio** in tow. As soon as he pledges his commitment to academics, he is immediately sidetracked when he falls in love with **Bianca** at first sight. By disguising himself as a classics instructor named Cambio, he convinces **Gremio** to offer him to **Baptista** as a tutor for Bianca. He wins her love, but his impersonation gets him into trouble when his father, **Vincentio**, visits Padua. Lucentio's idyllic, poetic view of love runs opposite to **Petruccio**'s pragmatism.

Lucetta

The Two Gentlemen of Verona
William Shakespeare

Julia's servant. She gives Julia a loveletter sent by **Proteus** and persuades her to read it and forget the rigidity of a lady's ethics. When Julia declares that she will travel to Milan to seek Proteus, Lucetta counsels her to wait for his return.

Lucia

A Tree Grows in Brooklyn
Betty Smith

A Sicilian woman who becomes illegitimately pregnant. Lucia is ill-treated by her father and family until **Aunt Sissy** offers to take her baby.

Luciana

The Comedy of Errors
William Shakespeare

Adriana's unmarried sister. In contrast to her shrewish sibling, Luciana advocates obedience and submission in a wife and tries to convince Adriana to beat away her "self-harming jealousy." **Antipholus of Syracuse**, whom Adriana and Luciana mistake for **Antipholus of Ephesus**, Adriana's husband, makes passes at her at dinner. Luciana rebukes him for not being faithful.

Luciana

Catch-22
Joseph Heller

A beautiful Italian girl with whom **John Yossarian** has an affair in Rome.

Lucifer

Inferno
Dante Alighieri

The three-headed prince of Hell, also known as **Satan** and **Dis**. He resides in the Judecca, the Fourth Ring of the Ninth Circle of Hell (Canto XXXIV). According to Christian legend, **Lucifer**, God's favorite angel, was thrown out of Heaven after rebelling against **God**. Dante imagines that in his fall, Lucifer plunged into the center of the Earth. An enormous giant, he has three faces but does not speak; his three mouths are busy chewing three of history's greatest traitors: **Judas**, the betrayer of Christ, and **Cassius** and **Brutus**, the betrayers of **Julius Caesar**.

Lucifer

Doctor Faustus
Christopher Marlowe

Mephastophilis's master. Lucifer is the prince of the devils and the ruler of hell.

Lucille

On the Road
Jack Kerouac

A New York acquaintance of **Sal Paradise**'s. When Sal is attending school in New York, he wants to marry Lucille, but she's already married.

Lucinda

Don Quixote
Miguel de Cervantes

Cardenio's wife and a model courtly woman. Docile and beautiful, Lucinda obliges her parents and her lover, **Ferdinand**.

Lucio

Measure for Measure
William Shakespeare

Claudio's bachelor friend. Lucio is a flamboyant "fantastic" who provides much of the play's comedic content.

Lucius of *Timon*

Timon of Athens
William Shakespeare

One of **Timon**'s friends. Lucius accepts Timon's gifts but refuses to give him a loan when Timon goes bankrupt.

Lucius of *Titus*

Titus Andronicus
William Shakespeare

Titus's last surviving son by the end of the play. Banished from Rome for trying to free his framed brothers, Lucius raises an army of Goth and returns as the voice of reason to become the new emperor.

Caius Lucius

Cymbeline
William Shakespeare

The Roman ambassador to Britain and, later, the general of the Roman invasion force.

Lucky

Johnny Got His Gun
Dalton Trumbo

One of the American prostitutes in the American House in Paris for soldiers overseas. Lucky and **Joe Bonham** became friends and spent time gossiping together.

Lucky

Waiting for Godot
Samuel Beckett

Pozzo's slave, who carries Pozzo's bags and stool.

Lucullus

Timon of Athens
William Shakespeare

One of **Timon**'s friends. Lucullus accepts Timon's gifts but refuses to lend him money.

Lucy

The House on Mango Street
Sandra Cisneros

One of the two girls who are **Esperanza**'s neighbors and best friends.

Sir William Lucy

Henry VI, Part I
William Shakespeare

An English soldier and messenger. During the climactic battle, Lucy asks the **Duke of York** and the **Duke of Somerset** for reinforcements for **Lord Talbot** at Bordeaux; when both lords refuse to send soldiers because of their brimming dispute with one another, Lucy scolds them.

Mr. Ludsbury

A Separate Peace
John Knowles

The master in charge of **Gene Forrester**'s dormitory. A stern disciplinarian, Mr. Ludsbury thrives on the unquestioning obedience of schoolboys and works hard to restore order after the anarchic summer session.

Lugulbanda

The Epic of Gilgamesh
Unknown

Third king of Uruk after the deluge (**Gilgamesh** is the fifth), later deified. Lugulbanda is the hero of a cycle of Sumerian poems and a minor god. Depending on the tradition, Lugalbanda is either Gilgamesh's father or his guardian deity.

Luis

In Our Time
Ernest Hemingway

A bullfighter who drinks and dances all day before a fight, even when his fellow matadors try to stop him.

Luke

The New Testament
Unknown

A traveling companion of **Paul**'s. Christian tradition dating back to the second century A.D. claims that Luke is the author of the Gospel that bears his name and of Acts of the Apostles.

Luke

Incidents in the Life of a Slave Girl
Harriet Ann Jacobs

An acquaintance of **Linda Brent**'s from home whom she meets on the street in New York. Luke has escaped by stealing money from his dead master, and Linda uses him as an example of how slaves cannot be judged by the same moral standards as free citizens.

Luke

The Handmaid's Tale
Margaret Atwood

Offred's husband in the time before the Republic of Gilead. Because Luke was married once before (he got a divorce while having an affair with Offred), their marriage is void under Gilead law. Offred's loving memories of Luke contrast with the regimented, passionless male-female relationships of Gilead.

Septimus Luker

The Moonstone
Wilkie Collins

A seedy London moneylender.

Teta Elzbieta Lukoszaite

The Jungle
Upton Sinclair

Ona's stepmother and a mother of six. The resilient, strong-willed old Teta Elzbieta survives many hardships in the novel and represents the redemptive power of family, home, and tradition.

Juozapas Lukoszaite

The Jungle
Upton Sinclair

Teta Elzbieta's crippled son, who was injured as a toddler when a wagon ran over his leg. While foraging for food at a local dump, Juozapas meets a rich lady who later helps the family.

Kotrina Lukoszaite

The Jungle
Upton Sinclair

Teta Elzbieta's daughter. Kotrina takes care of the children and the household and sells newspapers with her brothers when **Jurgis** is sent to prison.

Ona Lukoszaite

The Jungle
Upton Sinclair

Jurgis Rudkus's wife and **Teta Elzbieta**'s stepdaughter. A lovely, kind, optimistic girl, Ona is ruined by the forces of capitalism after she and Jurgis emigrate from Lithuania to Chicago. The family's dire financial straits force her to take on a job even when she becomes pregnant. Ona's boss, **Phil Connor**, rapes her, and although she survives the assault, she dies in childbirth not long afterward.

Stanislovas Lukoszaite

The Jungle
Upton Sinclair

Teta Elzbieta's teenage son. Terrified of frostbite, Stanislovas often refuses to go to work until **Jurgis** beats him. Stanislovas meets a grisly death at the workplace when he falls asleep in a storeroom and a swarm of rats attacks him.

Ada Lumb

Regeneration
Pat Barker

The mother of **Sarah Lumb**. She desires nothing more than for her daughters to be the beneficiaries of a stable pension from their deceased husbands. Ada is very involved in her daughter's life, and she cautions Sarah about the risks of pregnancy.

Sarah Lumb

Regeneration
Pat Barker

The girlfriend of **Billy Prior**. Sarah is a young working-class woman who works in a munitions factory in Scotland. Like her mother, she is very practical. She is not sure that true love between a man and a woman is possible, but she is willing to give it a try.

Patrice Lumumba

The Poisonwood Bible
Barbara Kingsolver

The charismatic first elected president of the Republic of Congo, who preached a gospel of peace and prosperity. He was beaten to death during a military coup orchestrated by the United States government.

Juan, Lucas, Mateo, and Pedro Luna

Bless Me, Ultima
Rudolfo A. Anaya

María Márez's brothers and **Antonio Márez**'s uncles. They are farmers. They struggle with **Gabriel Márez** to lay a claim to Antonio's future. They want him to become a farmer or a priest, but Gabriel wants Antonio to be a *vaquero* in the Márez tradition. Antonio's uncles are quiet and gentle, and they plant their crops by the cycle of the moon. When harvest time comes, Antonio, María, **Deborah Márez**, **Theresa Márez**, and **Ultima** settle into Juan's, because it is his turn to host his sister and her children. Antonio overhears Juan urge María to send Antonio to Juan's house for a summer before Antonio is "lost" like his older brothers, **Eugene Márez**, **León Márez**, and **Andrew Márez**, who are in the war. Pedro says that Lucas saw the **Trementina daughters** dancing the Black Mass, a blasphemous satanic ritual. Within the week, Lucas fell ill, having been cursed by the daughters. After **Tenorio Trementina** kills Ultima's owl, Pedro shoots Tenorio.

Prudencio Luna

Bless Me, Ultima
Rudolfo A. Anaya

The father of **María Luna**, **Pedro Luna**, **Juan Luna**, **Mateo Luna**, and **Lucas Luna**. He is a quiet man who prefers not to become involved in other people's conflicts. When **Tenorio Trementina** declares an all-out war against **Ultima**, he does not want his sons to get involved, even though Ultima once saved Lucas's life.

The Lunatic

Walk Two Moons
Sharon Creech

The mysterious young man who appears on **Phoebe**'s doorstep and lurks threateningly around her neighborhood. Mike turns out to be the adoptive son of the local police chief, **Sergeant Bickle**.

Carol Lundgren

The Big Sleep
Raymond Chandler

Geiger's young and handsome lover. Lundgren is both despicable and endearing: his crude, limited vocabulary annoys **Marlowe** while he is under his custody for killing **Brody**. The boy kills Brody thinking that Brody has killed Geiger, his lover.

Wang Lung

The Good Earth
Pearl S. Buck

The novel's protagonist. A poor farmer by birth, Wang Lung maintains a fierce attachment to the land. At the same time, he is ambitious and envies the wealth and decadent lifestyle of **Old Master Hwang**. By the end of the novel, his piety and love of the land only partially maintain his good character and moral standing.

Remus Lupin

The Harry Potter Series: Books 3 and *4*
J. K. Rowling

The Defense Against the Dark Arts teacher in **Harry Potter**'s third year at Hogwarts. In *Harry Potter and the Prisoner of Azkaban*, he is very competent and likable. He teaches Harry Potter how to defend himself against Dementors, creatures that have the ability to suck all good thoughts out from those around them. Remus is forced to leave Hogwarts at the end of the year on account of his being a werewolf. He is one of the creators of the Marauder's Map, a document that shows the grounds of Hogwarts, including the location of everyone on the premises.

Lupito

Bless Me, Ultima
Rudolfo A. Anaya

A war veteran who has been deeply affected by the war. After Lupito murders **Chávez**'s brother, the local sheriff, in one of Lupito's deranged moments, Lupito is killed by a mob in front of young **Antonio Márez**. Lupito's death provides the impetus for Antonio's serious moral and religious questioning.

Lurai

Island of the Blue Dolphins
Scott O'Dell

One of the birds that **Karana** tames.

Luster

The Sound and the Fury
William Faulkner

The son of **Frony** and the grandson of **Dilsey**. Luster is a young boy who looks after and entertains **Benjy**, despite the fact that he is only half Benjy's age.

Navigator Lustig

The Martian Chronicles
Ray Bradbury

The navigator for the third expedition to Mars.

Mr. Luttrell

Wide Sargasso Sea
Jean Rhys

One of **Annette**'s only friends after the death of her husband, **Alexander Cosway**. Mr. Luttrell lives at Nelson's Rest, the estate that neighbors the Cosway home. Suffering financial hardship in the wake of the Emancipation Act, he shoots his dog and swims out to sea, never to be seen again.

Luz

In Our Time
Ernest Hemingway

The Italian nurse and lover of a young American soldier in "A Very Short Story." She eventually leaves this soldier for an Italian major.

Pyotr Petrovich Luzhin

Crime and Punishment
Fyodor Dostoevsky

Avdotya Romanovna Raskolnikova's fiancé. Luzhin is stingy, narrow-minded, and self-absorbed. He longs to marry a beautiful, intelligent, but desperately poor girl like **Dunya** so that she will be indebted to him forever.

Lychordia

Pericles
William Shakespeare

Thaisa's nurse. Later, Lychordia is **Marina**'s nurse in Tarsus.

Captain Lydgate

Middlemarch
George Eliot

Tertius Lydgate's foppish cousin. He takes **Rosamond Vincy** out riding, and she suffers a miscarriage as a result of an accident on horseback.

Sir Godwin Lydgate

Middlemarch
George Eliot

Tertius Lydgate's uncle.

Tertius Lydgate

Middlemarch
George Eliot

The orphan son of a military man. He chose the medical profession at a young age, much to the chagrin of his wealthy, titled relatives. He comes to Middlemarch hoping to test new methods of treatment. He marries **Rosamond Vincy**, whose expensive habits get him into debt. He takes a loan from **Nicholas Bulstrode** and becomes embroiled in Bulstrode's scandal. **Dorothea Brooke** aids him in his darkest hour. He hopes to find the tissue that is the most basic building block of life.

Lydia

Johnny Tremain
Esther Forbes

The black washerwoman at a tavern where many British officers sleep. Lydia is a rebel sympathizer who, because of her connection to the British soldiers, gathers information for the rebel forces.

Lydia

A Prayer for Owen Meany
John Irving

Mrs. Wheelwright's maid, who loses a leg to cancer. Lydia spends the rest of her life in a wheelchair at 80 Front Street.

Anna Karenina
Leo Tolstoy

Countess Lydia Ivanovna

A morally upright woman who is initially **Anna Arkadyevna Karenina**'s friend and later her fiercest critic. Lydia Ivanovna harbors a secret love for Anna's husband, **Alexei Alexandrovich Karenin**, and induces him to believe in and rely on psychics.

The Handmaid's Tale
Margaret Atwood

Aunt Lydia

An **Aunt** of The Red Center whose slogans continue to echo in **Offred**'s head. Aunt Lydia argues that despite all the restrictions, women are treated with more respect under the Republic of Gilead than they were previously.

A Portrait of the Artist as a Young Man and *Ulysses*
James Joyce

Lynch

Stephen Dedalus's longtime friend, a medical student. Lynch often listens to Stephen theorizing on aestheticism. He is seeing **Kitty Ricketts**.

A Death in the Family
James Agee

Andrew Lynch

Brother of **Mary Follet**. Andrew Lynch, unlike his sister, is not religious in the least. He becomes upset that **Father Jackson** did not perform a full burial service for **Jay Follet** on account of Jay's not being baptized.

Love in the Time of Cholera
Gabriel García Márquez

Barbara Lynch

The woman who has a four-month affair with **Dr. Juvenal Urbino del Calle**. During the affair, Dr. Urbino del Calle suffers in anguish. **Fermina Daza** discovers the affair, and immediately leaves for **Hildebranda Sánchez**'s house.

A Death in the Family
James Agee

Catherine Lynch

Mother of **Mary Follet**. Catherine Lynch is a very kind old lady with a tinkling laugh.

A Death in the Family
James Agee

Hannah Lynch

Aunt of **Mary Follet** and sister of **Joel Lynch**. Hannah Lynch, like Mary, is very religious, and she is calm, practical, and considerate. She explains certain facts about **Jay Follet**'s death to **Rufus Follet** and **Little Catherine**.

Joel Lynch

A Death in the Family
James Agee

Father of **Mary Follet**. Joel Lynch is a tough, pragmatic man who has little patience for or belief in religion. He feels that Mary has married beneath her genteel upbringing, yet he remains very supportive of her. Joel says she will need to brace herself and hold herself together, especially for the children's sake. He tells her that he knows there will be financial difficulties and assures her that he will take care of her family.

Mrs. Rachel Lynde

Anne of Green Gables
L. M. Montgomery

The town busybody. Mrs. Rachel likes nothing better than to give her opinion and preach morals. She lives with her meek husband, **Thomas**, and an affectionate, quarrelsome friendship exists between her and **Marilla Cuthbert**. Mrs. Rachel is outspoken about everything from politics to fashion, and, although childless, she never fails to advise Marilla on how to raise Anne.

Laura Lyons

Hound of the Baskervilles
Sir Arthur Conan Doyle

A local young woman and the beautiful brunette daughter of **Mr. Frankland**, a local litigator who disowns her when she marries against his will. Subsequently abandoned by her husband, the credulous Laura turns to **Mr. Jack Stapleton** and **Sir Charles Baskerville** for help.

Lysander

A Midsummer Night's Dream
William Shakespeare

A young man of Athens, in love with **Hermia**. He cannot marry her openly because **Egeus**, her father, wishes her to wed **Demetrius**. Lysander convinces Hermia to run away into the forest to his aunt's house, where they can get married outside the jurisdiction of Athens. However, once in the woods, Lysander becomes the victim of **Puck**'s misapplied magic and wakes up in love with **Helena**. The fairies set things right, and at the end of the play he is indeed happily together with Hermia in Athens.

Lysimachus

Pericles
William Shakespeare

Governor of Mytilene. Lysimachus comes to **Marina**'s brothel, but she convinces him not to take her virginity. Impressed with her grace, he suggests that she talk to the grief-stricken **Pericles** when Pericles arrives in Mytilene. Lysimachus is betrothed to Marina at the end.

Lysistrata

Lysistrata
Aristophanes

An Athenian woman who is tired of war and frustrated with the treatment of women in Athens. She gathers the women of Sparta and Athens together to solve these social ills. Exhibiting no traces of sexual desire or flirtatious attributes, Lysistrata gains respect among the men. Smarter, wittier, and more serious than the women she unites, Lysistrata is more a mastermind than a participant in the action.

Thomas W. Lyster

Ulysses
James Joyce

A librarian at the National Library in Dublin and a Quaker. Lyster is the most solicitous of **Stephen Dedalus**'s listeners in Episode Nine.

Conrad Lyte

Babbitt
Sinclair Lewis

A speculator who colludes frequently with **Babbitt** on shady real estate deals.

Jonathan Lyte

Johnny Tremain
Esther Forbes

A wealthy Boston merchant and **Jonathan Tremain**'s great-uncle. Crooked and cruel, Lyte tries to make a profit by making friends on both sides of the colonial struggle, but as tensions mount in Boston, Lyte is exposed as a Tory. On the eve of war, Lyte and his family depart for London.

Lavinia Lyte

Johnny Tremain
Esther Forbes

Jonathan Lyte's beautiful, arrogant, and regal daughter. Enchanted by **Isannah Lapham**'s ethereal beauty, Lavinia takes the child away from her family, and slowly weakens the bond between Isannah and her sister **Priscilla Lapham**.

MAJOR MONSTERS

***SC-SC-SCARY*. WORSE THAN YOUR BOSS.**

Count Dracula	1	*Dracula*
Dragon	2	*Grendel*
Gollum	3	*The Lord of the Rings* trilogy
Grendel	4	*Grendel*
Mr. Edward Hyde	5	*Dr. Jekyll and Mr. Hyde*
The Monster	6	*Frankenstein*
Sauron	7	*The Lord of the Rings* trilogy

M. de Charlus

Swann's Way
Marcel Proust

One of **Charles Swann**'s closest friends and allies. He encourages **Odette** to think more highly of Swann and later becomes her "watchdog," ensuring she never cheats on Swann. **Marcel** hints that Charlus helps Swann not only out of friendliness, but an undeclared love for him.

M'Dear

The Bluest Eye
Toni Morrison

A quiet, elderly woman who serves as a doctor in the community where **Cholly Breedlove** grows up.

San Ma

The Kitchen God's Wife
Amy Tan

Jiang Sao-yan's senior wife. San Ma is stubborn and sneaky. She carries herself with arrogance and yet gives the impression of kindness as she shops with **Weili** (Winnie) for her dowry. She, like Winnie's father's other wives, is always full of gossip and jealousy.

Mucho Maas

The Crying of Lot 49
Thomas Pynchon

Oedipa Maas's husband. Mucho once worked in a used-car lot but recently became a disc jockey for KCUF radio in Kinneret. At the end of the novel, he goes crazy on LSD, alienating Oedipa.

Oedipa Maas

The Crying of Lot 49
Thomas Pynchon

The novel's protagonist. After her ex-boyfriend, **Pierce Inverarity**, names her executor of his immense estate, Oedipa begins to unravel a worldwide conspiracy in southern California. She functions as a type of detective, although the story is as much about her own self-discoveries as it is about the mystery she attempts to piece together.

M. Mabeuf

Les Misérables
Victor Hugo

A churchwarden in Paris who tells **Marius Pontmercy** the truth about his father. Mabeuf and Marius become friends during tough times, and Mabeuf later dies a heroic death on the barricade.

Mablung

The Two Towers
J. R. R. Tolkien

One of two warriors of **Faramir** who come upon **Samwise Gamgee**, **Frodo Baggins**, and **Gollum** as the three are making their way east to Mordor through Ithilien.

Faintly Macabre

The Phantom Tollbooth
Norton Juster

The woman who has been imprisoned since **Rhyme** and **Reason** disappeared. It was once her duty to select the words to use for every occasion, but she became corrupted by her power and began to horde the words for herself. Faintly tells **Milo** the story of the imprisoned princesses and inspires him to broach the subject with **King Azaz**.

Macalister

To the Lighthouse
Virginia Woolf

The fisherman who accompanies the Ramsays to the lighthouse. Macalister relates stories of shipwreck and maritime adventure to **Mr. Ramsay** and compliments **James Ramsay** on his handling of the boat while James lands it at the lighthouse.

General John Gordon Macarthur

And Then There Were None
Agatha Christie

The oldest guest. Macarthur is accused of sending a lieutenant, **Arthur Richmond**, to his death during World War I because Richmond was his wife's lover. Once the first murders take place, Macarthur, already guilt-ridden about his crime, becomes resigned to his death and sits by the sea waiting for it to come to him.

Mr. Macartney

Evelina
Fanny Burney

A tenant of the Branghtons, an impoverished Scottish poet who falls in love with **Sir John Belmont**'s daughter before he realizes that Sir Belmont is his father. He is **Evelina Anville**'s half-brother.

Mrs. Macartney

Evelina
Fanny Burney

Mr. Macartney's mother. She has an affair with **Sir John Belmont** sometime after his marriage to **Lady Caroline Evelyn Belmont** and flees to Scotland when she bears him an illegitimate son.

Macbeth

Macbeth
William Shakespeare

The main character in the play. Macbeth, a Scottish general and the Thane of Glamis, is led to wicked ambition after **the Three Witches** predict his rise to kingship. Macbeth is a brave soldier and a powerful man, but he is not a virtuous one. He has ambitions to the throne and is easily tempted into murder in order to fulfill them. Once he kills **King Duncan** and is crowned king of Scotland, he embarks on further atrocities in an attempt at securing his doomed reign. He becomes a nervous insomniac over his actions. He is ultimately overthrown by **Prince Malcolm**, Duncan's son, and beheaded by **Macduff**.

Lady Macbeth

Macbeth
William Shakespeare

Macbeth's wife. Lady Macbeth is a deeply ambitious woman who lusts for power and position. Early in the play, she seems to be the stronger and more ruthless of the two, urging her husband to kill **King Duncan** and seize the crown. After the bloodshed, she grows mad over her actions, continually washing out a spot of blood on her hands that isn't really there. She commits suicide just before Macbeth's final defeat.

Gerty MacDowell

Ulysses
James Joyce

A young working-class woman whom **Leopold Bloom** glimpses on the beach. Lame because of a childhood accident, Gerty fastidiously attends to her clothing and personal beauty regimen. She hopes to fall in love and marry and seldom thinks about her disability.

Macduff

Macbeth
William Shakespeare

A Scottish nobleman hostile to **Macbeth**'s kingship from the start. Macduff becomes a leader of the crusade to unseat Macbeth. He desires to place **Malcolm** on the throne, for Malcolm is the son and rightful heir to the murdered **King Duncan**. Macduff also desires vengeance for Macbeth's murder of **Lady Macduff** and of Macduff's son. On the battlefield, Macbeth believes he is protected from death by **the Three Witches**' prophesy that no man born of woman can harm him. However, Macduff informs the doomed Macbeth that he was not "of woman born" but was instead "untimely ripped" from his mother's womb. Macduff beheads Macbeth, ending the tyrant's grip on Scotland.

Lady Macduff

Macbeth
William Shakespeare

Macduff's wife. **Macbeth** sends murderers to kill her and her son.

Mr. Macey

Silas Marner
George Eliot

Raveloe's parish clerk. Mr. Macey is opinionated and smug, but he means well.

MacGowan

As I Lay Dying
William Faulkner

A despicable young employee at a Jefferson drugstore. MacGowan extorts a sexual favor from **Dewey Dell Bundren** in return for a fake abortion treatment.

Machevill

The Jew of Malta
Christopher Marlowe

The narrator of the Prologue. Machevill is based on Machiavelli, but he is more of an ironic than a genuine characterization of this author.

Mack

Cannery Row
John Steinbeck

The leader of a group of down-and-out but always scheming men who live together in the run-down fish-meal shack owned by **Lee Chong**, which they call the Palace Flophouse and Grill. Mack is a smart, charismatic man who can charm anyone into anything.

Barney MacKean

The Member of the Wedding
Carson McCullers

A friend of **Frankie Addams**'s. In the summer previous to the novella's action, Frankie and Barney "committed a queer sin" in Barney's garage. Frankie's reaction to the experience with Barney tells us how she is both ignorant and afraid of matters regarding sex.

Ira Mackel

Mourning Becomes Electra
Eugene O'Neill

A sly, cackling farmer who helps goad **Abner Small** into the allegedly haunted Mannon house.

Shreve MacKenzie

The Sound and the Fury and *Absalom, Absalom!*
William Faulkner

Quentin's roommate at Harvard. A young Canadian man, Shreve reappears in *Absalom, Absalom!*, which he and Quentin narrate from their dorm room at Harvard.

Thomas Mackenzie

Stranger in a Strange Land
Robert A. Heinlein

An old friend of **Jubal Harshaw**'s. He works for a stereovision (a kind of futuristic television) network as an executive.

Barbara Macklin

Walden Two
B. F. Skinner

Rogers's girlfriend. She neither likes nor appears to understand Walden Two.

Ernie Macmillan

Harry Potter and the Chamber of Secrets
J. K. Rowling

Justin Finch-Fletchley's friend, who thinks that **Harry Potter** is responsible for the suspicious occurrences at Hogwarts.

Captain MacMorris

Henry V
William Shakespeare

The Irish captain of **King Henry V**'s troops. The three foreign captains in the play, MacMorris, the Welsh **Captain Fluellen**, and the Scottish **Captain Jamy**, retain their respective heavy accents, broadly represent their nationalities, and prove the importance of each of the British nations.

Sam MacMurfee

All the King's Men
Robert Penn Warren

Willie's main political enemy within the state's Democratic Party, and governor before Willie. After Willie crushes him in the gubernatorial election, MacMurfee continues to control the Fourth District, from which he plots ways to claw his way back into power.

The MacNamara sisters

Angela's Ashes
Frank McCourt

Angela McCourt's cousins who live in New York. The MacNamara sisters are bossy, burly women who keep their husbands in check and interfere in everyone else's business.

Macon, Jr.

Song of Solomon
Toni Morrison

Milkman Dead's father and **Ruth Foster Dead**'s husband, also known as Macon Dead II, or Macon Dead, Jr. Traumatized by seeing his father, **Macon Dead I**, murdered during a skirmish over the family farm, Macon, Jr. has developed an obsession with becoming wealthy. In the process, he has become an emotionally dead slumlord. He is a horrible man, trying to force Ruth to abort Milkman by forcing her to stick needles into her womb, evicting **Henry Porter** for having a romantic involvement with **First Corinthians Dead**, and killing **Dr. Foster** by throwing away his pills. Macon, Jr.'s stories about his childhood help fuel Milkman's investigation into the history of the Dead family, which ends up being Milkman's salvation.

Father MacPhail

His Dark Materials
Robert Pullman

The President of the Consistorial Court. To prevent the second fall, Father MacPhail sends **Father Gomez** to assassinate **Lyra Belacqua**.

Cluny Macpherson

Kidnapped
Robert Louis Stevenson

Like **James of the Glens**, a former Highland chieftain stripped of his powers by the English government. Cluny Macpherson is marked for death by the English after leading Jacobite troops against the English army. Cluny now hides in a treehouse near the mountain of Ben Alder. When **David Balfour** and **Alan Breck Stewart** are on the run, they hide out with him for a little while.

Moody Spurgeon MacPherson

Anne of Green Gables
L. M. Montgomery

One of the boys in **Anne Shirley**'s class at the Avonlea school and a classmate of hers at Queen's Academy.

Claudia MacTeer

The Bluest Eye
Toni Morrison

The narrator of parts of the novel. An independent and strong-minded girl, Claudia is a fighter and rebels against adults' tyranny over children and against the black community's idealization of white beauty standards. She and **Frieda MacTeer**, her sister, plant marigold seeds and money in hopes that they can help **Pecola Breedlove** through her madness, but nothing grows. When she finds a group of boys harassing Pecola, she attacks them. When she learns that Pecola is pregnant, she and her sister come up with a plan to save Pecola's baby from the community's rejection.

Frieda MacTeer

The Bluest Eye
Toni Morrison

Claudia MacTeer's sister, who shares Claudia's independence and stubbornness. Because she is closer to adolescence, Frieda is more vulnerable to her community's equation of whiteness with beauty. Frieda is more knowledgeable about the adult world and sometimes braver than Claudia. **Henry Washington** touches Frieda's breasts one day, and people are worried that Frieda may have been "ruined." Frieda participates in the plan to plant marigold seeds and money to help **Pecola Breedlove**'s unborn child.

Mr. MacTeer

The Bluest Eye
Toni Morrison

Father of **Claudia MacTeer** and **Frieda MacTeer**, husband of **Mrs. MacTeer**. He works hard to keep his family fed and clothed. He is fiercely protective of his daughters. When **Henry Washington** touches Frieda's breasts, Mr. MacTeer attacks Henry and shoots at him with a gun lent to him by a neighbor.

Mrs. MacTeer

The Bluest Eye
Toni Morrison

Mother of **Claudia MacTeer** and **Frieda MacTeer**, wife of **Mr. MacTeer**. She is an authoritarian and sometimes callous woman who nonetheless steadfastly loves and protects her children. She is given to fussing aloud and to singing the blues.

Mad Hatter

Alice in Wonderland and *Through the Looking Glass*
Lewis Carroll

The crazy hat-seller trapped in a perpetual tea-time. He is seemingly fond of confusing people. He is rather impolite to **Alice**, and he rejoices when he frustrates her enough that she snaps at him in return. He reappears in *Through the Looking Glass* as "Hatta," one of the Anglo-Saxon messengers.

Madame

The Maids
Jean Genet

A woman who employs **Claire** and **Solange** as her maids. Madame is a wealthy older woman whose husband, the **Monsieur**, has been anonymously "denounced" to the police. She lives a lavish lifestyle, wearing furs and drinking champagne, but in Monsieur's absence she sometimes resigns herself to a self-pitying life of mourning. Still, she is aroused by his criminality and fantasizes about breaking him free from prison. She favors Claire, and is scared that the maids will desert her.

Owney Madden

Legs
William Kennedy

An underworld figure who provides **Jack** with financial support when Jack is down and out.

Madeleine

Herzog
Saul Bellow

Moses Herzog's beautiful but neurotic second wife and antagonist, the mother of his second child, **June**. Madeleine divorced Moses, leaving him for his best friend, **Valentine Gersbach**. She converted to Christianity, and later she turns her attention to the scholarly world of ideas.

Patricia Madigan

Angela's Ashes
Frank McCourt

A young diphtheria patient whom **Frank McCourt** meets in the hospital while he is recovering from typhoid. Patricia reads poems to Frank and jokes with him.

Madox

The English Patient
Michael Ondaatje

Almásy's best friend in the desert. Madox is a rational, level-headed man who, like Almásy, chose to live in the desert to study the features of the land and report back to the Geographical Society. Unlike Almásy, Madox includes his own emotional reactions in his writing and reports. Though he always carries a copy of *Anna Karenina*, the famous tale of adultery, he remains ever faithful to his wife back home. Madox sees the church as proclaiming a jingoistic pro-war message during World War II. He takes his own life in the church.

Bonzo Madrid

Ender's Game
Orson Scott Card

Ender Wiggin's Battle School enemy and the commander of Salamander Army. Too proud to accept the fact that Ender is smarter and better than him, he becomes cruel. His honor forces him to challenger Ender to a one-on-one fight, and Ender kills him in the ensuing struggle.

Tim Madsen

Into Thin Air
Jon Krakauer

A client with **Scott Fischer**'s guide service. Madsen is among the clients lost during the storm, and he stays behind to look after the ailing climbers while **Neal Beidleman** goes back to find **Anatoli Boukreev**, who then rescues Madsen's group.

Maduka

Things Fall Apart
Chinua Achebe

Obierika's son. Maduka wins a wrestling contest in his mid-teens. **Okonkwo** wishes he had promising, manly sons like Maduka.

Mae

Cat on a Hot Tin Roof
Tennessee Williams

A mean, agitated "monster of fertility" who schemes with her husband **Gooper** to secure **Big Daddy**'s estate. Mae appears primarily responsible for the burlesques of familial love and devotion that she and **the children** stage before Daddy and **Big Mama**, the children's grandparents. Mae affects refinement because of her family name and her crown as the Memphis cotton carnival queen. Mae tries to stop Mama from finding out that Daddy really has cancer and not a spastic colon. She also calls out **Maggie** on her lie about being pregnant.

Mae and Gooper's children

Cat on a Hot Tin Roof
Tennessee Williams

Kids who appear as grotesque, demonic "no-necked monsters" who intermittently interrupt the action onstage. Under Mae's direction, they offer up a burlesque image of familial love and devotion, overtly trying to win **Big Daddy**'s affection so that **Gooper** and **Mae** can win his money.

Maera

In Our Time
Ernest Hemingway

A bullfighter who tries to stop **Luis** from partying all day before a bullfight. Eventually, Maera is killed by a bull.

Miss Maestas

Bless Me, Ultima
Rudolfo A. Anaya

Antonio Márez's first-grade teacher. Although Antonio does not speak English well, Miss Maestas recognizes his bright spark of intelligence. Under her tutelage, Antonio unlocks the secrets of words. She promotes him from the first to the third grade at the end of the year.

Magdalena

The House on Mango Street
Sandra Cisneros

Esperanza's younger sister and closest companion. While Nenny is old enough to be Esperanza's playmate, she is too young to share in the changes Esperanza is experiencing.

Maggie

Cat on a Hot Tin Roof
Tennessee Williams

Brick's hard, nervous wife. Though she is seductive and vulnerable, she is utterly unable to lure her husband into having sex with her. Maggie's dispossession lies in her childlessness, which is contrasted against **Mae** and **Gooper**'s large number of children. Without a child, Maggie and Brick's place in **Big Daddy**'s household is not assured. While Maggie is struggling with the absence of Brick's desire, Brick is getting drunk, secretly mourning the loss of his friend **Skipper**. Maggie, in a lie to get the dying Daddy's money, claims she is pregnant with Brick's child. The play ends with Maggie locking up Brick's liquor and holding him captive until he has sex with her during her fertile time.

Aunt Maggie

Black Boy
Richard Wright

Ella Wright's sister, who sporadically lives with Ella, **Richard Wright**, and his brother **Alan Wright**. Maggie is Richard's favorite aunt.

Farmer Maggot

The Fellowship of the Ring
J. R. R. Tolkien

A farmer who drives **Frodo Baggins**, **Samwise Gamgee**, **Meriadoc Brandybuck**, and **Peregrin Took** to the Brandywine River ferry in his wagon while they are fleeing from **the Nazgûl**.

The Maginot Line

The Bluest Eye
Toni Morrison

See **Miss Marie**.

Examining Magistrate

The Stranger
Albert Camus

The magistrate who questions **Meursault** several times after his arrest. Deeply disturbed by Meursault's apparent lack of grief over his mother **Madame Meursault**'s death, the magistrate brandishes a crucifix at Meursault and demands to know whether he believes in God. When Meursault asserts his atheism, the magistrate states that the meaning of his own life is threatened by Meursault's lack of belief.

Magnet

Holes
Louis Sachar

Another boy at the Camp Green Lake. Magnet earned his nickname because of his ability to steal things.

Magua

The Last of the Mohicans
James Fenimore Cooper

The novel's villain, in contrast to the hero **Hawkeye**. Magua is a cunning Huron Native American nicknamed Le Renard Subtil ("Subtle Fox"). A former Huron chief, Magua was exiled from his tribe for alcoholism. He carries a grudge against **Colonel Munro**, who humiliated him by whipping him for drunkenness. When he learns that he is in the presence of Colonel Munro's daughter, **Cora Munro**, he chooses to be vengeful, determined to either marry or kill Cora, thus bruising the colonel's psyche. Throughout *The Last of the Mohicans,* Magua is playing off of as many factions as he can to get what he wants. When he kidnaps Cora and **Alice Munro**, he knows just how to use them to divide up the group of men who are stalking him. Though Magua is wounded and captured by Hawkeye, he still manages to escape and to stir the Delawares into a frenzy of hatred for Hawkeye and **Major Duncan Heyward**, who was originally guided and misled by Magua through the forest. In the end, Magua has a chance to kill Cora when he is cornered by Hawkeye, but he does not. He is then shot by Hawkeye in the confusion caused by another impatient Huron's stabbing of Cora.

Abel Magwitch

Great Expectations
Charles Dickens

A fearsome criminal. After **Pip** shows him kindness, Magwitch becomes Pip's secret benefactor.

Dr. Mahmoud

Stranger in a Strange Land
Robert A. Heinlein

A semantician on the Envoy mission to Mars who studies the Martian language. Mahmoud is a devout Muslim, raised in proper English society. He marries **Miriam**.

Mahony

Dubliners
James Joyce

The narrator's companion in "An Encounter." When Mahony and the narrator rest in a field, a strange old man approaches them. At one point Mahony runs away after a cat, leaving the narrator and the old man alone.

Maisie Maidan

The Good Soldier
Ford Madox Ford

A woman described by **John Dowell** as young, gentle, and "so submissive." She attended the same convent school as **Leonora Powys Ashburnham**, and preserves some of the strict morality that was once taught to her.

Maillotte

Wide Sargasso Sea
Jean Rhys

Like **Christophine**, a black servant who distinguishes herself by not being Jamaican. Maillotte is **Tia**'s mother and Christophine's only friend.

Solomon Maimon

The Chosen
Chaim Potok

An eighteenth-century Polish Jew who reminds **David Malter** of **Danny Saunders**. Solomon Maimon was an extremely gifted student who studied non-Jewish literature after the Talmud could not satisfy his hunger for knowledge. As a result of his heresy, he died rootless and alone.

Grandmother Majauszkiene

The Jungle
Upton Sinclair

Jurgis and **Ona**'s Lithuanian immigrant neighbor. A socialist and a concerned old woman, **Grandmother Majauszkiene** has seen generations of immigrants destroyed by the merciless labor practices of the Packingtown factories.

Major

The Contender
Robert Lipsyte

A bad influence on **Alfred Brooks**. Major and **Hollis** try to push Alfred in the direction of **James**. They invite Alfred to parties and encourage his involvement in crime and drugs.

Major de Spain

Go Down, Moses
William Faulkner

The proprietor of the old Sutpen plantation, also owns the hunting camp described in "The Old People" and "The Bear."

Judy Major

The Autobiography of Miss Jane Pittman
Ernest J. Gaines

The white girl to whom **Tee Bob Samson** is engaged.

Major Major Major Major

Catch-22
Joseph Heller

The lonely and awkward squadron commander. Born Major Major Major, he was promoted to the rank of major by a mischievous computer on his first day in the army. Major Major agrees to see people in his office only when he is not there.

Roland Major

On the Road
Jack Kerouac

Sal Paradise's Denver friend, with whom he lives for a while. A Hemingwayesque writer, Roland scorns "arty" types but snobbishly talks about Europe and fine wines.

Tony Makarios

His Dark Materials
Robert Pullman

One of the children stolen by the Gobblers. **Lyra Belacqua** finds Tony in a town outside of Bolvanger without his daemon, **Ratter**.

Malacoda

Inferno
Dante Alighieri

The leader of the Malabranche, the demons who guard the Fifth Pouch of the Eighth Circle of Hell (Canto XXI). Malacoda ("evil tail") intentionally gives **Virgil** and **Dante** bad directions.

Malcolm

Macbeth
William Shakespeare

The son of the murdered **King Duncan**, whose restoration to the throne signals Scotland's return to order following **Macbeth**'s reign of terror. After King Duncan's murder, Malcolm flees to England while his younger brother **Donalbain** flees to Ireland. Initially weak and uncertain of his own power, Malcolm becomes a serious challenge to Macbeth. With **Macduff**'s aid and the support of England, Malcolm leads a victorious charge against Macbeth, retaking the throne.

Malcolm X

The Autobiography of Malcolm X
Malcolm X & Alex Haley

The narrator and subject of the autobiography. As a young boy, Malcolm is bright and popular but feels excluded by white people. He becomes a ruthless hustler on the streets of Boston and New York but undergoes a change of heart during his time in prison. After his release, he develops into an aggressive and persuasive spokesman for the Nation of Islam. As an independent and international political leader, he is tolerant, meditative, and ambitious. He is assassinated in 1965.

Dr. Ian Malcolm

Jurassic Park
Michael Crichton

A mathematician who specializes in the emerging field of chaos theory. Malcolm is part of a new breed of mathematician, with a vibrant personality and a wardrobe that seems to consist only of black. One of the original consultants for Jurassic Park, he has always been skeptical that the idea could work. Once Malcolm actually gets to see the island, his predictions of the park's doom get more and more antagonistic, eliciting **John Hammond**'s anger.

Draco Malfoy

The Harry Potter Series: Books 1–4
J. K. Rowling

A slimy, smirking student and **Harry Potter**'s nemesis. Malfoy is a rich snob from a long line of wizards who feels entitled to the Hogwarts experience. In *Harry Potter and the Sorcerer's Stone*, he makes fun of the poorer **Ron Weasley** and advises Harry to choose his friends more carefully. In *Harry Potter and the Chamber of Secrets*, Malfoy is able to buy himself a position on the Slytherin House Quidditch team, but even though he has the fastest broomstick, he cannot play the game well. (Quidditch is a wizard sport.) In *Harry Potter and the Prisoner of Azkaban*, Malfoy is able to use his father's power as an intimidation tactic when he tries to have **Hagrid** fired and **Buckbeak** executed.

Lucius Malfoy

The Harry Potter Series: Books 1–4
J. K. Rowling

Draco Malfoy's father, a mean, hissing man who mistreats **Dobby**, his house-elf, and encourages meanness and bigotry in his son. He is the head of the school governing board, and he uses his power to temporarily remove **Albus Dumbledore** from power. Malfoy makes disparaging comments about wizards who lack pure wizard blood. Lucius Malfoy is a Death Eater, an associate of **Voldemort**'s.

Stephen Mallory

The Fountainhead
Ayn Rand

A gifted but disillusioned sculptor who feels alone and misunderstood until **Howard Roark** rescues him from his drunken doldrums. Mallory blames **Ellsworth Toohey** for the world's mediocrity and tries to kill him. Eventually Mallory regains his self-confidence through his work on Roark's buildings.

Dr. Mary Malone

His Dark Materials
Robert Pullman

A nun-turned-scientist who works in **Will Parry**'s Oxford, where she studies dark matter. Mary helps **Lyra Belacqua** escape from the men who are chasing Will. Mary then escapes to another world, where she meets the mulefa. It is Mary's job to bring Will and Lyra together.

Sir Thomas Malory

The Once and Future King
T. H. White

A page whom **King Arthur** asks to carry on the Arthurian ideals of justice. In real life, Sir Thomas Malory wrote the fifteenth-century text *Le Morte d'Arthur*, an account of the Arthurian legends that served as the basis for the novel.

David Malter

The Chosen
Chaim Potok

Reuven Malter's father. David Malter is a traditional Orthodox Jew and a teacher, scholar, writer, and humanitarian. He is notorious in the Hasidic community for his controversial biblical scholarship and his outspoken support of Zionism.

Reuven Malter

The Chosen
Chaim Potok

The narrator of the novel and one of its two protagonists. Reuven is intelligent, conscientious, and popular, skilled in softball, math, and Talmud study.

Albert Malvoisin

Ivanhoe
Sir Walter Scott

The leader of the Templar stronghold of Templestowe. Malvoisin urges **Brian de Bois-Guilbert** to put aside his love for **Rebecca** and stay the course of his career with the Templars.

Malvolio

Twelfth Night
William Shakespeare

The straitlaced steward—or head servant—in the household of Lady **Olivia**. His priggishness and haughty attitude earn him the enmity of **Sir Toby Belch**, **Sir Andrew Aguecheek**, and **Maria**, who play a cruel trick on him, making him believe that Olivia is in love with him. After he finds a forged letter, Malvolio dons crossed garters and yellow stockings, smiling like a maniac, thinking that this is the way to Olivia's heart. In his fantasies about marrying his mistress, he reveals a powerful ambition to rise above his social class, but in doing so, abandons his good sense.

Mama

A Raisin in the Sun
Lorraine Hansberry

Walter Lee Younger and **Beneatha Younger**'s mother. The matriarch of the family, Mama is religious, moral, sensitive, and maternal. She demands that members of her family respect themselves and take pride in their dreams. She wants to use her husband's insurance money as a down payment on a house with a backyard to fulfill her dream for her family to move up in the world. When Walter comes to her with his idea to invest in the liquor-store venture, she condemns the idea and explains that she will not participate in such un-Christian business. She cares deeply for Walter and shows this care by giving him the remaining insurance money. She cares deeply for **Ruth Younger** as well, consoling her when Walter ignores her. She is very proud when Walter stands up to **Mr. Karl Lindner** at the end of play, and declares to Ruth that Walter has finally become a man.

Mama

Where the Red Fern Grows
Wilson Rawls

Billy Colman's mama. She is part Cherokee. She is very religious and always enjoys answering Billy's questions about God. She wants very much to move to town so the children can get a good education, and, in the end, is able to do so because Billy makes a lot of money from his coon-hunting with **Old Dan** and **Little Ann**.

Mama

Roll of Thunder, Hear My Cry
Mildred D. Taylor

Mother of **Cassie Logan**, **Stacey Logan**, **Little Man Logan**, and **Christopher-John Logan**. She is a schoolteacher of the seventh grade until she gets fired because of **Harlan Granger**'s influence and **T.J. Avery**'s gossip.

Mama

Ellen Foster
Kaye Gibbons

Ellen's mother. She has suffered from poor health since having "romantic [rheumatic] fever" as a child. When she is at last out of the hospital, she is so depressed by her husband's cruelty and her bleak situation that she commits suicide by ingesting a bottle of her prescription medication.

Shabanu
Suzanne Fisher Staples

Mama

Shabanu and **Phulan**'s mother. Mama is beautiful, strong, and gentle. She raises her two daughters lovingly and with joy. Mama loves life in the desert. She is a wise woman who understands the constraints and challenges of society.

Ellen Foster
Kaye Gibbons

New Mama

Ellen's foster mother. She is everything Ellen wanted in a mother. New Mama is kind, caring, nurturing, always has enough money to pay for groceries, and has plenty of love to give Ellen and the other foster children she cares for.

Ellen Foster
Kaye Gibbons

Mama's Mama

Ellen's grandmother. She is old and miserly and treats Ellen with the utmost cruelty, as she vehemently hates Ellen's father and seeks vengeance on him through Ellen. After winning custody of Ellen in court, she immediately sends her to work the fields with the black field hands on the farms she owns in the scorching summer heat. At the end of the summer, she dies of illness, even after Ellen has taken extraordinary care of her.

Ragtime
E. L. Doctorow

Mameh

Wife of **Tateh** and mother to **the little girl**, Mameh does not appear in the novel. Having heard she performs sexual favors for her boss for money, Tateh disowns her and never sees her again. He later finds out she has died.

The Winter's Tale
William Shakespeare

Mamillius

The young prince of Sicilia, and **Leontes**'s and **Hermione**'s son. Mamillius dies of grief after his father wrongly imprisons his mother.

Paradise Lost
John Milton

Mammon

A devil known in the Bible as the epitome of wealth. Mammon always walks hunched over, as if he is searching the ground for valuables. In the debate among the devils, he argues against war, seeing no profit to be gained from it. He believes Hell can be improved by mining the gems and minerals they find there.

Mammy

Gone with the Wind
Margaret Mitchell

Scarlett O'Hara's childhood nurse. Mammy is an old, heavyset slave who was also nurse to Scarlett's mother, **Ellen O'Hara**. Loyal and well-versed in Southern etiquette, Mammy keeps Scarlett in line. After Ellen's death, Mammy becomes for Scarlett one of the only living reminders of the Old South.

The Man of Law

The Canterbury Tales
Geoffrey Chaucer

A successful lawyer commissioned by the king. He upholds justice in matters large and small and knows every statute of England's law by heart.

Man with the Red Eyes

A Wrinkle in Time
Madeleine L'Engle

A robot-like inhabitant of Camazotz. He tries to hypnotize **Meg Murry**, **Charles Wallace Murry**, and **Calvin O'Keefe** in the CENTRAL Central Intelligence building. He succeeds in gaining control of Charles Wallace's brain and tries to use Charles Wallace to convince Meg and Calvin to give in to **IT**. Charles Wallace, under the influence of the Man with the Red Eyes and IT, leads Meg and Calvin to **Mr. Murray**, who is trapped in a transparent column.

Man with the Red Tie

The Sound and the Fury
William Faulkner

The mysterious man with whom **Miss Quentin** allegedly elopes.

Leading Man

Six Characters in Search of an Author
Luigi Pirandello

The haughty actor taking on the role of **the Father**. At the beginning of the play, just before the six Characters interrupt the rehearsal, the Leading Man protests the absurdity of the fake Pirandello play they are rehearsing. Once the six Characters arrive, he flirts with the **Stepdaughter**. The Father and the Stepdaughter try to be polite, but comment that the Leading Man and **the Leading Lady** are no good at portraying the Characters.

The Whether Man

The Phantom Tollbooth
Norton Juster

A peculiar fellow who says everything three times. He is the caretaker of Expectations. He is so busy thinking about what could be and why that he never seems to go anywhere or get anything done.

Manager

The Metamorphosis
Franz Kafka

Gregor Samsa's manager. A suspicious, threatening man, he suggests that Gregor's absence from work is connected with the theft of funds from the company.

The Manager

Six Characters in Search of an Author
Luigi Pirandello

A comic figure who agrees to play the role of the Characters' author in realizing their drama. Somewhat slow-witted and of fiery temper, the Manager remains committed to the vulgar notions of reality and conventional stagecraft that the Characters, particularly **the Father**, dismiss as wholly unreal. The Manager acts as a blundering peacekeeper and liaison between the actors and the Characters.

The Manciple

The Canterbury Tales
Geoffrey Chaucer

A man in charge of getting provisions for a college or court. Despite his lack of education, this Manciple is smarter than the thirty lawyers he feeds.

Doctor Mandelet

The Awakening
Kate Chopi

Léonce Pontellier and **Edna Pontellier**'s family physician. Doctor Mandelet sympathizes with Edna's dissatisfaction with her life but worries about the possible consequences of her turmoil. Léonce asks Mandelet to observe Edna, to see why she is so despondent when it comes to fulfilling her role as his wife. After Edna's affair with **Alcée Arobin**, and during her resumption of her affair with **Robert Lebrun**, Doctor Mandelet, who is also **Adèle Ratignolle**'s doctor, walks Edna to the pigeon house.

Pastor Manders

Ghosts
Henrik Ibsen

A local priest from the nearby town. He often lectures others about morality and religion. Sometimes, his financial dealings regarding the orphanage seem suspect.

Gideon Mandoma

The Power of One
Bryce Courtenay

Nanny's son and the great-great-grandson of the Zulu chief Cetshwayo. **Peekay** boxes against him and emerges victorious in Sophiatown. Gideon continues to train at **Solly Goldman**'s gym and he and Peekay become great friends. Eventually, it is Gideon's influence that convinces **Singe 'n' Burn** to support Peekay in starting a night school for black boxers.

Doctor Manette

A Tale of Two Cities
Charles Dickens

Lucie Manette's father and a brilliant physician. Doctor Manette spent eighteen years as a prisoner in the Bastille. At first demented by his incarceration, he proves to be a kind, loving father who prizes his daughter's happiness above all things.

Lucie Manette

A Tale of Two Cities
Charles Dickens

A young French woman who grew up in England. Lucie was raised as a ward of Tellson's Bank. She is an archetype of compassion whose love transforms those around her, revitalizing her father and turning **Sydney Carton** from a "jackal" into a hero.

Alice Manfred

Jazz
Toni Morrison

Dorcas's aunt and legal guardian. She lives alone in Harlem, works as a seamstress and is deeply mistrustful of young people and the sinful lives they seem to be leading. Alice is overly protective and concerned for Dorcas, and hopes to shelter her from what she sees as a threatening world. Her own husband had an affair with another woman and died soon after. Alice becomes close to **Violet** after Violet slashes Dorcas's corpse's face at the funeral. Alice ends up moving back to Springfield after coming to terms with her past through her friendship with Violet.

Mangan's sister

Dubliners
James Joyce

The narrator's young love interest in "Araby." She represents the familiarity of Dublin, as well as the hope of love and the exotic appeal of new places.

Padma Mangroli

Midnight's Children
Salman Rushdie

Saleem's lover and, eventually, his fiancée. Padma plays the role of the listener in the storytelling structure of the novel.

Mrs. Mann

Oliver Twist
Charles Dickens

The superintendent of the juvenile workhouse where **Oliver Twist** is raised. Mrs. Mann beats and starves the children in her care.

Mannie

Go Down, Moses
William Faulkner

Rider's wife, whose death sends him into despair.

Mannie

Wide Sargasso Sea
Jean Rhys

A groom. Mannie is one of the new servants whom **Mr. Mason** brings to Coulibri.

Brigadier-General Ezra Mannon

Mourning Becomes Electra
Eugene O'Neill

The great Union general. The Brigadier-General Ezra Mannon is a spare, big-boned man of exact and wooden movements. **Lavinia Mannon** is incestuously obsessed with her father and his return. She knows that **Captain Adam Brant**, her illegitimate half-brother, and the lover of Lavinia's mother, **Christine Mannon**, will try to seek revenge on his scoundrel father, Ezra, for abusing Ezra's brother, **David Mannon**, who is the beloved of Brant's mother, **Marie Brantôme**. Lavinia challenges Brant and Christine, knowing about their affair, and threatens to tell Ezra. Brant seduces his half-sister to keep her quiet. Lavinia never gets to tell her father anything because he coldly spurns her when he arrives home, only trying to get the attentions of Christine, who doesn't care for Ezra because she has Brant. Christine poisons Ezra and kills him. He continues to exert his influence in symbolic form after his death. Ezra's various images will call his family to judgment from beyond the grave. Lavinia knows that she alone must be shut up like the dead in the tomb-like house with the ghosts of Ezra, Orin, and Christine.

Christine Mannon

Mourning Becomes Electra
Eugene O'Neill

A striking woman with a fine, voluptuous figure, flowing animal grace, and a mass of beautiful copper hair. Having long abhorred her husband, the **Brigadier-General Ezra Mannon**, Christine Mannon plots his murder with her lover, the illegitimate son of Ezra, **Captain Adam Brant**, upon Ezra's return from the Civil War. She loves incestuously, repudiating Ezra and clinging to her son, **Orin Mannon**. Orin becomes a substitute for Brant after Orin's arrival home from the Civil War. Her daughter **Lavinia Mannon**, who incestuously desires Ezra, drives Christine to suicide. When Orin kills Brant, Christine must submit to the rule of Lavinia, and must replace Brant totally with Orin. However, she madly shoots herself in Ezra's office, killing herself.

Lavinia Mannon

Mourning Becomes Electra
Eugene O'Neill

The daughter of the **Brigadier-General Ezra Mannon** and **Christine Mannon**, the sister of **Orin Mannon**, the half-sister of the illegitimate **Captain Adam Brant**. Her militaristic bearing, a mark of her identification with her father, symbolizes her role as a functionary of the Mannon clan or, to use Christine's terms, as their sentry. The severe Lavinia considers herself robbed of love at her mother's hands. She is in love with Ezra, who will not give her the time of day. She knows that Christine despises Ezra, but Ezra still seeks Christine out to love him after he returns from the Civil War. Because Ezra spurns Lavinia when he returns home, she cannot warm him that Christine and her lover, Brant, are plotting to kill Ezra. Brant also has sex with Lavinia to try to keep her quiet. Christine succeeds in poisoning and killing Ezra. Lavinia schemes to take Christine's place and become the wife of her father and mother of her brother. She ultimately does so upon her mother's death, reincarnating her in her own flesh, wearing green, acting with the sexuality of a woman from the exotic islands that Brant spoke about. After the suicide of the crazed Orin, this manor becomes her tomb. Lavinia condemns herself to live with the Mannon dead until she and all their secrets with her die. **Seth Beckwith** shuts her up in the tomb house.

Orin Mannon

Mourning Becomes Electra
Eugene O'Neill

The son of the **Brigadier-General Ezra Mannon** and **Christine Mannon** returned from war. He is the half-brother and murderer of the illegitimate **Captain Adam Brant**, the brother/lover/son of **Lavinia Mannon**. Orin possesses a boyish charm that generally invites the maternal favors of women. He is the counterpart to Aeschylus's Orestes from the *Orestia*. Because he loves Christine incestuously, he flies into a jealous rage upon the discovery of her love affair with Brant. This leads to Brant's death by Orin's pistol, and Christine's subsequent suicide. Orin then forces himself and his sister to judgment for their crimes by the ghosts of the Mannons in an attempt to rejoin his mother in death. Orin shoots himself after he realizes he cannot escape his son/brother/lover relationship with Lavinia to be with **Hazel Niles**.

Manolin

The Old Man and the Sea
Ernest Hemingway

A boy, presumably in his adolescence, who serves as apprentice and devoted attendant to the elderly fisherman **Santiago**. The old man first took Manolin out on a boat when he was only five years old. Due to Santiago's extraordinary run of bad luck, Manolin's parents force the boy to go out on a different fishing boat. Manolin, however, still cares deeply for the old man, whom he continues to view as a mentor. His love for Santiago is unmistakable as the two discuss baseball and as the young boy recruits help from villagers to improve the old man's impoverished conditions.

Medora Manson

The Age of Innocence
Edith Wharton

Countess Ellen Olenska's eccentric old aunt. Medora raised Ellen after the child's parents died. A penniless itinerant and widow, Medora is tolerated by society only because of her family connections.

Manuel

The Call of the Wild
Jack London

A gardener's helper on **Judge Miller**'s estate. Manuel kidnaps **Buck** and sells him to dog traders in order to pay off his gambling debts.

Manuel

Jurassic Park
Michael Crichton

Dr. Roberta Carter's paramedic. Distressed by the injuries to the InGen employee, he believes they may be caused by a hupia, a "night ghost."

Manuel

How the Garcia Girls Lost Their Accents
Julia Alvarez

Sofia's boyfriend while she lived on the Island; also her illegitimate cousin on her father's side of the family.

Manya

The Chosen
Chaim Potok

The loving Russian housekeeper who cooks and cleans the Malters' apartment.

The Shadout Mapes

Dune
Frank Herbert

A Fremen and servant of the Atreides. Mapes is the first among the Fremen to test **Jessica** and discover that she is a Bene Gesserit. Mapes is later killed when **Dr. Yueh** betrays the Atreides to the Harkonnens.

Father Mapple

Moby-Dick
Herman Melville

A former whaleman and now the preacher in the New Bedford Whaleman's Chapel. Father Mapple delivers a sermon on Jonah and the whale in which he uses the Bible to address the whalemen's lives.

Marc

Breath, Eyes, Memory
Edwidge Danticat

Martine's longtime lover in New York. Marc is a stocky, well-dressed Haitian lawyer, in love with his mother's cooking and with his own full name, Marc Jolibois Francis Legrand Moravien Chevalier. He is slightly patronizing.

Marcel

Swann's Way
Marcel Proust

The narrator of the novel and a representation of the author. Marcel suffers from nervous ailments and longs for the nightly comfort of his mother's kiss. He is fascinated by art and becomes an avid reader and lover of architecture, theater, painting and music. He loves to walk around Combray, spying on people and admiring the stunning hawthorn blossoms that inspire him to become a writer. After losing himself in books and his imagination, he is easily disappointed by the "real" world, especially with the women he loves. He even imagines the dark eyes of **Gilberte** and the **Duchess of Guermentes** to be blue so that they will be more beautiful to him.

Marcel's father

Swann's Way
Marcel Proust

Marcel's father, who prevents his son from kissing his "mamma" goodnight.

Marcel's grandparents

Swann's Way
Marcel Proust

Marcel's grandparents, who live in Combray. They worry about his health and encourage him to read. They were great friends with **Charles Swann**'s father and remain close to Swann, although they greatly disapprove of his marriage to **Odette**.

Marcel's mother

Swann's Way
Marcel Proust

The focal point of all **Marcel**'s anguish and happiness. Her nightly goodnight kiss brings him immense joy, but once it is over, he suffers terribly. She worries about his nervous disposition.

Marcellus

Hamlet
William Shakespeare

A night watchman at Elsinore. The play begins on a cold night atop the castle ramparts, where **Bernardo** and Marcellus are the first people to see **the Ghost** of King Hamlet, **Hamlet**'s father.

March Hare

Alice in Wonderland and *Through the Looking Glass*
Lewis Carroll

The **Mad Hatter**'s friend and companion, who is equally crazy and discourteous. He also reappears as an Anglo-Saxon messenger in *Through the Looking Glass* as Haigha.

Amy March

Little Women
Louisa May Alcott

The youngest March girl. Amy is an artist with a weakness for pretty possessions. Amy is more vain and difficult than her other sisters, but her flaws are partly charming, and certainly the product of youth. She spends time and money attempting to impress the rich girls from her art class with a fancy party; the failure of her party teaches her a lesson about pretending to be something she is not. Amy is able to confront her selfishness when she realizes with shame that she is more worried about getting her hands on the turquoise ring than she is about her ill sister, **Beth March**. When Amy marries **Laurie Laurence**, she serves as a mentor for Laurie.

Aunt March

Little Women
Louisa May Alcott

A rich widow and one of the March girls' aunts. **Josephine March** works as her companion. Though Aunt March is strict with Jo, Jo does like her; both women are stubborn and determined. Jo inherits Aunt March's old house.

Beth March

Little Women
Louisa May Alcott

The third March daughter. Beth is quiet and very virtuous, and she does nothing but try to please others. She adores music and plays the piano very well. Beth is rewarded for her efforts with a piano, sent by **Mr. Laurence**, and her gratitude trumps her shyness when she marches across to Mr. Laurence's house and gives him a kiss in thanks. When Beth goes to visit **the Hummels**, an impoverished neighboring family, she contracts scarlet fever.

Josephine March

Little Women
Louisa May Alcott

The protagonist of the novel, and the second-oldest March sister. Josephine, called Jo, wants to be a writer. She has a temper and a quick tongue, although she works hard to control both. She is a tomboy, and reacts with impatience to the many limitations placed on women and girls. She hates romance in her real life, and wants nothing more than to hold her family together.

Meg March

Little Women
Louisa May Alcott

The oldest March sister. She works as a nanny. Responsible and kind, Meg mothers her younger sisters. Meg cares a great deal about social etiquette and has formed a code for her blundering sister, **Josephine**

March. Meg's attraction to the luxury of **Annie Moffat**'s life and subsequent longing for finery and riches of her own sets her up as an example of how materialistic desires can corrupt a good person. When Meg agrees to marry **Mr. Brooke**, she demonstrates that at last she has overcome her own weakness for luxury and riches. John is not a rich man, and he will not provide Meg with the glamorous lifestyle she once coveted, but she loves him nonetheless.

Little Women
Louisa May Alcott

Mr. March

The March girls' father and **Marmee**'s husband. He serves in the Union army as a chaplain. When he returns home, he continues acting as a minister to a nearby parish.

The Outsiders
S. E. Hinton

Marcia

Cherry Valance's friend and **Randy Adderson**'s girlfriend. Marcia is a pretty, dark-haired Soc who befriends **Two-Bit Matthews** at the drive-in. Marcia and Two-Bit share a sense of humor and a taste for nonsensical musings. Their relationship is an example of a bridged gap between the Socs and the greasers.

A Connecticut Yankee in King Arthur's Court
Mark Twain

Marco

A humble charcoal-burner, fairly representative of the poor-spirited peasants of the day. When **the Yankee** and **King Arthur**, disguised as peasants, have dinner with Marco and **Dowley**, the Yankee realizes he has made a mistake in his conversation by causing all of the dinner guests to believe that he is going to turn them in for paying their workers overly generous wages. Marco and friends decide to kill Arthur and the Yankee, but the two men beat down the dinner guests. Marco and his wife disappear and return with a mob of villagers who chase Arthur and the Yankee into the woods, and the two men are rescued, but are later sold into slavery.

A View from the Bridge
Arthur Miller

Marco

The cousin of **Beatrice**. Marco comes to the U.S. to work and make money to send back to his wife and three children in Italy. He is caught in the storm of **Eddie Carbone**'s jealousy about **Catherine** and **Rodolpho**'s relationship. Because Eddie wants to remove Rodolpho from his life, he calls the immigration police on both Rodolpho and Marco. When Eddie later tries to apologize to Marco, he also tries to stab Marco in a twisted manner of redeeming himself. However, Marco turns the knife around and stabs and kills Eddie.

The Bell Jar
Sylvia Plath

Marco

A tall, dark, well-dressed Peruvian who takes **Esther Greenwood** on a date to a country club. Marco expresses dashing self-confidence, but also a hatred of women. Later that evening, he pushes Esther into the mud and climbs on top of her, ripping off her dress. After he calls her a slut, however, she begins to fight him, and she eventually escapes.

Marco

Herzog
Saul Bellow

Moses Herzog's son from his first marriage, who is away at camp throughout the novel. Moses fears that Marco blames his father for both divorces.

Uncle Marcos

The House of the Spirits
Isabel Allende

Nivea del Valle's favorite brother and **Clara**'s favorite uncle. He is an explorer and inventor. Uncle Marcos became famous for assembling a flying contraption in which he had sailed off over the mountains. He had been taken for dead, but then he reappeared. For this reason, Nivea has trouble believing that Marcos is actually dead when men bring his body back to the del Valle family from over the mountains.

Marcus Andronicus

Titus Andronicus
William Shakespeare

Roman Tribune of the People and **Titus**'s brother, who remains conspicuously separated from the bloodshed throughout the play. Every time he speaks, he is the sound of reason and calmness, standing in stark contrast to the ravenous and crazed speeches of the other characters. He is one of the few survivors at the end of the play.

Al Marcus

The Assistant
Bernard Malamud

The paper-bag seller who frequently visits the Bobers' grocery store. Although he has a terminal form of cancer, he keeps working diligently, unwilling to give up and die.

Maretha

The Piano Lesson
August Wilson

Berniece's daughter. Maretha, like her mother when she was young, is beginning to learn piano. She symbolizes the next generation of the Charles family, providing the occasion for a number of confrontations on what the family should do with its legacy.

Andrew, Eugene, and Leon Márez

Bless Me, Ultima
Rudolfo A. Anaya

Antonio Márez's older brothers. For most of Antonio's childhood, they are are fighting in World War II. When they return home, they suffer post-traumatic stress as a result of the war. Restless and depressed, they all eventually leave home to pursue independent lives, crushing **Gabriel Márez**'s dream of moving his family to California.

Antonio Márez

Bless Me, Ultima
Rudolfo A. Anaya

The precocious protagonist, Antonio is six years old at the beginning of the novel. His parents are **María Márez** and **Gabriel Márez**. Antonio is serious, thoughtful, and prone to moral questioning, and his experiences force him to confront difficult issues that blur the lines between right and wrong. He turns to both pagan and Catholic ideologies for guidance, but he doubts both traditions. With **Ultima**'s help, Antonio makes the transition from childhood to adolescence and begins to make his own choices and to accept responsibility for their consequences. Antonio's intense desire to know the truth leads him into a spiral of questioning and uncertainty regarding sin, innocence, death, the afterlife, forgiveness, and the nature of God. Ultima's guidance leads Antonio to resolve many of the conflicts within and around him. He realizes that he can determine his future and that he alone will decide what he becomes. Though the novel is narrated by the adult Antonio looking back over his childhood, we never learn what Antonio does decide to do with his life, whether he becomes a priest, a vaquero or something entirely different.

Bless Me, Ultima
Rudolfo A. Anaya

Deborah and Theresa Márez

Antonio Márez's older sisters.

Bless Me, Ultima
Rudolfo A. Anaya

Gabriel Márez

Antonio Márez's father. Gabriel and **María Márez**, Antonio's mother, have frequently conflicting views, which make it difficult for Antonio to accept either of their belief systems. At first glance, Gabriel appears to be a washed-up old vaquero, or cowboy, who lives in a state of nostalgic regret on a patch of barren land. Gabriel works a demeaning job, drinks himself into a stupor on a weekly basis, and frequently fights with María. But as *Bless Me, Ultima* progresses, the depth and dignity of Gabriel's relationship with the llano becomes clear. Even though he lives in a state of regret, he does so only out of his genuine fondness for the vaquero way of life. For the sake of María and his family, Gabriel leaves the llano, moves to the town of Guadalupe, and begins to attend church. At the conclusion of the novel, Gabriel volunteers to put aside the conflict with María's family, the Lunas, and help Antonio make his own choice about his future.

Bless Me, Ultima
Rudolfo A. Anaya

María Márez

Antonio Márez's mother. María and **Gabriel Márez**, Antonio's father, have frequently conflicting views, which makes it difficult for Antonio to accept either of their belief systems. María, the devoutly Catholic daughter of a farmer, wants Antonio to follow her Luna family tradition by becoming a priest. She convinced Gabriel, who is a cowboy, to move to the town of Guadalupe so that the their children could have an education.

Much Ado About Nothing
William Shakespeare

Margaret

One of **Hero**'s servingwomen. Margaret unwittingly helps **Don John** deceive **Claudio** into thinking that Hero is unfaithful when she dresses up like her mistress to have a romantic exchange with her lover, **Borachio**, by the window.

The Awakening
Kate Chopin

Margaret

Edna's oldest sister, who took care of both Edna and **Janet** after their mother died.

Margaret

Cat on a Hot Tin Roof
Tennessee Williams

See **Maggie**.

Margaret

Seize the Day
Saul Bellow

Tommy Wilhelm's estranged wife. She refuses to grant Tommy a divorce and is always demanding financial support for their two children.

Margaret of Anjou

Henry VI, Part I; Henry VI, Part II; Henry VI, Part III; and *Richard III*
William Shakespeare

Wife of **King Henry VI**; daughter of **Reignier**; mother of **Prince Edward**. Toward the end of *King Henry VI, Part I*, Margaret is captured by **William de la Pole, Duke of Suffolk**, who is so taken with her that he convinces Henry VI to wed her in what is a politically disadvantageous marriage. Suffolk hopes to use Margaret to control King Henry. But even before *King Henry VI, Part II* begins, Margaret becomes disillusioned with the weak king, and begins to plot with Suffolk and **Cardinal Beaufort** against the **Humphrey, Duke of Gloucester** to secure more control of the government. When **Richard Plantagenet, Duke of York** begins his rebellion, Margaret becomes Henry's backbone, urging him to fly to London for safety. By *King Henry VI, Part III*, Margaret is for all intents and purposes the actual ruler of England. Henry's staunchest supporter, Margaret is repeatedly denounced as an unnatural woman by her opponents, but is glorified by those who fight for her. After **King Edward IV** takes the throne, Margaret goes to France to seek military aid and eventually wins the **Earl of Warwick** over to her side. In *King Richard III*, the embittered Margaret, filled with hatred for Richard and the entire York line, spends much of her time prowling around the castle. She curses **Queen Elizabeth** and her clan, Richard, **Lord Hastings**, and **Lord Buckingham**. Reduced to depending on the charity of her family's murderers to survive, Margaret and her muttering curses symbolize the helpless, righteous anger of all of Richard's victims.

Margariz

Song of Roland
Unknown

One of the twelve Saracen lords picked to battle the twelve Frankish peers at Roncesvals. He gives **Olivier** a good blow, but God protects Olivier from being wounded.

Aunt Marge

Harry Potter and the Prisoner of Azkaban
J. K. Rowling

Vernon Dursley's visiting sister; a loud, beefy, nasty-tempered woman who adores attack dogs and enjoys insulting **Harry Potter** and his late parents.

Margie

The Iceman Cometh
Eugene O'Neill

One of **Rocky**'s tarts. She is feather-brained, sentimental, lazy, and reasonably content with life. Although she retains a degree of youthful prettiness, her trade is beginning to wear on her. She denies her status as a whore.

Margot

Chronicle of a Death Foretold
Gabriel García Márquez

The narrator's sister. She feels that **Santiago Nasar** would be a good catch for any girl, since he is young, handsome, and wealthy. She invites Santiago over for breakfast.

Mother Marguerite de Jesus

Cyrano de Bergerac
Edmond Rostand

A nun in **Roxane**'s convent. She admires and respects **Cyrano de Bergerac** and allows him to visit whenever he wishes.

Marheyo

Typee
Herman Melville

The senior man in the house where **Tommo** lives. Marheyo is kind and sympathetic. In the final scene, it is Marheyo who insists that Tommo should be free.

Maria of *Love's Labour's*

Love's Labour's Lost
William Shakespeare

One of three ladies attending the **Princess of France**. Maria, along with **Rosaline** and **Katherine**, helps catch the fancy of the three lords attending the **King of Navarre**. Maria is wooed by **Longaville**, who secretly sends her a sonnet and pearls.

Maria of *Twelfth Night*

Twelfth Night
William Shakespeare

Olivia's clever, daring young serving-woman. Maria is remarkably similar to her antagonist, **Malvolio**, who harbors aspirations of rising in the world through marriage. In recompense for her collaboration in the plot against Malvolio, **Sir Toby Belch**, Olivia's drunk uncle, agrees to marry her.

Maria

Dubliners
James Joyce

A quiet, prim maid and the protagonist of "Clay." Maria goes to visit **Joe Donnelly**, the man she nursed many years ago.

Maria

Steppenwolf
Hermann Hesse

The blond and blue-eyed lover of **the Steppenwolf**. Maria is a creature of the senses, talented in all the intricate arts of love and as voracious as she is generous. Her love reenergizes Harry with new hope and vitality. Harry's love affair with Maria makes him fond of aspects of sexuality and romance that he previously had seen as degrading and trivial.

Maria

The Power and the Glory
Graham Greene

Brigida's mother and the woman with whom **the Priest** had a brief but extremely significant affair. Maria is unhappy to see the priest return, although she helps him to escape capture when the police come to her village.

Maria

For Whom the Bell Tolls
Ernest Hemingway

A young woman with **Pablo**'s band who falls in love with **Robert Jordan**. Maria exudes a natural, glowing beauty, despite the fact that she has recently suffered a traumatic rape at the hands of Fascist soldiers and has had most of her hair shorn off. Though she is vulnerable and lays her emotions bare, she exhibits an inner strength, determination, and resilience that enable her to bear her difficult circumstances. Robert Jordan affectionately calls Maria "Rabbit."

Maria

All the Pretty Horses
Cormac McCarthy

The kind, quiet cook at **Don Hector**'s ranch. Though she never says so explicitly, she seems deeply sympathetic toward **John Grady Cole**.

Father Jose Dulce Maria

The House of the Spirits
Isabel Allende

A revolutionary priest from Tres Marias. He teaches and repeatedly helps **Pedro Tercero Garcia**, who is a revolutionary and an outcast.

Marian

Tess of the d'Urbervilles
Thomas Hardy

A milkmaid whom **Tess Durbeyfield** befriends at the Talbothays Dairy. Marian, **Izz Huett**, and **Retty** remain close to Tess throughout the rest of her life. They are all in love with **Angel Clare** and are devastated when he chooses Tess over them. Marian turns to drink but nevertheless remains helpful to Tess.

Marian

This Boy's Life
Tobias Wolff

The obnoxious, overweight housekeeper in the Seattle boarding-house. Marian and **Jack Wolff** have nothing but disdain for one another. Marian shares the ramshackle house with **Kathy** and **Rosemary Wolff**, and looks after Jack and Kathy's baby, **Willy**, while Kathy and Rosemary work. Rosemary ignores Marian's pleas for Rosemary to discipline Jack.

Mariana of *All's Well*

All's Well that Ends Well
William Shakespeare

A Florentine neighbor of the **Widow** and **Diana**. Mariana warns Diana to protect her chastity from the lecherous **Parolles** and the other soldiers.

Mariana of *Measure*

Measure for Measure
William Shakespeare

Lord Angelo's former fiancée. He called off the wedding after Mariana lost her dowry in the shipwreck that killed her brother, but is tricked into sleeping with her, believing he is sleeping with **Isabella**.

Marie

Uncle Tom's Cabin
Harriet Beecher Stowe

Augustine St. Clare's wife and **Evangeline St. Clare**'s mother, a self-centered woman.

Marie

The Power of One
Bryce Courtenay

A fifteen-year-old farm girl who works as a nurse in the Barberton hospital. **Peekay's mother** manages to turn her into a born-again Christian and Marie, in turn, tries to proselytize everyone she can.

Miss Marie

The Bluest Eye
Toni Morrison

One of the three local whores, along with **China** and **Poland**. Miss Marie (also known as **the Maginot Line**) is fat and affectionate. The whores live above the Breedlove apartment and befriend **Pecola Breedlove**. They are neither hookers with hearts of gold nor women whose innocence has been betrayed.

Marie-Claude

The Unbearable Lightness of Being
Milan Kundera

Franz's wife. A vulgar and pretentious Geneva socialite, she forced Franz to marry her by threatening suicide. She calmly allows Franz to move out but does not grant him a divorce, and after his death reclaims his body.

Mariequita

The Awakening
Kate Chopin

A young, pretty, flirtatious Spanish girl living on Grand Isle. Mariequita embodies the self-demeaning coquetry that **Edna Pontellier** shuns.

Marigold

The Black Prince
Iris Murdoch

Roger Saxe's mistress, who is pregnant with his child. Little is known about Marigold except that she is a dentist. Her presence in Roger's life testifies to the terrible state of his marriage.

Marin

The House on Mango Street
Sandra Cisneros

A Puerto Rican girl. Flirtatious, lively, and older than **Esperanza** and her friends, Marin shares her knowledge about makeup and boys. She lives with her aunt and uncle for a time, but is soon sent back to Puerto Rico.

Marina

Pericles
William Shakespeare

Pericles and **Thaisa**'s daughter. Born at sea during a storm, Marina is raised by **Cleon** and **Dionyza** in Tarsus. A model of beauty, grace, and chastity, Marina becomes famous for her virtue in Mytilene and eventually is reunited with her parents.

Marina Timofeyevna

Uncle Vanya
Anton Chekhov

A kind, elderly, and devout nurse. She resents the disruption of routine that the others have brought to the household. She delivers religious platitudes throughout the play and offers comfort to a number of characters (**Sofya**, **Astrov**, **Serbryakov**, etc.).

Mario

The Maids
Jean Genet

The milkman. Mario never appears onstage, but **Claire** and **Solange** frequently bring him up in their insults. Their plan is for Solange to get impregnated by him, but he seems to be carrying on affairs with both sisters.

Marjorie

In Our Time
Ernest Hemingway

Nick Adams's girlfriend and prospective bride back home. But in "The End of Something," he breaks it off with her, only to later question the wisdom of that action.

Lady Markby

An Ideal Husband
Oscar Wilde

A pleasant and popular woman. Lady Markby appears at the dinner party in Act I and visits **Lady Gertrude Chiltern** in Act II, both times with **Mrs. Cheveley**.

Jacob Marley

A Christmas Carol
Charles Dickens

Ebenezer Scrooge's former business partner, now deceased. When Marley was alive, he was just as self-absorbed and greedy as Scrooge. In death, he is doomed to eternally regret his misspent life.

The marlin

The Old Man and the Sea
Ernest Hemingway

An eighteen-foot fish that engages in an olympian struggle with the elderly Cuban fisherman **Santiago**. Santiago hooks the marlin on the first afternoon of his fishing expedition but is unable to pull the fish in because of its great size. The two engage in a three-day tug-of-war that often seems more like an alliance than a struggle. The exhausted Santiago finally succeeds in reeling the marlin in, killing it with a harpoon, and lashing it to the side of his boat. However, sharks devour the fish's carcass during the journey back to shore, leaving only a skeleton.

Francis Marloe

The Black Prince
Iris Murdoch

Christian Evandale's brother and **Bradley Pearson**'s ex-brother-in-law. Francis is a former doctor who is no longer allowed to practice after a scandal having to do with his handing out of perscriptions. Fallen, he is now a drunk who resorts to harassing his rich sister for money.

Marlow

Heart of Darkness and *Lord Jim*
Joseph Conrad

The protagonist of *Heart of Darkness* and the narrator of *Lord Jim*. Marlow is philosophical, independent-minded, and generally skeptical of those around him. He is also a master storyteller, eloquent and able to draw his listeners into his tale. Although Marlow shares many of his fellow Europeans' prejudices, he has seen enough of the world and has encountered enough debased white men to make him skeptical of imperialism. In *Lord Jim*, Marlow compulsively pieces together Jim's story and perpetuates it through various retellings.

Mr. and Mrs. Marlowe

The Member of the Wedding
Carson McCullers

Former boarders in **Frankie Addams**'s household. Frankie once caught the Marlowes having sex.

Philip Marlowe

The Big Sleep
Raymond Chandler

The novel's protagonist. Marlowe is a private detective who is asked to deal with a blackmailing case for the wealthy **General Sternwood**. Marlowe is a man of the streets, tough and clever, but he is honest and good-willed. Other characters even call him naïve in several instances. His dialogue and manner of speaking are particularly raw and witty.

Marmee

Little Women
Louisa May Alcott

The March girls' mother. Marmee is the moral role model for her girls. She counsels them through all of their problems and works hard but happily while her husband is at war.

Crime and Punishment
Semyon Zakharovich Marmeladov
Fyodor Dostoevsky

Sofya Semyonovna Marmeladova's father and **Katerina Ivanovna Marmeladova**'s husband. An alcoholic public official, Marmeladov understands that his drinking is ruining him and his family, but he cannot change. He dies after falling under the wheels of a carriage, perhaps in a drunken accident or perhaps in a suicide.

Crime and Punishment
Katerina Ivanovna Marmeladova
Fyodor Dostoevsky

Semyon Zakharovich Marmeladov's wife. Katerina Ivanovna has consumption, which gives her a persistent, bloody cough. She is very proud and repeatedly speaks of her aristocratic heritage.

Crime and Punishment
Polina Mikhailovna Marmeladova
Fyodor Dostoevsky

The oldest daughter of **Katerina Ivanovna Marmeladova** from her former marriage.

Crime and Punishment
Sofya Semyonovna Marmeladova
Fyodor Dostoevsky

Rodion Romanovich Raskolnikov's love and **Semyon Zakharovich Marmeladov**'s daughter. Sonya is forced to prostitute herself to support herself and the rest of her family. She is meek and easily embarrassed, but she maintains a strong religious faith. She is the only person with whom Raskolnikov shares a meaningful relationship.

Silas Marner
Silas Marner
George Eliot

The protagonist of the novel. Silas is a simple, honest, and kindhearted weaver. After losing faith in God and his fellow man, Silas lives for fifteen years as a solitary miser. After his money is stolen by **Dunstan Cass**, his faith and trust are restored by his adopted daughter, **Eppie**.

Typee
Marnoo
Herman Melville

A native who enjoys "taboo" status and who is able to therefore wander around the island. **Tommo** feels attracted to Marnoo just like all the Typees do. Marnoo ultimately is also a kind figure because it is he who tells other natives that Tommo is amongst the Typees, which eventually leads to Tommo's rescue.

My Ántonia
Jake Marpole
Willa Cather

One of the Burdens' hired hands. Jake goes out west with **Otto Fuchs**. Despite a quick temper, Jake is generally good-natured and innocent.

Colonel Gerineldo Márquez

One Hundred Years of Solitude
Gabriel García Márquez

The comrade-in-arms of **Colonel Aureliano Buendía**. He is the first to become tired of the civil war. Instead of fighting, he devotes himself to **Amaranta**, who steadily rebuffs his protestations of love even as she becomes more and more used to his presence. Withdrawn into himself, he becomes a shell of a man. It is only when he and Colonel Aureliano Buendía are captured and sentenced to execution by firing squad that Colonel Aureliano Buendía is forced to confront himself.

Marquis de Rollebon

Nausea
Jean-Paul Sartre

Although not a character in the novel per se, he is the subject of **Roquentin**'s research. He was a mysterious French aristocrat who meddled in politics during and after the French Revolution.

Marquise of Parolignac

Candide
Voltaire

A cunning, sexually licentious Paris socialite. She seduces **Candide** and steals some of his jeweled rings.

Mars

Greek Mythology
Unknown

The Roman name for the Greek god **Ares**.

Eddie Mars

The Big Sleep
Raymond Chandler

The novel's antagonist, the thoroughly corrupt leader of a gambling racket who has at least an indirect hand in almost all the murders that take place in the novel. Though Mars is a ruthless man, he will not taint his own hands with blood; instead, he hires others to do his dirty work. He maintains a hold on many of the characters in the book through his manipulative threats and offers of "protection."

Howard Marsellus

Dead Man Walking
Helen Prejean

The Pardon Board Chairman, who recognizes the arbitrary and biased nature of the death penalty but nevertheless continues to support executions. He is later convicted of taking bribes. Howard exposes to **Sister Helen Prejean** the corruption within the Pardon Board system.

Marsilla

Song of Roland
Unknown

The pagan king of Saragossa, the last Spanish city to hold out against the Frankish army. His vassal **Blancandrin** plans with the traitor **Ganelon** the ambush at Roncesvals and the death of **Roland**. While Roland does die that day, he chops off Marsilla's right hand. Badly weakened by this wound, Marsilla dies of grief when he hears of **Baligant**'s defeat. Marsilla's queen, **Bramimonde**, is later taken to Aix where she converts to Christianity.

Anthony Marston

And Then There Were None
Agatha Christie

A rich, athletic, handsome youth. Marston likes to drive recklessly and seems to lack a conscience. He killed two small children in a car accident caused by his speeding, but shows no remorse.

Martha

Who's Afraid of Virginia Woolf?
Edward Albee

The daughter of the president of New Carthage University and wife of **George**. While her marriage was once a loving relationship, it is now defined by sarcasm and frequent acrimony, due in part to her disappointment with her husband's aborted academic career. George and Martha engage in public and private humiliation and cruelty, drawing their guests, **Nick** and **Honey**, into their fights. Martha even attempts to have an affair with Nick. Only through a figurative exorcism on George's part can Martha accept her son's death.

Martha

I Am the Cheese
Robert Cormier

Adam Farmer's aunt, **Louise Farmer**'s sister. Martha is a cloistered nun in Maine. Adam is not meant to know about his aunt, because he is not supposed to have any knowledge of his past life as **Paul Delmonte.** Adam's mother has weekly phone calls with her, calling on the special telephone day that has become a Farmer family ritual.

Aunt Martha

Incidents in the Life of a Slave Girl
Harriet Ann Jacobs

Linda Brent's maternal grandmother and chief ally. She cares for her entire family, working tirelessly to buy her children's and grandchildren's freedom. Her unwavering piety leads her to attribute her enslavement to God's will and to patiently bear the loss of her children to slave traders. She is the only black woman in the book with her own home. She is essential to Linda's survival, but at times her maternal power threatens to suffocate her loved ones. She would rather see them in slavery than have them run away from her to freedom. She mourns the successful escape of her son, **Uncle Benjamin**, who has been dreadfully abused by his master.

Marthas

The Handmaid's Tale
Margaret Atwood

Infertile females who work as domestic servants.

Sister Marthe

Cyrano de Bergerac
Edmond Rostand

A nun in **Roxane**'s convent. She admires and respects **Cyrano de Bergerac** and allows him to visit whenever he wishes.

Martin

Candide
Voltaire

A cynical scholar whom **Candide** befriends. More knowledgeable and intelligent than either Candide or **Pangloss**, Martin is nonetheless a flawed philosopher. Since he always expects the worst, he often has trouble seeing the world as it really is.

Martin

The Old Man and the Sea
Ernest Hemingway

A café owner in **Santiago**'s village. The boy **Manolin** often goes to Martin for Santiago's supper.

Martin

Cloud Nine
Caryl Churchill

Victoria's husband. Martin often feels incompetent and frustrates himself by over-thinking his sex life. He does have a giving side, which he demonstrates in his relationship to **Lin**'s daughter **Cathy** and his own son **Tommy**. He is thoughtful but totally ineffectual and tries desperately to give Victoria enough space to live with Lin and **Edward** despite his own desires.

Martin

Fool For Love
Sam Shepard

A simple, innocent, and kind man who lives in a town near **May**'s hotel and works maintenance around town. He is an audience to May and **Eddie**'s conflicting stories and an involuntary sufferer to their verbal abuse and power struggle. Martin represents the hopeful but dull life ahead of May if she chooses to let go of Eddie for good. He is also an unknowing competitor to Eddie.

Elizabeth Martin

Emma
Jane Austen

Mr. Martin's kind sister and a close friend of **Harriet Smith**'s before Harriet met **Emma Woodhouse**. Harriet's feelings of guilt and her desire to rekindle her relationship with Elizabeth pose a dilemma for Emma, who finds the Martins pleasant, worthy people, but worries that Harriet may be tempted to accept Mr. Martin's offer if she again grows close with the family.

Mr. Robert Martin

Emma
Jane Austen

A twenty-four-year-old farmer. Mr. Martin is industrious and good-hearted, though he lacks the refinements of a gentleman. He lives at Abbey-Mill Farm, a property owned by **George Knightley**, with his mother and sisters.

Romola Martin

The Day of the Locust
Nathanael West

A woman who only appears as part of a brief flashback which consists of a near sexual encounter she and **Homer Simpson** had at the Iowa hotel where he worked as a bookkeeper.

Martine

Breath, Eyes, Memory
Edwidge Danticat

Sophie's mother, **Atie**'s sister and **Grandmè Ifé**'s daughter. Martine was raped at the age of sixteen by a masked Macoute in a cane field on her way home from school. The rape left Martine with a child, Sophie, and a lifetime of vivid nightmares. Martine emigrates to New York after Sophie's birth, where she works tirelessly at menial jobs. As a result, Sophie has the opportunity to leave Haiti and get an American education. Martine's continual struggle to be a good mother to Sophie and a sexually adequate lover to **Marc** remain powerfully informed by the twin violations of rape and of her own mother's practice of testing for virginity.

Meo Martinez

When the Legends Die
Hal Borland

Red Dillon's cook, **Thomas Black Bull**'s friend and a retired bronco rider. The illiterate Mexican man Meo and Tom become friends, as they understand each other's circumstances.

Martini

One Flew over the Cuckoo's Nest
Ken Kesey

Another hospital patient. Although Martini lives in a world of delusional hallucinations, **Randle McMurphy** includes him in the board and card games with the other patients.

Martino

Doctor Faustus
Christopher Marlowe

A friend of **Benvolio**'s who, along with **Frederick**, reluctantly joins Benvolio's scheme to kill **Faustus**.

Abel Martinson

Snow Falling on Cedars
David Guterson

Art Moran's young and relatively inexperienced deputy.

Young Martius

Coriolanus
William Shakespeare

Coriolanus and **Virgilia**'s son.

Marty

A Clockwork Orange
Anthony Burgess

A record shopper, who along with **Sonietta** chats up **Alex** as he purchases Beethoven's Ninth. They return to Alex's apartment to listen to records, where he rapes and beats them after getting them drunk.

André Marty

For Whom the Bell Tolls
Ernest Hemingway

The French Commissar of the International Brigades, the troops of foreign volunteers who serve on the Republican side in the Spanish Civil War. Marty has become blinded by political paranoia and is convinced that he is surrounded by enemies.

Bernard Marx

Brave New World
Aldous Huxley

Alpha male who fails to fit in because of his inferior physical stature. His insecurity about his size and status makes him discontented with the World State. When he discovers **Linda** and **John** the Savage at the New Mexico Savage Reservation, he relishes the chance to bring them to the World State, not only to gain vicarious attention, but to scandalize **the Director**, who had threatened to exile Bernard to Iceland. As Marx's social status improves, he becomes more outspoken against the World State, and is called alongside fellow dissident **Helmholtz Watson** to speak with **Mustapha Mond**, who exiles them both to colonies of freethinkers. Marx, whose discontent hypocritically stems from the desire to be accepted, considers this a tremendous punishment.

Carlo Marx

On the Road
Jack Kerouac

Sal Paradise's and **Dean Moriarty**'s close friend. Carlo is a brooding, sensual, and energetic poet.

Mary

The New Testament
Unknown

Jesus' mother, who becomes impregnated by the Holy Spirit. Mary is also one of the only people who remains with Jesus through the crucifixion.

Mary

The Adventures of Tom Sawyer
Mark Twain

Tom Sawyer's sweet, almost saintly cousin. Mary holds a soft spot for Tom. Like **Sid**, she is well-behaved, but unlike him, she acts out of genuine affection rather than malice.

Mary

Miss Lonelyhearts
Nathanael West

Shrike's wife. Mary has been having an ongoing affair with **Miss Lonelyhearts** and other men for some time, but Shrike allows this, as it saves him money. She enjoys the dreamy atmospheres of nightclubs and restaurants and clearly wishes to escape from her dreary home life.

Invisible Man
Mary
Ralph Ellison

A serene and motherly black woman with whom **the Narrator** stays after learning that the Men's House has banned him. Mary treats him kindly and even lets him stay for free. She nurtures his black identity and urges him to become active in the fight for racial equality.

The New Testament
Mary Magdalene
Unknown

A female follower of **Jesus** since the time of his Galilean ministry, when he exorcised her of seven demons. Mary Magdalene is a close friend of Jesus' and is one of the women who discover that his body is not in his tomb. Following this event, she witnesses the resurrected Jesus.

Anna Karenina
Marya Nikolaevna
Leo Tolstoy

Nikolai Dmitrich Levin's girlfriend and a former prostitute. They become involved after Nikolai Levin saves her.

The Caine Mutiny
Steve Maryk
Herman Wouk

A peacetime fisherman who decides that he wants to convert to the regular Navy after the war. Maryk is straightforward, blunt, and simple, but extremely loyal, dedicated, and knowledgeable about the sea and boat handling. Because of his naiveté, Maryk is taken in by **Thomas Keefer**'s constant complaining against **Philip Francis Queeg**, and is perhaps falsely convinced of Queeg's madness.

On the Road
Marylou
Jack Kerouac

Dean Moriarty's first wife. Marylou is a pretty but not particularly bright blonde from Colorado.

The Seagull
Masha
Anton Chekhov

The daughter of **Polina Andreyevna** and **Shamrayev**, the managers of **Sorin**'s farm. She always wears black because she is chronically depressed. A heavy drinker and snuff addict, Masha remains tormented by her repressed, unrequited love for the young playwright **Treplyov**. Meanwhile, the poor schoolteacher **Medvedenko** pursues Masha despite his vanilla, obsequious personality. Masha is critical and unsympathetic toward him, even though she herself suffers from unrequited love. Masha ultimately marries Medvedenko even though she never stops loving Treplyov.

Mashpia

My Name Is Asher Lev
Chaim Potok

The man at **Asher Lev**'s school who is in charge of the spiritual development of the students. Mashpia is kind and committed to his community. He expresses concern for the well-being of his students and is genuinely interested in their personal development.

B.F. Mason

The Heart Is a Lonely Hunter
Carson McCullers

A con artist who passes through town and preys on the black population by selling them false "government pensions." Mason is caught by the police, but not until after he has spent or hidden all his money.

Bertha Mason

Jane Eyre
Charlotte Brontë

Edward Rochester's secret wife. She is a formerly beautiful and wealthy Creole woman who has become insane, violent, and bestial. She lives locked in a secret room on the third story of Thornfield and is guarded by **Grace Poole**, whose occasional bouts of inebriation sometimes enable Bertha to escape. Bertha eventually burns down Thornfield, plunging to her death in the flames.

Mr. Mason

Wide Sargasso Sea
Jean Rhys

An elegant English visitor to Coulibri Estate who meets and marries **Annette**. Mr. Mason is a wealthy Englishman who comes to the West Indies to make money. Captivated by his second wife's beauty, he intends to become even more prosperous by restoring Coulibri. He is confident in his authority to control the servants, believing them harmless and lazy and dismissing his wife's fears of revolt. Mr. Mason effectively abandons Annette and **Antoinette** after the estate is destroyed in a fire.

Richard Mason

Jane Eyre
Charlotte Brontë

Bertha Mason's brother. During a visit to Thornfield, he is injured by his mad sister. After learning of **Edward Rochester**'s intention to marry Jane, Mason arrives with **Mr. Briggs** in order to thwart the wedding and reveal the truth of Rochester's prior marriage.

Richard Mason

Wide Sargasso Sea
Jean Rhys

Mr. Mason's son by his first marriage. After studying for several years in the Barbados, Richard moves to Spanish Town, where he negotiates **Antoinette**'s marriage arrangements after his father's death. He persuades **Rochester**, the unnamed English gentleman, to marry his stepsister for 30,000 pounds and rights to the girl's inheritance. Later, Richard visits the couple in England and hardly recognizes Antoinette as the madwoman locked in the attic.

Masson

The Stranger
Albert Camus

One of **Raymond**'s friends, who invites Raymond, **Meursault**, and **Marie** to spend a Sunday at his beach house with him and his wife. It is during this ill-fated trip at the beach that Meursault kills **the Arab**. Masson testifies to Meursault's good character when Meursault is put on trial for murder.

The Master

The Turn of the Screw
Henry James

The uncle of **Flora** and **Miles**, who are orphans. A dashing, charming man, the master asks the **governess** to assume complete responsibility for running Bly and to refrain from contacting him for any reason.

The Master

His Dark Materials
Robert Pullman

The Master of Jordan College in Oxford, where **Lyra Belacqua** has spent most of her life. The Master tries to poison **Lord Asriel** and gives Lyra the aleithiometer. His daemon is a raven.

Edward Henry Masterman

Murder on the Orient Express
Agatha Christie

Ratchett's valet, brought into the murder plot by **Cyrus Hardman**.

Cass Mastern

All the King's Men
Robert Penn Warren

The brother of **Jack**'s grandmother. During the middle of the nineteenth century, Cass had an affair with **Annabelle Trice**, the wife of his friend **Duncan**. After Duncan's suicide, Annabelle sold a slave, **Phebe**; Cass tried to track down Phebe, but failed. He became an abolitionist, but fought in the Confederate Army during the Civil War and was killed. Jack tried to use his papers as the basis of his Ph.D. dissertation, but walked away from the project when he was unable to understand Cass Mastern's motivations.

Gilbert Mastern

All the King's Men
Robert Penn Warren

Cass Mastern's wealthy brother.

President Masuda

Bel Canto
Ann Patchett

A government figure who never makes a direct appearance in the novel. The terrorists invade the party in the hopes of capturing him, but he has stayed home to watch an important episode of his favorite soap opera.

Matasaip

Island of the Blue Dolphins
Scott O'Dell

The chief during **Kimki**'s absence, who is in charge the day everyone leaves the island.

Mathemagician

The Phantom Tollbooth
Norton Juster

King Azaz's brother. He lives in a world of numbers, and unlike his brother, he has doubts about releasing **Rhyme** and **Reason**.

Don Mathias

The Jew of Malta
Christopher Marlowe

Abigail's lover and **Lodowick**'s friend. Mathias and Lodowick kill each other in a duel masterminded by **Barabas**, making Mathias the first innocent victim of Barabas's many plots to exact revenge.

Matt

White Fang
Jack London

Weedon Scott's musher. Matt feeds **White Fang** and works him on the sled after the two men rescue White Fang from a fight.

Keith Matthews

The Outsiders
S. E. Hinton

See **Two-Bit**.

"Professor" Matthews

Black Boy
Richard Wright

Aunt Maggie's second husband. The "Professor" is an outlaw. After Matthews apparently kills a white woman, he and Maggie flee to Detroit. Several years later, he deserts Maggie.

Mattie

The Bean Trees
Barbara Kingsolver

The owner of Jesus Is Lord Used Tires and a mother figure for **Taylor Greer**. She is wise and kind. She allows illegal immigrants to stay in her home, operating a kind of sanctuary. Her garden of beautiful vegetables and car parts is an inspiration for **Turtle**, whose first word is *bean* and who loves all kinds of vegetables.

Aunt Matty

A Day No Pigs Would Die
Robert Newton Peck

A very distant relation to **Robert Peck** whose name is Martha Plover. Robert's Aunt Matty comes by about once a month to have tea with **Aunt Carrie** and **Lucy Peck** and to share the town gossip. She is a former

English teacher, and she tries to tutor Robert in English grammar and sentence diagrams, but has a difficult time. Her intentions for Robert are good, even though she is forceful about things with him.

Maud

Cloud Nine
Caryl Churchill

Clive's mother-in-law. Always a traditionalist, Maud encourages the women around her to behave as she does. She has a penchant for crankiness when her relatives fall out of line. Maud adheres to the notion that women are meant to serve and honor their husbands by taking care of the home. Throughout the first act, Maud's presence stops each lover from carrying out their secret love affairs.

Maugrim

The Lion, the Witch, and the Wardrobe
C. S. Lewis

A wolf and the chief of **the White Witch**'s Secret Police. **Peter Pevensie** murders the evil wolf after Maugrim chases **Susan Pevensie** up a tree.

Matthew Maule the elder

The House of the Seven Gables
Nathaniel Hawthorne

A simple farmer in the 1600s. The elder Matthew Maule was hanged for witchcraft, most likely at the instigation of **Colonel Pyncheon**, who coveted and stole the elder Maule's land and built upon it the house of the seven gables. Before he died, Maule warned that God would give the Pyncheons blood to drink. This curse still haunts the Pyncheons, who are aware of their family history.

Matthew Maule the younger

The House of the Seven Gables
Nathaniel Hawthorne

The carpenter grandson of the original **Matthew Maule (the elder)** and the son of **Thomas Maule**. Thomas built the house of the seven gables. The younger Matthew Maule nurses a powerful grudge against the Pyncheon family, which follows from the curse that the elder Matthew Maule placed upon **Colonel Pyncheon**. Maule believes that the house of the seven gables is rightfully his and that the curse will never end until the house has been returned to the Maule family. **Gervayse Pyncheon** believes that the younger Matthew Maule knows where the deed to the Pyncheon family land in Maine is. The younger Maule turns a deaf ear to Gervayse's offers of money if he can produce the desired documentation, but he eventually agrees to help Gervayse in exchange for the house of the seven gables. Before giving the information, Maule asks to see Gervayse's young daughter, **Alice Pyncheon**. Maule uses Alice as a medium to contact the spirits of Colonel Pyncheon, the elder Matthew Maule, and Thomas Maule. The younger Maule declares that the secret will not be revealed until the deed no longer has value. He tells Pyncheon to keep the house of the seven gables and glories in the fact that he now has control over Alice. Over the next few years, Maule uses his power to toy with Alice. Alice suffers greatly from this indignity and she eventually dies after catching pneumonia while participating in Matthew's antics. Matthew Maule is broken with guilt by the way his petty antics, which were only meant to humble, have cost the innocent girl her life.

Thomas Maule

The House of the Seven Gables
Nathaniel Hawthorne

The son of **Matthew Maule (the elder)** and the father of **Matthew Maule (the younger)**. Thomas Maule is the carpenter forced to build a new house on land stolen from his own family by **Colonel Pyncheon**. People believe that Thomas stole the Pyncheons' deed to their Maine land and hid it somewhere in the house of the seven gables.

Maurice

The Catcher in the Rye
J. D. Salinger

The elevator operator at the Edmont Hotel. Maurice procures a prostitute for **Holden Caulfield**. He later comes up to Holden's hotel room to pin him against the wall while **Sunny** takes money from Holden.

Mavis

Ellen Foster
Kaye Gibbons

A kind field hand on **Ellen**'s grandmother's farm. Mavis takes Ellen under her wing and teaches her how to row the land and how to stay cool in the unbearable summer heat. She tells Ellen of how she had known her mother as a child and says that Ellen looks very much like her. Mavis has a large, happy family that Ellen admires and wants to emulate.

Boris A. Max

Native Son
Richard Wright

A Jewish lawyer who defends **Bigger Thomas**. Boris works for the Labor Defenders, an organization affiliated with the Communist Party. In Bigger's trial, he argues that institutionalized racism and prejudice—not inherent ethnic qualities—create violence in urban ghettos.

Miracle Max

The Princess Bride
William Goldman

The king's former leading miracle man. **Prince Humperdinck** fired him, and so he retired. Max distrusts everybody but prides himself on the talent of his younger life, and therefore is willing to take a chance with **Westley** to show off his still-impressive abilities with the dead.

Madame Maxime

Harry Potter and the Goblet of Fire
J. K. Rowling

The enormous and elegant headmistress of Beauxbatons, and the object of **Hagrid**'s affection.

Cory Maxson

Fences
August Wilson

The teenage son of **Troy Maxson** and **Rose Maxson**. A senior in high school, Cory is a good student, ambitious young man, and excellent football player—good enough that college recruiters are coming to see him play. While Rose sees Cory as hope for the future, Troy tries to keep Cory tied to the past. He refuses to let Cory play for the college recruiters, telling him he should have a job and learn a trade. Cory comes of age during the course of the play when he challenges and confronts Troy and leaves home.

Gabriel Maxson

Fences
August Wilson

Troy Maxson's brother, and uncle to **Lyons Maxson**, **Cory Maxson**, and **Raynell Maxson**. Gabriel was a soldier in the Second World War, during which he received a head injury that required a metal plate to be surgically implanted into his head. Because of the physical damage and his service, Gabriel receives checks from the government that Troy used in part to buy the house where the play takes place. Gabriel wanders around the Maxson family's neighborhood, singing and carrying a basket and trumpet.

Lyons Maxson

Fences
August Wilson

Troy Maxson's oldest son, fathered before Troy's time in jail, before he met **Rose Maxson**. Lyons is an ambitious jazz musician, but like most musicians, has a hard time making a living. For income, he mostly depends on his girlfriend **Bonnie** (who never appears on stage). Lyons drops by the Maxson house frequently on Troy's payday to ask for money.

Raynell Maxson

Fences
August Wilson

Troy Maxson's illegitimate child, mothered by **Alberta**, his lover. Her innocent need for care and support convinces **Rose Maxson** to take the child—and Troy—back into the house. Later, Raynell plants seeds, the symbol of nurturing and compassion, in the once barren dirt yard.

Rose Maxson

Fences
August Wilson

Wife of **Troy Maxson**, mother of **Cory Maxson**. Rose has been married to Troy for eighteen years at the outset of the play. She overlooks Troy's faults and sees his positive attributes. She is a fair judge of character, a realist, and unlike Troy, doesn't live in the past. She is aware they are on the brink of social change. She puts faith in her husband and hopes for a better future through her son, whom she sides with in his wish to play football. Her acceptance of Troy's illegitimate daughter, **Raynell Maxson**, as her own child further illustrates her compassion.

Troy Maxson

Fences
August Wilson

The protagonist and tragic-hero, husband of **Rose Maxson**, father to **Lyons Maxson**, **Cory Maxson**, and **Raynell Maxson**, and brother to **Gabriel Maxson**. Troy is an African-American man who works for the sanitation department, lifting garbage into trucks. Hardworking, strong, and prone to telling compelling, fanciful stories and twisting the truth, he is the family breadwinner and plays the dominant role in his over-thirty-year friendship with fellow sanitation worker **Jim Bono**. Once a baseball star in the Negro Leagues, he is convinced he would have been a legend in the Major Leagues as well; however, his ability diminished before baseball became integrated. While he possesses great familial love and responsibility, his affair and illegitimate child threaten that stability. Though Troy begins the play loved and admired, his death leaves behind his negative attributes as an inheritance.

May

Fool for Love
Sam Shepard

Eddie's lover and half-sister, and daughter of the **Old Man**. Simultaneously strong-willed and vulnerable, May lives alone in a seedy motel room on the outskirts of the Mojave Desert. May is a good match for Eddie in that she can keep up with his verbal gymnastics and power plays. Despite her wish for stability and independence, May is as vulnerable to their love and desire as Eddie is. While Eddie seems to have accepted the nature of their incestuous relationship, May feels ashamed and seems to be in denial of the situation.

Maylene

The Land
Mildred D. Taylor

A girl who lives near the lumbering camp where **Jessup** is the boss. Maylene is a sweet young girl who packs **Paul-Edward Logan** and **Mitchell Thomas** a lunch before their escape from the camp.

Harry Maylie

Oliver Twist
Charles Dickens

Mrs. Maylie's son. Harry is a dashing young man with grand political ambitions and career prospects, which he eventually gives up to marry **Rose Maylie**.

Mrs. Maylie

Oliver Twist
Charles Dickens

A kind, wealthy older woman. Mrs. Maylie is **Harry Maylie**'s mother and **Rose Maylie**'s adopted aunt.

Rose Maylie

Oliver Twist
Charles Dickens

Agnes Fleming's sister. Rose, who is raised by **Mrs. Maylie**, is beautiful, compassionate, and forgiving.

Mayor

Inherit the Wind
Jerome Lawrence & Robert E. Lee

The mayor of Hillsboro. The mayor supports **Matthew Harrison Brady** and welcomes him to town. Under pressure from a state capitol worried about media coverage of the trial by people like **Harry Y. Esterbrook**, the mayor instructs the judge to pass a lenient sentence at the trial's conclusion.

Mayor of London in *Henry VI, Part I*

Henry VI, Part I
William Shakespeare

The mayor of London. He struggles to keep peace between the **Cardinal Beaufort, Bishop of Winchester** and **Humphrey, Duke of Gloucester** and their men on the streets of London. When he orders them to cease fighting with weapons upon pain of death, they revert to throwing rocks. His inability to stop the lords' fights exemplifies the victory of civil strife over English authority.

Richard III
William Shakespeare

Lord Mayor of London in *Richard III*

The mayor of London, used as a pawn by **King Richard III** and the **Duke of Buckingham** during Richard's rise to power.

Cold Sassy Tree
Olive Anne Burns

Clayton McAllister

A brash, charming, and wealthy rancher from Texas. Clayton's shabby treatment of **Miss Love Simpson** makes her fear love and marriage.

Pnin
Vladimir Nabokov

Charles McBeth

A student of **Timofey Pnin**'s.

The Color of Water
James McBride

Andrew Dennis McBride

Ruth McBride Jordan's first husband and **James McBride**'s biological father. Dennis was a violinist from North Carolina whom Ruth met while working at her aunt's leather factory. He was gentle and strong, and fathered eight of Ruth's twelve children. He died from lung cancer at a young age.

The Color of Water
James McBride

Helen McBride

James McBride's older sister and **Ruth McBride Johnson**'s daughter. Helen is a strong-willed and pretty girl who runs away from home at the age of fifteen.

The Color of Water
James McBride

James McBride

Author and main narrator of the memoir, and the son of **Ruth McBride Jordan** and **Andrew Dennis McBride**. James is a writer, journalist, jazz musician, and composer. Like his mother, he places significant emphasis on his Christian faith and on family unity. As a young man, he expresses his confusion by succumbing to drugs and crime. Later, he becomes diligent and determined.

A Passage to India
E. M. Forster

Mr. McBryde

The Chandrapore police superintendent and the prosecutor of **Dr. Aziz**'s trial. Mr. McBryde shows some respect for Indians but elaborately explains why darker-skinned people are inferior. Like his casual friend

Cyril Fielding, McBryde defies the expectation of the British community, divorcing his wife for his mistress, **Miss Derek**.

Edward McCabe

Cat's Cradle
Kurt Vonnegut

A marine deserter, Edward McCabe hired **Bokonon** to transport him to Miami. However, they shipwrecked on San Lorenzo, which lacked a government at the time. Seeing the horrendous poverty and disease among the island's residents, Bokonon and McCabe set out to make the island into a utopia. McCabe and Bokonon quickly realized that no amount of legal and economic reform could improve the standard of living for the island's residents. Bokonon sought to comfort the island's citizens with a religion, Bokononism, based on lies. At his request, McCabe, now a dictator, outlawed Bokononism so that it would be more exciting and meaningful to its practitioners. The strain of playing their roles in this charade drove both Bokonon and McCabe a little insane.

McCann

A Portrait of the Artist as a Young Man
James Joyce

A fiercely political student at **Stephen Dedalus**'s school.

Amodeus McCaslin

Go Down, Moses
William Faulkner

Carothers McCaslin's son, **Theophilus McCaslin**'s twin brother. He raises his sister's son, **McCaslin Edmonds**, and tends to the house while his brother runs the plantation. He is nicknamed Buddy.

Carothers McCaslin

Go Down, Moses
William Faulkner

The patriarch of the McCaslin family and the founder of the McCaslin plantation. Most of the important characters are his descendents, through one of three branches: the male branch (**Isaac**, descended from Carothers's son **Buck**), the female branch (the Edmondses, descended from Carothers's daughter and her husband, **Edmonds**), and the black branch (**Tomey's Turl** and his descendents, including **Lucas Beauchamp**, descended from Carothers's affair with his slave-girl Tomey).

Isaac McCaslin

Go Down, Moses
William Faulkner

Carothers McCaslin's grandson, the son of **Buck McCaslin** and **Sophonsiba Beauchamp**; born in the late 1860s. Raised by his second-cousin **McCaslin Edmonds**. Taught to hunt as a young boy by **Sam Fathers**, he remains deeply committed to the wilderness and to hunting.

Theophilus McCaslin

Go Down, Moses
William Faulkner

Carothers McCaslin's son, **Amodeus McCaslin**'s twin brother, **Isaac McCaslin**'s father. He runs the McCaslin plantation while Amodeus tends the house. He eventually marries **Sophonsiba Beauchamp**, Isaac's mother. He is nicknamed Buck.

Mr. McChoakumchild

Hard Times
Charles Dickens

The unpleasant teacher at **Thomas Gradgrind**'s school. As his name suggests, McChoakumchild stifles children's imaginations and feelings.

Clarisse McClellan

Fahrenheit 451
Ray Bradbury

A beautiful girl who introduces **Guy Montag** to the world's potential for beauty and meaning with her gentle innocence and curiosity. She is an outcast from society because of her odd habits, which include hiking, playing with flowers, and asking questions.

Alphie McCourt

Angela's Ashes
Frank McCourt

Frank McCourt's youngest brother.

Angela McCourt

Angela's Ashes
Frank McCourt

Frank McCourt's humorous and loving "Mam." Angela is never overbearing or self-pitying, despite her difficult life. As she deals with her husband's alcoholism, the deaths of three of her children, and the necessity of begging for handouts from aid agencies, her expectations disintegrate. Despite the painful thwarting of her own hopes, however, Angela always puts her children's welfare above all else.

Eugene and Oliver McCourt

Angela's Ashes
Frank McCourt

Frank McCourt's younger twin brothers. Both Eugene and Oliver die within several months of one another, shortly after the McCourts arrive in Limerick. Their deaths devastate **Angela McCourt**, who is already grieving over the loss of her baby girl, **Margaret McCourt**.

Frank McCourt

Angela's Ashes
Frank McCourt

The book's author, narrator, and protagonist. As the teller of his own life story, McCourt writes from the perspective of an adolescent looking out onto the world rather than as an adult looking back on his childhood.

Malachy McCourt, Sr.

Angela's Ashes
Frank McCourt

An alcoholic who spends his wages and dole money on drink while his children starve. **Frank McCourt**'s treatment of his father is masterfully evenhanded, revealing not only the despair inflicted on the family by Malachy's drinking, but also the obvious love between Malachy and his sons.

Malachy McCourt, Jr.

Angela's Ashes
Frank McCourt

Frank McCourt's younger brother by one year. Malachy is named after his father, **Malachy McCourt Sr.**

Michael McCourt

Angela's Ashes
Frank McCourt

Frank's second-youngest brother, born in Limerick. Frank believes Michael was left by an angel on the seventh step of their house.

Mr. McEachern

Light in August
William Faulkner

Joe Christmas's adoptive father. McEachern is a stern, unfeeling, demanding man and a pious Presbyterian. Joe kills him by hitting him over the head with a chair at a local dance.

Mrs. McEachern

Light in August
William Faulkner

Joe Christmas's adoptive mother. Mrs. McEachern is a soft, clumsy, loving woman. Joe hates her.

Mr. McGarrity

A Tree Grows in Brooklyn
Betty Smith

The saloonkeeper in the bar where **Johnny Nolan** hangs out and gets drunk. Mr. McGarrity is a dreamer. Wishing he had a family like Johnny's, he lives vicariously through Johnny and misses him enough to help out the family after he dies.

Pat McGloin

The Iceman Cometh
Eugene O'Neill

Ed Mosher's drinking partner. He used to be a police lieutenant, but he was ruined by a graft scandal.

Minerva McGonagall

The Harry Potter Series: Books 1–4
J. K. Rowling

The head of Gryffindor House, a stern but deeply concerned witch. Her devotion to the letter of the law is impressive but a bit cold.

Miss McGoun

Babbitt
Sinclair Lewis

Babbit's young, unmarried secretary, with whom he briefly wishes he could have an affair. When Babbitt's reputation and business suffer during his brief rebellion against the values of Zenith's middle class, Miss McGoun resigns from her job to work for a rival real estate firm.

Bill McGovern

Alas, Babylon
Pat Frank

Elizabeth McGovern's father and **Lavinia McGovern**'s husband. After his wife's death, he and Lib move in with **Randy Bragg**.

Elizabeth "Lib" McGovern

Alas, Babylon
Pat Frank

Randy Bragg's girlfriend, and later his wife. A smart, resourceful, attractive woman, she moves to Fort Repose from the north with her parents, **Bill McGovern** and **Lavinia McGovern**. After her mother dies of diabetes, she and her father move in with Randy.

Lavinia McGovern

Alas, Babylon
Pat Frank

Elizabeth McGovern's mother, who suffers from diabetes.

Charles McKelvey

Babbitt
Sinclair Lewis

One of **Babbitt**'s college classmates who, along with his wife, **Lucile**, has become part of Zenith's upper class. The Babbitts try to become friends with the McKelveys, but the McKelveys treat them with snobbery and disdain.

Lucile McKelvey

Babbitt
Sinclair Lewis

Charles McKelvey's wife. Lucile likes to rub elbows with British aristocrats like **Sir Gerald Doak**. Like her husband, she treats the Babbitts with disdain.

Albert McKisco

Tender Is the Night
F. Scott Fitzgerald

An aspiring American writer with an inferiority complex and streak of cowardice. McKisco is forced into a duel with the mercenary soldier **Tommy Barban** after he takes exception to a comment Tommy makes about McKisco's wife, **Violet**. Both men survive the duel unscathed, and McKisco goes on to establish himself as a prize author.

Violet McKisco

Tender Is the Night
F. Scott Fitzgerald

Albert McKisco's obnoxious, self-important wife. Violet is obsessed with social status and her husband's career as a writer.

Lightfoot McLendon

Cold Sassy Tree
Olive Anne Burns

A pretty and studious young girl from the impoverished Mill Town. Lightfoot is the object of **Will Tweedy**'s affections. Although she marries **Hosie Roach**, Lightfoot feels affection for Will and parts from him with difficulty.

Randle McMurphy

One Flew over the Cuckoo's Nest
Ken Kesey

The novel's protagonist, a big, redheaded gambler, a con man, and a backroom boxer. He was sentenced to six months at a prison work farm, and when he was diagnosed as a psychopath he did not protest because he thought the hospital would be more comfortable. McMurphy is the obvious foil for the quiet and repressed **Chief Bromden** and the sterile, mechanical **Nurse Ratched**. His loud, free laughter stuns the other patients, who have grown accustomed to repressed emotions.

Mrs. McNab

To the Lighthouse
Virginia Woolf

An elderly woman who takes care of the house on the Isle of Skye, restoring it after ten years of abandonment during and after World War I.

Hector McQueen

Murder on the Orient Express
Agatha Christie

Ratchett's personal secretary. Hector is in cahoots with **Mary Debenham** and the Armstrong family. McQueen tries to hard to tell **Hercule Poirot** that Ratchett did not speak any French, making him an immediate suspect in the case.

Sergeant McShane

A Tree Grows in Brooklyn
Betty Smith

Katie Nolan's second husband, whom she is about to marry when the book ends. Sergeant McShane is a successful public figure who will support Katie and her children well.

McWatt

Catch-22
Joseph Heller

A polite and cheerful pilot who often flies **John Yossarian**'s planes.

Mrs. McWeeney

Girl, Interrupted
Susanna Kaysen

The evening nurse on **Susanna Kaysen**'s ward. Mrs. McWeeney's old-fashioned uniform, aphorisms, and severity alienate the girls.

General George Meade

The Killer Angels
Michael Shaara

The recently appointed commander of the Union armies. Cautious but intelligent, Meade arrives a bit late to the Battle of Gettysburg.

Mr. Meany

A Prayer for Owen Meany
John Irving

Owen Meany's father, a lumbering, simple man who runs a granite business. When Owen is eleven, his father and mother tell him he was a virgin birth.

Mrs. Meany

A Prayer for Owen Meany
John Irving

Owen Meany's mother, a melancholy woman who spends all her time indoors and almost never speaks.

Owen Meany

A Prayer for Owen Meany
John Irving

John Wheelwright's best friend, a dwarf with weirdly luminous skin and a high-pitched, nasal voice that is represented in all capital letters throughout the novel. Owen's father runs a granite quarry; some of Owen's eccentricities may be due to the inhalation of granite dust at an early age. Despite his tiny size, Owen is a powerful personality, often dominating situations and telling adults what to do even when he is a young child. Owen possesses a powerful and personal religious faith, believing himself to be God's instrument on Earth. When he and John are eleven, Owen accidentally kills John's mother when a foul ball he hits at a Little League game breaks her neck.

Bessie Mears

Native Son
Richard Wright

Bigger Thomas's girlfriend.

Meatball

The Caine Mutiny
Herman Wouk

A pudgy but good-humored sailor. He shows an uncanny understanding of the problems with **Philip Francis Queeg** and eventually looks up to **Willie Keith** as a voice of reason.

Medea

Medea
Euripides

A princess from Colchis on the Black Sea. Medea selflessly helps **Jason** defeat her own father and obtain the Golden Fleece. When Jason abandons her after several years, Medea's suicidal despair progresses to sadistic fury. In her passion for Jason, Medea kills his new wife and then her own children. Afterward, she rides off in a chariot drawn by dragons.

Medea

The King Must Die
Mary Renault

A priestess of the Mother who is living with Aigeus (**Aegeus**) when **Theseus** gets to Athens. Lady Medea wants the King to poison Theseus and thereby lift the curse of the Mother that has been laid on his house. When Aigeus recognizes Theseus as his son, he refuses.

Mrs. Medlock

The Secret Garden
Frances Hodgson Burnett

The head of the servants at Misselthwaite Manor. Mrs. Medlock is distinguished by her punctilious obedience of all of **Archibald Craven**'s odd rules. Beneath her rigid exterior, she is basically kind.

Medusa

Greek Mythology
Unknown

One of the three Gorgons, a horrible woman-beast with snakes for hair. Medusa's gaze turns men to stone. She is killed by **Perseus**.

Semyon Semyonovich Medvedenko

The Seagull
Anton Chekhov

A local schoolteacher who is poor and must support his family at home while later supporting his new family with **Masha**. He is a boring conversationalist because he spends most of his time complaining about his poverty. Medvedenko pursues the melancholy Masha, eventually winning her hand in marriage, though his new wife never stops loving the brooding playwright **Treplyov**.

Caroline "Carrie" Meeber

Sister Carrie
Theodore Dreiser

The protagonist of the novel, a young woman who travels to Chicago to stay with her sister and her brother-in-law. The cosmopolitan consumer world of Chicago enthralls the small-town Carrie. Her first job is a low-paid, arduous position in a factory. When she loses her job, her sister and brother-in-law are unable to support her, so she becomes **Charlie Drouet**'s mistress. Afterward, she becomes infatuated with another man, **George Hurstwood**. Carrie and Hurstwood move to New York, where they discover that married life is far less exciting than their affair. Carrie's material demands grow greater, and ultimately she leaves Hurstwood because he fails to provide her with the lavish life she wants. At the novel's end, Carrie becomes a famous, high-paid actress in New York City.

Meeker

Inherit the Wind
Jerome Lawrence & Robert E. Lee

The bailiff at the Hillsboro courthouse.

Dink Meeker

Ender's Game
Orson Scott Card

Ender Wiggin's platoon leader in Rat Army, and a squadron leader in the battles with the buggers. Dink is a very good strategist who always looks out for Ender. He tries to stop **Bonzo Madrid** and warns Ender of the plot to kill him.

Eliphalet Meeker

My Brother Sam Is Dead
Christopher & James Lincoln Collier

Father of **Sam Meeker** and **Tim Meeker**, and the owner of Meeker Tavern. Mr. Meeker wants nothing to do with the war and is angry at Sam for participating in it.

Sam Meeker

My Brother Sam Is Dead
Christopher & James Lincoln Collier

Tim Meeker's older brother. Sam is headstrong and often at odds with his father. He leaves Yale to fight the rebel cause and is ultimately framed as a cattle thief and shot publicly.

Susannah Meeker

My Brother Sam Is Dead
Christopher & James Lincoln Collier

Mother of **Sam Meeker** and **Tim Meeker**. Mrs. Meeker is very religious and hardworking.

Tim Meeker

My Brother Sam Is Dead
Christopher & James Lincoln Collier

The narrator. Tim greatly admires his older brother, **Sam Meeker**, and longs to be more involved in the excitement and danger of the war.

Mehevi

Typee
Herman Melville

The most important chief of the Typees. Mehevi is a noble and dignified figure whom everyone, including **Tommo**, treats with respect. Tommo spends almost every afternoon sitting and eating with him because he so enjoys Mehevi's company.

Melanie

Oranges Are Not the Only Fruit
Jeanette Winterson

Jeanette's first lover. Jeanette meets Melanie at a fish stand. Melanie's docility allows her later to marry, have children, and deny the existence of her lesbian love.

Melanthius

The Odyssey
Homer

A treacherous, opportunistic goatherd. Melanthius supports the suitors, especially **Eurymachus**. Melanthius abuses the beggar who appears in **Odysseus**'s palace, not realizing that the man is Odysseus himself.

Melantho

The Odyssey
Homer

Melanthius's sister, a maidservant in **Odysseus**'s palace. Melantho abuses Odysseus when he is disguised as a beggar. She is having an affair with **Eurymachus**.

Oliver Mellors

Lady Chatterley's Lover
D. H. Lawrence

The lover in the novel's title. Mellors is the gamekeeper on **Clifford Chatterley**'s estate, Wragby. He is aloof, sarcastic, intelligent and noble. He was born near Wragby, and worked as a blacksmith until he ran off to the army to escape an unhappy marriage. In the army he rose to become a commissioned lieutenant—but was forced to leave the army when he came down with pneumonia. Disappointed by a string of unfulfilling love affairs, Mellors lives in quiet isolation, from which he is redeemed by his relationship with **Lady Chatterley**: the passion unleashed by their lovemaking forges a profound bond between them. At the end of the novel, Mellors is fired from his job as gamekeeper and works as a laborer on a farm, waiting for a divorce from his old wife.

Boma Mellowbug

Pigs in Heaven
Barbara Kingsolver

One of Heaven's most eccentric personalities.

Melquíades

One Hundred Years of Solitude
Gabriel García Márquez

The gypsy leader who brings technological marvels to Macondo and befriends the Buendía clan. Melquíades is the first person to die in Macondo. He encourages **José Arcadio Buendía** to explore alchemy. **José Arcadio Segundo** also lives in the gypsy's old room, studying Melquíades's manuscripts. **Aureliano (II)** works in Melquíades's old laboratory and is visited occasionally by the ghost of Melquíades. Aureliano (II) finally translates the manuscripts at the end of the novel, and they contain the entire history of Macondo, foretold.

Count Melun

King John
William Shakespeare

A French nobleman. Mortally wounded in battle, Melun tips off the defecting English lords that **Lewis** plans to behead them if the French win the battle.

Bayonet and Silver Melville

The Shipping News
E. Annie Proulx

The owners of the ship *Tough Baby*. Silver and Bayonet Melville are bruised from fighting with each other, and they are drunks. They are also clients of **the aunt** who take the boat without paying her. However, once the head of Bayonet is found in a suitcase, the aunt receives a mysterious bundle of U.S. cash wrapped in a strip of the blue leather she used to upholster the ship. Silver and the ship's steward are later captured in Hawaii.

Melvin

Girl, Interrupted
Susanna Kaysen

Susanna Kaysen's therapist. Impressed by Susanna's intelligence, Melvin begins an advanced program of analysis with her.

Meme

One Hundred Years of Solitude
Gabriel García Márquez

The daughter of **Fernanda del Carpio** and **Aureliano Segundo**, Meme's real name is **Renata Remedios**. Meme falls madly in love with **Mauricio Babilonia**, a mechanic working for the banana plantation who courts her bluntly and shamelessly. Fernanda discovers them kissing in a movie theater and confines the lovesick Meme to the house. When Babilonia returns to Meme, a guard hired by Fernanda shoots him, shattering his spine and paralyzing him for the rest of his life. Meme is imprisoned in a convent. The product of her affair with Babilonia is **Aureliano (II)**.

Menas

Antony and Cleopatra
William Shakespeare

An ambitious young soldier under **Pompey**. Menas asks for permission to kill the triumvirs **Octavius Caesar**, **Antony**, and **Lepidus**. Though this would result in Pompey's controlling the entire empire, Pompey declines the request, saying that such an action would damage his honor.

Mencius

Walden
Henry David Thoreau

A Chinese sage of the fourth century B.C. and a disciple of **Confucius**. Mencius was best known for his anthology of sayings and stories collected under the title *The Book of Mencius*. Like his master's work, Mencius's combination of respect for social harmony and the inward reconciliation with the universe exerted a powerful influence on **Henry David Thoreau**.

Don Pedro de Mendez

Gulliver's Travels
Jonathan Swift

The Portuguese captain who takes **Gulliver** back to Europe after the voyage to the land of the **Houyhnhnms**.

Bel Canto
Ann Patchett

Oscar Mendoza

A South American contractor and one of the captives. Mendoza and the vice president, **Iglesias**, often chat, talking about their early love affairs, their adoration for **Coss**, and the affection they feel for one of the young terrorists, **Ishmael**.

The Iliad and *The Odyssey*
Homer

Menelaus

The King of Sparta, **Agamemnon**'s younger brother and **Helen**'s husband. The Trojan War begins when the Trojan **Paris** abducts Helen from Menelaus. Menelaus is quieter, less imposing, and more modest than Agamemnon. After the war, Menelaus helps **Telemachus** in his quest for his father, **Odysseus**.

The Aeneid
Virgil

Menelaus

See above.

Troilus and Cressida
William Shakespeare

Menelaus

A Greek commander, **Agamemnon**'s brother, and **Helen**'s abandoned husband.

Coriolanus
William Shakespeare

Menenius

A Roman patrician and a friend to **Coriolanus**. Menenius uses his wit and clever tongue to avoid conflict.

Night
Elie Wiesel

Dr. Josef Mengele

The historical Nazi physician who presided over the selection of arrivals at Auschwitz, where **Eliezer** was sent, who directed horrific experiments on human subjects.

Ulysses
James Joyce

John Henry Menton

A solicitor who employed **Patrick Dignam, Jr.** When **Leopold Bloom** and **Molly Bloom** were first courting, Menton was a rival for Molly's affections. He scorns Bloom.

Doctor Faustus
Christopher Marlowe

Mephastophilis

A devil who becomes **Faustus**'s servant. Mephastophilis delivers moving descriptions of what the devils have lost in their eternal separation from God and repeatedly reflects on the torment of eternal damnation, emerging as a tragic figure in his own right.

Valencia Merble

Slaughterhouse-Five
Kurt Vonnegut

Billy Pilgrim's pleasant, fat, loving wife. Valencia and Billy share a well-appointed home and have two children together, but Billy consistently distances himself from his family.

Mercadé

Love's Labour's Lost
William Shakespeare

A French lord. Mercadé appears at the end of the play to inform the **Princess of France** of her father's death.

Orest Mercator

White Noise
Don DeLillo

A nineteen-year-old senior at **Heinrich**'s high school who is training to set a new record for sitting in a cage with deadly snakes. Orest claims to be unafraid of dying.

Mercédès

The Count of Monte Cristo
Alexandre Dumas

Edmond Dantès's fiancée before he is wrongfully imprisoned. Though she marries **Fernand Mondego** while Dantès is in prison, she never stops loving Dantès. For all her avowed weakness and fear, Mercédès proves herself capable of great courage on three occasions: first, when she approaches Dantès to beg for the life of her son, **Albert de Morcerf**; second, when she reveals her husband's wickedness in order to save Dantès's life; and third, when she abandons her wealth, unwilling to live off a fortune that has been tainted by Fernand's misdeeds. In the end, **the Count of Monte Cristo** gives Mércedès **Louis Dantés**'s house in Marseilles as well as Louis's remaining money. Albert goes off to the army.

Mercedes

The Call of the Wild
Jack London

Hal's sister and **Charles**'s wife. Hal and Charles buy the sled-dog team that once belonged to **François** and **Perrault**. As a group, the three have no experience in the wild, and, thus, they make mistake after mistake.

Merchant

The Canterbury Tales
Geoffrey Chaucer

A fur and cloth trader. The merchant trades mostly with **Flanders**. He is part of a powerful and wealthy class in Chaucer's society.

Second Merchant

The Comedy of Errors
William Shakespeare

A tradesman to whom **Angelo** owes money. Angelo can only repay him once **Antipholus of Ephesus** pays him for a golden chain which he has mistakenly given to **Antipholus of Syracuse**. Antipholus of Ephesus's refusal to pay the Second Merchant leads to a false arrest and more general confusion.

Merchant of Ephesus

The Comedy of Errors
William Shakespeare

An Ephesian merchant and friend of **Antipholus of Syracuse**. He gives money to Antipholus and advises him to say he is from Epidamnum, since the new Ephesian law states that any Syracusan found in town will be executed.

Mercury

Greek Mythology
Unknown

The Roman name for the Greek messenger-god **Hermes**; the son of **Jupiter**.

Mercutio

Romeo and Juliet
William Shakespeare

A kinsman to **Prince Escalus**, **Romeo**'s close friend, and a friend of the Montague house. Mercutio overflows with imagination, wit, and at times a strange, biting satire and brooding fervor. After Romeo marries the Capulet daughter **Juliet**, Romeo no longer upholds the Montague feud against the Capulets and therefore won't allow **Tybalt** to goad him into a fight. Mercutio chides Romeo for his docility and steps into the fight, only to be murdered by Tybalt.

Max Mercy

The Natural
Bernard Malamud

A journalist who delights in exposing the seedy aspects of baseball. Mercy makes it his mission to pry into the private lives of baseball players and put their personal flaws on display.

Meredith

The Autobiography of Benjamin Franklin
Benjamin Franklin

Benjamin Franklin's business partner. Together they first found a new printing house, and later take over **Samuel Keimer**'s. Meredith, however, does not work very hard, and eventually leaves for the southern colonies.

Madame Merle

The Portrait of a Lady
Henry James

An accomplished, graceful, and manipulative woman who also happens to be **Gilbert Osmond**'s longtime lover. Madame Merle is a popular lady without a husband or a fortune. Motivated by her love for **Gilbert Osmond**, Merle manipulates **Isabel Archer** into marrying Osmond, delivering Isabel's fortune into his hands and ruining Isabel's life in the process. Unbeknownst to either Isabel or **Pansy Osmond**, Merle is Pansy's mother.

Merlin

A Connecticut Yankee in King Arthur's Court
Mark Twain

A hack magician with the fatal flaw of actually believing in his own sleight of hand. Merlin is deceptive and petty and terribly vindictive. As the **Yankee** gains power, Merlin tries many plots to foil him. Merlin simply wants to have **King Arthur**'s favor again.

Merlyn

The Once and Future King
T. H. White

A magician who has already lived the future. Merlyn is **King Arthur**'s tutor and friend. Arthur's creation of the Round Table and a more civilized England is largely due to Merlyn's influence. Although Merlyn is powerful, he is also kind and a little absentminded. Later on, he is less powerful under the influence of **Nimue**.

Mrs. Merridew

The Moonstone
Wilkie Collins

Rachel Verinder's conservative aunt.

Reverend Louis Merrill

A Prayer for Owen Meany
John Irving

The doubt-plagued Congregationalist minister in Gravesend, who often speaks to **Owen Meany** about matters of religious faith. At the end of the book, **John Wheelwright** learns that the Reverend Merrill is his father.

Billy Merrit

The Chosen
Chaim Potok

A young blind boy **Reuven Malter** meets in the hospital.

Roger Merrit

The Chosen
Chaim Potok

Billy Merrit's father. He was the driver in the car accident that led to his wife's death and Billy's blindness.

Marquise de Merteuil

Dangerous Liaisons
Pierre-Ambroise-François Choderlos de Laclos

The toast of all of Paris. She is considered wise and chaste, though she has had more lovers than most professionals. She is a self-described self-made woman. After her husband died, she set about educating herself and creating a reputation. She enters into an unsavory deal with her former lover **the Vicomte de Valmont**. Valmont must provide Merteuil with written proof that he has seduced **the Présidente de Tourvel**, a religious married woman, before Merteuil will sleep with Valmont again. Merteuil also wants revenge on her former lover, **the Comte de Gercourt**. He is soon meant to marry **Cécile Volanges**. Merteuil thinks that Valmont should deflower the young Cécile to spoil the secretly nasty Gercourt's prized chaste future bride. Because of Merteuil and Valmont's declarations of war upon each other, all plans fall by the wayside. Valmont ends up dead in a duel with the **Chevalier Danceny**, and Merteuil ends up horribly disfigured and ostracized. The ruined Merteuil flees to Holland.

Evelina
Fanny Burney

Lord Merton

A bold and ill-mannered young Lord whom **Evelina Anville** meets for the first time at the Pantheon. He flirts with Evelina even though he is engaged to be married to **Lady Louisa Orville**.

The Red Tent
Anita Diamant

Meryt

The kind Egyptian midwife who delivers **Dinah**'s son, **Re-mose**. Meryt becomes Dinah's closest friend and confidant in Egypt. Meryt is barren but has two adopted sons. With Meryt's friendship, Dinah learns to trust herself again.

Antigone 1946
Jean Anouilh

Messenger

A typical figure of Greek drama who also appears in Sophocles' *Antigone*. The Messenger is a pale and solitary boy who bears the news of death.

Bel Canto
Ann Patchett

Joachim Messner

A Swiss representative for the Red Cross who negotiates between the government and the terrorists. Messner is the one person allowed to come and go from the mansion. He punctuates the general happiness with frequent reminders that the situation will end badly.

The Power and the Glory
Graham Greene

The mestizo

A person whom **the Priest** meets about halfway through his journey and who continues to reappear throughout the last half of the novel. Impoverished, occasionally delirious and always calculating, the mestizo sees in the outlawed priest an opportunity to make money.

His Dark Materials
Robert Pullman

Metatron

An angel of the highest order. Metatron was a powerful human being before he became Lord Regent of "the Authority" (God). **Lord Asriel** and **Marisa Coulter** give their own lives to destroy him.

The Poisonwood Bible
Barbara Kingsolver

Methuselah

A parrot, left for **Nathan Price** and his family by **Brother Fowles**.

William Methwold

Midnight's Children
Salman Rushdie

An Englishman from whom the Sinais buy their house in Bombay.

Metzger

The Crying of Lot 49
Thomas Pynchon

A lawyer who works for Warpe, Wistfull, Kubitschek and McMingus. He has been assigned to help **Oedipa Maas** execute **Pierce Inverarity**'s estate. He and Oedipa have a brief affair in San Narciso.

Meursault

The Stranger
Albert Camus

The protagonist and the stranger to whom the novel's title refers. He is emotionally indifferent, even to the death of his mother **Madame Meursault** and to the marital propositions of his lover **Marie**. He also refuses to adhere to the accepted moral order of society. After Meursault kills **the Arab**, he is put on trial. However, the focus of his trial quickly shifts away from the murder itself and toward Meursault's attitudes and beliefs. Meursault's atheism, his lack of outward grief at his mother's funeral, and his lack of repentance for the crime of murder all represent serious challenges to the morals of his society. Consequently, society brands him an outsider and sentences him to death by the guillotine.

Madame Meursault

The Stranger
Albert Camus

The old woman whose death begins the action of the novel. Three years prior, **Meursault** sent her to an old-persons home. Meursault identifies with his mother and believes that she shared many of his attitudes about life, including a love of nature and the capacity to become accustomed to virtually any situation or occurrence. Most important, Meursault decides that, toward the end of her life, his mother must have embraced a meaningless universe and lived for the moment, just as he does.

Mexican girl

Ceremony
Leslie Marmon Silko

Betonie's grandmother. Wise even as a young girl, she begins the new ceremony along with **Descheeny**. She raises Betonie and ensures that he gains the tools he will need to continue the ceremony.

Mexican woman

A Streetcar Named Desire
Tennessee Williams

A vendor of Mexican funeral decorations who frightens **Blanche DuBois**.

Rachel Meyerson

Walden Two
B. F. Skinner

A member of Walden Two. She is in charge of "Clothing for Women" and helps **T.E. Frazier** give a tour of the community on the first day of the visit.

Mr. and Mrs. Wilkins Micawber

David Copperfield
Charles Dickens

An unlucky couple crippled by precarious finances. Although Mr. Micawber can't support his own family, he generously and industriously serves others. Mrs. Micawber stands by her husband despite his flaws.

Michael

Paradise Lost
John Milton

The chief of the archangels. Michael leads the angelic forces against **Satan** and his followers in the battle in Heaven and stands guard at the Gate of Heaven. He shows **Adam** the future of the world in Books XI and XII.

Brother Michael

A Portrait of the Artist as a Young Man
James Joyce

A kindly cleric who takes care of **Stephen Dedalus** and **Athy** at the infirmary.

Michaelis

Lady Chatterley's Lover
D. H. Lawrence

A successful Irish playwright with whom **Lady Chatterley** has an affair early in the novel. Michaelis asks Connie to marry him, but she decides against it, realizing that he is like all other intellectuals: a purveyor of vain ideas and empty words.

M. Michel

The Plague
Albert Camus

The concierge for the building where **Rieux** works, and the plague's first victim.

Pierre Michel

Murder on the Orient Express
Agatha Christie

Father of the suicidal nursemaid of **Daisy Armstrong**, and the conductor of the Orient Express. Pierre, like the other servants, does not initially receive much scrutiny. However, as the novel progresses, **Hercule Poirot** discovers his involvement in the murder.

Fatima Michele

Stranger in a Strange Land
Robert A. Heinlein

Miriam's daughter. Her paternity is ambiguous, though **Jubal Harshaw** suspects that Fatima was fathered by either **Valentine Michael Smith** or **Dr. "Stinky" Mahmoud**, who marries Miriam before Fatima is born.

Michie

Lucky Jim
Kingsley Amis

Miss O'Shaughnessy's boyfriend, and a pain to **Jim Dixon**. He is a junior history student at the college and takes his schooling very seriously. Much to Dixon's annoyance, he is particularly interested in Dixon's special subject course, a class that Dixon had created with the express purpose of luring pretty girls.

Mickey

The Chosen
Chaim Potok

A sickly six-year-old boy whom **Reuven Malter** meets while in the hospital.

Lady Middleton

Sense and Sensibility
Jane Austen

A distant relation of the Dashwoods. Lady Middleton lives at Barton Cottage with her husband, **Sir John Middleton**, and their four spoiled children.

Sir John Middleton

Sense and Sensibility
Jane Austen

A jovial but vulgar man who invites **Mrs. Dashwood** and her daughters, his distant relations, to stay at Barton Cottage after Mr. and Mrs. **John Dashwood** inherit Norland.

The midwife

Tristram Shandy
Laurence Sterne

The local delivery-nurse who is commissioned to assist at **Mrs. Shandy**'s labor.

Miep

Anne Frank: Diary of a Young Girl
Anne Frank

See **Miep Gies**.

Miguel

The Day of the Locust
Nathanael West

Earle's Mexican companion and would-be roommate—if they ever had a house. Miguel keeps gamecocks and is quite proud of them. Much to Earle's dismay, Miguel and **Faye** are powerfully attracted to each other. Like Earle, Miguel can quickly turn violent.

Miguel

The House of the Spirits
Isabel Allende

Amanda's younger brother. Miguel first sees **Alba** at her birth, and when he meets her again eighteen years later he falls in love with her. Their relationship lasts through the end of the book. Miguel is also a revolutionary who joins the guerrillas after the Military Coup, which puts **Esteban Garcia** into power.

Flora Miguel

Chronicle of a Death Foretold
Gabriel García Márquez

The pretty but uninteresting woman that **Santiago Nasar** was betrothed to marry.

Nahir Miguel

Chronicle of a Death Foretold
Gabriel García Márquez

The father of **Flora Miguel**. He warns **Santiago Nasar** that **Pedro Vicario** and **Pablo Vicario** are waiting to kill him.

Mike

Johnny Got His Gun
Dalton Trumbo

Kareen's crotchety father. Mike worked as a coal miner for twenty-eight years and then worked on the railroad.

Mike

The Fountainhead
Ayn Rand

A tough, ugly electrician. He admires **Howard Roark**'s ability instantly and helps construct buildings Roark designs.

Mike

A View from the Bridge
Arthur Miller

A Longshoreman and friend of **Eddie Carbone**'s. Mike hangs out with **Louis** outside Eddie's home. Louis and Mike praise Eddie for keeping the illegal immigrants **Marco** and **Rodolpho**.

Agafya Mikhailovna

Anna Karenina
Leo Tolstoy

Konstantin Dmitrich Levin's former nurse, now his trusted housekeeper.

Liberius Avercievich Mikulitsin

Dr. Zhivago
Boris Pasternak

Son of **Avercius Mikulitsin** and a leader of the partisan army. He lives near the Varykino estate. He treats **Yury Andreyevich Zhivago** well as long as the doctor does what he deems right for the cause of the Revolution.

Mildred

Happy Days
Samuel Beckett

A young girl. **Winnie** tells Mildred's story about undressing her doll in the middle of the night. It is unclear if Mildred is the young Winnie or a pure fantasy.

Mildred's Aunt

The Hairy Ape
Eugene O'Neill

A stuffy, fat, middle-aged aristocratic woman who is intensely critical of **Mildred**'s involvement in social work.

Miles

The Turn of the Screw
Henry James

The orphaned ten-year-old nephew of the **governess**'s employer. Miles is expelled from school, perhaps because he engaged in homosexual conduct with some classmates or imparted inappropriate sexual knowledge to them. It is also implied that **Peter Quint** either sexually molested Miles or gave him information about sex. Miles is an extraordinarily beautiful, clever child. He grows uncomfortable with the **governess**'s attentions. It is possible that the governess smothers him to death.

Rosa Millard

The Unvanquished
William Faulkner

Grandmother of **Bayard**. Granny Millard is a stubborn old woman who at first seems difficult to like: she is quick to punish others and rigidly moral, even though her morality does not prevent her from lying and cheating when she has to. She sets up an audacious mule-stealing scam against the Yankees that lasts for almost a year. But despite these apparent flaws, Faulkner portrays her as a tireless crusader for her family and for the poor people of the county.

Chief Tee Ah Millatoona

One Flew over the Cuckoo's Nest
Ken Kesey

Chief Bromden's father, also known as the Pine That Stands Tallest on the Mountain, chief of the Columbia Indians. He married a Caucasian woman and took her last name. She made him feel small and drove him to alcoholism.

The Miller

The Canterbury Tales
Geoffrey Chaucer

A member of the pilgrimage who threatens **the Host**'s notion of propriety when he drunkenly insists on telling the second tale. The Miller seems to enjoy overturning all conventions: he ruins the Host's carefully planned storytelling order; he rips doors off hinges; and he tells a tale that is somewhat blasphemous.

The Miller sisters

Jazz
Toni Morrison

Alice Manfred's neighbors. They take care of **Dorcas** and a few other children in the afternoons. They disapprove of the styles and fashions of the era and worry, like Alice, about moral corruption.

Daisy Miller

Daisy Miller
Henry James

A young, beautiful American girl traveling in Europe. **Winterbourne** falls in love with her, as does **Mr. Giovanelli**. But because she does not conform to the social etiquette of her European setting, Daisy is eventually shunned from society. Owing to her reckless behavior, she dies of Roman fever.

Dr. Miller

Go Ask Alice
Anonymous

The psychiatrist at **Alice**'s mental hospital. He is sympathetic to Alice's case.

Hugh Miller

All the King's Men
Robert Penn Warren

Willie Stark's attorney general. An honorable man who resigns following the **Byram White** scandal.

Judge Miller

The Call of the Wild
Jack London

Buck's original master. Judge Miller is the owner of a large estate in California's Santa Clara Valley. Buck is treated well as the prized animal of the estate, but is eventually illegally sold by **Manuel** to some sled-dog traders.

Lee Miller

I Never Promised You a Rose Garden
Joanne Greenberg

One of **Deborah**'s fellow patients at the mental hospital. When the normally silent **Sylvia** speaks, Lee hurries to inform the medical staff. Deborah admires her for having the courage to participate in reality for Sylvia's benefit even though Sylvia will probably not thank her for it.

Mrs. Miller

Tom Jones
Henry Fielding

A faithful friend to **Tom** and a caring and concerned mother to **Nancy** and **Betty**. Feisty and active, Mrs. Miller carries through on her promises and becomes Tom's biggest advocate to **Allworthy**.

Mrs. Miller

Daisy Miller
Henry James

Daisy Miller and **Randolph Miller**'s mother. Mrs. Miller is a nervous woman who is constantly ill. Members of society disapprove of her disregard for Daisy's behavior.

Nancy Miller

Tom Jones
Henry Fielding

The daughter of **Mrs. Miller** who becomes **Nightingale**'s wife.

Randolph Miller

Daisy Miller
Henry James

Daisy Miller's younger brother, who is about nine or ten years old. Randolph is greedy and self-righteous about his own country.

Millie

Pigs in Heaven
Barbara Kingsolver

Annawake Fourkiller's sister-in-law. Millie and her husband **Dellon** are an example of the way the Cherokee value all kinds of family configurations. Though divorced, they continue to have children together.

Miss Millie

The Color Purple
Alice Walker

The wife of the mayor of the town where **Celie** lives. Miss Millie is racist and condescending, but she admires the cleanliness and good manners of **Sofia**'s children, so she asks Sofia to be her maid. Sofia refuses and ends up fighting the mayor. Sofia is sent first to jail, then to Miss Millie's, where she ends up working as her maid as a punishment. Miss Millie is responsible for separating Sofia from her children.

Aubrey Mills

A Portrait of the Artist as a Young Man
James Joyce

Stephen Dedalus's friend. Together they play imaginary adventure games.

Milly

House Made of Dawn
N. Scott Momaday

Abel's lover in Los Angeles. Milly, who has a plain face and a constant laugh, is a social worker on Abel's case. She starts visiting Abel and his roomate, **Ben Benally**, socially, which makes Abel begin to appreciate her. Milly and Abel eventually become lovers, and she nurtures him even when he loses his job and starts drinking heavily.

Milo

The Phantom Tollbooth
Norton Juster

The main character, a bored little boy. Milo takes a trip through the mysterious make-believe tollbooth that appears in his bedroom one day and learns lessons that enable him to find his way through a number of demon encounters. In the end, Milo is inspired and fascinated by his world.

Ross Milton

Across Five Aprils
Irene Hunt

Jethro Creighton's friend. Milton defends Jethro from remarks about **Bill Creighton**'s loyalties. Milton also takes an interest in Jethro's education, giving him a textbook to accelerate his knowledge in proper grammar and speech. Milton accompanies **Jenny Creighton** to Washington, DC, to see **Shadrach Yale**.

Mina

Dicey's Song
Cynthia Voigt

Dicey's schoolmate. Mina is a pretty, well-liked, and intelligent girl who takes an interest in Dicey because she is so different from the other students. Mina persists good-naturedly in her attempts to befriend Dicey despite the other girl's aloofness.

Milo Minderbinder

Catch-22
Joseph Heller

A fantastically powerful mess officer. Milo controls an international black-market syndicate and is revered all over the world. Ruthlessly money-hungry, he bombs his own soldiers as part of a contract with Germany. Milo takes his official job very seriously, so **John Yossarian**'s division eats well.

Minerva

The Aeneid
Virgil

The Roman name for the Greek goddess **Athena**. She protects the Greeks during the Trojan War and helps them conquer Troy. Like **Juno**, Minerva dislikes the Trojans because **Paris** judged **Venus** the most beautiful goddess.

Mineu

Annie John
Jamaica Kincaid

The boy that **Annie** played with when she was a young girl. He tricked her into sitting naked on a red anthill, so that she was stung all over. When she meets him later in life, she remembers this incident as a time when her mother stood up for her.

Hosain, Conte di Minghetti

Tender Is the Night
F. Scott Fitzgerald

A wealthy man from southwestern Asia and the second husband of **Mary North**. **Dick** and **Nicole Diver** inadvertently insult Hosain's sister in a misunderstanding about their child's bath.

Mrs. Manson Mingott

The Age of Innocence
Edith Wharton

May Welland and the **Countess Ellen Olenska**'s grandmother. Mrs. Mingott is a fat and fiery old aristocratic lady who wields great influence over the New York clan. While her moral standards are irreproachable, she has some unorthodox social views. She insists on family solidarity and continues to support Ellen financially when she leaves New York to return to Europe.

Minimus

Animal Farm
George Orwell

Poetic pig who writes verse about **Napoleon**. He pens the banal patriotic song "Animal Farm, Animal Farm" to replace the earlier idealistic hymn "Beasts of England," which **Old Major** passes on to the others.

The Minister

Giants in the Earth
O. E. Rölvaag

An unnamed character who arrives in the settlement one day and holds divine services at **Per Hansa**'s house. The minister comforts Per and **Beret Hansa**, and his sermon and communion service succeed in restoring Beret's sanity. However, Beret replaces her former depression with religious mania.

Minister of the Interior

A Clockwork Orange
Anthony Burgess

Government official who orders Ludovico's Technique to be used on **Alex**. The Minister believes Ludovico's Technique will ease the overburdened prison system by reprogramming young offenders like Alex, and shows little concern for its effect on the offenders themselves. He worries that Alex might be used as a rallying point for dissidents like **F. Alexander** and after Alex's suicide attempt tries to buy his cooperation with a new stereo and a position at the National Gramodisc Archives.

Willie Mink

White Noise
Don DeLillo

Shadowy project manager behind Dylar, the drug **Babette** has been taking to relieve her of her fear of death. Willie runs drug experiments from his motel room, trading sex for drugs. He loses his mind and spends his days staring vacantly at a soundless television. He becomes the epitome of the white noise that haunts the novel, and the focal point of **Jack Gladney**'s fear of death.

Minnie

A Room with a View
E. M. Forster

Mr. Beebe's rambunctious thirteen-year-old niece, who stays with the Honeychurches during a diphtheria epidemic.

Minnie

Mourning Becomes Electra
Eugene O'Neill

Louisa Ames' meek middle-aged cousin and most eager listener. She sneaks around the **Mannon** property to spy along with Louisa and her husband, **Amos Ames**.

Minnie

Flowers for Algernon
Daniel Keyes

A female mouse bought by **Fay Lillman** as a companion for **Algernon**.

Minnie May

Anne of Green Gables
L. M. Montgomery

Diana Barry's little sister. When Minnie May falls ill with the croup, **Anne Shirley** saves her life. As a result, **Mrs. Barry** gains a new respect for Anne and permits Diana to reestablish her friendship with Anne.

Detective Minogue

The Assistant
Bernard Malamud

The father of **Ward Minogue** and the detective who investigates the crimes on the **Bobers**' block. Detective Minogue is a sympathetic character who treats the Bobers kindly.

Ward Minogue

The Assistant
Bernard Malamud

Detective Minogue's wicked son. Although his father is a detective, Ward Minogue has long violated the law. His father takes Ward's failings seriously, beating him and ejecting him from his household. Ward is racist and cruel, with no redeeming qualities. He attempts to rape **Helen Bober**. He hits **Morris Bober** out of malice.

Minos

The King Must Die
Mary Renault

The King of Crete. When **Theseus** arrives as a bull-dancer, the current Minos is sick with leprosy. Minos no longer believes in the gods, but he aids Theseus because he wants to stop **Asterion** and save his daughter **Ariadne**.

Minos

Inferno
Dante Alighieri

A giant beast who judges the sinners in the Second Circle of Hell (Canto V). The number of times Minos curls his tail around himself corresponds to the Circle of Hell appropriate for each sinner. In Greek mythology, Minos was the wise and just king of Crete.

Minotaur

Greek Mythology
Unknown

The half-man, half-bull monster that terrorizes **Minos**'s Labyrinth. **Theseus** kills it.

Harry Minowitz

The Heart Is a Lonely Hunter
Carson McCullers

A boy, several years older than **Mick Kelly**, who lives next door to the Kellys. Harry and Mick become friends after Mick's party, though they later have a sexual encounter that largely ruins their relationship. Harry is Jewish and frequently worries about the Nazi regime in Germany; aside from **Biff Brannon**, Harry is one of the only characters who pays close attention to world events.

Claire Minton

Cat's Cradle
Kurt Vonnegut

Wife of **Horlick Minton**.

Horlick Minton

Cat's Cradle
Kurt Vonnegut

Husband of **Claire Minton** and the new American ambassador to San Lorenzo. **John** meets the Mintons on the plane to San Lorenzo. Horlick delivered a speech that argued against the murderous consequences of patriotism and nationalism. Shortly after, he died in an accident.

Count Mippipopolous

The Sun Also Rises
Ernest Hemingway

A wealthy Greek count and a veteran of seven wars and four revolutions. Count Mippipopolous meets **Lady Brett Ashley** at a cafe, becomes infatuated with her, and initiates an affair. The count stands out as stable and sane amid the careless, amoral, pleasure-seeking crowd that revolves around Brett, **Jake Barnes**, and their friends.

Miranda

The Tempest
William Shakespeare

Prospero's daughter. Miranda was brought to the island at an early age and has never seen anyone other than her father and **Caliban**.

Lieutenant-Colonel Miranda

For Whom the Bell Tolls
Ernest Hemingway

A Republican staff office brigade commander in the Spanish Civil War. Miranda's only goal in the war is not to be demoted from his current rank.

Miriam

Stranger in a Strange Land
Robert A. Heinlein

One of **Jubal Harshaw**'s three beautiful, extremely competent live-in secretaries. Her colleagues are **Anne** and **Dorcas**, and she marries **Dr. "Stinky" Mahmoud** and gives birth to **Fatima Michele**.

Captain Mirvan

Evelina
Fanny Burney

The rude and rough-mannered husband of **Mrs. Mirvan** who returns after nearly seven years in the service. The anti-Gallic Captain spends most of his time finding ways to torment **Madame Duval**.

Maria Mirvan

Evelina
Fanny Burney

Evelina Anville's pleasant and amiable childhood friend.

Mrs. Mirvan

Evelina
Fanny Burney

The polite, delicate, and genteel wife of **Captain Mirvan**. Mrs. Mirvan assumes the responsibility of watching over **Evelina Anville** when she comes to visit her daughter, **Maria Mirvan**.

The Miss Guests

The Mill on the Floss
George Eliot

Stephen Guest's two sisters. They are unattractive and snobbish.

Missouri

Alas, Babylon
Pat Frank

The wife of **Two-Tone Henry**. She lives with him on the Henry farm and cleans houses for a living.

Harold Mitchell

A Streetcar Named Desire
Tennessee Williams

Stanley Kowalski's army friend, coworker, and poker buddy. He courts **Blanche DuBois** until he finds out that she lied to him about her sordid past. Though he is clumsy and unrefined, Mitch is more sensitive and gentlemanly than Stanley and his other friends. Blanche and Mitch are an unlikely match: nevertheless, they bond over their lost loves, and when the asylum takes Blanche away against her will, Mitch is the only person besides **Stella Kowalski** who despairs over the tragedy.

Mr. Mitchell

This Boy's Life
Tobias Wolff

The gym teacher at Concrete high who organizes the "smokers." Mr. Mitchell forces **Jack Wolff** and **Arthur Gayle** to battle one another in the ring.

Rummy Mitchens

Major Barbara
George Bernard Shaw

A poor woman. Like **Price**, Rummy has embellished her down-and-out condition to pander to the workers of the Army.

Mithoo

Shabanu
Suzanne Fisher Staples

The camel **Shabanu** helps birth. Mithoo's mother dies of a snakebite. Because no other female camels will nurse the orphaned baby, Shabanu takes him under her protection.

Mit-sah

White Fang
Jack London

Gray Beaver's son. Mit-sah runs **White Fang** and the other dogs, including **Lip-lip**, on a sled.

Mittelstaedt

All Quiet on the Western Front
Erich Maria Remarque

One of **Paul Bäumer**'s classmates. Mittelstaedt becomes a training officer and enjoys tormenting **Kantorek**, his former schoolteacher, when Kantorek is conscripted as a soldier.

Pyotr Aleksandrovich Miusov

The Brothers Karamazov
Fyodor Dostoevsky

A wealthy landowner, the cousin of **Fyodor Pavlovich Karamazov**'s first wife, and briefly the guardian of the young **Dmitri Fyodorovich Karamazov**. Considering himself a political intellectual, Miusov utterly despises Fyodor Pavlovich.

Hatsue Miyamoto

Snow Falling on Cedars
David Guterson

Kabuo Miyamoto's wife, whose maiden name is Hatsue Imada. Hatsue and **Ishmael Chambers** became friends as small children, and by the time they entered their adolescence, Ishmael had fallen in love with her. Hatsue, however, always experienced doubt regarding the nature of her feelings for Ishmael. Throughout her life, Hatsue is torn between her Japanese culture and family background and her desire for a world without societal pressures and prejudices.

Kabuo Miyamoto

Snow Falling on Cedars
David Guterson

Hatsue Miyamoto's husband, a Japanese-American fisherman who stands trial for the murder of **Carl Heine**. When Kabuo was a boy, his family worked as sharecroppers on the strawberry farm owned by **Carl Heine, Sr.** Like his father, **Zenhichi Miyamoto**, Kabuo is a master at kendo, the Japanese art of stick fighting. Kabuo considers himself a murderer because he killed enemy soldiers in World War II, in which he fought for the United States Army. Since the war, Kabuo has been consumed with his dream to repurchase his family's land.

Zenhichi Miyamoto

Snow Falling on Cedars
David Guterson

Kabuo Miyamoto's father. When Kabuo was eight years old, Zenhichi began training him in the Japanese martial art of kendo, or stick fighting, and emphasized the discipline and self-restraint of the art.

Joseph Mobutu

The Poisonwood Bible
Barbara Kingsolver

Dictator after Lumumba was assassinated. For thirty years he kept his nation in abject poverty, while he himself lived like a king.

Moby Dick

Moby-Dick
Herman Melville

The great white sperm whale. Moby Dick, also referred to as the White Whale, is considered by Captain **Ahab** to be the incarnation of evil and a fated nemesis. Moby Dick is responsible for Ahab's missing leg, and hunting and killing the whale is Ahab's one mad obsession.

Nance Mockridge

The Mayor of Casterbridge
Thomas Hardy

A peasant in Casterbridge. She is instrumental in planning the skimmity-ride, the traditional English spectacle whose purpose was to express public disapproval of adultery. Nance Mockridge and **Mother Cuxsom** are excited about the humiliation of those who usually hold their heads high in Casterbridge society. The skimmity-ride causes **Lucetta Templeman** to suffer an epileptic fit and die.

Queen Modthryth

Beowulf
Unknown

A wicked queen of legend who punishes anyone who looks at her the wrong way.

Annie Moffat

Little Women
Louisa May Alcott

A wealthy friend of **Meg March**'s. Annie is fashionable and social, and she wears stylish clothing that Meg envies.

Ned Moffat

Little Women
Louisa May Alcott

The older brother of **Meg March**'s friend, **Annie Moffat**.

Luke Moggs

The Mill on the Floss
George Eliot

Jeremy Tulliver's employee, the miller at the mill on the Floss. Luke is practically a family member, and he sits by Mr. Tulliver's sickbed.

Nazir Mohammad

Shabanu
Suzanne Fisher Staples

Former owner of the land that **Bibi Lal**'s family farms. Nazir Mohammad is rich, fat, and greedy. He owns a great deal of land, which he leases out to tenant farmers who must then pay him for use of the land with part of their crop. He wants to make Bibi Lal's family pay as well, even though they bought the land from him.

Reverend Mother Gaius Helen Mohiam

Dune
Frank Herbert

Spiritual leader of the Bene Gesserit. Mohiam is old and serves as **Emperor Shaddam IV**'s truthsayer, a person who can tell the emperor whether someone is lying. Before **Paul Atreides** leaves for Arrakis, Mohiam puts him through a severe test of endurance.

Moira

The Handmaid's Tale
Margaret Atwood

Offred's best friend from college. A lesbian and a staunch feminist, Moira is one of the few to repeatedly defy the Republic of Gilead, making several escape attempts from the Red Center. When Moira is caught escaping, the **Eyes of God** torture her. She chooses to work as a prostitute in a club, because she can live longer in the club than she can in the Colonies.

Moll's mother

Moll Flanders
Daniel Defoe

A convicted felon. Moll's mother was transported to the American colonies soon after her daughter was born. She reappears as Moll's mother-in-law midway through the novel, when **Moll** travels to Virginia with the husband who turns out to be her half-brother. She leaves her daughter a sizable inheritance when she dies, which Moll reclaims in America at the end of the novel.

Mollie

Animal Farm
George Orwell

The vain, flighty mare who pulls **Mr. Jones**'s carriage. Mollie craves the attention of human beings and loves being groomed and pampered. She has a difficult time with her new life on Animal Farm, missing work and secretly consorting with **Mr. Pilkington**'s workers in exchange for ribbons and sugar. Eventually, she flees to another farm and is never spoken of again by the animals.

Mikey Molloy

Angela's Ashes
Frank McCourt

Frank McCourt's cross-eyed school friend who has fits and is an expert on sex-related topics. Mikey's father, **Peter**, is the champion pint drinker of Limerick, while his mother, **Nora**, is well-known for her frequent visits to the insane asylum.

Molly

The Autobiography of Miss Jane Pittman
Ernest J. Gaines

The older black woman who works in the Big House at the ranch where **Joe Pittman** goes to break horses. Molly has become so completely indoctrinated into slavery that she cannot envision life without it, and she dies shortly after leaving the house.

Molly

Great Expectations
Charles Dickens

Jaggers's housekeeper and **Estella**'s mother.

Fly Molo

Ender's Game
Orson Scott Card

One of **Ender Wiggin**'s toon leaders in Dragon Army. Fly Molo also fights with Ender during the battles against the buggers.

Moloch

Paradise Lost
John Milton

A rash, irrational, and murderous devil. Moloch argues in Pandemonium that the devils should engage in another full war against God and his servant angels.

Molvik

Wild Duck
Henrik Ibsen

A tenant who lives below the Ekdals. A drunken student of theology, he lives under the care of **Relling**, keeping himself alive through what Relling would call a "life-illusion" of demonic possession.

Mom

True West
Sam Shepard

Mother to **Austin** and **Lee**. Mom is a powerless parental figure who exerts much less control over her children than the absent, drunk, and penniless father. Generally withdrawn from reality, Mom has just returned from a trip to Alaska. When her sons begin to attack each other, she is unable to deal with the confrontation, and, before leaving for a motel, quietly asks Austin not to kill Lee.

Momentilla

The Rape of the Lock
Alexander Pope

The sylph who is assigned to guard **Belinda**'s watch.

Momma

I Know Why the Caged Bird Sings
Maya Angelou

Annie Henderson, **Maya Johnson** and **Bailey Johnson**'s paternal grandmother. Momma raises them for most of their childhood. She owns the only store in the black section of Stamps, Arkansas, and it serves as the central gathering place for the black community. She has owned the store for about twenty-five years, starting it as a mobile lunch counter. Momma is the moral center of the family and especially of Maya's life. She raises the children according to stern Christian values and strict rules. Despite the affection she feels for her grandchildren, she cares more about their well-being than her own needs, extracting them from the Stamps community when racist pressures begin to affect Bailey negatively. Momma considers herself a realist regarding race relations. She stands up for herself but believes that white people cannot be spoken to without risking one's life.

Momma

Homecoming and *Dicey's Song*
Cynthia Voigt

The Tillerman children's mother. She is loving and beautiful but not reliable or practical. Having watched the sad marriage of her own mother (**Gram**), Momma decided early in life never to marry. Momma has struggled to raise her children on her own, but eventually buckles under the pressure. She spends half of *Homecoming* and most of *Dicey's Song* in a mental hospital in Boston. The children remember her as hardworking and loving, and question their individual roles in the decline of Momma's health.

Mommy

American Dream
Edward Albee

Wife of **Daddy**, daughter of **Grandma**. Mommy is the household's sadistic disciplinarian, dismissing her mother and infantilizing her husband, whom she has married for the money. Mommy's speech distinguishes itself as the most violent in the household in its shrillness, scorn, and derision.

Mona

Lolita
Vladimir Nabokov

Lolita's favorite friend at the Beardsley School for Girls. Mona has already had an affair with a Marine and appears to be flirting with **Humbert Humbert**. Mona refuses to divulge any of Lolita's secrets, and even helps Lolita lie to Humbert when he discovers that she has been missing her piano lessons.

Monaco

Fallen Angels
Walter Dean Myers

A soldier of Italian descent on **Richie Perry**'s squad. Monaco always takes the dangerous position of point man.

Mon-a-nee

Island of the Blue Dolphins
Scott O'Dell

An otter that **Karana** finds injured after **the Aleuts** have left her island. Karana cares for Mon-a-nee until her return to the sea, and later sees her with her babies playing in the ocean.

Algernon Moncrieff

The Importance of Being Earnest
Oscar Wilde

A good friend of **Jack Worthing**'s. Algernon lives in a nice flat in a prestigious part of London. He is **Lady Bracknell**'s nephew and, it turns out, Jack's younger brother. Algernon falls in love with **Cecily Cardew**.

Mustapha Mond

Brave New World
Aldous Huxley

One of ten World Controllers, in charge of West Europe. Mond was once an ambitious young scientist performing illicit research. When his work was discovered, he was given the choice of going into exile or training to become a World Controller and now censors scientific discoveries and exiles people for unorthodox beliefs. Mond is the most articulate and intelligent proponent of the World State. He explains to **John**, **Bernard Marx** and **Helmholtz Watson** that happiness and stability come at the price of truth and beauty.

Mike Monday

Babbitt
Sinclair Lewis

An ex-prize fighter who is now an evangelist. Mike Monday is invited to Zenith to speak because he has a reputation for distracting the working class from concerns about wages and working conditions.

Fernand Mondego

The Count of Monte Cristo
Alexandre Dumas

Edmond Dantès's rival for **Mercédès**'s affections. Mondego, with the help of **Danglars**, frames Dantès for treason and then marries Mercédès. Mondego becomes a wealthy and powerful man by betraying **Ali Pacha** to the Turks. He becomes the **Count de Morcerf**. After **the Count of Monte Cristo** proves to Mércèdes and **Albert de Morcerf**, Mondego's and Mércèdes' son, that Mondego is a dishonorable criminal, Mércèdes and Albert distance themselves from the man.

Monique

Lolita
Vladimir Nabokov

A French nymphet prostitute. Initially, **Humbert Humbert** is attracted to her, but he breaks off their affair when Monique starts to mature.

The Monk

The Canterbury Tales
Geoffrey Chaucer

One of the travelers on the pilgrimage to Canterbury. Most monks of the Middle Ages lived in monasteries according to the Rule of Saint Benedict, which demanded that they devote their lives to "work and prayer." This Monk cares little for the Rule; his devotion is to hunting and eating. He is large, loud, and well-clad in hunting boots and furs.

Monks

Oliver Twist
Charles Dickens

Oliver Twist's half-brother. A sickly, vicious young man, prone to violent fits and teeming with inexplicable hatred. With **Fagin**, he schemes to give Oliver a bad reputation.

Monks's Mother

Oliver Twist
Charles Dickens

An heiress. **Monks**'s mother lived a decadent life and alienated her husband, **Mr. Leeford**. She destroyed her husband's will, which left part of his property to **Oliver Twist**.

Monroe

Cold Mountain
Charles Frazier

Ada Monroe's dead father and the old preacher of Cold Mountain. His wife died giving birth their daughter. Monroe moved with his daughter to Black Cove to speed his recovery from consumption. A kind man and unconventional preacher, Monroe recognizes in hindsight that he has been overly protective of Ada.

Ada Monroe

Cold Mountain
Charles Frazier

The female protagonist and **Inman**'s lover. Ada is a highly educated, literate, and intensely private young woman. She has experienced the hardship and loss of her father's death, and has been left penniless and in charge of the farm. Ada feels alienated from small-town society and rejects its restrictive mentality.

Monsieur

The Maids
Jean Genet

The husband of **Madame**. Monsieur never appears onstage—he has been wrongfully sent to prison by an anonymous letter from **Claire**—but his presence looms over the play.

The monster

Frankenstein
Mary Shelley

The eight-foot-tall, hideously ugly creation of **Victor Frankenstein**. Intelligent and sensitive, the monster attempts to integrate himself into human social patterns, but all who see him shun him. His feeling of abandonment compels him to seek revenge against his creator.

Guy Montag

Fahrenheit 451
Ray Bradbury

A third-generation fireman who suddenly realizes the emptiness of his life and starts to search for meaning in the books he is supposed to be burning. His biggest regret in life is his poor relationship with his wife, **Mildred Montag**. He is determined to break free from the oppression of ignorance. He quickly forms unusually strong attachments with anyone who seems receptive to true friendship, including **Clarisse McClellan**.

Mildred Montag

Fahrenheit 451
Ray Bradbury

Guy Montag's brittle, sickly wife. She is obsessed with watching television and refuses to engage in frank conversation with her husband about their marriage or her feelings, including her suicide attempt.

Montague

Romeo and Juliet
William Shakespeare

Romeo's father, the patriarch of the Montague clan and the bitter enemy of **Capulet**. At the beginning of the play, he sends his nephew **Benvolio** to discover the root of Romeo's melancholy.

Lady Montague

Romeo and Juliet
William Shakespeare

Romeo's mother, **Montague**'s wife. She dies of grief after Romeo is exiled from Verona.

Marquess of Montague

Henry VI, Part III
William Shakespeare

The brother of **Richard Neville, Earl of Warwick** and a supporter of the Yorkist claim to the throne. Though initially loyal to **King Edward**, Montague is critical of Edward's marriage to **Elizabeth Woodville, Lady Grey**, believing an alliance with France through a political wedding would behoove England. He eventually joins Warwick in deserting Edward, and fights for the Lancastrian side. Montague and Warwick die in the same battle.

Montano

Othello
William Shakespeare

The governor of Cyprus before **Othello**. He first appears in Act II, as he recounts the status of the war and awaits the Venetian ships.

General Montcalm

The Last of the Mohicans
James Fenimore Cooper

Commander of the French forces. General Montcalm is also known as Marquis Louis Joseph de Saint-Veran. Montcalm enlists the help of Native American tribes to navigate the unfamiliar forest terrain in the war against their common enemy, the British. Montcalm urges **Major Duncan Heyward** to surrender Fort William Henry, under siege by the French, reminding Heyward that France's bloodthirsty Native American allies are difficult to hold in check. Montcalm tells **Colonel Munro** that if the English surrender, they will get to keep their arms, baggage, and colors, and the French will ensure that the Native Americans do not attack them. However, when the surrender occurs, one frenzied Native American man sparks an all-out massacre of the surrendering English.

Count of Monte Cristo

The Count of Monte Cristo
Alexandre Dumas

See **Edmond Dantès**.

Montfleury

Cyrano de Bergerac
Edmond Rostand

A fat, incompetent actor whom **Cyrano de Bergerac** bans from the stage.

Sir John Montgomery

Henry VI, Part III
William Shakespeare

A supporter of **King Edward IV**. After Edward is rescued and brought to York, Montgomery approaches the would-be king and says that he will fight for him. Along with Richard of Gloucester (later **Richard III**) and **Lord Hastings**, Montgomery helps convince Edward to revive his forces and make another push for the crown.

Montjoy

Henry V
William Shakespeare

The French herald who acts as a liaison between the English and French. Twice Montjoy is sent, first by **King Charles VI** and then by the **Constable of France**, to encourage **King Henry V** to surrender. His third and final mission is to inform Henry that the English have won.

Montoya

The Sun Also Rises
Ernest Hemingway

A bullfighting expert and the owner of a Pamplona inn. Montoya sees bullfighting as sacred and respects and admires **Jake Barnes** for his genuine enthusiasm about the sport. Montoya takes a paternal interest in the gifted young bullfighter **Pedro Romero** and seeks to protect him from the corrupting influences of tourists and fame.

Domingo Montoya

The Princess Bride
William Goldman

Inigo Montoya's father. Domingo was a great sword-maker who was killed by **Count Rugen**.

Inigo Montoya

The Princess Bride
William Goldman

Vizzini's man of steel. Inigo is the world's youngest sword-fighting wizard and an extremely skilled and dangerous man. He has spent his life learning the sword in order to avenge his father's death at the hands of **Count Rugen**.

Mona Aamons Monzano

Cat's Cradle
Kurt Vonnegut

The adopted daughter of **"Papa" Monzano**. Monzano adopted the unusually beautiful girl to raise his popularity, and he turned her into a national erotic symbol. **Frank Hoenikker** successfully convinced **John** to become President of San Lorenzo when he mentioned that Mona would marry him. The Books of **Bokonon** predicted that Mona would marry the next president, and Mona was a devout Bokononist. Mona committed suicide by swallowing *ice-nine* after it killed almost all life on earth.

Papa Monzano

Cat's Cradle
Kurt Vonnegut

The ailing dictator of the small island republic of San Lorenzo, and **Mona Aamons Monzano**'s adopted father. He gave **Frank Hoenikker** a comfortable post as Major General in exchange for *ice-nine*. He also planned to install Frank as his successor, but Frank convinced **John** to become the President of San Lorenzo following Monzano's death. Stricken by terminal cancer, Monzano committed suicide by swallowing *ice-nine*.

Father Moody

The Virgin Suicides
Jeffrey Eugenides

The local Catholic priest who visits the Lisbon house after **Cecilia Lisbon**'s death.

Mad-Eye Moody

Harry Potter and the Goblet of Fire
J. K. Rowling

A grizzled, eccentric, skilled retired Auror (dark-wizard catcher) who comes to teach Defense Against the Dark Arts in **Harry Potter**'s fourth year at Hogwarts. He takes a liking to Harry Potter and subtly helps him with his tasks. In the end, we find that he is really young **Bartemius Crouch** in disguise. His unveiling as a villain leaves everyone's instincts, including those of **Albus Dumbledore**, in an insecure state.

Moon Orchid

The Woman Warrior
Maxine Hong Kingston

Brave Orchid's sister. At Brave Orchid's urging, Moon Orchid comes to America in the 1960s to find her estranged husband, who left China thirty years earlier. Moon Orchid is timid and incapable.

Mrs. Mooney

Dubliners
James Joyce

Polly's mother and the proprietress of the boarding house. Mrs. Mooney's guests call her "the Madam." Separated from her husband, Mrs. Mooney firmly governs her own life, as well as Polly's.

Moon-Watcher

2001: A Space Odyssey
Arthur C. Clarke

One of the most innately gifted man-apes. Moon-Watcher demonstrates the ability to walk upright and to engage in crude planning. His mind is pushed along a bit further by the black monolith.

Moony

Harry Potter and the Prisoner of Azkaban
J. K. Rowling

Remus Lupin's werewolf name.

Mrs. Moore

A Passage to India
E. M. Forster

An elderly Englishwoman; mother of **Ronny Heaslop** (first marriage) and **Ralph Moore** and **Stella Moore** (second marriage). Mrs. Moore travels to India to visit Ronny, oversee his marriage to **Adela Quested**, and discover the "real India." An unsettling experience in the Marabar caves and its echoes leave Mrs. Moore with a sense of dread, and she slowly withdraws from human relationships. She eventually understands that no one real India exists; India is complex and multifarious. She dies on the journey back to England.

A Passage to India
E. M. Forster

Ralph Moore

Mrs. Moore's sensitive son.

A Passage to India
E. M. Forster

Stella Moore

Mrs. Moore's daughter; later **Cyril Fielding**'s wife.

Snow Falling on Cedars
David Guterson

Art Moran

The local sheriff. Art initially believes that **Carl Heine**'s death is an accident, but he begins to suspect **Kabuo Miyamoto** of murder after hearing the coroner's offhand comment that Carl's head wound resembles wounds inflicted by Japanese soldiers skilled in the martial art of kendo.

The Once and Future King
T. H. White

Mordred

The son of **King Arthur** and his half-sister, **Morgause**. Cold, calculating, and vicious, Mordred is raised by Morgause to hate Arthur. He thrives on slander and insinuation, which he prefers to open confrontation. He is ultimately the cause of Arthur's decline. Mordred hatches a plot with **Gawaine** to have **Lancelot** and **Guenever** killed because of their affair.

Utopia
Sir Thomas More

More

A fictional character sharing the same name as *Utopia*'s author, Sir Thomas More. In service to **King Henry VIII** of England, More travels to Antwerp, where he meets **Peter Giles** and **Raphael Hythloday**.

A Man for All Seasons
Robert Bolt

Alice More

More's wife. Alice spends most of the play questioning why her husband refuses to give in to **King Henry**'s wishes. Her attitude shifts from anger to confusion. Eventually, More shows her that he cannot go to his death until he knows that she understands his decision. When she visits her husband in prison, Alice finally shows him unconditional love, saying that the fact that "God knows why" More must die is good enough for her.

A Man for All Seasons
Robert Bolt

Sir Thomas More

The protagonist of the play. More's historical refusal to swear to Parliament's Act of Supremacy is the play's main subject, but Bolt intentionally does not depict More as the saint or martyr of legend. Bolt's More is a man who gives up his life because he cannot stifle his conscience, which dictates that he must follow his Catholic notions of rectitude and of God. More makes no move to speak out against **King Henry**'s divorce or indicate his opinion on the matter. Only after **Cromwell** uses a sham trial to condemn him does More reveal his true opinions.

Annie Morel

Sons and Lovers
D. H. Lawrence

Paul Morel's older sister. When their mother, **Gertrude Morel**, lies dying toward the end of the novel, Annie and Paul decide to give her an overdose of morphia pills.

Arthur Morel

Sons and Lovers
D. H. Lawrence

Paul Morel's younger brother.

Gertrude Morel

Sons and Lovers
D. H. Lawrence

The protagonist in the first half of the novel. She becomes unhappy with her husband, **Walter Morel**, and devotes herself to her children.

Paul Morel

Sons and Lovers
D. H. Lawrence

The protagonist in the second half of the book. After his brother **William Morel**'s death, Paul becomes his mother's favorite and struggles throughout the novel to balance his love for her with his relationships with other women.

Walter Morel

Sons and Lovers
D. H. Lawrence

Gertrude Morel's husband, a coal miner.

William Morel

Sons and Lovers
D. H. Lawrence

The oldest Morel son. He is **Gertrude Morel**'s favorite until he falls ill and dies.

Chuck Morello

The Iceman Cometh
Eugene O'Neill

The day bartender at **Harry Hope**'s saloon. He wants to marry his lover **Cora** and buy a farm in New Jersey, but their engagement ends before the end of the play.

Ettore Moretti

A Farewell to Arms
Ernest Hemingway

An American soldier from San Francisco. Ettore, like **Frederic Henry**, fights for the Italian army in World War I. Quick to instigate a fight, Ettore is an obnoxious braggart who pursues the glory and honor that Henry finds absurd.

J. P. Morgan

Ragtime
E. L. Doctorow

A wealthy financier with an interest in Egyptian culture, art, and religion. **Coalhouse Walker** and his followers take over his residence and library in his absence.

Mr. Joseph Morgan

A Lesson Before Dying
Ernest J. Gaines

The white superintendent of schools. Despite his benevolent façade, Mr. Joseph believes that black children should receive only a small amount of religious and patriotic education, and should primarily work the fields as farm hands.

Morgause

The Once and Future King
T. H. White

The mother of **Gawaine**, **Gaheris**, **Gareth**, and **Agravaine**, and the half-sister of **King Arthur**. Morgause is cruel and petty, but her little whims have a huge impact on Arthur and England. Her seduction of Arthur is the first step in Arthur's destruction. She conceives a child with Arthur during the seduction, and this baby is **Mordred**, who hates Arthur. Morgause is killed by Agravaine when he catches her in bed with a man.

S. Morgenstern

The Princess Bride
William Goldman

The fictional Florinese author of *The Princess Bride*.

Dean Moriarty

On the Road
Jack Kerouac

Sal Paradise's friend. A reckless, energetic, womanizing young man from Colorado, Dean has been in and out of jail. While Dean is deeply flawed, Sal usually considers him a larger-than-life savior figure.

Justine Moritz

Frankenstein
Mary Shelley

A young girl adopted by **Victor Frankenstein**'s family. Justine is wrongfully convicted and executed for **William Frankenstein**'s murder, which was in fact committed by **the monster**.

Julia and Kate Morkan

Dubliners
James Joyce

The aging sisters who throw an annual dance party in "The Dead." Julia's gray and sullen appearance, combined with her remote attitude, make her seem sapped of life. Kate is vivacious and constantly frets over her sister's and her guests' happiness.

Catherine Morland

Northanger Abbey
Jane Austen

The protagonist. Catherine is seventeen years old and has spent all her life in her family's modest home in the rural area of Fullerton. Her naiveté about the world and about the motivations of the people she meets is an endless source of frustration for her. Nonetheless, Catherine is very intelligent, and occasionally witty, and she learns from her mistakes.

James Morland

Northanger Abbey
Jane Austen

The brother of **Catherine Morland** and a fellow student of **John Thorpe**'s at Oxford University. James is mild-mannered and caring, like his sister. He falls for **Isabella Thorpe** and becomes engaged to her, but breaks off the engagement when she begins a flirtation with **Frederick Tilney**.

Mr. and Mrs. Morland

Northanger Abbey
Jane Austen

Catherine Morland and **James Morland**'s parents from the rural town of Fullerton. We visit the Morlands only briefly, at the beginning and end of the novel. Mr. and Mrs. Morland are simple and practical people, especially compared to **Mrs. Thorpe** and **General Tilney**. Both James Morland and Catherine Morland must get their parents' approval before they can marry their prospective spouses.

The Mormon Mother

Angels in America
Tony Kushner

A dummy from the diorama at the Mormon Visitor's Center. She is silent while her husband and son speak. The Mormon mother comes to life, however, and accompanies **Harper Pitt** while sharing painful truths about life and change.

Captain Moro

For Whom the Bell Tolls
Ernest Hemingway

An overconfident Fascist commander. He is in charge of taking the hilltop occupied by **El Sordo** and his guerrilla band, but he falls into the guerrillas' trap and is shot and killed before planes bomb the guerrillas' position.

Prince of Morocco

The Merchant of Venice
William Shakespeare

A Moorish prince. The prince seeks **Portia**'s hand in marriage, asking her to ignore his dark countenance, but he picks the wrong chest.

Jean Morrel

Childhood's End
Arthur C. Clarke

George Greggson's wife, **Jeffrey Greggson** and **Jennifer Greggson**'s mother. Jean has an interest in the paranormal and may have psychic powers herself.

Maximilian Morrel

The Count of Monte Cristo
Alexandre Dumas

The brave and honorable son of **Monsieur Morrel**. Protected by **Edmond Dantès**, Maximilian and his beloved **Valentine Villefort** remain uncorrupted by power or wealth. Maximilian wants to marry Valentine, but she is betrothed to **Franz d'Epinay**. After a long-buried family secret comes to light, Franz calls the marriage off. Later, believing that Valentine is dead after her step-mother's attempt to kill her, Maximilian reveals to **the Count of Monte Cristo** that he is preparing to kill himself. In an attempt to stop him, Monte Cristo reveals that he is really Edmond Dantès, the man who saved Monsieur Morrel from ruin. Monte Cristo plays upon his gratitude to extract a promise: for one month Maximilian will remain alive and never stray from Monte Cristo's side. If Maximilian is still unhappy at the end of this month, Monte Cristo will help him to commit suicide. At the end of that month, Maximilian still believes that Valentine is dead. Dantès give Maximilian a potion to drink. Maximilian, thinking the potion will kill him, does not know that it will only put him to sleep. Dantès, seeing that Maximilian was really ready to die for his love, tells the finally awoken Valentine that she must never leave Maximilian's side.

Monsieur Morrel

The Count of Monte Cristo
Alexandre Dumas

Edmond Dantès's former boss and **Maximilian Morrel**'s father. Monsieur Morrel, a kind, honest ship owner, tries to free Dantès from prison and later tries to save **Louis Dantès** from death. Edmond, after escaping from prison, acting as **Abbé Busoni**, saves Monsieur Morrel from ruin by giving him the money to keep his ship business going.

Bob Morris

Jurassic Park
Michael Crichton

An EPA investigator who visits **Dr. Alan Grant** and **Dr. Ellie Sattler** in Montana. Morris is digging up dirt to support his suspicion of **John Hammond**, InGen, and the activity on Isla Nublar.

Isaac Morris

And Then There Were None
Agatha Christie

A shady character hired by **Judge Lawrence Wargrave** to make the arrangements for the island. Morris allegedly peddled drugs to a young woman and drove her to suicide.

Quincey Morris

Dracula
Bram Stoker

A plainspoken American from Texas and another of **Lucy Westenra**'s suitors. Quincey proves himself a brave and good-hearted man, never begrudging **Arthur Holmwood** his success in winning Lucy's hand. Quincey ultimately sacrifices his life in order to rid the world of Dracula's influence.

Morrison

Major Barbara
George Bernard Shaw

The longtime family butler who hesitantly announces **Andrew Undershaft**'s return to the household.

L. T. Morrison

Roll of Thunder, Hear My Cry
Mildred D. Taylor

A big, burly man with streaks of white hair who comes to work on the Logan farm. The Ku Klux Klan is possibly looking around for him in order to lynch him. After the ambush on L.T., **Papa**, and **Stacey Logan** by members of the **Wallace** family, L.T. moves the Wallace truck out of the road with his sheer strength. He is usually cool under pressure, and talks **Uncle Hammer** out of assaulting **Lillian Jean Simms** and her father with a rifle.

Mortimer

Hound of the Baskervilles
Sir Arthur Conan Doyle

Family friend and doctor to **Sir Charles Baskerville** and his family. Mortimer dresses sloppily but is a good man and the executor of Charles's estate. Mortimer is also a phrenology enthusiast and hopes to someday have the opportunity to study **Sherlock Holmes**'s head.

Edmund Mortimer, Earl of March

Henry IV, Part I and *Henry VI, Part I*
William Shakespeare

The son-in-law of Welsh rebel **Owen Glendower**; uncle of **Richard Plantagenet**. In *King Henry IV, Part I*, Mortimer professes his claim to the throne of England: before **King Henry IV** overthrew **King Richard II**, Richard II proclaimed Mortimer heir to the throne. Henry IV decries Mortimer as a traitor, insinuating that he has purposely lost a battle against his new father-in-law, Glendower. Mortimer joins the Percy faction and Glendower in the plot to overthrow the King. Following his defeat, Mortimer is not seen again until *King Henry VI, Part I*, when his nephew, Richard Plantagenet (later **Duke of York**) comes to visit him in the Tower of London. Mortimer has been imprisoned there for years. He dies, passing his claim to the throne and his titles to Plantagenet, who later becomes the Duke of York. By bringing up King Henry IV's usurpation of Richard II, Mortimer evokes the unnatural reign of the Lancastrian line and paves the way for the Yorkist challenge.

Cardinal John Morton

Utopia
Sir Thomas More

Chancellor to Henry VIII. **Raphael Hythloday** once spent a fictional evening discussing the societal problems of England with Morton and **the Lawyer**. The real Morton was instrumental in furthering Sir Thomas More's education at Oxford.

Mosca

Volpone
Ben Jonson

Volpone's parasite. Though initially Mosca behaves in a servile manner toward Volpone, Mosca conceals a growing independence gained from abetting Volpone's confidence game.

Don Apolinar Moscote

One Hundred Years of Solitude
Gabriel García Márquez

Father of **Remedios Moscote** and the government-appointed magistrate of Macondo. He is driven out of town by **José Arcadio Buendía**. When he returns, José Arcadio Buendía forces him to forfeit much of his authority over the village. When he finally succeeds in bringing armed soldiers to help govern Macondo, he disturbs the self-governing peace that the town has always enjoyed. He is a Conservative and helps rig the election so that his party will win.

Remedios Moscote

One Hundred Years of Solitude
Gabriel García Márquez

The child-bride of **Colonel Aureliano Buendía**. He falls in love with her, but when she dies suddenly, possibly of a miscarriage, he feels no great sorrow.

Moseley

As I Lay Dying
William Faulkner

A Mottson druggist. Moseley indignantly refuses **Dewey Dell Bundren**'s request to help her abort. Moseley's stern lecture to Dewey Dell is sanctimonious but caring.

Moses

The Old Testament
Unknown

Israel's reluctant savior during the exodus from Egyptian bondage to the promised land. Moses mediates between **God** and the people, transforming the Israelites from an oppressed ethnic group into a nation founded on religious laws. Moses's legendary miracles before **Pharaoh**, along with his doubts and insecurities, make him the great mortal hero of the Old Testament. He is the only man ever to know God "face to face." Born in Egypt, Moses is raised by **Pharaoh's daughter**, who takes pity on the abandoned Hebrew baby. After an impulsive murder, Moses flees west, where he begins a life as a shepherd and stumbles into God in the form of a burning bush. He reluctantly agrees to return to Egypt and demand the Israelites' release. Each event in the journey from Egypt to Mount Sinai, where God delivers his laws to the Israelites, propels Moses further into the roles of prophet, priest, ruler, and savior of Israel.

Moses

Animal Farm
George Orwell

Raven who spreads stories of Sugarcandy Mountain, the paradise to which animals supposedly go when they die.

Moshe the Beadle

Night
Elie Wiesel

Eliezer's Cabbala teacher. A poor Sighet Jew, Moshe is deported before the rest of the community. He manages to escape and return to tell his story to the townspeople, but they take him for a lunatic.

Ed Mosher

The Iceman Cometh
Eugene O'Neill

A man at **Harry Hope**'s saloon. He is a born grafter, con man, and practical joker. He wants to return to the circus.

Sir Oswald Mosley

The Remains of the Day
Kazuo Ishiguro

The leader of the British Union of Fascists. He visited Darlington Hall several times.

Suzanne Mosley

Ordinary People
Judith Guest

A girl in **Conrad Jarrett**'s trigonometry class. Conrad feels bad for Suzanne Mosley because she has particular difficulty with math. **Jeannine Pratt** reveals at the end *Ordinary People* that Suzanne has a crush on Conrad.

Dave Moss

Glengarry Glen Ross
David Mamet

An angry real estate salesman. Moss harbors a great deal of resentment toward the company. He tends to lash out angrily when under pressure. His sheer aggression makes him a more successful salesman than **George Aaronow** or **Shelly Levene**, but he has none of **Ricky Roma**'s verbal agility.

Margaret Moss

The Mill on the Floss
George Eliot

Jeremy Tulliver's sister, and "Aunt Gritty" to **Tom Tulliver** and **Maggie Tulliver**. A patient, loving woman, she is especially fond of Maggie. She has eight children and the family is very poor. Mr. Tulliver did not want Margaret to marry **Mr. Moss** and is still cross about their relationship.

Mr. Moss

The Mill on the Floss
George Eliot

Margaret Moss's husband. Mr. Moss does not have much character, mainly because he works too much.

Mote

A Midsummer Night's Dream
William Shakespeare

One of four fairies, along with **Cobweb**, **Mustardseed**, and **Peaseblossom**, whom **Titania** orders to attend to **Bottom** after she falls in love with him.

Moth

Love's Labour's Lost
William Shakespeare

The Spanish knight **Armado**'s page. The diminutive Moth counsels Armado on the effects of love and serves as a verbal sparring partner for the Spaniard.

The mother

Six Characters in Search of an Author
Luigi Pirandello

One of the six characters, the center of their conflict. Dressed in modest black and a thick widow's veil, she bears the anguish of the characters' drama, serving as its horrified spectator. Particularly agonizing to her is the aloofness of her estranged **Son**, whom she approaches to no avail throughout the play. **The Father** saw that the Mother was attracted to his secretary, and allowed her to run off with him. After they had three children, the secretary left the Mother and she was forced to return to the Father with a bastard entourage.

Mother

Dandelion Wine
Ray Bradbury

Douglas Spaulding and **Tom Spaulding**'s mother. She is a strong-minded, kind woman who cares greatly for her children. She worries that some harm may come to Douglas while he is off in the wilderness with **John Huff** and **Charlie Woodman**.

Mother

Ragtime
E. L. Doctorow

Part of the upper-class family living in New Rochelle. Disappointed by her marriage to **Father**, she marries **Tateh** after Father's death. She often feels guilt over her treatment of her brother, referred to in the novel as **Mother's Younger Brother**. Throughout the novel she experiences many changes through her care for the child of **Coalhouse** and **Sarah**, as well as her newfound awareness of her sexuality.

Mother

Fallen Angels
Walter Dean Myers

Richie Perry and **Kenny**'s mother. She is a depressive alcoholic who has barely functioned since her husband left her years earlier. Though Richie and his mother have never gotten along well, they realize how much they need each other while Richie is in Vietnam. They try to repair their damaged relationship through their letters.

Motor Boat

Their Eyes Were Watching God
Zora Neale Hurston

One of **Tea Cake** and **Janie Mae Crawford**'s friends in the Everglades. He stays around despite an approaching hurricane. Miraculously, even though Janie and Tea Cake flee the house and Motor Boat stays, they all survive the storm.

Joe Mott

The Iceman Cometh
Eugene O'Neill

A black man who dreams of reopening his colored gambling house. He wears a once flashy suit and sports a scar across his left cheek.

Wesley Mouch

Atlas Shrugged
Ayn Rand

Originally **Hank Rearden**'s "Washington Man," or lobbyist. Wesley Mouch is a mediocre bureaucrat who rises to the role of economic dictator through his betrayal of Rearden and his well-placed connections with the corrupt socialist government. Under Mouch's new post as the head of the Bureau of Economic Planning and National Resources, a number of statements are issued urging the use of emergency powers to balance the economy. This starts the corrupt nationalization of industry that eventually destroys society.

Mouldy

Henry IV, Part II
William Shakespeare

One of the Army recruits that **Sir John Falstaff** inspects in Gloucestershire. Mouldy and **Bullcalf** bribe Falstaff to let them off the hook, and thus are not selected for military service.

Dr. Lester Mount

Death Be Not Proud
John Gunther

Assistant to **Dr. Tracy Putnam**. Dr. Lester Mount helps **Johnny** throughout his illness.

Mousqueton

The Three Musketeers
Alexandre Dumas

Porthos's manservant. Like his master, he enjoys the finer things in life. While **Athos**, **Aramis**, Porthos, **d'Artagnan**, and the **Lord de Winter** attend **Madame Bonacieux**'s funeral, Athos sends **Bazin**, **Planchet**, **Grimaud**, and Mousqueton to Armentieres to scout the **Lady de Winter**'s exact location.

Mowanna

Typee
Herman Melville

The puppet king placed in power by the colonial French to rule the Marquesas.

Lord Thomas Mowbray

Henry IV, Part II
William Shakespeare

A conspirator, along with **Lord Hastings** and the **Archbishop of York**, who plots to overthrow **King Henry IV**. Though they file their grievances with Prince **John of Lancaster** and agree to disband their armies after a tentative truce, the prince goes back on his word and arrests the rebels, sending them off to be executed.

Mow-Mow

Typee
Herman Melville

A fierce one-eyed chieftain.

Moy

Sister Carrie
Theodore Dreiser

Along with **Fitzgerald**, the joint owner of a popular saloon in Chicago. The saloon serves as a gathering place for Chicago's glitterati. Fitzgerald and Moy are good to **Hurstwood**, the saloon's manager, first providing him with gainful employment and then choosing not to prosecute when he steals thousands of dollars from them.

Mozart

Steppenwolf
Hermann Hesse

The renowned classical composer. **The Steppenwolf**, who has a lifelong obsession with Mozart, encounters him in the Magic Theater as the ultimate representative of "the immortals." This eccentric, personal Mozart is as modern as he is a man of the past, and is also thoroughly unceremonious and jocular.

Mr. ___

The Color Purple
Alice Walker

Celie's husband, who abuses her for years. Mr. ___, whose first name is Albert, shows no human connection to Celie. He pines for **Shug Avery** during his marriage to Celie and hides **Nettie**'s letters to Celie in his trunk for decades. After Celie finally defies Mr. ___, he undergoes a deep personal transformation, reassessing his life and eventually becoming friends with Celie.

Mr. K

The Martian Chronicles
Ray Bradbury

The practical, short-tempered Martian husband of **Mrs. K**, whom he calls Ylla. Mr. K is suspicious of his wife's dreams of a visiting rocket. He learns when the rocket will land from his wife's sleep-talking, and he leaves her at home and kills the rocket's passengers, including Captain **Nathaniel York**.

Mrs. K

The Martian Chronicles
Ray Bradbury

A Martian housewife who is married to **Mr. K**, whom she calls Yll. Her situation is much like that of the bored American housewife of the 1950s. She dreams of Captain **Nathaniel York** coming down in his rocket, and unwittingly alerts her husband to the exact time of York's arrival.

Mrs. Prior

Regeneration
Pat Barker

Billy Prior's mother. Mrs. Prior is a nervous woman who always protected her son, even to the point of making him more sensitive than was socially acceptable at the time. Unlike **Mr. Prior**, she wants Billy to achieve in life and ascend the social ladder.

Theophilus Msimangu

Cry, the Beloved Country
Alan Paton

Stephen Kumalo's host and guide in Johannesburg. A tall, young minister at the Mission House in Sophiatown, Msimangu has an acute understanding of the problems that face South Africa. He helps Kumalo understand the people and places that they encounter, and is unfailingly sympathetic to Kumalo, making Kumalo's quest his top priority. He sometimes speaks unkindly, but he quickly repents.

Mudd

Catch-22
Joseph Heller

A squadron member who was killed in action before his assignment to the squadron was processed. Mudd is officially listed as never having arrived. His belongings remain in **John Yossarian**'s tent.

Elijah Muhammad

The Autobiography of Malcolm X
Malcolm X & Alex Haley

The spiritual leader of the Nation of Islam. **Malcolm X** treats Elijah with immense respect even before he knows him, writing him letters daily while still in prison. Though he seems like a benevolent father figure, Elijah Muhammad becomes a jealous and defensive leader as his health fails and as Malcolm becomes more powerful.

Muhe Ca

The Martian Chronicles
Ray Bradbury

A Martian encountered by **Toma's Gomez**. Muhe Ca seems to be from the past, but may simply be from another plane or dimension. He is friendly and has a deep love for the sort of festival he describes to Gomez.

Mulciber

Paradise Lost
John Milton

The devil who builds Pandemonium, **Satan**'s palace in Hell. Mulciber's character is based on a Greek mythological figure known for being a poor architect, but in Milton's poem he is one of the most productive and skilled devils in Hell.

Robert Muldoon

Jurassic Park
Michael Crichton

Former big-game hunter and zoo consultant who serves as the park's game warden. Muldoon's primary task is to keep the dinosaurs from eating people or each other. Though irked that **John Hammond** refuses give him more firepower to handle large species like the tyrannosaurus, Muldoon is more concerned about the raptors, which he thinks should be terminated.

Müller

All Quiet on the Western Front
Erich Maria Remarque

One of **Paul Bäumer**'s former classmates. A hardheaded, practical young man, he plies his friends in the Second Company with questions about their postwar plans. When **Franz Kemmerich** is dying, Müller arranges to receive his boots.

Gerhard Müller

Slaughterhouse-Five
Kurt Vonnegut

The nonfictional taxi driver who takes **Kurt Vonnegut** and **Bernard V. O'Hare** back to their Dresden slaughterhouse. Müller later sends O'Hare a Christmas card bearing tidings of peace, and Vonnegut dedicates the novel in part to Müller.

Malachi Mulligan

Ulysses
James Joyce

Stephen Dedalus's medical student friend and roommate at the Martello tower. Plump, well-read, and well-liked, Buck ridicules everything with bawdy humor. Stephen intensely resents Buck's ease with people and comfort in life.

Midas Mulligan

Atlas Shrugged
Ayn Rand

The most successful banker of all time and the owner of the valley where **John Galt**'s strikers of the mind live. Midas Mulligan withdrew from society after realizing that he cannot thrive in a system that rewards need over ability, the system that the government "looters" are promoting. Mulligan bides his time in the strikers' valley, refusing to use his mind or money to condone the corrupt action of the government, which is destroying society and the economy through its corrupt rules and nationalization of industries.

Fern Mullins

Main Street
Sinclair Lewis

The new high school teacher in Gopher Prairie. Fern, who is physically active and intelligent, becomes **Carol**'s friend. She leaves town, however, when a student, **Cy Bogart**, falsely accuses Fern of corrupting him.

Corinne Mulvaney

We Were the Mulvaneys
Joyce Carol Oates

Seemingly the perfect mother—loving, funny, and supportive. Corinne is a truly happy housewife, content to care for her children, her home, her pets, and her husband. Though she is the glue that holds the family together, once things start to go wrong, Corinne does little to right them. Christian acceptance and forbearance—virtues that she taught to her daughter **Marianne Mulvaney**—help Corinne accept her terrible choice and the consequences that follow.

Judd Mulvaney

We Were the Mulvaneys
Joyce Carol Oates

A child of eleven at the beginning of the novel who grows up to become a journalist and the narrator of his family's story. As a child too young to understand the events at the beginning of the novel, Judd is an outsider rather than a fully conscious participant in the family tragedy, which makes him best suited to recount it.

Marianne Mulvaney

We Were the Mulvaneys
Joyce Carol Oates

The novel's emotional center. Sweet, good, pious, pretty, and popular, Marianne is a high school junior at the beginning of the story. Her rape sets in motion the tragic chain of events. She accepts responsibility for the rape because she was drunk at the time. She even accepts her father's banishment and her mother's acquiescence. Her self-blame grows into extreme self-doubt and self-loathing as she squanders her many gifts, including her beauty. Only when Marianne meets **Whit West**, who loves and cares for wounded creatures, is she able to accept love.

Mike Mulvaney Sr.

We Were the Mulvaneys
Joyce Carol Oates

The leader of the Mulvaney family. A Catholic from a working-class family in Pittsburgh, Mike Sr. has worked hard to become a small-town businessman. At the beginning of the novel, he seems to have it all—an adoring wife, a beautiful home, four happy and healthy children, a thriving business, and the respect of his community. The ruin of his daughter **Marianne Mulvaney** leads Michael Sr. to throw all of this success away. Unable to stand the sight of Marianne after her rape, he banishes his favorite child. His world subsequently falls to pieces as he loses his home and business, systematically alienates everyone in his life, and takes to drink. He dies an utter failure at the age of sixty-one.

Mike Mulvaney, Jr.

We Were the Mulvaneys
Joyce Carol Oates

The oldest Mulvaney son. He peaked in high school as a football star and an all-around, attractive, popular good guy. As the first-born son, Mike, Jr. was expected to make something of his life, but instead he runs away and joins the Marines to escape his family tragedy. He marries, has children, and drifts from the picture.

Patrick Mulvaney

We Were the Mulvaneys
Joyce Carol Oates

In many ways the hero of the novel, who transforms from a scowling scholar to a man of action. Patrick is the first family member to see **Marianne Mulvaney** after the rape, and he blames himself for failing to notice that something is wrong with her. In the first years of her exile, he is the only Mulvaney to keep in touch with her. After **Mike Mulvaney, Jr.** disappears from the scene, Patrick must restore the family honor. With his brother **Judd Mulvaney**, Patrick avenges the family in a satisfying but ultimately merciful fashion.

Mumtaz

Midnight's Children
Salman Rushdie

Saleem's mother, and the daughter of **Aadam Aziz**. Born Mumtaz, she changes her name to Amina after her marriage to **Ahmed**. A loving, devoted mother, she inherits her father's skepticism and her mother's determination. Despite being married to Ahmed, she is never able to forget her first husband, **Nadir Khan**.

Aunt Juley Mund

Howards End
E. M. Forster

The sister of **Margaret Schlegel** and **Helen Schlegel**, and **Theobald Schlegel**'s deceased mother. Though good-hearted, Aunt Juley is a meddling, conventional woman.

Mundin

How the Garcia Girls Lost Their Accents
Julia Alvarez

Yolanda's favorite cousin. When they were children, Mundin asked Yolanda to prove she was a girl in exchange for pink modeling clay. He later protects **Sofia** and **Manuel** from getting into trouble for having sex.

Lord Munodi

Gulliver's Travels
Jonathan Swift

An aristocrat of Lagado, the capital of Balnibarbi, the land that supports the **Laputians**. Munodi hosts **Gulliver** on Gulliver's third voyage. Unlike the other Laputians, Munodi is practical. He fell from grace with the ruling Laputian elite when he proposed implementing a practical agriculture model.

Alice Munro

The Last of the Mohicans
James Fenimore Cooper

Colonel Munro's younger daughter and **Cora Munro**'s half-sister. Fair, girlish, and faint of heart, Alice is a foil for the dark and fiery Cora. Alice and **Major Duncan Heyward** are in love. Despite being kidnapped by **Magua**, hidden in a cave, hidden in the clothes of a dead Native American woman, and almost being killed by a group of Delawares, Alice survives the conflict and lives out her love for Heyward.

Colonel Munro

The Last of the Mohicans
James Fenimore Cooper

Commander of the British forces at the eventually surrendered Fort William Henry and **Cora Munro**'s and **Alice Munro**'s father. A massive and powerful man, Colonel Munro has become withdrawn and ineffectual in the war against the French and their Native American allies. Colonel Munro wants to see his daughters, who want to see him, and **General Webb** charges **Major Duncan Heyward** with the task of bringing them to him at Fort William Henry. After meeting with **General Montcalm**, Munro surrenders the fort to the French, which results in a massacre of the surrendered English by frenzied Native Americans. At the end, Colonel Munro and **Chingachgook** wait by the beaver pond to rescue Cora, kidnapped by **Magua**. This battle that follows results in Cora's, **Uncas**'s and Magua's deaths.

Cora Munro

The Last of the Mohicans
James Fenimore Cooper

Colonel Munro's elder daughter, **Alice Munro**'s half-sister. A solemn, poised girl, Cora Munro inherits her dark complexion from her mother, the colonel's first, West Indian, wife. Cora cautiously returns the Mohican **Uncas**'s love, but **Magua** wants to marry Cora to get revenge on the colonel, who once had Magua publicly whipped. Cora is guided by **Major Duncan Heyward**, led around and kidnapped by Magua, and imprisoned by the Delawares. In the end, Magua, given a choice to kill Cora, does not. However, Cora ends up being stabbed to death by an impatient Huron Native American in the battle for her freedom by **Hawkeye** and Heyward.

Murad

Shabanu
Suzanne Fisher Staples

Hamir's younger brother and **Shabanu**'s betrothed. Shabanu remembers that when they were younger, Murad was kind to her and treated her with respect.

George Murchison

A Raisin in the Sun
Lorraine Hansberry

A wealthy, African-American man who courts **Beneatha Younger**. The Youngers approve of George, but Beneatha dislikes his willingness to submit to white culture and forget his African heritage.

Murellus

Julius Caesar
William Shakespeare

A tribune who condemns the plebeians for their fickleness in cheering **Julius Caesar**, when once they cheered for Caesar's enemy **Pompey**. Murellus and **Flavius** are punished for removing the decorations from Caesar's statues during Caesar's triumphal parade.

Muriel

Animal Farm
George Orwell

White goat that learns to read from scraps of newspaper in the rubbish bin. **Clover** has Muriel read from the Seven Commandments whenever she suspects **Napoleon**'s pig government of violating one of its tenets. However, neither has the memory or reasoning to realize that **Squealer** has surreptitiously amended the Commandments to allow for abuse of the other animals.

Lex Murphy

Jurassic Park
Michael Crichton

John Hammond's granddaugher and **Tim Murphy**'s younger sister. Whereas Tim handles the shocks, scares, and predicaments of Jurassic Park with astonishing grace, Lex is prone to cry or whine when the chips are down.

Tim Murphy

Jurassic Park
Michael Crichton

John Hammond's grandson and **Lex Murphy**'s older brother. Tim is an expert on dinosaurs. When the dinosaurs at Jurassic Park start attacking the park's guests, the events are often related from Tim's perspective. Tim is noticeably more mature than his sister.

Anna Murray

Narrative of the Life of Frederick Douglass
Frederick Douglass

Frederick Douglass's wife. Anna is a free black woman from Baltimore who becomes engaged to Douglass before he escapes to freedom. After his escape, Anna and Douglass marry in New York and then move to New Bedford, Massachusetts.

Mina Murray

Dracula
Bram Stoker

Jonathan Harker's fiancée and **Lucy Westenra**'s best friend. Mina is a practical young woman who works as a schoolmistress. Mina is in many ways the heroine of the novel, embodying purity, innocence, and Christian faith—virtues she maintains despite her suffering at **Count Dracula**'s hands. She is intelligent and resourceful, and her research leads **Van Helsing**'s men to Castle Dracula.

Theodore Murrell

All the King's Men
Robert Penn Warren

The "Young Executive," as Jack characterizes him; **Jack's mother**'s husband for most of the novel.

Charles Wallace Murry

A Wrinkle in Time
Madeleine L'Engle

Meg Murry's extraordinarily intelligent younger brother. He is capable of reading minds and understanding other creatures in a way that Meg, **Dennys Murry**, and **Sandy Murry** cannot. Charles Wallace seems to know **Mrs. Whatsit** from some point in his past, and he is the child who gets the adventure to find **Mr. Murry** started. Before tessering, or transporting via the fifth dimension, to Camazotz, Mrs. Whatsit strengthens in Charles Wallace the natural resilience of his childhood. However, he is too confident in his mental and mind-reading abilities, and his brain is taken over by **the Man with the Red Eyes** and **IT**. After rescuing Mr. Murry and being helped by **Aunt Beast** on Ixchel, Meg goes back to Camazotz and rescues Charles Wallace by loving him, which is a thing that IT cannot do.

Dennys Murry

A Wrinkle in Time
Madeleine L'Engle

Son of **Mrs. Murry** and the missing **Mr. Murry**, and **Meg Murry** and **Charles Wallace Murry**'s athletic and socially successful brother. His twin is **Sandy Murry**. The twins encourage Meg to let them fight off the bullies who make fun of Charles Wallace. The twins do not accompany Meg and Charles Wallace on their interplanetary adventure.

Meg Murry

A Wrinkle in Time
Madeleine L'Engle

Daughter of **Mrs. Murry** and the missing **Mr. Murry**. A homely, awkward, but loving high school student who is sent on an adventure through time and space with her brother, **Charles Wallace Murry**, and her friend, **Calvin O'Keefe**, to rescue Mr. Murry from the evil force, **the Black Thing**, that is attempting to take over the universe. On Camazotz, Meg resists the power of **the Man with the Red Eyes** and **IT**, and is led by the brainwashed Charles Wallace to their missing father. She breaks Mr. Murry free, and she, Mr. Murry, and Calvin leave the planet without Charles Wallace. Upon leaving the planet, the three have to tesseract, or transport via the fifth dimension, through the Black Thing, which is surrounding Camazotz. This nearly kills Meg, but she is saved by **Aunt Beast**'s love and care on the planet Ixchel. Once back on planet Camazotz, Meg realizes that IT does not know how to love. In loving her brother intensely in that moment, she saves him, and the Murry children, Mr. Murry, and Calvin are all suddenly and safely back on Earth.

Mr. Murry

A Wrinkle in Time
Madeleine L'Engle

Father of **Meg Murry**, **Charles Wallace Murry**, **Dennys Murry**, and **Sandy Murry**, and husband to **Mrs. Murry**. Mr. Murry is a physicist who works for a top-secret government agency on experiments with travel in the fifth dimension. In trying to tesser to Mars (i.e., travel through a tesseract, or a wrinkle in time), he is captured and imprisoned on the dark planet of Camazotz. Charles Wallace coordinates a plan with **Mrs. Whatsit**, **Mrs. Who**, and **Mrs. Which** to save Mr. Murry and fight the evil power that is imprisoning him, **IT**. Meg saves her father and after one year, Mr. Murry finally returns home.

Mrs. Murry

A Wrinkle in Time
Madeleine L'Engle

Mother to **Meg Murry**, **Charles Wallace Murry**, **Dennys Murry**, and **Sandy Murry**, and wife to **Mr. Murry**. An experimental biologist who works out of a lab in the Murry home, she is at once a brilliant scientist and a loving mother who cooks meals for her family on her Bunsen burner. After meeting **Mrs. Who**, **Mrs. Which**, **Mrs. Whatsit**, and the **Happy Medium**, Meg succeeds in rescuing Mrs. Murry's husband.

Sandy Murry

A Wrinkle in Time
Madeleine L'Engle

Son of **Mrs. Murry** and the missing **Mr. Murry**, and **Meg Murry**'s and **Charles Wallace Murry**'s athletic and socially successful brother. His twin is **Dennys Murry**. The twins encourage Meg to let them fight off the bullies who make fun of Charles Wallace. The twins do not accompany Meg and Charles Wallace on their interplanetary adventure.

Mr. Murthwaite

The Moonstone
Wilkie Collins

A famous traveler to India. He is fluent in languages spoken there and his thin, tanned appearance allows him to pass for a native. Murthwaite has a good understanding and a healthy respect for the Indians in pursuit of the diamond.

Charles Musgrove

Persuasion
Jane Austen

Mary Elliot Musgrove's husband and heir to the great house at Uppercross. Charles Musgrove is a relatively good-natured man who patiently endures his wife's trials. He would have preferred to marry **Anne Elliot**.

Henrietta Musgrove

Persuasion
Jane Austen

The younger sister of **Charles Musgrove** and the older sister of **Louisa Musgrove**, Henrietta is also young and fun-loving. Though she is not as decisive as Louisa, Henrietta sees the charms both of her cousin **Charles Hayter** and of the dashing **Captain Wentworth**.

Louisa Musgrove

Persuasion
Jane Austen

Charles Musgrove's younger sister. Louisa is young, accomplished, and headstrong. She falls easily in love and admires the Navy excessively.

Mary Elliot Musgrove

Persuasion
Jane Austen

The youngest Elliot sister. Mary is married to **Charles Musgrove** and has two small boys. She is high-strung, often hysterical, and always aware of imagined slights. Mary is more focused on social climbing than mothering.

Mr. and Mrs. Musgrove

Persuasion
Jane Austen

The parents of **Charles Musgrove**, **Henrietta Musgrove**, and **Louisa Musgrove**. The Musgroves have provided a balanced, happy home for their children at Uppercross. They are a landed family, second in rank in the parish only to the Elliots. They are practical and want only happiness for their children.

Mustapha

Midnight's Children
Salman Rushdie

Saleem's uncle, the brother of **Mumtaz**. He marries **Sofia**.

Mustardseed

A Midsummer Night's Dream
William Shakespeare

One of four fairies, along with **Cobweb**, **Mote**, and **Peaseblossom**, whom **Titania** orders to attend to **Bottom** after she falls in love with him.

M. Myriel

Les Misérables
Victor Hugo

The bishop of Digne. Myriel's compassion earns him the love of his parishioners, and he becomes a clergyman of wide renown. He defends the needs of the poor and argues that most petty criminals steal to survive, not because they are inherently malicious. He initiates **Jean Valjean**'s spiritual renewal by saving Valjean from arrest and making him promise to live as an honest man.

Myrrhine

Lysistrata
Aristophanes

The second-strongest woman after **Lysistrata**. She seduces her husband, **Kinesias**, but she refuses sex with him at the last minute.

Moaning Myrtle

The Harry Potter Series: Books 2 and *4*
J. K. Rowling

A ghost who haunts the girls' toilet. In *Harry Potter and the Chamber of Secrets*, we discover that Myrtle was killed by the Chamber of Secrets basilisk (a snake-like creature whose eyes turn people to stone) fifty years earlier. She has a small crush on **Harry Potter**.

Prince Lev Nikolayevich Myshkin

The Idiot
Fyodor Dostoevsky

The novel's hero. He feels great compassion for **Anastassya Filippovna Barashkova** and is in love with **Aglaya Ivanovna Yepanchina**. Myshkin is a descendant of an old noble line and a distant relative of **Lizaveta Prokofyevna Yepanchina**. He is young epileptic who comes to Russia after four years spent in a sanitarium in Switzerland. Myshkin is naïve, impractical, and immensely kind, which leads most characters in the novel to consider him an "idiot" and take advantage of him. After Anastassya's murder, he goes mad and returns to Switzerland.

9

FAT FELLOWS AND FEMALES

LARGE AND IN CHARGE. THESE CHARACTERS WANT TO KNOW IF YOU ARE GOING TO EAT YOUR DESSERT.

Bilbo Baggins	1	*The Hobbit, The Fellowship of the Ring*
Dudley Dursley	2	*Harry Potter* series, Books I-IV
Sir John Falstaff	3	*Henry IV, Parts One and Two, Henry V, The Merry Wives of Windsor*
Kind Henry VIII	4	*Henry VIII*
Big Hettie	5	*The Power of One*
Piggy	6	*Lord of the Flies*
Tweedledee and Tweedledum	7	*Alice in Wonderland, Through the Looking Glass*
The Wife of Bath	8	*The Canterbury Tales*
Wash Williams	9	*Winesburg, Ohio*

Salomé
Oscar Wilde

Naaman

A "huge Negro." Naaman stands silently in the background until executing **Jokanaan**. He also executed **Herod**'s deposed elder brother.

Like Water for Chocolate
Laura Esquivel

Nacha

The ranch cook. Of unspecified indigenous background, she is the prime caretaker for **Tita** throughout her childhood, and provides her with the love and support that **Mama Elena** fails to give. She is also the source for most of the recipes in the novel. Nacha dies on the day of **Rosaura**'s wedding but returns throughout the narrative as a spiritual guide for Tita.

Herzog
Saul Bellow

Nachman

A childhood friend of **Moses Herzog**'s. A sentimental, romantic poet, Nachman fell deeply in love with an unstable woman who was taken from him and placed in an institution.

Ellen Foster
Kaye Gibbons

Nadine

Ellen's aunt on her mother's side. Nadine is false and pretentious and lies to herself that she is wealthy and successful to gain confidence. She is forced to take in Ellen for a short period of time, though she eventually kicks her out of the house on Christmas day. She dotes on her daughter **Dora** and treats Dora like a small child, although she is the same age as Ellen.

Endgame
Samuel Beckett

Nagg

Nagg is **Nell**'s husband and **Hamm**'s father. Contained in an ashbin next to his similarly trapped wife, he emerges now and then to cry for food or to try unsuccessfully to kiss Nell and tell her the same story he always tells. At times he is childlike, barely verbal, but he can also be profound and articulate.

Song of Roland
Unknown

Naimes

A Gascon lord who paid homage to **Charlemagne**. He became known as a wise advisor in medieval legends. He is prudent and loyal, but his prudence sometimes leads him astray, as when he urges moderation and mercy toward **Marsilla**. He fights nobly in the battle against **Baligant**'s army.

Hiroshima
John Hersey

Mrs. Hatsuyo Nakamura

A tailor's widow living in Hiroshima. Mrs. Nakamura narrowly escapes disaster when the explosion destroys her house. She and her three children cope with illness and radiation poisoning for years after the bomb, and she faces tremendous difficulties finding work and housing in the years after the explosion.

Toshio Nakamura

Hiroshima
John Hersey

Mrs. Hatsuyo Nakamura's son. Toshio has terrible dreams following the death of his friend in the explosion.

Nakht-re

The Red Tent
Anita Diamant

Brother of **Re-nefer** and esteemed scribe in Egypt. Nakht-re acts as **Re-mose**'s father and provides **Dinah** with a home for many years.

Nalda

Annie John
Jamaica Kincaid

The girl who dies after having a disease where she eats mud. **Annie's mother** prepares Nalda's dead body for the funeral.

Namonee

Typee
Herman Melville

A Typee warrior whose head **Tommo** shaves. Later Namonee is injured in a battle with the Happars.

Nana

The House of the Spirits
Isabel Allende

The housekeeper and nurse for **Nivea del Valle**, **Severo del Valle**, **Clara**, and **Rosa the Beautiful**. Nana is especially close to Clara. After Severo and Nivea's deaths, Nana moves to Clara and **Esteban Trueba**'s household as their housekeeper. There, she competes with **Ferula** for the attention of Clara.

Nancy

Oliver Twist
Charles Dickens

A young prostitute and one of **Fagin**'s former child pickpockets. Nancy is **Bill Sikes**'s lover. She gives her life for **Oliver Twist** by revealing **Monks**'s plots.

Aunt Nancy

Incidents in the Life of a Slave Girl
Harriet Ann Jacobs

Linda Brent's maternal aunt, and **Mrs. Flint**'s slave. Aunt Nancy is slowly killed by Mrs. Flint's abuse.

Vicomte de Nanjac

An Ideal Husband
Oscar Wilde

Attaché at the French Embassy in London. He is famous for his ties and Anglomania. He appears in Act I at **Sir Robert Chiltern**'s dinner party as a comic figure, his malapropisms and awkward speech contrasting with the polished repartee of the other guests.

Island of the Blue Dolphins
Scott O'Dell

Nanko

A young man of the tribe that **Karana**'s sister, **Ulape**, has a crush on. Nanko mistakenly thought he saw **Ramo** board the boat the day Ramo and Karana are left behind, and this error indirectly leads to the two siblings' being stranded on the island.

The Power of One
Bryce Courtenay

Nanny

Nanny is **Peekay**'s Zulu wet nurse. She brings Peekay up telling him stories of warriors and women washing by the baboon's water hole. When Peekay arrives in Barberton, he is distraught to find that Nanny has been dismissed after refusing to remove the charms and amulets that conflict with **Peekay's mother**'s born-again Christian beliefs.

Volpone
Ben Jonson

Nano

A dwarf. Nano is also **Volpone**'s jester, keeping Volpone amused with songs and jokes written by **Mosca**.

The Red Tent
Anita Diamant

Naphtali

Issachar's twin; son of **Jacob** by **Leah**.

The Red and the Black
Stendhal

Napoleon

Former emperor of France. Though not in the novel, Napoleon is a model for **Julien Sorel**. Julien dreams of rising to the top of French society and uses Napoleon's military techniques to seduce women.

War and Peace
Leo Tolstoy

Napoleon

French emperor and military leader who invades Russia. Defeated at Baradino by **General Kutuzov**. He is small, plump, and extremely arrogant.

Animal Farm
George Orwell

Napoleon

Pig who emerges as the leader of Animal Farm after the Rebellion. Napoleon initially takes a backseat to **Snowball**, his more idealistic compatriot. Once he solidifies his base of power, he drives Snowball into exile, controlling the animals with propaganda from **Squealer** and force from his attack dogs. As the years pass, Napoleon becomes more tyrannical, systematically altering the farm's Commandments until the previously egalitarian laws have been replaced with "All animals are created equal, but some are more equal than others." By the end, Napoleon and his gang stand on hind legs, wear clothing, and consort with humans, and the other animals cannot tell pig from human.

Narciso

Bless Me, Ultima
Rudolfo A. Anaya

The town drunk. Narciso is good friends with **Gabriel Márez** because they both share a deep and passionate love for the llano. **Cico** tells Antonio that Narciso has magic and plants his vegetables by the light of the moon. Narciso respects and loves **Ultima** deeply. **Tenorio Trementina** kills Narciso because he supports Ultima.

Doctor Narlikar

Midnight's Children
Salman Rushdie

A gynecologist and businessman.

Judge Narragansett

Atlas Shrugged
Ayn Rand

The legal mind that champions the freedom of individuals to produce and trade free of government intervention. Judge Narragansett is one of the strikers of the mind who lives in the valley of the strikers, led by **John Galt**. Narragansett withdraws from society after realizing that he cannot thrive in a system that rewards need over ability, the system that the government "looters" promote. The judge bides his time in the strikers' valley, refusing to use his mind or money to condone the corrupt action of the government. The judge, like many of the strikers, knows that once the looters cause the collapse of society, the strikers in the valley will start to rebuild the country.

Narrator of "Araby"

Dubliners
James Joyce

An amorous boy devoted to his neighbor **Mangan's sister**. When she tells him about a bazaar called Araby, the narrator decides to go there and find her a gift, but he arrives too late to buy anything.

Narrator of "An Encounter"

Dubliners
James Joyce

A young boy who endures an awkward conversation with a perverted old man while skipping school and frolicking through Dublin with his friend **Maloney**.

Narrator

The Fall of the House of Usher
Edgar Allan Poe

Roderick Usher's best boyhood friend. He is contacted by Roderick during his emotional distress. The narrator knows little about the house of Usher and is the first outsider to visit the mansion in many years.

Narrator

The Murders in the Rue Morgue
Edgar Allan Poe

A friend and housemate of **C. Auguste Dupin**'s. Though he attempts to provide an objective chronicle of the crime, he can't help celebrating Dupin's brilliance.

A Room of One's Own
Virginia Woolf

Narrator

The fictionalized narrator of the essay. Like Woolf, the narrator is a writer who lives on an inheritance.

Dubliners
James Joyce

Narrator of "The Sisters"

A reserved and contemplative boy who quietly deals with the death of his friend, **Father Flynn**. The narrator and the priest had an ambiguous relationship that worried many around them.

Ethan Frome
Edith Wharton

Narrator

An engineer. As a stranger to Starkfield, he is the connection between the closely guarded story of **Ethan Frome**'s tragedy and the reader.

Invisible Man
Ralph Ellison

Narrator

The nameless protagonist of the novel. A black man in 1930s America, the narrator considers himself invisible because people never see his true self beneath the roles that stereotype and racial prejudice compel him to play. Though the narrator is intelligent, the experiences that he relates demonstrate that he was naive in his youth. As the novel progresses, the narrator's illusions are gradually destroyed through his experiences. Shedding his blindness, he struggles to arrive at a conception of his identity that honors his complexity as an individual without sacrificing social responsibility.

The Little Prince
Antoine de Saint-Exupéry

Narrator

A lonely pilot. While stranded in the desert, he befriends **the Little Prince**. They spend eight days together in the desert before the Little Prince returns to his home planet.

The Scarlet Letter
Nathaniel Hawthorne

Narrator

A surveyor of the Salem Custom House some 200 years after the novel's events take place. The narrator discovers an old manuscript in the building's attic that tells the story of **Hester Prynne**. When the narrator loses his job, he decides to write a fictional treatment of the narrative.

The Time Machine
H. G. Wells

Narrator

Mr. Hillyer, **the Time Traveller**'s dinner guest. His curiosity is enough to make him return to investigate the morning after the first time travel.

Narrator

Tom Jones
Henry Fielding

The ironic, intrusive narrator. He is assumed to be Fielding himself, since he reflects on his process of creating *Tom Jones*.

Narrator of Episode Twelve

Ulysses
James Joyce

A debt collector, though this is the most recent of many different jobs. He enjoys feeling like he is "in the know" and has gotten most of his gossip about the Blooms from his friend **"Pisser" Burke**, who knew them when they lived at the City Arms Hotel.

Ibrahim Nasar

Chronicle of a Death Foretold
Gabriel García Márquez

Santiago Nasar's father, an Arab. He seduced **Victoria Guzman** when she was a teenager. After his father died, Santiago abandoned his studies at the end of secondary school in order to take over the family ranch.

Santiago Nasar

Chronicle of a Death Foretold
Gabriel García Márquez

The protagonist of the story. He is killed the day after **Angela Vicario**'s wedding. On the day he is killed, he wakes up at 5:30 a.m. to wait for the boat that is bringing the bishop. He is the only child of a marriage of convenience. He inherited his sixth sense from his mother. From his father, **Ibrahim Nasar**, he learned his love of firearms, horses, and falconry, as well as the qualities of valor and prudence.

Nately

Catch-22
Joseph Heller

A good-natured young soldier in **John Yossarian**'s squadron. Nately comes from a wealthy home. He tries to keep Yossarian from getting into trouble.

Nately's whore

Catch-22
Joseph Heller

The beautiful prostitute with whom **Nately** falls in love in Rome.

Nathaniel

Love's Labour's Lost
William Shakespeare

A curate who, along with the schoolmaster **Holofernes**, provides learned commentary on **Berowne**'s misplaced letter to **Rosaline**. He plays the role of Alexander the Great in the highly comedic masque of the Nine Worthies at the end of the play. Nathaniel and Holofernes's pompous speech is thought to be a satirical send-up of the academics, critics and other notables of Shakespeare's day.

Naumann

Middlemarch
George Eliot

Will Ladislaw's painter friend in Rome. He uses **Edward Casaubon** as a model for Thomas Aquinas as a ruse to draw a sketch of **Dorothea Brooke**.

Nausicaa

The Odyssey
Homer

The beautiful daughter of King **Alcinous** and Queen **Arete** of the Phaeacians. She discovers **Odysseus** on the beach at Scheria and, out of budding affection for him, ensures his warm reception at her parents' palace.

The Nawab Bahadur

A Passage to India
E. M. Forster

A wealthy Indian who supports the English. He renounces his role as mediator between the local Indians and the colonial English in protest after **Dr. Aziz**'s trial.

Widow Nazaret

Love in the Time of Cholera
Gabriel García Márquez

The woman whom **Transito Ariza** tries put in her son **Florentino Ariza**'s bed. Florentino intends to offer his bed to the Widow and sleep on the floor, but before he can do so, the twenty-eight-year-old widow crawls into his bed, strips, and seduces him. After that night, the widow no longer dresses in mourning. Florentino continues to sleep with her, and she proceeds to sleep with any man who will have her. After his first encounter with the Widow, Florentino convinces himself that he has survived his torturous romance with **Fermina Daza**. He proceeds to sleep with many women and keeps a notebook of his encounters.

Nazgûl

The Lord of the Rings trilogy
J. R. R. Tolkien

Nine Minions of the Dark Lord **Sauron**. They ceaselessly search for the One Ring. These wraiths were once Kings of Men, promised power by receiving Nine Rings of Power from Sauron. The Rings consumed the Kings. The Ringwraiths—also known as the Black Riders, the Nine, or the Nazgûl (the Elvish term)—take the form of cloaked riders on terrifying black horses. In *The Fellowship of the Ring*, they pursue **Frodo Baggins**, the Ring-bearer, incessantly, and are especially drawn to him at moments when he puts the Ring on his finger. In *The Two Towers*, the Nazgûl continue to rely on intimidation and terror. In *The Return of the King*, the leader and most powerful of the nine Ringwraiths, the Black Captain, is struck down by a small Hobbit, **Meriadoc Brandybuck**.

Tata Ndu

The Poisonwood Bible
Barbara Kingsolver

The village chief. He is wary of **Nathan Price** and his proselytizing, afraid that a move toward Christianity will effect a moral decline in his village. He tries in many subtle and tactful ways to inform the Prices that their presence is not welcome, but Nathan ignores these signals.

Lavinia Nebbs

Dandelion Wine
Ray Bradbury

A woman who will not let fear dictate her life. She is unwilling to let the mania surrounding **the Lonely One** affect her. She starts the evening rational but is reduced to panic on the walk home when she admits her fear. At her house, she stabs and kills the Lonely One with a pair of sewing scissors.

Ned

My Brother Sam Is Dead
Christopher & James Lincoln Collier

A local black man who is beheaded by the British.

Dennis Nedry

Jurassic Park
Michael Crichton

Jurassic Park's computer technician. **Lewis Dodgson** of the Biosyn Corporation hires Nedry to steal fifteen of the park's dinosaur embryos. His computer hacking is responsible for all the problems that send Jurassic Park into turmoil.

Dan Needham

A Prayer for Owen Meany
John Irving

John Wheelwright's stepfather. A young drama teacher who marries John's mother only a year before she dies, Dan remains in Gravesend on the academy faculty and helps raise John as though he were his own son.

John Nefastis

The Crying of Lot 49
Thomas Pynchon

A scientist obsessed with perpetual motion. He has tried to invent a type of Maxwell's Demon. **Oedipa Maas** visits him to see the machine after learning about him from **Stanley Koteks**. John shows her the machine but scares her off by propositioning her.

Negro woman

A Streetcar Named Desire
Tennessee Williams

The woman who sits on the steps talking to **Eunice Hubbell** when **Blanche DuBois** arrives. She finds **Stanley Kowalski**'s openly sexual gestures toward **Stella Kowalski** hilarious.

Neighborhood boys

The Virgin Suicides
Jeffrey Eugenides

The indistinct group that narrates the novel. The neighborhood boys attend high school with the Lisbon girls. Still haunted by the suicides in middle age, they reconstruct the story to make sense of the girls' actions, motives, and desires in their final year of life.

Peter Neilsen

Number the Stars
Lois Lowry

Part of the Resistance movement. He was engaged to **Lise Johansen**, the oldest of **Mr. Johansen**'s and **Mrs. Johansen**'s three daughters, before she died. He visits the Johansen family occasionally at night, bringing them the resistance newspaper and gifts and breaking Nazi-imposed curfew to see them. Peter is the young, brave, effective leader of the plan to get **Mr. Rosen**, **Mrs. Rosen**, and **Ellen Rosen** to safety. He is determined to help the Jews and defy the Nazis at all costs.

Nel

Sula
Toni Morrison

Sula's best friend. Nel is quiet and unassuming, while Sula is spontaneous and aggressive. Following the death of **Chicken Little**, Nel feels the guilt that Sula does not have. Nel's guilt causes her to submit to conventional womanhood, marrying **Jude Greene** and settling into her position as a submissive wife. As Nel and Sula are becoming close again, she finds out that Sula and Jude are having sex. This causes Jude to abandon Nel and their children, and breaks up the friendship between Nel and Sula. When Sula falls seriously ill, Nel decides to go and see her for the first time in three years. Nel finally gathers the courage to ask her why she slept with Jude. In the resulting conversation, they dance around the topic of morality and obligation. Sula does not deny her actions, but refuses to accept total responsibility for the rupture of their friendship. She also refuses to accept total responsibility for the end of Nel's marriage. Sula states that she slept with Jude, but Jude chose to abandon his marriage.

Nell

The Comedy of Errors
William Shakespeare

Antipholus of Ephesus's prodigiously fat maid and wife of **Dromio of Ephesus**. Nell helps bar the entry of her husband and master from the house during dinner. Dromio of Syracuse has a long, bawdy dialogue with his master about Nell's large body.

Nell

Endgame
Samuel Beckett

Nagg's wife and **Hamm**'s mother. She and her husband are contained in ashbins. She seems resigned to her life of routine, calling the daily attempt to kiss Nagg a "farce." Her death midway through the play triggers a downward spiral for the characters' fragile cohabitation.

Nellie

Maggie: A Girl of the Streets
Stephen Crane

A "woman of brilliance and audacity" who lures **Pete** away from **Maggie**. Nellie promises the sophistication and worldliness that Pete craves. In the novel's penultimate scene, it becomes clear that Nellie has nothing but contempt for Pete and that she is using him for money.

Nellie

The Red Pony
John Steinbeck

A mare who is bred with a stallion, **Sun Dog**, in hopes that she will produce a colt to replace **Gabilan**, the deceased red pony of the novella's title. The birth is difficult, and the ranch-hand **Billy Buck** is forced to kill Nellie and cut the colt out of her with a knife.

Nelly

The Hours
Michael Cunningham

The cook in the Woolf household. In contrast to **Virginia Woolf**'s distracted relationship with the house and its workings, Nelly is relentlessly domestic and doesn't understand Virginia's focus on writing and indifference to her own household.

Nelson

The Poisonwood Bible
Barbara Kingsolver

An orphan and **Anatole Ngemba**'s best student. He works for **Nathan Price** and his family, helping them to get along in the Congo in exchange for a place to sleep and some eggs to sell in the marketplace so that he can save up for a wife. Unusually bright, Nelson picks up English quickly and helps the girls learn the native language and customs.

Dr. Nelson

Stranger in a Strange Land
Robert A. Heinlein

The medical doctor of the Envoy mission to Mars. He becomes **Michael Valentine Smith**'s primary doctor on Earth.

Miss Nelson

Annie John
Jamaica Kincaid

Annie's homeroom teacher, who praises Annie's essay about her mother.

Professor Harold Nemur

Flowers for Algernon
Daniel Keyes

The scientist in charge of the experiment that heightens **Charlie Gordon**'s intelligence. An arrogant careerist, Nemur treats Charlie as a laboratory animal rather than a human being. Nemur has a tendency to imply that he created Charlie. Nemur is tormented by his wife, who seems even more fixated on his career than he is.

Neptune

The Aeneid
Virgil

The Roman name for the Greek god **Poseidon**. God of the sea and generally an ally of **Venus** and **Aeneas**. Neptune calms the storm that opens the epic and conducts Aeneas safely on the last leg of his voyage.

Nerissa

The Merchant of Venice
William Shakespeare

Portia's lady-in-waiting and confidante. Nerissa marries **Graziano** and escorts Portia to Venice by disguising herself as a law clerk.

Evelyn Nesbit

Ragtime
E. L. Doctorow

A symbol of sex and beauty at the turn of the century. She endures the trial of her husband **Harry Thaw** for the murder of her ex-husband **Stanford White**. In the novel, she develops an interest in **Tateh** and his little girl, and attempts to help them escape the poverty of life as an immigrant on the Lower East Side.

Nessus

Inferno
Dante Alighieri

A Centaur (mythological half-man, half-horse creature) who carries **Dante** through a ring of boiling blood in the First Ring of the Seventh Circle of Hell (Canto XII).

Nestor

The Iliad and *The Odyssey*
Homer

King of Pylos and the oldest Greek warrior in the Trojan War. Nestor is very wise and often advises the military commanders, especially **Agamemnon**. He and **Odysseus** are the Greeks' most persuasive orators.

Nestor

Troilus and Cressida
William Shakespeare

The oldest of the Greek commanders.

Agostino Neto

The Poisonwood Bible
Barbara Kingsolver

A Congolese doctor-poet and the first president of the independent nation of Angola. **Anatole Ngemba** was engaged in a vigorous correspondence with him, and was asked to serve in his government.

Nettie

The Color Purple
Alice Walker

Celie's younger sister, whom **Mr.** ___ initially wanted to marry. Nettie is highly intellectual and from an early age recognizes the value of education. She meets a husband-and-wife pair of missionaries, **Samuel** and **Corrine**. With them, she moves to Africa to preach. Nettie becomes the caretaker of Samuel and Corrine's adopted children, **Adam** and **Olivia** (who, Nettie later learns, are Celie's biological children, stolen and sold by **Alphonso**), and faithfully writes letters to Celie for decades, but Mr. ___ silences Nettie's communication with Celie by keeping the letters in his trunk for years and years.

Sophie Neveu

The Da Vinci Code
Dan Brown

A cryptologist with the French Judicial Police, and the female protagonist of the novel. Sophie, who is about thirty years old, is attractive, single, compassionate, and very intelligent. Her grandfather instilled in her a love of puzzles and codes, and after training in cryptology, Sophie becomes determined to crack her grandfather's code. She and **Robert Langdon**'s goals never diverge. In this way, they echo **Leah Teabing**'s and Langdon's ideas about the partnership of Jesus and Mary Magdalene, of whom Sophie is a descendent.

Christopher Newman

The American
Henry James

The novel's hero and protagonist. Newman is a "superlative American": tall, pleasant, temperate, liberal, athletic, independent, and direct. Forced to earn a living at a young age, Newman has accumulated a substantial fortune through a combination of diligence and luck. Now forty-two, he travels to Paris to enjoy the fruits of his labors and to find a wife to complete his fortune. Newman is curious about but unimpressed with the intricate Parisian social system—an attitude that causes him trouble. Yet, though often unaware of what he has provoked, Newman is far from a simplistic hero. His moral reasoning, honest love, and unfailing allegiance mark him as mature, consistent and self-aware, even out of his element.

Howie Newsome

Our Town
Thornton Wilder

The town's milkman.

Newson

The Mayor of Casterbridge
Thomas Hardy

The sailor who buys **Susan Henchard** and **Elizabeth-Jane Newson** from **Michael Henchard** when he drunkenly auctions off his family. Henchard believes that Elizabeth-Jane is the daughter whom he auctioned off eighteen years before, but Henchard learns that the daughter he auctions off died after Newson bought her. Elizabeth-Jane is really Newson's daughter.

Elizabeth-Jane Newson

The Mayor of Casterbridge
Thomas Hardy

The daughter of **Susan Henchard** and **Newson**, and the woman whom **Michael Henchard** believes is his daughter until Susan tells him the truth in a letter. Elizabeth-Jane bears the same name as the child born to Susan and Henchard, who actually dies shortly after Henchard drunkenly sells Susan and his daughter to Newson. As she follows her mother across the English countryside in search of a relative she does not know, Elizabeth-Jane proves a kind, simple, and uneducated girl. Once in Casterbridge, however, she undertakes intellectual and social improvement. This self-education comes at a painful time, for not long after she arrives in Casterbridge, Susan dies, leaving her in the custody of a man who has learned that she is not his biological daughter and therefore wants little to do with her. Her resolve and brilliance in a gray world cause her to finally be able to forgive Henchard after her harsh words to him at her wedding celebration, and seek him out after her reunion with Newson and the beginning of her new married life.

Newspapermen

The Chairs
Eugène Ionesco

Among the last invisible guests to arrive at the house of the **Old Man** and **Old Woman**. They are all eager to hear the **Orator** deliver the Old Man's message.

Anatole Ngemba

The Poisonwood Bible
Barbara Kingsolver

The English-speaking schoolteacher in the village of Kilanga and the translator for **Nathan Price**'s weekly sermons. He marries **Leah Price** and becomes active in subversive political activities against the dictatorial Mobutu regime.

Elisabet Ngembe

The Poisonwood Bible
Barbara Kingsolver

Anatole Ngemba's aunt. She moves in with **Leah Price** and Anatole and becomes Leah's only female companion.

Martin-Lothaire, Natan, Pascal, and Patrice Ngembe

The Poisonwood Bible
Barbara Kingsolver

Leah Price and **Anatole Ngembe**'s sons.

Nicholas

The Canterbury Tales
Geoffrey Chaucer

In **the Miller**'s Tale, Nicholas is a poor astronomy student who boards with an elderly carpenter, **John**, and the carpenter's too-young wife, **Alisoun**. Nicholas dupes John and sleeps with Alisoun right under John's nose, but **Absolon**, the foppish parish clerk, gets Nicholas in the end.

Nick

Who's Afraid of Virginia Woolf?
Edward Albee

Husband to **Honey**. Nick is the newest member of the biology faculty at New Carthage University, good-looking, Midwestern, and clean-cut. During a nightcap at **George** and **Martha**'s, he and his wife become an audience and then pawns in a sadistic game of jealousy and humiliation.

Nick

The Handmaid's Tale
Margaret Atwood

One of the **Guardians of the Faith**. He is the **Commander**'s gardener and chauffeur and possibly a member of **Mayday**, the **Eyes of God**, or both. After **Serena Joy** arranges for Nick and **Offred** to meet so that Offred can conceive, Nick and Offred begin a covert sexual affair. At the end of the novel, Nick orchestrates Offred's escape from the Commander's house, but we do not know whether he delivers her to the Eyes or the resistance.

Nearly-Headless Nick

The Harry Potter Series: Books 2–4
J. K. Rowling

The friendly Gryffindor ghost. In *Harry Potter and the Chamber of Secrets* **Ron Weasley**, **Harry Potter**, and **Hermione Granger** attend his deathday party.

Dayton Nickles

A Yellow Raft in Blue Water
Michael Dorris

Lee's best friend in high school and **Christine**'s lover. Though originally Dayton had rejected Christine because he thought of her as a sister, after Lee's death the two formed a bond, and they had an off-and-on romance.

Nicolas

The House of the Spirits
Isabel Allende

Jaime's twin brother, and the son of **Clara** and **Esteban Trueba**. Nicolas inherits **Uncle Marcos**'s penchant for travel and invention. Nicolas dates **Amanda**, whom he impregnates. He is not really interested in her, however, and after Jaime performs an abortion for her, Nicolas distances himself from her. Nicolas is eccentric, and he eventually pursues spiritual enlightenment, embarrassing Esteban Trueba. He opens a center for the attainment of Nothingness and is eventually sent out of the country by his ashamed father, who gives him enough money to live on.

Marshall Nicolls

The Heart Is a Lonely Hunter
Carson McCullers

A black pharmacist friend of **Dr. Benedict Mady Copeland**'s. Mr. Nicolls urges **Jake Blount** not to become involved when **Willie Copeland** gets in trouble.

Night Swan

Ceremony
Leslie Marmon Silko

Josiah's girlfriend. Night Swan is a strong, smart, sexy, self-aware woman. A former cantina dancer, she also seduces **Tayo** in order to teach him his first lesson about miscegenation and change.

Nightingale

Tom Jones
Henry Fielding

A foppish city gentleman. Nightingale possesses the traits of loyalty and compassion—although not always in affairs of love. It takes a little time for **Tom** to convince Nightingale not to abandon **Nancy**, since Nightingale is caught up in his image in London. Nightingale transforms and follows Tom's principles of Honour.

Bernard Nightingale

Arcadia
Tom Stoppard

The modern fool and fop. A fame-hunting historian, he leaps over careful research in favor of flashy and radical theories, publicizing from scant evidence the idea that Lord Byron killed **Ezra Chater** in a dual.

The theory, eventually proved false by **Hannah Jarvis**, brings Bernard great shame and embarrassment, as does the scandal of finding Bernard and the young heiress **Chloe Covery** in a carnal embrace.

James Nightshade

Something Wicked This Way Comes
Ray Bradbury

William Halloway's best friend. In turmoil throughout the book, Jim wants to help Will and **Charles Halloway** fight the carnival, but he also longs to ride the carousel and instantly grow up. Jim is fiercely independent and afraid of nothing, but these traits threaten to get him into problems at the carnival that he'll be unable to escape.

Jim's mother

Something Wicked This Way Comes
Ray Bradbury

A single mother who was beaten by her husband and lost two of her children. She is still fragile, and has only **James Nightshade**. She tries to protect him but knows that he will leave her someday.

Captain Peter Niles

Mourning Becomes Electra
Eugene O'Neill

An artillery captain for the Union. He is straightforward and good-natured, failing to apprehend the machinations afoot in the Mannon house until the very end of the trilogy. In the end, he falls under the control of **Lavinia Mannon**, cutting off his sister, **Hazel Niles**, but comes to see the light when **Orin Mannon** kills himself and Hazel comes to attack Lavinia.

Hazel Niles

Mourning Becomes Electra
Eugene O'Neill

A longtime friend of the Mannon children, **Orin Mannon** and **Lavinia Mannon**. Hazel is a pretty, healthy, dark-haired girl and Orin's would-be sweetheart. Hazel haplessly attempts to rescue Orin from his fate and regain her brother, **Captain Peter Niles**, who fell under the control of Lavinia. Orin is made crazy by his realization that he cannot take his ghosts outside of his relationship with Lavinia, and he kills himself. Afterward, Hazel reconnects with Peter, and Lavinia is left to live with her dead in the Mannon house.

Nim

The Merry Wives of Windsor
William Shakespeare

One of **Sir John Falstaff**'s men. Nim wants to stay honest, and he refuses to deliver Falstaff's seductive letter to **Mistress Alice Ford**. He and **Pistol** decide to let the husbands know of Falstaff's scheme.

Nimue

The Once and Future King
T. H. White

Merlyn's lover, who eventually traps him in a cave for centuries. Despite her faults, Nimue is a good woman, and she promises to take care of **King Arthur** on Merlyn's behalf.

Ninsun

The Epic of Gilgamesh
Unknown

The mother of **Gilgamesh**. Ninsun is a minor goddess, noted for her wisdom. Her husband is **Lugulbanda**.

Monsieur Nioche

The American
Henry James

Noémie Nioche's father, an old, minor aristocrat who has fallen on bad times. Nioche's decent forlornness appeals to **Christopher Newman**'s democratic instincts, and the help Newman gives Noémie is meant not for her directly but to assuage her father's fears. Newman's attempts ultimately prove futile, however, as Nioche becomes progressively more resentful of his petty, prodigious, and increasingly popular daughter.

Noémie Nioche

The American
Henry James

A free-spirited and ruthless Parisian copyist whose painting **Christopher Newman** agrees to buy. Noémie is acutely aware of her many charms and uses them tirelessly to her advantage. Noémie habitually humiliates her father, **Monsieur Nioche**, sending him on menial errands, berating his mistakes, and giving him an occasional stipend gleaned from her rich admirers. When **Valentin de Bellegarde** and **Kapp** agree to duel over her, she is thrilled.

Nippers

Bartleby, the Scrivener
Herman Melville

Another scrivener employed by **the Lawyer**, the opposite of his fellow scrivener **Turkey**. Nippers is young and works best in the afternoon.

Frank No Deer

When the Legends Die
Hal Borland

A mixed-blood Native American from a reservation in New Mexico. He steals from **George Black Bull**, **Thomas Black Bull**'s father, and in the end pays for this crime with his life. After he is murdered, the Black Bull family is forced to flee their home and seek refuge in the wilderness.

Noah

The Old Testament
Unknown

The survivor of **God**'s great flood. Noah obediently builds the large ark, or boat, that saves the human race and the animal kingdom from destruction.

Richard Noakes

Arcadia
Tom Stoppard

A gardener who excels at frustrating **Lady Croom**. He does so with his improbable garden plans, his spying and gossiping, and his introduction of a noisy steam engine into the estate.

Miss Noble

Middlemarch
George Eliot

Mrs. Farebrother's sister. She steals small items of food to give to the poor. She becomes fond of **Will Ladislaw**.

Nolan

The Shipping News
E. Annie Proulx

The only living kinsmen of **Quoyle** and **the aunt**. True to legend, he is a madman who seems capable of malicious acts. When Quoyle goes to visit Nolan in the asylum, he brings him a framed picture of a poodle. Quoyle later hears that Nolan has stabbed everyone at the asylum with the broken glass from the poodle picture.

Cornelius (Neeley) Nolan

A Tree Grows in Brooklyn
Betty Smith

Mary Frances Nolan's younger brother. Growing up, Neeley and Francie grow to be close friends. He looks just like his father, and his mother thinks of him as someone who can be like **Johnny Nolan**, without Johnny's faults. Indeed, he is musical, but hardworking, and does not like alcohol.

Doctor Nolan

The Bell Jar
Sylvia Plath

Esther Greenwood's psychiatrist at the private mental hospital. Esther comes to trust and love Dr. Nolan, who encourages Esther's unusual thinking.

Johnny Nolan

A Tree Grows in Brooklyn
Betty Smith

Mary Frances Nolan's father. Johnny is a young Irish singer-waiter, talented but weak. He is a dreamer without the resources or abilities to make his dreams reality. He loves his children, but is an alcoholic. Francie dreads his drunkenness, but loves her father more than her mother, **Katie Nolan**. Like Katie and **Mary Rommely**, Johnny knows that an education will allow his children to live a better life than he has.

Katie Nolan

A Tree Grows in Brooklyn
Betty Smith

Mary Frances Nolan's mother. Katie is hard and detached ever since she had her two children and realized she could not depend on her husband **Johnny Nolan** to support her family. Katie is extremely hardworking, saves money as best she can, and will do anything to give her children a better life.

Mary Frances (Francie) Nolan

A Tree Grows in Brooklyn
Betty Smith

The protagonist of the novel. Francie is the daughter of second-generation Americans living in Brooklyn, New York, in the early twentieth century. She is a combination of her hardworking, practical mother and her imaginative, dreaming father. Growing up without luxury, and sometimes without friends, she loves to read and creates new worlds through her writing.

Alice Nolina

Animal Dreams
Barbara Kingsolver

Codi Nolina and **Hallie Nolina**'s mother, wife of **Doc Homer Nolina**. Called Alice only by Doc Homer, and Althea by the rest of the town of Grace, she died shortly after Hallie's birth from complications arising from the pregnancy. Alice's life was characterized by her extreme stubbornness. Doc Homer tells Codi that her mother is not from the town of Grace, partly out of shame from her family thinking that his family was a bad one.

Codi Nolina

Animal Dreams
Barbara Kingsolver

The protagonist and narrator of the novel. After losing her mother at age three and her unborn child at age fifteen, Codi Nolina does not want to love anything for fear of losing it. She aimlessly follows her medical student boyfriend **Carlo** to rural Crete while she and Carlo and Codi's sister **Hallie Nolina** are based out of Tucson. After Hallie leaves Tucson for Nicaragua, and Codi leaves Carlo, Codi returns to her hometown of Grace, where her father, **Doc Homer Nolina**, is suffering from Alzheimer's disease. It is not until Codi understands her own relationship to her community, mostly through women like **Viola Domingos** and **Doña Althea**, and finds a profession that she enjoys on her own that she can build on a sense of belonging and purpose with **Loyd Peregrina**. She finds out by the time of Hallie's murder in Nicaragua and Doc Homer's descent into complete confusion from his brain disease that despite her understanding her mother was from Grace, and was the cousin of Doña Althea. By the end, Codi is pregnant with Loyd's child again, and feels she has a place among the memories of her mother in Grace.

Doc Homer Nolina

Animal Dreams
Barbara Kingsolver

Codi Nolina's and **Hallie Nolina**'s father, **Alice Nolina**'s husband. Doc Homer Nolina is the person from whose perspective the secondary third-person narrator interjects. Although he serves as the sole town doctor for Grace his entire life, Doc Homer always feels like an outsider. **Doña Althea** and Alice's families thought Doc Homer's family was a bad one, and so he never tells Codi or Hallie that their mother was from Grace. Despite his gruff manner and uncommunicative style, Doc Homer loves his two daughters desperately. As he loses his mind to Alzheimer's disease, he also loses many of his inhibitions and is finally able to voice his care for and understanding of Codi.

Hallie Nolina

Animal Dreams
Barbara Kingsolver

Codi Nolina's younger sister. She leaves for Nicaragua at the beginning of the novel, and even when she faces the horrible destruction of life and land there, she finds enormous happiness in trying to help improve cultivation practices. Contrary to Codi, Hallie feels at home absolutely anywhere. Hallie is kidnapped in Nicaragua and later found dead. Hallie's funeral and Codi's subsequent burial of the sisters' afghan give Codi a sense of belonging to Grace and her own history there.

No-Name Woman

The Woman Warrior
Maxine Hong Kingston

Kingston's unnamed aunt. No-Name Woman kills herself and her illegitimate child in China. Kingston imagines a history for her aunt, portraying her as a timid woman who gave in to a forbidden passion and was then driven to suicide by the condemnation of her village.

Johnny Nonsuch

The Return of the Native
Thomas Hardy

The son of **Susan Nonsuch**. He has the knack of being in the right place at the right time: he reports **Eustacia Vye** and **Damon Wildeve**'s tryst to **Diggory Venn**, and is also the one who tells **Clym Yeobright** of his mother's damning last words.

Duke of Norfolk

Henry VIII
William Shakespeare

A lord of the court and member of the Council. At first, Norfolk does not believe the **Duke of Buckingham**'s criticism of **Cardinal Wolsey**, and he urges the duke to hold his tongue. After Buckingham's fall, he becomes suspicious; after **Queen Katherine**'s fall, he plots with the other lords to bring down the Cardinal, and takes part in reading the charges against him. Following Wolsey's demise, Norfolk receives a promotion. He takes part in a plot to bring down **Cranmer, Archbishop of Canterbury**.

Duke of Norfolk

A Man for All Seasons
Robert Bolt

More's close friend. Norfolk is ultimately asked by **Cromwell**, and even encouraged by More himself, to betray his friendship with More. When Cromwell interrogates More and sets up a sham trial, Norfolk subtly tries to help More but ultimately bows to political and social pressures. He ultimately sanctions More's execution.

Thomas Mowbray, Duke of Norfolk

Richard II
William Shakespeare

A nobleman accused by **Henry Bolingbroke** of conspiring to kill the late **Thomas of Woodstock, Duke of Gloucester**. Banished by **King Richard II**, Mowbray dies in exile.

Nori

The Hobbit
J. R. R. Tolkien

One of the dwarf companions on **Bilbo Baggins**'s quest.

Sara Noriega

Love in the Time of Cholera
Gabriel García Márquez

An older woman whom **Florentino Ariza** meets at a poetry festival and with whom he conducts a long-term affair. She is the only woman besides **Fermina Daza** to ever reject him.

Norma

This Boy's Life
Tobias Wolff

Dwight's eldest daughter, for whom **Jack Wolff** harbors a secret infatuation. Norma is sweet and chipper in her youth and loves **Bobby Crow**, a good-hearted boy from school whom she calls "Bobo." Later, Norma decides that Bobby is not ambitious, and she marries **Kenneth**.

Norman

Tuesdays with Morrie
Mitch Albom

An old, long-estranged friend of **Morrie Schwartz**'s. He eventually moved away and did not send his regards to Morrie or **Charlotte** although he knew that Charlotte would be undergoing a serious surgery. Morrie refuses to accept his apology, which Morrie later regrets.

Norris

The Big Sleep
Raymond Chandler

The **Sternwoods**' butler.

Elsie Norris

Oranges Are Not the Only Fruit
Jeanette Winterson

A member of the church. Elsie is energetic, outgoing, and entertaining. Despite her genuine religiousness, she is also quite eccentric. Elsie serves as a loving mother figure to **Jeanette** when Jeanette's own mother is neglectful.

Mrs. Norris

Mansfield Park
Jane Austen

Sister to **Fanny Price**'s mother and **Lady Bertram**; wife of the first parson at Mansfield Parsonage. With no children of her own, Mrs. Norris is an officious busybody, always trying to derive glory from her association with the family. She is horribly cruel to Fanny, always reminding the girl of her "place" in the family.

Mrs. Norris

The Harry Potter Series: Books 2 and *3*
J. K. Rowling

Argus Filch's beloved cat, petrified by the basilisk (a snake-like creature whose eyes turn people to stone) in *Harry Potter and the Chamber of Secrets*.

Abe North

Tender Is the Night
F. Scott Fitzgerald

A dear friend of **Dick Diver**'s and a once brilliant musician who drinks away his career. Abe leaves the expatriate community in France to which he and his wife, **Mary**, belong and moves back to America. Ultimately, Abe is killed in a fight at a speakeasy in New York.

Mary North

Tender Is the Night
F. Scott Fitzgerald

Abe North's lovely and kind wife. Mary weds the wealthy **Conte di Minghetti** after Abe passes away. She becomes enraged at **Dick** and **Nicole Diver** after they inadvertently insult her second husband in a misunderstanding over their child's bath.

Earl of Northumberland

Henry VI, Part III
William Shakespeare

A supporter of **King Henry VI** and ally of **Queen Margaret**. Though loyal to Henry, he is disgusted when the king agrees to relinquish the crown to the Yorkists following his death. Before Margaret and **Lord Clifford** stab the **Duke of York**, Northumberland admits to being moved by York's words, earning Margaret's scorn. His death is alluded to by **King Edward IV** at the end of the play.

Henry Percy, Earl of Northumberland

Richard II; Henry IV, Part I; and *Henry IV, Part II*
William Shakespeare

An initial supporter of Bolingbroke (**Henry IV**); father of Henry Percy (**Hotspur**), husband of **Lady Northumberland**, father-in-law of **Lady Kate Percy**, and brother of the **Earl of Worcester**. Following the death of **John of Gaunt**, Northumberland acknowledges the ruinous reign of **King Richard II**; when Northumberland reveals that Bolingbroke has come to England with an army, he and two other nobles decide to join forces with him to return England to its former glory. Northumberland and his son both swear fealty to Bolingbroke, and become major players in the rebellion. After Henry ascends to the throne, however, Northumberland plots with his son and brother to rebel against the crown. Refusing to send troops to the Battle of Shrewsbury in *King Henry IV, Part I*, Northumberland greatly disappoints the other rebel leaders. In the failed uprising, he has lost both his son and his brother, as he learns at opening of *King Henry IV, Part II*. He swears revenge, and sends letters to begin plans for the second stage of rebellion, with the **Archbishop of York**, **Thomas Mowbray**, **Lord Bardolph**, and **Lord Hastings**. Due in part to the advice from his wife and daughter-in-law, he again does not send troops to battle, and his defeat is mentioned only in passing toward the end of the play.

Lady Northumberland

Henry IV, Part II
William Shakespeare

The **Earl of Northumberland**'s wife. Along with **Lady Kate Percy**, she convinces her husband not to fight in the upcoming rebellion, but to flee to Scotland.

Mr. Norton

Invisible Man
Ralph Ellison

One of the wealthy white trustees at **the Narrator**'s college. Mr. Norton is a narcissistic man who treats the narrator as proof that he is liberal-minded and philanthropic.

Father Tom Novak

A Yellow Raft in Blue Water
Michael Dorris

A new cleric at the Holy Martyrs Mission who recruits **Rayona** into the God Squad. Father Tom is the only person on the reservation who seems to think Rayona is worth his time. Their close relationship ends awkwardly when Father Tom's friendship turns to lechery.

The Second Nun

The Canterbury Tales
Geoffrey Chaucer

The Second Nun is not described in the General Prologue, but she tells a saint's life for her tale.

The Nun's Priest

The Canterbury Tales
Geoffrey Chaucer

Like **the Second Nun**, **the narrator** fails to describe the Nun's Priest in the General Prologue. He tells the story of **Chanticleer** and **the fox**.

Nunkie

Their Eyes Were Watching God
Zora Neale Hurston

A girl in the Everglades who flirts relentlessly with **Tea Cake**. **Janie Mae Crawford** grows extremely jealous of Nunkie, but Tea Cake reassures her that Nunkie means nothing to him.

Nurse

Romeo and Juliet
William Shakespeare

Juliet's nurse. She breast-fed Juliet when she was a baby and has cared for Juliet her entire life. A vulgar, long-winded, and sentimental character, the Nurse provides comic relief with her inappropriate remarks and speeches. Until a disagreement near the play's end, the Nurse is Juliet's faithful confidante and loyal intermediary in Juliet's affair with **Romeo**.

Nurse

Moll Flanders
Daniel Defoe

A widow in Colchester who takes care of the child **Moll** from the age of three through her teenage years. The sudden death of this nurse precipitates Moll's placement with a local wealthy family.

Nurse

Antigone 1946
Jean Anouilh

Anouilh's addition to the *Antigone* legend. Fussy, affectionate, and reassuring, she suffers no drama or tragedy but exists in the day-to-day tasks of caring for the two sisters. Though she is an ineffectual biddy, her comforting presence returns **Antigone** to her girlhood.

Nurse

A Streetcar Named Desire
Tennessee Williams

The woman who accompanies the doctor to collect **Blanche DuBois** and bring her to an institution. She possesses a severe, unfeminine manner and has a talent for subduing hysterical patients.

Francis Nurse

The Crucible
Arthur Miller

A wealthy, influential man in Salem, husband of the upright **Rebecca Nurse**. Francis Nurse is well-respected by most people in Salem, but he is an enemy of **Thomas Putnam** and **Ann Putnam**. Over the years, he gradually bought up the 300 acres that he once rented, and some people resent his success. Francis is present during much of the witch trials because Rebecca is arrested for witchcraft. Francis tries to help get to the bottom of matters like **Giles Corey**'s accusation that the witch trials are just a ploy by Thomas Putnam to gain more land.

Rebecca Nurse

The Crucible
Arthur Miller

Francis Nurse's wife. Rebecca Nurse is a wise, sensible, and upright woman, held in tremendous regard by most of the Salem community. However, she falls victim to the witch hunt hysteria when **Thomas Putnam** and **Ann Putnam**, enemies of the Nurses, accuse Rebecca of killing seven of Ann's children through witchcraft and she refuses to confess. Rebecca assures everyone that **Ruth Putnam** and **Betty Parris** are probably only suffering from a childish fit derived from overstimulation. For holding to her beliefs and not falsely confessing, Rebecca is eventually hanged, even though **John Proctor** presents a petition signed by ninety-one residents attesting to Rebecca's upright character.

Nutbeem

The Shipping News
E. Annie Proulx

An English castaway on the Newfoundland shore. Nutbeem ostensibly covers foreign correspondence for **Jack Buggit**'s newspaper and tracks down sexual-abuse stories. He loves talking about his boat; he made it himself to sail across the Atlantic. The men of the town drunkenly destroy it.

Nwakibie

Things Fall Apart
Chinua Achebe

A wealthy clansman who takes a chance on **Okonkwo** by lending him 800 seed yams—twice the number that Okonkwo requests. Nwakibie's loan helps Okonkwo build up the beginnings of his personal wealth, status, and independence.

Nwoye

Things Fall Apart
Chinua Achebe

Okonkwo's oldest son, whom Okonkwo believes is weak and lazy. Okonkwo continually beats Nwoye, hoping to correct the faults that he perceives in him. Influenced by **Ikemefuna**, Nwoye begins to exhibit more masculine behavior, which pleases Okonkwo. He maintains doubts about some of the laws and rules of his tribe and eventually converts to Christianity. Okonkwo believes that Nwoye is afflicted with the same weaknesses that his father, **Unoka**, possessed in abundance.

Harold Nye

In Cold Blood
Truman Capote

The youngest of **Alvin Dewey**'s principal KBI assistants.

Nym

Henry V
William Shakespeare

A commoner from London who serves in the war. Though he almost comes to blows with **Pistol** over the affections of **Mistress Quickly**, Nym is friends with both Pistol and **Bardolph**. During the war, Nym and Bardolph steal goods around towns in France, are arrested, and hanged.

17

SUICIDES

THEY TOOK THE OTHER WAY OUT.

Cathy Ames	1	*East of Eden*
Jose Arcadio	2	*One Hundred Years of Solitude*
Emma Bovary	3	*Madame Bovary*
Cleopatra	4	*Antony and Cleopatra*
Dido	5	*The Aeneid*
Hedda Gabler	6	*Hedda Gabler*
Judas Iscariot	7	*The New Testament*
Javert	8	*Les Misérables*
Dr. Henry Jekyll	9	*Dr. Jekyll and Mr. Hyde*
Juliet	10	*Romeo and Juliet*
Anna Karenina	11	*Anna Karenina*
Willy Loman	12	*Death of a Salesman*
Lady Macbeth	13	*Macbeth*
Romeo	14	*Romeo and Juliet*
The Lisbon Sisters	15	*The Virgin Suicides*
George Wilson	16	*The Great Gatsby*
Virginia Woolf	17	*The Hours*

O'Brien

1984
George Orwell

Mysterious and powerful member of the Inner Party. O'Brien appears to **Winston Smith** in a dream, and eventually Smith comes to believe that O'Brien is a member of the Brotherhood, a legendary rebel group founded by **Emmanuel Goldstein**. Winston and his lover **Julia** confide their anti-Party sentiments to O'Brien, who responds enthusiastically. However, when Winston is captured by the Thought Police, O'Brien takes part in his interrogation as an active member of the Party. It is left unclear if O'Brien was ever a member of the Brotherhood, or if he was really captured and converted.

Tim O'Brien

The Things They Carried
Tim O'Brien

The narrator and protagonist of the collection of stories. O'Brien is a pacifist who contends with his guilt and confusion about Vietnam by writing.

Jim O'Connor

The Glass Menagerie
Tennessee Williams

An old acquaintance of **Tom Wingfield** and **Laura Wingfield**'s. Jim O'Connor was a popular athlete in high school and is now a shipping clerk at the shoe warehouse in which Tom works. When Jim is invited to dinner by Tom, **Amanda Wingfield** goes a little crazy getting ready for Jim's arrival, thinking of Jim as Laura's long-awaited gentleman caller. Even though Laura is incredibly nervous when Jim comes to dinner, he calms her down. They waltz and he kisses her, then mentions his girlfriend **Betty**. Jim talks as if he is trying to convince himself as much as all the others that he has the self-confidence he needs to succeed.

Hildy O'Dair

A Tree Grows in Brooklyn
Betty Smith

Katie Nolan's best friend when she was a young girl. Hildy dated **Johnny Nolan** before Katie and Johnny fell in love.

Mr. O'Halloran

Angela's Ashes
Frank McCourt

Frank McCourt's headmaster and teacher during his final year at school. "Hoppy" encourages Frank to go to America and find good employment rather than stay in a dead-end job in Ireland.

Carreen O'Hara

Gone with the Wind
Margaret Mitchell

Scarlett O'Hara's youngest sister. Carreen is a good-natured girl who turns to religion after the war and joins a convent.

Ellen O'Hara

Gone with the Wind
Margaret Mitchell

Scarlett O'Hara's mother, and a descendent of the aristocratic Robillard family. Ellen marries **Gerald O'Hara** and devotes herself to running Tara, the family plantation, after her father forbids her love affair with **Philippe**, her cousin. Even after Ellen's death, Scarlett struggles with the competing desires to please her mother and please herself.

Gerald O'Hara

Gone with the Wind
Margaret Mitchell

Scarlett O'Hara's father. Gerald is a passionately loyal Confederate who immigrated to America from Ireland as a young man. His strong will, tendency to drink, and selfishness echo in Scarlett's nature. Scarlett also inherits Gerald's love for the South and for his plantation, Tara.

Scarlett O'Hara

Gone with the Wind
Margaret Mitchell

The novel's protagonist. Scarlett is a pretty, coquettish Southern belle who grows up on the Georgia plantation of Tara in the years before the Civil War. Selfish, shrewd, and vain, Scarlett inherits the strong will of her father, **Gerald O'Hara**, but also desires to please her well-bred, genteel mother, **Ellen**. When hardships plague Scarlett, she shoulders the troubles of her family and friends.

Suellen O'Hara

Gone with the Wind
Margaret Mitchell

Scarlett O'Hara's younger sister. Suellen is a selfish, petty girl who marries **Will Benteen** after Scarlett steals **Frank** from her.

Bernhard V. O'Hare

Slaughterhouse-Five
Kurt Vonnegut

A wartime pal of **Kurt Vonnegut**'s. Vonnegut visits him and his wife, **Mary O'Hare**, in Pennsylvania while trying to do research and collect remembrances for his Dresden book.

Mary O'Hare

Slaughterhouse-Five
Kurt Vonnegut

Bernhard O'Hare's wife. Mary gets upset with **Kurt Vonnegut** because she believes he will glorify war in his novel; Vonnegut, however, promises not to do so.

Calvin O'Keefe

A Wrinkle in Time
Madeleine L'Engle

A popular boy and talented athlete in **Meg Murry**'s high school who accompanies Meg and **Charles Wallace Murry** on their adventure. No one in his large family really cares about him, but he nonetheless demonstrates a strong capacity for love and affection and shows a burgeoning romantic interest in Meg.

After meeting the **Happy Medium** and before going to the planet Camazotz, **Mrs. Whatsit** strengthens Calvin's innate ability to communicate with people of all different types.

J. J. O'Molloy

Ulysses
James Joyce

A lawyer who is out of work and money. O'Molloy is thwarted in his attempts to borrow money from friends. He sticks up for **Leopold Bloom** in **Barney Kiernan**'s pub in Episode Twelve.

Miss O'Shaughnessy

Lucky Jim
Kingsley Amis

Michie's girlfriend and one of the pretty college girls that **Jim Dixon** lusts after. Dixon tries to lure her and her female friends to take his special subject course next fall, but he is fired before he has a chance to teach the class.

Sugar-Boy O'Sheean

All the King's Men
Robert Penn Warren

Willie Stark's driver and bodyguard. Sugar-Boy is a crack shot with a .38 special and a brilliant driver. A stuttering Irishman, Sugar-Boy follows Willie blindly.

Gabriel Oak

Far from the Madding Crowd
Thomas Hardy

One of the protagonists. Gabriel Oak is a farmer, shepherd, and bailiff. He is humble, honest, loyal, and exceptionally skilled with animals and farming. At first, Gabriel is prosperous and **Bathsheba Everdene** is not very successful. When Gabriel pursues Bathsheba romantically, she spurns him. After a disaster where all his pregnant sheep are led off of a cliff, Gabriel becomes poor and travels to Weatherbury, where he ends up working for Bathsheba. When Bathsheba and **William Boldwood** are involved in a romance, Bathsheba asks Gabriel what he thinks of it. Gabriel tells her that Boldwood is unworthy, and Bathsheba then accuses Gabriel of being jealous. Finally, she orders him to leave the farm, and he agrees. Gabriel is soon asked back to the farm and made a bailiff. As **Sergeant Francis Troy** moves onto the scene, replacing Boldwood and marrying Bathsheba, Gabriel becomes aware of a coming doom. He then single-handedly saves Bathsheba's wheat and barley during a storm. In a private conversation with Gabriel, Bathsheba reveals that she was pressured into marrying Troy. Later, Gabriel is the one responsible for transporting the dead body of **Fanny Robin** after **Joseph Poorgrass** fails to do so. After Boldwood shoots Troy, Gabriel ends up marrying Bathsheba. He tells her that he is leaving because he doesn't like the rumors about himself and Bathsheba. And for the first time in her life, Bathsheba tells a man that she wants him. Gabriel agrees to stay with her as a result.

Thorin Oakenshield

The Hobbit
J. R. R. Tolkien

A Dwarf who leads his fellow **Dwarves** on a trip to the Lonely Mountain to reclaim their treasure from **Smaug**. **Gandalf** convinces **Bilbo Baggins** to come along for the adventure. Smaug's bounty is Thorin Oakenshield's inheritance, as it belonged to **Thror**, Thorin's grandfather, the great King under the Mountain. Once Thorin gets his hands on Smaug's treasure, he becomes irrationally greedy and obsessed with wealth.

Sally Oates

Silas Marner
George Eliot

Silas Marner's neighbor and the cobbler's wife. Silas eases the pain of Sally's heart disease and dropsy with a concoction he makes out of foxglove.

Obadiah

Tristram Shandy
Laurence Sterne

Servant to **Walter Shandy**.

Willie Oban

The Iceman Cometh
Eugene O'Neill

A man who left Harvard Law School upon the ruin of his prominent industrialist father. He dreams of starting his legal career and speaks with mocking suavity.

Oberon

A Midsummer Night's Dream
William Shakespeare

The king of the fairies, husband of **Titania**. The confusion and mischief that sets the play in action stems from a fight Oberon has with his wife. Titania refuses to relinquish control of a young Indian prince whom Oberon wants for a page. His desire for revenge on Titania leads him to send **Puck** to obtain the love-potion flower that eventually creates havoc with the four Athenian lovers.

Obiageli

Things Fall Apart
Chinua Achebe

The daughter of **Okonkwo**'s first wife. **Ezinma** has a great deal of influence over her even though the two are close in age.

Obie

The Chocolate War
Robert Cormier

Secretary of **the Vigils**. Obie is perhaps the only one who understands how horribly cruel **Archie Costello** is, and is the one member of the Vigils who doubts what they are doing. He does not want to involve **Jerry Renault** in any trouble or cruel behaviors because he feels sorry for the fact that Jerry's mother recently died.

Obierika

Things Fall Apart
Chinua Achebe

Okonkwo's close friend, whose daughter's wedding provides cause for festivity early in the novel. Obierika sells Okonkwo's yams to ensure that Okonkwo won't suffer financial ruin while in exile, and he comforts Okonkwo whenever he is depressed. Like **Nwoye**, Obierika questions some of the tribe's traditional strictures.

Anna Karenina
Leo Tolstoy

Darya Aleksandrovna Oblonskaya

Stepan Arkadyich Oblonsky's wife, **Anna Arkadyevna Karenina**'s sister-in-law and **Ekaterina Alexandrovna Shcherbatskaya**'s older sister. Dolly is one of the few people who behave kindly toward Anna after her affair becomes public. The novel opens with the painful revelation that Dolly's husband has betrayed her, and her even more painful awareness that he is not very repentant.

Anna Karenina
Leo Tolstoy

Stepan Arkadyich Oblonsky

Anna Arkadyevna Karenina's brother. A pleasure-loving aristocrat and minor government official, his affair with his children's governess nearly destroys his marriage to **Darya Alexandrovna Oblonskaya**. Stiva and Anna share a common tendency to place personal fulfillment over social duties. Stiva is incorrigible, proceeding from his affair with the governess—which his wife, Dolly, forgives—to a liaison with a ballerina.

The Things They Carried
Tim O'Brien

Kathleen O'Brien

Tim O'Brien's daughter. Although O'Brien alludes to having multiple children, Kathleen is the only one we meet. Her youth and innocence force O'Brien to try to explain the meaning of the war.

Prometheus Bound
Aeschylus

Oceanus

A follower of **Zeus**. Oceanus agrees that Zeus is too harsh and sympathizes with **Prometheus**, but he suggests that it's better to accept injustice than to fight it.

Dubliners
James Joyce

Mat O'Connor

One of the political workers from "Ivy Day in the Committee Room." Quiet and reserved, O'Connor tempers the men's conversation by praising the dead politician **Parnell**, but he shows little interest in his own political work.

Antony and Cleopatra
William Shakespeare

Octavia

Octavius Caesar's sister. Octavia marries **Antony** in order to cement an alliance between the two triumvirs. She is a victim of Antony's deception, and her meekness, purity, and submission make her the paradigm of Roman womanhood and **Cleopatra**'s polar opposite. Under the guise of sending Octavia to broker a peace with Caesar, Antony flees for Egypt to rejoin Cleopatra.

Odell

Cold Mountain
Charles Frazier

A peddler. He meets **Inman** at an inn and tells him the sad tale of his lifelong search for **Lucinda**, the slave-girl that he loves. Odell's story parallels Inman's own quest to return to **Ada Monroe** and acts as a reminder that the Southern army was fighting in part to uphold the legality of slavery.

Odette

Swann's Way
Marcel Proust

The love of **Charles Swann**'s life and the cause of his most wretched suffering. Though devoid of intelligence, class, and even beauty, Odette is an expert seductress who lures Swann into an affair and marriage that he will never escape. Swann falls in love with her after detecting a resemblance between her face and that of the girl in the Boticelli painting *Jethro's Daughter*. Odette leads a torrid life and takes lovers behind Swann's back, including other guests at the **Verdurins**, the **Comte de Forcheville**, and even other women. Though unable to love Swann, Odette thinks very highly of him.

Odin

Norse Mythology
Unknown

The counterpart of **Zeus** in Norse mythology, a quiet, brooding figure. Odin trades one of his eyes and suffers for nine nights to attain the insights of the Well of Wisdom, which he passes on to men along with the mystical powers of the runes and poetry. He rewards fallen warriors with a place in Valhalla, the Hall of the Slain.

Odon

Pale Fire
Vladimir Nabokov

An actor and a friend of Charles the Beloved, aka **Charles Kinbote**. Odon helps Charles escape from Zembla. In America, Odon's mother **Sylvia** takes Charles in.

Odysseus

The Iliad and *The Odyssey*
Homer

The protagonist of the *Odyssey*. He is the king of Ithaca and the great Greek warrior, speaker, and commander. He is the husband of Queen **Penelope** and the father of Prince **Telemachus**. In the *Iliad*, Odysseus helps mediate between **Agamemnon** and **Achilles** during their quarrel. Though a strong and courageous warrior, Odysseus is most renowned for his cunning and intellect. He is a favorite of the goddess **Athena**, who often sends him divine aid, but a bitter enemy of **Poseidon**, who frustrates his journey at every turn. In the *Odyssey*, he struggles for ten years to return home to his wife and kingdom in Ithaca. In the *Aeneid*, Shakespeare's *Troilus and Cressida*, and other texts that follow the Roman tradition, Odysseus is known as **Ulysses**. Odysseus is also a prominent figure in Greek mythology.

Oedipus

Oedipus trilogy (Oedipus Rex, Oedipus at Colonus, Antigone)
Sophocles

King of Thebes, wife and son of **Jocasta**, son of **Laius**, and father of **Antigone** and **Ismene**. Oedipus is renowned for his intelligence and cleverness—he saved Thebes and became its king by solving the riddle of the **Sphinx**. Yet he is stubbornly blind to the truth about himself. He was taken from the house of Laius as a baby and left in the mountains with bound feet. On his way to Thebes, Oedipus killed his biological father without learning his identity, then proceeded to marry Jocasta, his biological mother. He is later exiled by his brother-in-law **Creon** and blinds himself. Oedipus also appears in Greek mythology.

Alas, Babylon
Pat Frank

Bubba Offenhaus

The owner of the local funeral parlor.

Notes from Underground
Fyodor Dostoevsky

Officer

A military officer who treats **the Underground Man** dismissively in a tavern one night, thereby making himself the object of the Underground Man's obsessive desire for revenge for several years. The Underground Man resents the officer for his rank, wealth, physical prowess, and confidence, but is also intimidated by him for these same reasons, and therefore can never make a move against him.

The Handmaid's Tale
Margaret Atwood

Offred

The novel's narrator and protagonist. Offred is one of the **Handmaids** in the fictional future Republic of Gilead. She remembers but never reveals her real name, which has been discarded in favor of "of Fred," a name that announces her as being a child-bearer for Fred, one of the Commanders of the Faithful of Gilead. As a Handmaid, Offred is not only denied friends, she is denied a family. In her former life she was married to **Luke** and had a young daughter. Before Gilead, Offred used to think of her body as an instrument of pleasure or of transportation. Now, others define her body as nothing more than a uterus. She hates facing menstruation every month because it means failure. Her captivity becomes familiar, and the prospect of a new, free life becomes scary.

The Handmaid's Tale
Margaret Atwood

Offred's mother

A single mother and a feminist activist. At **the Red Center**, **Offred** sees a video of her mother as a young woman protesting violence against women in a Take Back the Night march.

Babbitt
Sinclair Lewis

Jake Offutt

A corrupt Zenith politician. Offutt and **Thompson** carry out shady business deals with **Babbitt**'s help.

The Handmaid's Tale
Margaret Atwood

Ofglen

One of the **Handmaids** of the Republic of Gilead and **Offred**'s shopping partner. Ofglen is a member of Mayday, the underground resistance. Soon after the Particution, Ofglen hangs herself before the **Eyes of God** can arrest her.

Song of Roland
Unknown

Oger

One of **Charlemagne**'s fiercest and most reliable vassals. Danish.

His Dark Materials
Robert Pullman

King Ogunwe

An African king from **Lyra Belacqua**'s world who is working with **Lord Asriel** to overthrow "the Authority," or God.

The Big Sleep
Raymond Chandler

Bernie Ohls

The D.A.'s chief investigator. Ohls is a friend of **Marlowe**'s and tells the detective about the Sternwood job.

Murder on the Orient Express
Agatha Christie

Greta Ohlsson

Daisy Armstrong's Swedish nurse. She is delicate, and after the murder, she spends most of the novel weeping.

Kidnapped
Robert Louis Stevenson

Robin Oig

A son of the famous Scottish nationalist Rob Roy Macgregor. Robin Oig is also a foe of **Alan Breck Stewart**, since Rob Roy was a Campbell like **Colin Roy Campbell of Glenure**, whom Alan and **David Balfour** are accused of having murdered. When Robin encounters Alan, the two men prepare to duel, but the owner of the house intervenes and suggests that they duel by playing the bagpipes. When Robin plays an air from Alan's country, Alan softens. They exchange airs the rest of the night, and become friends.

The Hobbit
J. R. R. Tolkien

Oin

One of the dwarf companions on the **Bilbo Baggins**' quest.

Things Fall Apart
Chinua Achebe

Ojiugo

Okonkwo's third and youngest wife, and the mother of **Nkechi**. Okonkwo beats Ojiugo during the Week of Peace.

No Longer At Ease
Chinua Achebe

Clara Okeke

Obi's fiancée. Clara is a young Nigerian woman whom Obi met at a dance in London and later on the boat ride back to Nigeria. She is strong-minded and has also studied abroad to become a nurse. Clara is an osu, an outcast whose marriage to Obi is socially forbidden. Her social standing therefore causes a huge struggle between Clara and Obi regarding their relationship and marriage.

Joseph Okeke

No Longer At Ease
Chinua Achebe

A friend of **Obi**'s and a clerk in the Survey Department. Though he gives Obi a place to stay, he also tells the Umuofia Progressive Union that Obi's fiancee **Clara** is an osu, or outcast.

Sam Okoli

No Longer At Ease
Chinua Achebe

The Minister of State. Sam Okoli is a good-looking and popular politician. He becomes friends with **Clara**, and through Clara he also befriends **Obi**. When Clara needs an abortion, Obi borrows the money from Sam.

Okonkwo

Things Fall Apart
Chinua Achebe

An influential clan leader in Umuofia. Okonkwo has been embarrassed since childhood of his lazy and effeminate father, **Unoka**, which gives him a strong drive for success. Okonkwo's hard work and prowess in war have earned him a position of high status in his clan, and he attains wealth sufficient to support three wives and their children. His tragic flaw is that he is terrified of appearing weak like his father. As a result, he behaves rashly, bringing a great deal of trouble and sorrow upon himself and his family.

Hannah Okonkwo

No Longer At Ease
Chinua Achebe

Obi's mother. Hannah is a strong-willed woman with whom Obi has a special relationship. Obi's mother refuses to allow her son to marry **Clara** and threatens to kill herself. However, Obi loves Hannah for the folk stories she shared with him, and he goes on to share her stories with his schoolmates.

Isaac Okonkwo

No Longer At Ease
Chinua Achebe

Obi's father, a devout Christian. He left home at an early age, against the will of his father, because he wanted to join the other Christians. Isaac's Christianity is the most important aspect of his life, and it colors most everything he does and says.

Obi Okonkwo

No Longer At Ease
Chinua Achebe

The novel's protagonist. A young man who has returned to Nigeria after having studied in England. Obi's background puts him in an awkward position, torn between his mother country and the colonizing English. The novel follows his idealistic beginnings to his unfortunate end, in which he is put on trial for taking a bribe.

O-lan

The Good Earth
Pearl S. Buck

Wang Lung's first wife. Sold to **Old Master Hwang** as a slave at the age of ten and then bought by **Wang Lung**, O-lan achieves respectability as the mother of three sons. Strong and hardworking, O-lan is a resourceful woman and a devoted wife. Nonetheless, Wang Lung eventually grows tired of her and takes on the beautiful yet petulant **Lotus** as his concubine.

Old Major

Animal Farm
George Orwell

Prize-winning boar whose vision of a socialist utopia serves as the inspiration for the animals' rebellion. Three days after proclaiming that "All men are enemies. All animals are comrades," Major dies, leaving **Snowball** and **Napoleon** to struggle for control of his legacy. Orwell based Major on both the German political economist Karl Marx and the Russian revolutionary leader Vladimir Ilych Lenin.

Old Man

Electra
Sophocles

The faithful servant to whom **Electra** entrusted **Orestes** as a young boy. The Old Man smuggled Orestes to Phocia, where he served as the boy's tutor and guardian. A voice of wisdom and practicality, he advises Orestes on exacting revenge for **Agamemnon**'s death, paying strict attention to detail, focus, and timing.

Old Man

The Canterbury Tales
Geoffrey Chaucer

A figure from **the Pardoner**'s Tale. When **the three Rioters** encounter him, his body is completely covered except for his face. Before the old man tells the Rioters where they can find "Death," one of the Rioters rashly demands why the old man is still alive. The old man answers that he is doomed to walk the earth for eternity.

Old Man

Doctor Faustus
Christopher Marlowe

An enigmatic figure who in the final scene urges **Faustus** to repent and to ask God for mercy.

Old Man

Miss Lonelyhearts
Nathanael West

An old man whom **Miss Lonelyhearts** and his friend **Ned Gates** find in a toilet in the park one night. His real name is George B. Simpson, and he is interrogated mercilessly and mockingly by the two men.

Old Man

The Chairs
Eugène Ionesco

The protagonist of the play. The Old Man has been married to the **Old Woman** for seventy-five years, and he entertains her nightly with the same story. He spends his time with a few hobbies, but mostly devotes himself to his "message," with which he will save humanity. The Old Man and Old Woman are waiting for the arrival of the **Orator**, who will deliver the Old Man's message.

Old Man

Fool for Love
Sam Shepard

Eddie's and **May**'s father. The Old Man appears only in the minds of May and Eddie—the spectre of a man who had little contact with his children, and whose selfish decisions and history still have a role in their lives. **Martin** does not hear or see him.

Old man at gas station

I Am the Cheese
Robert Cormier

A man who gives **Adam Farmer** a map at the outset of his journey. He is paranoid about identity crimes and lack of privacy. Like all of Adam's encounters on his bike journey, it turns out that the old man is just another person on the institution grounds.

Old Woman

The Canterbury Tales
Geoffrey Chaucer

In **the Wife of Bath's** Tale, the ugly old woman helps **Arthur's knight** in a quest, in exchange for his promise to do whatever she wants. She tells him he must marry her, and he begrudgingly agrees. She then asks him to choose whether he would like her to be beautiful and unfaithful or ugly and faithful, and when Arthur's knight relinquishes the choice to his wife, she rewards him by becoming both beautiful and faithful.

Old Woman

Candide
Voltaire

A daughter of a pope and **Cunégonde**'s servant. The old woman's misfortunes have made her cynical about human nature, but she does not pity herself. She is wise, practical, and loyal to her mistress.

Old Woman

The Chairs
Eugène Ionesco

Married to the **Old Man** for seventy-five years. On the island, her only entertainment is listening to her husband's stories and imitations, which she keeps fresh by erasing her memory nightly. As many invisible guests arrive to hear the **Orator** speak, the Old Woman places chairs for them and also ends up echoing many of the Old Man's statements.

Countess Ellen Olenska

The Age of Innocence
Edith Wharton

May's cousin and **Mrs. Manson Mingott**'s granddaughter. Ellen was educated and raised in Europe. There, she married a Polish count, who cheated on her and prompted her to leave him. Upon her return to her New York family, she hopes to be reintegrated to American life, but finds only judgment and stifling mores. Her behavior is deemed too unorthodox for Old New York. To **Archer**, however, she is free and truly alive.

Father Olguin

House Made of Dawn
N. Scott Momaday

The priest at the mission in Walatowa. He serves as a role model for **Abel**, and introduces Abel to **Angela St. John**. Father Olguin, who is from Mexico, is small, swarthy, has graying hair, and is missing one eye.

Olin

Black Boy
Richard Wright

A white southerner who works with **Richard Wright** at the optical shop in Memphis, Tennessee. Racist and destructive, Olin pretends to be Richard's friend but secretly tries to get him and **Harrison** to kill each other.

Olive

Seize the Day
Saul Bellow

The woman with whom **Tommy Wilhelm** is in love. We never meet Olive. She is a Christian but is willing to marry Tommy outside the church after he divorces his wife. **Margaret**, however, will not grant him a divorce.

Oliver

As You Like It
William Shakespeare

The oldest son of **Sir Rowland de Bois** and sole inheritor of the de Bois estate. Oliver is a loveless young man who begrudges his brother, **Orlando**, a gentleman's education. He admits to hating Orlando without cause or reason and goes to great lengths to ensure his downfall. When **Duke Frederick** employs Oliver to find his missing brother, Oliver finds himself living in despair in the Forest of Arden, where Orlando saves his life. This display of undeserved generosity prompts Oliver to change into a better, more loving person. His transformation is evidenced by his love for the disguised **Celia**, whom he takes to be a simple—and therefore classless and poor—shepherdess.

Bill Oliver

Death of a Salesman
Arthur Miller

An old employer of **Biff Loman**. Biff plans to ask Oliver for a loan to buy a ranch, but when he meets with Oliver, he does not even remember him.

Rosamond Oliver

Jane Eyre
Charlotte Brontë

The beautiful daughter of **Mr. Oliver**, Morton's wealthiest inhabitant. Rosamond gives money to the school in Morton where **Jane Eyre** works. Although she is in love with **St. John Rivers**, she becomes engaged to the wealthy **Mr. Granby**.

Olivia

Twelfth Night
William Shakespeare

A wealthy, beautiful, and noble Illyrian lady, niece to **Sir Toby Belch**. Olivia is courted by **Orsino** and **Sir Andrew Aguecheek**, but to each of them she insists that she is in mourning for her brother, who has recently died, and will not marry for seven years. **Viola**'s arrival in the masculine guise of Cesario enables Olivia to break free of her self-indulgent melancholy.

Olivia

The Autobiography of Miss Jane Pittman
Ernest J. Gaines

An older black woman on the Samson plantation. She offers to drive the other protesters in her car.

Olivia

The Color Purple
Alice Walker

Celie and **Alphonso**'s biological daughter, who is adopted by **Samuel** and **Corrine**. Olivia develops a close sisterly relationship with **Tashi**, an Olinka village girl. Eventually, Olivia has a joyful reunion with Celie.

Olivier

Song of Roland
Unknown

A gallant warrior, one of the twelve peers of France, and **Roland**'s best friend. At Roncesvals, Olivier sees how the Franks will be overwhelmed by the sheer numbers of the Saracens and urges Roland to blow his oliphant and call back to **Charlemagne** for aid. Roland is too proud to do so, angering Olivier, but the two end their quarrel before dying, remaining the greatest of companions.

Hans Olsa

Giants in the Earth
O. E. Rölvaag

Per Hansa's best friend and **Beret Hansa**'s childhood friend. Hans was a fisherman in Norway along with Per until Per persuaded him to move to America. The two friends become neighbors in the Dakota Territory. Hans is naturally good-natured, physically strong, and mentally slow. He prospers along with Per, but they both die from the fierce winter.

Sofie Olsa

Giants in the Earth
O. E. Rölvaag

Hans Olsa and **Sorine Olsa**'s daughter.

Sorine Olsa

Giants in the Earth
O. E. Rölvaag

Hans Olsa's wife. Sorine is a kindhearted spirit who continually helps **Per Hansa** and **Beret Hansa** through their troubles. She becomes almost a second mother to Beret's youngest child, **Peder Victorious,** when Beret sinks into depression and insanity.

Mr. Omo

No Longer At Ease
Chinua Achebe

The administrative assistant at **Obi**'s office. Accustomed to the rule of the English, Mr. Omo is submissive to his boss **Mr. Green** and respectful of "old ways." He has worked for the Civil Service for thirty years and has a son studying law in England.

One Eye

White Fang
Jack London

White Fang's father. One Eye is full wolf and kills his rivals to mate with **Kiche** after the famine is over. One Eye is killed by a lynx while out hunting for food for White Fang, his brothers and sisters, and Kiche.

Operator

I Am the Cheese
Robert Cormier

A mysterious figure. Each time **Adam Farmer** tries to call **Amy Hertz**, he seems to connect through the same operator. It is the same operator, as Adam is actually riding around the grounds of an institution, believing in his mind that it is two years before the present date.

Ophelia

Hamlet
William Shakespeare

Polonius's daughter, **Laertes**'s sister, and **Hamlet**'s sometime love. A sweet and innocent young girl, Ophelia obeys both Polonius and Laertes. Ophelia is smart and loving, but madness overtakes her when Hamlet spurns her. In her madness, she commits suicide by drowning.

Miss Ophelia

Uncle Tom's Cabin
Harriet Beecher Stowe

Augustine St. Clare's cousin from the North who comes to help him manage the household. Ophelia opposes slavery but she finds actual slaves somewhat distasteful and harbors considerable prejudice against them. Through her relationship with **Topsy**, an unruly slave child whom she tries to educate, Ophelia realizes her prejudices and learns to see slaves as human beings. The change in Ophelia is brought about partly by **Evangeline St. Clare**'s support with Topsy's lessons.

Orator

The Chairs
Eugène Ionesco

A man who looks like a pompous nineteenth-century artist who is scheduled to deliver the **Old Man**'s message. He has an actor's regal bearing and hands out autographs. However, just after the Old Man and **Old Woman** commit suicide, the Orator reveals himself to be a mute.

Orcs

The Fellowship of the Ring and *The Two Towers*
J. R. R. Tolkien

Servants of **Sauron**. Hordes of Orcs, which are unable to withstand daylight and therefore emerge almost exclusively at night, pursue the Fellowship of the Ring through the Mines of Moria and beyond. In *The Fel-*

lowship of the Ring, **Saruman** creates a special race of Orcs, **the Uruk-hai**, who can withstand daylight, and who kidnap **Meriadoc Brandybuck** and **Peregrin Took**. In *The Two Towers*, a huge number of Orcs come to defend Saruman's tower of Orthanc and the gates of Mordor.

Orestes

The Libation Bearers
Aeschylus

Clytemnestra and **Agamemnon**'s son and **Iphigenia** and **Electra**'s brother. Orestes is sent away as an infant while Clytemnestra and her lover, **Aegisthus**, plot to kill Agamemnon to avenge the sacrifice of Iphigenia. He is compelled by the god **Apollo** to preserve the social order by punishing Clytemnestra and Aegisthus for Agamemnon's brutal murder. After he carries out this matricide, Orestes is pursued by **the Furies** until he atones for his crime. This act brings the suffering of the House of **Atreus** to an end. Orestes is also a figure in Greek mythology.

Orestes

Electra
Sophocles

See above.

Orestes

The Flies
Jean-Paul Sartre

The protagonist of the play. Orestes wants to belong to Argos, his birthplace, having been raised in Athens and taught by **Tutor** never to commit himself to anything. Yet when he sees the servile life **the Argives** live and that his sister **Electra** has been made into a slave, Orestes decides to disobey both the Tutor's advice and the laws of the gods. He murders both the new king **Aegistheus** and his mother **Clytemnestra**, freeing the city from their corrupt reign. Orestes does not feel remorse for the murders he commits. He threatens the order of the gods because **Jupiter** has no power over humans who know that they are free.

Ori

The Hobbit
J. R. R. Tolkien

One of the dwarf companions on **Bilbo Baggins**'s quest.

Ork

Grendel
John Gardner

An old, blind, Scylding priest. Ork is a theologian who studies the theories behind religion. Mistaking **Grendel** for the Destroyer, the supreme Scylding deity, Ork describes ultimate wisdom as a vision of a universe in which nothing is lost or wasted. Ork is one of only a few priests in the novel for whom religion is more than an empty show.

Orlando

As You Like It
William Shakespeare

The youngest son of **Sir Rowland de Bois** and younger brother of **Oliver** and **Jaques de Bois**. When the aging **Adam** tells him of his brother's plot to destroy him, Orlando and his new servant escape to the Forest of Arden. Orlando proves himself a proper gentleman first by taking care of Adam, who is close to starvation, and later by risking his life to save the treacherous Oliver from a hungry lioness. He falls in love with **Rosalind**, but his simplicity in the matters of love forces him to rely on romantic clichés as he litters the forest with his attempts at poetry.

Orlando

Orlando
Virginia Woolf

The protagonist, a wealthy nobleman who is adventurous and artistic. Based on Woolf's real-life love interest Vita Sackville-West, Orlando also has values deeply rooted in his home and in his long and noble ancestry. By changing sexes halfway through the novel (from male to female) Orlando is able to reflect upon the differing positions and experiences of each and realizes herself to be composed of not one, but many selves.

Bastard of Orléans

Henry VI, Part I
William Shakespeare

A French commander who introduces **Charles, Dauphin of France** to **Joan of Arc**. He delivers the first wound to **John Talbot** in the battle before Bordeaux.

Duke of Orléans

Henry V
William Shakespeare

A French nobleman and military leader. Like the **Dauphin** and the other French nobles, Orléans does not take the English seriously, and instead of preparing for battle, mocks the English. Orléans is taken prisoner following the Battle of Agincourt.

Dolge Orlick

Great Expectations
Charles Dickens

The day laborer in **Joe Gargery**'s forge. He attacks **Mrs. Joe** and almost murders **Pip**.

Captain Orlov

Island of the Blue Dolphins
Scott O'Dell

The Russian leader of **the Aleut** expedition to Ghalas-at. Orlov is snide and deceptive.

Oronte

The Misanthrope
Molière

Courts **Célimène**, the same woman **Alceste** courts. He wants to make friends with Alceste, and recites a poem to him that Alceste insults bluntly. Though he appears confident, he reveals his insecurities when criticized. His love for Célimène is not stronger than his pride, and he abandons her after she insults him.

Orpheus

Greek Mythology
Unknown

A Muse's son and the greatest mortal musician of all time. Orpheus is famous for his journey to **Hades** to retrieve his dead wife, **Eurydice**. He loses her forever by ignoring Hades's orders not to turn around to ensure that she is behind him. Orpheus also travels on the Argo and protects **Jason** from the Sirens. He is killed by a pack of roving Maenads, and his head floats to Lesbos, where it becomes a magical icon.

Catch-22
Joseph Heller

Orr

John Yossarian's maddening tent-mate. A handyman, Orr continually makes little improvements to their tent. His plane often crashes, but he always manages to survive.

Twelfth Night
William Shakespeare

Orsino

A powerful nobleman in the country of Illyria. Duke Orsino is lovesick for the beautiful Lady **Olivia**, but becomes more and more fond of his handsome new page boy, Cesario, who is actually a woman—**Viola**.

Evelina
Fanny Burney

Lord Orville

A handsome young man who wins **Evelina Anville**'s heart. He is courteous, delicate, and unwaveringly polite, the embodiment of everything that Evelina strives for in herself. Lord Orville is introduced into Evelina's life shortly after her encounter with the ugly **Mr. Lovel**.

Evelina
Fanny Burney

Lady Louisa Orville

Lord Orville's sister and **Lord Merton**'s fiancée. Lady Louisa is an indolent woman whose delicacy manifests itself as physical and constitutional weakness. Unlike her brother, Lady Louisa is snobbish and impolite.

On the Beach
Nevil Shute

John Osborne

A scientist with CSIRO, the Commonwealth Scientific and Industrial Research Organization. He joins the crew of the *Scorpion* and befriends **Dwight Towers** and **Peter Holmes**. More than any other character, John faces the reality of his impending death and uses his last few months to fulfill his dreams. Traveling on the submarine and racing his Ferrari give him the chance to break from his mundane lifestyle. Attracted to wealth and exclusivity, Osborne joins the fancy and formal Pastoral Club.

The Portrait of a Lady
Henry James

Gilbert Osmond

A gentleman who seduces **Isabel Archer** and marries her for her money. An art collector, Osmond poses as a disinterested aesthete, but in reality he is desperate for the recognition and admiration of those around him. He treats everyone who loves him as simply an object to be used to fulfill his desires; he teaches his daughter **Pansy Osmond** to be unswervingly subservient to him, and treats his longtime lover **Madame Merle** as a mere tool.

Pansy Osmond

The Portrait of a Lady
Henry James

Gilbert Osmond's placid, submissive daughter, raised in a convent. Pansy believes that her mother died in childbirth; in reality, her mother is Osmond's longtime lover, **Madame Merle**. When **Isabel Archer** becomes Pansy's stepmother, she learns to love the girl.

Osric

Hamlet
William Shakespeare

The foolish courtier who summons **Hamlet** to his duel with **Laertes**.

Ostrinski

The Jungle
Upton Sinclair

A Polish immigrant. He inspires **Jurgis Rudkus** with a rousing speech at a socialist political meeting and later teaches Jurgis about socialism.

Oswald

King Lear
William Shakespeare

The steward, or chief servant, in **Goneril**'s house. Oswald obeys his mistress's commands and helps enact her conspiracies.

Oswald

Ivanhoe
Sir Walter Scott

Cedric the Saxon's porter.

Othello

Othello
William Shakespeare

The play's protagonist and hero. A Christian Moor and general of the armies of Venice, Othello is an eloquent and physically powerful figure, respected by all those around him. In spite of his elevated status, he is nevertheless easy prey to insecurities because of his age, his life as a soldier, and his race. He possesses a "free and open nature," which his ensign **Iago** uses to twist his love for his wife **Desdemona** into a powerful and destructive jealousy. As a result of Iago's manipulations, Othello murders Desdemona in a jealous rage.

Jacques Othon

The Plague
Albert Camus

Othon's small son. The first recipient of **Castel**'s plague serum, though he dies of the plague anyway. His death prompts a religious crisis for **Paneloux**.

M. Othon

The Plague
Albert Camus

A conservative magistrate whom **Tarrou** considers "public enemy number one" for being so inflexible. His son **Jacques Othon** dies of the plague, prompting him to help plague victims in the quarantine until he too contracts the plague and dies.

James Otis

Johnny Tremain
Esther Forbes

The founder of the Boston Observers, a secret rebel organization that meets in **Mr. Lorne**'s print shop. James Otis's fellow club members acknowledge his intellectual brilliance, but his mental instability frightens and endangers them.

Otto

How the Garcia Girls Lost Their Accents
Julia Alvarez

A man **Sofia** met while traveling in Colombia. They fell in love, he wrote her love letters, and she ran away from home to be with him in Germany.

Sir Harry Otway

A Room with a View
E. M. Forster

A local in **Lucy Honeychurch**'s town. He buys the two villas, Cissie and Albert, and lets one of them out to the Emersons.

Ourang-Outang

"The Murders in the Rue Morgue"
Edgar Allan Poe

The orangutan responsible for the grisly murders, which he commits after escaping his sailor owner. It is **C. Auguste Dupin** who uncovers Ourang-Outang's crime by a process of deduction.

Ouranos

Greek Mythology
Unknown

God of the sky and heavens. Born out of **Gaea**, Ouranos becomes Gaea's husband and proceeds to father all the original creatures of the earth, including the **Titans**, the **Cyclopes**, and the **Furies**.

Ed Overbrook

Babbitt
Sinclair Lewis

One of **Babbitt**'s college classmates. Ed and his wife want to become friends with the Babbitts in order to climb the social ladder. The Babbitts, however, treat the Overbrooks with the same snobbery and disdain that they themselves receive from the more successful **McKelveys**.

Mistress Overdone

Measure for Measure
William Shakespeare

The madam of a Vienna brothel.

The Overlords

Childhood's End
Arthur C. Clarke

An alien race that comes to Earth in the late twentieth century and takes control of the planet. They eliminate disease, war and hatred, and create a world government that broadens into a utopia. This peaceful mission is overseen by **Karellen**. Physically, the average Overlord is much taller and broader than a human, with large wings, horns on its head, and a barbed tail.

The Overmind

Childhood's End
Arthur C. Clarke

The alien being that the Overlords serve. The Overmind is not a creature of matter. It is a collective consciousness, a massive entity of thought and energy that crosses the galaxy trying to "increase its awareness of the universe." It incorporates entire races into itself, eliminating their individuality while greatly enhancing their power.

Evelyn Owen

The Member of the Wedding
Carson McCullers

Frankie Addams's only friend. She moves away to Florida, leaving Frankie alone.

Wilfred Owen

Regeneration
Pat Barker

In real life, the most famous of the Great War poets. Owen died in 1918, just before the end of the war. In the novel, Owen is depicted as a young man still unsure of himself and his work, though his confidence is growing. A closeted homosexual, he seems to develop a crush on **Siegfried Sassoon**. Owen is deeply affected by the war, and he works to express it in his own words.

Owl Eyes

The Great Gatsby
F. Scott Fitzgerald

An eccentric, bespectacled drunk whom **Nick Carraway** meets at one of **Gatsby**'s parties.

Madame Oxentiel

His Dark Materials
Robert Pullman

The Gallivespian who becomes the leader of the Gallivespian spies after **Lord Roke** is killed.

Earl of Oxford

An ally and supporter of **King Henry VI** and **Queen Margaret**. In France, Oxford argues with the **Earl of Warwick** over the rightful claim to the throne. After Warwick joins the Lancaster side, Oxford and Warwick lead the return attack in England against **King Edward IV**. Oxford and **Somerset** help protect **Henry Tudor, Earl of Richmond** by sending him to Brittany to escape the war. When he is captured by the Yorkists after the final battle, Oxford is sent away to Hames Castle as a prisoner.

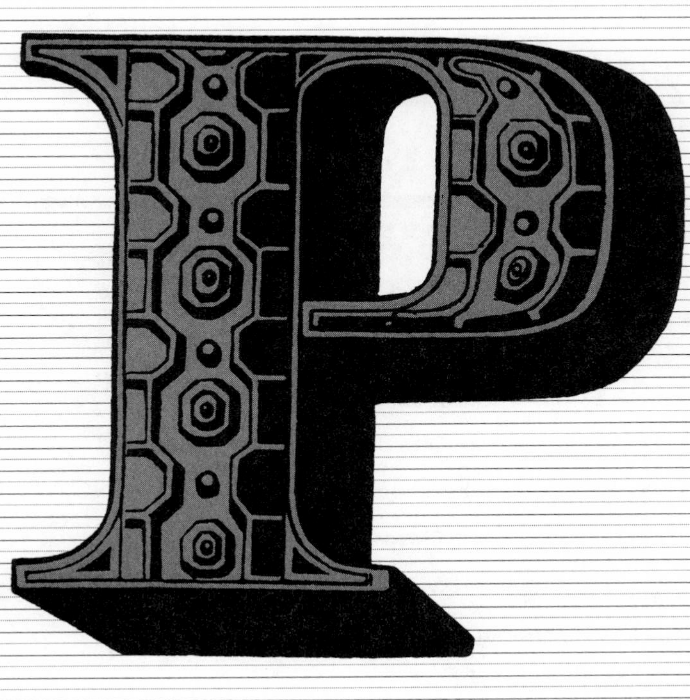

18

CERTIFIABLE CRAZIES

NUTS AND FRUITS AND FLAKES, EVERY LAST ONE OF THEM.

Ahab	1	*Moby-Dick*
Cathy Ames	2	*East of Eden*
Don Quixote	3	*Don Quixote*
Blanche DuBois	4	*A Streetcar Named Desire*
Harper	5	*Angels in America*
Miss Havisham	6	*Great Expectations*
Humbert Humbert	7	*Lolita*
Hungry Joe	8	*Catch-22*
King Lear	9	*King Lear*
Kurtz	10	*Heart of Darkness*
Lady Macbeth	11	*Macbeth*
Bertha Mason	12	*Jane Eyre*
Mad Hatter	13	*Alice in Wonderland, Through the Looking Glass*
Ophelia	14	*Othello*
Queen of Hearts	15	*Alice in Wonderland, Through the Looking Glass*
Clare Quilty	16	*Lolita*
Roderick Usher	17	*"The Fall of the House of Usher"*
John Yossarian	18	*Catch-22*

Pablo

Steppenwolf
Hermann Hesse

A jazz saxophone player and bandleader. Popular among the denizens of the world of pleasure, he is introduced to **the Steppenwolf** by **Hermine**. Laconic and unabashedly modern, at first Pablo inspires the Steppenwolf only with disdain.

Pablo

Tortilla Flat
John Steinbeck

One of **Danny**'s *paisanos* and the first person to join the group after the original founders. Although Pablo is not a smart or righteous man, he demonstrates a keen insight for the messages that life tries to teach.

Pablo

For Whom the Bell Tolls
Ernest Hemingway

The leader of the guerrilla camp that **Robert Jordan** directs in the operation to blow up the Fascist-controlled bridge. Pablo is a rash, sometimes brutal man and feels responsible only to himself. Pablo used to be a great fighter and a great man but has now started drinking. He openly opposes the bridge-destruction mission and throws Robert Jordan's explosives into a river the night before it is to take place. However, the deed makes Pablo feel lonely, so he returns to the camp to help the guerrillas complete the mission.

General Pace

Ender's Game
Orson Scott Card

The chief of the I.F. military police. Pace unsuccessfully pleads with **Colonel Graff** to intervene in **Bonzo Madrid**'s plot to kill **Ender Wiggin**. Bonzo goes through with the plot, and is killed by Ender as a result.

Madame Pace

Six Characters in Search of an Author
Luigi Pirandello

The Stepdaughter's exploitative Madame. Pace is a fat, older woman. Conjured out of nowhere in Act II, Pace is an apparition, her birth is an exercise in what **the Father** describes as the magic of the stage. Pace runs a bordello that the Father frequents, one day finding **the Mother** working there. Their reunion marks the beginning of the Characters' drama.

Ali Pacha

The Count of Monte Cristo
Alexandre Dumas

A Greek nationalist leader betrayed by **Fernand Mondego**. Ali Pacha is killed by the Turks, and his wife and daughter, **Haydée**, are sold into slavery.

Paddy

The Hairy Ape
Eugene O'Neill

An old and wise Irishman who works with **Yank** as a fireman aboard the Ocean Liner. Paddy, known for drunkenness, thinks the firemen are forced to do slave labor.

Padfoot

The Harry Potter Series: Books 3 and *4*
J. K. Rowling

Sirius Black's animagus name when he transforms into a large black dog.

Johannes Pafuri

Cry, the Beloved Country
Alan Paton

One of three young men present at the attempted robbery of **Arthur Jarvis**'s house. According to **Absalom Kumalo**'s testimony, Pafuri is the ringleader of the group, deciding the time of the robbery and having his weapon blessed to give them good luck.

Page

The Spanish Tragedy
Thomas Kyd

A messenger boy who brings **Lorenzo**'s empty box to the execution, which is believed to hold a pardon for **Pedringano**. After the page looks inside, he does not tell anyone that it is empty out of fear for his own life. Pedringano's belief that he will be pardoned stops him from exposing Lorenzo as one of **Horatio**'s murderers before it is too late.

Page

Salomé
Oscar Wilde

A friend of the **Young Syrian**'s who senses his impending death.

Page

Antigone 1946
Jean Anouilh

Creon's attendant. He sees all, understands nothing, and is no help to anyone.

Anne Page

The Merry Wives of Windsor
William Shakespeare

The daughter of **Master George Page** and **Mistress Margaret Page**. Doggedly pursued in marriage by **Doctor Caius** and **Abraham Slender**, Anne manages to trick her parents and elope with **Fenton**, the man of her choosing. Though Fenton admits he first wooed her for the money, his newfound love for her wins Anne's heart.

Clara Page

This Side of Paradise
F. Scott Fitzgerald

Monsignor Darcy's widowed third cousin, whom **Amory Blaine** visits often in Philadelphia. Although Amory loves her, **Clara** claims that she has never been in love and has no intention of remarrying.

Master George Page

The Merry Wives of Windsor
William Shakespeare

Mistress Alice Page's husband and **Anne Page**'s father. Unlike his friend **Master Frank Ford**, Page is not jealous of his wife, so **Sir John Falstaff**'s plan to seduce their wives does not threaten him. He refuses to allow **Fenton**, the suitor of his daughter's choosing, marry Anne. Without consulting his daughter or his wife, he endorses **Abraham Slender** for his daugher's hand. After Ford learns to trust his wife, Page learns his own lesson at the end of the play when Fenton and Anne come in married.

Mistress Margaret Page

The Merry Wives of Windsor
William Shakespeare

Master George Page's wife, **Anne Page**'s mother, and **Mistress Margaret Ford**'s friend. The central plot of the play begins when Mistress Ford and Mistress Page receive wooing letters from **Sir John Falstaff,** who secretly hopes to bed them and then gain financial rewards. The two ladies quickly discover the trickery, and plot to humiliate the fat knight.

Stamp Paid

Beloved
Toni Morrison

Considered by the community to be a figure of salvation, like **Baby Suggs**. Stamp Paid is welcomed at every door in town. An agent of the Underground Railroad, he helps **Sethe** to freedom and later saves **Denver**'s life as Sethe is about to kill her. While a slave, Stamp was forced to give his wife to his master's son to sleep with, and he concluded that this was a gift so terrible that it freed him forever of all emotional and moral obligation. By the end of the book he realizes that he may still owe protection and care to the residents of 124 Bluestone Road. Angered by the community's neglect of Sethe, Denver, and **Paul D**, Stamp begins to question the nature of a community's obligations to its members.

Painter

Timon of Athens
William Shakespeare

One of **Timon**'s hangers-on who receives money from Timon for his art. The painter seeks out Timon after his fall, hearing that Timon has found gold in the wilderness.

Patty Paiwonski

Stranger in a Strange Land
Robert A. Heinlein

A devout Fosterite. Patty works in a traveling carnival displaying the head-to-toe tattoos applied by her late husband. She longs to share the joy she has learned from **the Reverend Foster** and, later, **Valentine Michael Smith**.

Palamon

The Canterbury Tales
Geoffrey Chaucer

One of two imprisoned Theban soldiers in **the Knight**'s Tale. Brave, strong, and sworn to everlasting friendship with his cousin **Arcite**, Palamon and Arcite both fall in love with the fair maiden **Emelye**. Arcite and Palamon agree to compete in a tournament for Emelye's hand. While Palamon prays to the gods for love, Arcite prays for victory. Arcite wins the tournament but is killed by the gods shortly thereafter, leaving Palamon free to marry Emelye.

Palamon

The Two Noble Kinsmen
William Shakespeare

Arcite's cousin and **Creon**'s nephew. Sullen and proud, Palamon is a formidable warrior. Governed by a strong sense of honor, he fights with Creon against **Theseus** even though he hates Creon. Palamon quickly becomes enraged with Arcite when Arcite declares his love for **Emilia**.

Dominic Palazzolo

The Virgin Suicides
Jeffrey Eugenides

An overly suave Italian boy of romantic temperament, who lives with his relatives in the neighborhood. Dominic speaks little English but is desperately in love with local rich girl **Diana Porter**. To prove his love, he jumps from the roof of his relatives' house, emerging unharmed and satisfi ed.

Finito de Palencia

For Whom the Bell Tolls
Ernest Hemingway

Pilar's former lover, a bullfighter who died from complications from wounds received in a bullfight.

Pallas

The Aeneid
Virgil

Evander's son, who is entrusted to **Aeneas**'s care. **Turnus** eventually slays Pallas in battle, an event that causes Aeneas and Evander great grief. Aeneas kills Turnus to avenge Pallas's death.

The Palmer

Ivanhoe
Sir Walter Scott

A religious pilgrim who wears a palm emblem to indicate that he has made a pilgrimage to the Holy Land. In reality, the Palmer is **Ivanhoe** in his first disguise.

Pancha

The House of the Spirits
Isabel Allende

A peasant girl at Tres Marias. She is raped by **Esteban Trueba**, taken into his house as a housekeeper, and thrown out when she becomes pregnant with his illegitimate son. That son then has a son called **Esteban Garcia**, who despises his grandfather and later becomes a fascist military dictator.

Pandarus

The Iliad
Homer

A Trojan archer whose shot at **Menelaus** breaks the temporary truce between the Trojans and the Greeks.

Pandarus

Troilus and Cressida
William Shakespeare

Cressida's uncle. He serves as a go-between for **Troilus** and Cressida, acting as a cheerful, bawdy pimp for his niece.

Pander

Pericles
William Shakespeare

A pimp. Pander buys **Marina** from the pirates for his brothel.

Pandora

Greek Mythology
Unknown

Woman of Greek myth. Married to **Epimetheus**, **Prometheus**'s simple-minded brother, Pandora has been entrusted with a box that the gods have told her never to open. When she peeks inside the box, she unleashes evil into the world but also frees Hope.

Cardinal Pandulph

King John
William Shakespeare

The Pope's emissary. Pandulph excommunicates **King John** when John refuses to bow to Church authority, and he pressures **King Philip** and **Lewis** to wage war on the English. He cites the imminent murder of **Arthur** and the robbing of the monasteries as reasons for civil unrest against John. Pandulph agrees to call off the French offensive after John pledges allegiance to the Pope, but is unable to quench the war he started. He eventually succeeds in negotiating peace between the French and the English after part of **Lewis**'s navy is sunk.

Father Paneloux

The Plague
Albert Camus

A Jesuit priest who gives two public sermons during the novel. Paneloux initially argues that the plague is God's punishment for the people's sins, but then suggests that it is the supreme test of faith in God. His conviction in a just God is rocked when **Jacques Othon**, an innocent boy, dies of the plague.

Pangle

Cold Mountain
Charles Frazier

A fellow outlier and friend of **Stobrod Thewes**'s.

Pangloss

Candide
Voltaire

A philosopher and **Candide**'s tutor. An exaggerated parody of overly optimistic Enlightenment philosophers, his belief that this world is "the best of all possible worlds" is the primary target of the novel's satire. While Pangloss's own experiences contradict this belief, he remains faithful to it nonetheless.

Pantalaimon

His Dark Materials
Robert Pullman

Lyra Belacqua's daemon. Pantalaimon usually can only speak to Lyra. In the beginning, he takes thousands of different shapes, as all daemons do before their humans become adults. When Lyra's character is fully formed, Pantalaimon takes the fixed shape of a pine marten.

Panthino

The Two Gentlemen of Verona
William Shakespeare

Antonio's servant. Like **Lucetta**, Panthino advises his master on familial matters, resulting in Antonio's sending **Proteus** to Milan. Panthino also tells **Launce** to follow Proteus.

Sancho Panza

Don Quixote
Miguel de Cervantes

The peasant laborer who joins **Don Quixote** on his adventures as his squire. Greedy but generous, cowardly but loyal, Sancho is a common man of "old Christian" values and a simple foil to Don Quixote's intellectual and strict agenda. Sancho dispenses wisdom in loopy proverbs.

Teresa Panza

Don Quixote
Miguel de Cervantes

Sancho's good-hearted wife. Teresa speaks in wise proverbs and endures Sancho's exploits.

Paolo da Rimini

Inferno
Dante Alighieri

A lover condemned to the Second Circle of Hell, with the Lustful, for an adulterous affair that began when Paolo and **Francesca** began reading about **Lancelot** and **Guinevere** (Canto V). Paolo is Francesca's husband's brother.

Pap

The Adventures of Huckleberry Finn
Mark Twain

Huckleberry Finn's father, the town drunk and ne'er-do-well in St. Petersburg, Missouri. The illiterate Pap disapproves of Huck's education and beats him frequently. Pap kidnaps Huck from the **Widow Douglas** and tries unsuccessfully to extort the money Huck won from **Injun Joe**. As a result of a court ruling, Huck ends up in Pap's custody. Huck escapes from Pap after his father nearly murders him in a drunken rampage. Huck feigns his own murder and escapes down the river with **Jim**. At the end of *The Adventures of Huckleberry Finn*, Jim tells Huck that Pap was found dead in a flood. Pap represents both the general debasement of white society and the failure of family structures in the novel.

Papa

Where the Red Fern Grows
Wilson Rawls

Billy Colman's papa. He is poor, but is working hard so his family can move to the city. Once Billy buys **Old Dan** and **Little Ann**, he starts to treat Billy like a man. Billy's father is able to move the family to the city because Billy makes so much money with his coon-hunting.

Papa

Roll of Thunder, Hear My Cry
Mildred D. Taylor

Father of **Cassie Logan**, **Stacey Logan**, **Little Man Logan**, and **Christopher-John Logan**, and husband of **Mama (Mary Logan)**. He values his independence highly, leaving to work on the railroad in order not to lose ownership of Logan land. His leg is crushed by a wheel in an ambush by members of **the Wallace Family (Kaleb, Dewberry, etc.)**. Papa successfully averts a lynch mob's attack on the Logan family farm and house by setting part of their cotton field ablaze.

Papillon

Rhinoceros
Eugène Ionesco

Papillon is the head of **Berenger**'s office. Work at the office is temporarily suspended when **Boeuf** as a rhinoceros breaks the office staircase, but is suspended indefinitely when Papillon also turns into a rhinoceros.

Paquette

Candide
Voltaire

A chambermaid and later a prostitute. **Candide** is moved by Paquette's misery and gives her a large sum of money, which she quickly squanders.

Joe Paradise

Babbitt
Sinclair Lewis

A guide at a wilderness resort in Maine where the Babbitts vacation every year. **Babbitt** idealizes Paradise until he learns that Paradise is just as materialistic and ignorant as any Zenith businessman.

Sal Paradise

On the Road
Jack Kerouac

The narrator, a young, penniless New York writer. Sal sets out to travel across America and experience life in order to become a better writer.

Doctor Parcival

Winesburg, Ohio
Sherwood Anderson

A doctor who enjoys chatting with **George Willard** and hinting about a criminal past. He suffers from paranoia, believing that the secret of life is "that everyone in the world is Christ."

The Pardoner

The Canterbury Tales
Geoffrey Chaucer

One of the pilgrims travelling to Canterbury. Pardoners granted papal indulgences—reprieves from penance in exchange for charitable donations to the Church. Many pardoners, including this one, collected profits for themselves. Chaucer's Pardoner excels in fraud, carrying a bag full of fake relics.

Paris

The Iliad, The Aeneid
Homer

A Trojan prince, the son of **Priam** and **Hecuba**, and the brother of **Hector**. The handsomest of men, he unwittingly starts the Trojan War by choosing **Aphrodite** over **Hera** and **Athena** as the fairest goddess. To reward him for the so-called "Judgment of Paris," which incurs Hera's eternal wrath, **Aphrodite** arranges for Paris to marry the beautiful **Helen**. Helen, however, is already married to the Greek king **Menelaus**, and so Paris kidnaps her, the event that sparks the conflict between the Greeks and Trojans. During the decade-long war, Paris is weak and unheroic, preferring to make love to Helen while others fight for him. Paris is also a figure in Greek mythology.

Paris

Troilus and Cressida
William Shakespeare

A Trojan prince who steals **Menelaus**'s wife **Helen**, precipitating the Trojan War.

Paris

Romeo and Juliet
William Shakespeare

A kinsman of **Prince Escalus**, and the suitor of **Juliet** most preferred by **Capulet**. When Capulet promises Paris that he can marry Juliet, Paris behaves presumptuously toward Juliet, acting as if they are already married.

Memo Paris

The Natural
Bernard Malamud

The spoiled niece of **Pop Fisher**. **Roy Hobbs** swiftly falls in love with her, though she continually rebuffs his advances. His infatuation with her and her constant rejections eventually lead to Roy's slump. Memo is an unhappy person, never able to get over the death of her boyfriend, **Bump Baily**.

Charles Parker

The Heart Is a Lonely Hunter
Carson McCullers

A fruit vendor who is the cousin and employer of **Spiros Antonapoulos**. At the beginning of the novel, Mr. Parker coldly sends Antonapoulos away to the insane asylum without consulting **John Singer** about the decision.

Sam Parkhill

The Martian Chronicles
Ray Bradbury

A member of the fourth expedition, and **Jeff Spender**'s antagonist. He is eager to conquer the Martian landscape. After settlement begins in earnest, he leaves the military and opens a hot-dog stand just in time for Mars to be evacuated. He is a violent, careless man.

Parolles

All's Well that Ends Well
William Shakespeare

Bertram's companion. He almost comes to blows with **Lafew**, and agrees that Bertram should go to war rather than stay in France with his new wife, **Helena**. Parolles is a coward, liar, braggart, and bad influence on Bertram. The **First Lord Dumaine** and the **Second Lord Dumaine** contrive a plot to reveal his character: thinking he's been captured and blindfolded by the enemy in war, Parolles tearfully denounces his friends, only to be released and discover those same friends playing a trick on him. He slinks back to France as a beggar, pleading with Lafew for shelter.

Betty Parris

The Crucible
Arthur Miller

Reverend Parris's daughter. Betty falls into a strange stupor after Parris catches her and the other girls dancing in the forest with **Tituba**. Her illness and that of **Ruth Putnam** fuel the first rumors of witchcraft. When Betty comes out of her stupor, she cries that **Abigail Williams** did not tell Parris about drinking blood as a charm to kill **Elizabeth Proctor**, **John Proctor**'s wife. Abigail strikes Betty across the face and warns the other girls to confess only that they danced and that Tituba conjured Ruth's dead sisters. Later, Betty is in a stupor again, and when the crowd around her recites a psalm, Betty goes into hysterics. When **Rebecca Nurse** comes to see Betty, Betty quiets in Rebecca's gentle presence.

Reverend Parris

The Crucible
Arthur Miller

The minister of Salem's church. Reverend Parris is a paranoid, power-hungry, yet self-pitying figure. Parris's daughter, **Betty Parris**, along with **Ruth Putnam**, fall into strange stupors, having been allegedly bewitched after they are discovered dancing with **Tituba** in the forest. His alliance with **Judge Hathorne** and **Deputy Governor Danforth** causes many innocent people in Salem to be accused of witchcraft. When Parris invites **Reverend John Hale** of Beverly to come to Salem as a witchcraft expert, he ensures not only fervor about the Devil's presence in Salem, but also a feeling of divisiveness along political and land ownership lines. After the trials, Abigail and **Mercy Lewis** rob Parris and disappear from Salem. Parris knows that at no point can he, Danforth, or Hathorne admit that they were wrong in executing people in the witch trials, or they will admit that they had been taken in by a group of lying young girls. Parris is eventually voted out of office.

Don Parritt

The Iceman Cometh
Eugene O'Neill

A gangly, awkward boy who has come to **Larry Slade** in order to hide from the police. Parritt confesses that he betrayed his mother because he hated her. Parritt's mother was once Larry's lover, so Parritt remembers Larry from his childhood and almost regards him as a father.

Elaine Parry

His Dark Materials
Robert Pullman

Will Parry's mother and **John Parry**'s wife.

Miss Helena Parry

Mrs. Dalloway
Virginia Woolf

Clarissa Dalloway's aunt. Aunt Helena is a relic of the strict English society that Clarissa finds so confining. A great botanist, she enjoys talking about orchids and Burma. She is a formidable old lady, over eighty, who found **Sally Seton**'s behavior as a youth shocking.

Will Parry

His Dark Materials
Robert Pullman

A strong-willed and stubborn twelve-year-old boy and **Lyra Belacqua**'s companion for the second two books in the series. Will possesses the subtle knife, which can cut through the fabric of the universe to other worlds. Will eventually discovers that he has a daemon named **Kirjava**, whose settled form is a cat. Because he lacks true parental figures, Will is free to explore another world. He is driven by his search for his father.

Roger Parslow

His Dark Materials
Robert Pullman

Lyra Belacqua's best friend from Oxford. The Gobblers steal Roger, which prompts Lyra to join the Gyptian party. **Lord Asriel** kills Roger. When Lyra and **Will Parry** go to the world of the dead, Lyra is looking for Roger. Roger's daemon is Salcilia.

The Parson

The Canterbury Tales
Geoffrey Chaucer

One of the pilgrims travelling to Canterbury. The only devout churchman in the company. The pastor of a sizable town, he preaches the Gospel and makes sure to practice what he preaches.

Parsons

1984
George Orwell

A obnoxious neighbor and coworker of **Winston Smith**'s. Parsons has a dull wife and a group of suspicious, ill-mannered children who are members of the Junior Spies. His children torment Winston and their father about potential thoughtcrimes, eventually turning Parsons over to the Ministry of Love. Parsons and Winston briefly encounter each other during their imprisonment.

Colonel Parsons

My Brother Sam Is Dead
Christopher & James Lincoln Collier

One of **Sam**'s officers in Redding.

Mrs. Virgie Parsons

The Bean Trees
Barbara Kingsolver

Lou Ann Ruiz's grumpy neighbor, who sometimes babysits for the children. She lives with a blind woman named **Edna Poppy**. She makes insensitive remarks about immigrants.

Partridge

Tom Jones
Henry Fielding

The teacher **Allworthy** accuses of being **Tom**'s father. Although pathetic, bumbling, and cowardly, Partridge remains a loyal servant to Jones. Although Partridge creates problems for Tom and **Sophia** by boosting Tom's reputation and defiling Sophia's, Tom cannot help forgiving Partridge, who always has the best of intentions.

Partridge

The Shipping News
E. Annie Proulx

Quoyle's first friend in the novel. A copy editor for the local paper, Partridge gets Quoyle his first job as a reporter. Quoyle keeps in touch with Partridge throughout *The Shipping News*.

Mrs. Partridge

Walk Two Moons
Sharon Creech

Mrs. Cadaver and **Mr. Birkway**'s mother. Mrs. Partridge lives with her daughter next door to **Phoebe**. Mrs. Partridge, despite her blindness, can guess people's ages by feeling their faces.

Parvati-the-witch

Midnight's Children
Salman Rushdie

One of midnight's children, and a friend to **Saleem**.

Gines de Pasamonte

Don Quixote
Miguel de Cervantes

An ungrateful galley slave freed by **Don Quixote**.

Pascal

The Poisonwood Bible
Barbara Kingsolver

A Congolese boy who befriends **Leah Price**. Later in life, Leah hears that he was killed by Mobutu's soldiers while walking on the road.

Mr. Patch-Withers

A Separate Peace
John Knowles

The substitute headmaster of the Devon School during the summer session. **Mr. Patch-Withers** runs the school with a lenient hand.

Parvati Patil

Harry Potter and the Goblet of Fire
J. K. Rowling

A pretty but vain Gryffindor girl who goes to the Yule Ball with **Harry Potter**.

Patrick

The English Patient
Michael Ondaatje

Hana's father, the only parent who was present to raise her while she was growing up. Like Hana, Patrick leaves Canada to join the war effort. Hana is extremely close to her father, and the news of his death sparks her initial emotional breakdown.

Patroclus

The Iliad
Homer

Achilles's beloved friend and advisor. Patroclus is devoted to both Achilles and the Greek cause. He is killed in battle by **Hector**.

Patroclus

Troilus and Cressida
William Shakespeare

A Greek warrior, and **Achilles**'s close friend and lover.

Patron-Minette

Les Misérables
Victor Hugo

A four-person Parisian crime ring, Patron-Minette so close-knit that its four members—Montparnasse, Babet, Claquesous, and Gueulemer—are described as four heads of the same violent beast. They specialize in ambushes. Whenever anyone in their area wants to plan a robbery, he presents his plan to Patron-Minette, and the four men refine and execute it. Patron-Minette assists in **M. Thénardier** and **M'me. Thénardier**'s ambush of **Jean Valjean**.

Patterson

The Heart Is a Lonely Hunter
Carson McCullers

Jake Blount's employer and the owner of the carnival. Patterson spends most of his time smoking marijuana.

Mr. and Mrs. Patterson

The Sound and the Fury
William Faulkner

One of the Compsons' next-door neighbors. **Uncle Maury** has an affair with Mrs. Patterson until Mr. Patterson intercepts a note Maury has sent to her.

Paul

A Lesson Before Dying
Ernest J. Gaines

The sheriff's deputy at the Bayonne jail and the only white person in the novel who truly sympathizes with the black struggle in the South.

Paul A

Beloved
Toni Morrison

The brother of **Paul F** and **Paul D**. They were all slaves at Sweet Home, along with **Halle**, **Sethe**, **Sixo**, and, earlier, **Baby Suggs**. Paul A is hanged by **schoolteacher** for trying to escape from Sweet Home.

Paul D

Beloved
Toni Morrison

Brother of **Paul A** and **Paul F**. He represses his painful memories and believes that the key to survival is not becoming too attached to anything. **Sethe** welcomes him to 124 Bluestone Road, where he becomes her lover and the object of **Denver**'s and **Beloved**'s jealousy. Beloved charms Paul D, against his will, into their secret sexual union multiple times. Though his union with Sethe provides him with stability and allows him to come to terms with his past, Paul D continues to doubt fundamental aspects of his identity and his value as a person. After finding out that Sethe committed infanticide, he leaves 124. After the exorcism, however, he comes back to help Denver take care of Sethe.

Paul F

Beloved
Toni Morrison

The brother of **Paul A** and **Paul D**. They were all slaves at Sweet Home, along with **Halle**, **Sethe**, **Sixo**, and, earlier, **Baby Suggs**.

Paul of Tarsus

The New Testament
Unknown

The great missionary who directs the spread of Christianity after the death of **Jesus**. More than half of the books in the New Testament have been attributed to Paul of Tarsus. In these books, Paul uses his robust intellect to develop Christianity's first sophisticated theology, treating such complex issues as the relationship between faith and works and the balance between unity and diversity.

Mr. Paul

On the Beach
Nevil Shute

A dairy farmer who provides milk and cream to the Holmes family. Mr. Paul asks **Peter Holmes** to help make a trailer with motorcycle wheels so that he can pull his wife into town, wanting to help her enjoy her last days.

Paul's mother

The Land
Mildred D. Taylor

A woman of African-American and Native-American ancestry. Born a slave on **Edward Logan**'s farm, **Paul-Edward Logan**'s father, Edward, takes her as his mistress, much to the distress and consternation of his white wife. When Mr. Logan's white wife dies, Paul's mother becomes like a wife to him, though she retains separate living quarters and regards herself primarily as his servant. She grows to feel tenderly toward Mr. Logan, and, after Emancipation, she chooses to stay with him, regarding her housewifely duties strictly as her work. From an early age, she tries to instill in Paul an understanding of the significance of his race. Paul sometimes becomes frustrated with his mother for letting Mr. Logan impose his will and his body upon her. Paul's mother dies when Paul is fourteen.

Paulina

The Winter's Tale
William Shakespeare

A noblewoman of Sicilia. Paulina fiercely defends **Hermione**'s virtue, and unrelentingly condemns **Leontes** after Hermione's death. She brings about the (apparently) dead Hermione's resurrection.

Pauline

A Yellow Raft in Blue Water
Michael Dorris

Ida's sister, and **Foxy**'s mother. Pauline leaves her parents while Ida and **Clara** are away in Colorado taking care of the pregnancy and goes to work with the nuns at the Holy Martyrs Mission.

Fra Pavel

His Dark Materials
Robert Pullman

A priest who can read the alethiometer even though he works for the Church.

Russian Pavel

My Ántonia
Willa Cather

Russian Peter's housemate, a tall, gaunt, and nervous man. Pavel is an immigrant who falls ill under the care of the Shimerdas. He had been ostracized and forced to leave his native Russia after a frightful incident involving a wolf attack on a wedding party.

Pavlo

One Day in the Life of Ivan Denisovich
Aleksandr Solzhenitsyn

The deputy foreman of **Ivan Denisovich Shukhov**'s Gang 104. The Ukrainian Pavlo is strict but kind. His patience and mercy toward the inmates earn him the devotion of many members of the gang, including Shukhov, who notes that a prisoner will not work hard for a distant boss but will break his back for a foreman he admires.

Dr. Oliver Payne

His Dark Materials
Robert Pullman

Dr. Mary Malone's colleague in the Dark Matter research unit.

Peabody

As I Lay Dying
William Faulkner

An obese rural doctor. Peabody attends to **Addie Bundren** and later to **Cash Bundren**. He is extremely critical of the way **Anse Bundren** treats his children.

Peace

Lysistrata
Aristophanes

Lysistrata's handmaid.

BoyBoy Peace

Sula
Toni Morrison

Eva Peace's husband. He abandoned her when their three children were small. Later, BoyBoy briefly visits, and Eva receives him without outward signs of animosity. It appears that he had come into a considerable sum of money. During his visit he never asks about his children, and when he leaves with his sophisticated city girlfriend, Eva looks forward to the long-standing hatred she will hold for him.

Eva Peace

Sula
Toni Morrison

A woman abandoned by her husband, **BoyBoy Peace**, when their children were young. She struggled to keep her family away from starvation, but she succeeded only through the kindness of her neighbors. Eva later became the matriarch of a busy household that included **Hannah Peace**, **Sula Peace**, **Ralph Peace**, **Tar Baby**, **the Deweys**, and a constant stream of boarders. Eva tries to save her daughter, Hannah, who is on fire, by jumping on top of her. Hannah dies, and Eva is only narrowly saved by **Old Willy Fields**. Eva kills her war-troubled and heroin-addicted son, **Plum**, because he wants to climb back into her womb. When Sula returns to the Bottom, she puts Eva in a nursing home. **Nel** visits Eva in the nursing home, but she is confronted with a sad, shriveled woman, a shadow of the vibrant matriarch Eva once was.

Hannah Peace

Sula
Toni Morrison

Eva Peace's oldest child. She moved back in with her mother after her husband, **Rekus**, died when their daughter, **Sula Peace**, was three years old. She has frequent, brief affairs with the men who take her fancy. Hannah catches fire and burns to death despite attempts by Eva, **Mr. Suggs**, and **Mrs. Suggs** to save her.

Pearl Peace

Sula
Toni Morrison

Eva Peace's second child. Pearl marries at age fourteen and moves to Flint, Michigan. She occasionally writes unremarkable letters about the everyday details of marriage and motherhood.

Ralph Peace

Sula
Toni Morrison

See **Plum**.

Sula Peace

Sula
Toni Morrison

Hannah Peace's daughter. When they are young girls, Sula and **Nel** become close friends. Nel's mother, **Helene**, disapproves of the friendship because Sula's mother has a loose reputation. Sula lives in a multi-generational household run by women. Whereas Nel's household is static and repressive, Sula's household is vibrant, active, and subject to constant change. Nel and Sula have radically different personalities: Nel is quiet and unassuming, while Sula is spontaneous and aggressive. One day, while Sula is swinging **Chicken Little** around with her hands, she accidentally loses her grip and throws Chicken Little into the water, where he drowns. At the funeral of Chicken Little, Sula feels no guilt and Nel has quite a bit. Sula later watches Hannah burn to death. Sula goes off to college for ten years but comes back to put Eva in a nursing home and have an affair with **Jude Greene**, Nel's husband. Things start going wrong in the Bottom, and people start blaming Sula. Nel is destroyed by Sula's betrayal. When Sula falls seriously ill, Nel decides to go and see her for the first time in three years after their estrangement. Sula affirms that Jude simply filled a space in her head. Even in their strained relations, the strong and independent Sula thinks of Nel in her last thoughts.

Maureen Peal

The Bluest Eye
Toni Morrison

A light-skinned, wealthy black girl who is new at the local school. She accepts everyone else's assumption that she is superior and is capable of both generosity and cruelty. Maureen's presence causes a group of boys to stop harassing **Pecola Breedlove**.

Peanut

The Kitchen God's Wife
Amy Tan

The bratty daughter of **Winnie**'s Uncle. Peanut and Winnie grow up together, and as a youth Peanut proves to be vain, conceited, selfish, and insecure. Later in life, Peanut leaves her marriage and becomes an adamant communist.

Pear Blossom

The Good Earth
Pearl S. Buck

A slave purchased by **Wang Lung** during the famine years, when she is a young girl. She becomes **Lotus**'s personal servant.

Pearl

The Scarlet Letter
Nathaniel Hawthorne

Hester Prynne's illegitimate daughter. Pearl is a young girl with a moody, mischievous spirit and an ability to perceive things that others do not. She quickly discerns the truth about the love affair between her mother and **Reverend Arthur Dimmesdale**. The townspeople say that she barely seems human and spread rumors that her unknown father is actually the Devil.

Pearl

The Iceman Cometh
Eugene O'Neill

One of **Rocky Pioggi**'s tarts. Though she retains a degree of youthful prettiness, her trade is beginning to wear on her.

Pearl

This Boy's Life
Tobias Wolff

Dwight's coddled youngest child, who is nearly the same age as **Jack Wolff**. Pearl and Jack despise one another, particularly when they are young, and do everything possible to get on each other's nerves. Pearl especially enjoys seeing Jack bear the brunt of Dwight's pressure and anger brought on by Dwight's feelings of inferiority.

Aunt Pearl

The Contender
Robert Lipsyte

The woman who takes care of **Alfred Brooks** in the wake of his parents' deaths. Aunt Pearl is a positive familial force in his life, although she disapproves of his boxing. The violence of the sport worries her, and she wishes Alfred would devote himself to safer, more productive activities. However, she allows Alfred to do it because she understands what it means to pursue a dream.

Nat Pearl

The Assistant
Bernard Malamud

The most socially and educationally successful character in the novel. He is a first-generation American who graduated from college and is now attending law school. He uses **Helen Bober** for sexual favors, then refuses to marry her because she is poor.

Bradley Pearson

The Black Prince
Iris Murdoch

The protagonist and the author of the novel, the ex-husband of **Christian Evandale**, **Arnold Baffin**'s best friend, and **Julian Baffin**'s lover. Bradley starts as a cold and occasionally cruel character. He ignores his depressed sister and it is his neglect, in part, that leads to her suicide. Initially, Bradley acts only with self-interest, but after he falls in love with Julian Baffin and is later wrongfully convicted of Arnold's murder, he becomes content and generous and is finally able to write a master novel.

Ray Pearson

Winesburg, Ohio
Sherwood Anderson

A married farm hand, about fifty years old, with a good reputation. He works alongside **Hal Winters**.

Pease

Black Boy
Richard Wright

Along with **Reynolds**, one of a pair of white Southerners who run **Richard Wright** off his job at the optical shop in Jackson, Mississippi.

Peaseblossom

A Midsummer Night's Dream
William Shakespeare

One of four fairies, along with **Cobweb**, **Mote**, and **Mustardseed**, whom **Titania** orders to attend to **Bottom** after she falls in love with him.

Haven Peck

A Day No Pigs Would Die
Robert Newton Peck

Father of **Robert Peck**, husband of **Lucy Peck**. Haven Peck is a hardy Shaker farmer who is illiterate but wise. Haven is the sole provider for the Peck family. His main goals in life are to make Robert into a good man and to own his own land.

Lucy Peck

A Day No Pigs Would Die
Robert Newton Peck

Robert Peck's mother and **Haven Peck**'s wife. Whereas Haven is eager for Robert to grow up, Lucy Peck always treats Robert like a boy. She lavishes love and care on him, heals his wounds, mends his pants, and helps him through his broken heart. She is very close with **Aunt Carrie**, who helps her run the house, and with whom Lucy gossips.

Robert Peck

A Day No Pigs Would Die
Robert Newton Peck

The narrator of *A Day No Pigs Would Die*. Robert is a curious and playful boy. He doesn't really have any friends except for his pig, **Pinky**. Robert's father, **Haven Peck**, serves as his role model, teacher, and inspiration. Robert is the first person in his family to receive an education. With Haven gone, Robert will have to provide for the family and take over responsibility for their finances.

Peddler

Silas Marner
George Eliot

An anonymous peddler who comes through Raveloe some time before the theft of **Silas**'s gold. The peddler is a suspect in the theft because of his gypsylike appearance.

Pedringano

The Spanish Tragedy
Thomas Kyd

Bel-Imperia's servant. Pedringano is easily bribed, and he betrays Bel-Imperia and is one of the gang of four murderers who kill **Horatio**. His lack of moral consideration leads him to trust **Lorenzo**, who ends up betraying him.

Pedro

Like Water for Chocolate
Laura Esquivel

Tita's true love, and the eventual father of **Roberto** and **Esperanza**. Denied marriage to **Tita** by Mama Elena, he agrees to marry **Rosaura**, breaking Tita's heart. Nevertheless, he asserts his love for Tita throughout the novel.

Don Pedro, Prince of Aragon

Much Ado About Nothing
William Shakespeare

Leonato's longtime friend and **Don John**'s brother. The powerful Don Pedro is also close to the soldiers who have been fighting under him: **Benedick** and the young **Claudio**. He woos **Hero** on behalf of Claudio, and later conspires with the others to trick Benedick into falling in love with **Beatrice**. Despite his age and experience, not to mention his long hostility with his illegitimate brother, Don Pedro believes Don John's lie about Hero's infidelity and is complicit in Claudio's public humiliation of Hero at the wedding altar.

Peduzzi

In Our Time
Ernest Hemingway

An Italian man in "Out of Season." Peduzzi has a tendency to drink too much.

Peekay

The Power of One
Bryce Courtenay

The novel's protagonist and narrator. Peekay is a white English South African who recounts his life growing up in South Africa during World War II and the beginning of the apartheid era. An extremely precocious student and a naturally brilliant boxer, Peekay is loved by almost all who meet him. He becomes a legend amongst black South Africans, who believe that he has come to avenge them against the Afrikaners. Each side, however, wishes to claim Peekay for themselves. Peekay's generosity and altruism lead him to devise ways of helping black prisoners write and receive letters, and to teach black men to box.

Peekay's mother

The Power of One
Bryce Courtenay

Suffers from a nervous breakdown during **Peekay**'s youth, and is absent for many years afterward. She returns to live with Peekay and his **Granpa** in Barberton, where she becomes a seamstress and a born again Christian. She spends most of her time zealously trying to proselytize people.

Margaret Peel

Lucky Jim
Kingsley Amis

A close friend of **Jim Dixon**'s who imagines herself to be his lover. She goes to great lengths to secure his sympathy, even staging a suicide attempt. Margaret has her moments of straightforward discussion with Dixon, but can just as quickly become clingy, condescending, or aggressive. She is better adjusted to the academic life in the college than Dixon, where she holds a slightly higher post than he.

Peeves

The Harry Potter Series: Books 2–4
J. K. Rowling

A poltergeist that causes harmless trouble at Hogwarts.

Peewee

Fallen Angels
Walter Dean Myers

Richie Perry's closest friend in Vietnam. Peewee copes with the fear and uncertainty of the war with comical bravado, though he occasionally allows his true emotions to peek through the bluster.

Francine Pefko

Cat's Cradle
Kurt Vonnegut

Worked with **Naomi Faust** at the Research Laboratory, transcribing documents that neither of them really understood.

Clara Peggotty

David Copperfield
Charles Dickens

David Copperfield's nanny and caretaker. Peggotty is gentle and selfless, helping David whenever he is in need. She is faithful to David and his family all her life.

Peggy

Native Son
Richard Wright

An Irish immigrant who has worked as **Mr. Dalton** and **Mrs. Dalton**'s cook for years. Peggy considers the Daltons to be marvelous benefactors to black Americans. Though she is actively kind to **Bigger Thomas,** she is also extremely patronizing.

Mrs. Pegler

Hard Times
Charles Dickens

Josiah Bounderby's mother. Mrs. Pegler makes an annual visit to Coketown in order to admire her son's prosperity from a safe distance.

Serafina Pekkala

His Dark Materials
Robert Pullman

A witch, the head of her clan. Serafina once loved **Farder Coram**, whose child she bore. Her daemon is Kaisa, a snow goose.

Peleg

Moby-Dick
Herman Melville

A well-to-do retired whaleman of Nantucket and a Quaker. Peleg, like the other owner of the *Pequod*, **Bildad**, is portrayed as a conniving cheapskate and a bitter taskmaster. Peleg and Bildad take care of hiring the crew. Both believe in Captain **Ahab**'s competence and believe him harmless, since he has a young wife and an infant child waiting for him at home. They don't know that he is keeping a band of men of questionable character hidden in the *Pequod*, including the mysterious and terrifying **Fedallah**. Bildad and Peleg see their ship out of harbor, and then take a small boat back to the Nantucket shore.

The Iliad
Homer

Peleus

Achilles's father and **Zeus**'s grandson. Although his name recurs frequently in the *Iliad*, Peleus never appears in person. **Priam** powerfully invokes Peleus's memory when he convinces Achilles to return **Hector**'s corpse.

The Once and Future King
T. H. White

King Pellinore

The first knight **King Arthur** meets. An amiable bumbler whose lifelong quest is to hunt **the Questing Beast**, King Pellinore becomes an accomplished knight after his marriage. Even after he is killed, his legacy of kindness lives on in his children.

King John
William Shakespeare

Pembroke

An English nobleman who defects, along with **Lord Bigot** and **William, Earl of Salisbury**, to the French after **Arthur**'s death. Pembroke and the other two lords return to the English after they discover that **Lewis** plans to kill them after defeating **King John**'s forces in battle.

Holes
Louis Sachar

Mr. Pendanski

The man in charge of Tent D, **Stanley Yelnats**'s tent at Camp Green Lake. He seems to be friendly but is just as mean as the **Warden** and **Mr. Sir**.

The Once and Future King
T. H. White

Uther Pendragon

The king of England during **King Arthur**'s childhood. Uther Pendragon is actually Arthur's father. Arthur was taken by **Merlyn** as a little boy to live with **Sir Ector**. Once Pendragon dies, the next king is determined by a trial, the famous sword in the stone, which Arthur wins. Thus, Arthur is eventually placed on the throne after Uther's death.

The Odyssey
Homer

Penelope

Odysseus's wife and **Telemachus**'s mother. Penelope yearns for the husband who left twenty years ago. Though she has not seen Odysseus in twenty years, and despite pressure the suitors place on her to remarry, Penelope never loses faith in her husband.

The Moonstone
Wilkie Collins

Penelope

Gabriel Betteredge's daughter, and **Rachel Verinder**'s maid. She was raised, along with her mistress, in **Lady Verinder**'s household.

Dr. Wilder Penfield

Death Be Not Proud
John Gunther

A renowned brain surgeon who operates on **Johnny**.

Mrs. Peniston

The House of Mirth
Edith Wharton

Lily Bart's wealthy aunt and guardian. Upon hearing rumors that Lily had an affair and gambles on Sundays, Mrs. Peniston disinherits her niece and leaves most of her estate to other relatives.

Pennyways

Far from the Madding Crowd
Thomas Hardy

The bailiff on **Bathsheba Everdene**'s farm. Pennyways is caught stealing grain and dismissed. Later, Pennyways recognizes **Sergeant Francis Troy** at Greenhill Fair, where Troy is working in the circus act. Pennyways agrees not to tell anyone about Troy's reappearance after his presumed death, as Troy wants to surprise Bathsheba.

Pentheus

The Bacchae
Euripides

King of Thebes, son of Agave, grandson of **Cadmus**, and first cousin of **Dionysus**. Pentheus is a stern patriach, a military man who preserves law and order.

Rosina Pepita

Orlando
Virginia Woolf

A Spanish woman in Turkey whose marriage to **Orlando** lasts only a day before she falls into a deep trance.

Peppino

The Count of Monte Cristo
Alexandre Dumas

An Italian shepherd who is arrested for being an accomplice to **Luigi Vampa** and his bandits. Although he only provided the bandits with food, he is sentenced to a public beheading. **The Count of Monte Cristo** promises to buy Peppino's freedom, and Vampa pledges his everlasting loyalty in return. At the execution, Peppino is granted a reprieve. Monte Cristo watches impassively as the other condemned man is brutally executed.

Kate, Lady Percy

Henry IV, Part I and *Henry IV, Part II*
William Shakespeare

Hotspur's wife and the **Earl of Northumberland**'s daughter-in-law. Suspecting her husband of plotting rebellion, Lady Percy pleads with Hotspur to tell her what he's planning. Hotspur lashes out, declaring that war is more important than love. In *King Henry IV, Part II*, she helps convince her father-in-law Northumberland not to fight in the upcoming rebellion, but to flee to Scotland.

Perdita

The Winter's Tale
William Shakespeare

The daughter of **Leontes** and **Hermione**. Because her father believes her to be illegitimate, she is abandoned as a baby on the coast of Bohemia and brought up by a shepherd. Unaware of her royal lineage, she falls in love with the Bohemian Prince **Florizel**.

Leander Peregrina

Animal Dreams
Barbara Kingsolver

Loyd Peregrina's twin brother and best friend. Leander Peregrina died when he was fifteen. Loyd and his brother moved to Whiteriver to be with their father. Leander was killed in a fight in a bar; he died of puncture wounds and internal hemorrhaging.

Loyd Peregrina

Animal Dreams
Barbara Kingsolver

Codi Nolina's love interest. A Native American with mixed Apache, Pueblo and Navajo ancestry, Loyd is deeply connected to his Native American roots. In high school, Codi was pregnant with and miscarried Loyd's baby, but he does not know this until years later. Loyd introduces Codi to his family and his mother, **Inez**, who welcome her warmly but make her feel out of place. Loyd had a twin brother who was killed, **Leander Peregrina**, and a loyal dog, **Jack**. Codi ends up becoming pregnant with Loyd's baby deliberately at the end of *Animal Dreams*. In his relationship with Codi, Loyd often takes the role traditionally assigned to the woman, expressing a desire to settle down and have children while Codi seems restless and terrified of birth due to her past traumatic experiences.

Peregrine

Volpone
Ben Jonson

A young English traveler who meets and befriends **Sir Politic Would-be** upon arriving in Venice. Peregrine is amused by the gullible Would-be, but is also easily offended.

Alice Pereira

Midnight's Children
Salman Rushdie

Mary Pereira's sister, who works for **Ahmed Sinai**.

Mary Pereira

Midnight's Children
Salman Rushdie

A midwife and servant, who switches **Shiva** and **Saleem** at birth.

Perez

All the Pretty Horses
Cormac McCarthy

A wealthy, powerful prisoner. He tries to force **John Grady Cole** and **Lacey Rawlins** to ally themselves with him or pay him bribes to arrange for their freedom. When the Americans refuse, he has Rawlins stabbed and presumably pays an assassin to try to kill John Grady.

Thomas Perez

The Stranger
Albert Camus

A resident at the old-persons home where **Madame Meursault** lived. Before Madame Meursault's death, she and Perez had become so inseparable that the other residents joked that they were fiancés.

Pericles

Pericles
William Shakespeare

The prince of Tyre; **Thaisa**'s husband and **Marina**'s father. Pericles wins Thaisa with his virtue and jousting skills but loses her in a storm. At the end he is reunited with Thaisa and Marina.

Perico

The Old Man and the Sea
Ernest Hemingway

The owner of the bodega in **Santiago**'s village. Perico provides Santiago with newspapers that report the exploits of Santiago's hero, the New York Yankees' center fielder **Joe DiMaggio**.

Pyotr Ilyich Perkhotin

The Brothers Karamazov
Fyodor Dostoevsky

A friend of **Dmitri Fyodorovich Karamazov**'s. Perkhotin is a young official who follows Dmitri on the night of **Fyodor Pavlovich Karamazov**'s murder.

Mr. Perls

Seize the Day
Saul Bellow

A breakfast companion of **Dr. Adler**'s, a salesman whom **Tommy Wilhelm** resents for playing the "buffer."

Mr. Perpich

Hatchet
Gary Paulsen

Brian Robeson's old English teacher. Mr. Perpich repeatedly insists on the importance of a positive attitude. His message continues to stay with Brian in his times of discouragement when Brian is stranded in the Canadian woods.

Perrault

The Call of the Wild
Jack London

A French Canadian. Perrault, together with **François**, turns **Buck** into a sled dog. François and Perrault run the pack of dogs all over the North country. Perrault exits Buck's life abruptly upon being reassigned to work somewhere else along with François.

Caroline Perry

The Land
Mildred D. Taylor

Paul-Edward Logan's first and only love and **Mitchell Thomas**'s wife. Paul first meets the kind-hearted Caroline when she is defending a black boy from the taunting of peers. Caroline is industrious, independent, forthright, and strong-willed. She becomes pregnant with Mitchell's child, and when Mitchell is killed by **Digger Wallace**, Mitchell's dying wish is that Paul marry Caroline and raise their child. After Mitchell's death, Caroline refuses to leave the forty acres, and she and Paul marry. In *Roll of Thunder, Hear My Cry*, she is **Big Ma**.

Mr. Perry

Emma
Jane Austen

An apothecary and associate of **Emma Woodhouse**'s father's.

Nathan Perry

The Land
Mildred D. Taylor

Caroline Perry's younger brother. Nathan is fascinated by **Paul-Edward Logan**'s skill as a carpenter and goes to live with Paul on the forty acres and learn his trade. Paul is concerned for him because Nathan insists on befriending **Wade Jamison**, a white boy.

Rachel Perry

The Land
Mildred D. Taylor

Mother of **Caroline Perry**. Rachel Perry is hardworking and cautious. As a child, her owner's wife took her name away, insisting that Rachel's mother call her by another name. Consequently, Rachel is deeply suspicious of all whites, including the white-looking **Paul-Edward Logan**. She warms up to him after he presents the Perry family with a beautiful rocking chair that he built.

Richie Perry

Fallen Angels
Walter Dean Myers

The narrator and protagonist, a high school graduate from Harlem. Though he is smart and ambitious, his alcoholic single mother cannot afford to send him to college, so he joins the army to escape an uncertain future. Richie is sent to Vietnam, and during his months there, he suffers numerous harrowing combat experiences and tries to grapple with the meaning of war, heroism, and good and evil.

Sam Perry

The Land
Mildred D. Taylor

Father of **Caroline Perry**.

Persephone

Greek Mythology
Unknown

The beautiful and passive daughter of **Demeter**, whom **Hades** kidnaps to be his wife.

Perseus

Greek Mythology
Unknown

Zeus's son by the beautiful princess **Danaë**. Danaë's father, forewarned that Perseus will someday kill him, locks the infant and his mother in a trunk and casts it into the sea. Perseus survives, comes of age, and sets out to kill the monster **Medusa** and bring back her head. As predicted, he kills his grandfather, though unwittingly, by hitting him with a stray discus.

Pertelote

The Canterbury Tales
Geoffrey Chaucer

Chanticleer's favorite wife in **the Nun's Priest**'s Tale. When **the fox** takes Chanticleer away, she mourns him in classical Greek fashion, burning herself and wailing.

Aunt Pet

The Member of the Wedding
Carson McCullers

A relative of **Frankie Addams** and **Royal Quincy Addams**. At the end of the novella, Frankie and her father get ready to move into a suburban house with Aunt Pet and **Uncle Ustace**.

Pete

Maggie: A Girl of the Streets
Stephen Crane

A bartender with bourgeois pretensions who seduces and then abandons **Maggie**. Pete affects bravado and wealth, and to the downtrodden Maggie, he seems to promise a better life. But Pete is easily drawn away from Maggie by the manipulative and relatively sophisticated **Nellie**.

Pete

A Clockwork Orange
Anthony Burgess

A mild-mannered member of **Alex**'s gang. Unlike **Dim** or **Georgie**, Pete never directly betrays Alex. He gets married and becomes an office worker, and Alex's encounter with Pete and his wife Georgina in a café inspires Alex to consider the appeal of commitment and adulthood.

Peter

The New Testament
Unknown

The first of **Jesus**' disciples, who recognizes Jesus as the Messiah before the other apostles. As a result, Jesus makes him the "rock"—renaming Simon "Peter," which means rock—on which his church would be built. Although he denies his association with Jesus after Jesus' arrest, Peter later realizes his mistake and weeps bitterly. He goes on to become one of the leaders of the church in Jerusalem. Simon Peter is a model of faithful discipleship. The Catholic Church still claims apostolic succession from Peter.

Peter

Romeo and Juliet
William Shakespeare

A Capulet servant who invites guests to **Capulet**'s feast and escorts the Nurse to meet with **Romeo**.

Peter

Incidents in the Life of a Slave Girl
Harriet Ann Jacobs

A family friend who helps **Linda Brent** escape. Peter urges Linda to risk the escape he has planned, rather than remaining in her attic hideaway.

Peter

The Color of Water
James McBride

Ruth McBride Jordan's first boyfriend. Peter was the first black person with whom Ruth was genuinely close. Because of the heated racial atmosphere of the times, Peter and Ruth had to see one another secretly. Ruth became pregnant by Peter during her adolescence, but chose not to have the baby.

Peter

Tuesdays with Morrie
Mitch Albom

Mitch Albom's younger brother. Peter lives in Spain and flies to various European cities seeking treatment for his pancreatic cancer. He has grown estranged from his family and refuses their attempts to help. He is reluctant when Mitch first tries to reestablish a relationship with him, but eventually warms.

Russian Peter

My Ántonia
Willa Cather

Russian Pavel's housemate, and a fat, happy man. Like Pavel, Peter was forced into exile from his native Russia following a wolf attack on a wedding party. Peter eventually finds himself severely in debt and sells off his belongings, leaving America for a job as a cook in a Russian labor camp.

Jules Peterson

Tender Is the Night
F. Scott Fitzgerald

A black man who is found dead in **Rosemary Hoyt**'s room because of **Abe North** and a case of mistaken identity with another black man.

Petit-Gervais

Les Misérables
Victor Hugo

A small boy who is robbed by **Jean Valjean** shortly after leaving Digne. After Valjean takes his silver coin, the boy runs off crying and Valjean is struck by the wickedness of his act. He tries in vain to find the boy and return the coin.

Peto

Henry IV, Part I and *Henry IV, Part II*
William Shakespeare

A criminal and highwayman, friend to **Sir John Falstaff** and Prince Harry (the future **Henry V**). Along with **Bardolph** and **Edward Poins**, Peto drinks with Falstaff and Hal in the Boar's Head Tavern in Eastcheap, accompanies them in highway robbery, and goes with them to war. Like Falstaff, Peto gets richer and gains prestige after the Battle of Shrewsbury.

Crime and Punishment
Nastasya Petrovna
Fyodor Dostoevsky

A servant in the house where **Rodion Romanovich Raskolnikov** rents his "closet." Nastasya brings him tea and food when he requests it and helps care for him in his illness after the murders.

The Taming of the Shrew
Petruccio
William Shakespeare

A gentleman from Verona. Loud, boisterous, eccentric, quick-witted, and frequently drunk, Petruccio wishes for nothing more than a woman with an enormous dowry, and he finds **Katherine** to be the perfect fit. Disregarding everyone who warns him of her shrewishness, he eventually succeeds not only in wooing Kate, but in silencing her tongue and temper with his own.

Wild Duck
Pettersen
Henrik Ibsen

Werle's servant, who appears at the dinner party in Act I.

The Harry Potter Series: Books 3 and *4*
Peter Pettigrew
J. K. Rowling

The fourth in the group of friends that included **James Potter**, **Sirius Black**, and **Remus Lupin**. In *Harry Potter and the Prisoner of Azkaban*, we learn that Pettigrew betrayed **Lily Potter** and James, turning their whereabouts over to **Voldemort**, then blowing up a dozen Muggles (non-magical people), framing Sirius, and turning himself into a rat so that he could escape.

The Lion, the Witch, and the Wardrobe
Edmund Pevensie
C. S. Lewis

The brother of **Peter Pevensie**, **Lucy Pevensie**, and **Susan Pevensie**. His greed for the enchanted Turkish Delight given to him by **the White Witch** leads him to act as a traitor against his siblings. Edmund joins forces with the White Witch, but eventually sees the error of his ways and returns to the good side.

The Lion, the Witch, and the Wardrobe
Lucy Pevensie
C. S. Lewis

The youngest sister of **Susan Pevensie**, **Peter Pevensie,** and **Edmund Pevensie**. She is the first of the children to venture into Narnia. Later, she urges her siblings to search for her friend, **Tumnus**, when they find that the faun's home is ransacked. In the beginning, she is the protagonist, although **Aslan** fills that role later in the novel. She is known as Queen Lucy the Valiant when Aslan makes her one of the rulers of Narnia.

The Lion, the Witch, and the Wardrobe
Peter Pevensie
C. S. Lewis

The oldest brother of **Edmund Pevensie**, **Susan Pevensie**, and **Lucy Pevensie**. He matures into a young man during his first few days in Narnia. He immediately proves himself after protecting Susan by killing **Maugrim**. **Aslan** knights him and eventually crowns him the High King of Narnia. During his reign he is known as King Peter the Magnificent.

Susan Pevensie

The Lion, the Witch, and the Wardrobe
C. S. Lewis

The sister of **Edmund Pevensie**, **Lucy Pevensie**, and **Peter Pevensie**. When she becomes queen at Cair Paravel, she is known as Queen Susan the Gentle.

Pew

Treasure Island
Robert Louis Stevenson

An old, blind beggar and pirate. Pew's inner power and charisma captivate young Jim even while striking fear into the villagers. Pew presents **Billy Bones** with a black spot, an ultimatum to give up the sea chest's contents to the pirate gang. Billy dies soon after Pew's visit, and Pew then dies in a carriage accident.

Fatty Pfaff

Arrowsmith
Sinclair Lewis

One of **Martin Arrowsmith**'s fellow medics at medical school. Fatty tries his hardest to learn but lacks intelligence. Nonetheless, he does graduate and eventually becomes an obstetrician.

Phaedra

The King Must Die
Mary Renault

Minos's daughter. She falls in love with **Theseus** when she is a young girl. Theseus promises that they will get married when Phaedra is older. According to legend, he does so, and she causes the troubles that lead to the death of his son.

Phebe

All the King's Men
Robert Penn Warren

The slave who brings **Annabelle Trice** her husband's wedding ring following his suicide. As a result, Annabelle sells her.

Pheidippides

The Clouds
Aristophanes

The spendthrift and arrogant son of **Strepsiades**. Pheidippides is fascinated by himself—his own material needs and later his sharp intellect—and his egotism makes him cruel and ruthless.

C. Paul Phelps

Dead Man Walking
Helen Prejean

The head of the Louisiana Department of Corrections. He supports the death penalty even if he doesn't personally believe in it. A kind and compassionate man, Phelps helps institute a number of necessary prison reforms.

Mrs. Phelps

Fahrenheit 451
Ray Bradbury

One of **Mildred Montag**'s vapid friends. She is emotionally disconnected from her life, appearing unconcerned when her third husband is sent off to war, but she breaks down crying when **Guy Montag** reads her a poem.

Sally and Silas Phelps

The Adventures of Huckleberry Finn
Mark Twain

Tom Sawyer's aunt and uncle. Sally is **Aunt Polly**'s sister. **Huckleberry Finn** coincidentally encounters Sally Phelps and Silas Phelps in his search for **Jim** after **the duke** and **the dauphin** have sold him. Essentially good people, the Phelpses nevertheless hold Jim in custody and try to return him to his rightful owner, who turns out to be the dead **Miss Watson**. Silas and Sally are the unknowing victims of Tom and Huck's mischief as they try to free Jim. Aunt Sally wants to take Huck in at the end, but Huck wants to travel with Tom to Oklahoma for more adventures.

Philadelphy

The Unvanquished
William Faulkner

Loosh's wife. Philadelphy does not share his vengefulness and feels sad and guilty, but she is unable to sway him from his course.

Philario

Cymbeline
William Shakespeare

An Italian gentleman who houses **Posthumus** during his exile from Britain.

Philarmonus

Cymbeline
William Shakespeare

A soothsayer in the service of **Caius Lucius**.

Philemon

Pericles
William Shakespeare

Cerimon's assistant.

Philinte

The Misanthrope
Molière

A polite and tactful man who is well-adapted to the society of the play. He lacks the sharp wit and cleverness of many of the other characters, but is appealing in his selflessness.

King Philip of France

King John
William Shakespeare

The ruler of France, and **Lewis**'s father. Philip champions **Arthur**'s claim to the throne and threatens war unless **King John** abdicates. Philip changes his mind and makes a tenuous peace with the English in exchange for a lucrative marriage for Lewis to the daughter of the King of Spain, **Blanche**. He changes his mind again when **Cardinal Pandulph** demands that Philip oppose the English on behalf of the pope.

Uncle Phillip

Incidents in the Life of a Slave Girl
Harriet Ann Jacobs

Linda Brent's other uncle, instrumental in her escape. Uncle Phillip is a reliable, moderate man, remaining in the South with his family long after his mother, **Aunt Martha**, buys his freedom.

Mr. Phillips

Anne of Green Gables
L. M. Montgomery

The schoolmaster at Avonlea during **Anne Shirley**'s first year at Green Gables. Mr. Phillips is an inattentive teacher and a capricious disciplinarian. Mr. Phillips spends class time flirting with his oldest student, **Prissy Andrews**.

Wendell Phillips

Narrative of the Life of Frederick Douglass
Frederick Douglass

President of the American Anti-Slavery Society. Phillips considers **Frederick Douglass** a close friend. He admires Douglass's bravery in publishing his history without pseudonyms, but also fears for Douglass's safety.

Richard Phillotson

Jude the Obscure
Thomas Hardy

The schoolmaster who first introduces **Jude Fawley** to the idea of studying at the university. He later marries **Susanna Bridehead**. Susanna likes Phillotson despite his age, but is surprised at her inability to find him attractive. She even comes to be repulsed by him and later admits to jumping out of the window for fear that he would enter her bed. Phillotson tries very hard to preserve at least the external appearance of a typical marriage.

Philostrate

A Midsummer Night's Dream
William Shakespeare

Theseus's master of the revels. Philostrate is responsible for organizing the entertainment for the duke's marriage celebration.

Phineas

A Separate Peace
John Knowles

See **Finny**.

Phipps

An Ideal Husband
Oscar Wilde

Lord Goring's butler. Absolutely impassive, Phipps reveals nothing of his intellect or emotions.

Phlegyas

Inferno
Dante Alighieri

The boatman who rows the dead across the river Styx, from the Fifth to the Sixth Circle of Hell (Canto VIII).

Phoebe

As You Like It
William Shakespeare

A young shepherdess who disdains the affections of **Silvius**. When **Rosalind**, disguised as the male youth Ganymede, chastises her for her cruelty, Phoebe is immediately smitten. Rosalind ultimately tricks her into marrying Silvius.

Phoebus de Chateaupers

Hunchback of Notre Dame
Victor Hugo

The captain of the King's Archers. He saves **La Esmerelda** from **Quasimodo**. He does not love her, but he tries to seduce her and a number of other women as well. After **Claude Frollo** stabs Phoebus, he recovers from his wounds even though they are severe. He fails to speak up when La Esmerelda is sentenced to death for his murder. He ends up marrying **Fleur-de-Lys de Gondelaurier**.

Phoenix

The Iliad
Homer

A kindly old warrior who helped raise **Achilles**.

Photo engraver

The Chairs
Eugène Ionesco

The invisible husband of **Belle**. He gives the **Old Woman** a painting when they arrive, and she flirts with him.

Phulan

Shabanu
Suzanne Fisher Staples

Shabanu's older sister. Phulan is more beautiful and graceful than Shabanu, but she is not as clever, critical, or capable. She and Shabanu have a close relationship, although Shabanu is envious of Phulan's beauty and maturity. Phulan enjoys being indoors and doing housework, and her life centers on her upcoming marriage to her cousin, **Hamir**.

Phutatorius

Tristram Shandy
Laurence Sterne

A part of a colloquy of learned men whom **Walter**, **Toby**, and **Parson Yorick** consult about the possibility of changing **Tristram**'s name.

The Physician

The Canterbury Tales
Geoffrey Chaucer

One of the pilgrims travelling to Canterbury. He knows the cause of every malady and can cure most of them. Though the Physician keeps himself in perfect physical health, **the narrator** calls into question the Physician's spiritual health.

Henri Pichot

A Lesson Before Dying
Ernest J. Gaines

A stubborn white man with a sense of duty who owns the plantation where **Grant Wiggins** spent his childhood. Pichot enjoys his position of power in the quarter.

Dr. Almus Pickerbaugh

Arrowsmith
Sinclair Lewis

The director of the Department of Public Health in the small city of Nautilus, Iowa. **Martin Arrowsmith** attains a position in public health under the garrulous Dr. Pickerbaugh, who comes across as a far better salesman and commercialist than doctor or researcher. Pickerbaugh campaigns for cleanliness, writes bad poetry about health and sanitation for his eight daughters to sing, and spends a great deal of time on pointless, extracurricular public relations endeavors. Ultimately, Pickerbaugh campaigns for a seat in the U.S. Congress, wins the election, and moves to Washington.

Orchid Pickerbaugh

Arrowsmith
Sinclair Lewis

Dr. Pickerbaugh's eldest daughter. Orchid is a flirtatious and beautiful girl who admires **Martin Arrowsmith**'s eccentricities and intelligence. Martin, in turn, becomes infatuated with her, arousing the jealousy of his wife, **Leora**. However, Martin's pining turns out to be all for naught when Dr. Pickerbaugh moves to Washington and takes Orchid with him.

Colonel Pickering

Pygmalion
George Bernard Shaw

Scholar of Indian languages, author of "Spoken Sanscrit." Pickering covers the cost of Higgins's experiment with **Eliza**, and, through his good manners and kindness, teaches her to respect herself as Higgins teaches her enunciation.

General George Pickett

The Killer Angels
Michael Shaara

An officer in the Confederate army and a perfumed dandy. Last in his class at West Point, Pickett has nonetheless risen to the rank of major general, and he leads an entire division. He is in love with a girl half his age. His division has not seen action in battle yet, and he longs for a chance to prove himself and his men.

Grandparents Pickford

Walk Two Moons
Sharon Creech

Salamanca Tree Hiddle's mother's parents. Sal's Grandparents Pickford are prim, proper, and easily shocked.

Professor Pieixoto

The Handmaid's Tale
Margaret Atwood

One of the transcribers of **Offred**'s audio diary. Pieixoto is the keynote speaker at the year 2195 symposium portrayed in the epilogue.

Pierre

Wide Sargasso Sea
Jean Rhys

Antoinette's mentally and physically disabled younger brother. It is suggested that Pierre's illness is a result of inbreeding and physical decline in the Cosway family. When the house at Coulibri is set on fire, Pierre is trapped in his burning room and he dies soon after.

Pierre

Oranges Are Not the Only Fruit
Jeanette Winterson

Ex-lover of **Jeanette's mother**.

Geel Piet

The Power of One
Bryce Courtenay

A Cape Colored man who works in the Barberton prison. He becomes **Peekay**'s personal boxing trainer in Barberton and develops a close relationship with both Peekay and **Doc**. Geel Piet is brutally murdered by one of the Barberton prison warders, **Borman**, who grows suspicious of Peekay and Geel Piet's close relationship. Together Peekay and Geel Piet had been running a black market within the prison.

Piggy

Lord of the Flies
William Golding

Ralph's "lieutenant." A whiny intellectual boy, Piggy's inventiveness frequently leads to innovation such as a makeshift sundial. **Roger** causes Piggy's death by rolling a rock on top of him.

Pigwidgeon

Harry Potter and the Goblet of Fire
J. K. Rowling

Ron Weasley's tiny, excitable pet owl.

Pikes

The Martian Chronicles
Ray Bradbury

William Stendahl's partner. He used to be an actor in fantasy movies. He now works as a master craftsman of robots, and helps Stendahl build Usher II.

Pilar

For Whom the Bell Tolls
Ernest Hemingway

Pablo's part-gypsy "woman." A large, robust, fiercely patriotic woman, Pilar exercises great influence over the band of guerrilleros. She pushes Robert Jordan and **Maria**'s romance, commands the allegiance of the guerrilla fighters, and organizes the guerrilleros' brief alliance with **El Sordo**. She unites the band of guerrilla fighters into a family, cooks for all, and sews Robert Jordan's packs. Pilar, though practical, often relies on intuitive, mystical, gypsy folk wisdom and claims a deep connection to the primitive forces of fate.

Pontius Pilate

The New Testament
Unknown

The prefect of Judea by the authority of the Roman Empire during the time of **Jesus**' trial in Jerusalem. It was Pilate who ultimately decided that Jesus be executed.

Nurse Pilbow

One Flew over the Cuckoo's Nest
Ken Kesey

A strict Catholic with a prominent birthmark on her face that she attempts to scrub away. Nurse Pilbow is afraid of the patients' sexuality.

Barbara Pilgrim

Slaughterhouse-Five
Kurt Vonnegut

Billy Pilgrim's daughter. Barbara marries at age twenty-one and is soon faced with the sudden death of her mother, **Valencia Merble**, and the apparent mental breakdown of her father.

Billy Pilgrim

Slaughterhouse-Five
Kurt Vonnegut

The protagonist. A World War II veteran, POW survivor of the firebombing of Dresden, prospering optometrist, husband, and father. He believes he has "come unstuck in time." His fragmented experience of time structures the novel as short episodic vignettes and shows how the difficulty of recounting traumatic experiences can require unusual literary techniques.

Robert Pilgrim

Slaughterhouse-Five
Kurt Vonnegut

Billy Pilgrim's son. Robert is a failure and a delinquent at school, though he cleans up his life enough to become a Green Beret in the Vietnam War.

Pilia-Borza

The Jew of Malta
Christopher Marlowe

Bellamira's pimp. Pilia-Borza is crude but not easily deceived, as shown by his reluctance to dine with **Barabas**. Ironically, he is still poisoned by Barabas along with Bellamira and **Ithamore**.

Mr. Pilkington

Animal Farm
George Orwell

Easygoing gentleman farmer who runs Foxwood, a neighboring farm. **Mr. Frederick**'s bitter enemy, Pilkington participates in the Battle of Cowshed, but by the end of the book enters into a business arrangement with the tyrannical new "Manor Farm" run by **Napoleon**.

Dr. Pillsbury

Looking Backward
Edward Bellamy

A skilled mesmerist whose help **Julian West** enlists in his efforts to battle insomnia. Doctor Pillsbury never fails to put Julian into a deep sleep and trains **Sawyer**, Julian's servant, to bring Julian out of a mesmerized state.

Pilon

Tortilla Flat
John Steinbeck

One of the group of paisanos' cofounding members. Whenever the group faces a difficult situation or a need, Pilon usually is the one to find a solution. Although he lives an unscrupulous life, the spiritual Pilon always tries to do what is right.

Pinabel

Song of Roland
Unknown

Ganelon's closest companion. A mighty and eloquent Frankish baron, Pinabel defends Ganelon at his trial. He at first convinces **Charlemagne**'s council of barons to let Ganelon live, but he is challenged by **Thierry** to a trial by combat. Though Thierry is the weaker warrior, divine intervention allows Thierry to kill Pinable and seal Ganelon's fate.

Doctor Pinch

The Comedy of Errors
William Shakespeare

A schoolteacher, conjurer, and would-be exorcist. **Adriana**, fearing her husband has gone mad, employs him to expel a demon from **Antipholus of Ephesus**'s body. Antipholus loses his temper and smacks the buffoonish Doctor Pinch, causing an uproar.

Pinkie

Ceremony
Leslie Marmon Silko

A childhood friend of **Tayo**'s, and **Emo**'s drinking buddy and sidekick. Pinkie is eventually betrayed and killed by Emo.

Pinky

A Day No Pigs Would Die
Robert Newton Peck

Robert Peck's pig. He receives Pinky as a gift for helping **Benjamin Tanner**'s cow, **Apron**, give birth. Robert pictures Pinky as a brood sow, but Pinky's barrenness means that she will eventually have to be killed so that the Pecks will be able to eat. With **Haven Peck** gone and no pigs from Pinky, Robert will have to give up school and resign himself to the life of a farmer in order to pay off the debt that the Pecks owe on their land.

Rocky Pioggi

The Iceman Cometh
Eugene O'Neill

The night bartender at **Harry Hope**'s saloon. He is in his late twenties, tough, sentimental, and good-natured. He refuses to admit to himself that he is a pimp.

Pious woman

The Power and the Glory
Graham Greene

A person **the Priest** meets during his night in jail. The pious woman is too proud of herself and her convictions to be truly pious. She looks down on the priest for having sympathy for the other prisoners in the cell.

Pip

Moby-Dick
Herman Melville

A young boy who fills the role of a cabin boy or jester on the *Pequod*. Pip goes insane after being left to drift alone in the sea for some time, a punishment handed to him by **Starbuck**. He dies with everyone else in the chase and battle with Moby Dick.

Pip

Great Expectations
Charles Dickens

The protagonist and narrator of the novel. In the beginning of the book, Pip is a young orphan raised by his sister and brother-in-law in the marsh country of Kent. He is passionate, romantic, and somewhat unrealistic. Pip also has a powerful conscience and real commitment to improving himself, both morally and socially.

Pipkin

Watership Down
Richard Adams

The smallest of the rabbits. Pipkin is **Fiver**'s friend and is fiercely loyal to **Hazel**. Hazel can often count on Pipkin to follow him without questioning or hesitating.

M. Pirard

The Red and the Black
Stendhal

The director of the seminary at Besançon and **Julien Sorel**'s protector. At first, M. Pirard intimidates Sorel, but soon Pirard realizes how intelligent Sorel is and takes him under his wing. Pirard defends Sorel from the attacks of the priests in the seminary, and eventually promotes Sorel to tutor. Pirard shuns politics, but the Church has become so corrupt that he resigns. He is a powerful figure in Sorel's life, eventually introducing Sorel to the **Marquis de la Mole**, who brings Sorel into Parisian society.

The pirate

Tortilla Flat
John Steinbeck

A somewhat slow-witted *paisano* who becomes an odd addition to **Danny**'s group. Danny and his friends grow to like the pirate, however, and one day he turns over to them the stash of money he has been saving.

Pirithous

The Two Noble Kinsmen
William Shakespeare

Theseus's close friend. Together, Pirithous and Theseus have gone on many heroic quests.

Pisanio

Cymbeline
William Shakespeare

Posthumus's loyal servant. When Pisanio's master goes into exile, Pisanio is left behind in Britain and acts as a servant to **Imogen** and the **Queen**.

Pistol

The Merry Wives of Windsor
William Shakespeare

One of **Sir John Falstaff**'s men. Pistol wants to stay honest and refuses to deliver Falstaff's seductive letter to **Mistress Margaret Page**. He and **Nim** decide to let the husbands know about Falstaff's scheme.

Pistol

Henry IV, Part II and *Henry V*
William Shakespeare

Friend of **Sir John Falstaff** and husband of **Mistress Quickly**. A braggart and "swaggerer," he joins the Eastcheap crowd in *King Henry IV, Part II*: he gets into a fight with **Doll Tearsheet** at the tavern before being driven out by Falstaff and **Bardolph**. In *King Henry V*, he almost comes to blows with **Nym** over the affections of Quickly before going off to war in France. He pleads to **Captain Fluellen** to pardon Bardolph, who has been arrested for stealing. When Fluellen refuses, the two share an enmity that lasts through the end of the play.

Pistorius

Demian
Hermann Hesse

An organist at a church in the town of **Emil Sinclair**'s boarding school, and a foil for **Max Demian**—he is Sinclair's mentor during a period of time when Demian is absent from his life. Sinclair stalks him, secretly listening to him play music. They eventually meet when Sinclair follows him to a bar. He teaches Sinclair a lot about **Abraxas**.

Piter

Dune
Frank Herbert

Baron Vladimir Harkonnen's counselor. As a Mentat, Piter is trained to think logically, rationally, and mathematically to be the perfect adviser. He is ambitious and scheming.

Prudencia Pitre

Love in the Time of Cholera
Gabriel García Márquez

Twice widowed, one of many of **Florentino Ariza**'s lovers. Intuitive and direct, she comforts Florentino after **Fermina Daza** rejects him for a second time.

Hannah Pitt

Angels in America
Tony Kushner

Joe Pitt's mother. Hannah moves from Salt Lake City to New York after Joe confesses his homosexuality in a late-night phone call. Hannah tends sternly to **Harper Pitt** but blossoms after she encounters **Prior Walter**, becoming his companion and friend. Her chilly demeanor is melted by Prior and by a remarkable sexual encounter with the **Angel**.

Harper Pitt

Angels in America
Tony Kushner

Joe Pitt's wife. She is a Valium-addicted agoraphobe trapped in a failing marriage who hallucinates and invents imaginary characters to escape her troubles. Through a dream encounter with Prior, she learns that her husband is gay and begins to take control of her own destiny.

Joe Pitt

Angels in America
Tony Kushner

A Mormon, Republican lawyer at the appeals court, husband of **Harper Pitt**, son of **Hannah Pitt**. Joe grapples with his latent homosexuality and eventually leaves Harper for **Louis Ironson**, who in turn leaves him. Louis is at first drawn to Joe's ideology but ultimately turns on him because he is a conservative and an intimate of the hated **Roy Cohn**. His initial naiveté is challenged by Roy's unethical behavior and his painful love affair.

King Pittheus

The King Must Die
Mary Renault

Theseus's grandfather and king of Troizen. A good judge of character, Pittheus believes Theseus will make a good ruler.

Joe Pittman

The Autobiography of Miss Jane Pittman
Ernest J. Gaines

Miss Jane Pittman's husband. His toughness gave him the courage to leave **Colonel Dye**'s plantation after finding another job.

Miss Jane Pittman

The Autobiography of Miss Jane Pittman
Ernest J. Gaines

The protagonist of the novel. She is a spunky woman who has always stood up for herself. From the very beginning of the novel to the very end, Jane attempts to make herself as emotionally and physically free as possible. She is a physically strong woman who becomes a community leader because of her strength, insight, and character.

Sandy Pittman

Into Thin Air
Jon Krakauer

An NBC employee who is along on the expedition to dispatch media files. This is her third attempt to climb Everest, and she was at one time in contention to be the first woman to successfully climb the highest mountain in each of the seven continents. **Lopsang Jangbu Sherpa** virtually drags her up the mountain at one point, but she reaches the top.

Mr. Pivart

The Mill on the Floss
George Eliot

A man who lives down the Floss from the Tullivers. He begins a dispute with **Jeremy Tulliver** over the river water.

Planchet

The Three Musketeers
Alexandre Dumas

D'Artagnan's manservant. Planchet goes along for the journey with d'Artagnan to his appointment for a tryst with **Madame Bonacieux**, and is then sent away before the two actually meet. Planchet also takes **Aramis**'s letter to **Lord de Winter**, warning him of the **Lady de Winter**'s plans on his life and her criminal history. While **Athos**, Aramis, **Porthos**, d'Artagnan, and the Lord de Winter attend Madame Bonacieux's funeral, Athos sends **Bazin**, Planchet, **Grimaud**, and **Mousqueton** to Armentieres to scout the Lady's exact location.

The plantation owner

Moll Flanders
Daniel Defoe

A man who marries **Moll** under the delusion that she has a great fortune. Together they move to Virginia, where he has his plantations. There, Moll learns that he is actually her half-brother, and she leaves him to return to England.

Ezekiel Platt

My Brother Sam Is Dead
Christopher & James Lincoln Collier

Sam Meeker and **Tim Meeker**'s cousin in New Salem. Ezekiel's family hosts Tim and **Eliphalet Meeker** when they travel to Verplancks Point.

Mr. Platt

My Brother Sam Is Dead
Christopher & James Lincoln Collier

Tim Meeker and **Sam Meeker**'s uncle in New Salem.

The Plowman

The Canterbury Tales
Geoffrey Chaucer

The Parson's brother. A member of the peasant class, he pays his tithes to the Church and leads a good Christian life.

Plum

Sula
Toni Morrison

Eva Peace's youngest and best-loved child, born **Ralph Peace**. Plum fights in World War I, returning home with troubling memories and a heroin addiction. He wants to reenter Eva's womb. One night, Eva enters his bedroom to rock him in her arms. Afterward, she pours kerosene over him and burns him to death.

Sir Plume

The Rape of the Lock
Alexander Pope

Thalestris's "beau," who ineffectually challenges **the Baron**.

Pluto

Greek Mythology
Unknown

The Roman name for the Greek god **Hades**.

Ned Plymdale

Middlemarch
George Eliot

A young man who unsuccessfully courts **Rosamond Vincy**.

Selina Plymdale

Middlemarch
George Eliot

A good friend of **Harriet Bulstrode**'s, and **Ned Plymdale**'s mother.

Dr. Pavin Pnin

Pnin
Vladimir Nabokov

Timofey Pnin's father. Dr. Pnin, a St. Petersburg ophthalmologist, once treated Leo Tolstoy. He is pleased by his son's successful academic career.

Timofey Pnin

Pnin
Vladimir Nabokov

The hero of the novel. A bundle of eccentricities, Pnin moves to America and learns to speak broken English. Never far from Pnin's mind is his deep love for his former wife, **Liza Pnin Wind**, who has left him and several successive husbands. While many of Pnin's academic colleagues are petty and sinister, Pnin retains his warm innocence and hope.

Herbert Pocket

Great Expectations
Charles Dickens

Pip's best friend after Pip becomes a gentleman. He is the son of **Matthew Pocket**, **Miss Havisham**'s cousin, and he hopes to become a merchant so that he can afford to marry **Clara Barley**. Pip first meets Herbert Pocket in the garden of Satis House, when, as a pale young gentleman, Herbert challenges him to a fight. Years later, they meet again in London, and Herbert becomes Pip's key companion.

Poet

Timon of Athens
William Shakespeare

One of **Timon**'s hangers-on, who receives money from Timon for his art. When Timon goes bankrupt and retires to the wilderness, **the Painter** and the Poet follow Timon into the wilderness once they hear that he has found gold there.

Poet

The House of the Spirits
Isabel Allende

A friend of **Clara**'s. Never given a more specific name, the Poet is a frequent visitor to the big house on the corner, where **Esteban Trueba** and Clara live with their family. When the Poet dies, there is a public outpouring of grief, but that feeling and event are immediately quashed by **Esteban Garcia**'s fascist regime.

Edward Poins

Henry IV, Part I and *Henry IV, Part II*
William Shakespeare

A criminal and highwayman, friend to **Sir John Falstaff** and Prince Harry (the future **Henry V**). Along with **Bardolph** and **Peto**, Poins drinks with Falstaff and Hal in the Boar's Head Tavern in Eastcheap, accompanies them in highway robbery, and goes with them to war. Poins's greatest moment comes when he convinces Hal to double-cross Falstaff at the robbery of Gad's Hill; they dress up like bandits and steal the money that Falstaff and his cronies had themselves just stolen. The shrewdest of the Falstaffian followers, Poins becomes something of a confidant to Hal, who uses Poins as a sounding board for his inner struggle in *King Henry IV, Part II*. Hal and Poins disguise themselves and go to the tavern to spy on Falstaff.

Hercule Poirot

Murder on the Orient Express
Agatha Christie

A retired Belgian police officer. Poirot is Christie's most famous detective.

Poland

The Bluest Eye
Toni Morrison

One of the three local whores, along with **the Maginot Line**, also known as **Miss Marie**, and **China**. They live above the Breedlove apartment and befriend **Pecola Breedlove**.

Polina Andreyevna

The Seagull
Anton Chekhov

The mother of **Masha** and the wife of **Shamrayev**, who manages **Sorin**'s estate. Unhappy in her loveless marriage, she is often embarrassed by Shamrayev's arguments with **Arkadina**, their employer's famous sister. She loves **Dorn** but is unsatisfied by his aloof affection for her. Polina Andreyevna sees her own misery in her daughter Masha's unrequited love for **Treplyov**.

Polixenes

The Winter's Tale
William Shakespeare

The king of Bohemia and boyhood friend of **Leontes**, King of Sicilia. He is falsely accused of having an affair with Leontes's wife, **Hermione**, and barely escapes Sicilia with his life. Much later in life, he sees his only son, **Florizel**, fall in love with **Perdita**, whom he believes a lowly shepherd's daughter but who is, in fact, Leontes's daughter.

Guy Pollock

Main Street
Sinclair Lewis

An intelligent, middle-aged bachelor lawyer who befriends **Carol**. Although Carol admires Guy briefly, she discovers, to her disappointment, that he maintains a defeatist attitude and feels content doing nothing important with his life.

Polly

Dubliners
James Joyce

Mrs. Mooney's daughter. Polly has an affair with **Mr. Doran**.

Polly

Girl, Interrupted
Susanna Kaysen

A disfigured patient. Before entering McLean, Polly poured gasoline over her face and upper body and set herself on fire. Polly appears to be at peace for her first year at the hospital. When she realizes the extent of her injuries, she is inconsolable. **Susanna Kaysen** notes that while everyone at McLean is ill, Polly is the only patient trapped forever by the consequences of her illness.

Aunt Polly

The Adventures of Tom Sawyer and *The Adventures of Huckleberry Finn*
Mark Twain

Tom Sawyer's aunt and guardian, **Sally Phelps**'s sister. In *The Adventures of Tom Sawyer*, Aunt Polly is introduced as a simple, kindhearted woman who struggles to balance her love for her nephew with her duty to discipline him. She generally fails in her attempts to keep Tom under control because, although she worries about Tom's safety, she seems to fear constraining him too much. Above all, Aunt Polly wants to be appreciated and loved. She has a sense of when Tom is trying to deceive her. When Tom breaks Aunt Polly's heart by doing something wrong, she explains to him that the burden of her heavy sorrow is a punishment in itself. In *The Adventures of Huckleberry Finn*, Aunt Polly appears at the end of the novel and properly identifies **Huckleberry Finn**, who has pretended to be Tom, and Tom, who has pretended to be his own younger brother, **Sid**.

Polonius

Hamlet
William Shakespeare

The Lord Chamberlain of **Claudius**'s court, and the father of **Laertes** and **Ophelia**. Polonius is a pompous, conniving old man who gives long-winded advice and repeatedly tries to decipher Hamlet's odd behavior. When Polonius eavesdrops on Hamlet behind an arras in **Queen Gertrude**'s chamber, Hamlet stabs him to death, mistaking him for Claudius. Hamlet then hides Polonius's body.

Polydamas

The Iliad
Homer

A young Trojan commander. Polydamas is calm and prudent. He gives the Trojans sound advice, but **Hector** seldom acts on it.

Polynices

Oedipus trilogy (Oedipus Rex, Oedipus at Colonus, Antigone)
Sophocles

Oedipus's son and brother, who arrives at Colonus seeking his father's blessing in his battle with his brother for control of Thebes.

Polyphemus

The Odyssey
Homer

Poseidon's son, one of the Cyclops, a race of uncivilized, one-eyed giants. Polyphemus imprisons **Odysseus** and his crew and tries to eat them, but Odysseus blinds him through a clever ruse and manages to escape. In later myths, Polyphemus becomes a pitiful character who recovers his sight, only to chase after the cruel, mocking nymph **Galatea**. Polyphemus is also a figure in Greek mythology.

Pompey

Antony and Cleopatra
William Shakespeare

The son of a great general who was one of **Julius Caesar**'s partners in power. Pompey is young and popular with the Roman people, and he possesses enough military might to stand as a legitimate threat to the triumvirs **Octavius Caesar**, **Antony**, and **Lepidus**. He fancies himself honorable for refusing to allow his man **Menas** to kill the unsuspecting triumvirs.

Pompey

Measure for Measure
William Shakespeare

A clown who works for **Mistress Overdone**.

Johnny Pom-Pom

Tortilla Flat
John Steinbeck

A man who, though not a member of **Danny**'s inner circle of friends, helps the group in many parts of the novel. Johnny Pom-Pom is just another paisano trying to scrape his way through life and helping his friends when he can.

Edna Pontellier

The Awakening
Kate Chopin

The Awakening's protagonist. The respectable young wife of a New Orleans businessman, **Léonce Pontellier**, Edna Pontellier finds herself dissatisfied with her marriage into Creole aristocracy and her limited lifestyle. In a series of awakenings over the course of the novella, she emerges from her semiconscious existence as a devoted wife and mother, discovering her own identity and acting on her desires for emotional and sexual satisfaction. Her desires awakened, Edna's urges for music, sexual satisfaction, art, and freedom can no longer be hidden.

Etienne and Raoul Pontellier

The Awakening
Kate Chopin

Léonce Pontellier's and **Edna Pontellier**'s sons. Edna neglects her children in order to pursue her newfound autonomy, sending them away to their grandmother for much of the novella.

Léonce Pontellier

The Awakening
Kate Chopin

Edna Pontellier's husband, a wealthy New Orleans businessman and a Creole aristocrat. Léonce Pontellier is often away on business and spends little time with his family. Léonce is kind and loving but aloof. When he worries about Edna's strange actions and newfound freedoms, he calls **Doctor Mandelet** in to observe Edna at a dinner party.

Colonel Georges Pontmercy

Les Misérables
Victor Hugo

An officer in Napoléon's army and **Marius Pontmercy**'s father. Pontmercy is severely wounded at the Battle of Waterloo, and mistakenly believing that Thénardier has saved his life, he asks that Marius honor this debt.

Marius Pontmercy

Les Misérables
Victor Hugo

The son of **Georges Pontmercy**, a colonel in Napoléon's army. Marius has grown up under the care of his ninety-year-old maternal grandfather, **Monsieur Gillenormand**, a staunch supporter of the monarchy. Shortly after Marius turns eighteen, Gillenormand tells him that Marius's father is ill. Marius rides out to Vernon the following morning but arrives a few minutes after his father dies. Since Marius has always believed that his father did not love him, he finds his death difficult to grieve. Marius devours history books and bulletins about his father's exploits in Napoléon's army and comes to admire the dead Pontmercy. To the chagrin of his grandfather, Marius also becomes a passionate follower of Napoléon. Gillenormand learns of Marius's new political views, and the two get into a heated argument. Marius moves out, refusing any help or money from his family. Marius manages both to fight on the barricades and successfully court the love of his life, **Cosette**.

Ponzo

On the Road
Jack Kerouac

Terry and **Rickey**'s friend; a smelly seller of manure. Big and eager to please, Ponzo is in love with Terry.

Frank Poole

2001: A Space Odyssey
Arthur C. Clarke

Along with **David Bowman**, one of two astronauts awake for the entire journey to Saturn. Poole is mechanically skilled and is the one who makes extra-vehicular trips, one of which ultimately results in his death.

Grace Poole

Jane Eyre
Charlotte Brontë

Bertha Mason's keeper at Thornfield. Grace's drunken carelessness frequently allows Bertha to escape.

Grace Poole

Wide Sargasso Sea
Jean Rhys

A woman who answers an advertisement placed by **Mrs. Eff** for a servant to look after the deranged **Antoinette**. Grace is promised twice as much as the other household servants as long as she keeps her mouth shut and guards Antoinette well. Sharing Antoinette's garret, Grace drinks frequently, often falling asleep with the garret key in plain view of her prisoner.

Mr. Poole

Dr. Jekyll and Mr. Hyde
Robert Louis Stevenson

Dr. Henry Jekyll's butler. Mr. Poole is a loyal servant, having worked for the doctor for twenty years. When he is concerned that something has happened to Jekyll, he seeks help from **Mr. Gabriel John Utterson**.

Joseph Poorgrass

Far from the Madding Crowd
Thomas Hardy

A shy, timid farm laborer on **Bathsheba Everdene**'s farm in Weatherbury. Joseph Poorgrass is supposed to carry **Fanny Robin**'s coffin from Casterbridge back to Weatherbury, but takes a break along the way to have a drink at Buck's Head. His delay causes **Gabriel Oak** to have to come get the body, postponing the funeral. As a result, Bathsheba discovers Fanny and **Sergeant Francis Troy**'s baby in the coffin with Fanny.

Pope

Doctor Faustus
Christopher Marlowe

The head of the Roman Catholic Church and a powerful political figure in **Faustus**'s Europe.

Popé

Brave New World
Aldous Huxley

Savage on the New Mexico Savage Reservation. Popé was **Linda**'s lover, and he gave her a copy of *The Complete Works of Shakespeare*. As a result, Shakespeare became the centerpiece of **John**'s education and view of society.

Mr. Pope

Orlando
Virginia Woolf

An eighteenth-century poet famous for his polemical satires and mock-epics, "The Dunciad" and "The Rape of the Lock." In the novel, **Orlando** places Pope on a pedestal when she meets him at a gathering of "brilliant" people, but Orlando soon learns that the famous writer is a regular person, driven by petty jealousies, praise, and ego.

Popo

The Joy Luck Club
Amy Tan

An-mei's maternal grandmother. When **An-mei's mother** married **Wu Tsing** and became a third concubine, Popo disowned her. When Popo fell terminally ill, An-mei returned and, following superstitious healing methods, sliced off a piece of her flesh to put in a broth for Popo.

Edna Poppy

The Bean Trees
Barbara Kingsolver

The blind woman who lives with **Mrs. Virgie Parsons**. She is much warmer than her roommate. **Taylor** does not realize that Edna is blind throughout the novel.

Porfiry Petrovich

Crime and Punishment
Fyodor Dostoevsky

The magistrate in charge of investigating the murders of **Lizaveta Ivanovna** and her sister **Alyona Ivanovna**. Porfiry Petrovich has a shrewd understanding of criminal psychology and is exquisitely aware of **Rodion Romanovich Raskolnikov**'s mental state at every step along the way from the crime to the confession.

Pork

Gone with the Wind
Margaret Mitchell

Gerald O'Hara's first slave. Pork is loyal and devoted to the O'Haras.

Big Joe Portagee

Tortilla Flat
John Steinbeck

One of **Danny**'s *paisanos*. Large, slow-witted, lazy, and weak-willed, Big Joe has to be pushed to do good things, but he is a force to be reckoned with once he finally gets motivated. Big Joe often causes trouble by accident, not meaning harm but simply forgetting what he originally was told to do.

Porter

Macbeth
William Shakespeare

The drunken doorman of **Macbeth**'s castle.

Ed Porter

When the Legends Die
Hal Borland

A supporter of **Thomas Black Bull**, Ed runs the cobbler's shop at the school. He notices Tom's skill at basketmaking.

Henry Porter

Song of Solomon
Toni Morrison

First Corinthians Dead's lover and a member, along with **Guitar Bains**, of the Seven Days vigilante group, which murders white people. Porter is a yardman. When **Macon, Jr.** finds out that First Corinthians is dating Henry, he evicts Henry unfairly. In the end, First Corinthians moves into a small house with Henry on the South Side of Chicago.

Porthos

The Three Musketeers
Alexandre Dumas

The third of the Three Musketeers, along with **Athos** and **Aramis**. Porthos is loud, brash, and self-important. He is extremely vain, but a valiant fighter and a courageous friend. His mistress is **Madame de Coquenard**, the wife of a wealthy attorney.

Portia

Julius Caesar
William Shakespeare

Brutus's wife; the daughter of a noble Roman who took sides against **Julius Caesar**. Portia, accustomed to being Brutus's confidante, is upset to find him reluctant to speak his mind when she finds him troubled. Brutus later hears that Portia has killed herself out of grief that **Antony** and **Octavius** have become so powerful.

Portia

The Merchant of Venice
William Shakespeare

A wealthy heiress from Belmont. Portia's beauty is matched only by her intelligence. Bound by a clause in her father's will that forces her to marry whichever suitor chooses correctly from among three chests, Portia is nonetheless able to marry her true love, **Bassanio**. Portia, in the disguise of a young law clerk, saves **Antonio** from **Shylock**.

Portia

The Heart Is a Lonely Hunter
Carson McCullers

Dr. Benedict Mady Copeland's daughter. She works as a servant in **Mick Kelly**'s household. Portia is loving and faithful, and she values her relationships with her family highly. She always tries to include her father in family gatherings, even though he is estranged from much of the family.

Portuguese captain

Robinson Crusoe
Daniel Defoe

A sea captain. **The Portuguese captain** picks up Crusoe and the slave boy **Xury** from their boat after they escape from their Moorish captors. He is polite, personable, and extremely generous to Crusoe.

Poseidon

The Iliad and *The Odyssey*
Homer

Zeus's brother and second to him in power. Poseidon is god of the seas and patron of the seafaring Phaeacians. His rage causes earthquakes and much other damage. Poseidon supports the Greeks in the war against the Trojans, but after **Odysseus** blinds his son, the Cyclops **Polyphemus**, Poseidon punishes Odysseus by complicating his journey home. In the *Aeneid* and other Roman texts, Poseidon is known as **Neptune**. Poseidon also appears in Greek mythology.

Poseidon

The King Must Die
Mary Renault

The god of the sea. **Theseus** is convinced that Poseidon is his father.

Amy and Isaac Post

Incidents in the Life of a Slave Girl
Harriet Ann Jacobs

Abolitionist antislavery friends of **Linda Brent**'s in Rochester. They appear in the book under their real names. They show Linda that it is possible for white people to treat her as an equal.

Posthumus

Cymbeline
William Shakespeare

An orphaned gentleman adopted and raised by **Cymbeline**. He marries **Imogen** in secret. Although Posthumus is deeply in love with Imogen, he is nevertheless willing to think the worst of her when she is accused of infidelity.

Harry Potter

The Harry Potter Series: Books 1–4
J. K. Rowling

A powerful young wizard. As an infant, Harry's parents were brutally slain by the evil wizard **Lord Voldemort**, who also tried to murder Harry. Though Voldemort was nearly destroyed by his attempt on Harry's life, Harry survived with only a scar in the shape of a lightning bolt on his forehead. Harry is closely connected to his archnemesis and has become famous in the wizard community for surviving the attack. Soon after, Harry was left on the doorstep of his Muggle, or non-magical, relatives the Dursleys. Harry grows up enduring the abuse of his adopted family and suppressing his latent magical powers until he is rescued as an adolescent and spirited away to Hogwarts School of Witchcraft and Wizardry, a boarding school for young wizards. In *Harry Potter and the Sorcerer's Stone*, Harry befriends the disciplined and spirited **Hermione Granger** and the downtrodden **Ron Weasley**. He adapts to life in the house of Gryffindor, adjusts to his notoriety in the wizarding community, becomes enemies with the imperious **Draco Malfoy**, and discovers his prodigious skill at Quidditch, a popular wizard sport. He also finds himself in the midst of a plot by the weakened Voldemort to recover the magical Sorcerer's Stone, which Harry thwarts with the aid of his friends. In *Harry Potter and the Chamber of Secrets*, Harry returns to Hogwarts only to discover that the mysterious Chamber of Secrets has been opened. Students and staff members alike are found transformed into stone, and Harry soon discovers that a basilisk roams the halls of Hogwarts at the bidding of Voldemort, who has used young **Ginny Weasley** as a vessel through which he commits magical crimes. In *Harry Potter and the Prisoner of Azkaban*, the accused murderer **Sirius Black**, who was implicated in the death of Harry's parents, has escaped from the wizard prison Azkaban and has set his sights on Hogwarts and Harry. Ultimately, Harry discovers the truth. His godfather Sirius was falsely accused and **Peter Pettigrew**, a servant of Voldemort's posing as Ron's pet rat, is the true killer. In *Harry Potter and the Goblet of Fire*, Harry participates in the Triwizard Tournament, discovers his latent feelings for his fellow student **Cho Chang**, quarrels with the invasive gossip columnist **Rita Skeeter**, and finally battles and defeats a newly powerful Voldemort, who kills his friend **Cedric Diggory** during their standoff.

James Potter

The Harry Potter Series: Books 3 and 4
J. K. Rowling

Harry Potter's father, killed by **Voldemort**. He and **Lily Potter** return as ghosts to protect Harry from Voldemort. Harry also learns more about his father from **Sirius Black**, who reveals Harry's similarities to his parents with bittersweet fondness.

Lily Potter

The Harry Potter Series: Books 3 and 4
J. K. Rowling

Harry Potter's mother, who sacrificed herself to save Harry from **Voldemort**. She and **James Potter** return as ghosts to protect Harry from Voldemort.

Muff Potter

The Adventures of Tom Sawyer
Mark Twain

A hapless drunk and friend of **Injun Joe**'s. Muff Potter is kind and grateful toward **Tom Sawyer** and **Huckleberry Finn**, who bring him presents after he is wrongly jailed for **Dr. Robinson**'s murder. Huck and Tom witness the murder of Dr. Robinson and know that Joe is framing Potter for Robinson's death. Potter's naïve trust eventually pushes Tom's conscience to the breaking point, compelling Tom to tell the truth at Potter's trial about who actually committed the murder, even though Tom is terrified that Injun Joe will kill him.

Yvette Pottier

Mother Courage
Bertolt Brecht

A camp prostitute, Yvette is the only character who will make her fortune through the war, marrying and inheriting the estate of a lecherous old colonel. Yvette returns obese and grotesque after her years of marriage.

Hezekiah Potts

Their Eyes Were Watching God
Zora Neale Hurston

The delivery boy and assistant shopkeeper at **Jody Starks**'s store. After Jody's death, Hezekiah begins to mimic Jody's affectations. **Janie Mae Crawford** is only amused by the mimicry, not threatened.

Mr. Poulter

The Mill on the Floss
George Eliot

A man hired by **Mr. Stelling** to give **Tom Tulliver** exercise. Mr. Poulter drinks and talks about the war in which he fought.

Jotham Powell

Ethan Frome
Edith Wharton

The hired man on the Frome farm. Powell's main duty is helping **Ethan Frome** cut, load, and haul lumber. Markedly reticent, Powell is sensitive to the tensions between the Fromes but loath to involve himself in them.

Jack Power

Dubliners and *Ulysses*
James Joyce

A Dubliner friendly with **Tom Kernan**, **Simon Dedalus**, **Martin Cunningham**, and others. He rescues Kernan from his accident in *Dubliners*' "Grace." For all his reforming efforts, Mr. Power's dedication to Kernan appears shallow, for he is too acutely aware of Kernan's dwindling social status in comparison to his own success. In *Ulysses*, he is not very nice to **Leopold Bloom**.

Colonel Powys

The Good Soldier
Ford Madox Ford

The father of **Leonora Powys Ashburnham**. Colonel Powys is a retired Army officer living in Ireland with his wife and seven daughters. He helped arrange the marriage between Leonora and **Captain Edward Ashburnham**. He values saving money and managing it strictly, and he passed these financial tendencies down to his daughter.

Pozzo

Waiting for Godot
Samuel Beckett

Lucky's master. He and Lucky help **Vladimir** and **Estragon** pass the time in both acts. In Act I, Pozzo is on his way to sell Lucky at the fair. In Act II, Pozzo is blind and does not remember the events of the previous act.

Ernie Prang

Harry Potter and the Prisoner of Azkaban
J. K. Rowling

The driver of the Knight Bus. The conversation between Ernie and **Stan Shunpike** during the bus ride reaffirms Harry's fame among wizards.

Praskovia

Pnin
Vladimir Nabokov

The "sturdy sixty-year-old woman" who runs The Pines. Praskovia ensures that the guests are fed and provided with clean sheets. She has volcanic energy and dresses in baggy homemade shorts, a matronly blouse, and rhinestones.

Jeannine Pratt

Ordinary People
Judith Guest

A new student at Lake Forest. Jeannine Pratt is in the school choir with **Conrad Jarrett**. She and Conrad become close friends and begin to date seriously, forming a deep emotional and sexual relationship by the end of the novel.

Mrs. Pratt

Lolita
Vladimir Nabokov

The headmistress of the Beardsley School for Girls. **Humbert Humbert** is unimpressed with her school's emphasis on social skills and her resistance to traditional academic approaches.

Mrs. Rachel Pratt

Pudd'nhead Wilson
Mark Twain

Judge Driscoll's widowed sister and **Valet de Chambre**'s, or "Tom"'s surrogate mother. Mrs. Rachel Pratt helps to keep "Tom" in the judge's good graces, since "Tom" gambles away all of the judge's money and goes to St. Louis to be a ne'er-do-well.

Preacher

When the Legends Die
Hal Borland

Baptizes **Thomas Black Bull**. He later feels responsible for his development.

Sister Helen Prejean

Dead Man Walking
Helen Prejean

The author and narrator, a Catholic nun who grew up in a loving, affluent household. She realizes that in order to live up to her faith and ideals, she must shoulder the struggles of the poor as if they are her own, and so becomes a social activist in 1981. Her work with the poor eventually leads her to the criminal justice system, where she becomes a spiritual advisor to two death row inmates, first **Patrick Sonnier** and then **Robert Willie**. After witnessing the executions, Prejean dedicates her life to abolishing the death penalty and other abuses of the American judicial system. After witnessing Willie's execution, Prejean reaches out to support the victims' families, just as she supports the men on death row.

Aleksii Antedilluvianovich Prelapsarianov

Angels in America
Tony Kushner

The World's Oldest Living Bolshevik, who delivers the tirade that marks the beginning of *Perestroika*. Prelapsarianov criticizes the pettiness of modern American life, the pointless quality of life in the absence of a governing theory.

Preston

Dicey's Song
Cynthia Voigt

The nurse at **Momma**'s mental hospital. Preston is strong, warm, and compassionate. She speaks gently to **Dicey** and **Gram** and suggests they cremate Momma to bring her home with them more easily.

Willard Pretty Dog

A Yellow Raft in Blue Water
Michael Dorris

Lee's father and **Ida**'s lover. Ida had had a crush on him from her youth. When Willard comes back from World War II horribly scarred, he begins an affair with Ida thanks to matchmaking by **Father Hurlburt**. After his looks are restored through reconstructive surgery, Willard is willing to stay with Ida out of duty, but when Ida realizes this, she sends him home.

Billy Pretty

The Shipping News
E. Annie Proulx

A man who covers the home stories for *The Gammy Bird*. He is firmly against the all-powerful oil industry and yearns for the good old days of local fishermen and abundant natural resources.

Prévan

Dangerous Liaisons
Pierre-Ambroise-François Choderlos de Laclos

A boastful army officer. One night at a dinner party, Prévan brags within **the Vicomte de Valmont**'s earshot that Prévan can seduce **the Marquise de Merteuil**. Valmont informs Merteuil, and she sets about a plan to ruin Prévan. Through an elaborate scheme involving her servants, Merteuil successfully accuses Prévan of a rape that he did not commit. He is shamed and thrown out of his position in the army. When Merteuil is ruined and revealed as a very sinister woman, Prévan is cleared of all wrongdoing and given back his position in the army.

Priam

The Iliad
Homer

The king of Troy, husband of **Hecuba**, and father of fifty Trojan warriors, including **Hector** and **Paris**. Though too old to fight, Priam is level-headed, wise, and benevolent. He treats **Helen** kindly, though he laments the war that her beauty has sparked. Priam is slain before **Aeneas**'s eyes as the Greeks sack Troy.

Priam

The Aeneid
Virgil

See above.

Priam

Troilus and Cressida
William Shakespeare

The King of Troy, and the father of **Hector**, **Paris**, **Helenus**, **Troilus**, and **Cassandra**, among others.

Adah Price

The Poisonwood Bible
Barbara Kingsolver

Leah Price's twin sister. Adah is born with a condition called "hemiplegia," which prevents her from using the left side of her body. Rather than view herself with pity, Adah places herself in voluntary exile from the world.

Bronterre O'Brien Price

Major Barbara
George Bernard Shaw

A young, unemployed, and opportunistic "poser." Price appears incapable of honesty and altruism.

Fanny Price

Mansfield Park
Jane Austen

The protagonist. The daughter of a drunken sailor and a woman who married beneath her station, Fanny comes to live at Mansfield Park with her wealthy uncle and aunt, **Sir Thomas Bertram** and **Lady Bertram**, who take Fanny in as an act of charity to her parents. Although she is mistreated and constantly reminded of her "place" as a charity ward, Fanny eventually becomes an indispensable member of the family. Modest, always proper, and, as she grows older, quite beautiful, Fanny is secretly in love with her cousin **Edmund Bertram**. Slick **Henry Crawford** proposes to her, to no avail.

Leah Price

The Poisonwood Bible
Barbara Kingsolver

Adah Price's twin sister, an idealistic fourteen-year-old tomboy who worships her father, **Nathan Price**, and believes fully in his God. As she confronts the political and daily realities in the Congo, she loses her religious faith and begins to despise her father. She ends up spending her life working, with her husband **Anatole Ngembe**, to improve the life of the Congolese. She is the mother of **Martin-Lothaire Ngembe**, **Natan Ngembe**, **Pascal Ngembe**, and **Patrice Ngembe**.

Nathan Price

The Poisonwood Bible
Barbara Kingsolver

An overzealous Baptist minister. Nathan is driven by the overwhelming guilt he feels as the only member of his army regimen to escape the Battaan Death March. Certain that God despises him as a coward, he is determined to remain unswerving in the face of all obstacles on his mission to save as many souls as he can.

In the process he imperils the souls, as well as the lives, of his wife, **Orleanna Price**, and his four daughters, **Adah Price**, **Leah Price**, **Rachel Price**, and **Ruth May Price**.

Orleanna Price

The Poisonwood Bible
Barbara Kingsolver

Nathan Price's wife, and mother of **Adah Price**, **Leah Price**, **Rachel Price**, and **Ruth May Price**. Once a carefree, nature-loving, beautiful girl, Orleanna has been beaten down by her husband's dour and fanatical views. Though she fears for her children's safety, she is kept passive by a combination of fear, loyalty, and the belief that God really is on her husband's side. As the danger to her children becomes more tangible, however, Orleanna slowly regains her ability to act on her own, but it takes the death of her youngest daughter to force her to take full control of her own and her daughters' fates.

Rachel Price

The Poisonwood Bible
Barbara Kingsolver

Nathan Price and **Orleanna Price**'s daughter. At the start of the book, Rachel is a materialistic, egotistical, and stupid girl of fifteen. As we watch her age to fifty, little changes in her personality. Her appearance remains her chief concern, and her own well-being is the only force that can motivate her. With her good looks, she catches a string of wealthy husbands, one of whom leaves her a luxury hotel deep in the heart of the French Congo.

Ruth May Price

The Poisonwood Bible
Barbara Kingsolver

Nathan Price and **Orleanna Price**'s daughter. When she is five years old, she enters the Congo with a fierce and adventurous attitude. Without speaking the language she manages to befriend all of the children in the village. After a bad bout with malaria, however, she becomes quiet and spiritless. Obsessively frightened by green mamba snakes, she is ultimately killed by one.

Susan Price

Mansfield Park
Jane Austen

Fanny Price's younger sister. Fanny and Susan get reacquainted when Fanny returns to her family's home. Susan is a smart girl with essentially good manners who is stuck in a terrible home. After Fanny brings Susan back to Mansfield Park, Susan becomes a new favorite of **Sir Thomas Bertram** and **Lady Bertram**.

William Price

Mansfield Park
Jane Austen

Fanny Price's brother. **Sir Thomas Bertram** has gotten William a commission in the Navy, and **Henry Crawford**, when trying to seduce Fanny, gets her brother a promotion. William and Fanny are extremely close, and he impresses everyone as a bright, capable young man.

Fourth priest

Grendel
John Gardner

A young priest. He is overjoyed at the news of **Ork**'s encounter with the Destroyer. The fourth priest has a vision of the universe to which **Beowulf** alludes in his battle with **Grendel**.

Priest

Don Quixote
Miguel de Cervantes

Don Quixote's friend. Tales of chivalry are a guilty pleasure for the priest. He enjoys Don Quixote's madness but tricks him into going home.

Priest

A Farewell to Arms
Ernest Hemingway

A kind young man who provides spiritual guidance to **Frederic Henry** and the few other soldiers interested in it. Often the butt of the officers' jokes, the priest responds with good-natured understanding.

Priest

The Power and the Glory
Graham Greene

The protagonist. He spends the majority of the novel on the run from the police, especially **the Lieutenant**, friendless and homeless and searching for some sense of purpose in his life. His decadent, indulgent life as a parish priest takes place before the novel begins, but it is present in his thoughts as a source of deep humiliation. He meets his daughter, **Brigida**, the product of a secret affair with one of his parishioners, **Maria**, and finds that his love for her makes it impossible for him to repent the sin of conceiving her.

Priest

The Pearl
John Steinbeck

The local village priest. The priest is just as interested in exploiting **Kino**'s wealth as everyone else, hoping that he can find a way to persuade Kino to give him some of the money he will make from the sale of the large pearl he finds.

Primitivo

For Whom the Bell Tolls
Ernest Hemingway

An elderly guerrilla fighter. Despite his gray hair and broken nose, Primitivo has not learned the cynicism needed for survival in the war.

Prince S.

The Idiot
Fyodor Dostoevsky

The good-looking fiancé of **Adelaida Ivanovna Yepanchina**. He later on becomes her husband. Prince S. is hardworking, knowledgeable, and very rich.

Little Prince

The Little Prince
Antoine de Saint-Exupéry

The hero of the story. He leaves his home planet and **the Rose** that he loves, journeying around the universe until he lands on Earth and befriends **the Narrator**. He is insatiably curious; the Narrator often repeats that the Little Prince never stops asking a question until it's been answered. Though the prince is sociable during his travels, he never stops loving and missing the Rose.

Princess of France

Love's Labour's Lost
William Shakespeare

The daughter of the French King, who lies sick in bed. She is sent to the court to demand the return of Aquitaine, a region (fictitiously) under the control of Navarre. When the **King of Navarre** demands payment from France for expenses disbursed by his father during the wars, the Princess claims the her country has already paid it off. The receipts cannot be found, and the Princess—along with her three ladies, **Rosaline**, **Maria**, and **Katherine**—must stay in Navarre, ultimately tempting the lords away from their restrictive oath. When the Princess is informed of her father's death at the end of the play, she tells the King that to win her love, he must live like a hermit for an entire year. The King readily agrees to it, giving *Love's Labour's Lost* an ambiguous ending.

The Principal

Lucky Jim
Kingsley Amis

A powerful figure in the college whom **Jim Dixon** accidentally crosses when he imitates his notably clipped, consonantal accent while giving his drunken lecture on "Merrie England"—the breaking point of his academic career.

Billy Prior

Regeneration
Pat Barker

An initially difficult (and purely fictional) patient of **Dr. W.H.R. Rivers**'s who becomes **Sarah Lumb**'s lover. Prior initially has a bad attitude and suffers from mutism and severe asthma. Though he gives the staff a hard time, he truly wants to get better.

Mr. Prior

Regeneration
Pat Barker

Billy Prior's father. Mr. Prior, unlike his wife, is a rough, working-class man who believes that his son must grow up the hard way. He believes it is presumptuous and wrong for Billy to reach beyond his class and station.

Prioress

The Canterbury Tales
Geoffrey Chaucer

A pilgrim traveling to Canterbury, a modest and quiet head of a convent who aspires to have exquisite taste.

Miss Prism

The Importance of Being Earnest
Oscar Wilde

Cecily Cardew's tutor. Miss Prism lost **Jack Worthing** when he was a baby, accidentally putting him in her handbag instead of in his stroller.

Prison Chaplain

A Clockwork Orange
Anthony Burgess

A kind man. He lets **Alex** choose the music for services after Alex shows an interest in the Bible (for its violent and sexually charged stories). He opposes Alex undergoing Ludovico's Technique, which will prohibit violence through physical illness.

Prissy

Gone with the Wind
Margaret Mitchell

The daughter of **Dilcey**, a slave at Twelve Oaks. Prissy is a foolish, lazy young slave prone to telling lies. The late discovery of Prissy's lie that she knows how to assist at childbirth forces **Scarlett O'Hara** to deliver **Melanie Hamilton Wilkes**'s baby herself.

Rainie and Ruben Pritchard

Where the Red Fern Grows
Wilson Rawls

The two Pritchard brothers. They come from a strange, disliked family. The Pritchard Brothers are beaten often by their family. Rainie and Ruben get **Old Dan**, **Little Ann**, and **Billy Colman** to "tree" a "ghost coon" that lives on the Pritchard land, and then sinisterly bring out their own dog, Old Blue, to get the coon. Old Dan and Little Ann almost kill Old Blue. Then Ruben almost axes Billy's two dogs. However, Billy saves the dogs, and Ruben falls on his own axe, killing himself. Ruben's death is a source of tremendous guilt for Billy.

Elizabeth Proctor

The Crucible
Arthur Miller

John Proctor's wife. Elizabeth Proctor fires **Abigail Williams** when she discovers that her husband, John Proctor, is having an affair with Abigail. Elizabeth is virtuous, but often cold. Abigail seeks to destroy Elizabeth by helping to strengthen the accusation against Elizabeth of witchcraft. Because Elizabeth does not know that John Proctor has confessed to his affair with Abigail in court, Elizabeth lies to the court after his confession. Elizabeth is pregnant when she is sentenced to a hanging, so the court tells John that she will be spared until the baby is born. In the end, however, Elizabeth is not hanged, but her husband is. She eventually remarries a few years after John's execution.

John Proctor

The Crucible
Arthur Miller

A local farmer who lives just outside town. John Proctor is **Elizabeth Proctor**'s husband. A stern, honest, upright, harsh-tongued man, John hates hypocrisy. Nevertheless, he has a hidden sin—his affair with **Abigail Williams**. When the witch hunt begins, he hesitates to expose Abigail as a fraud because he worries that his secret will be revealed and his good name ruined. Once the trials begin, John Proctor realizes that he can stop Abigail's rampage through Salem but only if he confesses to his adultery. His confession succeeds only in leading to his arrest and conviction as a witch. Proctor redeems himself and provides a final denunciation of the witch trials in his final act.

Proculeius

Antony and Cleopatra
William Shakespeare

One of **Octavius Caesar**'s soldiers, who proves untrustworthy.

Prometheus

Prometheus Bound
Aeschylus

The only Titan to side with **Zeus** in his struggle against **Cronus**. He is later punished for giving fire to humans. Zeus devises a cruel torture for Prometheus, chaining him to a rock where every day an eagle comes to pick at his innards, but the Titan never surrenders. Intelligent, rebellious, and loyal, Prometheus is the rare example of a tragic hero whose faults, such as stubbornness and excessive pride, ennoble him. Prometheus also appears in Greek mythology.

Prompter

Six Characters in Search of an Author
Luigi Pirandello

An ever-present member of the Crew who holds the book in the first rehearsal and attempts to record the Characters' drama in shorthand.

Prongs

Harry Potter and the Prisoner of Azkaban
J. K. Rowling

James Potter's animagus name, when he is a stag. An animagus is a wizard that can take animal form.

Prosecutor

The Stranger
Albert Camus

The lawyer who argues against **Meursault** at the murder trial. During his closing arguments, the prosecutor characterizes Meursault as a cool, calculating monster. The prosecutor demands and obtains the death penalty for Meursault, arguing that Meursault's moral indifference threatens all of society and must therefore be stamped out.

Proserpina

Greek Mythology
Unknown

The Roman name for the Greek goddess **Persephone**.

Prospero

The Tempest
William Shakespeare

The play's protagonist, and **Miranda**'s father. Twelve years before the events of the play, Prospero was the duke of Milan. His brother, **Antonio**, in concert with **Alonso**, king of Naples, usurped him, forcing him to flee in a boat with his daughter. Prospero has spent twelve years on the island refining his magic.

Miss Pross

A Tale of Two Cities
Charles Dickens

The servant who raised **Lucie Manette**. Miss Pross is brusque, tough, and fiercely loyal to her mistress.

Prostitute

A Streetcar Named Desire
Tennessee Williams

A woman whom **Blanche DuBois** sees moments before **Stanley Kowalski** rapes her.

Proteus

The Two Gentlemen of Verona
William Shakespeare

Valentine's best friend, **Julia**'s suitor, and one of the title gentlemen of Verona. After being sent to Milan by his father **Antonio**, Proteus falls in love with Valentine's sweetheart **Silvia** and betrays both his former love Julia and his best friend in pursuit of her. He entrusts himself to the **Duke of Milan** by informing him of Valentine and Silvia's plan to elope, and then, with his friend exiled, sets about to woo the forlorn Silvia. He sends Julia, disguised as the page Sebastian, to deliver a ring that Julia had given him to Silvia; he sends **Launce** to present her with his servant's beloved dog, **Crab**; and he attempts to rape Silvia in the woods. While he pursues love at any cost, he is magnanimously forgiven by Valentine, who still cherishes their friendship above all things.

Lucas Prout

Babbitt
Sinclair Lewis

A conservative mattress manufacturer who defeats **Seneca Doane** in Zenith's mayoral race. **Babbitt** campaigns fervently for Prout by making political speeches. In return for his help, Prout awards him with some insider information about future plans for road development in Zenith.

Provost

Measure for Measure
William Shakespeare

The keeper of the prison where **Claudio** is held.

Wavey Prowse

The Shipping News
E. Annie Proulx

The "tall and quiet" woman in **Quoyle**'s life. She is passionately devoted to her son, **Herry**, and just like Quoyle, she is haunted by the memories of a past, abusive lover.

Prudence

Walk Two Moons
Sharon Creech

Phoebe's older sister. Prudence resembles Phoebe in her primness and her self-absorption. She thoughtlessly demands **Mrs. Winterbottom**'s help in her life even while rejecting her advice and love.

Hester Prynne

The Scarlet Letter
Nathaniel Hawthorne

The book's protagonist and the wearer of the titular scarlet letter. The letter, a patch of fabric in the shape of an "A," signifies that Hester is an "adulterer." As a young woman, Hester married an elderly scholar, **Roger Chillingworth**, who sent her ahead to America to live but never followed her. While waiting for him, she had an affair with a Puritan minister named **Reverend Arthur Dimmesdale**, after which she gave birth to **Pearl**. Hester is passionate but also strong—she endures years of shame and scorn. Her alienation puts her in the position to make acute observations about her community, particularly about its treatment of women.

Ivan Petrovich Ptitsyn

The Idiot
Fyodor Dostoevsky

A usurer. Ptitsyn is suitor and later husband to **Varvara Ardalyonovna Ivolgina**.

Murray "The Goose" Pucinski

Legs
William Kennedy

A short, stocky man with an eye patch, he is **Jack**'s strong man. They met in the army when they were both in prison.

Puck

A Midsummer Night's Dream
William Shakespeare

Oberon's assistant and jester. Also known as Robin Goodfellow, Puck is a mischievous sprite who delights in playing pranks on mortals. His antics, both accidental (smearing the love potion on the wrong Athenian lover's eyes) and intentional (transforming **Nick Bottom**'s head into that of an ass), propel the plot. Unlike the folk myth of malevolent fairies, Puck is light-hearted and whimsical.

Uncle Puffs

Midnight's Children
Salman Rushdie

Jamila Singer's agent.

Mr. Pullet

The Mill on the Floss
George Eliot

A gentleman farmer, and **Mrs. Pullet**'s husband. The couple was originally the most wealthy of the Dodson family, until **Mr. Deane** began rising in the business world. Mr. Pullet does not have much to say for himself. He covers for this fact by sucking on peppermints.

Mrs. Pullet

The Mill on the Floss
George Eliot

Elizabeth Tulliver, **Mrs. Guest**, and **Mrs. Deane**'s sister. Elzabeth is closer to her than to her other sisters, and they share a love of fine household goods.

Uncle Pumblechook

Great Expectations
Charles Dickens

Joe Gargery's pompous, arrogant uncle. A merchant obsessed with money, Pumblechook shamelessly takes credit for **Pip**'s rise in social status.

Joseph K. Pumphrey

Babbitt
Sinclair Lewis

One of **Babbitt**'s many friends and associates. Pumphrey is a professor of business English.

Pumpkin

Johnny Tremain
Esther Forbes

A British soldier stationed in Boston. Pumpkin wants to abandon his duties and buy a farm. Because he is poor, he can only achieve his dream in America. **Jonathan Tremain** helps him desert from the army, but Pumpkin is captured and executed.

Ed Punch

The Shipping News
E. Annie Proulx

Editor of the first paper where **Quoyle** is hired. Ed Punch has a habit of continually firing and hiring Quoyle.

Archibald Purdy

Babbitt
Sinclair Lewis

A grocer in Zenith. When Purdy needs to purchase a lot to expand his store, he falls victim to the collusion of **Conrad Lyte** and **Babbitt**, who buy the lot when they hear of Purdy's plans to extract an exorbitant price for it.

Jerry Purdy

Sons and Lovers
D. H. Lawrence

Walter Morel's bosom friend. Walter goes for a walk to Nottingham with Jerry, during which he takes the nap on the ground that eventually causes his illness.

Ida Putiak

Babbitt
Sinclair Lewis

An ignorant, pretty manicurist. **Babbitt** tries to have an affair with Ida, but she rebuffs his romantic overtures after they go on a disastrous dinner date.

Ann Putnam

The Crucible
Arthur Miller

Thomas Putnam's wife. Ann Putnam gave birth to eight children, but only **Ruth Putnam** survived. The other seven died before they were a day old, and Ann is convinced that they were murdered by supernatural means. Ann is one of those responsible for wanting **Tituba** to try to conjure spirits: she wants Tituba to contact her dead babies to ask them who their murderer was. **Elizabeth Proctor** is eventually arrested for the supernatural murders of these babies. **Giles Corey** is convinced that Ann's husband is fueling the witch trials so that he can try to grab for more land.

General Putnam

My Brother Sam Is Dead
Christopher & James Lincoln Collier

The leader of the Rebels staying in Redding. Putnam is a rigid and unemotional man who sentences **Sam Meeker** to death as an example to the rest of the troops.

Ruth Putnam

The Crucible
Arthur Miller

Ann Putnam and **Thomas Putnam**'s lone surviving child out of eight. Like **Betty Parris**, Ruth Putnam falls into a strange stupor after **Reverend Parris** catches Ruth, **Abigail Williams** and other girls dancing in the woods at night with **Tituba**. Ann had sent Ruth to Tituba so that she could find out who murdered her children by having Tituba contact the dead babies.

Thomas Putnam

The Crucible
Arthur Miller

A wealthy, influential citizen of Salem, and husband of **Ann Putnam**. Thomas Putnam uses the witch trials to increase his own wealth by accusing people of witchcraft and then buying up their land.

Dr. Tracy Putnam

Death Be Not Proud
John Gunther

A specialist in tumors. **Dr. Tracy Putnam** originally removes half of **Johnny**'s tumor.

Josie Pye

Anne of Green Gables
L. M. Montgomery

A member of the notorious Pye family. Josie lives up to her family's bad reputation and inspires the dislike of her classmates. **Anne Shirley** tries to cultivate charitable feelings toward Josie but cannot manage to do so.

Pylades

The Libation Bearers
Aeschylus

The silent companion to **Orestes** and the representative of the god **Apollo**. Though omnipresent, Pylades only speaks when Orestes hesitates to kill his mother, **Clytemnestra**. Reminding Orestes of his duties to Apollo, Pylades says it's better to make mortal than divine enemies.

Pylades

Electra
Sophocles

See above.

Pylas

The King Must Die
Mary Renault

The king of Megara's son. He is a superior warrior who becomes a close friend of **Theseus** Pylas's and dies young.

Alice Pyncheon

The House of the Seven Gables
Nathaniel Hawthorne

The daughter of **Gervayse Pyncheon**. When Gervayse tries to get information about the missing Pyncheon deed to Maine land from **Matthew Maule (the younger)**, the younger Maule uses Alice as a medium to contact the spirits of **Colonel Pyncheon**, **Matthew Maule (the elder)**, and **Thomas Maule**. Over the next few years, the younger Matthew uses his power to toy with Alice. One night, after she is summoned by the younger Matthew and trudges through the dark and snow wearing only a light evening gown, she catches pneumonia and dies. Matthew Maule is broken with guilt over his petty antics, which have cost the innocent girl her life.

Clifford Pyncheon

The House of the Seven Gables
Nathaniel Hawthorne

The brother of **Hepzibah Pyncheon**, the relative of **Phoebe Pyncheon** and of **Judge Jaffrey Pyncheon**. Once a beautiful young man, Clifford was broken by the thirty years he spent in prison for allegedly murdering his uncle, **Old Jaffrey Pyncheon**, a crime the Judge committed and framed Clifford for. Clifford returns home more idiot than man, but Hepzibah and Phoebe gradually bring him back to his wits. The Judge threatens to have Clifford committed to a mental asylum unless the two can speak. When Hepzibah returns from not finding Clifford in his empty room, she sees that the Judge has been mysteriously murdered. Clifford is temperamental and brash, and despite his nearly imbecilic state, he still manages to be cruel to his adoring sister, even after three decades of separation.

Colonel Pyncheon

The House of the Seven Gables
Nathaniel Hawthorne

A bastion of the town's Puritan community two centuries before the action of *The House of the Seven Gables* unfolds. Colonel Pyncheon's greed and heartlessness are responsible for the Pyncheon curse. The Colonel accused **Matthew Maule (the elder)** of witchcraft because he coveted the tract of land that the elder Matthew owned. The Colonel then had **Thomas Maule**, the elder Matthew's son, build the house of the seven gables. Before he died, the elder Matthew said that God would have the Pyncheons drink blood, cursing them.

Gervayse Pyncheon

The House of the Seven Gables
Nathaniel Hawthorne

The grandson of **Colonel Pyncheon** and father of **Alice Pyncheon**, who tries to find the deed to the Pyncheon land in Maine. Gervayse believes that the Maule family may know where the missing deeds to the land are, since **Matthew Maule (the younger)** had a father, **Thomas Maule**, who was working on the stolen Pyncheon house when these deeds disappeared. Gervayse's attempts to retrieve the deed eventually end up costing his daughter her life.

The House of the Seven Gables
Nathaniel Hawthorne

Hepzibah Pyncheon

The current occupant of the house of the seven gables. Hepzibah Pyncheon is **Clifford Pyncheon**'s sister, a cousin to **Judge Jaffrey Pyncheon**, and a relative of **Phoebe Pyncheon**'s. Hepzibah is the last in a long line of Pyncheon aristocrats. Hepzibah personifies the pitfalls of this aristocracy, both financially, as evidenced by her having to open and tend a shop, and spiritually, as shown by the permanent scowl on her face. Hepzibah is strongly devoted to Clifford, even though he is absent for thirty years and refuses even to look at her when he returns. By the end of the novel, Clifford comes to trust Hepzibah when they flee from the mysterious death of the Judge in the house of the seven gables. After the Judge's death, Clifford, Hepzibah, Phoebe, **Uncle Venner**, and **Holgrave** move to the Judge's lavish estate out of town.

The House of the Seven Gables
Nathaniel Hawthorne

Judge Jaffrey Pyncheon

The wealthy, popular cousin of **Hepzibah Pyncheon** and **Clifford Pyncheon**, and a relative of **Phoebe Pyncheon**'s. His status as a pillar of the community disguises a dark and greedy nature. Most likely the true culprit in the death of **Old Jaffrey Pyncheon**, the Judge covets the rest of the dead man's missing Maine property. The Judge framed Clifford for the death of Old Jaffrey, and now that Clifford is out of prison after thirty years believes that Clifford knows where the deed to the property is. He continually tries to enter the house of the seven gables, but Hepzibah blocks him. When he finally does, it seems that the curse of the house causes his mysterious death. The Judge's ties to the dubious Pyncheon past are most clearly revealed by his resemblance to **Colonel Pyncheon**'s portrait and by his own death from apoplexy, a sudden hemorrhage, which killed both the Colonel and the Judge's uncle, Old Jaffrey. In the public's perception, the Judge is a model of austerity and morality, and Hawthorne devotes much of the novel to unveiling the dark truths that such popular perceptions hide. After the Judge's death, Phoebe, Hepzibah, **Uncle Venner**, and **Holgrave** move into the Judge's lavish out-of-town estate.

The House of the Seven Gables
Nathaniel Hawthorne

Old Jaffrey Pyncheon

The uncle of **Clifford Pyncheon**, **Hepzibah Pyncheon**, and **Judge Jaffrey Pyncheon**. Old Jaffrey Pyncheon dies of an apoplectic fit after finding young Jaffrey, later the Judge, rummaging through his notes. Young Jaffrey went on to destroy a will that left the Pyncheon property to Clifford. Aware that his uncle's death might arouse suspicion, young Jaffrey arranged the evidence to point toward Clifford, and though he may not have intended for his cousin to be accused of murder, young Jaffrey kept quiet when Clifford was put on trial.

The House of the Seven Gables
Nathaniel Hawthorne

Judge Pyncheon's son

Judge Jaffrey Pyncheon's estranged son, whose death from cholera in Europe leaves the Judge's inheritance to **Clifford Pyncheon**.

Phoebe Pyncheon

The House of the Seven Gables
Nathaniel Hawthorne

A vibrant and beautiful young woman who brings a note of cheer to the gloomy Pyncheon house. Within the novel's morally ambiguous maelstrom, Phoebe emerges as a voice of reason. **Clifford**, **Holgrave**, Phoebe, **Hepzibah**, and **Uncle Venner** all move into **Judge Jaffrey Pyncheon**'s lavish out-of-town estate after his death.

Pyotr Ivanovich

The Death of Ivan Ilych
Leo Tolstoy

Ivan Ilych Golovin's closest friend and fellow judge. Peter serves as a representative of Ivan's social milieu. He tends to view his relationships with people as instrumental to the achievement of his ends, and he goes to great lengths to avoid what is discomforting.

Pyrrhus

The Aeneid
Virgil

Achilles's son, also called Neoptolemus. **Aeneas** briefly recalls Pyrrhus's role murdering **Priam** and his sons during the siege of Troy.

16

VILE VILLAINS

VERY, VERY BAD. DANGEROUS. FREQUENTLY CRAZY.

Cathy Ames	1	*East of Eden*
Big Brother	2	*1984*
Alec D'Urberville	3	*Tess of the D'Urbervilles*
Uriah Heep	4	*David Copperfield*
Iago	5	*Othello*
Injun Joe	6	*The Adventures of Tom Sawyer*
Judas Iscariot	7	*The New Testament*
Morgan le Fay	8	*The Once and Future King*
Simon Legree	9	*Uncle Tom's Cabin*
Lady Macbeth	10	*Macbeth*
Dr. Joseph Mengele	11	*Night*
Nurse Ratched	12	*One Flew Over the Cuckoo's Nest*
Satan	13	*Paradise Lost*
Sauron	14	*The Lord of the Rings* trilogy
Lord Voldemort	15	*Harry Potter* series, books I-IV
Lady de Winter	16	*The Three Musketeers*

Cliff Quackenbush

A Separate Peace
John Knowles

The manager of the crew team. The boys at the Devon School have never liked Quackenbush; thus, he frequently takes out his frustrations on anyone whom he considers his inferior.

Quaquenga

The Light in the Forest
Conrad Richter

True Son's Indian mother. True Son favors Quaquenga to **Myra Butler**. She is described as loving and protective of her son.

Quasimodo

Hunchback of Notre Dame
Victor Hugo

The hunchback of Notre Dame. Quasimodo is an abandoned child left at Notre Dame and adopted by **Archdeacon Claude Frollo**. Hideously deformed, he has a giant humpback, a protrusion coming out of his chest, and a giant wart that covers one of his eyes. He is also deaf. His heart is pure, and this purity is linked to the cathedral itself. Indeed, his love for Notre Dame's bells represents his only form of communication. He falls in love with **La Esmeralda**, and when she is about to be hanged, he saves her and takes her to Notre Dame. He adores her and cares for her, but she cannot help but recoil in horror each time she looks at him. They form an uneasy friendship. Years later, when a gravedigger stumbles across La Esmerelda's remains, he finds the skeleton of Quasimodo curled around her.

Captain Philip Francis Queeg

The Caine Mutiny
Herman Wouk

The controversial captain of the *Caine*. He acts stubbornly, rashly, and harshly in many circumstances, but whether the symptoms actually add up to a clinical case of paranoia, as his men claim, is not clear.

Queen

Cymbeline
William Shakespeare

Cymbeline's wife and **Imogen**'s stepmother. A villainous woman, the queen will stop at nothing to see her son **Cloten** married to Imogen.

Queen of Hearts

Alice in Wonderland
Lewis Carroll

A monstrous, violently domineering woman. She seems to hold the ultimate authority in Wonderland, although her continuous death sentences are never actually carried out.

Queenie

Cold Sassy Tree
Olive Anne Burns

The Tweedys' cook and **Loomis**'s wife. However jovial she seems, Queenie suffers from the prejudices of white Southerners.

Queequeg

Moby-Dick
Herman Melville

Starbuck's skilled harpooner and "squire," and **Ishmael**'s best friend. Each mate takes on a squire aboard the *Pequod,* someone who would do the harpooning for them on the boats that chase whales. Queequeg was once a prince from a South Sea island who stowed away on a whaling ship in search of adventure. He is brave and generous, and he enables Ishmael to see that race has no bearing on a man's character. Queequeg and Ishmael become "married" when they each take a social smoke. They share a bed in the Spouter Inn, where Queequeg wakes with his arm over Ishmael in a loving way. At one point, Queequeg falls ill and is sure he is going to die, so he has a coffin built for himself and lies in it. However, he comes out alive and well, making Ishmael think that he can will himself out of deathly illness because he is a savage. Queequeg dies with all the rest of the crew of the *Pequod*, save Ishmael, in the chase and battle with Moby Dick.

Quentin

The Hours
Michael Cunningham

Vanessa Bell's middle child, age thirteen. He is kind, stalwart, and inherently good. **Virginia** feels a sense of kinship with him.

Miss Quentin

The Sound and the Fury
William Faulkner

Caddy's illegitimate daughter. She is raised by the Compsons after **Caddy**'s divorce. A rebellious, promiscuous, and miserably unhappy girl, Miss Quentin eventually steals money from Jason and leaves town with a member of a traveling minstrel show.

Adela Quested

A Passage to India
E. M. Forster

A young, intellectually minded Englishwoman; briefly **Ronny Heaslop**'s fiancée. Adela travels to India to see the "real India." In the Marabar Caves, Adela's confusion about her feelings for Ronny and about her chaotic experiences in India crystallize into something she perceives as a physical attack, which she blames on **Dr. Aziz**.

Questing Beast

The Once and Future King
T. H. White

A magical creature that only a Pellinore, like **King Pellinore** can hunt. The Questing Beast needs to be hunted to survive, and after a series of comic mishaps, it is hunted by Sir Palomides instead of King Pellinore. At one point, the men invent a fake beast to hunt, and the real Questing Beast falls in love with it.

Mistress Quickly

Henry IV, Part I; Henry IV, Part II; Henry V;
and *The Merry Wives of Windsor*
William Shakespeare

The hostess of the seedy Boar's Head Tavern in Eastcheap, London, and wife of **Pistol**. Mistress Quickly has a dim wit but a good heart—she is consistently taken in by **Sir John Falstaff**'s lies in *King Henry IV, Part I,* not only about marriage but about repaying bar tabs. Before the commoners from the tavern go off to war in *King Henry V,* Quickly tells of Falstaff's death in humorous but touching terms. The comic relief that she and the other tavern denizens provided through the Henry plays comes to an end in *King Henry V*. While **Bardolph** and **Nym** are hanged for stealing, Mistress Quickly dies of a venereal disease.

Bill Quigley

Dead Man Walking
Helen Prejean

A death-row attorney in Louisiana. He is a deeply religious man who has dedicated his life to working for the poor. Bill Quigley assists in **Patrick Sonnier**'s case.

Clare Quilty

Lolita
Vladimir Nabokov

Humbert Humbert's shadow and double. Quilty is a successful but clearly insane playwright and child pornographer who takes a liking to **Lolita** from an early age. He bribes Lolita to leave Humbert and come and work for him. Humbert murders him at the end of the novel.

Ivor Quilty

Lolita
Vladimir Nabokov

Clare Quilty's overweight uncle, a dentist and lifelong friend of the Haze family. Dreamy and well-liked, Ivor thinks of his nephew with kind indulgence. **Humbert Humbert** finds Clare Quilty by visiting Ivor at his office.

Peter Quince

A Midsummer Night's Dream
William Shakespeare

A carpenter. He is the nominal leader of the craftsmen's attempt to put on a play for **Theseus**'s marriage celebration. Quince is often shoved aside by the abundantly confident **Bottom**. During the craftsmen's play, Quince plays the Prologue.

Josiah Quincy

Johnny Tremain
Esther Forbes

A prominent Whig lawyer. Quincy successfully defends **Johnny** against **Jonathan Lyte**'s charge of theft.

Peter Quint

The Turn of the Screw
Henry James

The deceased valet of the governess's employer. It is implied that **Peter Quint** impregnated **Miss Jessel** and had a close, perhaps sexual relationship with **Miles**. Peter Quint died after slipping and injuring his head on the roads near Bly.

Mrs. Quintana

Animal Dreams
Barbara Kingsolver

Doc Homer Nolina's assistant. Mrs. Quintana cares for Doc Homer over the years.

Professor Quirrell

Harry Potter and the Sorcerer's Stone
J. K. Rowling

Professor of Defense Against the Dark Arts at Hogwarts in **Harry Potter**'s first year there. It turns out that Quirrell has faked his withdrawing meekness and is actually a cold-blooded conniver. Quirrell is possessed by **Voldemort**, and he ultimately dies.

Edgar Quisenberry

Alas, Babylon
Pat Frank

The president of the Fort Repose bank. When the banking system collapses after the war, he commits suicide.

Alonso Quixano

Don Quixote
Miguel de Cervantes

See **Don Quixote**.

Quoyle

The Shipping News
E. Annie Proulx

A pathetic newspaper reporter and the protagonist of *The Shipping News*. Quoyle is lonely and resigned to seeing himself as a failure, and is therefore vulnerable to the hurt of a cruel lover, **Petal Bear**, who sells their children, **Sunshine** and **Bunny**, to a child molester. Quoyle's transformation begins as he makes his life on Newfoundland, whisked there by **the aunt**. Assigned car-wreck stories and the shipping news by **Jack Buggit**, Quoyle is forced to face two old fears daily: Petal's death and his fear of water. With a larger sense of self-worth, Quoyle is able to stand up to the sins of his ancestors—specifically, the sins of his abusive father, **Guy**—and overpowers a long blood line of hurt and malice. He finally realizes that with **Wavey Prowse** he will have a love without pain.

16

AMAZING ANIMALS

YOU WOULDN'T NECESSARILY WANT THEM AS PETS, BUT THERE'S NO DOUBTING THAT THESE ANIMALS ARE ALL PRETTY CLEVER.

Bigwig	1	*Watership Down*
Boxer	2	*Animal Farm*
Buck	3	*The Call of the Wild*
Buckbeak	4	*Harry Potter and the Prisoner of Azkaban*
Dapple	5	*Don Quixote*
Fiver	6	*Watership Down*
Gabilan	7	*The Red Pony*
Hazel	8	*Watership Down*
Houyhnhnms	9	*Gulliver's Travels*
The Marlin	10	*The Old Man and the Sea*
Napolean	11	*Animal Farm*
Ourang-Outang	12	*"The Murders in the Rue Morgue"*
Rocinante	13	*Don Quixote*
Snowball	14	*Animal Farm*
Shadowfax	15	*The Lord of the Rings* trilogy
White Fang	16	*White Fang*

Lieutenant Rabbitt

The Caine Mutiny
Herman Wouk

A loyal senior officer through the reigns of **Captain De Vriess** and **Philip Francis Queeg**. When Rabbitt receives orders to leave the *Caine*, he is the envy of the ship.

Rabscuttle

Watership Down
Richard Adams

El-ahrairah's faithful friend. Rabscuttle gets in and out of trouble with the prince of rabbits and often plays a key role in his adventures.

Rachael

Hard Times
Charles Dickens

A simple, honest Hand who loves **Stephen Blackpool**.

Rachel

The Red Tent
Anita Diamant

Most beautiful of **Laban**'s daughters. Rachel is the mother of **Joseph** and **Benjamin**. She suffers many miscarriages and begins to apprentice as a midwife with **Inna**. She passes this knowledge on to **Dinah**. Rachel is considered the true love of **Jacob**'s life. Though initially jealous, Rachel changes significantly with the birth of her son and her growing success as a midwife. After Jacob, **Simon**, and **Levi**'s massacre of the men of Shechem, Rachel dies giving birth to Benjamin.

Rachel

The House on Mango Street
Sandra Cisneros

One of the two girls who are **Esperanza**'s neighbors and best friends. Rachel and **Lucy**, Hispanic girls from Texas, share Esperanza's love of words.

Mazer Rackham

Ender's Game
Orson Scott Card

Ender Wiggin's last teacher, and a hero of the first and second bugger invasions. Rackham is forced to deceive Ender into thinking he is playing mere games and explains to him that no one but a child could have won the war.

Sheindl Rackover

My Name Is Asher Lev
Chaim Potok

The woman who helps out around the Lev household when **Asher Lev**'s mother is ill. She is often reprimanding Asher for not acting like the Ladover version of a "good" boy.

Radine

Farewell to Manzanar
Jeanne Wakatsuki Houston

Jeanne's white best friend at Cabrillo Homes in Long Beach after the war. Radine's popularity and recognition in high school underscore the fundamental difference between her and Jeanne, whose Japanese ancestry makes her an outsider.

Arthur "Boo" Radley

To Kill a Mockingbird
Harper Lee

A recluse who never sets foot outside his house. Arthur "Boo" Radley dominates the imaginations of **Jem Finch**, **Scout Finch**, and **Dill Harris**. He leaves little presents for Scout and Jem and emerges at an opportune moment to save the children from the murderous and drunken hands of **Bob Ewell**.

Nathan Radley

To Kill a Mockingbird
Harper Lee

Boo Radley's cruel older brother. Nathan cold-heartedly cuts off an important element of Boo's relationship with **Jem Finch**, **Dill Harris**, and **Scout Finch** when he plugs up the knothole in which Boo leaves presents for the children.

Yevgeny Pavlovich Radomsky

The Idiot
Fyodor Dostoevsky

A young and dashing suitor to **Aglaya Ivanovna Yepanchina**. Radomsky retires from the military just before he takes part in the novel's action. A man of reason, he frequently visits **Prince Lev Nikolayevich Myshkin** in the Swiss sanitarium at the end of the novel.

Rafael

For Whom the Bell Tolls
Ernest Hemingway

A gypsy member of the guerrilla band. Frequently described as well-meaning but "worthless," Rafael proves his worthlessness by leaving his lookout post at a crucial moment. Rafael has few loyalties and does not believe in political causes.

Rafe

Doctor Faustus
Christopher Marlowe

An ostler friend of **Robin**'s. He is known as "Dick" in some editions.

John Raffles

Middlemarch
George Eliot

An old business partner of **Nicholas Bulstrode**'s. Bulstrode bribed him to keep the existence of the daughter and grandchild of his first wife (**Will Ladislaw**) secret. He comes back to blackmail Bulstrode. He is **Joshua Rigg Featherstone**'s stepfather. He dies at Stone Court because Bulstrode interferes with **Tertius Lydgate**'s medical treatment.

Ragueneau

Cyrano de Bergerac
Edmond Rostand

A pastry chef with a deep love for poetry. Ragueneau gives away pastries in return for poems. After his business fails, he becomes **Roxane**'s porter.

Rahim-sahib

Shabanu
Suzanne Fisher Staples

Nazir Mohammad's older brother. Rahim is a judicious and kind man. He is a politician and a respected holy man. He has three wives and falls in love with **Shabanu** the first time he sees her, despite the fact that she is young enough to be his granddaughter.

Railway Switchman

The Little Prince
Antoine de Saint-Exupéry

The railway switchman works at the hub for the enormous trains that rush back and forth carrying dissatisfied adults from one place to the other. He agrees with **the Little Prince** that the children are the only ones who appreciate and enjoy the beauty of the train rides.

Andy Rainbelt

Pigs in Heaven
Barbara Kingsolver

The social worker responsible for **Turtle Greer**'s case. He is kind and gentle, without the professional airs that Taylor associates with social workers.

Mikhail Osipovich Rakitin

The Brothers Karamazov
Fyodor Dostoevsky

A young seminary student whom **Alexei Fyodorovich Karamazov** considers a friend, but who secretly despises him. Cynical and sarcastic, Rakitin is too sophisticated to have real religious faith, so he satisfies himself with adopting various fashionable philosophical theories. He quotes Nietzsche and claims to be a socialist. Deeply threatened by Alyosha's apparently genuine moral purity, Rakitin secretly longs to see Alyosha become corrupted. As a result, he tries very hard to introduce Alyosha to **Agrafena Alexandrovna Svetlova**, whom he believes will shake Alyosha's faith.

Iofur Raknison

His Dark Materials
Robert Pullman

The pretender to the throne of the bears. Iofur Raknison tricked **Iorek Byrnison** into killing another bear so that Iorek would be exiled. Iofur wants to be human and wants a daemon. Iorek kills Iofur.

Ralph

Lord of the Flies
William Golding

The novel's protagonist. Ralph is an English boy who is elected leader of a group of boys marooned on an island. Ralph attempts to coordinate the boys' efforts to build a miniature civilization on the island until they can be rescued. Ralph eventually loses support and becomes hunted by **Jack**'s tribe after **Simon** and **Piggy** are killed.

James Ralph

The Autobiography of Benjamin Franklin
Benjamin Franklin

A Philadelphia poet, **Benjamin Franklin**'s friend and traveling companion to England. Neither well-liked nor respected as a poet, Ralph at one point asks Franklin to pass off one of Ralph's poems as Franklin's own, which Franklin does to very high praise. In England, Ralph leeches off Franklin and borrows large sums of money that he never repays. Franklin and Ralph end up going separate ways when Franklin attempts to seduce Ralph's girlfriend and is rejected.

Tito Ralph

Tortilla Flat
John Steinbeck

The jailer of Tortilla Flat. Although Tito Ralph is not part of **Danny**'s inner circle, he is a good friend of the *paisanos*.

The ram

Grendel
John Gardner

The first creature **Grendel** encounters in the novel. The ram stands at the edge of a cliff and will not budge despite Grendel's repeated protests.

Raymond Rambert

The Plague
Albert Camus

A Parisian journalist in Oran who researches the sanitary conditions of the Arab population. Trapped in Oran by the quarantine, Rambert struggles to find a way to escape to Paris and rejoin his wife.

Eleanor Ramilly

This Side of Paradise
F. Scott Fitzgerald

A young, wild girl, educated in France, whom **Amory Blaine** meets on a rainy haystack in Maryland. Eleanor and Amory have an intense summer romance, though Amory feels incapable of love because he is still recovering from his failed relationship with **Rosalind Connage**. One day, Amory predicts that Eleanor, on her deathbed, will renounce her paganism and call for a priest. His assertion ignites an incident that spoils their romance just before Amory leaves for New York. Several years later, the two exchange wistful and lovely poems in memory of their love.

Dolores Engracia "Sweets" Ramirez

Tortilla Flat
John Steinbeck

A single, landowning woman in Tortilla Flat who spends her days pursuing men. She has her eye on **Danny** and becomes involved with him.

Island of the Blue Dolphins
Scott O'Dell

Ramo

Karana's younger brother. He is confident, proud, and often rash. His rashness causes him to be left behind when his tribe leaves Ghalas-at, and his unfounded confidence leads to his death when he is attacked by wild dogs.

Herzog
Saul Bellow

Ramona

Moses Herzog's Argentinean lover. She is beautiful, well-educated, and the epitome of "sex and swagger."

To the Lighthouse
Virginia Woolf

Andrew Ramsay

The oldest of the Ramsays' sons. Andrew is a competent, independent young man, and he looks forward to a career as a mathematician.

To the Lighthouse
Virginia Woolf

Cam Ramsay

One of the Ramsays' daughters, who is mischievous as a young girl. She sails with **James Ramsay** and **Mr. Ramsay** to the lighthouse in the novel's final section.

To the Lighthouse
Virginia Woolf

James Ramsay

The Ramsays' youngest son. James loves his mother deeply and feels a murderous antipathy toward his father, with whom he must compete for **Mrs. Ramsay**'s love and affection. At the beginning of the novel, **Mr. Ramsay** refuses the six-year-old James's request to go to the lighthouse, saying that the weather will be foul; ten years later, James finally makes the journey with his father and his sister **Cam Ramsay**. By this time, he has grown into a willful and moody young man who has much in common with his father, whom he still detests.

To the Lighthouse
Virginia Woolf

Mr. Ramsay

Mrs. Ramsay's husband, a prominent metaphysical philosopher. Mr. Ramsay loves his family but often acts like a tyrant. He tends to be selfish and harsh due to his persistent personal and professional anxieties. He fears, more than anything, that his work is insignificant in the grand scheme of things and that he will not be remembered by future generations. Well aware of how blessed he is to have such a wonderful family, he nevertheless tends to punish his wife, children, and guests by demanding their constant sympathy, attention, and support.

Mrs. Ramsay

To the Lighthouse
Virginia Woolf

Mr. Ramsay's wife. A beautiful and loving woman, Mrs. Ramsay is a hostess who takes pride in making memorable experiences for the guests at the family's summer home on the Isle of Skye. She lavishes particular attention on her male guests, whom she believes have delicate egos and need constant support and sympathy. She is a dutiful and loving wife but often struggles with her husband's difficult moods and selfishness.

Nancy Ramsay

To the Lighthouse
Virginia Woolf

One of the Ramsays' daughters. Nancy accompanies **Paul Rayley** and **Minta Doyle** on their trip to the beach. Like her brother **Roger Ramsay**, Nancy is adventurous.

Prue Ramsay

To the Lighthouse
Virginia Woolf

The oldest Ramsay girl, a beautiful young woman. **Mrs. Ramsay** delights in contemplating Prue's marriage, which she believes will be blissful.

Roger Ramsay

To the Lighthouse
Virginia Woolf

One of the Ramsays' sons. Roger is wild and adventurous, like his sister **Nancy Ramsay**.

Rose Ramsay

To the Lighthouse
Virginia Woolf

One of the Ramsays' daughters. Rose has a talent for making things beautiful. She arranges the fruit for her mother's dinner party and picks out her mother's jewelry.

Steve Randle

The Outsiders
S. E. Hinton

Sodapop Curtis's best friend since grade school. Steve Randle is a greaser who works with Sodapop at the gas station.

Lyuba Ranevskaya

The Cherry Orchard
Anton Chekhov

A middle-aged Russian woman, the owner of the estate and the cherry orchard around which the story revolves. Her feelings of love often cloud her judgment, and she is unable to control her spending. She loses the cherry orchard to the middle-class businessman **Lopakhin**.

Dr. Rank

A Doll's House
Henrik Ibsen

A close friend of the Helmers'. A doctor and a pillar of the community, Dr. Rank is in love with **Nora** and is dying of syphilis, which his father contracted from his mistresses. Though Nora and Rank flirt with each other, Nora distances herself from Rank when he makes his affections towards her overt.

Mr. Rankeillor

Kidnapped
Robert Louis Stevenson

David Balfour's lawyer. Mr. Rankeillor helps David against **Ebenezer Balfour**. **Alan Breck Stewart** comes to Ebenezer's door pretending to be holding David for ransom. David and Mr. Rankeillor are hiding just within earshot when Ebenezer admits that he was hoping that he sold David into slavery. In the wake of this admission, Rankeillor works out a deal: Ebenezer keeps one-third of the income of the House of Shaw and the estate, and David gets two-thirds of the income.

Ransome

Kidnapped
Robert Louis Stevenson

The cabin boy of the *Covenant*. Ransome is younger than **David Balfour**, but has led a tough life at sea. **Mr. Shuan** often beats him. Shuan beats Ransome to death, and David must become the new cabin boy.

Raphael

Paradise Lost
John Milton

One of the archangels in Heaven who acts as one of God's messengers. Raphael informs **Adam** of **Satan**'s plot to seduce them into sin, and also narrates the story of the fallen angels, as well as the fall of Satan.

Mr. Rappaport

Seize the Day
Saul Bellow

A blind old man at the stock exchange. He asks **Tommy Wilhelm** for assistance on his venture to the cigar store and Tommy accompanies him.

Ras the Exhorter

Invisible Man
Ralph Ellison

A stout, flamboyant, charismatic, angry man with a flair for public agitation. A maverick, Ras frequently opposes the Brotherhood and **the Narrator**, often violently, and incites riots in Harlem. Ras represents the black nationalist movement, which advocates the violent overthrow of white supremacy.

Rashaverak

Childhood's End
Arthur C. Clarke

One of **the Overlords**. Rashaverak's speciality is psychological research, and he takes special interest in **Rupert Boyce**'s library of paranormal research. Like all Overlords, he is much taller and more broadly built than a human, with large wings, horns on his head, and a barbed tail.

Rashid the rickshaw boy

Midnight's Children
Salman Rushdie

A boy who informs **Aadam Aziz** that **Nadir Khan** needs a place to hide.

Rodion Romanovich Raskolnikov

Crime and Punishment
Fyodor Dostoevsky

The protagonist of the novel, who has murdered **Lizaveta Ivanovna** and **Alyona Ivanovna**, and who is in love with **Sofya Semyonovna Marmeladova**. A former student, Raskolnikov is now destitute. He believes that an evil action is justified if it leads to an ultimate good. He also believes that certain extraordinary men can commit such evil actions without qualms. Raskolnikov murders the pawnbroker and then her sister (as she has accidentally witnessed the act) in an attempt to prove to himself that he is such an extraordinary man.

Avdotya Romanovna Raskolnikova

Crime and Punishment
Fyodor Dostoevsky

Rodion Romanovich Raskolnikov's sister. Dunya is as intelligent, proud, and good-looking as her brother, but she is also moral and compassionate. She is decisive and brave, ending her engagement with **Pyotr Petrovich Luzhin** when he insults her family and fending off **Arkady Ivanovich Svidrigailov** with gunfire.

Pulcheria Aleksandrovna Raskolnikova

Crime and Punishment
Fyodor Dostoevsky

Avdotya Romanovna Raskolnikova and **Rodion Romanovich Raskolnikov**'s mother. Pulcheria Alexandrovna is deeply devoted to her son and willing to sacrifice everything, even her own and her daughter's happiness, so that he might be successful. Even after Raskolnikov has confessed, she is unwilling to admit to herself that her son is a murderer.

Rasputin

The Power of One
Bryce Courtenay

A Russian man who lives next door to **Peekay** in the mining camp in Northern Rhodesia. He buys sweets for the mining kids on Wednesday western nights, and he loves to make rabbit (or cat) stew for Peekay. When Peekay is knocked unconscious in a mining accident, Rasputin comes to the rescue, killing himself in order to save his friend.

Nurse Ratched

One Flew over the Cuckoo's Nest
Ken Kesey

The head of the hospital ward and the novel's antagonist. Nurse Ratched is a middle-aged former army nurse who rules her ward with an iron hand. She selects her staff members for their submissiveness and systematically destroys her patients' self-esteem and masculinity. She maintains her power by the strategic use of shame and guilt, as well as by a determination to "divide and conquer" her patients.

Ratchett

Murder on the Orient Express
Agatha Christie

The assumed name of a man called Cassetti, who kidnapped and murdered the young **Daisy Armstrong** for money. The Armstrong family murders Ratchett because he escaped punishment in the U.S.

Lieutenant Ratcliffe

Billy Budd, Sailor
Herman Melville

The HMS *Bellipotent*'s brusque boarding officer. Lieutenant Ratcliffe visits the merchant marine *Rights-of-Man* to look for crewmembers and presses **Billy Budd** into service aboard the *Bellipotent*.

Sir Richard Ratcliffe

Richard III
William Shakespeare

A supporter of **King Richard III**. Ratcliffe carries out gruesome tasks for Richard, like delivering **Lord Rivers**, **Lord Grey**, and **Sir Thomas Vaughan** to their execution, and carrying out the beheading of **Lord Hastings**. He fights alongside Richard during the final battle with **Richmond**'s army.

Adèle Ratignolle

The Awakening
Kate Chopin

Edna Pontellier's close friend. Adèle Ratignolle epitomizes the conventional feminine ideal of the era, idolizing her children and worshipping her husband. Although Adèle leads a conservative life, her free manner of discourse and expression inspires Edna to abandon her reserve. Adèle's uninhibited conversation reminds Edna of the romantic dreams and fantasies of her youth, and Edna gradually begins to uncover the desires that had been suppressed for so many years. Later in the novel, it is apparent that Adèle still views a woman's life in terms of the service she performs for her family and society. When she suspects Edna of having an affair with **Alcée Arobin** she reminds Edna of her duty to her children.

Rawler

One Flew over the Cuckoo's Nest
Ken Kesey

A patient on the Disturbed ward who commits suicide by cutting off his testicles.

Nannie Land Rawley

Prodigal Summer
Barbara Kingsolver

Garnett Walker's neighbor. Nannie is a bright, independent seventy-five-year-old who raises apples and organic vegetables and argues with Garnett about pesticides. As a younger woman, Nannie had a long affair with the widowed **Ray Dean Wolfe**, **Deanna Wolfe**'s father. **Rachel Carson Rawley** was their child.

Rachel Carson Rawley

Prodigal Summer
Barbara Kingsolver

Nannie Land Rawley's daughter. Rachel was born with Down syndrome and a hole in her heart; she died at about age fifteen.

Babe Rawlins

On the Road
Jack Kerouac

Ray Rawlins's sister and **Tim Gray**'s girlfriend.

Lacey Rawlins

All the Pretty Horses
Cormac McCarthy

John Grady Cole's best friend and his companion on the trip into Mexico. At age seventeen, he is tall and thin, with long arms. Rawlins is louder, more impatient, and less introspective than Cole. While he is faithful to Cole, he does not subscribe to Cole's code of absolute loyalty and strictly moral action. Rawlins and Cole stick together until their jail ordeal; afterward, Rawlins returns to Texas.

Ray Rawlins

On the Road
Jack Kerouac

Babe Rawlins's brother and **Sal Paradise**'s Denver acquaintance.

Major Rawls

A Prayer for Owen Meany
John Irving

Owen Meany's military contact in Phoenix, who kills **Dick Jarvits** after Dick kills Owen.

Dwayne Ray

The Bean Trees
Barbara Kingsolver

Lou Ann Ruiz's son. He was born on New Year's Day.

John Ray, Jr.

Lolita
Vladimir Nabokov

The author of the foreword and the editor of **Humbert Humbert**'s memoir. After receiving the memoir, John Ray, Jr. makes minor edits and attempts to prove that *Lolita* is not obscene. He also contends that the work has value to psychiatrists and provides a valuable lesson to parents raising their children.

Paul Rayley

To the Lighthouse
Virginia Woolf

A young friend of the Ramsays who visits them on the Isle of Skye. Paul is a kind, impressionable young man who follows **Mrs. Ramsay**'s wishes in marrying **Minta Doyle**.

Mr. Dolphus Raymond

To Kill a Mockingbird
Harper Lee

A wealthy white man who lives with his black mistress and mulatto children. Dolphus Raymond cynically pretends to be a drunk so that the citizens of Maycomb will have an explanation for his behavior. In reality, he is simply jaded by the hypocrisy of white society and prefers living among blacks.

The Autobiography of Miss Jane Pittman
Ernest J. Gaines

Jules Raynard

A good friend of **Robert Samson**'s who is also **Tee Bob Samson**'s godfather, or Parrain. Jules Raynard is a true gentleman who refuses to let violence against **Mary Agnes LeFarbe** follow Tee Bob's death. Raynard's wisdom leads to Mary Agnes's flight.

A Yellow Raft in Blue Water
Michael Dorris

Rayona

The daughter of **Christine** and **Elgin Taylor**. Rayona is unusually tall and thin and is very self-conscious about her physical appearance. She loves her parents but is repeatedly disappointed by them, and she often feels unloved and unwanted. She dreams about having a perfect family, and invents one based on a letter she finds on the ground while working as a custodian at Bearpaw Lake. Eventually, Rayona becomes satisfied with her real family and abandons her fantasy of an ideal one.

Crime and Punishment
Fyodor Dostoevsky

Dmitri Prokofych Razumikhin

Rodion Romanovich Raskolnikov's friend. A poor ex-student, he responds to his poverty not by taking from others but by working harder. To some extent, he serves as Raskolnikov's replacement, stepping in to advise and protect **Pulcheria Alexandrovna Raskolnikova** and **Avdotya Romanovna Raskolnikova**.

My Brother Sam Is Dead
Christopher & James Lincoln Collier

Betsy Read

Sam Meeker's girlfriend and the daughter of **Colonel Read**, a prominent local Patriot. Betsy is a bold, nosy teenage girl, very loyal to Sam and to the Rebel cause.

My Brother Sam Is Dead
Christopher & James Lincoln Collier

Colonel Read

Betsy Read's father, a staunch and aging Patriot.

The Autobiography of Benjamin Franklin
Benjamin Franklin

Deborah Read

Benjamin Franklin's sweetheart and eventually his wife. Their courtship is interrupted by Franklin's eighteen-month stay in England, during which time Deborah Read marries another man. Her husband disappears, and she then marries Franklin.

Atlas Shrugged
Ayn Rand

Hank Rearden

The greatest of the nation's industrialists, the husband of **Lillian Rearden**. Hank Rearden is a steel baron and **Dagny Taggart**'s lover for most of *Atlas Shrugged*. Because he truly loves his job of producing metal, Rearden continues to fight for his mills and inadvertently props up the government's ("looters'") regime. When he sees **the Wet Nurse** die in his arms at the hands of the government and his former friend **Fran-**

cisco d'Anconia save Rearden's own life, he has a realization about how he is helping the government by loving his own business. He also mistakenly believes in a separation of the mind and body, which makes him see physical desire as base and low, and the things of the mind as unrelated to the physical world. Once he understands the ideal of the mind and body working together, he is able to embrace the cause of the strikers.

Lillian Rearden

Atlas Shrugged
Ayn Rand

Hank Rearden's lifeless, beautiful wife. Lillian Rearden is dominated by a hatred of the good, and her purpose in life is to destroy her husband. In an attempt to hurt Rearden, Lillian has sex with **James Taggart**. She uses the evidence she gets from Jim about the affair between **Dagny Taggart** and Rearden to try to blackmail the two so that they cooperate with the corrupt government.

Philip Rearden

Atlas Shrugged
Ayn Rand

Hank Rearden's parasitic brother. Philip Rearden lives off of Hank Rearden's accomplishments while simultaneously criticizing Hank for pursuing them. When Hank resolves to let his family abuse him no longer, Philip gets resentful and tries to get even with Hank by giving the corrupt government information regarding Hank's doings.

Reason

The Phantom Tollbooth
Norton Juster

One of the two princesses adopted by **King Azaz**. When Azaz and the Mathemagician asked them to determine whether numbers or letters are more important, **Rhyme** and Reason say each is equally valuable. The brothers then imprison the two princesses in the Castle in the Air.

Reba

Song of Solomon
Toni Morrison

Pilate Dead's daughter and **Hagar**'s mother, also known as Rebecca. Reba has a strong sexual drive but is attracted to abusive men. Nevertheless, because the powerful Pilate is her mother, the few men who dare mistreat her are punished.

Rebeca

One Hundred Years of Solitude
Gabriel García Márquez

The earth-eating orphan girl who mysteriously arrives at the **Buendía** doorstep. The Buendías raise her as one of their own children, first conquering her self-destructive habits of eating dirt and whitewash. She is afflicted with an insomnia that also causes memory loss. Eventually, the entire town becomes infected with insomnia and the associated amnesia. She and **Amaranta** both fall in love with a stranger, **Pietro Crespi**. Rebeca and Pietro Crespi become engaged, and Amaranta's threat to destroy Rebeca's wedding deeply troubles Rebeca. After Pietro Crespi, Rebeca becomes enthralled by **José Arcadio**'s masculinity, and they begin a torrid affair. The affair ends in marriage, and they are exiled from the house. After her husband's death, Rebeca becomes a hermit, living the rest of her life in solitary grief.

Rebecca

The Red Tent
Anita Diamant

Jacob's mother. Rebecca is the Oracle of Mamre: she can see the future and has healing powers. She is the matriarch of the family and schemes to give **Isaac**'s blessing to Jacob, her favorite son, instead of to **Esau**. She appears cruel and heartless to **Dinah**, who spends three months waiting on her after **Tabea** is banished.

Rebecca

Ivanhoe
Sir Walter Scott

A beautiful Jewish maiden, the daughter of **Isaac of York**, who tends to **Ivanhoe** when he is wounded in the tournament at Ashby. Though she knows that she and Ivanhoe can never marry (he is a Christian and she is a Jew), she falls in love with him.

Rebecca

Rebecca
Daphne du Maurier

In life, the beautiful, much-loved, accomplished wife of **Maxim de Winter** and the mistress of Manderley. Now a ghost, she haunts the mansion, and her presence torments **the Heroine** after her marriage to Maxim.

Red

Bless Me, Ultima
Rudolfo A. Anaya

One of a group of exuberant boys who frequently curse and fight. Red is a Protestant, so he is often teased by the other boys, who are **Abel**, **Bones**, **Ernie**, **Horse**, **Lloyd**, and **the Vitamin Kid**.

Red Horse

Grendel
John Gardner

Hrothulf's mentor and advisor. A crotchety old man, Red Horse believes that all governments are inherently evil and that revolution does nothing but replace one corrupt system with another.

Red King

Through the Looking Glass
Lewis Carroll

The man whom **Tweedledum** and **Tweedledee** claim is the dreaming architect of the Looking-Glass world.

Red Leg Daddy

I Know Why the Caged Bird Sings
Maya Angelou

One of **Daddy Clidell**'s con-men friends. These men teach **Maya Johnson** that it is possible to use white prejudice to gain advantage over whites. The other con-men friends are **Cool Clyde**, **Tight Coat**, **Just Black**, **Stonewall Jimmy**, and **Spots**.

Red Pepper

Billy Budd, Sailor
Herman Melville

The HMS *Bellipotent*'s forecastleman. Red Pepper thinks that **Billy Budd** should denounce the mutineers who want to pay Billy Budd for joining them.

Red Queen

Through the Looking Glass
Lewis Carroll

A domineering and often unpleasant woman. She expects **Alice** to abide by her rules of proper etiquette.

The Red Whiskers

Billy Budd, Sailor
Herman Melville

Billy Budd's adversary aboard his first ship, the *Rights-of-Man*. When the Red Whiskers punches Billy, Billy responds with a forceful blow of his own, and the Red Whiskers's hatred of Billy turns to love.

Redcrosse

The Faerie Queene
Edmund Spenser

The hero of Book I. His real name is discovered to be George, and he ends up becoming St. George, the patron saint of England.

Ben Redmond

The Unvanquished
William Faulkner

Colonel Sartoris's business partner turned enemy, who murders him and is in turn driven out of Jefferson by **Bayard**.

Mary Redmond

When the Legends Die
Hal Borland

Thomas Black Bull's caretaker while he is in the hospital after his bronco-riding accident, and a colleague of **Dr. Ferguson**'s.

Tom Redruth

Treasure Island
Robert Louis Stevenson

One of **Jim Hawkins**'s sailor companions on the ship. Tom is killed by pirate gunfire and buried with great ceremony on the island.

Eliza Reed

Jane Eyre
Charlotte Brontë

Jane Eyre's cousin, **Georgiana Reed** and **John Reed**'s sister, and **Mrs. Reed**'s daughter. Not as beautiful as her sister, Eliza devotes herself somewhat self-righteously to the Church and eventually goes to a convent in France where she becomes the Mother Superior.

Georgiana Reed

Jane Eyre
Charlotte Brontë

Jane Eyre's cousin, **Eliza Reed** and **John Reed**'s sister, and one of **Mrs. Reed**'s two daughters. The beautiful Georgiana treats Jane cruelly when they are children, but later in their lives she befriends her cousin and confides in her. Georgiana attempts to elope with a man named **Lord Edwin Vere**, but her sister Eliza alerts Mrs. Reed of the arrangement and sabotages the plan. After Mrs. Reed dies, Georgiana marries a wealthy man.

Henry Reed

I Know Why the Caged Bird Sings
Maya Angelou

The valedictorian of **Maya Johnson**'s eighth-grade class.

John Reed

Jane Eyre
Charlotte Brontë

Jane Eyre's cousin, **Mrs. Reed**'s son, and **Eliza Reed** and **Georgiana Reed**'s brother. John treats Jane with appalling cruelty during their childhood and later falls into a life of drinking and gambling. John commits suicide midway through the novel when his mother ceases to pay his debts for him.

Mrs. Reed

Jane Eyre
Charlotte Brontë

John Reed, **Eliza Reed**, and **Georgiana Reed**'s mother, and **Jane Eyre**'s cruel aunt, who raises her at Gateshead Hall until Jane is sent away to school at age ten. Later in her life, Jane attempts reconciliation with her aunt, but the old woman continues to resent her because her husband, **Uncle Reed**, had always loved Jane more than his own children.

Uncle Reed

Jane Eyre
Charlotte Brontë

Mrs. Reed's late husband. In her childhood, **Jane Eyre** believes that she feels the presence of his ghost. Because he was always fond of Jane and her mother (his sister), Uncle Reed made his wife promise that she would raise Jane as her own child. It is a promise that Mrs. Reed does not keep.

Doctor Reefy

Winesburg, Ohio
Sherwood Anderson

An aging doctor with a declining practice. He marries a young female patient, but she dies after less than a year. He also develops a close relationship with **Elizabeth Willard** during her last months.

The Reeve

The Canterbury Tales
Geoffrey Chaucer

One of the pilgrims traveling to Canterbury. The reeve's job was similar to a steward of a manor, and this reeve performs his job shrewdly—his lord never loses so much as a ram, and the vassals under his command are kept in line. However, he steals from his master.

Regan

King Lear
William Shakespeare

King Lear's middle daughter and the wife of the duke of **Cornwall**. Regan is as ruthless as her older sister **Goneril**, seeking power aggressively and disregarding her father's desires. The two sisters alternate between goading each other into acts of cruelty and jealously competing over **Edmund**. Goneril ends up poisoning Regan.

Terrance Regan

The Big Sleep
Raymond Chandler

An ex-bootlegger and husband of **Vivian Sternwood**. Though long dead, he remains one of the novel's main characters because much of the novel revolves around him and the search for him. **General Sternwood** wants Regan found because he had been a good friend to the General. In the end, Regan is one of the very few characters who is saved from the plight of the novel and its aftermath—he exists only in "the big sleep," far away from the everyday reality of a seedy Los Angeles.

Ed Regis

Jurassic Park
Michael Crichton

The park publicist. Ed feels annoyed that he must babysit visitors to the park.

Rehoboam

The Old Testament
Unknown

One of the opposing kings who divides Israel into the northern kingdom of Israel and the southern kingdom of Judah. Rehoboam and **Jeroboam** introduce rampant worship of idols and false gods into their kingdoms.

Hilda Reid

Lady Chatterley's Lover
D. H. Lawrence

Lady Chatterley's older sister by two years, the daughter of **Sir Malcolm Reid**. Hilda shared Connie's cultured upbringing and intellectual education. She remains unliberated by the raw sensuality that changed Connie's life. She disdains Connie's lover, **Oliver Mellors**, as a member of the lower classes, but in the end she helps Connie leave **Clifford Chatterley**.

Sir Malcolm Reid

Lady Chatterley's Lover
D. H. Lawrence

The father of **Connie (Lady Chatterley)**, and **Hilda**. He is an acclaimed painter, an aesthete and unabashed sensualist who despises **Clifford Chatterley** for his weakness and impotence, and who immediately warms to **Oliver Mellors**.

Reignier, Duke of Anjou

Henry VI, Part I
William Shakespeare

Charles, Dauphin of France's ally. Reignier fights alongside Charles and the other French nobles throughout the play. When his daughter, **Margaret of Anjou**, is captured by **William de la Pole, Earl**

of Suffolk, he expresses regret that he cannot ransom her; though he is a major lord and the King of Naples and Jerusalem, he has no money. Suffolk offers him an alternative: his daughter will be wed to **King Henry VI**. Reignier agrees to the match, providing that he be allowed to keep two French territories, Maine and Anjou. He later urges Charles to agree to a peace accord with the English.

Frank Reilly

Flowers for Algernon
Daniel Keyes

An employee at Donner's Bakery who often picks on **Charlie Gordon**. With **Joe Carp**, Frank plays tricks on Charlie and makes him the butt of jokes that he does not understand.

Reinhold

Childhood's End
Arthur C. Clarke

An American working on building an interstellar spaceship.

Mademoiselle Reisz

The Awakening
Kate Chopin

A reclusive pianist, and an unconventional and unpopular older woman. A small, homely woman, Mademoiselle is distant and reserved in her interaction with the other guests on Grand Isle. Mademoiselle Reisz's influence is instrumental in **Edna Pontellier**'s awakening. She is unmarried, childless, and passionate about her music, which inspires Edna. Edna is drawn to the older woman, whose lifestyle she envies, despite finding her disagreeable and difficult.

Rekus

Sula
Toni Morrison

Hannah Peace's husband and **Sula Peace**'s father. He dies when Sula is three years old.

Public Relation

One Flew over the Cuckoo's Nest
Ken Kesey

A fat, bald bureaucrat who wears a girdle. Public Relation leads tours of the ward, claiming that it is nice and pleasant.

Reldresal

Gulliver's Travels
Jonathan Swift

Principal Secretary of Private Affairs of Lilliput. Friendly to **Gulliver**, Reldresal explains to him the intricacies of Lilliputian politics.

Relling

Wild Duck
Henrik Ibsen

Hjalmar's longtime antagonist from the Hoidal. Relling pits himself against **Gregers**'s idealism, calling Gregers's sentiments "quackery."

Remedios the Beauty

One Hundred Years of Solitude
Gabriel García Márquez

The daughter of **Santa Sofía de la Piedad** and **Arcadio**, Remedios the Beauty becomes the most beautiful woman in the world. She remains unconcerned with love and with men throughout the novel and seems unworldly. One day she floats off the ground and up to heaven, disappearing forever.

Re-mose

The Red Tent
Anita Diamant

Dinah's only child. Re-mose is born of **Shalem** and Dinah but raised in Egypt with **Re-nefer** and **Nakht-re** as his Egyptian parents. Dinah is his nurse. Re-mose is a strong and determined young man, and he unknowingly becomes the scribe for his own uncle **Joseph**, the vizier.

Rena

Breath, Eyes, Memory
Edwidge Danticat

Sophie's therapist and the instigator of the sexual-phobia group. She has spent two years in the Peace Corps in the Dominican Republic and is an initiated Santeria priestess.

M. de Rênal

The Red and the Black
Stendhal

The mayor of the town of Verrières. M. de Rênal is a conservative supporter of the Restoration, and, as a result, is conceited, obtuse, and greedy. He is concerned only with his title and rank, even though he is constantly manipulated and ridiculed. **Julien Sorel** sees M. de Rênal as an adversary and seduces M. de Rênal's wife, **Mme de Rênal**. When **Elisa** tells **M. Valenod** about the affair, M. de Rênal is quick to believe the explanation given by Mme. de Rênal and Julien Sorel, which clears them of any wrong-doing. M. de Rênal considers killing Julien Sorel and his wife when he does believe they are having an affair, as his honor and name are much more important to him than love.

Mme. de Rênal

The Red and the Black
Stendhal

An aristocrat and the wife of the town mayor, **M. de Rênal**. Mme. de Rênal is **Julien Sorel**'s first love interest. After Sorel gets engaged to **Mathilde de la Mole**, the **Marquis de la Mole** is sent a letter by Mme. de Rênal denouncing Julien as a womanizer ambitious to make his fortune by seducing rich aristocrats. The Marquis de la Mole withdraws all of his support for Sorel, condemns Sorel's proposed marriage to Mathilde and asks Sorel to move to America. Sorel goes back to the town of Verrières, where he shoots Mme. de Rênal from behind, wounding her. He is put in prison, and while the still-in-love Mme. de Rênal does all she can to have clemency granted to Sorel before his punishment of death, Sorel wants to die, and so refuses the offers of clemency. Mme. de Rênal confesses that she was forced by her confessor to write the letter to the Marquis de la Mole, and Sorel forgives her.

Jerry Renault

The Chocolate War
Robert Cormier

The protagonist of the story. He single-handedly takes on the biggest bullies in at the Trinity School—**the Vigils** and **Brother Leon**. He is the only one at his school who refuses to sell the chocolates that have gotten Brother Leon into his current predicament. He is physically beaten and stripped of his dignity, and in the end he can no longer cling to his principles of doing what is right.

Re-nefer

The Red Tent
Anita Diamant

The wife of **Hamor**, and **Shalem**'s mother. Re-nefer is a doting mother who connives to bring **Dinah** and Shalem together, eventually becoming Dinah's mother-in-law. Re-nefer smuggles Dinah out of Shechem to Egypt after **Simon** and **Levi** massacre Re-nefer's people. Re-nefer then raises Dinah's son as her own, and Dinah must be her only son's nurse.

Renfield

Dracula
Bram Stoker

A patient at **John Seward**'s mental asylum who is eventually murdered by **Count Dracula**. A behemoth and a refined gentleman, Renfield consumes living creatures—flies, spiders, birds, and so on—which he believes provide him with strength and vitality.

Reuben

The Red Tent
Anita Diamant

The eldest of **Jacob**'s sons by **Leah**. Reuben is known for his kindness and good counsel and is among **Dinah**'s favorite brothers. Reuben eventually develops a deep love for his aunt **Bilhah**, and the discovery of their affair results in his banishment.

Revenge

The Spanish Tragedy
Thomas Kyd

Andrea's companion throughout the play. Revenge is a spirit that talks of the living characters as if they were performing a tragedy for his entertainment.

Paul Revere

Johnny Tremain
Esther Forbes

A master silversmith and one of the leaders of the Revolutionary forces in Boston.

Rex

Holes
Louis Sachar

See **X-Ray**.

Reynaldo

All's Well that Ends Well
William Shakespeare

The **Countess of Roussillon**'s steward. He informs the Countess of **Helena**'s love for **Bertram**.

Reynaldo

Hamlet
William Shakespeare

Polonius's servant. Polonius sends Reynaldo to France so that he can spy on Polonius's son **Laertes**.

Reynolds

Black Boy
Richard Wright

Along with **Pease**, one of a pair of white Southerners who run **Richard Wright** off his job at the optical shop in Jackson, Mississippi.

General John Reynolds

The Killer Angels
Michael Shaara

Union. An intelligent infantry general who has a gift for positioning troops. Reynolds refuses to become the commander of the Union army, a position that is then given to **General George Meade**. Reynolds is killed shortly after the action begins at Gettysburg.

Rhyme

The Phantom Tollbooth
Norton Juster

One of the two princesses adopted by **King Azaz**. When Azaz and the Mathemagician asked them to determine whether numbers or letters are more important, Rhyme and **Reason** say each is equally valuable. The brothers then imprison the two princesses in the Castle in the Air.

Riach

Kidnapped
Robert Louis Stevenson

The second officer of the *Covenant* under **Captain Hoseason**. Riach is kinder to **David Balfour** than the other sailors are to David. He helps **Alan Breck Stewart** escape after the ship wrecks on the Torran Rocks and Hoseason tries to take his money.

Herr Ribbentrop

The Remains of the Day
Kazuo Ishiguro

The German ambassador during World War II, who makes several trips to Darlington Hall. Herr Ribbentrop uses **Lord Darlington** to exert Nazi influence on British heads of state.

King Richard I

Ivanhoe
Sir Walter Scott

The King of England and the head of the Norman royal line, the Plantagenets. He is known as "Richard the Lion-Hearted" for his valor and courage in battle, and for his love of adventure. He spends much of the novel disguised as the **Black Knight**. Richard has a reckless disposition and is something of a thrill-seeker. His courage and prowess are beyond reproach, but he comes under criticism—even from his loyal knight **Ivanhoe**—for putting his love of adventure ahead of the well-being of his subjects.

King Richard II

Richard II
William Shakespeare

The ruler of England at the start of the play, cousin to **Henry Bolingbroke**, and nephew to **John of Gaunt**, **Edmund of Langley, Duke of York**, and the late **Thomas of Woodstock, Duke of Gloucester.** Having ascended to the throne at an early age, Richard is thought to have been corrupted by bad advisers, like **Bagot**, **Bushy**, and **Green**. Toward the start of the play, he makes two poor decisions that bring about his downfall: he exiles the popular Bolingbroke for six years, and with money from renting out English land to nobles, he takes his army to fight in the Irish Wars. Following Gaunt's bitter rebuke of him for being implicit in Gloucester's death, Richard decides to take over Gaunt's land, an action that precipitates Bolingbroke's return to reclaim his inheritance. As Bolingbroke grows stronger with more lords defecting, Richard becomes increasingly ineffectual and wistful. Richard, deposed by Bolingbroke and sent to prison in Pomfret Castle, is eventually assassinated by **Sir Piers Exton**.

King Richard III

Henry VI, Part II; Henry VI, Part III; and *Richard III*
William Shakespeare

Son of **Richard Plantagenet, Duke of York** and the **Duchess of York**; brother of **King Edward IV**, **George, Duke of Clarence**, and **Edmund, Earl of Rutland**. Richard first appears at the end of *King Henry IV, Part II*, when York returns from Ireland to begin his rebellion for the crown. Joining his father, Richard exchanges hot words with **Lord Clifford**; at the Battle of St. Albans, Richard kills the **Duke of Somerset**. When the battle continues in *King Henry VI, Part III*, Richard begins to scheme his way to the throne. A fierce supporter of the Yorkist cause, Richard has a hump back, lame leg, and shriveled arm, and takes his physical deformities as proof that he will not succeed with women or in the world of the court. Even while he fights on his brother's side, Richard is plotting against the many people who stand in his way to the throne. When York is killed, Edward weeps, but Richard plots revenge, chasing the younger Lord Clifford alone across the battlefield; when he kills **Henry VI** in the Tower, Richard declares himself free of family and brotherhood, and stands alone in his quest for the crown. In *King Richard III*, Richard is both the central character and villain. He schemes and connives to get closer to the crown until finally he has it, seducing **Lady Anne**, having his brother Clarence murdered, executing **Lord Rivers** and **Lord Grey**, and contracting the murders of **Prince Edward** and the young **Richard, Duke of York**. When he becomes king, his real nature, that of a cruel monstrous tyrant, becomes much more apparent. Always self-reliant, Richard tries to reassert his strength the night before his final battle with **Henry Tudor, Earl of Richmond**'s army.

Richard

Go Tell It on the Mountain
James Baldwin

Elizabeth's intelligent, bitter, and fragile first love, and **John Grimes**'s biological father. He committed suicide after a racist incident with the police, not knowing that Elizabeth was pregnant with his son.

Richard Rich

A Man for All Seasons
Robert Bolt

A low-level functionary whom **More** helps to establish. Rich seeks to gain employment, but More denies him a high-ranking position and suggests that Rich become a teacher. Rich, however, goes to work for **Norfolk** instead, eventually falling in with **Cromwell** as a lackey. Cromwell offers him a post as the attorney general of Wales in exchange for perjuring himself at More's sham trial. Rich's meteoric rise to wealth and power is simultaneous with More's fall from favor.

Dr. Richard

The Plague
Albert Camus

The chairman of the Oran medical association. Richard is skeptical in the face of **Rieux** and **Castel**'s suggestion that the city is in the grips of the plague. He refuses to alarm the public with immediate, decisive action.

Winnie Richards

White Noise
Don DeLillo

Brilliant and stealthy neuroscientist at the College. Winnie goes out of her way to be invisible. She helps **Jack Gladney** find out about **Dylar** and **Willie Mink**.

Cardinal Richelieu

The Three Musketeers
Alexandre Dumas

King Louis XIII's most influential advisor. Cardinal Richelieu is the most powerful and important man in France. He is furiously self-absorbed, but also an extremely effective leader of the state. Richelieu works hard to maintain the reputation and power of the king, since this is the stock on which his own status is based. He is responsible for putting the **Lady de Winter** up to her sinister tasks, and **Athos**, **Porthos**, **Aramis**, and **d'Artagnan** swear to fight against the Cardinal's forces because they are Royalists. The Cardinal shares a mutual hatred for **Queen Anne**. Even though d'Artagnan swears to fight the Cardinal, in the end, he accepts a promotion to lieutenant Musketeer from the powerful man.

Cardinal Richelieu

Cyrano de Bergerac
Edmond Rostand

A historical figure referenced as **Comte de Guiche**'s uncle. He does not appear in the play. The advisor to the king, the historical Richelieu was a skilled political manipulator and the most powerful man in France.

Richie

Go Ask Alice
Anonymous

Alice's college boyfriend until she leaves home the first time. She sells drugs to help Richie someday attend medical school, and eventually discovers him conducting a homosexual affair with his roommate **Ted**.

Richie

The Hours
Michael Cunningham

Laura Brown's son. Richie will grow up to be **Richard Brown**, novelist. At three years old, Richie's entire world is his mother. He is sensitive and gets upset easily.

Henry Tudor, Earl of Richmond

Henry VI, Part III and *Richard III*
William Shakespeare

A distant cousin of **King Henry VI** and future King Henry VII. In the midst of a deadly war between the Yorkist faction in *King Henry VI, Part III*, Henry VI is mesmerized by the young Richmond. To ensure his safety, the **Duke of Oxford** sends him to Brittany, out of harm's way. In *King Richard III*, Richmond, who has been biding his time in France, begins gathering forces once **King Richard III** ascends to the throne. Spurred on by nobles fleeing Richard, Richmond sets sail for England. The night before the two armies meet, the two leaders dream of the ghosts of Richard's victims; while they curse Richard, they praise Richmond, saying that he will be victorious and "beget a happy race of kings." Richmond does defeat Richard, and accepts the crown of England. He marries **Elizabeth of York**, the daughter of **King Edward IV** and **Queen Elizabeth**, thus uniting the Houses of York and Lancaster and ending the Wars of the Roses.

Seth Richmond

Winesburg, Ohio
Sherwood Anderson

A sensitive, deep-thinking young man, and a friend of **George Willard**'s.

Kitty Ricketts

Ulysses
James Joyce

One of the prostitutes working in **Bella Cohen**'s brothel. Kitty seems to have a relationship with **Lynch** and has spent part of the day with him. Her clothing reflects her upper-class aspirations.

Rickey

On the Road
Jack Kerouac

Terry's wild, alcoholic, happy-go-lucky brother, whom **Sal Paradise** meets in Sabinal.

Ricky

Holes
Louis Sachar

See **Zigzag**.

Tom Riddle

The Harry Potter Series: Books 2 and *4*
J. K. Rowling

The last remaining descendent of Salazar Slytherin. Tom's past and appearance resemble **Harry Potter**'s. Tom grew up to become **Voldemort**. Through his old diary he enchants **Ginny Weasley** to perform his dark tasks.

Sean Rideheart

Animal Dreams
Barbara Kingsolver

An art collector from Tucson. Sean Rideheart becomes interested in the peacock piñatas being sold by the Stitch and Bitch Club, led by **Doña Althea**. He tells the women that if Grace and its trees can be declared a historic reserve and get listed on the National Register of Historic Places, it will receive national protection from the kind of destruction the polluted water and the dam wreak on the town.

Rider

Go Down, Moses
William Faulkner

A huge black man who works at the sawmill and lives in a house on Carothers Edmonds's property. His wife, **Mannie**, dies young.

Paul Riesling

Babbitt
Sinclair Lewis

Babbitt's college classmate and closest friend. When Riesling was young, he wanted to become a professional violinist, but like Babbitt, he became mired in the conventional lifestyle of the middle-class businessman. He is harshly critical of the monotonous, hypocritical character of Zenith's middle class. His wife, **Zilla**, is equally dissatisfied with this life and vents her frustration on Riesling by constantly nagging him. One day, Riesling snaps and shoots her during an argument—an offense for which he is sentenced to three years in prison. The loss of his friend devastates Babbitt and prompts him to embark on a rebellion against the middle-class lifestyle.

Zilla Riesling

Babbitt
Sinclair Lewis

Paul Riesling's wife. Bored and embittered with their monotonous, conventional, middle-class lifestyle, Zilla vents her frustration by constantly nagging her husband. During an argument, Riesling snaps and shoots her. After he is sent to prison for three years, Zilla "gets religion" but uses it to give moral justification to her resentful desire to see Riesling suffer for shooting her.

Dr. Bernard Rieux

The Plague
Albert Camus

The novel's protagonist and narrator. A humanist and atheist, Rieux follows his own code of social ethics. He struggles to convince the authorities to enact sanitation measures to contain the plague, then doggedly battles the plague despite indications that his efforts are fruitless. Separated from his wife during the quarantine, Rieux does not allow his personal distress to distract him from the work of alleviating Oran's collective suffering.

Jacob Riis

Ragtime
E. L. Doctorow

A famous journalist and advocate of the poor who wrote *How the Other Half Lives*, which exposed life in the tenements.

Mr. Riley

The Mill on the Floss
George Eliot

The auction manager in St. Ogg's. **Jeremy Tulliver** looks up to him as a high-class man of wisdom and intelligence, but Mr. Riley is more likely middle class and not particularly wise.

Aunt Rina

Hedda Gabler
Henrik Ibsen

Tesman's sick aunt. Rina helped **Aunt Julle** raise **Tesman**.

Rinaldi

A Farewell to Arms
Ernest Hemingway

A surgeon in the Italian army and **Frederic Henry**'s closest friend. The mischievous, wry, and oversexed Rinaldi is a skilled doctor, but his primary practice is seducing beautiful women.

Rinehart

Invisible Man
Ralph Ellison

A surreal figure who never appears in the book except by reputation. Rinehart possesses a seemingly infinite number of identities, among them pimp, bookie, and preacher who speaks on the subject of "invisibility."

Ringo

The Unvanquished
William Faulkner

A black slave born the same month as **Bayard**, who is his best friend and constant companion. Ringo is the smarter of the two boys, and displays savvy and entrepreneurism as well as a sense of humor that Bayard lacks. He is bold and courageous, and he accompanies Bayard on his most dangerous and difficult adventures. Even after the slaves are freed, he continues to serve Bayard with the same unfailing devotion as before.

Three Rioters

The Canterbury Tales
Geoffrey Chaucer

The three protagonists of **the Pardoner**'s Tale. All three indulge in and represent the vices against which the Pardoner has railed in his Prologue: Gluttony, Drunkeness, Gambling, and Swearing. These traits define the three and eventually lead to their downfall.

Rita

Lolita
Vladimir Nabokov

An alcoholic floozy whom **Humbert Humbert** lives with after he loses **Lolita Haze**. Rita has many encounters with the law and becomes paranoid that Humbert will leave her.

Rita

The Handmaid's Tale
Margaret Atwood

One of the **Marthas** of the Republic of Gilead at the house hold of **the Commander**. Rita is less content with her lot than **Cora**.

Mr. Ritchie

On the Beach
Nevil Shute

The Prime Minister of Australia. Mr. Ritchie explains the submarine's mission to the crew.

Doris Rivera

I Never Promised You a Rose Garden
Joanne Greenberg

A hospital legend for having left the mental ward to live a normal life in the outside world. When Doris is recommitted to the hospital, the other patients are bitterly disappointed, because they secretly hope they can get well and return to the outside world.

Diana Rivers

Jane Eyre
Charlotte Brontë

Jane Eyre's cousin, and **Mary Rivers** and **St. John Rivers**'s sister. Diana, a kind and intelligent woman, urges Jane not to go to India with St. John.

Dr. W. H. R. Rivers

Regeneration
Pat Barker

The protagonist of the novel and a practicing psychiatrist at Craiglockhart War Hospital. Originally an anthropologist, Dr. Rivers has spent a good part of his life studying the culture and customs of man. Though he is dedicated to doing his duty by healing the men so that they may return to fight, Rivers feels conflicted about the amount of control and influence he has over his patients.

Lord Rivers

Henry VI, Part III and *Richard III*
William Shakespeare

Brother to **Elizabeth Woodville, Lady Grey** (later Queen Elizabeth), uncle to the **Marquess of Dorset** and **Lord Grey**, and brother-in-law to **King Edward IV**. Though he survivies the Lancaster-York battle, the megalomaniacal Richard III executes Rivers and Grey.

Mary Rivers

Jane Eyre
Charlotte Brontë

Jane Eyre's cousin and **St. John Rivers** and **Diana Rivers**'s sister. Mary is a kind and intelligent young woman who is forced to work as a governess after her father loses his fortune. Like her sister, she serves as a model for Jane of an independent woman who is also able to maintain close relationships with others and a sense of meaning in her life.

St. John Rivers

Jane Eyre
Charlotte Brontë

Diana Rivers and **Mary Rivers**'s brother, and **Jane Eyre**'s cousin. Along with his sisters, St. John serves as Jane's benefactor after she runs away from Thornfield, giving her food and shelter. The minister at Morton, St. John is cold, reserved, and often controlling in his interactions with others.

Hosie Roach

Cold Sassy Tree
Olive Anne Burns

A twenty-one-year-old boy from Mill Town who attends **Will Tweedy**'s school despite his advanced age.

Howard Roark

The Fountainhead
Ayn Rand

The protagonist and hero. Roark is a brilliant architect of absolute integrity. Though not without friends and colleagues, Roark relies on himself alone. Born poor, Roark supported himself throughout high school and college by working odd jobs on construction sites. He brings fiery intensity to all his work and loves **Dominique Francon** with violent passion. He rapes her and cures her of her frigidity. He sees marriage as a meaningless formality, he feels no jealousy toward **Peter Keating** about his marriage to Dominique, and he feels no compunction about committing adultery with her. He considers all value systems but his own utterly irrelevant.

Rob

Tuesdays with Morrie
Mitch Albom

One of **Morrie Schwartz**'s two adult sons. Though they live far away, Rob and his brother **Jon** often travel to Boston to visit Morrie, especially as his condition worsens.

Pearl Robbins

Arrowsmith
Sinclair Lewis

The secretary to **Dr. A. DeWitt Tubbs** at the Mcgurk Institute in New York. Beautiful and talented, **Pearl** has learned the "business" and even attempts to attain the directorship when Tubbs resigns. When **Max Gottlieb** is named head of the institute, Pearl basically runs it because of Gottlieb's lack of attention to commercial matters.

Robert

Moll Flanders
Daniel Defoe

The younger of the two brothers who fall in love with **Moll**. He eventually marries her in spite of his family's disapproval. However, he dies after five years.

Robert

Something Wicked This Way Comes
Ray Bradbury

Miss Foley's nephew. **Mr. Cooger** pretends to be him.

Robert

Ceremony
Leslie Marmon Silko

Auntie's husband. Robert is a mild-mannered quiet man who has little power in the family. He generally minds his own business, adhering to the old traditions. Robert shows his deep caring for **Tayo** as he welcomes him home from the war and as he warns him of **Emo**'s impending attack.

Roberto

Like Water for Chocolate
Laura Esquivel

The first child of **Rosaura** and **Pedro**, Roberto dies in America after being taken away from **Tita**'s care.

Dread Pirate Roberts

The Princess Bride
William Goldman

The most feared pirate name on the seas. Dread Pirate Roberts captured **Westley**, and passed the name on to him.

John Roberts

The Heart Is a Lonely Hunter
Carson McCullers

A black postman friend of **Dr. Benedict Mady Copeland**'s. Mr. Roberts also urges **Jake Blount** not to try to defend **Willie**, as he says it will only lead to trouble.

Marion Roberts

Legs
William Kennedy

Jack's girlfriend, she is a stereotypical Broadway dancer. She has a perfect body and knows how to wield her sex appeal, but she is not exceptionally intelligent. She loves to party and hates being left alone when Jack has to do business or go home to his wife.

Mr. Roberts

Harry Potter and the Goblet of Fire
J. K. Rowling

A confused Muggle (non-magical person) who owns the site where the Weasleys camp during the Quidditch World Cup.

Brian Robeson

Hatchet
Gary Paulsen

The protagonist of *Hatchet*. He must learn to survive in the harsh Canadian wilderness after surviving a plane crash. He starts out as a New York City boy who takes for granted the daily conveniences of urban life, and transforms himself into a man of the wilderness, completely self-sufficient and very knowledgeable about his surrounding natural environment. His respect and love for nature only grow with time, as does his ability to come to terms with his parents' divorce. He is eventually rescued and returned to civilization.

Brian's father

Hatchet
Gary Paulsen

Divorced from **Brian's mother**. He is unaware that she is having an affair. One month after the divorce, Brian is on the plane, heading north to visit his father and to bring him some special equipment from New York but crash lands and must learn to survive in the Canadian wilderness.

Hatchet
Gary Paulsen

Brian's mother

The wife of **Brian's father**. She has recently filed for divorce because of her extramarital affair with **the man with short blond hair.** She gives a hatchet to Brian when he departs for Canada.

Doctor Faustus
Christopher Marlowe

Robin

An ostler who provides comic contrast to **Faustus**.

Far from the Madding Crowd
Thomas Hardy

Fanny Robin

A young orphaned servant girl at **Bathsheba Everdene**'s farm in Weatherbury. Fanny runs away from Bathsheba's farm. **Sergeant Francis Troy** has a romance with Fanny, eventually almost marrying her. Fanny dies giving birth to Troy's child at the poor house in Casterbridge. Bathsheba's jealousy regarding Fanny turns to reserved compassion when she discovers the dead child of Troy and Fanny in the coffin along with Fanny.

Lord Jim
Joseph Conrad

Robinson

Along with **Chester**, one of two disreputable characters who offer **Jim**, through **Marlow**, a job taking a wreck of a ship to a desolate island to collect guano. The guano-collecting mission, under someone else's command, leaves port and is never heard from again; it is thought to have been wiped out by a hurricane.

The Adventures of Tom Sawyer
Mark Twain

Dr. Robinson

A respected local physician. Dr. Robinson shows his more sordid side on the night of his murder: he hires **Injun Joe** and **Muff Potter** to dig up Hoss Williams's grave because he wants to use the corpse for medical experiments. Injun Joe kills Dr. Robinson and blames the murder on the drunk Potter.

Winesburg, Ohio
Sherwood Anderson

Enoch Robinson

A man from Winesburg who moves to New York. In the grip of a terrible loneliness, he becomes slightly unhinged and populates his apartment with imaginary people.

Fallen Angels
Walter Dean Myers

Johnny Robinson

A boy from **Richie Perry**'s neighborhood in Harlem who is killed in Vietnam.

Tom Robinson

To Kill a Mockingbird
Harper Lee

The generous field hand wrongfully accused of rape by **Mayella Ewell** and **Bob Ewell**. **Atticus Finch** defends Tom in court, even though Atticus knows that it will turn the whole community against Atticus. Tom is unfairly convicted of raping Mayella, and is shot seventeen times while trying to escape prison.

Comte de Rochefort

The Three Musketeers
Alexandre Dumas

Cardinal Richelieu's private spy. He is a dangerous man who in the end arrests **d'Artagnan**, bringing him to a private audience with the Cardinal. He plans with the **Lady de Winter** for a personal carriage to take the Lady's unknowing prisoner, **Madame Bonacieux**, away. The Comte de Rochefort is also known as the Man from Meung.

Rochelle

Sula
Toni Morrison

Helene Wright's mother. She is a Creole prostitute in New Orleans. Rochelle played little part in Helene's upbringing.

Rochester

Wide Sargasso Sea
Jean Rhys

Antoinette's English husband who, though never named in the novel, narrates at least a third of the story. Rochester, the youngest son of a wealthy Englishman, travels to the West Indies for financial independence, as his older brother will inherit his father's estate. When Rochester arrives in Spanish Town, he comes down with a fever almost immediately. When **Mr. Mason** offers him a hefty sum of money to marry Antoinette, he succumbs to the pressure, though he knows nothing of the girl or her family. He realizes his mistake during his honeymoon on one of the Windward Islands. Eventually, he abandons the Caribbean lifestyle he has come to hate and returns to England, where he locks his mad wife in an upstairs garret.

Edward Rochester

Jane Eyre
Charlotte Brontë

Jane Eyre's employer and the master of Thornfield. Rochester is a wealthy, passionate man with a dark secret—his marriage to **Bertha Mason**—that provides much of the novel's suspense. Rochester is unconventional, ready to set aside polite manners, propriety, and consideration of social class in order to interact with Jane frankly and directly. He is rash and impetuous and has spent much of his adult life roaming about Europe in an attempt to avoid the consequences of his youthful indiscretions.

Rocinante

Don Quixote
Miguel de Cervantes

Don Quixote's worn-out barn horse. Slow and faithful.

Rocky

Ceremony
Leslie Marmon Silko

Tayo's cousin and adoptive brother. He represents for Tayo and his family the perfect success of a Native American to integrate into white society. Much to everyone's dismay, Rocky dies in the Philippines during World War II.

Roderigo

Othello
William Shakespeare

A jealous suitor of **Desdemona**'s. Young, rich, and foolish, Roderigo is convinced that if he gives **Iago** all of his money, Iago will help him to win Desdemona's hand. His efforts to woo Desdemona are repeatedly frustrated, especially after **Othello** marries Desdemona and then takes her to Cyprus. Roderigo is so desperate and trustful that Iago convinces him to kill **Cassio**, another potential suitor of Desdemona's.

Jem Rodney

Silas Marner
George Eliot

A somewhat disreputable character and a poacher. Jem sees **Silas Marner** in the midst of one of Silas's fits. Silas later accuses Jem of stealing his gold.

Rodolpho

A View from the Bridge
Arthur Miller

Beatrice's young, illegal immigrant cousin, and the brother of **Marco**. Rodolpho prefers singing jazz to working on the ships and desires all the privileges of Western society. Unlike his Italian brother Marco, Rodolpho does not seek revenge on **Eddie Carbone** for calling Immigration or abusing his fiance **Catherine** in front of him. He does end up marrying Catherine, despite having to go to jail because of Eddie's call to the Immigration Bureau, and despite Eddie's attempted murder of Marco and Marco's subsequent murder of Eddie.

Jan Rodricks

Childhood's End
Arthur C. Clarke

A young, brilliant man with a strong interest in astronomy and space exploration. He is bitter that the Overlords have never allowed mankind to explore space.

Leonard Rodriguez

Farewell to Manzanar
Jeanne Wakatsuki Houston

Jeanne's classmate at her new high school in San Jose. Leonard's willingness to be friends with Jeanne despite her outsider status contrasts with their teachers' inherent prejudice against Japanese people.

Roger

Lord of the Flies
William Golding

Jack's "lieutenant." A sadistic, cruel boy, Roger brutalizes the littluns and murders **Piggy** by rolling a boulder onto him.

Roger

Go Ask Alice
Anonymous

A straight, square boy on whom **Alice** has an overwhelming crush. He plans to attend military school.

Roger

Ellen Foster
Kaye Gibbons

Stella's baby son who likes to crawl into **Ellen**'s room and chew on objects he finds on the floor.

Rogers

Walden Two
B. F. Skinner

A former classmate of **Professor Burris**, **Steve Jamnik**'s friend and **Barbara Macklin**'s boyfriend. After returning from service in WWII, he decides to try to find a better life than standard American capitalism can offer him.

Ben Rogers

The Adventures of Tom Sawyer
Mark Twain

One of **Tom Sawyer**'s friends, whom Tom persuades to whitewash **Aunt Polly**'s fence by making the task look enviable.

Ethel Rogers

And Then There Were None
Agatha Christie

Thomas Rogers's wife. Ethel is a frail woman, and the death of **Anthony Marston** makes her faint. **Judge Lawrence Wargrave** believes her husband dominates her and that he masterminded their crime.

Thomas Rogers

And Then There Were None
Agatha Christie

The dignified butler. Rogers continues to be a proper servant even after his wife, **Ethel Rogers**, is found dead and the bodies begin piling up. The recording accuses Rogers and his wife of letting their former employer die because they stood to inherit money from her.

Parfyon Semyonovich Rogozhin

The Idiot
Fyodor Dostoevsky

Madly and passionately in love with **Anastassya Filippovna Barashkova**. After receiving a large inheritance, he attempts to woo her by bringing her 100,000 rubles. She runs between him and **Prince Lev Nikolayevich Myshkin** until the end, when Rogozhin kills her.

Roland

Song of Roland
Unknown

The hero. Roland is only mentioned in passing in historical records, as the prefect of the Breton Marches, among those who fell at Roncesvals. He is a skillfull and bold warrior, one of the twelve peers of France and **Charlemagne**'s nephew and favorite. To Roland, the Frankish campaign in Spain is a crusade, and he therefore allows no compromise with the Saracens. Roland's stepfather **Ganelon** resents Roland's boastfulness, popularity, and success on the battlefield. Ganelon plots the Saracen ambush of the Franks at Roncesvals, masterminding Roland's death. Roland dies a martyr's death at Roncesvals and is directly taken up to Paradise by saints and angels. The rest of the poem recounts how Charlemagne avenges Roland's death.

Roland

The Caine Mutiny
Herman Wouk

One of **Willie Keith**'s roommates in midshipmen's school, and **Thomas Keefer**'s brother. Roland understands the way the military works.

Ricky Roma

Glengarry Glen Ross
David Mamet

A big-shot real estate salesman with a quick tongue. Roma is the top name on the board at his office, which means he is currently the most successful salesman. Rather than trying to force customers to submit to his sales tactics, as the others do, he lures people into thinking they want what he is selling.

Romeo

Romeo and Juliet
William Shakespeare

The son and heir of **Montague** and **Lady Montague**. A young man of about sixteen, Romeo is handsome, intelligent, and sensitive. At the beginning of the play he is madly in love with an unseen character named **Rosaline**, but the instant he lays eyes on **Juliet** he falls in love with her. **Friar Lawrence** questions the impetuousness of Romeo's love, but soon marries Romeo to Juliet even though she is a Capulet. Romeo kills himself when he believes that his beloved is dead. Romeo is also an affectionate and devoted friend to **Mercutio**, **Friar Lawrence**, and to his cousin **Benvolio**.

Pedro Romero

The Sun Also Rises
Ernest Hemingway

A beautiful, nineteen-year-old bullfighter. His prodigious talents in the ring charm aficionados and casual spectators alike. Romero becomes embroiled in a passionate affair with **Lady Brett Ashley**, but Brett ultimately breaks off the affair because she fears she will ruin the young bullfighter and his career.

Mary Rommely

A Tree Grows in Brooklyn
Betty Smith

Francie Nolan's maternal grandmother, who came to America from Poland. She believes in the supernatural, tells ghost stories and fairy tales, and is a devout Catholic. Mary is convinced that **Katie Nolan** will have a better life because Katie can read and write.

Romulus

The Prince
Niccolò Machiavelli

Founder and first king of Rome.

Rontu

Island of the Blue Dolphins
Scott O'Dell

The leader of the pack of wild dogs that lives on Ghalas-at. He was brought to the island by **the Aleuts**, and is **Karana**'s companion, though she initially blames him for her brother's death.

Rontu-Aru

Island of the Blue Dolphins
Scott O'Dell

Literally "son of **Rontu**." **Karana** befriends this dog after Rontu's death.

Margaret Roper

A Man for All Seasons
Robert Bolt

More's well-educated and inquisitive daughter. Also called Meg, Margaret is in love with and later marries **William Roper**. She shows that she understands her father perhaps better than anyone else in the play. However, like her mother **Alice**, Margaret questions her father's stubborn refusal to bow down to **King Henry**'s will.

William Roper

A Man for All Seasons
Robert Bolt

An overzealous young man who is a staunch Lutheran at the beginning of the play and later converts to Catholicism. Roper is **Margaret**'s boyfriend and, after he converts to Catholicism, her husband. Roper's high-minded ideals contrast with **More**'s level-headed morality. Each of Roper's scenes shows him taking a public stance on a new issue, in opposition to More, who prefers to keep his opinions to himself.

Antoine Roquentin

Nausea
Jean-Paul Sartre

The protagonist of the novel. He is also the narrator, writing down his observations in diary format. After traveling around most of Africa and the Far East, he returned to Bouville to complete his historical research on the **Marquis de Rollebon**. He has lost interest in his research, and thinks the physical characteristics of objects and people are just a comforting facade to mask the "nothingness" of existence. By the end of the novel he has disavowed the past, embraced his existence, and discovered that there is no purpose to existence. Rather than surrender to despair, he decides to assert his freedom and moves to Paris to write a novel.

Rosa the Beautiful

The House of the Spirits
Isabel Allende

The oldest daughter of **Severo del Valle** and **Nivea del Valle**. She is engaged to **Esteban Trueba** but dies before they can marry, accidentally poisoned by mysterious brandy intended for Severo at his political celebration.

Rosalba

Love in the Time of Cholera
Gabriel García Márquez

The young woman who travels aboard the ship to Villa de Leyva with two other women, presumably her mother and sister, and carries her baby in a bird cage. **Florentino Ariza** is convinced that it is she who one night seizes him, drags him into her cabin, and robs him of his virginity. Florentino's encounter with Rosalba instigates his sexual promiscuity and his belief that he can relieve his desire for **Fermina Daza** by having sex with countless other women.

Rosalind

As You Like It
William Shakespeare

The daughter of **Duke Senior** and cousin of **Celia**. Rosalind is independent, strong-willed, good-hearted, and clever. When the tyrannical **Duke Frederick** exiles her, Rosalind resourcefully uses her trip to the Forest of Arden as an opportunity to take control of her own destiny. With Celia in voluntary exile along with her, Rosalind disguises herself as Ganymede, a handsome young man, and offers herself as a tutor in the ways of love to her beloved **Orlando**. In chastising **Phoebe** for spurning the love of **Silvius,** and mentoring Orlando, Rosalind teaches those around her to think, feel, and love better than they have previously.

Rosaline

Love's Labour's Lost
William Shakespeare

One of three ladies attending the **Princess of France**. Rosaline, along with **Maria** and **Katherine**, helps catch the fancy of the three lords attending the **King of Navarre**.

Rosaline

Romeo and Juliet
William Shakespeare

The woman with whom **Romeo** is infatuated at the beginning of the play. Rosaline never appears onstage.

Rosaura

Like Water for Chocolate
Laura Esquivel

The second daughter of **Mama Elena**, she marries **Pedro**, much to the despair of **Tita**. Her first child, **Roberto**, dies as an infant; her second, **Esperanza**, prohibited like Tita from ever marrying, weds **Alex**. She suffers from digestive problems that make her overweight and give her bad breath and flatulence. When she dies, her funeral is poorly attended because of the unbearable smell still emanating from her body.

The rose

The Little Prince
Antoine de Saint-Exupéry

A coquettish flower who has trouble expressing her love for **the Little Prince** and consequently drives him away. Throughout the story, she occupies the prince's thoughts and heart.

Rose

Pigs in Heaven
Barbara Kingsolver

Cash Stillwater's girlfriend in Wyoming. She always seems to be trying a little too hard to attract the attention of men.

Rose Dear

Jazz
Toni Morrison

Violet's mother and **True Belle**'s daughter. Her husband abandons the family for long stretches at a time, squandering their money and getting them further into debt. When she and her children are driven into utter poverty, Rose Dear loses faith and commits suicide by throwing herself into a well.

Rose of Sharon

The Grapes of Wrath
John Steinbeck

The oldest of **Ma** and **Pa Joad**'s daughters, and **Connie**'s wife. An impractical, petulant, and romantic young woman, Rose of Sharon begins the journey to California pregnant with her first child. She has notions of establishing a life with Connie in a city, but the harsh realities of migrant life soon disabuse Rose of Sharon of these ideas, as her husband abandons her and her child is stillborn.

Rose the Nose

Ender's Game
Orson Scott Card

Ender Wiggin's commander in Rat Army. Rose the Nose tries to control Ender, but, after **Dink Meeker** advises him to stick up for himself, Ender is able to make Rose the Nose back down.

Simon Rosedale

The House of Mirth
Edith Wharton

A dedicated social climber who owns many stocks and lots of property. At the end of the novel, Rosedale asks **Lily Bart** to marry him, an opportunity that she passes up at first. Later on, he becomes her friend and visits her after she becomes very poor and very sick.

Madame de Rosemonde

Dangerous Liaisons
Pierre-Ambroise-François Choderlos de Laclos

The aunt of **the Vicomte de Valmont**. She corresponds with, and offers advice to, **the Présidente de Tourvel** when Tourvel is having difficulties with Valmont.

Ellen Rosen

Number the Stars
Lois Lowry

Annemarie Johansen's schoolmate and best friend. She is Jewish. The only child of **Mrs. Rosen** and **Mr. Rosen**, Ellen Rosen is very quiet and more serious than her best friend. To Ellen, the events of the war are terrifying, and she cannot reflect upon them in the way that Annemarie can. **Mrs. Johansen** takes care of Ellen for a short time while Mr. and Mrs. Rosen prepare for the family's escape to Sweden.

Mr. Rosen

Number the Stars
Lois Lowry

Father of **Ellen Rosen**, husband of **Mrs. Rosen**. Mr. Rosen is a teacher and has instilled in his daughter the importance of education. He hides with his family on **Henrik**'s boat after the staged funeral for **Great-aunt Birte**. The Rosens safely escape the Nazis and are transported to Sweden.

Mrs. Rosen

Number the Stars
Lois Lowry

Ellen Rosen's mother, **Mr. Rosen**'s wife, and **Mrs. Johansen**'s friend. The two mothers often have coffee together in the afternoon. Mrs. Rosen fears the ocean, but she overcomes her fear when **Henrik** takes her family across the water to Sweden to escape the Nazis.

Ethel Rosenberg

Angels in America
Tony Kushner

A real-life Jewish woman who was executed for treason during the McCarthy era. The Ethel of the play returns as a ghost to take satisfaction in the death of her persecutor, **Roy Cohn**. Ethel hates Roy with a "needlesharp" passion, yet on his deathbed she musters enough compassion to sing to him.

Rosencrantz

Hamlet
William Shakespeare

Rosencrantz and **Guildenstern** are courtiers and former friends of **Hamlet**'s from Wittenberg. **Claudius** and **Gertrude** summon the pair so that they can discover the cause of Hamlet's strange behavior. Sensing their hidden purpose, Hamlet has them murdered by making them the targets of a contract killing originally meant for Hamlet himself.

Eliot Rosewater

Slaughterhouse-Five
Kurt Vonnegut

A war veteran who occupies the bed near **Billy Pilgrim** in the mental ward of a veterans' hospital. Rosewater helps Billy find escape in the science-fiction novels of **Kilgore Trout**.

Rosie

Bless Me, Ultima
Rudolfo A. Anaya

The woman who runs the local brothel in a ramshackle mansion. **Antonio Márez** is devastated when he finds out that his brother **Andrew Márez** frequents the brothel.

Edward Rosier

The Portrait of a Lady
Henry James

A hapless American art collector who lives in Paris. Rosier falls in love with **Pansy Osmond** and does his best to win her father **Gilbert Osmond**'s permission to marry her. But though he sells his art collection and appeals to **Madame Merle**, **Isabel Archer**, and the **Countess Gemini**, Rosier is unable to change Osmond's mind.

Roskus

The Sound and the Fury
William Faulkner

Dilsey's husband and the Compsons' servant. Roskus suffers from a severe case of rheumatism that eventually kills him.

Madam Rosmerta

Harry Potter and the Prisoner of Azkaban
J. K. Rowling

The barmaid at the Three Broomsticks in Hogsmeade.

Ross

Macbeth
William Shakespeare

A Scottish nobleman.

Ross

Black Boy
Richard Wright

A black Communist whom **Richard Wright** wishes to profile for his series of biographical sketches. Ross is somewhat uneasy around Richard, and suspicious of his deviations from Party doctrine.

Lord Ross

Richard II
William Shakespeare

An early supporter of **Henry Bolingbroke**. Following the death of **John of Gaunt**, Ross, along with the **Earl of Northumberland** and **Lord Willoughby**, acknowledge the ruinous reign of **King Richard II**; when Northumberland reveals that Bolingbroke has come to England with an army, the three decide to join forces with him to return England to its former glory.

Count Ilya Andreyevich Rostov

War and Peace
Leo Tolstoy

Natasha Ilyinichna Rostova, **Vera Ilyinichna Rostova**, **Nikolai Ilyich Rostov** and **Pyotor Ilyich Rostov**'s father and **Countess Natalya Rostova**'s husband. A loving, friendly, and financially carefree nobleman who lives with his large family at Otradnoe, their estate south of Moscow. The old count piles up debts through luxurious living, eventually depriving his children of their inheritance—a failing for which he seeks his children's forgiveness before he dies.

Nikolai Ilyich Rostov

War and Peace
Leo Tolstoy

The impetuous eldest son of **Count Ilya Andreyevich Rostov** and **Countess Natalya Rostova**. He joins the Russian forces in 1805 and spends much of the novel on the front. Nikolai accumulates gambling debts that become burdensome for his family. However, upon his father's death, he supports his mother and cousin Sonya on his meager salary while continuing to pay off the family's debts. Nikolai eventually marries the heiress **Marya Nikolayevna Bolkonskaya**, saving his family from financial ruin.

Pyotor Ilyich Rostov

War and Peace
Leo Tolstoy

The youngest son of **Count Ilya Andreyevich Rostov** and **Countess Natalya Rostova**. He begs to join the Russian army. Pyotor Ilyich, who is close to his sister **Natasha Ilyinichna Rostova** and beloved by his mother, is killed in partisan fighting after the French begin their withdrawal from Moscow.

Countess Natalya Rostova

War and Peace
Leo Tolstoy

Count Ilya Andreyevich Rostov's wife. The countess is as neglectful of money matters as her husband, maintaining standards of luxury that prove a burden to her son **Nikolai Ilyich Rostov** when he supports her after the count's death. The death of her youngest son, **Pyotor Ilyich**, deeply affects the countess, sinking her into a gloom from which she never again emerges.

Natasha Ilyinichna Rostova

War and Peace
Leo Tolstoy

The youngest daughter of **Count Ilya Andreyevich Rostov** and **Countess Natalya Rostova**. Natasha is full of joyful vitality. From infancy to adulthood, Natasha charms everyone who meets her, winning the hearts of **Prince Andrei Nikolayevich Bolkonsky**, **Anatole Vasilievich Kuragin** and finally **Pierre Bezukhov**. Yet, despite her charms, Natasha never comes across as a show-off or a flirt angling for men's attentions. She changes radically by the end of the novel, growing wise in a way that makes her Pierre's spiritual equal.

Sonya Rostova

War and Peace
Leo Tolstoy

The humble cousin of **Natasha Ilyinichna Rostova** and **Nikolai Ilyich Rostov**, who lives with the Rostovs as a ward. Sonya and Nikolai were childhood sweethearts, but as adults, Sonya gives up Nikolai so that he can marry a rich woman and save the Rostov finances.

Vera Ilyinichna Rostova

War and Peace
Leo Tolstoy

The eldest daughter of **Count Ilya Andreyevich Rostov** and **Countess Natalya Rostova**. Vera is a somewhat cold, unpleasant young woman, and her only proposal of marriage comes from an officer who is candid about his need for her dowry.

Arnold Rothstein

Legs
William Kennedy

The Jewish mob boss under whom **Jack** begins his tutelage. When Rothstein tells Jack that he needs a new haircut, Jack murders and robs a man to pay for one.

Mrs. Rothwell

Oranges Are Not the Only Fruit
Jeanette Winterson

Near-deaf member of **Jeanette**'s church who almost drowns in Blackpool.

Rouault

Madame Bovary
Gustave Flaubert

Emma Bovary's father, a simple, essentially kindly farmer with a weakness for drink. He is devoted both to Emma and to the memory of his first wife, whom he loved deeply.

Cecil Rountree

Babbitt
Sinclair Lewis

The chairman of the program committee for the annual convention of the State Association of Real Estate Boards. At **Rountree**'s urging, **Babbitt** writes a speech to deliver at the convention.

Countess of Roussillon

All's Well that Ends Well
William Shakespeare

Bertram's mother, **Helena**'s guardian, and the mistress of Roussillon. A wise, discerning old woman, the countess supports Helena, giving her her blessing to go to the **King of France**'s court. When Helena returns without Bertram, and she receives letters from her son denouncing the new marriage, the Countess condemns Bertram's behavior.

Rowena

Pudd'nhead Wilson
Mark Twain

The town belle and the daughter of the **Widow Cooper**, or Aunt Patsy.

Lady Rowena

Ivanhoe
Sir Walter Scott

A beautiful Saxon lady. She is the ward of **Cedric the Saxon**, and the love of his son **Ivanhoe**. Ivanhoe and Rowena are prevented from marrying until the end of the book because Cedric would rather see Rowena married to **Athelstane**—a match that could reawaken the Saxon royal line. Rowena represents the chivalric ideal of womanhood: She is fair, chaste, virtuous, loyal, and mild-mannered.

Sir Rowland de Bois

As You Like It
William Shakespeare

The father of **Oliver** and **Orlando**, friend of **Duke Senior**, and enemy of **Duke Frederick**. Upon Sir Rowland's death, the vast majority of his estate was handed over to Oliver, according to the custom of primogeniture.

Roxana

Pudd'nhead Wilson
Mark Twain

A slave nicknamed Roxy. Roxana begins as a slave owned by **Percy Northumberland Driscoll**. Only one-sixteenth black, she looks white. She gives birth to a son, **Valet de Chambre**, called Chambers. **Colonel Cecil Burleigh Essex** is Chambers's father. Roxy switches her son with Percy's son, **Thomas a Beckett Driscoll**. Chambers becomes "Tom," and Tom becomes "Chambers." Roxy is freed when Percy dies, and she goes to work on a riverboat. When work stops on the riverboat, she returns to the town of Dawson's Landing, and starts hounding "Tom," eventually revealing to him the truth about his real parents. She pressures "Tom" for money, forces him to sell her as a slave and then forces him to buy her back again. After the trial of "Tom" gets him "sold down the river," Roxy spends most of her time in church repenting. The real Tom still pays Roxy a stipend as his "mother" and as his father's former slave.

Roxane

Cyrano de Bergerac
Edmond Rostand

Cyrano de Bergerac's cousin. She is a beautiful and intellectual heiress who appreciates Cyrano's wit and courage and has a soft spot for romantic poetry. Though she initially falls in love with **Baron Christian de Neuvillette** for his good looks, she later comes to love him because of the soul expressed in his letters—which she thinks are Christian's, but are actually written by Cyrano. After Christian's death, she joins a convent, and Cyrano visits her and reads to her.

Roy

Go Tell It on the Mountain
James Baldwin

John Grimes's younger half-brother, and **Gabriel** and **Elizabeth**'s son. He is outspoken and unconcerned with the metaphysical questions that plague John. His wild youth closely resembles that of his father, and he shares many traits with his deceased half-brother **Royal**, Gabriel's unacknowledged son.

Roy

Ellen Foster
Kaye Gibbons

Julia's husband. Roy is a progressively minded hippy who keeps an organic garden with which **Ellen** is fascinated.

Roy

This Boy's Life
Tobias Wolff

The alcoholic and abusive ex-husband of **Rosemary Wolff**. He follows her and **Jack Wolff** from Sarasota to Salt Lake City after she has fled from him. Roy is extremely possessive of Rosemary and checks up on her obsessively.

Dr. Royson

I Never Promised You a Rose Garden
Joanne Greenberg

The doctor who takes over **Deborah**'s case temporarily while **Dr. Fried** is away one summer. Dr. Royson and Deborah do not get along because he focuses on trying to logically prove to her that Yr is Deborah's own creation, not a real kingdom.

Marty Rubin

The Caine Mutiny
Herman Wouk

May Wynn's agent. He is a wholehearted supporter and friend to May and **Willie Keith**. Willie suspects him of having an affair with May. Marty sets May up with the jobs that allow her to support her family, he finds an apartment she can afford, and in the end, he helps Willie find May when she does not want to be found.

Ruckly

One Flew over the Cuckoo's Nest
Ken Kesey

A Chronic patient. Like **Ellis**, Ruckly was once an Acute who became a Chronic after a botched lobotomy.

Antanas Rudkus

The Jungle
Upton Sinclair

Jurgis and **Ona**'s young son. Antanas, named after his grandfather **Dede Antanas**, is Jurgis's last hope after Ona's death. However, Antanas dies tragically by drowning in mud on the street.

Dede Antanas Rudkus

The Jungle
Upton Sinclair

Jurgis Rudkus's father. A proud old man, Dede Antanas is humiliated when he must pay a middleman to help him find a job. The unsafe and unsanitary conditions at the workplace quickly lead to Dede Antanas's death.

Jurgis Rudkus

The Jungle
Upton Sinclair

The novel's protagonist. He immigrates to Chicago from Lithuania along with his sweetheart, **Ona Lukoszaite**. Although Jurgis is optimistic when he settles in Packingtown, the city's meatpacking district, his determination, health, family, and faith in the American Dream are slowly destroyed by Packingtown's miserable living and working conditions. Frustrated by an injury that leaves him unable to work, he becomes a beggar and ends up in and out of jail. Ultimately, after living on charity for some time, Jurgis regains hope when he stumbles upon a socialist rally and is inspired by the orator's political speech.

Rudolph

Ellen Foster
Kaye Gibbons

Ellen's uncle on her father's side. With his brother **Ellis**, Rudolph agrees to spy on Ellen and her father for Ellen's grandmother.

Rudy

How the Garcia Girls Lost Their Accents
Julia Alvarez

Yolanda's first boyfriend. He becomes frustrated when she does not want to have sex.

Mr. Rudyard

Homecoming
Cynthia Voigt

A farmer in southern Maryland. The children meet Rudyard when they offer to work picking tomatoes for him. They soon realize that Rudyard intends to hurt them.

Major Rufford

The Good Soldier
Ford Madox Ford

Nancy Rufford's father. A violent man, Rufford beat his wife severely and was eventually separated from her. During the action of the novel, he is stationed in India.

Nancy Rufford

The Good Soldier
Ford Madox Ford

A young woman who becomes the ward of **Leonora Powys Ashburnham** and **Captain Edward Ashburnham** after her mother abandons her and her father leaves for India. Having been educated in a convent school with nuns, Nancy remains naive and unworldly. She offers to sleep with Edward but tells him she could never love him. She helps drive him to suicide, and goes mad. After she succumbs to insanity, **John Dowell** becomes her caretaker.

Count Rugen

The Princess Bride
William Goldman

Prince Humperdinck's right-hand man. Count Rugen has six fingers on his right hand. He murdered **Inigo Montoya**'s father, and in the end is slain by Inigo.

Angel Ruiz

The Bean Trees
Barbara Kingsolver

Lou Ann Ruiz's husband. Lou Ann met him when he worked in the rodeo in Kentucky. After a pickup-truck accident, Angel's leg is replaced by a prosthetic limb, and his disability wounds his pride terribly. When Lou Ann gets pregnant, she stops having sex with him. Convinced that his amputation repulses her, Angel leaves her.

Cornelia Ruiz

Tortilla Flat
John Steinbeck

A restless girl and Tortilla Flat's primary source of gossip. Cornelia goes through husbands almost as quickly as **Danny**'s *paisanos* go through gallons of wine.

Lou Ann Ruiz

The Bean Trees
Barbara Kingsolver

A Kentucky woman who settled in Tucson with her baby, **Dwayne Ray**. Her husband, **Angel Ruiz**, has just walked out on her when the story begins, and **Taylor Greer** and **Turtle** move in with her.

Rumanian Rostipov

The House of the Spirits
Isabel Allende

An itinerant doctor who diagnoses **Clara**'s dumbness. He realizes that Clara has stopped speaking because she does not want to speak.

Bertram Copeland Rumfoord

Slaughterhouse-Five
Kurt Vonnegut

A Harvard history professor and the official U.S. Air Force historian. Rumfoord is laid up by a skiing accident in the same Vermont hospital as **Billy Pilgrim** after his plane crash. He is reluctant to believe that Billy was present during the Dresden raid.

Lily Rumfoord

Slaughterhouse-Five
Kurt Vonnegut

Betram Copeland Rumfoord's young trophy wife and research assistant. Lily Rumfoord is frightened of **Billy Pilgrim**.

Bobby Rupp

In Cold Blood
Truman Capote

Nancy Clutter's steady boyfriend. Bobby lives near the Clutters.

Rushworth

Mansfield Park
Jane Austen

Maria Bertram's fiancé and then husband. Rushworth is an idiot and a bore, but quite wealthy.

Lady Russell

Persuasion
Jane Austen

The former best friend of **Anne Elliot**'s deceased mother. Lady Russell is a woman of considerable birth and wealth who serves as advisor to the Elliot family. A practical woman, she is conscious of class interactions and finances.

Russian trader

Heart of Darkness
Joseph Conrad

A Russian sailor who has gone into the African interior as the trading representative of a Dutch company. He is a devoted disciple of **Kurtz**'s.

Orlando
Virginia Woolf

Rustum

The old gypsy man of the tribe in the hills of Turkey who welcomes **Orlando** into the tribe. Rustum later distrusts her when he finds her beliefs differ so much from those of the gypsies.

Stranger in a Strange Land
Robert A. Heinlein

Ruth

Sam's wife. She is an early member of **Valentine Michael Smith**'s Church of All Worlds. The unhappy couple join the church because Sam wants to learn the Martian language, but the two end up rediscovering their love for each other and becoming high-level church members.

The Remains of the Day
Kazuo Ishiguro

Ruth and Sarah

Two Jewish maids at Darlington Hall. **Lord Darlington** orders **Stevens** to fire them because of their religion.

The Red Tent
Anita Diamant

Ruti

Laban's mistreated young wife. She produces his two male heirs, **Kemuel** and **Beor**. She is either murdered by Laban or driven to suicide by him.

Henry VI, Part III
William Shakespeare

Edmund, Earl of Rutland

Richard Plantagenet, Duke of York's youngest son, and the younger brother of **King Edward IV**, **George, Duke of Clarence**, and **King Richard III**. Though he pleads for his life, Rutland is killed by **Lord Clifford** the younger in revenge for York's killing of Clifford's father.

Black Like Me
John Howard Griffin

Don Rutledge

White photographer. He photographs **John Howard Griffin** in New Orleans, coming to terms with his own social and racial preconceptions in the process.

This Side of Paradise
F. Scott Fitzgerald

Dawson Ryder

A handsome young man from an old-money family. **Rosalind Connage** marries Dawson a few years after she leaves **Amory Blaine** because he is too poor.

Noel Ryland

Babbitt
Sinclair Lewis

A car salesman in Zenith. **Babbitt** thinks Ryland is an example of taking "civilization too far" because he graduated from Princeton University and reads foreign poetry.

Ryna

Song of Solomon
Toni Morrison

Milkman Dead's great-grandmother and **Solomon**'s wife. When Solomon abandons her, flying across the ocean to Africa, Ryna goes mad, left to suffer in the cotton fields, and leaves **Macon Dead I** an orphan.

Lee Rynor

A Tree Grows in Brooklyn
Betty Smith

A soldier about to leave for France when **Francie Nolan** meets him. Passionate and sweet, Lee knocks Francie off her feet and professes that he returns her love. Two days later, he marries his fiancée from his hometown.

14

CHARMING CRIMINALS

THEY LIE. THEY CHEAT. THEY STEAL. THEY KILL. WE ADORE THEM. WE CANNOT HELP OURSELVES.

Artful Dodger	1	*Oliver Twist*
Kate Barlow	2	*Holes*
Gentleman Brown	3	*Lord Jim*
Edgemond Dantes	4	*The Count of Monte Cristo*
Jack "Legs" Diamonds	5	*Legs*
Dread Pirate Roberts	6	*The Princess Bride*
Moll Flanders	7	*Moll Flanders*
Jay Gatsby	8	*The Great Gatsby*
Locksley	9	*Ivanhoe*
Philip Lombard	10	*And Then There Were None*
Abel Magwitch	11	*Great Expectations*
Oedipus	12	*The Oedipus Plays*
Long John Silver	13	*Treasure Island*
Jean Valjean	14	*Les Misérables*

Midnight's Children
Salman Rushdie

Commander Sabarmati

The husband of **Lila Sabarmati**. He murders his unfaithful wife and her lover.

Midnight's Children
Salman Rushdie

Lila Sabarmati

Commander Sabarmati's wife, who is murdered by him for having an affair with **Homi Catrack**.

The Unbearable Lightness of Being
Milan Kundera

Sabina

Tomas's favorite mistress and closest friend. A talented painter with a distaste for communism, she is as beautful and original as her artwork. In her striving for "lightness" Sabina betrays, successively, her father's home, her art school, her lovers (including **Franz**), and ultimately her country. She cares deeply for both Tomas and **Tereza**, even if she cannot understand why Tomas would trade his freedom for domesticity. She herself ends up alone in California.

The Fellowship of the Ring
J. R. R. Tolkien

Lobelia Sackville-Baggins

A relative of **Bilbo Baggins**'s who buys Bag End, Underhill, in the Shire, from **Frodo Baggins** when he leaves the Shire to go on his quest.

A Death in the Family
James Agee

Great-Aunt Sadie

Great aunt of **Rufus Follet** and **Little Catherine** on **Jay Follet**'s side. **Great-Aunt Sadie** has a failing memory, and she lives in the woods with Rufus's **Great-Great-Grandmother Follet**.

Frankenstein
Mary Shelley

Safie

The Turkish woman with whom **Felix De Lacey** is in love.

A Connecticut Yankee in King Arthur's Court
Mark Twain

Sir Sagramor le Desirous

Haughty, block-headed knight. Sir Sagramor le Desirous angers quickly and holds a grudge. Sir Sagramor challenges **the Yankee** to a duel four years in the future. The Yankee goes out and adventures in order to gain experience and credibility for the duel. The Yankee defeats Sir Sagramor. Later, Sir Sagramor appears again, and the second time the Yankee simply shoots and kills Sir Sagramor with a revolver.

Sailor

"The Murders in the Rue Morgue"
Edgar Allan Poe

The owner of **Ourang-Outang**. The sailor witnesses the two murders but is unable to restrain the orangutan.

Jeremiah de Saint-Amour

Love in the Time of Cholera
Gabriel García Márquez

A children's photographer. He is **Dr. Juvenal Urbino del Calle**'s only worthy competitor at chess. The novel begins with Jeremiah's suicide; he kills himself with gold cyanide because he refuses to grow old.

Marquis de Saint-Méran

The Count of Monte Cristo
Alexandre Dumas

The former father-in-law of **Gérard de Villefort**. The marquis and his wife, the **Marquise de Saint-Méran**, die from brucine poisoning. **Madame d'Villefort** is behind the "accidental" poisonings.

Marquise de Saint-Méran

The Count of Monte Cristo
Alexandre Dumas

The former mother-in-law of **Gérard de Villefort**. The marquise and her husband, the **Marquis de Saint-Méran**, die from brucine poisoning. **Madame d'Villefort** is behind the "accidental" poisonings. The night of the Marquis de Saint-Méran's death, the Marquise de Saint-Méran becomes sick, and the next morning she announces that she is going to die. The marquise yearns to see **Valentine Villefort** married before she dies and orders that the marriage contract be signed the day after **Franz d'Epinay** returns to France. Valentine longs to tell her grandmother that she loves another man but knows that her aristocratic grandmother would never allow her to marry a man from a family as common as **Maximilian Morrel**'s.

The saints

Go Tell It on the Mountain
James Baldwin

The saved members of **Gabriel**'s church, Temple of the Fire Baptized.

Sakina

Shabanu
Suzanne Fisher Staples

Bibi Lal's youngest daughter. Sakina tells **Shabanu** and **Phulan** the story of **Hamir**'s death.

Sal's aunt

On the Road
Jack Kerouac

Sal Paradise's only relative. She is supportive and kind, and she sends him money throughout his travels. When not traveling, Sal lives at her house in Paterson, New Jersey, and sometimes on Long Island.

Salamano

The Stranger
Albert Camus

One of **Meursault**'s neighbors.

Coach Salan

Ordinary People
Judith Guest

The swimming coach at Lake Forest. Salan wants to see **Conrad Jarrett** do well, and he is disappointed when Conrad quits the team.

Salerio

The Merchant of Venice
William Shakespeare

A Venetian gentleman and friend to **Antonio**, **Bassanio**, and **Lorenzo**. Salerio escorts the newlyweds **Jessica** and Lorenzo to Belmont, and returns with Bassanio and **Graziano** for Antonio's trial. He is often almost indistinguishable from his companion **Solanio**.

The Salesclerk

The Little Prince
Antoine de Saint-Exupéry

The salesclerk sells pills that quench thirst on the grounds that people can save up to fifty-three minutes a day if they don't have to stop to drink.

John, Earl of Salisbury

Richard II
William Shakespeare

King Richard II's loyal supporter. Salisbury unsuccessfully manages Richard's Welsh army. Later, he is beheaded for conspiring to kill the new **King Henry IV** (Bolingbroke).

Richard Neville, Earl of Salisbury

Henry VI, Part II
William Shakespeare

Father of **Richard Neville, Earl of Warwick**. When the battlelines are drawn early in the play, Salisbury sides with his son and **Richard Plantagenet, Duke of York** to defend **Humphrey, Duke of Gloucester** and the "public good" against the other lords in the court. Shortly after, both Salisbury and Warwick readily support York's claim to the throne. When York returns from Ireland, Salisbury, and Warwick join him in his quest for the crown, and fight against the King and his lords.

Thomas Montague, Earl of Salisbury

Henry V and Henry VI, Part I
William Shakespeare

An English nobleman and military leader who serves valiantly under **King Henry V** in *Henry V*. He is killed during the siege of Orléans in *Henry VI, Part I*.

William, Earl of Salisbury

King John
William Shakespeare

An English nobleman who defects, along with **Lord Bigot** and **Pembroke**, to the French after **Arthur**'s death. However, Salisbury and the other two lords return to the English after they discover that **Lewis** plans to kill them after defeating **King John**'s forces in battle. Salisbury functions as the English lords' leader and spokesman.

Sally

Incidents in the Life of a Slave Girl
Harriet Ann Jacobs

A family friend who lives with **Aunt Martha** and helps **Linda** to escape into hiding.

Sally

The House on Mango Street
Sandra Cisneros

Esperanza's neighbor. Sally, who is Esperanza's age, is sexually bold and seems glamorous to Esperanza. Before eighth grade, Sally elopes with an older man.

Sally

The Hours
Michael Cunningham

Clarissa Vaughn's live-in lover of eighteen years. Sally produces an interview show on public television. She is kind, steady, and smart.

Old Sally

Oliver Twist
Charles Dickens

An elderly pauper who is the nurse at Oliver's birth. Old Sally steals **Agnes Fleming**'s gold locket.

The Lady Salmakia

His Dark Materials
Robert Pullman

A Gallivespian spy who accompanies **Lyra Belacqua** and **Will Parry** to the world of the dead.

Abigail Salmon

The Lovely Bones
Alice Sebold

The mother of **Susie Salmon** and **Lindsey Salmon**, wife of **Jack Salmon**. She seems to have wandered into her role as wife and mother almost by mistake. Abigail decides to leave her family, spurred by her fleeting romance with **Detective Len Fenerman**. In the end, she returns to her family and resumes her role as wife and mother with more confidence and self-awareness.

Jack Salmon

The Lovely Bones
Alice Sebold

Husband of **Abigail Salmon** and father of **Susie** and **Lindsey Salmon**. As Lindsey and Abigail retreat into themselves after Susie Salmon's death, Jack keeps the family operating emotionally. But he can be incapable of taking action when necessary. Jack knows before anyone else that **George Harvey** killed Susie, but all he does with this knowledge is call the police station.

Lindsey Salmon

The Lovely Bones
Alice Sebold

Susie Salmon's precociously intelligent and charismatic sister. Lindsey is a wonder child: she is blond and beautiful, she reads French philosophy for fun, she breezes her way through math and science classes, and she is the only girl to play on the boys' soccer team. She breaks into **George Harvey**'s house to search for clues about her sister's disappearance, and narrowly misses being caught when Harvey returns home unexpectedly.

Susie Salmon

The Lovely Bones
Alice Sebold

The narrator. She is raped and murdered in the first scene of the novel. Susie resides on the border between our world and the next, a kind of ambassador to the afterlife. Over the course of the novel, she comes to understand that her family will survive without her.

Salomé

Salomé
Oscar Wilde

Protagonist of the tragedy; **Herodias**'s daughter. Salomé first appears disgusted by the court, mortified by its crude, painted guests and the incestuous gaze of her stepfather **Herod**. Soon thereafter she is seduced by the imprisoned prophet **Jokanaan**'s voice and has him drawn from his tomb, against Herod's order.

Sam

Lord of the Flies
William Golding

One of a pair of twins closely allied with **Ralph**. Sam and **Eric** are always together, and the other boys often treat them as a single entity, calling them "Samneric." At the end of the novel, they fall victim to **Jack**'s manipulation and coercion.

Sam

Stranger in a Strange Land
Robert A. Heinlein

Ruth's husband, and an early member of **Valentine Michael Smith**'s Church of All Worlds. Sam joins the church to learn the Martian language, but he ends up rediscovering his love for his wife, and the two become high level church members.

Sam

The Color of Water
James McBride

Ruth McBride Jordan's brother, he is two years older than she is. **Fishel Shilsky** was particularly hard on the timid, sensitive Sam, expecting him to fulfill many duties at the family store. Sam found the burden too weighty and ran away at fifteen. He was killed in the army during World War II.

Sam

Holes
Louis Sachar

Kate Barlow's great love in 1888. Sam was a victim of racist laws, which prevented him from attending school or being with Kate. Sam is killed by **Charles Walker**, or Trout, of Green Lake, after he and Kate kiss. Kate becomes a violent criminal.

Sam Pearl

The Assistant
Bernard Malamud

Nat Pearl and **Betsy Pearl**'s father. He owns the candy store on the block. He is relatively successful and makes money betting on horses.

Big Sam

Gone with the Wind
Margaret Mitchell

The gigantic slave and foreman of the field hands at Tara. Big Sam saves **Scarlett O'Hara** from her attacker in Shantytown.

Sammy the Pimp

The Autobiography of Malcolm X
Malcolm X & Alex Haley

A Harlem pimp and drug dealer, and a friend of **Malcolm X**'s. Malcolm and Sammy work together until tension develops between them over Malcolm's assault on one of Sammy's girlfriends.

Sampson

Romeo and Juliet
William Shakespeare

Capulet servants. They hate the Montagues.

Gregor Samsa

The Metamorphosis
Franz Kafka

The protagonist. He is a young traveling salesman who wakes up one morning transformed into a bug.

Grete Samsa

The Metamorphosis
Franz Kafka

Gregor Samsa's younger sister. Before Gregor's transformation, Grete is devoted to him. Afterward, motivated by devotion to his memory, she takes on sole responsibility for his care. Grete finally voices the family's impatience with Gregor's situation.

Samson

The Old Testament
Unknown

One of Israel's judges. He is an epic hero who thwarts the neighboring Philistines with his superhuman strength. Samson's long hair is both the source of his strength and the symbol of his religious devotion to **God** as a Nazirite.

Samson

As I Lay Dying
William Faulkner

A farmer with whom the Bundrens spend the first night of their journey. Samson thinks that the Bundrens' problems are punishment for their behavior.

Samson d'Arnault

My Ántonia
Willa Cather

A blind black pianist. D'Arnault comes to Black Hawk on a blustery March weekend and gives a concert at the Boys' Home that brings down the house.

Miss Amma Dean Samson

The Autobiography of Miss Jane Pittman
Ernest J. Gaines

The wife of **Robert Samson**, mother of **Tee Bob Samson** and mistress of the Samson plantation. Miss Amma Dean maintains the racial social order on the plantation.

Robert Samson

The Autobiography of Miss Jane Pittman
Ernest J. Gaines

Tee Bob Samson and **Timmy**'s father, **Miss Amma Dean Samson**'s husband, and the master of the Samson Plantation. He seduces a black woman and fathers a child, Timmy, whom he refuses to accept as his own because he is black. Samson's inability to see beyond the old southern order leads to the death of his other son, Tee Bob.

Tee Bob Samson

The Autobiography of Miss Jane Pittman
Ernest J. Gaines

Robert Samson's son and **Timmy**'s half-brother. Even though he is a white man of privilege and heir to the Samson plantation, Tee Bob's awakening to the reality of their racist system leads him to kill himself.

Kuzma Kuzmich Samsonov

The Brothers Karamazov
Fyodor Dostoevsky

An old merchant. He brings **Agrafena Alexandrovna Svetlova** to the town after her former lover betrays her.

Samuel

The Old Testament
Unknown

The last of Israel's judges and the prophet who anoints both **Saul** and **David** kings. Samuel fulfills political and priestly duties for Israel, but he ushers in Israel's monarchy mainly as a prophet.

Samuel

The Moonstone
Wilkie Collins

Lady Verinder's footman.

Samuel

Bless Me, Ultima
Rudolfo A. Anaya

One of **Antonio Márez**'s closer friends. He is also **the Vitamin Kid**'s brother. Unlike most of Antonio's friends, Samuel is gentle and quiet. Samuel tells Antonio a story that **Jasón Chávez's Indian** originally told that explains why eating carp is sin.

Samuel

The Color Purple
Alice Walker

A minister. Along with his wife, **Corrine**, he adopts **Celie**'s biological children, **Olivia** and **Adam**. Samuel takes Corrine, **Nettie**, and the children to Africa for missionary work. After Corrine's death, Samuel marries Nettie. He comes back with Nettie to meet Celie with the children in a joyous reunion.

Bayardo San Roman

Chronicle of a Death Foretold
Gabriel García Márquez

The wealthy man who marries **Angela Vicario**. Despite his relentless pursuit of Angela, which includes the purchase of **Xius**'s farmhouse, Bayardo returns Angela to her home on her wedding night when he finds that she is not a virgin.

General Petronio San Roman

Chronicle of a Death Foretold
Gabriel García Márquez

Bayardo San Roman's father. He drives up to meet **Angela Vicario**'s family in a Model T Ford. He is impressively bedecked with medals from his heroism in the civil wars of the past century.

Fermina Sánchez

Love in the Time of Cholera
Gabriel García Márquez

Fermina Daza's mother. Fermina Sánchez dies when Fermina Daza is a small child, leaving **Lorenzo Daza** and **Aunt Escolastica** to take care of Fermina Daza.

Hildebranda Sánchez

Love in the Time of Cholera
Gabriel García Márquez

Fermina Daza's older cousin and best friend. She helps **Florentino** and Fermina Daza communicate via secret telegrams while Fermina is away on her years-long journey. Fermina Daza seeks refuge at Hildebranda's ranch when **Dr. Juvenal Urbino del Calle** cheats on Fermina Daza with **Barbara Lynch**.

Clay Sanders

A Day No Pigs Would Die
Robert Newton Peck

The man for whom **Haven Peck** slaughtered pigs. He is not seen until Haven's funeral.

Mitchell Sanders

The Things They Carried
Tim O'Brien

A soldier in the war. His ability to tell stories and to discuss their nuances makes a profound impression on O'Brien.

Sandra

How the Garcia Girls Lost Their Accents
Julia Alvarez

The second-oldest daughter. Sandi felt stifled and frustrated as a child, and lost her artistic vision after she suffered a broken arm. She has a mental breakdown as an adult.

Gus Sands

The Natural
Bernard Malamud

A rich and powerful bookie who tries to bribe **Roy Hobbs** into throwing the final game for the pennant. Gus is a good friend of **Memo Paris** and, in Hobbs's eyes, a rival.

Lord Sands

Henry VIII
William Shakespeare

A lord of the court. At **Cardinal Wolsey**'s dinner party, Sands flirts with **Anne Boleyn** before **King Henry VIII** meets her.

Mr. Sands

Incidents in the Life of a Slave Girl
Harriet Ann Jacobs

Linda Brent's white lover and the father of her children. Mr. Sands feels no real love or responsibility for his mixed-race children. His repeated promises to Linda to free them are easily broken when he finds it convenient.

Sandy

A Connecticut Yankee in King Arthur's Court
Mark Twain

A pretty but somewhat flighty damsel. She comes to **King Arthur**'s court seeking assistance and becomes attached to **the Yankee**. The Yankee finds her terribly annoying at first, but she proves to be quite useful and pleasant. The two eventually marry and have children after the Yankee sets up a nineteenth-century-style civilization in the sixth century.

Sandy

The Outsiders
S. E. Hinton

Sodapop Curtis's girlfriend. Sandy is pregnant with another man's child and moves to Florida to live with her grandmother. She returns Sodapop's letter, unopened, which, along with **Ponyboy Curtis**'s and **Darry**'s fighting, causes him to have a breakdown.

Jerry Sanford

My Brother Sam Is Dead
Christopher & James Lincoln Collier

A young local boy and **Tim Meeker**'s friend. Jerry is captured by the British and dies on a prison ship.

Ausencia Santander

Love in the Time of Cholera
Gabriel García Márquez

The older woman with whom **Florentino Ariza** conducts an affair. He meets her through her husband, Florentino's colleague. Florentino is more attracted to her beautiful house than he is to her. After they drag Ausencia's drunken husband to bed, Florentino and Ausencia go to bed themselves, and they continue the affair for seven years. One afternoon, she discovers that all of her belongings have been stolen. Florentino visits her less after the robbery.

Santiago

The Old Man and the Sea
Ernest Hemingway

The old Cuban fisherman of the novella's title. Despite his expertise, Santiago has been unable to catch a fish for eighty-four days. On the next day, however, he hooks an eighteen-foot **marlin** and embarks on a lengthy struggle to reel the fish in. After three days of exhausting effort, he lands the fish, which he sees as his brother as much as his rival. Paradoxically, although Santiago ultimately loses the fish to scavenging sharks, the marlin represents his greatest victory.

Faustino Santos

Chronicle of a Death Foretold
Gabriel García Márquez

The local butcher. He alerts a local police officer that **Pedro Vicario** and **Pablo Vicario** are talking about murdering **Santiago Nasar**.

Jiang Sao-yan

The Kitchen God's Wife
Amy Tan

Winnie's father. Jiang Sao-yan is a wealthy and powerful man at the beginning of the story who forces his daughter to live with his brother and his wives so as not to be reminded of Winnie's mother. He ends up a weak man with no memory and a lack of will.

Sara

Cold Mountain
Charles Frazier

An eighteen-year-old widow who offers **Inman** food and shelter. Inman feels bound to help when Federal soldiers steal her hog, the only thing she and her baby have to live on.

Sara Goulding

Ulysses
James Joyce

The wife of **Richie Goulding** and the mother of **Walter Goulding**.

Sarah

Silas Marner
George Eliot

Silas Marner's fiancé in Lantern Yard. Sarah is put off by Silas's strange fits and marries **William Dane** after Silas is disgraced.

Sarah

Ragtime
E. L. Doctorow

The mother of **Coalhouse**'s child. She dies attempting to fight for Coalhouse's cause.

Bayard Sartoris

The Unvanquished
William Faulkner

The novel's narrator and protagonist. The novel traces his coming of age from the time he is twelve until he is a grown man and the head of his family. Bayard is decent, honorable, courageous and intelligent, a model southern aristocrat for the post-war era. As a boy, he is occasionally given to impetuousness and rashness. In the course of the novel he matures profoundly.

Colonel John Sartoris

The Unvanquished
William Faulkner

Father of **Bayard**, the patriarch of the Sartoris family. Colonel Sartoris commands his own regiment on the Virginia front until he is demoted by his troops so he can return home to care for his family; even then, he raises an "irregular" brigade who terrorize the far more numerous Yankees in Mississippi with their dashing assaults. He is hot-blooded and arrogant but heroic, and Bayard worships him. When he dies at the end of the novel, his son begins to assume his grandeur and valor.

Saruman

The Lord of the Rings trilogy
J. R. R. Tolkien

The head of **Gandalf**'s order of Wizards. Saruman advises the other wizards not to challenge the growing power of **Sauron**. Gandalf, who suspects that Saruman intends to join Sauron's forces outright, confirms his suspicions when he travels to Saruman's tower, Orthanc, in *The Fellowship of the Ring*. Saruman imprisons Gandalf at the top of Orthanc, where Gandalf is rescued by **Gwaihir**, the Windlord. In *The Two Towers*, Saruman takes over the realm of Isengard completely, destroying the nature and the forest around his stronghold. He plots to seize the Ring and breeds a new race of evil **Orcs** that do not fear sunlight, **the Uruk-hai**. Beseeched by **Meriadoc Brandybuck** and **Peregrin Took**, **Treebeard** and his army of Ents from the nearby Entwash help destroy Saruman's stronghold. Saruman is also revealed as the manipulator of **Théoden**, king of Rohan, through Saruman's servant, **Gríma Wormtongue**. In *The Return of the King*, Saruman is seen as the deposed wizard and the enactor of the Shire's brief police state. Saruman's power is so diminished that the Hobbits easily overthrow his regime when **Frodo Baggins** returns from his Quest, after which the dejected Gríma Wormtongue kills Saruman.

Dr. Terufumi Sasaki

Hiroshima
John Hersey

A young surgeon at the Red Cross Hospital in Hiroshima. Dr. Sasaki treats thousands of the dying and wounded after the bombing and eventually operates on **Toshiko Sasaki**'s fractured and infected leg. After the war, he studies radiation sickness and other effects of the bomb.

Toshiko Sasaki

Hiroshima
John Hersey

A young clerk who works in a tin works factory. Miss Sasaki becomes trapped in the wreckage of a factory when a bookcase crashes onto her. For weeks she receives no real medical care for her leg, which is badly fractured and infected. She is eventually treated by **Dr. Terufumi Sasaki**, but she remains crippled for the rest of her life. After the war, with the guidance of **Father Wilhelm Kleinsorge**, she becomes a nun.

Sasha

Orlando
Virginia Woolf

A Russian princess, a Muscovite who travels by ship to England to the court of King James I. When **Orlando** first catches sight of her, he is unable to tell whether she is a man or a woman. She deceitfully seduces Orlando and then runs away with a Russian seaman.

Sass

Wide Sargasso Sea
Jean Rhys

A servant at Coulibri. He has been there ever since his mother abandoned him there as a child. Sass leaves the estate when **Annette**'s money runs out, but he returns when **Mr. Mason** arrives. Annette distrusts Sass, believing him to be greedy and self-serving.

Siegfried Sassoon

Regeneration
Pat Barker

In real life, and in the novel, a distinguished soldier and Great War poet who is treated by **Dr. W.H.R. Rivers**. Though he strongly opposes the war, Sassoon has not had a breakdown, and he feels uncomfortable around the other patients in the hospital. In the end, Sassoon returns to his duty.

Satan

Paradise Lost
John Milton

Head of the rebellious angels who have just fallen from Heaven. As the poem's antagonist, Satan is the originator of sin—the first to be ungrateful for **God the Father**'s blessings. He embarks on a mission to Earth that eventually leads to the fall of **Adam** and **Eve** but also worsens his eternal punishment. He can assume any form, adopting both glorious and humble shapes.

Jean de Satigny

The House of the Spirits
Isabel Allende

Blanca's husband. Jean de Satigny is a French immigrant who wants to join the Trueba family through business or marriage. He is able to marry Blanca thanks to his revelation of her affair with **Pedro Tercero Garcia** and her subsequent pregnancy by Pedro Tercero. They never consummate their marriage. He is eccentric and hires a lot of incompetent Indian servants to help around the house, does a lot of cocaine and opium, and works on his photography secretively. When Blanca peeks into his photography studio and finds him recording "erotic" poses on film with his Indian servants, she leaves him.

Sattamax

His Dark Materials
Robert Pullman

The wisest and eldest of the mulefa. Sattamax asks for **Dr. Mary Malone**'s help in figuring out what is happening in the world of the mulefa.

Dr. Ellie Sattler

Jurassic Park
Michael Crichton

Dr. Alan Grant's partner on the Montana fossil dig, and an attractive paleobotanist.

Saturn

Greek Mythology
Unknown

The Roman name for the Greek god **Cronus**.

Titus Andronicus
William Shakespeare

Saturninus

The late Emperor's eldest son and **Bassianus**'s brother. Saturninus is less deserving of the throne, but **Titus** supports him for emperor because he is the firstborn. He tries to choose Titus's daughter **Lavinia** for an empress, but Lavinia elopes with Bassianus. Saturninus chooses **Tamora** instead, a combination that wreaks havoc on Titus's family and all of Rome. Saturninus is killed by Titus's son **Lucius**, who takes the throne.

The Faerie Queene
Edmund Spenser

Satyrane

The son of a human and a satyr (a half-human, half-goat creature). He is "nature's knight," the best a man can become through his own natural abilities without the enlightenment of Christianity and God's grace. Satyrane is significant in both Book I and Book III, generally as an aide to the protagonists.

The Old Testament
Unknown

Saul

Israel's first king. After **God** chooses Saul to be king, Saul loses his divine right to rule Israel by committing two religious errors. Saul's plot to murder **David** highlights David's mercy to Saul in return.

The Chosen
Chaim Potok

Danny Saunders

One of the novel's two protagonists. The son of **Reb Saunders**, Danny is a brilliant scholar with a photographic memory and a deep interest in Freud and psychoanalysis. Danny attends his father's Hasidic yeshiva, but he reads secular books in secret at the public library. As the heir to a Hasidic dynasty, Danny feels an obligation to remain within his cloistered, extremely conservative Jewish community. At the same time, he longs to study intellectual ideas in the outside world.

The Chosen
Chaim Potok

Reb Isaac Saunders

Danny Saunders's father. Reb Saunders is the pious and zealous patriarch of a Hasidic dynasty. Reb Saunders's home is also the center of study and prayer for his followers, who join him at his table every Shabbat. He is a wise, learned, and deeply religious sage who raises Danny in silence, speaking to him only when discussing the Talmud. Reb Saunders is fervently committed to his strict and limited Hasidic worldview, and he imposes his views on everyone around him.

The Chosen
Chaim Potok

Levi Saunders

Danny Saunders's sickly younger brother. Unlike Danny, Levi is not raised in silence.

Mrs. Saunders

Cloud Nine
Caryl Churchill

A widow who is unafraid to wield her sexuality. She has an affair with **Clive** in which Mrs. Saunders openly says she only wants him for sex. **Harry** proposes to her out of a need to hide his sexuality, and rather than seeking the security of marriage she opts for the freedom to strike out on her own.

Jacques Saunière

The Da Vinci Code
Dan Brown

The curator at the Louvre, and **Sophie Neveu**'s grandfather. His murder sets off the chain of events in the novel. Saunière's scholarly passions include Leonardo Da Vinci, goddess iconography, and puzzles. He is also secretly the head of the Priory of Sion, the secret brotherhood charged with protecting the Grail, and a descendent of Jesus and Mary Magdalene.

Sauron

The Hobbit and *The Lord of the Rings trilogy*
J. R. R. Tolkien

The embodiment of evil throughout the ages of Middle-earth. In *The Hobbit*, Sauron is presented as an evil sorcerer in Mirkwood. In *The Fellowship of the Ring*, we learn that Sauron created the magic ring, the One Ring that allows its holder to have power over all the lesser Ring-wearers and their races. The Dark Lord Sauron was a servant of Morgoth, the Great Enemy, who took his master's place after the First Age. Sauron is never seen at any point in *The Lord of the Rings*; he is represented only by images of his Great Eye or the Dark Tower where he resides. He fervently desires the One Ring, which was lost to him when **Isildur** defeated him at the end of the Second Age. Isildur soon became corrupted by the Ring, which fell into the Great River, Anduin, where **Gollum** finds it. It eventually falls into the hands of **Bilbo Baggins** and then **Frodo Baggins**, who is the Ring-bearer within a Fellowship meant to destroy it. In *The Two Towers*, the Dark Lord of Mordor increases his power through his manipulations of **Saruman** and his corruptions of **Humans** in Rohan and Gondor. In *The Return of the King*, the destruction of the Ring ultimately empties Sauron of his power and begins the Age of Men on Middle-earth.

Margaret Saville

Frankenstein
Mary Shelley

Robert Walton's sister. Saville is the recipient of letters from her seafaring brother.

Tony Savo

The Chosen
Chaim Potok

A patient **Reuven Malter** befriends while in the hospital. Tony Savo is a former boxer. He warns Reuven to watch out for religious fanatics like **Danny Saunders**.

Janet Savory

White Noise
Don DeLillo

Heinrich's mother and **Jack Gladney**'s ex-wife. Janet now lives in an ashram and is known as Mother Devi.

Sawyer

Looking Backward
Edward Bellamy

Julian West's African-American servant in the nineteenth century.

Luke Sawyer

The Land
Mildred D. Taylor

A shop owner in Vicksburg. Luke Sawyer is a skilled and honest businessman. He takes **Paul-Edward Logan** on as a furniture maker and treats him fairly.

Tom Sawyer

The Adventures of Tom Sawyer and *The Adventures of Huckleberry Finn*
Mark Twain

The protagonist of *The Adventures of Tom Sawyer*. Tom Sawyer is a mischievous boy with an active imagination who spends most of the novel getting himself, and often his friends, into and out of trouble. When the novel begins, Tom envies **Huckleberry Finn**'s lazy lifestyle and freedom. As Tom's adventures proceed, however, critical moments show Tom moving away from his childhood concerns and making mature, responsible decisions.

Priscilla Saxe

The Black Prince
Iris Murdoch

The sister of **Bradley Pearson** and wife of **Roger Saxe**. Priscilla spends the majority of the book in an unloving marriage that she had tricked her husband into with a false claim of pregnancy. Priscilla's greatest regret is the abortion that left her unable to have children. She leaves her husband and comes to her brother for support, but when he fails to provide her with it she kills herself.

Roger Saxe

The Black Prince
Iris Murdoch

Priscilla Saxe's husband, **Marigold**'s lover and **Bradley Pearson**'s brother-in-law. Roger made Priscilla get an abortion, and the operation seems to have left Priscilla barren. As Roger really wants a child, he looks for love outside of their marriage. He drives Priscilla away with his cruelty so that he and Marigold can have bastard children. Although Priscilla tricked him into marrying her, he stayed with her for twenty years, despite their unhappiness.

Sayan Kötör

His Dark Materials
Robert Pullman

John Parry's daemon. Sayan, who is also known as Stanislas Grumman, is an Osprey.

Lord Saye

Henry VI, Part II
William Shakespeare

A nobleman loyal to **King Henry VI**. Blamed by **Jack Cade**'s rebels for losing the French counties, Saye remains behind when Henry VI and **Queen Margaret** flee London. Saye is captured by the rebels, and accused by Cade not only of losing the French territories, but also of building a grammar school and paper-mill, and hanging illiterate men. Saye defends himself, but has nothing to do with the loss of France.

Scabbers

Harry Potter and the Prisoner of Azkaban
J. K. Rowling

Ron Weasley's aging rat; the animal form of **Peter Pettigrew**.

Scanlon

One Flew over the Cuckoo's Nest
Ken Kesey

A patient at the hospital. The only Acute besides **Randle McMurphy** who was involuntarily committed.

Alvah Scarret

The Fountainhead
Ayn Rand

The *Banner*'s editor-in-chief. Scarret believes every word his newspaper publishes, and **Gail Wynand** uses him to gauge public opinion.

Scarus

Antony and Cleopatra
William Shakespeare

A young soldier serving under **Antony**. Scarus garners fantastic wounds in the battle against **Octavius Caesar**'s army and begs for the opportunity to win more.

Miss Scatcherd

Jane Eyre
Charlotte Brontë

Jane Eyre and **Helen Burns**'s sour and vicious teacher at Lowood. Miss Scatcherd behaves with particular cruelty toward Helen.

Scyld Scefing

Beowulf
Unknown

The legendary Danish king from whom **Hrothgar** is descended. Scyld Scefing is the mythical founder who inaugurates a long line of Danish rulers and embodies the Danish tribe's highest values of heroism and leadership.

Scyld Scefing

Grendel
John Gardner

The legendary king from whom **Hrothgar** is descended. In Scyld Scefing's honor, the Danes are sometimes referred to as the Scyldings.

Madame Schächter

Night
Elie Wiesel

A Sighet Jewish woman deported in the same cattle car as **Eliezer**. Every night on the journey, Madame Schächter screams that she sees furnaces in the distance.

Anna Schaeffer

My Name Is Asher Lev
Chaim Potok

An international socialite and gallery owner. She is interested in art and artists and even more interested in using them to make money.

Lieutenant Scheisskopf

Catch-22
Joseph Heller

The officer who trains **John Yossarian**'s squadron in America. Scheisskopf loves elaborate military parades; he is promoted to corporal and general over the course of the novel.

Lieutenant Scheisskopf's Wife

Catch-22
Joseph Heller

Lieutenant Scheisskopf's wife. She conducts affairs with all the men in Scheisskopf's squadron, including **John Yossarian**.

Anna Pavlovna Scherer

War and Peace
Leo Tolstoy

A wealthy St. Petersburg society hostess and matchmaker for **Anatole Vasilievich Kuragin** and his sister **Helene Vasilievna Kuragina**. Her party in 1805 opens the novel.

Rich Schields

The Joy Luck Club
Amy Tan

Waverly's fiancé. Waverly wants to tell her mother about their engagement, but she is afraid that **Lindo** will dislike Rich, who is white.

Peter Schiff

Anne Frank: Diary of a Young Girl
Anne Frank

The love of **Anne Frank**'s sixth-grade year. Peter Schiff is one year older than Anne. She dreams about him in the annex. When she becomes infatuated with **Peter van Daan**, she melds the two Peters in her mind.

Father Schiffer

Hiroshima
John Hersey

A Jesuit priest. He is badly injured in the blast and evacuated, along with **Father LaSalle**, with the help of **Father Wilhelm Kleinsorge** and **Reverend Mr. Kiyoshi Tanimoto**.

Richard Schiller

Lolita
Vladimir Nabokov

The man **Lolita** marries after escaping **Clare Quilty**. Dick is a simple, good-natured war veteran with bad hearing in one ear. He is unaware of Lolita's sexual relationship with **Humbert Humbert** and thinks that Humbert is simply Lolita's father.

Helen Schlegel

Howards End
E. M. Forster

Margaret Schlegel's sister. She is a passionate, flighty girl of twenty-one who lives for art, literature, and "human relations." Helen, who is prettier than Margaret, is much less grounded and far more prone to excessive and dramatic behavior.

Margaret Schlegel

Howards End
E. M. Forster

The protagonist of the novel. She is a twenty-nine-year-old woman of mixed English and German heritage living in London in the early years of the twentieth century. Margaret is the sister of **Helen Schlegel** and **Theobald Schlegel** and later **Henry Wilcox**'s wife. Margaret is idealistic, imaginative, and committed to "personal relations."

Theobald "Tibby" Schlegel

Howards End
E. M. Forster

Margaret Schlegel and **Helen Schlegel**'s younger brother. A peevish sixteen-year-old who grows up and attends Oxford, Tibby is prone to acting out the flaws of the Schlegel family–their excessive aestheticism, indulgence in luxury, and indolence–but shows real improvement by the end of the novel.

Nicholas Schliemann

The Jungle
Upton Sinclair

A fervent socialist whom Sinclair uses as a mouthpiece for his own political philosophy in the novel.

Hildegarde Schmidt

Murder on the Orient Express
Agatha Christie

A slow-minded woman who unquestioningly carries out the **Princess Dragomiroff**'s orders. Hildegarde pretends to be the princess's maid, but is truly the Armstrong's cook.

Schmitz

The Assistant
Bernard Malamud

German owner of the grocery store across the street. Schmitz's store hurts the Bobers' business.

Konrad Schneider

Childhood's End
Arthur C. Clarke

A scientist building an interstellar spaceship for the Soviet Union.

Scholars

Doctor Faustus
Christopher Marlowe

Faustus's colleagues at the University of Wittenberg. The scholars bookend the play, appearing in the beginning to express dismay at the direction of Faustus's studies, and at the end to marvel at his achievements and to hear his agonized confession.

Schoolmaster

The Two Noble Kinsmen
William Shakespeare

A pretentious man who organizes the morris dance. He is mocked by the countrymen and gently ridiculed by **Theseus**.

Schoolteacher

Beloved
Toni Morrison

The owner of Sweet Home, following **Mr. Garner**'s death. Cold, sadistic, and vehemently racist, schoolteacher replaces what he views as Garner's too-soft approach with an oppressive regime of rigid rules and punishment on the plantation. When **Sixo** and others try to escape, schoolteacher has Sixo burned, **Paul A** hanged, and a bit placed in **Paul D**'s mouth. Along with his nephews, schoolteacher rapes **Sethe**, causing **Halle** to go mad.

Schwartz

The Death of Ivan Ilych
Leo Tolstoy

Ivan Ilych Golovin's colleague and friend. Schwartz is a well-dressed, playful, thoroughly proper man. At Ivan's funeral, he is immune to all depressing influences and maintains his jovial and lighthearted demeanor.

Morrie Schwartz

Tuesdays with Morrie
Mitch Albom

Mitch Albom's favorite professor from Brandeis University. Morrie suffers from ALS, a debilitating, incurable disease that ravages his body, but, cruelly, leaves him intellectually lucid. He had taught sociology at Brandeis, and continues to teach it to Mitch, instructing him on "The Meaning of Life" and how to accept death and aging. He does not suffocate his emotions, but shares them openly, and rejects the popular cultural norms in favor of creating his own system of beliefs.

Joan Schwartzen

The Day of the Locust
Nathanael West

A woman who only appears in the scenes at the **Estees**' party. Joan tries to be playful and flirtatious but comes off as shrill and menacing.

His Dark Materials
Robert Pullman

Lee Scoresby

A Texan aeronaut from New Denmark in **Lyra Belacqua**'s world. Lee Scoresby has a balloon and is old friends with **Iorek Byrnison**. Lee gives his life to save **John Parry** and help Lyra. His daemon is **Hester.**

The Epic of Gilgamesh
Unknown

Scorpion-Man

Guardian, with his wife, of the twin-peaked mountain called Mashu, which **Shamash** the sun god travels through every night. The upper parts of the scorpion-men's bodies are human, and the lower parts end in a scorpion tail.

White Fang
Jack London

Judge Scott

Weedon Scott's father. Judge Scott does not truly believe in **White Fang** until after White Fang saves his life by attacking **Jim Hall**.

White Fang
Jack London

Weedon Scott

White Fang's first loving master. Weedon Scott saves White Fang from the fight with the bulldog that **Beauty Smith** put him up to. Weedon brings White Fang back to California to live with **Judge Scott** and the rest of his family.

To Kill a Mockingbird
Harper Lee

Scout

See **Jean Louise Finch**.

A Christmas Carol
Charles Dickens

Ebenezer Scrooge

The protagonist of the novel. Scrooge is a mean, greedy, unkind old man who fails to see the meaning of Christmas. On Christmas Eve, three spirits visit him and show him Christmases past, present, and yet to come. After seeing himself as an objective observer would, he changes his ways.

Henry V
William Shakespeare

Lord Scroop

One of three noblemen bribed by French agents to kill **King Henry V** before he sets sail for France. Along with the **Earl of Cambridge** and **Sir Thomas Grey**, Scroop is found out and sentenced for execution, despite his pleas for mercy.

Sir Stephen Scroop

Richard II
William Shakespeare

King Richard II's supporter and bearer of bad news. He informs the king that **Henry Bolingbroke** has returned from exile with an army, that the English people support Bolingbroke, that Richard's supporters **Bushy** and **Green** have been executed, and that many lords, including the **Duke of York**, have sided with Bolingbroke.

Mike Scully

The Jungle
Upton Sinclair

A wealthy and corrupt Chicago political boss. He owns the dump where many of the poor immigrant children forage for food. Scully rigs elections and profits from the housing scam to which **Jurgis Rudkus**'s family falls victim. Jurgis briefly works as one of Scully's henchmen.

Lois Seager

All the King's Men
Robert Penn Warren

Jack's sexy first wife. He leaves her when he begins to perceive her as a person rather than simply as a machine for gratifying his desires.

Molly Seagrim

Tom Jones
Henry Fielding

The rugged, unfeminine daughter of **Black George**. She seduces **Tom**. Feisty and aggressive, Molly enjoys the company of men and fights fiercely for her rights.

Seamus

Angela's Ashes
Frank McCourt

The hospital janitor. He helps **Frank McCourt** and **Patricia Madigan** communicate, and later recites poetry to Frank in the eye hospital.

Sebastian

The Tempest
William Shakespeare

Alonso's brother. Like **Antonio**, Sebastian is both aggressive and cowardly. He is easily persuaded to kill his brother, and he tells a ridiculous story about lions when **Gonzalo** catches him with his sword drawn.

Sebastian

Twelfth Night
William Shakespeare

Viola's lost twin brother. When he arrives in Illyria, traveling with **Antonio**, his close friend and protector, Sebastian discovers that many people think that they know him. Furthermore, the beautiful Lady **Olivia**, whom he has never met, wants to marry him.

The Hairy Ape
Eugene O'Neill

Secretary

A worker at the I.W.W. office in New York City. When **Yank** visits the office to join the I.W.W., the Secretary comes to believe that Yank works for the government. He tells Yank he is the biggest joke they have dealt with and instructs the men to throw Yank out.

The Moonstone
Wilkie Collins

Superintendent Seegrave

The local police superintendent. Seegrave's methods of detection are unperceptive. He suspects the servants first and bullies them into cooperation with the case.

Flowers for Algernon
Daniel Keyes

Burt Selden

A friendly graduate student. He assists **Dr. Strauss** and **Professor Harold Nemur** in conducting their experiments. Burt oversees the testing of both **Charlie Gordon** and **Algernon**. He introduces Charlie to some of the students and faculty at Beekman College.

The House of Mirth
Edith Wharton

Lawrence Selden

A detached observer of the New York society that **Lily Bart** aspires to join. Selden is a lawyer by profession, but he is not particularly wealthy, which prevents Lily from marrying him even though they love one another. Throughout the novel, Selden struggles between his desire to remain detached from society and his wish to court Lily and convince her to marry him. At the end of the novel, he resolves finally to propose marriage to Lily, but his decision comes too late–he finds her dead in her apartment.

Antony and Cleopatra
William Shakespeare

Seleucus

Cleopatra's treasurer. He betrays her to **Caesar**.

Nausea
Jean-Paul Sartre

Self-Taught Man

A lonely man whom **Roquentin** meets at the Bouville Library while researching the **Marquis de Rollebon.** He is later chased out of town for fondling a small boy in public.

The Jew of Malta
Christopher Marlowe

Selim-Calymath

The Turkish leader and son of the Ottoman Emperor. Calymath awards **Barabas** the governorship of the island following Barabas's help in its capture. Calymath then becomes embroiled in Maltese politics as Barabas and **Ferneze** scheme against one another. Ultimately, Ferneze's tactics result in Calymath's capture.

Selmes

The Good Soldier
Ford Madox Ford

A young man from Fordingbridge. His father has been ruined by a fraudulent solicitor. **Captain Edward Ashburnham**, meeting Selmes along a path one day, offers to give him his old horse. This act of charity enrages **Leonora Powys Ashburnham** but enthralls **Nancy Rufford**.

Genevieve Selsor

The Martian Chronicles
Ray Bradbury

A large, childish, impatient woman who eats constantly. Though she may be the last woman on Mars, **Walter Gripp** runs away from her shortly after his desperate attempts to find her.

Mrs. Selwyn

Evelina
Fanny Burney

A country gentlewoman and an acquaintance of **Reverend Mr. Arthur Villars** and **Mrs. Beaumont**.

Sempronius

Timon of Athens
William Shakespeare

One of **Timon**'s friends. Sempronius accepts Timon's gifts but refuses to give him a loan.

Duke Senior

As You Like It
William Shakespeare

The father of **Rosalind** and the rightful ruler of the dukedom in which the play is set. Having been banished by his usurping brother, **Duke Frederick**, Duke Senior now lives in exile in the Forest of Arden with a number of loyal men, including **Lord Amiens** and the melancholy **Jaques**. Duke Senior proves to be a kind and fair-minded ruler.

The Senses Taker

The Phantom Tollbooth
Norton Juster

A man who spends his days in the Castle in the Air trying to rob people of their senses by bombarding them with detailed questions.

Serberine

The Spanish Tragedy
Thomas Kyd

Balthazar's manservant. Along with **Lorenzo**, Balthazar, and **Pedringano**, he kills **Horatio**. Lorenzo suspects Serberine of informing **Hieronimo** of the crime and has him killed by Pedringano.

Aleksandr Vladimirovich Serebryakov

Uncle Vanya
Anton Chekhov

A failed scholar who is deeply embittered by the onset of old age. Plagued by gout and rheumatism, the pompous and egotistical Serebryakov finds himself detestable in his infirmity and bemoans his residence in the provinces and his tomb-like estate, tormented by the meaningless chatter and indifference of his family.

Sofya Aleksandrovna Serebryakova

Uncle Vanya
Anton Chekhov

Serebryakov's daughter by his first marriage. Gentle but homely, she has steadfastly given herself to the maintenance of the estate and pines hopelessly after the brooding Dr. **Astrov** amidst her drudgery.

Yelena Andreyevna Serebryakova

Uncle Vanya
Anton Chekhov

Serebryakov's beautiful wife. She is characterized throughout the play by her infectious idleness and lack of interest in any serious work. Raised in the St. Petersburg Conservatory, she sacrificed a budding music career to marry the aging Serebryakov, whom she does not love but to whom she remains bound by conscience, convention, and inertia.

Serena

Miss Julie
August Strindberg

Miss Julie's canary, beheaded by **Jean**.

Servilius

Timon of Athens
William Shakespeare

One of **Timon**'s servants. Timon sends Servilius to ask for a loan from Timon's friends.

Shri Ramram Seth

Midnight's Children
Salman Rushdie

A seer that **Mumtaz** visits while pregnant.

Sethe

Beloved
Toni Morrison

The protagonist of *Beloved*. A former slave, Sethe escaped from Sweet Home Plantation after being brutally raped by **schoolteacher** and his gang. She barely survives, giving birth to **Denver** while on the run. Sethe is extremely devoted to her children, but she kills **Beloved** and almost kills **Denver** when she sees schoolteacher approaching 124 Bluestone Road. Despite her distrust of men, she welcomes **Paul D** into her home, where she is tormented by the reincarnation of her murdered daughter. She quickly succumbs to Beloved's demands and allows herself to be consumed by Beloved. Only with the help of Denver and the community can Sethe break free. After Beloved is gone, Paul D comes to care for Sethe.

Anton Antonich Setochkin

Notes from Underground
Fyodor Dostoevsky

The head of **the Underground Man**'s department in the ministry. Anton Antonich is the closest thing to a friend that the Underground Man has. The Underground Man occasionally borrows money from Anton Antonich and visits his home on Tuesdays when he has an urge to be social.

Sally Seton

Mrs. Dalloway
Virginia Woolf

A close friend of **Clarissa Daloway**'s in their youth. Sally was a wild, rambunctious girl who smoked cigars. Clarissa now realizes she was in love with Sally, who had the kind of personality Clarissa admired but could never match. Sally is now married to the wealthy Lord Rosseter and has five sons. Though long ago Sally and Clarissa plotted to reform the world together, now both are married, a fate they once considered a "catastrophe."

Septimius Severus

The Prince
Niccolò Machiavelli

Roman emperor (a.d. 193–211).

Sewall

Johnny Tremain
Esther Forbes

A poor relative of the Lytes'. He works as a clerk in **Jonathan Lyte**'s office. Sewall is kind and brave; he runs off to join the Minute Men.

John Seward

Dracula
Bram Stoker

A talented young doctor and former pupil of **Van Helsing**'s. Seward is the administrator of an insane asylum not far from **Count Dracula**'s English home. Throughout the novel, Seward conducts ambitious interviews with one of his patients, **Renfield**, in order to understand better the nature of life-consuming psychosis. Although **Lucy Westenra** turns down Seward's marriage proposal, his love for her remains, and he dedicates himself to her care when she suddenly takes ill. After her death, he remains dedicated to fighting the count.

Shabanu

Shabanu
Suzanne Fisher Staples

Eleven-year-old desert girl who narrates the story. Shabanu lives in the Cholistani desert with her family. She loves the desert and the sense of freedom it gives her more than anything in the world. She is willful and independent but also compassionate, tender, and insightful. She chafes under the constraints of the restrictive world around her.

Frank Shabata

O Pioneers!
Willa Cather

Marie Shabata's jealous, unhappy husband. When he seduced Marie away from her family, Frank Shabata was a handsome, dashing young man. Gradually, Frank becomes resentful and melancholy, and his marriage to Marie begins to unravel, leading her to pursue a relationship with **Emil Bergson**. When Frank discovers them together, he kills them both.

Marie Shabata

O Pioneers!
Willa Cather

The pretty, vivacious young Bohemian wife of **Frank Shabata**, and **Emil Bergson**'s love interest. Marie's insistent cheer and friendly effervescence make her an easy friend for her neighbor, **Alexandra Bergson**. Near the novel's end, the jealous Frank kills both Marie and Emil.

Emperor Shaddam IV

Dune
Frank Herbert

The ruler of the Imperium. The emperor is arguably the most powerful man in the known universe, although he is often at the mercy of the Spacing Guild, which has a monopoly on space travel.

Hazel Shade

Pale Fire
Vladimir Nabokov

John Shade and **Sibyl Shade**'s daughter. As a child, Hazel is overweight and unpopular. Hazel drowns.

John Shade

Pale Fire
Vladimir Nabokov

A college professor and the author of the four-canto poem "Pale Fire." Shade is sixty-one years old and grateful for his wife **Sibyl Shade**'s attentions to him. He funnels his frustrations into poetry. "Pale Fire" examines his life, his thoughts on eternity, the afterlife, his daughter **Hazel Shade**'s death, and his love for his wife. He is aware that **Charles Kinbote** hopes he will incorporate tales about Charles the Beloved into his poem, but he refuses to be pressured.

Sybil Shade

Pale Fire
Vladimir Nabokov

John Shade's wife. Sybil loathes her next-door neighbor **Charles Kinbote**. She is suspicious of his demands on her husband's time.

Shadow

Henry IV, Part II
William Shakespeare

One of the Army recruits that **Sir John Falstaff** inspects in Gloucestershire. Because Shadow does not bribe Falstaff, he, **Feeble**, and **Wart** have to serve in the military.

Shadowfax

The Lord of the *Rings trilogy*
J. R. R. Tolkien

The swiftest of all horses, whom **Gandalf** tames for his own use. Shadowfax is a borrowed horse from **Théoden**, king of Rohan.

Shadrack

Sula
Toni Morrison

A World War I veteran in 1917. Shadrack suffers a traumatic experience in the war. When **Sula Peace** accidentally kills **Chicken Little**, she immediately runs to Shadrack's house, where he comforts her.

Shagrat

The Two Towers and *The Return of the King*
J. R. R. Tolkien

A warrior of the **Orcs**. Along with **Gorbag**, he carries the body of **Frodo Baggins**, recently paralyzed by **Shelob**, into Mordor. At the end of *The Two Towers*, this leaves **Samwise Gamgee** shut out of Mordor, thinking that Frodo is dead.

Shaheed

Midnight's Children
Salman Rushdie

Farooq, Shaheed, and **Ayooba** are **Saleem**'s fellow soldiers in the Pakistani army.

Yamil Shaium

Chronicle of a Death Foretold
Gabriel García Márquez

An Arab man. He warns **Cristo Bedoya** about the Vicario twins' plan to murder **Santiago Nasar**.

Judith Shakespeare

A Room of One's Own
Virginia Woolf

The imagined sister of William Shakespeare. Judith Shakespeare suffers greatly and eventually commits suicide because she can find no socially acceptable outlets for her genius.

Shalem

The Red Tent
Anita Diamant

Dinah's first love and first husband, the prince of Shechem, son of **Hamor** and **Re-nefer**, father of **Re-mose**. Shalem's passion for Dinah leads him to agree to **Jacob**'s absurd bride-price and the agreement to have himself and every man in Shechem circumcised. Shalem is killed brutally by **Simon** and **Levi**.

Justice Shallow

Henry IV, Part II
William Shakespeare

A justice of the peace (minor local law officer). Shallow, along with his cousin **Justice Silence**, comes to the tavern in Gloucestershire to present **Sir John Falstaff** with the possible army recruits they've rounded up.

Robert Shallow

The Merry Wives of Windsor
William Shakespeare

A Justice of the law and uncle of **Abraham Slender**. He urges his nephew to try to seduce **Anne Page**.

Shamash

The Epic of Gilgamesh
Unknown

The sun god and the ancient patron of travelers. Shamash, the brother of **Ishtar**, protects **Gilgamesh** and **Enkidu** in their quests for glory. He sends the "thirteen winds" to blind **Humamba** and intercedes in vain on Enkidu's behalf when **Enlil** decrees his death.

Shamhat

The Epic of Gilgamesh
Unknown

The temple prostitute. She tames **Enkidu** by seducing him away from his natural state.

Ilya Afanasyevich Shamrayev

The Seagull
Anton Chekhov

Father to **Masha** and husband to **Polina Andreyevna**. He acts as the manager of **Sorin**'s farm and household. Shamrayev adores **Arkadina**'s fame and fortune and close ties to Russian artists. When it comes to running the farm, Shamrayev is argumentative about his control. He is cruel and unsympathetic to his daughter Masha's admirer and future husband **Medvedenko**.

Bobby Shandy

Tristram Shandy
Laurence Sterne

Tristram's older brother. He dies in London while away at school. His death affects the family greatly.

Elizabeth Shandy

Tristram Shandy
Laurence Sterne

Tristram's mother. Mrs. Shandy is singularly passive and uncontentious, which makes her a dull conversational partner for her argumentative husband.

Tristram Shandy
Laurence Sterne

Captain Toby Shandy

Tristram's uncle, and brother to **Walter Shandy**. After sustaining a groin wound in battle, he retires to a life of obsessive attention to the history and science of military fortifications. His temperament is gentle and sentimental.

Tristram Shandy
Laurence Sterne

Tristram Shandy

Both the fictionalized author of the novel and the child whose conception, birth, christening, and circumcision form one major sequence of the narrative. The adult Tristram Shandy relates certain aspects of his family history, including things that took place before his own birth, drawing from stories and hearsay as much as from his own memories.

Tristram Shandy
Laurence Sterne

Walter Shandy

Tristram's philosophy-minded father. Walter Shandy's love for abstruse and convoluted intellectual argumentation and his readiness to embrace any tantalizing hypothesis lead him to propound a great number of absurd pseudo-scientific theories.

Shane
Jack Schaefer

Shane

The protagonist. He is a stoic, mysterious man. He is **Bob Starrett**'s hero and quickly becomes **Joe Starrett**'s companion. Shane is loyal to the very end, never compromising any of the Starretts or placing them in danger.

Grendel
John Gardner

The shaper

A harpist and storyteller in **Hrothgar**'s court. The Shaper provides the Danes with an image of the world as essentially connected and purposeful—an image that **Grendel** finds incredibly seductive, despite his awareness that the glorious stories of Hrothgar's court are built on a foundation of lies.

Grendel
John Gardner

The shaper's assistant

The young apprentice who takes over the Shaper's duties upon his death.

Shabanu
Suzanne Fisher Staples

Sharma

Mama's dearest and liveliest cousin. Sharma lives in the desert with her daughter, **Fatima**. She left her husband because he abused her, and she now lives an independent life raising goats and sheep in the desert.

Shaw

A Streetcar Named Desire
Tennessee Williams

A supply man. He is **Stanley Kowalski**'s coworker and his source for stories of **Blanche DuBois**' disreputable past in Laurel, Mississippi.

George Bernard Shaw

The Remains of the Day
Kazuo Ishiguro

Famous Irish playwright. He came to dine at Darlington Hall.

Ekaterina Alexandrovna Shcherbatskaya

Anna Karenina
Leo Tolstoy

A beautiful young woman. She is courted by both **Konstantin Dmitrich Levin** and **Alexei Kirillovich Vronsky** and ultimately marries Levin. Kitty is sensitive and overprotected, shocked by some of the crude realities of life. Despite her indifference to intellectual matters, Kitty displays great courage and compassion in the face of death when caring for Levin's dying brother **Nikolai Dmitrich Levin**.

Princess Shcherbatskaya

Anna Karenina
Leo Tolstoy

The mother of **Ekaterina Alexandrovna Shcherbatskaya** and **Darya Alexandrovna Oblonskaya**. Princess Shcherbatskaya initially urges Kitty to choose **Alexei Kirillovich Vronsky** over **Konstantin Dmitrich Levin**.

Prince Alexander Dmitrievich Shcherbatsky

Anna Karenina
Leo Tolstoy

The father of **Ekaterina Alexandrovna Shcherbatskaya** and **Darya Alexandrovna Oblonskaya**. A practical aristocrat, Prince Shcherbatsky favors **Nikolai Dmitrich Levin** over **Alexei Kirillovich Vronsky** as a potential husband for Kitty.

Sammy Shecker

Bless the Beasts and Children
Glendon Swarthout

A New York City native, the son of a rich and famous comedian. Living in his father's shadow, Sammy often attempts to use humor to hide pain.

Ab Sheehan

Angela's Ashes
Frank McCourt

Angela McCourt's brother and **Frank McCourt**'s uncle. Uncle Ab was dropped on his head as a child, which damaged his brain. Frank moves in with him when he fights with his mother and **Laman Griffin**.

Reverend Shegog

The Sound and the Fury
William Faulkner

The pastor who delivers a powerful sermon on Easter Sunday at the local black church in Jefferson.

Sheila

Go Ask Alice
Anonymous

A sophisticated older woman, into drugs and kinky sex, who gets **Chris** a job in her hip San Francisco boutique. At a party, Sheila and her boyfriend brutally rape **Alice** and Chris.

Shel

Orlando
Virginia Woolf

A brave, gallant seaman. He sweeps **Orlando** off her feet in the nineteenth century when he sees her hurt on the moor. Shel is in love with Orlando and hastens to marry her, but he is torn between love for a woman and his duty as a seaman. When the wind changes, he must return to his ship to sail around Cape Horn.

Arthur Shelby

Uncle Tom's Cabin
Harriet Beecher Stowe

Uncle Tom's Kentucky owner. Shelby sells Tom to the cruel **Mr. Haley** to pay off his debts. An educated, kind, and basically good-hearted man, Shelby nonetheless tolerates and perpetuates slavery.

Emily Shelby

Uncle Tom's Cabin
Harriet Beecher Stowe

Arthur Shelby's wife. Emily is a loving, Christian woman who does not believe in slavery. She uses her influence with her husband to try to help the Shelbys' slaves.

George Shelby

Uncle Tom's Cabin
Harriet Beecher Stowe

Arthur Shelby and **Emily Shelby**'s good-hearted son. He loves **Uncle Tom** and promises to rescue him from the cruelty into which his father sold him. After Tom dies, George resolves to free all the slaves on the family farm in Kentucky.

Bob Sheldon

The Outsiders
S. E. Hinton

Boyfriend of **Cherry Valance**. Bob Sheldon is the dark-haired Soc who beats up **Johnny Cade** before the novel begins. Johnny murders Bob to keep Bob from drowning **Ponyboy Curtis**. Bob's death causes tension between the Socs and the greasers, resulting in a big rumble, which the greasers win.

Shelob

The Two Towers
J. R. R. Tolkien

An unimaginably ancient, enormous female spider that lives in the tunnels near Mordor. **Gollum** leads **Frodo Baggins** and **Samwise Gamgee** into Shelob's lair, where the spider paralyzes Frodo and nearly kills both Hobbits before Sam drives her away with the Phial of **Galadriel**.

Shen

Ender's Game
Orson Scott Card

A small recruit in **Ender Wiggin**'s launch group. He and Ender become friends through their mutual dislike of **Bernard**. Shen is one of Ender's commanders in the battles with the buggers.

Curly Shepard

The Outsiders
S. E. Hinton

The brother of **Tim Shepard**. He cannot go to the rumble because he was put in a reformatory for six months after robbing a liquor store.

Tim Shepard

The Outsiders
S. E. Hinton

The leader of another band of greasers and a friend of **Dally**'s. Tim Shepard and Dally respect each other, despite occasional conflicts. **Ponyboy Curtis** sees Tim's gang as real street hoods and criminals, and realizes that his own gang is little more than a group of friends fighting to survive.

Stan Shephard

On the Road
Jack Kerouac

Tim Gray's enthusiastic friend. Stan accompanies **Dean Moriarty** and **Sal Paradise** to Mexico, in part to escape his controlling grandfather.

Shepherd

Henry VI, Part I
William Shakespeare

The alleged father of **Joan of Arc**. At her trial, Joan denies any connection to the shepherd; he in turn curses her and tells the English to burn her.

Shepherd

The Winter's Tale
William Shakespeare

An old and honorable sheep-tender. The shepherd finds **Perdita** as a baby and raises her as his own daughter.

Lenny Shepherd

The Bell Jar
Sylvia Plath

Doreen's love interest. Lenny is a New York DJ and smooth older man.

Bill Sheppard

Pnin
Vladimir Nabokov

One of the brothers who rents an upstairs room to **Timofey Pnin**. Bill is a retired groundskeeper of the college who is totally deaf in one ear.

Bob Sheppard

Pnin
Vladimir Nabokov

One of the brothers who rents an upstairs room to **Timofey Pnin**. When Bob's wife dies, he moves in with his brother, **Bill Sheppard**. Bob rushes to Pnin's aid when he falls down the stairs.

Sher Dil

Shabanu
Suzanne Fisher Staples

The puppy **Dadi** buys **Shabanu** to compensate for selling **Guluband**. Sher Dil grows up to be an excellent herding dog.

Sherburn

The Adventures of Huckleberry Finn
Mark Twain

Man who shoots a rowdy, insulting drunk in one of the river towns where **Huckleberry Finn** and **Jim** stop.

Ang Dorje Sherpa

Into Thin Air
Jon Krakauer

Rob Hall's number-one Sherpa. Ang performs with near heroics frequently during the ascent, always helping other climbers and exhausting himself with the effort he exerts for others. He attempts to find Hall during the summit, but cannot climb high enough.

Lopsang Jangbu Sherpa

Into Thin Air
Jon Krakauer

Scott Fischer's main Sherpa. Lopsang is exceedingly loyal to Fischer, and helps secure ropes and haul supplies all the way up the mountain. He pulls **Sandy Pittman** up the mountain when she is too tired to climb herself. Lopsang tries and fails to save Fischer after the storm hits.

Vida Sherwin

Main Street
Sinclair Lewis

Gopher Prairie's high school teacher. Vida becomes one of Carol's best friends. Because she once loved **Will Kennicott** herself, Vida develops a love-hate relationship with Carol. They gradually drift apart when Vida marries **Raymond Wutherspoon** and devotes herself to housework.

Shiduri

The Epic of Gilgamesh
Unknown

A goddess who inhabits a tavern at the edge of the world. Shiduri shares her sensuous, worldly wisdom with **Gilgamesh**, advising him to cherish the pleasures of this world. She eventually tells him how to find **Ur-Shanabi**.

Mrs. Shigemura

Snow Falling on Cedars
David Guterson

Hatsue Miyamoto's teacher. When Hatsue was thirteen, her parents sent her to Mrs. Shigemura for training in social graces. Mrs. Shigemura told Hatsue to avoid white men.

Fishel Shilsky

The Color of Water
James McBride

Ruth McBride Jordan's father. He was racist, demanding, harsh, unloving, and greedy. He sexually abused Ruth. He finalized his separation from Ruth when he told her never to return home if she married a black man.

Hudis Shilsky

The Color of Water
James McBride

Ruth McBride Jordan's mother. She suffered from polio her entire life. Soft-spoken and meek, she deferred to Ruth's father, **Fishel Shilsky**, in virtually all matters. While she came from a well-to-do background, her family had little to do with her because of her handicap. Ruth felt guilty her entire life that she hadn't taken better care of Mameh.

Ambrosch Shimerda

My Ántonia
Willa Cather

The Shimerdas' oldest son. **Mrs. Shimerda** and her daughters dote on Ambrosch. Ambrosch shares his mother's curt and presumptuous attitude. He becomes the unquestioned head of the family after **Mr. Shimerda**'s suicide.

Ántonia Shimerda

My Ántonia
Willa Cather

Jim Burden's childhood friend. Intelligent, optimistic, loyal, and kindhearted, Ántonia has a difficult life after her father, **Mr. Shimerda**, commits suicide.

Marek Shimerda

My Ántonia
Willa Cather

The younger of the two Shimerda brothers. Marek is physically deformed and mentally unstable.

Mr. Shimerda

My Ántonia
Willa Cather

The patriarch of a Bohemian immigrant family. A melancholy man given to artistic and scholarly pursuits, Mr. Shimerda feels out of place in Nebraska and eventually commits suicide.

Mrs. Shimerda

My Ántonia
Willa Cather

The matriarch of a Bohemian immigrant family. Mrs. Shimerda is a brusque, bossy, and often curt woman. After **Mr. Shimerda** commits suicide, she is forced to make do with the little that she has in an attempt to provide for her family.

Yulka Shimerda

My Ántonia
Willa Cather

The youngest of the Shimerda children. Yulka is a pretty young girl who later helps **Ántonia Shimerda** raise her baby.

The Shipman

The Canterbury Tales
Geoffrey Chaucer

A pilgrim travelling to Canterbury. Brown-skinned from years of sailing, the Shipman has seen every bay and river in England, and exotic ports in Spain and Carthage as well.

Anne Shirley

Anne of Green Gables
L. M. Montgomery

The protagonist of the novel. Anne is an orphan who is adopted by **Matthew Cuthbert** and **Marilla Cuthbert** and grows up on their farm, Green Gables. The novel follows Anne as she makes social blunders and tries to quickly absorb the rules of social conduct, religion, and morality that other children have grown up learning.

Peter Shirley

Major Barbara
George Bernard Shaw

A "half hardened, half worn-out" old-timer. Shirley has just lost his job to a younger laborer.

Shirrifs

The Return of the King
J. R. R. Tolkien

Hobbit policemen. They attempt to arrest **Frodo Baggins**, **Samwise Gamgee**, **Peregrin Took**, and **Meriadoc Brandybuck** as they reenter the Shire. The returning Hobbits of the Fellowship quickly defeat the Shirrifs and Chief.

Shiva

Midnight's Children
Salman Rushdie

A boy who is born at the same moment as **Saleem**. They are switched at birth. Shiva possesses an amazing ability to fight.

Shock

The Rape of the Lock
Alexander Pope

Belinda's lapdog.

Earle Shoop

The Day of the Locust
Nathanael West

A tall, skinny cowboy from Arizona. Earle never has much money and rarely even has a home, spending his days in Hollywood standing in front of Hodge's saddlery store. He dates **Faye** for part of the novel.

Shorty

Black Boy
Richard Wright

The black elevator man in the building in Memphis where **Richard Wright** works. Shorty is witty, intelligent, and confident, but he demeans himself to earn money.

Shorty

The Autobiography of Malcolm X
Malcolm X & Alex Haley

Malcolm X's best friend during his Boston years. Shorty is a musician who at first leads and then follows Malcolm into a life of crime. While Malcolm converts to an aggressive hustler lifestyle, Shorty leads a comparatively normal life.

Broad Shoulders

Miss Lonelyhearts
Nathanael West

An anonymous person who pens the longest letter **Miss Lonelyhearts** receives during the novel. Broad Shoulders writes poorly, in a wrenching torrent of run-on sentences and misspellings that detail her life of suffering.

Diddy Shovel

The Shipping News
E. Annie Proulx

The friendly harbormaster. Diddy Shovel gives **Quoyle** the "shipping news" and lets him know about any interesting new vessels in the harbor.

Roza Shpolyanski

Pnin
Vladimir Nabokov

Another guest at the Pines during **Timofey Pnin**'s summer visit. Madame Roza finds Pnin delightful, and she is especially pleased by his expert croquet technique.

Shreve

Absalom, Absalom!
William Faulkner

Quentin Compson's roommate at Harvard. He is a young man from Edmonton in Alberta, Canada. The roommates discuss the story of the Sutpens.

Officer Shrift

The Phantom Tollbooth
Norton Juster

An officer who is twice as wide as he is tall. In Dictionopolis, he works as a police officer, judge, and jailer all at the same time. Officer Shrift has a habit of sentencing people to millions of years in prison then immediately forgetting about them.

Shrike

Miss Lonelyhearts
Nathanael West

Miss Lonelyhearts's editor at the newspaper. He is cynical, hedonistic, grandiloquent, and a womanizer. He is married to **Mary**, who he claims beats him and refuses to give up her virginity. Still, Shrike lets Mary go out with other men to save money. He mocks Miss Lonelyhearts most when it comes to religion, ridiculing his identification with Jesus and forcing him to dispense false hopes to his readership.

Mr. Shuan

Kidnapped
Robert Louis Stevenson

The first officer of the *Covenant* under **Captain Hoseason**. Mr. Shuan is monstrous when drinking and kills the cabin boy, **Ransome**, in a drunken rage. Shuan is later himself killed by **Alan Breck Stewart** in the battle of the Round-House, where Alan is assisted by **David Balfour**.

Ivan Denisovich Shukhov

One Day in the Life of Ivan Denisovich
Aleksandr Solzhenitsyn

An inmate of a Stalinst labor camp, along with **Tsezar Markovich**, **Fetyukov**, and **Alyoshka**, somewhere in Siberia in 1951. He is a working-class, somewhat uneducated man and the hero of the novel.

Stan Shunpike

Harry Potter and the Prisoner of Azkaban
J. K. Rowling

The teenage, pimply, nosy conductor of the Knight Bus.

Shylock

The Merchant of Venice
William Shakespeare

A Jewish moneylender. Angered by his mistreatment at the hands of Venice's Christians, particularly **Antonio**, Shylock schemes to take revenge by demanding a pound of Antonio's flesh in payment for **Bassanio**'s defaulted debt.

Sicinius

Coriolanus
William Shakespeare

A Roman tribune. He is a clever politician and **Brutus**'s ally in the struggle against **Coriolanus**.

Sid

The Adventures of Tom Sawyer
Mark Twain

Tom Sawyer's half-brother. Sid is a goody-goody who enjoys getting Tom into trouble.

Siddhartha

Siddhartha
Hermann Hesse

Kamala's lover, **Vasudeva**'s student, and a friend of **Govinda**'s. When the novel begins, Siddhartha is a handsome young Brahmin distinguished in his town for his cleverness and superior bearing. As we follow his life's path, he transforms into a bearded, long-haired, loincloth-wearing ascetic, then into an opulently dressed businessman well-versed in the ways of pleasure, and finally into a simple ferryman.

Father Siemes

Hiroshima
John Hersey

A Jesuit priest. He writes a report for the Holy See in Rome about the atomic bomb and expresses mixed views about the morality of using such a powerful weapon.

Sigemund

Beowulf
Unknown

A figure from Norse mythology, famous for slaying a dragon. Sigemund's story is told in praise of **Beowulf**.

Signa

O Pioneers!
Willa Cather

Alexandra Bergson's maid. She takes care of Alexandra during the difficult months after **Emil Bergson**'s death. Signa marries **Nelse Jensen**.

Norse Mythology
Unknown

Sigurd

The son of Sigmund. He is a fierce warrior who braves a ring of fire for the love of the beautiful woman-warrior **Brynhild**. He is the prototype for Siegfried in Wagner's Ring Cycle.

Oliver Twist
Charles Dickens

Bill Sikes

A brutal, professional burglar brought up in **Fagin**'s gang. Sikes murders his lover **Nancy**.

The Da Vinci Code
Dan Brown

Silas

A monk of Opus Dei and the murderer of **Jacques Saunière**. When he falls into the orbit of Bishop **Manuel Aringarosa**, Silas devotes himself to the strict Catholic ways of Opus Dei.

Anne Frank: Diary of a Young Girl
Anne Frank

Hello Silberberg

A boy with whom **Anne Frank** has an innocent, though romantic, relationship before she goes into hiding.

Henry IV, Part II
William Shakespeare

Justice Silence

A justice of the peace (minor local law officer). Silence, along with his cousin **Justice Shallow**, comes to the tavern in Gloucestershire to present **Sir John Falstaff** with the possible army recruits they've rounded up.

The Woman Warrior
Maxine Hong Kingston

The silent girl

A classmate of **Kingston**'s. Like Kingston, the silent girl is quiet and unpopular. Kingston torments the girl.

Inherit the Wind
Jerome Lawrence & Robert E. Lee

Sillers

An employee at the local feed store and a member of the jury.

The Martian Chronicles
Ray Bradbury

Silly

A worker in **Mr. Teece**'s store. He is a young man, but he hopes to start his own hardware store on Mars.

Rab Silsbee

Johnny Tremain
Esther Forbes

Jonathan Tremain's best friend. With his quiet, unassuming confidence, Rab becomes Johnny's model and guide as Johnny struggles to find a new identity. Rab introduces Johnny to the world of revolutionary politics.

Dean Silva

Arrowsmith
Sinclair Lewis

A professor of internal medicine and the dean of the faculty at **Martin Arrowsmith**'s medical school. He believes more in the practice of medicine than in research and is supportive of Martin.

Joe Silva

Mourning Becomes Electra
Eugene O'Neill

A fat, boisterous Portuguese fishing captain. He helps goad **Abner Small** into the allegedly haunted, boarded-up Mannon house.

Silver

Watership Down
Richard Adams

A rabbit that **Bigwig** convinces to leave the Owsla. **Hazel** counts on Silver both to fight well and to make the best decision for the group's welfare.

Long John Silver

Treasure Island
Robert Louis Stevenson

The cook on the voyage to Treasure Island. Silver is the secret ringleader of the pirate band. Silver is deceitful and disloyal, yet he is always kind toward **Jim Hawkins** and is genuinely fond of the boy.

Mattie Silver

Ethan Frome
Edith Wharton

Zenobia Frome's cousin. She comes to assist the Fromes with their domestic tasks.

Terry Silver

This Boy's Life
Tobias Wolff

Jack Wolff's delinquent friend from Salt Lake City. Together with Jack, **Terry Silver** and **Terry Taylor** egg passersby from the roof of an apartment building and watch the Mickey Mouse Club while making vulgar remarks about one of the show's stars.

Ned Silverton

The House of Mirth
Edith Wharton

A young, rich man who accompanies **Lily Bart** and the Dorsets on their Mediterranean cruise. On the cruise, Ned has an affair with **Bertha Dorset**, which he manages to conceal from most of society.

Silvia

The Two Gentlemen of Verona
William Shakespeare

Daughter to the **Duke of Milan** and **Valentine**'s beloved. **Proteus**, too, falls in love with Silvia, unrequitedly. Silvia commiserates with **Julia** (who is dressed as a page boy), about Proteus's mistreatment of Julia. When the Duke banishes **Valentine**, she escapes to seek him with the help of **Sir Eglamour**. Silvia's loyalty to Valentine and sympathy for Julia stands in contrast to the men's fickle attitudes toward their loves and responsibilities: Proteus quickly betrays both Valentine and Julia; Sir Eglamour runs away when he and Silvia are beset by outlaws; even Valentine lacks honor, offering Silvia to his best friend as a make-up gift after stopping Proteus from raping her.

Silvius

As You Like It
William Shakespeare

A young shepherd who is desperately in love with the disdainful **Phoebe**. When **Rosalind** reveals herself at the end of the play, Phoebe, who had been in love with the disguised Rosalind, readily turns to Silvius.

Boris Simeonov-Pischik

The Cherry Orchard
Anton Chekhov

A nobleman and landowner. Like **Ranevsky**, he experiences financial difficulties. Pischik is always certain he will find money somehow to pay for the mortgages that are due. However, he continually borrows money from Ranevsky.

Daisy Simmons

Mrs. Dalloway
Virginia Woolf

Peter Walsh's lover in India. She is married to a major in the Indian army. Daisy is twenty-four years old and has two small children. Peter is in London to arrange her divorce.

Dr. Simmons

Their Eyes Were Watching God
Zora Neale Hurston

A friendly white doctor. He chats amiably with **Tea Cake** and hears his story about fighting with the dog, but afterward, he pulls **Janie Mae Crawford** aside and tells her that he thinks that the dog who bit Tea Cake was rabid.

Jody Simmons

Johnny Got His Gun
Dalton Trumbo

The night-shift manager at the Los Angeles bakery where **Joe Bonham** worked.

Ralph Simmons

A Farewell to Arms
Ernest Hemingway

An opera student of dubious talent whom **Frederic Henry** meets in Milan. Simmons is the first person Henry goes to see after he flees from battle. Simmons gives Henry civilian clothes so that he can travel to Switzerland without drawing suspicion.

Simms

The Heart Is a Lonely Hunter
Carson McCullers

A religious fanatic. He writes quotes from the Bible on brick walls around town. Simms starts coming to the carnival where **Jake Blount** works so that he may preach from a soapbox. Jake often makes fun of Simms.

Jeremy Simms

Roll of Thunder, Hear My Cry
Mildred D. Taylor

A white boy. He is often beaten for walking to school with and associating with **Cassie Logan**, **Little Man Logan**, **Christopher-John Logan**, and **Stacey Logan**. His sister is **Lillian Jean Simms**, who is often rude to Cassie. He has two big brothers, **Melvin Simms** and **R. W. Simms**, who use **T. J. Avery** by pretending they are his friend and then framing him for a robbery that they commit.

Lillian Jean Simms

Roll of Thunder, Hear My Cry
Mildred D. Taylor

A prissy seventh-grader. Lillian Jean Simms is the sister of **Jeremy Simms**, **Melvin Simms**, and **R. W. Simms**. She is often rude to **Cassie Logan**.

Melvin and R. W. Simms

Roll of Thunder, Hear My Cry
Mildred D. Taylor

The two older Simms brothers. They are also brothers to **Jeremy Simms** and to **Lillian Jean Simms**. The brothers pretend to befriend **T. J. Avery** but make fun of him behind his back. They take advantage of T.J. and frame him for a robbery in the town of Strawberry, which turns into an event with a lynch mob that is a direct threat to the Logan family, as the mob threatens to hang T.J., **L.T. Morrison**, and **Papa** at the Logan house. The terror is averted by Papa and L.T.

Simon

The Red Tent
Anita Diamant

A son of **Jacob** by **Leah**, brother to **Levi**. They sell their own brother, **Joseph**, into slavery, and are responsible for counseling Jacob with their greedy influence. Concerned that their own legacies and power might diminish, they reject **Dinah**'s marriage to **Shalem** and slaughter Shalem and all of the men of Shechem in their sleep after taking a disgustingly huge bride-price from **Hamor**.

Simon

Lord of the Flies
William Golding

A shy, sensitive boy in the group. Simon is attacked by all those involved in the ritual and savage dance of Jack's tribe. Before Simon is murdered, he has a conversation with **the Lord of the Flies**, the sow's head planted on a spear by Jack's tribe.

Simon

The Unbearable Lightness of Being
Milan Kundera

Tomas's son by his first wife. He is a dreamer and has always idealized his father, who did not wish to know him. After Prague Spring, a time of increased political and artistic freedom, Simon joins a dissident group and regains contact with Tomas through the **Editor with a big chin**. After his father's death, he turns to Christianity.

Ida Simon

The Autobiography of Miss Jane Pittman
Ernest J. Gaines

A woman on the plantation. She takes care of **Mary Agnes LeFarbre** after she thinks Mary Agnes was ravished.

Alberta Simonds

Chronicle of a Death Foretold
Gabriel García Márquez

Bayardo San Roman's mother. She is a mulatto woman from Curacao, who in her youth had been proclaimed the most beautiful woman in the Antilles.

Simonides

Pericles
William Shakespeare

King of Pentapolis and **Thaisa**'s father. Impressed with **Pericles**'s jousting skill, Simonides tests Pericles by insulting his honor before blessing Pericles's marriage to Thaisa.

Simonov

Notes from Underground
Fyodor Dostoevsky

A former schoolmate of **the Underground Man**. He is the only one with whom the Underground Man currently maintains a relationship. The Underground Man sees Simonov as an honest, independent man who is less narrow-minded than most people.

Saunder Simpcox

Henry VI, Part II
William Shakespeare

A peasant who pretends that he regained his sight through a miracle. **Humphrey, Duke of Gloucester** sees through the trick. Gloucester orders Simpcox to be beaten with whips and paraded through town.

Peter Simple

The Merry Wives of Windsor
William Shakespeare

Abraham Slender's servant. **Sir Hugh Evans** sends him to deliver a letter to **Anne Page** on behalf of Slender's romantic endeavors. **Doctor Caius** discovers him hiding in a closet and sends him back to Evans with a challenge for a duel.

Dr. Simpson

Jurassic Park
Michael Crichton

A leading world authority on lizards who works at Columbia University.

Homer Simpson

The Day of the Locust
Nathanael West

A large, broad man who has recently moved to Hollywood after working as a hotel bookkeeper in Iowa. His days consist mainly of eating, sleeping, and sitting until he meets **Faye Greener** and unhappily falls in love. Homer's meekness makes him a doormat for Faye and others.

Miss Love Simpson

Cold Sassy Tree
Olive Anne Burns

A pretty, affectionate, and strong-willed woman. Miss Love has succeeded despite a troubled childhood. In addition to charm and a sense of humor, she possesses a business acumen that wins her an important role in running Rucker's store.

Sam Simpson

The Natural
Bernard Malamud

The scout who first discovers **Roy Hobbs**. Unfortunately, Sam dies on the way to Hobbs's first tryout and is therefore not present to prevent Hobbs from being attacked by **Harriet Bird**.

Sergeant Simpson

Fallen Angels
Walter Dean Myers

The leader of **Richie Perry**'s squad. When Richie first arrives in Vietnam, Sergeant Simpson is near the end of his tour of duty. Later, under great pressure from **Captain Stewart**, Simpson extends his tour by thirty days, but he survives and returns home.

Sin

Paradise Lost
John Milton

Satan's daughter. She sprang full-formed from Satan's head when he was still in Heaven. Sin has the shape of a woman above the waist, that of a serpent below, and her middle is ringed about with Hell Hounds, who periodically burrow into her womb and gnaw her entrails. She guards the gates of Hell.

Aadam Sinai

Midnight's Children
Salman Rushdie

Saleem's son.

Ahmed Sinai

Midnight's Children
Salman Rushdie

Saleem's father and **Mumtaz**'s husband.

Saleem Sinai

Midnight's Children
Salman Rushdie

The son of poor parents, switched with another child at birth. **Mumtaz** and **Ahmed Sinai** raise him in relative comfort and wealth, unlike **Shiva**, who is born at the exact same moment. Saleem possesses supernatural powers, the most unusual of which is his ability to read others' thoughts.

Sinbad the Sailor

The Count of Monte Cristo
Alexandre Dumas

See **Edmond Dantès**.

Emil Sinclair

Demian
Hermann Hesse

The protagonist of the novel. He is friends with **Max Damian** and in love with **Frau Eva**. The book is a chronicle of his intellectual development from the time he was ten until his late teens. The book recounts the story of Sinclair's interactions with Demian and a host of other characters who are instrumental in his intellectual transformation from a religious boy who follows others' commands to a man who seeks to fulfill the deepest desires of his soul.

Sing

Song of Solomon
Toni Morrison

Milkman Dead's grandmother and **Macon Dead I**'s wife. Sing is an Indian woman also known as Singing Bird. After Macon Dead I is orphaned by **Solomon**'s flight and **Ryna**'s madness, he is taken in by a Native American woman named **Heddy**. Sing is one of his adoptive siblings. Eventually, Sing and Macon Dead I run away together and fall in love, producing **Macon, Jr.** and **Pilate Dead**.

John Singer

The Heart Is a Lonely Hunter
Carson McCullers

A deaf-mute. He makes a living engraving silver pieces in a jewelry shop. A diligent worker and a kind person, he is also a good and attentive listener.

Picture Singh

Midnight's Children
Salman Rushdie

A snake charmer and a friend to **Saleem**.

Pooran Singh

Out of Africa
Isak Dinesen

The blacksmith on the farm. Singh is an Indian from Kashmir who has not seen his family in many years, but who frequently sends money to them.

Ray Singh

The Lovely Bones
Alice Sebold

Susie Salmon's family neighbor. When Susie returns to Earth for a tantalizing few hours, she comes not to see her sister again or hug her father—as much as she loves them—but to make love with Ray.

Dave Singleman

Death of a Salesman
Arthur Miller

An old salesman. He briefly met **Willy Loman** and inspired him to become a salesman as well. Singleman's dignified success and graceful, respected position as an older man deluded Willy into believing that "selling was the greatest career a man could want" because of its limitless potential and its honorable nature.

Mrs. Sinico

Dubliners
James Joyce

The neglected wife of a ship captain. She falls in love with **Mr. Duffy** in "A Painful Case." After Mr. Duffy shuns her, Mrs. Sinico starts drinking and eventually commits suicide.

Sinon

The Aeneid
Virgil

The Greek youth who persuades the Trojans to accept the wooden horse, then lets out the warriors hidden inside the horse's belly.

Raymond Sintes

The Stranger
Albert Camus

A local pimp and **Meursault**'s neighbor. Raymond becomes angry when he suspects his mistress is cheating on him, and he enlists Meursault's help in punishing her. After Raymond beats his mistress, he exchanges blows with her brother **the Arab**. He testifies on Meursault's behalf during the trial.

Mr. Sir

Holes
Louis Sachar

One of the counselors at Camp Green Lake. He is tough and mean and is constantly eating sunflower seeds. After he thinks **Stanley Yelnats** has stolen his sunflower seeds, which was really **Magnet**'s doing, he stops giving Stanley water.

Murray Jay Siskind

White Noise
Don DeLillo

One of the New York émigré professors teaching at the College-on-the-Hill. He is an ex-sportswriter who speaks in a hyper-inflated intellectual rhetoric. Image- and media-obsessed, Murray aspires to create a department around Elvis the same way **Jack Gladney** did around Hitler.

Peter Sissen

The Virgin Suicides
Jeffrey Eugenides

The first boy to set foot inside the Lisbon house. Peter Sissen is invited to dinner for helping **Mr. Lisbon** install a model of the solar system in his high school math classroom. For months afterward, Peter regales the boys with his eyewitness account of the Lisbon house and its feminine secrets.

Aunt Sissy

A Tree Grows in Brooklyn
Betty Smith

Katie Nolan's oldest sister. The first of **Mary Rommely**'s daughters, Aunt Sissy is the only daughter who has not learned to read and write. Her sisters always end up forgiving her foibles. **Francie Nolan** absolutely adores her.

Sixo

Beloved
Toni Morrison

A slave at Sweet Home along with **Paul A**, **Paul D**, **Paul F**, **Halle**, **Sethe**, and, earlier, **Baby Suggs**. Sixo is the only slave who does not pine away after Sethe before she marries Halle. He instead frequently walks thirty miles to meet his great love. Sixo tries to escape from Sweet Home and fails. For that, **schoolteacher** burns him alive.

Ruta Skadi

His Dark Materials
Robert Pullman

The queen of the Latvian witches and a former lover of **Lord Asriel**'s. Ruta Skadi's daemon is **Sergi**, a bluethroat.

Rita Skeeter

Harry Potter and the Goblet of Fire
J. K. Rowling

A nosy, middle-aged reporter. She buzzes around, absorbing gossip to use in her reputation-ruining articles.

Skipper

Cat on a Hot Tin Roof
Tennessee Williams

The deceased friend of **Brick**. Brick's drinking problem is often blamed on Skipper, who is suspected to be Brick's lover from the past. Skipper once made a drunken confession to Brick over the phone, and Brick hung up on Skipper and never spoke to him again. **Maggie** drove a jealous wedge between Brick and Skipper.

Skipper

This Boy's Life
Tobias Wolff

Dwight's second-eldest child, a few years older than **Jack Wolff**. Skipper is reserved and polite. He spends months transforming a beat-up 1949 Ford, only to have it destroyed in a sandstorm on his way to Mexico.

Sky

A Yellow Raft in Blue Water
Michael Dorris

Evelyn's husband. He owns a gas station near Bearpaw Lake and helps out **Rayona**. Sky is kind and giving, but also rather simpleminded.

Slackbridge

Hard Times
Charles Dickens

A crooked orator. He convinces the Hands to unionize and turns them against **Stephen Blackpool** when he refuses to join the union.

Larry Slade

The Iceman Cometh
Eugene O'Neill

A bitter retired Syndicalist-Anarchist. He had an affair with **Don Parritt**'s mother but argued with her, declared her a whore and stormed out. He takes care of **Don Parritt** when Parritt is on the run from the police.

Slamecksan

Gulliver's Travels
Jonathan Swift

A Lilliputian political party.

Emmie Slattery

Gone with the Wind
Margaret Mitchell

A young woman whose poor white family lives in the swamp bottom near Tara. Emmie is considered "white trash," and **Scarlett O'Hara**'s class-conscious, genteel society dislikes Emmie.

Mr. Sleary

Hard Times
Charles Dickens

The proprietor of the circus where **Sissy**'s father was an entertainer.

Abraham Slender

The Merry Wives of Windsor
William Shakespeare

Robert Shallow's nephew and the third suitor for **Anne Page**'s hand. Slender speaks nothing but nonsense to Anne, but **Master George Page** favors him as a good match for his daughter. Though there is much vying for support among the elders concerning Anne's rightful match, both Slender and his main rival **Doctor Caius** are duped at the end of the play when **Fenton** marries Anne.

Slim

Of Mice and Men
John Steinbeck

A highly skilled mule driver. He is the acknowledged "prince" of the ranch where **Lennie** and **George** work. The other characters often look to the quiet and insightful Slim for advice.

Charlie Sloane

Anne of Green Gables
L. M. Montgomery

One of the first people to recognize **Anne Shirley**'s charms. Charlie admires Anne from afar from the time they are children.

Dr. Slop

Tristram Shandy
Laurence Sterne

The local male midwife. At **Walter**'s insistence, he acts as a backup at **Tristram**'s birth.

Christopher Sly

The Taming of the Shrew
William Shakespeare

The principal character in the play's brief Induction, which leads into the play. Sly is a drunken tinker, tricked by a mischievous nobleman into thinking that he is really a lord. As he sits, tricked and dazed, he is treated to the feature presentation by a troupe of players.

Uncle Whittier Smail

Main Street
Sinclair Lewis

Aunt Bessie's husband. Along with his wife, he proves to be a great annoyance to **Carol** when they move to Gopher Prairie.

Abner Small

Mourning Becomes Electra
Eugene O'Neill

The shrill, goat-bearded clerk of the town hardware store. He breaks into the allegedly haunted, boarded-up Mannon house on a wager.

Liddy Smallbury

Far from the Madding Crowd
Thomas Hardy

Bathsheba Everdene's maid and confidante. Bathsheba tells Liddy Smallbury all of her little comments about the men in her life. Liddy gossips with the other servants about the goings-on with Bathsheba, **Sergeant Francis Troy**, and **William Boldwood**.

Smaug

The Hobbit
J. R. R. Tolkien

The great dragon who lives in the Lonely Mountain. Years ago, Smaug heard of the treasure that the **Dwarves** had amassed in the mountain under **Thror**'s reign, and he drove them away to claim the gold for himself. Smaug is killed by **Bard**, who knows the weak spot in the hollow of Smaug's left breast.

Pavel Fyodorovich Smerdyakov

The Brothers Karamazov
Fyodor Dostoevsky

The son of **Stinking Lizaveta** and **Fyodor Pavlovich Karamazov**, Smerdyakov is raised by **Grigory Kutuzov Vasilievich** and his wife and is made to work in Fyodor Pavlovich's house as a servant. Cursed with epilepsy, Smerdyakov also has a mean temperament, sometimes exhibiting outright malice and sometimes hiding behind a mask of groveling servitude. He is particularly interested in discussing philosophy with **Ivan Fyodorovich Karamazov**, whose advocacy of an antireligious amorality paves the way for Smerdyakov to murder Fyodor Pavlovich.

Lieutenant Smit

The Power of One
Bryce Courtenay

A boxing coach at the Barberton prison. He is also the brother of the well-known boxer, Jackhammer Smit. **Peekay** and Lieutenant Smit become fast friends. Smit avenges **Geel Piet**'s death for Peekay by beating up **Borman**.

Smith the Weaver

Henry VI, Part II
William Shakespeare

A follower of **Jack Cade**'s rebellion. Along with Cade and his other followers, the Weaver calls for the creation of a realm where the simplest working man is the most honored, and literate people will be executed.

Beauty Smith

White Fang
Jack London

An ugly man. Beauty tricks **Gray Beaver** into selling **White Fang** to Beauty. Beauty Smith trains White Fang to become a fighting dog. **Weedon Scott** saves White Fang from Beauty's cruel ownership.

Harriet Smith

Emma
Jane Austen

A pretty but unremarkable seventeen-year-old woman of uncertain parentage. She lives at the local boarding school. Harriet becomes **Emma Woodhouse**'s protégé and the object of her matchmaking schemes.

Harry Smith

The Remains of the Day
Kazuo Ishiguro

A resident of Moscombe and a passionate politician. During dinner at the Taylors' house, Harry tells **Stevens** that he believes that people exhibit dignity only when they accept their responsibility to vote and strongly exercise their own opinions.

Reverend James Smith

Things Fall Apart
Chinua Achebe

The missionary who replaces **Mr. Brown**. Unlike Mr. Brown, Reverend Smith is uncompromising and strict. He demands that his converts reject all of their beliefs, and he shows no respect for indigenous customs or culture. He is indirectly responsible, through **Enoch**, for the climactic clash between the African and English cultures.

Lucrezia Smith

Mrs. Dalloway
Virginia Woolf

Septimus Warren Smith's twenty-four-year-old Italian wife. She loves Septimus, but it is difficult for her to bear the burden of his mental illness alone. Grown thin with worry, she feels isolated and continually wishes to share her unhappiness with somebody. She trims hats for her neighbor, **Mrs. Filmer**.

Miss Smith

Maggie: A Girl of the Streets
Stephen Crane

A woman who appears in the closing scene. Miss Smith helps to whip **Mary Johnson** up into a sentimental fit of mourning for her lost daughter, **Maggie**.

Mr. Smith

Evelina
Fanny Burney

One of **Mr. Branghton**'s more prosperous tenants. Although he tries his best to look refined, Mr. Smith is vulgar, obvious, and rude.

Mrs. Smith

Persuasion
Jane Austen

The girlhood friend of **Anne Elliot**, currently living in Bath. After her husband went into debt and left her a widow, Mrs. Smith was left with nothing. Now crippled by an illness, Mrs. Smith rekindles her former friendship with Anne and provides her with information that helps Anne learn more of **Mr. William Elliot**.

Perry Edward Smith

In Cold Blood
Truman Capote

Along with **Richard Eugene Hickock**, one of the two murderers of **Herbert Clutter** and his family. His legs were badly injured in a motorcycle accident.

Robert Smith

Song of Solomon
Toni Morrison

An insurance agent and member of the Seven Days vigilante group. Smith's attempt to fly off the roof of Mercy Hospital begins the novel's exploration of flight as a means of escape. Later, it is revealed that **Solomon**, **Milkman Dead**'s great-grandfather, flew across the Atlantic to Africa to escape slavery.

Septimus Warren Smith

Mrs. Dalloway
Virginia Woolf

A World War I veteran suffering from shell shock. He is married to an Italian woman named **Lucrezia Smith**. Though he is insane, Septimus views English society in much the same way **Clarissa Dalloway** does, and struggles both to maintain his privacy and to communicate with others. Before the war, he was a young and idealistic aspiring poet. After the War he regards human nature as evil and believes he is guilty of not being able to feel. Rather than succumb to the society he abhors, he commits suicide.

Tex John Smith

In Cold Blood
Truman Capote

Perry Edward Smith's father. Tex is a kindly backwoodsman who never comes to see his son in jail. Perry's mother is **Flo Buckskin**, whom Tex met and married on the rodeo circuit.

Valentine Michael Smith

Stranger in a Strange Land
Robert A. Heinlein

Human born on Mars to two Earth explorers. Orphaned as an infant, Mike is raised by the Martian race. When he is brought to Earth as an adult, he brings knowledge of telekinesis and mind-reading abilities, as well as a Martian worldview. Mike develops a deep curiosity about Earthling ways, and he endeavors to understand the human concepts that he has been raised without. He forms an intimate relationship with **Gillian Boardman** and becomes something of an adopted son to **Jubal Harshaw**.

Winston Smith

1984
George Orwell

Minor member of the ruling Party of Oceania. Winston has come to hate all that **Big Brother** and the Party represent. Eventually he shares his thoughts with his lover **Julia** and the sympathetic ear of **O'Brien**, whom Winston believes is part of **Emmanuel Goldstein**'s subversive Brotherhood. When he is captured by the Thought Police and betrayed by O'Brien and Julia, he reverts dejectedly back to blind obedience to Big Brother.

Treasure Island
Robert Louis Stevenson

Captain Smollett

The captain of the voyage to Treasure Island. Captain Smollett is suspicious of the crew that **Squire Trelawney** has hired. Smollett believes in rules and does not like **Jim Hawkins**'s disobedience.

The Return of the King
J. R. R. Tolkien

Snaga

An **Orc** whom **Samwise Gamgee** and **Frodo Baggins** encounter as he fights **Shagrat**, another orc, in the tower of Cirith Ungol.

The Little Prince
Antoine de Saint-Exupéry

The Snake

The first character **the Little Prince** meets on Earth. Ultimately the snake sends the prince back to the heavens by biting him.

The Harry Potter Series: Books 1–4
J. K. Rowling

Severus Snape

The Potions teacher. A slimy, ill-tempered man, Snape is the head of Slytherin House and gets great pleasure out of trying to get **Harry Potter** into trouble. He once was a Death Eater, a follower of **Voldemort**. Now that Snape is no longer a Death Eater, **Albus Dumbledore** trusts him as one of the good wizards.

Henry IV, Part II
William Shakespeare

Snare

Along with **Fang**, one of the incompetent officers of the law whom **Mistress Quickly** calls to arrest **Sir John Falstaff**.

The Brothers Karamazov
Fyodor Dostoevsky

Ilyusha Snegiryov

The son of a military captain. He once saw his father beaten up by **Dmitri Fyodorovich Karamazov**. Proud and unwilling to be cowed by the larger boys who pick on him, Ilyusha befriends **Alexei Fyodorovich Karamazov**, but becomes ill and dies toward the end of the novel.

Silas Marner
George Eliot

Mr. Snell

The landlord of the Rainbow, a local tavern.

Ab Snopes

The Unvanquished
William Faulkner

A shiftless, lower-class farmer. Ab Snopes betrays **Granny Millard** twice, first to the Yankees and then to the bandit **Grumby**.

Tom Snout

A Midsummer Night's Dream
William Shakespeare

A tinker. In the craftsmen's play for **Theseus**'s marriage celebration, he ends up playing the part of Wall.

Col. Rutherford Snow

Babbitt
Sinclair Lewis

The owner of Zenith's local newspaper. **Snow** helps other members of the Good Citizen's League in the attempt to coerce **Babbitt** into conforming with middle-class Zenith's values.

Snowball

Animal Farm
George Orwell

Pig who, alongside **Napoleon**, takes control of the farm after the animals oust **Mr. Jones**. But while Snowball was planning a socialist utopia, Napoleon was consolidating power. Shortly before an election for leadership of the farm, Napoleon stages a coup, sending his attack dogs to run Snowball off the farm. Though Snowball is never seen again, he is vilified and blamed for every mishap that befalls the farm, invoked as a bogeyman in **Squealer**'s propaganda, and marginalized in his revisionist history.

Snowden

Catch-22
Joseph Heller

A young gunner who died on a mission over Avignon. The circumstances of Snowden's death—a shattering experience for **John Yossarian**, who witnessed it—are slowly revealed over the course of the novel.

Snug

A Midsummer Night's Dream
William Shakespeare

A joiner. He is chosen to play the lion in the craftsmen's play for **Theseus**'s marriage celebration.

John Erik Snyte

The Fountainhead
Ayn Rand

A supposedly progressive architect. In reality, John Erik Snyte's designs are a composite of the designs of five architects.

Mrs. Louella Soames

Our Town
Thornton Wilder

A gossipy woman who sings in the church choir with **Mrs. Myrtle Webb** and **Mrs. Julia Gibbs**.

Socrates

The Republic
Plato

The master-sophist and spokesman for the "new education" of rhetoric, atheism, and science. His dialogues are the source of Plato's entire body of philosophy. The crux of these dialogues is the Socratic elenchus. Sometimes called the dialectic, the elenchus is a cross-examination meant to amend or improve the beliefs of Socrates's conversational partner.

Socrates

The Clouds
Aristophanes

See above.

Tiny Soderball

My Ántonia
Willa Cather

One of the hired girls in Black Hawk. She is a friend to **Ántonia Shimerda** and **Lena Lingard**. After working with **Mrs. Gardener** in the Boys' Home, Tiny travels west and makes a small fortune during the Alaskan gold rush.

Sofia

Midnight's Children
Salman Rushdie

Mustapha's wife.

Sofia

The Color Purple
Alice Walker

A large, fiercely independent woman who befriends **Celie** and marries **Harpo**. Sofia refuses to submit to whites, men, or anyone else who tries to dominate her. **Miss Millie**, the mayor's wife, admires the cleanliness and good manners of Sofia's children, so she asks Sofia to be her maid. Sofia violently refuses, causing a fight that lands her in jail, followed by a long period of servitude in Miss Millie's house. By the time she is free, her children have grown up or barely recognize her.

Sofia

How the Garcia Girls Lost Their Accents
Julia Alvarez

The youngest daughter of the Garcia family. Sofia's wild and rebellious streak comes out during her adolescence, when she challenges her father's authority and runs away to Germany to marry **Otto**.

Solange

The Maids
Jean Genet

Claire's older sister. She has a more resentful attitude toward **Madame**, and in their roleplaying fantasies she maintains her role as a maid. She gets aroused when Claire plays the Madame and heaps sadistic abuse upon her, but she is not afraid to fight back with violence. The maids have been planning to get Solange impregnated by **Mario**.

Solanio

The Merchant of Venice
William Shakespeare

A Venetian gentleman, and frequent companion to **Salerio**.

Soldier

The Member of the Wedding
Carson McCullers

An unnamed military man who is in town on a three-day leave. His attempts to have sex with **Frankie Addams** open her eyes to the dangers of both war and sexuality.

The soldier in white

Catch-22
Joseph Heller

A body covered in bandages that stays at the same ward as **John Yossarian** and **Dunbar** in the Pianosa hospital.

The Tattered Soldier

The Red Badge of Courage
Stephen Crane

A twice-shot soldier whom **Henry Fleming** encounters in the column of wounded men.

Soldiers

The Flies
Jean-Paul Sartre

The king's enforcers. They rarely have any need to act because the **Argives** are so obedient.

Solinus

The Comedy of Errors
William Shakespeare

The Duke of Ephesus. While he adheres to the new Ephesian law that mandates the execution of any Syracusan found in the country, he is moved by **Egeon**'s tale of woe. Solinus grants Egeon the entire day to seek help from any Ephesian friends to raise the thousand-mark ransom for his life. In the face of the two sets of twins' reunions at the end of the play, kindly waives the execution as well as the penalty.

Sol-leks

The Call of the Wild
Jack London

An older, more experienced dog on **Buck**'s team. Buck learns from Sol-leks how to be a sled dog by being placed between Sol-leks and **Dave**.

Solomon

The Old Testament
Unknown

David's son and the third king of Israel. Solomon builds the opulent Temple in Jerusalem and ushers in Israel's greatest period of wealth and power. **God** grants Solomon immense powers of knowledge and discernment in response to Solomon's humble request for wisdom. Solomon's earthly success hinders his morality, however, and his weakness for foreign women and their deities leads to Israel's downfall.

Solomon

Song of Solomon
Toni Morrison

Milkman Dead's great-grandfather. He supposedly flew back to Africa but dropped his son Jake, or **Macon Dead I**, shortly after taking off. The song about Solomon's flight is one of the clues given to Milkman about his past.

Henry and Sam Solum

Giants in the Earth
O. E. Rölvaag

American-born settlers of Norwegian origin. The brothers join **Per Hansa**, **Hans Olsa**, and **Syvert Tonseten** to form a small settlement along Spring Creek. They frequently serve as interpreters because the other men do not know English. Henry becomes the settlement's schoolteacher.

2nd Duke of Somerset

Henry VI, Part I and *Henry VI, Part II*
William Shakespeare

King Henry VI's cousin, and Richard Plantagenet (later **Duke of York**)'s long-standing enemy. Somerset's disagreement with Plantagenet at the Temple Garden in *King Henry VI, Part I*, eventually leads to the Wars of the Roses, in which the Houses of Lancaster and York fought over the rightful inheritance of the throne. As once predicted, this internal strife leads to the empire's foreign downfall: when Somerset delays sending his cavalry to York, York is unable to move out reinforcements during the climactic battle near Bordeaux. This leads to **Lord Talbot**'s death and an English defeat in France. In *King Henry VI, Part II*, Somerset plots with **Cardinal Beaufort** and the **1st Duke of Buckingham** to wrest power from **Humphrey, Duke of Gloucester**. When York returns from Ireland with an army and demands that Somerset be named a traitor, Henry VI is forced to acquiesce, and he puts Somerset in the Tower of London. As York comes to meet the King and **Queen Margaret**, he spies Somerset freed, and declares a rebellion against the throne. Somerset fights for Henry VI, but is killed by York's son and future monarch, **King Richard III**.

4th Duke of Somerset

Henry VI, Part III
William Shakespeare

A supporter of **King Edward IV**'s. But following Edward's marriage to **Lady Elizabeth Grey**, Somerset follows **George, Duke of Clarence** and **Richard Neville, Earl of Warwick** in deserting the Yorkist side. He is captured at the end of the play and sent away to be beheaded.

The Son

Six Characters in Search of an Author
Luigi Pirandello

A tall, severe man of twenty-two. He is estranged from his family. He is the first witness to **the Boy** and **the Child**'s demise. His role as a Character is his ashamed refusal to participate in the spectacle. He protests to **the Manager** that he is an unrealized character.

True Son

The Light in the Forest
Conrad Richter

The novel's protagonist. True Son is a fifteen-year-old boy who, after being raised by Lenni Lenape (Delaware) Indians for eleven years, is forced to return to his white family in Pennsylvania. Strong-willed, rebellious, and passionate, True Son longs to be a noble Indian warrior like his adoptive father, **Cuyloga**. His stubborn teenage nature prevents him from adapting easily to white culture, yet he eventually forges a strong relationship with his younger brother, **Gordie**.

Gustaf Sondelius

Arrowsmith
Sinclair Lewis

A public speaker about medical issues. He becomes one of **Martin Arrowsmith**'s heroes. Sondelius turns Martin's interests toward public health and later helps Martin in his plague research.

Sonia

Annie John
Jamaica Kincaid

A dimwitted girl at **Annie**'s school. Annie pesters Sonia until she discovers that Sonia's mother has died.

Sonietta

A Clockwork Orange
Anthony Burgess

A record shopper. Along with **Marty**, she chats up **Alex** as he purchases Beethoven's Ninth. They return to Alex's apartment to listen to records, where he rapes and beats them after getting them drunk.

Eddie Sonnier

Dead Man Walking
Helen Prejean

Patrick Sonnier's brother. Eddie and Patrick have been convicted of murdering two teenagers. During their trials, Patrick and Eddie accused each other of pulling the trigger; only Patrick has been sentenced to death. Eddie confesses to murdering **David LeBlanc** and **Loretta Bourque**. He is haunted by his role in the murders and by the knowledge that his brother will be executed for a crime he did not commit.

Elmo Patrick Sonnier

Dead Man Walking
Helen Prejean

The first death row inmate counseled by **Sister Helen Prejean**. Patrick has been sentenced to death for the murder of two teenagers, a crime he committed with his brother **Eddie Sonnier**. Patrick has been a model prisoner since his incarceration. He is eager for Prejean's approval. For the first time in his life, Patrick experiences love when Prejean and her friends show genuine affection for him. Although put to death for a crime that his brother actually committed, Patrick, transformed by love, dies with dignity. His last words are an apology to **Lloyd LeBlanc**, the father of one of the murdered teenagers.

Sons of Jacob

The Handmaid's Tale
Margaret Atwood

Jews.

Soothsayer

Antony and Cleopatra
William Shakespeare

An Egyptian fortuneteller who follows **Antony** to Rome and predicts that his fortune will always pale in comparison to **Octavius Caesar**'s. The soothsayer also predicts the fortune of **Cleopatra**'s servant **Alexas**, saying that Alexas will outlive Cleopatra.

Sophia

The Autobiography of Malcolm X
Malcolm X & Alex Haley

Malcolm X's white girlfriend. Malcolm and Sophia do not love each other but rather use each other as status symbols. The emptiness of her relationship with Malcolm shapes Malcolm's skepticism about interracial romance.

Sophie

Jane Eyre
Charlotte Brontë

Adéle Varens's French nurse at Thornfield.

Sophie

Breath, Eyes, Memory
Edwidge Danticat

Martine's daughter, **Atie**'s charge, **Grandmè Ifé**'s granddaughter, **Joseph**'s wife and **Brigitte**'s mother. A child of rape, Sophie is raised in Croix-des-Rosets, Haiti, by her maternal aunt Atie before being called to New York by her mother at the age of twelve.

Bertha Sørby

Wild Duck
Henrik Ibsen

Werle's housekeeper and fiancée. A charming and sociable woman, she believes that she and Werle will build their marriage—a second for them both—on a foundation of truth and honesty.

Julien Sorel

The Red and the Black
Stendhal

The central character. Julien Sorel is the son of a provincial carpenter. An admirer of **Napoleon**, Sorel dreams of rising in the ranks of French society. When he is caught having an affair with **Mme. de Rênal** by **Elisa**, **M. Chélan** sends Sorel to the monastery at Besançon. There, **M. Pirard** favors Sorel, eventually introducing Sorel to the **Marquis de la Mole** and Parisian society. He impregnates and is engaged to **Mathilde de la Mole**, gaining a new noble name, Julien de la Vernaye, and a new societal rank. However, the Mme. de Rênal sends a condemning letter about Sorel to the Marquis, and he is thrown out of his newly attained high life. Sorel goes back to the town of Verrières and shoots and wounds Mme. de Rênal. For this, Sorel is sent to jail and set to be killed. He rejects all offers of clemency given to him, and refuses help to escape from Mathilde and **Fouqué**. While in jail, Sorel renounces hypocrisy as the malaise of his century and finds solace in his love for Mme. de Rênal.

Bea Sorenson

Main Street
Sinclair Lewis

Carol's maid and good friend. Arriving in Gopher Prairie on the same day as Carol, Bea makes a very different assessment of Gopher Prairie, finding the town beautiful and exciting. Bea marries **Miles Bjornstam** and, later in the novel, dies tragically.

George Sorenson

One Flew over the Cuckoo's Nest
Ken Kesey

A hospital patient, a big Swedish former seaman. **Randle McMurphy** recruits Sorenson as captain for the fishing excursion. He is nicknamed "Rub-a-Dub George" by the aides because he has an intense phobia of dirtiness. McMurphy receives his first electroshock treatment for defending Sorenson.

Pyotr Nikolayevich Sorin

The Seagull
Anton Chekhov

The sixty-year-old owner of the estate where the play takes place. He spent his life working for a government office and retired to his country farm. Sorin is the brother of the famed actress **Arkadina** and the uncle of the struggling playwright **Treplyov**. His health deteriorates during the course of the play. He is disappointed with his life's decisions; he laments his failed life goals of finding love and of becoming a successful writer.

Transito Soto

The House of the Spirits
Isabel Allende

A prostitute. **Esteban Trueba** first encounters her while restoring Tres Marias. Transito borrows money from Esteban Trueba to move to the city and establish a brothel there. After the death of **Clara**, Esteban Trueba can be at peace with his loss by having sex with Transito. In good faith, Transito pays back her debt to Esteban Trueba many years later by helping him secure **Alba** after she is captured by the fascist government of **Esteban Garcia**.

Sounder

Sounder
William Armstrong

A dog owned by **the boy**. Sounder and the boy's father are taken from the family at the same time, and they both eventually find their way back after having sustained serious injury. After the boy finds his father dead in the woods, he knows that Sounder will soon die too. A few months after the return of the father, Sounder crawls under the cabin and dies.

Soundkeeper

The Phantom Tollbooth
Norton Juster

The previous ruler of the Valley of Sound. The Soundkeeper becomes dismayed with the lack of appreciation of beautiful sounds and the rise of Dr. **Dischord**'s terrible practice. In protest, she cuts off sound and retreats to the fortress where she keeps all sounds made since the beginning of time.

Mr. Sowerberry

Oliver Twist
Charles Dickens

The undertaker to whom **Oliver Twist** is apprenticed. Though Mr. Sowerberry makes his living arranging cut-rate burials for paupers, he is a decent man who is kind to Oliver.

Mrs. Sowerberry

Oliver Twist
Charles Dickens

Mr. Sowerberry's wife. Mrs. Sowerberry is a mean, judgmental woman who henpecks her husband.

Dickon Sowerby

The Secret Garden
Frances Hodgson Burnett

A common moor boy. Two years older than **Colin Craven** and **Mary Lennox**, Dickon has lived on Missel Moor his entire life, and has a uniquely intimate relationship with the land. He has the power to charm both animals and people: all the creatures who come close to him are instantly tamed, and he counts a fox, a crow, and two wild squirrels among his pets. It is Dickon who brings Mary the tools and seeds that she requires to make the garden "come alive." He is the brother of **Martha Sowerby** and the son of **Susan Sowerby**.

Martha Sowerby

The Secret Garden
Frances Hodgson Burnett

Mary Lennox's friend and maidservant. Martha is distinguished by her frankness and levelheaded approach to all aspects of life. She expects Mary to dress and feed herself, and is not at all deferential. Her Yorkshire bluntness, her simplicity and her kindness are a great help to Mary upon the her arrival at Misselthwaite. She is the daughter of **Susan Sowerby** and sister of **Dickon Sowerby**.

Susan Sowerby

The Secret Garden
Frances Hodgson Burnett

The mother of **Martha Sowerby** and **Dickon Sowerby**.

The Spaniard

Robinson Crusoe
Daniel Defoe

One of the men from the Spanish ship that is wrecked off **Crusoe**'s island, and whose crew is rescued by the cannibals and taken to a neighboring island. The Spaniard is doomed to be eaten as a ritual victim of the cannibals until Crusoe saves him. In exchange, he becomes a new "subject" in Crusoe's "kingdom."

Spareribs

The Heart Is a Lonely Hunter
Carson McCullers

A neighborhood boy. He owns the BB gun with which **Bubber Kelly** accidentally shoots **Baby Wilson**.

Mrs. Sparsit

Hard Times
Charles Dickens

Josiah Bounderby's housekeeper. Once a member of the aristocratic elite, Mrs. Sparsit fell on hard times when her marriage collapsed. A selfish, manipulative, dishonest woman, Mrs. Sparsit hopes to sabotage Bounderby's marriage so she can marry him herself.

Douglas Spaulding

Dandelion Wine
Ray Bradbury

The protagonist of the book. He is a boy with a vivid imagination and a compassionate nature. He cares deeply about his family, especially his brother, **Tom Spaulding**, and his friends. Douglas has trouble understanding why things do not always work out well, and death is particularly troublesome to him.

Grandma Spaulding

Dandelion Wine
Ray Bradbury

Douglas Spaulding and **Tom Spaulding**'s grandmother. Grandma Spaulding shares the same zest for life as **Grandpa Spaulding** and the rest of the family. Grandma Spaulding is a brilliant spontaneous chef, capable of concocting magnificent feasts.

Grandpa Spaulding

Dandelion Wine
Ray Bradbury

Douglas Spaulding and **Tom Spaulding**'s grandfather. Grandpa Spaulding finds pleasure in the little things, like dandelions.

Great-grandma Spaulding

Dandelion Wine
Ray Bradbury

The matriarch of the Spaulding family. She is happy with the world and the life that she has lived and she dies contentedly. She tries to pass on to **Tom Spaulding** and **Douglas Spaulding** her understanding of life as a process that must end even though people live on in their families.

Tom Spaulding

Dandelion Wine
Ray Bradbury

Douglas Spaulding's brother. His responses to situations help Douglas maintain a balance between taking an adult perspective and seeing things from a child's point of view. Tom sees things that other characters in the book do not see.

Rosanna Spearman

The Moonstone
Wilkie Collins

One of **Lady Verinder**'s housemaids. Rosanna was a thief before repenting and entering the Reformatory from which Lady Verinder hired her.

Speed

The Two Gentlemen of Verona
William Shakespeare

Valentine's page. Speed is quick-witted and adept at puns. Along with **Lucetta** and **Launce**, Speed is an advocate of moderation in matters of the heart.

Speedwell

Watership Down
Richard Adams

The third rabbit **Blackberry** brings with him. Speedwell, like **Acorn**, gains faith in the group as events unfold. He mates with **Clover** to give the warren its first litter.

Elsie Speers

Tender Is the Night
F. Scott Fitzgerald

The twice-widowed mother of **Rosemary Hoyt**. Mrs. Speers is her daughter's best friend in Europe and also oversees Rosemary's career.

Spelling Bee

The Phantom Tollbooth
Norton Juster

A self-taught master of spelling who enjoys randomly spelling the words he hears or speaks.

Mr. Spencer

The Catcher in the Rye
J. D. Salinger

The history teacher of **Holden Caulfield** at Pencey Prep. Mr. Spencer tries unsuccessfully to shake Holden out of his academic apathy.

Mrs. Spencer

Anne of Green Gables
L. M. Montgomery

A worker at the asylum where **Anne Shirley** lived. Mrs. Spencer brings Anne to **Matthew Cuthbert** and **Marilla Cuthbert** instead of the boy orphan they requested.

Jeff Spender

The Martian Chronicles
Ray Bradbury

The archaeologist for the fourth expedition. He reveres Mars and quickly leaves the crew to explore the planet by himself. Finally, he decides that he should kill off the crew in an effort to preserve Mars. He kills several, including **Cheroke**, but doesn't have the heart to finish, and is shot by **Captain Wilder**.

Dora Spenlow

David Copperfield
Charles Dickens

David Copperfield's first wife and first real love. Dora is foolish and giddy, more interested in playing with her dog, Jip, than in keeping house with David. She behaves like a spoiled child, but David cannot bear to displease her.

Speranski

War and Peace
Leo Tolstoy

A brilliant liberal advisor to the tsar. Until his fall from grace, **Speranski** attempts to reform and modernize the Russian state.

Sphinx

Greek Mythology
Unknown

A beast with the head of a woman and the body of a winged lion. The Sphinx blocks entry to the city of Thebes, refusing to budge until someone answers her riddle and eating anyone who fails. When **Oedipus** solves the riddle, the Sphinx kills herself.

Spitz

The Call of the Wild
Jack London

The original leader of **François**'s and **Perrault**'s dog team and **Buck**'s archrival. A fierce "devil-dog" used to winning fights with other dogs, Spitz is finally defeated and killed by Buck.

Doctor Spivey

One Flew over the Cuckoo's Nest
Ken Kesey

A mild-mannered doctor who may be addicted to opiates. **Nurse Ratched** chose Doctor Spivey as the doctor for her ward because he is as easily cowed and dominated as the patients. He often supports **Randle McMurphy**'s unusual plans for the ward.

Spoade

The Sound and the Fury
William Faulkner

A Harvard senior from South Carolina.

Spoon

The Contender
Robert Lipsyte

A role model to **Alfred Brooks**. Spoon was a boxer, but he gave up boxing in order to go back to school. He encourages Alfred to get a high school diploma.

Spots

I Know Why the Caged Bird Sings
Maya Angelou

One of **Daddy Clidell**'s con-men friends. These men teach **Maya Johnson** that it is possible to use white prejudice to gain advantage over whites. The other con-man friends are **Cool Clyde**, **Tight Coat**, **Red Leg Daddy**, **Stonewall Jimmy**, and **Just Black**.

Luther Spotted Dog

When the Legends Die
Hal Borland

Tom's roommate at school.

Pastor Spratt

Oranges Are Not the Only Fruit
Jeanette Winterson

The pastor who converted **Jeanette's mother** and whom she idolizes. **Jeanette** and her mother frequently discuss his crusades in the tropics.

Professor Sprout

Harry Potter and the Chamber of Secrets
J. K. Rowling

The Herbology teacher at Hogwarts in **Harry Potter**'s second year.

Square

Tom Jones
Henry Fielding

The philosopher who lives with **Allworthy**. He justifies his questionable behavior (such as making love to **Molly Seagrim**) by contorting his philosophical notions. Square's transformation at the end of the novel allows Allworthy to forgive **Tom**.

Squeak

Billy Budd, Sailor
Herman Melville

John Claggart's most cunning corporal. Squeak fuels Claggart's contempt for **Billy Budd** and tries by various maneuvers to make Billy's life miserable.

Squeak

The Color Purple
Alice Walker

Harpo's lover after **Sofia** leaves him. In trying to get Sofia out of jail, dressed as a white woman, Squeak is raped brutally by a prison warden who is her uncle. Squeak eventually undergoes a transformation much like **Celie**'s. She demands to be called by her real name, Mary Agnes, and she pursues a singing career.

Squealer

Animal Farm
George Orwell

Pig who spreads propaganda among the other animals. Alongside **Snowball** and **Napoleon**, he composes the tenets of Animalism, an expansion of **Old Major**'s pro-animal, anti-human speech. As the book progresses, Squealer uses his silver tongue and fabricated statistics to placate the other animals and to justify the increasingly totalitarian and cruel actions Napoleon inflicts upon the farm.

Squid

Holes
Louis Sachar

A boy at the camp. Squid is as tough as **X-Ray**, although he often follows X-Ray's directions. Squid often taunts **Stanley Yelnats** about receiving letters from, and writing to, his mother.

Squire

The Canterbury Tales
Geoffrey Chaucer

The Knight's son and apprentice. The Squire is curly-haired, youthfully handsome, and loves dancing and courting.

Clifford St. Clair

The Joy Luck Club
Amy Tan

Ying-ying's second husband. He never learned to speak Chinese fluently, and Ying-ying never learned to speak English fluently.

Lena St. Clair

The Joy Luck Club
Amy Tan

The only child of **Ying-ying** and **Clifford St. Clair**. When she married **Harold Livotny**, Lena unwittingly began to follow her mother's passive example, believing herself incapable of control in her marriage and her career.

Ying-ying St. Clair

The Joy Luck Club
Amy Tan

A member of the Joy Luck Club. As a child, Ying-ying was headstrong and independent, but as she matured she grew passive, allowing her American husband, **Clifford**, to incorrectly translate her feelings and thoughts.

Augustine St. Clare

Uncle Tom's Cabin
Harriet Beecher Stowe

Uncle Tom's master in New Orleans and **Evangeline St. Clare**'s father. St. Clare is a flighty and romantic man. He carouses and drinks every night. St. Clare sees the evil of slavery but nonetheless tolerates and practices it. He promises that he will free Uncle Tom after his daughter's death, but he keeps Tom. Because St. Clare does not keep his word, Tom is sold to a very cruel master, **Simon Legree**, when St. Clare is killed in a bar fight.

Angela St. John

House Made of Dawn
N. Scott Momaday

Abel's lover in Walatowa. A pale, brunette white woman who has recently married and who arrives at the Benevides house at Walatowa for rest and relaxation. When Abel goes to work at Angela's house to chop firewood, her fascination with his work eventually leads to their love affair.

Henrietta Stackpole

The Portrait of a Lady
Henry James

Isabel Archer's fiercely independent American friend. She is a feminist journalist who refuses to believe that women need men to be happy. After Isabel leaves for Europe, Henrietta fights a losing battle to keep her true to her American outlook, constantly encouraging her to marry **Caspar Goodwood**. At the end of the book, Henrietta disappoints Isabel by giving up her independence and marrying **Mr. Bantling**.

Miss Muriel Stacy

Anne of Green Gables
L. M. Montgomery

Anne Shirley's teacher. Miss Stacy becomes the Avonlea schoolteacher after the unpopular **Mr. Phillips** departs. Her unorthodox, liberal teaching methods worry the conservative Avonlea trustees and **Mrs. Rachel**, but all of her students love her. She is a role model and mentor for Anne.

Dr. Robert Stadler

Atlas Shrugged
Ayn Rand

The disillusioned head scientist at the State Science Institute. He allows the government looters to appropriate his mind. Stadler is convinced by **Dr. Floyd Ferris** that the deadly sonic super-weapon, the Thompson Harmonizer, is needed for the keeping of the peace amongst a hysterical public. Once he realizes how powerful **John Galt** has become, he tries to destroy the weapon but accidentally activates it during a scuffle, destroying the countryside for hundreds of miles in all directions.

Sir Humphrey Stafford

Henry VI, Part II
William Shakespeare

A nobleman. Along with his brother, he leads the effort to suppress **Jack Cade**'s rebellion in Kent. Both die in battle.

Stafford's brother

Henry VI, Part II
William Shakespeare

A nobleman. Along with his brother **Stafford**, he leads the effort to suppress **Jack Cade**'s rebellion in Kent. Both die in battle.

Stage Manager

Our Town
Thornton Wilder

The play's host and omniscient narrator. The Stage Manager interacts with both the audience and the characters. He cues and stops scenes, provides background information, and comments on the action of the play.

Madame Stahl

Anna Karenina
Leo Tolstoy

A seemingly devout invalid woman whom **Ekaterina Alexandrovna Shcherbatskaya** and her family meet at a German spa. **Varvara Andreevna** is her protégée. Madame Stahl appears righteous and pious, but **Prince Alexander Dmitrievich Shcherbatsky** and others doubt her motivations.

Valentine Stamarowski

The Virgin Suicides
Jeffrey Eugenides

A polite Polish boy who lives in a mansion a block away from the Lisbons' house.

Lord Stanley, Earl of Derby

Richard III
William Shakespeare

Richmond's stepfather. A devoted friend of **Lord Hastings**, Stanley begins to fear for their lives after dreaming that a boar (**King Richard III**'s heraldic symbol) killed him. After Hastings is executed for the fabricated charge of treason, Stanley begins to help Richmond secretly. Stanley continues to help the rebels in secret, and outrightly joins Richmond right before the armies clash, giving the king no time to execute his son.

Dr. Stanpole

A Separate Peace
John Knowles

Devon's resident doctor. Dr. Stanpole operates on **Finny** after both of Finny's accidents. Dr. Stanpole breaks the news to Gene that Finny is dead.

Adam Stanton

All the King's Men
Robert Penn Warren

Anne Stanton's brother. He is a brilliant surgeon and **Jack Burden**'s closest childhood friend. Jack persuades Adam to put aside his moral reservations about Willie and become director of the new hospital Willie is building, and Adam later cares for **Tom Stark** after his injury. But Adam learns that his father illegally protected Judge Irwin after he took a bribe, and he learns that his sister has become **Willie Stark**'s lover. Driven mad with the knowledge, Adam assassinates Willie in the lobby of the Capitol toward the end of the novel.

Anne Stanton

All the King's Men
Robert Penn Warren

Jack Burden's first love, **Adam Stanton**'s sister, and, for a time, **Willie Stark**'s mistress. The daughter of Governor Stanton, Anne is raised to believe in a strict moral code, a belief that is threatened and nearly shattered when Jack shows her proof of her father's wrongdoing.

Governor Joel Stanton

All the King's Men
Robert Penn Warren

Adam and **Anne**'s father, governor of the state when **Judge Irwin** was attorney general. He protects the judge after he takes the bribe to save his plantation.

Miss Beryl Stapleton

Hound of the Baskervilles
Sir Arthur Conan Doyle

A Latin beauty. She is allegedly **Mr. Jack Stapleton**'s sister, but is actually his wife. Eager to prevent another death but terrified of her husband, she provides enigmatic warnings to **Sir Henry Baskerville** and **Dr. Watson**.

Mr. Jack Stapleton

Hound of the Baskervilles
Sir Arthur Conan Doyle

Sir Henry Baskerville's neighbor. He hides his marriage to **Miss Beryl Stapleton** in order to seduce **Laura Lyons** and involve her in his scheme to murder **Sir Charles Baskerville** and Sir Henry Baskerville with his fearsome hound.

Starbuck

Moby-Dick
Herman Melville

The first mate of the *Pequod*. Starbuck questions **Ahab**'s judgment, first in private and later in public. He is a religious man who believes that Christianity offers a way to interpret the world around him. Starbuck believes that it is rational and necessary to fear whales, and his reverence for nature inclines him toward superstition. Starbuck leaves **Pip** out at sea alone as a punishment for his repeated mistakes upon a whale-hunting boat, which drives Pip insane. Starbuck dies with all the other men from the *Pequod*, save **Ishmael**, during the battle with **Moby Dick**.

Lucy Stark

All the King's Men
Robert Penn Warren

Willie's wife. She is constantly disappointed by her husband's failure to live up to her moral standards. Lucy eventually leaves Willie. They are in the process of reconciling when Willie is murdered.

Tom Stark

All the King's Men
Robert Penn Warren

Willie's arrogant, hedonistic son. He is a football star for the state university. Tom lives a life of drunkenness and promiscuity before he breaks his neck in a football accident. Permanently paralyzed, he dies of pneumonia shortly thereafter. Tom is accused of impregnating **Sibyl Frey**, whose child is adopted by **Lucy** at the end of the novel.

Willie Stark

All the King's Men
Robert Penn Warren

Jack Burden's boss. He rises from poverty to become the governor and most powerful political figure of his state. Willie takes control through a combination of political reform and underhanded guile. Willie believes that everyone and everything is bad, and that moral action involves making goodness out of the badness. Willie is married to **Lucy Stark**, with whom he has a son, **Tom Stark**. His voracious sexual appetite leads him into a number of affairs, including one with **Sadie Burke** and one with **Anne Stanton**. Willie is murdered by **Adam Stanton** toward the end of the novel.

Jody Starks

Their Eyes Were Watching God
Zora Neale Hurston

Janie Mae Crawford's second husband. Jody travels from Georgia to Eatonville to satisfy his ambition. A consummate politician and businessman, he becomes the postmaster, mayor, storekeeper, and biggest landlord in Eatonville. He treats Janie as an object rather than a person, and their marriage deteriorates. Janie ultimately rebels against Jody's suppression of her.

Starletta

Ellen Foster
Kaye Gibbons

Ellen's black best friend. She lives with her mother and father in a ramshackle cabin and often provides Ellen with refuge from her father.

Candy Starr

One Flew over the Cuckoo's Nest
Ken Kesey

A beautiful, carefree prostitute from Portland. Candy accompanies **Randle McMurphy** and the other patients on the fishing trip, and then comes to the ward for a late-night party that McMurphy arranges.

Captain Starr

My Brother Sam Is Dead
Christopher & James Lincoln Collier

A local Patriot who is killed by the British.

Walter Starr

A Death in the Family
James Agee

A friend of **Jay Follet** and **Mary Follet**. He is kind to **Rufus Follet** and **Little Catherine**.

Bob Starrett

Shane
Jack Schaefer

The narrator of the book. **Shane** teaches Bob to accept responsibility for his actions.

Shane
Joe Starrett Jack Schaefer

Shane's good friend, companion, and coworker. The two men are undyingly loyal to one another, even though both love the same woman, **Marian Starrett**. The bond between the two men is so great that Joe is not jealous of Shane's taking him out of the spotlight in public or with Joe's son **Bob Starrett**.

Shane
Marian Starrett Jack Schaefer

The only significant female character in the book. A good wife, mother, and cook, she embraces Shane wholeheartedly, though she does not fall out of love with **Joe Starrett**.

Great Expectations
Startop Charles Dickens

A friend of **Pip**'s and **Herbert Pocket**'s. Startop is a delicate young man who helps with **Abel Magwitch**'s escape.

A Midsummer Night's Dream
Robin Starveling William Shakespeare

A tailor. He is chosen to play Thisbe's mother in the craftsmen's play for **Theseus**'s marriage celebration and ends up playing the part of Moonshine.

Miss Lonelyhearts
Gas station attendant Nathanael West

A worker at a gas station near **Betty**'s farm. The attendant openly reveals his anti-Semitic beliefs when **Miss Lonelyhearts** talks to him while gassing up the car.

My Ántonia
Widow Steavens Willa Cather

The Burdens' tenant at their old farmhouse. She develops a close relationship with **Ántonia Shimerda** in the time surrounding the breaking of Ántonia's engagement.

Inherit the Wind
Tommy Stebbins Jerome Lawrence & Robert E. Lee

A boy who drowned while swimming in a river when he was eleven years old. **Bertram Cates** befriended Tommy Stebbins. According to **Reverend Jeremiah Brown**, Stebbins was damned when he died because he was never baptized. Brown's harsh condemnation of Stebbins disgusted Cates, who, as a result, stopped attending church.

Anne Steele

Sense and Sensibility
Jane Austen

Lucy Steele's older, unmarried sister. Anne accidentally reveals her sister's secret engagement to **Edward Ferrars**.

Lucy Steele

Sense and Sensibility
Jane Austen

Mrs. Jennings's cousin. She breaks her secret, four-year engagement to **Edward Ferrars** after Edward is disinherited, and instead marries his brother, **Robert Ferrars**.

James Steerforth

David Copperfield
Charles Dickens

A villain. Steerforth charms both women and men because he enjoys the feeling of power it gives him. He also abuses **David Copperfield**, although David is too enraptured with him and too grateful for his patronage to notice.

Mrs. Steerforth

David Copperfield
Charles Dickens

James Steerforth's mother. Mrs. Steerforth is a cruel, haughty woman. She loves her son and disdains **David Copperfield**.

Stefano

The Tempest
William Shakespeare

A drunken butler, a minor member of the shipwrecked party. Along with **Trinculo** the jester, he provides a comic foil to the other, more powerful pairs of **Prospero** and **Alonso** and **Antonio** and **Sebastian**.

Steffie

White Noise
Don DeLillo

Jack Gladney's quiet, media-obsessed daughter. Steffie repeats brand names in her dreams, and lips the words to commercials. She seeks out comfort and familiarity through small gestures, such as wearing the same hat, or sitting in a bath tub for hours.

Stein

Lord Jim
Joseph Conrad

The owner of a large trading post. He sends first **Cornelius** and then **Jim** to Patusan. Stein was forced to flee Europe as a young man after becoming involved in revolutionary activities. Having made his way to the East Indies, he has become successful as a trader.

Stein

Night
Elie Wiesel

A distant relative from Antwerp, Belgium, whom **Eliezer** and his father, **Clomo**, encounter in Auschwitz. Eliezer's father lies to Stein and tells him that his family is alive and well in Antwerp.

Maurie Stein

Tuesdays with Morrie
Mitch Albom

A good friend of **Morrie Schwartz**'s. He sends some of Morrie's aphorisms to a *Boston Globe* reporter who eventually publishes a feature story on Morrie. The reporter's article prompts **Ted Koppel** to ask Morrie for an interview.

Stella

Ellen Foster
Kaye Gibbons

Ellen's foster sister at her new mama's house. Stella is a big flirt and sits at the back of the bus with the boys on the way to school. As a seventh-grader, she is a mother to a fatherless baby, **Roger**, and is the youngest mother Ellen has ever known.

Mr. Stelling

The Mill on the Floss
George Eliot

The clergyman tutor of **Tom Tulliver** and, later, **Philip Wakem**. He teaches exactly as he was taught.

William Stendahl

The Martian Chronicles
Ray Bradbury

A rich man, and a lover of fantasy authors. Censors on Earth ban his beloved authors and destroy his library. Bitter, he moves to Mars, where, with the help of **Pikes**, he builds a house called "Usher II," after the house in Poe's story "The Fall of the House of Usher." When **Garrett** comes from a Martian censorship agency to condemn his building, Stendahl lures him into the house, chains him to a wall in his catacombs, and builds a wall over him, smothering him, in a recreation of the Poe story, "The Cask of Amontillado."

The Stepdaughter

Six Characters in Search of an Author
Luigi Pirandello

One of the characters, dashing, impudent, and beautiful. The Stepdaughter wants to realize the Characters' drama just as much as **the Father**, but she protests when **the Manager** attempts to sentimentalize their first meeting. In reality, the Father first met the Stepdaughter in **Madame Pace**'s bordello, where he tried to seduce the girl. The Manager is attempting to change the drama by portraying the meeting as a more loving and benevolent one. The Stepdaughter is seductive, exhibitionistic and dangerously cruel.

Stephen

The New Testament
Unknown

A leader of the Hellenists, a faction of the Jewish Christians, in Jerusalem during the years after **Jesus**' ascension. Stephen preaches against the temple. When brought for trial before the Jewish court, Stephen seals his fate by issuing a ringing condemnation of the Jewish leadership.

Stephen Lally, Jr.

Bless the Beasts and Children
Glendon Swarthout

The older brother of **Billy Lally**. Stephen Lally, Jr. demonstrates borderline-psychotic behavior. Engaged in fierce sibling rivalry, he often acts vengeful toward his brother and his fellow campers.

Uncle Stephen

This Boy's Life
Tobias Wolff

Rosemary Wolff's brother and **Jack Wolff**'s uncle, who lives in Paris. After Jack writes to **Uncle Stephen** with an exaggerated tale of his grim family situation, Stephen invites Jack to live with him and his family in Paris, but only if Jack will agree to forfeit his name so that Stephen can officially adopt him. Jack cannot stand the idea of having another mother and decides not to go.

Grace Stepney

The House of Mirth
Edith Wharton

Lily Bart's competetive cousin. She inherits much of **Mrs. Peniston**'s fortune. When Lily asks Grace for financial assistance, Grace flatly refuses.

Jack Stepney

The House of Mirth
Edith Wharton

Lily Bart's cousin. Jack married **Gwen Van Osburgh**, and is a regular member of society, wealthy and well-regarded. Later he agrees to shelter Lily for the night after she is kicked off the yacht by **Bertha Dorset**.

The Steppenwolf

Steppenwolf
Hermann Hesse

A middle-aged recluse. He lives alone in a bourgeois lodging house. Harry Haller refers to himself as a "Steppenwolf" because he feels like a lonely wolf of the steppes, removed from the obsessions and conventions common to most people. His life begins to change after he meets **Hermine**, a beautiful courtesan, and **Pablo**, a jazz musician. These characters induct Harry into a demimonde of sensuality and hedonistic abandon.

Carmen Sternwood

The Big Sleep
Raymond Chandler

Vivian's younger sister. Carmen is flirtatious and wears provocative clothing. Beneath her innocent, thumb-sucking, childlike veneer, she is the murderess of **Rusty Regan**.

General Sternwood

The Big Sleep
Raymond Chandler

A rich and very ill oil baron. He has fathered two wild daughters—**Vivian** and **Carmen Sternwood**—and hired **Marlowe** as a private detective.

Vivian Sternwood

The Big Sleep
Raymond Chandler

The elder of **General Sternwood**'s wild daughters. Vivian is seductive but dangerous, a beautiful and smart temptress whose dark eyes hide many secrets. She is a gambler and a drinker and an accomplice to murder. She may have murdered her husband to conceal the truth from her father.

Stevens

The Remains of the Day
Kazuo Ishiguro

The protagonist and narrator. Stevens is the epitome of perfect English butler. His fidelity to his former master, **Lord Darlington**, prevents him from accepting the fact that Darlington was a Nazi sympathizer and supporter.

Gavin Stevens

Go Down, Moses
William Faulkner

A white lawyer. He helps **Molly** and **Miss Worsham** bring **Samuel Beauchamp**'s body back from Illinois.

Mr. William Stevens

The Remains of the Day
Kazuo Ishiguro

A veteran butler. He comes to work at Darlington Hall when he is in his seventies and struggling with arthritis. He and his son **Stevens** only communicate very formally until the night the elder Stevens is on his deathbed.

Stewart

Homecoming
Cynthia Voigt

Windy's roommate. Stewart is quieter and more serious than Windy, but just as generous and open-hearted. Stewart drives the children to Bridgeport in his car.

Alan Breck Stewart

Kidnapped
Robert Louis Stevenson

A flamboyant but skilled warrior from the Scottish Highlands. Alan Breck Stewart is a Jacobite rebel, and he is fiercely loyal to his clan and countrymen, especially **James of the Glens** and **Cluny Macpherson**. He and **David Balfour**, whom he befriends in the Round-House battle onboard the *Covenant*, are on the run because they are wanted for the murder of **Colin Roy Campbell of Glenure**, which they did not commit. A Jacobite, he believes that the Scottish Stuarts are the true kings of England. Alan assists David in tricking **Ebenezer Balfour** so that David can reclaim part of the fortune of the House of Shaw.

Captain Stewart

Fallen Angels
Walter Dean Myers

The commander of **Richie Perry**'s company. He sends Richie's company on numerous dangerous missions.

Stilgar

Dune
Frank Herbert

A leader of the Fremen, the native people of Arrakis who live in the desert. He becomes a mentor to **Paul Atreides**. Stilgar is wise, experienced, and familiar with the legends and folklore of the Fremen.

Kevin Stillman

Ordinary People
Judith Guest

A member of **Joe Lazenby**'s carpool. Kevin Stillman can be very cruel to **Conrad Jarrett**.

Cash Stillwater

Pigs in Heaven
Barbara Kingsolver

A Cherokee man living in Wyoming. Cash suffers the losses of the women in his family, including his dead wife and daughter **Alma**. As **Turtle Greer**'s biological grandfather, he also suffers as the result of her disappearance from the Nation.

Stilson

Ender's Game
Orson Scott Card

The bully who torments **Ender Wiggin** before Ender is chosen for Battle School. During **Colonel Graff**'s trial, Ender learns that he killed Stilson in their fight.

Stilwell

The Caine Mutiny
Herman Wouk

Creator of much controversy on the *Caine*, and **Philip Francis Queeg**'s unfortunate scapegoat. Stilwell chooses to risk his military career in order to save his marriage.

Simon Stimson

Our Town
Thornton Wilder

The choirmaster. His alcoholism and other "troubles" have been material for Grover's Corners gossip for a while. By the end of the play, Mr. Stimson has hanged himself in his attic.

Dolores Stockland

I Know Why the Caged Bird Sings
Maya Angelou

Big Bailey Johnson's prim-and-proper live-in girlfriend in Los Angeles. **Maya Johnson** spends the summer with them and drives Dolores into a jealous rage.

Mrs. Katherine Stockmann

An Enemy of the People
Henrik Ibsen

Dr. Stockmann's wife. She is loyal and practical and often encourages her husband to think of his family when he is being rash. **Morten Kiil** is her adoptive father.

Peter Stockmann

An Enemy of the People
Henrik Ibsen

Dr. Thomas Stockmann's brother. He is mayor of the town as well as chairman of the baths committee. He is a cautious but sometimes ruthless politician.

Petra Stockmann

An Enemy of the People
Henrik Ibsen

The daughter of **Thomas** and **Katherine**, Petra is as idealistic as her father. She is a hardworking teacher, and she is frustrated that the law requires her to teach things she doesn't believe in.

Doctor Thomas Stockmann

An Enemy of the People
Henrik Ibsen

The medical officer of the town baths. Thomas is the brother of **Peter Stockmann**, the town's mayor. He declares that the bath waters are contaminated, only to be stifled and labeled an enemy of the people.

Joe Stoddard

Our Town
Thornton Wilder

The town undertaker.

Alfred Stoecklein

In Cold Blood
Truman Capote

An employee of River Valley Farm. He and his wife live on the property.

Alphonse Stompanato

White Noise
Don DeLillo

Chairman of the American environments department at the College-on-the-Hill. Alphonse is a strong, tough, imposing personality, typical of the cadre of smart, biting New York émigrés teaching at the College.

Harvey Stone

The Sun Also Rises
Ernest Hemingway

A drunken expatriate gambler who is perpetually out of money. A friend of **Jake Barnes**'s, Harvey is intelligent and well-read but unable to escape his drinking and gambling habits.

Jurassic Park
Dr. Richard Stone Michael Crichton

The head of the Tropical Diseases Laboratory at Columbia University. Dr. Stone analyzes the lizard carcass and concludes it poses no threat of infection.

I Never Promised You a Rose Garden
Carla Stoneham Joanne Greenberg

A patient at the mental hospital. When Carla was young, her mother shot Carla, Carla's brother, and then herself. Over the course of their three years at the hospital together, she and **Deborah** become friends.

Fahrenheit 451
Stoneman Ray Bradbury

With **Black**, a fireman who works with **Guy Montag**.

I Know Why the Caged Bird Sings
Stonewall Jimmy Maya Angelou

One of **Daddy Clidell**'s con-men friends. The other con-men friends are **Cool Clyde**, **Tight Coat**, **Red Leg Daddy**, **Just Black**, and **Spots**.

Inherit the Wind
Storekeeper Jerome Lawrence & Robert E. Lee

The owner of a store across the square from the courthouse.

Childhood's End
Stormgren Arthur C. Clarke

The secretary-general of the United Nations when **the Overlords** arrive on Earth. Stormgren is the only human to have any personal contact with the Overlords during the first few years of the Overlords' reign on Earth. He reports directly to **Karellen** once every few weeks.

The Catcher in the Rye
Stradlater J. D. Salinger

The roommate of **Holden Caulfield** at Pencey Prep. Stradlater is handsome, self-satisfied, and popular, but Holden calls him a "secret slob," because he appears well groomed, but his toiletries, such as his razor, are disgustingly unclean. Stradlater is sexually active and quite experienced for a prep school student.

Flowers for Algernon
Dr. Strauss Daniel Keyes

Professor Harold Nemur's partner. He is the neurologist and psychiatrist who performs the operation that briefly raises **Charlie Gordon**'s intelligence. Dr. Strauss conducts therapy sessions with Charlie after the operation. Unlike Nemur, Dr. Strauss maintains interest in and concern for Charlie's emotional development.

Watership Down
Richard Adams

Strawberry

The only rabbit to leave the warren of the snares. Strawberry is larger than the other rabbits, but he knows little of the wild. Eager to learn and help the others, he designs the Honeycomb and shares his knowledge of building with them.

Legs
William Kennedy

Clem Streeter

A local upstate bumpkin. He happens to be moving a small truck of hard cider as **Jack** drives by one evening. Streeter is taken to Jack's farm and tortured so that he will reveal the location of his sill.

The Clouds
Aristophanes

Strepsiades

An Athenian citizen. He is burdened by the debts his son, **Pheidippides**, has incurred. Strepsiades is primarily concerned with shirking his debts instead of honoring them.

David Copperfield
Charles Dickens

Doctor and Annie Strong

A couple who exemplify the best of married life. Doctor Strong and Annie are faithful and selfless. Their deep love for each other enables them to survive **Uriah Heep**'s scheming.

The Things They Carried
Tim O'Brien

Lee Strunk

A soldier in the platoon. A struggle with **Dave Jensen** over a jackknife results in Strunk's broken nose.

A Tale of Two Cities
Charles Dickens

Mr. Stryver

An ambitious lawyer. Stryver dreams of climbing the social ladder. Unlike his associate, **Sydney Carton**, Stryver is bombastic, proud, and foolish.

The Killer Angels
Michael Shaara

General J. E. B. Stuart

The cavalry leader assigned by **General Robert E. Lee** to track the movements of the Union army. A fun-loving publicity hound, Stuart is off joyriding for the first two days of the battle, and it is his negligence that causes the Confederate army to lose track of the Union troops in the first place.

Stubb

Moby-Dick
Herman Melville

The second mate of the *Pequod*. Stubb, chiefly characterized by his mischievous good humor, is easygoing and popular. He has worked in the dangerous occupation of whaling for so long that the possibility of death has ceased to concern him.

Stuck

Jazz
Toni Morrison

A friend of **Joe Trace**'s. He lives in New York City along with **Gistan**.

Charles Brandon, Duke of Suffolk

Henry VIII
William Shakespeare

A lord of the court and member of the Council. Following the execution of the **Duke of Buckingham** and the fall of **Queen Katherine**, Suffolk plots with the other lords to bring down **Cardinal Wolsey**. After Wolsey falls out of favor with the king and court, Suffolk gets a promotion; he is a member of the Council that tries **Cranmer, Archbishop of Canterbury**.

Michael de la Pole, Earl of Suffolk

Henry V
William Shakespeare

An English nobleman and military leader who dies, along with his cousin the Duke of York (*Richard II*'s **Aumerle**), at the Battle of Agincourt.

William de la Pole, Earl of Suffolk

Henry VI, Part I and *Henry VI, Part II*
William Shakespeare

An English nobleman. In *King Henry VI, Part I*, Suffolk captures **Margaret of Anjou** and is smitten with her, but woos her on behalf of **King Henry VI**. After successfully arranging the match between the King and Margaret, Suffolk divulges that he plans to use his connection to the future Queen of England to control King Henry and the government. After Margaret expresses her disillusionment with Henry's weakness and religious devotion at the beginning of *King Henry VI, Part II*, Suffolk works with her and **Cardinal Beaufort** to depose and arrest **Humphrey, Duke of Gloucester**. After Suffolk and Beaufort's men assassinate Gloucester, Suffolk is decried by the commoners, who suspect his guilt. He is banished by Henry, and in a tearful good-bye to Margaret, agrees to sail to France. When pirates board his ship and kidnap him, Suffolk realizes that his ransomer's name, **Walter Whitmore**, was part of a prophecy he heard long ago. When he reveals his own name, the **Captain** and Whitmore scorn him and his actions in England and sentence him to be decapitated.

Lord Suffolk

The English Patient
Michael Ondaatje

A member of the old English aristocracy. Once the war begins, he takes it upon himself to defuse bombs and train other men to do so. The nobleman's death is a large loss for **Kip**.

Baby Suggs

Beloved
Toni Morrison

Halle's mother and **Sethe**'s mother-in-law. After Halle buys Baby Suggs her freedom, she travels to Cincinnati, where she becomes a source of emotional and spiritual inspiration for the city's black residents. She holds religious gatherings, where she teaches her followers to love their voices, bodies, and minds. After Sethe's act of infanticide, Baby Suggs stops preaching and retreats to a sickbed to die. Baby Suggs continues to be a source of inspiration long after her death: the memory of her grandmother motivates **Denver** to leave 124 Bluestone Road and find help for Sethe.

Mr. and Mrs. Suggs

Sula
Toni Morrison

Eva Peace's neighbors. Not long after **BoyBoy Peace** abandoned her, Eva left her children with Mr. Suggs and Mrs. Suggs, promising that she would return within a few hours. She returned in eighteen months.

Professor Sullivan

Childhood's End
Arthur C. Clarke

An oceanographic scientist. Sullivan's lab is deep under the ocean. **The Overlords** often ask Sullivan to perform such tasks as stuffing entire whales for exhibition in the Overlords' museums on their homeworld.

Summoner

The Canterbury Tales
Geoffrey Chaucer

The Summoner brings people accused of violating Church law to the ecclesiastical court. This Summoner is a lecherous man whose face is scarred by leprosy. He gets drunk frequently, is irritable, and is not particularly qualified for his position. He spouts the few words of Latin he knows in an attempt to sound educated.

Lieutenant Sunderstrom

On the Beach
Nevil Shute

The *Scorpion*'s radio and electric officer. **Dwight Towers** sends him ashore to investigate the mysterious radio signals coming from Santa Maria Island.

Sunny

The Catcher in the Rye
J. D. Salinger

The prostitute whom **Holden Caulfield** hires through **Maurice**. She steals money from him because she feels Holden has underpaid her, even though nothing happens between them.

Sunshine

The Shipping News
E. Annie Proulx

The younger of **Quoyle**'s daughters. Sunshine is more easy-going in manner than **Bunny**. Like Bunny, she loves her father dearly. Sunshine and Bunny were sold to a child molester by their mother **Petal Bear** and later rescued.

Earl of Surrey

Henry IV, Part II
William Shakespeare

A nobleman and ally of **King Henry IV**. He talks about the state of the kingdom with the King and the **Earl of Warwick**.

Earl of Surrey

Henry VIII
William Shakespeare

A son-in-law of the **3rd Duke of Buckingham**'s, a lord of the court, and member of the Council. Because of Buckingham's demise, Surrey turns against **Cardinal Wolsey**. Following **Queen Katherine**'s fall, Surrey plots with the other lords against the Cardinal and takes the lead part in reading the charges against Wolsey. He is a member of the Council that tries **Cranmer, Archbishop of Canterbury**.

Susanna's husband

Girl, Interrupted
Susanna Kaysen

A man introduced to **Susanna** prior to her hospitalization. He stays in touch with her throughout her time at McLean. His marriage proposal allows Susanna to leave the hospital. They are married only a short time.

Susannah

Tristram Shandy
Laurence Sterne

Chambermaid to **Mrs. Shandy**. She is present at **Tristram**'s birth, complicit in his mis-christening, and partly to blame for his accidental circumcision by the fallen window shade.

Ray Sutcliffe

The Land
Mildred D. Taylor

A man at the east Texas horse race. He sees **Paul-Edward Logan** win a race with one of **Edward Logan**'s horses and is impressed. Ray Sutcliffe offers Paul the chance to ride his horse in a race and then neglects to pay him afterward. **Mitchell Thomas** forcibly takes the money from Sutcliffe.

Clytemnestra Sutpen

Absalom, Absalom!
William Faulkner

Daughter of **Thomas Sutpen** and a slave woman. She grows up on Sutpen's Hundred as a servant to **Judith Sutpen** and **Henry Sutpen** and remains at the plantation until burning the manor house down in 1910, causing her own death.

Ellen Coldfield Sutpen

Absalom, Absalom!
William Faulkner

Thomas Sutpen's second wife, mother of **Henry Sutpen** and **Judith Sutpen**. A flighty and excitable woman, she dies relatively young of natural causes.

Henry Sutpen

Absalom, Absalom!
William Faulkner

Son of **Thomas Sutpen** with **Ellen Coldfield Sutpen**. He grows up on Sutpen's Hundred, then attends the University of Mississippi beginning in 1859. There he befriends **Charles Bon**, whom he later murders in order to prevent Bon's marrying **Judith Sutpen**.

Judith Sutpen

Absalom, Absalom!
William Faulkner

Thomas Sutpen's daughter with **Ellen Coldfield Sutpen**. She grows up on Sutpen's Hundred, where she is engaged to **Charles Bon** in 1860. The engagement is cut short when **Henry Sutpen** murders Bon. She is strong and, like her father, swift to action.

Thomas Sutpen

Absalom, Absalom!
William Faulkner

Owner and founder of the plantation Sutpen's Hundred. He is married to **Ellen Coldfield Sutpen**; father of **Henry Sutpen**, **Judith Sutpen**, and **Clytemnestra Sutpen**, also of **Charles Bon**. A willful, powerful man, he achieves his ends through shrewdness and daring but lacks compassion. He is murdered by **Wash Jones** in 1869. The novel's subject is the rise and fall of his family.

Agrafena Alexandrovna Svetlova

The Brothers Karamazov
Fyodor Dostoevsky

A beautiful young woman. She is brought to the town by **Kuzma Kuzmich Samsonov** after a lover betrays her. Proud, fiery, and headstrong, Grushenka is an almost universal object of desire among the men in the town and is the source of much of the antagonism between **Fyodor Pavlovich Karamazov** and **Dmitri Fyodorovich Karamazov**. She is reputed to be sexually promiscuous, but in reality, she is much too proud to give herself to lovers. She devotes herself instead to increasing her wealth by making shrewd investments, but after she meets **Alexei Fyodorovich Karamazov**, a hidden vein of gentleness and love begins to emerge in her character.

Arkady Ivanovich Svidrigailov

Crime and Punishment
Fyodor Dostoevsky

Avdotya Romanovna Raskolnikova's depraved former employer. Svidrigailov appears to believe, almost until the end of the novel, that he can make Dunya love him. The death of his wife has made him generous, but he is a threatening presence to both Dunya and Raskolnikov.

Nikolai Ivanovich Sviyazhsky

Anna Karenina
Leo Tolstoy

A friend of **Konstantin Dmitrich Levin**'s who lives in a far-off province.

Ralph Swain

On the Beach
Nevil Shute

A young crew member on the submarine. He jumps ship just off his home town in Washington state so that he can spend his last days there. After visiting his house and seeing the bodies of his family, Yeoman Swain spends his final days fishing.

The Swangers

Cold Mountain
Charles Frazier

Ada Monroe's closest neighbors and friends. The Swangers oppose the war, although both their sons are off fighting. Deeply religious, the couple was offended by **Monroe**'s assumptions when he first arrived at Cold Mountain that they did not know the Bible. The Swangers send **Ruby Thewes** to help out at the farm after realizing that Ada intends to run it herself.

Charles Swann

Swann's Way
Marcel Proust

A friend of **Marcel**'s family in Combray. He is a celebrity in the Parisian social scene. A wealthy stockbroker, Swann becomes an expert art critic and dealer. Swann is also a womanizer who falls hopelessly in love with **Odette**, even though she is not his "type." Swann's idealization of Odette keeps him from seeing her as she really is.

Eddie Swanson

Babbitt
Sinclair Lewis

A salesman and **Babbitt**'s neighbor.

Louetta Swanson

Babbitt
Sinclair Lewis

Eddie Swanson's young, pretty wife. **Babbitt** tries to flirt with Louetta, but she rebuffs his attentions. Only after Babbitt becomes a member of **Tanis Judique**'s group of Bohemian friends does Louetta return his flirtatious advances.

Neil Swanson

When the Legends Die
Hal Borland

In charge of the stables and livestock, Swanson hires **Thomas Black Bull**, only to treat him meanly when he discovers his lack of farming skills.

Sweet

Song of Solomon
Toni Morrison

A prostitute with whom **Milkman Dead** has a brief affair. Unlike Milkman's affairs with other women, especially **Hagar**, his relationship with Sweet is mutually respectful and entirely reciprocal.

Sweetness

Jazz
Toni Morrison

Nephew of **Malvonne Edwards**. Sweetness no longer lives with his aunt in **Joe Trace** and **Violet**'s apartment building. For unknown reasons he had stolen a bag of addressed and stamped letters and hid it in his room before moving away.

Kate Swift

Winesburg, Ohio
Sherwood Anderson

A Winesburg schoolteacher. She sees a "spark of genius" in **George Willard** and tries to encourage it, but she is also looking for love, and she briefly allows him to embrace her in the newspaper office.

Swimmer

Cold Mountain
Charles Frazier

A Cherokee boy whom **Inman** met in his youth. Inman recalls Swimmer's tales about gateways to an invisible spirit world found atop high mountains.

Syaudi

The Joy Luck Club
Amy Tan

The son of **An-mei's mother** and **Wu-Tsing** who **Second Wife** took as her own. **An-mei** learned that Syaudi was her brother through **Yan Chang**, her mother's servant.

Sybil

Invisible Man
Ralph Ellison

A white woman whom **the Narrator** attempts to use to find out information about the Brotherhood. Sybil instead uses the narrator to act out her fantasy of being raped by a "savage" black man.

Aunt Sybil

Lolita
Vladimir Nabokov

Humbert Humbert's maternal aunt. After Humbert's mother is killed by lightning while picnicking, Aunt Sybil moves in and becomes Humbert's governess and his father's housekeeper.

Allan Sykes

On the Beach
Nevil Shute

The director of the State Fisheries and Game Department. Sykes is initially reluctant to move up the starting date of the fishing season, but he ultimately caves and opens the waters for fishing.

Sylvia

I Never Promised You a Rose Garden
Joanne Greenberg

A patient at the mental hospital who is normally silent and withdrawn. When violently attacked by **Helene**, Sylvia makes no outward sign of distress. While the staff rushes to contain Helene, only **Deborah** understands why Sylvia needs attention as much as Helene.

Syme

1984
George Orwell

An intelligent, outgoing man who works with **Winston Smith** at the Ministry of Truth. Syme specializes in language and is working on a new edition of the Newspeak dictionary. Winston believes Syme is too intelligent to stay in the Party's favor, and his suspicions are confirmed when one day Syme is "vaporized" and all references to him are deleted.

Mr. Syme

The Outsiders
S. E. Hinton

Ponyboy Curtis's English teacher. Mr. Syme expresses concern over Ponyboy's falling grades. He offers to raise Ponyboy's grade if he turns in a well-written autobiographical theme. This assignment inspires Ponyboy to write about the greasers and the Socs, and his autobiographical theme turns into the novel *The Outsiders*.

Richard Sympson

Gulliver's Travels
Jonathan Swift

Gulliver's cousin. He publishes Gulliver's account of his travels. **Sympson**'s fictional prefatory note, "The Publisher to the Readers," warns that half of Gulliver's original manuscript has been excised as irrelevant prior to publication.

The Young Syrian

Salomé
Oscar Wilde

A former prince and captain of **Herod**'s guard. The Syrian is a handsome, languorous youth mesmerized by **Salomé**. The Syrian raises **Jokanaan** from his cistern at Salomé's request and kills himself when she professes her love for the prophet.

Jokubas Szedvilas

The Jungle
Upton Sinclair

The kind proprietor of a failing Packingtown delicatessen and **Jonas**'s acquaintance from Lithuania. The street-smart Jokubas introduces Jurgis's family to the harsh realities of poor immigrant life in Chicago.

STELLAR SIDEKICKS

THE RIGHT HAND. THE SECOND FIDDLE. NUMBER TWO. CONTENT TO STAY OUT OF THE LIMELIGHT, BUT INDISPENSABLE.

Jack Burden	1	*All the King's Men*
Enkidu	2	*Gilgamesh*
Samwise Gamgee	3	*The Lord of the Rings* trilogy
Jim	4	*Huckleberry Finn*
Dean Moriarty	5	*On the Road*
Professor Pangloss	6	*Candide*
Sancho Panza	7	*Don Quixote*
Patroclus	8	*The Illiad*
Dr. Watson	9	*The Hound of the Baskervilles*

T. P.

The Sound and the Fury
William Faulkner

One of **Dilsey**'s sons. T.P. gets drunk with Benjy and fights with Quentin at Caddy's wedding.

T. R.

Cold Sassy Tree
Olive Anne Burns

Will Tweedy's dog, named after Theodore Roosevelt.

Tabea

The Red Tent
Anita Diamant

Dinah's cousin by **Esau**'s wife **Basemath**. Tabea is Dinah's first girlfriend of her own age. Tabea is banished by their grandmother **Rebecca** for not being initiated into womanhood properly.

Maxwell Taber

One Flew over the Cuckoo's Nest
Ken Kesey

A former patient who stayed in **Nurse Ratched**'s ward before **Randle McMurphy** arrived. When Taber questioned the nurse's authority, she punished him with electroshock therapy. After the treatments made him completely docile, he was allowed to leave the hospital. He is considered a successful cure by the hospital staff.

Billy Tabeshaw

In Our Time
Ernest Hemingway

A Native American who comes with **Dick Boulton** to chop wood. Billy is quiet and sensitive.

Tadzio

Death in Venice
Thomas Mann

The subject of **Gustav von Aschenbach**'s affection, an intensely beautiful but sickly Polish boy who stays with his mother, sisters, and governess at the same hotel in Venice as Aschenbach. Tadzio is pure and innocent but also aware of Aschenbach's interest in him. To the old man this boy embodies every possible virtue.

Dagny Taggart

Atlas Shrugged
Ayn Rand

The protagonist. She is the onetime lover of **Francisco D'Anconia** and **Hank Rearden** and vice president in charge of operations of Taggart Transcontinental Railroad. Dagny Taggart is **John Galt**'s greatest love and worst enemy. Her brilliant management style and unwavering commitment to her own railroad enable her to remain in the world of the "looters"—the people and government agencies that seize property from capitalists—and to keep her railroad running despite the growing chaos. When she realizes the looters are in fact agents of death, she withdraws and is the last to join the strike.

James Taggart

Atlas Shrugged
Ayn Rand

Dagny Taggart's brother and president of Taggart Transcontinental Railroad. An inferior businessman, Jim excels at influence peddling and becomes highly skilled at manipulating the system. Though he claims to be motivated by both personal wealth and public service, his true motive is destruction of the productive. Finally, watching **John Galt**'s torture by **Dr. Floyd Ferris** brings Jim face to face with his own depravity. The realization causes him to go mad.

Tai

Midnight's Children
Salman Rushdie

A boatman. Tai is a friend of **Aadam Aziz**'s.

Tainor

Island of the Blue Dolphins
Scott O'Dell

One of the birds that **Karana** tames.

Huang Taitai

The Joy Luck Club
Amy Tan

Tyan-yu's mother. When **Lindo** came to live in her household at the age of twelve, Taitai trained her to be the epitome of the obedient wife. Domineering and tyrannical, Taitai made Lindo's life miserable and blamed her for the fact that Lindo and Tyan-yu had no children.

Florry Talbot

Ulysses
James Joyce

One of the prostitutes in **Bella Cohen**'s brothel. Florry is plump and slow but eager to please.

John Talbot

Henry VI, Part I
William Shakespeare

Lord Talbot's son. John arrives at the battlefield of Bordeaux to experience war firsthand. When Talbot realizes that their army is doomed, he urges John to flee. John dies in battle before his father, who himself apparently dies of grief.

Lord Talbot

Henry VI, Part I
William Shakespeare

General of the English troops in France and father of **John Talbot**. Talbot has a fearsome reputation, and he recaptures several towns taken by **Joan of Arc** and the French forces. At Bordeaux, Talbot is trapped between two armies. Because of the **Duke of York** and the **Duke of Somerset**'s personal quarrel, reinforcements do not come in time. His son John dies in battle, and Talbot dies of grief.

Tall engineer

The Unbearable Lightness of Being
Milan Kundera

The stranger with whom **Tereza** has a brief affair. He is a mysterious character who saves Tereza from a difficult situation early on, seduces her, then vanishes. Some friends warn her he may have been a police agent gathering potential blackmail material.

Tamb'Itam

Lord Jim
Joseph Conrad

A Malay who came to Patusan and was enslaved by the **Rajah Allang**. Freed by **Doramin**, he becomes **Jim**'s loyal servant and adviser. He escapes with **Jewel** after Jim's death and is the one to give **Marlow** the most complete account of Jim's final days.

Tamenund

The Last of the Mohicans
James Fenimore Cooper

The Delaware Native American sage. Wise and revered, Tamenund has outlived three generations of warriors. When warriors bring **Major Duncan Heyward**, **Hawkeye**, **Cora Munro**, and **Alice Munro** to the sage for judgment, Tamenund hears the pronouncements of **Uncas**. Uncas uses his newfound power to convince the Delawares that Magua has maliciously deceived them. However, since Cora is Magua's rightful prisoner, Magua escapes with her, which leads to Magua's, Uncas's, and Cora's eventual deaths. At the funeral, Tamenund gives a wise speech.

Dr. Tamkin

Seize the Day
Saul Bellow

Tommy Wilhelm's friend and fellow resident of the Hotel Gloriana. Dr. Tamkin claims to be many things, including a psychologist, a poet, a member of the Detroit Purple Gang, the head of a medical clinic in Toledo, the coinventor of an unsinkable ship, a technical consultant in television, and a widower. Although most distrust Dr. Tamkin, Tommy likes him and takes his psychoanalytical advice. Tommy also enters into a joint stock-market venture with Dr. Tamkin, entrusting the old, East-European, Jewish doctor with the last of his money.

Tammuz

The Epic of Gilgamesh
Unknown

The god of vegetation and fertility, also called the Shepherd. Born a mortal, Tammuz is the husband of **Ishtar**.

Tamora

Titus Andronicus
William Shakespeare

Queen of the Goths, and **Chiron** and **Demetrius**'s mother. After **Titus** murders her eldest son in a traditional sacrifice, Tamora plots Titus's ruin. At the end of the play, Titus kills Tamora, first feeding her the remains of Chiron and Demetrius baked into pies.

Mr. Tanaka

Hiroshima
John Hersey

A man who hates all Christians. He accuses **Reverend Mr. Kiyoshi Tanimoto** of being an American spy.

Reverend Mr. Kiyoshi Tanimoto

Hiroshima
John Hersey

A Methodist pastor living in Hiroshima. Kiyoshi helps bring many of the nameless dying and wounded to safety as fires rage around the city. In the years following the war, he becomes a staunch peace activist and tours America giving speeches and appearing on television.

Koko Tanimoto

Hiroshima
John Hersey

The daughter of **Mr. Tanimoto**. Koko is exposed to radiation as a baby during the explosion and is unable to have children when she grows up.

Benjamin Tanner

A Day No Pigs Would Die
Robert Newton Peck

A neighbor and friend to the Pecks. He gives **Pinky** to **Robert Peck** in gratitude for helping with his cow **Apron**'s birth to **Bib** and **Bob**. Mr. Tanner also brings Robert to the Rutland fair, where Pinky wins a prize for being the best-behaved pig raised by a child.

Bess Tanner

A Day No Pigs Would Die
Robert Newton Peck

Benjamin Tanner's good-natured wife, and a neighbor to the Pecks. She likes **Robert Peck** quite a bit and is instrumental in getting him invited to the Rutland fair.

Charles Tansley

To the Lighthouse
Virginia Woolf

A young philosopher and pupil of **Mr. Ramsay**'s who stays with the Ramsays on the Isle of Skye. Tansley is a prickly and unpleasant man who is insecure about his humble background.

Tar Baby

Sula
Toni Morrison

A white alcoholic who lives in a room in **Eva Peace**'s home. He stays in his room, drinking himself to death.

Jean Tarrou

The Plague
Albert Camus

A visitor vacationing in Oran during the outbreak of the plague. Like **Rieux**, Tarrou is an atheist who embraces personal social responsibility, and he contributes to the anti-plague effort. Tarrou believes that life and death have no intrinsic moral meaning.

Tashi

The Color Purple
Alice Walker

An Olinka village girl. She befriends **Olivia** and marries **Adam**. Tashi defies white imperialist culture and embodies the struggle of traditional cultural values against colonization. She chooses to undergo two painful African traditions—facial scarring and genital mutilation—as a way to physically differentiate her culture from imperialist culture. Adam, in a show of solidarity with Tashi, also undergoes facial scarring after the two are married. Adam and Tashi come home to **Celie** in a joyous reunion and meeting.

Tashtego

Moby-Dick
Herman Melville

Stubb's harpooner, or "squire." Tashtego is a Gay Head Indian from Martha's Vineyard, one of the last of a tribe about to disappear. Tashtego performs many of the skilled tasks aboard the ship, such as tapping the case of spermaceti in the whale's head. He accidentally falls into the "case," or cavern in the whale's head strapped alongside the ship, and has to be "delivered" by **Queequeg** out of the head like a baby when the head starts sinking.

Mama Tataba

The Poisonwood Bible
Barbara Kingsolver

The live-in helper for **Brother Fowles**. She is so outraged by **Nathan Price**'s insistence on baptism, as well as by the contemptuous manner in which he treats her helpful suggestions, that she abandons the Prices, forcing them to fend for themselves.

Miss Effie Belle Tate

Cold Sassy Tree
Olive Anne Burns

Rucker Blakeslee's next-door neighbor. Miss Effie Belle Tate loves snooping and gossiping.

Heck Tate

To Kill a Mockingbird
Harper Lee

The sheriff of Maycomb. Heck Tate is a major witness at **Tom Robinson**'s trial. Heck warns **Atticus Finch** that a lynch mob might be coming to kill Tom Robinson before the trial. Later on, Heck refuses to acknowledge that **Jem Finch** or **Boo Radley** may have killed the drunken, violent **Bob Ewell**, who was responsible for Tom Robinson's unfair conviction.

Tateh

Ragtime
E. L. Doctorow

A Jewish immigrant from Latvia. In the first part of the novel he lives with his daughter on the Lower East Side, working as a peddler and a silhouette artist. He later leaves with his daughter to travel to Lawrence, Massachusetts, where he becomes a filmmaker. He marries **Mother** at the end of the novel.

Taube

Herzog
Saul Bellow

Moses Herzog's stepmother and **Jonah Herzog**'s second wife. Twice widowed, she lives alone in the old house she used share with Jonah.

Fred Tayama

Farewell to Manzanar
Jeanne Wakatsuki Houston

A leader of the Japanese American Citizens League and suspected collaborator with the U.S. government. On December 5, 1942, Tayama is severely beaten, and the arrest of his attackers leads to the December Riot at Manzanar.

Elgin Taylor

A Yellow Raft in Blue Water
Michael Dorris

Christine's husband and **Rayona**'s father. Elgin has good intentions but never follows through. He and Christine have an on-and-off relationship.

Mrs. Florida Taylor

I Know Why the Caged Bird Sings
Maya Angelou

Mr. Taylor's wife of forty years.

Johnny Taylor

Their Eyes Were Watching God
Zora Neale Hurston

A young man whom **Janie Mae Crawford** kisses under a pear tree when she starts to feel sexual desire at age sixteen. This incident prompts **Nanny Crawford** to force Janie to marry the more socially respectable **Logan Killicks**, who treats Janie like a piece of livestock.

Mr. Taylor

I Know Why the Caged Bird Sings
Maya Angelou

An acquaintance of **Maya Johnson**'s family. Mr. Taylor is devastated by the loss of his wife, **Mrs. Florida Taylor**. He comes to stay at **Momma**'s store and house one night after Mrs. Taylor's death.

Mr. Taylor

The Remains of the Day
Kazuo Ishiguro

A man whom **Stevens** runs into when he is crossing a field, in search of help, after his car runs out of gas near the town of Moscombe.

Owen Taylor

The Big Sleep
Raymond Chandler

The Sternwoods' chauffeur, a young man. Taylor is in love with **Carmen Sternwood** and tries to run away with her, but he is jailed because **Vivian**, Carmen's sister, presses charges. The only way Taylor can see to save Carmen and her name is to murder **Geiger**.

Terry Taylor

This Boy's Life
Tobias Wolff

Jack Wolff's delinquent friend from Salt Lake City. Together with Jack, **Terry Silver** and Terry Taylor egg passersby from the roof of an apartment building and watch the Mickey Mouse Club while making vulgar remarks about one of the show's stars.

Tayo

Ceremony
Leslie Marmon Silko

The novel's protagonist. He is the nephew of **Auntie** and **Josiah**, **Harley**'s friend and **Betonie**'s student. Educated in white schools, Tayo has always maintained a belief in the Native American traditions. Tayo is able to make use of his double consciousness (of white and Native American life) to cure himself and his community.

Tea Cake

Their Eyes Were Watching God
Zora Neale Hurston

Janie Mae Crawford's third husband and first real love. Twelve years younger than Janie, Tea Cake impresses her with his quick wit and zest for living. Tea Cake contracts rabies when fighting with a dog in a flood in order to save Janie's life. His paranoid delusions cause him to attempt to shoot Janie, who anticipates this and kills him first.

Leigh Teabing

The Da Vinci Code
Dan Brown

The novel's antagonist. He is a knight, a Royal Historian, and an extremely wealthy man crippled since childhood from polio. The Holy Grail has been Teabing's one passion for years. This obsession eventually turns him into a murderer. He creates an alter ego, the Teacher, who carries out his evil plot. Initially, Teabing is a welcome benefactor for **Sophie Neveu** and **Robert Langdon**, but it soon becomes clear that Teabing will go to any lengths to get what he wants.

The teacher

Sounder
William Armstrong

The only person outside of **the boy**'s family who treats him with kindness. The teacher seems to implicitly understand the boy's plight, and the teacher knows that books bring the boy pleasure.

Teague

Cold Mountain
Charles Frazier

The leader of a band of the Home Guard, a local militia charged with rounding up the deserters. Teague is a cunning sadist who is mentioned by both **the Swangers** and **the captive** with fear and disgust.

Teapot

Sula
Toni Morrison

A neglected, malnourished child living in the Bottom. When **Sula Peace** comes back to town, Teapot falls off a porch and Sula is blamed by Teapot's mother.

Doll Tearsheet

Henry IV, Part II
William Shakespeare

Sir John Falstaff's favorite prostitute and a good friend of **Mistress Quickly**'s. Doll has a bottomless repertoire of insults and is fiercer and smarter than most of the law officers hanging around Eastcheap, almost coming to blows the with swaggering **Pistol**. Towards the end of the play, Doll is taken away to prison for her part in the death of a man that she and Pistol beat up.

Ted

Go Ask Alice
Anonymous

Richie's college roommate, who has a hidden homosexual relationship with him.

Uncle Ted

A Death in the Family
James Agee

Aunt Kate's husband. Uncle Ted is a distant relative and close friend of **Mary Follet** and **Jay Follet**.

Mr. Teece

The Martian Chronicles
Ray Bradbury

A racist white storeowner. He sometimes participates in lynchings. He is shocked that the Negroes plan to emigrate to Mars. He tries to stop **Silly** from leaving because of his work contract, but his friends persuade him to let him go. When he tries to stop **Belter** from leaving because of an unpaid debt, the other Negroes band together and pay back the money.

Lawrence Teft III

Bless the Beasts and Children
Glendon Swarthout

Quiet, rebellious fourteen-year-old from Mamaroneck, New York. His parents have high expectations that he constantly fails to meet. He has an explosive temper and violent tendencies. He resents all manifestations of authority.

Ilya Ilich Telegin

Uncle Vanya
Anton Chekhov

An impoverished landowner who works on the estate. He is nicknamed "Waffles" for his pockmarked face. Telegin is largely a comic figure, pathetic in his love life, cowed by conflict in the household, and prone to making the occasional inappropriate interjections.

Telemachus

The Odyssey
Homer

Odysseus's son. An infant when his father left for Troy some twenty years earlier, Telemachus possesses courage and a good heart, but he initially lacks the poise and self-confidence to oppose his mother **Penelope**'s suitors.

Téllez

Bless Me, Ultima
Rudolfo A. Anaya

A rancher friend of **Gabriel Márez**'s from the town of Agua Negra. He challenges **Tenorio Trementina** when Tenorio speaks badly of **Ultima**. Not long afterward, a curse is laid on his home. Ultima performs a Comanche funeral ceremony on Téllez's land, and ghosts cease to haunt his home.

Temple

A Portrait of the Artist as a Young Man
James Joyce

A student who openly admires and imitates **Stephen Dedalus**.

Alfred Temple

The Adventures of Tom Sawyer
Mark Twain

A well-dressed new boy in town. Like **Amy Lawrence**, Alfred Temple gets caught in the crossfire of **Tom Sawyer** and **Becky Thatcher**'s love games.

Maria Temple

Jane Eyre
Charlotte Brontë

A kind teacher at Lowood. She treats **Jane Eyre** and **Helen Burns** with respect and compassion. Miss Temple helps clear Jane of **Mrs. Reed**'s accusations against her.

The Mayor of Casterbridge
Thomas Hardy

Lucetta Templeman

Michael Henchard's ex-lover, and **Donald Farfrae**'s first wife. During the eighteen years between Henchard's sale of **Susan Henchard** and their daughter and their reunion, Henchard meets, courts, and proposes to marry Lucetta Templeman. Her indiscreet affair with Henchard makes her the pariah of her hometown of Jersey. After settling in High-Place Hall in Casterbridge, Lucetta quickly becomes enamored with Henchard's archrival and **Elizabeth-Jane Newson**'s forbidden love interest, Farfrae. Lucetta's life is peaceful until all of Casterbridge learns of Lucetta's past relationship with Henchard, whereupon **Nance Mockridge** and company make her the subject of a shameful "skimmity-ride," where the two are humiliated in effigy form for their scandalous behavior. She suffers an epileptic fit and dies at the sight of the skimmity-ride.

The Power and the Glory
Graham Greene

Mr. Tench

An Englishman living in Mexico and working as a dentist. Mr. Tench is living a life of apathy and vacancy. Estranged from his wife and filled with a low-level loathing of Mexico, Tench is the first character in the novel to interact with **the Priest**.

The Idiot
Fyodor Dostoevsky

Ippolit Terentyev

Ippolit is a friend of **Nikolai Ardalyonovich Ivolgin** and the son of Madame Terentyeva, the mistress of **Ardalyon Ivolgin**. He is in love with **Aglaya Ivanovna Yepanchina**. Sick with consumption, Ippolit is well aware of his approaching death and feels like an outcast of nature.

The Unbearable Lightness of Being
Milan Kundera

Tereza

Tomas's wife. She grew up in a small Czech town. Seeking escape from that small world, Tereza worships books, culture, and kindness and has a childlike helplesness that had originally attracted Tomas to her. Identifying Tomas as a kindred spirit and outsider, she falls in love instantly and permanently. Her husband's womanizing drives Tereza to the brink of insanity, and even causes her to return to Prague from the free West in an attempt to leave him. She finds some fulfillment in her dog, Karenin, and in her work as a photographer, especially during the Soviet tank occupation, where she does dangerous and politically dissident work as a photojournalist.

The Unbearable Lightness of Being
Milan Kundera

Tereza's mother

Tereza's mother. Doomed to a frustrating marriage by her pregnancy with Tereza and then consigned to continual disappointments in her romantic life, she renounces youth and beauty for a harsh, shameless vulgarity. Bitter and jealous of Teresa's youth, she took pleasure in embarrassing and torturing the shy, unhappy girl. To the end, their relationship remained strained.

Pilar Ternera

One Hundred Years of Solitude
Gabriel García Márquez

A local whore and madam. Pilar Ternera tells both the past and the future on a deck of cards. She seduces a teenager, **José Arcadio**, because she is attracted to the huge size of his penis. Eventually, he impregnates her with **Arcadio** and leaves the town to follow a gypsy girl. Later, José Arcadio's brother, **Aureliano** sleeps with her, and she helps Aureliano in his campaign to marry **Remedios**. When her son wants to sleep with her, she sends him a young virgin named **Santa Sofía de la Piedad** instead. Later, **Colonel Aureliano Buendía** impregnates her with **Aureliano José**. In her old age, she comforts **Aureliano (II)** by offering him her reliable wisdom and intuition. She survives until the very last days of Macondo.

Terry

On the Road
Jack Kerouac

A pretty Mexican girl with whom **Sal Paradise** spends fifteen days in California. Terry comes from a family of grape-pickers in Sabinal. She is trying to escape her abusive husband with her son **Johnny**.

Terry

Hatchet
Gary Paulsen

Brian Robeson's good friend back in New York.

Jørgen Tesman

Hedda Gabler
Henrik Ibsen

An amiable, if naïve, young scholar. Jørgen is **Hedda Tesman**'s husband. Raised by his **Aunt Julle**, Tesman has always been in awe of Hedda, and can hardly believe that she consented to marry him. As the play opens, he hopes for a professorship and a steady income and knows that only **Ejlert Løvborg** could stand in his way. His focus on work over marriage alienates and bores Hedda.

Miss Juliane Tesman

Hedda Gabler
Henrik Ibsen

Jørgen Tesman's aunt. She raised Tesman after the death of his parents. Aunt Julle is happy to see Tesman settled and hopes he and his wife **Hedda Tesman** will have a baby. She comes from a lower-class background than Hedda and does not get along with Hedda, despite her best efforts. Aunt Julle lives with the ailing **Aunt Rina**.

Mr. Tetley

Something Wicked This Way Comes
Ray Bradbury

The owner of the United Cigar Store.

Thaisa

Pericles
William Shakespeare

Simonides's daughter, **Pericles**'s wife, and **Marina**'s mother. She apparently dies in childbirth at sea, but is revived by **Cerimon**. Believing Pericles dead, Thaisa becomes a priestess at **Diana**'s temple in Ephesus.

Thalestris

The Rape of the Lock
Alexander Pope

Belinda's friend. She is named for the Queen of the Amazons and represents the historical Gertrude Morley, a friend of Pope's and the wife of Sir George Browne (rendered as her "beau," **Sir Plume**, in the poem). Thalestris eggs Belinda on in her anger and demands that the lock be returned.

Thaliart

Pericles
William Shakespeare

The villain hired by **Antiochus** to kill **Pericles**.

Thanthalteresco

Childhood's End
Arthur C. Clarke

One of **the Overlords**. He visits and inspects the commune of New Athens.

Becky Thatcher

The Adventures of Tom Sawyer
Mark Twain

Judge Thatcher's pretty, yellow-haired daughter. Becky initially shies from **Tom**'s attentions, but she soon warms to him. Naïve at first, Becky soon matches Tom as a romantic strategist, and the two go to great lengths to make each other jealous. When Tom takes the blame for Becky's ripping **Mr. Dobbins**'s secret anatomy book, she likes him again, and the two go off on an adventure in what turns out to be **Injun Joe**'s cave, getting lost and then found again.

Jim Thatcher

When the Legends Die
Hal Borland

A supporter of **Bessie** and **Thomas Black Bull**. He is a kind store owner who trades with the Indians.

Judge Thatcher

The Adventures of Tom Sawyer and *The Adventures of Huckleberry Finn*
Mark Twain

Becky Thatcher's father, the county judge. A local celebrity, Judge Thatcher inspires the respect of all the townspeople. In *The Adventures of Tom Sawyer*, he takes responsibility for issues affecting the community as a whole, such as closing **Injun Joe**'s cave for safety reasons and taking charge of **Huckleberry Finn** and **Tom Sawyer**'s treasure money. In *The Adventures of Huckleberry Finn*, Judge Thatcher shares responsibility for Huck with the **Widow Douglas**. When Huck discovers that **Pap** has returned to town, he wisely signs his fortune over to the judge for one dollar. When Pap kidnaps Huck and takes him to a cabin deep in the woods, the Widow Douglas and Judge Thatcher try to apply for custody of Huck by dealing with a new judge in St. Petersburg, Missouri, their town. However, the judge denies their request, refusing to break up a father and son.

Harry K. Thaw

Ragtime
E. L. Doctorow

Evelyn Nesbit's husband. He murders her ex-husband and rival, architect **Stanford White.** Evelyn begins to question his love for her after talking to **Emma Goldman** about his treatment of her.

Mrs. Thayer

Pnin
Vladimir Nabokov

The librarian of the college. She suggests that **Timofey Pnin** could find a nice, quiet room of his own with the Clementses.

The Everpresent Wordsnatcher

The Phantom Tollbooth
Norton Juster

A bird who flutters around the Mountains of Ignorance turning the words of others around to illustrate his own cleverness.

The Lonely One

Dandelion Wine
Ray Bradbury

The antagonist in the book, a force that everyone in the town fears. The adults fear the man whom **Lavinia Nebbs** stabs and kills. For the children, The Lonely One represents the evil force that always lurks in the dark and can never be killed.

The old man

The Martian Chronicles
Ray Bradbury

An old man working at a gas station where **Tomas Gomez** stops. He believes that people should take Mars as it is and appreciate it for being different.

The Vain Man

The Little Prince
Antoine de Saint-Exupéry

The sole resident of the second planet **the Little Prince** visits. The Vain Man is lonely and craves admiration from all who pass by.

Eponine Thénardier

Les Misérables
Victor Hugo

M. Thénardier and **M'me. Thénardier**'s eldest daughter. Eponine is eventually redeemed by her love for **Marius Pontmercy**.

M. Thénardier

Les Misérables
Victor Hugo

A cruel, money-obsessed man. He first appears as **Cosette**'s keeper and tormentor. Thénardier extorts money from whomever he can, and he frequently serves as an informant to whoever will bid the highest. His schemes range from robbery to fraud to murder, and he has strong ties to the criminal underworld in Paris.

Mme Thénardier

Les Misérables
Victor Hugo

M. Thénardier's wife. She is just as evil as her husband and takes special pleasure in abusing **Cosette**. In later years, she becomes her husband's most devoted accomplice and is particularly enthusiastic about his schemes to rob **Valjean** and Cosette.

Théoden

The Two Towers and *The Return of the King*
J. R. R. Tolkien

The King of Rohan, or King of the Riddermark, uncle of **Éowyn** and **Éomer**. In *The Two Towers*, Théoden-king is the keeper of the Golden Hall. Théoden is a good man, but his wily, long-time two-faced counselor, **Gríma Wormtongue**, has fallen under the influence of **Saruman**, and is controlling Théoden via Saruman's powers. Gríma has misled Théoden, urging him to support the evil Saruman. **Gandalf** reveals the truth of Wormtongue's deception to Théoden, who then supports the members of the Fellowship. Théoden then agrees to use his Rohirrim, the Riders of Rohan, to support the cause of Gondor in the war against **Sauron**. He tells Éowyn that she must rule in his absence in Rohan. In *The Return of the King*, Théoden sacrifices his own life on the battlefield for the sake of the West. **Meriadoc Brandybuck** valiantly defends Théoden-king before Théoden's death, and kills the Lord of **the Nazgûl** to try to save the King of Rohan.

Theodore

Holes
Louis Sachar

See **Armpit**.

Sister Therese

The Poisonwood Bible
Barbara Kingsolver

Leah Price's friend in the French mission.

Alex Therien

Walden
Henry David Thoreau

A laborer in his late twenties who often works in the vicinity of **Henry David Thoreau**'s abode. He holds great appeal for Thoreau as an untutored backwoods sage.

Thersites

Troilus and Cressida
William Shakespeare

A cynical Greek soldier who has a vicious, abusive tongue. Thersites rails against both war and warriors.

Theseus

Oedipus trilogy (Oedipus Rex, Oedipus at Colonus, Antigone)
Sophocles

The son of King Aegeus of Athens. Brave and proud, he believes that he is the son of the god **Poseidon** and determines to become worthy of this parentage. A renowned and powerful warrior, Theseus takes pity on **Oedipus** and defends him against **Creon**. King of Eleusis at age seventeen, Theseus often serves as an intermediary between gods and men, and he would rather die than dishonor himself before the gods. He abandons **Ariadne**, and later doubts his own son, which leads to his tragic demise. Theseus also appears in Greek mythology, notably as the slayer of the monstrous **Minotaur**.

Theseus

The King Must Die
Mary Renault

See above.

Theseus

The Canterbury Tales
Geoffrey Chaucer

A great conqueror and the duke of Athens in **the Knight's Tale**. The most powerful ruler in the story, he is often called upon to make final judgments and to help people in distress. His father **Egeus** helps him to unite **Palamon** and **Emelye** even though they are mourning over the death of **Arcite**.

Theseus

The Prince
Niccolò Machiavelli

King of Athens; hero of Attica. According to Greek myth, he killed the **Minotaur** in the Cretan labyrinth.

Theseus

A Midsummer Night's Dream
William Shakespeare

The heroic duke of Athens, engaged to **Hippolyta**. His approaching wedding day gives the rustics, including **Peter Quince** and **Nick Bottom**, reason to prepare a sketch to perform.

Theseus

The Two Noble Kinsmen
William Shakespeare

The duke of Athens. A warrior of mythical strength, Theseus has recently subdued the Amazons and won their queen, **Hippolyta**, for his bride. Theseus is related to Hercules and is a close quest companion of **Pirithous**.

Thetis

The Iliad
Homer

A sea-nymph. She is the devoted mother of **Achilles**, the greatest of all Greek warriors. Thetis enlists **Zeus**'s help against the Trojans at the request of her angry son.

Ruby Thewes

Cold Mountain
Charles Frazier

The daughter of **Stobrod Thewes**. Uneducated, Ruby possesses a store of knowledge about the natural world that she gleaned while younger, when her father would leave her for weeks at a time to go drinking. Ruby speaks plainly and insists on being treated like an equal. She possesses a warm and loyal heart underneath her gruff exterior. She supports her father when he returns as an army deserter to seek her help.

Stobrod Thewes

Cold Mountain
Charles Frazier

Ruby Thewes's father. Despite his drunk and disreputable past, Stobrod partially redeems himself through music. As an outlier living in a cave on Cold Mountain, Stobrod looks to his daughter for help in evading **Teague**'s Home Guard.

Simon Thibault

Bel Canto
Ann Patchett

The French ambassador to the South American country where the novel is set. Because he longs for his wife, Thibault is the hostage most unhappy about the long standoff.

Thierry

Song of Roland
Unknown

The single dissenting voice at the council of barons convened to judge **Ganelon**. Thierry argues that by betraying **Roland** while in Charlemagne's service, Ganelon has also betrayed Charlamagne himself. Ganelon's friend **Pinabel** fights Thierry in a trial by combat. Though Pinabel is the mightier warrior, God intervenes and gives Thierry the victory. As a result, Franks realize that Ganelon is a traitor and they kill him.

Thitpan

The Light in the Forest
Conrad Richter

Little Crane's brother. A bloodthirsty and ruthless man, Thitpan has no compassion for whites and feels justified in killing white children.

Felix Tholomyès

Les Misérables
Victor Hugo

Fantine's lover in Paris. Tholomyès is a wealthy student who thinks much less of his relationship with Fantine than she does. He gets Fantine pregnant and then abandons her as a joke. Tholomyès is **Cosette**'s absent biological father.

Bigger Thomas

Native Son
Richard Wright

The protagonist. Bigger is a poor, uneducated black man who has always felt trapped. He hates and fears whites, and views them as a single overwhelming force that controls his life. He murders **Mary Dalton** in a moment of panic.

Buddy Thomas

Native Son
Richard Wright

Bigger Thomas's younger brother. Initially Buddy does not rebel against the forces that oppress him, but he begins to take a more antagonistic attitude toward racial prejudice.

Dean Thomas

Harry Potter and the Goblet of Fire
J. K. Rowling

One of **Harry Potter**'s Gryffindor roommates.

Mitchell Thomas

The Land
Mildred D. Taylor

Paul-Edward Logan's best friend. Mitchell is the son of a worker, **Willie Thomas**, on the farm of Paul's father, **Edward Logan**. Mitchell resents Paul when they are children because of Paul's privileged life. Finally, they come to an understanding where Mitchell will teach Paul how to fight if Paul will teach Mitchell how to read and write. Mitchell enjoys the unfettered life that he and Paul lead when they work in the lumber camp together. Though Mitchell enjoys courting ladies, he has no desire to settle down until he marries **Caroline Perry**. Mitchell has a more difficult time remaining calm when confronted with the attacks of racist whites than Paul does, and his volatility ultimately plays a significant role in his own murder by **Digger Wallace**.

Mrs. Thomas

Anne of Green Gables
L. M. Montgomery

Anne Shirley's first foster parent. After the death of her alcoholic husband, Mrs. Thomas gives up Anne.

Mrs. Thomas

Native Son
Richard Wright

Bigger Thomas's devoutly religious mother. Mrs. Thomas has accepted her precarious, impoverished position in life and warns Bigger at the beginning of the novel that he will meet a bad end if he fails to change his ways.

Vera Thomas

Native Son
Richard Wright

Bigger Thomas's younger sister. Vera, like Bigger, lives her life in constant fear.

Willie Thomas

The Land
Mildred D. Taylor

Mitchell Thomas' father. He beats Mitchell frequently, and when Mitchell runs away, he beats his wife and younger children as well.

Henry T. Thompson

Babbitt
Sinclair Lewis

Babbitt's father-in-law and business partner. Babbitt thinks Thompson is "old-fashioned" and "provincial" because he didn't graduate from college. However, he is just as eager as Babbitt to take advantage of shady business opportunities in Zenith's real estate market.

Mr. Thompson

Atlas Shrugged
Ayn Rand

The Head of State, the head of the looters who are seizing property from capitalists in a great nationalization of industry. He believes that everyone, including **John Galt**, is willing to cut a deal in exchange for power. The super-weapon, Project X, is called the Thompson Harmonizer.

Thor

Number the Stars
Lois Lowry

The kitten that **Kirsten Johansen** finds outside Uncle **Henrik**'s house.

Henry David Thoreau

Walden
Henry David Thoreau

Amateur naturalist, essayist, lover of solitude, and poet. Thoreau was a student and protégé of the great American philosopher and essayist **Ralph Waldo Emerson**. Strongly influenced by Transcendentalism, Thoreau believed in the perfectibility of mankind through education, self-exploration, and spiritual awareness.

John Thoreau

Walden
Henry David Thoreau

Elder brother to **Henry David Thoreau**. The two brothers oversaw and taught at the Concord Academy, a progressive independent school, from 1838 to 1841. John Thoreau's failing health was a contributing factor in the demise of the school, and he died in 1842 from complications related to lockjaw.

Mr. Thorne

Incidents in the Life of a Slave Girl
Harriet Ann Jacobs

A Southerner visiting Brooklyn. He betrays Linda's whereabouts to **Dr. Flint**.

John Thornton

The Call of the Wild
Jack London

Buck's final master. John Thornton is a gold hunter experienced in the ways of the Klondike. Thornton and Buck protect each other and are devoted to each other.

Thorold

His Dark Materials
Robert Pullman

Lord Asriel's old servant. Thorold's daemon, like all servants' demons, is a dog.

Isabella Thorpe

Northanger Abbey
Jane Austen

One of **Mrs. Thorpe**'s three daughters, the sister of **John Thorpe**. Isabella is **Catherine Morland**'s best friend for the first half of the novel. Isabella is attractive and very spirited, but–like her mother–she is a gossip and often concerned with superficial things. She enjoys flirting with many young men, which bothers the more reserved Catherine. Ultimately, Isabella's nature causes her to lose both **James Thorpe** and her other boyfriend, **Frederick Tilney**.

John Thorpe

Northanger Abbey
Jane Austen

The brother of **Isabella Thorpe**. John is conceited and arrogant. John tries to woo **Catherine Morland**, but his arrogance quickly turns her against him.

Mrs. Thorpe

Northanger Abbey
Jane Austen

The widowed mother of **Isabella Thorpe** and of two other daughters. Like her daughter, Mrs. Thorpe is concerned primarily with gossip, fashion, and money.

Thrasymachus

The Republic
Plato

One of **Socrates**'s key interlocutors in *The Republic*. Thrasymachus claims that the unjust enjoy happier lives, which forces Socrates to address the question of whether it is better to live justly or unjustly.

Threarah

Watership Down
Richard Adams

The Chief Rabbit in the old home warren. He listened to **Fiver**'s warnings but did not do anything about them. Threarah's decision was prudent—as moving a warren is often worse than staying put—but in this case he was wrong.

Thror

The Hobbit
J. R. R. Tolkien

Thorin Oakenshield's grandfather. Thror mined Moria, a series of caves under the Mountain, and discovered a wealth of gold and jewels. He became King of **Dwarves** under the Mountain, but before long, the dragon **Smaug** came and killed or scattered all of Thror's people. The dragon has been guarding the treasure ever since, and Thorin wants to get back what is rightfully his.

Lotario Thugut

Love in the Time of Cholera
Gabriel García Márquez

A German telegraph operator who acts as a father figure to **Florentino Ariza**. He gives Florentino violin lessons and initiates his loss of innocence when, after leaving the telegraph office to own and manage a transient hotel, he kindly gives Florentino a room free of charge. Florentino enjoys a fast life, drinking in the taverns and sleeping with the "birds," or prostitutes, who live at the hotel.

Peter Thump

Henry VI, Part II
William Shakespeare

Thomas Horner's servant. He accuses his master of supporting **Richard Plantagenet, Duke of York**'s claim to the crown. Peter and Horner are sentenced by the **Duke of Gloucester** to fight in single combat against each other. When Peter unexpectedly wins, Henry VI claims that Horner's defeat 'proves' his guilt. Horner's death marks the beginning of a public Yorkist threat to King Henry's throne.

Sir Thurio

The Two Gentlemen of Verona
William Shakespeare

Silvia's wealthy yet boorish suitor. Because of his fortune, Thurio is the **Duke of Milan**'s favorite for Silvia's hand, but is one-upped first by **Valentine** (whom Silvia loves) and then by **Proteus** (who woos Silvia for himself). When Valentine threatens his life over Silvia in the forest, Thurio admits that he does not love her.

Thwackum

Tom Jones
Henry Fielding

The vicious tutor of **Blifil** and **Tom** who constantly beats Tom and praises Blifil.

Tia

Wide Sargasso Sea
Jean Rhys

Maillotte's daughter and **Antoinette**'s only childhood friend.

The Chevalier Tialys

His Dark Materials
Robert Pullman

A Gallivespian spy who accompanies **Lyra Belacqua** and **Will Parry** to the world of the dead.

Tiberinus

The Aeneid
Virgil

The river god associated with the Tiber River, where Rome will eventually be built. At Tiberinus's suggestion, **Aeneas** travels upriver to make allies of the Arcadians.

Tibi

Night
Elie Wiesel

A Zionist, and brother of **Yosi**, whom **Eliezer** meets in Buna. Together with Eliezer, they make a plan to move to Palestine after the war.

Carl Tiflin

The Red Pony
John Steinbeck

A rancher and **Jody**'s father. He finds it difficult to show regret or to praise Jody.

Jody Tiflin

The Red Pony
John Steinbeck

The protagonist of the novel and the only son of **Carl Tiflin**. Jody's experiences with his father's horses and his conversations with his **grandfather** teach him a number of important lessons.

Mrs. Tiflin

The Red Pony
John Steinbeck

Jody's mother and **Carl**'s wife. Mrs. Tiflin usually stays in the house, cooking meals and keeping house for the men of the ranch. She is often quick to scold Jody but shows understanding when a horse of Jody's is in danger. Mrs. Tiflin usually leaves decisions up to Carl, except when Carl tries to treat her father, Jody's **grandfather**, with disrespect.

Tight Coat

I Know Why the Caged Bird Sings
Maya Angelou

One of **Daddy Clidell**'s con-men friends. These men teach **Maya Johnson** that it is possible to use white prejudice to gain advantage over whites. The other con-men friends are **Cool Clyde**, **Just Black**, **Red Leg Daddy**, **Stonewall Jimmy**, and **Spots**.

Tilda

I Never Promised You a Rose Garden
Joanne Greenberg

One of **Dr. Fried**'s former patients. Dr. Fried treated Tilda in Nazi Germany before immigrating to the United States. Tilda once escaped the hospital, only to return to tell Dr. Fried that the outside world was crazier than the one inside the hospital.

Big Tildy

Cold Mountain
Charles Frazier

The prostitute whom **Solomon Veasey** spends a night with at the inn. Big Tildy is strong and seems capable of overpowering most men. As a black woman who is not a slave, she does not conform to social conventions.

Dicey Tillerman

Homecoming and *Dicey's Song*
Cynthia Voigt

The protagonist of both *Homecoming* and *Dicey's Song*. Dicey is a thirteen-year-old girl with a haircut that makes her look like a boy and a fierce determination to survive and keep her family together. As the oldest child of a mentally unwell single mother (**Momma**), Dicey is used to playing the role of an adult in her family, but when their mother abandons them in a parking lot in Rhode Island near the beginning of *Homecoming*, Dicey must shoulder even greater responsibility. She is willing to take any risks necessary to protect her siblings and keep them together. In *Dicey's Song*, Dicey continues to resent school and social conventions. She reflexively shuns friendships and instead devotes her time to her job and to an old sailboat in her grandmother (**Gram**)'s barn.

James Tillerman

Homecoming and *Dicey's Song*
Cynthia Voigt

Dicey Tillerman's ten-year-old brother. James is a serious and cerebral boy who has always been an outsider despite his desire to be liked. James often frustrates Dicey with his abstract and philosophical musings. He looks up to Dicey and relies on her to make decisions, but can also act rebelliously and selfishly.

Maybeth Tillerman

Homecoming and *Dicey's Song*
Cynthia Voigt

Dicey Tillerman's nine-year-old sister. Maybeth is a pretty young girl troubled by an overwhelming shyness. In Provincetown, her shyness interfered so severely with her studies that she was held back in school, and the label of mental retardation always lingered around her ominously. The Tillermans know otherwise, because of Maybeth's musical abilities and keen perceptiveness about other people. Maybeth is a capable musician who reads music much more fluently than words. Maybeth's gentleness causes her family to want to protect her from the outside world.

Sammy Tillerman

Homecoming and *Dicey's Song*
Cynthia Voigt

Dicey Tillerman's six-year-old brother, a stubborn and belligerent child. Early in *Homecoming*, Dicey finds herself reminiscing about a younger Sammy, who was wildly joyful and uninhibited. Sammy is a fierce fighter and as quick and vehement as Dicey about defending his family members. Throughout *Homecoming*, Sammy repeatedly refuses to go on walking, he steals food and a wallet, and in Bridgeport, he engages in fights with the other schoolchildren, greatly upsetting **Eunice**. In Crisfield, Sammy forces the crisis between Dicey and **Gram** when he disappears all afternoon without permission.

Little Tilly

A Tree Grows in Brooklyn
Betty Smith

Child in the Nolan's neighborhood.

Eleanor Tilney

Northanger Abbey
Jane Austen

Henry Tilney's younger sister. Eleanor is a shy, quiet young woman. She shares an interest in reading with her brother, but for the most part her reserve prevents her from having many friends. Like her brothers, Eleanor is often subject to the somewhat tyrannical behavior of her father, **General Tilney**.

Frederick Tilney

Northanger Abbey
Jane Austen

The oldest sibling in the Tilney family, often referred to as simply "Captain Tilney." Unlike his brother **Henry Tilney** or his sister **Eleanor Tilney**, Frederick is flirtatious and mischevious. Frederick flirts with **Isabella Thorpe** and leads her to break off her engagement with **James Morland**, then abandons her in Bath.

General Tilney

Northanger Abbey
Jane Austen

A widower, and the domineering father of **Henry Tilney**, **Eleanor Tilney** and **Captain Tilney**. He takes great pride in his home, Northanger Abbey, which he has refurbished himself.

Henry Tilney

Northanger Abbey
Jane Austen

A twenty-six-year-old parson in a small village called Woodston. Henry is intelligent, well-tempered, and attuned to the motivations and behavior of those around him. He is often amused at the folly of others, but he takes care to instruct them gently, particularly in the case of the naïve **Catherine Tilney**.

Tim

Go Ask Alice
Anonymous

One of **Alice**'s younger siblings. Tim develops into a mature young man.

Tiny Tim

A Christmas Carol
Charles Dickens

Bob Cratchit's youngest son. Tiny Tim, a cripple, is patient, kind, and pious.

Time Traveller

The Time Machine
H. G. Wells

The unnamed protagonist of the novella. The Time Traveller is an inventor. He likes to speculate on the future and the underlying structures of what he observes.

Corporal Timlon

Johnny Got His Gun
Dalton Trumbo

The corporal in charge of the English regiment stationed next to **Joe Bonham**'s regiment.

Timmy

The Autobiography of Miss Jane Pittman
Ernest J. Gaines

The unacknowledged son of **Robert Samson**. Timmy looks and acts just like Robert Samson, but because Timmy is the son of a black woman he cannot claim his father's name. Timmy's knowledge of his parentage makes him slightly more obstinate than other blacks. His father exiles him from the plantation eventually because of Timmy's attitude.

Timon

Timon of Athens
William Shakespeare

The play's protagonist. After spending all his money on gifts for friends, Timon goes bankrupt, and his friends will not lend him money. Convinced that humanity has turned against him, Timon declares his hatred for mankind and goes to the forest, where, to his dismay, he becomes a sought-after guru. Timon ends his days filled with vitriol.

Mr. Timoney

Angela's Ashes
Frank McCourt

An old eccentric. **Frank McCourt** reads him Jonathan Swift's satirical essay "A Modest Proposal." Mr. Timoney becomes a close friend of Frank's, in part because he respects Frank and treats him like an adult.

Timothy

The New Testament
Unknown

The traveling companion and fellow missionary of **Paul**. Timothy coauthors letters with Paul—such as 1 Corinthians and Philippians—and serves as his emissary throughout the Christian communities of the Mediterranean.

Timothy

The Martian Chronicles
Ray Bradbury

Dad's eldest son in the story "The Million-Year Picnic." He takes his responsibility as role model to his younger brothers very seriously. He soon understands that the family's "picnic" on Mars is actually a permanent move, and works with his father to help his younger brothers accept this charge.

Timothy the Taborer

The Two Noble Kinsmen
William Shakespeare

The tabor player for the morris dance.

Tinor

Typee
Herman Melville

The industrious wife of **Marheyo**. Tinor is an expert at preparing "poee-poee," the classic breadfruit dish of the island.

Tiresias

The Odyssey
Homer

The blind soothsayer of Thebes. Tiresias meets **Odysseus** in the underworld and allows the Greek warrior to communicate with other souls in Hades, then shows him how to get back to Ithaca.

Tiresias

The Bacchae
Euripides

The blind soothsayer of Thebes. Tiresias persuades **Cadmus** to worship Dionysus.

Tiresias

Oedipus trilogy (Oedipus Rex, Oedipus at Colonus, Antigone)
Sophocles

The blind soothsayer of Thebes. Though **Oedipus** and **Creon** claim to trust Tiresias, they refuse to believe his grim prophecies.

Tita

Like Water for Chocolate
Laura Esquivel

The protagonist of the novel. Tita is the youngest daughter of **Mama Elena**, prohibited by family tradition from marrying so that she will be free to take care of her mother later in life. Tita is tortured when the man she loves, **Pedro**, is betrothed to her sister **Rosaura**. Tita spends much of her time as the cook for the ranch. Her food is often a direct cause of physical and emotional unrest, and serves as a medium through which emotions can be transmitted.

Titania

A Midsummer Night's Dream
William Shakespeare

The beautiful queen of the fairies and wife of **Oberon**. Their lovers' quarrel sets into motion the events of the play. Titania has a brief, potion-induced love for **Nick Bottom**, whose head the mischievous **Puck** has transformed into that of an ass.

Titans

Greek Mythology
Unknown

The original gods, children of **Gaea** and **Ouranos**, and parents of the six original Olympians. Defeated by **Zeus** and his siblings in a war for control of the universe, most of the Titans are imprisoned in the bowels of the earth, with the exception of **Prometheus**, who sided with Zeus, and his two brothers, **Epimetheus** and **Atlas**.

Titorelli

The Trial
Franz Kafka

The Court Painter, a position inherited from his father. He knows a great deal about the comings and goings of the Court's lowest level. He offers to help **Joseph K.** and manages to unload a few identical landscape paintings on the accused man.

Tituba

The Crucible
Arthur Miller

Reverend Parris's slave from Barbados. Tituba agrees to perform voodoo at **Abigail Williams**'s request. She also honors **Ann Putnam**'s request via **Ruth Putnam** to conjure the spirits of Ann's dead babies in order to find out who supernaturally murdered them. Like the other girls, Tituba at one point is involved in naming names of witches in a frenzy to Parris and **Reverend John Hale**.

Titus Andronicus

Titus Andronicus
William Shakespeare

Roman general and the play's tragic hero. He is **Lavinia** and **Lucius**'s father. His staunch reverence for tradition forces him into unwise and at times horrific acts. He supports the unbalanced **Saturninus** as emperor over the more suitable **Bassianus**. He also earns **Tamora**'s hatred by killing her son in a ritual sacrifice. He kills his son **Lucius** for disobedience and kills his daughter Lavinia so that she won't have to live with the shame of being raped. Titus seeks vengeance and dies exacting it, killing Tamora only to be killed by Saturninus.

Kuprik Tiverzin

Dr. Zhivago
Boris Pasternak

A former railway strike leader who becomes a leader in the Red Army, along with **Liberius Avercievich Mikulitsin** and **Pavel Pavlovich Antipov**.

Tjaden

All Quiet on the Western Front
Erich Maria Remarque

One of **Paul Bäumer**'s friends in the Second Company. He bears a deep grudge against **Corporal Himmelstoss**.

Toby

Typee
Herman Melville

A young, quiet man who agrees to accompany **Tommo** on his adventure.

Tock

The Phantom Tollbooth
Norton Juster

Milo's friend, and a "watchdog." A giant clock makes up part of his body, and he makes ticking noises.

Tom

The Martian Chronicles
Ray Bradbury

The deceased son of **LaFarge** and **Anna**. However, a Martian who can take the form of the person an individual most wants to see assumes Tom's shape. It craves love and wants to be accepted by the elderly couple. It is terrified of going to town, and it dies there when many different people perceive it in a variety of forms.

Tom

Homecoming
Cynthia Voigt

One of the two boys who takes the Tillermans across the Chesapeake Bay on a sailboat.

Crazy Tom

Ender's Game
Orson Scott Card

One of **Ender Wiggin**'s leaders in Dragon Army. He is one of Ender's platoon leaders during the battles of the Third Invasion.

Uncle Tom

Uncle Tom's Cabin
Harriet Beecher Stowe

The protagonist. Even under the worst conditions, **Uncle Tom** always prays to God and finds a way to keep his faith. As the novel progresses, the cruel treatment that Tom suffers at the hands of **Simon Legree** threatens his belief in God, but Tom withstands his doubts and dies the death of a Christian martyr.

Uncle Tom

Black Boy
Richard Wright

One of **Ella Wright**'s brothers. Like **Aunt Addie**, Uncle Tom dislikes **Richard Wright** and leaps at any opportunity to beat or ridicule him.

Tomas

The Unbearable Lightness of Being
Milan Kundera

The protagonist of the novel. He is a brilliant Prague surgeon and intellectual. Having divorced early and lost contact with his ex-wife and son, Tomas is a light-hearted womanizer who lives for his work. After falling in love with and marrying the emotionally needy **Tereza**, Tomas finds himself trapped between the womanizing he cannot give up and his genuine love for his new wife. He is unwilling to identify himself as a political liberal or as a faithful husband. Consequently, most of the characters misinterpret Tomas; the police and his hospital colleagues think him a dissident, and dissidents think him a coward.

Juan Tomás

The Pearl
John Steinbeck

The older brother of **Kino**. Deeply loyal to his family, Juan Tomás supports Kino in all his endeavors but warns him of the dangers involved in possessing the highly valuable pearl he finds while diving one day. Juan Tomás remains sympathetic to Kino and his wife, **Juana**, sheltering them when they need to hide.

Tomey

Go Down, Moses
William Faulkner

The slave who becomes **Carothers McCaslin**'s lover and may also be Carothers's daughter if **Isaac** is right in thinking that Carothers also had an affair with Tomey's mother, **Eunice**. Tomey gives birth to **Turl**, Carothers's son, not long after her mother commits suicide by drowning.

Tomey's Turl

Go Down, Moses
William Faulkner

Carothers McCaslin's son with the slave-girl **Tomey**. He marries Tennie and becomes **Lucas Beauchamp**'s father.

Tomlinson

Cry, the Beloved Country
Alan Paton

One of a trio of powerful black politicians in Johannesburg. The others are **Dubula** and **John Kumalo**.

Miss Marie Tomlinson

No Longer At Ease
Chinua Achebe

Mr. Green's secretary. She is kind to Obi.

Tommo

Typee
Herman Melville

The narrator. He is an adventurous fellow in his early twenties who longs for liberty so much that he flees his whaling ship in order to live amongst the natives. When he lives with the Typees, he falls in love with the native beauty **Fayaway**, and is attended to by a tribe-appointed servant, **Kory-Kory**.

Tommy

Cloud Nine
Caryl Churchill

Victoria and **Martin**'s son. The onstage characters establish his presence by yelling at him, telling him not to do whatever he's doing.

Kjersti Tonseten

Giants in the Earth
O. E. Rölvaag

Syvert Tonseten's kind and good-natured wife. Kjersti often helps **Sorine Olsa** take care of **Per Hansa** and **Beret Hansa**'s household, and she aids Beret during childbirth. Kjersti often regrets having no child of her own.

Syvert Tonseten

Giants in the Earth
O. E. Rölvaag

Norwegian immigrant who becomes **Per Hansa** and **Hans Olsa**'s neighbor in the Dakota Territory. Although Tonseten is not as physically strong as Per or Hans, he is bright and humorous, with a quick mind. As the community grows, Tonseten is elected justice of the peace.

Tonton Macoutes

Breath, Eyes, Memory
Edwidge Danticat

Creole for "Uncle Bogeyman." The Tonton Macoutes are the private militia first conscripted under Francois Duvalier, Haitian president from 1957–1971, and formally known as the VSN (Volontaires de la Sécurité Nationale). They are widely feared as torturers, assassins and agents of arbitrary cruelty.

Tony

A View from the Bridge
Arthur Miller

A friend of **Eddie Carbone** and **Beatrice**. He assists **Marco** and **Rodolpho** off the ship and brings them safely to Beatrice's home.

Tony

Tuesdays with Morrie
Mitch Albom

Morrie Schwartz's home care worker, who helps him in and out of his swimming suit.

Ellsworth Toohey

The Fountainhead
Ayn Rand

Howard Roark's antithesis. Ellsworth Toohey is a man with a lust for power but no talent. He has always despised others' achievements and has dedicated himself to squelching ambition by encouraging selflessness and altruism.

Peregrin "Pippin" Took

The Lord of the Rings trilogy
J. R. R. Tolkien

A young and somewhat rash Hobbit. In *The Fellowship of the Ring*, he gets drunk at the Prancing Pony Inn, calling attention to **Frodo Baggins** when he should not. In *The Two Towers*, Pippin and **Meriadoc Brandybuck** are cut off from the rest of the Fellowship during a battle with **Orcs**. While Pippin and Merry are separated from the Fellowship, and after they escape from the Orcs, they stumble into Entwash and convince **Treebeard** to fight against **Saruman**. In *The Return of the King*, Pippin abandons his troublesome ways and acts as the intermediary between **Gandalf** and **Denethor**, the mad Steward of Gondor.

Reverend Tooker

Cat on a Hot Tin Roof
Tennessee Williams

A guest at **Big Daddy**'s birthday party.

Topsy

Uncle Tom's Cabin
Harriet Beecher Stowe

A slave girl whom **Miss Ophelia** tries to reform. Topsy gradually learns to love and respect others by following the example of **Evangeline St. Clare**.

Mr. Torrelli

Tortilla Flat
John Steinbeck

The bootlegger and tradesman of Tortilla Flat. He is the target for much of the *paisanos*' frustration.

Mrs. Torrelli

Tortilla Flat
John Steinbeck

The wife of **Torrelli**, the bootlegger of Tortilla Flat. When Torelli is not around, the *paisanos* have to go through Mrs. Torrelli to get their wine and other goods. Despite Torrelli's efforts to keep his wife pure, she often barters herself rather than conduct transactions with money alone.

Torrey

Girl, Interrupted
Susanna Kaysen

A methamphetamine-addicted patient from Mexico. Torrey's parents, embarrassed by their daughter, arrive to retrieve her after a short time. **Lisa** plans to help Torrey escape, but **Valerie** thwarts the plan with a dose of Thorazine.

John Big Bluff Tosamah

House Made of Dawn
N. Scott Momaday

The Priest of the Sun. He provides **Abel** with spiritual guidance. He runs the Pan-Indian rescue mission in Los Angeles.

Afanassy Ivanovich Totsky

The Idiot
Fyodor Dostoevsky

A rich aristocrat. He tries to arrange the marriage between **Anastassya Filippovna Barashkova** and **Gavril Ardalyonovich Ivolgin** to get her off his hands.

Mr. Touchett

The Portrait of a Lady
Henry James

Ralph Touchett's father and the proprietor of Gardencourt. He is an elderly American banker who has made his life and his vast fortune in England. Before Mr. Touchett dies, Ralph convinces him to leave half his fortune to his niece **Isabel Archer**, which will enable her to preserve her independence.

Mrs. Touchett

The Portrait of a Lady
Henry James

Isabel Archer's aunt and **Ralph Touchett**'s mother. Mrs. Touchett is an indomitable, independent old woman who first brings Isabel to Europe. Mrs. Touchett is separated from her husband, **Mr. Touchett**, residing in Florence while he stays at Gardencourt. After Isabel inherits her fortune and falls under the sway of **Madame Merle** and **Gilbert Osmond**, Mrs. Touchett's importance in her niece's life gradually declines.

Ralph Touchett

The Portrait of a Lady
Henry James

Isabel Archer's cousin. He is ill with lung disease throughout the entire novel. Ralph loves life, but he is kept from participating in it vigorously by his ailment; as a result, he acts as a dedicated spectator, resolving to live vicariously through his beloved cousin Isabel. It is Ralph who convinces **Mr. Touchett** to leave Isabel her fortune, and it is Ralph who is the staunchest advocate of Isabel remaining independent.

Touchstone

As You Like It
William Shakespeare

A clown in **Duke Frederick**'s court. He accompanies **Rosalind** and **Celia** in their flight to the Forest of Arden. Touchstone falls in love with the shepherdess **Audrey**.

Madame de Tourvel

Dangerous Liaisons
Pierre-Ambroise-François Choderlos de Laclos

The chaste and religious wife of a member of Parliament. She is seduced by, and falls in love with, **Vicomte de Valmont**. After Valmont finally gains Tourvel's company through **Father Anselme** and has his way with her, he no longer wants her.

Dwight Towers

On the Beach
Nevil Shute

The decent, soft-spoken captain of the American nuclear submarine. Dwight befriends **Moira Davidson, Peter Holmes**, and **John Osborne** during his time in Australia. Although Dwight is considered a practical, rational man, he continues to believe—or at least pretends to believe—that his family in America survived the nuclear attack. He refuses to break rules, and he remains loyal to the Navy and his wife, **Sharon Towers**, until the end of his life.

Helen and Junior Towers

On the Beach
Nevil Shute

Dwight Towers's children. They were killed, along with their mother, in the war.

Sharon Towers

On the Beach
Nevil Shute

Dwight Towers's wife. Sharon was killed during the war in America, but Dwight constantly thinks of her and remains loyal to her to the end.

Townspeople

Rhinoceros
Eugène Ionesco

The Old Gentleman, the Grocer, the Grocer's Wife, the Housewife, the Café Proprietor, and the Waitress who appear in the first act. They are characterized largely by their trivial concerns, though the Old Gentleman is very interested in the **Logician**'s reasoning. The appearance of the first rhinoceros is marked by their idle wonderment.

Aunt Toyo

Farewell to Manzanar
Jeanne Wakatsuki Houston

Papa's aging aunt in Hiroshima, Japan. **Woody** visits Toyo in 1946 and is impressed by the dignity of her graceful manner. Woody comes to see this dignity in the face of difficulty as a Wakatsuki family trait.

Leora Tozer

Arrowsmith
Sinclair Lewis

Martin Arrowsmith's loyal wife. Leora is opinionated and yet completely supportive and understanding of Martin and his career. Caring and loving, she is his constant companion until her death from the same plague Martin is researching. Leora's death plunges Martin into loneliness and unhappiness, and although he marries again, the second marriage does not fill the void that Leora's death leaves.

Joe Trace

Jazz
Toni Morrison

Violet's husband. Joe Trace is a good-looking man in his late fifties who, despite having lived in Harlem for twenty years, retains the boyish innocence and dignified comportment of a hardworking outdoorsman. Joe works hard, shuttling between a job as a cosmetics salesman and a waiter. He treats Violet well, but when she becomes depressed and starts sleeping with a wooden doll, he cannot maintain a sense of completion. He tries to secure Dorcas's affection by adoring her. When Dorcas scorns him and chooses **Acton** over him, his pain is compounded by a deeper anguish as he watches the third woman in his life abandon him. Joe murders Dorcas.

Tommy Traddles

David Copperfield
Charles Dickens

David Copperfield's schoolmate. Traddles works hard but faces great obstacles because he lacks money and connections. He eventually succeeds in making a name and a career for himself.

Dr. Traeger

Death Be Not Proud
John Gunther

The family physician. He advises **John Gunther** and **Frances** on **Johnny**'s condition.

Tralfamadorians

Slaughterhouse-Five
Kurt Vonnegut

Aliens. They are shaped like toilet plungers, each with one hand containing an eye in its palm. They abduct **Billy Pilgrim** and **Montana Wildhack**, and their philosophies of time and death influence the narrative style of the novel.

Tramecksan

Gulliver's Travels
Jonathan Swift

A Lilliputian political party. **High-Heels** policies are influenced by the ancient constitution of Lilliput. Though more numerous than **Low-Heels**, High-Heels are underrepresented in government.

Tranio

The Taming of the Shrew
William Shakespeare

Lucentio's servant. Tranio accompanies his master from Pisa and immediately dissuades him from rigidly studying, instead convincing him to lose himself in more visceral delights. He assumes Lucentio's identity and bargains with **Baptista** for **Bianca**'s hand.

Transgressor of the Unspeakable Word

Anthem
Ayn Rand

A martyr for the word "I." He represents the way to die properly for the cause of egoism.

Adam Trask

East of Eden
John Steinbeck

The son of **Cyrus Trask**, half-brother of **Charles**, and father of **Aron** and **Cal**. The protagonist of the first half of the novel. For much of the boys' childhood, Adam proves a less than ideal father, distant from his sons and unable to see his own favoritism for Aron over Cal. Ultimately, Adam's housekeeper, **Lee**, causes him to realize Cal's potential, and Adam redeems Cal by blessing him at the end of the novel.

Alice Trask

East of Eden
John Steinbeck

Cyrus Trask's second wife and the **Charles**'s mother. Alice is a quiet, deferential woman who almost never shows emotion. Alice dies while **Adam** is away in the Army.

Aron Trask

East of Eden
John Steinbeck

The son of **Adam Trask** and **Cathy Ames** and the twin brother of **Cal**. Aron's deep morality makes it painful for him to hear about or witness evil. As a result, Aron retreats into the church as a protection from the harsh realities of the world. When Cal reveals to Aron that their mother, Cathy, is a prostitute, Aron is so devastated that he leaves Stanford University and joins the army, and soon dies in World War I.

Caleb Trask

East of Eden
John Steinbeck

The son of **Adam Trask** and **Cathy Ames** and the twin brother of **Aron**. Cal is a manipulative, tempestuous boy who is fiercely jealous of his brother, Aron. Cal struggles throughout the second half of the novel to control his temptations and to lead a moral life. He becomes fiercely jealous of Aron because of Adam's obvious preference for him, and ultimately sets in motion the events that lead to Aron's death. Although Cal does make several poor moral choices as he grows up, he eventually takes **Lee**'s advice and recognizes the validity of *timshel*, the idea that each individual has the power to choose between good and evil in life.

Charles Trask

East of Eden
John Steinbeck

The son of **Cyrus Trask** and the half-brother of **Adam**. Charles is a violent, cynical, manipulative man who works his father's farm and greedily amasses a large fortune. Although Charles is deeply jealous of his brother, he also needs Adam and misses him terribly when he is not at home. He is one of the only characters capable of inspiring fear in the thoroughly evil **Cathy Ames**. When Charles dies, he leaves half of his sizable fortune to Adam and the other half to Cathy.

Cyrus Trask

East of Eden
John Steinbeck

The patriarch of the Trask family and the father of **Adam** and **Charles**. Cyrus lies so convincingly about his military heroics during the Civil War that the government appoints him to a powerful position in the Army administration. Cyrus leaves his (probably stolen) fortune to his sons upon his death.

Mrs. Trask

East of Eden
John Steinbeck

The first wife of **Cyrus Trask** and the mother of **Adam**. She is a deeply pious woman. She contracts syphilis from Cyrus after he sleeps with a black prostitute in the South during the Civil War. Mrs. Trask commits suicide shortly thereafter.

Travers

Henry IV, Part II
William Shakespeare

The **Earl of Northumberland**'s servant. He delivers the real information of the Battle of Shrewsbury; that **King Henry IV** has prevailed and that **Hotspur** is dead.

Glady Treadwell

White Noise
Don DeLillo

Sister of **Old Man Treadwell**. Glady dies of a lingering dread caused by being lost in a shopping mall for four days.

Old Man Treadwell

White Noise
Don DeLillo

Blind old man to whom **Babette** reads tabloids.

Treebeard

The Return of the King
J. R. R. Tolkien

The Ent whom **Fangorn** tells to keep the corrupt **Saruman** imprisoned at Isengard in the tower of Orthanc.

Sibyll Trelawney

The Harry Potter Series: Books 3 and *4*
J. K. Rowling

The Divination Professor at Hogwarts. She is an insect-like, dramatic woman who loves predicting deaths but is not at all accurate in her predictions.

Squire Trelawney

Treasure Island
Robert Louis Stevenson

A local Bristol nobleman. Trelawney arranges the voyage to the island to find the treasure. The pirates easily trick him into hiring them as his crew.

Charles Tremain

Johnny Tremain
Esther Forbes

Jonathan Tremain's father. Charles Tremain, known in Boston as Charles Latour, was a French soldier taken as a British prisoner during the French and Indian War. While he was held as a prisoner in Boston, he met and wooed Johnny's mother. After they married, Johnny's parents traveled to France, where Charles died of cholera.

Jonathan Tremain

Johnny Tremain
Esther Forbes

The protagonist of the novel. Johnny is the fourteen-year-old prize apprentice of the Boston silversmith **Ephraim Lapham**. Johnny is a talented craftsman, but he is also arrogant, rash, and slightly cruel. When Johnny's hand is disfigured in an accident, he can no longer work as a silversmith. As the rebellious colonists begin to fight England for their identity, Johnny finds a new life among the leaders of the Boston Whig party.

Lavinia Lyte Tremain

Johnny Tremain
Esther Forbes

Jonathan Tremain's mother. Lavinia Tremain defied her wealthy family's wishes when she married **Charles Tremain**, a French prisoner of war being held in Boston. When her husband died, she raised Johnny on her own by sewing to make money. She revealed her wealthy origins to her son only on her deathbed.

Tenorio Trementina and the Trementina daughters

Bless Me, Ultima
Rudolfo A. Anaya

A malicious saloon-keeper and barber in El Puerto. The **Trementina daughters** are witches and place a curse upon **Lucas Luna**, which **Ultima** lifts. Ultima seems to be responsible for the Trementina's daughters' deaths. Tenorio detests **Ultima** and vows to kill her. He finally achieves this by killing her owl familiar, her spiritual guardian, but he is then killed by **Pedro Luna** as he is about to shoot at **Antonio Márez**.

Gus Trenor

The House of Mirth
Edith Wharton

A lonely, moody man. He has a particular liking for **Lily Bart** even though he is married to **Judy Trenor**. Lily asks him to invest her money for her in the stock market. Instead, Trenor invests his own money and gives Lily the profits. When Lily finds out that the money is not truly hers, she resolves to pay Trenor back rather than agree to be his friend.

Judy Trenor

The House of Mirth
Edith Wharton

A close friend of **Lily Bart**. Judy Tenor regularly hosts large bridge parties and gives Lily a place to stay for up to weeks at a time.

Konstantin Gavrilovich Treplyov

The Seagull
Anton Chekhov

One of the play's four protagonists. Treplyov is **Arkadina**'s only son. He struggles to find his voice as a playwright in the shadow of his mother's succcess as an actress. He also desires the success of his wife's lover, the famed writer **Trigorin**. Treplyov is a dreamer and a compassionate soul whose love for the young actress **Nina** goes unrequited. When Nina runs off with Trigorin only to return to Treplyov as a fallen woman who still won't love him, Treplyov commits suicide.

Monsieur de Treville

The Three Musketeers
Alexandre Dumas

The head of **King Louis XIII**'s Musketeers. Monsieur de Treville is an honorable and distinguished gentleman and close friend to the King. Treville is a rival of **Cardinal Richelieu** for favor and influence with the King.

Annabelle Trice

All the King's Men
Robert Penn Warren

Cass Mastern's lover, the wife of **Duncan Trice**. When the slave **Phebe** brings her Duncan's wedding ring following his suicide, Annabelle says that she cannot bear the way Phebe looked at her, and sells her.

Duncan Trice

All the King's Men
Robert Penn Warren

Cass Mastern's hedonistic friend in Lexington, **Annabelle Trice**'s husband. When he learns that Cass has had an affair with Annabelle, Duncan takes off his wedding ring and shoots himself.

Boris Alexeyevich Trigorin

The Seagull
Anton Chekhov

Arkadina's lover. Trigorin is one of the four protagonists of *The Seagull* and is an esteemed Russian novelist. Like Arkadina, Trigorin is a member of the the elite Russian intelligensia and artistic community. He begins as a dutiful lover to Arkadina but becomes tempted by the youthful beauty, optimism, and flattery of **Nina**. He is an obsessive-compulsive writer and is somewhat aloof to the family and friends on the estate. Trigorin virtually crushes **Treplyov** by being such a famous writer and by stealing Nina's affections from Treplyov.

Corporal Trim

Tristram Shandy
Laurence Sterne

Manservant and sidekick to **Uncle Toby**. Trim colludes with Captain Toby in his military shenanigans.

Trinculo

The Tempest
William Shakespeare

A jester.

Lizzie Tristram

The American
Henry James

Tom Tristram's wife and **Christopher Newman**'s first friend and advocate in Paris. Mrs. Tristram is intelligent and compassionate, but her marriage to the boorish Tom has left her somewhat incomplete. She is neither beautiful nor truly brave. Newman instantly likes her, and she is immediately taken by him. It is Mrs. Tristram who first discerns Newman's wish to marry, and suggests her childhood friend, **Claire de Bellegarde**.

Tom Tristram

The American
Henry James

An old acquaintance of **Christopher Newman**'s who briefly served with him in the Civil War before moving to Paris six years before the novel begins. Tristram lives on the Avenue d'Iéna, the wealthy American district, with his wife **Lizzie Tristam** and their several children. He is dull, unaware, and unappreciative of artistic or personal genius, preferring to spend his time in the Occidental Club smoking and thinking about clothes, style, cigars and card games with other Americans.

The Terrible Trivium

The Phantom Tollbooth
Norton Juster

A demon with no facial features. He lives in the Mountains of Ignorance and preys upon travelers, convincing them to undertake tasks that can never be completed.

Pyotr Trofimov

The Cherry Orchard
Anton Chekhov

A student at the local university. He knows **Ranevsky** from tutoring her son **Grisha** before he died. Trofimov's utopian idealism contrasts with **Lopakhin**'s practicality and materialism.

Troilus

Troilus and Cressida
William Shakespeare

A Trojan prince, **Hector** and **Paris**'s younger brother. An honorable and valiant warrior, Troilus is desperately in love with **Cressida**.

Trolls

The Hobbit
J. R. R. Tolkien

Short-tempered and dull-witted monsters who will eat just about anything.

Miss Betsey Trotwood

David Copperfield
Charles Dickens

David Copperfield's eccentric, kindhearted aunt. She becomes a mother figure for David.

Clopin Trouillefou

Hunchback of Notre Dame
Victor Hugo

King of the vagabonds. He leads the vagabonds into battle, crying out that they have come to rescue **La Esmerelda**. Unfortunately, **Quasimodo** can't hear them, and he assumes that they have come to kill La Esmerelda. He throws a large wooded beam from the belfry and kills many of them.

Kilgore Trout

Slaughterhouse-Five
Kurt Vonnegut

A bitter, unappreciated author of several cleverly ironic science-fiction novels that have a great influence on **Billy Pilgrim**. Trout appears in many of **Kurt Vonnegut**'s works.

Sergeant Francis Troy

Far from the Madding Crowd
Thomas Hardy

The antagonist. Sergeant Francis Troy is handsome and irresponsible. He treats women very badly. In the end, Troy is jealously shot and killed by **Boldwood**.

Trudolyubov

Notes from Underground
Fyodor Dostoevsky

A former schoolmate of **the Underground Man** and a distant relation of **Zverkov**'s. Trudolyubov is an honest man who treats the Underground Man with some degree of politeness.

True Belle

Jazz
Toni Morrison

Violet's grandmother. True Belle leaves her family and moves with her mistress, **Vera Louise Gray**, to Baltimore in order to raise the woman's half-black baby boy, **Golden Gray**. When she learns that her daughter, **Rose Dear**, is in trouble back in Virginia, True Belle goes to help.

Esteban Trueba

The House of the Spirits
Isabel Allende

The patriarch of the Trueba family. He is the husband of **Clara**, son of **Dona Ester Trueba**, illegitimate grandfather of **Esteban Garcia**, sometime lover of **Transito Soto**, father of **Jaime**, **Nicolas**, and **Blanca**, grandfather of **Alba**. Esteban Trueba builds a vast fortune, marries Clara and becomes a senator. Esteban Trueba's penchant for turning his violence on his workers at Tres Marias and his family creates deep tensions in the family. Esteban achieves his material goals but is not able to be close to anyone. As he ages, Esteban begins to see the negative outcomes of his actions. He helps to rescue **Pedro Tercero Garcia**, once an object of Esteban Trueba's hate, and becomes close with Alba, writing the stories of their lives with the help of Clara's notebooks, until his death at 90.

Dona Ester Trueba

The House of the Spirits
Isabel Allende

A direct descendant of one of Peru's oldest families. In her youth, Dona Ester falls in love with and marries the lower-class immigrant **Trueba**. The money she brings to the marriage quickly runs out, her husband dies, and she is afflicted by severe arthritis that confines her to a wheelchair. Trueba and Dona Ester produce a son, **Esteban Trueba**. Dona Ester dies shortly after Esteban Trueba has finished restoring Tres Marias.

Jim Trueblood

Invisible Man
Ralph Ellison

An uneducated black man who impregnated his own daughter and who lives on the outskirts of **the Narrator**'s college campus.

Trujillo

How the Garcia Girls Lost Their Accents
Julia Alvarez

Real-life Dominican dictator. In the novel, he lives next door to the de la Torre compound and takes walks with his grandson through the adjoining grounds. His secret police also threatened **Carlos**'s and others' lives.

Borthrop Trumbell

Middlemarch
George Eliot

An auctioneer in Middlemarch.

Louise Trunnion

Winesburg, Ohio
Sherwood Anderson

A local girl with whom **George Willard** has one of his first sexual experiences.

Ts'ai Yen

The Woman Warrior
Maxine Hong Kingston

A Chinese poet born in 175 a.d. After barbarians captured Ts'ai Yen and forced her to fight their battles, she brought her people, the Han, a song called "Eighteen Stanzas for a Barbarian Reed Pipe."

Ts'eh

Ceremony
Leslie Marmon Silko

A sacred figure in Laguna cosmology incarnated as a woman to help **Tayo** in his ceremony.

Tsezar Markovich

One Day in the Life of Ivan Denisovich
Aleksandr Solzhenitsyn

A fellow prisoner in **Ivan Denisovich Shukhov**'s Gang 104. He is of uncertain national background and mysterious connections. Tsezar receives regular food parcels that make him the envy of the gang. He is worldly, a man of cultivated artistic interests and luxurious tastes.

Wu Tsing

The Joy Luck Club
Amy Tan

A wealthy Chinese merchant. He took **An-mei's mother** as his third concubine, or "Fourth Wife." Wu Tsing, a coward, was manipulated by **Second Wife**. After An-mei's mother killed herself, he feared the vengeance of her ghost and promised to raise **An-mei** in wealth and status.

Tubal

The Merchant of Venice
William Shakespeare

One of **Shylock**'s friends, a Venetian Jew.

Dr. A. Dewitt Tubbs

Arrowsmith
Sinclair Lewis

The director of the McGurk Institute in New York. Tubbs is one of the many "salesmen" in the medical industry. **Martin Arrowsmith** has difficulty working with Tubbs, whom he views as unintelligent, and is annoyed by the constant pressure to publish that Tubbs puts on him.

Esmar Tuek

Dune
Frank Herbert

One of the head smugglers on Arrakis.

Staban Tuek

Dune
Frank Herbert

The son of **Esmar Tuek**. Staban assumes control of his family's smuggling operations after his father's death.

Cora Tull

As I Lay Dying
William Faulkner

Vernon Tull's wife. A deeply religious woman, Cora stays with **Addie Bundren** during Addie's last hours.

Vernon Tull

As I Lay Dying
William Faulkner

The Bundrens' wealthier neighbor. Tull both criticizes and helps the Bundrens. He hires **Darl Bundren, Jewel**, and **Cash Bundren** for odd jobs and helps the Bundrens cross the river despite their overt hostility to him.

Tullio

His Dark Materials
Robert Pullman

Angelica's older brother. Tullio attempts to steal the subtle knife from **Giacomo Paradisi** and then fights **Will Parry** for it, cutting off two fingers on Will's hand. Tullio is killed by **Specters**.

Elizabeth Tulliver

The Mill on the Floss
George Eliot

Maggie Tulliver and **Tom Tulliver**'s mother, and **Jeremy Tulliver**'s wife. Mrs. Tulliver is a dull-witted, stout, blond woman. Her maiden name is Dodson, and Mrs. Tulliver still maintains that the respectable ways of the Dodson family are better than the ways of Mr. Tulliver. Her husband's bankruptcy makes her confused and listless.

Jeremy Tulliver

The Mill on the Floss
George Eliot

Maggie Tulliver's and **Tom Tulliver**'s father. Mr. Tulliver works the mill on the Floss river, which is on land his family has held for generations. Mr. Tulliver is fond of Maggie, especially her cleverness, and he often takes her side in family quarrels. Mr. Tulliver senses the changing economic world around him and is puzzled by it. Tulliver is an affectionate man, yet his bitterness toward **Lawyer Wakem** consumes and changes him in the end.

Maggie Tulliver

The Mill on the Floss
George Eliot

The protagonist. She is the daughter of **Jeremy Tulliver** and **Elizabeth Tulliver** and the sister of **Tom Tulliver**. The novel tracks Maggie as she grows from an impetuous, clever child into a striking, unconventional young woman.

Tom Tulliver

The Mill on the Floss
George Eliot

Jeremy Tulliver and **Elizabeth Tulliver**'s older son and **Maggie Tulliver**'s brother. Tom has affection for Maggie, but he dislikes her impetuous way of doing what she wants. When Mr. Tulliver goes bankrupt, Tom must go to work at a young age and with little experience. Tom brings the family out of debt working for his uncle, **Mr. Deane**, at Guest & Co. Tom may be in love with **Lucy Deane**, but he focuses only on his work.

Tumnus

The Lion, the Witch, and the Wardrobe
C. S. Lewis

A faun. **Lucy Pevensie** meets Tumnus on her first excursion into Narnia. He initially intends to kidnap her and bring her to **the White Witch**, but he spares her life. For his crime, the Witch ransacks his home and petrifies him. Later, **Aslan** rescues Tumnus by breathing on his stone statue. Tumnus and Lucy become fast friends.

Turkey

Bartleby, the Scrivener
Herman Melville

The Lawyer's eldest employee.

Turkish Astronomer

The Little Prince
Antoine de Saint-Exupéry

The first human to discover **the Little Prince**'s home, Asteroid B-612. When the Turkish astronomer first presents his discovery, no one believes him on account of his Turkish costume. Years later, he makes the same presentation wearing Western clothes, and his discovery is well-received.

Mr. Turkle

One Flew over the Cuckoo's Nest
Ken Kesey

The black nighttime orderly for **Nurse Ratched**'s ward. Mr. Turkle is kind to **Chief Bromden** and goes along with the nighttime ward party.

Franklin Turnbo

Pigs in Heaven
Barbara Kingsolver

A lawyer on the Cherokee Nation. He is **Annawake Fourkiller**'s boss. A self-described "born-again" Cherokee, he feels guilty that he is not a better mentor for Annawake.

Turner

Fallen Angels
Walter Dean Myers

A soldier briefly in **Richie Perry**'s squad.

Mr. Turner

Their Eyes Were Watching God
Zora Neale Hurston

An Everglades resident. He runs a small restaurant with his wife, **Mrs. Turner**. **Tea Cake** plans to meet Mr. Turner in order to tell him to keep his wife away from **Janie Mae Crawford**.

Mrs. Turner

Their Eyes Were Watching God
Zora Neale Hurston

An Everglades resident who runs a small restaurant with her husband, **Mr. Turner**. She worships **Janie Mae Crawford** because of her Caucasian features. She cannot understand why a woman like Janie would marry a man as dark as **Tea Cake**, and she wants to introduce Janie to her brother.

Turnus

The Aeneid
Virgil

The ruler of the Rutulians in Italy and **Aeneas**'s major mortal antagonist. Turnus is **Lavinia**'s leading suitor until Aeneas arrives. This rivalry incites him to wage war against the Trojans, despite **Latinus**'s willingness to let the Trojans settle in Latium.

Turpin

Song of Roland
Unknown

The archbishop who fights and dies alongside **Roland** at Roncesvals. Turpin represents Christendom's turn towards militant activity at the time of the Crusades. He is the last to die besides Roland. **Charlemagne**'s men take Turpin, **Olivier** and Roland back to France for burial.

A Passage to India

Mr. Turton E. M. Forster

The stern collector (or governor) of Chandrapore.

A Passage to India

Mrs. Turton E. M. Forster

Mr. Turton's wife, the epitome of the snobby and prejudiced colonial wife.

Island of the Blue Dolphins

Tutok Scott O'Dell

One of the Aleuts who comes with a hunting party to the island and becomes friends with **Karana**. Though she belongs to the enemy tribe, the two girls are able to bridge their differences. Tutok is the first human contact Karana has in many years, and reminds her just how lonely she has been upon the island.

The Flies

Tutor Jean-Paul Sartre

The Tutor who raised and educated **Orestes**. The Tutor believes that he has given Orestes complete freedom by teaching him to avoid commitments and attachments to others. Orestes finally rejects this as a false view of freedom.

Anna Karenina

Elizaveta Fyodorovna Tverskaya Leo Tolstoy

A wealthy friend of **Anna Arkadyevna Karenina** and **Alexei Kirillovich Vronsky**'s cousin. Betsy has a reputation for wild living and moral looseness.

Johnny Tremain

Mr. Tweedie Esther Forbes

A silversmith. He becomes **Ephraim Lapham**'s business partner after **Jonathan Tremain**'s accident. When none of her daughters will marry him, **Mrs. Lapham** marries Tweedie to ensure that the silver shop stays in the Lapham family.

Through the Looking Glass

Tweedledee and Tweedledum Lewis Carroll

A pair of little fat brothers dressed as schoolboys. They are fond of dancing and poetry. They are very affectionate with one another but fight over extremely trivial matters.

Hoyt Tweedy

Cold Sassy Tree
Olive Anne Burns

Will Tweedy's father. Hoyt is a stern, pious man who loves his family and has a weak spot for modern technology. Although Hoyt is **Rucker Blakeslee**'s son-in-law and a devoted employee, he proves himself capable of standing up to his boss and defending his wife, **Mary Willis**, when the occasion calls for it.

Mary Toy Tweedy

Cold Sassy Tree
Olive Anne Burns

Will Tweedy's younger sister.

Will Tweedy

Cold Sassy Tree
Olive Anne Burns

The novel's narrator and protagonist. Will is a fourteen-year-old boy growing up Cold Sassy, Georgia at the very beginning of the twentieth century. Although he comes from a conventional family, Will is a free spirit and often feels compelled to defy the rules governing his life. Following his grandmother's death and his grandfather's second marriage, Will begins to grapple with issues of love and death, and his perspective on life begins to change.

Oliver Twist

Oliver Twist
Charles Dickens

The novel's protagonist. Oliver is between nine and twelve years old when the main action of the novel occurs. Even though he is surrounded by coarse people who treat him cruelly, Oliver is a pious, innocent child whose charms draw the attention of several wealthy benefactors.

Two-Bit

The Outsiders
S. E. Hinton

The joker of **Ponyboy Curtis**'s group. Two-Bit, whose real name is **Keith Matthews**, is a wisecracking greaser who regularly shoplifts. He instigates the hostilities between the Socs and the greasers by flirting with **Marcia**, the girlfriend of a Soc. This flirting leads to a confrontation between **Bob Sheldon**, **Randy Adderson**, **Johnny Cade**, and Ponyboy.

Huang Tyan-yu

The Joy Luck Club
Amy Tan

Lindo's first husband, in China. Huang's mother was **Huang Taitai**. When Tyan-yu and Lindo were babies, a matchmaker arranged their marriage. Pampered and self-centered, Tyan-yu makes Lindo's life extremely unpleasant when she comes to live with his family at the age of twelve. When Lindo is sixteen, they get married, but Tyan-yu remains very much a boy.

Tybalt

Romeo and Juliet
William Shakespeare

Juliet's cousin and **Lady Capulet**'s nephew. **Capulet** scolds Tybalt for taking offense at **Romeo** crashing the Capulet party, but Tybalt never forgets the incident. He later challenges Romeo to fight, and initially Romeo refuses. When **Mercutio** steps in on Romeo's behalf and is slain by Tybalt, Romeo kills Tybalt.

Millie Tydings

Dicey's Song
Cynthia Voigt

The butcher and owner of Crisfield's market. She is one of **Gram**'s oldest acquaintances. Millie is slow with words and numbers, but **Dicey** grows to respect the older woman for her steadiness and constancy of heart.

Walter Tyke

Middlemarch
George Eliot

An Evangelical Protestant minister. He is supported by **Nicholas Bulstrode**. He wins the election for the chaplaincy at the New Hospital, beating out **Camden Farebrother**.

Annie Tyler

Their Eyes Were Watching God
Zora Neale Hurston

A wealthy widow. Annie Tyler dates a young rascal, **Who Flung**, in Eatonville. Who Flung takes Annie's money and flees at the first opportunity. Early in her marriage to **Tea Cake**, **Janie Mae Crawford** fears that Tea Cake will turn out to be like Who Flung.

Miss Lizzie Tynmore

A Tree Grows in Brooklyn
Betty Smith

Poor piano instructor who lives with her sister in the Nolans' building. Lizzie is proper and punctual and never has quite enough to eat.

Edmund Tyrone

Long Day's Journey into Night
Eugene O'Neill

The younger son of **James Tyrone** and **Mary Tyrone**. He is ten years younger than his brother **Jamie Tyrone**. An intellectual and romantic dreamer, he learns during the play that he is afflicted with consumption (tuberculosis), which means that he will have to spend up to a year in a sanatorium. Mary always holds out hope that he will become a success one day.

James Tyrone

Long Day's Journey into Night
Eugene O'Neill

The husband of **Mary Tyrone** and the father of **Jamie Tyrone** and **Edmund Tyrone**. He had been a famous actor who toured the U.S. with his wife. Because his Irish father abandoned him at age ten, forcing him to work immediately to support himself, he has a strong work ethic and an appreciation for money that leads to strong financial prudence, bordering on stinginess. After Mary gave birth, Tyrone hired a very cheap doctor who foolishly gave her morphine, resulting in her addiction to the drug.

Jamie Tyrone

Long Day's Journey into Night
Eugene O'Neill

The elder son of **Mary Tyrone** and **James Tyrone**. Jamie is in his early thirties. Because he squanders money on booze and women, he has to rely on his parents for support. He dropped out of several colleges and has very little ambition, much to the dismay of his parents. Jamie is jealous of Edmund.

Mary Tyrone

Long Day's Journey into Night
Eugene O'Neill

The wife of **James Tyrone** and mother of **Jamie Tyrone** and **Edmund Tyrone**. Mary blames herself for breaking her vow never to have another baby after **Eugene**, her second baby who died at two years old from measles. She struggles with a morphine addiction that has lasted over two decades. Mary has a deep distrust of doctors, who first prescribed her morphine, and when a doctor says that her son Edmund has tuberculosis, she insists that he has nothing more than a bad cold.

Sir James Tyrrel

Richard III
William Shakespeare

A murderer. **King Richard III** hires him to kill his young cousins, **Prince Edward** and **Richard, Duke of York**, in the Tower of London. Tyrrel contracts two lowlifes to carry out the deed; and he expresses sincere remorse after the murders are carried out.

Andrei Prokofievich Tyurin

One Day in the Life of Ivan Denisovich
Aleksandr Solzhenitsyn

The foreman of **Ivan Denisovich Shukhov**'s Gang 104. Tyurin is a strict but fair man.

Tzipora

Night
Elie Wiesel

The youngest of **Eliezer**'s three sisters, all of whom perished in the concentration camps.

Han Tzu

Ender's Game
Orson Scott Card

One of **Ender Wiggin**'s leaders from Dragon Army. He works with his commander again in the war with the buggers.

15

IRREFUTABLE

JERKS

AWFUL. REPREHENSIBLE. IRRITATING. SMACKABLE.

1. **Holden Caufield** — *The Catcher in the Rye*
2. **John Claggart** — *Billy Budd, Sailor*
3. **Jason Compson IV** — *The Sound and Fury*
4. **Archie Costello** — *The Chocolate War*
5. **Kenneth** — *This Boy's Life*
6. **Krogstad** — *A Doll's House*
7. **Laban** — *The Red Tent*
8. **Lee** — *True West*
9. **Monsieur Lheureux** — *Madame Bovary*
10. **Draco Malfoy** — *Harry Potter* series, Books I-IV
11. **Iago** — *Othello*
12. **Stanley Kowalski** — *A Streetcar Named Desire*
13. **Chip Lambert** — *The Corrections*
14. **James Steerforth** — *David Copperfield*
15. **Charles Walker** — *Holes*

Uchendu

Things Fall Apart
Chinua Achebe

The younger brother of **Okonkwo**'s mother. Uchendu receives Okonkwo and his family warmly when they travel to Mbanta and he advises Okonkwo to be grateful for the comfort that his motherland offers him lest he anger the dead. All but one of his six wives are dead, and he has buried twenty-two children.

Uglúk

The Two Towers
J. R. R. Tolkien

An warrior of the **Orcs**, and captor of **Meriadoc Brandybuck** and **Peregrin Took**. **Aragorn**, **Gimli**, and **Legolas** pursue Uglúk and his fellow Orcs in order to try to save the Hobbits, who are being kept alive to be brought to **Saruman**. Uglúk is killed in battle at the hands of **Éomer**.

Count Ugolino

Inferno
Dante Alighieri

A traitor. He is condemned to gnaw the head of traitor **Archbishop Ruggieri** in Antenora, the Second Ring of the Ninth Circle of Hell (XXXIII). Count Ugolino is condemned because he ate the corpses of his dead children when dying of hunger.

Ulape

Island of the Blue Dolphins
Scott O'Dell

Karana's older sister. Ulape is extremely feminine, whereas Karana is more of a tomboy. When she is left behind on the island, Karana often finds herself wondering what happened to her sister.

Ulrica

Ivanhoe
Sir Walter Scott

A Saxon crone. She has lived her life as a consort to the Norman rulers of Torquilstone. At the end of the battle for the castle, she burns it to the ground, taunting **Reginald Front-de-Boeuf** and singing a death song as the flames slowly engulf her.

Ultima

Bless Me, Ultima
Rudolfo A. Anaya

An elderly curandera, or healer, endowed with the spiritual power of her ancestors. When **Antonio Márez** is six, Antonio's parents, **Gabriel Márez** and **María Márez**, invite Ultima to come live with them. Ultima fights against the curses of **Tenorio Trementina** and the **Trementina daughters**, and for this, Tenorio kills her owl, and consequently, kills Ultima. Before she dies, Ultima tells Antonio that **Ultima's teacher** taught her to do good works with her powers, but not to interfere with destiny.

Ultima's teacher

Bless Me, Ultima
Rudolfo A. Anaya

A man also known as *el hombre volador*, or "the flying man." He gave **Ultima** the owl that became her spirit familiar, her guardian.

Ulysses

The Aeneid
Virgil

One of the captains of the Greek army that takes Troy. Like **Aeneas**, Ulysses must make a long and treacherous voyage before he finds home again. References to his whereabouts help situate Aeneas's wanderings in relation to Ulysses's. In the Greek tradition, Ulysses is known as **Odysseus**.

Ulysses

Inferno
Dante Alighieri

The great hero of the Homeric epics *The Iliad* and *The Odyssey*. Ulysses is imprisoned among the False Counselors in the Eighth Pouch of the Eighth Circle of Hell for his participation in the Trojan horse ruse (Canto XXVI).

Ulysses

Troilus and Cressida
William Shakespeare

A Greek commander. A highly intelligent, even philosophical man, Ulysses is renowned for his cunning.

Umbriel

The Rape of the Lock
Alexander Pope

The chief gnome, who travels to the Cave of Spleen and returns with bundles of sighs and tears to aggravate **Belinda**'s vexation.

Una

The Faerie Queene
Edmund Spenser

Redcrosse's future wife. She is one of the major protagonists in Book I. She is meek, humble, and beautiful, but strong when necessary. She represents Truth, which Redcrosse must find in order to be a true Christian.

Unbaby

The Handmaid's Tale
Margaret Atwood

A malformed or otherwise "defective" baby, discarded at birth.

Uncas

The Last of the Mohicans
James Fenimore Cooper

Chingachgook's son, and the last Mohican Native American. A noble, proud, self-possessed young man, Uncas falls in love with **Cora Munro**, a woman of mixed race and **Colonel Munro**'s daughter. **Hawkeye** mentors Uncas. Uncas eventually becomes a natural leader of men by combining the skill of Hawkeye with the spirituality of a revered Native American leader.

Underground man

Notes from Underground
Fyodor Dostoevsky

The anonymous narrator and protagonist of the novel. He lives with his servant, **Appalon**, and tries to save **Liza**, a prostitute. He is a minor civil servant living in nineteenth-century St. Petersburg who has retired into a state of total alienation and isolation from society. Severely misanthropic, the Underground Man believes himself to be more intelligent and perceptive than most other people in the world, but he also despises himself and frequently feels himself to be inferior or humiliated.

Andrew Undershaft

Major Barbara
George Bernard Shaw

A great arms industrialist of Europe. Undershaft was a foundling who inherited a great armory, and he intends to bequest the armory to another foundling rather than to his biological son **Stephen Undershaft.** Long estranged from his family, his return to the Undershaft household ruffles the entire family, especially his daughter **Barbara**, whose Christian sensibilities directly conflict with Andrew's worship of expediency and the dollar.

Lady Britomart Undershaft

Major Barbara
George Bernard Shaw

Stephen, **Barbara**, and **Sarah Undershaft**'s mother. Upon **Andrew Undershaft**'s arrival, the family—and Stephen Undershaft in particular—will abandon her, as she is too set in her ways to participate in the revolution he brings.

Sarah Undershaft

Major Barbara
George Bernard Shaw

Barbara's younger sister. Sarah is a "slender, bored, and mundane" society girl.

Stephen Undershaft

Major Barbara
George Bernard Shaw

Lady Britomart's only son. Stephen is a "gravely correct young man" who takes himself and his sense of morality very seriously. He remains in some awe from his mother but quickly comes to assert his majority in planning his future. He resents that his father **Andrew Undershaft** chooses not to bequest the family armory to him.

Mr. Underwood

To Kill a Mockingbird
Harper Lee

The publisher of Maycomb's newspaper. Mr. Underwood respects **Atticus Finch** and proves to be his ally. After **Tom Robinson** is shot while trying to escape, Mr. Underwood writes a long editorial condemning Tom's death as the murder of an innocent man.

Unferth

Beowulf
Unknown

A Danish warrior who is jealous of **Beowulf**. Though Unferth is quick to point out Beowulf's potential cowardice during his legendary swimming race against **Breca**, Unferth's unwillingness to fight **Grendel** proves his cowardice and inferiority to Beowulf.

Unferth

Grendel
John Gardner

A Scylding hero who is unable to defeat **Grendel** in battle. Unferth believes wholeheartedly in the heroic ideals of his warrior culture. When Grendel denies Unferth the opportunity to embody those ideals, he becomes a bitter and broken man.

Unoka

Things Fall Apart
Chinua Achebe

Okonkwo's father. Okonkwo has been ashamed of him since childhood. By the standards of the clan, Unoka was a coward and a spendthrift.

Unwoman

The Handmaid's Tale
Margaret Atwood

Any female enemy of the state.

Horace Updike

Babbitt
Sinclair Lewis

A man who tries to seduce **Lucile McKelvey**.

Uranus

Greek Mythology
Unknown

The Latin form of the Greek god **Ouranos**.

Dr. Juvenal Urbino del Calle

Love in the Time of Cholera
Gabriel García Márquez

The City of the Viceroy's most educated doctor and most esteemed public figure, as he made advances against the cholera epidemic. Unlike **Florentino Ariza**, who is of the peasant class, Dr. Urbino del Calle is entirely passionless, taking pleasure in little but chess, medicine, and foreign books. He does not make much of Florentino's pining away for **Fermina Daza**, nor does he care if Florentino is waiting for Dr. Urbino del Calle to die. When he is enfeebled by his old age, having to be dressed and cared for by his wife, Dr. Urbino del Calle suffers a fatal fall from a mango tree when he tries to recapture his escaped, beloved parrot.

Ofelia Urbino

Love in the Time of Cholera
Gabriel García Márquez

The miserable daughter of **Fermina Daza** and **Dr. Juvenal Urbino del Calle**. Fermina Daza banishes Ofelia Urbino from Fermina Daza's home when Ofelia protests her mother's courtship with **Florentino Ariza**.

Uriel

Paradise Lost
John Milton

An angel who guards the planet Earth. Uriel is the angel whom **Satan** tricks when he is disguised as a cherub. Uriel, as a good angel and guardian, tries to correct his error by making the other angels aware of Satan's presence.

Ur-Shanabi

The Epic of Gilgamesh
Unknown

The guardian of the mysterious "stone things." Urshanabi ferries people across the waters of death to **Utanapishtim**'s dwelling. He loses this privilege when he accepts **Gilgamesh** as a passenger, so he returns with him to Uruk.

Ursula

Much Ado About Nothing
William Shakespeare

One of **Hero**'s serving women. She conspires with Hero and **Margaret** to trick **Beatrice** into falling in love with **Benedick**. Unlike Margaret, Ursula is of a slightly higher class and carries herself with more decorum.

Uruk-hai

The Two Towers
J. R. R. Tolkien

A fearsome breed of **Orcs** specially created by **Saruman** to be able to withstand daylight. Saruman keeps breeding these Orcs so that he can win battles in the name of **Sauron** against Minas Tirith, Rohan, and all of the Good Peoples of Middle-earth.

Madeline Usher

"The Fall of the House of Usher"
Edgar Allan Poe

Roderick Usher's cataplectic twin sister.

Roderick Usher

"The Fall of the House of Usher"
Edgar Allan Poe

The owner of the mansion. He is the last male in the Usher line and the doppelganger, or character double, of his twin sister, **Madeline Usher**. Roderick is intellectual and bookish, and Madeline ill and bedridden. Roderick is unable to distinguish fantasy from reality.

Uncle Ustace

The Member of the Wedding
Carson McCullers

A relative of **Frankie Addams** and **Royal Quincy Addams**. At the end of the novella, Frankie and her father get ready to move into a suburban house with **Aunt Pet** and Uncle Ustace.

Utnapishtim

The Epic of Gilgamesh
Unknown

A king and priest of Shurrupak. By the god **Ea**'s connivance, Utnapishtim survived the great deluge that destroyed most life on earth, when he built a great boat that carried him, his family, and one of every living creature to safety. The gods granted him and his family eternal life. Utnapishtim received a promise from the gods that henceforth only individuals would die and that humankind as a whole would endure. For this reason, he counsels **Gilgamesh** to accept the inevitability of death.

Utnapishtim's wife

The Epic of Gilgamesh
Unknown

An unnamed woman. She softens her husband, **Utnapishtim**, toward **Gilgamesh**, persuading him to disclose the secret of the magic plant called "How-the-Old-Man-Once-Again-Becomes-a-Young-Man."

General Utopus

Utopia
Sir Thomas More

Ancient warrior and founder of Utopia. He conquered the savages who once lived on the isthmus Utopia now occupies, and then set his army and new subjects to work cutting the land away to make Utopia an island.

Mr. Gabriel John Utterson

Dr. Jekyll and Mr. Hyde
Robert Louis Stevenson

A prominent lawyer. He is a friend of **Dr. Henry Jekyll** and **Dr. Hastie Lanyon**. Utterson is reserved and dignified, but he has a furtive curiosity about the sordid side of life.

Okagbue Uyanwa

Things Fall Apart
Chinua Achebe

A famous medicine man. **Okonkwo** summons him for help in dealing with **Ezinma**'s health problems.

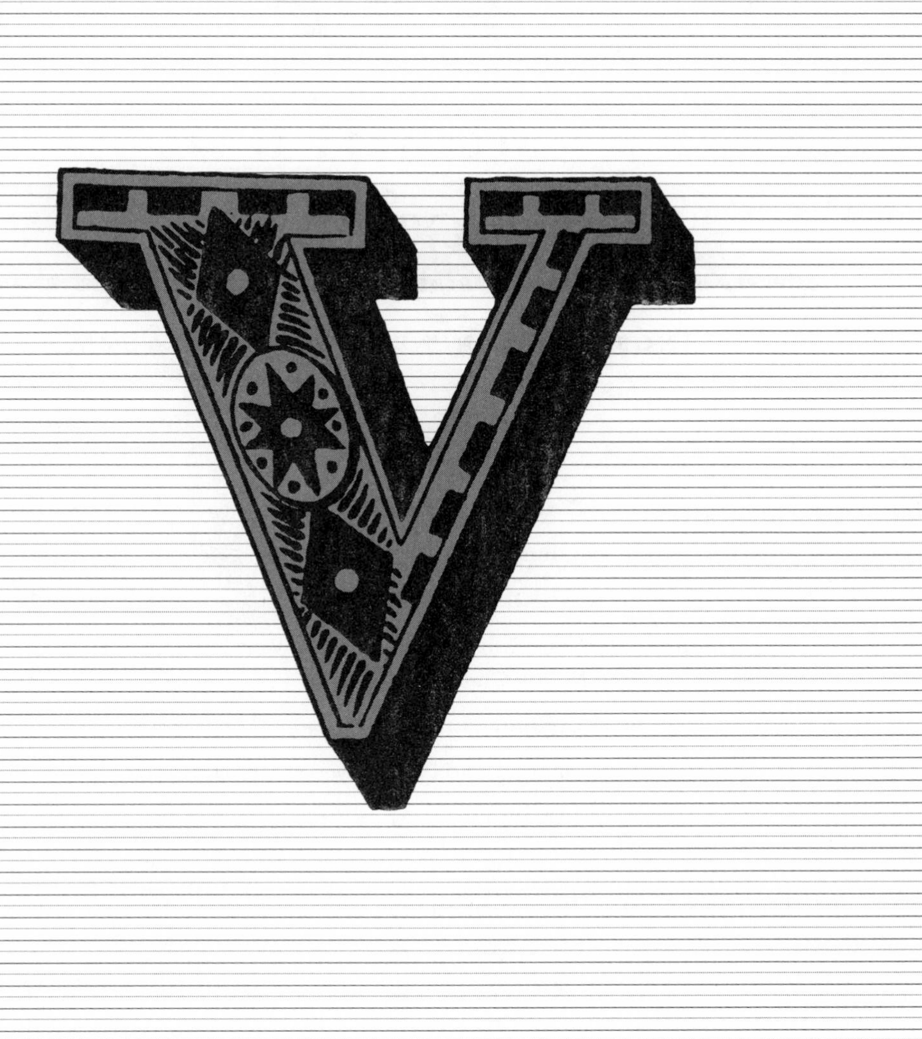

15

MURDER VICTIMS

THINGS JUST DON'T END WELL FOR THEM.

Agamemnon	1	*Agamemnon*
Banquo	2	*Macbeth*
Billy Budd	3	*Billy Budd, Sailor*
Julius Caesar	4	*Julius Caesar*
Claudius	5	*Hamlet*
Bonnie, Herbert, Kenyon, and Nancy Clutter	6	*In Cold Blood*
Clytemnestra	7	*Electra*
Macon Dead I	8	*Song of Solomon*
Desdemona	9	*Othello*
Horatio	10	*Spanish Tragedy*
Brigadier-General Ezra Mannon	11	*Mourning Becomes Electra*
Polonius	12	*Hamlet*
Rebecca	13	*Rebecca*
Susie Salmon	14	*The Lovely Bones*
Jaques Sauniere	15	*The Da Vinci Code*

David Vaccaro

Dead Man Walking
Helen Prejean

Robert Willie's accomplice in the murder of **Faith Hathaway**.

Cherry Valance

The Outsiders
S. E. Hinton

The girlfriend of **Bob Sheldon**. Cherry Valance is a Soc cheerleader whom **Ponyboy Curtis** meets at the movies. Cherry's real name is Sherry, but people call her Cherry because of her red hair. Ponyboy and Cherry have a great deal in common, and Ponyboy feels comfortable talking to her. In the days preceding the rumble, Cherry becomes a spy for the greasers.

Erik Valborg

Main Street
Sinclair Lewis

A young tailor in his twenties. He finds himself ridiculed by the townspeople because of his attractive feminine appearance and interest in books. **Erik** embarks on a romantic friendship with **Carol Kennicott**, much to her delight, but leaves Gopher Prairie to avoid creating a scandal.

Valdes

Doctor Faustus
Christopher Marlowe

One of **Faustus**'s magician friends who teach him black magic.

Tommy Valdon

I Know Why the Caged Bird Sings
Maya Angelou

An eighth-grader who writes **Maya Johnson** a valentine. Maya reacts with hostility at first, distrusting any man's advances after her rape by **Mr. Freeman**. She softens when Tommy writes her another letter showing that his interest in her is sincere.

M. Valenod

The Red and the Black
Stendhal

A bourgeois liberal and **M. de Rênal**'s nemesis. M. Valenod has made his fortune by running the local poorhouse, cheating the less fortunate of society out of what little money they have. He is jealous of **Julien Sorel**'s affair with **Mme. de Rênal** and proudly takes revenge upon Sorel by voting for Sorel's execution after Sorel shoots and wounds Mme. de Rênal.

Valentine

The Two Gentlemen of Verona
William Shakespeare

Proteus's noble best friend, **Silvia**'s sweetheart, and one of the title gentlemen of Verona. Banished from Milan after Proteus betrays him to the **Duke of Milan** by revealing his plan to elope with Silvia, Valentine becomes king of the outlaws. Even after Proteus's cruel betrayal and attempted rape of Silvia, Valentine offers her to him as a make-up gift.

Dr. Valentini

A Farewell to Arms
Ernest Hemingway

A cheerful, energetic, and competent Italian surgeon who operates on **Frederic Henry**'s leg.

Valeria

Coriolanus
William Shakespeare

A Roman noblewoman. Valeria is close friends with **Virgilia** and **Volumnia**.

Valeria

Lolita
Vladimir Nabokov

Humbert Humbert's first wife. He married her to cure himself of his addiction to nymphets. Humbert finds her intellectually inferior and often bullies her. When he plans to move to America, Valeria leaves him to marry a Russian taxi driver. They both die in California years later.

Valerie

The Bell Jar
Sylvia Plath

A friend of **Esther Greenwood**'s in the private mental hospital. Valerie has had a lobotomy.

Valerie

The Princess Bride
William Goldman

Miracle Max's wife. Valerie has lost her hearing but still knows how to subtly coerce her husband.

Valerie

Girl, Interrupted
Susanna Kaysen

The head nurse on **Susanna Kaysen**'s ward. The girls like and respect Valerie for her fairness and willingness to speak up on their behalf.

Valerius

The Two Noble Kinsmen
William Shakespeare

A messenger from Creon to **Palamon** and **Arcite**.

Joe Valery

East of Eden
John Steinbeck

An escaped convict employed as a bouncer at **Cathy Ames**'s brothel. As Cathy degenerates into madness, Joe assumes increasing influence and control over her brothel. Before Cathy kills herself, she informs the police about Joe's earlier jailbreak. Just as Joe is about to leave town with Cathy's money, he is found and gunned down by a deputy.

Valet

No Exit
Jean-Paul Sartre

A taciturn representative of the devil. He shows each prisoner to their room, answers their questions, and promptly leaves. There is a call bell in the room, but he doesn't always answer it.

Valet de Chambre

Pudd'nhead Wilson
Mark Twain

Roxana's son. Valet de Chambre is also known as Chambers. At three months old he is switched by his mother with **Thomas a Becket Driscoll**, a white child of Roxy's master, **Percy Northumberland Driscoll**. After the switch, Chambers is known as "Tom," and Tom is known as "Chambers." Raised as a white heir to a substantial estate, "Tom" is spoiled, vicious, and dissolute. When Roxy returns to the town of Dawson's Landing she starts hounding "Tom," eventually revealing to him the truth about his real parents. She pressures him for money, forces him to sell her as a slave and then forces him to buy her back again. Tom steals **Luigi Capello**'s knife and kills **Judge Driscoll** with it, blaming Luigi and **Angelo Capello**. He is eventually incriminated by **Pudd'nhead Wilson**'s fingerprinting system and revealed as Chambers.

Jean Valjean

Les Misérables
Victor Hugo

Cosette's adopted father. Valjean is an ex-convict who leaves behind a life of hatred and deceit and makes his fortune with his innovative industrial techniques. Valjean is followed by the police inspector **Javert**, but convinces Javert to release him. Valjean preaches forgiveness, explaining that love is the most important thing that exists.

Valkyries

Norse Mythology
Unknown

The female warriors who select and ferry dead warriors to Valhalla.

Vicomte de Valmont

Dangerous Liaisons
Pierre-Ambroise-François Choderlos de Laclos

A rich playboy. He was at one time the **Marquise de Merteuil**'s lover and confidant. He was also once the lover of **the Intendante**, who left him for **the Comte de Gercourt**. The Comte de Gercourt left Merteuil for the Intendante. **Madame Volanges** has arranged that her daughter, **Cécile Volanges** will marry Gercourt, so Merteuil suggests that Valmont deflower Cécile in revenge. In the end, to defend the honor of Cécile, **the Chevalier Danceny** kills Valmont in a duel. Valmont's aunt, **Madame de Rosemonde**, does not press charges because she knows if she does, damning evidence will also come out against her dead nephew.

Luigi Vampa

The Count of Monte Cristo
Alexandre Dumas

A famous Roman bandit. Luigi Vampa pledges undying loyalty to **Edmond Dantès**, who is playing the part of **the Count of Monte Cristo**, because Monte Cristo buys the freedom of **Peppino**, a man who was sentenced to public beheading for feeding Vampa and his bandits. Later, Monte Cristo and Vampa make a deal in which Vampa kidnaps **Albert de Morcerf** so that Monte Cristo can save Albert, gaining trust and friendship from Morcerf, whose father, **Fernand Mondego**, is one of Dantès' enemies.

Miss Van Campen

A Farewell to Arms
Ernest Hemingway

The superintendent of nurses at the American hospital in Milan where **Catherine Barkley** works. Miss Van Campen is strict, cold, and unpleasant. She disapproves of **Frederic Henry** and remains on cool terms with him throughout his stay in the hospital.

Mr. Van Daan

Anne Frank: Diary of a Young Girl
Anne Frank

The father of the family who hides in the annex along with **Anne Frank**, **Edith Frank**, **Margot Frank**, and **Otto Frank**. Mr. Van Daan had worked with Otto Frank as an herbal specialist in Amsterdam. Mr. Van Daan is temperamental, especially with his wife, with whom he fights frequently and openly. He died in the gas chambers at Auschwitz in October or November of 1944.

Peter van Daan

Anne Frank: Diary of a Young Girl
Anne Frank

The teenage son of **Mr. Van Daan** and **Petronella van Daan**. **Anne Frank** first sees Peter as obnoxious, but during their time in the annex, Anne and Peter develop a romantic attraction, which **Otto Frank** discourages. **Edith Frank** forbids Anne from going upstairs to see Peter because Petronella is jealous. Peter is Anne's first kiss and her one confidant and source of affection and attention in the annex. Peter died on May 5, 1945, at the concentration camp at Mauthausen, only three days before the camp was liberated.

Petronella van Daan

Anne Frank: Diary of a Young Girl
Anne Frank

Mr. van Daan's wife. **Anne Frank** initially describes Mrs. van Daan as a friendly, teasing woman, but later calls her an instigator. She argues frequently with **Edith Frank**. Mrs. van Daan also teases Anne for her relationship with **Peter van Daan**. Mrs. van Daan did not survive the war, but the exact date of her death is unknown.

Henry and Louisa van der Luyden

The Age of Innocence
Edith Wharton

Elderly descendants of pre-Revolutionary Dutch aristocracy. They are the last word in social authority. Very quiet and non-adventurous people, they rarely make public appearances and even more rarely invite guests to their solemn Madison Avenue mansion.

Van Helsing

Dracula
Bram Stoker

A Dutch professor. Called upon to cure the ailing **Lucy Westenra**, Van Helsing's contributions are essential in the fight against **Count Dracula**. Unlike his comrades, Van Helsing is not blinded by the limitations of Western medicine: he knows that he faces a force that cannot be treated with traditional science and reason. Knowledgeable about vampire folklore, Van Helsing becomes the leader of the group that hunts Dracula down and destroys him.

Mrs. Van Hopper

Rebecca
Daphne du Maurier

A vulgar, gossipy and wealthy American woman. She employs **the Heroine** as a companion while she travels from one European resort town to another.

Alexander Van Ness

Snow Falling on Cedars
David Guterson

A local boat builder and member of the jury in **Kabuo Miyamoto**'s trial. Van Ness does not believe the evidence proves Kabuo's guilt beyond a reasonable doubt, and he refuses to convict the fisherman of murder until the other jurors convince him of Kabuo's guilt.

Peter Van Ryberg

Childhood's End
Arthur C. Clarke

Stormgren's assistant and the deputy-general of the United Nations.

Captain Willem van Tromp

Stranger in a Strange Land
Robert A. Heinlein

Captain of the Envoy mission that discovers **Valentine Michael Smith** on Mars.

Kommandant van Zyl

The Power of One
Bryce Courtenay

Head of the Barberton prison. A simple man, he enjoys "braais" (barbecues), "tiekiedraais" (dances), and often commissions **Doc** to give piano concerts. He is notorious for taking the credit for inventions of other people.

Mrs. Josephine Vanbruuker-Brown

Alas, Babylon
Pat Frank

The former secretary of health, education and welfare. She becomes president of the U.S.A. after nuclear weapons wipe out Washington.

Eileen Vance

A Portrait of the Artist as a Young Man
James Joyce

The Dedaluses' young neighbor. **Stephen Dedalus**'s childish wish to marry the Protestant Eileen Vance angers **Dante**.

Mrs. Vance

Sister Carrie
Theodore Dreiser

Carrie's neighbor in New York City for a time. As Mrs. Vance and Carrie become friends, Carrie notices Mrs. Vance's status as a wealthy, well-kept wife and subsequently becomes dissatisfied with **Hurstwood**'s modest income.

Vanderdendur

Candide
Voltaire

A cruel slave owner and unscrupulous merchant. After he steals one of **Candide**'s jewel-laden sheep, his ship sinks in a battle.

James Vane

The Picture of Dorian Gray
Oscar Wilde

Sibyl Vane's brother, a sailor bound for Australia. James cares deeply for his sister and worries about her relationship with **Dorian Gray**. Distrustful of his mother's motives, he believes that **Mrs. Vane**'s interest in Dorian's wealth prevents her from properly protecting Sibyl.

Mrs. Vane

The Picture of Dorian Gray
Oscar Wilde

Sibyl Vane and **James Vane**'s mother. Mrs. Vane is a faded actress who has consigned herself and her daughter to a tawdry theater company, the owner of which has helped her to pay her debts. She considers **Dorian Gray** a wonderful match for her daughter because of his wealth.

Sibyl Vane

The Picture of Dorian Gray
Oscar Wilde

A poor, beautiful, and talented actress with whom **Dorian Gray** falls in love. Sibyl's love for Dorian compromises her ability to act, as her experience of true love in life makes her realize the falseness of affecting emotions onstage.

Captain Vangs

Typee
Herman Melville

The Captain of the **Dolly**. Captain Vangs is a cruel captain who overworks his crew and fails to care for their needs. While Captain Vangs tries to enslave his crew in a barren landscape without food, **Mehevi** offers up food and feasts to his people in the lush Polynesian valley.

Duke of Vanholt

Doctor Faustus
Christopher Marlowe

A German nobleman whom **Faustus** visits.

Vanita

Midnight's Children
Salman Rushdie

Saleem's biological mother, who dies during labor.

Adèle Varens

Jane Eyre
Charlotte Brontë

Jane Eyre's pupil at Thornfield. Adèle is a lively, somewhat spoiled child from France. **Rochester** brought her to Thornfield after her mother, **Celine Varens**, abandoned her. Although Celine was once **Edward Rochester**'s mistress, he does not think he is Adèle's father.

Celine Varens

Jane Eyre
Charlotte Brontë

A French opera dancer with whom **Edward Rochester** once had an affair. Although Rochester does not believe Celine's claims that he fathered her daughter, **Adèle Varens**, he nonetheless brought the girl to England after Celine abandons her. Rochester had broken off his relationship with Celine after learning that Celine was unfaithful to him and interested only in his money.

Junior Varney

I Am the Cheese
Robert Cormier

A known thief who steals **Adam Farmer**'s bike. Junior Varney is another resident of the institution where Adam is.

Varvara Andreevna

Anna Karenina
Leo Tolstoy

A pure and high-minded young woman who becomes **Ekaterina Alexandrovna Shcherbatskaya**'s friend at the German spa. Varenka, who is a protégée of **Madame Stahl**, nearly receives a marriage proposal from **Sergei Ivanovich Koznyshev**.

Varya

The Cherry Orchard
Anton Chekhov

Ranevksy's adopted daughter. She is in love with the businessman **Lopakhin**, but she doubts that he will ever propose to her. Varya is hardworking and responsible. She is the estate's manager, so she will lose her job if Ranevsky loses the estate. She is left in tears at the end of the play when Lopakhin neglects to propose to her when he levels the orchard.

Vasudeva

Siddhartha
Hermann Hesse

Siddhartha's mentor. Vasudeva is one of the many names of the god Krishna. He carries Siddhartha twice across the symbolic river and ends up making him an apprentice ferryman, so that Siddhartha may stay with him to learn the river's secrets. He is kind and wise, always speaking exactly what is in Siddhartha's mind and what Siddhartha knows to be the truth. Upon Siddhartha's enlightenment, the elder ferryman leaves him to the river and goes off into the woods to die.

Richard III
William Shakespeare

Sir Thomas Vaughan

A friend of **Queen Elizabeth**'s. **King Richard III** has Vaughan executed along with **Lord Rivers** and **Lord Grey**.

The Hours
Michael Cunningham

Clarissa Vaughn

One of the three major characters. She is an editor who lives in a lovely apartment in the West Village of Manhattan with her lover, **Sally**. She is cheerfully domestic, but at the same time, she is going through a mid-life crisis, in which she remembers her youth and feels wistful at its vanishing. Clarissa roughly corresponds to *Mrs. Dalloway*'s title character.

Little Women
Louisa May Alcott

Frank Vaughn

One of the Vaughn siblings. Frank is sickly.

Little Women
Louisa May Alcott

Fred Vaughn

One of the Vaughn siblings. Fred is **Laurie Laurence**'s friend, but he soon develops a romantic interest in **Amy March**.

Little Women
Louisa May Alcott

Grace Vaughn

The youngest sister of the Vaughn family. Grace and **Amy March** become friends on a picnic.

Little Women
Louisa May Alcott

Kate Vaughn

One of **Laurie Laurence**'s British friends. At first, Kate turns up her nose at the bluntness and poverty of the Marches. She later overcomes her initial prejudice and decides that she likes them.

Henry VIII
William Shakespeare

Sir Nicholas Vaux

A lord of the court. Saddled with unpleasant responsibility of escorting the **Duke of Buckingham** to his execution, Vaux orders his ship to be fitted with furniture that would suit the greatness of the duke.

Solomon Veasey

Cold Mountain
Charles Frazier

A preacher. **Inman** exposes him for trying to murder his pregnant lover, **Laura Foster**. Veasey reunites with Inman on his journey west, proving to be an unintentionally dangerous, though humorous, traveling companion.

Nikolay Nikolayevich Vedenyapin

Dr. Zhivago
Boris Pasternak

The uncle of **Yury Andreyevich Zhivago**. He becomes a famous writer and settles in Switzerland but later returns to Russia.

Maurice Venice

Seize the Day
Saul Bellow

The fraudulent talent scout from **Tommy Wilhelm**'s past. Maurice Venice initially is attracted to Tommy because of his good looks, but later refuses to work with him after a failed screen test.

Diggory Venn

The Return of the Native
Thomas Hardy

A semi-nomadic "reddleman," a man who travels selling the dye that farmers use to mark their sheep. As a consequence of his exposure to the dye, his entire body and everything he owns are dyed red. He watches over **Thomasin Yeobright**'s interests throughout the novel, but also preserves his own interests: he has long been in love with her, and at the end of the novel they marry. Venn is clever and insightful, and can be a devious schemer.

Uncle Venner

The House of the Seven Gables
Nathaniel Hawthorne

A colorful figure in the small New England village. Uncle Venner preaches a philosophy of undaunted optimism in spite of his poverty. He provides friendship to the lonely **Clifford Pyncheon** and **Hepzibah Pyncheon**, as well as to **Phoebe Pyncheon** and **Holgrave.** In the end, Uncle Venner moves with Phoebe, Clifford, Hepzibah, and Holgrave into **Judge Jaffrey Pyncheon**'s lavish out-of-town estate.

Ventidius

Antony and Cleopatra
William Shakespeare

A Roman soldier under **Antony**'s command. Ventidius leads the legions to victory against the kingdom of Parthia. Although a competent fighter, he cautiously decides not to push his troops further into battle, for fear that winning too much glory would sour his relationship with Antony.

Ventidius

Timon of Athens
William Shakespeare

One of **Timon**'s friends. Timon pays to get Ventidius out of prison, but Ventidius feels no obligation to help Timon in turn.

Venus

The Aeneid
Virgil

The Roman name for the Greek goddess **Aphrodite**; the goddess of love, beauty, and romance, and one of **Jupiter**'s daughters. Venus's son is the great Trojan warrior **Aeneas**, and so Venus remains on the side of the Trojans throughout the Trojan War.

The Verdurins

Swann's Way
Marcel Proust

The couple who introduce **Odette** to **Charles Swann** and then to the **Comte de Forcheville**. They have no class, intelligence, culture, or social distinction.

Captain Edward Fairfax Vere

Billy Budd, Sailor
Herman Melville

Captain of H.M.S. *Bellipotent*. A bachelor of aristocratic lineage, the Honorable Edward Fairfax Vere has made his mark as a distinguished sailor. When **John Claggart** accuses **Billy Budd** of mutinous plans in front of Vere, Billy speechlessly punches and kills Claggart. Vere feels sympathy toward Billy, but convenes a drumhead court to try him and urges the surprised jury to disregard their own feelings of compassion and punish Billy according to the letter of the law. Vere is racked with guilt after putting the law ahead of his conscience.

Verges

Much Ado About Nothing
William Shakespeare

Dogberry's deputy. Though they successfully apprehend **Borachio** and **Conrad**, Verges and Dogberry's verbal gaffes make it impossible to warn **Leonato** of the treachery in time.

Lady Verinder

The Moonstone
Wilkie Collins

Rachel Verinder's mother, and an honest and just mistress to her household in Yorkshire. She suffers from heart disease and dies.

Rachel Verinder

The Moonstone
Wilkie Collins

Lady Verinder's only daughter. She receives the Moonstone on her eighteenth birthday, only to have it stolen that night. Rachel is a straightforward and impassioned heroine. She is in love with **Franklin Blake**.

Katerina Ivanovna Verkhovtseva

The Brothers Karamazov
Fyodor Dostoevsky

Dmitri Fyodorovich Karamazov's fiancée, whom he abandons after falling in love with **Agrafena Alexandrovna Svetlov**a. The proud and sensitive daughter of a military captain, Katerina anguishes over her ill treatment by Dmitri, which leads her to adopt an attitude of martyrdom toward those around her.

She insists on humiliating herself with an unfailing loyalty to the people who hurt her, and though she loves **Ivan Fyodorovich Karamazov**, she is unable to act on her love until the end of the novel.

André Vernet

The Da Vinci Code
Dan Brown

The president of the Paris branch of the Depository Bank of Zurich. Vernet was a friend of **Jacques Saunière**'s, and sworn protector of his secret. The immaculately groomed Vernet lives among the rich but wishes only to be immersed in culture.

John Vernon

Henry VI, Part I
William Shakespeare

A follower of the **Richard Plantagenet, Duke of York**.

Sir Richard Vernon

Henry IV, Part I
William Shakespeare

A relative and ally of the **Earl of Worcester**. Vernon is the bad-news messenger who delivers information to **Hotspur** and Worcester.

Versh

The Sound and the Fury
William Faulkner

One of **Dilsey**'s sons.

Madame Alexandra Vesant

Stranger in a Strange Land
Robert A. Heinlein

An acquaintance of **Jubal Harshaw**'s from decades earlier when she worked under a master astrologer. Becky Vesey has taken on the professional name Madame Vesant and become an astrologer herself, catering to wealthy customers, including **Agnes Douglas**. Her primary avocation is investing her earnings in the stock market.

Vasenka Veslovsky

Anna Karenina
Leo Tolstoy

A young, pleasant, somewhat dandyish man whom **Stepan Arkadyich Oblonsky** brings to visit **Konstantin Dmitrich Levin**. The attention Veslovsky lavishes on **Ekaterina Alexandrovna Shcherbatskaya** make Levin jealous.

The Veteran

Invisible Man
Ralph Ellison

An institutionalized black man. He claims to have graduated from **the Narrator**'s college. The veteran exposes the blindness and hypocrisy of the narrator and **Mr. Norton**.

Angela Vicario

Chronicle of a Death Foretold
Gabriel García Márquez

The dishonored bride of **Bayardo San Roman**. Her husband returns her to her family upon discovering she is not a virgin. Her family learns that she lost her virginity to **Santiago Nasar**. Her brothers, **Pablo Vicario** and **Pedro Vicario**, head out to kill Santiago. She ends up in a town called Guarija, making her living as an embroiderer.

Pablo Vicario

Chronicle of a Death Foretold
Gabriel García Márquez

The twin of **Pedro Vicario**. He insists they follow through with their plan to kill **Santiago Nasar**. He is betrothed to **Prudencia Cotes**, whom he marries when he is released from jail.

Pedro Vicario

Chronicle of a Death Foretold
Gabriel García Márquez

The twin of **Pablo Vicario**. It is his idea to kill **Santiago Nasar**. He spent some time in the army, and after being released from prison he joins the army once more and is never heard from again.

Poncio Vicario

Chronicle of a Death Foretold
Gabriel García Márquez

Angela Vicario's father. He used to work as a goldsmith until the strain of the profession made him go blind. He dies shortly after his twin sons, **Pedro Vicario** and **Pablo Vicario**, are sent to prison.

The Viceroy

The Spanish Tragedy
Thomas Kyd

The King's counterpart in Portugal. He is defeated in battle, wallows in self-pity when he believes his son **Balthazar** to be dead, and is easily led astray by **Villuppo** into condemning **Alexandro**.

Dr. Vickerson

Arrowsmith
Sinclair Lewis

A country doctor in **Martin Arrowsmith**'s hometown of Elk Mills. Although he is an alcoholic and highly disorganized, Vickerson supports Martin in the direction of scholarship and medicine.

Vicomte de Valvert

Cyrano de Bergerac
Edmond Rostand

Comte de Guiche's protégé. He is an insolent young nobleman. De Guiche wants to marry Valvert and **Roxane**, a scheme that would give de Guiche access to Roxane. **Cyrano** defeats Valvert in a duel after Valvert insults Cyrano's nose.

Victoire

Dangerous Liaisons
Pierre-Ambroise-François Choderlos de Laclos

The **Marquise de Merteuil**'s chambermaid. Victoire helps Merteuil in the plan to ruin **Prévan**.

Victor

The Picture of Dorian Gray
Oscar Wilde

Dorian Gray's servant. Although Victor is trustworthy, Dorian becomes suspicious of him and sends him out on needless errands to ensure that he does not attempt to steal a glance at Dorian's portrait.

Victor

On the Road
Jack Kerouac

A kind, polite Mexican who serves as **Sal Paradise**, **Dean Moriarty**, and **Stan Shephard**'s guide in Gregoria.

Victoria

A Death in the Family
James Agee

A woman who helps deliver **Little Catherine**.

Victoria

Cloud Nine
Caryl Churchill

A two-year-old baby played by a dummy. Like others in her family, Victoria is prone to dependence and uncertainty. She is usually non-confrontational, preferring the role of peacemaker. The second act marks her search for independence, first leaving her husband **Martin** to become **Lin**'s lesbian lover, then taking her brother **Edward** into their home for a sexual threesome, and then finally leaving everyone for a job in Manchester.

Peder Victorious

Giants in the Earth
O. E. Rölvaag

Per Hansa and **Beret Hansa**'s youngest child. Peder Victorious is born on Christmas Day during their first winter in the Dakota Territory. He provides a source of amusement for the settlement during the lonely winter.

Victory

Jazz
Toni Morrison

Joe Trace's adoptive brother. Victory accompanies Joe and **Henry LesTroy** on their hunting expeditions.

América Vicuna

Love in the Time of Cholera
Gabriel García Márquez

The fourteen-year-old girl who is entrusted to **Florentino Ariza** by her parents. He seduces her despite his age and his position as her legal guardian and protector. He ends the affair abruptly because he finds out that **Fermina Daza**'s husband, **Dr. Juvenal Urbino del Calle**, has died, and it is finally time to pursue Fermina Daza. Without giving América a reason, Florentino abandons her, and she commits suicide.

Vidal

House Made of Dawn
N. Scott Momaday

Abel's brother, who dies in his youth.

The Vigils

The Chocolate War
Robert Cormier

A gang of kids. They run the school by scaring, commanding and torturing other students. They possess a Mafia-like presence. **Archie Costello** is the leader of the Vigils. **Obie** is the secretary. **Brother Leon** seeks out the help of the Vigils so that he can get out of financial trouble.

Rosemary Villanucci

The Bluest Eye
Toni Morrison

A white, comparatively wealthy girl who lives next door to **Claudia MacTeer**, **Frieda MacTeer**, **Mr. MacTeer**, and **Mrs. MacTeer**. She makes fun of Claudia and Frieda and tries to get them into trouble, and they sometimes beat her up.

Reverend Mr. Arthur Villars

Evelina
Fanny Burney

Evelina Anville's benevolent, loving, and fiercely protective guardian. Mr. Villars was the tutor of Evelina's grandfather, **Mr. Evelyn**, and the guardian of her mother, **Lady Caroline Evelyn Belmont**. He adopts Evelina when her mother dies in childbirth and raises her in the seclusion of his home in Berry Hill. Mr. Villars is Evelina's primary correspondent.

Edward de Villefort

The Count of Monte Cristo
Alexandre Dumas

The spoiled son of **Madame d'Villefort** and **Gérard de Villefort**. Edward is an innocent victim of **Edmond Dantès**'s revenge on Villefort. By exposing Madame d'Villefort as a cold-hearted woman willing to kill her daughter, Edmond drives the woman to kill herself and her son.

Gérard de Villefort

The Count of Monte Cristo
Alexandre Dumas

The corrupt and ambitious public prosecutor who sentences **Edmond Dantès** to life in prison. His father is **Noirtier de Villefort**, his wife is **Madame d'Villefort**, and his children are **Edward d'Villefort** and **Valentine Villefort**. Villefort wants his daughter, Valentine, to marry **Franz D'Epinay**, but Valentine is truly in love with **Maximilian Morrel**. Villefort is responsible for the birth of **Benedetto**, along with **Madame Danglars**. He tries to bury Benedetto as a baby after smothering the child, but unbeknownst to Villefort, the baby is rescued by **Signor Bertuccio**. Later, **the Count of Monte Cristo** takes revenge on Villefort through Benedetto. Villefort goes mad after finding his wife and son dead, believing his daughter to be dead, and being asked to repent by Edmond Dantès.

Madame de Villefort

The Count of Monte Cristo
Alexandre Dumas

Gérard de Villefort's murderous wife. Devoted wholly to her son **Edward d'Villefort**, Madame d'Villefort turns to crime in order to secure his fortune. She does not want Gérard de Villefort's daughter from another marriage, **Valentine Villefort**, to gain the family fortune. However, **the Count of Monte Cristo** exposes Madame d'Villefort as willing to murder her step-daughter. Gérard de Villefort is a public prosecutor, so he tells her that in order to save the honor of his name, he does not want to publicly prosecute her. Rather, he asks her to kill herself. She does, and she kills her son, Edward, as well.

Noirtier de Villefort

The Count of Monte Cristo
Alexandre Dumas

Gérard de Villefort's father, **Valentine Villefort**'s grandfather. Noirtier is a brilliant and willful former French revolutionary. Because he suffered a stroke, he only has his senses of sight and hearing. The only person with whom he can communicate is Valentine, who knows what he is thinking just from looking at his eyes. Noirtier is the only Villefort besides Valentine who does not want her to marry **Franz d'Epinay**. Noirtier gives Valentine small doses of the poison brucine, to build up her tolerance, because he is sure that **Madame d'Villefort** will try to poison Valentine with it.

Valentine de Villefort

The Count of Monte Cristo
Alexandre Dumas

Gérard de Villefort's saintly and beautiful daughter. Valentine is engaged to **Franz d'Epinay**, but she does not want to marry him. The only other person in her family who does not want her to marry Franz is her grandfather, **Noirtier de Villefort**, who cannot speak. Valentine and **Maximilian Morrel** are in love, and this love is protected by **Edmond Dantès** as **the Count of Monte Cristo**. Fearing that her stepmother, **Madame d'Villefort** will try to poison Valentine with brucine, Noirtier builds up Valentine's tolerance to the poison. Madame d'Villefort does try to poison Valentine, and after this happens, Monte Cristo gives her a pill that make her sleep for one month.

Villuppo

The Spanish Tragedy
Thomas Kyd

A nobleman who betrays **Alexandro**.

Father Vincent

Cry, the Beloved Country
Alan Paton

An Anglican priest from England. He stays at the Sophiatown Mission and offers to help **Stephen Kumalo** with his troubles. Father Vincent counsels Kumalo when he is brokenhearted over his son **Absalom Kumalo**, and he presides over the wedding between Absalom and **Absalom's girlfriend**.

Fred Vincy

Middlemarch
George Eliot

The oldest son of **Walter Vincy** and **Lucy Vincy**. His father sends him to college because he wants Fred to become a clergyman, but Fred doesn't want to work in the Church. He gets himself into debt by gambling. He causes financial difficulty for the Garths because he cannot pay the debt co-signed by **Caleb Garth**. He wants to marry **Mary Garth**, but she won't have him unless he finds a steady occupation other than the Church. He hopes to inherit Stone Court from his uncle, **Peter Featherstone**. These hopes are disappointed, so he works for Caleb Garth.

Lucy Vincy

Middlemarch
George Eliot

Walter Vincy's wife, **Fred Vincy** and **Rosamond Vincy**'s mother. She is the daughter of an innkeeper, much to Rosamond's chagrin. She dotes on her son and doesn't want him to marry **Mary Garth**. She is the sister of **Peter Featherstone**'s second wife.

Rosamond Vincy

Middlemarch
George Eliot

The daughter of **Walter Vincy** and **Lucy Vincy**. She marries **Tertius Lydgate** because she thinks he is rich. She dreams of leaving Middlemarch and living an exciting, aristocratic lifestyle, but her expensive tastes get Lydgate deeply into debt.

Walter Vincy

Middlemarch
George Eliot

Lucy Vincy's husband, **Fred Vincy** and **Rosamund Vincy**'s father. Vincy is a modestly well-off businessman in manufacturing and the mayor of Middlemarch. Fred and Rosamond's expensive tastes infuriate him. He refuses to lend Rosamond and **Tertius Lydgate** money to pay Lydgate's debt. He is **Harriet Bulstrode**'s brother.

Vindarten

Childhood's End
Arthur C. Clarke

An Overlord who befriends **Jan Rodricks** on **the Overlords**' homeworld. Like all Overlords, he is much taller and more broadly built than a human, with large wings, horns on his head, and a barbed tail.

M. Vinteuil

Swann's Way
Marcel Proust

The composer of **Charles Swann** and **Odette**'s favorite sonata, which rouses Swann's feelings for Odette even when he tries not to think of her.

Mlle. Vinteuil

Swann's Way
Marcel Proust

The daughter of **M. Vinteuil**. She breaks her father's heart when she begins a sordid affair with another woman.

Viola

Twelfth Night
William Shakespeare

A young woman of aristocratic birth, and the play's protagonist. Washed up on the shore of Illyria when her ship is wrecked in a storm, Viola decides to make her own way in the world. She disguises herself as a young man, calling herself "Cesario," and becomes a page to Duke **Orsino**. She ends up falling in love with him—even as **Olivia**, the woman Orsino is courting, falls in love with Cesario. Her poignant plight is the central conflict in the play. The strength of Viola's spirit separates her from the rest of Illyria.

Violet

Jazz
Toni Morrison

Wife of **Joe Trace**. When Violet is a child, her mother, **Rose Dear**, throws herself in a well after all of the family's belongings are repossessed due to Violet's father's absence. Violet is then raised by her grandmother, **True Belle**. When Violet marries Joe Trace, she seeks to escape the hard-knocks lifestyle of her childhood by moving to New York City. Her relationship with Joe becomes strained when she falls into depression. Violet herself has no children and, after several miscarriages, she longs for a child. When she finds out that Joe has cheated on her with **Dorcas**, Violet projects all of her anger, sadness and frustration by slashing Dorcas's face at her funeral as she lies in her open casket. After she causes the scene at the funeral, she becomes very friendly with **Alice Manfred**, Dorcas's aunt. She and Joe eventually repair their marriage.

Miss Violet

Bless Me, Ultima
Rudolfo A. Anaya

Antonio Márez's third-grade teacher.

Virgil

Inferno
Dante Alighieri

An ancient Roman poet and **Dante**'s guide through Hell. The historical Virgil lived in the first century b.c. and is widely considered the greatest of the Latin poets. Dante's fictional Virgil is wise and resourceful but unable to protect Dante from Hell's dangers.

Virgilia

Coriolanus
William Shakespeare

Coriolanus's loyal wife.

Vitamin Kid

Bless Me, Ultima
Rudolfo A. Anaya

One of an exuberant group of boys who frequently curse and fight. The other boys in the group are **Abel**, **Bones**, **Ernie**, **Horse**, **Lloyd**, and **Red**.

Vittoria

The Da Vinci Code
Dan Brown

A woman in **Robert Langdon**'s past. She appears only in his memory and demonstrates the difficulty he has holding onto relationships.

Vivian

A Lesson Before Dying
Ernest J. Gaines

Grant Wiggins's beautiful, loving, and intelligent girlfriend. Vivian is a schoolteacher at the black Catholic school in Bayonne. She is married and has two children but is in the process of divorcing her husband.

Vizzini

The Princess Bride
William Goldman

A Sicilian man of genius. Vizzini is the brains behind the trio, which includes **Fezzik** and **Inigo Montoya**, hired by **Prince Humperdinck** to kidnap and murder **Buttercup**. He is calculating, smug, ruthless, and rather pitiful. He is killed quickly in a battle of wits against **Westley**.

Vladimir

Waiting for Godot
Samuel Beckett

One of the play's two main characters. He is more contemplative than **Estragon** and has some authority over him.

Vladimir Ivanovich

The Death of Ivan Ilych
Leo Tolstoy

Ivan Ilych Golovin's son. Vasya is the youngest member of the Golovin household. Sensitive and quiet, Vasya has not yet been corrupted by the beliefs and values of his parents' social world. He is the only other person besides **Gerasim** who truly understands Ivan and his illness.

Cécile Volanges

Dangerous Liaisons
Pierre-Ambroise-François Choderlos de Laclos

A young girl, fresh out of the convent. Cécile Volanges is preyed upon by the **Marquise de Merteuil** and **the Vicomte de Valmont**. **Madame Volanges** has arranged the marriage of Cécile to the **Comte de Gercourt**, a former lover of Merteuil, who left Merteuil for **the Intendante**. Merteuil wants revenge, and beseeches Valmont to deflower the young girl. Cécile also falls in love with **the Chevalier Danceny**. Thanks to Valmont's rape of Cécile, she can no longer marry Gercourt since she is no longer a virgin. As a result, she returns to the convent.

Madame Volanges

Dangerous Liaisons
Pierre-Ambroise-François Choderlos de Laclos

The mother of **Cécile Volanges**, who arranges an advantageous marriage for her daughter to **the Comte de Gercourt**. Madame Volanges lives a respectable life, and corresponds frequently with **the Présidente de Tourvel**, warning her against associating with **the Vicomte de Valmont**. Madame Volanges also trusts **the Marquise de Merteuil**, who is secretly playing with Cécile behind the scenes, like Valmont.

Lord Voldemort

The Harry Potter Series: Books 1–4
J. K. Rowling

An evil wizard. **Harry Potter**'s arch-nemesis. When Harry was an infant, Voldemort brutally murdered Harry's parents and then turned his death curse on Harry. However, Harry resisted the dark magic and the spell backfired, destroying Voldemort and leaving a lightning-shaped scar on Harry's forehead. For years, the wizard community believed Voldemort to be dead, referring to him in whispered tones only as "He Who Must Not Be Named." In *Harry Potter and the Sorcerer's Stone*, the weakened Voldemort takes over the body of **Professor Quirrell** in an attempt to get the magical Sorcerer's Stone, but is thwarted by Harry and his friends. In *Harry Potter and the Chamber of Secrets*, Voldemort uses the diary of his younger self, Tom Riddle, to enchant **Ginny Weasley** and use her to open the mysterious Chamber of Secrets, wreaking havoc on Hogwarts until Harry and his friends discover the deception. In *Harry Potter and the Goblet of Fire*, Voldemort returns to life with the aid of his former followers, the Death Eaters, and makes another failed attempt on Harry's life. Voldemort is pure evil. Greatly weakened by his attack on Harry, he is left bodiless and must commit his misdeeds through other people. Over time, he becomes strengthened through the Death Eaters' machinations and is able to take on physical form once again. However, the Ministry of Magic, the governing body of wizards, refuses to believe that he has returned to life. Harry must rely on his own wits to keep the evil wizard at bay. The two are inextricably linked, bonded by their explosive contact when Harry was a baby, as well as by similarities in their academic careers at Hogwarts and the physical connection between their two wands. Though Voldemort remains primarily in the shadows, he is bent on destroying Harry and Hogwarts, and his growing power over the course of the series foreshadows the inevitable showdown that will occur between the two wizards.

Volpone

Volpone
Ben Jonson

The protagonist of the play. He is lustful, lecherous, and greedy. He is also energetic and has an unusual gift for rhetoric. He worships his money, all of which he has acquired through cons, such as the one he plays on **Voltore**, **Corbaccio**, and **Corvino**. Volpone has no children, but he has something of a family: his parasite, **Mosca**; his dwarf, **Nano**; his eunuch, **Castrone**, and his hermaphrodite, **Androgyno**. Volpone begins to lust feverishly after **Celia** upon first setting eyes on her.

Voltimand

Hamlet
William Shakespeare

Along with **Cornelius**, a courtier sent to Norway to prevent **Fortinbras**'s impending attack on Denmark.

Voltore

Volpone
Ben Jonson

One of the "carrion-birds" who continually circle around **Volpone**, giving him gifts in hopes of being chosen as his heir. Voltore is a lawyer by profession, adept in speech and, by implication, adept in deceit.

Volumnia

Coriolanus
William Shakespeare

Coriolanus's mother. Volumnia is devoted to her son. She raised him to be a warrior and delights in his military exploits. Coriolanus often allows his iron-willed mother to dominate him, as when she convinces him to halt his attack on Rome.

Bodo von Falternfels

Pnin
Vladimir Nabokov

An Austrian hired while **Timofey Pnin** is away teaching a course in Washington.

Dr. Schlichter von Koenigswald

Cat's Cradle
Kurt Vonnegut

Papa Monzano's attending physician. A former S.S. officer who served at Auschwitz, he joins **Julian Castle**'s staff at the San Lorenzo Charity hospital to atone for the atrocities he committed. After "Papa" commits suicide by swallowing *ice-nine*, Dr. von Koenigswald's hands are contaminated with the substance. He washes them, and the *ice-nine* spreads throughout his body, killing him instantly.

Kurt Vonnegut

Slaughterhouse-Five
Kurt Vonnegut

The novel's author and a minor character. Vonnegut himself was a prisoner of war during the firebombing of Dresden, and he periodically inserts himself in the narrative, as when he becomes the incontinent soldier in the latrine in the German prison camp.

Elizabeth "Bep" Voskuijl

Anne Frank: Diary of a Young Girl
Anne Frank

A worker in **Otto Frank**'s office. Bep Voskuijl helps the family by serving as a liaison to the outside world. After the war and the timeline of the diary, she remained in Amsterdam until her death in 1983.

Mr. Voskuijl

Anne Frank: Diary of a Young Girl
Anne Frank

The father of **Otto Frank**'s coworker, **Bep Voskuijl**.

Maria Vasilyevna Voynitskaya

Uncle Vanya
Anton Chekhov

Voynitsky's mother. She is still enthralled with the professor, and passes her days usually annotating pamphlets on various social issues.

Ivan Petrovich Voynitsky

Uncle Vanya
Anton Chekhov

The play's protagonist. Vanya is a bitter, broken man who has wasted his life toiling on the estate of his brother-in-law, **Serebryakov**. He is consumed with his lost life and obsessed with what might have been—a prime object of this obsession being the elusive **Yelena**.

Vresac

Dangerous Liaisons
Pierre-Ambroise-François Choderlos de Laclos

The lover of the **Comtesse de B—**. He almost catches the Comtesse in a compromising position with **the Vicomte de Valmont** at their estate.

Countess Vronskaya

Anna Karenina
Leo Tolstoy

Alexei Kirillovich Vronsky judgmental mother.

Alexei Kirillovich Vronsky

Anna Karenina
Leo Tolstoy

A wealthy and dashing military officer whose love for **Anna Arkadyevna Karenina** prompts her to desert her husband, **Alexei Alexandrovich Karenin**, and son, **Sergei Alexeich Karenin**. Vronsky is passionate and caring toward Anna but clearly disappointed when their affair forces him to give up his dreams of career advancement.

Vulcan

The Aeneid
Virgil

The Roman name for the Greek god **Hephaestus**, the god of fire and the forge. Vulcan is **Venus**'s husband, and the son of **Jupiter** and **Juno**. In the *Aeneid*, Venus urges Vulcan to craft a superior set of arms for **Aeneas**. The arms serve Aeneas well in his battle with **Turnus**.

Captain Vye

The Return of the Native
Thomas Hardy

Eustacia Vye's grandfather and guardian, a former captain in the British navy. A reclusive and silent man.

Eustacia Vye

The Return of the Native
Thomas Hardy

A woman who is transported to Egdon Heath to live with her grandfather. Eustacia despises the heath and searches for a way to escape. She has an amorous relationship with **Damon Wildeve**. They fill their time with childish squabbling and arguments, which seem more about self-interest than any real affection. Later, Eustacia enters into a tragic marriage with **Clym Yeobright** when she realizes that he is the more interesting and urbane of the two men.

Cecil Vyse

A Room with a View
E. M. Forster

The man who becomes **Lucy Honeychurch**'s fiancé for a short period of time. Cecil is pretentious and despises all the country people of Lucy's town, finding them unsophisticated and coarse in comparison to the affluent London society he is used to. He treats people without kindness or respect.

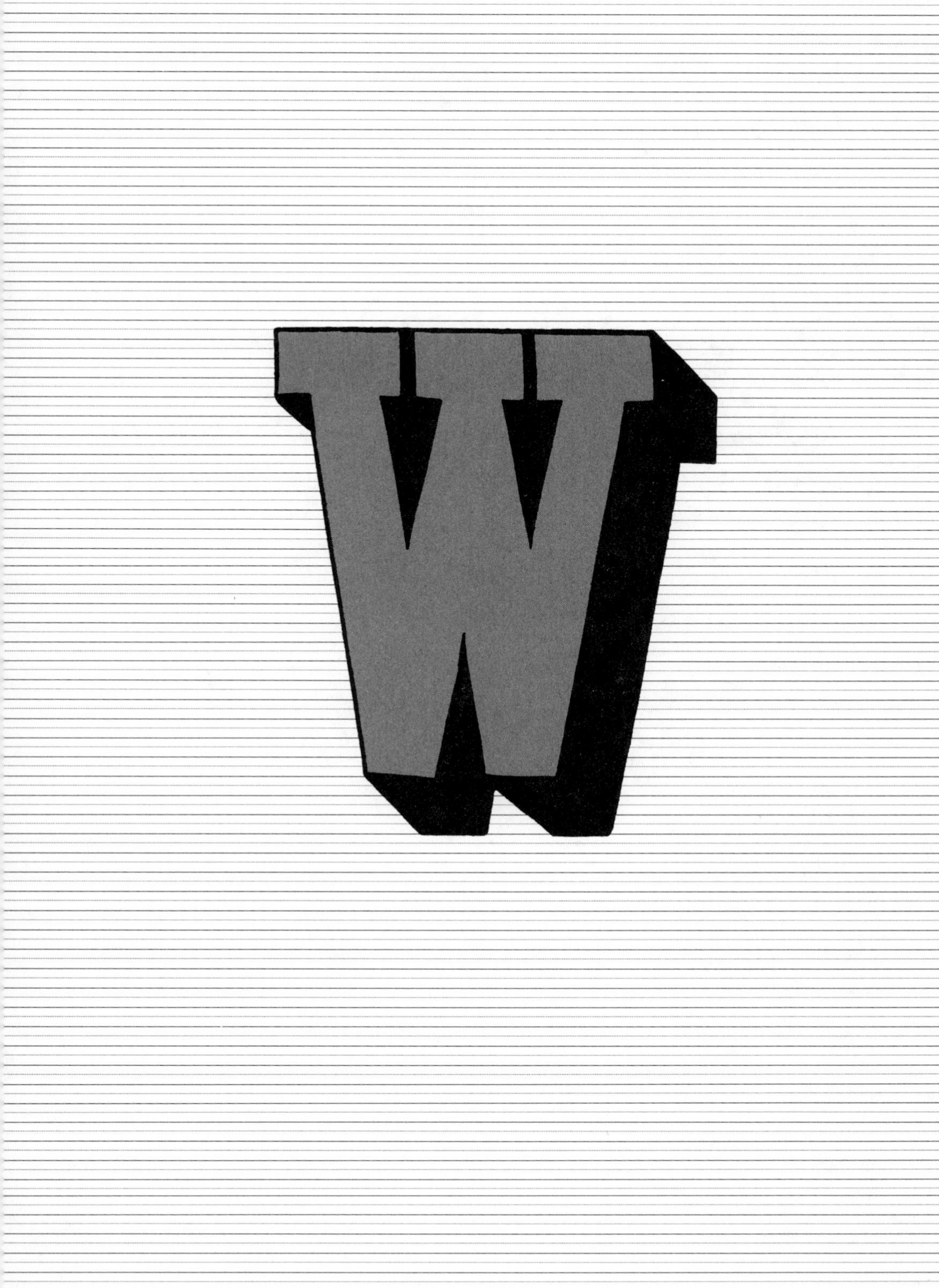

GHASTLY GHOSTS

WHO SAYS THAT BEING DEAD HAS TO KEEP YOU OUT OF THE STORY?

Banquo	1	*Macbeth*
Beloved	2	*Beloved*
The Ghost	3	*Hamlet*
Ghosts of Christmas Past, Present, and Future	4	*A Christmas Carol*
Julius Caesar	5	*Julius Caesar*
Peter Quint	6	*The Turn of the Screw*
Rebecca	7	*Rebecca*

Wade

Girl, Interrupted
Susanna Kaysen

Georgina's boyfriend and a patient at McLean. Wade fascinates the girls with stories of his father's exploits as a CIA agent. Wade's fits of uncontrollable rage ultimately land him on the maximum security ward.

Widow Wadman

Tristram Shandy
Laurence Sterne

A neighbor who has marital designs on **Captain Toby Shandy**, and with whom he has a brief and abortive courtship.

Wagner

Doctor Faustus
Christopher Marlowe

Faustus's servant. Wagner uses his master's books to learn how to summon devils and work magic.

Howard Wagner

Death of a Salesman
Arthur Miller

Willy Loman's boss. Howard inherited the company from his father, whom Willy regarded as "a masterful man" and "a prince." He essentially fires Willy, despite Willy's wounded assertions that he helped Howard's father name him.

Wainwright

Childhood's End
Arthur C. Clarke

Leader of the Freedom League, a religiously based group that opposes Earth's domination by **the Overlords**, despite the Overlords' clearly friendly and beneficial attitude.

Agnes Wainwright

The Grapes of Wrath
John Steinbeck

The daughter of the couple who shares the Joads' boxcar toward the end of the novel. Agnes becomes engaged to **Al Joad**, who leaves his family in order to stay with her.

Bill Wakatsuki

Farewell to Manzanar
Jeanne Wakatsuki Houston

The oldest Wakatsuki child. Along with **Woody**, Bill serves as one of **Papa**'s crew before the war on his sardine boats. In the camp, he is the leader of a dance band called The Jive Bombers.

Eleanor Wakatsuki

Farewell to Manzanar
Jeanne Wakatsuki Houston

The second Wakatsuki child and **Jeanne**'s oldest sister. Eleanor leaves the camp with her husband, **Shig**, to relocate to Reno, Nevada, but returns to the camp when Shig is drafted. She gives birth to a baby boy, which leads **Mama** and **Papa** to a reconciliation.

George Ko Wakatsuki

Farewell to Manzanar
Jeanne Wakatsuki Houston

Jeanne's father and the patriarch of the American branch of the Wakatsuki family. Papa is a first-generation Japanese immigrant with a strong sense of honor. His experience shows how unfair accusations hurt many Japanese families: when the FBI accuses Papa of being a Japanese spy, his relationship with his family deteriorates and he becomes an alcoholic.

Jeanne Wakatsuki

Farewell to Manzanar
Jeanne Wakatsuki Houston

The protagonist. Jeanne is the youngest of the Wakatsuki children and **Papa**'s favorite. She observes and comments on her own and her family's experiences before, during, and after the wartime internment. In the beginning of the narrative she is a naïve seven-year-old, but as she grows older, she loses her naïveté and comes to understand the true nature of the camps, her family, and herself.

Kiyo Wakatsuki

Farewell to Manzanar
Jeanne Wakatsuki Houston

The ninth Wakatsuki child and **Jeanne**'s closest brother. Kiyo shares many experiences with Jeanne, including being ambushed by children in the Japanese ghetto on Terminal Island and being spat at by an old woman in Long Beach.

Rigu Sukai Wakatsuki

Farewell to Manzanar
Jeanne Wakatsuki Houston

Jeanne's mother. Patient and caring with her children and husband, Mama places a high value on privacy and dignity. Despite **Papa**'s violent treatment of her while at Manzanar, she is the first member of the Wakatsuki family to make amends with Papa, demonstrating her commitment to family.

Woodrow Wakatsuki

Farewell to Manzanar
Jeanne Wakatsuki Houston

The third Wakatsuki child. Woody is the most fatherly of **Jeanne**'s brothers and takes charge when Papa is detained for a year at Fort Lincoln. Woody demonstrates his loyalty to America by joining the U.S. army.

Mr. and Mrs. Wakefield

The Remains of the Day
Kazuo Ishiguro

An American couple who are friends of **Mr. Farraday** and come to visit Darlington Hall. When Mrs. Wakefield asks **Stevens** if he worked for Lord Darlington, he denies it, raising doubts in her mind about the legitimacy of Mr. Farraday's purchase of the mansion.

Lawyer Wakem

The Mill on the Floss
George Eliot

Philip Wakem's father, **Jeremy Tulliver**'s enemy, and a powerful, increasingly wealthy member of St. Ogg's society. He remembers his late wife lovingly and is very indulgent but close to his deformed son.

Philip Wakem

The Mill on the Floss
George Eliot

The sensitive and intelligent son of **Lawyer Wakem**. Philip first meets **Maggie Tulliver** when he is at school with **Tom Tulliver**. He falls in love with her the year that they meet in secret during Maggie's father's bankruptcy. Philip has had a hunched back since birth. Philip's love of art, music, and knowledge go some way toward counteracting the severe sadness he feels about his deformity.

M. Waldman

Frankenstein
Mary Shelley

The professor of chemistry who sparks **Victor Frankenstein**'s interest in science. Waldman dismisses the alchemists' conclusions as unfounded but sympathizes with Victor's interest in a science that can explain the "big questions," such as the origin of life.

Bill Walker

Major Barbara
George Bernard Shaw

A man who appears at the Army shelter to reclaim his converted girlfriend and bully its staff. The swaggering, menacing Bill is quickly cowed and disgraced by the shining Major **Barbara**.

Charles Walker

Holes
Louis Sachar

The son of the richest family in the Green Lake of 1888, where **Kate Barlow** is the school teacher. He is spoiled and stupid and gets upset when he is denied access to something he wants. When Kate Barlow refuses to go out with him he becomes very angry. Charles leads the citizens of Green Lake to burn down the schoolhouse and kill **Sam** after Sam kisses Kate. Later, in 1908, Charles and his wife, the redhead **Linda Miller**, tie up Kissin' Kate Barlow and make her walk on hot sand until she dies from the bite of a yellow-spotted lizard.

Coalhouse Walker

Ragtime
E. L. Doctorow

A ragtime pianist and the father of **Sarah**'s child.

Crystal Gail Walker

Prodigal Summer
Barbara Kingsolver

Jewel Walker's ten-year-old daughter. Crystal is a tough tomboy whose lack of femininity worries most of her relatives. Crystal and **Lusa Maluf Landowski** get along because Lusa respects Crystal as she is. Crystal threatens her little brother **Lowell Walker**'s life, but protects him when he gets in trouble.

Garnett Walker

Prodigal Summer
Barbara Kingsolver

A widower near the age of eighty. Garnett is a retired teacher devoted to developing a disease-resistant hybrid American chestnut. At first he loathes his closest neighbor, **Nannie Land Rawley**, but over time his feelings for her change.

Jewel Walker

Prodigal Summer
Barbara Kingsolver

Cole Widener's youngest sister. Jewel is divorced from **Sheldon Walker** and dying of cancer. She worries about the future of **Crystal Gail Walker** and **Lowell Walker**, her children. Jewel is the first of Cole's relatives to befriend **Lusa Maluf Landowski**.

Lowell Walker

Prodigal Summer
Barbara Kingsolver

Jewel Walker's son. Lowell hopes to develop a friendship with his grandfather, **Garnett Walker**. He is quieter and more reflective than his sister, **Crystal Gail Walker**.

Mrs. Walker

Daisy Miller
Henry James

An American who admires European society and customs. Mrs. Walker warns **Daisy Miller** about her flirtatious and uncultivated behavior.

Mrs. Walker

A Prayer for Owen Meany
John Irving

The Episcopalian Sunday school teacher who always blames **Owen Meany** when the other students lift him up and pass him around. Mrs. Walker also acts in **Dan Needham**'s Gravesend Players productions.

Sheldon Walker

Prodigal Summer
Barbara Kingsolver

The alcoholic father of **Crystal Gail Walker** and **Lowell Walker**. Shel gladly surrenders his rights to the children in order to avoid paying child support.

Digger Wallace

The Land
Mildred D. Taylor

A drunken ne'er-do-well. Digger resents **Paul-Edward Logan**'s and **Mitchell Thomas**'s mounting successes. When Digger comes to take his brother, **John Wallace**, away from the forty acres, Digger shoots Mitchell in the back as a tree is falling, and Mitchell later dies. Digger also shoots Paul's best horse, which puts Paul into even deeper financial worry. Much later on, Digger is found dead, presumably having drowned as a result of his own drunkenness.

John Wallace

The Land
Mildred D. Taylor

The meek younger brother of **Digger Wallace**. John works at the forty acres. He was in the band of men in the woods who accused **Mitchell Thomas** and **Paul-Edward Logan** of stealing chickens.

The Wallaces

Roll of Thunder, Hear My Cry
Mildred D. Taylor

Proprietors of a general store on **Harlan Granger**'s land. They are violent, brutal people. They are responsible for the burning of a black man and his subsequent death. Led by **Big Ma**, a boycott is started so that the black members of the community will not have to buy their goods from the very people who are killing them. However, Harland Granger and other brutal powerful whites start threatening black workers and farmers if they do not start buying again from the Wallace store. *The Land* features two members of this family: **Digger Wallace** and **John Wallace**.

Maria Wallis

Tender Is the Night
F. Scott Fitzgerald

An American woman and an acquaintance of **Nicole Diver**'s. Nicole runs into Maria at the train station near their villa on the Riviera, but Maria snubs her and, for an unknown reason, pulls out a gun and fatally shoots an Englishman in the crowd. **Dick Diver** tries to help Maria by visiting her in jail—a clear attempt to impress his mistress, **Rosemary Hoyt**.

Walowick

Fallen Angels
Walter Dean Myers

A slightly racist soldier in **Richie Perry**'s squad who appears to overcome his prejudices as the bond among the squad members deepens.

Peter Walsh

Mrs. Dalloway
Virginia Woolf

An old friend of **Clarissa Dalloway**'s, once an impetuous young man who disdained English snobbery. When Clarissa rejected his proposal of marriage, he went to India. Now he has a new young lover, **Daisy Simmons**. Stormy, unpredictable Peter acts as a foil to **Richard Dalloway**, who is stable, generous, and rather simple.

Prior Walter

Angels in America
Tony Kushner

The AIDS-stricken boyfriend that **Louis Ironson** abandons after his disease is revealed. Prior becomes a prophet when he is visited by the **Angel**, but he eventually rejects his prophecy and demands a blessing of additional life. He proves wiser than the collected Angels in Heaven, rejecting their doctrine of stasis in favor of the painful necessity of movement and migration. Prior is as genuinely decent and moral as Louis is flawed. His AIDS infection renders him weak and victimized, but he manages to transcend that mere victimhood, surviving and becoming the center of a new, utopian community at the play's end.

Prior I

Angels in America
Tony Kushner

Prior Walter's ancestor who, along with **Prior II**, is summoned from the dead to help prepare the way for the Angel's arrival. He is a medieval farmer who died of the plague.

Prior II

Angels in America
Tony Kushner

Prior Walter's ancestor who, along with **Prior I**, is summoned from the dead to help prepare the way for the Angel's arrival. More sophisticated and cosmopolitan than Prior I, he is a seventeenth-century Londoner who died of the plague.

Mr. Walters

The Adventures of Tom Sawyer
Mark Twain

The somewhat ridiculous Sunday-school superintendent.

Robert Walton

Frankenstein
Mary Shelley

The Arctic seafarer whose letters open and close the book. Walton picks the bedraggled **Victor Frankenstein** up off the ice, helps nurse him back to health, and hears Victor's story. He records the incredible tale in a series of letters addressed to his sister, **Margaret Saville**, in England.

Wamai

Out of Africa
Isak Dinesen

The young Kikuyu boy who is killed during the shooting accident.

Wamba

Ivanhoe
Sir Walter Scott

Cedric the Saxon's jester, a witty, incisive Saxon clown, whose barbed comments often mask nuggets of wry wisdom.

Wang Chwun Hwa Chwun and Wang Chwun Yu

The Joy Luck Club
Amy Tan

One of **Suyuan**'s twin daughters by her first husband, **Wang Fuchi**. Chwun Hwa and her sister **Yu** are the half-sisters of **Jing-mei**. When an officer told Suyuan she should go to Chungking with her daughters, Suyuan knew the Japanese were going to invade Kweilin. Suyuan was forced to leave her daughters by the side of the road.

Wang Lung's first daughter

The Good Earth
Pearl S. Buck

A girl who suffers from severe malnutrition as an infant during a famine year. She grows up retarded and never learns to speak. **Wang Lung** is very attached to her and makes arrangements for her care after his death.

Wang Lung's second daughter

The Good Earth
Pearl S. Buck

The twin sister of **Wang Lung's third son**. After **Wang Lung** begins to criticize **O-lan**'s big feet, she binds the second daughter's feet. The second daughter is promised in marriage to **Liu**'s son.

Wang Lung's father

The Good Earth
Pearl S. Buck

A traditional and morally severe man.

Wang Lung's first son

The Good Earth
Pearl S. Buck

An extravagant and arrogant man, obsessed with appearances. He grows up spoiled and rejects his father's values.

Wang Lung's first son's wife

The Good Earth
Pearl S. Buck

The daughter of **Liu**, a wealthy local grain merchant. Spoiled and reckless, she urges her husband to spend money on luxury items. She has bound feet.

Wang Lung's second son

The Good Earth
Pearl S. Buck

A crafty, enterprising, and miserly man. Though he is more responsible than his older brother, both brothers reject their father **Wang Lung**'s traditional values.

Wang Lung's second son's wife

The Good Earth
Pearl S. Buck

The daughter of a modest landowning village family. She becomes enemies with **Wang Lung's first son's wife**.

Wang Lung's third son

The Good Earth
Pearl S. Buck

The twin brother of **Wang Lung's second daughter**. He dreams of glory and becomes a soldier against his father **Wang Lung**'s wishes.

Wang Lung's uncle

The Good Earth
Pearl S. Buck

Wang's father's younger brother; a cunning scoundrel and thief. Out of filial piety, **Wang Lung** shows his uncle respect and supports him in difficult times despite the uncle's despicable nature.

Wang Lung's uncle's son

The Good Earth
Pearl S. Buck

A prodigal scoundrel and a sexual predator.

Wang Lung's uncle's wife

The Good Earth
Pearl S. Buck

The village gossip. Like her husband and son, she is lazy and manipulative.

Wanyangerri

Out of Africa
Isak Dinesen

The young Kikuyu boy who has his jaw blown off during the shooting incident.

Lord Warburton

The Portrait of a Lady
Henry James

An aristocratic neighbor of the Touchetts' who falls in love with **Isabel Archer** during her first visit to Gardencourt. Warburton remains in love with Isabel even after she rejects his proposal and later tries to marry **Pansy Osmond** simply to bring himself closer to Isabel.

Ward

Ordinary People
Judith Guest

The brother of **Beth Jarrett**. Ward and his wife, **Audrey**, live in Houston and host Beth and **Calvin Jarrett** when the two play in a lawyers-only golf tournament in Houston.

Warden

Brave New World
Aldous Huxley

The talkative chief administrator for the New Mexico Savage Reservation. He is an Alpha.

Warden

Holes
Louis Sachar

The ultimate symbol of cruel authority at Camp Green Lake. The Warden rewards only those who do what she wants and uses her power to threaten everyone else. She has hidden cameras and microphones that she uses to spy on the boys. She is a descendent of **Charles Walker**, or Trout, and the redhead Linda Miller, and is making the boys dig holes in an attempt to dig up **Kate Barlow**'s treasure, which is hidden in the ground on Trout and Linda's land, which they took from Kate.

Comte de Wardes

The Three Musketeers
Alexandre Dumas

An agent of **Cardinal Richelieu**. The **Lady de Winter** is in love with him. In order to get information from the Lady, **d'Artagnan** impersonates the Comte de Wardes and has sex with the Lady.

Judge Lawrence Wargrave

And Then There Were None
Agatha Christie

A recently retired judge. Wargrave is a highly intelligent old man with a commanding personality. As the characters begin to realize that a murderer is hunting them, Wargrave's experience and air of authority make him a natural leader for the group. He lays out evidence, organizes searches, and ensures that weapons are locked away safely.

Wargs

The Hobbit
J. R. R. Tolkien

Evil wolves who join forces with the **Goblins** against the **Dwarves**, **Humans**, and **Elves** at the Battle of the Five Armies over the Arkenstone.

Dain Waris

Lord Jim
Joseph Conrad

Doramin's son and **Jim**'s best friend. The two are soul mates, and Dain Waris serves as Jim's second-in-command. He leads the initial attack on **Gentleman Brown**, but is not entirely successful, lacking Jim's charisma as a leader of men. He is killed when **Cornelius** leads Brown down the river channel behind his camp, after Jim foolishly frees Brown and his men.

Warren

The Shipping News
E. Annie Proulx

The aunt's dog. Warren is named after the aunt's dead lover, **Irene Warren**. Speaking about "Warren" provides the aunt with a way to talk to others about her love without always revealing who her love was.

Baby Warren

Tender Is the Night
F. Scott Fitzgerald

Nicole Warren's spinsterish, anglophile older sister. **Baby** controls the sisters' inheritance and is always on the lookout for her sister's well-being. Baby does not believe that **Dick Diver** is a good match for her sister, but she sees their undeniable chemistry and does not interfere with their romance.

Constable Bill Warren

Our Town
Thornton Wilder

A local policeman whose personal knowledge of the town's citizens bespeaks the close-knit nature of the town.

Devereux Warren

Tender Is the Night
F. Scott Fitzgerald

Nicole and **Baby Warren**'s wealthy, alcoholic father. Devereux sexually abuses Nicole and then places her in a mental clinic in Zurich.

Doctor Warren

Johnny Tremain
Esther Forbes

One of the leaders of the Revolutionary forces in Boston. He fixes **Jonathan Tremain**'s disfigured hand at the end of the novel.

Irene Warren

The Shipping News
E. Annie Proulx

The aunt's lesbian partner who died of cancer. The aunt tells **Quoyle** that she used to have a "significant other" named "Warren." As soon as she died, the aunt bought her dog **Warren** and started the upholstery business.

Mary Warren

The Crucible
Arthur Miller

The servant in **John Proctor**'s household and a member of **Abigail Williams**'s group of girls. She is a timid girl, easily influenced by those around her. However, she does come to speak out against Abigail in front of **Judge Hathorne** and **Deputy Governor Danforth**. For this, Abigail starts acting like Mary Warren is bewitching her and her group of willing followers in court.

Tom Warrups

My Brother Sam Is Dead
Christopher & James Lincoln Collier

An Indian living on **Colonel Read**'s land who allows **Sam Meeker** to hide out in his teepee.

Wart

Henry IV, Part II
William Shakespeare

One of the Army recruits that **Sir John Falstaff** inspects in Gloucestershire. Because Wart does not bribe Falstaff, he, **Feeble**, and **Shadow** have to serve in the military.

Richard Beauchamp, Earl of Warwick

Henry IV, Part II; Henry V; and Henry VI, Part I
William Shakespeare

A nobleman and ally of several of the Henrys. Throughout *Henry IV, Part II*, Warwick is a calming force for **Henry IV**. When Henry worries late at night about the rebels' troops and **King Richard II**'s prophecy of the **Earl of Northumberland**'s mutiny, Warwick dismisses rumor. When Henry lies on his deathbed, Warwick calms the princes down and helps reconcile the King with **Prince Harry**. Warwick later advises **Henry V**. In *Henry VI, Part I*, Warwick judges several trials. He accompanies the **Duke of Somerset** and **Richard Plantagenet, Duke of York** to the Temple Garden to settle their dispute, but ends up plucking a white rose in support of York. However, in other matters he remains quite the objective arbiter: He helps forge a (temporary) peace between **Humphrey, Duke of Gloucester** and **Cardinal Beaufort, Bishop of Winchester**, he hears the case against **Joan of Arc**, and he assists in the peace negotiations with the French lords.

Richard Neville, Earl of Warwick

Henry VI, Part II and *Henry VI, Part III*
William Shakespeare

Son of **Richard Neville, Earl of Salisbury**; supporter of **Richard Plantagenet, Duke of York**; and brother of the **Marquess of Montague**. When the battle lines are drawn among the bickering nobles early in *King Henry VI, Part II*, Warwick sides with his father and York to defend **Humphrey, Duke of Gloucester**. Shortly after, both Warwick and Salisbury readily support York's claim to the throne. After Gloucester is murdered, Warwick reports to **King Henry VI** that the commoners suspect **William de la Pole, Duke of Suffolk** and **Cardinal Beaufort**; he proves to Henry VI that Gloucester was strangled, and argues with Suffolk and **Queen Margaret**. When York returns from Ireland, Salisbury and Warwick join him in his quest for the crown and fight against the King and his lords. He continues the fight in *King Henry VI, Part III*, ultimately putting York's son **King Edward IV** on the throne following the duke's death. While Warwick is negotiating with **King Louis XI** in France for a marriage between **Lady Bona** and Edward, word comes that the newly crowned king has taken **Elizabeth Woodville, Lady Grey** as his bride. Embarassed and betrayed, Warwick joins Queen Margaret's Lancastrian faction and marries one of his daughters to **Prince Edward**. Warwick and the **Earl of Oxford** lead the armies back to England and capture Edward IV. Fatally wounded in a battle with the Yorkist forces, Warwick gives a touching soliloquy before dying. Warwick's shifting allegiance is symbolic of the tumultuous period of the Wars of the Roses.

Mr. and Mrs. Washburn

Their Eyes Were Watching God
Zora Neale Hurston

One of **Nanny Crawford**'s white employers after she becomes a free woman. Nanny lives in a house in the Washburns' backyard, and they help raise **Janie Mae Crawford** along with their own children.

Booker T. Washington

Ragtime
E. L. Doctorow

A well-educated and famous orator and black civil rights leader. He believes friendship and cooperation between whites and blacks is essential to the success of blacks in America.

Henry Washington

The Bluest Eye
Toni Morrison

The MacTeers' boarder. He has a reputation for being a steady worker and a quiet man. Middle-aged, he has never married and has a lecherous side. He entertains the local whores, **Miss Marie**, **China**, and **Poland**. One day, he touches **Frieda MacTeer**'s breasts and runs away after **Mr. MacTeer** shoots at him for doing so.

Gen Watanabe

Bel Canto
Ann Patchett

Hosokawa's interpreter. Watanabe, who is in his twenties, has a great gift for languages, and the hostages and the terrorists rely on him to communicate with each other. Despite his facility with languages, Watanabe struggles when trying to express himself. When Watanabe falls in love with **Carmen**, one of the terrorists, he finds his own voice.

Belle Watling

Gone with the Wind
Margaret Mitchell

An Atlanta prostitute with whom **Rhett Butler** has a long-term affair. Belle earns the gratitude of the Atlanta Ku Klux Klan by providing them with an alibi for a murder.

Dr. Watson

Hound of the Baskervilles
Sir Arthur Conan Doyle

Sherlock Holmes's sidekick and the novel's narrator. Watson tries his hand at Holmes's game, expressing his eagerness to please and impress the master by solving such a baffling case.

Helmholtz Watson

Brave New World
Aldous Huxley

An Alpha lecturer at the College of Emotional Engineering. Helmholtz is a prime example of his caste, successful in sex, sports and his job. Still, he feels empty and wishes to use his writing abilities for something more meaningful. He befriends **Bernard Marx** out of a mutual dissatisfaction with the World State. Helmholtz eventually accepts exile to the Falkland Islands.

Miss Watson

The Adventures of Huckleberry Finn
Mark Twain

The sister of the **Widow Douglas**. Miss Watson and the widow are two wealthy sisters who live together in a large house in St. Petersburg, Missouri, and who adopt **Huckleberry Finn**. The gaunt and severe Miss

Watson is a prominent representative of hypocritical religious and ethical values. Miss Watson dies toward the end of the narrative and frees her slave, **Jim**, in her will.

Pheoby Watson

Their Eyes Were Watching God
Zora Neale Hurston

Janie Mae Crawford's best friend in Eatonville. Pheoby gives Janie the benefit of the doubt when the townspeople gossip viciously about Janie returning from the Everglades after **Tea Cake**'s death.

Sam Watson

Their Eyes Were Watching God
Zora Neale Hurston

Pheoby Watson's husband. Sam Watson is a source of great humor and wisdom during the conversations on **Jody Starks**'s porch between the townsmen.

Wealhtheow

Beowulf
Unknown

Hrothgar's wife, the gracious Queen of the Danes.

Wealtheow

Grendel
John Gardner

Hrothgar's wife and queen of the Danes. Originally a Helming princess, Wealtheow represents love, altruism, and an ideal image of womanhood, bringing balance and harmony to her adopted community.

Roland Weary

Slaughterhouse-Five
Kurt Vonnegut

A stupid, cruel soldier taken prisoner by the Germans along with **Billy Pilgrim**. Unlike Billy, who is totally out of place in the war, Weary is a deluded glory-seeker who fancies himself part of the Three Musketeers and saves Billy's life out of a desire to be heroic.

Arthur Weasley

The Harry Potter Series: Books 2–4
J. K. Rowling

Ron Weasley's father, who works in the Misuse of Muggles Artifacts Office within the Ministry of Magic. A thoroughly likeable man, Mr. Weasley treats **Harry** as if he were one of his own children.

Bill Weasley

Harry Potter and the Goblet of Fire
J. K. Rowling

Ron Weasley's second-eldest brother, who was a prefect and Head Boy at Hogwarts, who works in Gringotts Bank in Egypt.

Harry Potter and the Goblet of Fire
J. K. Rowling

Charlie Weasley

The eldest Weasley offspring, who currently works with dragons in Romania, and who comes to Hogwarts to help out.

The Harry Potter Series: Books 2–4
J. K. Rowling

Fred and George Weasley

Ron Weasley's older twin brothers. Fred and George are beaters for the Gryffindor House Quidditch team. The twins are troublemakers. In *Harry Potter and the Prisoner of Azkaban*, they are responsible for passing the Marauder's Map onto **Harry Potter**. The Marauders Map shows, in great detail, the grounds of Hogwarts, including the location of everyone on the premises. In *Harry Potter and the Goblet of Fire*, they become involved in trying to set up a line of practical jokes called Weaslies' Wizard Wheezes.

The Harry Potter Series: Books 2–4
J. K. Rowling

Ginny Weasley

Ron Weasley's younger sister. Ginny is a shy red-haired girl with an enormous crush on **Harry Potter**. She finds **Tom Riddle**'s diary. The magic diary manipulates her into opening the Chamber of Secrets and releasing the monstrous basilisk.

The Harry Potter Series: Books 2–4
J. K. Rowling

Molly Weasley

Ron Weasley's mother. Molly is very maternal and kind, but also quite strict.

The Harry Potter Series: Books 2–4
J. K. Rowling

Percy Weasley

Ron Weasley's brother. Percy is a prefect who is in charge of a group of younger students. He is annoying, nagging, and pompous, but has good intentions.

The Harry Potter Series: Books 1–4
J. K. Rowling

Ron Weasley

A modest boy who comes from an impoverished wizard family. Ron is **Harry Potter**'s first friend at Hogwarts, and they become close. He lacks Harry's gusto and charisma, but his loyalty and help are useful to Harry throughout their adventures. Ron's mediocrity despite his wizard background reminds us that success at Hogwarts is based solely on talent and hard work, not on family connections. In *Harry Potter and the Sorcerer's Stone*, Ron's willingness to be beaten up by the monstrous chess queen shows how selfless and generous he is.

Into Thin Air
Jon Krakauer

Beck Weathers

A climber left for dead, along with the Japanese woman **Yasuko Namba**, when their group gets lost on the way down the mountain. Only Weathers survives, though he is blinded.

Ben Weatherstaff

The Secret Garden
Frances Hodgson Burnett

A gruff elderly gardener who is only permitted to stay at Misselthwaite because he was a favorite of the late **Lilias Craven**. He helps the children keep the secret of the garden. Ben himself clandestinely tended the garden during the ten years in which it was locked, out of love and loyalty for his late mistress.

Mr. Weaver

Death Be Not Proud
John Gunther

An older neighbor in the country and a chemistry teacher at Andover. Mr. Weaver helps **Johnny** with his ammonia experiment, in which Johnny discovers a new property of the substance.

Emily Webb

Our Town
Thornton Wilder

Mrs. Myrtle Webb and **Mr. Charles Webb**'s daughter; **George Gibbs**'s schoolmate and next-door neighbor, later his fiancée and wife. Emily is a good student and conscientious daughter. After Emily dies, she says that she still feels like one of the living, and against the advice of the other dead souls, she decides to go back and relive one happy day from her life.

General Webb

The Last of the Mohicans
James Fenimore Cooper

Commander of the British forces at Fort Edward. General Webb gives **Hawkeye** a letter to deliver to **Colonel Munro** at Fort William Henry. The letter states that Munro should surrender the fort to the French **General Montcalm**. Webb also charges **Major Duncan Hawkeye** with the task of escorting the colonel's two daughters, **Cora Munro** and **Alice Munro**, to Fort William Henry, to see their father.

Mr. Charles Webb

Our Town
Thornton Wilder

Emily Webb's father and the publisher and editor of the *Grover's Corners Sentinel*.

Mrs. Myrtle Webb

Our Town
Thornton Wilder

Emily Webb's mother. Usually no-nonsense, she worries during Emily's wedding that she has not taught her daughter enough about marriage.

Wally Webb

Our Town
Thornton Wilder

Emily Webb's younger brother. His untimely death from a burst appendix on a Boy Scout trip underscores the brief and fleeting nature of life.

Florence Wechek

Alas, Babylon
Pat Frank

Randy Bragg's neighbor, and **Alice Cooksey**'s friend. Florence is a gossipy older woman who runs the telegraph office in Fort Repose.

Weena

The Time Machine
H. G. Wells

One of the Eloi, the peaceful, docile people who inhabit the surface of the future Earth visited by **The Time Traveller**.

Bertrand Welch

Lucky Jim
Kingsley Amis

The oldest son of **Professor Ned Welch** and **Celia Welch**, **Carol Goldsmith**'s lover, **Christine Callaghan**'s boyfriend, and **Jim Dixon**'s enemy. Bertrand lives in London, where he has begun a career as a painter. He tries to present himself as cultured, witty, and cosmopolitan, but comes off more as pretentious, elitist and snooty. Bertrand is dating Christine, in part to get a job with her uncle, **Gore-Urquhart**, as the wealthy patron's personal assistant.

Celia Welch

Lucky Jim
Kingsley Amis

The wife of **Professor Ned Welch** and the driving force behind her husband's social ambition. Mrs. Welch accompanies the musical parties held at her house on the piano. She is unwilling to forgive **Jim Dixon** for anything.

Jack Welch

This Boy's Life
Tobias Wolff

A simple, gentle boy with whom **Jack Wolff** is sometimes made to wrestle in gym class. **Jack Welch**'s father owns a farm from which Jack Wolff and **Chuck Bolger** are caught stealing gasoline.

Professor Ned Welch

Lucky Jim
Kingsley Amis

The husband of **Celia Welch**, the father of **Bertrand Welch**, and a professor at the college in charge of **Jim Dixon**'s career. He is an absent-minded man who rambles on about old English music, the recorder, and children's artwork, not noticing whether or not his audience cares. He and his wife have some social pretensions, and they often try to attract the local press to musical events at their house.

May Welland

The Age of Innocence
Edith Wharton

The dewy-eyed and artless young debutante who marries **Newland Archer**. Though May seems unassailably innocent, Archer comes to regard her as the living embodiment of New York society: incapable of thinking on her own, conditioned to act as she is expected. She remains a loyal wife even after she suspects that Newland is having an affair with **Countess Ellen Olenska**.

Joe Welling

Winesburg, Ohio
Sherwood Anderson

The agent for Standard Oil in Winesburg. Joe seizes on strange ideas and talks about them for hours on end.

Wells

A Portrait of the Artist as a Young Man
James Joyce

A bully who taunts **Stephen Dedalus**. He pushes Stephen into a filthy cesspool, which lands him in the infirmary.

Floyd Wells

In Cold Blood
Truman Capote

An inmate at Lansing prison. After **Perry Edward Smith** leaves on parole, he becomes **Richard Eugene Hickock**'s cellmate. He is a former employee of **Herbert Clutter**'s, and he tells Dick about the ranch and the layout of the house.

Wemmick

Great Expectations
Charles Dickens

Jaggers's clerk and **Pip**'s friend. At work, Wemmick is cynical and sarcastic, but at home in Walworth, he is jovial, wry, and tender to his "**Aged Parent**."

Florry Wendy

A Tree Grows in Brooklyn
Betty Smith

A ten-year-old girl. She sits on her fire escape and watches **Francie** get ready for her date.

Captain Frederick Wentworth

Persuasion
Jane Austen

The object of **Anne Elliot**'s affections. Captain Wentworth is a gallant Naval officer who has made his own fortunes by climbing the Naval ranks. He values constancy, practicality, and firmness of mind in women. Though Captain Wentworth is almost universally liked and respected for his gentle nature and kind attentions to others, **Sir Walter Elliot** disdains him for his "lower" birth.

Werenro

The Red Tent
Anita Diamant

A messenger and slave of **Rebecca**'s. Werenro invites **Jacob**'s family to Rebecca's for the barley festival and during their meeting, **Dinah** becomes entranced with Werenro's red hair and strange costume. Werenro is nearly killed after being attacked and brutally raped while traveling one day. She manages to live and ekes out a pitiful existence as a traveling singer. She and Dinah are reunited later in Egypt when Dinah recognizes her song.

Gregers Werle

Wild Duck
Henrik Ibsen

The impassioned, idealistic son of **Haakon Werle**. He has returned from self-imposed exile to avenge his father's crimes against the Ekdal family. Vengeance consists of the unmasking of **Hjalmar**'s family life. When he finally realizes that he has failed to redeem his friends, he will make a melancholic exit from a world in which he has no place.

Haakon Werle

Wild Duck
Henrik Ibsen

A wealthy industrialist who is responsible for the ruin of his former partner, **Old Ekdal**, and his family. Werle has attempted to make amends by becoming the Ekdals' provider. He also hides a liaison with **Hjalmar**'s wife **Gina**, a liaison that drove him to facilitate Gina and Hjalmar's marriage as a guard against public scandal.

West Indian Archie

The Autobiography of Malcolm X
Malcolm X & Alex Haley

An older Harlem hustler who pays **Malcolm X** for helping him run an informal gambling system in Harlem. They later have a violent break after a misunderstanding. Archie's photographic memory and aptitude in math exemplify the wasted potential of the black ghetto.

John Henry West

The Member of the Wedding
Carson McCullers

The six year-old first cousin of **Frankie Addams**. He spends much of his time hanging around the Addams house. Intelligent beyond his years and highly circumspect, he is quick with an insightful comment. John Henry's sudden death from meningitis at the end of the novel represents the death of Frankie's childhood.

Julian West

Looking Backward
Edward Bellamy

The narrator. Born into an aristocratic nineteenth-century family, Julian West suffers from insomnia and builds a sleeping chamber under his house to shield himself from the street noises in Boston. One night, he falls asleep with the aid of **Dr. Pillsbury**, a skilled mesmerist. Julian's house burns down during the night, but he is protected by his underground chamber. He is assumed dead, but 100 years later **Dr. Leete** discovers the chamber while preparing the site for the construction of a laboratory. Julian has not aged a day because his body has been in a state of suspended animation. Julian awakes to an entirely different world—one without war or poverty. Through Dr. Leete, Julian learns how these problems have been solved by basing the economy on public rather than private capital.

Lucy Westenra

Dracula
Bram Stoker

Mina Murray's best friend and an attractive, vivacious young woman. The first to fall under **Count Dracula**'s spell, Lucy becomes a vampire, which compromises her much-praised chastity and virtue, and banishes her soul from the promise of eternal rest. Determined that such an end is unfit for an English lady of Lucy's caliber, **Van Helsing**'s crew hunts down the demon she has become and kills it. They follow the rituals of vampire slaying and save Lucy's soul.

Mrs. Westenra

Dracula
Bram Stoker

Lucy Westenra's mother. A brittle woman of failing health, Mrs. Westenra inadvertently sabotages her daughter's safety by interfering with **Van Helsing**'s folk remedies. She dies of shock when a wolf leaps through Lucy's bedroom window.

Louisa Lily Denys Western

Sons and Lovers
D. H. Lawrence

A girl **William Morel** sees in London and to whom he becomes engaged. The rest of the family is less than impressed with Louisa when William brings her home, and William shortly becomes sick of her as well.

Mrs. Western

Tom Jones
Henry Fielding

The foil of her brother **Squire Western** and aunt of **Sophia**. Mrs. Western is a caricature of the artificial city lady who always acts out of expediency. Mrs. Western's sole aim in the novel is to improve the Western name by marrying off Sophia to the richest, most prosperous man she can find.

Sophia Western

Tom Jones
Henry Fielding

Daughter of the violent **Squire Western**. Like **Tom**, Sophia lavishes gifts on the poor, and she treats people of all classes with such respect that one landlady cannot believe she is a "gentlewoman." Sophia manages to reconcile her love for Tom, her filial duty to her father, and her hatred for **Blifil** through her courage and patience.

Squire Western

Tom Jones
Henry Fielding

Father of **Sophia**. Squire Western is a caricature of the rough-and-ready, conservative country gentleman. Affectionate at heart, the Squire nevertheless acts with extreme violence toward his daughter by constantly incarcerating her and even verbally and physically abusing her.

Haie Westhus

All Quiet on the Western Front
Erich Maria Remarque

One of **Paul Bäumer**'s friends in the Second Company. A gigantic, burly man, Westhus was a peat-digger before the war. He plans to serve a full term in the army after the war ends, since he finds peat-digging so unpleasant.

Westley

The Princess Bride
William Goldman

Buttercup's beloved farm boy. Westley is a brave, multitalented man who leaves to seek his fortune, is reportedly murdered by the **Dread Pirate Roberts**, and returns, costumed as the Man in Black, to rescue Buttercup from everything that threatens her. Westley beats **Vizzini**, **Fezzik**, and **Inigo**.

Abbot of Westminster

Richard II
William Shakespeare

A clergyman loyal to **King Richard II**. He is beheaded for conspiring to assassinate the newly crowned **King Henry IV** (Bolingbroke).

1st Earl of Westmorland

Henry IV, Part I; Henry IV, Part II; and *Henry V*
William Shakespeare

A nobleman and ally of **King Henry IV**. He warns Henry IV of **Owen Glendower** and the new threat to England in the beginning of *King Henry IV, Part I*. When war begins, he inspects and scoffs at **Sir John Falstaff**'s ragtag bunch of beggar-soldiers. In *King Henry IV, Part II*, Westmoreland meets with the rebels **Lord Thomas Mowbray**, **Lord Hastings**, and the **Archbishop of York**, accusing the latter of using his religious authority to support a rebellion. Westmoreland delivers the official list of the rebels' grievances to **John, Duke of Lancaster** and later orders their arrest for treason. In *Henry V*, Westmorland's offhanded comment about wishing for more troops from England during the battle of Agincourt sparks Henry V's famous St. Crispian's Day speech. He helps broker the peace between France and England following the war.

2nd Earl of Westmorland

Henry VI, Part III
William Shakespeare

A supporter of **King Henry VI** and ally of **Queen Margaret**. Though loyal to Henry, he is disgusted when the king agrees to relinquish the crown to the Yorkists following his death.

Mr. Weston

Emma
Jane Austen

Widower and proprietor of Randalls. When the novel begins, Mr. Weston has just married **Miss Taylor**, **Emma Woodhouse**'s former governess. Mr. Weston has a son, **Frank**, from his first marriage to **Miss Churchill**. Mr. Weston is warm, sociable, and perpetually optimistic.

Mrs. Weston

Emma
Jane Austen

Formerly Miss Taylor, **Emma Woodhouse**'s beloved governess and companion. Known for her kind temperament and her devotion to Emma, Mrs. Weston lives at Randalls with her husband, **Frank Churchill**'s father.

Wet nurse

Atlas Shrugged
Ayn Rand

A young bureaucrat sent by the government to watch over **Hank Rearden**'s mills. The Wet Nurse starts out as a cynical follower of the looters' code. The looters are the corrupt government officials who nationalize and regulate all industries, making a system based on "need" instead of on ability and merit. The looters make the Wet Nurse, whose real name is Tony, the Deputy Director of Distribution. The Wet Nurse is supposed to determine the amounts of orders, but realizes through this corrupt system that he respects and admires the producers, and that "fair share" doesn't really mean "fair." The Wet Nurse is shot and killed, dying in Rearden's arms, after refusing to help government goons enter Rearden's mills to start a riot.

Piet Wetjoen

The Iceman Cometh
Eugene O'Neill

Cecil Lewis's drinking partner. Wetjoen dreams of returning to South Africa, having left in disgrace for his cowardice during the Boer war.

Horace Whaley

Snow Falling on Cedars
David Guterson

The Island County coroner and a World War II veteran. Horace is shattered by his experience as a wartime doctor and feels like a shell of his former self. He envies **Carl Heine**'s strength and vitality even as he examines Carl's corpse.

Whammer

The Natural
Bernard Malamud

A talented but aging baseball player whom **Roy Hobbs** meets on his way to his first major league tryout. After both **the Whammer** and Hobbs reveal their prowess at a carnival, **Sam Simpson** bets the Whammer that Hobbs can strike him out. Hobbs does so, and the Whammer retreats back to the train, now an "old man."

Mrs. Whatsit

A Wrinkle in Time
Madeleine L'Engle

The youngest of the three celestial beings, along with **Mrs. Who** and **Mrs. Which**, who accompany **Meg Murry**, **Charles Wallace Murry**, and **Calvin O'Keefe** on their adventure to save **Mr. Murry**. Meg initially comes to know Mrs. Whatsit as the tramp who stole bed-sheets from **Mrs. Buncombe** and then sought shelter from a storm in the **Mrs. Murry**'s warm kitchen. Charles Wallace later figures out that Mrs. Whatsit gave up her existence as a star in order to fight **the Dark Thing**. When Meg goes back down to Camazotz to rescue Charles after the children have rescued Mr. Murry, Mrs. Whatsit enables the force of Meg's innate love.

Wheaties

Bless the Beasts and Children
Glendon Swarthout

The Bedwetters' camp counselor before **John Cotton** took pity on them and became their leader.

Harriet Wheelwright

A Prayer for Owen Meany
John Irving

John Wheelwright's maternal grandmother, a domineering, aristocratic woman who loves her family very deeply. Descended from John Adams, and having married into the most prominent family in Gravesend, Mrs. Wheelwright is the matriarch of the town in her old age.

John Wheelwright

A Prayer for Owen Meany
John Irving

Owen Meany's best friend, the narrator of the novel. The son of **Tabitha Wheelwright** and **Reverend Louis Merrill** (though he does not know who his father is until late in the story), John is raised by the aristocratic Wheelwright family.

Tabitha Wheelwright

A Prayer for Owen Meany
John Irving

John Wheelwright's mother, who keeps the identity of John's father a secret from him. Killed by a foul ball hit by **Owen Meany** in a 1953 Little League game.

Mrs. Which

A Wrinkle in Time
Madeleine L'Engle

The oldest of the three celestial beings who accompany the children on their adventure. Her companion beings are **Mrs. Whatsit** and **Mrs. Who**. Mrs. Which has difficulty materializing and is usually just a shimmering gleam. She often speaks in languages foreign to **Charles Wallace Murry**, **Meg Murry**, and **Calvin O'Keefe**, before translating what she says into English for them. She seems to be the most powerful of the three celestial beings. She instructs the children on how to manage the difficult task they have in rescuing **Mr. Murry**. As a gift to all three children before they go down to Camazotz, Mrs. Which gives them the command to go to the town on Camazotz and stay strong together.

Whipper

I Am the Cheese
Robert Cormier

A troublemaker. Whipper lives in the town of Carver, and with his two friends, harasses **Adam Farmer** by throwing things at him and approaching him like a bully. It turns out that Adam and Whipper are actually both at an institution and all of their interactions are actually taking place on the grounds there.

Hugh Whitbread

Mrs. Dalloway
Virginia Woolf

Clarissa Dalloway and **Peter Walsh**'s old friend, married to **Evelyn Whitbread**. An impeccable Englishman and upholder of English tradition, Hugh is vain, pompous, and gluttonous, and makes Clarissa feel young and insecure.

Corporal Whitcomb

Catch-22
Joseph Heller

The Chaplain's atheist assistant. Corporal Whitcomb believes that the chaplain has hurt his chances of advancing and implicates the chaplain in the Washington Irving scandal. The corporal is later promoted to sergeant.

White benefactress

Incidents in the Life of a Slave Girl
Harriet Ann Jacobs

An upper-class white friend of **Aunt Martha**'s who hides **Linda Brent** for a while.

White Fang

White Fang
Jack London

The main character. White Fang's mother, **Kiche**, is half wolf, half dog. His father, **One Eye**, is full wolf. White Fang starts his life in the wild, but becomes more and more of a dog after he and Kiche go to the Native American camp, where **Gray Beaver**, Kiche's former owner, lives. Because other dogs and humans are mean to White Fang, he turns his skills into fighting skills, becoming fierce and unloved. He is sold by a drunken and broke Gray Beaver to the evil **Beauty Smith**, who makes White Fang fight. It is only when he meets **Weedon Scott** and his friend **Matt** that White Fang becomes a loving dog. Weedon Scott ends up taking White Fang to California, where White Fang lives peacefully with **Judge Scott** and Weedon, eventually having a litter with **Collie**.

White King

Through the Looking Glass
Lewis Carroll

A bumbling and ineffectual ruler. He honors his promise to send all of his horses and all of his men with amazing swiftness when **Humpty Dumpty** falls off his wall.

White Knight

Through the Looking Glass
Lewis Carroll

A knight who is kind, gentle, and noble, despite his extreme clumsiness. He is terribly sentimental and enjoys **Alice**'s company immensely. Alice listens kindly to the awkward but gentle Knight, who obviously cherishes her company and regrets having to let her go.

White Queen

Through the Looking Glass
Lewis Carroll

A sweet but fairly stupid queen. She allows herself to be dominated in the presence of her red counterpart, the **Red Queen**.

White Rabbit

Alice in Wonderland
Lewis Carroll

A nervous character of somewhat important rank in Wonderland. He generally is in a hurry. The appearance of the White Rabbit marks the novel's transition from the real to the unreal.

White Witch

The Lion, the Witch, and the Wardrobe
C. S. Lewis

Evil queen of Narnia. She places a spell on the land so that it is always winter and never Christmas. The White Witch is the "Emperor's hangman," as **Mr. Beaver** says, and she has the right to kill any Narnian traitor. She wields a wand that turns creatures and people to stone. The wand also produces the Turkish Delight that enslaves **Edmund Pevensie** and makes him greedy. The Witch kills **Aslan**, and it is only after he rises from the dead that he defeats her.

Byram B. White

All the King's Men
Robert Penn Warren

The State Auditor during **Willie**'s first term as governor. His acceptance of graft money propels a scandal that eventually leads to an impeachment attempt against Willie. Willie protects White and blackmails his enemies into submission, a decision that leads to his estrangement from **Lucy** and the resignation of **Hugh Miller**.

Helen White

Winesburg, Ohio
Sherwood Anderson

A local girl, who is romantically connected to both **Seth Richmond** and **George Willard**.

Mrs. White

Oranges Are Not the Only Fruit
Jeanette Winterson

A very religious member of **Jeanette**'s church. With **Jeanette's mother**, Mrs. White represents one of the church members who holds unbending ideas about sin and goodness.

Randy White

A Prayer for Owen Meany
John Irving

The headmaster at Gravesend Academy, who is responsible for **Owen Meany**'s expulsion shortly before graduation. Mr. White loses his job as a result of the incident.

Stanford White

Ragtime
E. L. Doctorow

A famous architect. Stanford White dies at the hands of **Harry Thaw**.

Whitfield

As I Lay Dying
William Faulkner

The local minister. Whitfield has had an affair with **Addie Bundren** and fathered **Jewel**.

Charles S. Whitman

Ragtime
E. L. Doctorow

The District Attorney of New York. He helps to negotiate **Coalhouse**'s evacuation of **Morgan**'s property.

Walter Whitmore

Henry VI, Part II
William Shakespeare

A pirate who, with his **Captain**, attacks **William de la Pole, Duke of Suffolk**'s ship. Because he has lost his eye in the battle, Whitmore declares that will kill his hostage, Suffolk. When the Captain and Whitmore find out Suffolk's identity, they scorn him for his traitorous actions and order his beheading.

Whittaker

The Caine Mutiny
Herman Wouk

The African-American steward's mate on the *Caine*. Whittaker, an enlisted sailor, must provide coffee for the officers whenever they want it and prepare the meals.

Abel Whittle

The Mayor of Casterbridge
Thomas Hardy

One of the workers in **Michael Henchard**'s hay yard. Abel Whittle is the source of the first disagreement between the business partners Henchard and **Donald Farfrae**, as Farfrae thinks that Henchard is too rough with Whittle when he is constantly late for work. When **Elizabeth-Jane Newson** tracks down Henchard to make amends with him, she tracks him to Whittle's house. Whittle notifies her that he has just died and left a will.

Mrs. Who

A Wrinkle in Time
Madeleine L'Engle

The second of the three celestial beings who accompany the children on their adventure. Her companions are **Mrs. Whatsit** and **Mrs. Which**. She usually speaks in quotations from famous thinkers and writers because she finds it too difficult to craft her own sentences. When **Charles Wallace Murry**, **Meg Murry**, and **Calvin O'Keefe** first meet Mrs. Who, she is sewing the stolen sheets of **Mrs. Buncombe** in the haunted house in their neighborhood. Before the children go down to Camazotz, Mrs. Who gives them gifts. Her gifts emphasize the intelligence and wit the children must use to rescue Mr. Murry.

Mr. Whymper

Animal Farm
George Orwell

The human solicitor whom **Napoleon** hires to represent Animal Farm in human society. Mr. Whymper's entry into the Animal Farm community initiates contact between Animal Farm and human society, alarming the common animals.

Dr. Wick

Girl, Interrupted
Susanna Kaysen

An older female psychiatrist on the hospital staff. Dr. Wick is from Africa and is entirely unfamiliar with the American youth culture of her patients. Vulgarity and frank discussion of sex embarrass Dr. Wick, whose efforts at treatment are dubiously effective.

Terry Wickett

Arrowsmith
Sinclair Lewis

A laboratory scientist at the McGurk Institute in New York. Much like **Martin Arrowsmith**'s mentor, **Max Gottlieb**, **Terry** is completely committed to his work, to the point that he does not have a family or much of a social life. Martin initially dislikes Terry, who is stubborn and seen as cold. By the end of the novel, he becomes a symbol of freedom and independence for Martin, and the two reach an underst anding and ultimately become research partners.

Agnes Wickfield

David Copperfield
Charles Dickens

David Copperfield's true love and second wife. Agnes, the daughter of **Mr. Wickfield**, is calm and gentle. She patiently endures David's other romances, hiding her love for him. Agnes always comforts David with kind words or advice.

George Wickham

Pride and Prejudice
Jane Austen

A handsome, fortune-hunting militia officer. Wickham's good looks and charm attract **Elizabeth Bennet** initially, but **Fitzwilliam Darcy**'s insights into Wickham's disreputable past reveals his true nature to Elizabeth even as it draws her closer to Darcy.

Cole Widener

Prodigal Summer
Barbara Kingsolver

Lusa Maluf Landowski's young husband. Cole dies in a traffic accident, leaving Lusa the family farm.

Widow

All's Well that Ends Well
William Shakespeare

Diana's mother. She generously invites the disguised **Helena** to stay with her while in Florence. With Diana and Helena, the Widow helps contrive the plot to trick **Bertram** into giving up his ring and sleeping with Helena.

Widow

Robinson Crusoe
Daniel Defoe

A friend of **Crusoe**'s. The widow keeps 200 pounds safe for Crusoe during his thirty-five years of journeying. She returns it loyally to Crusoe upon his return to England.

The Wife of Bath

The Canterbury Tales
Geoffrey Chaucer

A seamstress from Bath, England, who tells a tale about her five husbands. She has been married five times and had many other affairs in her youth, making her well practiced in the art of love. She presents herself as someone who loves marriage and sex, but, from what we see of her, she also takes pleasure in rich attire, talking, and arguing. She has traveled on pilgrimages to Jerusalem three times and elsewhere in Europe.

The Wife of Bath's first three husbands

The Canterbury Tales
Geoffrey Chaucer

Three rich and old men. **The Wife of Bath** could order them around, use sex to get what she wanted, and trick them into believing lies.

The Wife of Bath's fourth husband

The Canterbury Tales
Geoffrey Chaucer

The **Wife of Bath** says comparatively little about her fourth husband. She loved him, but he was a reveler who had a mistress.

The Wife of Bath's fifth husband

The Canterbury Tales
Geoffrey Chaucer

A twenty-year-old former student with whom **the Wife of Bath** was madly in love. He reads her a book about wicked wives, and his stories frustrate her so much that one night she rips a page out of his book. He delivers the Wife a deafening smack on her ear in retaliation. When the Wife delivers a smack in return, the two adopt a shaky and loving peace.

Barb Wiggin

A Prayer for Owen Meany
John Irving

Dudley Wiggin's insufferable wife, a former stewardess.

Ender Wiggin

Ender's Game
Orson Scott Card

The younger brother of **Peter Wiggin** and **Valentine Wiggin**. At age six, Ender is chosen by **Colonel Graff** and the International Fleet to help save mankind from the buggers. Ender is afraid of his brother and loves his sister. Wherever he goes, Ender makes things happen, and by age nine he is given his own army to command. Ender is angry at the various people who manipulate him during his fleet training.

Peter Wiggin

Ender's Game
Orson Scott Card

Ender Wiggin and **Valentine Wiggin**'s older brother. Peter is a cruel and evil child, gifted in manipulation. Peter tortures Ender endlessly until Ender is sent to Battle School. He believes that the buggers will soon be defeated, creating a whole new political reality, and, under the pseudonym Locke, he uses the computer networks to spread his ideas.

Reverend Dudley Wiggin

A Prayer for Owen Meany
John Irving

The brash, ridiculous Episcopalian rector in Gravesend, who puts on the ill-fated 1953 Christmas pageant in which **Owen Meany** plays the baby Jesus. His wife **Barb Wiggin** is a former stewardess.

Valentine Wiggin

Ender's Game
Orson Scott Card

Ender Wiggin's older sister. The only person in the world who truly loves Ender, she protects him from **Peter Wiggin**, their sadistic older brother. Along with Peter, Valentine takes an active interest in the world's political situation. Writing under the pseudonym Demosthenes, she begins to exert influence over the changing situation. After the Third Invasion, Valentine convinces Ender to go with her to colonize the bugger worlds, and she writes a history of the world during their travels. Later, she joins Ender in his search for a new world for the buggers.

Grant Wiggins

A Lesson Before Dying
Ernest J. Gaines

The protagonist and narrator of the novel, an elementary school teacher in his mid-twenties. Grant is intelligent and willful, but a life spent in a segregated, racist community has made him bitter, hypocritical, and depressed. His defeatist attitude makes him shun responsibility, and he resents **Tante Lou** and **Miss Emma** for forcing him to help **Jefferson**. Over the course of the novel, however, Grant learns to accept responsibility for his own life, for his relations with other people, and for his role as an educator and agent of change in his needy community.

Wiglaf

Beowulf
Unknown

A young kinsman and retainer of **Beowulf** who helps him in the fight against the **dragon** while all of the other warriors run away. Wiglaf adheres to the heroic code better than Beowulf's other retainers, thereby proving himself a suitable successor to Beowulf.

Charles Wilcox

Howards End
E. M. Forster

The oldest Wilcox son, a self-centered, aggressive, moralistic young man who represents the negative aspects of the Wilcoxes' materialistic pragmatism. He is married to **Dolly Wilcox**. Charles is sentenced to three years in prison at the end of the novel for killing **Leonard Bast**.

Dolly Wilcox

Howards End
E. M. Forster

Charles Wilcox's wife, a scatterbrained, insecure girl who often causes trouble by revealing secrets.

Evie Wilcox

Howards End
E. M. Forster

The youngest Wilcox daughter, a self-centered, petulant young girl who, at eighteen, marries **Percy Cahill**.

Henry Wilcox

Howards End
E. M. Forster

The patriarch of the Wilcox family, a prominent London businessman. Henry is married to **Ruth Wilcox** and later to **Margaret Schegel**. Stuffy, conventional, and chauvinistic, Henry typifies the Wilcox family, which represents the pragmatic, materialistic aspect of the English upper classes.

Mr. Wilcox

A Day No Pigs Would Die
Robert Newton Peck

The county coroner who arranges **Haven Peck**'s funeral.

Paul Wilcox

Howards End
E. M. Forster

The youngest Wilcox son, who travels to Nigeria to make his fortune in the British colony. Before he leaves, he has a brief romance with **Helen Schlegel**.

Ruth Wilcox

Howards End
E. M. Forster

Henry Wilcox's wife, who dies in the first half of the novel. Gentle, selfless, loving, and strangely omniscient, Mrs. Wilcox seems to represent the past of England. Howards End belongs to her, and she attempts to leave it to **Margaret Schlegel** when she dies, an attempt that is blocked by Henry and **Charles Wilcox**.

Wild

Jazz
Toni Morrison

A dark-skinned woman who roams through the woods near Vienna, Virginia. She is called "Wild" because she bites **Henry LesTroy**'s arm as he helps her to deliver her child, **Joe Trace**. Her origins are mysterious. **Golden Gray** accompanies Wild into the woods and the two of them make their home in a secret hovel.

Wild Bob

Slaughterhouse-Five
Kurt Vonnegut

A deranged army colonel whom **Billy Pilgrim** meets in the German rail yard.

Taggart Wilde

The Big Sleep
Raymond Chandler

The local district attorney.

Wilder

White Noise
Don DeLillo

Babette's innocent youngest son. Wilder never speaks and yet remains an essential source of comfort for both **Jack Gladney** and Babette, even when he cries for hours on end.

Captain Wilder

The Martian Chronicles
Ray Bradbury

The captain of the fourth expedition to Mars. When Jeff Spender tries to murder the crew, Wilder kills him, but tries to carry on Spender's mission to preserve Mars. Wilder is sent off to explore Jupiter and Pluto. He returns to a desolated Mars, where he finds **Hathaway** living with a family of robots.

Damon Wildeve

The Return of the Native
Thomas Hardy

A local innkeeper. At the start of the novel, he puts off his marriage to **Thomasin Yeobright** in order to pursue a relationship with the woman he truly wants, **Eustacia Vye**. They fill their time with childish squabbling and arguments. When Damon is jilted by Eustacia, he marries Thomasin and has a daughter with her. He drowns at the end of the novel just before making an escape with Eustacia.

Montana Wildhack

Slaughterhouse-Five
Kurt Vonnegut

A nubile young actress who is kidnapped by the **Tralfamadorians** to be **Billy Pilgrim**'s mate inside the zoo. Billy wins Montana's trust and love and fathers a child by her in Tralfamadore. Billy likely is delusional about his experiences with Montana, whose presence may have been imaginatively triggered by a visit to an adult bookstore in Times Square.

Tommy Wilhelm

Seize the Day
Saul Bellow

The novel's protagonist, a forty-four-year-old man who is living temporarily in New York City. In a state of marital and financial turmoil, he has moved to a hotel on the Upper West Side to ask for his father's assistance. Tommy has worked many an odd jobs after a stint in acting but ended up with a steady position in sales. He has recently been laid off, however, and has a strained relationship with his father, is separated from his wife, and is in love with a woman he cannot marry. A constant disappointment to his father, Tommy has also invested the last of his money in a joint investment venture bound to fail.

George Wilkens

Go Down, Moses
William Faulkner

The black man who marries **Lucas Beauchamp**'s daughter.

Jonas Wilkerson

Gone with the Wind
Margaret Mitchell

The Yankee overseer of Tara whom **Gerald O'Hara** fires for impregnating **Emmie Slattery**. Jonas works for the Freedmen's Bureau after the war and marries Emmie. He raises taxes on Tara to try to force out the O'Haras, prompting **Scarlett O'Hara**'s marriage to **Frank Kennedy**.

Ashley Wilkes

Gone with the Wind
Margaret Mitchell

The handsome, chivalrous, and honorable heir to the Twelve Oaks plantation near Tara. Ashley bewitches **Scarlett O'Hara** through most of the novel. After the war, Ashley becomes resigned and sad, and he regrets not marrying Scarlett. Committed to his honor and Southern tradition, he cannot adjust to the post-war South.

India Wilkes

Gone with the Wind
Margaret Mitchell

Ashley Wilkes's cold and jealous sister. India never forgives **Scarlett O'Hara** for stealing **Stuart Tarleton** from her during their youth. At one point India catches Scarlett embracing Ashley Wilkes and gossips about it, causing a great debate among all of Atlanta society.

Melanie Hamilton Wilkes

Gone with the Wind
Margaret Mitchell

The frail, good-hearted wife of **Ashley Wilkes**. Melanie provokes **Scarlett O'Hara**'s jealous hatred throughout most of the novel. After the two women suffer together through the Civil War, however, a strong bond forms between them.

Professor Wilkins

The Unvanquished
William Faulkner

Bayard's mentor and landlord at the University of Mississippi. When Bayard receives word of his father's death, Professor Wilkins awkwardly tries to lend him a pistol.

The Wilkses

The Adventures of Huckleberry Finn
Mark Twain

A family who is swindled by **the duke** and **the dauphin**. Through a series of quickly-thought-out plans, **Huckleberry Finn** causes the fortune that the con men stole from the Wilks family to be buried with the body of Peter Wilks. The real English Wilks brothers appear, and the duke and the dauphin are run out of town.

Will

Homecoming
Cynthia Voigt

The owner of the circus. Will saves the children from **Rudyard** and drives them to Crisfield. Will is a caring and philosophical man who enjoys the rootlessness life in the circus affords him.

Will's mother

Something Wicked This Way Comes
Ray Bradbury

A truly happy and content woman who is present mostly in **William Halloway**'s thoughts. She is protected from the carnival by Will and her husband, **Charles Halloway**.

Willard

Regeneration
Pat Barker

A patient who comes to Craiglockhart relatively late in the novel. Although there is nothing physically wrong with his spine, Willard is paralyzed from the waist down. Willard quickly grows frustrated by his feelings of powerlessness, but by the end of the novel he recovers his ability to walk.

Buddy Willard

The Bell Jar
Sylvia Plath

Esther Greenwood's college boyfriend, he is an athletic, intelligent, good-looking man who graduated from Yale and went to medical school. Buddy cares for Esther but has conventional ideas about women's roles and fails to understand Esther's interest in poetry.

Elizabeth Willard

Winesburg, Ohio
Sherwood Anderson

George Willard's mother, and **Tom Willard**'s wife. She lives in the family's run-down boarding house, where she is constantly ill and has become an invalid.

George Willard

Winesburg, Ohio
Sherwood Anderson

A young man who works as a reporter in Winesburg, Ohio. As a result of either chance meetings or other people's decisions to confide in him, George is the figure who links many of the novel's disparate stories together.

Mrs. Willard

The Bell Jar
Sylvia Plath

A friend of **Esther Greenwood**'s mother, **Mrs. Greenwood**, and the mother of Esther's sometime boyfriend, **Buddy Willard**. Mrs. Willard, who feels protective of her son, has traditional ideas about the roles men and women should play.

Professor Willard

Our Town
Thornton Wilder

A professor at the State University who gives the audience a report on Grover's Corners.

Tom Willard

Winesburg, Ohio
Sherwood Anderson

George Willard's father and **Elizabeth Willard**'s husband, a middle-aged man with frustrated political ambitions.

Eddie Willers

Atlas Shrugged
Ayn Rand

Dagny Taggart's assistant at Taggart Transcontinental Railroad and a hard worker dedicated to the preservation of the rail service. Through his friendship and everyday lunch with the mysterious track worker in the cafeteria, Eddie Willers unwittingly provides the mysterious man with information about Dagny and the railroad. It turns out that this mysterious man is **John Galt**.

William

As You Like It
William Shakespeare

A young country boy who is in love with **Audrey**. **Touchstone** comically scares him into leaving Audrey by threatening to kill him.

William

Incidents in the Life of a Slave Girl
Harriet Ann Jacobs

Linda Brent's brother, to whom she is close. William's escape from **Mr. Sands**, his relatively "kind" master, shows that even a privileged slave desires freedom above all else.

Father William

The Bean Trees
Barbara Kingsolver

The priest who works with **Mattie**, transporting illegal immigrants to and from her house.

Abigail Williams

The Crucible
Arthur Miller

Reverend Parris's niece. Abigail Williams was once the servant for the Proctor household, but **Elizabeth Proctor** fired her after she discovered that Abigail was having an affair with her husband, **John Proctor**. Abigail is smart, wily, sexual, a good liar, and vindictive when crossed. She tells lies, manipulates her friends and the entire town, and eventually sends nineteen innocent people to their deaths. The witch trials, then, in which the girls are allowed to act as though they have a direct connection to God, empower the previously powerless Abigail. Once shunned and scorned by the respectable townsfolk, Abigail now finds that she has clout, and she takes full advantage of it. When **Reverend John Hale** returns to Salem after the worst of the trials are over, and some citizens are about to be hanged; Parris tells Hale that **Mercy Lewis** and Abigail robbed Parris and then vanished from Salem.

Cold Sassy Tree
Olive Anne Burns

Campbell Williams

Loma Williams's husband. Campbell, called Camp, fails at home and at work. He wants to please but finds himself hampered by his own incompetence.

The Martian Chronicles
Ray Bradbury

Captain Williams

The leader of the second expedition. A clever man, he quickly realizes that he and his three men have been placed in an insane asylum. He is killed by a Martian who thinks that he and his crew are secondary hallucinations.

Cold Sassy Tree
Olive Anne Burns

Loma Williams

Mary Willis's younger sister. Loma is a bossy, jealous, and often petulant young woman. She dreams of being a writer or an actress and chafes against her dead-end marriage to the useless **Campbell Williams**.

Henry V
William Shakespeare

Michael Williams

An English soldier. The night before the Battle of Agincourt, **King Henry V** disguises himself and argues with Williams, **John Bates**, and **Alexander Court** about the worthiness of the French war. Though he disagrees heatedly with them, and ends up exchanging gloves with Williams as the promise of a future fight, When the King confronts him after the Battle of Agincourt, Williams apologizes, but insists that he cannot be held responsible, because the King came disguised. Approving of Williams's courage, Henry orders his glove filled with crowns.

Black Like Me
John Howard Griffin

Sterling Williams

A soft-spoken, articulate black man who shines shoes for a living. Williams is **John Howard Griffin**'s contact in the black society of New Orleans, and first helps him make the transition from being a white man to being a black man.

The Member of the Wedding
Carson McCullers

T.T. Williams

Berenice Sadie Brown's latest beau, who is well off and works in a restaurant. He and Berenice eventually agree to marry.

Winesburg, Ohio
Sherwood Anderson

Wash Williams

The Winesburg telegraph operator. A fat, filthy man, he despises the world.

Williamson

The Martian Chronicles
Ray Bradbury

A member of the crew that **Captain Wilder** took to Jupiter and Pluto. He goes to investigate whether **Hathaway**'s real family might be dead.

John Williamson

Glengarry Glen Ross
David Mamet

The manager of the real estate office. Williamson's job is to oversee the operations of the office and assign the salesmen their leads. The salesmen dislike him because of his status as "company man"—he merely follows orders from the unseen **Mitch** and **Murray**, and the salesmen do not think he really understands the business. Nonetheless, when he sees an opportunity to scam—bargaining with **Shelly Levene** to break company policy by selling him two leads—he is quite willing to put company loyalty aside.

Willie

Happy Days
Samuel Beckett

Married to **Winnie**. Willie crawls in and out of his hole behind her and is generally offstage. He ignores Winnie most of the time, either sleeping or reading his newspaper.

Willie

The Heart Is a Lonely Hunter
Carson McCullers

Dr. Benedict Mady Copeland's son and **Portia**'s brother, who works in the kitchen at **Biff Brannon**'s cafe. Willie always carries his trademark harmonica and plays it wherever he goes. He is a sweet young man, but not very bright, and he gets into trouble primarily by being in the wrong place at the wrong time.

Boy Willie

The Piano Lesson
August Wilson

Berniece's brash, impulsive, and fast-talking brother. Coming from Mississippi, he plans to sell the family piano and buy the land his ancestors once worked as slaves. By selling the piano, he will avenge his property-less father, Boy Charles, as well as symbolically prove that he and his family are the equal of the white man. In the final scene, he solidifies his link in the family by engaging in a battle with the ghost of the piano's previous owner.

Elisabeth Willie

Dead Man Walking
Helen Prejean

Robert Willie's mother. A hardworking woman, she has a terrible time dealing with her son's execution.

Robert Willie

Dead Man Walking
Helen Prejean

The second death-row inmate **Sister Helen Prejean** counsels. Robert has been sentenced to death for the rape and murder of **Faith Hathaway**. Strong-willed and defiant, Willie has been in and out of jail since he was fourteen years old. He is a complicated figure, at once contrite and defiant. Unlike **Patrick Sonnier**,

Robert knows his execution is inevitable and approaches it with false bravado. In the end, he opens himself up to Prejean's love, believing that he has accepted the truth and that it will set him free. He dies peacefully after apologizing to Faith's family.

In Cold Blood
Truman Capote

Willie-Jay

Assistant to the chaplain of Lansing, the Kansas state prison. Willie-Jay becomes a kind of mentor to **Perry Edward Smith**.

Cold Sassy Tree
Olive Anne Burns

Mary Willis

Rucker Blakeslee's older daughter. Mary Willis is conventional and nervous, but kind. The death of her mother deeply affects Mary Willis. She mourns for a long time and finds it difficult to forgive her father for remarrying so quickly.

Evelina
Fanny Burney

Sir Clement Willoughby

A duplicitous, upper-class rake who pursues **Evelina Anville** relentlessly. Lord Clement is a skilled social chameleon ruled by his passions, with no honor or integrity, who acts as a foil to **Lord Orville**. Lord Clement is an intelligent and educated gentleman whose manners are entirely assumed.

Sense and Sensibility
Jane Austen

John Willoughby

An attractive but deceitful young man. Willoughby wins **Marianne Dashwood**'s heart, then abandons her for the wealthy **Miss Sophia Grey**.

Richard II
William Shakespeare

Lord Willoughby

An early supporter of **Henry Bolingbroke**. Following the death of **John of Gaunt**, Willoughby, along with the **Earl of Northumberland** and **Lord Ross**, acknowledge the ruinous reign of **King Richard II**; when Northumberland reveals that Bolingbroke has come to England with an army, the three decide to join forces with him to return England to its former glory.

The Count of Monte Cristo
Alexandre Dumas

Lord Wilmore

See **Edmond Dantès**.

Uncle Wilse

The Light in the Forest
Conrad Richter

A radical white supremacist and leader of the infamous Paxton boys, **True Son**'s large-set and powerful uncle. He believes strongly in the extermination of the Indian race. Like his nephew True Son, Wilse is stubborn, passionate about his feelings, and willing to use violence against those he perceives as enemies.

Wilson

The Red Badge of Courage
Stephen Crane

A loud private; **Henry Fleming**'s friend in the regiment. Wilson and Henry grow close as they share the harsh experiences of war and gain a reputation as the regiment's best fighters.

Wilson

The Dumb Waiter
Harold Pinter

The unseen boss of **Gus** and **Ben**. Though Wilson never shows up onstage, it is clear that he is more powerful and of a higher social class than Gus and Ben. The messages that Gus and Ben receive may or may not be from Wilson or his henchmen. These messages include a mysterious delivery of an envelope full of matches, numerous written notes delivered by means of a dumb waiter, and unintelligible calls made through a speaking tube. Wilson may also own the café in which the play is set.

Baby Wilson

The Heart Is a Lonely Hunter
Carson McCullers

Lucile Wilson's daughter. Baby is an obedient and pleasant, although somewhat prissy, little girl with blond curls and blue eyes. She becomes petulant and rude to her mother after her accident in the second half of the novel.

George Wilson

The Great Gatsby
F. Scott Fitzgerald

The lifeless, exhausted owner of a run-down auto shop at the edge of the "valley of ashes," a dismal industrial zone between New York City and the Long Island suburbs. George, who loves and idealizes his wife, **Myrtle**, is devastated that she is having an affair with the boorish **Tom Buchanan** and consumed with grief when she is killed in a roadside accident. Mistakenly believing that **Jay Gatsby** was Myrtle's lover and the driver of the car that killed her, George shoots Gatsby and then turns the gun on himself.

Ivy Wilson

The Grapes of Wrath
John Steinbeck

A man traveling to California with his wife, **Sairy Wilson**. The Wilsons meet the Joad family on Route 66 and lend the Joads their tent so that **Grampa Joad** can have a comfortable place to die. In return, the Joads fix the Wilsons' broken-down car.

Reverend Mr. John Wilson

The Scarlet Letter
Nathaniel Hawthorne

Boston's scholarly yet grandfatherly clergyman. He is a stereotypical Puritan, a stiff American patriarch. Like **Governor Bellingham**, Wilson follows the community's rules strictly but can be swayed by **Reverend Arthur Dimmesdale**'s eloquence. Unlike Dimmesdale, Wilson preaches hellfire and damnation and advocates harsh punishment of sinners.

Leroy Wilson

The Heart Is a Lonely Hunter
Carson McCullers

Lucile Wilson's ex-husband. Leroy frequently abused Lucile and then bragged about it to other men, prompting **Biff Brannon** to beat him up.

Lucile Wilson

The Heart Is a Lonely Hunter
Carson McCullers

Biff Brannon's sister-in-law. Mrs. Wilson has huge ambitions for her daughter, **Baby Wilson**, to be famous. Mrs. Wilson is raising Baby alone, for her former husband, **Leroy Wilson**, used to beat her.

Myrtle Wilson

The Great Gatsby
F. Scott Fitzgerald

The passionate, voluptuous wife of the garage owner **George Wilson**. **Myrtle**, desperate to improve her lot in life, has an affair with the boorish **Tom Buchanan**, who treats her as a mere object of desire and breaks her nose one night in a bout of drunken anger. Myrtle is killed when Tom's wife, **Daisy**, inadvertently strikes her with Gatsby's car on a Long Island road.

Pudd'nhead Wilson

Pudd'nhead Wilson
Mark Twain

The town eccentric in Dawson's Landing. Pudd'nhead Wilson first comes to Dawson's Landing intending to set up a law practice as David Wilson. His sense of humor proves too much for the townspeople, though, and his law practice goes nowhere; he earns the name Pudd'nhead. He fills his time with odd surveying and accounting jobs, and dabbles in a number of quasi-scientific hobbies, most notably fingerprinting and palmistry. **Judge Driscoll** is his closest friend, and the two of them are the members of Dawson's Landing's "Freethinker's Society." He eventually gets elected mayor. In the end, it is Pudd'nhead's fingerprinting system that proves that "Tom" is the murderer of Judge Driscoll, and not **Luigi Capello** and **Angelo Capello**.

Sairy Wilson

The Grapes of Wrath
John Steinbeck

A sickly woman traveling to California with her husband, **Ivy Wilson**. When the Wilsons encounter the Joad family on Route 66, the two families combine forces, hoping to make the trip easier. The Wilsons and Joads travel together until Sairy's health forces her and Ivy to stop.

Stark Wilson

Shane
Jack Schaefer

A man brought into town by **Fletcher** after it is clear that **Shane** and **Joe Starrett** will not back down. Stark Wilson kills a short-fused town framer, Ernie Wright. Shane wants to make sure to warn the townspeople not to have any confrontation with him, as Wilson will use it as an excuse to shoot them.

William Wilson

"William Wilson"
Edgar Allan Poe

The narrator who murders his double, also named William Wilson. The first William Wilson suffers from a split personality: he takes a figment of his imagination and gives it physical shape. William Wilson loses his personal identity when he discovers a classmate who shares not only his full name but also his physical appearance and manner of speaking. When the narrator attempts to murder his double in the story's final moments, he actually ends up killing himself.

Wilson-Harris

The Sun Also Rises
Ernest Hemingway

A British man whom **Jake Barnes** and **Bill Gorton** befriend while fishing in Spain. The three men, all World War I veterans, are quick to bond over their shared war experiences.

Eric Wind

Pnin
Vladimir Nabokov

The doctor who lures **Liza Pnin Wind** away from **Timofey Pnin**. Although Liza is carrying Eric's child when she returns to Pnin, he gratefully takes her back, and they soon board a ship for America. Eric follows them to America, planning to marry Liza after Pnin has paid her passage.

Liza Pnin Wind

Pnin
Vladimir Nabokov

Timofey Pnin's ex-wife. Eternally unsatisfied, Liza goes through several husbands over the course of the novel. She is brusque with Pnin, who loves her despite her unkindness.

Victor Wind

Pnin
Vladimir Nabokov

The son of **Liza Pnin Wind** and **Eric Wind**, who are both specialists in abnormal psychology.

John Windmuller

Lolita
Vladimir Nabokov

The lawyer to whom **John Farlow** entrusts the Haze estate. Jack handles the estate but wants nothing to do with the "sordid" business regarding **Humbert Humbert**'s manuscript and the impending trial.

Windy

Homecoming
Cynthia Voigt

A garrulous and friendly Yale undergraduate who takes the Tillermans in one rainy night in New Haven. Windy explains his generosity by telling the children of his own experiences as a young runaway.

Tim Winer

The Virgin Suicides
Jeffrey Eugenides

The neighborhood brain. Tim is overly smart and physically weak. When the boys need plots, insight, codes, anatomical remarks on fish flies, or handwriting analysis, they turn to Tim.

Amanda Wingfield

The Glass Menagerie
Tennessee Williams

Laura Wingfield and **Tom Wingfield**'s mother. A proud, vivacious woman, Amanda Wingfield clings to memories of a vanished, genteel past. Amanda's constant wait for gentleman callers to appear in the Depression-wreck St. Louis becomes an incessant annoyance. Amanda nags Tom constantly and refuses to see Laura for who she truly is, but Amanda also reveals a willingness to sacrifice for her loved ones. She subjects herself to the humiliating drudgery of subscription sales in order to enhance Laura's marriage prospects. Like her children, Amanda withdraws from reality into fantasy.

Laura Wingfield

The Glass Menagerie
Tennessee Williams

Amanda Wingfield's daughter and **Tom Wingfield**'s younger sister. Laura Wingfield has a bad leg, on which she has to wear a brace, and she walks with a limp. Painfully shy, she has largely withdrawn from the outside world and devotes herself to old records and her collection of glass figurines. Amanda uses the contrast between herself and Laura to emphasize the glamour of her own youth as a Southern belle and to fuel her hope of recreating that youth through Laura. Tom and **Jim O'Connor** both see Laura as an exotic creature, completely and rather quaintly foreign to the rest of the world. When Tom abandons his home just as **Mr. Wingfield** did, he finds that he cannot leave the memory of Laura behind.

Mr. Wingfield

The Glass Menagerie
Tennessee Williams

Amanda Wingfield's husband, **Laura Wingfield** and **Tom Wingfield**'s father. Mr. Wingfield was a handsome man who worked for a telephone company. He abandoned his family years before the action of the play and never appears onstage.

Tom Wingfield

The Glass Menagerie
Tennessee Williams

Amanda Wingfield's and **Mr. Wingfield**'s son, and **Laura Wingfield**'s older brother. An aspiring poet, Tom works at a shoe warehouse to support the family. He is frustrated by the numbing routine of his job and escapes it through movies, literature, and alcohol. Tom invites **Jim O'Connor** over for dinner, exciting both Laura's residual affections for her high school crush and Amanda's excitement to receive a "gentleman caller" for her daughter. When they learn that Jim is engaged to be married, Amanda attacks Tom for being a selfish dreamer lost in his own world. After he cruelly abandons his mother and sister, just as his father did, he cannot leave the memory of Laura behind.

Wining Boy

The Piano Lesson
August Wilson

A wandering, washed-up recording star who drifts in and out of his brother **Doaker Charles**'s household whenever he finds himself broke. A comic figure, he functions as one of the play's primary storytellers, recounting anecdotes from his travels.

Wee Willie Winkie

Midnight's Children
Salman Rushdie

Saleem's biological father.

Winky

Harry Potter and the Goblet of Fire
J. K. Rowling

Once **Bartemius Crouch**'s house-elf, and now a free elf working at Hogwarts. She is a squeaky, hysterical, unconfident figure.

Winnie

Happy Days
Samuel Beckett

The protagonist, married to **Willie**. Winnie is buried in a mound of earth that grows higher each day as Willie lies in a hole behind her. She fills up her days with talk that Willie ignores, performing rituals with implements from her black bag. She punctuates her babble with the nearly constant optimistic proclamation that today will be a "happy day."

Winnie's mother

The Kitchen God's Wife
Amy Tan

The woman who mysteriously disappeared from **Winnie**'s life and changed it forever. She had been a modern Shanghai woman who had wanted to marry for love and was, instead, forced to take on the position of second wife to a man whom she did not love.

Ned Winsett

The Age of Innocence
Edith Wharton

Newland Archer's bohemian journalist friend.

Dallas Winston

The Outsiders
S. E. Hinton

See **Dally**.

Lady de Winter

The Three Musketeers
Alexandre Dumas

A mysterious, beautiful, dangerous, and ultimately evil agent of **Cardinal Richelieu**, and the sister-in-law of the **Lord de Winter**. She is responsible for the kidnapping of **d'Artagnan**'s beloved, **Madame Bonacieux**. D'Artagnan becomes obsessed with the Lady, also known as the Woman from Meung, or Milady. D'Artagnan has sex with the Lady, posing as the man she loves, the **Comte de Wardes**, in order to gain information about Madame Bonacieux's whereabouts. **Athos** seems to have a possible secret past with the Lady. In a drunken stupor, Athos confesses that he married a young woman of humble background, breaking the rules of social conduct for idealistic love. One day, he discovered that this woman was branded with the Fleur-de-Lis on her left shoulder, a symbol put on the most heinous of criminals. The young woman was a fraud; all she wanted was money and social power. In mad sadness, Athos hung his wife. After d'Artagnan manipulates the Lady sexually, Athos and d'Artagnan become convinced that the Lady de Winter is somehow Athos's presumed-dead wife. Athos finds the Lady and confronts her. Athos, **Aramis**, **Porthos**, and d'Artagnan end up defeating the Lady, putting her on trial, and having her beheaded, but not until after the Lady has killed Madame Bonacieux and manipulated **John Felton** into killing **George Villiers, the Duke of Buckingham**.

Lord de Winter

The Three Musketeers
Alexandre Dumas

Lady de Winter's brother-in-law. **D'Artagnan** almost slays the Lord de Winter, but stops so that he can learn more about his sister-in-law. Lord de Winter is a foppish gentlemen, not given to intrigue or action, but he rises to the occasion when **Planchet** takes **Aramis**'s letter to the Lord, warning him of the Lady's plans on his life and her criminal history. The Lord follows the urgings of the letter and imprisons the Lady when she gets to Britain.

Mr. Winterbottom

Walk Two Moons
Sharon Creech

Phoebe's father. Like his wife, Mr. Winterbottom fills his role as husband and father exactingly. He diligently works at his nine-to-five job as a mapmaker and comes home, withdrawn, distant, and largely unspeaking, responding mechanically to his wife's questions. **Mrs. Winterbottom**'s sudden departure challenges his understanding and expectations of her.

Mrs. Winterbottom

Walk Two Moons
Sharon Creech

Phoebe's mother. Like her daughter, Mrs. Winterbottom is obsessed with propriety. She works diligently as a housewife and mother, baking, sewing, cooking, cleaning, chatting pleasantly at the dinner table, but becomes increasingly saddened by her family's disregard of her. Convinced that her life has become insignificant and meaningless, she one day disappears in an attempt to reconcile herself to her past and her true self.

Phoebe Winterbottom

Walk Two Moons
Sharon Creech

Salamanca Tree Hiddle's best friend in Euclid, Ohio. Phoebe, who lives next door to **Margaret Cadaver**, is a high-strung girl obsessed with propriety and order. Phoebe lives within a sort of manufactured drama, transforming every insignificant event into a menacing portent. Despite her stiff exterior, Phoebe desperately needs the love and security her family provides for her.

Winterbourne

Daisy Miller
Henry James

The protagonist of the story. Winterbourne is a twenty-seven-year-old American who has been living in Geneva since he was a boy, and so seems more European than American. He falls in love with **Daisy Miller** while visiting his aunt, **Mrs. Costello**. He remains sympathetic to Daisy even after she has been dropped by society.

Ex-Pfc. Wintergreen

Catch-22
Joseph Heller

The mail clerk at the 27th Air Force Headquarters. Wintergreen holds enormous power because his position allows him to intercept and forge documents. He often goes AWOL (Absent Without Leave), and is then punished with demotions.

Hal Winters

Winesburg, Ohio
Sherwood Anderson

A farm hand who works alongside **Ray Pearson**. His fights and relationships with women give him a bad reputation.

Aaron Winthrop

Silas Marner
George Eliot

Dolly Winthrop's son. He eventually marries **Eppie**.

Dolly Winthrop

Silas Marner
George Eliot

The wheelwright's wife and **Aaron Winthrop**'s mother. Dolly helps **Silas Marner** with **Eppie** and later becomes Eppie's godmother and mother-in-law. She is kind, patient, and devout.

Three Witches

Macbeth
William Shakespeare

Three strange women who plot mischief against **Macbeth** using charms, spells, and prophecies. The Three Witches' predictions about Macbeth's imminent reign prompt him to murder **King Duncan**, order the deaths of **Banquo** and **Fleance**, and blindly believe in his own immortality.

Wives

The Handmaid's Tale
Margaret Atwood

The wives of the **Commanders of the Faithful**.

Deanna Wolfe

Prodigal Summer
Barbara Kingsolver

A forest ranger living in a cabin on Zebulon Mountain. Deanna is a devoted ecologist who champions the rights of coyotes. As a child, she thought of **Nannie Land Rawley** as her surrogate mother and role model.

Ray Dean Wolfe

Prodigal Summer
Barbara Kingsolver

Deanna Wolfe's father. Ray Dean's wife died young, and he raised Deanna with the help of **Nannie Land Rawley**, with whom he had another daughter, **Rachel**. Although Ray Dean proposed marriage to Nannie several times over a period of years, she never accepted, preferring her independence.

Arthur Wolff

This Boy's Life
Tobias Wolff

Jack Wolff's biological father. He has a millionaire wife in Connecticut. He is a compulsive liar who makes promises to Jack that he cannot keep. Jack changes his name from **Toby Wolff** so that he can shed the name his father gave him, as well as any connection with his father. When Jack goes to stay with **Arthur Wolff** for the summer, Arthur leaves for a vacation with his girlfriend on the day after Jack's arrival.

Geoffrey Wolff

This Boy's Life
Tobias Wolff

Jack Wolff's kind older brother. He is a student at Princeton while Jack is still in high school. Geoffrey Wolff has grown up in his father's custody and goes for years without seeing Jack. Six years after their last meeting, he and Jack begin corresponding, and Jack asks Geoffrey advice about getting into boarding schools, telling him about the terrible situation with **Dwight**.

Jack Wolff

This Boy's Life
Tobias Wolff

The author and protagonist of the autobiography, Jack Wolff leads the reader through his troubled boyhood. Despite his grim upbringing, Jack remains hopeful and is convinced that he is capable of a better life. In elementary school, Jack changes his name from **Toby Wolff** to Jack. His mother, **Rosemary Wolff**, begrudgingly allows him to do this, knowing that Toby is trying to shed the name that his father, **Arthur Wolff**, gave him. Jack relies on his imagination and intelligence to escape from the grim circumstances of his childhood, which is riddled with domestic violence, alcohol abuse, criminal activity, and emotional neglect. Jack's imagination is what drives him to overcome the adversity he must endure at home, especially at the hands of **Dwight**. Whichever school Jack attends, he has a knack for befriending the school's most notorious troublemakers. At heart, Jack remains a kind person—as evidenced by his sweet relationship with **Arthur Gayle**—and is especially caring and compassionate toward his mother. Jack is more mature than most boys of his age, and feels he must accept responsibility even for situations and events that he could not have controlled, such as his father's abandonment of the family. As a young boy especially, Jack feels inadequate and unworthy of any good fortune that presents itself to him. However, as he grows older, Jack realizes that he deserves more than the meager attention and care he is given. Jack ends up finding himself in boarding school after escaping Dwight's abuse, but he is forced to leave because of bad grades halfway through his senior year. He enlists in the armed forces, and goes to fight in Vietnam.

Rosemary Wolff

This Boy's Life
Tobias Wolff

Jack Wolff's mother. Rosemary Wolff struggles financially to support herself and her son, and though she is neglectful at times, she shows that she loves Jack very much. Rosemary marries **Dwight**, who seems gentle and kind at first, but is actually terrible and abusive. In her attempts to assume a conventional, family-oriented lifestyle, Rosemary betrays herself and suffers for it. Rosemary's restraint is the direct result of her own abusive childhood. Like Jack, Rosemary never loses faith that her situation will improve, however tragic her circumstances.

Toby Wolff

This Boy's Life
Tobias Wolff

See **Jack Wolff**.

Cardinal Wolsey

Henry VIII
William Shakespeare

King Henry VIII's right-hand man. Wolsey is a schemer who controls England's relationships with other countries and steals from fallen lords. The **Duke of Buckingham** tries to warn the other lords about Wolsey's megalomania, but the Cardinal beats him to the punch, arresting the duke for treason. After Buckingham's downfall, Wolsey engineers a divorce between Henry and **Queen Katherine**, attempting to forge a new marriage between the King and the Princess of France. However, Wolsey inadvertantly introduces Henry to **Anne Boleyn** at his dinner party, sending the King head over heels. His plan temporarily shot, Wolsey writes a letter to the pope urging him to deny the divorce until Henry is over Anne. Henry learns of the Cardinal's betrayal: he intercepts not only the letter to the Vatican, but also an inventory of lands and possessions Wolsey has been accumulating. The King fires him, removes his royal protection, and takes his possessions. Wolsey sees that his arrogance and machinations were wrong. Wolsey soon dies, and is the recipient of a lovely eulogy from **Griffith**, who convinces Katherine to forgive him.

Cardinal Wolsey

A Man for All Seasons
Robert Bolt

The Lord Chancellor of England, who dies suddenly following his inability to obtain a dispensation from the pope that would annul **King Henry**'s marriage to Catherine. Wolsey's sudden death serves as a warning to anyone who would court the king's disapproval. **Thomas More** takes Wolsey's place as Lord Chancellor and is just as inept at pleasing the fickle and willful king.

Woman

The Power and the Glory
Graham Greene

A nameless woman, mother of **the boy**. She tries to keep her child in touch with the Catholic faith by reading him stories of saints' lives, including that of the martyr **Juan**.

Woman

Death of a Salesman
Arthur Miller

Willy Loman's mistress when **Happy Loman** and **Biff Loman** were in high school. When Biff catches Willy in his hotel room with her, he loses faith in his father, and his dream of passing math and going to college dies.

Wonderboy

The Natural
Bernard Malamud

Roy's bat. When Roy was a boy, he came across a tree that had been struck by lightning, and he decided to make a bat out of it.

Canning Woo

The Joy Luck Club
Amy Tan

Suyuan's second husband and father of her daughter, **Jing-mei**. Canning met Suyuan in the hospital in Chungking, where she was recovering from her flight from Kweilin. After Suyuan's death, he travels to China with Jing-mei to meet Suyuan's children.

Suyuan Woo

The Joy Luck Club
Amy Tan

Jing-mei's mother and the founder of the Joy Luck Club, a group of women who come together once weekly to play mahjong. She started the club in China, in the early days of her first marriage. During her flight from a war-torn area of China, Suyuan lost her twin daughters, **Chwun Yu** and **Chwun Hwa**. In San Francisco, Suyuan revived the Joy Luck Club with **Lindo**, **An-mei**, and **Ying-ying**.

Jerry Wood

The Outsiders
S. E. Hinton

The teacher who accompanies **Ponyboy Curtis** to the hospital after Ponyboy and **Johnny Cade** save the children from the fire at the abandoned church in Windrixville.

Oliver Wood

The Harry Potter Series: Books 2 and *3*
J. K. Rowling

The Gryffindor Quidditch captain and keeper.

Ian Woodall

Into Thin Air
Jon Krakauer

The leader of the South African expedition, rumored to be dishonest, corrupt, and somewhat crazy. **Jon Krakauer**'s group has a number of unpleasant encounters with Woodall, including during the storm when Woodall refuses to loan his radio for use in a rescue attempt.

Emma Woodhouse

Emma
Jane Austen

The protagonist. In some ways, the twenty-year-old Emma is mature for her age. Because her mother is dead and her older sister is married, she is already the head of her father's household. She cares for her father and oversees the social goings-on in the village of Highbury. Emma's misplaced confidence in her abilities as a matchmaker and her prudish fear of love constitute the central focus of the novel.

Mr. Woodhouse

Emma
Jane Austen

Emma Woodhouse's father and the patriarch of Hartfield, the Woodhouse estate. Though nervous, frail, and prone to hypochondria, Mr. Woodhouse is also known for his friendliness and his attachment to his daughter. He is so resistant to change that he is unhappy to see his daughters or Emma's governess marry. In this sense, he impedes Emma's growth and acceptance of her adult destiny.

Charlie Woodman

Dandelion Wine
Ray Bradbury

Douglas Spaulding and **John Huff**'s good friend. Charlie introduces the boys to **Colonel Freeleigh**. Charlie is always looking for thrills and adventure.

Thomas of Woodstock, Duke of Gloucester

Richard II
William Shakespeare

Uncle to **King Richard II** and brother to **John of Gaunt, Duke of Lancaster** and **Edmund of Langley, Duke of York.** Gloucester is dead at the start of the play, killed in a conspiracy that involved **Thomas Mowbray** and Richard. His murder is the origin of the shame that will haunt Richard II's reign.

Woodville

Henry VI, Part I
William Shakespeare

The lieutenant of the Tower of London. Under orders from the **Cardinal Beaufort, Bishop of Winchester,** Woodville bars **Humphrey, Duke of Gloucester** from entering the Tower.

Jim Woodward

When the Legends Die
Hal Borland

Thomas Black Bull's employer. After Tom's riding accident, he hires Tom to herd his flock of sheep at Pagosa. This new lifestyle, away from the rodeo, finally brings peace to Tom's life.

Wooer

The Two Noble Kinsmen
William Shakespeare

The **Jailer's daughter**'s fiancé. He loves her, but remains calm when she falls in love with **Palamon**.

Leonard Woolf

The Hours
Michael Cunningham

The husband of **Virginia Woolf**. He is an editor and a kind man who thinks his wife is the most important writer of her generation. Although he can be testy and curmudgeonly with his assistants, Leonard is never angry with Virginia, only worried when she refuses to eat.

Virginia Woolf

The Hours
Michael Cunningham

A writer who is tormented by headaches and voices. One of the three major characters closely based on the renowned author. Every third chapter is devoted to her life and is set in 1923, in London. She is wildly intelligent and respected, but her family protects her and fears for her sanity. She is in the process of writing *Mrs. Dalloway*, a book that she hopes will be her masterwork.

Mr. Wopsle

Great Expectations
Charles Dickens

The church clerk in **Pip**'s country town. Sometime after Pip becomes a gentleman, Mr. Wopsle moves to London and becomes an actor.

Thomas Percy, Earl of Worcester

Henry IV, Part I
William Shakespeare

Hotspur's uncle and the **Earl of Northumberland**'s brother. Shrewd and manipulative, Worcester is the mastermind behind the Percy mutiny against **King Henry IV**. He directs the meeting of the rebels, telling Hotspur to gather the **Earl of Douglas** and the Scottish powers and to meet him and **Owen Glendower** and **Lord Edmund Mortimer** in Wales. He decides not to tell Hotspur of King Henry's truce offering.

Wormtail

The Harry Potter Series: Books 3 and *4*
J. K. Rowling

Peter Pettigrew's animagus name, when he is a rat. An animagus is a wizard or witch that can change into animal form.

Gríma Wormtongue

The Two Towers and *The Return of the King*
J. R. R. Tolkien

The wicked and deceitful advisor of King **Théoden**. In *The Two Towers*, Gríma Wormtongue, who is secretly in the employ of **Saruman**, is exposed by **Gandalf** at Rohan. Wormtongue flees to Saruman's headquarters. In *The Return of the King*, the mad Wormtongue turns on the fallen and pitiful Saruman and kills him.

Miss Worsham

Go Down, Moses
William Faulkner

An old white woman with whom **Molly Beauchamp**'s brother lives. She asks **Gavin Stevens** to bring **Samuel Beauchamp**'s body back from Illinois.

Jack Worthing

The Importance of Being Earnest
Oscar Wilde

The central figure of the play. Jack loves **Gwendolen Fairfax** and wishes to marry her. When he is in the city, he goes by Ernest; when he is in the country, he goes by Jack. Jack is the legal guardian of **Cecily Cardew**. In the end, it is revealed that Jack is **Algernon Montcrieff**'s older brother.

Lord Henry Wotton

The Picture of Dorian Gray
Oscar Wilde

A nobleman and a close friend of **Basil Hallward**'s. Urbane and witty, Lord Henry is perpetually armed and ready with well-phrased epigrams criticizing the moralism and hypocrisy of Victorian society. His pleasure-seeking philosophy of "new Hedonism," which espouses garnering experiences that stimulate the senses without regard for conventional morality, plays a vital role in **Dorian Gray**'s development.

Lady Politic Would-be

Volpone
Ben Jonson

A would-be courtesan. She was the impetus for the Would-bes' move to Venice because of her desire to learn the ways of the sophisticated Venetians. She is very well read and very inclined to let anyone know this, or anything else about her.

Sir Politic Would-be

Volpone
Ben Jonson

An English knight who resides in Venice. He occupies the central role in the subplot, which centers on his relationship with **Peregrine**, another English traveler much less gullible than the good knight.

General Woundwort

Watership Down
Richard Adams

The head of the Efrafa warren and the only rabbit bigger and stronger than **Bigwig**. Militant and vengeful, Woundwort tries to destroy **Hazel**'s warren and in doing so almost destroys his own. Woundwort runs his warren in such a manner because he does not want it to be discovered by humans. The problem is that his method of saving his rabbits from humans also makes the rabbits' lives miserable.

Mr. Wrench

Middlemarch
George Eliot

A Middlemarch doctor. He misdiagnoses **Fred Vincy** when Fred catches typhoid fever. **Tertius Lydgate** treats Fred's illness, and the Vincys fire Mr. Wrench. Mr. Wrench becomes Lydgate's enemy as a result.

Alan Wright

Black Boy
Richard Wright

Richard Wright's younger brother.

Ella Wright

Black Boy
Richard Wright

Richard Wright's mother. Although she is hard on her son, Ella loves him. Despite her ill health and partial paralysis, Ella maintains an optimistic outlook on life.

Helene Wright

Sula
Toni Morrison

The daughter of a New Orleans Creole prostitute, **Rochelle**. Helene's strictly religious grandmother, **Cecile**, raises her until she is safely married off to **Wiley Wright** at age sixteen. Helene lives a comfortable middle-class life in the Bottom. After nine years of marriage, she gives birth to her only child, **Nel**.

Nathan Wright

Black Boy
Richard Wright

Richard Wright's father and **Ella Wright**'s husband. Although Nathan is physically intimidating and frequently beats Richard, he abandons the family and proves to be simple, weak, and pathetic.

Richard Wright

Black Boy
Richard Wright

Author, narrator, and protagonist. Richard is an unpredictable bundle of contradictions: he is timid yet assured, tough yet compassionate, enormously intelligent yet ultimately modest. Growing up in an abusive family environment in the racially segregated and violent American South, Richard finds his salvation in reading, writing, and thinking. He grows up feeling insecure about his inability to meet anyone's expectations, particularly his family's wish that he accept religion. Even though he remains isolated from his environment and peers, at the autobiography's end Richard has come to accept himself.

Wiley Wright

Sula
Toni Morrison

Cecile's grand-nephew and **Helene Wright**'s husband. He is a seaman and is often away from home.

Dr. Henry Wu

Jurassic Park
Michael Crichton

A scientist whom **John Hammond** has hired directly out of graduate school to begin work on developing a dinosaur-cloning process. Wu has next to no knowledge about dinosaurs as a species.

Raymond Wutherspoon

Main Street
Sinclair Lewis

A rather spineless man who marries **Vida Sherwin**. Raymond becomes more courageous and upstanding due to his wife's prodding. He enlists in World War I and comes back to Gopher Prairie a hero.

Ellis Wyatt

Atlas Shrugged
Ayn Rand

An oil tycoon who sparks the growth of Colorado's industry through his innovations in reviving spent oil wells. When the government burdens Colorado with impossible regulations and demands based on socialist ideas of provision based on "need," Ellis Wyatt refuses to cooperate and withdraws, joining **John Galt**'s strikers of the mind in the valley. Leaving nothing behind for the government looters, he sets fire to his wells, creating the spectacular and symbolic Wyatt's Torch.

George Wyatt

The Unvanquished
William Faulkner

A former member of **Colonel Sartoris**'s regiment who tries to incite Bayard to violence against Redmond. When he learns that Bayard has intentionally confronted Redmond unarmed, he is astonished and angry at first but eventually admits that his choice was honorable.

Beatrice Wyld

Sons and Lovers
D. H. Lawrence

A friend of the Morel family who ridicules **Miriam Leivers** and flirts with **Paul Morel**. She eventually marries **Arthur Morel** when he returns from the army.

Gail Wynand

The Fountainhead
Ayn Rand

Owner of the *Banner*. Gail Wynand is a ruthless media tycoon who compromises his principles to gain power. Born in the slums of New York, he is entirely self-taught and self-made. He initially sought power to rule the incompetent and corrupt, but has become like them in acquiring wealth. His faith in humanity is restored when he meets the incorruptible **Howard Roark**. Wynand becomes Roark's great ally and friend, but he ultimately betrays him.

May Wynn

The Caine Mutiny
Herman Wouk

An stunningly beautiful lounge singer, and **Willie Keith**'s love interest. Though uneducated and from a lower class than Willie, May is insightful, assertive, and endearing.

ADORABLE ORPHANS

PARENTLESS, THESE CHARACTERS HAVE TO FIND THEIR OWN WAY IN THE WORLD.

Isabella Archer	1	*The Portrait of a Lady*
Cecily Cardew	2	*The Importance of Being Earnest*
Jane Eyre	3	*Jane Eyre*
Elizabeth Lavenza	4	*Frankenstein*
Pip	5	*Great Expectations*
Harry Potter	6	*Harry Potter* series, Books I-IV
Anne Shirley	7	*Anne of Green Gables*
Oliver Twist	8	*Oliver Twist*

Xanthias

The Clouds
Aristophanes

A household slave to **Strepsiades**. He is obedient, but will stand up for himself when challenged.

Xanthos

The King Must Die
Mary Renault

The **Queen of Eleusis**'s brother and the war leader in Eleusis. Greedy and unkind, Xanthos tries to have **Theseus** killed. Theseus, aided by his opponent's own men, kills Xanthos instead.

Xius

Chronicle of a Death Foretold
Gabriel García Márquez

A widower who owned the most beautiful house in town. Bayardo wants to buy it because it was **Angela Vicario**'s favorite house. The widower insists that the house isn't for sale, but Bayardo keeps offering more and more money until he gives in. The house held all of his dead wife's possessions, and he dies of sadness soon after.

X-Ray

Holes
Louis Sachar

The unofficial leader of the group of boys in Tent D at Camp Green Lake. Although he is small and cannot see well, he manages to take charge and have the other boys follow his orders. X-Ray is able to maintain his position at the head of the group through a system of rewards and allies. Every time that **Stanley Yelnats** does something nice for X-Ray, X-Ray is nice to Stanley and stands up for him when the other boys pick on him. When Stanley becomes friends with **Zero**, X-Ray's system is threatened and he becomes hostile towards Stanley.

Xury

Robinson Crusoe
Daniel Defoe

A nonwhite slave boy. During his enslavement at Sallee, **Crusoe** demonstrates trust in Xury, by keeping him on board the ship they occupy during their escape. Nevertheless, Crusoe later sells Xury to the Portuguese captain.

EVIL MASTERMINDS

FROM YOUR LEAKING SINK TO THE MURDERS OF THOUSANDS... THEY'RE BEHIND IT ALL.

Big Brother	1	*1984*
Marisa Coulter	2	*His Dark Materials* trilogy
Roger Chillingworth	3	*The Scarlet Letter*
Kurtz	4	*Heart of Darkness*
Lady Macbeth	5	*Macbeth*
The Marquise de Merteuil	6	*Dangerous Liaisons*
Richard III	7	*Richard III*
Satan	8	*Paradise Lost*

Uncle Yaakov

My Name Is Asher Lev
Chaim Potok

Asher Lev's uncle, who dies when Lev is six years old. His death causes Lev's mother to become ill. He is often referenced by Lev's mother, who seems to carry on a relationship with her memories of him.

Mr. Yacobowski

The Bluest Eye
Toni Morrison

The local grocer, a middle-aged white immigrant. He has a gruff manner toward little black girls.

Yahoos

Gulliver's Travels
Jonathan Swift

Filthy anthropomorphic beasts who live in servitude to the **Houyhnhnms** and perform manual labor. They live naked, the men covered by hair, the women with low-hanging breasts. Their lasciviousness and primitive eating habits repel **Gulliver**. By the end of his journey, Gulliver, full of bitterness and self-loathing, refers to himself—and later to any human—as a Yahoo.

Shadrach Yale

Across Five Aprils
Irene Hunt

Jethro Creighton's teacher and friend. Shadrach helps Jethro learn to read and speak and encourages the furthering of his education. Shadrach goes to fight in the war, leaving both Jethro and **Jenny Creighton** to miss him intensely. Shadrach is wounded and nearly dies. Jenny visits him, helps him recover, and the two marry.

Yank

The Hairy Ape
Eugene O'Neill

The play's antagonist. Yank works as a fireman on a Transatlantic Ocean Liner. Yank, whose real name is Bob Smith, was born in New York City and was brought up in a lower-class family. Yank is a burly, sometimes menacing figure. The play follows his quest to find a sense of belonging in modern, industrial society. When Yank is working in the stockhole, he declares that he is part of the engines. When Yank is walking on Fifth Avenue, he points to a skyscraper and says that he is the skyscraper. When a wealthy young woman, **Mildred**, goes to watch firemen working in the stockhole of the Ocean Liner, she becomes faint. Yank tells the men he has fallen in hate with her. In a futile attempt to get revenge on Mildred, Yank goes on a rampage on Fifth Avenue, ends up in jail, is thrown out of the office of the I.W.W., and eventually ends up talking to a gorilla in a cage in the zoo. The gorilla springs on Yank, crushes and kills him with his massive arms, and then tosses Yank into his cage.

The Yankee

A Connecticut Yankee in King Arthur's Court
Mark Twain

The central character and narrator, "The Boss." The Yankee is practical, business-minded, hardworking, determined, resourceful, intelligent, and possessed of an unbelievably good memory. Through the novel, the Yankee makes a close friend out of **Clarence**, who helps him set up a secret nineteenth-century-style civilization, turning Camelot into an electrified, modern city, only to be destroyed in a power ploy by the Church. The Yankee helps **King Arthur** to see that slavery is terrible after the two men become slaves after traveling the countryside as peasants. He constantly outwits **Merlin**, the jealous court magician, defeats **Sir Launcelot** in a joust, and kills **Sir Sagramor le Desirous**. The Yankee marries **Sandy** and has children with her, but is spellbound by a sleeping spell that Merlin casts, causing him to sleep for thirteen centuries, which returns him to his own time.

Alvin Yark

The Shipping News
E. Annie Proulx

Wavey Prowse's uncle, and a shipmaker with a good reputation in Killick-Claw.

Yasha

The Cherry Orchard
Anton Chekhov

The young manservant who has been traveling with **Ranevsky** ever since she left for France. He is always complaining about how uncivilized Russia is when compared to France. A rakish character, Yasha exploits **Dunyasha**'s love for him, and openly tells the butler **Firs** that Firs is so old he should die. Most of the characters besides Ranevsky regard him as repulsive and obnoxious.

Yashvin

Anna Karenina
Leo Tolstoy

Alexei Kirillovich Vronsky's wild friend from the army. Yashvin has a propensity for losing large sums of money at gambling.

Yates

Mansfield Park
Jane Austen

Tom Bertram's friend, who proposes the amateur theatricals at Mansfield. He shows an interest in **Julia Bertram**, which continues in London. After **Maria Bertram** runs off with **Henry Crawford**, Julia and Yates elope and marry. The family later rehabilitates them.

Dr. Kurt Yavitch

Babbitt
Sinclair Lewis

A histologist from Zenith. He is a friend of **Seneca Doane**'s.

Dr. Lewis Yealland

Regeneration
Pat Barker

A foil for **Dr. W.H.R. Rivers**, who works at the National Hospital in London and uses electroshock therapy to treat his patients.

Yellin

The Princess Bride
William Goldman

The Chief of all Enforcement in Florin City. Along with **Count Rugen**, Yellin is **Prince Humperdinck**'s only confidant.

Yellow man

Cold Mountain
Charles Frazier

The kind slave who gives **Inman** food and shelter after he gets shot by the Home Guard.

Elya Yelnats

Holes
Louis Sachar

Stanley Yelnats's great-great-grandfather and the reason that Stanley's family has such bad luck. After becoming disillusioned with the woman he thought he loved in Latvia, Elya travels to America, forgetting to fulfill a promise that he made to the gypsy, **Madame Zeroni**, who curses him as a result. Elya passes down generations of bad luck to his family.

Mr. Yelnats

Holes
Louis Sachar

Stanley Yelnats's father. He is an inventor who is smart and persistent, but unlucky because of the curse of **Madame Zeroni**. Eventually he discovers a cure for foot odor and is able to hire the lawyer, Ms. Morengo, to get Stanley out of Camp Green Lake.

Mrs. Yelnats

Holes
Louis Sachar

Stanley Yelnats's mother. She does not believe in curses and always tries to point out the luck that the Yelnats have had.

Stanley Yelnats

Holes
Louis Sachar

The protagonist. He is an overweight boy who does not have any friends from school and is often picked on by his classmates and the school bully, **Derrick Dunne**. He is convicted of a crime he did not commit and is sent to the Camp Green Lake juvenile detention center. Nonviolent and generally kind, Stanley has a difficult time in school and at the camp. Stanley's family is cursed with bad luck, and although they do not have much money, they always try to remain hopeful. As the novel progresses, Stanley slowly develops physical strength and personal strength. He identifies the people who threaten him, like the **Warden**, and while he tries not to get in trouble, he also stands up for his own rights and the rights of his friends. Stanley gradually develops the self-confidence necessary to disregard the opinions of the majority of the boys and form a friendship with **Zero**, the least popular kid in the camp. Through this friendship, he succeeds in eradicating his family curse.

Stanley Yelnats the elder

Holes
Louis Sachar

The son of **Elya Yelnats** and the great-grandfather of the protagonist **Stanley Yelnats**. **Kate Barlow** robbed Stanley Yelnats the elder of his fortune while he was moving from New York to California.

Clym Yeobright

The Return of the Native
Thomas Hardy

The "Native" of the novel's title. Clym is the son of **Mrs. Yeobright** and the cousin of **Thomasin Yeobright**. He goes abroad to work as a diamond merchant in Paris but comes home when he realizes that he does not want to be materially wealthy. He is pursued by **Eustacia Vye** and eventually marries her, but their marriage turns sour when her ambition to move to Paris conflicts with his plan to stay on Egdon Heath and teach. Clym is intelligent, cultured and deeply introspective. As a pathologically honest person, he is almost incapable of seeing trickery or imagining deviousness in others. Clym represents to the mind of the narrator the typical modern man: he is philosophically and intellectually progressive, but he is also portrayed as stoic and largely joyless. When he loses his eyesight, he responds with more than his characteristic stoicism. He resigns himself to his fate and develops a kind of joy that was previously foreign to him. At the end of the novel, weakened by a degenerative eye condition and by the trauma of losing his mother and Eustacia, he becomes an itinerant preacher, sermonizing about simple moral topics.

Mrs. Yeobright

The Return of the Native
Thomas Hardy

Clym Yeobright's mother, and **Thomasin Yeobright**'s aunt and guardian. A proper, class-conscious, proud woman, Mrs. Yeobright objects to the marriage of both her charges. There is an element of jealousy in Mrs. Yeobright's hatred of **Eustacia Vye**. She becomes increasingly irrational, essentially asking Clym to choose between a marriage and his mother.

Thomasin Yeobright

The Return of the Native
Thomas Hardy

Clym Yeobright's cousin and **Mrs. Yeobright**'s niece and ward. Thomasin is an innocent and good-hearted, if somewhat vacuous woman who seems genuinely to care for **Damon Wildeve**, who is merely using her to make Eustacia Vye jealous. She eventually marries Wildeve and has a child, whom she names Eustacia. At the end of the novel, she marries **Diggory Venn**, who has long loved her.

Yeoman

The Canterbury Tales
Geoffrey Chaucer

The servant who accompanies **the Knight** and **the Squire**.

Ivan Fyodorovich Yepanchin

The Idiot
Fyodor Dostoevsky

The father of **Alexandra Ivanovna Yepanchina**, **Adelaida Ivanovna Yepanchina** and **Aglaya Ivanovna Yepanchina**, and the husband of **Lizaveta Prokofyevna Yepanchina**. Yepanchin is a wealthy and respected member of St. Petersburg society. At the beginning of the novel he lusts after **Anastassya Filippovna Barashkova**.

Adelaida Ivanovna Yepanchina

The Idiot
Fyodor Dostoevsky

The middle daughter of **Ivan Fyodorovich Yepanchin** and **Lizaveta Prokofyevna Yepanchina**. Adelaida, like her older sister, **Alexandra Ivanovna Yepanchina**, is very cultivated and expresses a talent for painting. She is engaged to **Prince S**.

Aglaya Ivanovna Yepanchina

The Idiot
Fyodor Dostoevsky

The youngest daughter of **Ivan Fyodorovich Yepanchin** and **Lizaveta Prokofyevna Yepanchina**. Aglaya is haughty and childlike in her caprices, but also very romantic and idealistic. She falls in love with **Prince Lev Nikolayevich Myshkin**, but is unable to accept his compassionate love for **Anastassya Filippovna Barashkova**. Aglaya ends up running away with a man claiming to be a Polish count, who later abandons her.

Alexandra Ivanovna Yepanchina

The Idiot
Fyodor Dostoevsky

The oldest daughter of **Ivan Fyodorovich Yepanchin** and **Lizaveta Prokofyevna Yepanchina**. Although Alexandra's parents worry about her marriage, she feels very calm. Highly educated and well-read, she has a talent for music.

Lizaveta Prokofyevna Yepanchina

The Idiot
Fyodor Dostoevsky

A distant relative of **Prince Lev Nikolayevich Myshkin** and the wife of **Ivan Fyodorovich Yepanchin**. In her willfulness and eccentricity, Lizaveta is very similar to her daughter **Aglaya Ivanovna Yepanchina**. Her greatest anxiety in life is finding suitable husbands for her three daughters.

Semyon Yepikhodov

The Cherry Orchard
Anton Chekhov

A clerk at the **Ranevsky** estate. He is a source of amusement for all the other workers, who refer to him as "Simple Simon." Yepikhodov provides comic relief, with his self-conscious pose as the hopeless lover and romantic, often contemplating suicide. He loves **Dunyasha**, to whom he has proposed.

Yeste

The Princess Bride
William Goldman

Madrid's most famous swordmaker, for whom **Inigo Montoya**'s father made back-order swords.

Ying-ying's Amah

The Joy Luck Club
Amy Tan

Ying-ying's childhood nursemaid. She loved Ying-ying as if she were her own child and tried to instill traditional Chinese values in her.

Uncle Yitzchok

My Name Is Asher Lev
Chaim Potok

Asher Lev's uncle, with whom he lives while his parents are in Europe. He is a wealthy, kind man with no distinct personality. He appreciates his nephew's talent in his manner as a layman.

Yolanda

How the Garcia Girls Lost Their Accents
Julia Alvarez

The rebellious tomboy of the family in the Dominican Republic. Once in the U.S., she develops into a poet. Her difficulties with men and a painful divorce lead to a mental breakdown.

Limping Lucy Yolland

The Moonstone
Wilkie Collins

A close friend of **Rosanna Spearman**'s. She is loyal and quick to be indignant on Rosanna's behalf, even toward upper-class men such as **Franklin Blake**.

Parson Yorick

Tristram Shandy
Laurence Sterne

The village parson, and a close friend of the Shandy family. Yorick is lighthearted and straight-talking; he detests gravity and pretension.

Archbishop of York

Henry IV, Part I and Henry IV, Part II
William Shakespeare

A powerful northern clergyman who symapthizes with **Hotspur** and the rest of the Percy clan in their uprising against **King Henry IV** in *Henry IV, Part I*. In *Henry IV, Part II*, York, along with **Lord Hastings** and **Lord Thomas Mowbray**, leads the rebellion against **King Henry IV**. Though the rebel leaders file their grievances with **Prince John of Lancaster** and agree to disband their armies after a tentative truce, the prince goes back on his word and arrests the rebels, sending them off to be executed.

Duchess of York

Richard II
William Shakespeare

Wife to **Edmund of Langley, Duke of York** and mother to the **Duke of Aumerle**. When she and her husband discover that their son plans to assassinate the newly crowned **King Henry IV**, she rushes to the king to plead for Aumerle's life, while her husband pleads to the king for Aumerle's traitorous execution.

Duchess of York

Richard III
William Shakespeare

Widow of **Richard Plantagenet, Duke of York** and mother of **King Edward IV**, **George, Duke of Clarence**, and **King Richard III**. The Duchess is the mother-in-law of Queen Elizabeth (**Elizabeth Woodville, Lady Grey**), and is very protective of Elizabeth and her children, the Duchess's grandchildren. She is fully aware of Richard's deceit and guilt in the increasing murders and executions; in her very first appearance in the play, the Duchess rues that she ever gave birth to Richard. After Richard rises to the throne, she bitterly curses him.

Richard II

Edmund of Langley, Duke of York

William Shakespeare

Uncle to **Richard II** and Henry Bolingbroke (**Henry IV**), brother to **John of Gaunt**, and father to the **Duke of Aumerle**. Following Gaunt's death, York is left lord governor of England when Richard II leads an army to Ireland, but he is faced with a dilemma when Bolingbroke returns from his exile with an army. When he finally meets Henry's forces near Berkeley Castle, he rebukes Henry for challenging the crown but declares his neutrality on the issue, effectively helping Bolingbroke usurp the crown. When he later discovers that his son, Aumerle, is plotting to kill the newly crowned Henry IV, he puts his national loyalty above his familial loyalty and rushes to Henry to reveal the conspiracy and plead for his son's execution.

Richard III

Richard, Duke of York

William Shakespeare

The younger son of **King Edward IV** and **Queen Elizabeth**, younger brother of **Prince Edward**, and half-brother of **Lord Grey** and the **Marquess of Dorset**. Following the imprisonment of Elizabeth's sons from her first marriage, the Queen takes the young Duke of York to sanctuary. However, King Richard III soon places both him and Prince Edward in the Tower for their "safety." After his ascent to the throne, the paranoid king contracts **Sir James Tyrrel** to kill the two young heirs to the throne.

Henry VI, Part I; Henry VI, Part II; and *Henry VI, Part III*

Richard Plantagenet, Duke of York

William Shakespeare

Son of the **Earl of Cambridge**; nephew of **Edmund Mortimer**; husband of the **Duchess of York**; father of **King Edward IV**, **King Richard III**, **George, Duke of Clarence**, and **Edmund, Earl of Rutland**. Plantagenet first appears in *King Henry VI, Part I*, asserting that he has been born into nobility, though his father was put to death for treason in *King Henry V*. He argues this point with the **Duke of Somerset** in the Temple Garden, as other lords present pluck red (Somerset) or white (Plantagenet/York) roses to declare their allegiance. This dispute will soon set off the violent Wars of the Roses. When Mortimer dies, Plantagenet inherits his claim to the throne, which becomes the basis of his ultimate rebellion against Henry VI. Leaving the dead Mortimer, Plantagenet pleads to **King Henry VI** just for the reinstatement of his title; the king agrees and bestows on him the honor of Duke of York. Though the King tries to quell the York-Somerset dispute, York is offended when Henry puts on a red rose. As foretold, this internal strife leads to the empire's foreign downfall: when Somerset delays sending his cavalry to York, York is unable to move out reinforcements during the climactic battle near Bordeaux. This leads to **Lord Talbot**'s death and ultimately the English defeat in France. In *King Henry VI, Part II*, though he first sides with the **Richard Neville, Earl of Salisbury** and his son **Richard Neville, Earl of Warwick** to defend **Humphrey, Duke of Gloucester** and the public good, York maintains his own designs on the throne. After convincing Salisbury and Warwick of his rightful claim to the crown of England, York begins to pave his way to the throne by helping the other nobles depose Gloucester. York uses his army from Ireland to announce his own rebellion against King Henry and begin the Wars of the Roses with the Battle of St. Albans. He continues the quest for the crown in *King Henry VI, Part III*. York leads his army to London to depose the king. He loses the battle, however; after his youngest son Rutland is killed, York is captured by **Queen Margaret**'s forces. The Queen and the younger **Lord Clifford** mock York before stabbing and killing him. After York's death, two of his sons, Edward IV and Richard III, will go on to become monarchs before the Tudor dynasty begins, ending the York-Lancaster dispute.

Nathaniel York

The Martian Chronicles
Ray Bradbury

The captain of the first expedition. He appears only in **Ylla**'s dreams as a seductive, handsome man.

Mr. Yoshida

Hiroshima
John Hersey

The former head of the Nobori-cho Neighborhood Association. He is pinned by the wreckage of his house but manages to free himself.

Satsue Yoshiki

Hiroshima
John Hersey

Father Wilhelm Kleinsorge's cook, nurse, and close friend in the years leading up to his death.

Yosi

Night
Elie Wiesel

A Zionist, and brother of **Tibi**, whom **Eliezer** meets in Buna. Together with Eliezer, they make a plan to move to Palestine after the war.

John Yossarian

Catch-22
Joseph Heller

The protagonist and hero of the novel. Yossarian is a captain in the Air Force and a lead bombardier in his squadron. He wants to live and hates the war. He has decided to live forever or die trying.

Young Catherine

Wuthering Heights
Emily Brontë

Catherine and **Edgar Linton**'s daughter. Like her mother, young Catherine is headstrong, impetuous, and occasionally arrogant. However, Edgar's influence has made young Catherine a gentler and more compassionate woman than her mother. Through **Heathcliff**'s meddling, she marries **Linton Heathcliff**.

Young Collector

A Streetcar Named Desire
Tennessee Williams

A teenager who comes to the Kowalskis' door to collect for the newspaper when **Blanche DuBois** is home alone. The boy leaves bewildered after Blanche hits on him and gives him a passionate farewell kiss.

Young man

Cry, the Beloved Country
Alan Paton

A young white man who works at the reformatory and attempts to reform **Absalom Kumalo**. He cares deeply for his students.

Young man

American Dream
Edward Albee

A blond Midwestern beauty, self-described as a "type," and dubbed by **Grandma** as the "American Dream." He is the product of the murder of his lost identical twin who stands against him in his physical deformity. As he tells Grandma, he has suffered the progressive loss of all feeling and desire, losses that correspond to the mutilations **Mommy** inflicted on his brother to punish his bodily excesses.

Young student

The Unbearable Lightness of Being
Milan Kundera

Franz's mistress after Sabina leaves him. The student loves Franz simply and completely and with her he finds true happiness. Because **Marie-Claude** refuses to grant him a divorce they are never able to marry and his young mistress cannot claim any rights to Franz after his death.

Comrade Young

Black Boy
Richard Wright

An escapee from a mental institution. Young shows up at a meeting of the John Reed Club, a revolutionary artists' organization that **Richard Wright** joins in Chicago.

Beneatha Younger

A Raisin in the Sun
Lorraine Hansberry

Mama's daughter and **Walter Lee Younger**'s sister. Beneatha, also known as "Bennie," is an intellectual. She attends college and is better-educated than the rest of the Younger family. Some of her personal beliefs and views have distanced her from conservative Mama. She dreams of being a doctor and struggles to determine her identity as a well-educated black woman. Throughout the play, she searches for her identity. She dates two very different men: **Joseph Asagai** and **George Murchison**. She is at her happiest with Asagai, her Nigerian boyfriend. She is at her most depressed and angry with George, her pompous, affluent African-American boyfriend. In the end, Beneatha intends to accept Asagai's proposal of marriage and move to Nigeria with him.

Lena Younger

A Raisin in the Sun
Lorraine Hansberry

See **Mama**.

Ruth Younger

A Raisin in the Sun
Lorraine Hansberry

Wife of **Walter Lee Younger** and mother of **Travis Younger**. Ruth takes care of the Youngers' small apartment. Her marriage to Walter has problems, but she hopes to rekindle their love. Her weariness makes her seem older than she really is. She fights with Walter about his going out and getting drunk, but the two also recognize that a distance is growing between them, and they try to repair it. When she finds out she is pregnant, she considers having an abortion because she doesn't know how she and Walter can support another child. **Mama** tells Ruth that Walter has become a man at the end of the play when Walter stands up to **Mr. Karl Lindner**.

Travis Younger

A Raisin in the Sun
Lorraine Hansberry

The young, sheltered son of **Walter Lee Younger** and **Ruth Younger**. Travis earns some money by carrying grocery bags and likes to play outside with other neighborhood children, but he has no bedroom and sleeps on the living-room sofa. **Mama**'s dream is to have a house with a big yard where Travis can play.

Walter Lee Younger

A Raisin in the Sun
Lorraine Hansberry

The protagonist of the play. Walter is a dreamer. He wants to be rich and devises plans to acquire wealth with his friends, particularly **Willy Harris**. When the play opens, he wants to invest his father's insurance money in a new liquor-store venture. As **Mama**'s only son, **Ruth Younger**'s defiant husband, **Travis Younger**'s caring father, and **Beneatha Younger**'s belligerent brother, Walter serves as both protagonist and antagonist of the play. Most of his actions and mistakes hurt the family greatly. Once he begins to listen to Mama and Ruth express their dreams of owning a house, he realizes that buying the house is more important for the family's welfare than getting rich quickly. Walter's and the family's hopes are crushed when **Bobo** informs them that Willy has run away with the money that Walter was going to invest in their liquor store business plan. After refusing the money that **Mr. Karl Lindner** offers the family not to move in to a white neighborhood, Walter feels forced to call back and accept the deal after his money is stolen. Walter finally becomes a man when he stands up to Mr. Lindner, and, at the last moment, proudly declines the offer yet again.

Dr. Yueh

Dune
Frank Herbert

The Atreides's doctor. Dr. Yueh betrays the Atreides and murders **the Shadout Mapes** under orders from **Baron Vladimir Harkonnen**.